# *Introduction to*
# PSYCHOLOGY

*Eleventh Edition*

Ben.

# Introduction to
# PSYCHOLOGY

*Eleventh Edition*

**Rita L. Atkinson**
*University of California, San Diego*

**Richard C. Atkinson**
*University of California, San Diego*

**Edward E. Smith**
*University of Michigan*

**Daryl J. Bem**
*Cornell University*

With the Assistance of
**Susan Nolen-Hoeksema**
*Stanford University*

Harcourt Brace College Publishers

*Fort Worth   Philadelphia   San Diego   New York   Orlando   Austin   San Antonio*
*Toronto   Montreal   London   Sydney   Tokyo*

Publisher *Ted Buchholz*
Acquisitions Editor *Christina N. Oldham*
Developmental Editor *Sarah Helyar Smith*
Senior Project Editor *Steve Welch*
Production Manager *Erin Gregg*
Book Designer *Nick Welch*
Photo/Permissions Editor *Molly Shepard*

On the cover: John Sloan, *The Red Lane*, 1918, oil on canvas, 32" × 26". Courtesy a private collection.

*Address for Editorial Correspondence*: Harcourt Brace College Publishers, 301 Commerce Street, Suite 3700, Fort Worth, TX 76102.

*Address for Orders*: Harcourt Brace & Company 6277 Sea Harbor Drive, Orlando, FL 32887. 1-800-782-4479, or 1-800-433-0001 (in Florida).

*Copyrights and Acknowledgements and Illustration Credits appear on pp. A-61–A-66, which constitute a continuation of this copyright page.*

Printed in the United States of America

Library of Congress Catalog Card Number 92-73450

ISBN: 0-15-500287-2

3  4  5  6  7  8  9  0  1  048  9  8  7  6  5  4  3  2

# Preface

With the publication of this eleventh edition, *Introduction to Psychology* celebrates its fortieth anniversary. In the years since the publication of the first edition, authored by Ernest R. Hilgard in 1953, this textbook has become one of the most widely used in the history of college publishing. More psychology students have used it than any other introductory textbook, and many studying from it today have parents who were introduced to psychology by an earlier edition. It has been translated into a number of languages, including Russian, Spanish, French, Chinese, German, and Portuguese.

We believe that the success of the book stems from a continuing commitment to present the substantive knowledge and methodological contributions of psychology as accurately and as clearly as possible, without oversimplifying or glossing over difficult concepts. To this end, we prefer to present integrated essays about individual topics rather than snippets of fact and theory to be memorized for the final examination. Indeed, our ultimate focus has always been on what we want our readers to retain long *after* the final examination, and it is this criterion that has informed our larger agenda.

The first goal of this agenda is to inspire a general appreciation for an empirical approach to human behavior and a specific enthusiasm for the field of psychology itself. Psychology is both broad and ambitious. Nourished by biology at its border with the natural sciences and by sociology and anthropology at its border with the social sciences, psychology deals with complex questions about human nature once considered solely the province of literature and philosophy. Above all, this book seeks to convey the excitement of psychology as an intellectual human enterprise.

Second, we seek to produce intelligent consumers of psychological information. All of us are bombarded daily by claims and assertions about human behavior. We believe that an introduction to psychology should instill an open-minded but inquiring skepticism about all such claims. We hope that "alumni" of this book who encounter assertions about lie detection, hypnosis, sexual orientation, extrasensory perception, and so forth will remember the kinds of questions that need to be asked about the evidence—even if they no longer remember the specific evidence they once read about here.

Third, we are concerned with psychology's role in promoting human welfare and solving social problems. As many discussions in this book illustrate, the discipline of psychology has often contributed to these goals. The use of psychotherapy to treat behavioral and emotional disorders is but one example. Psychological research on learning led to the development of computer-aided instruction; research on memory has contributed to our understanding of eyewitness testimony; and research in social psychology has helped to design programs for reducing prejudice and intergroup conflict. Examples like these will be found in every chapter of the book.

One psychologist has suggested that "the secrets of our trade need not be reserved for highly trained specialists. . . . Our responsibility is less to assume the role of experts and try to apply psychology ourselves than to give it away to the people who really need it. . . . I can imagine nothing we could do that would be more relevant to human welfare . . . than to discover how best to give psychology away" (Miller, 1969). We agree. For forty years

*Introduction to Psychology* has been our vehicle for giving psychology away.

In the ninth edition we introduced an appendix called "How to Read a Textbook: The PQRST Method." Our readers report that this appendix proved helpful, and we recommend that students read it before beginning the text. Another learning aid, new to this edition, is the use of boldface type to highlight important terms and concepts. The reader who understands these boldface terms should be well prepared for an examination on the material. A further aid is the *Study Guide and Unit Mastery Program* prepared by John G. Carlson of the University of Hawaii. This workbook, which is discussed later in the preface, can be used by students in preparing either for a traditional course or for a course taught by the unit mastery method.

The eleventh edition has been revised and updated throughout. New developments related to neurotransmitter–neuroreceptor systems, theories of consciousness, neural networks and connectionism, gender differences, genetic and evolutionary influences on behavior, and the functional mapping of the brain to locate specific areas for cognition, emotions, and language have been integrated into every section of the book. Rather than pinpointing all of these additions for every chapter, we will mention only some of the major changes.

Chapter 1, "Psychology as a Scientific and Human Endeavor," includes a new Critical Discussion of ethical issues in psychological research and an expanded section on interdisciplinary approaches, focusing on cognitive science and evolutionary psychology. In Chapter 3. "Psychological Development," the section on cognitive development has been rewritten to provide a clearer treatment of Piaget's theories and of the alternative approaches that explain how children's understanding of the world changes with age. New research on gender identity and sex typing is discussed and amplified by a Critical Discussion entitled "Can Sex Education Prevent Childhood Sexism?"

Chapter 5, "Perception," introduces the distinction between bottom-up processes (driven by stimulus input) and top-down processes (driven by knowledge and expectations) in the recognition of objects. (The role these processes play in acquiring concepts is discussed in Chapter 9). This chapter also intoduces the reader to connectionism as a model for pattern recognition and includes a new Critical Discussion on the breakdown of recognition that occurs in some forms of brain damage.

Chapter 7, "Learning and Conditioning," has been revised and reorganized to reflect the current synthesis of behavioral, cognitive, and ethological approaches to learning. This chapter includes new material on complex learning. In Chapter 8, "Memory," a Critical Discussion further illustrates the neural network approach by describing a connectionist model of long-term memory. Also included is a new section on implicit memory, presenting evidence that memories for facts and events may involve a different storage system than memories for skills.

Chapter 10, "Basic Motives," has an expanded discussion of obesity, anorexia, and bulimia as well as a new section on sexual perversions. Chapter 11, "Emotion," presents the latest cross-cultural work on emotional expression and a new section on precognitive emotions.

Chapter 13, "Personality Through the Life Course," which was new to the tenth edition, has been expanded to include a major discussion of how genetic, environmental, and cultural factors interact to determine personality. This chapter includes a new section on personality development in adolescence and concludes with a discussion of the factors that contribute to personality stability and change throughout adulthood.

Chapter 15, "Stress and Coping," has been completely reorganized to reflect the growing field of health psychology. It includes new sections on how stress affects health, how personality styles mediate stress responses, and the effectiveness of strategies for coping with stress. Two new Critical Discussions are "Sexual Abuse as a Major Stressor" and "Can Psychological Interventions Affect the Course of Cancer?"

Chapter 16, "Abnormal Psychology," has been revised to include the latest research on genetic and biological contributions to mental disorders. The sections on schizophrenia and obsessive–compulsive disorders have been rewritten, and new case histories have been added.

Chapter 18, "Social Beliefs and Attitudes," now includes an enlightening discussion of why stereotypes persist in the face of nonconfirming data. The section on attitudes has been rewritten to describe the functions that attitudes serve for the individual, and how these functions influence both the consistency among attitudes and the ease with which an attitude can be changed. The section on interpersonal attraction concludes with a discussion of passionate versus companionate love and a three-component theory of love. Chapter 19, "Social Interaction and Influence," contains a new section on group decision making and a Critical Discussion concerning ethical issues in Milgram's obedience experiments.

Although we four authors are now at universities spread across the country, we were originally colleagues at Stanford University, where we gained much of our enthusiasm for psychology from Ernest R. Hilgard. In keeping with the Stanford connection, we asked Susan Nolen-Hoeksema of that university to prepare a draft of Chapter 15. Professor Nolen-Hoeksema's research focuses on strategies for coping with stress. We are pleased with her contribution and feel that the new version of the chapter "Stress and Coping" is an exciting addition to the book.

# Ancillaries

The primary ancillaries accompanying this edition have been carefully updated and coordinated both with the textbook and with each other to ensure accuracy and maximum usefulness. The highly successful *Study Guide and Unit Mastery Program*, by John G. Carlson of the University of Hawaii at Manoa, offers for each chapter study practice with vocabulary, ideas, and concepts set within a unit mastery framework, as well as sample quizzes. A considerably enhanced *Instructor's Manual*, by John G. Carlson and Tracy Trevorrow, also of the University of Hawaii at Manoa, includes creative lecture suggestions, insightful student-involving activities, discussion and essay questions, updated lists of videos and films, specifically tailored transparency masters, and an instructor's guide to the unit mastery system featured in the *Study Guide*.

The *Test Item File*, by Vivian Jenkins of the University of Southern Indiana, has been greatly improved and expanded and is available in both printed and computerized versions. First, the core items, comprising half of the items in each chapter, have been validated and approved by The Psychological Corporation. The validated items, which are clearly identified in the item keys, enable instructors to create exams with confidence that they will accurately test students' knowledge. The balance of the items, which have been carefully written, allow instructors to expand or adjust their exams according to the needs of individual classes. Second, in response to requests from instructors, half of all items are now conceptual in format. These conceptual items, which are also identified in the item keys, test students' understanding of concepts, asking them to apply factual knowledge to given situations and to generalize information. Third, the total number of items in the testbank has been increased by 50 percent so instructors can use it over many sections without concern of duplicating earlier exams. Each chapter now contains 150 items, in addition to 75 entirely new items for the statistical appendix.

Additional ancillaries available for the Introductory Psychology course include the creative *Dynamic Concepts of Psychology* laser disc, an extensive overhead transparency package, a comprehensive videotape library, exciting and innovative interactive software, and the resourceful *Whole Psychology Catalog*.

To keep abreast of research developments, we relied on experts to review material pertinent to their areas of specialization. Several specialists commented on each chapter. These reviewers and others who contributed valuable suggestions are listed following the preface. Those who provided critiques for previous editions are not listed, but they have our continuing appreciation.

In addition to those listed below, we would like to thank the staff at Harcourt Brace Jovanovich, who contributed their skills in helping us put the new edition together.

*Rita L. Atkinson*
*Richard C. Atkinson*
*Edward E. Smith*
*Daryl J. Bem*

# Acknowledgments

Ruth L. Ault
*Davidson College*

Don Baucum
*Birmingham-Southern College*

Karl A. Blendell
*Siena College*

John G. Carlson
*University of Hawaii*

Eugene R. Cilden
*Linfield College*

Paul Chara
*Loras College*

Hank Davis
*University of Guelph*

M. Robin DiMatteo
*University of California, Riverside*

James A. Duke
*Linfield College*

Jack Dutro
*Grays Harbor College*

Linda Enloe
*Idaho State University*

G. William Farthing
*University of Maine, Orono*

Howard Flock
*York University*

Nelson Freedman
*Queen's University at Kingston*

William C. Gordon
*University of New Mexico*

Paul Greene
*Iona College*

Philip M. Groves
*University of California, San Diego*

Norman Haltmayer
*Kilgore College*

W. H. Jack
*Franklin Pierce College*

G. Christian Jernstedt
*Dartmouth College*

Lawrence L. Jesky
*Seton Hill College*

Craig H. Jones
*Arkansas State University*

Michael Kaufman
*Daley College*

Kenneth Kotovsky
*Carnegie Mellon University*

Kevin M. McConkey
*Macquarie University*

Douglas Medin
*University of Michigan*

Howard B. Orenstein
*Western Maryland College*

Marcia Ozier
*Dalhousie University*

John B. Pittenger
*University of Arkansas, Little Rock*

John Polich
*Scripps Research Institute*

Jerome Sattler
*San Diego State University*

Barry Schwartz
*Swarthmore College*

Lance Shotland
*Penn State*

Steven Sloman
*Brown University*

Anna Smith
*Troy State University*

Eliot R. Smith
*Purdue University*

Michael D. Spiegler
*Providence College*

Cheryl L. Spinweber
*University of California, San Diego*

Timothy J. Strauman
*University of Wisconsin, Madison*

Harald Taukulis
*University of New Brunswick, Saint John*

Vernon Tupper
*Charles Stuart University, Mitchell*

Joseph W. Waterman
*University of Lowell*

Wilse B. Webb
*University of Florida*

Alexandria M. Weida
*University of Lowell*

Fred Whitford
*Montana State University*

Frank R. Williams
*Kilgore College*

Eugene Winograd
*Emory University*

Larry A. Wise
*Mt. Hood Community College*

# Contents in Brief

**Part I**    *Psychology as a Scientific and Human Endeavor*

1   Nature of Psychology    2

**Part II**    *Biological and Developmental Processes*

2   Biological Basis of Psychology    34
3   Psychological Development    70

**Part III**    *Consciousness and Perception*

4   Sensory Processes    126
5   Perception    164
6   Consciousness and Its Altered States    202

**Part IV**    *Learning, Remembering, and Thinking*

7   Learning and Conditioning    252
8   Memory    288
9   Thought and Language    330

**Part V**    *Motivation and Emotion*

10   Basic Motives    372
11   Emotion    416

**Part VI**    *Personality and Individuality*

12   Assessment of Mental Abilities    450
13   Personality Through the Life Course    488
14   Personality Theory and Assessment    524

**Part VII**    *Stress, Psychopathology, and Therapy*

15   Stress and Coping    576
16   Abnormal Psychology    616
17   Methods of Therapy    666

**Part VIII**    *Social Behavior*

18   Social Beliefs and Attitudes    712
19   Social Interaction and Influence    730

# Contents

**Preface V**

**Part I**    *Psychology as a Scientific and Human Endeavor*

### 1   Nature of Psychology   2

*Scope of Psychology*   4
*Perspectives in Psychology*   6
*Methods of Psychology*   13
    *Critical Discussion: Ethical Issues in*
      *Psychological Research*   20
*Fields of Psychology*   22
*Overview of the Book*   27

**Part II**    *Biological and Developmental Processes*

### 2   Biological Basis of Psychology 34

*Components of the Nervous System*   35
*Structure of the Brain*   42
    *Critical Discussion: Pictures of the Living Brain*   46
*Cerebral Hemisphere*   48
*Asymmetries in the Brain*   52
    *Critical Discussion: Language and the Brain*   56
*Autonomic Nervous System*   58
*Endocrine System*   60
*Genetic Influences on Behavior*   62

### 3   Psychological Development 70

*Basic Questions About Development*   71
*Capacities of the Newborn*   76

*Critical Discussion: Can Newborns Imitate? 78*

*Cognitive Development in Childhood 83*

*Social Development in Childhood 97*

*Critical Discussion: Can Sex Education Prevent Childhood Sexism? 108*

*Adolescent Development 111*

*Critical Discussion: Teenage Pregnancy and Contraceptive Use 116*

*Development as a Lifelong Process 116*

**Part III** *Consciousness and Perception*

Page 116-177

this

## 4 Sensory Processes 126

*Common Properties of Sensory Modalities 127*

*Critical Discussion: Decision Processes in Detection 132*

*Visual Sense 134*

*Auditory Sense 145*

*Critical Discussion: Artificial Ears and Eyes 152*

*Other Senses 151*

## 5 Perception 164

*Functions of Perception 165*

*Localization 166*

*Recognition 173*

*Critical Discussion: Breakdown of Recognition 186*

*Perceptual Constancies 187*

*Perceptual Development 191*

## 6 Consciousness and its Altered States 202

*Aspects of Consciousness 203*

*Divided Consciousness 207*

*Sleep and Dreams 210*

*Critical Discussion: Theories of Dream Sleep 218*

*Psychoactive Drugs 219*

*Critical Discussion: Drug Dependence 232*

Meditation   231

Hypnosis   235

Psi Phenomena   240


# Part IV   *Learning, Remembering, and Thinking*

## 7   Learning and Conditioning 252

Perspectives on Learning   253

Classical Conditioning   254

　　Critical Discussion: Neural Basis of Elementary Learning   264

Operant Conditioning   264

　　Critical Discussion: Economics of Reward   276

Complex Learning   278


## 8   Memory 288

Distinctions About Memory   289

Short-Term Memory   291

Long-Term Memory   298

　　Critical Discussion: Connectionist Models of Memory 304

Implicit Memory   311

　　Critical Discussion: Childhood Amnesia   312

Improving Memory   317

Constructive Memory   322


## 9   Thought and Language 330

Concepts and Categories   331

　　Critical Discussion: Linguistic Relativity Hypothesis   338

Reasoning   339

Language and Communication   344

Development of Language   350

　　Critical Discussion: Brain Localization   356

Imaginal Thought   359

Thought in Action: Problem Solving   361

# Part **V** *Motivation and Emotion*

## 10 Basic Motives 372

*Survival Motives and Homeostasis* 373
*Hunger* 377
*Obesity and Anorexia* 382
*Adult Sexuality* 393
*Early Sexual Development* 404
*Maternal Behavior* 407
   *Critical Discussion: Instincts and Maternal-Infant Behavior* 408
*Curiosity Motives* 410
*Common Principles for Different Motives* 413

## 11 Emotion 416

*Components of an Emotion* 417
*Arousal and Emotion* 418
   *Critical Discussion: Using Arousal to Detect Lies* 420
*Cognition and Emotion* 424
*Expression and Emotion* 429
*General Reactions to Being in an Emotional State* 435
*Aggression as an Emotional Reaction* 437

# Part **VI** *Personality and Individuality*

## 12 Assessment of Mental Abilities 450

*Ability Tests* 451
*Characteristics of a Good Test* 455
*Test of Intellectual Ability* 457
   *Critical Discussion: Coaching and Test Sophistication* 466
*Predictive Validity* 466
   *Critical Discussion: Sext Differences in Specific Abilities* 470
*Nature of Intelligence* 470
   *Critical Discussion: Multiple Intelligences* 476

*Genetic and Environmental Influences  478*

    *Critical Discussion: Race and Intelligence  484*

*Ability Tests in Perspective  482*


# 13  Personality Through the Life Course 488

*Childhood: Shaping of Personality  489*

    *Critical Discussion: Minnesota Study of Twins Reared Apart  492*

    *Critical Discussion: The Debate over Maternal Employment and Daycare  498*

*Adolescence: Constructing an Identity  508*

*Adulthood: Continuity of Personality  511*

    *Critical Discussion: Studying Personality the Long Way  512*


# 14  Personality Theory and Assessment 524

*Trait Approach  525*

*Psychoanalytic Approach  533*

*Social-Learning Approach  540*

*Phenomenological Approach  544*

*Personality Assessment  551*

    *Critical Discussion: Testimonial Validity and Other Nonsense  554*

*Consistency Paradox  564*

    *Critical Discussion: Are Our Intuitions about Consistency Wrong?  566*


# Part VII  *Stress, Psychopathology, and Psychotherapy*

## 15  Stress and Coping 576

*Characteristics of Stressful Events  578*

    *Critical Discussion: Sexual Abuse as a Major Stressor  582*

*Psychological Reactions to Stress  583*

*Physiological Reactions to Stress  587*

*How Stress Affects Health  591*

*Appraisals and Personality Styles as Mediators of Stress Responses  596*

*Coping Skills  602*

*Managing Stress  610*

    *Critical Discussion: Can Psychological Interventions Affect the Course of Cancer?  612*

## 16   Abnormal Psychology 616

*Abnormal Behavior*   617

*Anxiety Disorders*   624

*Mood Disorders*   635

   *Critical Discussion: Depression and Suicide*   638

   *Critical Discussion: Illusion and Well-Being*   644

*Personality Disorders*   658

   *Critical Discussion: Insanity as a Legal Defense*   662

## 17   Methods of Therapy 666

*Historical Backgrounds*   667

*Techniques of Psychotherapy*   673

*Effectiveness of Psychotherapy*   693

   *Critical Discussion: The Placebo Response*   698

*Biological Therapies*   698

*Enhancing Mental Health*   703

# Part  VIII  *Social Behavior*

## 18   Social Beliefs and Attitudes 712

*Intuitive Science of Social Beliefs*   713

   *Critical Discussion: Information Processing Biases:*
   *Cognitive or Motivational?*   726

*Attitudes*   725

*Interpersonal Attraction*   737

   *Critical Discussion: Passion through Misattribution*   742

## 19   Social Interaction and Influence 748

*Presence of Others*   749

   *Critical Discussion: Social Impact Theory*   758

*Interpersonal Influence*   759

   *Critical Discussion: Ethical Issues in Milgram's*
   *Obedience Experiments*   768

*Group Decision Making*   778

# APPENDIX I

*How to Read a Textbook: The PQRST Method* A-1

# APPENDIX II

*Brief History of Psychology* A-5

*Roots of Contemporary Psychology* A-5
*Schools of Psychology* A-7
*Recent Developments* A-11

# APPENDIX III

*Statistical Methods and Measurement* A-15

*Descriptive Statistics* A-15
*Statistical Inference* A-19
*Coefficient of Correlation* A-24
*Glossary* A-29

Copyrights and Acknowledgments and
   Illustration Credits A-61
References A-67
Index A-111

# Part I

*Psychology as a Scientific and Human Endeavor*

1 Nature of Psychology

NOTE TO THE STUDENT
*A method for effectively reading a textbook is described in Appendix I; you may wish to read the appendix before starting this chapter.*

*Flowers in a Garden*, 1897, by John Joseph Enneking (1841–1916), Oil on canvas, 30" × 22". Courtesy of Dr. and Mrs. John J. McDonough, via the Surovek Gallery, Palm Beach, Florida.

# Chapter 1

# Nature of Psychology

**Scope of Psychology 4**

**Perspectives in Psychology 6**
*Origins of Psychological Perspectives*
*Modern Perspectives*
*Relations among Perspectives*

**Methods of Psychology 13**
*Experimental Method*
*Correlational Method*
*Observational Method*
*Critical Discussion: Ethical Issues in Psychological Research*

**Fields of Psychology 22**
*Specializations within Psychology*
*Interdisciplinary Approaches*

**Overview of the Book 27**

Detail, *Flowers in a Garden*, 1897, by John Joseph Enneking.

No one today can afford *not* to know psychology; it touches virtually every aspect of your life. For example: How does the way your parents raised you affect the way you raise your own children? What is the best way to break a drug dependency? Can a man care for an infant as ably as a woman? Can you recall childhood experiences in more detail under hypnosis? How should instruments in a nuclear power plant be designed to minimize human error? What effect does prolonged stress have on your immune system? How effective is psychotherapy in treating depression? Can learning be improved by the use of drugs that facilitate neural transmission? Psychologists are working on these and many other questions.

Psychology also affects our life through its influence on laws and public policy. Psychological theories and research have influenced laws concerning discrimination, capital punishment, pornography, sexual behavior, and the conditions under which individuals may not be responsible for their actions. For example, laws pertaining to sexual deviancy have changed markedly in the past 40 years as research has shown that many sexual acts previously classed as perversions are "normal" in the sense that most people engage in them. Consider also the effect of television violence on children. Only since psychological studies provided evidence of the harmful effects of such programs has it been possible to modify television programming policies. Programs designed for children now contain less violence, and an effort is made to restrict particularly brutal television to late-evening viewing hours.

Because psychology affects so many aspects of our life, it is essential that even those who do not intend to specialize in the field know something about its basic facts and research methods. An introductory course in psychology should give you a better understanding of why people think and act as they do, and provide insights into your own attitudes and reactions. It should also help you evaluate the many claims made in the name of psychology. Everyone has seen newspaper headlines like these:

■ New drug discovered to improve memory
■ Anxiety controlled by self-regulation of brain waves
■ Proof of mental telepathy found
■ Hypnosis effective in the control of pain
■ Emotional stability closely related to family size
■ Homosexuality linked to parental attitudes
■ Transcendental meditation facilitates problem solving
■ Multiple personality linked to childhood abuse

You can judge the validity of such claims in part by knowing what psychological facts have been firmly established; you can then assess whether the new claim is compatible with these established facts. You can also judge the validity in part by knowing the kind of evidence necessary to give credence to a new "discovery," so that you can determine whether the arguments in support of the new claim meet the usual standards of evidence. This book reviews the current state of knowledge in psychology—that is, it tries to present the most important, established facts in the field. It also examines the nature of research—that is, how a psychologist designs a research program that is capable of providing strong evidence for or against a hypothesis.

In this chapter, we first consider the kinds of *topics* that are studied in psychology. Next we discuss the *perspectives* that psychologists adopt in investigating these topics. Then we describe the *research methods* used in psychological investigations, and after that discussion, we turn to the various specializations or *fields of psychology*. Finally, we briefly overview the contents of the rest of the book.

# Scope of Psychology

Psychology can be defined as the *scientific study of behavior and mental processes*. An astonishing variety of topics is covered by this definition. To get a better grasp on this variety, we briefly describe five representative problems psychologists examine. (All of these problems will be discussed in more detail at various points in the text.)

**LIVING WITH A DIVIDED BRAIN**  The human brain is divided into a left and a right hemisphere. Normally, the two hemispheres are connected by a band of neural fibers. But some people who suffer from severe epilepsy have had these fibers surgically disconnected and are living with a divided brain (this separation prevents a seizure that originates in one hemisphere from spreading to the other). Casual interaction with such people would not indicate anything unusual. But psychological experiments show that a split-brain person can have unusual perceptual and conscious experiences, and these experiences tell us a good deal about normal consciousness.

In a standard experiment, a split-brain person is seated in front of a screen that hides his hands from view (see Figure 1-1). The word "nut" is flashed very briefly on the screen in such a way that its image goes only to the right hemisphere of the person's brain. Because the right hemisphere controls the left side of the body, the subject can use his left hand to pick out a nut from a pile of tools hidden from view. But the subject cannot tell the experimenter what word flashed on the screen, because speech is controlled by the left hemisphere and the image of "nut" was not transmitted to that hemisphere. When asked what his left hand is doing, the split-brain person cannot answer! The normal unity of conscious experience has been disrupted.

**CONDITIONED FEAR**  Suppose a rat is placed in an enclosed compartment and periodically subjected to mild electric shock through the floor. Just before the shock occurs a tone sounds. After the tone and shock have been presented in succession a number of times, the tone alone will produce reactions that are indicative of fear, including crouching and defecating. The animal is said to have a **conditioned fear** of what was once an innocuous stimulus.

Many human fears may be learned this way, particularly in early childhood. Suppose a young child is subjected to repeated physical or emotional abuse by a particular relative. After a number of painful experiences, the mere sound of the relative's voice may elicit a fear reaction in the child. Such a fear, learned with little thought or conscious awareness, is hard to combat by verbal assurances ("There's nothing to be afraid of now."). But the fear

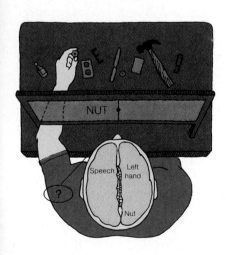

**FIGURE 1-1**
**Testing the Abilities of the Two Hemispheres** *The split-brain subject correctly retrieves an object by touch with the left hand when its name is flashed to the right hemisphere, but he cannot name the object or describe what he has done.*

may be reduced by a form of therapy that is based on the principles of conditioning, discussed in Chapters 7 and 17.

**CHILDHOOD AMNESIA** Most adults, even elderly ones, can recall events from their early years. But only up to a certain point. Virtually no one can recall many events from the first 3 years of life. Consider a significant event like the birth of a sibling. If the birth occurred after you were 3 years old you may have some memory of it, the amount you recall being greater the older you were at the time of the birth. But if the birth occurred before age 3, most people have trouble recalling a single incident about the event (see Figure 1-2).

This phenomenon, discovered by Sigmund Freud, is called **childhood amnesia.** It is particularly striking because our first three years are so rich in experience. So much is new in a way that it never will be again; we develop from helpless newborns to crawling, babbling infants to walking, talking children. But these remarkable transitions leave little trace on our memory.

**OBESITY** Roughly 35 million Americans are obese, which technically means they are 30 percent or more above the appropriate weight for their body structure and height. Unfortunately, obesity can be a stigma in our society. Obesity is also dangerous—it contributes to a higher incidence of diabetes, high blood pressure, and heart disease. At the other end of the spectrum, some people (especially young women) suffer from **anorexia nervosa,** a disorder in which people severely restrict their eating, sometimes to the point of self-imposed starvation. Anorexia can even result in death.

Psychologists are interested in what factors lead people to eat too much or too little. One factor seems to be a history of deprivation. If rats are first deprived of food, then allowed to feed back to normal weights, and finally allowed to eat as much as they want, they eat more than other rats who have no history of deprivation. In this instance prior deprivation leads to subsequent overeating. This may explain why many cases of anorexia paradoxically record binge eating as well: the deprivation required to stay thin eventually leads to overeating.

**EXPRESSION OF AGGRESSION** Many people believe that they can lessen their aggressive feelings by expressing them either directly or vicariously. Psychological research indicates the opposite is more often the case. To study vicarious expression of aggression, researchers have looked at children's viewing of television. In one experiment, one group of children watched violent cartoons, while another group watched nonviolent cartoons for the same amount of time. The children who watched violent cartoons became more aggressive in their interactions with peers, whereas the children who viewed nonviolent cartoons showed no change in aggression. Moreover, these effects of television violence can be lasting: the more violent programs a boy watches at age 9, the more aggressive he is likely to be at age 19 (see Figure 1-3).

These five problems—split-brain perception, conditioned fear, childhood amnesia, weight control, and expression of aggression—will surface again in our discussion of perspectives in psychology.

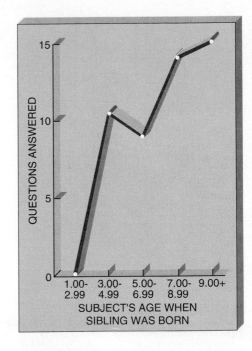

**FIGURE 1-2**
**Recall of an Early Memory** *In an experiment on childhood amnesia, college-age subjects were asked 20 questions about the events surrounding the birth of a younger sibling. The average number of questions answered is plotted as a function of the subject's age when the sibling was born. If the birth occurred before the fourth year of life, no subject could recall a thing about it; if the birth occurred after that, recall increased with age at the time of the event.* (After Sheingold & Tenney, 1982)

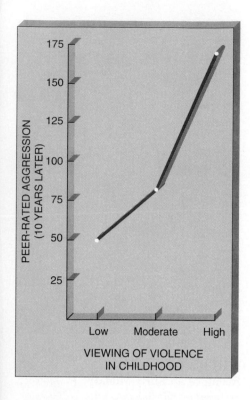

**FIGURE 1-3**
**Relationship between Childhood Viewing of Violent Television and Adult Aggression** *Preference for viewing violent TV programs by boys at age 9 is related to aggressive behavior as rated by peers at age 19.* (After Eron, Huesmann, Lefkowitz, & Walder, 1972)

# Perspectives in Psychology

Any topic in psychology can be approached from a variety of perspectives. Indeed, this is true of any action a person takes. Suppose you walk across the street. From a **biological perspective,** this act can be described as the firing of the nerves that activate the muscles that move the legs that transport you across the street. From a **behavioral perspective,** the act can be described without reference to anything within your body; rather, the green light is interpreted as a stimulus to which you respond by crossing the street. One may also take a **cognitive perspective** of crossing the street, focusing on the *mental processes* involved in producing the behavior. From a cognitive perspective, your action might be explained in terms of your goals and plans: your goal is to visit a friend, and crossing the street is part of your plan for achieving that goal.

While there are many possible ways to describe any psychological act, the following five perspectives represent the major approaches to the modern study of psychology. These five include the three mentioned above—biological, behavioral, and cognitive—plus two others: **psychoanalytic** and **phenomenological** (see Figure 1-4). Because some of these perspectives arose in reaction to other views, we first consider the origin of psychological perspectives, and then describe the five contemporary perspectives.

## Origins of Psychological Perspectives*

The roots of modern psychology can be traced to the fourth and fifth centuries B.C. The great Greek philosophers Socrates, Plato, and Aristotle posed fundamental questions about mental life. For example: Do people perceive reality correctly? What is consciousness? Are people inherently rational or irrational? Are people capable of free choice? These questions, as important now as they were two thousand years ago, deal with the nature of *mind* and mental processes, rather than with the nature of *body* or *behavior,* and are precursors to a cognitive perspective.

The biological perspective has an equally long history. Hippocrates, usually credited as the "father of medicine," lived at roughly the same time as Socrates, and was much interested in *physiology* (the branch of biology that studies the normal functions of the living organism and its parts). He made many important observations about how the brain controls various organs of the body, which set the stage for the modern approach to physiology and the biological perspective in psychology.

Two millennia later, in the latter part of the nineteenth century, scientific psychology was born. The fundamental idea behind its inception was that mind and behavior—like the planets or chemicals or human organs—could be the subject of scientific analysis. That is, by systematically varying the situations presented to people, their minds and behaviors could be analyzed into more basic components. The beginning of psychology involved some mixing of the questions of philosophy and the methods of physiology,

---

*A fuller history of psychology is presented in Appendix II.

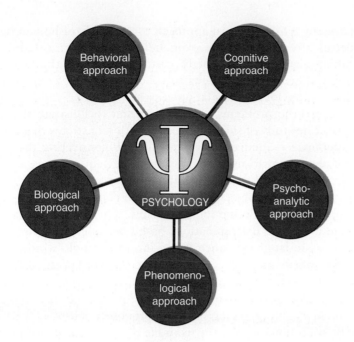

**FIGURE 1-4**
**Perspectives in Psychology** *The analysis of psychological phenomena can be approached from several perspectives. Each offers a somewhat different explanation of why individuals act as they do, and each can make a contribution to our conception of the total person. The Greek letter psi, ψ, is sometimes used as an abbreviation for psychology.*

but these two approaches were distinct enough to emerge as the cognitive and biological perspectives to psychology.

The nineteenth-century version of the biological perspective differed markedly from the current version because relatively little was then known about the nervous system. Still, the development of this perspective has been more continuous than that of the cognitive perspective. The nineteenth-century cognitive perspective focused mainly on mental experiences, and its data were largely self-observations in the form of **introspections.** Introspection refers to an individual's observation and recording of the nature of his or her own perceptions, thoughts, and feelings; for example, self-reflections on one's immediate sensory impressions of a stimulus, such as the flash of a colored light. This extreme reliance on introspection, particularly for very rapid mental events, proved unworkable. Even after receiving extensive training in introspecting, different people produced very different introspections about simple sensory experiences, and little could be made of these differences. Introspectionism is not a critical part of the current cognitive perspective. As we will see, reactions by some psychologists to introspection played a role in the development of other modern perspectives.

## Modern Perspectives

Because the five perspectives of interest are discussed throughout the book, we provide here only a brief description of some main points. Also keep in mind that these approaches need not be mutually exclusive; rather, they may focus on different aspects of the same complex phenomenon.

**BIOLOGICAL PERSPECTIVE** The human brain contains well over 10 billion nerve cells and an almost infinite number of interconnections. It may well be the most complex structure in the universe. In principle, all psychological events correspond in some manner to the activity of the brain and

*Chop 1.*
*Pg 267*

*Biol. Psychology*

nervous system. The biological approach to the study of human beings and other species attempts to relate overt behavior to electrical and chemical events taking place inside the body, particularly within the brain and nervous system. This approach seeks to specify the *neurobiological* processes that underlie behavior and mental processes.

We can use the problems described earlier to illustrate the biological perspective. The study of split-brain patients demonstrates that normal conscious experience is mediated by neural fibers connecting the two hemispheres of the brain; it also tells us where certain abilities are localized within the brain. Recall that if a word is presented only to the right hemisphere of a split-brain subject, the person can correctly select by touch the named object from a pile hidden from view. This indicates that the right hemisphere can make discriminations based on touch, and also that it can understand some language, since it can interpret single words. Recall further that the split-brain subject cannot name the word presented. This indicates that only the left hemisphere has the power of speech.

The biological perspective has also made progress in the study of learning and memory. Neurobiologists have proposed cell-by-cell accounts of learning by conditioning, as in the example of a rat being conditioned to fear a tone. The gist of these accounts is that conditioning involves changes in connections between **neurons,** or nerve cells, where these neural changes are themselves mediated by alterations in the amount of certain chemicals produced in the brain. The biological approach to memory has emphasized the importance of certain brain structures, including the **hippocampus,** which is involved in consolidating memories. Childhood amnesia may be partly due to an immature hippocampus, since this brain structure is not fully developed until a year or two after birth.

*By studying the brain activity of animals, researchers gain insight into the human brain. In this single-cell recording experiment a microelectrode, which monitors the electrical activity of a single neuron, is implanted in the visual system of an anesthetized monkey.*

The biological perspective has had similar successes in the study of motivation and emotion, particularly with other species. We know from work with rats, cats, and monkeys that there are certain regions in the brain that when electrically stimulated produce excessive overeating and obesity, and other nearby regions that when stimulated produce aggressive behavior. While human obesity and aggression involve far more than stimulation of these particular regions, these studies with animals provide some idea of the contribution that biology alone makes to human motives and emotions.

**BEHAVIORAL PERSPECTIVE**  A person eats breakfast, rides a bike, talks, blushes, laughs, and cries. These are forms of behavior—the activities of an organism that can be observed. With the behavioral approach, a psychologist studies individuals by looking at their behavior rather than at their brain and nervous system.

The view that behavior should be the sole subject matter of psychology was first advanced by the American psychologist John B. Watson in the early 1900s. Before that, the dominant nonbiological approach was the nineteenth-century cognitive perspective, with its emphasis on introspection. Watson noted that introspections have a private quality that distinguishes them from observations in other fields of science. Any qualified scientist can replicate an observation in the natural sciences, whereas the introspective observation can be reported by only one observer—the person engaging in the introspection. In contrast, other people *can* observe your behavior, including verbal behavior about your perceptions and feelings. Watson maintained that only by studying what people do—their behavior—is an objective science of psychology possible.

**Behaviorism,** as Watson's position came to be called, helped shape the course of psychology during the first half of this century. One offshoot of behaviorism, **stimulus-response psychology,** is still influential. Stimulus-response psychology (S-R psychology) studies the relevant stimuli in the environment, the responses that are elicited by these stimuli, and the rewards or punishments that follow these responses.

Again we can use our sample problems to illustrate the approach. In conditioned fear, the critical stimuli are the tone and the electric shock (recall that the tone consistently precedes the shock), and the relevant responses include withdrawal, defecation, and other specific behaviors associated with fear. Conditioning involves coming to respond to the tone in a fashion similar to how the organism naturally responds to the shock. This change is a consequence of the tone reliably preceding the shock.

Similar analyses have proven useful in the areas of obesity and aggression. Some people may overeat (a specific response) only in the presence of specific stimuli, and learning to avoid these stimuli is now part of many weight-control programs. With regard to aggression, children are more likely to express aggressive responses, such as hitting another child, when such responses are rewarded—the other child withdraws—then when their responses are punished—the other child counterattacks.

A strict behavioral approach does not consider the individual's mental processes. Psychologists other than behaviorists will often record what a person says about his or her conscious experiences (a verbal report), and from this objective data draw inferences about the person's mental activity. But, by and large, behavioral psychologists have chosen not to conjecture about the mental processes that intervene between the stimulus and the response

*Language is a uniquely human activity.*

(Skinner, 1981).* Today, few psychologists would regard themselves as strict behaviorists. Nevertheless, many modern developments in psychology have evolved from the work of behaviorists.

**COGNITIVE PERSPECTIVE**  The modern cognitive perspective is in part a reaction to behaviorism and in part a return to the cognitive roots of psychology. Like the nineteenth-century version, the modern study of cognition is concerned with mental processes, such as perceiving, remembering, reasoning, deciding, and problem solving. Unlike the nineteenth-century version, however, modern cognitivism is not based on introspection. Thus, the modern study of cognition is premised on the assumptions that: (a) only by studying mental processes can we fully understand what organisms do; and (b) we can study mental processes in an objective fashion by focusing on specific behaviors, just as the behaviorists do, but interpreting them in terms of underlying mental processes. In making these interpretations, cognitive psychologists often rely on an analogy between the mind and a computer. Incoming information is processed in various ways: it is selected, compared and combined with other information already in memory, transformed, rearranged, and so on.

The cognitive perspective (which from here on refers to the modern version) developed partly in reaction to the narrowness of the S-R view. To conceive of human actions solely in terms of stimulus and response may be adequate for the study of simple forms of behavior, but this approach neglects too many important areas of human functioning. People can reason, plan, make decisions on the basis of remembered information, and, perhaps most striking of all, use language to communicate with one another. But these more complex phenomena are somewhat neglected by the behavioral perspective.

We can use our sample problems to illustrate the cognitive approach. The rat learning to fear a tone may actually be developing a hypothesis that "If you hear a tone, a painful shock is coming." And it is this hypothesis that is responsible for the animal's reactions. The phenomenon of childhood amnesia also lends itself to a cognitive analysis. Perhaps we cannot remember events from the first few years of life because we change the way we organize our experience in memory. Such changes may be particularly pronounced around age 3 because at that point there is a great increase in our language abilities, and language offers us a new way of organizing our memories.

Cognitive analyses can also be used in the study of obesity and aggression. Some obese people fit the following pattern: they diet successfully for a while, then break down and overeat so excessively that they eventually consume more calories than they would have had they not dieted at all. The critical factor here seems to be a breakdown of a plan, and the feelings of lack of control that ensue from this loss of cognitive control. With regard to aggression, the importance of cognition or knowledge is straightforward. If someone insults you, you are far more likely to return the verbal aggression if the person is an acquaintance than if he or she is a mental patient you do not know. In both cases, acquaintance and mental patient, the stimulus

---

*Throughout this book you will find references, cited by author and date, that document or expand the statements made here. Detailed publishing information on these studies appears in the reference list at the end of the book. The reference list also tells you the pages in this book on which the citation appears.

situation is roughly the same; what differs is what you know about the other person, and it is this *knowledge* that controls your behavior.

**PSYCHOANALYTIC PERSPECTIVE** The psychoanalytic conception of human behavior was developed by Sigmund Freud in Europe about the same time behaviorism was evolving in the United States. Freud was a physician by training, but he knew about the cognitive developments then going on in Europe. In some respects his psychoanalysis was a blend of nineteenth-century versions of cognition and physiology. In particular, Freud combined then-current cognitive notions of consciousness, perception, and memory, with ideas about biologically based instincts to forge a bold new theory of human behavior.

The basic assumption of Freud's theory is that much of our behavior stems from unconscious processes. By **unconscious process** Freud meant beliefs, fears, and desires a person is unaware of but that nevertheless influence behavior. He believed that many of the impulses that are forbidden or punished by parents and society during childhood are derived from innate instincts. Because each of us is born with these impulses, they exert a pervasive influence that must be dealt with in some manner. Forbidding them merely forces them out of awareness into the unconscious, where they remain to affect dreams, slips of speech, or mannerisms, and to manifest themselves as emotional problems, symptoms of mental illness, or, on the other hand, socially approved behavior such as artistic and literary activity.

Freud believed that all of our actions have a cause but that the cause is often some unconscious motive rather than the rational reason we may give. Freud's view of human nature was essentially negative; he believed that we are driven by the same basic instincts as animals (primarily sex and aggression) and that we are continually struggling against a society that stresses the control of these impulses. While most psychologists do not completely accept Freud's view of the unconscious, they would probably agree that individuals are not fully aware of some important aspects of their personality.

The psychoanalytic perspective suggests new ways of looking at some of our sample problems. According to Freud (1905), childhood amnesia arises because some emotional experiences in the first few years of life are so traumatic that allowing them to enter consciousness years later (that is, remembering them) would cause the individual to be overwhelmed by anxiety. With regard to obesity, it is known that some people overeat when anxious. The psychoanalytic perspective suggests that these people may be responding to an anxiety-producing situation by doing the one thing that has brought them comfort all their lives—namely, eating. And of course, psychoanalysis has much to say about the expression of aggression. Freud claimed that aggression is an instinct, which means that people aggress to express an inborn desire. While this proposal is not widely accepted in human psychology, it is in agreement with the views of some biologists and psychologists who study aggression in animals.

**PHENOMENOLOGICAL PERSPECTIVE** Unlike the other approaches we have considered, the phenomenological perspective focuses almost entirely on *subjective experience*. It is concerned with the individual's personal view of events—the individual's **phenomenology**. This approach developed partly as a reaction to what phenomenologists perceived as the overly mechanistic quality of the other perspectives to psychology. Thus, phenomenological psychologists tend to reject the notion that behavior is con-

*Sigmund Freud*

trolled by external stimuli (behaviorism), or by just the processing of information in perception and memory (cognitive psychology), or by unconscious impulses (psychoanalytic theories). Also, phenomenological psychologists have different goals than psychologists operating from the other perspectives: they are concerned more with describing the inner life and experiences of individuals than with developing theories or predicting behavior.

Some phenomenological theories are called *humanistic* because they emphasize those qualities that distinguish people from animals: for example, the drive toward self-actualization. According to humanistic theories, an individual's principal motivational force is a tendency toward growth and **self-actualization.** All of us have a basic need to develop our potential to the fullest, to progress beyond where we are now. Although we may be blocked by environmental and social obstacles, our natural tendency is toward actualizing our potential.

Phenomenological or humanistic psychology has been more aligned with literature and the humanities than with science. For this reason, it is difficult to give detailed descriptions of what the phenomenological perspective would say about our sample problems, such as conditioned fear and childhood amnesia, because these are not the kinds of problems that phenomenologists study. In fact, some humanists reject scientific psychology altogether, claiming that its methods can contribute nothing to an understanding of human nature. This position, which is incompatible with our definition of psychology, seems far too extreme. The humanistic view makes a valuable point as a warning that psychology needs to focus its attention on solving problems relevant to human welfare rather than studying isolated bits of behavior that happen to lend themselves to an easy scientific analysis. But to assume that problems of mind and behavior can be solved by discarding all that we have learned about scientific methods of investigation seems fallacious.

## Relations among Perspectives

The biological perspective is at a different level than the other perspectives. The biological perspective uses concepts and principles that are drawn from physiology and other branches of biology, whereas the other perspectives rely on concepts and principles that are purely psychological (concepts such as perception, memory, the unconscious, and self-actualization).

There is a way, though, in which the biological perspective makes direct contact with the more psychological perspectives. Biologically oriented researchers attempt to explain psychological concepts and principles in terms of their biological counterparts. For example, researchers might attempt to explain the conditioning of fear *solely* in terms of changes in neural connections in a certain region of the brain. Because this attempt involves reducing psychological notions to biological ones, this kind of explanation is called **reductionism.** Throughout this book we will present examples in which reductionism has been successful; that is, situations in which what was once understood at only the psychological level is now understood at the biological level.

If reductionism can be successful, why bother with psychological explanations at all? To put it another way, is psychology just something to do until the biologists get around to figuring everything out? The answer is a resounding *No*. First and foremost, there seem to be many principles that can be stated *only* at the psychological level.

To illustrate, consider a principle about human memory, namely, that memory preserves the meaning of a message and not the actual symbols used to communicate the meaning. So, two minutes after being presented some lines of text, people have no memory for the exact words used, although they do remember the meaning of the message. This principle seems to hold regardless of whether the message is read or heard. But because some of the biological (brain) processes involved are different for reading and listening, any attempt to reduce our psychological principle to the biological level would end up with two separate subprinciples—one for reading and one for listening. The single overarching principle would therefore be lost. There are many examples of this sort, and they justify the need for a psychological level of explanation that is distinct from the biological level (Fodor, 1981).

A second reason for having a psychological level of explanation is that psychological concepts and principles can be used to direct biological researchers in their work. Given that the brain contains billions of brain cells and countless interconnections, biological researchers cannot hope to find something of interest by arbitrarily selecting some brain cells to study. Rather, they must have a way of directing their search to relevant groups of brain cells. Psychological findings can supply this direction. For example, if psychological research indicates that conditioning is a slow process that is hard to undo, then biological psychologists can direct their attention to brain processes that are relatively slow but that permanently alter neural connections (Churchland & Sejnowski, 1988).

Perspectives at the psychological level—particularly behavioral, cognitive, and psychoanalytic—are sometimes mutually compatible, and sometimes competitive. The perspectives tend to be compatible when they focus on different aspects of the same phenomenon. For example, with regard to obesity there may be different reasons why people overeat, some of which are biological (for example, a genetic predisposition to be obese), some of which are behavioral (for example, the stimuli of a holiday-meal situation trigger overeating), and some of which are psychoanalytic (for example, eating is a familiar means of reducing anxiety). The perspectives are competitive when they offer different explanations for the very same phenomenon. This kind of conflict will arise many times throughout this book. Such a conflict may indicate only that our knowledge of the relevant phenomenon is imperfect. As more is learned about the phenomenon, the views may become compatible with one another. An initial conflict among the views may thus be just another step in the ongoing process of scientific psychology.

## Methods of Psychology

Now that we have some idea of the topics studied in psychology and the perspectives adopted in studying them, we can consider the research methods used to investigate them.

As mentioned earlier, psychology can be defined as the *scientific study of behavior and mental processes*. The term "scientific" means that the research methods used to collect data are (a) *unbiased*, in that they do not favor one hypothesis over another; and (b) *objective*, in that they allow other qualified people to repeat the observations and obtain the same results. The various methods to be considered next have these two characteristics. While some of the methods are used more by certain perspectives than others, each method can be used with each perspective. The only exception is that some phenomenological psychologists reject scientific methods entirely.

## Experimental Method

**CONTROL OF VARIABLES**  The typical scientific method is the **experimental method.** The investigator carefully controls conditions—often in a laboratory—and takes measurements in order to discover *relations among variables* (a variable is something that can occur with different values). For example, an experiment might seek to discover the relation between the variables of learning ability and age; to the extent that learning ability changes systematically with increasing age, an orderly relation between these two variables has been found.

The ability to exercise precise control over variables distinguishes the experimental method from other methods of scientific observation. If the experimenter seeks to discover whether learning ability depends on the amount of sleep a person has had, the amount of sleep can be controlled by arranging to have several groups of subjects spend the night in the laboratory. Two groups might be allowed to go to sleep at 11:00 P.M. and 1:00 A.M., respectively, and a third group might be kept awake until 4:00 A.M. By waking all the subjects at the same time, for example, 7:00 A.M., and giving each the same learning task, the experimenter can determine whether the subjects with more sleep learn more than those with less sleep.

In this study, the amount of sleep is called the **independent variable** because it is independent of what the subject does (the subject does not determine how much sleep he or she gets, the experimenter does). The amount learned is called the **dependent variable** because its values ultimately depend on the values of the independent variable. The dependent

*A researcher in a sleep laboratory monitors the brain activity of a sleeping woman.*

variable is almost inevitably some measure of the subject's behavior. The phrase "is a function of" is used to express the dependency of one variable on another. Thus, for this experiment we could say that the subjects' ability to learn a new task *is a function of* the amount of sleep they had.

An experiment concerned with the effect of marijuana on memory may make clearer the distinction between independent and dependent variables. When subjects arrived at the laboratory, they were given an oral dose of marijuana in a cookie. All subjects were given the same type of cookie and the same instructions. But the dosage level of the marijuana was different: one group of subjects received 5 milligrams of THC, the active ingredient in marijuana, a second group received 10 milligrams of THC, a third group got 15 milligrams, and a fourth group 20 milligrams.

After consuming the marijuana, the subjects were required to memorize several lists of unrelated words. One week later, the subjects were brought back to the laboratory and asked to recall as many words as possible. Figure 1-5 shows the percentage of words recalled for each of the four groups. Note that recall decreases as a function of the amount of marijuana taken at the time the subject studied the lists.

The experimenters had worked out a careful plan before bringing the subjects to the laboratory. Except for the dosage of marijuana, they held all conditions constant: the general setting for the experiment, the instructions to the subjects, the material to be memorized, the time allowed for memorization, and the conditions under which recall was tested. The only factor permitted to vary across the four groups was the dosage of marijuana—the independent variable. The dependent variable was the amount of material recalled one week later. The marijuana dosage was measured in milligrams of THC; memory was measured by the percentage of words recalled. The experimenters could plot the relation between the independent and dependent variables as shown in Figure 1-5. Finally, the experimenters used enough subjects (a sample of 20 per group) to justify expecting similar results if the experiment were repeated with a different sample of subjects. The letter $N$ is generally used to denote the number of subjects in each group; in this study, $N = 20$.

The experimental method can be used outside the laboratory as well as inside. For example, it is possible to investigate the effects of different psychotherapeutic methods by trying these methods on separate but similar groups of emotionally troubled individuals. The experimental method is a matter of logic, not of location. Still, most experiments take place in special laboratories, chiefly because precision instruments are usually necessary to control the presentation of stimuli and to obtain exact measures of behavior.

**EXPERIMENTAL DESIGN**  The expression **experimental design** refers to the procedure used in collecting data. The simplest experimental designs are those in which the investigator manipulates one independent variable and studies its effect on one dependent variable (as was the case in the above marijuana study). Because everything is held constant except the independent variable, at the end of the experiment a statement like this can be made: "With everything else constant, when X is increased, Y also increases." Or, in other cases: "When X is increased, Y decreases." Almost any content can fit into this kind of statement, as is indicated by the following examples: (a) "When the dosage of THC is increased, the recall of memorized material decreases"; (b) "The more televised aggression children are exposed to, the more aggressively they will act with other children"; (c)

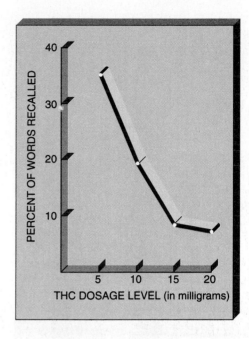

**FIGURE 1-5**
**Marijuana and Memory** *Subjects memorized word lists after taking varying dosages of THC (the active ingredient in marijuana). Recall tests administered a week later measured how much of the memorized material was retained. The figure shows the relationship between dosage level (independent variable) and recall score (dependent variable).* (After Darley et al., 1973a)

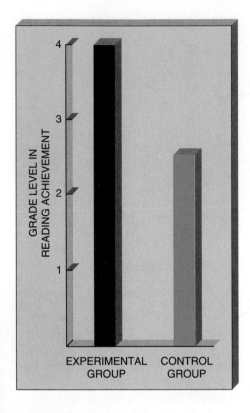

**FIGURE 1-6**
**Experimental and Control Groups**
*Each day, grade-school children in the experimental group participated in a computer-assisted instruction (CAI) program in reading. The computer was programmed to present different types of materials and instructions to each student, depending on the difficulty a student was having at any point in the reading curriculum. CAI has the advantage of working with each student in a highly individualized way, concentrating on those areas in which the student is having the most difficulty. The control group had no supplementary CAI in reading. At the end of the third grade, all students in both groups were given a standardized reading test. In this experiment, the independent variable is the presence or absence of CAI; the dependent variable is the student's score on the reading test. As the figure indicates, students in the experimental group scored higher on the test than students in the control group, suggesting that CAI had been beneficial* (After Atkinson, 1974). *Similar experiments indicate that CAI benefits learning of other subject matters as well* (Reiser et al., 1989).

"When the physical frequency of a tone is increased, the perceived pitch increases"; or (d) "The more prolonged stress one is under, the greater the likelihood of ulcers."

Sometimes an experiment focuses only on the influence of a single condition, which can be either present or absent (an independent variable with two values, presence and absence). The experimental design calls for an **experimental group** with the condition present and a **control group** with the condition absent. The results of such an experiment are presented in Figure 1-6. Inspecting the figure, we see that the experimental group, which received computer-assisted learning, scored higher on reading achievement tests than the control group, which did not receive such instruction.

Limiting an investigation to only one independent variable is too restrictive for some problems. It may be necessary to study how several independent variables interact to produce an effect on one or even several dependent variables. Studies involving the simultaneous manipulation of several variables are called **multivariate experiments** and are frequently used in psychological research.

**MEASUREMENT** Psychologists using the experimental method often find it necessary to make statements about amounts or quantities. Sometimes the variables can be measured by physical means—for example, hours of sleep deprivation, dosage level of a drug, or time required to press a brake pedal when a light flashes. Other times variables have to be scaled in a manner that places them in some sort of order; in rating a patient's feelings of aggression, a psychotherapist might use a five-point scale ranging from "never" through "rarely," "sometimes," "often," and "always." Thus, for purposes of precise communication, numbers are assigned to variables; this process is referred to as **measurement.**

Experiments usually involve making measurements on not just one subject, but on a sample of many subjects. The outcome of the research is therefore data in the form of a set of numbers that must be summarized and interpreted. Basic to this task is **statistics,** the discipline that deals with sampling data from a population of individuals and then drawing inferences about the population from that sample. Statistics plays an important role not only in experimental research, but in other methods as well.* The most common statistic is the **mean,** which is simply the technical term for an arithmetic average. It is the sum of a set of scores divided by the number of scores. In studies involving an experimental and control group, there are two means to be compared: a mean for the scores of the subjects in the experimental group, and a mean for the scores of the subjects in the control group. The difference between these two means is, of course, what interests us.

If the difference between the means is large, we may accept it at face value. But what if the difference is small? What if our measures are subject to error? What if a few extreme cases are producing the difference? Statisticians have solved these problems by developing tests of the *significance of a difference.* A psychologist who says that the difference between the experimental group and the control group is "statistically significant" means that a

---

*This discussion is designed to give the reader a brief introduction to the problems of measurement and statistics. A more thorough discussion is provided in Appendix III.

statistical test has been applied to the data and that the observed difference is trustworthy. In other words, the statistical test indicates that the difference observed is, in fact, due to the effect of the independent variable rather than an unlucky accident of chance factors or a few extreme cases.

## Correlational Method

**NATURALLY OCCURRING DIFFERENCES** Not all problems are susceptible to the experimental method. There are many situations where the investigator has no control over which subjects go in which conditions. For example, if we want to test the hypothesis that anorexic people are more sensitive to changes in taste than normal-weight people, we cannot select a group of normal-weight subjects and require half of them to become anorexic! Rather, we select people who are already anorexic or already of normal weight and see if they also differ in taste sensitivity. More generally, we can use the **correlational method** to determine whether some variable that is not under our control is associated, or *correlated*, with another variable of interest.

**COEFFICIENT OF CORRELATION** In the above example, there were only two values of the weight variable—anorexic and normal. It is more common to have many values of each variable, and to determine the degree to which values on one variable are correlated with values on another. This determination is made by using a statistic called the **coefficient of correlation,** symbolized by the lowercase letter $r$. The correlation coefficient is an estimate of the degree to which two variables are related and is expressed as a number between 0 and 1. No relation is indicated by 0; a perfect relation is indicated by 1. As $r$ goes from 0 to 1, the strength of the relation increases.

The nature of a correlation coefficient can be made clearer by examining a graphic presentation of data from an actual study. In this study, subjects were tested for their susceptibility to hypnosis and were given a score: a low score indicated minimal susceptibility, whereas a high score indicated that they were easily hypnotized. Several weeks later, they were tested again to obtain a second measure of their susceptibility to hypnosis. The study was concerned with how effectively one can predict hypnotizability on one occasion from performance on a prior occasion. Each tally mark in Figure 1-7 represents the results for one subject on the two tests. For example, note that two subjects made scores of 1 on both test days (the two tallies in the box to the lower left), and two subjects made scores of 13 on both days (box to upper right). One subject (see lower right portion of diagram) made a score of 11 on the first test but only 5 on the second test, and so on.

If all subjects had exactly the same score on both tests, all of the tallies would have fallen in the diagonal squares (in yellow), and the coefficient of correlation would have been $r = 1$. Enough tallies fell to either side, however, so that the correlation was $r = .86$. A correlation of .86 indicates that the first test of hypnotizability is a very good, but not perfect, predictor of hypnotizability on a later occasion. The numerical method for calculating a correlation coefficient is described in Appendix III. At this point, however, we will set forth some rules of thumb that will help you interpret correlation coefficients when you encounter them in later chapters.

A correlation can be either + or −. The sign of the correlation indicates whether the two variables are positively or negatively correlated. For example, suppose the number of times a student is absent from class correlates

**FIGURE 1-7**
**Scatter Diagram Illustrating Correlation** *Each tally indicates the scores of one subject on two separate tests of hypnotic susceptibility. Tallies in the yellow area indicate identical scores on both tests; those between the dark blue lines indicate a difference of no more than one point between the two scores. The correlation of r = +.86 means that the performances were fairly consistent on the 2 days. There were 49 subjects in this study; thus, N = 49.*
(After Hilgard, 1961)

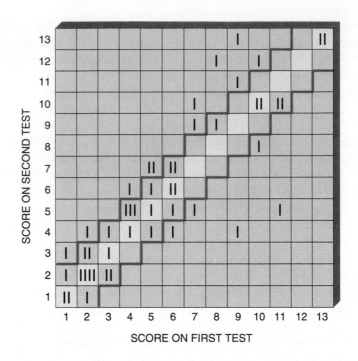

$-.40$ with the final course grade (the more absences, the lower the grade). Then the correlation between the number of classes *attended* and the course grade would be $+.40$. The strength of the relation is the same, but the sign indicates whether we are looking at classes missed or classes attended.

As the strength of the relation between two variables increases, $r$ goes from 0 to 1. To appreciate this, consider a few known correlation coefficients:

- A correlation coefficient of about .75 between grades received in the first year of college and grades received in the second year.
- A correlation of about .70 between scores on an intelligence test given at age 7 and a retest of intelligence at age 18.
- A correlation of about .50 between the height of a parent and the adult height of the child.
- A correlation of about .40 between scores on scholastic aptitude tests given in high school and grades in college.
- A correlation of about .25 between scores on paper-and-pencil personality inventories and judgments of these individuals' personalities by psychological experts.

In psychological research, a correlation coefficient of .60 or more is judged to be quite high. Correlations in the range from .20 to .60 are of practical and theoretical value and useful in making predictions. Correlations between 0 and .20 must be judged with caution and are only minimally useful in making predictions.

**TESTS** One familiar use of the correlation method involves tests that measure some aptitude, achievement, or other psychological trait. The test presents a uniform situation to a group of people who vary in some trait (such as mathematical ability, manual dexterity, or anxiety). The variation in scores on the test can then be correlated with variations on another variable.

For example, people's scores on a mathematical ability test can be correlated with their subsequent grades in a college math course; if the correlation is high, then the test score may be used to determine which of a new group of students should be placed in advanced sections.

The test is an important research instrument in psychology. It enables the psychologist to obtain large quantities of data from people with minimal disturbance of their daily routines and without elaborate laboratory equipment. The construction of tests requires many steps, which will be explored in some detail in later chapters.

**CAUSE-AND-EFFECT RELATIONS** There is an important distinction between experimental and correlational studies. In a typical experimental study, one variable (the independent variable) is systematically manipulated to determine its effect on some other variable (the dependent variable). Such cause-and-effect relations cannot be inferred from correlational studies. The fallacy of interpreting correlations as implying cause and effect can be illustrated with a couple of examples. The softness of the asphalt in the streets of a city may correlate with the number of sunstroke cases reported that day, but this does not mean that soft asphalt gives off some kind of poison that sends people to hospitals. Rather, variations in the two variables—softness of asphalt and number of sunstroke cases—are both being caused by a third factor—the heat of the sun. Another common example is the high positive correlation obtained for the number of storks seen nesting in French villages and the number of childbirths recorded in the same villages. We shall leave it to the reader's ingenuity to figure out possible reasons for such a correlation without postulating a cause-and-effect relation between storks and babies. These examples provide sufficient warning against giving a cause-and-effect interpretation to a correlation. When two variables are correlated, variation in one may *possibly* be the cause of variation in the other, but in the absence of experimental evidence, no such conclusion is justified.

## Observational Method

**DIRECT OBSERVATION** In the early stages of research on a given topic, laboratory experiments and correlational studies may be premature and progress can best be made by observing the phenomenon of interest as it occurs naturally. Careful observation of animal and human behavior is the starting point for a great deal of research in psychology. For example, observation of primates in their native environment may tell us things about their social organization that will help in later laboratory investigations (see Figure 1-8). Study of preliterate tribes reveals the range of variation in human institutions, which would go unrecognized if we confined our study to people of our own culture. Motion pictures of newborn babies reveal the details of movement patterns shortly after birth and the types of stimuli to which babies are responsive.

In making observations of naturally occurring behavior, however, there is a risk that interpretive anecdotes may be substituted for objective descriptions. We may be tempted, for example, to say that an animal known to have been without food for a long time is "looking for food" when all we observe is heightened activity. Investigators must be trained to observe and record accurately to avoid projecting their own biases into what they report.

*Critical*

# DISCUSSION

## Ethical Issues in Psychological Research

Because psychologists employ live subjects in their studies, they need to be sensitive to ethical issues that can arise in the conduct of research. Accordingly, the American Psychological Association (APA) and its counterparts in Canada and Great Britain have established guidelines for the care and treatment of both human and animal subjects (American Psychological Association, 1990). In the United States, federal regulations require any institution that conducts federally funded research to establish an internal review board, which reviews proposed studies to ensure that all subjects will be treated properly.

The first principle governing the ethical treatment of human subjects is *minimal risk*. The federal guideline specifies that the risks anticipated in the research should be no greater than those ordinarily encountered in daily life. Obviously a person should not be exposed to physical harm or injury, but deciding how much psychological stress is ethically justified in a research project is not always so clearcut. In everyday life, of course, people are often impolite, they lie, and they make others anxious. When is it ethically justifiable for a researcher to do these same things to a subject in order to satisfy the goals of a research project? These are precisely the kinds of questions that the review boards consider on a case-by-case basis.

The second principle governing the ethical treatment of human subjects is *informed consent*. Subjects must enter a study voluntarily and be permitted to withdraw from it at any time without penalty if they so desire. They must also be told ahead of time about any aspects of the study that could be expected to influence their willingness to cooperate.

Like the principle of minimal risk, the requirement of informed consent is not always easy to implement. In particular, informed consent is sometimes at odds with another common requirement of research: that subjects be unaware of the hypotheses being tested in a study. If a study plans to compare subjects who learn lists of familiar words with subjects who learn lists of unfamiliar words, no ethical problem arises by simply telling subjects ahead of time that they will be learning lists of words: they do not need to know how the words vary from one subject to another. Nor are any serious ethical issues raised even if subjects are given a "surprise quiz" on words they didn't expect to be tested on. But what if the study seeks to compare subjects

Observational methods can require the use of a laboratory if the problem being studied is partly a biological one. For example, in their extensive study of the physiological aspects of human sexuality, Masters and Johnson (1966) developed techniques that permitted direct observation of sexual responses in the laboratory. The data included (a) observations of behavior, (b) recordings of physiological changes, and (c) responses to questions asked about the subject's sensations before, during, and after sexual stimulation.

**FIGURE 1-8**
**Baboons Observed in Their Natural Habitat** *Field studies can often tell us more about social behavior than experimental studies. Professor Shirley Strum has observed the same troop of baboons in Kenya for more than 20 years, identifying individual animals and making daily recordings of their behaviors and social interactions. Her data have provided remarkable information about the mental abilities of baboons and the role of friendships in their social system.*

who learn words while in a neutral mood with subjects who learn words while they are angry or embarrassed? Clearly the research would not yield valid conclusions if subjects had to be told ahead of time that they would be intentionally angered (by being treated rudely) or intentionally embarrassed (by being led to believe that they had accidentally broken a piece of equipment).

Accordingly, the guidelines specify that if such a study is permitted to proceed at all, subjects must be debriefed about it as soon as possible following their participation. The reasons for keeping them in ignorance—or deceiving them—about the procedures must be explained, and any residual anger or embarrassment must be dealt with so the subjects leave with their dignity intact and their appreciation for the research enhanced rather than diminished. The review board must be convinced that the debriefing procedures are adequate to this task.

A third principle of ethical research is the subjects' *right to privacy*. Information about a person that might be acquired during a study must be treated as confidential and not made available to others without his or her consent. One common practice is to separate the names or other identifying information about the subjects from the data once they have been collected. The data are then identified only by code or case numbers. In that way, nobody other than the experimenter has access to how any given subject responded.

About 7 to 8 percent of all psychological studies involve animals (mostly rodents and birds), and very few of these subject animals to painful or harmful procedures. Nevertheless, concern and controversy over the use, care, and treatment of animal subjects in research has increased in recent years, and both federal and APA guidelines require that any painful or harmful procedures imposed upon animals must be thoroughly justi-

fied in terms of the knowledge to be gained from the study. Specific rules also govern the living conditions and maintenance procedures that laboratory animals are entitled to.

Aside from the specific guidelines, the governing ethical principle should be that those who participate in psychology studies should be considered as full partners in the research enterprise. Some of the research discussed in this text was conducted before the ethical guidelines were formulated and would not be permitted by most review boards today. We will see a particularly notable example in Chapter 19 when we discuss the controversial studies of obedience by Stanley Milgram (1963, 1974).

While Masters and Johnson would be the first to agree that human sexuality has many dimensions in addition to the biological one, their observations about the anatomical and physiological aspects of sexual response have been very helpful in understanding the nature of human sexuality, as well as in solving certain sexual problems.

**SURVEY METHOD**   Some problems that are difficult to study by direct observation may be studied by indirect observation through the use of questionnaires or interviews. That is, rather than observe if people engage in a particular behavior, researchers simply ask them if they do. Since people may be trying to present themselves in a favorable light, this method is more open to bias than direct observation. Still, the **survey method** has produced many important results. For example, prior to the Masters and Johnson research on sexual response, most of the information on how people behave sexually (as opposed to how laws, religion, or society said they should behave) came from extensive surveys conducted by Alfred Kinsey and his associates 20 years earlier. Information from thousands of individual interviews was analyzed to form the basis of *Sexual Behavior in the Human Male* (Kinsey, Pomeroy, & Martin, 1948) and *Sexual Behavior in the Human Female* (Kinsey, Pomeroy, Martin, & Gebhard, 1953).

Surveys have also been used to observe people's political opinions, product preferences, health care needs, and so on. The Gallup poll and the United States census are probably the most familiar surveys. An adequate survey requires a carefully pretested questionnaire, interviewers trained in its use, a sample of people selected to ensure they are representative of the population to be studied, and appropriate methods of data analysis to ensure that the results are properly interpreted.

*"How would you like me to answer that question? As a member of my ethnic group, income group, or religious category?"*
Drawing by D. Fradon, ©1969 *The New Yorker Magazine*, Inc.

**CASE HISTORIES**  Still another means of indirectly observing someone is to obtain a biography of him or her. Now the researcher is asking people about what they have done in the past, rather than observing the behaviors of interest. Biographies for scientific use are known as **case histories,** and are important sources of data for psychologists studying individuals. There can also be case histories of institutions or groups of people.

Most case histories are prepared by *reconstructing the biography* of a person on the basis of remembered events and records. Reconstruction is necessary because the individual's history often does not become a matter of interest until that person develops some sort of problem; at such a time, knowledge of the past is important in understanding present behavior. The retrospective method may result in distortions of events or in oversights, compared to what direct observation would have uncovered, but it is often the only approach available.

# Fields of Psychology

We have tried to gain some understanding of the nature of psychology by looking at its topics, perspectives, and methods. We can further our understanding of what psychology is by looking at what different kinds of psychologists *do*. We will first consider different specializations within psychology, and then discuss interdisciplinary approaches.

## Specializations within Psychology

About half the people who have advanced degrees in psychology work in colleges and universities. In addition to teaching, they may devote much of their time to research or counseling. Other psychologists work in the public schools, in hospitals or clinics, in research institutes, in government agencies, or in business and industry. Still others are in private practice and offer their services to the public for a fee. Table 1-1 gives the number and proportion of psychologists engaged in different specialized fields over a decade. Table 1-2 gives the number and proportion in terms of employment settings (where psychologists work). Table 1-3 shows the dramatic increase in the number of women in psychology in recent years.

We now turn to a brief description of some of these specializations.

**BIOLOGICAL PSYCHOLOGY**  This is the specialization of those who adopt a biological perspective. As discussed earlier, **biological psychologists** (also referred to as *physiological psychologists*) seek to discover the relationship between biological processes and behavior. For example: How do sex hormones influence behavior? What area of the brain controls speech? How do drugs like marijuana and LSD affect personality and memory?

**EXPERIMENTAL PSYCHOLOGY**  The term "experimental" is really a misnomer because psychologists in other areas of specialization also carry out experiments. But **experimental psychologists** are usually behaviorist and cognitive psychologists who use experimental methods to study how people (and other animals) react to sensory stimuli, perceive the world, learn and remember, reason, and respond emotionally.

| FIELD | 1977 | | 1987 | | |
|---|---|---|---|---|---|
| | NO. | % | NO. | % | CHANGE |
| Clinical | 13,378 | 39.8% | 28,147 | 49.9% | +10.1% |
| Counseling | 2,712 | 8.1% | 2,735 | 4.9% | –3.2% |
| School | 1,084 | 3.2% | 2,001 | 3.5% | +0.3% |
| Developmental | 1,728 | 5.1% | 2,903 | 5.1% | 0 |
| Educational | 1,622 | 4.8% | 1,438 | 2.6% | –2.2% |
| Social and Personality | 2,450 | 7.3% | 3,066 | 5.4% | –1.9% |
| Industrial/ Organizational | 1,974 | 5.9% | 2,714 | 4.8% | –1.1% |
| Experimental, Comparative, & Physiological | 4,598 | 13.7% | 4,959 | 8.8% | –4.9% |
| Other | 4,106 | 12.2% | 8,415 | 14.9% | +2.7% |
| Total | 33,652 | | 56,378 | | |

**TABLE 1-1**
**Fields of Specialization** *The number and percentage of all psychologists in the United States with doctoral-level degrees, in 1977 and a decade later in 1987. Also shown are percent changes over the decade.* (After Pion, 1991)

| SETTING | 1977 | | 1987 | | |
|---|---|---|---|---|---|
| | NO. | % | NO. | % | CHANGE |
| Academic Settings | 17,247 | 51.3% | 23,122 | 41.0% | –10.3% |
| Hospitals/Clinics | 5,386 | 16.0% | 7,155 | 12.7% | –3.3% |
| Nonprofit Organizations | 1,272 | 3.8% | 2,501 | 4.4% | +0.6% |
| Self-employed | 3,637 | 10.8% | 14,272 | 25.3% | +14.5% |
| Business & Industry | 1,891 | 5.6% | 3,109 | 5.5% | –0.1% |
| Government | 2,556 | 7.6% | 3,585 | 6.4% | –1.2% |
| Other | 1,663 | 4.9% | 2,634 | 4.7% | –0.2% |
| Total | 33,652 | | 56,378 | | |

**TABLE 1-2**
**Employment Setting** *The data base is the same as in the previous table, but is categorized by the principal employment setting of psychologists.* (After Pion, 1991)

**DEVELOPMENTAL, SOCIAL, AND PERSONALITY PSYCHOLOGY** The categories of developmental psychology, social psychology, and personality psychology overlap. **Developmental psychologists** are concerned with human development and the factors that shape behavior from birth to old

**TABLE 1-3**
**Recipients of Doctoral Degrees** *The number of individuals in the United States earning doctoral degrees in psychology in 1975 and fifteen years later in 1990, categorized by field of specialization. The percentages indicate the proportion of women and men receiving doctoral degrees.* (After Kohout, 1991)

| FIELD | 1975 | | | | 1990 | | | |
|---|---|---|---|---|---|---|---|---|
| | WOMEN | | MEN | | WOMEN | | MEN | |
| | NO. | (%) | NO. | (%) | NO. | (%) | NO. | (%) |
| Clinical, Counseling, & School | 371 | (32.4) | 773 | (67.6) | 1,114 | (59.4) | 760 | (40.6) |
| Developmental | 99 | (54.7) | 82 | (45.3) | 111 | (70.3) | 47 | (29.7) |
| Educational | 44 | (32.8) | 90 | (67.2) | 69 | (70.4) | 29 | (29.6) |
| Experimental, Comparative, & Physiological | 126 | (25.3) | 371 | (74.7) | 80 | (40.6) | 117 | (59.4) |
| Industrial/ Organizational | 10 | (15.9) | 53 | (84) | 53 | (42.7) | 71 | (57.2) |
| Personality/ Social | 81 | (27.5) | 214 | (72.5) | 102 | (61.8) | 63 | (38.2) |
| Other | 142 | (32.5) | 295 | (67.5) | 377 | (58) | 274 | (42.3) |
| Subtotal | 873 | (31.5) | 1,878 | (68.5) | 1,906 | (58.3) | 1,361 | (41.6) |

age. They might study a specific ability, such as how language develops in the growing child, or a particular period of life, such as infancy, the preschool years, or adolescence.

Because human development takes place in the context of other persons—parents, siblings, playmates, and school companions—a large part of development is social. **Social psychologists** are interested in the ways interactions with other people influence attitudes and behavior. They are concerned also with the behavior of groups, and are well known to the general public for their work in public opinion surveys and in market research.

To the extent that personality is a product of developmental and social factors, the province of personality psychology overlaps both of these categories. **Personality psychologists** focus on differences between individuals. They are interested in ways of classifying people for practical purposes, as well as in studying each individual's unique qualities.

**CLINICAL AND COUNSELING PSYCHOLOGY** The greatest number of psychologists are **clinical psychologists,** which means they are engaged in the application of psychological principles to the diagnosis and treatment of emotional and behavioral problems—mental illness, drug addiction, mental retardation, marital and family conflict, and other less serious adjustment problems. Many clinical psychologists have a psychoanalytic perspective, though the behavioral, cognitive, and phenomenological perspectives are also well represented. **Counseling psychologists** serve many of the same functions as clinical psychologists, although they usually deal with less serious problems. They often work with high school or university students, providing help with problems of social adjustment and vocational and educational goals.

SCHOOL AND EDUCATIONAL PSYCHOLOGY The elementary and secondary schools have a great need for psychologists. Because the beginnings of serious emotional problems often appear in the early grades, many elementary schools employ psychologists whose training combines courses in child development, education, and clinical psychology. These **school psychologists** work with individual children to evaluate learning and emotional problems. In contrast, **educational psychologists** are specialists in learning and teaching. They may work in the schools, but more often they are employed by a university's school of education, where they do research on teaching methods and help train teachers and school psychologists.

INDUSTRIAL AND ENGINEERING PSYCHOLOGY **Industrial psychologists** (sometimes called **organizational psychologists**) typically work for a particular company. They are concerned with such problems as selecting people most suitable for particular jobs, developing job training programs, and figuring out the determinants of consumer behavior. **Engineering psychologists** (sometimes called *human factors engineers*) seek to improve the relationship between people and machines; they help design machines to minimize the number of human errors. In computer systems, the design of the *person-machine interface*, the point at which the person interacts with the machine, is especially important.

## Interdisciplinary Approaches

There are disciplines other than psychology that are interested in mind and behavior—biology, linguistics, and philosophy, to name just a few. Increasingly, researchers from these other disciplines are combining with psychologists to forge new, interdisciplinary approaches to the study of psychological phenomena. Two interdisciplinary approaches of particular interest

*Counseling psychologists often work with families to help them resolve problems.*

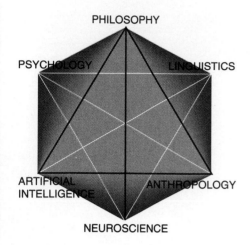

**FIGURE 1-9**
**Cognitive Science**
*The figure shows the fields involved in cognitive science and their interrelationships. Artificial intelligence refers to a branch of computer science concerned with (a) using computers to simulate human thought processes; and (b) devising computer programs that act "intelligently" and can adapt to changing circumstances. This figure was included in an unpublished report commissioned by the Sloan Foundation (New York City) in 1978; the report was prepared by leading researchers in cognitive science.*

are: **cognitive science,** which is concerned with the nature of cognitive processes, and **evolutionary psychology,** which is concerned with how evolution has shaped mental and behavioral processes.

**COGNITIVE SCIENCE** Cognitive Science describes those areas of psychological research that (a) are concerned with cognitive processes like perceiving, remembering, reasoning, deciding, and problem solving; and (b) overlap with other disciplines interested in these processes, such as philosophy and computer science. The field's major objectives are to discover how information is represented in the mind (**mental representations**); what types of computations can be carried out on these representations to bring about perceiving, remembering, reasoning, and so on; and how these computations are realized biologically in the brain. In addition to psychology, the disciplines involved are neuroscience, anthropology, linguistics, philosophy, and artificial intelligence. (The latter is a branch of computer science concerned with developing computers that act intelligently and computer programs that can simulate human thought processes.) The diagram in Figure 1-9 lists the contributing disciplines.

A central idea behind **cognitive science** is that the human cognitive system can be understood as though it were a giant computer engaged in a complex calculation. Just as a computer's complex calculation can be broken down into a set of simpler computations, such as storing, retrieving, and comparing symbols or representations, so a person's action can be decomposed into elementary mental components. Moreover, the elementary mental components may also involve storing, retrieving, and comparing symbols. There is a further parallel between a computer's calculations and mental computations. A computer's activity may be analyzed at different levels—including the level of hardware with its emphasis on chips, and the level of representation-and-algorithm with its emphasis on data structures and processes; similarly, human cognitive activity may also be analyzed at the level of "hardware" or neurons, and the level of mental representations and processes. The ideas of *mental computation* and *levels of analysis*, then, are among the cornerstones of cognitive science (Osherson, 1990).

One recent development within cognitive science that deserves special mention is **connectionism.** The hallmark of this approach is that mental representations and processes are described in terms that are similar to neurons and their interconnections. Thus, instead of talking about the storage, retrieval, and comparison of symbols, connectionist researchers talk about the activation of a unit and the spread of its activation to other units it is connected to. While the units and connections involved have some properties of real neurons (for example, they are subject to activation and inhibition), they do not have all the properties of neurons. Hence the units in a connectionist network are to be thought of at a more abstract level than neurons, and in this way a distinction between levels of analysis is maintained (Churchland, 1990).

**EVOLUTIONARY PSYCHOLOGY** While cognitive science deals with the *content* of the cognitive mechanisms that underlie mind and behavior, **evolutionary psychology** is concerned with the *origins* of cognitive and other psychological mechanisms. In addition to psychology, some of the major disciplines involved are branches of anthropology, biology, and psychiatry. The key idea behind evolutionary psychology, is that, just like biological mechanisms, psychological mechanisms must have evolved over millions of years by a process of natural selection. To say that a psychological mechanism has evolved by natural selection is to say that it has a genetic basis, and that it has proved useful in the past in solving some problems of survival or in increasing the chances of reproducing. To illustrate, consider a liking for sweets. Such a preference can be thought of as a psychological mechanism, and it has a genetic basis. Moreover, we have this preference because in our evolutionary past it succeeded in increasing our ancestors' chances of survival (the fruit that tasted the sweetest had the highest nutritional value), which increased the chances of the continued survival of the relevant genes (Symons, 1991).

There are a couple of ways in which adopting an evolutionary perspective can affect the study of psychological issues. For one thing, from an evolutionary perspective certain topics are of particular importance because of their link to survival or successful reproduction. Such topics include, among others, how we select our heterosexual mates, how we deal with those who have dominance over us, and how we handle our own aggressive feelings, and these topics are among the most investigated by evolutionary psychologists (Buss, 1991). An evolutionary perspective can also provide some new insights about familiar topics. We can illustrate this point by reconsidering a couple of our sample problems. Recall that in our description of obesity, we noted that a history of deprivation can lead to overeating in the future. Evolution theory provides an interpretation of this puzzling phenomenon. Until very recently in evolutionary history, people experienced deprivation *only* when food was scarce. An adaptive psychological mechanism for dealing with scarcity is a propensity to overeat when food *is* available. Hence evolution may have selected for the tendency to overeat following deprivation. Another example concerns conditioned fear. An interesting fact about such fears is that people are far more likely to learn to fear some things than others. For example, we are more likely to learn to fear snakes, spiders, and darkness than to fear cars, guns, and electrical outlets, even though the latter three objects in fact currently pose far greater threats to our survival than do the former three. All of this makes sense from the perspective of evolutionary theory. For much of evolutionary history, snakes, spiders, and darkness are what posed threats to people, and hence a tendency to readily learn to fear them may have been selected (Buss, 1991; Seligman, 1971).

Though only recently developed, evolutionary psychology and cognitive science have already influenced many areas of scientific psychology, and this influence will be apparent in many of the chapters that follow.

## Overview of the Book

Psychologists today are in the process of investigating thousands of different phenomena ranging from microelectrode studies of how individual brain cells change during learning to studies of the effects of population density and overcrowding on social behavior. Deciding how to classify these investigations topically and how to present the topics in the most meaningful order is difficult. Should we know how people perceive the world in order to understand how they learn new things? Or does learning determine how we perceive our environment? Should we discuss what motivates a person to action so that we can understand his or her personality? Or can motivation be better understood if we first look at the way personality develops over the course of a lifetime? Despite such unresolved questions, we have tried to arrange the topics in this book so that the understanding of the issues in each chapter will provide a background for the study of problems in the next.

To understand how people interact with their environment, we need to know something about their biological equipment. In Part II ("Biological and Developmental Processes"), the first chapter describes how the nervous and endocrine systems function to integrate and control behavior. Because behavior also depends on the interaction between inherited characteristics and environmental conditions, this chapter includes a discussion of genetic influences on behavior. The second chapter in Part II provides an overview of the individual's psychological development from infancy through adolescence and adulthood. By noting how abilities, attitudes, and personality develop, and the problems that must be faced at different stages of life, we can appreciate more fully the kinds of questions to which psychology seeks answers.

With this as background, we move on to Part III ("Perception and Consciousness"), where we will survey how humans and other species acquire information about the external world. Such information must first be registered by the sense organs, which mediate the sensations of light, sound, touch, and taste. We first discuss the nature of sensory information, and then consider how such information is organized into meaningful patterns and recognized as instances of familiar objects or events. Organization and recognition are parts of the *process* of perception. The *products* of perception often emerge in consciousness, and we will examine the characteristics of human consciousness under both normal and altered states.

In Part IV ("Learning, Remembering, and Thinking"), we will first consider how organisms learn about their environment, ranging from the learning of simple relations like "shock follows tone" to the complex knowledge taught in college courses. We will also consider how such information is remembered and used for purposes of reasoning and problem solving. In addition, we take up the critical problem of language—how we communicate what we know.

Part V ("Motivation and Emotion") deals with the forces that energize and direct behavior. Such forces include basic motives such as hunger and sex, as well as emotions such as joy, fear, and anger.

The ways in which individuals differ from one another is the substance of Part VI ("Personality and Individuality"). We will consider differences in both mental abilities and personality, paying close attention to how these differences are measured.

Dealing with stress and emotional problems are the major topics in Part VII ("Stress, Psychopathology, and Therapy"). We will consider the kinds of emotional problems that virtually everyone faces at some point, as well as more severe forms of mental disorders like schizophrenia. In addition, we discuss the various therapies that have been developed to deal with such problems and disorders.

Part VIII ("Social Behavior") is concerned with social interactions. We will discuss how we think, feel, and act in social situations, and how social situations in turn influence our thoughts, feelings, and actions. We will discuss how we perceive and interpret the behaviors of other people; how beliefs and attitudes are shaped; and how groups influence their members and vice versa.

1. *Psychology* may be defined as the *scientific study of behavior and mental processes*. The variety of topics covered by this definition is illustrated by considering five specific problems: (a) *split-brain perception*, where people with disconnected left and right hemispheres experience the world differently from people with connected hemispheres; (b) *conditioned fear*, wherein an organism learns to fear what was once a neutral stimulus; (c) *childhood amnesia*, the inability to remember events from the first few years of life; (d) *causes of obesity*, including psychological and biological factors; and (e) the *expression of aggression*, and whether such expression leads to more or less aggression.

2. The *roots of psychology* can be traced to the fourth and fifth centuries B.C. The Greek philosophers Socrates, Plato, and Aristotle posed fundamental questions about the mind, while Hippocrates, the "father of medicine," made many important observations about how the brain controlled other organs. *Scientific psychology* was born in the latter part of the nineteenth century, when the idea took hold that mind and behavior could be the subject of scientific analysis.

3. The study of psychology can be approached from several viewpoints. The *biological perspective* relates our actions to events taking place inside the body, particularly the brain and nervous system. The *behavioral* perspective considers only those external activities of the organism that can be observed and measured. The *cognitive* perspective is concerned with mental processes such as perceiving, remembering, reasoning, deciding, and problem solving, and with relating these processes to behavior. The *psychoanalytic* perspective emphasizes unconscious motives stemming from sexual and aggressive impulses repressed in childhood. The *phenomenological* perspective focuses on the person's subjective experiences and motivation toward self-actualization. A particular area of psychological investigation often can be analyzed from a number of these viewpoints.

4. The *biological* perspective differs from the other viewpoints in that its principles are drawn from biology. Often biological researchers attempt to explain psychological principles in terms of biological ones. While such *reductionism* can be successful, there are some principles that can be stated only at psychological levels. Also, psychological research is often needed to direct the work of researchers taking the biological perspective.

5. When applicable, the *experimental method* is preferred for studying problems because it seeks to control all variables except the ones being studied. The *independent variable* is the one manipulated by the experimenter; the *dependent variable* (usually some measure of the subject's behavior) is the one being studied to determine if it is affected by changes in the independent variable. In a simple *experimental design*, the experimenter manipulates one independent variable and observes its effect on one dependent variable.

6. In many experiments, the independent variable is something that is either present or absent. The simplest experimental design includes an *experimental group* (with the condition present for one group of subjects) and a *control group* (with the condition absent for another group of subjects). If the difference in *means* between the experimental and control groups is *statistically significant*, we know that the experimental condition had a reliable effect; that is, the difference is due to the independent variable, not to chance factors or a few extreme cases.

7. If an investigator has no control over which subjects go in which conditions, a *correlational method* may be used. This method determines whether a naturally occurring difference is associated with another difference of interest. The degree of correlation between two variables is measured by the *correlation coefficient, r.* It is a number between 0 and 1. No relationship is indicated by 0; a perfect relationship is indicated by 1. As *r* goes from 0 to 1, the strength of the relationship increases. The correlation coefficient can be positive or negative, depending on whether one variable increases with another (+) or one variable decreases as the other increases (–).

8. Another approach to research is the *observational* method, in which one observes the phenomenon of interest. Researchers must be trained to observe and record accurately to avoid projecting their own biases into what they report. Phenomena that are difficult to observe directly may be observed indirectly by *surveys* (questionnaires and interviews) or by *reconstructing a case history.*

9. Psychology as a profession includes numerous areas of specialization: biological psychology; experimental psychology; developmental, social, and personality psychology; clinical and counseling psychology; school and educational psychology; and industrial and engineering psychology.

10. There are a number of interdisciplinary approaches to the study of mind and behavior, including *cognitive science* and *evolutionary psychology.* Cognitive science deals with the nature of intelligent processes, and in addition to psychology involves the disciplines of neuroscience, anthropology, linguistics, philosophy, and artificial intelligence. Its key ideas are that mental processes may be understood as *computations,* and that mental activity may be analyzed at various levels. Evolutionary psychology is concerned with the origin of psychological mechanisms. Its key idea is that such mechanisms have evolved over millions of years by a process of *natural selection.* This approach has led psychologists to look at topics of particular evolutionary significance, such as mate selection.

## *Further* **READING**

The topical interests and theories of any contemporary science can often be understood best according to their history. Several useful books are Hilgard, *Psychology in America: A Historical Survey* (1987); Wertheimer, *A Brief History of Psychology* (3rd ed., 1987); and Schultz, *A History of Modern Psychology* (4th ed., 1987). A brief history of psychology is presented in Appendix II.

The various conceptual approaches to psychology are discussed in Medcof and Roth (eds.), *Approaches to Psychology* (1988); Anderson, *Cognitive Psychology and Its Implications* (3rd ed., 1990); Peterson, *Personality* (1988); Royce and Mos (eds.), *Humanistic Psychology: Concepts and Criticism* (1981); Bower and Hilgard, *Theories of Learning* (5th ed., 1981); and Lundin, *Theories and Systems of Psychology* (3rd ed., 1985).

The methods of psychological research are presented in Wood, *Fundamentals of Psychological Research* (3rd ed., 1986); Snodgrass, Levy-Berger, and Haydon, *Human Experimental Psychology* (1985); Ray and Ravizza, *Methods Toward a Science of Behavior and Experience* (3rd ed., 1988); and Elmes, Kantowitz, and Roediger, *Research Methods in Psychology* (3rd ed., 1989).

A simple but elegant introduction to basic concepts in statistics is Phillips, *How to Think About Statistics* (revised ed., 1992).

A general introduction to cognitive science is given in Gardner, *The Mind's New Science: A History of the Cognitive Revolution* (1985) and in Osherson, *Invitation to Cognitive Science* (Vols. 1–3) (1990). For an advanced treatment, see Posner, *Foundations of Cognitive Science* (1989). For an introduction to evolutionary psychology, see Barkow, Cosmides, and Tooky, *The Adapted Mind* (1990).

To find out more about career opportunities in psychology and the training required to become a psychologist, write to the American Psychological Association (1400 North Uhle Street, Arlington, Va., 22201) for a copy of their booklet, *A Career in Psychology*.

# Part  II

## Biological and Developmental Processes

2 Biological Basis of Psychology

3 Psychological Development

Predergast, Maurice. *The East River*. 1901. Watercolor and pencil on paper, $13\frac{3}{4}" \times 19\frac{3}{4}"$.
Collection, The Museum of Modern Art, New York. Gift of Abby Aldrich Rockefeller.

# Chapter 2

# Biological Basis of Psychology

**Components of the Nervous System 35**
*Neurons and Nerves*
*Action Potentials*
*Synaptic Transmission*
*Neurotransmitters and Neuroreceptors*
*Critical Discussion: Molecular Psychology*

**Organization of the Nervous System 42**

**Structure of the Brain 44**
*Central Core*
*Limbic System*
*Critical Discussion: Pictures of the Living Brain*

**Cerebral Hemispheres 48**
*Structure of the Cerebrum*
*Cortical Areas and Their Functions*

**Asymmetries in the Brain 52**
*Split-Brain Subjects*
*Hemispheric Specialization*
*Critical Discussion: Language and the Brain*

**Autonomic Nervous System 58**

**Endocrine System 60**

**Genetic Influences on Behavior 62**
*Chromosomes and Genes*
*Genetic Studies of Behavior*
*Environmental Influences on Gene Action*

Detail, *The East River*.

Behavior, from blinking an eye to playing tennis to writing a computer program, depends on the integration of numerous processes within the body. This integration is provided by the nervous system, with help from the endocrine system. Consider, for example, all the processes that must coordinate effectively for you to stop your car at a red light. First you must see the light; this means that the light must register on one set of your sense organs, your eyes. Neural impulses from your eyes are relayed to your brain, where the stimulus is analyzed and compared with information about past events stored in your memory: you recognize that a red light in a certain context means "stop." The process of moving your foot to the brake pedal and pressing it is initiated by the motor areas of the brain that control the muscles of your leg and foot. In order to send the proper signals to these muscles, the brain must know where your foot is as well as where you want it to go. The brain maintains a register of the position of body parts relative to one another, which it uses to plan directed movements. You do not stop the car with one sudden movement of your leg, however. A specialized part of your brain receives continual *feedback* from leg and foot muscles so that you are aware of how much pressure is being exerted and you can alter your movements accordingly. At the same time, your eyes and some of your other body senses tell you how quickly the car is stopping. If the light turned red as you were speeding toward the intersection, some of your endocrine glands would also be activated, leading to increased heart rate, more rapid respiration, and other metabolic changes associated with fear; these processes speed your reactions in an emergency. Your stopping at a red light may seem quick and automatic, but it involves numerous complex messages and adjustments. The information for these activities is transmitted by large networks of nerve cells.

Many aspects of behavior and mental functioning can be better understood with some knowledge of the underlying biological processes. Our nervous system, sense organs, muscles, and glands enable us to be aware of and to adjust to our environment. Our perception of events depends on how our sense organs detect stimuli and how our brain interprets information coming from the senses. Much of our behavior is motivated by such needs as hunger, thirst, and the avoidance of fatigue or pain. Our ability to use language, to think, and to solve problems depends on a brain that is incredibly complex. Indeed, the specific patterns of electrical and chemical events in the brain are the very basis of our most intricate thought processes.

Some of the research relating psychological events to biological processes will be discussed in later chapters when we talk, for example, about perception, memory, or motivation. This chapter attempts only to provide an overview of the nervous system.

## Components of the Nervous System

The basic unit of the nervous system is a specialized cell called the **neuron.** It is important to understand neurons because they undoubtedly hold the secrets of how the brain works. We know their role in the transmission of nerve impulses, and we know how some neural circuits work; but we are just beginning to unravel their more complex functioning in memory, emotion, and thought.

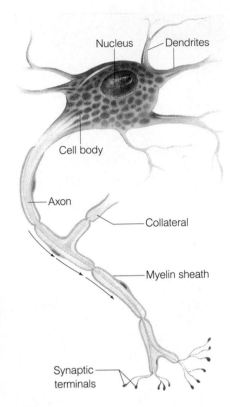

**FIGURE 2-1**
**Schematic Diagram of a Neuron**
*Arrows indicate the direction of the nerve impulse. Some axons are branched; the branches are called collaterals. The axons of many neurons are covered with a myelin sheath that helps to increase the speed of the nerve impulse.*

# Neurons and Nerves

Although neurons differ markedly in size and appearance, they have certain common characteristics (see Figure 2-1). Projecting from the cell body are a number of short branches called **dendrites** (from the Greek word *dendron*, meaning "tree"). The dendrites and cell body receive neural impulses from adjacent neurons. These messages are transmitted to other neurons (or to muscles and glands) by a slender tubelike extension of the cell called an **axon**. At its end the axon branches into a number of fine collaterals that end in small swellings called **synaptic terminals.**

The synaptic terminal does not actually touch the neuron that it will stimulate. Rather, there is a slight gap between the synaptic terminal and the cell body or dendrites of the receiving neuron. This junction is called a **synapse** and the gap itself is called the **synaptic gap.** When a neural impulse travels down the axon and arrives at the synaptic terminals, it triggers the secretion of a chemical called a **neurotransmitter.** The neurotransmitter diffuses across the synaptic gap and stimulates the next neuron, thereby carrying the impulse from one neuron to the next. The axons from a great many neurons (perhaps as many as 1,000) may synapse on the dendrites and cell body of a single neuron (see Figure 2-2).

Although all neurons have these general features, they vary greatly in size and shape (see Figure 2-3). A neuron in the spinal cord may have an axon three to four feet long, running from the tip of the spine to the big toe; a neuron in the brain may cover only a few thousandths of an inch.

There are three types of neurons. **Sensory neurons** transmit impulses received by **receptors** to the central nervous system. The receptors are specialized cells in the sense organs, muscles, skin, and joints that detect physical or chemical changes and translate these events into impulses that travel

**FIGURE 2-2**
**Synapses at the Cell Body of a Neuron** *Many different axons, each of which branches repeatedly, synapse on the dendrites and cell body of a single neuron. Each branch of an axon ends in a swelling called a synaptic terminal, which contains chemicals that are released and transmit the nerve impulse across the synapse to the dendrites or cell body of the receiving cell.*

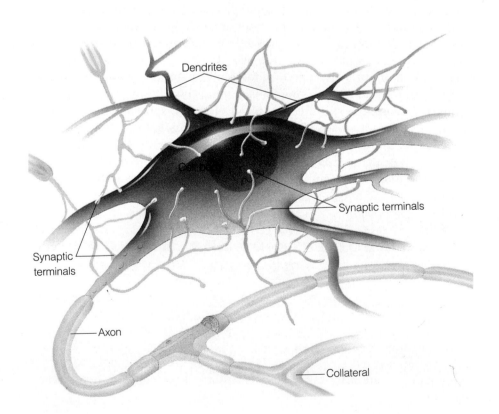

along the sensory neurons. **Motor neurons** carry outgoing signals from the brain or spinal cord to the effector organs, namely the muscles and glands. **Interneurons** receive the signals from the sensory neurons and send impulses to other interneurons or to motor neurons. Interneurons are found only in the brain, eyes, and spinal cord.

A **nerve** is a bundle of elongated axons belonging to hundreds or thousands of neurons. A single nerve may contain axons from both sensory and motor neurons.

In addition to neurons, the nervous system consists of a large number of nonneural cells, called **glial cells,** that are interspersed among—and often surround—neurons. The name is derived from the Greek word *glia* (meaning glue), because one of their principal functions is to hold the neurons in place. Glial cells are not specialized to receive or transmit signals. Rather, they provide structural and metabolic support, and serve in other ways to ensure that neurons can perform their functions. Estimates of the number of neurons and glial cells in the human nervous system vary widely, depending on the method used to make the determination; as yet, there is no agreement among scientists on the best estimate. In the human brain alone, the estimates range from 10 billion to 1 trillion neurons; whatever the estimate for neurons, the number of glial cells is probably 10 times that number (Groves & Rebec, 1992). These are astronomical figures, but this number of cells is undoubtedly necessary to support the complexities of human behavior.

## Action Potentials

Information moves along a neuron in the form of an electrochemical impulse that travels from the dendritic area down to the end of the axon. The ability to generate this traveling impulse, or **action potential,** is unique to neurons and is due to a multitude of **ion channels** and **ion pumps** that are embedded in the cell membrane. Ion channels are donut-shaped protein molecules that form pores across the cell membrane. These protein structures regulate the flow of electrically charged ions, such as sodium ($Na^+$), potassium ($K^+$), calcium ($Ca^{++}$) or chloride ($Cl^-$), by opening and closing their pores. Each ion channel is selective, permitting (usually) only one type of ion to flow through it when open. Separate protein structures, called ion pumps, help to maintain an uneven distribution of the various ions across the cell membrane by pumping them into or out of the cell. In this way, the resting neuron maintains high concentrations of $Na^+$ outside the cell and low concentrations inside. The overall effect of these ion channels and pumps is to make the cell membrane highly polarized, with a positive charge on the outside and a negative charge on the inside.

When the resting neuron is stimulated, the voltage difference across the cell membrane is reduced. If the voltage drop is large enough, $Na^+$ channels open briefly at the point of stimulation and $Na^+$ ions flood into the cell. This process is called **depolarization;** now the inside of that area of the cell membrane becomes positive relative to the outside. Neighboring $Na^+$ channels sense the voltage drop and in turn open causing the adjacent area to depolarize. This self-propagating process of depolarization (repeating itself down the length of the cell body) gives rise to the neural impulse. As the impulse travels down the neuron, the $Na^+$ channels close behind it and the various ion pumps are activated to quickly restore the cell membrane to its resting state.

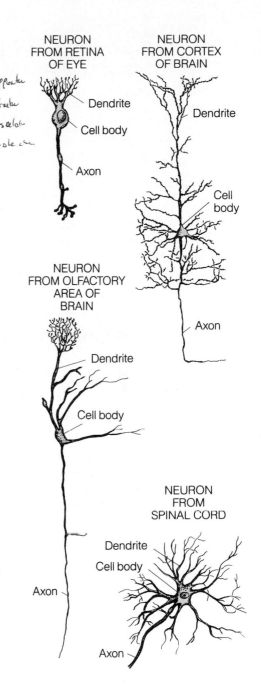

**FIGURE 2-3**
**Shapes and Relative Sizes of Neurons** *The axon of a spinal cord neuron (not shown in its entirety in the figure) may be several feet long.*

The speed of the action potential as it travels from the dendritic region to the end of the axon can vary from about 2 to 200 miles per hour, depending on the diameter of the axon, with larger ones generally being faster. The speed can also be affected by whether or not the axon of the neuron is covered with a thin fatty tissue, called the **myelin sheath.** The sheath consists of a series of short segments separated by small gaps (refer back to Figure 2-1). The insulating function of the myelin sheath allows the nerve impulse to virtually jump from gap to gap, thus greatly increasing the speed of transmission. The myelin sheath is characteristic of higher animals, and is particularly prevalent in those areas of the nervous system where speed of transmission is critical. *Multiple sclerosis*, a disease characterized by severe sensory and motor nerve dysfunction, is due to degeneration of the myelin sheath.

## Synaptic Transmission

The synaptic junction between neurons is of tremendous importance because it is there that nerve cells transfer signals. A single neuron discharges, or fires, when the stimulation reaching it via multiple synapses exceeds a certain threshold level. The neuron fires in a single, brief pulse and is then inactive for a few thousandths of a second. The strength of the neural impulse is constant and cannot be triggered by a stimulus unless it reaches threshold level; this is referred to as the **all-or-none principle** of action. The nerve impulse, once started, travels down the axon to its many axon terminals.

As we have said, neurons do not connect directly at a synapse; there is a slight gap across which the signal must be transmitted (see Figure 2-4). Although in a few areas of the nervous system the electrical activity in one neuron can stimulate another neuron directly, neurotransmitters are responsible for transmitting the signal in the vast majority of cases. When a nerve impulse moves down the axon of a neuron and arrives at a synaptic terminal, it stimulates **synaptic vesicles** in the terminal. These vesicles are small spherical or irregularly shaped structures that contain neurotransmitters; when stimulated they discharge the neurotransmtters. The neurotransmitter molecules diffuse across the synaptic gap and bind to **neuroreceptor molecules** in the cell membrane of the receiving neuron. The neurotransmitter molecule and the neuroreceptor molecule fit together in the same way that one piece of a jigsaw puzzle fits another, or the way a key fits a lock. This *lock-and-key action* of the two molecules causes a change in the permeability of the receiving neuron. When locked to their receptors some neurotransmitters have an excitatory effect and increase permeability in the direction of depolarization; others are inhibitory and decrease the permeability.

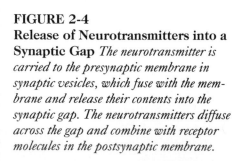

**FIGURE 2-4**
**Release of Neurotransmitters into a Synaptic Gap** *The neurotransmitter is carried to the presynaptic membrane in synaptic vesicles, which fuse with the membrane and release their contents into the synaptic gap. The neurotransmitters diffuse across the gap and combine with receptor molecules in the postsynaptic membrane.*

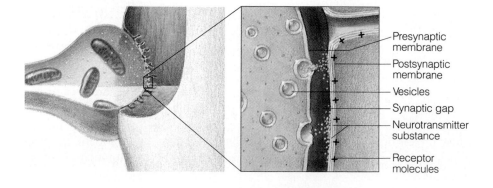

- Presynaptic membrane
- Postsynaptic membrane
- Vesicles
- Synaptic gap
- Neurotransmitter substance
- Receptor molecules

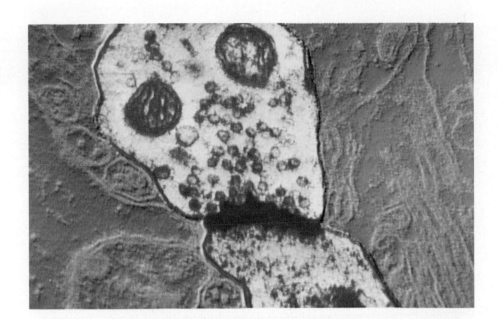

*A micrograph of a synapse between two neurons in the cerebral cortex. The synaptic gap appears deep red. Vesicles containing neurotransmitters are seen as small red and yellow spheres. The two larger circles are the sites of energy production in the nerve cell (magnification: × 17,600).*

A given neuron may receive many thousands of synapses from a network of other neurons. Some of these neurons release neurotransmitters that are *excitatory*, while others release neurotransmitters that are *inhibitory*. Depending on their pattern of firing, different axons will release their neurotransmitter substances at different times. If—at a particular moment and at a particular place on the cell membrane—the excitatory effects on the receiving neuron become large relative to the inhibitory effects, then depolarization occurs and the neuron fires an all-or-none impulse.

Once a neurotransmitter substance is released and diffuses across the synaptic gap, its action must be very brief. Otherwise, it will exert its effects for too long, and precise control will be lost. The brevity of the action is achieved in one of two ways. For some neurotransmitters, the synapse is almost immediately cleared of the chemical by **reuptake,** the process in which the neurotransmitter is reabsorbed by the synaptic terminals from which it was released. Reuptake cuts off the action of the neurotransmitter and spares the axon terminals from having to manufacture more of the substance. The effect of other neurotransmitters is terminated by **degradation,** the process in which enzymes in the membrane of the receiving neuron react with the neurotransmitter to break it up chemically and make it inactive.

## Neurotransmitters and Neuroreceptors

Over 50 different neurotransmitters have been identified, and others surely will be discovered in the future. Moreover, some neurotransmitters can bind to more than one type of receptor molecule, causing different effects. For example, there are neurotransmitters that are excitatory at some sites in the nervous system and inhibitory at other sites because two different types of receptor molecules are involved.

**Acetylcholine** (ACh) is a neurotransmitter found at many synapses throughout the body. In general, it is an excitatory transmitter, but it can be inhibitory depending on the type of receptor molecule in the membrane of the receiving neuron. ACh is particularly prevalent in an area of the brain

## Molecular Psychology

When the neural impulse reaches the end of an axon, neurotransmitter molecules are released that cross the synaptic gap and combine with receptor molecules in the membrane of the receiving neuron. The lock-and-key action of the two molecules changes the electrical properties of the target cell, either causing it to fire or preventing it from firing.

To serve its function, every key requires a lock and every neurotransmitter requires a receptor. Many commonly used drugs—from tranquilizers such as Valium to street drugs such as heroin and crack—interact with receptor molecules in very much the same way as neurotransmitters. Molecules of these drugs are shaped enough like those of the neurotransmitters to work as if they were keys to the lock of receptor molecules.

A good example of look-alike molecules are **opiates,** a class of drugs that includes heroin and morphine. In molecular shape, opiates resemble a group of neurotransmitters in the brain called **endorphins,** which have the effect of blocking pain. The discovery that opiates mimic naturally occurring substances in the brain has prompted considerable research on the chemical control system in the body that copes with stress and pain. Individuals who appear indifferent to pain may have an unusual ability to increase the production of these natural painkillers when they are needed. Research with one of the endorphins, called *enkephalin,* has helped explain why a painkiller like morphine can be addictive. Under normal conditions, enkephalin occupies a certain number of opiate receptors. Morphine relieves pain by binding to the receptors that are left unfilled. Too much morphine can cause a drop in enkephalin production, leaving opiate receptors unfilled. The body then requires more morphine to fill the unoccupied receptors and to reduce pain. When morphine is discontinued, the opiate receptors are left unfilled, causing painful withdrawal symptoms. The fact that the brain synthesizes substances that resemble opiates has been invoked to explain all sorts of effects. Joggers tout the theory that physical exertion increases enkephalin production to induce a "runner's high." Acupuncturists say their needles actuate enkephalins that act as natural anesthetics. There is, however, no definitive evidence to support these claims.

Drugs that influence mental functioning and mood, such as opiates, are called **psychoactive drugs**. By and large, they produce their effects by altering one of the various neurotransmitter-receptor systems. Different drugs can have different actions at the same

called the hippocampus, which plays a key role in the formation of new memories (Squire, 1987). Alzheimer's disease, a devastating disorder that affects many older people, involves impairment of memory and other cognitive functions. It has been demonstrated that brain cells producing ACh tend to degenerate in Alzheimer patients, and consequently the brain's production of ACh is reduced; the less ACh the brain produces, the more serious the memory loss.

ACh is also released at every synapse at which a nerve terminates at a skeletal muscle fiber. The ACh is directed onto small structures called *end plates,* located on the muscle cells. The end plates are covered with receptor molecules that, when activated by ACh, trigger a molecular linkage inside the muscle cells that results in their contraction. Certain drugs that affect ACh can produce muscle paralysis. For example, botulinum toxin, which forms from bacteria in improperly canned foods, blocks receptors for ACh at nerve-muscle synapses and can cause death when the muscles for breathing become paralyzed. Some nerve gases developed for warfare and many pesticides cause paralysis by destroying the enzyme that degrades ACh once the neuron has been fired; when the degradation process fails there is an uncontrolled buildup of ACh in the nervous system so that normal synaptic transmission becomes impossible.

**Norepinephrine** (NE) is a neurotransmitter that is produced mainly by neurons in the brain stem. Two well-known drugs, **cocaine** and **amphetamines,** prolong the action of NE by slowing down its reuptake process. Because of the delay in the reuptake, the receiving neurons are activated for a longer period of time, thus causing the stimulating psychological

synapse. One drug might mimic the effect of a specific neurotransmitter, another might occupy the receptor site so that the normal neurotransmitter is blocked out, and still others might affect the reuptake or degradation processes. The drug action will either increase or decrease the effectiveness of neural transmission.

Two drugs, **chlorpromazine** and **reserpine,** have proved effective in treating schizophrenia (a mental illness to be discussed in Chapter 16). Both drugs act on norepinephrine and dopamine systems, but their antipsychotic action is primarily due to their effect on the neurotransmitter dopamine. It appears that chlorpromazine blocks dopamine receptors, whereas reserpine reduces dopamine levels by destroying storage vesicles in the synaptic terminals. The effectiveness of these drugs in treating schizophrenia has led to the **dopamine hypothesis,** which postulates that schizophrenia is due to an excess of dopamine activity in critical cell groups within the brain. The key evidence for the hypothesis is that antipsychotic drugs seem to be clinically effective to the extent that they block the transmission of impulses by dopamine molecules. The dopamine hypothesis has wide support, but as yet, efforts to demonstrate an increase in dopamine concentrations in schizophrenics, as compared with nonschizophrenics, have not been conclusive.

Research on neurotransmitter-receptor systems has increased our understanding of how drugs work. In an earlier period, psychoactive drugs were discovered almost entirely by accident and their development took years of research. Now, as we gain more knowledge about neurotransmitters and receptors, new drugs can be designed and developed in a systematic way.

During the last 10 years, a great deal has been learned about the molecular basis of interneural communication. The emerging picture is that thousands of different types of molecules are involved—not just transmitter and receptor molecules but also the enzymes that manufacture and degrade them and various other molecules that modulate their action (Groves & Rebec, 1992). Of course, each time a new molecule is identified, we have discovered the potential for at least two diseases or forms of mental illness; some people will surely have too much of that molecule and others too little. Research on these problems has proved so productive that the field has been given the name *molecular psychology* (Franklin, 1987). The basic idea behind this new discipline is that mental processes and their aberrations can be analyzed in terms of the molecular interplay that takes place between neurons.

effects of these drugs. In contrast, **lithium** is a drug that speeds up the reuptake of NE, causing a person's mood level to be depressed. Any drug that causes NE to increase or decrease in the brain is correlated with an increase or decrease in the individual's mood level.

Another prominent neurotransmitter is **gamma-aminobutyric acid (GABA).** This substance is one of the major inhibitory transmitters in the nervous system. For example, the drug *picrotoxin* blocks GABA receptors and produces convulsions because (without GABA's inhibiting influence) there is a lack of control in muscle movement. The tranquilizing properties of certain drugs used to treat patients suffering from anxiety are related to a facilitation of GABA inhibitory activity.

Some mood-altering drugs, such as **chlorpromazine** and **LSD,** create their effects by causing an excess or deficiency of specific neurotransmitters. Chlorpromazine, a drug used to treat schizophrenia, blocks the receptors for the neurotransmitter **dopamine** and allows fewer messages to get through. Too much dopamine at the synapse may cause schizophrenia; too little dopamine results in Parkinson's disease. LSD is similar in chemical structure to the neurotransmitter **serotonin,** which affects emotion. Evidence shows that LSD accumulates in certain brain cells, where it mimics the action of serotonin and overstimulates the cells.

The excitatory neurotransmitter **glutamate** is present in more neurons of the central nervous system than any other transmitter. There are at least three subtypes of glutamate receptors, and one in particular is believed to play a role in learning and memory. It is called the **NMDA receptor** after the chemical (N-methyl D-aspartate) that is used to detect it. Neurons in the

**FIGURE 2-5**

**NMDA Receptors and LTP** *The diagram illustrates a possible mechanism by which NMDA receptors could effect a long-term change in the strength of a synaptic connection (LTP). When neurotransmitters (blue triangles) are released from the first signaling neuron, they activate non-NMDA receptors in the receiving neuron that partially depolarize the cell membrane. This partial depolarization sensitizes the NMDA receptors so that they can now be activated by glutamate transmitters (brown squares) coming from the second signaling neuron. Activating the NMDA receptors causes their associated calcium channels to open. As the calcium ions flow into the cell, they interact with various enzymes (purple circles) presumably in ways that restructure the cell membrane. This restructuring makes the receiving neuron more sensitive to neurotransmitters from the first neuron, so that in time it can activate the receiving neuron on its own, thus inducing LTP.*

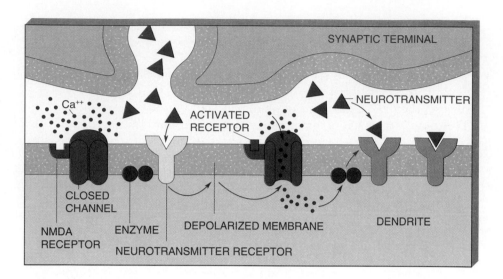

hippocampus (an area near the center of the brain) are particularly rich in NMDA receptors, and several lines of evidence indicate that this area is critical in the formation of new memories.

The NMDA receptor is not like other receptors in that successive signals from two different neurons are required in order to activate it. The signal coming from the first neuron sensitizes the cell membrane in which the NMDA receptor is embedded. Once sensitized, a second signal (glutamate transmitters coming from another neuron) will activate the receptor. When such converging signals occur, the NMDA receptor allows a very large number of calcium ions to flow into the neuron. That influx of ions appears to cause a long-term change in the membrane of the neuron making it more responsive to the initial signal when it reoccurs at a later time—a phenomenon known as **long-term potentiation,** or **LTP** (see Figure 2-5).

Such a mechanism, in which two convergent signals strengthen a synapse, provides a possible explanation of how separate events become associated in memory. For example, in an associative learning experiment, the sound of a bell is immediately followed by the sight of food. When a dog sees the food, it salivates. But with repeated pairings of the bell and food, the dog learns to salivate to the sound of the bell alone—possibly indicating that the "bell" signal and the "food" signal have converged at the synapses causing salivation. With enough pairing of the bell and food, those synapses are strengthened by LTP so that eventually the bell alone will cause the dog to salivate. The NMDA mechanism offers an intriguing theory of how events are associated in memory—a theory that is being actively pursued by researchers (Zalutsky & Nicoll, 1990).

# Organization of the Nervous System

All parts of the nervous system are interrelated. But for purposes of discussion, the nervous system can be separated into two major divisions, each having two subdivisions.

The **central nervous system** includes all the neurons in the brain and spinal cord. The **peripheral nervous system** consists of the nerves connecting the brain and spinal cord to the other parts of the body. The peripheral nervous system is further divided into the *somatic system* and the *autonomic system*.

The sensory nerves of the **somatic system** transmit information about external stimulation from the skin, muscles, and joints to the central nervous system; they make us aware of pain, pressure, and temperature variations. The motor nerves of the somatic system carry impulses from the central nervous system to the muscles of the body, where they initiate action. All the muscles we use in making voluntary movements, as well as involuntary adjustments in posture and balance, are controlled by these nerves.

The nerves of the **autonomic system** run to and from the internal organs, regulating such processes as respiration, heart rate, and digestion. The autonomic system, which plays a major role in emotion, is discussed later in this chapter.

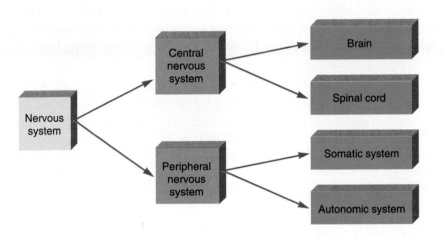

Most of the nerve fibers connecting various parts of the body to the brain are gathered together in the *spinal cord*, where they are protected by the bony spinal vertebrae. The spinal cord is remarkably compact—barely the diameter of your little finger. Some of the simplest stimulus-response reflexes are carried out at the level of the spinal cord. One example is the knee jerk, the extension of the leg in response to a tap on the tendon that runs in front of the kneecap. Frequently a doctor uses this test to determine the efficiency of the spinal reflexes. The natural function of this reflex is to ensure that the leg will extend when the knee is bent by the force of gravity, so the organism remains standing. When the knee tendon is tapped, the attached muscle stretches, and a signal from sensory cells embedded in the muscle is transmitted through sensory neurons to the spinal cord. There the sensory neurons synapse directly with motor neurons, which transmit impulses back to the same muscle, causing it to contract and the leg to extend. Although this response can occur solely in the spinal cord without any assistance from the brain, it can be modulated by messages from higher nervous centers. If you grip your hands just before the knee is tapped, the extension movement is exaggerated. Or if you consciously want to inhibit the reflex just before the doctor taps the tendon, you can do so. The basic mechanism is built into the spinal cord, but it can be modified by higher brain centers.

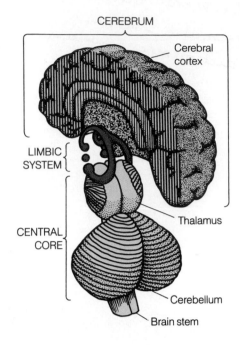

**FIGURE 2-6**
**Three Concentric Layers of the Human Brain** *The central core and the limbic system are shown in their entirety, but the left cerebral hemisphere has been removed. The cerebellum of the central core controls balance and muscular coordination; the thalamus serves as a switchboard for messages coming from the sense organs; the hypothalamus (not shown but located below the thalamus) regulates endocrine activity and such life-maintaining processes as metabolism and temperature control. The limbic system is concerned with actions that satisfy basic needs and with emotion. The cerebral cortex (an outer layer of cells covering the cerebrum) is the center of higher mental processes, where sensations are registered, voluntary actions initiated, decisions made, and plans formulated.*

# Structure of the Brain

Some brain structures are clearly demarcated. Others gradually merge into each other; this leads to debate about their exact boundaries and the functions they control. For descriptive purposes, it will be useful to think of the human brain as composed of three concentric layers: (a) a *central core;* (b) the *limbic system;* and (c) the *cerebral hemispheres* (together known as the *cerebrum*). Figure 2-6 shows how these layers fit together; it can be compared with the more detailed labeling of the cross section of the human brain in Figure 2-7.

## Central Core

The **central core** includes most of the brain stem. The first slight enlargement of the spinal cord as it enters the skull is the **medulla,** a narrow structure that controls breathing and some reflexes that help the organism maintain an upright posture. Also, at this point the major nerve tracts coming up from the spinal cord cross over so that the right side of the brain is connected to the left side of the body, and the left side of the brain to the right side of the body.

**CEREBELLUM** Attached to the rear of the brain stem, slightly above the medulla, is a convoluted structure, the cerebellum. The cerebellum is concerned primarily with the coordination of movement. Specific movements may be initiated at higher levels, but their smooth coordination depends on the cerebellum. Damage to the cerebellum results in jerky, uncoordinated movements.

**THALAMUS AND HYPOTHALAMUS** Located just above the brain stem inside the cerebral hemispheres are two egg-shaped groups of nerve cell nuclei that make up the thalamus. One region of the thalamus acts as a relay station and directs incoming information to the cerebrum from the sense receptors for vision, hearing, touch, and taste. Another region of the thalamus plays an important role in the control of sleep and wakefulness.

The **hypothalamus** is a much smaller structure, located just below the thalamus. Centers in the hypothalamus govern eating, drinking, and sexual behavior. The hypothalamus regulates endocrine activity and maintains **homeostasis.** Homeostasis refers to the normal level of functioning characteristic of the healthy organism, such as normal body temperature, heart rate, and blood pressure. Under stress, homeostasis is disturbed and processes are set into motion to correct the disequilibrium. For example, if we are too warm, we perspire; and if we are too cool, we shiver. Both of these processes tend to restore normal temperature and are controlled by the hypothalamus.

The hypothalamus also plays an important role in emotion and in our response to stress-producing situations. Mild electrical stimulation of certain areas in the hypothalamus produces feelings of pleasure, while stimulation of adjacent regions produces sensations that are unpleasant or painful. By its influence on the pituitary gland, which lies just below it (see Figure 2-7), the hypothalamus controls the endocrine system and in turn the production of hormones. This control is particularly important when the body must mobilize a complex set of physiological processes (the "fight-or-flight" response) to deal with emergencies. The hypothalamus has been called the "stress center" in recognition of its special role in mobilizing the body for action.

The hypothalamus, as noted, plays a key role in governing sexual behavior. There is even evidence to suggest that homosexuality is related to the structure of this part of the brain. If one measures the volume of a specific group of cells in the anterior region of the hypothalamus, its size is found to be more than twice as large in heterosexual men as in women. However, for homosexual men the size of this group of cells is equal to that for women (LeVay, 1991). This research suggests that the size difference may not only correlate with sexual orientation but play a role in causing it. Either interpretation—cause or consequence of an individual's sexual orientation—raises the possibility that a biological difference is a factor in homosexuality.

**RETICULAR SYSTEM**  A network of neural circuits that extends from the lower brain stem up to the thalamus, traversing through some of the other central core structures, is the reticular system. This system plays an important role in controlling our state of arousal. When an electric current of a certain voltage is sent through electrodes implanted in the reticular system of a cat or dog, the animal goes to sleep; stimulation by a current with a more rapidly changing waveform awakens the sleeping animal.

The reticular system also plays a role in our ability to focus attention on particular stimuli. All of the sense receptors have nerve fibers that feed into the reticular system. The system appears to act as a filter, allowing some of the sensory messages to pass to the cerebral cortex (to conscious awareness) while blocking others. Thus, our state of consciousness at any moment appears to be influenced by a filtering process in the reticular system.

## Limbic System

Around the central core of the brain are a number of structures that together are called the **limbic system** (refer back to Figure 2-6). This system is closely interconnected with the hypothalamus and appears to impose

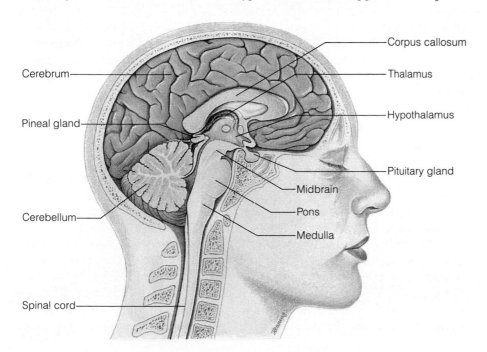

Cerebrum

Pineal gland

Cerebellum

Spinal cord

Corpus callosum

Thalamus

Hypothalamus

Pituitary gland

Midbrain

Pons

Medulla

**FIGURE 2-7**
**Human Brain** *This schematic drawing shows the main structures of the central nervous system. (Only the upper portion of the spinal cord is shown.)*

## *Critical*
# DISCUSSION

## *Pictures of the Living Brain*

A number of techniques have been developed to obtain detailed pictures of the living human brain without causing the patient distress or damage. Before these techniques were perfected, the precise location and identification of most types of brain injury could be determined only by exploratory neurosurgery, by a complicated neurological diagnosis, or by autopsy after the patient's death. The new techniques depend on sophisticated computer methods that have become feasible only recently.

One such technique is **computerized axial tomography** (abbreviated CAT or simply CT). This procedure involves sending a narrow X-ray beam through the patient's head and measuring the amount of radiation that gets through. The revolutionary aspect of the technique is that measurements are made at hundreds of thousands of different orientations (or axes) through the head. These measurements are then fed into a computer and, by making appropriate calculations, a cross-sectional picture of the brain is reconstructed that can be photographed or displayed on a television monitor. The cross-sectional slice can be at any level and angle desired. The term "computerized axial tomography" refers to the critical role of the computer, the many axes at which measurements are made, and the resulting image that is a cross-sectional slice through the brain (*tomo* is from the Greek word meaning "slice" or "cut").

A newer and even more powerful technique involves **magnetic resonance imaging** (abbreviated MRI). Scanners of this sort use strong magnetic fields, radio-frequency pulses, and computers to compose the image. In this procedure the patient lies in a dough-

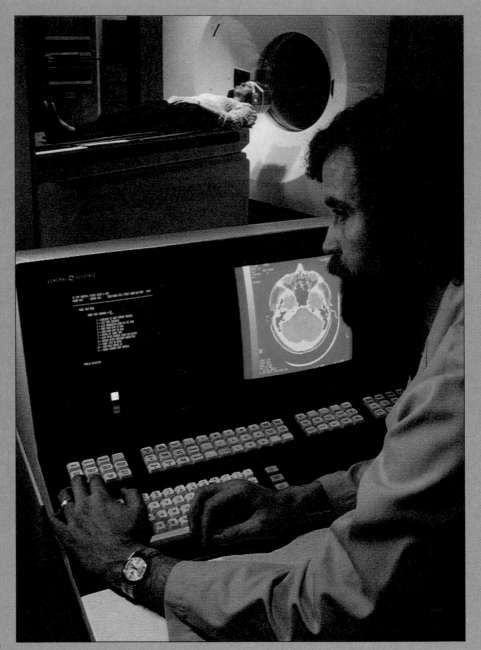

*A technician administers an MRI scan, which generates a computerized cross section of the patient's brain.*

nut-shaped tunnel surrounded by a large magnet that generates a powerful magnetic field. When the anatomic part to be studied is placed in a strong magnetic field and exposed to a certain radio-frequency pulse, the tissues emit a signal that can be measured. As with the CT scanner, hundreds of thousands of such measurements are made and then manipulated by a computer into a two-dimensional image of the anatomic part. Among scientists, the technique is usually called *nuclear magnetic resonance* because what is being measured are variations in the energy level of hydrogen atom nuclei in the body caused by

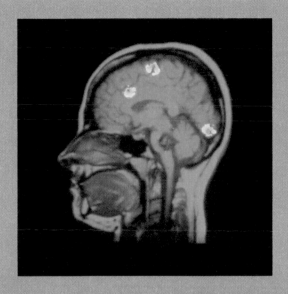

*PET image shows three areas in the left brain active during a language task.*

*Red areas indicate maximum brain activity; blue areas show minimum activity.*

the radio-frequency pulses. However, many physicians prefer to drop the term "nuclear" and simply call it magnetic resonance imaging, since they fear the public may confuse the reference to the nucleus of an atom with nuclear radiation.

MRI offers greater precision than the CT scanner in the diagnosis of diseases of the brain and spinal cord. For example, an MRI cross section of the brain shows features characteristic of multiple sclerosis that are not detected by a CT scanner; previously, diagnosis of this disease required hospitalization and a test in which dye is injected into the canal around the spinal cord. MRI is also useful in the detection of abnormalities in the spinal cord and at the base of the brain, such as herniated disks, tumors, and birth malformations.

While CT and MRI provide a picture of the anatomical detail of the brain, it is often desirable to assess the level of neural activity at different spots in the brain. A computer-based scanning procedure called **positron emission tomography** (abbreviated PET) provides this additional information. This technique depends on the fact that every cell in the body requires energy to conduct its various metabolic processes. In

the brain, neurons utilize glucose (obtained from the bloodstream) as their principal source of energy. A small amount of a radioactive tracer compound can be mixed with glucose so that each molecule of glucose has a tiny speck of radioactivity (that is, a label) attached to it. If this harmless mixture is injected into the bloodstream, after a few minutes the brain cells begin to use the radio-labeled glucose in the same way they use regular glucose. The PET scan is essentially a highly sensitive detector of radioactivity (it is not like an X-ray machine, which *emits* X rays, but rather like a Geiger counter, which *measures* radioactivity). Neurons of the brain that are most active require the most glucose and, therefore, will be the most radioactive. The PET scan measures the amount of radioactivity and sends the information to a computer that draws a color cross-sectional picture of the brain, with different colors representing different levels of neural activity. The measurement of radioactivity is based on the emission of positively charged particles called *positrons*— hence the term "positron emission tomography."

Comparing PET scans of normal individuals with those of persons who

have neurological disorders indicates that a variety of brain problems (epilepsy, blood clots, brain tumors, and so on) can be identified using this technique. For psychological research, the PET scan has been used to compare the brains of schizophrenics with those of nonschizophrenics and has revealed differences in the metabolic levels of certain cortical areas (Andreasen, 1988). It has also been used to investigate the brain areas activated during such higher mental functions as listening to music, doing mathematics, or speaking, the goal being to identify the brain structures involved (Posner, Petersen, Fox, & Raichle, 1988).

The CT, MRI, and PET scanners are proving to be invaluable tools for studying the relationship between the brain and behavior. These instruments are an example of how progress in one field of science forges ahead because of technical developments in another. (Pechura and Marrin, 1991).

additional controls over some of the instinctive behaviors regulated by the hypothalamus and brain stem. Animals that have only rudimentary limbic systems (for example, fish and reptiles) carry out activities such as feeding, attacking, fleeing from danger, and mating by means of stereotyped behaviors. In mammals, the limbic system seems to inhibit some of the instinctive patterns, allowing the organism to be more flexible and adaptive to changes in the environment.

One part of the limbic system, the **hippocampus,** plays a special role in memory. Surgical removal of the hippocampus or accidental damage to the structure demonstrates that it is critical for the storage of new events as lasting memories, but it is not necessary for the retrieval of older memories. Upon recovery from such an operation, the patient will have no difficulty recognizing old friends or recalling earlier experiences; he will be able to read and perform skills learned earlier in life. However, he will have little, if any, recall of events that occurred in the year or so just prior to the operation. He will not remember events and people he meets after the operation at all. For example the patient will fail to recognize a new person with whom he may have spent many hours earlier in the day. He will do the same jigsaw puzzle week after week, never remembering having done it before, and will read the same newspaper over and over without remembering the contents (Squire, 1992).

The limbic system is also involved in emotional behavior. Monkeys with lesions in some regions of the limbic system react with rage at the slightest provocation, suggesting that the destroyed area was exerting an inhibiting influence. Monkeys with lesions in other areas of the limbic system no longer express aggressive behavior and show no hostility, even when attacked. They simply ignore the attacker and act as if nothing had happened.

Describing the brain in terms of three concentric structures—the central core, the limbic system, and the cerebrum (to be discussed in the next section)—must not lead us to think of these structures as independent of one another. We might use the analogy of a network of interrelated computers. Each has specialized functions, but they must work together to produce the most effective result. Similarly, the analysis of information coming from the senses requires one kind of computation and decision process (for which the cerebrum is well adapted), differing from that which controls a reflexive sequence of activities (the limbic system). The finer adjustments of the muscles (as in writing or playing a musical instrument) require another kind of control system, in this case mediated by the cerebellum. All these activities are organized into an integrated system that maintains the integrity of the organism.

## Cerebral Hemispheres

The **cerebrum** is more highly developed in human beings than in any other organism. Its outer layer is called the **cerebral cortex;** in Latin, *cortex* means "bark." The cerebral cortex (often simply called the cortex) of a preserved brain appears gray because it consists largely of nerve cell bodies and unmyelinated fibers—hence the term "gray matter." The inside of the cerebrum, beneath the cortex, is composed mostly of myelinated axons and appears white.

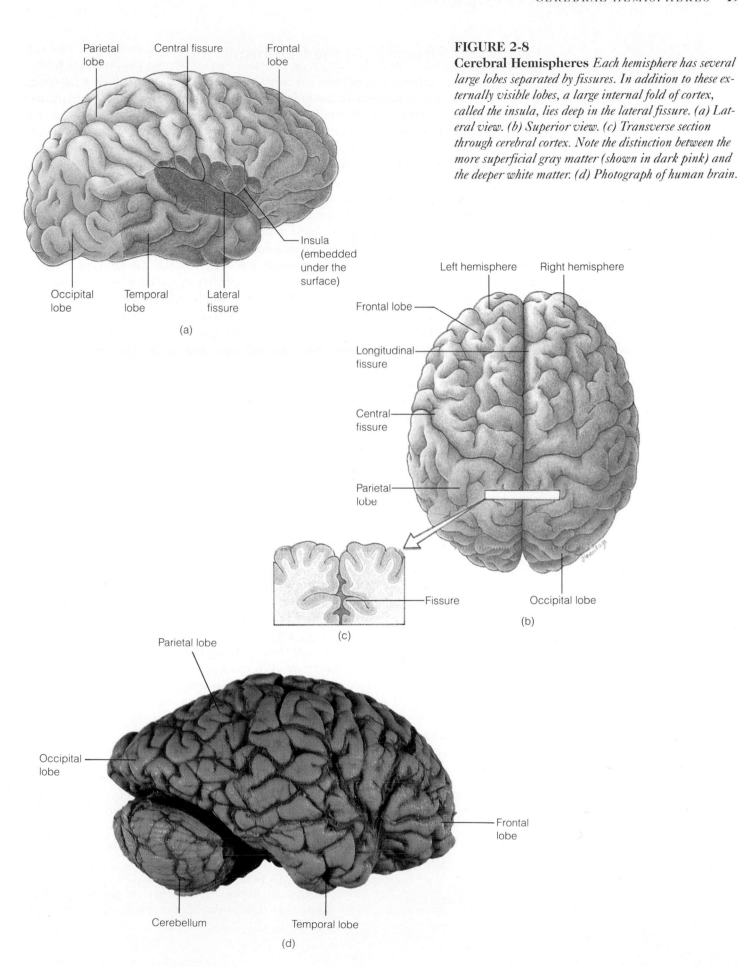

Parietal lobe
Central fissure
Frontal lobe
Occipital lobe
Temporal lobe
Lateral fissure
Insula (embedded under the surface)

(a)

**FIGURE 2-8**

**Cerebral Hemispheres** *Each hemisphere has several large lobes separated by fissures. In addition to these externally visible lobes, a large internal fold of cortex, called the insula, lies deep in the lateral fissure. (a) Lateral view. (b) Superior view. (c) Transverse section through cerebral cortex. Note the distinction between the more superficial gray matter (shown in dark pink) and the deeper white matter. (d) Photograph of human brain.*

Left hemisphere
Right hemisphere
Frontal lobe
Longitudinal fissure
Central fissure
Parietal lobe
Occipital lobe

(b)

Fissure

(c)

Parietal lobe
Occipital lobe
Frontal lobe
Cerebellum
Temporal lobe

(d)

## Structure of the Cerebrum

The cortex of a lower mammal, such as the rat, is small and relatively smooth. As we ascend the phylogenetic scale to the higher mammals, the amount of cortex relative to the amount of total brain tissue increases, and the cortex becomes progressively more wrinkled and convoluted, so that its actual surface area is far greater than it would be if it were a smooth covering of the cerebrum.

All of the sensory systems (for example, vision, audition, and touch) project information to specific areas of the cortex. The movements of body parts (motor responses) are controlled by another area of the cortex. The rest of the cortex, which is neither sensory nor motor, consists of association areas. These areas are concerned with other aspects of behavior—memory, thought, and language—and occupy the largest area of the human cortex.

Before discussing some of these locations, we need to introduce a few landmarks in describing areas of the **cerebral hemispheres.** The two hemispheres are basically symmetrical, with a deep division between them running from front to rear. So, our first classification is the division into **right** and **left hemispheres.** Each hemisphere is divided into four *lobes:* the **frontal, parietal, occipital,** and **temporal.** The divisions between these lobes are shown in Figure 2-8. The frontal lobe is separated from the parietal lobe by the **central fissure,** running from near the top of the head sideways to the ears. The division between the parietal lobe and the occipital lobe is less clear-cut; for our purpose, it suffices to say that the parietal lobe is at the top of the brain behind the central fissure and that the occipital lobe is at the rear of the brain. The temporal lobe is demarcated by a deep fissure at the side of the brain, the **lateral fissure.**

## Cortical Areas and Their Functions

**MOTOR AREA** The motor area controls the voluntary movements of the body; it lies just in front of the central fissure (see Figure 2-9). Electrical stimulation at certain spots on the motor cortex produces movement of specific body parts; when these same spots on the motor cortex are injured, movement is impaired. The body is represented on the motor cortex in approximately upside-down form. For example, movements of the toes are mediated near the top of the head, whereas tongue and mouth movements are mediated near the bottom of the motor area. Movements on the right side of the body are governed by the motor cortex of the left hemisphere; movements on the left side, by the right hemisphere.

**SOMATOSENSORY AREA** In the parietal lobe, separated from the motor area by the central fissure, lies an area that if stimulated electrically produces a sensory experience somewhere on the opposite side of the body. It is as though a part of the body were being touched or moved. This is called the somatosensory area (body-sense area). Heat, cold, touch, pain, and the sense of body movement are all represented here.

Most of the nerve fibers in the pathways that radiate to and from the somatosensory and motor areas cross to the opposite side of the body. Thus, the sensory impulses from the right side of the body go to the left

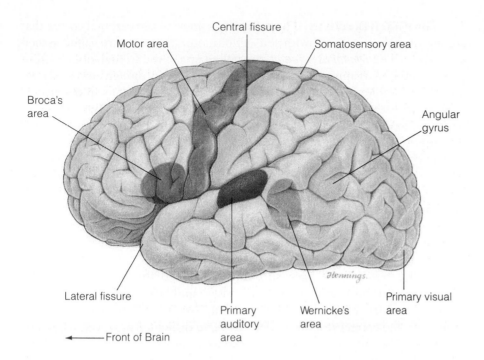

*Central fissure*

Motor area

Somatosensory area

Broca's area

Angular gyrus

*Hennings.*

Lateral fissure

Primary auditory area

Wernicke's area

Primary visual area

◄──── Front of Brain

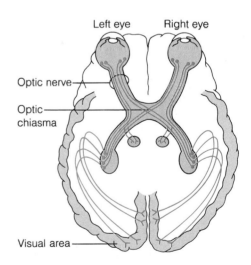

**FIGURE 2-9**
**Localization of Function in the Left Cortex** *A major part of the cortex is involved in generating movements and in analyzing sensory inputs. These areas (which include motor, somatosensory, visual, auditory, and olfactory areas) are present on both sides of the brain. Other functions are found on only one side of the brain. For example, Broca's area and Wernicke's area are involved in the production and understanding of language, and the angular gyrus is involved in matching the visual form of a word with its auditory form; these functions exist only on the left side of the human brain.*

somatosensory cortex, and the muscles of the right foot and hand are controlled by the left motor cortex.

It seems to be a general rule that the amount of somatosensory or motor area associated with a particular part of the body is directly related to its sensitivity and use. For example, among four-footed mammals the dog has only a small amount of cortical tissue representing the forepaws, whereas the raccoon—which makes extensive use of its forepaws in exploring and manipulating its environment—has a much larger representative cortical area, including regions for the separate fingers of the forepaw. The rat, which learns a great deal about its environment by means of its sensitive whiskers, has a separate cortical area for each whisker.

**VISUAL AREA** At the back of each occipital lobe is an area of the cortex known as the visual area. Figure 2-10 shows the optic nerve fibers and neural pathways leading from each eye to the visual cortex. Notice that some of the optic fibers from the right eye go to the right cerebral hemisphere, whereas others cross over at a junction called the optic chiasma and go to the opposite hemisphere; the same arrangement holds true for the left eye. Fibers from the right sides of *both* eyes go to the right hemisphere of the brain, and fibers from the left sides of both eyes go to the left hemisphere. Consequently, damage to the visual area of one hemisphere (say, the left) will result in blind fields in the left sides of both eyes, causing a loss of vision to the right side of the environment. This fact is sometimes helpful in pinpointing the location of a brain tumor or other abnormalities.

**AUDITORY AREA** The auditory area (found on the surface of the temporal lobe at the side of each hemisphere) is involved in the analysis of complex auditory signals. It is particularly concerned with the temporal patterning of sound, as in human speech. Both ears are represented in the auditory areas on both sides of the cortex; however, connections to the contralateral side are stronger.

Left eye    Right eye

Optic nerve

Optic chiasma

Visual area

**FIGURE 2-10**
**Visual Pathways** *Nerve fibers from the inner, or nasal, half of the retina cross over at the optic chiasma and go to opposite sides of the brain. Thus, stimuli falling on the right side of each retina are transmitted to the right hemisphere, and stimuli impinging on the left side of each retina are transmitted to the left hemisphere.*

**ASSOCIATION AREAS**  The many large areas of the cerebral cortex that are not directly concerned with sensory or motor processes are called association areas. The *frontal association areas* (the parts of the frontal lobes in front of the motor area) appear to play an important role in thought processes required for problem solving. In monkeys, for example, lesions in the frontal lobes destroy the ability to solve a delayed-response problem. In this kind of problem, food is placed in one of two cups while the monkey watches, and the cups are covered with identical objects. An opaque screen is then placed between the monkey and the cups; after a specified period of time the screen is removed, and the monkey is allowed to choose one of the cups. Normal monkeys can remember the correct cup after delays of several minutes, but monkeys with frontal lobe lesions cannot solve the problem if the delay is more than a few seconds. This delayed-response deficit following brain lesions is unique to the frontal cortex; it does not occur if lesions are made in other cortical regions (French & Harlow, 1962).

Human beings who have suffered damage to the frontal association areas can perform many intellectual tasks normally, including delayed-response problems. Their ability to use language probably enables them to remember the correct response. They do have difficulty, however, when it is necessary to shift frequently from one strategy to another while working on a problem (Milner, 1964).

The *posterior association areas* are located near the various primary sensory areas and appear to consist of subareas, each serving a particular sense. For example, the lower portion of the temporal lobe is related to visual perception. Lesions in this area produce deficits in the ability to recognize and discriminate different forms. A lesion here does not cause loss of visual acuity, as would a lesion in the primary visual area of the occipital lobe; the individual "sees" the forms (and can trace the outline) but cannot identify the shape or distinguish it from a different form (Goodglass & Butters, 1988).

## Asymmetries in the Brain

On casual examination, the two halves of the human brain look like mirror images of each other. But closer examination reveals asymmetries. When brains are measured during autopsies, the left hemisphere is almost always larger than the right hemisphere. Also, the right hemisphere contains many long neural fibers that connect widely separate areas of the brain, whereas the left hemisphere contains many shorter fibers that provide rich interconnections within a limited area (Geschwind & Galaburda, 1987).

As early as 1861, the French physician Paul Broca examined the brain of a patient who had suffered speech loss, and he found damage in an area of the left hemisphere just above the lateral fissure in the frontal lobe. This region, known as **Broca's area** and shown in Figure 2-9, is involved in the production of speech. Destruction of the equivalent region in the right hemisphere usually does not result in speech impairment. The areas involved in understanding speech and in the ability to write and understand written words are also usually located in the left hemisphere. Thus, a person who suffers a stroke that damages the left hemisphere is more likely to show language impairment than one whose damage is confined to the right hemisphere. A few left-handed people have speech centers located in the right hemisphere, but the great majority have language functions in the left hemisphere (the same as right-handed individuals).

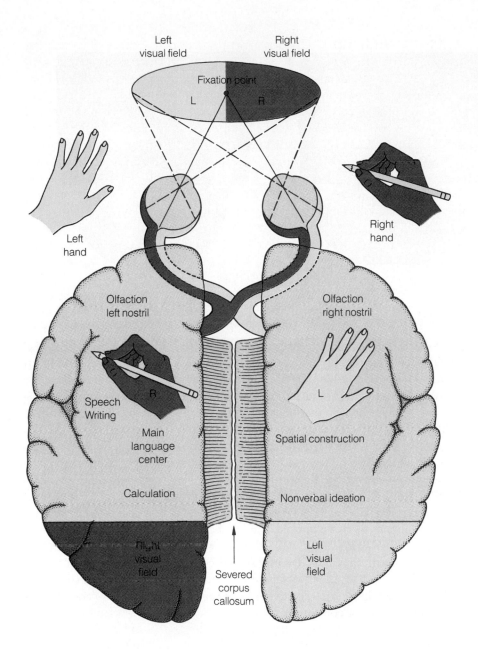

Left
visual field

Right
visual field

Fixation point

L     R

Left
hand

Right
hand

Olfaction
left nostril

Olfaction
right nostril

Speech
Writing

R

Main
language
center

Spatial construction

Calculation

Nonverbal ideation

Right
visual
field

Left
visual
field

Severed
corpus
callosum

**FIGURE 2-11**
**Sensory Inputs to the Two Hemispheres** *With the eyes fixated straight ahead, stimuli to the left of the fixation point go to the right cerebral hemisphere, and stimuli to the right go to the left hemisphere. The left hemisphere controls movements of the right hand, and the right hemisphere controls the left hand. Hearing is largely crossed in its input, but some sound representation goes to the hemisphere on the same side as the ear that registered it. The left hemisphere controls written and spoken language and mathematical calculations. The right hemisphere can understand only simple language; its main ability seems to involve spatial construction and pattern sense.*

Although the left hemisphere's role in language has been known for some time, only recently has it been possible to investigate what each hemisphere can do on its own. In the normal individual, the brain functions as an integrated whole; information in one hemisphere is immediately transferred to the other by way of a broad band of connecting nerve fibers called the **corpus callosum.** This connecting bridge can cause a problem in some forms of epilepsy, because a seizure starting in one hemisphere may cross over and trigger a massive discharge of neurons in the other. In an effort to prevent such generalized seizures in some severe epileptics, neurosurgeons have surgically severed the corpus callosum. The operation has proved successful for some individuals, resulting in a decrease in seizures. In addition, there appear to be no undesirable aftereffects; the patients seem to function in everyday life as well as individuals whose hemispheres are still connected. It took some very special tests to demonstrate how mental functions

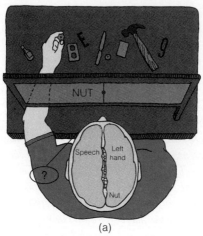
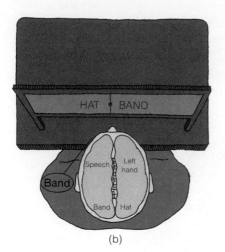
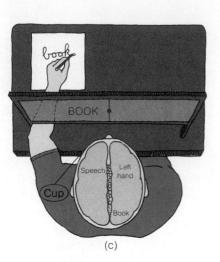

(a)       (b)       (c)

**FIGURE 2-12**
**Testing the Abilities of the Two Hemispheres** *(a) The split-brain subject correctly retrieves an object by touch with the left hand when its name is flashed to the right hemisphere, but he cannot name the object or describe what he has done. (b) The word "hatband" is flashed so that "hat" goes to the right cerebral hemisphere and "band" goes to the left hemisphere. The subject reports that he sees the word "band" but has no idea what kind of band. (c) A list of common objects (including "book" and "cup") is initially shown to both hemispheres. One word from the list ("book") is then projected to the right hemisphere. When given the command to do so, the left hand begins writing the word "book," but when questioned the subject does not know what his left hand has written and guesses "cup."*

are affected by separating the two hemispheres. A little more background information is needed to understand the experiments we are about to describe.

We have seen that the motor nerves cross over as they leave the brain, so that the left cerebral hemisphere controls the right side of the body and the right hemisphere controls the left. We noted also that the area for the production of speech (Broca's area) is located in the left hemisphere. When the eyes are fixated directly ahead, images to the left of the fixation point go through both eyes to the right side of the brain and images to the right of the fixation point go to the left side of the brain (see Figure 2-11). Thus, each hemisphere has a view of that half of the visual field in which "its" hand normally functions; for example, the left hemisphere sees the right hand in the right visual field. In the normal brain, stimuli entering one hemisphere are rapidly communicated, by way of the corpus callosum, to the other, so that the brain functions as a unit. We will see what happens when the corpus callosum in an individual is severed—leaving a **split brain**—and the two hemispheres cannot communicate.

## Split-Brain Subjects

Roger Sperry pioneered work in this field and was awarded the Nobel prize in 1981 for his research in neuroscience. In one of Sperry's test situations, a subject (who has undergone a split-brain operation) is seated in front of a screen that hides his hands from view (see Figure 2-12a). His gaze is fixed at a spot on the center of the screen and the word "nut" is flashed very briefly (one-tenth of a second) on the left side of the screen. Remember that this visual image goes to the right side of the brain, which controls the left side of the body. With his left hand, the subject can easily pick up the nut from a pile of objects hidden from view. But he cannot tell the experimenter what word flashed on the screen because speech is controlled by the left hemisphere and the visual image of "nut" was not transmitted to that hemisphere. When questioned, the split-brain subject seems unaware of what his left hand is doing. Since the sensory input from the left hand goes to the right hemisphere, the left hemisphere receives no information about what the left hand is feeling or doing. All information is fed back to the right hemisphere, which received the original visual input of the word "nut."

It is important that the word be flashed on the screen for no more than one-tenth of a second. If it remains longer, the subject can move his eyes so that the word is also projected to the left hemisphere. If the split-brain subject can move his eyes freely, information goes to both cerebral hemispheres; this in one reason why the deficiencies caused by severing the corpus callosum are not readily apparent in a person's daily activities.

Further experiments demonstrate that the split-brain subject can communicate through speech only what is going on in the left hemisphere. Figure 2-12b shows another test situation. The word "hatband" is flashed on the screen so that "hat" goes to the right hemisphere and "band" to the left. When asked what word he saw, the subject replies, "band." When asked what kind of band, he makes all sorts of guesses—"rubber band," "rock band," "band of robbers," and so forth—and only hits on "hatband" by chance. Tests with other word combinations (such as "keycase" and "suitcase") show similar results. What is perceived by the right hemisphere does not transfer to the conscious awareness of the left hemisphere. With the corpus callosum severed, each hemisphere seems oblivious to the experiences of the other.

If the split-brain subject is blindfolded and a familiar object (such as a comb, toothbrush, or keycase) is placed in his left hand, he appears to know what it is; for example, he can demonstrate its use by appropriate gestures. But he cannot express his knowledge in speech. If asked what is going on while he is manipulating the object, he has no idea. This is true as long as any sensory input from the object to the left (talking) hemisphere is blocked. But if the subject's right hand inadvertently touches the object or if it makes a characteristic sound (like the jingling of a keycase), the speaking hemisphere immediately gives the correct answer.

Although the right hemisphere cannot speak, it does have some linguistic capabilities. It recognized the meaning of the word "nut," as we saw in our first example, and it can write a little. In the experiment illustrated in Figure 2-12c, a split-brain subject is first shown a list of common objects such as cup, knife, book, and glass. This list is displayed long enough for the words to be projected to both hemispheres. Next, the list is removed, and one of the words (for example, "book") is flashed briefly on the left side of the screen so that it goes to the right hemisphere. If the subject is asked to write what he saw, his left hand will begin writing the word "book." If asked what his left hand has written, he has no idea and will guess at any of the words on the original list. The subject knows he has written something because he feels the writing movements through his body. But because there is no communication between the right hemisphere that saw and wrote the word and the left hemisphere that controls speech, the subject cannot tell you what he wrote (Nebes & Sperry, 1971; Sperry, 1968, 1970).

## Hemispheric Specialization

Studies with split-brain subjects indicate that the two hemispheres function differently. The left hemisphere governs our ability to express ourselves in language. It can perform many complicated logical and analytic activities and is skilled in mathematical computations. The right hemisphere can comprehend very simple language. It can respond to simple nouns by

# Language and the Brain

A great deal of our information about brain mechanisms for language comes from observations of patients suffering from brain damage. The damage may be due to tumors, penetrating head wounds, or the rupture of blood vessels. The term **aphasia** is used to describe language deficits caused by brain damage.

As already noted, Broca observed in the 1860s that damage to a specific area on the side of the left frontal lobe was linked to a speech disorder called *expressive aphasia*. Individuals with damage in Broca's area have difficulty enunciating words correctly and speak in a slow, labored way. Their speech often makes sense, but it includes only key words. Nouns are generally expressed in the singular, and adjectives, adverbs, articles, and conjunctions are apt to be omitted. However, these individuals have no difficulty understanding either spoken or written language.

In 1874, Carl Wernicke, a German investigator, reported that damage to another site in the cortex (also in the left hemisphere, but located in the temporal lobe) was linked to a language disorder called *receptive aphasia*. People with damage in this location, *Wernicke's area*, are not able to comprehend words; they can hear words, but they do not know their meaning. They can produce strings of words without difficulty and with proper articulation, but there are errors in word usage and their speech tends to be meaningless.

Based on an analysis of these defects, Wernicke developed a model for language production and understanding. Although the model is 100 years old, its general features still appear to be correct. Norman Geschwind has built on these ideas and developed the theory known as the *Wernicke-Geschwind model* (Geschwind, 1979). According to the model, Broca's area is assumed to store *articulatory codes* that specify the sequence of muscle actions required to pronounce a word. When these codes are transferred to the motor area, they activate the muscles of the lips, tongue, and larynx in the proper sequence and produce a spoken word (see figure).

Wernicke's area, on the other hand, is where auditory codes and the meanings of words are stored. If a word is to be spoken, its auditory code must be activated in Wernicke's area and transmitted by a bundle of nerves to Broca's area, where it activates the corresponding articulatory code. In turn, the articulatory code is transmitted to the motor area for the production of the spoken word.

If a word spoken by someone else is to be understood, it must be transmitted from the auditory area to Wernicke's area, where the spoken form of the word is matched to its auditory code, which in turn activates the word's meaning. When a written word is presented, it is first registered in the visual area and then relayed to the *angular gyrus*, which associates the visual form of the word with its auditory code in Wernicke's area; once the word's auditory code has been found, so has its meaning. Thus, the meanings of words are stored along with their acoustical codes in Wernicke's area. Broca's area stores articulatory codes, and the angular gyrus matches the written form of a word to its auditory code; neither of these two areas, however, stores information about word meaning. The meaning of a word is retrieved only when its acoustical code is activated in Wernicke's area.

The model explains many of the language deficits shown by aphasics. Damage restricted to Broca's area disrupts speech production but has less effect on the comprehension of spoken or written language. Damage to Wernicke's area disrupts all aspects of language comprehension, but the individual can still articulate words properly (since Broca's area is intact) even though the output is meaningless. The model also predicts that individuals with damage in the angular gyrus will not be able to read but will have no problem in comprehending speech or in speaking. Finally,

selecting objects such as a nut or comb, and it can even respond to associations of these objects. For example, if the right hemisphere is asked to retrieve from a group of objects the one used "for lighting fires," it will instruct the left hand to select a match. But the right hemisphere cannot comprehend more abstract linguistic forms; if it is presented with such simple commands as "wink," "nod," "shake head," or "smile," it seldom responds.

The right hemisphere can add simple two-digit numbers but can do little beyond this in the way of calculation. However, the right hemisphere appears to have a highly developed spatial and pattern sense. It is superior to the left hemisphere in constructing geometric and perspective drawings. It can assemble colored blocks to match a complex design much more effectively than the left hemisphere. When split-brain subjects are asked to use their right hand to assemble the blocks according to a picture design, they make numerous mistakes. Sometimes they have trouble keeping their left

if damage is restricted to the auditory area, a person will be able to read and to speak normally; but he or she will not be able to comprehend spoken speech.

There are some research findings that the Wernicke-Geschwind model does not adequately explain. For example, when the language areas of the brain are electrically stimulated in the course of a neurosurgical operation, both receptive and expressive functions may be disrupted at a single site. This suggests that some brain areas may share common mechanisms for producing and understanding speech. We are still a long way from a comprehensive model of language function, but there can be no doubt that some aspects of language function are highly localized in the brain (Geschwind & Galaburda, 1987).

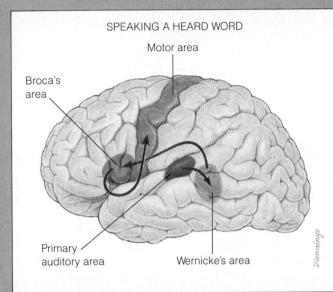

SPEAKING A HEARD WORD

Motor area

Broca's area

Primary auditory area

Wernicke's area

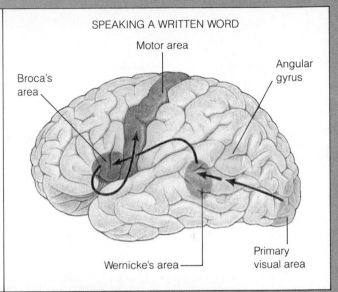

SPEAKING A WRITTEN WORD

Motor area

Broca's area

Angular gyrus

Wernicke's area

Primary visual area

**Wernicke-Geschwind Model** *The left panel illustrates the sequence of events when a spoken word is presented and the individual repeats the word in spoken form. Neural impulses from the ear are sent to the primary auditory area, but the word cannot be understood until the signal is next transmitted to Wernicke's area. In Wernicke's area, the word's acoustical code is retrieved and transmitted via a bundle of nerve fibers to Broca's area. In Broca's area, an articulatory code for the word is activated, which in turn directs the motor area. The motor area drives the lips, tongue, and larynx to produce the spoken word. In the right panel, a written word is presented and the individual is to speak the word. The visual input to the eye is first transmitted to the primary visual cortex and then relayed to the angular gyrus. The angular gyrus associates the visual form of the word with the related acoustical code in Wernicke's area. Once the acoustical code is retrieved and the meaning of the word is established, speaking the word is accomplished through the same sequence of events as before.*

hand from automatically correcting the mistakes being made by the right hand.

Studies with normal individuals tend to confirm the different specializations of the two hemispheres. For example, verbal information (such as words or nonsense syllables) can be identified faster and more accurately when flashed briefly to the left hemisphere (that is, in the right visual field) than to the right hemisphere. In contrast, the identification of faces, facial expressions of emotion, line slopes, or dot locations occurs more quickly when flashed to the right hemisphere. And **electroencephalogram** (EEG) studies indicate that electrical activity from the left hemisphere increases during a verbal task, whereas during a spatial task, EEG activity increases in the right hemisphere (Springer & Deutsch, 1989; Kosslyn, 1988).

One should not infer from this discussion that the two hemispheres work independently of each other. Just the opposite is true. The hemispheres differ in their specializations, but they integrate their activities at all times. It is this interaction that gives rise to mental processes greater than and different from each hemisphere's special contribution. As noted by Levy,

> These differences are seen in the contrasting contributions each hemisphere makes to all cognitive activities. When a person reads a story, the right hemisphere may play a special role in decoding visual information, maintaining an integrated story structure, appreciating humor and emotional content, deriving meaning from past associations and understanding metaphor. At the same time, the left hemisphere plays a special role in understanding syntax, translating written words into their phonetic representations and deriving meaning from complex relations among word concepts and syntax. But there is no activity in which only one hemisphere is involved or to which only one hemisphere makes a contribution. (1985, p. 44)

# Autonomic Nervous System

We noted earlier that the peripheral nervous system consists of two divisions. The somatic system controls the skeletal muscles and receives information from the skin, muscles, and various sensory receptors. The autonomic system controls the glands and the smooth muscles, which include the heart, the blood vessels, and the lining of the stomach and intestines. These muscles are called "smooth" because that is how they look when examined under a microscope. (Skeletal muscles, in contrast, have a striped appearance.) The autonomic nervous system derives its name from the fact that many of the activities it controls are autonomous, or self-regulating—such as digestion and circulation—and continue even when a person is asleep or unconscious.

The **autonomic nervous system** has two divisions, the **sympathetic** and the **parasympathetic,** which are often antagonistic in their actions. Figure 2-13 shows the contrasting effects of the two systems on various organs. For example, the parasympathetic system constricts the pupil of the eye, stimulates the flow of saliva, and slows the heart rate; the sympathetic system has the opposite effect in each case. The normal state of the body (somewhere between extreme excitement and vegetative placidity) is maintained by the balance between these two systems.

The sympathetic division tends to act as a unit. During emotional excitement, it simultaneously speeds up the heart, dilates the arteries of the skeletal muscles and heart, constricts the arteries of the skin and digestive organs, and causes perspiration. It also activates certain endocrine glands to secrete hormones that further increase arousal.

Unlike the sympathetic system, the parasympathetic division tends to affect one organ at a time. If the sympathetic system is thought of as dominant during violent and excited activity, the parasympathetic system may be thought of as dominant during quiescence. It participates in digestion and, in general, maintains the functions that conserve and protect bodily resources.

While the sympathetic and parasympathetic systems are usually antagonistic to one another, there are some exceptions to this principle. For example, the sympathetic system is dominant during fear and excitement; however, a not-uncommon parasympathetic symptom during extreme fear is the

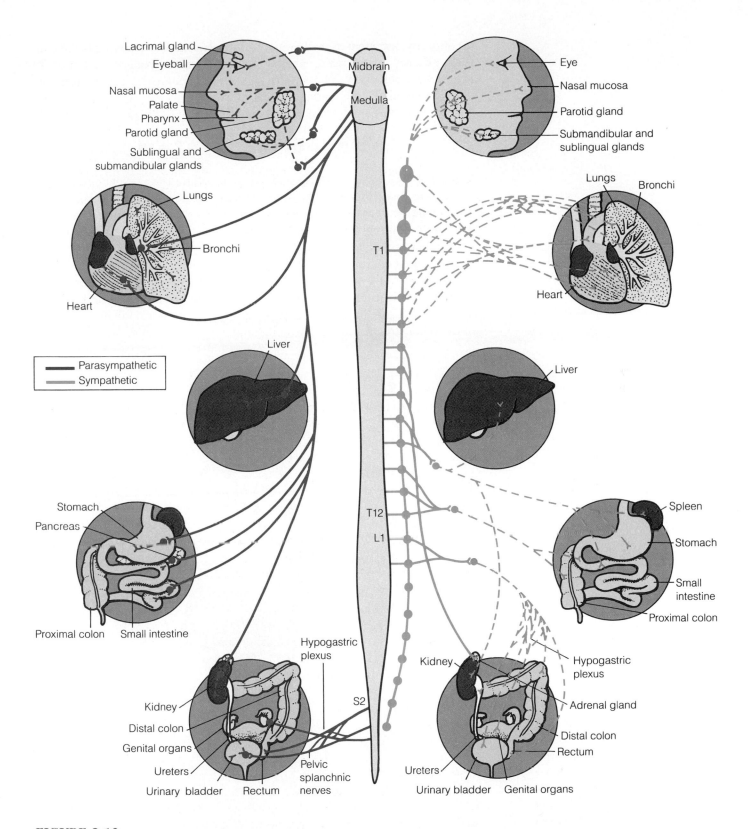

**FIGURE 2-13**

**Motor Fibers of the Autonomic Nervous System** *In this diagram the sympathetic division is indicated in blue and the parasympathetic is in red. Solid lines indicate preganglionic fibers and dashed lines indicate postganglionic fibers. Neurons of the sympathetic division originate in the thoracic and lumbar regions of the spinal cord; they form synaptic junctions with ganglia lying just outside the cord. Neurons of the parasympathetic division exit from the medulla region of the brain stem and from the lower (sacral) end of the spinal cord; they connect with ganglia near the organs stimulated. Most internal organs are innervated by both divisions, which function in opposition to each other.*

involuntary discharge of the bladder or bowels. Another example is the complete sex act in the male, which requires erection (parasympathetic) followed by ejaculation (sympathetic). Thus, although the two systems are often antagonistic, they interact in complex ways.

# Endocrine System

We can think of the nervous system as controlling the fast-changing activities of the body by its ability to directly activate muscles and glands. The **endocrine system** is slower acting and indirectly controls the activities of cell groups throughout the body by means of chemicals called **hormones.** These hormones are secreted by the various endocrine glands into the bloodstream (see Figure 2-14). The hormones then travel through the body, acting in various ways on cells of different types. Each target cell is equipped with receptors that recognize only the hormone molecules meant to act on that cell; the receptors pull the appropriate hormone molecules out of the bloodstream and into the cell. Some endocrine glands are activated by

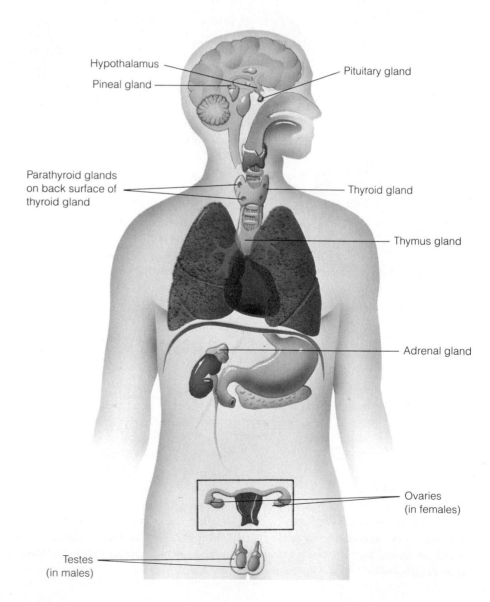

Hypothalamus

Pineal gland

Pituitary gland

Parathyroid glands on back surface of thyroid gland

Thyroid gland

Thymus gland

Adrenal gland

Ovaries (in females)

Testes (in males)

**FIGURE 2-14**
**Some of the Endocrine Glands** *Hormones secreted by the endocrine glands are as essential as the nervous system to the integration of the organism's activity. The endocrine system and the nervous system, however, differ in the speed with which they can act. A nerve impulse can travel through the organism in a few hundredths of a second. Seconds, or even minutes, may be required for an endocrine gland to produce an effect; the hormone, once released, must travel to its target site via the bloodstream—a much slower process.*

the nervous system, while others are activated by changes in the internal chemical state of the body.

One of the major endocrine glands, the **pituitary,** is partly an outgrowth of the brain and lies just below the hypothalamus (refer back to Figure 2-7). The pituitary gland has been called the "master gland" because it produces the largest number of different hormones and controls the secretion of other endocrine glands. One of the pituitary hormones has the crucial job of controlling body growth. Too little of this hormone can create a dwarf, while oversecretion can produce a giant. Other hormones released by the pituitary trigger the action of other endocrine glands, such as the thyroid, the sex glands, and the outer layer of the adrenal gland. Courtship, mating, and reproductive behavior in many animals are based on a complex interaction between the activity of the nervous system and the influence of the pituitary on the sex glands.

The relationship between the pituitary gland and the hypothalamus illustrates the complex interactions that take place between the endocrine system and the nervous system. In response to stress (fear, anxiety, pain, emotional events, and so forth) certain neurons in the hypothalamus secrete a substance called **corticotropin-release factor** (CRF). The pituitary is just below the hypothalamus and CRF is carried to it through a channel-like structure. The CRF stimulates the pituitary to release **adrenocorticotrophic hormone** (ACTH), which is the body's major stress hormone. ACTH, in turn, is carried by the bloodstream to the adrenal glands and to various other organs of the body, causing the release of some 30 hormones, each of which plays a role in the body's adjustment to emergency situations. This sequence of events indicates that the endocrine system is under the control of the hypothalamus and thereby under the control of other brain centers via the hypothalamus.

The **adrenal glands** play an important role in determining an individual's mood, level of energy, and ability to cope with stress. The inner core of the adrenal gland secretes **epinephrine** and **norepinephrine** (also known as **adrenaline** and **noradrenaline**). Epinephrine acts in a number of ways to prepare the organism for an emergency, often in conjunction with the sympathetic division of the autonomic nervous system. Epinephrine, for example, affects the smooth muscles and the sweat glands in a way similar to that of the sympathetic system. It causes constriction of the blood vessels in the stomach and intestines and makes the heart beat faster (as anyone who has ever had a shot of adrenaline knows).

Norepinephrine also prepares the organism for emergency action. When it reaches the pituitary in its travels through the bloodstream, it stimulates the gland to release a hormone that acts on the outer layer of the adrenal glands; in turn, this second hormone stimulates the liver to increase the blood-sugar level so the body has energy for quick action.

The hormones of the endocrine system and the neurotransmitters of neurons have similar functions; they both carry *messages* between cells of the body. A neurotransmitter carries messages between adjacent neurons, and its effect is highly localized. In contrast, a hormone may travel a long distance through the body and act in various ways on many different types of cells. The basic similarity between these chemical messengers (despite their differences) is shown by the fact that some serve both functions. Epinephrine and norepinephrine, for example, act as neurotransmitters when released by neurons, and as hormones when released by the adrenal gland.

# Genetic Influences on Behavior

To understand the biological foundations of psychology, we need to know something about hereditary influences. The field of **behavior genetics** combines the methods of genetics and psychology to study the inheritance of behavioral characteristics (Plomin, 1991). We know that many physical characteristics—height, bone structure, hair and eye color, and so on—are inherited. Behavioral geneticists are interested in the degree to which psychological characteristics—mental ability, temperament, emotional stability, and so on—are transmitted from parent to offspring.

## Chromosomes and Genes

The hereditary units we receive from our parents and transmit to our offspring are carried by structures known as **chromosomes**, which are found in the nucleus of each cell in the body. Most body cells contain 46 chromosomes. At conception, the human being receives 23 chromosomes from the father's sperm and 23 chromosomes from the mother's ovum. These 46 chromosomes form 23 pairs, which are duplicated each time the cells divide (see Figure 2-15).

Each chromosome is composed of many individual hereditary units called **genes**. A gene is a segment of **deoxyribonucleic acid (DNA)**, which is the actual carrier of genetic information. The DNA molecule looks like a twisted ladder or a double-stranded helix (spiral), as shown in Figure 2-16. All DNA has the same chemical composition, consisting of a simple sugar (deoxyribose), phosphate, and four bases—adenine, guanine, thymine, and cytosine (A, G, T, C). The two strands of the DNA molecule are composed of phosphate and sugar, and the strands are held apart by pairs of bases. Due to the structural properties of these bases, A always pairs with T and G always pairs with C. The bases can occur in any sequence along a strand, and these sequences constitute the genetic code. The fact that many different arrangements of bases are possible is what gives DNA the ability to express many different genetic messages. The same four bases specify the characteristics of every living organism and, depending on their arrangement, determine whether a creature turns out to be a bird, a lion, a fish, or Michelangelo.

A segment of the DNA molecule, the gene, will give coded instructions to the cell, directing it to perform a specific function (usually to manufacture a particular protein). Although all cells in the body carry the same genes, the specialized nature of each cell is due to the fact that only 5 to 10 percent of the genes are active in any given cell. In the process of developing from a fertilized egg, each cell switches on some genes and switches off all others. When "nerve genes" are active, for example, a cell develops as a neuron because the genes are directing the cell to make the products that allow it to perform neural functions (which would not be possible if the genes irrelevant to a neuron, such as "muscle genes," were not switched off).

Genes, like chromosomes, exist in pairs. One gene of each pair comes from the sperm chromosomes and one gene comes from the ovum chromosomes. Thus, a child receives only half of each parent's total genes. The total number of genes in each human chromosome is around 1,000—perhaps higher. Because the number of genes is so high, it is extremely unlikely that

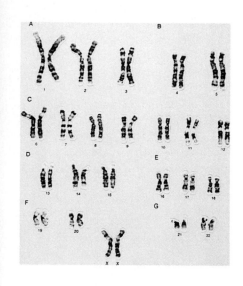

**FIGURE 2-15**
**Chromosomes** *This photo (greatly enlarged) shows the 46 chromosomes of a normal human female. A human male would have the same pairs 1 through 22, but pair 23 would be XY rather than XX.*

two human beings would have the same heredity, even if they were siblings. The only exception is *identical twins*, who, because they developed from the same fertilized egg, have exactly the same genes.

**DOMINANT AND RECESSIVE GENES**   Either gene of a gene pair can be a **dominant gene** or a **recessive gene**. When both members of a gene pair are dominant, the individual manifests the form of the trait specified by these dominant genes. When one gene is dominant and the other recessive, the dominant gene again determines the form of the trait. Only if the genes contributed by the both parents are recessive is the recessive form of the trait expressed. The genes determining eye color, for example, act in a pattern of dominance and recessiveness; blue is recessive and brown is dominant. Thus, a blue-eyed child may have two blue-eyed parents, or one blue-eyed parent and one brown-eyed parent (who carries a recessive gene for blue eyes), or two brown-eyed parents (each of whom carries a recessive gene for blue eyes). A brown-eyed child, in contrast, never has two blue-eyed parents.

Some of the characteristics that are carried by recessive genes are baldness, albinism, hemophilia, and a susceptibility to poison ivy. Not all gene pairs follow the dominant-recessive pattern, and as we shall see, most human characteristics are determined by many genes acting together, rather than by a single gene pair.

Even though most human characteristics are not determined by the actions of a single gene pair, there are some striking exceptions. Of special interest from a psychological viewpoint are diseases like *phenylketonuria* (PKU) and *Huntington's disease* (HD), both of which involve deterioration of the nervous system and correlated behavioral and cognitive problems. Geneticists have identified the gene responsible for PKU and they have been able to establish the approximate location of the gene responsible for HD.

PKU results from the action of a recessive gene that is inherited from each parent. The infant cannot digest an essential amino acid (phenylalanine), which then builds up in the body, poisoning the nervous system and causing irreversible brain damage. PKU children are severely retarded and usually die before the age of 30. If the PKU disorder is discovered at birth and the infants are placed on a diet that controls the level of phenylalanine, their chances of surviving with good health and intelligence are fairly high. Until the PKU gene was located, the disorder could not be diagnosed until an infant was at least 3 weeks old. Now it is possible to determine prenatally whether the fetus has the PKU gene so that the proper diet can begin at birth.

HD is caused by a single dominant gene. The long-term course of the disease involves a degeneration of certain areas in the brain and the ultimate outcome is death. Victims gradually lose their ability to talk and to control their movements, and they show a marked deterioration in memory and mental ability. The disease usually strikes when a person is 30 to 40 years of age. Before then there are no symptoms or other evidence of the disease. Once HD strikes, victims will typically live for 10 to 15 years with progressive deterioration and the agonizing experience of knowing what is happening to them.

Although the Huntington gene has not yet been isolated, geneticists have established that it is located on a specifiable part of a particular chromosome. As a consequence of this work, it is now possible to test individuals at risk and tell them with 99 percent accuracy whether or not they carry the

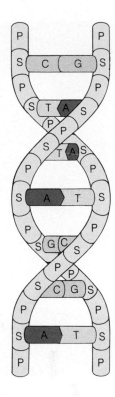

**FIGURE 2-16**
**Structures of the DNA Molecule**
*Each strand of the molecule is made up of an alternating sequence of sugar (S) and phosphate (P); the rungs of the twisted ladder are made up of four bases (A, G, T, C). The double nature of the helix and the restriction on base pairings make possible the self-replication of DNA. In the process of cell division, the two strands of the DNA molecule come apart with the base pairs separating; one member of each base pair remains attached to each strand. Each strand then forms a new complementary strand using excess bases available in the cell; an A attached to a strand will attract a T, and so forth. By this process, two identical molecules of DNA come to exist where previously there was one.*

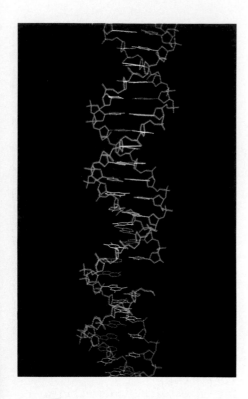

*A computer-generated graphic of DNA*

gene. When the gene is eventually isolated and its DNA structure established, the protein produced by the gene can be determined. It is this protein that must in some way be responsible for HD and will provide a key for treating the disease.

**SEX-LINKED GENES** Male and female chromosomes appear the same under a microscope, except for pair 23, which determines the sex of the individual and carries genes for certain traits that are sex-linked. A normal female has two similar-looking chromosomes in pair 23, called X chromosomes. A normal male has one X chromosome in pair 23 and one that looks slightly different, called a Y chromosome (refer back to Figure 2-15). Thus, the normal female chromosome pair 23 is represented by the symbol XX and the normal male pair by XY.

When most body cells reproduce, the resulting cells have the same number of chromosomes (46) as the parent cell. However, when sperm and egg cells reproduce, the chromosome pairs separate, and half go to each new cell. Thus, egg and sperm cells have only 23 chromosomes. Each egg cell has an X chromosome, and each sperm cell has either an X or a Y chromosome. If an X-type sperm is the first to enter an egg cell, the fertilized ovum will have an XX chromosome pair and the child will be a female. If a Y-type sperm fertilizes the egg, the 23rd chromosome pair will be XY and the child will be a male. The female inherits one X chromosome from the mother and one from the father; the male inherits his X chromosome from the mother and his Y chromosome from the father. Thus, it is the father's chromosome contribution that determines a child's sex (see Figure 2-17).

The X chromosome may carry either dominant or recessive genes; the Y chromosome carries a few genes dominant for male sexual characteristics but otherwise seems to carry only recessive genes. Thus, most recessive characteristics carried by a man's X chromosome (received from his mother) are expressed since they are not blocked by dominant genes. For example, color blindness is a recessive sex-linked characteristic. A man will be color-blind if he inherits a color-blind gene on the X chromosome he receives from his mother. Females are less often color-blind, because a color-blind female has to have both a color-blind father and a mother who is either color-blind or who carries a recessive gene for color blindness. A number of genetically determined disorders are linked to the 23rd chromosome pair; these are called *sex-linked disorders*.

**FIGURE 2-17**
**Sex of Offspring** *Females have XX cells and all of their eggs contain a single X chromosome. Males have XY cells; half of their sperm are X-bearing and half are Y-bearing. The sex of the offspring is determined by the sex chromosome contained in the sperm that fertilizes the egg.*

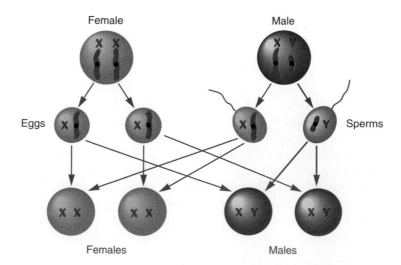

## Genetic Studies of Behavior

Some traits are determined by single genes, but most human characteristics are determined by many genes: they are **polygenic.** Traits such as intelligence, height, and emotionality do not fall into distinct categories, but show continuous variation. Most people are neither dull nor bright; intelligence is distributed over a broad range, with most individuals located near the middle. Sometimes a specific genetic defect can result in mental retardation, but in most instances, a person's intellectual potential is determined by a large number of genes that influence the factors underlying different abilities. Of course, what happens to this genetic potential depends on environmental conditions.

**SELECTIVE BREEDING** One method of studying the heritability of traits in animals is by selective breeding. Animals that are high or low in a certain trait are mated with each other. For example, to study the inheritance of learning ability in rats, the females that do poorly in learning to run a maze are mated with males that do poorly; the females that do well are mated with the males that do well. The offspring of these matings are tested on the same maze. On the basis of performance, the brightest are mated with the brightest and the dullest with the dullest. (To ensure that environmental conditions are kept constant, the offspring of "dull" mothers are sometimes given to "bright" mothers to raise so that genetic endowment rather than adequacy of maternal care is being tested.) After a few rodent generations, a " bright" and a "dull" strain of rats can be produced (see Figure 2-18).

Selective breeding has been used to show the inheritance of a number of behavioral characteristics. For example, dogs have been bred to be excitable or lethargic; chickens, to be aggressive and sexually active; fruit flies, to be more drawn or less drawn to light; and mice, to be more attracted or less attracted to alcohol. If a trait is influenced by heredity, it should be possible to change it by selective breeding. If selective breeding does not alter a trait, we assume that the trait is primarily dependent on environmental factors (Plomin, 1986).

**TWIN STUDIES** Since, ethically, breeding experiments cannot be carried out with human beings, we must look instead at similarities in behavior among individuals who are related. Certain traits often run in families. But families are not only linked genetically, they also share the same environment. If musical talent runs in the family, we do not know whether inherited ability or parental emphasis on music is more important to this development. Sons of alcoholic fathers are more likely than sons of nonalcoholic fathers to develop alcoholism. Do genetic tendencies or environmental conditions play the major role? In an effort to answer questions of this sort, psychologists have turned to studies on twins.

Identical twins develop from a single fertilized egg and thus share the same heredity; they are also called **monozygotic** since they come from a single zygote, or fertilized egg. Fraternal twins develop from different egg cells and are no more alike genetically than are ordinary siblings; they are also called **dizygotic,** or two-egged. Fraternal twins are about twice as common as identical twins. As Figure 2-19 indicates, there are other types of twins, but they are extremely rare.

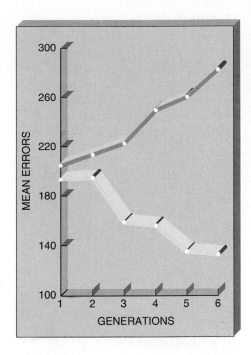

**FIGURE 2-18**
**Inheritance of Maze Learning in Rats** *Mean error scores of "bright" and "dull" rats selectively bred for maze-running ability.* (After Thompson, 1954)

**FIGURE 2-19**
**Types of Twins** *Besides identical and fraternal twins, there may be "half-identical" twins. Half-identicals arise when a precursor to a true ovum divides into identical halves and is fertilized by two sperm. Thus they are more alike than fraternals, but less alike than identicals.*

IDENTICAL TWINS

1. Accounting for about 1 in 250 births, identical twins are created when a single egg is fertilized by one sperm.

2. The egg splits into halves. Each develops into a fetus with the same genetic composition.

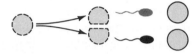

FRATERNAL TWINS

1. Twice as common as identicals, fraternals arise when two eggs are released at once.

2. If both are fertilized by separate sperm, two fetuses form. Genetically they are just ordinary siblings.

HALF-IDENTICAL TWINS

1. A rare type, half-identicals form when a precursor to an egg splits evenly and is fertilized by two sperm.

2. The fetuses have about half of their genes in common—those from the mother.

Studies comparing identical and fraternal twins help to sort out the influence of environment and heredity. Identical twins are found to be more similar in intelligence than fraternal twins, even when they are separated at birth and reared in different homes (see Chapter 12). Identical twins are also more similar than fraternal twins in some personality characteristics and in susceptibility to the mental disorder of schizophrenia (see Chapter 16). Twin studies have proved to be a useful method of investigating genetic influences on human behavior.

*Identical twins*

## Environmental Influences on Gene Action

The inherited potential with which an individual enters the world is very much influenced by the environment that he or she encounters. This interaction will be made clear in later chapters, but two examples will suffice to illustrate the point here. The tendency to develop diabetes is hereditary, although the exact method of transmission is unknown. Diabetes is a disease in which the pancreas does not produce enough insulin to burn carbohydrates as an energy source for the body. Scientists assume that genes determine the production of insulin. But people who carry the genetic potential for diabetes do not always develop the disease; for example, if one identical twin has diabetes, the other twin will develop the disorder in only about half the cases. Not all of the environmental factors that contribute to diabetes are known, but one variable that seems fairly certain is obesity. A fat person requires more insulin to metabolize carbohydrates than a thin person. Consequently, an individual who carries the genes for diabetes is more likely to develop the disorder if he or she is overweight.

A similar situation is found in the mental illness called **schizophrenia.** As we shall see in Chapter 16, substantial evidence indicates a hereditary component to the disorder. If one identical twin is schizophrenic, chances are high that the other twin will exhibit some signs of mental disturbance. But whether or not the other twin develops the full-blown disorder will depend on a number of environmental factors. The genes may predispose, but the environment shapes the outcome.

*Chapter* **SUMMARY**

1. The basic unit of the nervous system is a specialized type of cell called a *neuron.* Projecting from the cell body of the neuron are a number of short branches called *dendrites* and a slender tubelike extension call the *axon.* Stimulation of the dendrites and cell body leads to a neural impulse that travels down the length of the axon. *Sensory neurons* transmit signals from sense organs to the brain and spinal cord; *motor neurons* transmit signals from the brain and spinal cord to muscles and glands. A *nerve* is a bundle of elongated axons belonging to hundreds or thousands of neurons.

2. A stimulus moves along a neuron as an electrochemical impulse that travels from the dendrites to the end of the axon. This traveling impulse, or *action potential*, is due to a self-propagating mechanism called *depolarization* that changes the permeability of the cell membrane to different types of *ions* (electrically charged atoms and molecules) that float in and about the cell.

3. An action potential, once started, travels down the axon to many small swellings at the end of the axon called *synaptic terminals.* These terminals release chemical substances, called *neurotransmitters*, that are responsible for transferring the signal from one neuron to an adjacent one. The neurotransmitters diffuse across a small gap between the juncture of the two neurons (called the *synapse*) and bind to *neuroreceptors* in the cell membrane of the receiving neuron. Some neurotransmitter-receptor bindings cause the cell membrane to depolarize while others cause it to polarize. If depolarization reaches a threshold level, an action potential is fired down the length of the receiving neuron. The occurrence of the action potential is an all-or-none event. There are many different kinds

of neurotransmitter-receptor interactions and they help explain a range of psychological phenomena.

4. The nervous system is divided into the *central nervous system* (the brain and spinal cord) and the *peripheral nervous system* (the nerves connecting the brain and spinal cord to other parts of the body). Subdivisions of the peripheral nervous system are the *somatic system* (which carries messages to and from the sense receptors, muscles, and the body surface) and the *autonomic system* (which connects with the internal organs and glands).

5. The human brain is composed of three concentric layers: a *central core*, the *limbic system*, and the *cerebrum*.

   a. The central core includes the *medulla*, responsible for respiration and postural reflexes; the *cerebellum* is concerned with motor coordination; the *thalamus* is a relay station for incoming sensory information; and the *hypothalamus* is important in emotion and in maintaining homeostasis. The *reticular system*, which crosses through several of the above structures, controls the organism's state of wakefulness and arousal.

   b. The *limbic system* controls some of the instinctive activities (feeding, attacking, fleeing from danger, mating) regulated by the hypothalamus; it also plays an important role in emotion and memory.

   c. The *cerebrum* is divided into two *cerebral hemispheres*. The convoluted surface of these hemispheres, the *cerebral cortex*, plays a critical role in discrimination, decision making, learning, and thinking—the higher mental processes. Certain areas of the cerebral cortex represent centers for specific sensory inputs or for control of specific movements. The remainder of the cerebral cortex consists of *association areas*.

6. When the *corpus callosum* (the band of nerve fibers connecting the two cerebral hemispheres) is severed, significant differences in the functioning of the two hemispheres can be observed. The left hemisphere is skilled in language and mathematical abilities. The right hemisphere can understand some language but cannot communicate through speech; it has a highly developed spatial and pattern sense.

7. The *autonomic nervous system* is made up of the *sympathetic* and the *parasympathetic* divisions. Because its fibers mediate the action of the smooth muscles and of the glands, the autonomic system is particularly important in emotional reactions. The sympathetic division is active during excitement and the parasympathetic during quiescence.

8. The *endocrine glands* secrete hormones into the bloodstream that are important for emotional and motivational behavior. They complement the nervous system in integrating behavior, and their action is closely tied to the activity of the hypothalamus and the autonomic nervous system.

9. An individual's hereditary potential, transmitted by the *chromosomes* and *genes*, influences psychological and physical characteristics. Genes are segments of DNA *molecules*, which store genetic information. Some genes are *dominant*, some *recessive*, and some *sex-linked*. Most human characteristics are *polygenic*—that is, determined by many genes acting together, rather than by a single gene pair.

10. *Selective breeding* (mating animals that are high or low in a certain trait) is one method of studying the influence of heredity. Another method for sorting out the effects of environment and heredity is *twin studies*, in which the characteristics of *identical twins* (who share the same heredity)

are compared with those of *fraternal twins* (who are no more alike genetically than ordinary siblings). Behavior depends on the *interaction* between heredity and environment; the genes set the limits of the individual's potential, but what happens to this potential depends on the environment.

## *Further* **READING**

Introductions to physiological psychology are Carlson, *Foundations of Physiological Psychology* (1988); Groves and Rebec, *Introduction to Biological Psychology* (4th ed., 1992); Kolb and Whishaw, *Fundamentals of Human Neuropsychology* (2nd ed., 1985); Schneider and Tarshis, *An Introduction to Physiological Psychology* (3rd ed., 1986); and Rosenzweig and Leiman, *Physiological Psychology* (2nd ed., 1989).

For a review of the molecular basis of neural processes see Alberts et al., *Molecular Biology of the Cell* (2nd ed., 1989). Also see Squire, *Memory and Brain* (1987) for a discussion of the neural basis of memory and cognition.

A survey of genetic influences on behavior is provided by Plomin, De-Fries, and McClearn, *Behavioral Genetics: A Primer* (2nd ed., 1989). For a review of psychoactive drugs and their effects on the body, brain, and behavior, see Julien, *A Primer of Drug Action* (6th ed., 1992) and Julien, *Drugs and the Body* (1988).

For a survey of research on the function of the two cerebral hemispheres, see Springer and Deutsch, *Left Brain, Right Brain* (3rd ed., 1989) and Beaton, *Left Side/Right Side: A Review of Laterality Research* (1986).

# Chapter 3

# Psychological Development

## Basic Questions About Development 71
*Interaction between Nature and Nurture*
*Developmental Stages and Sensitive Periods*

## Capacities of the Newborn 76
*Hearing*
*Vision*
*Critical Discussion: Can Newborns Imitate?*
*Taste and Smell*
*Learning and Memory*
*Temperament*

## Cognitive Development in Childhood 83
*Piaget's Stage Theory*
*Evaluation of Piaget*
*Alternatives to Piaget*

## Social Development in Childhood 97
*Early Social Behavior*
*Attachment*
*Gender Identity and Sex Typing*
*Critical Discussion: Can Sex Education Prevent Childhood Sexism?*

## Adolescent Development 111
*Sexual Development*
*Sexual Standards and Behavior*
*Critical Discussion: Teenage Pregnancy and Contraceptive Use*
*Adolescent–Parent Conflict*
*Identity Development*

## Development as a Lifelong Process 116
*Early Adulthood*
*Middle Adulthood*
*The Aging Years*

Detail, *The East River.*

Of all mammals, human beings are the most immature at birth, requiring the longest period of learning, development, and interaction with others before they are self-sufficient. In general, the more complex an organism's nervous system is, the longer the time required to reach maturity. A lemur (a primitive primate) can move about on its own shortly after birth and is soon able to fend for itself; an infant monkey is dependent on its mother for several months, a chimpanzee for several years. But even a chimpanzee—one of our closest relatives—will be off on its own long before a human child born on the same day.

Development does not end once a person reaches physical maturity but continues throughout life, and developmental psychologists seek to describe and analyze the regularities of human development across the entire life span. They study *physical development*, such as changes in height and weight and the acquisition of motor skills; *perceptual development*, such as changes in seeing and hearing; *cognitive development*, such as changes in thought processes, memory, and language abilities; and *personality and social development*, such as changes in self-concept, gender identity, and interpersonal relationships. Some developmental psychologists focus on aspects of development that make all members of our species similar to one another; others focus on aspects of development that individualize us and make us different from one another.

This chapter provides an overview of psychological development and considers central questions that have arisen in this field of study. It focuses primarily on those aspects of development that make us similar to one another as a species. The development of particular psychological abilities and functions is treated in more detail in later chapters. Perceptual development is discussed in Chapter 5; concept acquisition and language development in Chapter 9; early sexual development in Chapter 10; and personality development in Chapter 13. In contrast to this chapter, Chapter 13 focuses primarily on those processes of development that make each of us different from one another.

## Basic Questions About Development

Developmental psychologists often study the average, or typical, rate of development. For instance, at what age does the average child begin to speak? How rapidly does a typical child's vocabulary increase with age? Such normative data are important for evaluating an individual child's development and for planning educational programs. But developmental psychologists are usually more deeply concerned with the how and why behind such data: How do certain behaviors develop and why do they appear when they do? Why do most children not walk or utter their first word until they are about a year old? What physiological developments and interactions with the environment must precede these accomplishments? Developmental psychologists also seek to discover how features of the environment influence development. For example, how do different child-rearing practices affect the emotional development of children? How does viewing television violence influence a child's own level of aggression?

Behind specific concerns like these lie two broader, more basic questions: (a) How do biological factors, such as genetically determined schedules, interact with events in the child's environment to determine the course

*Despite warnings of abnormal fetal development, some pregnant women continue to put their babies at risk by drinking and smoking.*

of development (the "nature–nurture" question)? and (b) Is development best understood as a continuous process of change or as a series of qualitatively distinct stages?

## Interaction between Nature and Nurture

The question of whether heredity ("nature") or environment ("nurture") is more important in determining the course of human development has been debated through the centuries. For example, the seventeenth-century British philosopher John Locke rejected the prevailing notion of his day that babies were miniature adults who arrived in the world fully equipped with abilities and knowledge and who simply had to grow in order for these inherited characteristics to appear. On the contrary, Locke believed that the mind of a newborn infant is a "blank slate" *(tabula rasa)*. What gets written on this slate is what the baby experiences—what he or she sees, hears, tastes, smells, and feels. According to Locke, all knowledge comes to us through our senses. It is provided by experience; no knowledge or ideas are built in.

The advent of Charles Darwin's theory of evolution (1859), which emphasizes the biological basis of human development, led to a return to the hereditarian viewpoint. With the rise of behaviorism in the twentieth century, however, the environmentalist position once again gained dominance. Behaviorists such as John B. Watson and B. F. Skinner argued that human nature is completely malleable: early training can turn a child into any kind of adult, regardless of his or her heredity. Watson stated the argument in its most extreme form: "Give me a dozen healthy infants, well-formed, and my own specified world to bring them up in, and I'll guarantee to take any one at random and train him to be any type of specialist I might select—doctor, lawyer, artist, merchant-chief, and, yes, even beggar-man and thief, regardless of his talents, penchants, tendencies, abilities, vocations, and race of his ancestors" (1930, p. 104).

Today most psychologists agree not only that both nature and nurture play important roles but that they interact continuously to guide development. For example, we shall see in Chapter 13 that the development of many personality traits, such as sociability and emotional stability, appear to be influenced about equally by heredity and environment; similarly, we shall see in Chapter 16 that mental disorders can have both genetic and environmental causes.

Even development that seems most obviously to be determined by innate biological timetables can be affected by environmental events. At the moment of conception, a remarkable number of personal characteristics are already determined by the genetic structure of the fertilized ovum. Our genes program our growing cells so that we develop into a person rather than a fish or chimpanzee. They decide our sex, the color of our skin, eyes, and hair, and general body size, among other things. These genetic determinants are expressed in development through the process of **maturation**—innately determined sequences of growth and change that are relatively independent of environmental events. But an environment that is decidedly atypical or inadequate in some way will affect maturational processes.

For example, the human fetus develops within the mother's body according to a fairly fixed time schedule, and fetal behavior, such as turning and kicking, also follows an orderly sequence that depends on the stage of growth. Premature infants who are kept alive in an incubator develop at much the same rate as infants who remain in the uterus to full term. The regularity of development before birth illustrates what we mean by maturation. However, if the uterine environment is seriously abnormal in some way, maturational processes can be disrupted. For example, if the mother contracts German measles during the first 3 months of pregnancy (when the fetus's basic organ systems are developing according to the genetically programmed schedule), the infant may be born deaf, blind, or brain-damaged (the type of defect depends on which organ system was in a critical stage of development at the time of infection). Maternal malnutrition, smoking, and consumption of alcohol and drugs are among the other environmental factors that can affect the normal maturation of the fetus.

Motor development after birth also illustrates the interaction between genetics and environment. As shown in Figure 3-1, all children go through the same sequence of motor behaviors in the same order. Unless we believe that all parents subject their offspring to the same training regimen (an unlikely possibility), we must assume that an innate timetable of maturation determines the order of the behaviors. But Figure 3-1 also shows that not all

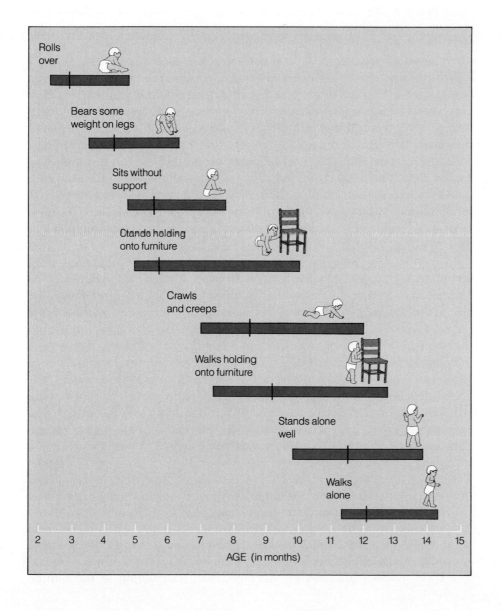

**FIGURE 3-1**
**Babies Develop at Different Rates**
*Although development is orderly, some infants reach each stage ahead of other infants. The left end of the bar indicates the age by which 25 percent of infants have achieved the stated performance; the right end gives the age by which 90 percent have accomplished the behavior. The vertical mark on each bar gives the age by which 50 percent have achieved it.* (After Frankenburg & Dodds, 1967)

**Motor Development in Infants** *Sitting alone, crawling, and standing alone are major developments in an infant's mobility.*

children go through the sequence at the same rate, and developmental psychologists began very early in the history of the discipline to ask whether learning and experience play an important role in such differences.

At first, the answer appeared to be no. One well-known study compared two groups of Hopi children in the southwestern United States. Hopi children raised by traditional parents were wrapped tightly by their parents and strapped to a flat cradle board for the first several months of life. Because they were unwrapped only once or twice a day to be washed and to have their clothes changed, they had little opportunity to move their arms and legs or to practice other motor behaviors such as rolling over. Yet, these children began to walk unaided at the same average age as Hopi children with less traditional parents who did not use cradle boards, suggesting that this basic motor skill does not depend upon practice for its development (Dennis & Dennis, 1940).

Early studies with twins arrived at similar conclusions (Gesell & Thompson, 1929; McGraw, 1935/1975). In these studies, one twin was given a lot of early practice on a particular skill (such as stair climbing). Later, the other twin was given a brief period of practice, and then the two twins were tested. In general, if the untrained twin had received even the briefest period of practice, the two performed almost equally well on the task. For basic motor skills, a small amount of practice later, when the muscles and nervous system are more mature, is apparently as good as a lot of practice earlier.

More recent studies, however, do indicate that practice or extra stimulation can accelerate the appearance of motor behaviors to some extent. For example, newborn infants have a stepping reflex; if they are held in an upright position with their feet touching a solid surface, their legs will make stepping movements that are very similar to walking. A group of infants who were given stepping practice for a few minutes several times a day during the first two months of life began walking five to seven weeks earlier than babies who had not had this practice (Zelazo, Zelazo, & Kolb, 1972). An observational study of babies among the Kipsigi in Kenya illustrates the same point. Kipsigi parents explicitly begin to teach their babies to sit up, stand, and walk shortly after birth. Kipsigi children begin to sit 5 weeks earlier and to walk 3 weeks earlier, on the average, than do children in the United

States. The conclusion that this earlier development is a consequence of the earlier practice is strengthened by the observation that Kipsigi children are *not* more precocious than American children on behaviors for which they have not received special early training (such as rolling over or crawling), and they are actually slower than American children in learning to negotiate stairs (Super, 1976).

The development of speech provides a final example of the interaction between genetically determined characteristics and the experiences provided by the environment. Almost all human infants are born with the ability to learn a spoken language; other species are not. In the normal course of development, human beings learn to speak. But they are not able to talk before they have attained a certain level of neurological development; no infant less than a year old speaks in sentences. Children reared in an environment in which people talk to them and reward them for making speech-like sounds will talk earlier than children who do not receive such attention. For example, children reared in middle-class American homes begin to speak at about 1 year of age. Children reared in San Marcos, a remote village in Guatemala, have little verbal interaction with adults and do not utter their first words until they are over 2 years old (Kagan, 1979). The language children speak, of course, will be that of their own culture. Thus, the development of speech has both genetic and environmental components. In Chapter 9, we shall see that some rather surprising features of language ability appear to be "wired into" the human brain at birth.

## Developmental Stages and Sensitive Periods

As we have noted, there are orderly sequences in development that depend on the maturation of the organism as it interacts with its environment. In explaining developmental sequences, a number of psychologists, such as Piaget, Kohlberg, Freud, and Erikson believe that there are discrete, qualitatively distinct steps or **stages of development**. We make use of the stage concept when we think of the life span as being divided into successive periods of infancy, childhood, adolescence, and adulthood. Parents use the term "stage" when they refer to a "negative stage" their 2-year-old is going through (saying no to every request) or a "rebellious stage" their adolescent is in (challenging parental authority). When psychologists refer to stages of development, they have a more precise concept in mind: the concept of stages implies that a) behaviors at a given stage are organized around a dominant theme; b) behaviors at one stage are qualitatively different from behaviors that appear at earlier or later stages; and c) all children go through the same stages in the same order. Environmental factors may speed up or slow down development, but the order of stages is invariant; a child cannot achieve a later stage without going through an earlier one first.

Although some psychologists believe that stage theories are a useful way of describing development, others do not accept the qualitative shifts in behavior that stage theories imply. Some of these critics argue that many of the tasks designed to test stage theories actually require several underlying information-processing skills if the child is to succeed on them (for example, attention, memory, specific factual knowledge). Because these component skills develop at different rates, development on the overall tasks may appear to be discontinuous—even though the underlying component skills themselves may be developing in a smooth and continuous manner. A closely related argument is that the tasks used to assess the stages are not narrowly designed enough to test only the specific ability under examination. A child may actually possess the requisite ability but fail the task because he or she lacks one of the other abilities it requires. As a result, children's abilities have been frequently underestimated by the stage theorists. We will examine the evidence for and against the stage theories as we proceed.

Closely related to the concept of stages is the idea that there may be **critical periods** in human development—crucial time periods in a person's life during which specific events must occur for development to proceed normally. Critical periods have been firmly established for some aspects of the physical development of the human fetus. For example, the period 6 to 7 weeks after conception is critical for the normal development of the fetus's sex organs. Whether the primitive sex organ develops into a male or female sexual structure depends on the presence of male hormones, regardless of the XX or XY arrangement of chromosomes. The absence of male hormones means that female sexual organs will develop in either case. If male hormones are injected later in development, they cannot reverse the changes that have already taken place.

During postnatal development, there is a critical period for the development of vision. If children who are born with cataracts have them removed before the age of 7, their vision will develop fairly normally. But if a child goes through the first seven years without adequate vision, extensive permanent disability will result (Kuman, Fedrov, & Novikova, 1983).

The existence of critical periods in the psychological development of the child has not been established. It is probably more accurate to say that there are sensitive periods—periods that are optimal for a particular kind of development. If a certain behavior is not well established during this sensitive period, it may not develop to its full potential. For example, the first year of life may be sensitive for the formation of close attachment to the parents. The preschool years may be especially significant for intellectual development and the acquisition of language. Children who have not had sufficient exposure to language prior to the age of 6 or 7 years may fail to acquire it altogether (Goldin-Meadow, 1982). The experiences of the child during such sensitive periods may shape his or her future course of development in a manner that will be difficult to change later.

## Capacities of the Newborn

Infancy (from the Latin word meaning "without language") is difficult to study because babies cannot explain what they are doing or tell us what they are thinking. Until recently, newborn infants were assumed to be helpless, unsensing, and unresponsive creatures who had little awareness of what was going on around them. Psychologist William James' notion that the newborn child experiences the world as a "buzzing, blooming confusion" was still prevalent as late as the 1960s. Parents were often told that their infants were essentially blind at birth and could not taste, smell, or feel pain.

Newborn infants may be physically weak and helpless when they are born, but they enter the world with all sensory systems functioning and well prepared to learn about their new environment. In fact, we shall see below that they have already begun to learn some things while still in the uterus. In order to reveal these early capacities, developmental psychologists have designed some very ingenious procedures.

The basic method used to study infant sensory and cognitive capacities is to introduce some change in the baby's environment and observe its effects on the baby's responses. For example, an investigator might present a tone or a flashing light and watch for indicators in the newborn that it has been sensed, such as a turn of the head, a change in heart rate or brain waves, or a change in the rate at which the baby sucks on a nipple. In some instances, the researcher will present two stimuli at the same time to determine if infants look longer at one than the other. If they do, it presumably shows that they can tell the stimuli apart, and may also indicate that they prefer one to the other.

Another method frequently used depends on the processes of **habituation** and **dishabituation.** A stimulus to which the newborn attends is presented repeatedly until the infant stops paying attention to it. This response pattern is called habituation—a reduction in the strength of a response to a repeated stimulus. Then some aspect of the stimulus is changed. If the infant continues to ignore the stimulus, despite the change, it can be concluded that the change is not psychologically significant to the baby. But if the infant's attention is renewed (that is, the baby dishabituates) the investigator can conclude that the baby did notice the change in the stimulus.

For example, while monitoring the infant's heart rate, an investigator presents a tone of a given pitch for a series of trials. When a baby—or anyone, for that matter—is presented with a new stimulus, the heart rate slows down. This reduction in heart rate is a sign that the infant is attending to the stimulus. After the tone is presented a number of times, the heart rate no longer decelerates at the onset of the sound; the heart rate response has habituated. We assume that the sound has become familiar and the infant ceases to attend to it. The experimenter then presents a new tone of higher pitch. If the infant's heart rate decelerates (that is, dishabituates), the investigator infers that the infant is attending to the new sound and is therefore able to detect the difference between the two tones.

## Hearing

Newborn infants will startle at the sound of a loud noise. They will also turn their heads toward the source of a sound. Interestingly, the head-turning response disappears at about 6 weeks and does not reemerge until 3 or 4 months of age, at which time the infants will also search with their eyes for the source of the sound. The temporary disappearance of the head-turning response probably represents a maturational transition from a reflexive response controlled by subcortical areas of the brain to a voluntary attempt to locate the sound source. By 6 months infants show a marked increase in their responsiveness to sounds that are accompanied by interesting sights (Field, 1987).

Studies using the habituation-dishabituation technique described above have shown that newborn infants can also detect the difference between very similar sounds, such as two tones that are only one note apart on the musical scale (Bridger, 1961). They can also distinguish sounds of the human voice from other kinds of sounds; and, as we will see in Chapter 9, they can distinguish a number of critical characteristics of human speech. For example, 1-month-old infants can tell the difference between the sounds of "p" and "b." Thus, human infants appear to be born with perceptual mechanisms already tuned to the properties of human speech that will help them in their mastery of language (Eimas, 1975).

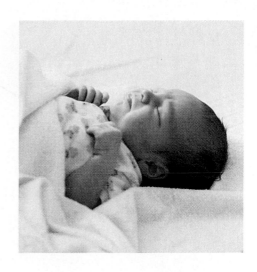

*The human infant may be helpless at birth, but all sensory systems are functioning.*

## Can Newborns Imitate?

For years, proud parents have claimed that their babies imitate their facial expressions—smiling, frowning, or sticking out the tongue in response to similar antics by the parents. It is beyond dispute that adults love to imitate babies, but the claim that young babies imitate adults has generally encountered skepticism from developmental psychologists.

Certainly the limited visual capacities and uncoordinated nature of a newborn infant would seem to rule out the possibility of very early imitation. Imitation would seem to require the infant to encode the visual image of the adult face into memory, translate this perception into corresponding motor commands, and then perform these commands. Moreover, because imitation requires individuals to reproduce a set of self-generated movements that they cannot themselves see or monitor visually, the famous Swiss psychologist, Piaget, believed that imitation cannot develop until the child is able to form mental images—at about 18 months (Piaget, 1962).

The controversy has not been fully settled, but there are some well-controlled observations that suggest that parents may have been right all along. In one set of studies, an adult made distinctive facial expressions such as opening the mouth or sticking out the tongue a few inches from the faces of babies who were only 12 to 20 days old. Independent photographs were taken of the infants and the adults. Judges who had not been present during the sessions were then asked to look at the photographs of the infants and to guess what kind of face the adult had made. They were able to do so at a level significantly above chance (Meltzoff & Moore, 1977, 1983). Even so, the data were not very strong or consistent, and not everyone who has attempted to find similar imitation has been successful (Abravanel & Sigafoos, 1984; Hayes & Watson, 1981; Jacobson, 1979; McKenzie & Over, 1983).

**Evidence for Early Imitation**
*An observer who watched the facial expressions of 36-hour-old infants was able to guess with significant accuracy the facial expression being modeled by the adult.*

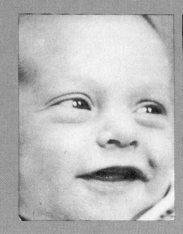

One possible source of some of the inconsistencies among these studies may be the variety of responses the infant is supposed to imitate. The infants in these studies were variously tested on their ability to imitate actions of the adult's hands or arms, eye blinks or tongue protrusions, or emotional facial expressions. It may be that infants can imitate some but not all of these responses. For example, facial expressions of several basic emotions appear to be innate (see Chapter 11), and it may be these that an infant comes best prepared to imitate.

This possibility was supported by a carefully designed study that used the habituation procedure we described earlier to examine an infant's imitation of an adult's emotional facial expressions. Of special interest is that the infants in this study were only 36 *hours* old! The adult "model" would hold the infant in

## Vision

The visual system is not well-developed at birth. Newborns have poor visual acuity and their ability to change focus is limited, so that objects appear fuzzy. They are very near-sighted, so they see things better at close distances. The infant's visual capacities improve rapidly over the first few months and by the time they are able to crawl on their own—at 7 or 8 months—they can see almost as well as an adult (Cornell & McDonnell, 1986).

Despite their visual immaturity, newborns spend a lot of time actively looking about. They scan the world in an organized way and pause when their eyes encounter an object or some change in the visual field. They are particularly attracted to areas of high visual contrast, such as the edges of an

her arms, do two knee bends, and click her tongue in order to get the infant's attention directed to her face. She would then hold her face in one of three facial expressions—happy, sad, or surprised—until the infant looked away. This was repeated with the same expression until the infant looked at the face for less than 2 seconds, that is, until the infant habituated to the expression. The procedure was then repeated with the two other expressions.

This procedure showed, first, that the infants could, indeed, discriminate the three different facial expressions: they habituated to the repeated presentation of each expression but then began to pay close attention again when the adult switched to a different facial expression. More importantly, the babies appeared to imitate these new expressions (see the photographs below). An observer who could not see the model and who did not know what expressions were being presented to the infant was able to determine at greater than chance accuracy the facial expression of the model from the facial movements of the infants (Field, Woodson, Greenberg, & Cohen, 1982). Even if these findings stand up to further investigation, it is not clear just how infants might manage this feat (Vinter, 1986).

It may be that this early form of imitation is a kind of reflex that disappears and is then replaced later in the first year of life with a more cognitively or socially mature form of imitation. We noted in the text that newborn infants have a reflexive head-turning response to sounds that disappears at about 6 weeks and gets replaced at 3 or 4 months of age by a more purposeful search with their eyes for the source of a sound. Imitation may follow this same pattern.

There is an amusing anecdote about this controversy. One of Piaget's graduate students had been testing 7-week-old babies and was convinced that they were imitating her. She went to him with her discovery:

"Do you remember what I am doing?" she said. "I am sticking out my tongue at the babies, and do you know what they are doing?"

"You may tell me," Piaget murmured.

"They are sticking their tongues right back at me! What do you think of that?"

The venerable professor puffed on his pipe for a moment as he contemplated the challenge to his theory. "I think that is very rude," he said. (*Time*, 1983)

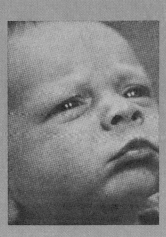  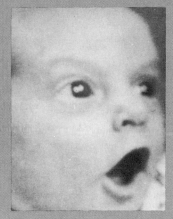 

object. Instead of scanning the entire object, as an adult would, they keep looking at areas that have the most edges. Crib ornaments and toys are now being designed with patterns of high contrast, using black and white or bright primary colors rather than the traditional baby pastels.

Newborn infants prefer to look at certain patterns over others. Using a specially constructed "looking chamber" (see Chapter 5), the investigator presents infants with pairs of stimuli that differ in a particular way—a yellow circle paired with a red circle, for example, or a gray square paired with a gray triangle. If the infants consistently look longer at one stimulus than the other (regardless of its position), the investigator can draw two conclusions: the infants can tell the difference between the stimuli, and they prefer one over the other. Using this method, investigators discovered that newborns prefer complex patterns to plain ones, prefer patterns with curved lines to

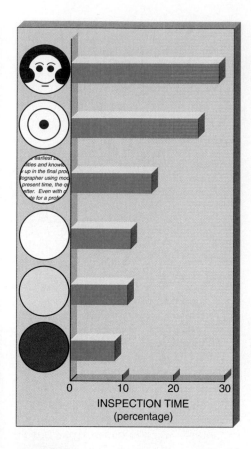

**FIGURE 3-2**
**Visual Preferences** *Newborns as young as 10 hours to 5 days old were shown disks that differed in particular ways—a face-like circle, a bull's eye, an array of fine print, and disks colored white, yellow, or red. Infants could tell the difference between them and preferred one pattern over another.* (After Fantz, 1961)

patterns with straight lines, can discriminate fine print from gray surfaces, and are especially interested in faces (Fantz, 1961) (see Figure 3-2).

The suggestion that newborns might have an unlearned preference for human faces aroused great interest. However, later research showed that infants are not attracted to faces per se but to stimulus characteristics such as curved lines, high contrast, interesting edges, movement, and complexity—all of which faces possess (Banks & Salapatek, 1983; Aslin, 1987).

Newborns look mostly at the outside contour of a face, but by 2 months they focus their attention on the inside of the face—the eyes, nose, and mouth (Haith, Bergman, & Moore, 1977). At this point a parent may notice with delight that the baby has begun to make eye contact.

## Taste and Smell

Infants can discriminate differences in taste shortly after birth. They much prefer sweet-tasting liquids to those that are salty, bitter, sour, or bland. The characteristic response of the newborn to a sweet liquid is a relaxed expression resembling a slight smile, sometimes accompanied by lip-licking. A sour solution produces pursed lips and a wrinkled nose. In response to a bitter-tasting solution, the baby will open its mouth with the corners turned down and stick out its tongue in what appears to be an expression of disgust.

Newborns can also discriminate among odors. They will turn their heads toward a sweet smell, and their heart rate and respiration will slow down, indicating attention. Noxious odors, such as ammonia or rotten eggs, cause them to turn their heads away; heart rate and respiration accelerate, indicating distress. Infants are even able to discriminate subtle differences in smells. After nursing for only a few days, an infant will consistently turn its head toward a pad saturated with its mother's milk in preference to one saturated with another mother's milk (Russell, 1976). The innate ability to distinguish among smells has a clear adaptive value: it helps infants avoid noxious substances, thereby increasing their likelihood of survival.

## Learning and Memory

Because the brain is not well-developed at birth, it was once thought that infants could neither learn nor remember. This is clearly not the case. Habituation itself is an indication of an elementary memory process. By paying less attention to a repeated stimulus, a baby indicates that he or she has seen or heard it before and is now becoming bored with it.

Evidence for early learning and remembering also comes from studies explicitly designed to test for these processes. In one, infants only a few hours old learned to turn their heads right or left, depending on whether they heard a buzzer or a tone. In order to taste a sweet liquid, the baby had to turn to the right when a tone sounded but to turn to the left when a buzzer sounded. In only a few trials, the babies were performing without error—turning to the right when the tone sounded and to the left when the buzzer sounded. The experimenter then reversed the situation so that the infant had to turn the opposite way when either the buzzer or the tone sounded. The babies mastered this new task very quickly (Siqueland & Lipsitt, 1966).

By the time they are 3 months old, infants have quite good memories. When a mobile over an infant's crib was attached by a ribbon to one of the baby's limbs, 3-month-old infants quickly discovered which arm or leg would move the mobile. When the infants were placed in the same situation eight days later, they remembered which arm or leg to move (Rovee-Collier & Hayne, 1987).

More startling is evidence that infants have already learned and remembered something from their pre-birth experiences in the uterus. We noted earlier that newborn infants can distinguish the sound of the human voice from other sounds. They also prefer the human voice over other sounds. Infants tested within a few days of birth will learn to suck on an artificial nipple in order to turn on recorded speech or vocal music, but they will not suck as readily in order to hear non-speech sounds or instrumental music (Butterfield & Siperstein, 1972). They also prefer heartbeat sounds and female voices to male voices, and they prefer their mothers' voices to those of other women. But they do not prefer their fathers' voices to those of other men (Brazelton, 1978; DeCasper & Fifer, 1980; DeCasper & Prescott, 1984) (see Figure 3-3).

These several preferences appear to have their source in the infant's prenatal experience with sounds. Microphones placed near the fetus's head in the uterus reveal that the average sound level is quite high, about the level we experience when we are in a moving car (Birnholz & Benacerraf, 1983). One of the major sounds heard against the background noise is the mother's heartbeat, and the newborn's familiarity with this sound is apparently comforting. Groups of newborn infants were exposed to recordings of a human heart beating at different rates. One group heard the sound of a heart beating at the rate of 80 beats per minute, the normal rate they would have heard in the uterus; a second group heard a heart beating at 120 times per minute; the third group heard no special sounds. Newborns who heard the normal heartbeat gained more weight and cried less during the 4-day experiment than did newborns who heard no special sounds. Newborns exposed to the accelerated heartbeat became so upset that the investigator discontinued that part of the experiment (Salk, 1973). A later study has con-

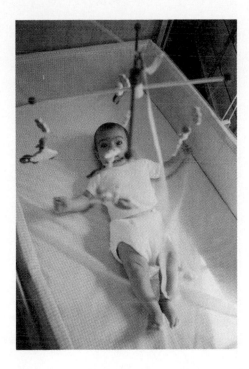

**Early Learning** *If a mobile is attached so the infant's movements activate the mobile, the infant soon discovers this relationship and seems to delight in activating the mobile with the appropriate kick. Two-month-old babies can learn to do this, but soon forget. Three-month-old babies can remember the correct action over several days.*

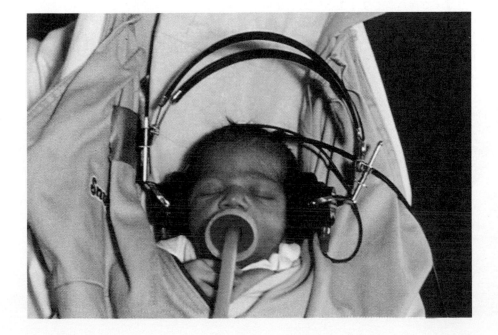

**FIGURE 3-3**
**Preference for Sounds** *A newborn can indicate a preference for certain sounds— like the mother's voice—by sucking more vigorously on a nipple when it causes the preferred sounds to be played through the earphones.*

firmed that the recorded sound of a heartbeat is rewarding to a newborn infant (DeCasper and Sigafoos, 1983).

The mother's voice can also be heard in the uterus, which would appear to explain why a newborn infant prefers her voice over others. And perhaps most startling of all is some evidence that the unborn infant may actually be learning in the uterus to discriminate some of the sound properties of individual words. In a quite extraordinary experiment, pregnant women recited speech passages from children's stories aloud each day during the last 6 weeks of pregnancy. For example, some women recited the first 28 paragraphs of the Dr. Seuss story *The Cat in the Hat*. Other pregnant women recited the last 28 paragraphs of the same story but with the main nouns changed so that it was now about "the dog in the fog" instead of the "cat in the hat." By the time the infants were born, they had heard one of the selected stories for a total of about 3-1/2 hours.

Two or three days after the infants were born, they were permitted to suck on a special pacifier wired to record sucking rates (like the apparatus shown in Figure 3-3). In this study, the pattern of sucking turned a tape recording of a story on or off. One sucking pattern turned on a recording of the story the infants had heard before birth; a contrasting pattern of sucking turned on a recording of one of the matched stories that the infant had not heard before. Some of the infants heard recordings of their own mother's voice; others heard recordings of an unfamiliar woman's voice. The results showed that the infants preferred the familiar story to the unfamiliar story—even when the two stories were read by an unfamiliar voice (DeCasper & Spence, 1986).

## Temperament

In discussing the capacities of the infant, we have focused on the ways in which infants are alike. But first-time parents are often surprised that their newborn seems to possess a distinctive personality from the very beginning; when they have a second child, they are often surprised at how different the second is from the first. These parental observations are valid. As

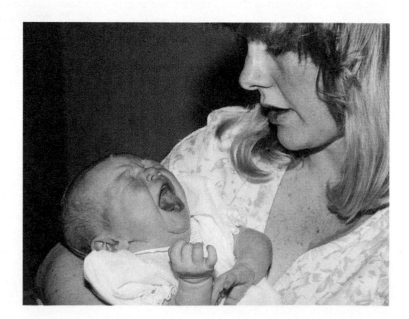

early as the first weeks of life, infants show individual differences in activity level, responsiveness to change in their environment, and irritability. One infant cries a lot; another cries very little. One endures diapering or bathing without much fuss; another kicks and thrashes. One is responsive to every sound; another is oblivious to all but the loudest noises. Infants even differ in "cuddliness." Some seem to enjoy being cuddled and mold their bodies to the person holding them; others stiffen and squirm and do less body adjusting (Korner, 1973). Such mood-related personality characteristics are called **temperaments,** and there is some evidence that they constitute early building blocks for the individual's later personality (Thomas & Chess, 1977).

The traditional view has been that parents shape their children's behavior. Parents of a fussy baby, for example, tend to blame themselves for their infant's difficulties. But research with newborns makes it increasingly clear that many temperamental differences are inborn, and that the relationship between parent and infant is reciprocal—in other words, the infant's behavior also shapes the parent's response. An infant who is easily soothed, who snuggles and stops crying when picked up, increases the parent's feelings of competency and attachment. The infant who stiffens and continues to cry, despite efforts to comfort it, makes the parent feel inadequate and rejected. The more responsive a baby is to the stimulation provided by the parent (snuggling and quieting when held, attending alertly when talked to or played with), the easier it is for the parent and child to establish a loving bond.

A child's temperament is not unchangeable or immune to environmental influences. Temperamental differences observed in infants often persist to some degree throughout childhood; thus, babies with "difficult" temperaments are more likely than "easy" babies to have school problems later on (Riese, 1987; Thomas & Chess, 1977). But temperamental traits can also change with development: an easygoing infant can become a tantrum-throwing toddler. Inborn temperament predisposes an infant to react in certain ways, but temperament and life experiences interact to form personality. In Chapter 13, we examine in detail the shaping and continuity of personality from infancy to old age.

In sum, the research we have described in this section on the capacities of the infant challenges the view of the newborn as a "blank slate." Clearly, the infant enters the world prepared to perceive and comprehend reality and to learn quickly the relations between events that are important for human development. He or she even has a head start on developing a distinctive personality.

# Cognitive Development In Childhood

## Piaget's Stage Theory

Although most parents are aware of the intellectual changes that accompany their children's physical growth, they would have difficulty describing the nature of these changes. The ways in which contemporary psychologists describe these changes have been most profoundly influenced by the Swiss psychologist Jean Piaget (1896–1980), widely acknowledged to be one of the century's most influential thinkers.

*Swiss psychologist Jean Piaget's careful observations of children led him to change the way psychology viewed cognitive development.*

Prior to Piaget, psychological thinking about children's cognitive development was dominated by the biological–maturation perspective, which gave almost exclusive weight to the "nature" component of development, and by the environmental–learning perspective, which gave almost exclusive weight to the "nurture" component. In contrast, Piaget focused on the interaction between the child's naturally maturing abilities and his or her interactions with the environment. Piaget saw the child as an active participant in this process rather than as a passive recipient of biological development or externally imposed stimuli. In particular, Piaget believed that the child should be viewed as an inquiring scientist who conducts experiments on the world to see what happens ("What does it feel like to suck on the teddy-bear's ear?" "What happens if I push my dish off the edge of the table?").

The results of these miniature experiments lead the child to construct "theories"—Piaget called them *schemata* (or the singular, **schema**)—of how the physical and social worlds operate. Upon encountering a novel object or event, the child attempts to understand it in terms of a pre-existing schema. (Piaget called this the process of **assimilation;** the child attempts to *assimilate* the new event to the pre-existing schema.) If the old schema is not adequate to accommodate the new event, then the child—like a good scientist—modifies the schema and thereby extends his or her theory of the world. (Piaget called this process of revising the schema **accommodation**.) (Piaget & Inhelder, 1969).

Piaget also differed from other psychologists earlier in this century in his experimental methodology. Piaget's first job as a postgraduate student in psychology was as an intelligence tester for Alfred Binet, inventor of the first IQ test (see Chapter 12). But Piaget found himself more interested in the children's *wrong* answers than in their intelligence test scores. Why did children make the errors they did? What distinguished their reasoning from that of adults? He began to observe his own three children closely as they played, frequently presenting them with simple scientific and moral problems and asking them to explain how they arrived at their answers. This informal clinical method of observing and interviewing a small number of children was quite alien to experimentally oriented American psychologists of the day. They criticized this approach as unscientific, and it was only slowly that they began to appreciate the importance of Piaget's work.

We emphasize these main features of Piaget's contribution here because even psychologists who believe he was simply wrong about many features of cognitive development nevertheless accept his general portrait of the child as an active, information-seeking organism and agree with his emphasis on the interaction between biological maturation and the environment. Similarly, many contemporary developmental psychologists use methods of empirical inquiry that strongly reflect Piaget's influence. For clarity, we will first present Piaget's theory and his interpretations of the evidence; we will postpone our discussion of empirical challenges, criticisms, and alternative interpretations to the subsequent section, "Evaluating Piaget."

On the basis of his observations, Piaget became convinced that children's abilities to think and to reason progress through a series of qualitatively distinct stages as they mature. He divided cognitive development into 4 major stages and a number of substages within each. The major stages and their prominent features are listed in Table 3-1.

| STAGE | CHARACTERIZATION |
| --- | --- |
| 1. Sensorimotor (birth–2 years) | Differentiates self from objects<br>Recognizes self as agent of action and begins to act intentionally: for example, pulls a string to set a mobile in motion or shakes a rattle to make a noise<br>Achieves object permanence: realizes that things continue to exist even when no longer present to the senses |
| 2. Preoperational (2–7 years) | Learns to use language and to represent objects by images and words<br>Thinking is still egocentric: has difficulty taking the viewpoint of others<br>Classifies objects by a single feature: for example, groups together all the red blocks regardless of shape or all the square blocks regardless of color |
| 3. Concrete operational (7–11 years) | Can think logically about objects and events<br>Achieves conservation of number (age 6), mass (age 7), and weight (age 9)<br>Classifies objects according to several features and can order them in series along a single dimension, such as size |
| 4. Formal operational (11 years and up) | Can think logically about abstract propositions and test hypotheses systematically<br>Becomes concerned with the hypothetical, the future, and ideological problems |

TABLE 3-1
**Piaget's Stages of Cognitive Development**
*The ages given are averages. They may vary considerably depending on intelligence, cultural background, and socioeconomic factors, but the order of progression is assumed to be the same for all children. Piaget has described more detailed phases within each stage; only a very general characterization of each stage is given here.*

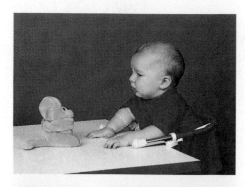

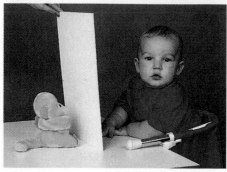

**FIGURE 3-4**
**Object Permanence** *When the toy is hidden by a screen, the infant acts as if the toy no longer exists. From this observation, Piaget concluded that the infant had not yet acquired the concept of object permanence.*

**SENSORIMOTOR STAGE** Noting the close interplay between motor activity and perception in infants, Piaget designated the first 2 years of life as the **sensorimotor stage.** During this period, infants are busy discovering the relationships between their actions and the consequences of these actions. They discover, for example, how far they have to reach to grasp an object, what happens when they push their food dish over the edge of the table, and that their hand is part of their body and the crib rail is not. Through countless "experiments," infants begin to develop a concept of themselves as separate from the external world.

An important discovery during this stage is the concept of **object permanence,** an awareness that an object continues to exist even when it is not present to the senses. If a cloth is placed over a toy that an 8-month-old is reaching for, the infant immediately stops and appears to lose interest. The baby seems neither surprised nor upset, makes no attempt to search for the toy, and acts as if the toy has ceased to exist (see Figure 3-4).

In contrast, a 10-month-old will actively search for an object that has been hidden under a cloth or behind a screen. The older baby seems to realize that the object exists even though it is out of sight and has thus attained the concept of object permanence. This implies that the baby possesses a *mental representation* of the missing object. But even at this age, search is limited. If the infant has had repeated success in retrieving a toy hidden in one place, he or she will continue to look for it in that spot even after watching an adult conceal it in a new location. The baby repeats the action that produced the toy earlier rather than looking for it where it was last seen. Not until about 1 year of age will a child consistently look for an object where it was last seen to disappear, regardless of what happened on previous trials.

**PREOPERATIONAL STAGE** By about 1-1/2 to 2 years of age, children have begun to use language. Words, as symbols, can represent things or groups of things, and one object can represent (symbolize) another. Thus, in play a 3-year-old may treat a stick as if it were a horse and ride it around the room; a block of wood can become a car; one doll can become a father and another, a baby.

Although 3- and 4-year-olds can think in symbolic terms, their words and images are not yet organized in a logical manner. Piaget calls the 2- to 7-years stage of cognitive development **preoperational,** because the child does not yet comprehend certain rules or *operations*. An operation is a mental routine for separating, combining, and otherwise transforming information mentally in a logical manner. For example, if water is poured from a tall narrow glass into a short wide one, adults know that the amount of water has not changed because they can reverse the transformation in their mind; they can imagine pouring the water from the short glass back into the tall glass, thereby arriving back at the original state. In the preoperational stage of cognitive development, a child's understanding of reversibility and other mental operations is absent or weak. As a result, according to Piaget, preoperational children have not yet attained **conservation.** They fail to understand that the amount of water is conserved when it is poured from the tall glass to the short one.

This lack of conservation is also illustrated by a procedure in which a child is given some clay to make into a ball that is equal to another ball of the same material. After doing this, the child declares them to be "the same." Then, leaving one ball for reference, the experimenter rolls the other into a long sausage shape while the child watches. The child can

**FIGURE 3-5**
**Concept of Conservation** *A 4-year-old acknowledges that the two balls of clay are the same size. But when one ball is rolled into a long thin shape, she says that it has more clay. Not until she is several years older will she state that the two different shapes contain the same amount of clay.*

plainly see that no clay has been added or subtracted. In this situation, children about 4 years of age say that the two objects no longer contain the same amount of clay: "The longer one contains more," they say (see Figure 3-5). Not until the age of 7 do the majority of children say that the clay in the longer object is equal in amount to that in the reference ball.

Piaget believed that a key feature of the preoperational stage is that children are unable to center attention on more than one aspect of the situation at a time. Thus, in the clay conservation task, the preoperational child cannot attend to both the length and the thickness of the clay ball simultaneously. Similarly, Piaget believed that preoperational thinking is dominated by visual impressions. A change in the visual appearance of the clay influences the preoperational child more than less obvious but more essential qualities, such as mass or weight.

The young child's reliance on visual impressions is made clear by an experiment on the conservation of number. If two rows of checkers are matched one for one against each other, young children will say, correctly, that the rows have the same number of checkers (see Figure 3-6). If the

**FIGURE 3-6**
**Conservation of Number** *When the two rows of seven checkers are evenly spaced, most children report that they contain the same amount. When one row is then clustered into a smaller space, children under 6 or 7 will say the original row contains more.*

checkers in one row are brought closer together to form a cluster, 5-year-olds say there are now more checkers in the straight row—even though no checkers have been removed. The visual impression of a long row of checkers overrides the numerical equality that was obvious when the checkers appeared in matching rows. In contrast, 7-year-olds assume that if the number of objects was equal before, it must remain equal. At this age, numerical equality has become more significant than visual impression.

**MORAL JUDGMENTS** Cognitive development affects not only the child's understanding of the physical world, but of the social world as well. Because understanding moral rules and social conventions is important in any society, Piaget was interested in how children come to understand such rules. He was skeptical that parental influence was as powerful in the development of this understanding as then-current theories claimed. Rather, he thought that children's understanding of moral rules and social conventions would have to match their overall level of cognitive development.

Interestingly, Piaget based his initial theorizing in this area on observations he made of children of different ages playing marbles, a popular game with most European children at the time. He asked these children questions about the origins, meaning, and importance of the game rules they were following. From their answers, he formulated four stages of children's developing understanding of rules. The first two stages fall within the preoperational period we are discussing in this section (Piaget, 1932/1965).

The first stage emerges at the beginning of the preoperational period when children begin to engage in symbolic play. Children at this stage will participate in a kind of "parallel play," playing amidst other children with shared objects but not in any socially organized way. Each child tends to follow a set of idiosyncratic rules, according to his or her own private wishes. For example, the child might sort the marbles of different colors into groups or roll the big ones across the room, followed by all the small ones. These "rules" give the child's play some regularity, but the child changes these rules frequently and arbitrarily, and they serve no collective purpose such as cooperation or competition.

*Although young children participate in parallel play with one another, it is only when they become older that they begin to understand the rules that govern social interaction.*

The second stage puts an abrupt end to this easygoing view of rules. Beginning about age five, the child develops a sense of obligation to follow rules, treating them as absolute moral imperatives handed down by some authority—possibly parents or God. Rules are permanent, sacred, and not subject to modification. Obeying them to the letter is more important than any human reason for changing them. For example, children at this stage reject the suggestion that the position of the starting line in the marble game might be changed to accommodate younger children who might want to play.

From this and other studies, Piaget came to the view that children at this stage subscribe to a **moral realism,** a confusion between moral and physical laws. Moral rules are predetermined and permanent aspects of the world—just like the law of gravity. When asked what would happen if they violated some moral rule (like lying or stealing), children at this stage often expressed the view that punishment would surely result—God would punish them or they would be hit by a car.

At this same stage, children judge an act more by its consequences than by the intentions behind it. For example, Piaget told children several pairs of stories. In one pair, a boy broke a teacup while trying to steal some jam when his mother was not home; another boy, who was doing nothing wrong, accidentally broke a whole trayful of teacups. "Which boy is naughtier?" Piaget asked. Preoperational children tended to judge as naughtier the person in the stories who did the most damage, regardless of the intentions or motivation behind the act. Similarly, a child who tells her mother that she saw a "dog as big as a cow" is judged to be naughtier than one who tells her mother that she received a good grade in school when she did not. Why? Because a dog could not be as big as a cow, and hence this is the bigger lie. Preoperational children do not differentiate between deliberate, opportunistic lies and harmless exaggerations or misstatements.

**OPERATIONAL STAGES**  Between the ages of 7 and 12, children master the various conservation concepts and begin to perform still other logical manipulations. They can order objects on the basis of a dimension, such as height or weight. They can also form a mental representation of a series of actions. Five-year-olds can find their way to a friend's house but cannot direct you there or trace the route with paper and pencil. They can find the way because they know they have to turn at certain places, but they have no overall picture of the route. In contrast, 8-year-olds can readily draw a map of the route. Piaget calls this period the **concrete operational stage:** although children are using abstract terms, they are doing so only in relation to concrete objects—that is, objects to which they have direct sensory access.

Piaget's third stage of moral understanding also begins about this time. The child begins to appreciate that some rules are social conventions—cooperative agreements that can be arbitrarily decided and changed if everyone agrees. Children's moral realism also declines: When making moral judgments, children now give weight to "subjective" considerations like a person's intentions, and they see punishment as a human choice, not an inevitable, divine retribution.

At about the age of 11 or 12, children arrive at adult modes of thinking, becoming able to reason in purely symbolic terms. Piaget called this the **formal operational stage.** In one test for formal operational thinking, the child tries to discover what determines the amount of time that a pendulum will swing back and forth (its period of oscillation). The child is presented with a

LEVEL I:   Preconventional Morality

Stage 1   Punishment orientation (Obeys rules to avoid punishment)

Stage 2   Reward orientation (Conforms to obtain rewards, to have favors returned)

LEVEL II:   Conventional Morality

Stage 3   Good-boy/good-girl orientation (Conforms to avoid disapproval of others)

Stage 4   Authority orientation (Upholds laws and social rules to avoid censure of authorities and feelings of guilt about not "doing one's duty")

LEVEL III:   Postconventional Morality

Stage 5   Social-contract orientation (Actions guided by principles commonly agreed on as essential to the public welfare; principles upheld to retain respect of peers and, thus, self-respect)

Stage 6   Ethical principle orientation (Actions guided by self-chosen ethical principles, which usually value justice, dignity, and equality; principles upheld to avoid self-condemnation)

**TABLE 3-2**
**Stages of Moral Reasoning** *Kohlberg believed that moral judgment develops with age according to these stages.* (After Kohlberg, 1969)

length of string suspended from a hook and several weights that can be attached to the lower end. He or she can vary the length of the string, change the attached weight, and alter the height from which the bob is released.

In contrast to children still in the concrete operational stage—who will experiment by changing some of the variables, but not in a systematic way—adolescents of even average ability will set up a series of hypotheses and proceed to test them systematically. They reason that if a particular variable (weight) affects the period of oscillation, the effect will appear only if they change one variable and hold all others constant. If this variable seems to have no effect on the time of swing, they rule it out and try another. Considering all the possibilities—working out the consequences for each hypothesis and confirming or denying these consequences—is the essence of what Piaget called formal operational thought.

The beginning of the formal operational stage also coincides with the fourth and final stage in children's understanding of moral rules. Youngsters show an interest in generating rules to deal even with situations they have never encountered. This stage is marked by an ideological mode of moral reasoning, which addresses wider social issues rather than just personal and interpersonal situations.

The American psychologist Lawrence Kohlberg extended Piaget's work on moral reasoning to include adolescence and adulthood (Kohlberg, 1969, 1976). He sought to determine if there are universal stages in the development of moral judgments by presenting moral dilemmas in story form. For example, in one story a man whose dying wife needs a drug he cannot afford pleads with a druggist to let him buy the drug at a cheaper price. When the druggist refuses, the man decides to steal the drug. Subjects then discuss the man's action.

By analyzing answers to several such dilemmas, Kohlberg arrived at six developmental stages of moral judgment grouped into three levels (see Table 3-2). The answers are scored on the basis of the reasons given for the decision, not on the basis of whether the action is judged right or wrong. For example, agreeing that the man should have stolen the drug because "If you let your wife die, you'll get in trouble" or disagreeing because "If you steal the drug, you'll be caught and sent to jail" are both scored at Stage 1. In both instances, the man's actions are evaluated as right or wrong on the basis of anticipated punishment.

Kohlberg believed that all children are at Level I until about age 10, when they begin to evaluate actions in terms of other people's opinions (Level II). Most youngsters reason at this level by age 13. Following Piaget, Kohlberg argues that only those who have achieved formal operational thought are capable of the kind of abstract thinking necessary for Level III, postconventional morality. The highest stage, Stage 6, requires formulating abstract ethical principles and upholding them to avoid self-condemnation.

Kohlberg reports that fewer than 10 percent of his adult subjects show the kind of "clear-principled" Stage-6 thinking exemplified by the following response of a 16-year-old to the man's dilemma: "By the law of society [the man] was wrong but by the law of nature or of God the druggist was wrong and the husband was justified. Human life is above financial gain. Regardless of who was dying, if it was a total stranger, man has a duty to save him from dying" (Kohlberg, 1969, p. 244).

Kohlberg has presented evidence for this sequence of stages in children from several cultures, including the United States, Mexico, Taiwan, and

Turkey (Colby, Kohlberg, Gibbs, & Lieberman, 1983; Nisan & Kohlberg, 1982). On the other hand, there is evidence that people use different rules for different situations and that the stages are not sequential (Kurtines & Greif, 1974). The theory has also been criticized for being "male centered," because it places a "masculine" style of abstract reasoning based on justice and rights higher on the moral scale than a "feminine" style of reasoning based on a care and concern for others (Gilligan, 1982).

## Evaluation of Piaget

It should be clear from even this brief summary of Piaget's ideas that his theory is a major intellectual achievement; it has revolutionized the way we think about children's cognitive development and has inspired an enormous amount of research over the decades. Many studies support Piaget's observations about the sequences in cognitive development.

But newer and more sophisticated methods of testing the intellectual functioning of infants and preschool children reveal that Piaget underestimated their abilities. As we noted earlier, many of the tasks designed to test stage theories actually require several underlying information-processing skills if the child is to succeed on them, such as attention, memory, and specific factual knowledge. A child may actually possess the requisite ability under examination but fail the task because he or she lacks one of the other required but irrelevant skills.

**OBJECT PERMANENCE**  These points are sharply illustrated by studies of object permanence, the awareness that an object continues to exist even when it is not present to the senses. As we described earlier, when infants younger than 8 months are shown a toy which is then hidden or covered while they watch, they act as if it no longer exists; they do not attempt to search for it. Even after 8 months, a baby that has repeatedly succeeded in retrieving a toy hidden in one place will continue to look for it in that spot even after watching an adult conceal it in a new location.

Note, however, that successful performance on this test requires the child not only to understand that the object still exists—object permanence—but also to remember where the object was hidden and to display some physical action that indicates he or she is searching for it. Because Piaget believed that early cognitive development depends on sensorimotor activities, he did not seriously entertain the possibility that the infant might know the object still exists but not be able to reveal this through searching behavior—that children's minds might be ahead of their motor abilities. Subsequent research has examined both the memory and the activity requirements of these object permanence tasks.

The memory requirements were examined in a study that used the procedure of hiding an object at location A and then visibly moving it and reconcealing it at location B while the baby watched. The investigator then imposed a short time delay before the child was permitted to search for the object. When they were allowed to search immediately, babies as young as 7-1/2 months looked correctly for the object at location B. But with as little as a 2-second delay, they looked incorrectly at location A—where the object had been found on previous occasions. Even 12-month-old children—who, according to Piaget, should have acquired object permanence—incorrectly looked at location A when the delay was extended to 10 seconds. In other

HABITUATION EVENT

TEST EVENTS

Possible Event

Impossible Event

**FIGURE 3-7**
**Testing Object Permanence** *Infants are shown a rotating screen until they no longer attend to it (habituation). A box is placed where it can be hidden by the screen and the infants then see either a possible event (the screen rotates until it would hit the box and then returns to its starting position) or an impossible event (the screen appears to pass right through the box). Infants attend more to the impossible event, indicating that they realize the hidden box still exists.* (Adapted from Baillargeon, 1987)

words, babies who have acquired object permanence will fail this test if the memory requirements are made too difficult. They realize that hidden objects still exist; they just lose track of where to look for them.

An even more damaging set of results for Piaget's theory of object permanence emerged from a set of studies that did not require the child to actively search for the hidden object. Infants were tested using a habituation procedure. As shown in the top section of Figure 3-7, the apparatus consisted of a screen hinged at one edge to the top of a table. The screen began in a position lying flat on the table. As the infant watched, the screen was rotated slowly away from the infant like a drawbridge, through its upright position at 90 degrees, and then continued until it had rotated through a complete 180-degree arc and was again lying flat on the table. The screen was then rotated in the opposite direction, toward the infant.

When the infants were first shown the rotating screen, they looked at it for almost a full minute; but after repeated trials, they lost interest and turned their attention elsewhere—the process of habituation. After the habituation procedure, a brightly painted box appeared on the table beyond the hinge where it would be hidden as the screen moved into its upright position. (The infant was actually seeing a reflected image of a box, not the actual box.) As shown in Figure 3-7, the infants were then shown either a possible event or an impossible event. One group of infants saw the screen rotate from its starting position until it reached the point where it should bump against the box; at that point, the screen stopped and then moved back to its starting position. The other group saw the screen rotate to the upright position but then continue to rotate all the way to the other side of the 180-degree arc just as though there were no box in the way.

The investigators reasoned that if the infants thought the box still existed even when it was hidden by the screen, they would be surprised when it seemed to pass through the box—an impossible event—and, hence, look at the screen longer than they would when the screen seemed to bump into the box before returning to its starting point. This is exactly what happened. Even though the impossible event was perceptually identical to the event to which the infants had just habituated, they found it more interesting than the possible but novel event. (Note that they had never before seen the screen stop half-way through the arc and then reverse direction.) (Baillargeon, Spelke, & Wasserman, 1985).

It should be noted that the infants in this experiment were only 4-1/2 months old; they thus displayed object permanence about 4–5 months earlier than Piaget's theory predicts. A replication of this study found that some infants as young as 3-1/2 months also had object permanence (Baillargeon, 1987).

**CONSERVATION** Piaget's conservation tasks provide a second instance in which the careful analysis of the component skills required for successful task performance has uncovered earlier competence than his theory anticipates. For example, if test conditions are carefully arranged in conservation experiments so that the children's responses do not depend on their language ability (their understanding of what the experimenter means by "more" or "longer"), then even 3- and 4-year-olds can show that they possess number conservation; that is, they can distinguish between the essential feature, the number of items in a set, and the irrelevant feature, the way in which the items are arranged spatially (Gelman & Gallistel, 1978).

In one study of number conservation, two sets of toys were lined up in one-to-one correspondence (as in Figure 3-6, described earlier). The experimenter identified one row as the child's and one as her own and then asked the child for the initial judgment of equality. For example, "These are your soldiers and these are my soldiers. What's more, my soldiers, your soldiers or are they both the same?" After this initial judgment, the experimenter spread out one of the rows of toys and repeated the question.

As Piaget and others had previously reported, 5-year-old children failed to conserve, stating that the spread-out row was "more soldiers." But the investigator introduced a second set of conditions. Instead of describing the toys as individual soldiers, she said: "This is my army and this is your army. What's more, my army, your army or are they both the same?" With this simple change of wording, most of the children were able to conserve, judging the two "armies" to be the same size, even when one of them was spread out. By prompting the children to interpret the display as an aggregate or collection rather than as a set of individual items, their judgments of equality were less likely to be influenced by irrelevant perceptual transformations. Moreover, when asked to justify their equality judgments, most of the children in the "army" condition showed they understood the underlying principle. Many explicitly referred to numbers (for example, counting the soldiers to demonstrate equal numbers); others noted that nothing had been added or taken away; and still others referred explicitly to the irrelevance of the transformation (for example, "You just spreaded them."). The same results were found when the objects were "football players" versus a "football team," "animals" versus an "animal party," or "pigs" versus a "pig family" (Markman, 1979).

**MORAL JUDGMENTS**   We saw earlier that preoperational children treat arbitrary rules of games and social conventions like divine moral prescriptions that cannot be changed by simple agreement among participants. More recent research suggests, however, that even preoperational children can and do make distinctions between social conventions and moral prescriptions.

In one study, for example, 7-year-old children were given a list of actions and asked to indicate which ones would be wrong even if there were no rule against them. There was widespread agreement among these children that lying, stealing, hitting, and selfishness would be wrong even if there were no rules against them. In contrast, they thought that there was nothing wrong with chewing gum in class, addressing a teacher by first name, boys entering the girls' bathroom, or eating lunch with the fingers—as long as there were no rules against these acts. Moreover, they could make a further distinction between rules governing conduct that affects other people and rules governing conduct that affects only oneself. For example, they believed that it was *legitimate* for a school to have rules against chewing gum in class, addressing a teacher by first name, and so forth. But they felt that it should be "the person's own business" and hence, that there should be no rules against watching TV on a sunny day (when parents want children out playing), interacting with a forbidden friend, and boys wearing long hair (Nucci, 1981).

In a similar study 7-year-old children were evenly divided in deciding whether it would be okay for a boy to wear a dress to school even if "the principal decided that there is no rule in the school against it." But 82 percent of them thought it would be okay for a boy to do so "in a country that had no rule against it" (Turiel, 1983). We will discuss the violation of gender norms later in the chapter.

# Alternatives to Piaget

There is general agreement among developmental psychologists that the kinds of findings we have reviewed here seriously challenge Piaget's theory and reveal that he underestimated children's abilities. But there is no consensus on which is the best alternative to pursue.

**INFORMATION-PROCESSING APPROACHES** We have already noted that many of the experiments challenging Piaget's views were inspired by investigators who view cognitive development as the acquisition of several separate information-processing skills. Accordingly, they believe that the standard Piagetian tasks fail to separate these several skills out from the critical skill that the task is allegedly designed to assess. But beyond that, information-processing theorists disagree among themselves about the challenge their views pose to Piaget.

For example, they disagree on one of the two big questions of this chapter: Is development best understood as a continuous process of change or as a series of qualitatively distinct stages? Some believe that the entire notion of stages should be abandoned (for example, Klahr, 1982). For them, the appearance of qualitative discontinuities in development is an illusion that arises from the careless mixing in the assessment tasks of information-processing skills at different stages of development; the separate skills develop smoothly and continuously.

But other information-processing theorists see themselves as modifying and extending the Piagetian stage model itself; they believe that gradual changes in information-processing skills do, in fact, lead to discontinuous, stage-like changes in children's thinking (for example, Case, 1985). These theorists are sometimes referred to as neo-Piagetians. Another group of neo-Piagetians agree that there are genuine stages but that they occur only within more narrow domains of knowledge. For example, a child's language skills, mathematical understanding, social reasoning, and so forth may all develop in stage-like fashion, but each domain proceeds at its own pace, relatively independently of the others (for example, Mandler, 1983).

**KNOWLEDGE-ACQUISITION APPROACHES** A number of developmental psychologists who question the existence of qualitative stages of cognitive development believe that after infancy, children and adults have essentially the same cognitive processes and capacities and that the difference between them is primarily the adult's more extensive knowledge base. By knowledge, they do not just mean a larger collection of facts, but a deeper understanding of how facts in a particular domain are organized.

This distinction between facts and the organization of facts is nicely illustrated by a study that compared a group of 10-year-olds who were competing in a chess tournament with a group of college students who were chess amateurs. When asked to memorize and recall lists of random numbers, the college students easily outperformed the 10-year-olds. But when tested on their ability to recall actual game positions of the chess pieces on the board, the 10-year-old chess experts did better than the 18-year-old chess amateurs (Chi, 1978). Thus, the relevant difference between the two groups is not different stages of cognitive development or different information-processing abilities (for example, memory capacity), but domain-specific knowledge. Because the 10-year-olds had a deeper grasp of the underlying structure of chess, they were able to organize and reconstruct the arrangements from memory by "chunking" the separate pieces of informa-

**FIGURE 3-8**
**Testing Conservation** *Children are told how doctors or scientists operated on an animal until it looked like a different animal (horse-to-zebra) or on an animal until it looked like a plant (porcupine-to-cactus). Children who say that the animal is "really" the new animal or plant are failing to show conservation; children who say that the animal is still "really" the original animal are showing conservation.*

tion into larger meaningful units (for example, a king-side attack by white) and by eliminating from consideration implausible placements of the pieces. An earlier study comparing adult chess masters with adult chess amateurs showed similar results (Chase & Simon, 1973). (We discuss experts versus amateur problem solvers in Chapter 9.)

Increasing knowledge of the world rather than a qualitative shift in cognitive development may also account for children's increasing ability to solve Piaget's conservation tasks as they get older. For example, the child who does not know that mass or number is the critical feature that defines what is meant by "more clay" or "more checkers" is likely to judge that the quantity has changed when only its visual appearance has changed. An older child may simply have learned the essential defining feature of "more." If this hypothesis is correct, then a child who fails to show conservation in one domain may show conservation in another, depending upon his or her understanding of the domain.

Evidence for this was obtained in a study in which kindergarten children were told about a series of "operations" that doctors or scientists had performed. Some operations altered an animal so that it looked like a different animal; other operations altered an animal so that it looked like a plant. Here is an example of each (see the stimulus photographs in Figure 3-8):

The doctors took a horse [shows child picture of horse] and did an operation that put black and white stripes all over its body. They cut off its mane and braided its tail. They trained it to stop neighing like a horse, and they trained it to eat wild grass instead of oats and hay. They also trained it to live in the wilds in Africa instead of in a stable. When they were all done, the animal looked just like this [shows picture of zebra]. When they were finished, was this animal a horse or a zebra? (Keil, 1989, p. 307)

This is a kind of porcupine that lives in the desert. It sleeps rolled up with its spikes out for protection. One scientist did an operation on it. He painted it yellowish green and gave it a shot that made it very sleepy. It went to sleep and didn't wake up for a whole year. This is what it looked like while it was sleeping. Did the scientist change it into a cactus plant or was it still a porcupine? (Keil, 1991, personal communication)

On operations that transformed one kind of animal to another, a majority of the children failed to conserve; about 65 percent agreed that the horse had been genuinely changed into a zebra. But when faced with the transformation of an animal to a plant, only about 25 percent agreed that the porcupine had been genuinely changed into a cactus (Keil, 1989). (Additional variations demonstrated that this could not be explained simply because the animals looked more like each other than plants and animals did.) The following transcript conveys a sense of how the children think about these transformations. Like most of the children, this particular child failed to conserve on the animal-to-animal transformation but did conserve on the animal-to-plant transformation.

### Horse-to-Zebra Transformation

INTERVIEWER: So, is it now a horse or a zebra?

CHILD: Where did they teach it to live?

I:  They taught it to live in Africa instead of a stable.

C: Well. I don't think horses live in Africa and zebras do. So it's a zebra.

I:  OK. You know what they did to it? [repeats the story] But now it's a zebra?

C: Yeah.

I:  Even though it came from a horse?

C: Yeah.

(Keil, 1986, pp. 148–149)

### Porcupine-to-Cactus Transformation

I:  So, is it now a porcupine or a cactus?

C: I think it's a porcupine still.

I:  Why is it still a porcupine and not a cactus?

C: Because maybe it still moves and cactuses don't move.

I:  OK. [repeats story] So what do you think?

C: It's a cactus. It looks like a cactus for years probably because they made it hibernate.

I:  But do you think it's a cactus or do you think it's a porcupine?

C: Still a porcupine.

I:  OK. Why do you think it's still a porcupine? What makes it still a porcupine?

C: They made it hibernate for years and after those years are all over, it will start waking up again.

I:  So even though it looks like this now . . . you think it's a porcupine?

C: Yes.

(Keil, 1986, p. 149)

Studies like these demonstrate that in some domains, preoperational children can ignore dramatic changes in visual appearance and conserve because they have learned that an invisible but essential defining feature of the object has remained unchanged. We will see a similar experiment in the later section on gender identity and sex typing, where we examine whether preoperational children believe that girls can be changed into boys and vice versa.

**SOCIOCULTURAL APPROACHES** Although Piaget emphasized the child's interaction with the environment, the environment he had in mind was the immediate physical environment. The child is seen as an inquiring physical scientist whose task it is to discover the true nature of the world and the universal rules of logical and scientific thought. The larger social and cultural context in which the child is embedded plays virtually no role in Piaget's theory. Even his discussion of social and moral rules implies that there is a universal, logical "right" way to think about such rules, which the child seeks to discover.

But not all knowledge is of this type. Much of what the developing child must learn is the particular and arbitrary ways in which his or her culture views reality, what roles different persons—and different sexes—are expected to play, and what rules and norms govern social relationships in his or her particular culture. In these areas, there are no universally valid facts or correct views of reality to be discovered. Thus, for cultural anthropologists and other social scientists who take a sociocultural approach to development, the child should be seen not as a physical scientist seeking "true" knowledge but as a newcomer to a culture who seeks to become a native by learning how to look at social reality through the lenses of that culture (Bem, 1987, 1993; Shweder, 1984). We will return to this theme in the section on gender identity and sex typing later in the chapter.

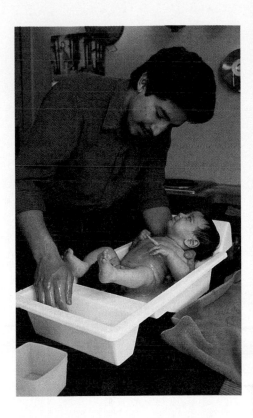

*Infants through the world begin to smile at about the same age—as do blind children—suggesting that maturation is more important than conditions of rearing in determining the onset of smiling.*

# Social Development In Childhood

Our first social contacts are with the persons who care for us in early infancy, usually the parents. The manner in which a caregiver responds to the infant's needs—patiently, with warmth and concern, or brusquely, with little sensitivity—will influence the child's relationships with other people. Some psychologists believe that a person's basic feelings of trust in others are determined by experiences during the first years of life (Erikson, 1963, 1976; Bowlby, 1973). In the discussions that follow, we will use the word "parent" to refer to the primary caregiver, while recognizing that others sometimes assume this role.

## Early Social Behavior

By two months of age, the average child will smile at the sight of its mother's or father's face. Delighted with this response, parents will go to great lengths to encourage repetition. Indeed, the infant's ability to smile at such an early age may have evolved historically precisely because it strengthened the parent-child bond. The first smiles tell the parents that the infant recognizes and loves them—which is actually not true in any personal sense at this age—and encourages them to be even more affectionate and stimulating in response. The infant smiles and coos at the parents; they pat, smile, and vocalize in return, thereby stimulating an even more enthusiastic response from the infant. A mutually reinforcing system of social interaction is thus established and maintained.

Infants all over the world begin to smile at about the same age, whether raised in a remote African village or a middle-class American home. This suggests that maturation is more important in determining the onset of smiling than are the conditions of rearing. Blind babies also smile at about the same age as sighted infants (in response to their parents' voices or touch rather than faces), which indicates that smiling is an innate response (Eibl-Eibesfeldt, 1970).

By their third or fourth month, infants show that they recognize and prefer familiar members of the household—by smiling or cooing more when seeing these familiar faces or hearing their voices—but infants are still fairly receptive to strangers. At about 7 or 8 months, however, this indiscriminate acceptance changes. Many infants begin to show wariness or actual distress at the approach of a stranger (even while being held by a parent) and, at the same time, to protest strongly when left in an unfamiliar setting or with an unfamiliar person. Parents are often disconcerted to find that their formerly gregarious infant, who had always happily welcomed the attentions of a baby-sitter, now cries inconsolably when they prepare to leave—and continues to cry for some time after they have left.

Although not all infants show this so-called "stranger anxiety"—it appears to be part of an infant's distinctive temperament—the number of infants who do show it increases dramatically from about 8 months of age until the end of the first year. Similarly, distress over separation from the parent—a distinct but related phenomenon also partially related to inborn temperament—reaches a peak between 14 to 18 months and then gradually declines. By the time they are 3 years old, most children are secure enough in their parents' absence to be able to interact comfortably with other children and adults.

The waxing and waning of these two fears appears to be only slightly influenced by conditions of child rearing. The same general pattern has been observed among American children reared entirely at home and among those attending a daycare center. Figure 3-9 shows that although the percentage of children who cry when their mothers leave the room varies across different cultures, the age-related pattern of onset and decline is very simi-

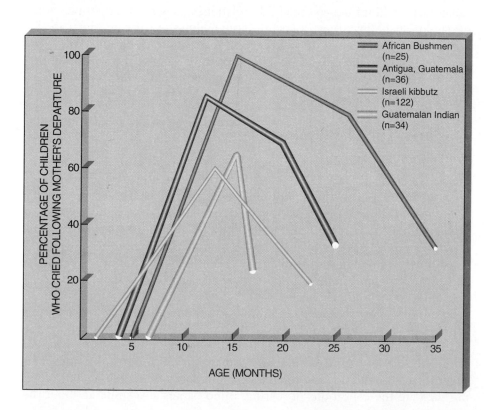

**FIGURE 3-9**
**Children's Stress at Mother's Departure** *Even though the percentages of children from different cultures who cry when their mothers leave the room varies from culture to culture, the age-related pattern of onset and decline of such distress is similar across cultures* (From Kagan, Kearsley, & Zelzao, 1978)

lar (Kagan, Kearsley, & Zelazo, 1978).

How do we explain the systematic timing of these fears among children who show them? Two factors seem to be important in both their onset and their decline. One is the growth of memory capacity. During the second half of the first year infants gain in their ability to remember past events and to compare past and present. This makes it possible for the baby to detect, and sometimes to fear, unusual or unpredictable events. The emergence of "stranger anxiety" coincides with the emergence of fears to a variety of stimuli that are unusual or unexpected; a weird-looking mask or a Jack-in-the-box that brings smiles to a 4-month-old often causes an 8-month-old to look apprehensive and distressed. As children learn that strangers and unusual objects are not generally harmful, such fears gradually diminish.

We also noted earlier the importance of memory in the strengthening of object permanence. As children approach the end of the first year, they are better able to recall the earlier presence of an object that has disappeared from view. It seems reasonable to assume that memory development is involved in so-called "separation anxiety." The infant cannot "miss" the parent unless he or she can recall that parent's presence a minute earlier and compare this with the parent's absence now. When the parent leaves the room, the infant is aware that something is amiss, which can lead to distress. As the child's memory improves for past instances of separation and return, the child becomes better able to anticipate the return of the absent parent, and anxiety declines.

The second factor is the growth of autonomy. One-year-olds are still highly dependent on care from adults, but children of 2 or 3 can head for the snack plate or toy shelf on their own. Also, they can use language to communicate their wants and feelings. Thus, dependency on caregivers in general and on familiar caregivers in particular decreases, and the issue of the parent's presence becomes less critical for the child.

## Attachment

An infant's tendency to seek closeness to particular people and to feel more secure in their presence is called **attachment.** The young of other species show attachment to their mothers in different ways. An infant monkey clings to its mother's chest as she moves about; puppies climb over each other in their attempts to reach the warm belly of their mother; ducklings and baby chicks follow their mother about, making sounds to which she responds and going to her when they are frightened. These early responses to the mother have a clear adaptive value: they prevent the organism from wandering away from the source of care and getting lost.

Psychologists at first theorized that attachment to the mother developed because she was the source of food, one of the infant's most basic needs. But some facts did not fit. For example, ducklings and baby chicks feed themselves from birth, yet they still follow their mothers about and spend a great deal of time with them. The comfort they derive from the mother's presence cannot come from her role in feeding. A series of well-known experiments with monkeys showed that there is more to mother-infant attachment than nutritional needs (Harlow & Harlow, 1969).

Infant monkeys were separated from their mothers shortly after birth and placed with two artificial "mothers" constructed of wire mesh with wooden heads. The torso of one mother was bare wire; the other was

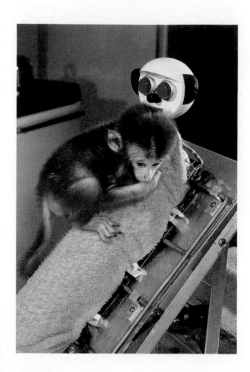

**FIGURE 3-10**
**A Monkey's Response to an Artificial Mother** *Although fed via a wire mother, the infant spends more time with the terry-cloth mother. The terry-cloth mother provides security and a safe base from which to explore strange objects.*

covered with foam rubber and terry cloth, making it more cuddly and easy to cling to (see Figure 3-10). Either mother could be equipped to provide milk by means of a bottle attached to its chest.

The experiment sought to determine whether the "mother" that was always the source of food would be the one to which the young monkey would cling. The results were clear-cut: no matter which mother provided food, the infant monkey spent its time clinging to the terry-cloth mother. This purely passive but soft-contact mother was a source of security. For example, the obvious fear of the infant monkey placed in a strange environment was allayed if the infant could make contact with the cloth mother. While holding on to the cloth mother with one hand or foot, the monkey was willing to explore objects that were otherwise too terrifying to approach. Similar responses can be observed in 1- to 2-year-old children who are willing to explore strange territory as long as a primary caregiver is close by.

Further studies revealed additional features that infant monkeys seek in their mothers. They prefer an artificial mother that rocks to an immobile one, and they prefer a warm mother to a cold one. Given a choice of a cloth mother or a wire mother of the same temperature, the infant monkeys always preferred the cloth mother. If the wire mother was heated, the newborns chose it over a cool cloth mother but only for the first 2 weeks of life. Later, the infant monkeys spent more and more time with the cloth mother.

The infant monkey's attachment to its mother is thus an innate response to certain stimuli provided by her. Warmth, rocking, and food are important, but contact comfort—the opportunity to cling to and rub against something soft—seems to be the most important attribute for monkeys.

Although contact with a cuddly, artificial mother provides an important aspect of "mothering," it is not enough for satisfactory development. Infant monkeys raised with artificial mothers and isolated from other monkeys during the first 6 months of life showed various types of bizarre behavior in adulthood. They rarely engaged in normal interaction with other monkeys later on (either cowering in fear or showing abnormally aggressive behavior), and their sexual responses were inappropriate. When female monkeys that had been deprived of early social contact were successfully mated (after considerable effort), they made poor mothers, tending to neglect or abuse their first-born infants—although they became better mothers with their later-born children. For monkeys, interaction with other members of their species during the first 6 months of life appears to be crucial for normal social development.

Although we should be careful in generalizing from research on monkeys to human development, there is evidence that the human infant's attachment to the primary caregiver serves the same functions: it provides the security necessary for the child to explore his or her environment, and it forms the basis for interpersonal relationships in later years. It has been hypothesized that the failure to form a secure attachment to one or a few primary persons in the early years is related to an inability to develop close personal relationships in adulthood (Bowlby, 1973).

Most of the research on attachment in humans has examined differences among infants in the security of their attachments to their mothers and whether those differences can be attributed to earlier patterns of interactions between the infant and mother, to the infant's inborn temperament, or to both. A few progressive researchers have even thought to examine infant-father attachments as well. The extensive research on individual differences in attachment is discussed in Chapter 13.

# Gender Identity and Sex Typing

With rare exceptions, the human species comes in two sexes, and most children acquire a firm sense of themselves as either male or female. They acquire what developmental psychologists call a **gender identity.** But most cultures elaborate the biological distinction between male and female into a sprawling network of beliefs and practices that permeate virtually every domain of human activity. Societies have both formal rules and informal norms that specify how men and women should behave; which roles they must, or are permitted to, fill; and even which personality characteristics they may "appropriately" possess. Different cultures may define the socially correct behaviors, roles, and personality characteristics differently from one another, and these may change over time within a culture—as they have in America over the past 25 years. But whatever its current definition, each culture still strives to transform male and female infants into masculine and feminine adults.

The acquisition of behaviors and characteristics that a culture considers sex-appropriate is called **sex typing.** Note that gender identity and sex typing are not the same thing. A girl may have a firm acceptance of herself as female and still not adopt all of the behaviors that her culture considers feminine or avoid all behavior labeled masculine.

But are gender identity and sex typing simply the product of cultural prescriptions and expectations or are they, in part, a product of "natural" development? Theories disagree on this point. We will examine four of them here.

**PSYCHOANALYTIC THEORY** The first psychologist to attempt a comprehensive account of gender identity and sex typing was Sigmund Freud, whose psychoanalytic theory contains a stage theory of **psychosexual development** within it (Freud, 1933/1964). Psychoanalytic theory is discussed

*Psychoanalytic theory proposes that a child models the behavior of a parent of the same sex to resolve an inner conflict with that parent, whereas social learning theory proposes that the modeling is strictly a result of observing that parent's behavior.*

in more detail in Chapter 14; here we will give only a sketch of the concepts relevant to his theory of gender identity and sex typing.

According to Freud, children begin to focus on the genitals at about age 3; he called this the beginning of the **phallic stage** of psychosexual development. Specifically, both sexes become aware that boys have a penis and that girls do not. During this same stage, they also begin to have sexual feelings toward their opposite-sex parent and feel jealous and resentful of their same-sex parent; Freud called this the **Oedipal conflict.** As they mature further, both sexes eventually resolve this conflict through **identification** with their same-sex parents, modeling their behaviors, attitudes, and personality attributes on those parents in an attempt to be like them. Thus, the process of forming a gender identity and becoming sex typed begins with the child's discovery of the genital differences between the sexes and ends with the child's identification with the same-sex parent (Freud, 1925/1961).

Psychoanalytic theory has always been controversial, and many object to its explicit assumption that "anatomy is destiny." The theory implies that rigid sex typing—even stereotyping—is universally inevitable and unmodifiable. More important, however, the empirical evidence does not support the conclusion that a child's discovery of genital sex differences or identification with the same-sex parent is an influential determinant of sex typing (Kohlberg, 1966; Maccoby & Jacklin, 1974; McConaghy, 1979).

**SOCIAL LEARNING THEORY**  In contrast to psychoanalytic theory, social learning theory has a much more straightforward account of sex typing. It emphasizes both the rewards and punishments that children receive for sex-appropriate and sex-inappropriate behaviors, respectively, and the ways in which children learn sex-typed behavior through their observation of adults (Bandura, 1986; Mischel, 1966). For example, children observe that adult male and female behaviors differ and develop hypotheses about what is appropriate for themselves (Perry & Bussey, 1984). Observational learning also enables children to imitate and thus to acquire sex-typed behaviors by modeling the significant same-sex adults they admire. Thus, like psychoanalytic theory, social learning theory has its own concept of modeling and identification, but it is based on observational learning rather than on inner conflict resolution. (Learning theory in general is discussed further in Chapter 7; social learning theory, in particular, is discussed further in Chapter 14.)

Two broader points are worth emphasizing about social learning theory. Unlike psychoanalytic theory, social learning theory treats sex-typed behaviors like any other learned behaviors; no special psychological principles or processes must be postulated to explain how children become sex typed. Second, if there is nothing special about sex-typed behaviors, then sex typing itself is neither inevitable nor unmodifiable. Children become sex typed because sex happens to be the basis on which their culture chooses to base reward and punishment. If a culture becomes less sex typed in its ideology, children will become less sex typed in their behavior.

Many lines of evidence support the general social learning account of sex typing. Parents do differentially reward and punish sex-appropriate and sex-inappropriate behaviors as well as serving as the child's first models of masculine and feminine behavior. From infancy on, most parents dress boys and girls differently and provide them with different toys (Rheingold & Cook, 1975). Observations made in the homes of preschool children have found that parents reward their daughters for dressing up, dancing, playing with dolls, and simply following them around but criticize them for manipulating objects, running, jumping, and climbing. In contrast, parents reward their sons for playing with blocks but criticize them for playing with dolls, asking for help, or even volunteering to be helpful (Fagot, 1978). Parents tend to demand more independence of boys and to have higher expectations of them; they also respond less quickly to boys' requests for help and focus less on the interpersonal aspects of a task. And finally, parents punish boys both verbally and physically more often than girls (Maccoby & Jacklin, 1974).

Some have suggested that in reacting differently to boys and girls, parents may not be imposing their own stereotypes on them but simply reacting to real innate differences between the behaviors of the two sexes (Maccoby, 1980). For example, even as infants, boys demand more attention than girls do, and research suggests that human males are innately more physically aggressive than human females (Maccoby & Jacklin, 1974). This could be why parents punish boys more often than girls.

There may be some truth to this, but it is also clear that adults approach children with stereotyped expectations that lead them to treat boys and girls differently. For example, adults viewing newborn infants through the window of a hospital nursery believe they can detect sex differences. Infants thought to be boys are described as robust, strong, and large-featured; identical looking infants thought to be girls are described as delicate, fine-featured, and "soft" (Luria & Rubin, 1974). In one study, college students viewed a videotape of a 9-month-old infant showing a strong but ambiguous emotional reaction to a Jack-in-the-box. The reaction was more often labeled "anger" when the child was thought to be a boy and "fear" when the same infant was thought to be a girl (Condry & Condry, 1976). When an infant was called "David" in another study, "he" was actually treated more roughly by subjects than when the same infant was called "Lisa" (Bem, Martyna, & Watson, 1976).

*Are you more comfortable with the boy's actions than with the girl's?*

Fathers appear to be more concerned with sex-typed behavior than mothers, particularly with their sons. They tend to react more negatively than mothers (interfering with the child's play or expressing disapproval) when their sons play with "feminine" toys. Fathers are less concerned when their daughters engage in "masculine" play, but they still show more disapproval than mothers do (Langlois & Downs, 1980).

But if parents and other adults treat children in sex-stereotyped ways, children themselves are the real "sexists." Peers enforce sex-stereotyping much more severely than parents. Indeed, parents who consciously seek to raise their children without the traditional sex-role stereotypes—by encouraging the child to engage in a wide range of activities without labeling any activity as masculine or feminine or by playing nontraditional roles within the home—are often dismayed to find their efforts undermined by peer pressure. Boys, in particular, criticize other boys when they see them engaged in "girls" activities. They are quick to call another boy a sissy if he plays with dolls, cries when he is hurt, or shows tender concern toward another child in distress. In contrast, girls seem not to object to other girls playing with "boys'" toys or engaging in masculine activities. (Langlois & Downs, 1980).

This points up a general phenomenon: the taboos in our culture against feminine behavior for boys are stronger than those against masculine behavior for girls. Being a male "sissy" is far less acceptable than being a female "tomboy." Four- and five-year-old boys are more likely to experiment with feminine toys and activities (such as dolls, a lipstick and mirror, hair ribbons) when no one is watching than when an adult or another boy is present. For girls, the presence of an observer makes little difference in their choice of play activities (Hartup & Moore, 1963; Kobasigawa, Arakaki, & Awiguni, 1966).

In addition to parental and peer influences, children's books and television programs play an important part in promoting sex-role stereotypes. Until recently, most children's books portrayed boys in active, problem-solving roles. They were the characters who displayed courage and heroism, persevered in the face of difficulty, constructed things, and achieved goals. Girls were usually much more passive. Female storybook characters were apt to display fear and avoidance of dangerous situations; they would give up easily, ask for help, and watch while someone else achieved a goal. Similar differences have been noted in the sex roles portrayed in children's television programs (Sternglanz & Serbin, 1974).

Attempts to modify children's sex-role stereotypes by exposing them to television programs in which the stereotypes are reversed (for example, the girls win in athletic events or a girl is elected president) have shown some success (Davidson, Yasuna, & Tower, 1979). But exposure to television cannot counteract real-life experiences.

This was apparent when 5- and 6-year-olds were shown films in which the usual sex-typed occupations were reversed: the doctors were women and the nurses were men. When questioned about the films afterward and shown pictures of the actors, the children tended to relabel the occupations of the characters, to identify the female actor as the nurse and the male actor as the doctor. On the other hand, having a mother who worked outside the home or being exposed to female physicians and male nurses in real life increased the likelihood that the child would accept the less conventional roles (Cordua, McGraw, & Drabman, 1979).

These several phenomena of sex typing are fairly well explained by social learning theory. On the other hand, there are some observations that social learning theory cannot easily explain. First, it treats the child as the passive recipient of environmental forces: society, parents, peers, and the media all "do it" to the child. This view of the child is inconsistent with the observation, implied above, that children themselves construct and enforce their own exaggerated version of society's gender rules on themselves and their peers more insistently than do most of the adults in their world. Second, there is an interesting developmental pattern to the child's view of gender rules. For example, a majority of 4-year-olds and a majority of 9-year-olds believe that there should be no sex-based restrictions on one's choice of occupation: let women be doctors and men be nurses if they wish. Between these ages, however, children hold more rigid opinions. Thus, about 90 percent of 6- and 7-year-olds believe that there *should* be sex-based restrictions on occupations (Damon, 1977).

Do these observations sound familiar? If you think these children sound like Piaget's preoperational moral realists, you are right. Which is why psychologist Lawrence Kohlberg (1966) developed a cognitive-developmental theory of sex typing based directly on Piaget's theory of cognitive development.

**COGNITIVE-DEVELOPMENTAL THEORY** In accounting for gender identity and sex typing, social learning theory puts its emphasis on the latter, describing how children acquire and come to prefer sex-typed behaviors because they are rewarded for them. This process begins long before gender identity emerges. Thus, children begin to show preferences for same-sex peers and sex-typed play activities when they are as young as 2 years old, well before they develop any conceptual awareness that these actions are correlated with sex (Jacklin & Maccoby, 1978). Although 2-year-olds can identify their own sex in a photograph of themselves and are usually able to identify the sex of a stereotypically dressed man or women in a photograph, they cannot accurately sort photographs into "boys" and "girls" or predict another child's toy preferences on the basis of sex (Thompson, 1975).

At about 2-1/2 years, however, a more conceptual awareness of sex and gender begins to emerge, and it is at this point that cognitive-developmental theory becomes relevant for explaining what happens next. In particular, the theory proposes that gender identity plays a critical role in sex typing. The sequence is: "I am a girl [boy]; therefore I want to do girl [boy] things" (Kohlberg, 1966). In other words, it is the motive to behave consistently with one's gender identity—not to obtain external rewards—that prompts children to behave in sex-appropriate ways. As a result they willingly take on the task of sex typing themselves—and their peers.

Gender identity itself develops slowly over the years from 2 to 7, in accord with the principles of the preoperational stage of cognitive development. In particular, preoperational children's overreliance on visual impressions and their consequent inability to conserve an object's identity when its appearance changes becomes relevant to their concept of sex. Thus, 3-year-olds can separate pictures of boys and girls, but many of them cannot say whether they themselves will be a mommy or a daddy when they grow up (Thompson, 1975). The understanding that a person's sex remains the same despite changes in age and appearance is called **gender constancy,** a direct analogue of object conservation with water, clay, and checkers.

For example, Kohlberg asked children if a doll's sex could be changed if they wanted it to. Most 4-year-olds said that it could be, whereas most 6-year-olds said it could not be. The children who showed gender constancy—who said the doll's sex could *not* be changed—also conserved on the clay conservation task described earlier in this chapter.

The preoperational child's moral realism is also pertinent here:

> The physical constancies underlying . . . gender . . . tend to be identified with divine or moral law, and the need to adapt to the physical realities of one's identity is viewed as a moral obligation. . . . [Children] view same-sex behavior as morally required, and . . . express punitive sentiments to children who deviate from sex-typed behavior. (Kohlberg, 1966, p. 122)

This, then, is why preoperational children seem to be even more sexist and less tolerant of gender nonconformity in themselves and others than are adults. This is why bewildered feminist parents of preoperational children find that their careful nonsexist childrearing practices do not seem to "take" despite their best efforts (but see the following Critical Discussion, "Can Sex Education Prevent Childhood Sexism?").

The cognitive-developmental theory of gender identity and sex typing is currently the most influential account of gender development within the field. But the shortcomings of Piaget's theory also apply to Kohlberg's special case of Piaget's theory. Thus, just as Piaget's more standard conservation tasks have been criticized, so too have the gender constancy tasks (Bem, 1989). For example, children who claim that a doll's sex can be changed at will may not understand that the experimenter wants them to pretend that the doll is a stand-in for a real person. Literally speaking, these children are right and the experimenter is wrong!

And just as developmental psychologists have shown that children can conserve at much younger ages than Piaget thought if the tasks are better designed, so too, it seemed to some researchers that children would display gender constancy long before they are 6 or 7 years of age if ambiguities, such as the one just cited, are removed. For example, in one study of gender constancy in the self, the investigators asked "If you wore [opposite-sex] clothes, what would you *really* be, a boy or a girl?" Over 90 percent of 4-, 5-, and 6-year olds responded correctly (Martin & Halverson, 1983). Another study took photos of some of the subject's classmates dressed up in opposite-sex clothes and then asked whether the child in each picture was a boy or a girl. Virtually all 3-, 4-, or 5-year olds responded correctly (Miller, 1984).

Earlier we saw that psychologists who adopt a knowledge acquisition approach to cognitive development believe that children often fail conservation tasks because they simply do not possess sufficient knowledge of the relevant domain. We saw, for example, children who conserved on animal-to-plant transformations but failed to conserve on animal-to-animal transformations. Children will ignore dramatic changes in visual appearance—and hence conserve—only when they understand that some essential defining feature of an object has not changed.

This suggests that a child's gender constancy might also depend on his or her understanding of maleness and femaleness. But what do we adults know about sex that children do not? One answer is genitalia. For all practi-

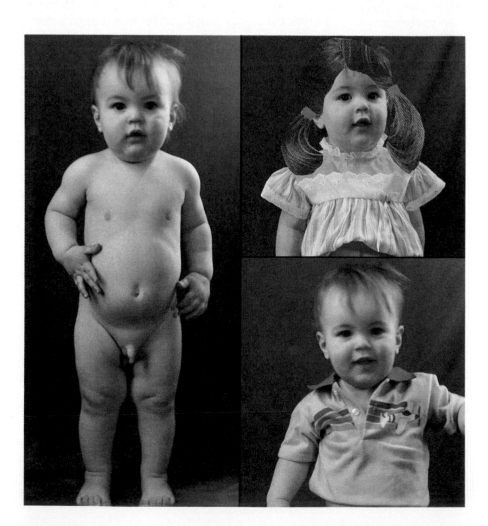

**FIGURE 3-11**
**Testing Gender Constancy** *After seeing the photograph of a nude toddler, children are asked to identify the sex of that same toddler from pictures in which the toddler is dressed in sex-inconsistent clothing and sex-consistent clothing. Children who can correctly identify the toddler's sex across all the pictures have attained gender constancy.* (From Bem, 1989, pp. 653–654)

cal purposes, genitalia constitute the essential defining feature of maleness and femaleness. Can young children who understand this conserve on a realistic gender constancy task?

In a study designed to test this possibility, three full-length, color photographs of toddlers between the ages of 1 and 2 were used as stimuli (Bem, 1989). As shown in Figure 3-11, the first photograph showed the toddler completely nude with the genitalia fully visible. The second photograph showed the same toddler dressed (and the boy be-wigged) like a child of the opposite sex; the third photograph showed the toddler dressed normally—like a child of his or her own sex.

(Because of the sensitive nature of child nudity in our culture, each photograph was taken in the toddler's own home with at least one parent present. Parents provided written consent to use the photographs in the research, and parents of the two children who appear in Figure 3-11 also gave written consent to have these photographs published. Finally, parents of the children who served as subjects in the study gave written permission for their children to participate in a study in which they would be asked questions about pictures of nude toddlers.)

Using these 6 photographs, children between 3 years and 5-1/2 years of age were tested for gender constancy. First the experimenter showed the child the photograph of the nude toddler, who was given a sex-ambiguous name (for example, "Gaw"), and asked the child to identify the toddler's sex:

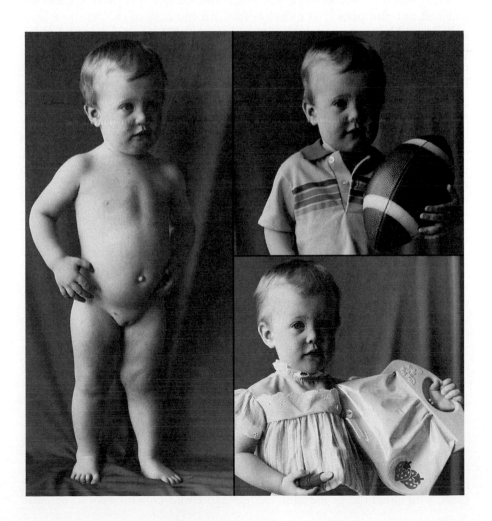

## *Critical* DISCUSSION

### *Can Sex Education Prevent Childhood Sexism?*

The experiment on gender constancy described in the text shows that children as young as 3 years old are able to understand that one's maleness and femaleness is a permanent biological fact; it

does not change just because one dresses like the opposite sex.

Sandra Bem, the researcher who conducted the study, and her husband (one of the authors of this text) believe that children who have a biologically grounded definition of sex may also have firmer gender identities—a more secure sense of themselves as male or female—because they do not have to fear that they will "lose" their maleness or femaleness if they engage in gender nonconforming behavior. Such children might thus be less sex-stereotyped in their own attitudes and behaviors, more able to resist social pressure to conform to society's gender rules, and more tolerant of others who do not conform.

In contrast, children who equate a person's sex with cultural indicators like clothing and hairstyle may be more sex-stereotyped as a result. Some support for this possibility comes from a study of 27-month-old children who were asked to identify the sex of conventionally clothed children in photographs taken from mail-order shopping catalogues. Children who could do this correctly—about half the children—were designated "early labelers."

Observations of these children revealed that, compared with the other children, early labelers spent twice as much of their time in sex-typed toy play. Moreover, their fathers were more likely than other fathers to believe that boys

"Is Gaw a boy or a girl?" Next the experimenter showed the child the sex-inconsistent photograph, making sure the child realized that this was the same toddler as in the nude photograph. The experimenter explained that the picture was taken one day when the toddler was playing dress-up and had put on opposite-sex clothes (and, in the case of the boy, put on a girl's wig). The nude photograph was removed and the child was asked to identify the sex of the toddler while looking only at the sex-inconsistent picture: "What is Gaw really—a boy or a girl?" Finally, the child was asked to identify the sex of the same toddler from the sex-consistent picture. This procedure was then repeated with the other set of 3 photographs. The children were also asked to explain their answers. A child was considered to have attained gender constancy only if he or she correctly identified the sex of the toddler all six times.

A set of photographs of different toddlers was used to assess whether the children knew that genitalia constitute the defining feature of sex. Again, children were asked to identify the sex of the pictured toddlers and to explain their answers. The easiest part of the test required the child to point out which of two nude toddlers was a boy and which a girl. The most difficult part of the test showed photographs of toddlers who were nude from the waist down but dressed in sex-inconsistent clothes from the waist up. In order to correctly identify the toddler's sex in these photographs, a child would have to know not only that genitalia indicate sex, but that when the genital indicators are in conflict with culturally defined indicators of sex (such as clothing, hairstyles, and toys), the genital indicators have priority. Note that the constancy task itself is even harder because children had to give priority to the genital indicators even when those indicators were no longer visible in the photograph (as in the second photograph of each set in Figure 3-11).

The results showed that 40 percent of the 3-, 4-, and early 5-year-old children displayed gender constancy. This is much earlier than predicted by the cognitive developmental theory of Piaget and Kohlberg. More importantly, a full 74 percent of those who passed the genital knowledge test displayed gender constancy, compared with only 11 percent (three children) of those who failed the gender knowledge test. Children who passed the gen-

and girls should have different kinds of toys, that children of different sexes should not see each other naked, and that children should not be given sexual information. They were also more likely to dread answering their children's questions about sex and to hold more traditional views about women. No such differences were observed among the mothers (Fagot & Leinbach, 1989). These findings are consistent with our earlier observation that fathers are more concerned with sex-typed behaviors than mothers.

The Bems thus believe that teaching children as early as possible that the genitalia are the essential defining feature of maleness and femaleness might immunize them against an unquestioning acceptance of the culture's gender rules. The preoperational child's "moral realism" might actually prompt these gender-liberated future citizens to be even more adamant and radical than their feminist parents in opposing sexism and sex stereotyping.

The difference between children with and without a genitally grounded gender constancy is amusingly illustrated by the Bems' own son, Jeremy, who naively decided to wear barrettes to nursery school one day. Several times another little boy insisted that Jeremy must be a girl because "only girls wear barrettes." After repeatedly asserting that "wearing barrettes doesn't matter; being a boy means having a penis and testicles," Jeremy finally pulled down his pants in order to make his point more graphically. The other boy was not impressed. He simply said, "Everybody has a penis; only girls wear barrettes!"

Freud believed that a child's early discovery of the genital differences between the sexes led inexorably to conventional sex typing. There is a certain delicious irony in the possibility that a child's early discovery of the genital differences between the sexes should become a feminist weapon against conventional sex typing.

der knowledge test were also more likely to show personal gender constancy: They correctly answered the question "If, like Gaw, you were playing dress-up games one day and you put on a girl's [boy's] wig . . . and girls' [boys'] clothes, what would you really be, a boy or a girl?

These results on gender constancy reveal that, like Piaget's general theory, Kohlberg's special theory about gender identity and sex typing underestimates the preoperational child's potential level of understanding. But there is a more important shortcoming of the theory: it fails to address why children should organize their self-concepts around their maleness or femaleness in the first place. Why should sex have priority over other potential categories of self-definition? It was this question that the next theory, gender schema theory, was designed to answer (Bem, 1985).

**GENDER SCHEMA THEORY**  We noted earlier that the sociocultural approach to psychological development views the developing child not as a physical scientist seeking universally true knowledge but as a newcomer to a culture who seeks to become a native by learning how to look at reality through the lenses of that culture.

We also noted that most cultures elaborate the biological distinction between male and female into a network of beliefs and practices that permeate virtually every domain of human activity. Accordingly, the child needs to learn many specific details of this network: What are the culture's rules and norms about sex-appropriate behaviors, roles, and personality characteristics? As we have seen, both social learning theory and cognitive-developmental theory provide reasonable explanations for how the developing child might acquire this information.

But the culture is also teaching the child a much deeper lesson, namely that the distinction between male and female is so important that it should become a set of lenses for looking at everything. Consider, for example, the child who first enters a daycare center offering a variety of new toys and activities. There are many potential criteria the child could use for deciding which toys and activities to try. Should she consider indoor or outdoor activities? Does he prefer a toy that involves artistic production or one that requires mechanical manipulation? How about an activity that one can do with

*Several theories attempt to account for the development of sex-typing in children.*

other children? Or one that can be done in solitude? But of all the potential criteria, the culture emphasizes one above all others: "Be sure to consider first and foremost whether the toy or activity is appropriate for your sex." At every turn, the child is encouraged to look at the world through the lenses of gender, and it is these lenses that Bem calls the **gender schema** (Bem, 1981, 1985, 1993). And it is because children learn to evaluate their behavioral alternatives through these lenses that gender schema theory is a theory of sex typing.

As anthropologists have pointed out, the natives of a culture are typically not aware of the lenses they wear. Lenses are transparent to the wearer—who looks *through* the lenses of the culture, not *at* them. For this same reason, parents and teachers do not teach children about the gender schema directly. Instead, the lesson is silently embedded in the daily practices of the culture.

Consider, for example, a teacher who wishes to treat children of both sexes equally. Accordingly, she lines them up at the drinking fountain by alternating boys and girls. If a boy is selected to be hall monitor on Monday, then a girl will be hall monitor on Tuesday. Equal numbers of boys and girls must be selected for the class play. This teacher believes she is teaching her students the importance of sex equality. She is right, but she is also unwittingly teaching them the importance of sex. The students learn that no matter how unrelated to sex an activity might seem, one cannot engage in it without attending to the male-female distinction. Even learning the pronouns of our language—he, she, him, her—requires wearing the lenses of gender.

Children also learn to apply the lenses of gender to themselves, to organize their self-concepts around their maleness or femaleness, and to judge their self worth in terms of their answer to the question: Am I masculine or feminine enough? It is in this way that gender schema theory is a theory of gender identity as well as a theory of sex typing.

Gender schema theory, then, is the answer to the question that Bem believes Kohlberg's cognitive-developmental theory of gender identity and sex typing fails to address: why should children organize their self-concepts around their maleness or femaleness in the first place? Like cognitive-developmental theory, gender schema theory views the developing child as an active agent in his or her own socialization. But like social learning theory, gender schema theory implies that sex typing is neither inevitable nor unmodifiable. Children become sex typed because sex happens to be a major focus around which their culture chooses to organize its view of reality. If the culture becomes less sex typed in its ideology, children will become less sex typed in their behaviors and self-concepts.

## Adolescent Development

**Adolescence** refers to the period of transition from childhood to adulthood. Its age limits are not clearly specified, but it extends roughly from age 12 to the late teens, when physical growth is nearly complete. During this period, the young person develops to sexual maturity and establishes an identity as an individual apart from the family.

### Sexual Development

**Puberty,** the period of sexual maturation that transforms a child into a biologically mature adult capable of sexual reproduction, takes place over a period of about 3 or 4 years. It starts with a period of very rapid physical growth (the **adolescent growth spurt**) accompanied by the gradual development of the reproductive organs and **secondary sex characteristics** (breast development in girls, beard growth in boys, and the appearance of pubic hair in both sexes).

**Menarche,** the first menstrual period, occurs relatively late in puberty—about 18 months after a girl's growth spurt has reached its peak velocity. The first menstrual periods tend to be irregular, and ovulation (the release of a mature egg) does not usually begin until a year or so after menarche. A boy's first ejaculation typically occurs about 2 years after the growth spurt begins. The first seminal fluid does not contain sperm; the number of sperm and their fertility gradually increase.

There is wide variation in the age at which puberty begins and the rate at which it progresses. Some girls attain menarche as early as 11, others as late as 17; the average age is 12 years, 9 months. Boys, on the average, experience their growth spurt and mature 2 years later than girls (see Figure 3-12). They begin to ejaculate semen with live sperm sometime between age 12 and 16; the average age is 14-1/2 years. The wide variation in the timing of puberty is strikingly apparent in seventh- and eighth-grade classrooms. Some of the girls may look like mature women with fully developed breasts and rounded hips, while others may still have the size and shape of little girls. Some of the boys may look like gangly adolescents, while others may look much as they did at the age of 9 or 10. (See the discussion of hormonal changes at puberty in Chapter 10.)

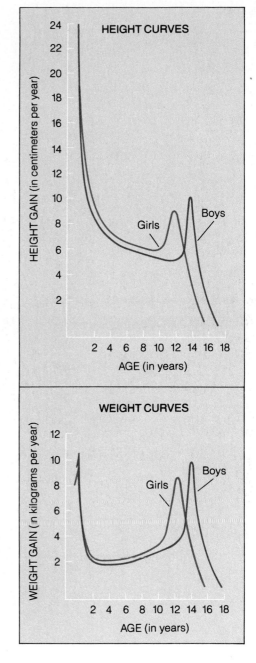

**FIGURE 3-12**
**Annual Gains in Height and Weight**
*The period of most rapid growth comes earlier for girls than for boys.* (After Tanner, 1970)

**PSYCHOLOGICAL EFFECTS OF PUBERTY** Conventional wisdom holds that adolescence is a period of "storm and stress" characterized by moodiness, inner turmoil, and rebellion. But research does not support this pessimistic view. A recent study followed more than 300 young adolescents as they progressed from the sixth through the eighth grades, assessing them and their parents twice a year through interviews and psychological tests. They were assessed again during their last year of high school (Petersen, 1988a). The data indicate that puberty does have significant effects on body image, self-esteem, moods, and relationships with parents and members of the opposite sex. However, most of the adolescents made it through this period without major turmoil.

Being an early or late maturer (one year earlier or later than average) affected the adolescents' satisfaction with their appearance and their body image. Early maturing boys tended to be more satisfied with their weight and their overall appearance than those who were less mature—a reflection of the importance of strength and physical prowess for males in our society. The reverse was true for girls. Those who were physically mature were generally less satisfied with their weight and appearance than their less mature classmates. Early maturing girls tended to be embarrassed by the fact that their bodies were more womanly in shape than those of their female classmates—particularly since the current standards for female attractiveness as promoted by the media emphasize the lean look.

With regard to mood, seventh- and eighth-grade boys who had reached puberty reported positive moods more often than their prepubertal male classmates did. Although pubertal status was less clearly related to mood among girls in this study, other studies indicate that early maturing girls experience more depression and anxiety (Brooks-Gunn & Ruble, 1983) and have lower self-esteem (Simmons & Blyth, 1988) than their less mature classmates. Puberty also affected the girls' relationship with their parents; girls who were developmentally advanced talked less with their parents and had fewer positive feelings about family relationships than did less-developed girls.

*There is wide variation in the age at which puberty begins and the rate at which it progresses. On average, boys experience their growth spurt and mature two years later than girls.*

In general, pubertal change appears to be a positive experience for boys but a negative one for girls. For both sexes, however, early adolescence was relatively trouble-free for more than half of those studied. About 30 percent of the group had only intermittent problems. Fifteen percent were caught in a "downward spiral of trouble and turmoil"; emotional and academic problems that were evident in the eighth grade continued or worsened into twelfth grade (Petersen, 1988a). The authors of this study conclude that for youngsters whose lives are already troubled, the changes that come with early adolescence add further burdens so that their problems are likely to persist.

## Sexual Standards and Behavior

The last 30 years have witnessed a revolutionary change in attitudes toward sexual activity in most Western societies. Views regarding premarital sex, homosexuality, and specific sexual acts are more permissive today than they have been at any time in recent history. We are exposed to sexual stimuli in the media to a greater extent than ever before. More satisfactory contraceptive methods and the availability of abortions have lessened fear of pregnancy. All these changes give the newly matured individual more freedom today. But they also cause more frequent conflict between young people and their parents because they produce wide divergences between successive generations in the norms for "appropriate" sexual behavior.

For women, the first major change in premarital sexual behavior actually occurred in the 1920s. In a set of famous studies conducted in the 1940s, Kinsey found that fewer than one-quarter of the women in his sample who had married prior to 1920 had had intercourse before marriage, compared with almost half of those married after 1920. These figures remained fairly constant until the middle 1960s when another significant increase occurred (Cannon & Long, 1971).

Table 3-3 lists the percent of young unmarried men and women over the years who have experienced sexual intercourse by age 19. The figures show that there has been an increase for both adolescent men and women, with women showing the more dramatic increase. And although men are more likely to have had sexual intercourse at all time periods, the difference between the sexes has been diminishing at a very rapid rate. This reflects, in part, the easing of the double standard (in which it is permissible for men but not women to engage in premarital intercourse). It also reflects a different pattern of sexual experience for male adolescents. Earlier in this century, they were much more likely to have their early sexual experiences with prostitutes or with one of the few "bad girls" in their community; today, they are more likely to have their early sexual experiences with a female peer, within a dating or longer-term relationship.

With the advent of AIDS (Acquired Immune Deficiency Syndrome) and the spread of venereal disease and genital infections (such as herpes), some health workers hoped that adolescents might begin to take a more cautious approach to sexual activity. And, as Table 3-2 suggests, there was, in fact, a leveling off in the increase of premarital intercourse during the early 1980s. But the 1988 figures reveal another sharp increase for female adolescents. The most dramatic increase has been among girls 15 years of age. In 1970, only 4.6 percent of 15-year-old female adolescents said they had had premarital intercourse; by 1988 that figure had risen to 25.6 percent, a five-fold increase (Centers for Disease Control, 1991). Of more concern to

| YEAR DATA COLLECTED | PERCENT PREMARITAL INTERCOURSE | |
| --- | --- | --- |
| | FEMALE | MALE |
| 1938–1949 | 20 | 45 |
| 1973 | 45 | 59 |
| 1976 | 55 | – |
| 1979 | 69 | 77 |
| 1983–1984 | 68 | 78 |
| 1988–1990 | 75 | 76 |

**TABLE 3-3**
**Premarital Intercourse of Male and Female Adolescents** *The table gives the percentage of unmarried 19-year-olds who reported having experienced sexual intercourse. The period of data collection is given in the first column. This and other evidence indicate a marked increase in premarital sexual experience over the past 20 years. For women, there was again an increase between 1984 and 1988, after a leveling off in the rate of increase during the early 1980s. Data for 1938–1949 are from Kinsey, Pomeroy & Martin (1948) and Kinsey, Pomeroy, Martin & Gebhard (1953); for 1973 from Sorenson (1973); for 1976 from Zelnick & Kantner (1977); for 1979 from Zelnick & Kantner (1980); for 1983–1984 from Mott & Haurin (1988), and for 1988–1990 from Centers for Disease Control (1991, 1992).*

*Sexual attitudes and behavior have changed dramatically during the 20th century in the industrialized countries.*

health officials than the simple increase of sexual activity, however, is the precautions that sexually active adolescents do or do not take in order to avoid pregnancy and sexually transmitted diseases. As the Critical Discussion, "Teenage Pregnancy and Contraceptive Use" notes, there is both discouraging and encouraging news here.

## Adolescent–Parent Conflict

Related to the traditional view that adolescence is inevitably a period of personal turmoil is the expectation that adolescents and their parents suffer from a "generation gap" characterized by stormy adolescent–parent relationships. As a result, parents often anticipate their youngsters' approaching puberty with trepidation.

Research yields no real evidence of a generation gap. Parents and their offspring have more similar values and attitudes than do adolescents and their friends (Lerner, Karson, Meisels, & Knapp, 1975), and they tend to agree about most important issues (Youniss & Smollar, 1985). And even though they consult their peers about areas of "adolescent culture"—such as how to dress, what music to listen to, and so forth—adolescents still continue to seek their parents' advice on important matters.

It is true, however, that family conflict in the form of nagging, squabbling, and bickering is more common during adolescence than during any other period of development, and it is more intense during early and middle adolescence (roughly ages 11 to 15) than it is in late adolescence. Puberty appears to play a central role in initiating this conflict. If physical maturity comes early, so does the arguing and bickering; if it is late, the period of heightened tension is delayed (Steinberg, 1987). Adolescents of both sexes have significantly more conflicts with their mothers than with their fathers, probably because mothers are more involved in regulating the everyday details of family life (Smetana, 1988).

In general, conflicts usually involve mundane aspects of daily life, such as chores, schoolwork, messy rooms, blaring stereos, personal appearance, and curfews. (More potentially explosive issues, such as sex, tend not to be discussed.) Significantly, these are precisely the areas that adolescents are most likely to believe should be under their personal jurisdiction. The parents view the same issues in conventional or pragmatic terms, that is, according to social customs or as necessary for the efficient running of the family (Smetana, 1988). Parents are often torn between the necessity of maintaining the family system and allowing their child increasing jurisdiction over his or her own behavior. Adolescents are caught between two worlds, one of dependence, the other of responsibility. They would like the power to decide for themselves, but are not certain they want the increased responsibility that accompanies adulthood. Their parents, who pay the bills and pick up the clothing tossed on the floor, demand that independence be matched by responsibility.

Most parents and teenagers manage to negotiate a new form of interdependence that grants the adolescent more autonomy, a more equal role in family decisions, and more responsibilities. If a teenager fails to negotiate a working relationship with his or her parents in early adolescence (if, for example, the parents are authoritarian and unwilling to grant more autonomy), then conflict may escalate into major difficulties by late adolescence (Petersen, 1988b). This may be why we mistakenly think of adolescent–parent conflict as more typical of the last years of high school when, in fact, conflict is more likely to peak earlier, at puberty.

Parents who provide explanations for their decisions, who relax parental control during adolescence, and who employ a democratic structure of decision making within the family give their offspring a sense of autonomy that reduces conflict and eases the transition to adulthood (Maccoby & Martin, 1983).

## Identity Development

A major task confronting the adolescent is to develop a sense of individual identity, to find answers to the questions "Who am I?" and "Where am I going?" The process also involves feelings about self-worth and competence. Although development of a self-concept starts in early childhood and continues throughout the life span, adolescence is a particularly critical period.

An adolescent's sense of identity develops gradually out of the various identifications of childhood. Young children's values and moral standards are largely those of their parents; their feelings of self-esteem stem primarily from their parents' view of them. As youngsters move into the wider world of junior high school, the values of the peer group become increasingly important, as do the appraisals of teachers and other adults. Adolescents try to synthesize these values and appraisals into a consistent picture. If parents, teachers, and peers project consistent values, the search for identity is easier.

In a simple society in which identification models are few and social roles are limited, the task of forming an identity is relatively easy. In a society as complex as ours, it is a difficult task for many adolescents. They are faced with an almost infinite array of possibilities of how to behave and what to do in life. As a result, there are large differences among adolescents in how the development of their identity proceeds. Moreover, any particular adolescent's identity may be at different stages of development in different areas of life (for example, sexual, occupational, ideological). Because one's identity is an integral part of one's overall personality, we discuss adolescent identity development in greater detail in Chapter 13 ("Personality through the Life Course").

*The values of the peer group become increasingly important as adolescents begin to define their personal identities.*

## *Teenage Pregnancy and Contraceptive Use*

One of the most troubling aspects of the increase in adolescent sexual activity is teenage pregnancy. The pregnancy rate for unmarried mothers under age 18 has been increasing rapidly in the United States since 1960. Close to one million American teenage girls become pregnant each year, and many of them are under age 15 (Hayes, 1987).

An adolescent girl who became pregnant 25 years ago usually married or gave up her baby for adoption. Abortion was not a legal option until 1973, when the Supreme Court ruled that the procedure could not be outlawed. Today, if a girl chooses not to abort her pregnancy (and some 45 percent of teenagers do decide to have an abortion), chances are she will keep the baby and raise it as a single parent. A decade ago, more than 90 percent of babies born out of wedlock were given up for adoption; today, almost 90 percent are kept by the mother.

Children raising children has enormous social consequences. Teenage mothers often do not complete high school, and many live below the poverty level, dependent on welfare. Their infants have high rates of illness and mortality and often experience emotional and educational problems later in life. Many are victims of child abuse at the hands of parents too immature to understand why their baby is crying or how their doll-like plaything has suddenly developed a will of its own.

*A poster prepared by the Children's Defense Fund for its campaign aimed at reducing teenage pregnancies.*

A 17-year follow-up study of some 300 adolescents born to teenage mothers indicates that teenage pregnancy can perpetuate a cycle of failure and early childbearing. Compared with the offspring of later child bearers, the adolescent children of teenage mothers had a much higher incidence of school failure, behavior problems, and delinquency. They were also more likely to engage in intercourse at an early age and to become pregnant or father a child (Furstenberg, Brooks-Gunn, & Morgan, 1987).

With effective methods of contraception more widely available than ever before, why do so many female adolescents have unplanned pregnancies? Part of the explanation is ignorance about the process of reproduction. Surveys find that fewer than half of the adolescents questioned know when in the menstrual cycle a woman is most likely to become pregnant (Morrison, 1985). Because low pregnancy risk due to "time of month" is a common reason adolescents give for not using contraception, this lack of information has important consequences. Other frequently reported bits of misinformation include the belief that one cannot become pregnant from the first intercourse, or if one has sex infrequently, or has intercourse standing up.

A second reason for the large number of unplanned pregnancies is an unwillingness to use reliable contraception even by those who are knowledgeable about the risks of pregnancy. In surveys, they mention the unplanned nature of

## Development As a Lifelong Process

Development does not end with the attainment of physical maturity. It is a continuous process extending from birth through adulthood to old age. Bodily changes occur throughout life, affecting the individual's attitudes, cognitive processes, and behavior. The kinds of problems people must cope with change throughout the life span, too.

Erik Erikson has proposed a series of eight stages to characterize development throughout life. He calls them **psychosocial stages** because he believes that the psychological development of individuals depends on the social relations established at various points in their lives. Each stage con-

intercourse and express generally negative attitudes toward contraception. A frequent theme is the feeling that being prepared robs sex of its spontaneity and is also somewhat immoral. Female adolescents who are uncomfortable admitting their sexuality to themselves prefer to be swept away romantically rather than to prepare for sex. They seem to feel that they can excuse their behavior if it was unplanned, but if they take birth control pills or carry a condom, then they must honestly acknowledge to themselves that they are sexually active. They also open themselves to the charge that they are promiscuous or are "looking for sex." Traditional sex roles also prompt female adolescents to relinquish decisions about contraception to the male. Another major barrier to the rational use of contraception is embarrassment and an inability of many adolescent couples to communicate openly with each other about their sexual activities.

As a result of these factors, teenage pregnancy rates in the United States are more than double that of any other industrialized country (see figure). American adolescents are not more sexually active than their foreign peers. Nor is the difference due to higher abortion rates abroad; indeed, abortion rates are much higher here (Brozan, 1985). Most experts attribute the high rates of teenage pregnancy in this country to a cultural ambivalence about teenage sex. The popular media encourage early experimentation with sex, conveying that to be sophisticated one must be sexually hip. Yet at the same time adult Americans are reluctant to acknowledge adolescent sexuality and to help teenagers prevent pregnancy. Television networks are unwilling to show programs dealing with contraception; many teenagers report that their parents are reluctant to discuss it; sex education in the schools is still a controversial topic; and high-school clinics that give birth control counseling and dispense contraceptives are even more controversial.

In contrast are countries like Sweden where schoolchildren receive instruction in reproductive biology starting at age 7 and are introduced to the various types of contraceptives by age 10 or 12. The aim is to demystify sex so that familiarity will make the child less likely to fall prey to unwanted pregnancy and venereal disease. These efforts appear to be successful; Sweden has one of the lowest rates of teenage pregnancy.

The current concern about preventing the spread of AIDS may finally be leading Americans to a more realistic concept of adolescent sexuality. One hopeful sign comes from a very recent survey of more than 11,000 high school students (Centers for Disease Control, 1992). It found that 78 percent of sexually active students—both male and female—used some method of contraception the last time they had intercourse. Forty percent of the females and 49 percent of the males reported using a condom—a method that also protects against sexually transmitted diseases, including AIDS. The rest used other methods, both reliable (for example, birth control pills) and unreliable (for example, withdrawal.)

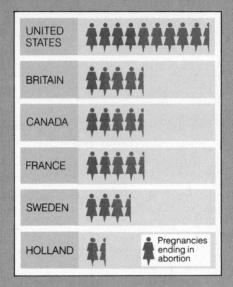

**Teenage Pregnancy Rates**
*Each figure represents 10 pregnancies out of every 1,000 female teenagers. The teenage pregnancy rate in the United States (9.5 percent) is more than double that of any of the other countries.*

fronts special problems or crises. These hypothesized stages are shown in Table 3-3.

Erikson believes that a person—child or adult—must successfully negotiate each crisis in order to be prepared for the psychosocial tasks that follow. Thus, infants must learn during the first year of life that their parents or caregivers can be trusted to provide food, comfort, and unconditional love. If and when such trust develops, then the child feels safe in trying out more autonomy in the second year. Parents who get exasperated when their toddler acts stubborn and defiant in the second year of life should congratulate themselves: their child trusts them enough to know that they will not withdraw their love when he or she is naughty. And, to the extent that parents encourage a sense of autonomy during the second year, their children learn

**TABLE 3-4**
**Stages of Psychosocial Development**
*Erikson defines eight major life stages in terms of the psychosocial problems, or crises, that must be resolved.* (After Erikson, 1963)

| STAGES | PSYCHOSOCIAL CRISES | FAVORABLE OUTCOME |
|---|---|---|
| 1. First year of life | Trust versus mistrust | Trust and optimism |
| 2. Second year | Autonomy versus doubt | Sense of self-control and adequacy |
| 3. Third through fifth years | Initiative versus guilt | Purpose and direction; ability to initiate one's own activities |
| 4. Sixth year to puberty | Industry versus inferiority | Competence in intellectual, social, and physical skills |
| 5. Adolescence | Identity versus confusion | An integrated image of oneself as a unique person |
| 6. Early adulthood | Intimacy versus isolation | Ability to form close and lasting relationships; to make career commitments |
| 7. Middle adulthood | Generativity versus self-absorption | Concern for family, society, and future generations |
| 8. The aging years | Integrity versus despair | A sense of fulfillment and satisfaction with one's life; willingness to face death |

to control their impulses and to feel pride in their accomplishments. Overprotection—restricting what the child is permitted to do—or ridiculing unsuccessful attempts may cause the child to doubt his or her abilities.

During the preschool years (ages 3 through 5), children progress from simple self-control to an ability to initiate activities and carry them out. Again, parental attitudes—encouraging or discouraging—can make children feel inadequate (or guilty, if the child initiates an activity that the adult views as shameful).

During the elementary-school years, children learn the skills valued by society. These include not only reading, writing, and physical skills, but also the ability to share responsibility and to get along with other people. To the extent that efforts in these areas are successful, children develop feelings of competence; unsuccessful efforts result in feelings of inferiority.

As we noted in the previous section, constructing a personal identity is the major psychosocial task of adolescence. In support of Erikson's hypothesis that each stage of development depends on the successful resolution of earlier stages, studies have found that adolescents who are actively concerned with their identities or who have already achieved an integrated identity score higher on measures of autonomy (Erikson's stage 2) than do those who have never gone through an identity crisis (Waterman & Waterman, 1972).

## Early Adulthood

During the early adult years, people commit themselves to an occupation, and many marry or form other types of intimate relationships. As Table 3-3 indicates, Erikson saw identity as a precursor to intimacy. He believed that adolescents who have not yet formed a satisfactory identity would find it difficult to become involved in an intimate, mutually satisfying relationship because their preoccupation with themselves would make it difficult to attend to the other person's needs. There is another point of view, however, that argues that adolescence begins not with a search for identity but with a need for intimacy and that the construction of self-identity is made possible by participating in intimate interpersonal relations (Sullivan, 1953). There is not enough research to decide between these two points of view; most likely, intimacy and identity interact throughout the periods of adolescence and early adulthood.

*In early adulthood, people strive to form close, lasting relationships and to make career commitments.*

## Middle Adulthood

For many people, the middle years of adulthood (roughly ages 40 to 65) are the most productive period. People in their forties are usually at the peak of their careers. Women who have devoted earlier years primarily to home responsibilities often turn to career or other activities as their children pass through and beyond adolescence.

Erikson uses the term *generativity* to refer to a concern with guiding and providing for the next generation. Feelings of satisfaction in middle adulthood come from helping teenage children become adults, providing for others who need help, and seeing one's contributions to society as valuable.

There is a widespread view that this is also a time of "midlife crisis"—a time when individuals begin to realize that they have not achieved the goals

*For many adults, the years of middle adulthood are their most productive period. But it can also be a time of transition as they begin to reassess their priorities.*

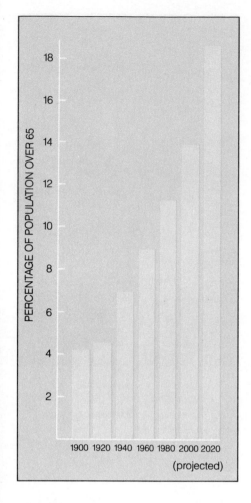

**FIGURE 3-13**
**Aging America.** *The percentage of the population in the United States over age 65 is increasing at a steady rate and is projected to continue to increase. For babies born in the United States today, life expectancy is an unprecedented 71.1 years for a boy and 78.3 years for a girl. For those who survive through middle age, the expected length of life is dramatically longer. A man who reaches 65 today can expect to live until 79.5 and a woman, to 83.7.* (U.S. Bureau of the Census, 1989)

they set for themselves as young adults or that they are not doing anything of much importance. Several longitudinal studies have reported that men in their early forties experience a period of emotional turmoil centered around conflicts about sexual relationships, family roles, and work values (Vaillant, 1977; Levinson et al, 1978). And a similar midlife crisis has been proposed for women (Sheehy, 1976). The transition to middle adulthood, according to this view, is a time of upheaval not unlike a second adolescence, during which life goals are reevaluated and questions such as "Who am I?" and "Where am I going?" become important again.

But many researchers question the concept of midlife crisis as a developmental stage that most people experience. They find little evidence that people in their forties report more symptoms of emotional distress than younger or older people (Costa & McCrae, 1980; Schaie & Willis, 1991). And studies of how middle-aged women react to events such as menopause and children leaving home report that few perceive these changes as traumatic (Neugarten, 1968).

It is true that middle age is often a time of transition. As people approach the midpoint in life, their view of the life span tends to change. Instead of looking at life in terms of time since birth, as younger people do, they begin to think in terms of years left to live. Having faced the aging or death of their parents, they begin to realize the inevitability of their own death. At this point, many people restructure their lives in terms of priorities, deciding what is important to do in the years remaining. A man who has spent his years building a successful business may leave it to return to school. A woman who has raised her family may develop a new career or become active in politics. A couple may leave their jobs in the city to purchase a small farm. Although some people find this kind of re-evaluation and change stressful enough to constitute a midlife crisis, most perceive it as a challenge rather than a threat.

## The Aging Years

People older than 65 now compose approximately 12 percent of the population, a percentage that is expected to approach 20 percent by the year 2020 (see Figure 3-13). Because of better medical care, improved diet, and increasing interest in physical fitness, more people are reaching the ages of 65, 75, and older in excellent health. Research has shown that aging does not mean inevitable physical and mental debility. Normal aging is a gradual process that brings some changes: slower reflexes, dimmer eyesight and hearing, decreased stamina. But the more extreme debilities that we associate with old age are the result of disease (such as Alzheimer's, which destroys mental and physical functioning); abuse of the body by improper diet or use of alcohol and cigarettes; and failure to keep physically and mentally active.

The belief that mental abilities decline with age has also been challenged by research findings. Elderly adults do not process information as quickly as younger people (Cerella, 1985), and they perform worse on some problem-solving tasks (Denny, 1980). But there is no evidence that the general ability to learn decreases with age (Schaie & Willis, 1986). Even brief training can improve the problem-solving skills of older people (Willis, 1985). The number of individuals in their 60s and 70s who work under demanding schedules and make important decisions (such as judges, corporate heads, and political leaders) attests to the fact that cognitive abilities need not diminish with age.

This is the bright side of the picture; for some older people the later years are not so happy. Those who are in poor health find that declining physical strength limits their activities and debilitating illnesses make them feel helpless. Mandatory retirement, which brings idle hours to be filled, may lessen feelings of worth and self-esteem, especially in a society in which one's contributions are usually evaluated in economic terms. The death of a spouse, siblings, and friends can make life unbearably lonely.

Erikson's last psychosocial crisis—integrity versus despair—is concerned with the way a person faces the end of life. Old age is a time of reflection, of looking back on the events of a lifetime. To the extent that an individual has successfully coped with the problems posed at each of the earlier stages of life, he or she has a sense of wholeness and integrity, of a life well-lived. If the elderly person looks back on life with regret, seeing it as a series of missed opportunities and failures, the final years will be ones of despair.

*Because of better medical care, improved diet, and increasing interest in physical fitness, more people are reaching older age in excellent health.*

## *Chapter* SUMMARY

1. Two central questions in developmental psychology are: a) How do biological factors ("nature") interact with environmental experiences ("nurture") to determine the course of development? and b) Is development best understood as a *continuous process* of change or as a series of qualitatively distinct *stages*? A related question is: Are there *critical* or *sensitive periods* during which specific experiences must occur for psychological development to proceed normally?

2. Genetic determinants express themselves through the process of *maturation*: innately determined sequences of growth or bodily changes that are relatively independent of the environment. Motor development, for example, is largely a maturational process because all children master skills such as crawling, standing, and walking in the same sequence and at roughly the same age. But even these can be modified by an atypical or inadequate environment.

3. Infants are born with all sensory systems functioning and well prepared to learn about the environment. There is even some evidence that newborns respond differentially to sounds they heard while still in the uterus. Newborns also show individual differences in *temperament*.

4. Piaget's theory describes stages in *cognitive development;* proceeding from the *sensorimotor stage* (in which an important discovery is *object permanence*), through the *preoperational stage* (symbols begin to be used), and the *concrete operational* stage (*conservation* concepts develop), to the *formal operational* stage (hypotheses are tested systematically in problem solving). The character of a child's *moral judgments* also corresponds to this sequence of stages.

5. New methods of testing reveal that Piaget's theory underestimates children's abilities, and alternative approaches have emerged. *Information-processing* approaches view cognitive development as reflecting the gradual development of processes such as attention and memory. Other theorists emphasize the child's increase in *domain-specific knowledge*. Still others focus on the influence of the *social and cultural context*.

6. Some early social behaviors, such as smiling, reflect innate responses that appear at about the same time in all infants, including blind infants. The emergence of many later social behaviors—including wariness of strangers and distress over separation from primary caregivers—appears to depend on the child's developing cognitive skills. An infant's *attachment* to primary caregivers forms the basis for close interpersonal relations in adulthood.

7. *Gender identity* is the degree to which one regards oneself as male or female. It is distinct from *sex typing,* the acquisition of those characteristics and behaviors society considers appropriate for one's sex. Freud's *psychoanalytic theory* holds that gender identity and sex typing develop from the children's early discovery of the genital differences between the sexes and children's eventual *identification* with the same-sex parent. *Social learning theory* emphasizes a) the *rewards and punishments* that children receive for sex-appropriate and sex-inappropriate behaviors and b) a process of *identification* with same-sex adults that is based on *observational learning.*

8. A *cognitive-developmental theory* of gender identity and sex typing developed by Kohlberg is based on Piaget's theory of cognitive development. Once children can identify themselves as male or female, they are motivated to acquire sex-typed behaviors. Their understanding of sex and gender corresponds to Piaget's stages of cognitive development, especially their understanding of *gender constancy,* the realization that a person's sex remains constant despite changes of age and appearance. Like its parent theory, cognitive-development theory underestimates children's degree of understanding.

9. *Gender schema theory,* developed by Sandra Bem, seeks to explain why children base their self-concept on the male–female distinction in the first place. It emphasizes the culture's role in teaching children to view the world through a set of *gender lenses.* Like cognitive developmental theory, gender schema theory sees children as active agents in promoting their own sex typing; like social learning theory, it rejects the conclusion that traditional sex typing is inevitable and unmodifiable.

10. Although the age at which sexual maturation *(puberty)* begins varies widely, on the average girls mature two years earlier than boys. Compared with their prepubertal classmates, early maturing boys report greater satisfaction with their appearance and more frequent positive moods; early maturing girls, in contrast, report more depression, anxiety, family conflict, and dissatisfaction with their appearance than do their less mature classmates. Survey data indicate that adolescents today are engaging in sexual intercourse at an earlier age than did their parents.

11. In their search for personal identity, adolescents try to synthesize the values and views of people important to them (parents, teachers, and peers) into a cohesive self-portrait. When these values are not consistent, adolescents may experience role confusion, trying out one social role after another before finding a sense of individual identity.

12. Development is a lifelong process: individuals change both physically and psychologically, and they encounter new adjustment problems throughout life. Erikson's *psychosocial stages* describe problems, or crises, in social relations that must be confronted at various points in life. These range from "trust versus mistrust" during the first year of life, through "intimacy versus isolation" in early adulthood, to "integrity versus despair" as individuals face death.

Comprehensive textbooks on development include Cole and Cole, *The Development of Children* (2nd ed., 1993); and Mussen, Conger, Kagan, and Huston, *Child Development and Personality* (7th ed., 1990). A general text on development through the life course is Goldhaber, *Life-Span Human Development* (1986). For a discussion of the major approaches to the study of development see Miller, *Theories of Developmental Psychology* (2nd ed., 1989).

Books focusing on infancy include Osofsky (ed.), *Handbook of Infant Development* (2nd ed., 1987); Lamb and Bornstein, *Development in Infancy: An Introduction* (2nd ed., 1987); and Rosenblith and Sims-Knight, *In the Beginning: Development in the First Two Years* (1989). A four-volume overview of the major theories and research in child development may be found in Mussen (ed.), *Handbook of Child Psychology* (4th ed., 1983).

*Cognitive Development* (2nd ed., 1985) by Flavell presents a thorough introduction to this topic. *The Development of Memory in Children* (3rd ed., 1989) by Kail provides a readable summary of research on children's memory. *Children's Thinking* (1986) by Siegler is written from the perspective of information-processing theories. For a brief introduction to Piaget, see Phillips, *Piaget's Theory: A Primer* (1981).

Two books on children's moral and social reasoning are Damon, *Social and Personality Development* (1983), and Turiel, *The Development of Social Knowledge*, (1983). Bem, *The Lenses of Gender* (1993) provides a sociocultural approach to issues of sex and gender.

Adolescent development is dealt with in Steinberg *Adolescence* (1985); and Kimmel and Wiener, *Adolescence: A Developmental Transition* (1985).

For the later years, see Woodruff and Birren, *Aging: Scientific Perspectives and Social Issues* (2nd ed., 1983); and Perlmutter and Hall, *Adult Development and Aging* (1985).

# Part  III

*Consciousness and Perception*

4 Sensory Processes

5 Perception

6 Consciousness and Its Altered States

# Chapter 4

# Sensory Processes

## Common Properties of Sensory Modalities 127
*Sensitivity*
*Sensory Coding*
*Critical Discussion: Decision Processes in Detection*

## Visual Sense 134
*Light and Vision*
*Visual System*
*Seeing Light*
*Seeing Color*

## Auditory Sense 145
*Sound Waves*
*Auditory System*
*Hearing Sound Intensity*
*Hearing Pitch*
*Critical Discussion: Artificial Ears and Eyes*

## Other Senses 151
*Smell*
*Taste*
*Skin Senses*
*Body Senses*

Detail, *Snowy Hill with Winding Road.*

Your face is your most distinctive part. The shape and size of your eyes, ears, nose, and mouth are what make you look so different from others. But the primary purpose of your facial features is not to make you recognizable; it is to enable you to sense the world. Our eyes see it, our ears hear it, our noses smell it, our mouths taste it, and these along with a few other senses provide us with most of the knowledge that we have about the world. The next time you look at your face in a mirror, think of it as an elaborate sensing system, mounted on the platform you call your body, that allows you to explore the outside world.

It is a remarkable fact that the world we know through our senses is not the same as the world that other species know through their senses. Each of our sense organs is tuned to receive a particular range of stimuli that is relevant to our survival, and is insensitive to stimuli outside this range. Different species have different ranges of sensitivity because they have different survival needs. Dogs, for example, are far more sensitive to smells than we are because they rely heavily on odors for activities critical to survival, like locating food, marking trails, and identifying kin.

In this chapter, we discuss some of the major properties of the senses, with an emphasis on human senses. Some of the research we review deals with psychological phenomena while other work deals with the biological bases of these phenomena. At both levels of analysis, we often make a distinction between sensation and perception. At the psychological level, sensations are experiences elicited by simple stimuli (a flashing red light, for example), while perceptions are *integrations* of those sensations (a fire engine, for example). At the biological level, *sensory processes* are those associated with the sense organs and peripheral levels of the nervous system, whereas *perceptual processes* are those associated with the higher levels of the nervous system.

This chapter deals with sensory processes. Chapter 5 deals with perceptual processes. The bulk of the present chapter is organized around the different senses: vision, hearing, smell, taste, touch (including pressure, temperature, and pain), and what are called the "body senses." In everyday life, a number of senses are often involved in any act—we see a peach, feel its texture, taste and smell it as we bite into it, and hear the sounds of our chewing. For purposes of analysis, however, we consider the senses one at a time. Before beginning our analysis of individual senses, or **sensory modalities,** we will discuss some properties that are common to all senses.

# Common Properties of Sensory Modalities

In this section we consider two properties common to all sensory modalities. The first one describes sensory modalities at a psychological level, while the second focuses on the biological level. (The Critical Discussion on decision processes in detection describes a third common property.)

## Sensitivity

One of the most striking aspects about our sensory modalities is that they are extremely sensitive at detecting changes in the environment. Some indication of this sensitivity is given in Table 4-1. For five of the senses, we have provided an estimate of the minimal stimulus that they can detect.

**TABLE 4-1**
**Minimum Stimuli** *Approximate minimum stimuli for various senses.* (After Galanter, 1962)

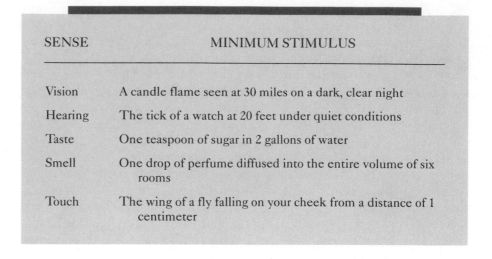

| SENSE | MINIMUM STIMULUS |
|---|---|
| Vision | A candle flame seen at 30 miles on a dark, clear night |
| Hearing | The tick of a watch at 20 feet under quiet conditions |
| Taste | One teaspoon of sugar in 2 gallons of water |
| Smell | One drop of perfume diffused into the entire volume of six rooms |
| Touch | The wing of a fly falling on your cheek from a distance of 1 centimeter |

What is most noticeable about these minimums is how low they are—that is, how sensitive the corresponding sensory modality is. This is particularly true for vision. A classic experiment by Hecht, Shlaer, and Pirenne (1942) demonstrated that human vision is virtually as sensitive as is physically possible. The smallest unit of light energy is a quantum. Hecht and his colleagues showed that a person can detect a flash of light that contains only 100 quanta. Furthermore, they showed that only 7 of these 100 quanta actually contact the critical molecules in the eye that are responsible for translating light into vision, and that each of these 7 quanta affects a different molecule. The critical receptive unit of the eye (a molecule) is therefore sensitive to the minimal possible unit of light energy.

**ABSOLUTE THRESHOLDS** Suppose you came across an alien creature, and you wanted to determine how sensitive it is to light. What would you do? Perhaps the most straightforward action would be to determine the minimum amount of light the creature could detect. This is the key idea behind measuring sensitivity. That is, the most common way to assess the sensitivity of a sensory modality is to determine the minimum magnitude of a stimulus that can be reliably discriminated from no stimulus at all—for example, the weakest light that can be reliably discriminated from darkness. This minimum magnitude is referred to as the absolute threshold.

The procedures used to determine such thresholds are called **psychophysical methods.** In one commonly used method, the experimenter first selects a set of stimuli with magnitudes varying around the threshold (for example, a set of dim lights varying in intensity). The stimuli are presented to a subject one at a time in random order, and the subject is instructed to say "yes" if the stimulus is detected and "no" if it is not. Each stimulus is presented many times, and the percentage of "yes" responses is determined for each stimulus magnitude.

Figure 4-1 is a graph of the percentage of "yes" responses as a function of stimulus magnitude (light intensity, for example). The data are typical of those obtained in this kind of experiment; the percentage of "yes" responses rises gradually as intensity is increased. The subject detects some stimuli with intensities as low as three units, yet occasionally fails to detect some with intensities of eight units. When performance is characterized by such a graph, psychologists have agreed to define the absolute threshold as the value of the stimulus at which it is detected 50 percent of the time.

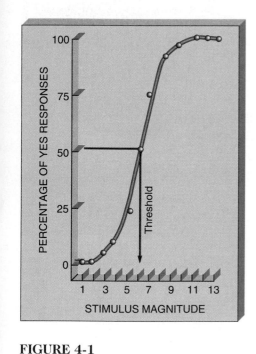

**FIGURE 4-1**
**Psychometric Function** *Plotted on the vertical axis is the percentage of times the subject responds, "Yes, I detect the stimulus"; on the horizontal axis is the measure of the magnitude of the physical stimulus. Such graphs are called* psychometric functions, *and they may be obtained for any stimulus dimension.*

Thus, for the data displayed in Figure 4-1, the absolute threshold is six units. (The absolute threshold may vary considerably from one individual to the next, and vary within an individual from time to time, depending on the person's physical and motivational state.)

**DETECTING CHANGES IN INTENSITY**    The world is constantly changing, and it is of obvious survival value to us to be able to spot these changes. Not surprisingly, psychologists have devoted a good deal of effort studying our ability to detect changes in intensity.

Just as there must be a certain minimum stimulus before we can perceive anything, so there must be a certain difference between two stimulus magnitudes before we can reliably distinguish one from the other. For instance, two tones must differ in intensity by a certain amount before one is heard as louder than the other; they must also differ in frequency by a certain amount before one is heard as different in pitch than the other. The minimum difference in stimulus magnitude necessary to tell two stimuli apart is called the **difference threshold** or the **just noticeable difference.** Like the absolute threshold, the just noticeable difference is defined statistically. Using an experimental method like the one we described earlier, the just noticeable difference is the amount of change necessary for a subject to detect a difference between two stimuli on 50 percent of the trials.

An experiment to determine a just noticeable difference, or **jnd** for short, might proceed as follows. A spot of light (standard) is flashed, and above it another spot of light (increment) is flashed for a shorter duration. The standard spot is the same on every trial but the increment spot varies in intensity from trial to trial. The subject responds "yes" or "no" to indicate whether or not the increment seems more intense than the standard. If the subject can discriminate an intensity of 51 watts in the increment from a standard of 50 watts on half the trials, then the jnd is 1 watt under these conditions.

Experiments like this have a long history. In 1834 Ernst Weber, a German physiologist, performed such a study and discovered one of the most robust findings in all of psychology. He found that the more intense the stimulus is to begin with, the larger the change must be for the subject to notice it. He measured jnds for intensity for several senses, including vision and hearing. He noted that a jnd increased with the intensity of the standard, and proposed that the jnd is a constant fraction of stimulus intensity (**Weber's law**). For example, if a jnd is 1 at an intensity of 50, it will be 2 at 100, 4 at 200, and so forth (the jnd always being 0.02 of the intensity of the standard in this example). This relation between the intensity of a standard and a jnd may be written as

$$\frac{\Delta I}{I} = k$$

where $I$ is the intensity of the standard, $\Delta I$ is the increase in the intensity for a jnd, and $k$ is a constant proportion, called **Weber's constant** (0.02 in our example).

Since Weber's pioneering study, many similar experiments have been performed. The results from a relatively recent one involving light intensities are presented in Figure 4-2. The data are given by the curved line, whereas the predictions from Weber's law are depicted by the straight line. While Weber's law does not match the data in detail, it does provide a very good approximation. This is true in general. Weber's law is useful in other ways as well. Thus, the values of Weber's constants can be used to contrast the sensitivity of different sensory modalities. The smaller the constant, the

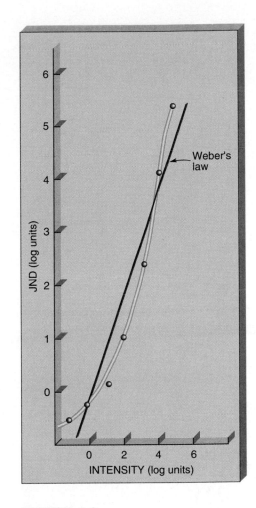

**FIGURE 4-2**
**Jnd for Light** *Here the subject's task was to detect the difference between a flash of intensity* I *and this same flash plus light of intensity* $\Delta$I. *The jnd (measured in logarithmic units) was determined at several different intensities (also measured in logarithmic units). The graph shows that the size of the jnd increases with intensity in a way that corresponds only roughly to Weber's law. In other cases, Weber's law holds more accurately.* (After Geisler, 1978)

| STIMULUS DIMENSION | WEBER'S CONSTANT |
|---|---|
| Sound frequency | .003 |
| Sound intensity | .15 |
| Light intensity | .01 |
| Odor concentration | .07 |
| Taste concentration | .20 |
| Pressure intensity | .14 |

**TABLE 4-2**
**Weber's Constant** *Approximate values of Weber's constant for various stimulus dimensions.*

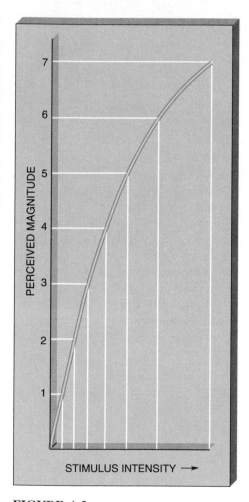

**FIGURE 4-3**
**Fechner's Law** *As the physical intensity of a stimulus increases, our perception of it increases rapidly at first, and then more slowly.*

more sensitive we are to a change in intensity in that modality. Table 4-2 provides Weber's constants for different modalities, and makes it clear, for example, that we are more sensitive to smell than taste. This means that as you add more spice to a dish you are cooking, you will be able to smell the difference before you can taste it.

Soon after Weber proposed his law, it was generalized by Gustav Fechner (1860), a German physicist. Fechner assumed not only that a jnd is a constant fraction of stimulus intensity, but also that one jnd is perceptually equal to any other jnd. (The perceived magnitude of a stimulus is therefore simply the number of jnds it is above the absolute threshold.) From these two assumptions, Fechner derived the relation that the perceived magnitude of a stimulus, $P$, is proportional to the logarithm of its physical intensity, $I$; that is,

$$P = c \log I.$$

This relation is known as **Fechner's law.** To see what it tells us, suppose $c = 1$. Then, doubling $I$, say from 10 to 20 units, increases $P$ only from 1 to approximately 1.3 units. Hence, doubling a light's intensity does not double its perceived brightness (a 100-watt bulb does not look twice as bright as a 50-watt bulb), doubling a sound's intensity does not double its perceived loudness, and so on for smell, taste, touch, and the other senses. More generally, as the physical intensity of a stimulus increases, its perceived magnitude increases rapidly at first, and then more and more slowly (see Figure 4-3). Like Weber's law, Fechner's law is only an approximation; modern researchers have proposed many variations on it to fit a wide variety of experimental results (Stevens, 1957). Nevertheless, the logarithmic relation has been useful in many practical applications of sensory psychology.

## Sensory Coding

Now that we know something about the sensitivity of the different senses, we can inquire into the biological bases of sensation.

**FROM RECEPTORS TO THE BRAIN**  The brain has a formidable problem in sensing the world. Each sense responds to a certain kind of stimulus—light energy for vision, mechanical energy for audition and touch, chemical energy for smell and taste. But the brain understands none of this. It speaks only the language of electrical signals associated with neural discharges. Somehow, each sensory modality must first translate its physical energy into electrical signals, so that these signals can eventually make their way to the brain. This translation process is called **transduction**. It is accomplished by specialized cells in the sense organs, called **receptors**. The receptors for vision, for instance, are located in a thin layer on the inside of the eye; each visual receptor contains a chemical that reacts to light, and this reaction triggers a series of steps that results in a neural impulse. The receptors for audition are fine hair cells located deep in the ear; the vibrations in the air that are the stimulus for sound succeed in bending these hair cells, which results in a neural impulse. Similar descriptions apply to the other sensory modalities.

A receptor is a specialized kind of nerve cell or **neuron** (see Chapter 2), and once activated, it passes its electrical signal to connecting neurons. The signal travels up the spinal cord until it reaches its receiving area in the cortex, with different receiving areas for different sensory modalities.

Somewhere in the brain—perhaps in the cortical receiving area, perhaps elsewhere—the electrical signal results in a sensory experience. Thus, when we experience a touch, the experience is "occurring" in our brain, not in our skin. However, the electrical impulses in our brain that directly mediate the experience of touch are themselves caused by electrical impulses in touch receptors that are located in the skin. Similarly, our experience of a bitter taste occurs in our brain, not in our tongue; but the brain impulses that mediate the taste experience are themselves caused by electrical impulses in taste receptors on the tongue. In this way, our sensory systems relate external events to subjective experience.

**CODING INTENSITY AND QUALITY**   In every sensory modality, we experience both the *intensity* of the stimulus and the *quality* (or nature) of the stimulus. For example, when we see a saturated red color patch, we experience the quality of redness at an intense level; when we hear a faint, high-pitched tone, we experience the quality of the pitch at a nonintense level. The receptors and their neural pathways to the brain must therefore code both intensity and quality. The question of interest is, how do the neurons accomplish this coding?

Researchers who study these coding processes need a way of determining which specific neurons are activated by which specific stimuli. The usual means is to record from single cells in the receptors and neural pathways to the brain while the subject is presented various inputs or stimuli. A typical *single-cell recording* experiment is illustrated in Figure 4-4. This is a vision experiment, but the procedure is similar for experiments that test other senses. An animal (in this case a monkey) is placed in a device that holds its head in a fixed position. The animal is anesthetized so it does not feel pain, and its eyes are prevented from moving. Facing the animal is a screen on which various stimuli can be projected. A thin wire (microelectrode), insulated except at its tip, is inserted into a selected area of the visual cortex through a small hole in the animal's skull. The electrode is positioned so that it will pick up the electrical responses of a single neuron while the animal's eyes are being exposed to various stimuli. These tiny electrical signals are amplified and displayed on an oscilloscope, which converts the electrical signals into a graph of the changing electrical voltage. Most neurons emit a series of nerve impulses that appear on the oscilloscope as vertical spikes. Even in the absence of a stimulus, many cells will respond at a slow rate *(spontaneous activity)*. If a stimulus is presented to which the neuron is sensitive, a fast train of spikes will be seen. The electrode can be moved to test different neurons.

With the aid of single-cell recordings, researchers have learned a good deal about how sensory systems code intensity and quality. The primary means for coding the intensity of a stimulus is in terms of the number of neural impulses in each unit of time, that is, the rate of neural impulses. We can illustrate with touch. If someone lightly touches your arm, a series of electrical impulses will be generated in a nerve fiber. If the pressure is increased, the impulses stay the same in size but increase in number (see Figure 4-5). The same story holds for other modalities. In general, the greater the intensity of the stimulus, the higher the rate of neural firing and the greater the perceived magnitude of the stimulus.

However, the intensity of a stimulus can also be coded by the *temporal pattern* of the electrical impulses. At low intensities, nerve impulses are relatively spaced in time and the exact time between successive impulses is

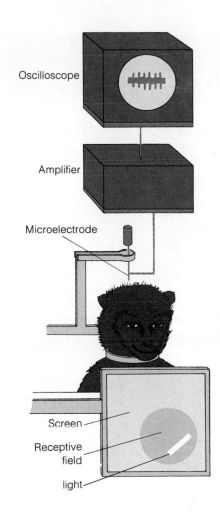

**FIGURE 4-4**
**Single-Cell Recording** *An anesthetized monkey is placed in a device that holds its head in a fixed position. A stimulus, often a flashing or moving bar of light, is projected onto the screen. A microelectrode implanted in the visual system of the monkey monitors activity from a single neuron, and this activity is amplified and displayed on an oscilloscope.*

Oscilloscope

Amplifier

Microelectrode

Screen

Receptive field

light

## Critical
## DISCUSSION

# Decision Processes in Detection

The notion of an absolute threshold dates back to the early 1800s. The key idea is that an absolute threshold is a fixed, sensory barrier; above the threshold people can detect a stimulus; below it they cannot. (This seemingly all-or-none property suggests that a threshold *should* be defined as the value of the stimulus that can be detected 100 percent of the time. The reason why the threshold is *in fact* defined by 50 percent detection is that on any trial of an experiment, numerous factors can go wrong: the sense organ may not function perfectly, the subject's attention may wander, and so on.) The idea of a threshold as a fixed barrier implies that what subjects do in experiments is report whether or not the stimulus passed the threshold. Detailed research on this issue, however, indicates that rather than observers simply reporting whether or not a stimulus crossed a fixed barrier, they are instead making a relatively complex decision about whether their sensory experience is due to a stimulus or to random activity in their sensory system.

**PROBLEMS WITH THRESHOLDS**
Researchers have long been aware of certain difficulties in establishing thresholds. To illustrate the problems, suppose we want to determine the likelihood that a subject will detect a weak auditory signal—a faint tone, briefly presented. On each trial of an experiment, the auditory signal is presented and the subject indicates whether or not she heard it. Suppose that on 100 such trials the subject reported hearing the signal 89 times. How should this result be interpreted? Because the subject knows that the same signal will be pre-

sented on each trial, and because she will often be uncertain whether to respond "yes" or "no" on a given trial, she may unconsciously tend toward "yes" answers to impress the experimenter with her ability. To deal with this problem, experimenters introduce *catch trials*—trials on which there are no signals—to see how the subject will respond.

The following results are typical of a subject's performance in an experiment involving several hundred trials, 10 percent of which were catch trials.

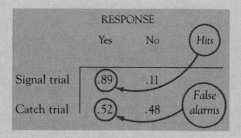

These results represent the proportion of times the subjects answered "yes" or "no" when the signal was or was not presented. For example, on 89 percent of the trials on which a signal was presented, the subject said "yes." We refer to this as the probability of a *hit*. The probability of a hit is a kind of measure of an absolute threshold: if it is around .5 (50 percent), the stimulus is at threshold, whereas if the probability is greater than .5 the stimulus is above threshold. If a subject says "yes" on a trial in which no signal was presented, the response is called a *false alarm*. In the example, the probability of a false alarm is .52. This result suggests that even a zero stimulus can cross the threshold, which seems at odds with the idea of an absolute threshold.

The notion of a threshold runs into more problems when we do an experiment that varies the percentage of catch trials. Suppose that the subject is tested for several days with the same auditory signal but with the percentage of catch trials varied from day to day. Results of an experiment in which the percentage of catch trials ranged from 10 to 90 percent are given in the table to the right.

These data show that hits and false alarms both decrease as the proportion of catch trials increases. Presumably, with more catch trials, subjects come to *expect* trials with no signals, and accordingly are biased to say "no." Given that expectancy affected the probability of a hit, it follows that expectancy can affect the absolute threshold. But again, this is at odds with the idea that a threshold is fixed and with the idea that it is a purely sensory barrier. Results like these have led to an alternative theory of how people detect sensory stimuli.

**THEORY OF SIGNAL DETECTION**
The alternative theory is referred to as the theory of signal detection. It assumes that there is always some random activity or *noise* in sensory systems; hence, *there is no such thing as a zero stimulus.* A person in a detection task is always in the position of deciding whether the sensory activity experienced is more likely to be due to a presented signal than to random noise in his or her sensory system. Thus, the task of detecting weak stimuli requires a decision process, rather than simply reporting whether or not a sensory barrier has been passed.

Two factors affect the decision that must be made. One factor is the subject's *sensitivity* to the stimulus—how well he can hear a faint tone or see a dim light. The other factor is the subject's *criterion*—how willing he is to say "yes." The subject's sensitivity is assumed to be influenced by the intensity of the stimulus, whereas his criterion is influenced by expectancies and motives. In particular, a subject's criterion will be lower when a stimulus is expected than when it is not (Green & Swets, 1966).

According to the theory of signal detection, one can get separate measures of a subject's sensitivity and criterion by plotting on the same graph the hit and false-alarm probabilities obtained in an experiment. We have plotted the probability of hits and false alarms from the table in the upper graph of the figure. Note, for example, that the point on the graph farthest to the right is for data obtained when 10 percent of the trials were catch trials; referring to the table, we see the hit probability plotted on the vertical axis is .89 and the false-alarm probability on the horizontal axis is .52. When all five points are plotted, an orderly picture emerges. The points fall on a symmetric, bow-shaped curve. The fact that these points fall on the same curve implies that they all reflect the same sensitivity. That is, while every point on this curve reflects a different performance (different hit and false-alarm probabilities), these differences reflect only the criterion and not the subject's sensitivity. Thus, if we performed other experiments with the same signal but different percentages of catch trials, the hit and false-alarm probabilities would differ from those in the table but would fall somewhere on this curve. This curve is called the **receiver-operating-characteristic curve** (or *ROC* curve for short) because it measures the operating characteristics of a person receiving signals.

While points along the same ROC curve indicate changes in criteria, different ROC curves indicate changes in sensitivity. The points that are plotted in the upper graph in the figure are for a particular signal intensity. When the signal is more intense, sensitivity is greater

and the ROC curve arches higher; when the signal is weaker, sensitivity is less and the ROC curve is closer to the diagonal line. The curvature of the ROC curve is therefore determined by the subject's sensitivity, and the measure used for the curvature is called $d'$. The lower graph in the figure gives ROC curves for values of $d'$ ranging from 0 to 2. Thus, hit and false-alarm probabilities can be converted into a $d'$ value that measures the subject's sensitivity to a particular signal. Manipulating the percentage of catch trials may affect hits and false alarms for a fixed signal, but the various probabilities will fall on an ROC curve corresponding to a particular $d'$ value (Egan, 1975).

Given this view of detecting signals, we need to reinterpret the threshold measurements obtained in other experiments. From the perspective of the theory of signal detection, a threshold is defined as the stimulus intensity at which $d'$ has a particular value, such as 1. Nevertheless, the older methods for determining thresholds remain convenient indicators of sensitivity.

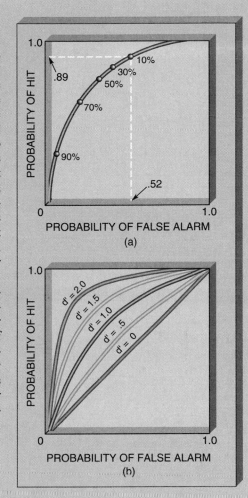

**Plotting ROC Curves from Data**
*(a) A plot of the same data from the table in the form of an ROC curve. The percentages on this curve indicate the percentages of catch trials. (b) ROC curves for several different values of d'. The more intense the signal, the higher the value of d'; the d' value for the data in the table is 1.18.*

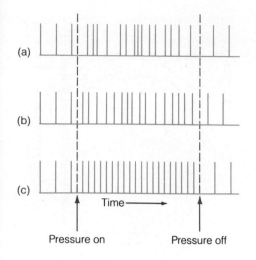

**FIGURE 4-5**
**Coding Intensity** *Response of a nerve fiber from the skin to (a) soft, (b) medium, and (c) strong pressure applied to the fiber's receptor. Increasing the stimulus strength increases both the rate and regularity of nerve firing in this fiber.* (After Goldstein, 1989)

variable. At high intensities, though, the time between impulses may be quite constant (see Figure 4-5). Thus, the regularity of neural firing may also serve as a code for intensity.

Coding the quality of a stimulus is a more complex matter, and one that will continually crop up in our discussion. The key idea behind coding quality is due to Johannes Müller, who in 1825 proposed that the brain can distinguish information from different sensory modalities—like lights and sounds—because they involve different sensory nerves (some nerves lead to visual experiences, others to auditory experiences, and so on). Müller's idea of **specific nerve energies** received support from subsequent research demonstrating that neural pathways originating in different receptors terminate in different areas of the cortex. There is now a good deal of consensus that the brain codes the qualitative differences between sensory modalities by the specific neural pathways involved.

But what about the distinguishing qualities *within* a sense? How do we tell red from green, or sweet from sour? It is likely that again the coding is based on the specific neurons involved. To illustrate, there is evidence that we distinguish sweet from sour tastes by virtue of the fact that each kind of taste has its own nerve fibers. Thus, *sweet fibers* respond primarily to sweet tastes, *sour fibers* primarily to sour tastes, and ditto for *salty fibers* and *bitter fibers*.

But *specificity* is not the only plausible coding principle. A sensory system may also use the pattern of neural firing to code the quality of a sensation. While a particular nerve fiber may respond maximally to a sweet taste, it may respond to other tastes as well, but to varying degrees. One fiber may respond best to sweet tastes, less to bitter tastes, and even less to salty tastes; a sweet-tasting stimulus would thus lead to activity in a large number of fibers, with some firing more than others, and this particular pattern of neural activity would be the system's code for sweet. A different pattern would be the code for bitter. As we will see when we discuss the senses in detail, both specificity and patterning are used in coding quality.

# Visual Sense

Humans are generally credited with the following senses: (a) vision; (b) audition; (c) smell; (d) taste; (e) touch (or the *skin senses*); and (f) the *body senses* (which are responsible for sensing the position of the head relative to the trunk, for example). Only the first three of these senses are capable of obtaining information that is at a distance from us (often vital to our survival), and of this group vision is the most finely tuned in the human species. In discussing vision, first we consider the nature of the stimulus energy to which vision is sensitive; next we describe the visual system with particular emphasis on how its receptors carry out the transduction process; and then we consider how the visual modality processes information about intensity and quality.

## Light and Vision

Each sense responds to a particular form of physical energy, and for vision the physical stimulus is light. Light is *electromagnetic radiation* (energy produced by oscillation of electrically charged matter) and belongs to the same continuum as cosmic rays, X rays, ultraviolet and infrared rays, and radio and television waves. Think of electromagnetic energy as traveling in waves, with wavelengths (the distance from one crest of a wave to the next) varying tremendously from the shortest cosmic rays (4 trillionths of a centimeter) to the longest radio waves (several miles). Our eyes are sensitive to only a tiny bit of this continuum—wavelengths of approximately 400 to 700 nanometers. Since a nanometer is one-billionth of a meter, visible energy makes up only a *very* small part of electromagnetic energy. Radiation within the visible range is called *light;* we are blind to all other wavelengths.

## Visual System

The human visual system consists of the eyes, several parts of the brain, and the pathways connecting them. (Go back to Figure 2-10 for a simplified illustration of the visual system.) Our primary concern will be with the inner workings of the eyes. The eye contains two systems, one for forming the image and the other for transducing the image into electrical impulses. The critical parts of these systems are illustrated in Figure 4-6.

The image-forming system consists of the cornea, the pupil, and the lens. Without them, we could see light but not pattern. The **cornea** is the transparent front surface of the eye: light enters here, and rays are bent inward by it to begin image formation. The **lens** completes the process of focusing the light on the **retina,** which is a thin layer at the back of the eyeball (see Figure 4-7). To focus objects at different distances, the lens changes shape. It becomes more spherical for near objects and flatter for far ones. In some eyes, the lens does not become flat enough to bring far objects in focus, although it focuses near objects well; people with such eyes are said to be *myopic* (nearsighted). In other eyes, the lens does not become spherical enough to focus on near objects, although it focuses well on far objects; people with such eyes are said to be *hyperopic* (farsighted). Such optical defects are common and can easily be corrected with eyeglasses or contact lenses. The **pupil,** the third component of the image-forming system, is a circular opening that varies in diameter in response to the light level. It is largest in dim light and smallest in bright light, thereby ensuring enough light to maintain image quality at different light levels.

All of the preceding serves to get light to the back of the eyeball, to the retina. There the transduction system takes over. The heart of the system is the receptors. There are two types of receptor cells, **rods** and **cones,** so called because of their distinctive shapes (see Figure 4-8). The two kinds of

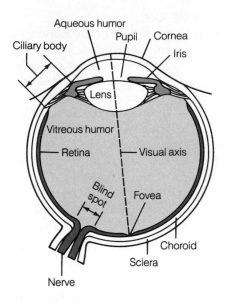

**FIGURE 4-6**
**Top View of Right Eye** *Light entering the eye on its way to the retina passes through the following:* cornea; aqueous humor; lens; *and* vitreous humor. *The amount of light entering the eye is regulated by the size of the* pupil, *a small hole toward the front of the eye formed by the* iris. *The iris consists of a ring of muscles that can contract or expand, thereby controlling pupil size. The iris gives the eyes their characteristic color (blue, brown, and so forth).*

**FIGURE 4-7**
**Image Formation in the Eye** *Each point on an object sends out light rays in all directions, but only some of these rays actually enter the eye. Light rays from the same point on an object pass through different places on the lens. If a sharp image is to be formed, these different rays have to come back together (converge) at a single point on the retina. For each point on the object, there will be a matching point in the retinal image. Note that the retinal image is inverted and is generally much smaller than the actual object. Note also that most of the bending of light rays is at the cornea.*

**FIGURE 4-8**
**Schematic Picture of the Retina** *This is a schematic drawing of the retina based on an examination with an electron microscope. The bipolar cells receive signals from one or more receptors and transmit those signals to the ganglion cells, whose axons form the optic nerve. Note that there are several types of bipolar and ganglion cells. There are also sideways or lateral connections in the retina. Neurons called horizontal cells make lateral connections at a level near the receptors; while neurons called amacrine cells make lateral connections at a level near the ganglion cells.* (After Dowling & Boycott, 1966)

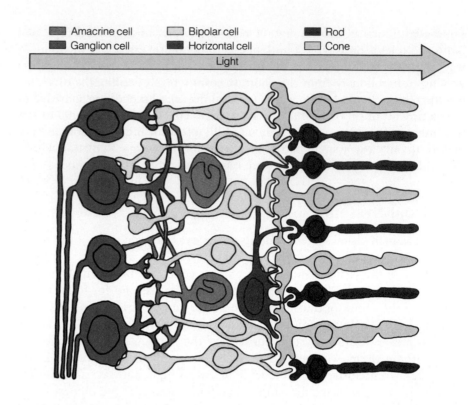

Amacrine cell   Bipolar cell   Rod
Ganglion cell   Horizontal cell   Cone
Light

receptors are specialized for different purposes. Rods are designed for seeing at night; they operate at low intensities and lead to colorless sensations. Cones are best for seeing during the day; they respond to high intensities and result in sensations of color. Curiously, the rods and cones are located in the layer of the retina farthest from the cornea (note the direction-of-light arrow in Figure 4-8). The retina also contains a network of neurons, plus support cells and blood vessels.

When we want to see the details of an object, we routinely move our eyes so that the object projects onto the center of our retina, onto a region called the **fovea.** The reason we do this has to do with the distribution of receptors across the retina. In the fovea, the receptors are plentiful and closely packed; outside of the fovea, in the *periphery*, there are fewer receptors. Not

**FIGURE 4-9**
**Locating Your Blind Spot** *(a) With your right eye closed, stare at the cross in the upper right-hand corner. Put the book about a foot from your eye and move it forward and back. When the blue circle on the left disappears, it is projected onto the blind spot. (b) Without moving the book and with your right eye still closed, stare at the cross in the lower right-hand corner. When the white space falls in the blind spot, the blue line appears to be continuous. This phenomenon helps us to understand why we are not ordinarily aware of the blind spot. In effect, the visual system fills in the parts of the visual field that we are not sensitive to; thus, they appear like the surrounding field.*

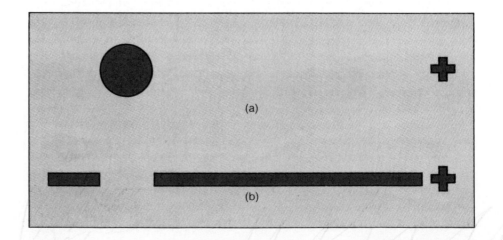

(a)

(b)

surprisingly, the fovea is the region of the eye that is best at seeing details (try reading this book while looking off the side of the page).

Given that light reflected from an object has made contact with a receptor cell, how exactly does the receptor transduce the light into electrical impulses? The rods and cones contain chemicals, called **photoreceptors,** that absorb light. The absorption of light by the photoreceptors starts a process that results in a neural impulse. Once this transduction step is completed, the electrical impulses must make their way to the brain via connecting neurons. The responses of the rods and cones are first transmitted to **bipolar cells,** and from bipolar cells to other neurons called **ganglion cells** (refer to Figure 4-8). The long axons of the ganglion cells extend out of the eye to form the **optic nerve** to the brain. At the place where the optic nerve leaves the eye, there are no receptors; we are blind to a stimulus in this region (see Figure 4-9). We do not notice this partial blindness—this hole in our visual field—because the brain automatically fills it in (Ramachandran & Gregory, 1991).

## Seeing Light

**SENSITIVITY** Our sensitivity to a light's intensity is determined by the rods and cones. There are two critical differences between rods and cones that explain a number of phenomena involving perceived intensity, or brightness. One difference is that, on the average, more rods connect to a single ganglion cell than do cones; rod-based ganglion cells therefore get more inputs than cone-based ones. Consequently, vision is more sensitive when based on rods than on cones. Secondly, rods and cones differ in where they are located. The fovea of the retina contains many cones but no rods, whereas the periphery (the rest of the retina) is rich in rods and relatively sparse in cones.

One consequence of these differences is that we are better able to detect a dim light in the rod-rich periphery than in the fovea. So while acuity (that is, seeing exactly *what* happened) is greater in the fovea than in the periphery, sensitivity (that is, seeing that *something* happened) is greater in the periphery. Greater sensitivity in the periphery may be established by measuring a subject's absolute threshold for light flashes presented in a dark room. The threshold is lower (which means sensitivity is greater) when the subject looks off to the side so that the light falls on the periphery, than when the subject looks directly at the flash so that the light falls on the fovea.

Another consequence of rod-cone differences is that, as night falls we become relatively more sensitive to blue lights. This happens because, with the coming of darkness vision shifts from cones to rods (since rods operate at low intensities), and rods are more sensitive than cones are to blue light. That is, our sensitivity to a light depends not only on whether it stimulates rods or cones, but also on the wavelength of the light; and for rods, maximum sensitivity occurs with shorter wave lengths, which are toward the blue end of the spectrum (see Figure 4-10).

**LIGHT ADAPTATION** Thus far we have emphasized that we are sensitive to change. The other half of the coin is that, if a stimulus does not change, we adapt to it. A good example of **light adaptation** occurs when you

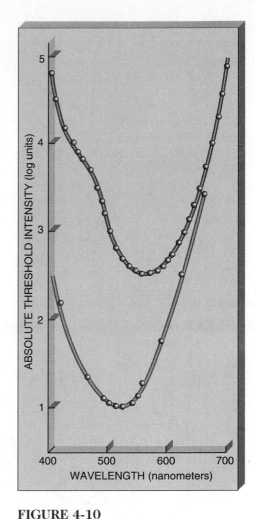

**FIGURE 4-10**
**Absolute Threshold for Light Intensity at Different Wavelengths** *The graph plots the absolute threshold as a function of wavelength (in nanometers). The curve is different depending on whether the subject looks directly at the flash, so the image falls on the central fovea, or off to the side, so that it falls on the periphery. The upper curve is attributed to the cones and the lower curve to the rods. Not only are the thresholds lower for the rods than for the cones, but the minimum thresholds for the rods and cones occur at different wavelengths, with the minimum for the rods being at a shorter wavelength. The thresholds are in log units; such units are often used for intensity.* (After Hecht & Hsia, 1945)

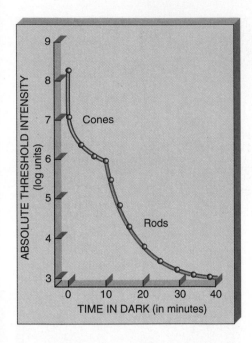

**FIGURE 4-11**

**The Course of Light Adaptation** *Subjects look at a bright light until the retina has become light adapted. When the subjects are then placed in darkness, they become increasingly sensitive to light, and their absolute thresholds decrease. This is called light adaptation. The graph shows the threshold at different times after the adapting light has been turned off. The purple data points correspond to threshold flashes whose color could be seen; the orange data points correspond to flashes that appeared white regardless of their wavelength. Note the sharp break in the curve at about 10 minutes; this is called the rod-cone break. A variety of tests show that the first part of the curve is due to cone vision and the second part to rod vision. (Data are approximate, from various determinations.)*

enter a dark movie theater from a bright street. At first you can see hardly anything in the dim light reflected from the screen. However, in a few minutes you are able to see well enough to find a seat. Eventually you are able to recognize faces in the dim light. When you re-enter the bright street, almost everything will seem painfully bright at first and it will be impossible to discriminate among these bright lights. Everything will look normal in less than a minute, though, because adaptation to this higher light level is rapid. Figure 4-11 shows how the absolute threshold decreases with time in the dark. The curve has two limbs. The upper limb is due to the cones and the lower limb to the rods. The rod system takes much longer to adapt, but it is sensitive to much dimmer lights.

As we adapt to a light, it appears to become dimmer. A dramatic illustration of this occurs when the image of an object on the retina is kept from moving across the receptors. Usually even when we are trying to look steadily at a single point our eyes are moving slightly, which means that the image is always moving over the retina. When this movement is eliminated, a visual object disappears within a few seconds. It takes delicate equipment to stabilize a retinal image completely (see Figure 4-12), but approximate stabilization will cause the image of an object to fade and almost disappear. This phenomenon appears to be a consequence of adaptation. That the visual system ceases to respond to an unchanging stimulus attests to the fact that it is designed to detect change.

## Seeing Color

All light is alike except for wavelength. Our visual system does something wonderful with wavelength—it turns it into color, with different wavelengths resulting in different colors. For example, *short-wavelength* lights, those 450–500 nanometers, appear blue; *medium-wavelength* lights, those roughly 500–570 nanometers, appear green; and *long-wavelength* lights, those about 620–700 nanometers, appear red (see Figure 4-13). In what follows, our discussion of color perception considers only wavelength. This is perfectly adequate for cases in which the origin of a color sensation is an object that emits light, such as the sun or a light bulb. Usually, however, the origin of a color sensation is an object that gives off light when a light source illuminates it. In these cases, our perception of the object's color is partly determined by the wavelengths the object reflects and partly by other factors. One such factor is the characteristic color of the object. Thus, we tend to see a rose as red even when it is illuminated by yellow-green light, yet if an un-

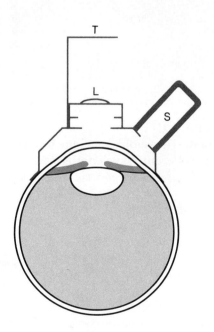

**FIGURE 4-12**

**Stabilized Image** *A device for stabilizing a retinal image using a contact lens. The target (T) is viewed through a powerful lens (L) mounted on a contact lens that is firmly attached to the cornea via a sucker (S). With each movement of the eyeball, the lens and target also move so that the projected image always falls on the same area of the retina. After a few seconds, the image of the target will fade and disappear.*

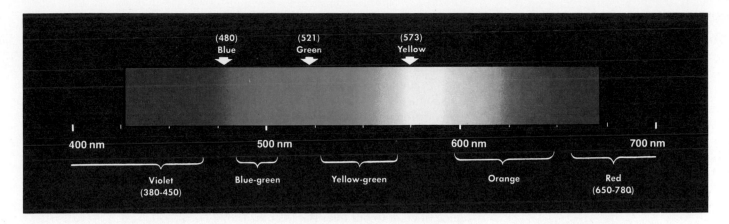

(480) Blue

(521) Green

(573) Yellow

400 nm   500 nm   600 nm   700 nm

Violet (380-450)   Blue-green   Yellow-green   Orange   Red (650-780)

familiar object were illuminated by this light we would see it as yellow-green. This effect of characteristic color is why our favorite blue jacket always looks navy blue to us, regardless of the changes in light.

**FIGURE 4-13**
**Solar Spectrum** *The numbers given are the wavelengths of the various colors in nanometers (nm).*

**COLOR APPEARANCE**  Seeing color is in some ways a subjective experience. But to study color scientifically we have to use a common vocabulary to describe it. Consider a spot of light seen against a dark background. Phenomenologically it can be described by three dimensions: brightness, hue, and saturation. Brightness, as we've seen, refers to the perceived intensity of the light. The other two dimensions say something about the color itself. Hue refers to the quality described by the color name, such as red or greenish-yellow. Saturation means the colorfulness or purity of the light: unsaturated colors appear pale or whitish (for example, pink); saturated colors appear to contain no white. Albert Munsell, an artist, proposed a scheme for specifying colored surfaces by assigning them one of 10 hue names and two numbers, one indicating saturation and the other brightness. The colors in the Munsell system are represented by the *color solid* (see Figure 4-14).

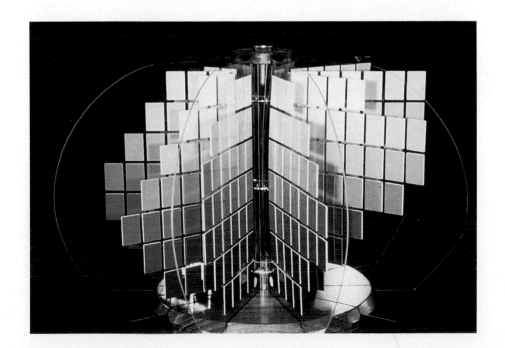

**FIGURE 4-14**
**Color Solid** *The three dimensions of color can be represented on a double cone. Hue is represented by points around the circumference, saturation by points along the radius, and lightness by points on the vertical axis. A vertical slice taken from the color solid will show differences in saturation and lightness of a single hue.*

Given a means for describing colors, we can ask how many different colors we are capable of seeing. Within the 400–700 nanometer range to which we are sensitive, we can discriminate about 150 different wavelengths. This means that, on the average, we can discriminate two wavelengths that are only 2 nanometers apart; that is, the jnd for wavelengths is 2 nanometers (see Figure 4-15). Given that each of the 150 discriminable colors can have many different values of brightness and many different values of saturation, the estimated number of colors that we can discriminate is over seven million! Furthermore, according to estimates of the National Bureau of Standards, we have names for about 7,500 of these colors (Judd & Kelly, 1965); it is hard to think of any other domain of experience that is so extensively coded in our language. These numbers give some indication of the importance of color to our lives (Goldstein, 1989).

COLOR MIXTURE   Remarkably, all the hues that we can discriminate can be generated by mixing together just a few basic colors. Suppose that we project different colored lights to the same region of the retina. The result of this light mixture will be a new color. For example, a mixture of 650-nanometer light (red) and 500-nanometer light (green) in the proper proportion will look yellow; in appearance the mixture will perfectly match a yellow light of 580 nanometers. Mixtures of lights other than this particular one can also result in a light that perfectly matches a yellow light of 580 nanometers. Thus, light mixtures whose physical components are grossly different can appear to be identical.

A cautionary note is in order. Here and throughout this section we are referring to mixing lights, called an **additive mixture;** we are *not* referring to mixing paints or pigments, a **subtractive mixture** (see Figure 4-16). The rules of color mixture are different for mixing colors (paints) and mixing lights. This is to be expected. In mixing paints, the physical stimulus is itself altered (the mixture takes place outside the eye) and hence is a topic of study for physics. In contrast, in mixing lights, the mixture occurs in the eye itself, and thus is a topic for psychology.

With regard to mixing lights, in general, *three widely spaced wavelengths can be combined to match almost any color of light.* To illustrate, a subject in an experiment on color matching might be asked to match the color of a test light by mixing together three other colored lights. As long as the three mixture lights are widely spaced in wavelength—for example, 450 (blue), 560 (green), and 640 nanometers (red)—the subject will always be able to match the test light. The subject will not, however, be able to match any test light

**FIGURE 4-15**
**Wavelength Discrimination** *This graph shows the difference threshold for wavelength at various wavelengths. In this experiment, lights of the two wavelengths were presented side by side, and the subjects had to judge whether they were the same or different. Over most of the range we can discriminate a change of 1 to 3 nanometers.* (After Wright, 1946)

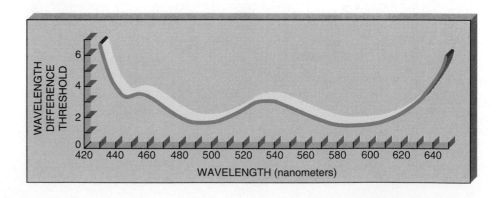

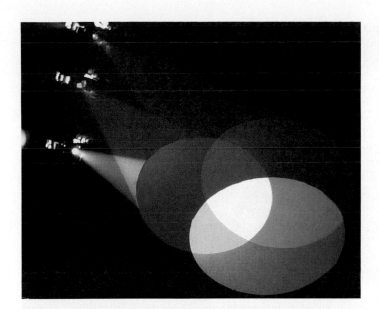 

**FIGURE 4-16**
**Additive and Subtractive Color Mixtures** *Additive color mixture (illustrated by the figure at the left) combines lights. Red and green lights are mixed to appear yellow; green and purple appear blue; and so on. In the center, where the three colors overlap, the mixture appears white.*

*Subtractive color mixture (illustrated in the figure at the right) takes place when pigments are mixed or when light is transmitted through colored filters placed one over another. Usually blue-green and yellow will mix to give green, and complementary colors like blue and yellow will combine to appear black.*

if he or she is provided only two mixture lights—for example, the 450- and 640-nanometer lights. The number three, therefore, is significant.

Because some lights that are grossly different physically look identical to humans, we have to conclude that we are blind to the differences. Without this blindness, color reproduction would be impossible. Realistic color reproduction in television or photography relies on the fact that a wide range of colors can be produced by mixing just a few colors. For example, if you examine your television screen with a magnifying glass you will find that it is composed of tiny dots of only three colors (blue, green, and red). Additive color mixture occurs because the dots are so close together that their images on your retina overlap. (See Figure 4-17 for a way of representing color mixtures.)

**COLOR DEFICIENCY** Most people match a wide range of colors with a mixture of three appropriately selected lights—such as blue, green, and red—and different people make very similar matches. Other people can match a wide range of colors by using mixtures of only two lights (dichromats) or, in rare cases, simply by adjusting the intensity of a single light (monochromats). Dichromats have a major weakness in discriminating wavelengths; monochromats are unable to discriminate wavelength at all. Both groups are called color-blind. (Screening for color blindness is done with tests like that shown in Figure 4-18, a simpler procedure than conducting color mixture experiments.) Most color deficiencies are genetic in origin. Color blindness occurs much more frequently in males (2%) than in females (.03%), because the critical genes are recessive genes on the X chromosome (Nathans, Thomas, & Hogness, 1986).

**THEORIES OF COLOR VISION** Over the years, two major theories of color vision have arisen. The first of these was initially proposed by Thomas Young in 1807. Fifty years later, Hermann von Helmholtz further developed Young's theory.

According to the **Young-Helmholtz** or **trichromatic theory,** even though there are many different colors that we can discriminate, there are

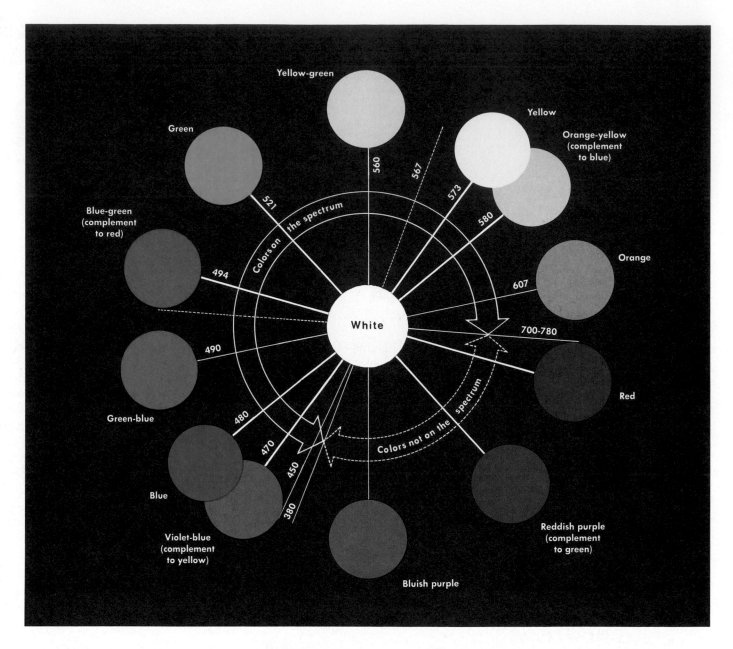

**FIGURE 4-17**
**Color Circle** *A simple way to represent color mixture is by means of the color circle.
The spectral colors (colors corresponding to wavelengths in our region of sensitivity)
are represented by points around the circumference of the circle. The two ends of the spectrum do not meet; the space between them corresponds to the nonspectral reds and purples, which can be produced by mixtures of long and short wavelengths. The inside of the
circle represents mixtures of lights. Lights toward the center of the circle are less saturated
(or whiter); white is at the very center. Mixtures of any two lights lie along the straight
line joining the two points. When this line goes through the center of the circle, the lights,
when mixed in proper proportions, will look white; such pairs of colors are called* complementary colors.

only three types of receptors (cones) for color. Each receptor is sensitive to a
wide range of wavelengths, but is most responsive in a narrow region. As
shown in Figure 4-19, the *short receptor* is maximally sensitive to short wavelengths (blues), the *medium receptor* is most sensitive to medium wavelengths

 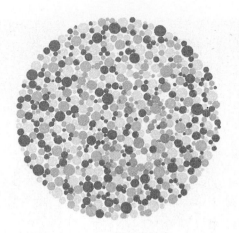

**FIGURE 4-18**
**Color Blindness** *Two plates used in color blindness tests. In the left plate, individuals with certain kinds of red-green blindness will see only the number 5; others see only the 7; still others, no number at all. Those with normal vision see 57. Similarly, in the right plate, people with normal vision see the number 15, whereas those with red-green blindness see no number at all.*

(greens and yellows), and the *long receptor* is maximally sensitive to long wavelengths (reds). The joint action of these three receptors determines the sensation of color. That is, a light of a particular wavelength stimulates the three receptors to different degrees, and the specific ratios of activity in the three receptors leads to the sensation of a specific color. Hence, with regard to our earlier discussion of coding quality, the trichromatic theory holds that the *quality* of color is coded by the *pattern* of activity of three receptors rather than by specific receptors for each color.

The trichromatic theory explains the facts about color vision that we mentioned previously. We can discriminate different wavelengths because they lead to different responses in the three receptors. We can match a mixture of three widely spaced wavelengths to any color, because the three widely spaced wavelengths will activate the three different receptors, and activity in these receptors is what lies behind perception of the test color. (Now we see the significance of the number three.) Trichromatic theory explains the various kinds of color blindness by positing that one or more of the three types of receptors is missing: dichromats are born missing one type of receptor, whereas monochromats are born missing two of the three types of receptors.

Despite its successes, the trichromatic theory cannot explain some well-established findings about the phenomenology of color. In 1878 Ewald Hering observed that all colors may be described phenomenologically as consisting of one or two of the following sensations: red, green, yellow, and blue. Hering also noted that nothing is perceived to be reddish-green or yellowish-blue; rather, a mixture of red and green may look yellow, and a mixture of yellow and blue may look white. These observations suggested that red and green form an *opponent pair*, as do yellow and blue, and that the colors in an opponent pair cannot be perceived simultaneously. Further support for the notion of opponent-pairs comes from studies in which a subject first stares at a colored light and then looks at a neutral surface. The subject reports seeing a color on the neutral surface that is the complement of the original one (see Figure 4-20).

These phenomenological observations led Hering to propose an alternative theory of color vision called **opponent-color theory.** Hering believed that the visual system contains two types of color-sensitive units. One type of unit responds to red or green, the other to blue or yellow. Each unit responds in opposite ways to its two opponent colors: the red-green unit, for example, increases its response rate when a red is presented and decreases it

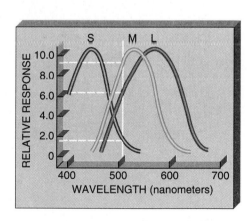

**FIGURE 4-19**
**Trichromatic Theory** *Response curves for the short-, medium-, and long-wave receptors proposed by trichromatic theory. These curves enable us to determine the relative response of each receptor to light of any wavelength. In the example shown here, the response of each receptor to a 500-nanometer light is determined by drawing a line up from 500 nanometers and noting where this line intersects each curve. (After Wald & Brown, 1965)*

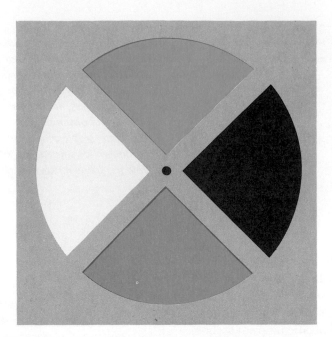

**FIGURE 4-20**

**Complementary Afterimages** *Look steadily for about a minute at the dot in the center of the colors, then transfer your gaze to the dot in the gray field at the right. You should see a blurry image with colors that are complementary to the original: the blue, red, green, and yellow are replaced by yellow, green, red, and blue.*

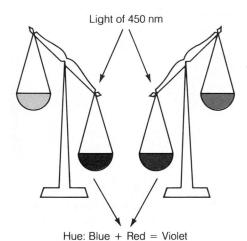

**FIGURE 4-21**

**Opponent-Process Theory** *The diagram shows how an opponent process responds to light of a particular wavelength. The light is in the short-wave region of the visible spectrum, 450 nanometers. This will affect both the blue-yellow and the red-green systems. It will tip the blue-yellow balance toward blue, and the red-green balance toward red. The resulting hue will be a mixture of red and blue (that is, violet).* (After Hurvich & Jameson, 1957)

when a green is presented. Because a unit cannot respond in two ways at once, reddish-greens and yellowish-blues cannot occur; white is perceived when both types of opponent units are in balance (see Figure 4-21). Opponent-color theory is thereby able to explain Hering's observations about color.

The theory also accounts for why we see the hues that we do. We perceive a single hue—red or green or yellow or blue—whenever only one type of opponent unit is out of balance, and we perceive combinations of hues when both types of units are out of balance. Opponent-color theory received a great impetus from the discovery of **color opponent cells** in the lateral geniculate nucleus of the thalamus (DeValois & Jacobs, 1984). These cells are spontaneously active, increasing their activity rate in response to one range of wavelengths and decreasing it in response to another. Thus, some cells at a higher level in the visual system fire more rapidly if the retina is stimulated by a blue light, and less rapidly when the retina is exposed to a yellow light; such cells seem to be the biological basis of the blue-yellow opponent pair.

The opponent-color theory and trichromatic theory competed for more than half a century; each could explain some facts but not others. Some researchers proposed that the theories might be reconciled in a two-stage theory in which the three types of receptors in the trichromatic theory feed into color-opponent units at a higher level in the visual system. The most completely developed theory of this kind is by Jameson and Hurvich (Hurvich, 1981). Figure 4-22 illustrates the basics of a two-stage color theory. The figure shows how the short, medium, and long receptors of trichromatic theory might connect with color-opponent cells to produce sensations of color. The blue-yellow opponent cell receives excitatory input from the short receptor and inhibitory input from the long receptor. If there is more excitation than inhibition, the opponent process yields blue; if inhibition dominates, the opponent process signals yellow; and if excitation equals inhibition, the process yields gray. A similar analysis applies to the red-green opponent cell. This theory accounts for much (though not all) of what is known about color vision. The analysis of color vision is one of the major theoretical accomplishments of psychology, and it serves as a prototype for the analysis of other sensory systems.

# Auditory Sense

Along with vision, audition is our major means of obtaining information about the environment. For most of us, it is the major channel of communication and the vehicle for music. As we will see, it all comes about because small changes in sound pressure level can move a membrane in our inner ear back and forth.

Our discussion of audition will follow the same plan as our discussion of vision. We will first consider the nature of the physical stimulus that audition is sensitive to, then describe the auditory system with particular emphasis on how the receptors execute the transduction process, and finally consider how the auditory system codes the intensity of sound and its quality.

## Sound Waves

Sound originates from the motion or vibration of an object, as when the wind rushes through the branches of a tree. When something moves, the molecules of air in front of it are pushed together. These molecules push other molecules and then return to their original position. In this way, a wave of pressure changes (a *sound wave*) is transmitted through the air, even though the individual air molecules do not travel far. This wave is analogous to the ripples set up by throwing a stone into a pond.

A sound wave may be described by a graph of air pressure as a function of time. A pressure-versus-time graph of one type of sound is shown in Figure 4-23. The graph depicts a **sine wave** (so called, because it corresponds to a sine-wave function in mathematics). Sounds that correspond to sine

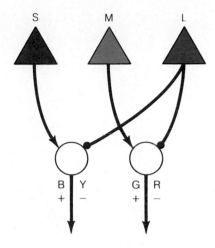

**FIGURE 4-22**
**Two-Stage Color Theory** *A simplified diagram showing how the short, medium, and long receptors connect with color-opponent cells to produce sensations of color. The blue-yellow opponent cell receives excitatory input from the short receptor and inhibitory input from the long receptor. If there is more excitation than inhibition, the process signals blue; if there is more inhibition than excitation, the process signals yellow; if excitation and inhibition are equal, the process yields a gray. The red-green opponent cell has similar dynamics* (Adapted from Hurvich and Jameson, 1974).

**FIGURE 4-23**
**Pure Tone** *As the tuning fork vibrates, it produces successive waves of compression and expansion of the air, which correspond to a sine wave. Such a sound is called a pure tone. It can be described by giving its frequency and intensity. If the tuning fork makes 100 vibrations per second, it produces a sound wave with 100 compressions per second and a frequency of 100 hertz. The intensity (or amplitude) of a pure tone is the pressure difference between the peaks and the troughs. The waveform of any sound can be decomposed into a series of sine waves of different frequencies with various amplitudes and phases. When these sine waves are added together, the result is the original waveform.*

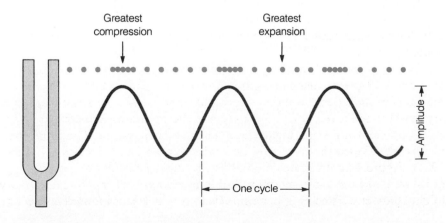

waves are called *pure tones*. They are important in the analysis of audition because more complex sounds can be analyzed into pure tones, that is, decomposed into a number of different sine waves. Pure tones vary with respect to their frequency (the number of cycles per second, called **hertz**), their intensity (the pressure difference between peak and trough), and the time at which they start. These physical aspects determine how we experience the tone. In particular, frequency underlies our sensation of pitch, and intensity our sensation of loudness. Sound intensity is usually specified in **decibels;** an increase of 10 decibels corresponds to a change in sound power of 10 times; 20 decibels, a change of 100 times; 30 decibels, a change of 1,000 times; and so forth. Table 4-3 shows the intensities of some familiar sounds, and indicates that some of them are so intense as to endanger our hearing.

## Auditory System

The auditory system consists of the ears, parts of the brain, and the various connecting neural pathways. Our primary concern will be with the ears;

**TABLE 4-3**
**Decibel Ratings and Hazardous Time Exposures of Common Sounds** *This table gives the intensities of common sounds in decibels. An increase of 3 decibels corresponds to a doubling of sound power. The sound levels given correspond approximately to the intensities that occur at typical working distances. The right-hand column gives the exposure times at which one risks permanent hearing loss.*

| DECIBEL LEVEL | EXAMPLE | DANGEROUS TIME EXPOSURE |
|---|---|---|
| 0 | Lowest sound audible to human ear | |
| 30 | Quiet library, soft whisper | |
| 40 | Quiet office, living room, bedroom away from traffic | |
| 50 | Light traffic at a distance, refrigerator, gentle breeze | |
| 60 | Air conditioner at 20 feet, conversation, sewing machine | |
| 70 | Busy traffic, office tabulator, noisy restaurant (constant exposure) | Critical level begins |
| 80 | Subway, heavy city traffic, alarm clock at 2 feet, factory noise | More than 8 hours |
| 90 | Truck traffic, noisy home appliances, shop tools, lawn-mower | Less than 8 hours |
| 100 | Chain saw, boiler shop, pneumatic drill | 2 hours |
| 120 | Rock concert in front of speakers, sandblasting, thunderclap | Immediate danger |
| 140 | Gunshot blast, jet plane | Any exposure is dangerous |
| 180 | Rocket launching pad | Hearing loss inevitable |

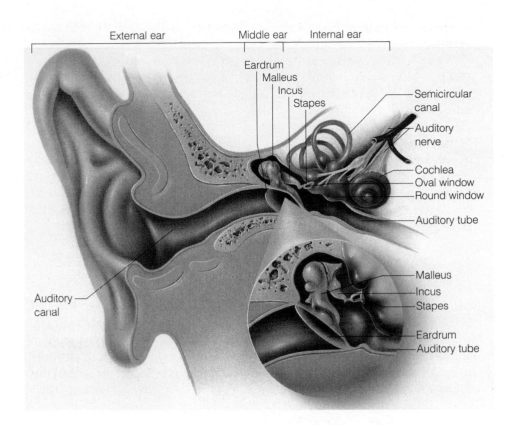

External ear | Middle ear | Internal ear

Eardrum
Malleus
Incus
Stapes

Semicircular canal

Auditory nerve

Cochlea
Oval window
Round window

Auditory tube

Auditory canal

Malleus
Incus
Stapes

Eardrum
Auditory tube

**FIGURE 4-24**
**A Cross-Section of the Ear** *This drawing shows the overall structure of the ear. The inner ear includes the cochlea, which contains the auditory receptors, and the vestibular apparatus (semicircular canals and vestibular sacs), which is the sense organ for our sense of balance and body motion.*

this includes not just the appendages on the sides of the head, but the entire hearing organ, most of which lies within the skull (see Figure 4-24).

As with the eye, the ear contains two systems. One system amplifies and transmits the sound to the receptors, whereupon the other system takes over and transduces sound into neural impulses. The *transmission system* involves the **outer ear,** which consists of the external ear (or *pinna*) along with the *auditory canal,* and the **middle ear,** which consists of the **eardrum** and a chain of three bones. The transduction system is housed in a part of the **inner ear** called the **cochlea,** which contains the receptors for sound.

Let us take a more detailed look at the transmission system (see Figure 4-25). At the outermost part of the middle ear is a taut membrane called the eardrum. It is set into vibration by sound waves funneled to it through the outer ear. The middle ear's job is to transmit these vibrations of the eardrum across an air-filled cavity to another membrane, the *oval window,* which is the gateway to the inner ear and the receptors. The middle ear accomplishes this transmission by means of a mechanical bridge built of three bones, called *malleus, incus,* and *stapes.* The vibrations of the eardrum move the first bone, which then moves the second, which in turn moves the third, which results in vibrations of the oval window. This mechanical arrangement not only transmits the sound wave, but amplifies it as well.

Now consider the transduction system. The cochlea is a coiled tube of bone. It is divided into sections of fluid by membranes, one of which, the **basilar membrane,** supports the auditory receptors (Figure 4-25). The receptors are called **hair cells** because they have hairlike structures that extend into the fluid. Pressure at the oval window (which connects the middle and inner ear) leads to pressure changes in the cochlear fluid, which in turn causes the basilar membrane to vibrate, resulting in a bending of the hair cells and an electrical impulse. By this complex process, a sound wave is transduced into an electrical impulse. The neurons that synapse with the

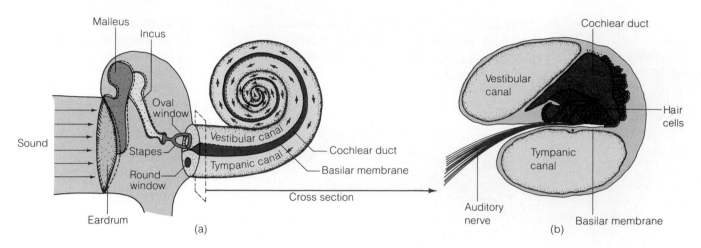

**FIGURE 4-25**
**Schematic Diagram of the Middle and Inner Ear** *(a) Movement of the fluid within the cochlea deforms the basilar membrane and stimulates the hair cells that serve as the auditory receptors. (b) Cross section of the cochlea showing the basilar membrane and the hair cell receptors.*

hair cells have long axons that form part of the acoustic nerve. Most of these auditory neurons are connected to a single hair cell. There are about 31,000 auditory neurons in the acoustic nerve, many fewer than the one million neurons in the optic nerve (Yost & Nielson, 1985). The auditory pathway from each ear goes to both sides of the brain and has synapses in several nuclei before reaching the auditory cortex.

## Hearing Sound Intensity

Recall that in vision, we are more sensitive to some wavelengths than others. There is a comparable phenomenon in audition. We are more sensitive to sounds of intermediate frequency than we are to sounds near either end of our frequency range. This is illustrated in Figure 4-26, which shows the absolute threshold for sound intensity as a function of frequency. The shape of this curve is largely a consequence of the transmission of sound by the outer and middle ear; these structures amplify the intermediate frequencies more than those at the extremes of the frequency range.

Many people have some deficit in hearing and consequently have a threshold higher than those shown in Figure 4-26. There are two basic kinds of hearing deficits. In one, thresholds are elevated roughly equally at all frequencies as the result of poor conduction in the middle ear **(conduction loss).** In the other kind of hearing loss, the threshold elevation is unequal, with large elevations occurring at higher frequencies. This pattern is usually a consequence of inner-ear damage, often involving some destruction of the hair cells **(sensory-neural loss).** Hair cells, once destroyed, do not regenerate. Sensory-neural loss occurs in many older people. That is why the elderly often have trouble hearing high-pitched sounds, which can result in their having more difficulty understanding female than male voices. Sensory neural loss is not reserved for the elderly, though. It occurs in young people who are exposed to excessively loud sound. Rock musicians, airport-runway crews, and pneumatic drill operators commonly suffer major, permanent hearing loss.

It is natural to assume that the perceived intensity of a sound is the same at both ears, but in fact there are subtle differences. A sound originating on our right side, for example, will be heard as more intense by our right than our left ear; this is because our head causes a "sound shadow," which decreases the intensity of the sound reaching the far ear. Rather than this

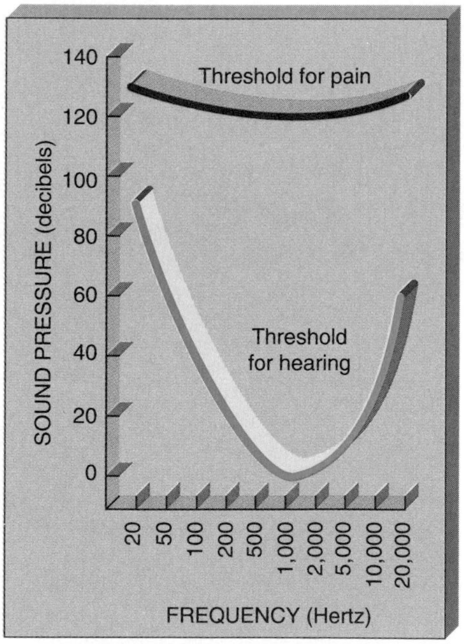

**FIGURE 4-26**
**Absolute Threshold for Hearing** *The lower curve shows the absolute intensity threshold at different frequencies. Sensitivity is greatest in the vicinity of 1,000 hertz. The upper curve describes the threshold for pain. (Data are approximate, from various determinations.)*

being a limitation on our hearing, we take advantage of this **interaural intensity** difference by using it to localize where the sound is coming from (as if we were reasoning "if the sound is more intense at my right than my left ear, it must be coming from my right side").

## Hearing Pitch

**PITCH AND FREQUENCY**  When hearing a pure tone, we experience not only its loudness but also its pitch. Just as color is the prime quality of light, so pitch is the prime quality of sound, ordered on a scale from low to high. And just as color is determined by the frequency of light, pitch is determined by the frequency of sound. As frequency increases, pitch increases. As with the wavelength of light, we are very good at discriminating the frequency of a sound. Young adults can hear frequencies between 20 and 20,000 hertz (cycles per second), with the jnd being less than 1 hertz at 100 hertz and increasing to 100 hertz at 10,000 hertz.

However, there is nothing analogous to color mixture in audition. When two or more frequencies are sounded simultaneously, we can hear the pitch associated with each frequency, provided that they are sufficiently separated. When the frequencies are close together, the sensation is more complex but still does not sound like a single, pure tone. In color vision, the fact that a mixture of three lights results in the sensation of a single color led to the idea of three types of receptors. The absence of a comparable phenomenon in audition suggests that, if there are receptors specialized for different frequencies, then there must be many different types of such receptors.

**THEORIES OF PITCH PERCEPTION**  As was the case with color vision, two different kinds of theories have been proposed to account for how the ear codes frequency into pitch.

The first kind of theory originated with Lord Rutherford, a British physicist, in 1886. He proposed that: a) a sound wave causes the entire basilar membrane to vibrate, and the rate of vibration matches the frequency of the sound; and b) the rate at which the membrane vibrates determines the rate of impulses of nerve fibers in the auditory nerve. Thus, a 1,000-hertz tone causes the basilar membrane to vibrate 1,000 times per second, which causes nerve fibers in the auditory nerve to fire at 1,000 impulses per second, and the brain interprets this as a particular pitch. Because this theory proposes that pitch depends on how the sound varies with time, it is called a **temporal theory** (it is also called a **frequency theory**).

Rutherford's hypothesis soon ran into a major problem. Nerve fibers were shown to have a maximum firing rate of about 1,000 impulses per second, so how do we perceive the pitch of tones whose frequency exceeds 1,000 hertz? Weaver (1949) proposed a way to salvage temporal theories. He argued that frequencies over 1,000 hertz could be coded by different groups of nerve fibers, each group firing at a slightly different pace. If one group of neurons is firing at 1,000 impulses per second, for example, and then 1 millisecond later a second group of neurons begins firing at 1,000 impulses per second, the combined rate of impulses per second for the two groups will be 2,000 impulses per second. This version of temporal theory received support from the discovery that the pattern of nerve impulses in the auditory nerve follows the waveform of the stimulus tone even though individual cells do not respond on every cycle of the wave (Rose, Brugge, Anderson, & Hind, 1967).

*Sitting in front of the speakers at a rock concert can cause permanent hearing loss.*

However, the ability of nerve fibers to follow the waveform breaks down at about 4,000 hertz; nevertheless, we can hear pitch at much higher frequencies. This suggests that there must be another means of coding the quality of pitch, at least for high frequencies.

The second kind of theory of pitch perception dates back to 1683 when Joseph Guichard Duverney, a French anatomist, proposed that frequency was coded into pitch mechanically by *resonance* (Green & Wier, 1984). To appreciate this proposal, it is helpful to first consider an example of resonance. When a tuning fork is struck near a piano, the piano string that is tuned to the frequency of the fork will begin to vibrate. To say that the ear works the same way is to say that: the ear contains a structure like a stringed instrument, with different parts of this structure being tuned to different frequencies, so that when a frequency is presented to the ear, the corresponding part of the structure vibrates. This idea proved to be essentially correct; the structure turned out to be the basilar membrane.

In the 1800s, Hermann von Helmholtz developed the resonance hypothesis into the **place theory** of pitch perception. It holds that each specific place along the basilar membrane will, when it responds, lead to a particular pitch sensation. The fact that there are many places on the membrane is compatible with there being many different receptors for pitch. Note that place theory does not imply that we hear with our basilar membrane; rather, the places on the membrane that vibrate most determine what neural fibers are activated, and that determines the pitch that we hear. This is an example of a sensory modality coding quality by the specific nerves involved.

How the basilar membrane actually moves was not established until the 1940s when Georg von Békésy measured its movement through small holes drilled in the cochlea. Working with the cochleas of guinea pigs and human cadavers, he showed that, while the whole membrane moves for most frequencies, the place of maximum movement depends on the specific frequency sounded. High frequencies cause vibration at the far end of the basilar membrane; as frequency increases, the vibration pattern moves toward the oval window (Békésy, 1960). For this and other research on audition, von Békésy received a Nobel prize in 1961.

Like temporal theories, place theories explain many phenomena of pitch perception, but not all. A major difficulty for place theory arises with low-frequency tones. With frequencies below 50 hertz, all parts of the basilar membrane vibrate roughly the same amount. This means that all receptors are equally activated, which implies that we have no way of discriminating between frequencies below 50 hertz. In fact, though, we can discriminate frequencies as low as 20 hertz.

Hence, place theories have problems explaining our perception of low-frequency tones, while temporal theories have problems dealing with high-frequency tones. This led to the idea that pitch depends on both place and temporal pattern with temporal theory explaining our perception of low frequencies, and place theory explaining our perception of high frequencies. It is not clear, however, where one mechanism leaves off and the other takes over. Indeed, it is possible that frequencies between 1000 and 5000 hertz are handled by both mechanisms (Goldstein, 1989).

# Other Senses

Senses other than vision and audition lack the richness of patterning and organization that have led sight and hearing to be called the "higher senses." Our symbolic experiences are expressed largely in visual and auditory terms: spoken language is to be heard, written language to be seen. Still, these other senses are vitally important.

In discussing each of these other senses, as with vision and audition we will consider: the nature of the stimulus energy to which the sensory modality is sensitive, how the receptors carry out the transduction process, and how the sensory modality codes intensity and quality.

## Smell

**EVOLUTIONARY SIGNIFICANCE**  Before turning to our usual considerations about a sensory modality, it is useful to view the sense of smell from an evolutionary perspective and consider its development in other species.

Smell is one of the most primitive and most important of the senses. The sense organ for smell has a position of prominence in the head appropriate to a sense intended to guide the organism. Smell has a more direct route to the brain than any other sense: the receptors, which are in the nasal cavity, are connected without synapse to the brain. Moreover, unlike the receptors for vision and audition, the receptors for smell are exposed directly to the environment—they are right there in the nasal cavity with no protective shield in front of them. (In contrast, the receptors for vision are behind the cornea, and those for audition are protected by the outer and middle ears.)

While smell (or **olfaction**) is not essential for our species, it is essential for the survival of many other animals. Not surprisingly, then, a larger area of the cortex is devoted to smell in other species than in our own. In fish, the

*A dog's acute sense of smell is helpful in law enforcement, as this drug-sniffing canine demonstrates.*

## *Artificial Ears and Eyes*

The science fiction fantasy of replacing defective sense organs with artificial, functioning ones is becoming a reality. Researchers have been working for several years on artificial replacements (called *prostheses*) for damaged eyes and ears, some of which have been approved by the United States Food and Drug Administration. This work has important implications for both the reduction of sensory handicaps and for our understanding of sensory processes.

Research on auditory prostheses has concentrated on devices that apply electrical stimulation to the auditory nerve. They are designed to aid people whose hair cells (the receptors) have been destroyed, and consequently suffer a total sensory-neural hearing loss, but whose auditory nerve is intact and functional. Most of these devices use an electrode, which is inserted through the round window into the cochlea, to stimulate the neurons along the basilar membrane (a *cochlea implant*). Because the electrode goes directly into the cochlea, the functional part of the ear is bypassed (including the receptors); the cochlea is simply a convenient place to stimulate auditory neurons where they are accessible and laid out in an orderly array.

In addition to the stimulating electrode, a cochlea implant has three other components that operate in sequence: (a) a microphone located near the external ear that picks up sound; (b) a small battery-operated electronic processor (worn on the outside of the body) that converts the sound into electrical signals; and (c) a transmission system that transmits the electrical signal through the skull and to the electrode implanted in the cochlea. The last step in this process is accomplished by radio transmission to avoid a wire through the skull.

A relatively simple device of this kind was developed in the early 1970s by William House (see the figure). The House implant extends only 6 millimeters into the cochlea and has only one electrode. The signal applied to this electrode is an electrical wave having essentially the same form as the sound wave. When sound is presented to a deaf patient using this device, he or she hears a complex noise that varies in loudness. These devices have been implanted in hundreds of profoundly deaf people. Most of the recipients believe that the device provides a marked improvement over their previously deaf state. With it, they at least hear sounds and have some ability to discriminate intensity.

More recent developments include devices with multiple electrodes. One of the most sophisticated of these, the Nucleus 22 Channel Cochlear Implant, has 22 electrodes. These extend further into the cochlea and are designed to independently stimulate several sets of neurons along the basilar membrane. Because the cochlea is only the size of a pea, with a solid bony shell and very delicate interior structures, there are difficult technical problems involved in designing and implanting the electrodes. Accompanying most of these multichannel implants is a more elaborate electronic processor that filters the sound into separate frequencies, one for each electrode. The sound wave in each frequency band is converted into an electrical signal and applied to one of the electrodes. Although results vary greatly, some patients show good performance, including word recognition scores of more than 70 percent (Loeb, 1985). Some cochlear implants have recently been performed with children, and again some of the results are encouraging (Staller, 1991).

The multiple-electrode devices are based on the place theory of pitch perception. In the normal ear, mechanical means are used to get different frequencies to vibrate specific parts of the basilar membrane, which lead to the activation of specific nerve fibers. In the multiple-electrode device, electronic filtering is used to accomplish this same task. The electronically filtered signal is sent to the identical place that it would be applied in the normal ear. To some extent the success of the device supports the theory.

However, use of the multiple-electrode devices has turned up some findings that don't fit well with place theory. According to the latter, when electrical stimulation is applied to a single small region on the basilar membrane, a sound with a particular pitch is heard and this pitch varies with place. However, the sound that is heard with a multiple-electrode device is not at all like a pure tone; it is more like the "quacking of ducks" or the "banging of garbage cans," even though it does have a crude pitch. Nor do results with multiple-electrode devices provide much support for temporal

olfactory cortex makes up almost all of the cerebral hemispheres; in dogs, about one-third; in humans, only about one-twentieth. These differences are related to differences in sensitivity among the species. Taking advantage of the superior smell capability of dogs, both the United States Postal Service and the Bureau of Customs have trained them to check unopened packages for heroin. And specially trained police dogs can sniff out hidden explosives.

Because smell is so well developed in other species, it is often used as a major means of communication. Insects and some higher animals secrete

theories of pitch. Temporal theorists might expect that the sensation would change when the frequency of electrical stimulation changes. In fact, this produces only slight changes. The results suggest that another factor, apart from place alone or temporal pattern alone, is involved in pitch perception. This may be a complex spatiotemporal pattern of stimulation along the basilar membrane that cannot be mimicked by a few electrodes (Loeb, 1985).

The development of artificial eyes for the blind has not progressed as far as the development of artificial ears. The problem is not one of picking up the optical image; a video camera can do this well. Rather, the problem is putting the image's information into the visual system in a form that the brain can use. Research has focused on the direct electrical stimulation of the visual cortex in volunteer subjects who are either blind or undergoing brain surgery. If we know what a person sees when different places in the cortex are electrically stimulated, then by controlling the electrical stimulation it should be possible to evoke different experiences. The next step would be to use a video camera to form an image of the scene in front of a blind person and then evoke an experience of that scene.

Results obtained thus far suggest we are a long way from developing an artificial eye. When a small region of the visual cortex is stimulated with a weak electrical signal, the person experiences rudimentary, visual sensations. These sensations have been described as small spots of light that are seen in front of the person in different directions. They range in size from that of a "grain of rice" to a "coin." Most are white, but some are colored. If several places in the visual cortex are stimulated simultaneously, the corresponding spots will usually be experienced together. Although multiple stimulation of the visual cortex provides the basis for a crude pattern vision (Dobelle, Meadejovsky, & Girvin, 1974), it is questionable whether this approach will lead to a successful prosthesis for damaged eyes. The neural input to the visual cortex is so complicated that it is unlikely to be adequately duplicated by artificial means.

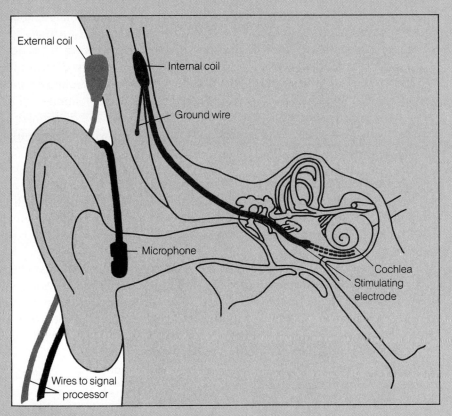

**Cochlear Implant** *This diagram illustrates the auditory prosthesis developed by William House and his associates. Sound is picked up by a microphone and filtered by a signal processor (not shown) worn outside the body. The electrical waveform produced by the processor is then transmitted by radio waves through the skull to the electrode inside the cochlea.*

chemicals, known as **pheromones,** that float through the air to be sniffed by other members of the species. For example, a female moth can release a pheromone so powerful that males are drawn to her from a distance of several miles. It is clear that the male moth responds only to the pheromone and not to the sight of the female; the male will be attracted to a female in a wire container even though she is blocked from view, but not to a female who is clearly visible in a glass container from which the scent cannot escape.

Insects use smell to communicate death as well as "love." After an ant dies, the chemicals formed from its decomposing body stimulate other ants to carry the corpse to a refuse heap outside the nest. If a living ant is experimentally doused with the decomposition chemicals, it is carried off by other ants to the refuse heap. When it returns to the nest, it is carried out again. Such premature attempts at burial continue until the "smell of death" has worn off (Wilson, 1963).

Do we humans have a remnant of this primitive communication system? Experiments indicate that we can use smell at least to tell ourselves from others, and males from females. In one study, subjects wore undershirts for 24 hours without showering or using deodorant. The undershirts were collected by the experimenter. He then presented each subject with three shirts to smell: one was the subject's own shirt, another was a male's, and the third was a female's. Based only on odor, most subjects could usually identify their own shirt and tell which of the other shirts was worn by males or females (Russell, 1976). Other studies suggest that we may communicate subtler matters by odor. Women who live or work together seem to communicate where they are in their menstrual cycle by means of smell, and over time this results in a tendency for their menstrual cycles to synchronize and begin at the same time (McClintock, 1971; Russell, Switz, & Thompson, 1980).

**OLFACTORY SYSTEM** The molecules given off by a substance are the stimulus for smell. The molecules leave the substance, travel through the air, and enter the nasal passage (see Figure 4-27). The molecules must also be soluble in fat, because the receptors for smell are covered with a fatlike substance.

The olfactory system consists of the receptors in the nasal passage, regions of the brain, and interconnecting neural pathways. The receptors for smell are located high in the nasal cavity. When the **cilia** (hairlike structures) of these receptors are contacted by molecules of odorant, an electrical impulse results; this is the transduction process. This impulse travels along nerve fibers to the **olfactory bulb,** a region of the brain that lies just below the frontal lobes. The olfactory bulb in turn is connected to the olfactory cortex on the inside of the temporal lobes.

**FIGURE 4-27**
**Olfactory Receptors** *(a) Detail of receptors interspersed among numerous supporting cells. (b) The placement of the olfactory receptors in the nasal cavity.*

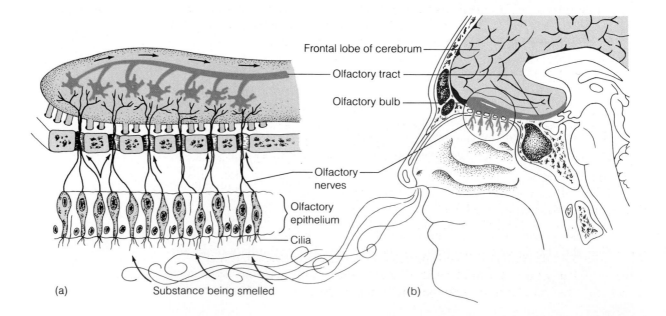

Frontal lobe of cerebrum
Olfactory tract
Olfactory bulb
Olfactory nerves
Olfactory epithelium
Cilia

(a)    Substance being smelled    (b)

**SENSING INTENSITY AND QUALITY** Human sensitivity to the intensity of a smell depends dramatically on the substance involved. Absolute thresholds can be as low as 1 part per 50 billion parts of air. Still, as noted earlier, we are far less sensitive to smell than other species. Dogs, for example, can detect substances in concentrations 100 times lower than concentrations humans can detect (Moulton, 1977). Our relative lack of sensitivity is not due to our having less sensitive olfactory receptors. Rather, we just have fewer of them: roughly 10 million receptors for people versus 1 billion for dogs.

Though we rely less on smell than other species, we are capable of sensing many different qualities of odor. Estimates vary, but a healthy person appears to be able to distinguish between 10,000 and 40,000 different odors, with women generally doing better than men (Cain, 1988). Professional perfumers and whiskey blenders can probably do even better—perhaps discriminating 100,000 different odors (Dobb, 1991). Our powers of discrimination, however, are not accompanied by a rich vocabulary for describing odors. Our descriptions sometimes borrow terms from other senses (we talk of a "sour" odor, or a "sharp" smell), and other times refer to the objects that produce the scent (as when we describe the smell of a newly mown lawn in terms of fresh-cut grass). As of now, no clear consensus exists on how to describe phenomenologically the qualities of different odors.

Still, progress has been made at the biological level on how the olfactory system codes the quality of odors. The situation is most unlike the coding of color in vision where three kinds of receptors suffice. In olfaction, many different kinds of receptors seem to be involved; an estimate of 1,000 kinds of olfactory receptors is not unreasonable in light of recent work (Buck & Axel, 1991). Rather than coding a specific odor, each kind of receptor may respond to many different odors (Matthews, 1972). So quality may be partly coded by the pattern of neural activity even in this receptor-rich sensory modality.

## Taste

Taste gets credit for a lot of experiences that it does not provide. We say that a meal "tastes" good; but when smell is eliminated by a bad cold our dinner becomes an impoverished experience, and we may have trouble telling red wine from vinegar. Still, taste (or **gustation**) is a sense in its own right. Even with a bad cold, we can tell salted from unsalted food.

In what follows, we will talk about the taste of particular substances, but note that the substance being tasted is not the only factor that determines its taste. Our genetic makeup and past experience also affect taste. For example, some people detect a bitter taste in caffeine and saccharine, whereas many do not, and this difference among people appears to be genetically determined (Bartoshuk, 1979). As another case in point, Indians living in the Karnataka province of India eat many sour foods, and experience citric acid and quinine as pleasant tasting: most of us experience the opposite. This particular difference between people seems to be a matter of past experience, for Indians who have been raised in a western country find citric acid and quinine unpleasant (Moskowitz et al., 1975).

**GUSTATORY SYSTEM** The stimulus for taste is a substance that is soluble in saliva, which is a fluid much like salt water. The gustatory system includes the receptors located on the tongue, parts of the brain, and

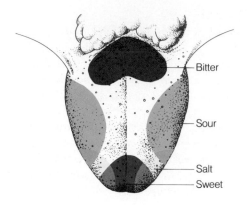

**FIGURE 4-28**
**Taste Areas** *Different areas of the tongue are sensitive to different tastes. The center of the tongue is relatively insensitive.*

interconnecting neural pathways. The taste receptors occur in clusters, called taste buds, on the bumps of the tongue and around the mouth. At the ends of the taste buds are short, hairlike structures that extend out and make contact with the solutions in the mouth. This contact results in an electrical impulse; this is the transduction process. The electrical impulse then travels to the brain.

**SENSING INTENSITY AND QUALITY** Sensitivity to different taste stimuli varies from place to place on the tongue. Sensitivity to salty and sweet substances is best near the front of the tongue; sour is best along the sides; and bitter is best on the soft palate (see Figure 4-28). In the center of the tongue is a region insensitive to taste (the place to put an unpleasant pill). While absolute thresholds for taste are generally very low, jnds for intensity are relatively high (Weber's constant is about 0.2). This means that if you are increasing the amount of spice in a dish you must add more than 20 percent or you will not taste the difference.

Unlike the case in olfaction, there is an agreed upon vocabulary for describing tastes. Any taste can be described as one or a combination of the four basic taste qualities: sweet, sour, salty, and bitter (McBurney, 1978). These four tastes are best revealed in sucrose (sweet), hydrochloric acid (sour), sodium chloride (salty), and quinine (bitter). When subjects are asked to describe the tastes of various substances in terms of just the four basic tastes, they have no trouble doing this; even if given the option of using additional qualities of their own choice, they tend to stay with the four basic tastes (Goldstein, 1989).

The gustatory system codes taste in terms of both the specific nerve fibers activated and the pattern of activation across nerve fibers. There appear to be four different types of nerve fibers, corresponding to the four basic tastes. While each fiber responds somewhat to all four basic tastes, it responds best to just one of them. Hence, it makes sense to talk of "salty fiber," whose activity signals saltiness to the brain.

*Food manufacturers employ tasters, who have highly discriminating senses of taste. Here, a taste expert samples varying blends of coffee.*

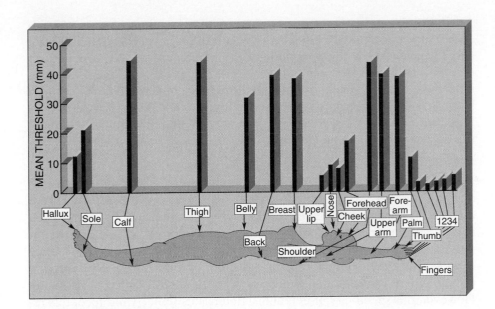

**FIGURE 4-29**
**Two-Point Threshold** *This graph shows the two-point threshold in millimeters at different places on the body surface. The threshold is determined by touching the skin with two thin rods separated by a small distance. The subject indicates whether one or two rods are sensed. The rod separation is adjusted to find the minimum separation at which two rods are sensed. The data given are for females, but male thresholds are very similar.* (After Weinstein, 1968)

## Skin Senses

Traditionally, touch was thought to be a single sense. Today, it is considered to include three distinct skin senses, one responding to pressure, another to temperature, and the third to pain. The reason for making this division is that each of the three skin senses: (a) responds to a distinct class of stimuli; (b) has the ability to discriminate among items within its class; (c) possesses a distinct set of receptors; and (d) leads to experiences that differ phenomenologically when the sense is stimulated. These are the standard criteria for telling senses apart.

**PRESSURE** The stimulus for sensed pressure is physical pressure on the skin. Although we are not aware of steady pressure on the entire body (such as air pressure), we can discriminate variations in pressure over the body surface. Some parts of the body are more effective than others at sensing the intensity of pressure; the lips, nose, and cheek are the most sensitive to pressure, while the big toe is least sensitive. These differences are closely related to the number of receptors that respond to the stimulus at each of these body loci. In sensitive regions, we can detect a force as small as 5 milligrams applied to a small area. However, like other sensory systems, the pressure system shows profound adaptation effects. If you hold your friend's hand for several minutes without moving, you will become insensitive to it and cease to feel the hand.

In addition to single points of pressure, we are also sensitive to patterns of pressure, which can be thought of as *qualities* of pressure. Most studies of pattern sensation have measured the **two-point threshold,** the minimum distance by which two very thin rods touching the skin must be separated before they are felt as two points rather than one. Like the pressure threshold, the two-point threshold varies greatly over the body surface, but the correlation between the two is not perfect. The two-point threshold is lowest in the fingers and highest on the calves (see Figure 4-29).

In the above discussion, we focused on what happens when we experience pressure in a passive way, that is, when we are being touched. But what about when we are actively exploring the environment, that is, when we are doing the touching. Such *active touching* results in a different experience than its passive counterpart, and involves the activity of the motor senses (see below), as well as the pressure sense. By active touch alone, we can readily identify familiar objects, even though most of us are rarely required to identify objects in this manner (Klatzky, Lederman, & Metzger, 1985).

**TEMPERATURE** The stimulus for temperature is the temperature of our skin. The receptors are neurons with free nerve endings just under the skin. In the transduction stage, *cold receptors* generate a neural impulse when there is a decrease in skin temperature, while *warm receptors* generate an impulse when there is an increase in skin temperature (Hensel, 1973; Duclauz & Kenshalo, 1980). Hence, different qualities of temperature can be coded primarily by the specific receptors activated (as pitch is coded in audition). However, this specificity of neural reaction has its limits. Cold receptors respond not only to low temperatures but also to very high temperatures (above 45 degrees centigrade). Consequently a very hot stimulus will activate both warm and cold receptors, which in turn evoke a hot sensation.

Because maintaining body temperature is crucial to our survival, it is important that we can sense small changes in our skin temperature. When the skin is at its normal temperature, we can detect a warming of only 0.4 degrees centigrade and a cooling of just 0.15 degrees centigrade (Kenshalo, Nafe, & Brooks, 1961). Our temperature sense adapts completely to moderate changes in temperatures, so that after a few minutes the stimulus feels neither cool nor warm. This adaptation explains the strong differences of opinion about the temperature of a swimming pool between those who have been in it for a while and those first dangling a foot in.

**PAIN** Any stimulus that is intense enough to cause tissue damage is a stimulus for pain. It may be pressure, temperature, electric shock, or irritant chemicals. The effect of such a stimulus is to cause the release of chemical substances in the skin, which in turn stimulate distinct high-threshold receptors (the transduction stage). These receptors are neurons with specialized free nerve endings, and researchers have distinguished at least four types (Brown & Deffenbacher, 1979).

With regard to variations in the quality of pain, perhaps the most important distinction is between the kind of pain we feel immediately upon suffering an injury, called **phasic** pain, and the kind we experience after the injury has occurred, called **tonic** pain. Phasic pain is typically brief and rapidly rises and falls in intensity; tonic pain, in contrast, is often long-lasting and steady. To illustrate, if you sprain your ankle, immediately you feel a sharp undulating pain (phasic pain), but a short while after you start to feel the steady pain due to the swelling (tonic pain). The two kinds of pain are mediated by two distinct neural pathways in the brain (Melzak, 1990).

Tonic pain can often be severe; in the cases of some cancer patients and burn victims, it can be downright excruciating. In our society, the major means for dealing with such severe pain is the administration of drugs, especially morphine. Physicians have long been reluctant to prescribe morphine before the pain starts—that is, to head it off—because they were afraid their patients would become addicted to the drug. Recent research, however,

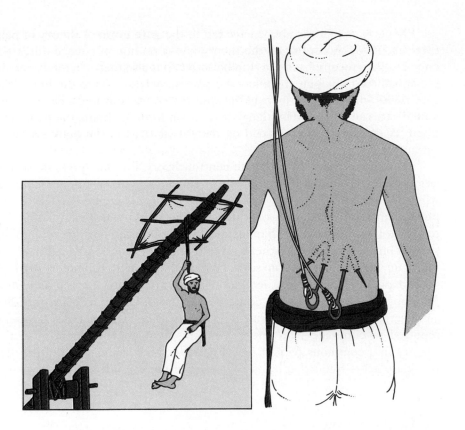

**FIGURE 4-30**
**Culture and Pain** *Right: two steel hooks in the back of the "celebrant" in the Indian hook-swinging ceremony. Left: the celebrant hangs onto the ropes as a cart takes him from village to village. As he blesses the village children and crops, he swings freely suspended by the hooks in his back.* (After Kosambi, 1967)

indicates that people who take morphine to combat chronic pain do not become addicted, unlike people who take it solely to induce pleasurable feelings (Melzak, 1990).

More than any other sensation, the intensity and quality of pain is influenced by factors other than the immediate stimulus. These factors include the person's culture, attitudes, and previous experience. The striking influence of culture is illustrated by the fact that some non-Western societies engage in rituals that would be unbearably painful to Westerners. A case in point is the hook-swinging ceremony practiced in some parts of India:

> The ceremony derives from an ancient practice in which a member of a social group is chosen to represent the power of the gods. The role of the chosen man (or "celebrant") is to bless the children and crops in a series of neighboring villages during a particular period of the year. What is remarkable about the ritual is that steel hooks, which are attached by strong ropes to the top of a special cart, are shoved under his skin and muscles on both sides of his back [see Figure 4-30]. The cart is then moved from village to village. Usually the man hangs on to the ropes as the cart is moved about. But at the climax of the ceremony in each village, he swings free, hanging only from the hooks embedded in his back, to bless the children and crops. Astonishingly, there is no evidence that the man is in pain during the ritual; rather, he appears to be in a "state of exaltation." When the hooks are later removed, wounds heal rapidly without any medical treatment other than the application of wood ash. Two weeks later the marks on his back are scarcely visible (Melzak, 1973).

Clearly, pain is as much a matter of mind as of sensory receptors.

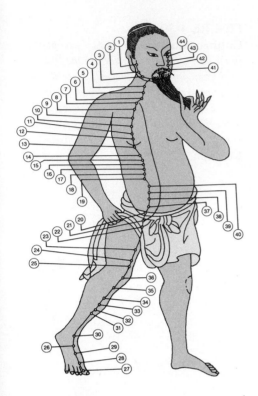

**FIGURE 4-31**
**Typical Acupuncture Chart** *The numbers indicate sites at which needles can be inserted, and then either twisted, electrified, or heated. An impressive analgesia results in many cases.*

Phenomena like the above have led to the **gate control theory** of pain (Melzak, 1973). According to the theory, the sensation of pain requires not only that pain receptors on the skin be active, but also that a "neural gate" in the spinal cord be open and allow the pain signals to pass to the brain (the gate closes when critical fibers in the spinal cord are activated). Because the neural gate can be closed by signals sent down from the brain, the perceived intensity of pain can be reduced by mental state, as in the hook-swinging ceremony.

Many phenomena fit with gate control theory. For one, pressure stimulation tends to close the neural gate (activate the critical fibers), which is why rubbing a hurt area may relieve pain. A more extreme version of this phenomenon is **stimulation-produced analgesia,** in which stimulation of a region in the midbrain acts like an anesthetic. One can perform abdominal surgery on a rat with no anesthetic other than an electrical stimulation of the midbrain, yet the rat shows no sign of experiencing pain (Reynolds, 1969). A related phenomenon is the reduction in pain resulting from *acupuncture.* Acupuncture is a healing procedure developed in China, in which needles are inserted into the skin at critical points; twirling these needles has been reported to eliminate pain entirely, making it possible to perform major surgery in a conscious patient (see Figure 4-31). Presumably, the needles stimulate nerve fibers that lead to a closing of the pain gate.

## Body Senses

In addition to skin senses, we also have a set of *body senses*, each of which informs us about our movements and orientation in space.

**KINESTHESIS** Kinesthesis is a sense of the position and movement of your head and limbs relative to your trunk. If you doubt whether you have such a sense, next time you wake in the middle of the night ask yourself where your arms are. Kinesthesis will enable you to answer correctly without looking. The receptors that are responsible for transduction are located in the muscles, tendons, joints, and skin. Often, kinesthesis does not work alone. When we actively control our limbs, kinesthesis is aided by signals from the motor center of the brain to the perceptual system. And when we actively touch something, kinesthesis can be involved along with the pressure sense.

**ORIENTATION AND BODY MOVEMENT** We sense the orientation of our body with respect to gravity, and we also sense the movement of our body through space (both linear and angular movement). These capacities are often grouped together because the receptors involved are all in the vestibular apparatus adjoining the inner ear.

The receptors for orientation and *linear movement* (movement in a straight line, as when running) are located in fluid-filled chambers. These chambers, called the **vestibular sacs,** consist of hair cells; when the cilia of these hair cells are bent by body tilt or linear acceleration, a neural impulse results (the transduction stage). Typically, our senses of orientation and linear movement do not lead to conscious sensations, as their main function is the largely unconscious regulation of motor activity.

The receptors for angular movements are sensitive to movement of our body or parts of it rotating through space, as when we do a somersault, or (for those of us who can) a twisting dive. The receptors are located in the **semicircular canals** (see Figure 4-24 again). Movement of the fluid in these canals bends the cilia of the hair cells embedded in the canals and causes them to respond (transduction), producing a sensation of acceleration. Extreme stimulation of this sense produces dizziness and nausea.

In many cases, then, the body senses do not give rise to conscious sensations of intensity and quality. In this respect, they are most unlike the other senses. Among the skin senses, pain in particular is notorious for filling one's consciousness. To a lesser extent, smells and tastes can also command our attention. And vision and hearing, our higher senses, are responsible for a good deal of the richness of conscious experience.

## *Chapter* SUMMARY

1.  Sensations result from processes associated with organs like the eye and ear, and presumably are elicited by simple stimuli (a red light, for example). The senses include vision, hearing *(audition)*, smell *(olfaction)*, taste *(gustation)*, the *skin senses* (including pressure, temperature, and pain), and the *body senses* (including our senses of orientation and body movement).

2.  One property common to all senses is a sensitivity for detecting change. Sensitivity to intensity is measured by the *absolute threshold*, the minimum amount of stimulus energy that can be reliably detected. Sensitivity to a change in intensity is measured by the *difference threshold* or *jnd*, the minimum difference between two stimuli that can be reliably detected. The amount of change needed for detection to occur increases with the initial intensity of the stimulus, and is approximately proportional to it *(Weber's law)*.

3.  Every sense modality must recode its physical energy into neural impulses. This *transduction* process is accomplished by the *receptors*. The receptors and connecting neural pathways code the *intensity* of a stimulus by the rate of neural impulses and their patterns; they code the *quality* of a stimulus by the specific nerve fibers involved and their pattern of activity.

4.  The stimulus for vision is electromagnetic radiation from 400 to 700 nanometers, and the sense organs are the eyes. Each eye contains a system for forming the image (including the *cornea, pupil,* and *lens*), and a system for transducing the image into electrical impulses. The transduction system is in the *retina,* which contains the visual receptors, the *rods* and *cones*.

5.  Cones operate at high intensities, lead to sensations of color, and are found only in the center (or *fovea*) of the retina; rods operate at low intensities, lead to colorless sensations, and predominate in the *periphery* of the retina. Our sensitivity to a light's intensity is mediated by properties of the rods and cones. For example, sensitivity is greater in the rod-rich periphery than in the fovea.

6.  Different wavelengths of light lead to sensations of different colors. Any color can be described phenomenologically by three dimensions: *brightness, hue,* and *saturation*. A mixture of three lights widely separated in wavelength can be made to match almost any color of light. There are four *basic color sensations:* red, yellow, green, and blue. Mixtures of these make up our experiences of color, except that we do not see reddish-greens and yellowish-blues. These facts can be explained by a

*two-stage theory.* It postulates three types of cones (each of which is maximally sensitive to wavelengths in a different region) followed at a higher level in the visual system by red-green and yellow-blue *opponent processes* (each of which responds in opposite ways to its two opponent colors).

7. The stimulus for audition is a wave of pressure changes (a *sound wave*), and the sense organs are the ears. The ear includes: the *outer ear* (the external ear and the *auditory canal*); the *middle ear* (the *eardrum* and a chain of bones); and the *inner ear.* The inner ear includes the *cochlea*, which is a coiled tube that contains the *basilar membrane*, which supports the *hair cells* that serve as the receptors for sound. Sound waves transmitted by the outer and middle ear cause the basilar membrane to vibrate, which results in a bending of the hair cells, and eventuates in a neural impulse.

8. *Pitch*, the most striking quality of sound, increases with the frequency of the sound wave. The fact that we can hear the pitches of two different tones sounded simultaneously suggests there may be many receptors, which respond to different frequencies. *Temporal theories* of pitch perception postulate that the pitch heard depends on the temporal pattern of neural responses in the auditory system, which itself is determined by the temporal pattern of the sound wave. *Place theories* postulate that each frequency stimulates one place along the basilar membrane, and each place, when stimulated, results in one pitch heard. There is room for both theories, as temporal theory explains our perception of low frequencies, while place theory accounts for our perceptions of high frequencies.

9. Smell is more important to nonhuman species than to humans. Many species use specialized odors *(pheromones)* for communication, and humans seem to have a remnant of this system. The stimuli for smell are the molecules given off by a substance. The molecules travel by air and activate the olfactory receptors located high in the *nasal cavity.* There are many different kinds of receptors (on the order of 1,000). Though we lack a vocabulary for describing odors, a normal person can discriminate 10,000 to 40,000 different odors.

10. Taste is affected not only by the substance being tasted, but also by genetic makeup and past experience. The stimulus for taste is a substance that is soluble in saliva. The receptors occur in clusters on the tongue *(taste buds)*. Sensitivity varies from place to place on the tongue. Any taste can be described as one or a combination of the four basic taste qualities: *sweet, sour, salty,* and *bitter.* Different qualities of taste are coded partly in terms of the specific nerve fibers activated—different fibers respond best to one of the four taste sensations—and partly in terms of the pattern of fibers activated.

11. Three *skin senses* are distinguished: *pressure, temperature,* and *pain.* Our sensitivity to pressure is greatest at the lips, nose, and cheeks, and least at the big toe. We are very sensitive to temperature, being able to detect a change of less than one degree centigrade. We code different kinds of temperatures primarily by whether *hot* or *cold receptors* are activated. Our sensitivity to pain is greatly influenced by factors other than the noxious stimulus, including culture, attitudes, and previous experience. These factors may have their influence by opening or closing a *neural gate* in the spinal cord; pain is experienced only when pain receptors are activated and the gate is open.

12. The *body senses* include *kinesthesis*, and the senses of *orientation* and *body*

*motion*. Kinesthesis is a sense of the position and movement of the limbs and head relative to the trunk; its receptors are located in the muscles, tendons, joints, and skin. We also sense our orientation with respect to gravity, as well as our movement through space (both *linear* and *angular movement*). These capacities are often grouped together because the receptors involved are all in the *vestibular apparatus* adjoining the inner ear.

## *Further* READING

There are several good general texts on sensory processes and perception. A particularly clear one is Goldstein, *Sensation and Perception* (3rd ed., 1989). Other useful texts include: Barlow and Mollon, *The Senses* (1982); Coren and Ward, *Sensation and Perception* (3rd ed., 1989); Schiffman, *Sensation and Perception* (3rd ed., 1990); and Sekuler and Blake, *Perception* (1985).

For treatments of color vision, see Boynton, *Human Color Vision* (1979); and Hurvich, *Color Vision* (1981). Introductory books on audition include Moore, *An Introduction to the Psychology of Hearing* (2nd ed., 1982); and Yost and Nielson, *Fundamentals of Hearing* (2nd ed., 1985). For smell, see Engen, *The Perception of Odors* (1982); for touch, *Tactual Perception*, edited by Schiff and Foulke (1982); and for pain, *The Psychology of Pain*, edited by Sternbach (2nd ed., 1986).

For reference there are four multivolume handbooks, each of which has several chapters on sensory systems. They are the *Handbook of Perception* (1974–1978), edited by Carterette and Friedman; the *Handbook of Physiology: The Nervous System:* Section 1, Volume 3, *Sensory Processes* (1984), edited by Darian-Smith; the *Handbook of Perception and Human Performance:* Volume 1, *Sensory Processes and Perception* (1986), edited by Boff, Kaufman, and Thomas; and *Stevens' Handbook of Experimental Psychology: Volume 1* (1988), edited by Atkinson, Herrnstein, Lindzey, and Luce.

# *Chapter* 5

# Perception

**Functions of Perception 165**

**Localization 166**
*Segregation of Objects*
*Perceiving Distance*
*Perceiving Motion*

**Recognition 173**
*Early Stages of Recognition*
*The Matching Stage and Connectionist Models*
*Recognizing Natural Objects and Top-Down Processing*
*Role of Attention*
*Critical Discussion: Breakdown of Recognition*

**Perceptual Constancies 187**
*Lightness and Color Constancy*
*Shape and Location Constancy*
*Size Constancy*

**Perceptual Development 191**
*Discrimination by Infants*
*Rearing with Controlled Stimulation*

Detail, *Snowy Hill with Winding Road.*

Information may enter our senses in bits and pieces, but that is not how we *perceive* the world. We perceive a world of objects and people, a world that bombards us with integrated wholes, not piecemeal sensations. Only under unusual circumstances do we notice the individual features and parts of stimuli; most of the time we see three-dimensional objects and hear words and music.

# Functions of Perception

Perception is the study of how we integrate sensations into percepts of objects, and how we then use these percepts to get around in the world (a **percept** is an outcome of a perceptual process). Inspired in part by the work of David Marr (1982), researchers are increasingly approaching the study of perception by asking what problems the perceptual system is designed to solve. Two general problems are repeatedly mentioned. The perceptual system must determine (a) *what* objects are out there (apples, tables, cats, and so on), and (b) *where* these objects are (arm's length on my left, hundreds of yards straight ahead, and so on). The same two problems are involved in auditory perception (*What* was that sound, a phone or a siren? *Where* was it coming from, the front or the back?).

In vision, determining what the objects are is referred to as the process of **pattern recognition,** or *recognition* for short. It is crucial for survival because often we have to know what an object is before we can infer some of its critical properties. So, once we know an object is an apple, we know it is edible; once we know an object is a wolf, we know not to perturb it. Determining where visual objects are is referred to as **spatial localization,** or *localization*. It is also necessary for survival. Localization is the means we use to navigate through our environment. Without such an ability, we would constantly be bumping into objects, failing to grasp things we are reaching for, and moving into the path of dangerous objects and predators.

Although visual recognition and localization are not completely independent (both tasks require some information about shape, for example), the idea that they are qualitatively different tasks is supported by the finding that they are carried out by different regions of the brain. Recognition of objects depends on a branch of the visual system that includes the cortical receiving area for vision (the first area in the cortex to receive visual information) and a region near the bottom of the brain. In contrast, localization of objects depends on a branch of the visual system that projects to a region of the cortex near the top of the brain. If the recognition branch of an animal's visual system is impaired, the animal can still perceive spatial relations between objects (one in front of the other, for example), but it cannot discriminate the actual objects—for example, it cannot tell a cube from a cylinder; if the location branch is impaired, the animal can distinguish a cube from a cylinder, but it does not know where they are in relation to each other (Mishkin & Appenzeller, 1987). More recent research has used brain scanning techniques to document the existence of separate object and location systems in the *human* brain. When people engage in a task that emphasizes object recognition, there is an increase in blood flow primarily in the recognition branch of the cortex; when they engage in a location task, blood flow increases mainly in the location branch (Haxby et al., 1990). In view of these results, and others, we will treat localization and recognition separately.

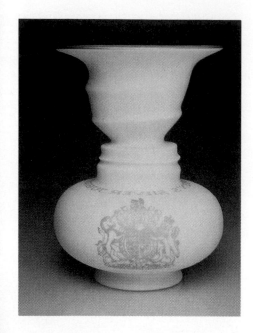

**FIGURE 5-1**
**Reversible Figure and Ground** *The reversible goblet illustrates figure-ground reversal. Note that you can perceive either the light portion (the vase) or the dark portion (two profiles) as a figure against a background, but only one at a time. This vase was a gift to Queen Elizabeth II on her silver jubilee and shows her profile and that of Prince Philip.*

In addition to localizing and recognizing objects, another goal of our perceptual system is to keep the appearance of objects constant, even though their impressions on our retinas are continually changing. Such **perceptual constancy** will be another concern to us. Finally, we will consider what is known about the development of the various aspects of perception. Throughout the chapter, we will be concerned primarily with visual perception, since this is the area that has been most investigated.

## Localization

To know where the objects in our environment are, we first have to *segregate* the objects from one another and from the background. Then the perceptual system can determine the position of the objects in a three-dimensional world, including their *distance* from us and their *movement* patterns. The idea that these three perceptual abilities—segregation, determining distance, and determining movement—belong together is supported by physiological findings indicating that all three abilities are mediated by the same branch of the visual system (Livingstone & Hubel, 1988). We will discuss each of these perceptual abilities in turn.

### Segregation of Objects

The image projected on our retina is a mosaic of varying brightnesses and colors. Somehow our perceptual system organizes the mosaic into a set of discrete objects projected against a background. This kind of organization was of great concern to **Gestalt psychology,** an approach to psychology that began in Germany early in this century. The Gestalt psychologists emphasized the importance of perceiving whole objects or forms, and proposed a number of principles of how we organize objects.

**FIGURE 5-2**
**The Slave Market with Disappearing Bust of Voltaire** *A reversible figure is in the center of this painting by Salvador Dali (1940). Two nuns standing in an archway reverse to form a bust of Voltaire.*

**FIGURE AND GROUND** If a stimulus contains two or more distinct regions, we usually see part of it as a *figure* and the rest as *ground*. The regions seen as a figure contain the objects of interest—they appear more solid than the ground and appear in front of the ground. This is the most elementary form of perceptual organization. Figure 5-1 illustrates that **figure-ground organization** can be reversible. The fact that either region can be recognized as a figure indicates that figure-ground organization is not part of the physical stimulus, but rather is an accomplishment of our perceptual system. Figure 5-2 illustrates a more complex reversible figure-ground effect. (Note that we can perceive figure-ground relations in senses other than vision. For example, we may hear the song of a bird against a background of outdoor noises, or the melody played by the violin against the harmonies of the rest of the orchestra.)

**GROUPING OF OBJECTS** We see not only objects against a ground, but a particular grouping of the objects as well. Even simple patterns of lines or dots fall into groups when we look at them. In the top part of Figure 5-3, we tend to see three pairs of lines, with an extra line at the right. But notice that the stimulus can be described equally well as three pairs beginning at the right with an extra line at the left. The slight modification of the lines shown in the lower part of the figure causes us to perceive the second grouping.

The Gestalt psychologists proposed a number of determinants of grouping. One is *proximity:* elements that are near to one another will tend to be grouped together. This principle explains the preferred grouping of the lines in the top part of Figure 5-3. *Closure,* or our tendency to group elements to complete figures with gaps, explains the grouping preferred in the bottom part of the figure. In the bottom part of the figure, closure is a stronger factor than proximity.

Many determinants of grouping were first noted by Max Wertheimer (1912), the founder of Gestalt psychology. Wertheimer's research strategy was to construct demonstrations such as the one in Figure 5-3, and leave it to the reader's intuition to verify the grouping. In modern times, researchers have used experiments to show that different ways of grouping objects have marked effects on perceptual performance. In one set of experiments, on each of the trials subjects were presented with a display (see Figure 5-4). The subject's task was to decide as quickly as possible whether or not the display contained a target letter, either a T or an F. On those trials where the display contained a target, subjects responded faster when the target was relatively far from the nontargets, as in the display on the top, than when the target was relatively close to the nontargets, as in the display on the bottom. When the target was close to the nontargets, the principle of proximity led the target and nontargets to be grouped together, which resulted in extra time being needed to extract the target.

The same task can be used to study another determinant of grouping, namely *good continuation,* our tendency to group together objects that form an unbroken contour. Look at the displays in Figure 5-5. The target F forms part of a contour with the nontargets in the display on the bottom but not in the display on the top. Because it requires extra time to extract the target from its grouping with the nontargets, subjects took longer to respond to the display on the bottom than to the one on the top. Still another determinant of grouping that deserves mention is *similarity,* our tendency to group together similar objects. If we replaced the F in the bottom display of Figure

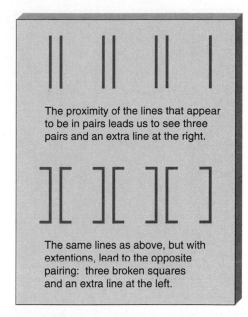

**FIGURE 5-3**
**Perceptual Grouping**

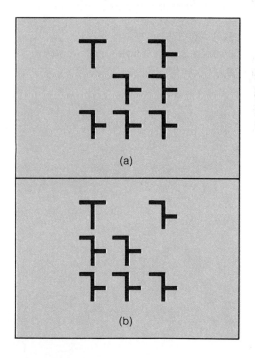

**FIGURE 5-4**
**Grouping by Proximity** *Subjects found the target T faster when it was relatively far from the nontargets (a) than when it was relatively close to the nontargets (b).* (After Banks & Prinzmetal, 1976)

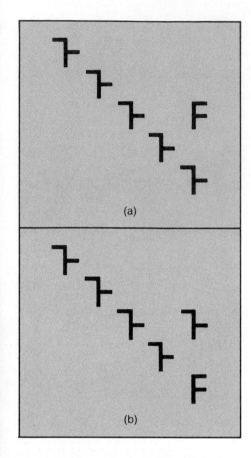

**FIGURE 5-5**
**Grouping and Good Continuation**
*Subjects found the target F faster when it did not form a part of the contour with the nontargets (a) than when it did form a part of the contour (b).* (After Prinzmetal & Banks, 1977)

5-5 with an O, subjects would be less likely to group it with the nontargets because an O is very dissimilar to the nontargets.

In addition to grouping whole objects into sets of objects, our perceptual system also groups features or parts into a single object. In such cases, there are other determinants of grouping. For example, we can group parts on the basis of common *distance* (two contours are likely to be parts of the same object only if they are at the same distance from the observer), or on the basis of their *motion* (two contours moving in the same direction are likely to be parts of the same object). These examples highlight the close connection between our ability to segment objects and parts on the one hand, and our abilities to determine distance and movement on the other.

Although perceptual grouping has been studied mainly in visual perception, the same determinants of grouping appear in audition. Proximity clearly operates in audition (though it is proximity in time rather than in space): four drumbeats with a pause between the second and third will be heard as two pairs. Similarity and good continuation are also known to play important roles in hearing tones and more complex stimuli (Bregman & Reidnicky, 1975).

## Perceiving Distance

To know where an object is, we must know its distance or *depth*. Although perceiving an object's depth seems effortless, it is a remarkable achievement given the physical structure of our eyes.

**DEPTH CUES**  The retina, the starting point of vision, is a two-dimensional surface. This means the retinal image is flat and has no depth at all. This fact has led many students of perception (artists as well as scientists) to the idea of distance cues, two-dimensional aspects that a perceiver uses to infer distance in a three-dimensional world. There are a number of distance cues that combine to determine perceived distance. The cues can be classified as monocular or binocular, depending on whether they involve one or both eyes.

People using only one eye can perceive depth remarkably well by picking up monocular depth cues. Figure 5-6 illustrates four of these cues. The first is **relative size.** If an image contains an array of similar objects that differ in size, people interpret the smaller objects as being further away (see Figure 5-6a). A second monocular cue is **superposition.** If one object is positioned so that it obstructs the view of the other, people perceive the overlapping object as being nearer (see Figure 5-6b). A third cue is **relative height.** Among similar objects, those that are higher in an image are perceived as being further away (see Figure 5-6c). A fourth cue is called **linear perspective.** When parallel lines appear to converge, they are perceived as vanishing in the distance (see Figure 5-6d). These four cues have been known to artists for centuries—they are called *pictorial cues* for this reason— and a single painting will often use more than one of the cues.

Another important monocular cue involves the use of motion. Have you ever noticed that if you are moving quickly—perhaps, on a fast-moving train—nearby objects seem to move quickly in the opposite direction while more distant objects move more slowly (though still in the opposite direction). The difference in speed with which these objects appear to move thus provides a cue as to their respective depths (this cue is referred to as **motion parallax).**

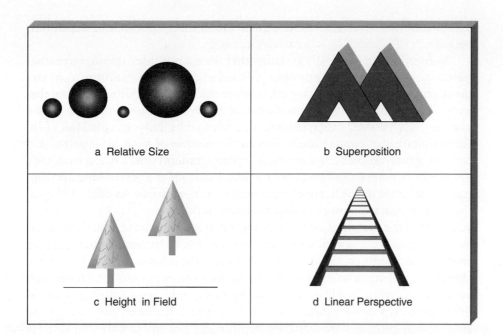

**FIGURE 5-6**
**Monocular Distance Cues** *The figure illustrates four monocular distance cues. These are used by artists to portray depth on a two-dimensional surface and are also present in photographs.*

Seeing with both eyes rather than one has advantages for **depth perception.** Because the eyes are separated in the head, each eye perceives a three-dimensional object from a slightly different angle. Consequently each eye has a slightly different view of the object. Fusing these different views gives rise to an impression of depth. This can be demonstrated by a device called a *stereoscope* (see Figure 5-7). The stereoscope displays a different photograph or drawing to each eye. If the two pictures are taken from slightly separated camera positions or drawn from slightly different perspectives, the viewer will experience vivid depth.

**Binocular parallax** is one cue that is responsible for this perception of depth. It hinges on the fact that any visible point will differ slightly in its direction to the two eyes. A related cue is **binocular disparity**; it is based on the difference between the retinal images on the two eyes when we look at an object from a distance. Both binocular parallax and binocular disparity are consequences of the fact that our eyes are separated. You can easily demonstrate these cues to yourself. Hold a pencil about a foot in front of you and, with only one eye open, line it up with a vertical edge of the wall opposite you. Then close that eye and open the other. The pencil will now appear in a different direction; the difference between these directions is binocular parallax. Also, the two edges that were lined up in the first eye will appear separated when you open the second eye, and indeed the images in the second eye are separated; the difference between the retinal images in the two eyes is binocular disparity. Binocular disparity is a particularly powerful cue. It leads to a vivid impression of depth even with completely meaningless stimuli, such as a random pattern of dots that contain no other depth cues (Julesz, 1971).

**DIRECT PERCEPTION** The idea behind distance cues is that the observer notes a critical cue—for instance, that one object appears larger than another—and then unconsciously infers distance information from the cue. This notion of **unconscious inference** was introduced by Helmholtz in 1909. While it continues to be a key idea in the study of perception (Rock,

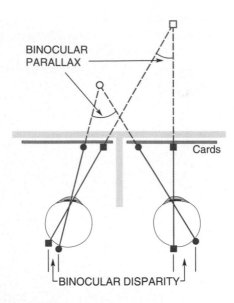

**FIGURE 5-7**
**A Stereoscope and Binocular Distance Cues** *A stereoscope is a device that presents different images to the two eyes. This very simple model holds a different card in front of each eye; a barrier between the eyes allows each eye to see only one card. If each card contains the same two symbols (here a circle and a square) separated by a different amount of space, the stimulus is the same as that produced by a circle and a square at different distances behind the cards. The dashed lines show how the images on the cards simulate two objects at different distances in space. When presented with stereo images such as these, people will experience vivid depth.* Binocular parallax *refers to the angle between the two lines of sight;* binocular disparity *refers to the difference between the separations of the retinal images of the symbols in the two eyes.*

1983), some psychologists have argued for another approach to depth perception.

Gibson (1950; 1966; 1979) claims that we do not infer depth, but rather perceive it directly. To appreciate Gibson's ideas, it is useful to consider *where* people routinely look for information about depth. Gibson argues that instead of looking for cues that characterize objects protruding in the air—such as relative size, superposition, and relative height—people look at information on the ground itself. The best example of such information is a **texture gradient** (see Figure 5-8). A texture gradient arises when we view a surface in perspective. The elements that make up the textured surface appear to be packed closer and closer together as the surface recedes. This gradient gives rise to a powerful impression of depth.

Unlike the standard distance cues, the gradient extends over a large visual area, and were you to move forward you could determine your distance to any other point on the gradient. The gradient information on the retina, therefore, remains constant or, to use Gibson's term, *invariant.* Depth perception, according to Gibson, is a matter of directly perceiving such invariants. Thus, when we perceive depth in a scene, we need not process the information provided by scattered depth cues, but instead we can directly perceive the depth information provided by the texture gradient (Goldstein, 1989).

Although Gibson's ideas about direct perception are controversial (Fodor & Pylyshyn, 1981), they have influenced many areas of perception. They will surface again in our discussion of localization.

## Perceiving Motion

If we are to move around our environment effectively, we need to know not only the locations of static objects, but also the trajectories of moving ones. We need to know, for example, not only that the object located a few feet in front of us is a softball, but also that it is coming at us at a fast clip. This brings us to the issue of how we perceive motion.

*The Holmes-Bates stereoscope, invented by Oliver Wendell Holmes in 1861 and manufactured by Joseph Bates, creates a vivid perception of depth.*

**STROBOSCOPIC MOTION**  What causes us to perceive motion? The simplest idea is that we perceive an object is in motion whenever its image moves across our retina. This answer turns out to be too simple, though, for we can see motion even when *nothing* moves on our retina. This phenomenon was demonstrated in 1912 by Wertheimer in his studies of **stroboscopic motion** (see Figure 5-9). Stroboscopic motion is produced most simply by flashing a light in darkness and then, a few milliseconds later, flashing another light near the location of the first light. The light will seem to move from one place to the other in a way that is indistinguishable from real motion.

The motion that we see in movies is stroboscopic. The film is simply a series of still photographs (frames), each slightly different than the preceding. The frames are projected on the screen in rapid sequence, with dark intervals in between. The rate at which the frames are presented is critical. In the early days of motion pictures, the frame rate was 16 per second. This was too slow, and as a consequence movement in these early films appears jerky and disjointed. Today, the rate is usually 24 frames per second.

**INDUCED MOTION**  Another case in which we perceive motion in the absence of movement across our retina is the phenomenon of **induced motion.** When a large object surrounding a smaller one moves, the smaller object may appear to be the one that is moving even if it is static. This phenomenon was first studied by the Gestalt psychologist, Duncker, in 1929.

**FIGURE 5-8**
**Examples of Texture Gradients** *The elements that make up the textured surface (rocks on left, people on right) appear to be packed closer and closer together as the surface recedes.*

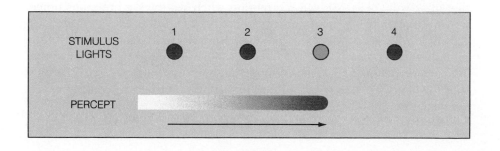

**FIGURE 5-9**
**Stroboscopic Motion** *The four circles in the top row correspond to four lights. If these are flashed one after the other with a short dark interval in between, they will appear to be a single light in continuous motion, such as that suggested in the second row. This is stroboscopic motion; motion in movies and on television is of this kind.*

Duncker had subjects sit in a darkened room and observe a small luminous circle inside a larger luminous rectangular frame. When the rectangle was moved to the right, subjects reported that the circle appeared to move to the left. This same phenomenon may be at play on a windy night when the moon seems to be racing through the clouds.

**REAL MOTION** Of course, our visual system is also sensitive to *real motion*—that is, motion induced by movement across the retina. Under optimal conditions, our threshold for seeing motion is strikingly low; an object need move only about one-fifth the diameter of a single cone in the retina in order for us to detect movement (Nakayama & Tyler, 1981).

We are much better at detecting motion when we can see an object against a structured background *(relative motion)* than when the background is dark or neutral and only the moving object can be seen *(absolute motion)*. According to Gibson (1966; 1979), there is a distinctive pattern of information produced in relative motion. Specifically, as the object moves, it covers and uncovers parts of the background. Gibson argues that we can use this pattern to directly perceive motion, just as we can directly perceive depth.

Some aspects of real movement are coded by specific cells in the visual cortex. These cells respond to some motions and not to others, and each cell responds best to one direction and speed of motion. Some evidence for the existence of such cells comes from studies of animals. The evidence is obtained by recording from single cells in the visual cortex while presenting stimuli with different patterns of motion (refer back to Figure 4-4). Such single-cell recording studies have found cortical cells tuned to particular directions of movement. There are even cells specifically tuned to detect an object moving toward the head, clearly useful for survival (Regan, Beverley, & Cynader, 1979).

There is also evidence for motion-detecting cells from studies with humans. Of course, these studies don't involve single-cell recording; rather, they involve a technique called **selective adaptation.** Selective adaptation is a loss in sensitivity to motion that occurs when we view motion; the adaptation is selective in that we lose sensitivity to the motion viewed and to similar motions, but not to motion that differs significantly in direction or speed. If we look at upward-moving stripes, for example, we lose sensitivity to upward motion but our ability to see downward motion is not affected (Sekuler & Ganz, 1963). Presumably, this selectivity occurs because the cortical cells specialized for upward motion have become fatigued, whereas those specialized for downward motion are functioning as usual.

As with other types of adaption, we do not usually notice the sensitivity loss but we do notice the aftereffect produced by adaptation. If we view a waterfall for a few minutes and then look at the cliff beside it, the cliff will appear to move upward. Most motions will produce such a **motion aftereffect** in the opposite direction.

However, there is more to the perception of real motion than the activation of specific cells. We can see motion when we track a luminous object moving in darkness (such as an airplane at night). Because our eyes follow the object, the image makes only a small, irregular motion on the retina (due to imperfect tracking), yet we perceive a smooth, continuous motion. Why? The answer seems to be that information about how our eyes are moving is sent to our visual system and influences the motion that we see. In essence, the visual system is being informed by the motor system that the latter is responsible for the lack of regular motion on the retina, and the visual system then corrects for this lack. In more normal viewing situations, there are both eye movements and large retinal-image movements. The visual system must combine these two sources of information to determine the perceived motion.

**MOTION AND EVENT PERCEPTION**   The motion of objects tells us not only about where the objects are, but also about what they are doing. Thus, our perception of motion is directly tied to our perception of events. A barking dog racing toward an intruder is perceived not just as a "moving dog" but as the event, "a dog is attacking."

Motion is particularly important in our perception of simple causal events. When two objects are in motion, we may perceive one as having *caused* the motion of the other. In a demonstration of this, Michotte (1963) used squares like those in Figure 5-10 as stimuli. When square A moves to square B, and then B immediately begins to move in the direction A was moving, subjects report that A caused B's movement; more specifically, A seems to launch B. (This perception of causality, however, obtains only when the interval between when A reaches B and when B starts to move is very brief, roughly, less than one-fifth of a second.) Furthermore, the perception of causality is not mediated by conscious inferences. The subject does not explicitly reason to herself that "A hit B and B moved, so A must have caused B to move." Rather, causality appears to be perceived without any intervening reasoning (Goldstein, 1989).

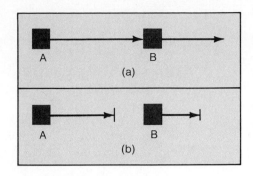

**FIGURE 5-10**
**Motion and the Perception of Causality** *When square A moves to square B, and B then immediately begins to move, subjects report that A "launches" B (a). The perception of causality is somewhat different when A stops before it reaches B (b).*

# Recognition

We turn now to the second major function of perception: recognizing what an object is. Recognizing an object amounts to assigning it to a category—that's a shirt, that's a cat, that's a daisy, and so on. Of course, we can also recognize people, which amounts to assigning the visual input to a particular individual—that's Ben Murphy, or this is Irene Paull. In either case, objects or people, recognition allows us to infer many hidden properties of the object—if it's a shirt then it's made of cloth and I can wear it; if it's a cat then it may scratch me if I pull its tail; if it's Ben Murphy he'll want to tell me one of those silly jokes, and so on. Recognition is what allows us to go beyond the information given.

What attributes of an object do we use to recognize it? Shape, size, color, texture, orientation, and so on? While all of these attributes may make some contribution, shape appears to play the critical role. We can recognize a cup, for example, regardless of whether it is large or small (a variation in size), or brown or white (a variation in color), or smooth or bumpy (a texture variation), or presented upright or tilted slightly (an orientation variation). In contrast, our ability to recognize a cup is strikingly affected by variations in shape; if part of the cup's shape is occluded, we may not recognize it at all. One piece of evidence for the importance of shape to recognition is that we can recognize many objects about as well from simple line drawings, which preserve only the shapes of the objects, as from detailed color photographs, which preserve many attributes of the objects (Biederman & Ju, 1988).

The critical question then becomes: How do we use the shape of an object to assign it to its appropriate category? In dealing with this question, first we focus on simple objects like letters of the alphabet, and later consider natural objects like animals and furniture.

## Early Stages of Recognition

Following Marr (1982), we may distinguish between *early* and *late* stages in recognizing an object. In early stages, the perceptual system uses information on the retina, particularly variations in intensity, to describe the object in terms of primitive components like lines, edges, and angles. The system uses these primitive components to construct a description of the object itself. In later stages, the system compares the object's description to shape descriptions of various categories of objects stored in visual memory and selects the best match. To recognize a particular object as the letter B, for example, is to say that the object's shape matches that of B's better than it matches that of other letters. For now, our concern is with the early stages, which construct the shape description of the object.

**FEATURE DETECTORS IN THE CORTEX**   Much of what is known about the primitive features of object perception comes from studies of other species (cats, monkeys) that use single-cell recordings in the visual cortex (refer back to Figure 4-4). These studies examine the sensitivity of specific cortical neurons when different stimuli are presented to the regions of the retina associated with these neurons; such a retinal region is called a **receptive field** of a cortical neuron. These single-cell studies were pioneered by Hubel and Wiesel (1968), who shared a Nobel prize in 1981 for their research.

Hubel and Wiesel identified three types of cells in the visual cortex that can be distinguished by the features to which they respond. **Simple cells** respond when the eye is exposed to a line stimulus (such as a thin bar or straight edge between a dark and a light region) at a particular orientation and position within their receptive field. Figure 5-11 illustrates how a simple cell will respond to a vertical bar and to bars tilted away from the vertical. The response decreases as the orientation varies from the optimal one. Other simple cells are tuned to other orientations and positions. A **complex cell** also responds to a bar or edge in a particular orientation, but it does not require that the stimulus be at a particular place within its receptive field. A complex cell responds to the stimulus anywhere within its receptive field, and it responds continuously as the stimulus is moved across its receptive

**FIGURE 5-11**

**Response of a Simple Cell** *This figure illustrates the response of a simple cortical cell to a bar of light. The stimulus is on the top, the response on the bottom; each vertical spike on the bottom corresponds to one nerve impulse. When there is no stimulus, only an occasional impulse is recorded. When the stimulus is turned on, the cell may or may not respond, depending on the position and orientation of the light bar. For this cell a horizontal bar produces no change in response, a bar at 45 degrees produces a small change, and a vertical bar produces a very large change.*

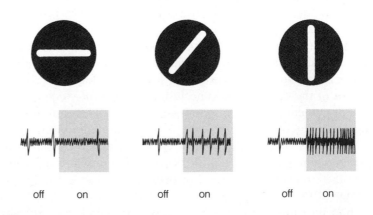

field. **Hypercomplex cells** require not only that the stimulus be in a particular orientation, but also that it be of a particular length. If a stimulus is extended beyond the optimal length, the response will decrease and may cease entirely. Since Hubel and Wiesel's initial reports, investigators have found cells that respond to shape features other than single bars and edges; for example, hypercomplex cells that respond to corners or angles of a specific length (DeValois & DeValois, 1980; Shapley & Lennie, 1985).

All of the cells described above are referred to as **feature detectors.** Because the edges, bars, corners, and angles to which these detectors respond can be used to approximate many shapes, the feature detectors might be thought of as the building blocks of shape perception. As we will see later, though, this proposal seems more true of simple shapes like letters than of complex shapes like those of tables and tigers.

**BEHAVIORAL INDICATORS OF FEATURES** In addition to single-cell recordings, researchers have developed behavioral tests of primitive features of objects that can be used with humans. One of the best-known techniques was devised by Treisman (for example, Treisman & Gormican, 1988). On each trial of the task, subjects are presented an array of items and have to decide as quickly as possible whether the array contains a target. For example, the target might be a curve and the nontargets straight lines, as illustrated in Figure 5-12. What varies from trial to trial is the number of nontargets—which can be between 3 and 30—and the question of interest is how this number affects the time to detect the target. If the target is defined by a primitive feature, a viewer might be able to search an array for it in parallel, rather than examining each nontarget in series. Consequently, the number of nontargets should have no effect on the time to detect a primitive feature. This is exactly what happens with arrays like that in Figure 5-12, which suggests that curvature is a primitive feature of objects. Phenomenologically, the curve seems to "pop out" of the array; for this reason, a demonstration of parallel search in this task is referred to as the **pop-out effect.**

Treisman has found pop-out effects for a number of other features. Two such features are the length of a line (a long line pops out from an array of short ones) and the amount of brightness contrast between neighboring dots (a high contrast pair pops out). These two features, like curvature, could well play a role in determining shape. Other features that pass the pop-out test, though, seem to have little to do with shape. Examples include color and orientation. These results indicate that the primitive features of objects are simple properties that characterize points and lines, with some but not all of these properties being related to shape.

**RELATIONS BETWEEN FEATURES** There is more to a description of a shape than just its features: relations between features must also be specified. The importance of such relations is illustrated in Figure 5-13. The features of a printed T include a vertical line and a horizontal line, but unless these lines are combined in the right way, the resulting pattern is not a T. The description of a T must include mention of the fact that the horizontal line is attached to the top of the vertical line at its center. It is this kind of relation between features that the Gestalt psychologists had in mind when they cautioned psychologists years ago that "the whole is greater than the sum of its parts."

A relation between features (for example, "horizontal line attached to top of vertical line at its center") is clearly not a primitive feature, and conse-

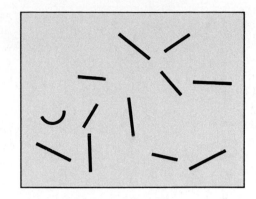

**FIGURE 5-12**
**Searching for a Curve** *The time it takes to find the curve does not depend on the number of straight lines surrounding it.* (After Treisman & Gormican, 1988)

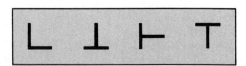

**FIGURE 5-13**
**Relations between Features** *All forms include the features of a vertical line and a horizontal line, but only the right-most form has the relation between features characteristic of the letter T.*

quently we would expect it to fail the pop-out test. And fail it does. When subjects are instructed to search for a target T embedded in a background of Ls, the time to find the target increases with the number of nontargets (Cave & Wolfe, 1989).

## The Matching Stage and Connectionist Models

Now that we have some idea of how an object's shape is described, we can consider how that description is matched to shape descriptions stored in memory to find the best match.

**SIMPLE NETWORKS**   Much of the research on the matching stage has used simple patterns, specifically handwritten or printed letters or words. Figure 5-14 illustrates a proposal about how we store shape descriptions of letters. The basic idea is that letters are described in terms of certain features, and that knowledge about what features go with what letter is contained in a network of connections (hence the term, **connectionist models**). What is appealing about connectionist models is that it is easy to conceive how these networks could be realized in an actual nervous system with its array of inter-connected neurons and receptors. Thus, *connectionism* offers a bridge between a model of how the mind might work and a neural model of how the brain works.

The bottom level of the network in Figure 5-14 contains the features—ascending diagonal, descending diagonal, vertical line, and right-facing curve, for example—and the top level contains the letters themselves. A connection between a feature and a letter means that the feature is part of the letter. The fact that the connections have arrowheads at their ends means they are *excitatory* connections; if the feature is activated, the activation spreads to the letter (in a manner analogous to how electrical impulses spread in a network of neurons).

The network in Figure 5-14 tells us that the category of K is described by an ascending diagonal, a descending diagonal, and a vertical line; Rs are described by a descending diagonal, a vertical line, and a right-facing curve, and Ps are described by a vertical line and a right-facing curve. (To keep the discussion simple, we will ignore relations between features.) To see how this network can be used to recognize (or match) a letter, consider what happens when the letter K is presented. It will activate the features of ascending diagonal, descending diagonal, and vertical line. All three of these features will activate the category K; two of them—the descending diagonal and vertical line—will activate the category R; and one of them—the verti-

**FIGURE 5-14**
**A Simple Network** *The bottom level of the network contains the features (ascending diagonal, descending diagonal, vertical line, and right-facing curve), the top level contains the letters, and a connection between a feature and a letter means the feature is part of the letter. Because the connections are excitatory, when a feature is activated the activation spreads to the letter.*

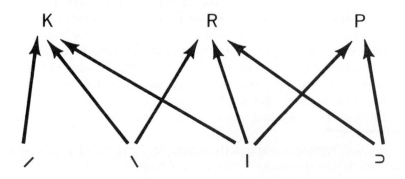

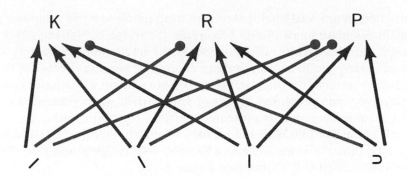

cal line—will activate P. Only the category K has all of its features activated, and consequently it will be selected as the best match.

The above model is too simple to account for many aspects of recognition. To see what the model lacks, consider what happens when the letter R is presented. It activates the features of descending diagonal, vertical line, and right-facing curve. Now both the categories R and P will have all their features activated, and the perceptual system has no way of deciding which of the two categories provides a better match. What the system needs to know to choose between these categories is that the presence of a descending diagonal means the input *cannot* be a P. This kind of negative knowledge is included in the augmented network in Figure 5-15. This network has everything the preceding one had, plus *inhibitory* connections (symbolized by solid circles at their ends) between features and letters that do not contain these features. When a feature is connected to a letter by an inhibitory connection, activating the feature *decreases* activation of the letter. When R is presented to the network in Figure 5-15, the descending diagonal sends inhibition to the category P, thereby decreasing its overall level of activation; now the category R will receive the most activation and consequently will be selected as the best match.

The preceding discussion illustrates some critical properties of connectionist networks, which many have claimed offer a revolutionary new way of understanding cognitive processes (Rumelhart & McClelland, 1986; McClelland & Rumelhart, 1986). The networks in Figures 5-14 and 5-15 are composed of only two kinds of entities: a) *nodes* designating features or patterns (such as the node for an upright line, or that for the letter R); and b) connections between nodes that are either excitatory or inhibitory. All connectionist networks are restricted to just nodes and connections.* Furthermore, the networks in Figures 5-14 and 5-15 allow an object to be compared to all stored categories *simultaneously* (the feature information is passed to all letter nodes at once); this is in contrast to comparing the object to the stored categories one at a time or *sequentially*. Simultaneous processing (also called **parallel processing**) is characteristic of connectionist models.

**NETWORKS WITH TOP-DOWN ACTIVATION** The basic idea behind the model we just considered—that a letter must be described by the features it lacks as well as the features it contains—was originally proposed by

---

*Each connection is usually accompanied by a number, or *weight*, indicating the strength of the connection.

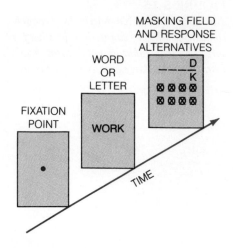

**FIGURE 5-16**
**Perception of Letters and Words** *This figure illustrates the sequence of events in an experiment that compares the perceptibility of a letter presented alone or in the context of a word. First, subjects saw a fixation point, followed by a word or a single letter, which was present for only a few milliseconds. Then the experimenter presented a stimulus that contained a visual mask in the positions where the letters had been, plus two response alternatives. The subjects' task was to decide which of the two alternatives occurred in the word or letter presented earlier. (After Reicher, 1969)*

researchers in artificial intelligence who were trying to write computer programs to simulate human letter perception (Selfridge & Neisser, 1960). Although the ideas were relatively successful for a time, ultimately they proved inadequate to explain findings about how context affects our ability to perceive letters. In particular, they could not explain why a letter is easier to perceive when presented as part of a word than when presented alone. Thus, if subjects are briefly presented a display containing either the single letter K or the word WORK, and are then asked whether the last letter was a K or a D, they are more accurate when the display contained a word than when it contained only a letter (see Figure 5-16).

To account for this result, our network of feature-letter connections has to be altered in a few ways. First, we have to add a level of words to our network, and along with it excitatory and inhibitory connections that go from letters to words (see Figure 5-17). In addition, we also have to add excitatory connections that go from words down to letters; these *top-down* connections explain why a letter is more perceptible when presented briefly in the context of a word than when presented briefly alone. When R is presented alone, for example, the features of vertical line, descending diagonal, and right-facing curve are activated, and this activation spreads to the node for R. Because the letter was presented very briefly, not all the features may have been fully activated, and the activation culminating at the R node may not be sufficient for recognition to occur. In contrast, when R is presented in RED, there is activation not only from the features of R to the R node, but also from the features of E and D to their nodes; all of these partially activated letters then partially activate the RED node, which in turn sends activation back to its letters via its top-down connections.

The upshot is that there is an additional source of activation for R when it is presented in a word—namely, that coming down from the word—and this is why it is easier to recognize a letter in a word than when it is presented alone. Many other findings about letter and word patterns have been shown to be consistent with this connectionist model (McClelland & Rumelhart, 1981).

**FIGURE 5-17**
**Network with Top-Down Activation**
*The network contains excitatory and inhibitory connections between letters and words (as well as between features and letters), and some of the excitatory connections go from words to letters.*

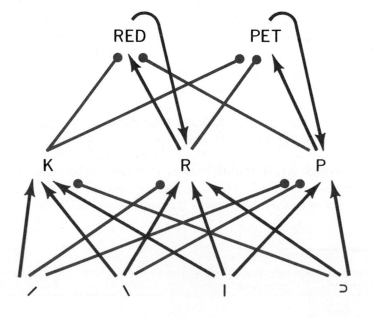

## Recognizing Natural Objects and Top-Down Processing

We know quite a bit about the recognition of letters and words, but what about more natural objects—animals, plants, people, furniture, and clothing?

**FEATURES OF NATURAL OBJECTS** The shape features of natural objects are more complex than lines and curves, and more like simple geometric forms. The features must be such that they can combine to form the shape of any recognizable object (just as lines and curves can combine to form any letter). The features of objects must also be such that they can be determined or constructed from more primitive features, such as lines and curves, because primitive features are the only information the system initially has available. These criteria have guided the search for a possible set of object features.

One proposal is that the features of objects include a number of geometric forms, such as cylinders, cones, blocks, and wedges, as illustrated in Figure 5-18a. These features are referred to as **geons** (an neologism of *geometric ions*), and they were developed by Biederman (1987). Biederman argues that a set of 36 geons like those in Figure 5-18a, combined according to a small set of spatial relations, is sufficient to describe the shapes of all objects that people can possibly recognize. To appreciate this point, note that the number of possible objects composed of just two geons is $36 \times 36$ (you can form a possible object by combining any two geons—see Figure 5-18b) while the number of possible three-geon objects is $36 \times 36 \times 36$. The sum of these two numbers is already on the order of 30,000, and we have yet to consider objects made up of 4 or more geons. Furthermore, geons like those in Figure 5-18a can be distinguished solely in terms of primitive features. For example, geon 2 in Figure 5-18a, the cube, differs from geon 3, the cylinder, in that the cube has straight edges whereas the cylinder has curved edges; straight and curved edges are primitive features.

Evidence that geons are features comes from experiments in which subjects try to recognize pictured objects that are presented briefly. The general finding is that recognition of an object is good to the extent the geons of the

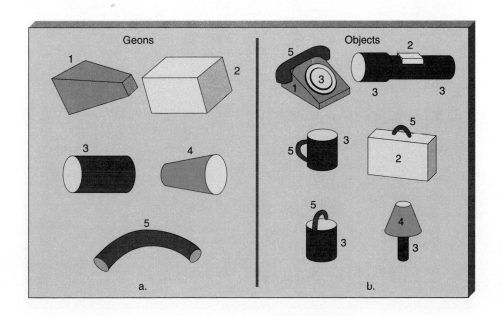

**FIGURE 5-18**
**A Possible Set of Features (Geons) for Natural Objects** *(a) Wedges, cubes, cylinders, and cones may be features of complex objects. (b) When the features (geons) are combined, they form natural objects. Note that when the arc (geon 5) is connected to the side of the cylinder (geon 3), it forms a cup; when connected to the top of the cylinder, it forms a pail. (After Biederman, 1990).*

object can be recovered. In one study, part of the shape of an object was deleted where this deletion either interfered with recovering the geons (see the right column of Figure 5-19) or not (middle column of Figure 5-19). Recognition of the objects was much better when there was no interference with the geons. Another experiment compared the recognition of simple and complex objects (see Figure 5-20). Fewer errors are committed on a complex object like an elephant, which is composed of many geons, than on a simple object like a lamp, which is composed of only a few geons. The more geons there are in an object, the more likely a few of them will be extracted, even when the object is briefly presented, and even a few geons can suffice to recognize a complex object.

As usual, the description of an object includes not just its features but also the relations between them. This is evident in Figure 5-18b. When the arc is connected to the side of the cylinder, it forms a cup; when connected to the top of the cylinder, it forms a pail. Once the description of an object's shape is constructed, it is compared to an array of geon descriptions stored in memory to find the best match. This matching process between the description of an object's shape and the array of descriptions stored in memory resembles the process described earlier in this chapter for letters and words (Hummel & Biederman, 1992).

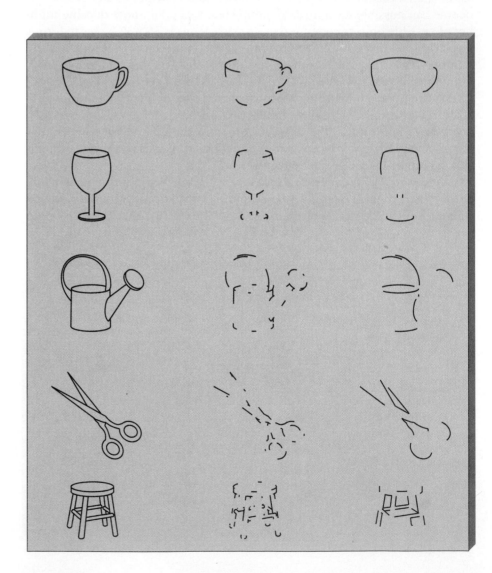

**FIGURE 5-19**
**Object Recognition and Geon Recovery** *Items used in experiments on object recognition. The left column shows the original intact versions of the objects. The middle column shows versions of the objects where regions have been deleted, but the geons are still recoverable. The right column shows versions of the objects where regions have been deleted, and the geons are not recoverable. Recognition is better for the middle versions than for the rightmost versions.* (After Biederman, 1987)

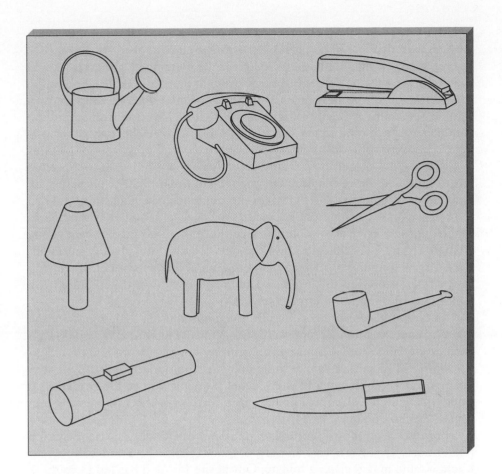

**FIGURE 5-20**
**Simple and Complex Objects** *Line drawings of objects varying in complexity, as measured by number of geons. As examples: the lamp contains 2 geons, the flashlight 3 geons, the watering can 4 geons, and the elephant at least 7 geons. The more geons it contained, the easier the object was to recognize when presented briefly.* (After Biederman, 1987)

**TOP-DOWN PROCESSES** A key distinction in perception is that between bottom-up and top-down processes. **Bottom-up processes** are driven solely by the input, whereas **top-down processes** are driven by a person's knowledge and expectations. To illustrate, recognizing that an object is a lamp on the basis of solely its geon description involves only bottom-up processes; one starts with primitive features of the input, determines the geon configuration of the input, and then compares this input description to stored object descriptions. In contrast, recognizing that the object is a lamp partly on the basis of its being on a nighttable next to a bed involves some top-down processes; one brings to bear information other than that in the input. While most of the processes considered thus far in this chapter are bottom-up ones, top-down processes also play a major role in object perception.

Top-down processes are what lie behind the powerful effects that context has on our perception of objects and people. You expect to see your chemistry study-mate Sarah at the library every weekday at 3 P.M., and when she enters the library at that moment you hardly need to look to tell that it's her. Your prior knowledge has led to a powerful expectation, and little input is needed for recognition. But should Sarah suddenly appear in your hometown during Christmas vacation, you may have substantial trouble recognizing her. She is *out of context*—your expectations have been violated, and you must resort to extensive bottom-up processing to tell that it is in fact her (we experience this as "doing a double take"). As this example makes clear, when the context is appropriate (that is, it predicts the input object), it facilitates perception; when inappropriate, the context impairs perception.

**FIGURE 5-21**
**Ambiguous Stimulus** *An ambiguous drawing that can be seen either as a young woman or as an old woman. Most people see the old woman first. The young woman is turning away, and we see the left side of her face. Her chin is the old woman's nose, and her necklace is the old woman's mouth.* (After Boring, 1930)

The effects of context are particularly striking when the stimulus object is *ambiguous*, that is, can be perceived in more than one way. An ambiguous figure is presented in Figure 5-21; it can be perceived either as an old woman or as a young woman (though the old woman is more likely to be seen initially). If you have been looking at unambiguous pictures that resemble the young woman in Figure 5-21 (that is, if young women are the context), you will tend to see the young woman first in the ambiguous picture. This effect of *temporal context* is illustrated with another set of pictures in Figure 5-22. Look at the pictures as you would look at a comic strip, from left to right and top to bottom. The pictures in the middle of the series are ambiguous. If you view the figures in the sequence just suggested, you will tend to see these ambiguous pictures as a man's face. If you view the figures in the opposite order, you will tend to see the ambiguous pictures as a young woman. Figure 5-23 illustrates how the *spatial context* provided by surrounding symbols influences our perception of an ambiguous symbol. If we look at the figure from top to bottom, we tend to see a 13 in the middle; if we look from left to right, we tend to see a B.

The stimulus object need not be ambiguous in order to demonstrate the effect of context. Suppose a person is first shown a picture of a scene, and is then briefly presented a picture of an unambiguous object to identify; identification will be more accurate if the object is appropriate to the scene. For example, after looking at a kitchen scene, a subject will correctly identify a briefly presented loaf of bread more often than he or she will a briefly presented mailbox (Palmer, 1975).

Because of top-down processing, our motives and desires can affect our perceptions. If we are very hungry, a quick glance at a red ball on our kitchen table may register a tomato. Our desire for food has led us to think about food, and these expectations have combined with the input (a red, round object) to yield the percept of a tomato. Our motives can also have a pernicious effect on perception. If we believe a man to be a child molester, for example, we are more likely to misperceive his innocent touching of a child as sexual.

Context effects and top-down processing also occur with more mundane materials, like letters and words. Earlier we mentioned that a letter is easier to perceive when presented as part of a word than when presented alone. This is a context effect, in that the word provides a context for the individ-

**FIGURE 5-22**
**Effect of Temporal Context** *What you see here depends on the order in which you look at the pictures. The pictures in the middle of the series are ambiguous. If you have been looking at pictures of a man's face, they will appear to be distorted faces. If you have been looking at pictures of a young woman, they will look like a young woman.* (After Fisher, 1967)

ual letter. A related context effect is that we can identify words more rapidly in the context of an appropriate sentence than when presented alone. Consider the sentence, "He swung the bat and hit the _____"; the last word is recognized as "ball" almost before the eye fixates it.

More generally, top-down processing plays a major role in reading. When we read, we do not scan a line of text in a smooth continuous motion. Rather, our eyes are still for a brief period, then jump to another position on the line, are still for another brief period, then jump again (perhaps to a different line), and so on. The periods during which the eyes are still, called *fixations*, are when our visual system extracts information. Both the number of fixations we make, and the durations of these fixations, are greatly influenced by how much we know about the text, and hence by the amount of top-down processing we can invoke. When the material is unfamiliar—say, unusual scientific material—there is little top-down processing. In such cases, we tend to fixate every word, except for certain function words like "a," "of," "the," and so on. As the material becomes more familiar, we can bring to bear our prior knowledge in top-down processes, and our fixations become wider spaced and shorter (Rayner, 1978; Just & Carpenter, 1980).

## Role of Attention

Most of the time we are bombarded with so many stimuli that we are unable to recognize all of them. Although a few objects intrude into our consciousness no matter what we do, within limits we select what we perceive. As you sit reading, stop for a moment, close your eyes, and attend to the various stimuli that are reaching you. Notice, for example, the tightness of your left shoe. What sounds do you hear? Is there an odor in the air? You probably were not aware of these inputs before, because you had not selected them for recognition. The process by which we select is called **selective attention.**

**SELECTIVE LOOKING** How exactly do we direct our attention to objects of interest? The simplest means is by physically reorienting our sensory receptors so as to favor those objects. For vision, this means moving our eyes until the object of interest falls on the most sensitive region of the retina.

Studies of visual attention often involve observing a subject looking at a picture or scene. If we watch the subject's eyes it is evident that they are not stationary; rather, they are scanning. As was the case in reading, scanning is not a smooth continuous motion, but, rather, it involves successive fixations. There are a number of techniques for recording these eye movements. The simplest method is to monitor the eyes with a television camera in such a way that what the eye is gazing at is reflected on the cornea of the eye so it appears on television superimposed on the image of the eye. From this superimposed image, the experimenter can determine the point in the scene where the eye is fixated. The procedure provides an unobtrusive method for monitoring eye movements, and researchers using the procedure can replay the television tape to measure the duration of each fixation.

The eye movements used in scanning a picture ensure that different parts of the picture will fall on the fovea so that all of its details can be seen. (As noted in the previous chapter, the fovea has the best resolution.) The points on which the eyes fixate are not evenly distributed, nor are they random. They tend to be places that are most informative about the picture, places where important features are located. For example, in scanning a

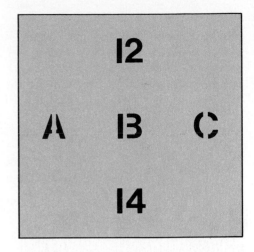

**FIGURE 5-23**
**Effect of Spatial Context** *The figure in the center is ambiguous, and the way we see it depends on whether we are attending to the row or the column.*

**FIGURE 5-24**
**Eye Movements in Viewing a Picture**
*Next to the picture of the young girl is a record of the eye movements made by a subject inspecting the picture.* (After Yarbus, 1967)

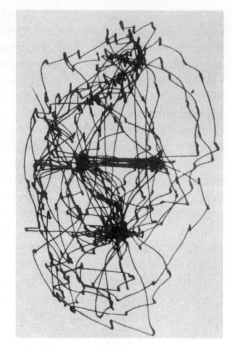

photograph of a face, many fixations are in the regions corresponding to the eyes, nose, and mouth) (see Figure 5-24). Perceiving the picture requires the perceptual system to combine these various glimpses into a single representation of the scene, a process akin to assembling a picture from a series of snapshots of its parts.

There are objects in which the various glimpses cannot be combined into a single representation: such *impossible figures* are illustrated in Figure 5-25. In either of these figures, recognition seems normal as we attend to each part, but the different glances will not fuse into a single, coherent picture. Consider the bottom object in Figure 5-25. When we attend to the right part, we see something like a perspective drawing of three rectangular beams joined together; when we attend to the left part, we see three round rods; when we try to put the products of our eye movements together, they will not gel. The problem is clearly one of integrating separate snapshots, for if the figure is made small enough that its image fits in the fovea, it tends to lose both its depth and its impossible quality, and it appears simply as lines on a flat surface (Hochberg, 1978).

**SELECTIVE LISTENING** In audition, the closest thing to eye movements is moving our head so that our ears are directed at the source of interest. This mechanism of attention is of limited use in many situations, though. Consider, for example, a crowded party. The sounds of many voices bombard our ears, and their sources are not far enough apart that reorienting our ears would allow us to selectively follow one conversation. We are able, however, to use purely mental means to selectively attend to the desired message. Some of the cues that we use to do this are the direction of the sound, the lip movements of the speaker, and the particular voice characteristics of the speaker (pitch, speed, and intonation). Even in the absence of any of these cues, we can, with difficulty, select one of two messages to follow on the basis of its meaning.

Research on what is called the *cocktail party phenomenon* indicates that we remember very little of messages that we do not attend to. A common procedure in this research is to put earphones on a subject and play one message through one ear and another message through the other ear. The subject is asked to repeat (or *shadow*) one of the messages as it is heard. After proceeding in this way for a few minutes, the messages are turned off and the listener is asked about the unshadowed message. The person can report very little about it. The listener's remarks are usually limited to the physical characteristics of the sound in the unshadowed ear—whether the voice was high or low, male or female, and so forth; he or she can say almost nothing about the content of the message (Moray, 1969).

The fact that we can report so little about unattended messages initially led researchers to the idea that nonattended stimuli are filtered out completely (Broadbent, 1958). However, there is now considerable evidence that our perceptual system processes nonattended stimuli to some extent, even though they never reach consciousness. One piece of evidence for partial processing of nonattended stimuli is that we are very likely to hear the sound of our own name even when spoken softly in a nonattended conversation. This could not happen if the entire nonattended message (such as another person's conversation across the room) were lost at lower levels of the perceptual system. Hence, a lack of attention does not block messages entirely, but rather *attenuates* them, much like a volume control that is turned down but not off (Treisman, 1969).

**EARLY VERSUS LATE SELECTION** When does selectivity occur? Does it happen in the early stages of recognition—when constructing a description of the input—or only during the later stages—when comparing the input's descriptions to those of stored objects? The issue is important because it concerns whether we can selectively ignore something before we know what it means—**early selection**—or only after we know its meaning—**late selection**.

There is now evidence for both early and late selection. Some evidence for early selection comes from studies that record electrical activity in the auditory cortex. These studies take as their starting point the findings that any auditory stimulus will trigger a sequence of brain waves, some of which occur early and are known to reflect processes prior to the determination of a stimulus' meaning. Thus, roughly 100 milliseconds after the onset of stimulus, there is a negative wave that is known to be insensitive to variations in meaning (hardly surprising given how early the wave occurs). This wave has been measured when human subjects are performing attentional tasks. Consider an experiment in which in one condition subjects monitored one ear for targets, whereas in another condition they monitored both ears for targets. In the latter condition, subjects should have had to divide their attention, that is, divide their selectivity. If selectivity occurs early, the difference between conditions should have been reflected in the early brain wave described above. In fact, the magnitude of this wave was less when a target occurred in the divided attention condition than when it occurred in the other condition (Hillyard, 1985).

Evidence for late selection comes from experiments that use strictly behavioral techniques, and that try to show that the meaning of nonattended stimuli gets through. In one experiment, subjects wearing earphones listened to sentences spoken to one ear and ignored everything said in the

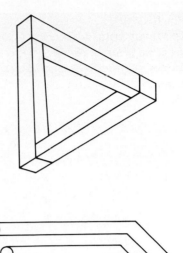

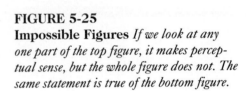

**FIGURE 5-25**
**Impossible Figures** *If we look at any one part of the top figure, it makes perceptual sense, but the whole figure does not. The same statement is true of the bottom figure.*

# Breakdown of Recognition

Recognizing an object is usually so automatic and effortless a process that we take it for granted. But the process can break down if people suffer brain damage (due to accidents or diseases like strokes). The general term for disorders in recognition is *agnosia*.

*ASSOCIATIVE AGNOSIA* Of particular interest is a type of agnosia called **associative agnosia**. This is a syndrome in which patients with damage to particular regions of the cortex have difficulty recognizing objects only when they are presented visually. For example, the patient may be unable to name a comb when presented a picture of it, but can name it when allowed to touch it. The deficit is exemplified by the following case:

> For the first three weeks in the hospital the patient could not identify common objects presented visually and did not know what was on his plate until he tasted it. He identified objects immediately on touching them [But] when shown a stethoscope, he described it as "a long chord with a round thing at the end," and asked if it could be a watch. He identified a can opener as "could be a key." Asked to name a cigarette lighter, he said, "I don't know." He said he was "not sure" when shown a toothbrush. Asked to identify a comb, he said, "I don't know." For a pipe, he said, "some type of utensil, I'm not sure." Shown a key, he said, "I don't know what that is; perhaps a file or a tool of some sort." (Reubens & Benson, 1971)

What aspects of object recognition have broken down in associative agnosia? Since these patients often do well on visual tasks other than recognition—such as drawing objects or determining whether two pictured objects match—the breakdown is likely to be in the later stages of recognition, where the input object is matched to stored object descriptions. One possibility is that the stored object descriptions have been lost or obscured (Damasio, 1985). A related possibility presupposes that recognition is accomplished by a connectionist network, and assumes the problem is due to an impairment in the nodes that encode visual knowledge (Farah, 1990).

*CATEGORY SPECIFIC DEFICITS* Some patients with associative agnosia have problems recognizing certain categories but not others. These category-specific deficits are of considerable interest because they may tell us something new about how normal recognition works.

The most frequent category-specific deficit is a loss just of the ability to recognize faces, called **prosopagnosia**. When this deficit arises, there is

other ear. The subjects were further required to paraphrase the sentence heard on the attended ear. Some of these sentences contained an ambiguous word, as in "The man walked by the bank," where "bank" could mean either a financial institution or a place by a river. How subjects paraphrased the sentence indicates how they interpreted the ambiguous word. At the same time the ambiguous word was occurring at the attended ear, a word related to one of its two meanings, say "river," was spoken to the unattended ear. Subjects' paraphrases of the attended sentence was biased by what was presented at the unattended ear: for example, with "river" on the unattended ear, a likely paraphrase might be "The man strolled by the water." This effect could arise only if subjects were determining the meaning of unattended words. Hence, selection in this task was accomplished late (Lackner & Garrett, 1973).

**CONJOINING FEATURES** Thus far we have discussed the role of attention in selecting one object or message from another, or selecting one part of an object from another part. But attention does more than select. It also conjoins, or "glues," the features of an object together. This idea can best be understood in reference to the case of looking *very briefly* at an array of objects, such as pieces of furniture in a living room. Even without paying attention, you may quickly register that there is a couch in the room, and that there is something gold in the room, but it takes a bit of attention to determine that it is the couch that is gold. That is, it takes attention to allocate color and other properties to shapes (Treisman & Schmidt, 1982).

always brain damage in the right hemisphere and often some lesser degree of damage in homologous regions of the left hemisphere. The deficit is illustrated by the following case:

> He could not identify his medical attendants. "You must be a doctor because of your white coat, but I don't know which one you are. I'll know if you speak." He failed to identify his wife during visiting hours . . . He failed to identify pictures of Churchill, Hitler, and Marilyn Monroe. When confronted with such portraits he would proceed deductively, searching for the 'critical' detail which would yield the answer. (Pallis, 1955)

Another kind of category-specific deficit involves an impairment in the ability to recognize most living things while recognition of nonliving things is relatively intact, or vice versa (one can recognize living things but not nonliving things). In these cases, "living things" include animals, plants, and foods, whereas "nonliving things" typically include human-made objects, particularly manipulable ones like tools. Thus, one patient with this kind of category-specific disorder might be unable to name pictures of familiar barnyard animals, but have no problem with household tools; another patient might show the reverse pattern.

Two of the suggested explanations of category-specific deficits have implications for normal recognition. One hypothesis is that the normal recognition system is organized around different classes of objects—one subsystem for faces, another for animals, a third for small objects, and so on—and these subsystems are localized in different regions of the brain. If a patient suffers only restricted brain damage, he or she may show a loss of one subsystem, but not others. Brain damage in a specific part of the right hemisphere, for example, might disrupt the face-recognition subsystem, but leave the other subsystems intact. A second proposal emphasizes the properties that are used to identify members of categories. According to this hypothesis, categories differ with respect to the kinds of properties that are used to identify their members. Thus, most objects (living or nonliving) are recognized mainly on the basis of their shape, but this is not true of faces, which tend to be recognized in terms of specific parts and their relations. Prosopagnosia, then, may involve a breakdown in the analysis of certain specific parts, while leaving shape analysis intact. Similarly, human-made objects often display straight edges, while animals and plants often have uneven shape outlines. Patients who cannot recognize living things but can recognize nonliving ones may have an impairment in analyzing irregular shapes but not regular ones; patients who manifest the opposite problem may have an impairment in analyzing regular shapes but not irregular ones (Damasio, 1985).

# Perceptual Constancies

We have emphasized that two major goals of our perceptual system are to determine *what* is out there and *where* it is, that is, to determine the identities and locations of the objects in our visual field. But there seems to be another goal of our perceptual system—to keep the appearance of objects constant even though their impressions on our retinas are changing. We have evolved so that we represent—and experience—objects as they really are in the world (real objects are constant in shape, size, color, and brightness), not as they impinge on our eyeball.

By and large, we perceive an object as remaining relatively constant regardless of changes in lighting, the position from which we view it, or its distance from us. Your car does not appear to grow larger as you walk toward it, distort in shape as you walk around it, or change in color when you view it in artificial light, even though the image on your retina does undergo these changes. This tendency toward constancy is referred to as **perceptual constancy.** Although constancy is not perfect, it is a salient aspect of visual experience.

## Lightness and Color Constancy

When an object is illuminated it reflects a certain amount of the light. The amount reflected is related to the apparent *lightness* of the object. The phenomenon of **lightness constancy** refers to the fact that the perceived

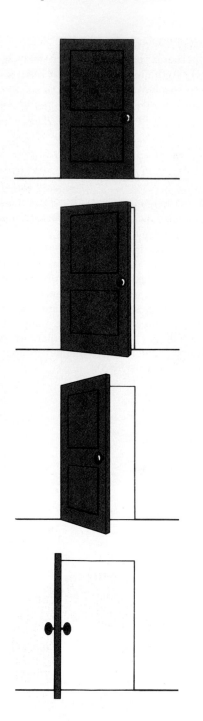

**FIGURE 5-26**
**Shape Constancy** *The various retinal images produced by an opening door are quite different, and yet we perceive a door of constant rectangular shape.*

lightness of a particular object may barely change even when the amount of reflected light changes dramatically. Thus, a black velvet shirt looks nearly as black in sunlight as in shadow, even though it reflects thousands of times more light when it is directly illuminated by the sun.

Although the above effect holds under normal circumstances, a change in the surroundings can destroy it. Attach a piece of the black velvet shirt to a white board and shine a bright light on both, and the velvet still looks black. So far nothing new. But now place an opaque black screen with a small opening in it between you and the velvet so that you can see only a small patch of the velvet. This screen reduces what you see through the opening to just the actual light reflected from the velvet, independent of its surroundings. Now the velvet looks white because the light that reaches your eye through the hole is more intense than that from the screen itself. This demonstration provides a clue as to why the lightness of an object remains constant. When we perceive objects in natural settings, several other objects are usually visible. Lightness constancy depends on the relations among the intensities of light reflected from the different objects. Thus, normally we continue to see black velvet as black even in sunlight because the velvet continues to reflect a lesser percentage of its light than does its surroundings. It is the relative percentage of light reflected that determines its brightness.

A similar story holds for color. The tendency for an object to remain roughly the same color with different light sources is called **color constancy.** As was the case with lightness constancy, color constancy can be eliminated by removing the object from its background. For example, if you look at a ripe tomato through a tube that obscures the surroundings and the nature of the object, the tomato may appear any color—blue, green, or pink—depending on the wavelengths reflecting from it. Hence color constancy, like lightness constancy, depends on a heterogeneous background (Land, 1977; Maloney & Wandell, 1986).

## Shape and Location Constancy

When a door swings toward us, the shape of its retinal image goes through a series of changes (see Figure 5-26). The door's rectangular shape produces a trapezoidal image, with the edge toward us wider than the hinged edge; then the trapezoid grows thinner, until finally all that is projected on the retina is a vertical bar the thickness of the door. Nevertheless, we perceive an unchanging door swinging open. The fact that the perceived shape is constant while the retinal image changes is an example of **shape constancy.**

Still another constancy involves the locations of objects. Despite the fact that a series of changing images strike the retina as we move, the positions of fixed objects appear to remain constant. We tend to take this **location constancy** for granted, but it requires that the perceptual system take account of both our movements and the changing retinal images. Consider the case in which we move our eyes over a static scene. The image moves across the receptors in the same way it would if the objects in the scene moved, yet we do not perceive movement in the scene. The visual system must receive information from the brain that the eyes are moving, and it must take this information into account in interpreting image motion. If your visual system is informed that your eyes just moved 5 degrees to the left, it subtracts this out from the visual signal. Some of this accounting is wired into the brain. Using single-cell recordings, researchers have found

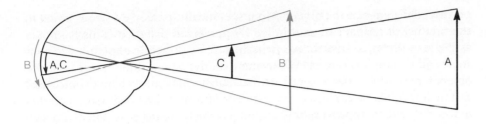

**FIGURE 5-27**
**Retinal Image Size** *This figure illustrates the geometric relationship between the physical size of an object and the size of its image on the retina. Arrows A and B represent objects of the same size, but one is twice as far from the eye as the other. As a result, the retinal image of A is about half the size of the retinal image of B. The object represented by arrow C is smaller than that of A, but its location closer to the eye causes it to produce a retinal image of the same size as A.*

cells in the brain that respond only when an external object moves, not when the eye moves over a static object (Robinson & Wurtz, 1976).

Shape constancy and location constancy also have implications for our earlier discussion of the goals of localization and recognition. In general, the constancies make the tasks of localization and recognition easier. If an object appeared to change its location every time we moved our eyes, determining its depth (an important part of localization) might be exceedingly difficult. If the shape of an object changed every time it or we move, then the description of the object that we construct in the early stages of recognition would also change, and recognition might be an impossible task.

## Size Constancy

The most studied of all the constancies is **size constancy,** the fact that an object's size remains relatively constant no matter what its distance. As an object moves farther away from us, we generally do not see it as decreasing in size. Hold a quarter a foot in front of you and then move it out to arm's length. Does it appear to get smaller? Not noticeably so. Yet the retinal image of the quarter when it is 24 inches away is half the size of the retinal image of the quarter when it is 12 inches away (see Figure 5-27). We certainly do not perceive the quarter as becoming half its size as we move it an arm's length. Like other constancies, however, size constancy is not perfect; *very* distant objects appear to be smaller than the same objects close up, as any one knows who has looked down from a tall building or from an airplane in flight.

**DEPENDENCE ON DEPTH CUES**  The moving quarter example indicates that when we perceive the size of an object, we consider something in addition to the size of the retinal image. That additional something is the *perceived distance* of the object. As long ago as 1881, Emmert was able to show that size judgments depend on distance. Emmert used an ingenious method that involved judging the size of afterimages.

Emmert first had subjects fixate on the center of an image for about 1 minute (see Figure 5-28 for an example of such an image). Then subjects looked at a white screen and saw an afterimage. Their task was to judge the size of the afterimage; the independent variable was how far away the screen was. Because the retinal size of the afterimage was the same regardless of the distance of the screen, any variations in the judged size of the afterimage had to be due to its perceived distance. When the screen was far away, the afterimage looked large; when the screen was near, the afterimage looked small. Emmert's experiment is so easy to do that you can perform it on yourself.

Based on such experiments, Emmert proposed that the perceived size of an object increases with both: (a) the retinal size of the object; and (b) the

**FIGURE 5-28**
**Emmert's Experiment** *Hold the book at normal reading distance under good light. Fixate on the cross in the center of the figure for about 1 minute, then look at a distant wall. You will see an afterimage of the two circles that appears larger than the stimulus. Then look at a piece of paper held close to your eyes; the afterimage will appear smaller than the stimulus. If the afterimage fades, blinking can sometimes restore it.*

perceived distance of the object. More specifically, perceived size is equal to the product of retinal size multiplied by perceived distance. This is known as the **size-distance invariance principle.** The principle explains size constancy in the following way. When the distance to an object increases, the object's retinal size decreases; but if distance cues are present, perceived distance will increase. Hence, the product of retinal size and perceived distance will remain approximately constant, which means that perceived size will remain approximately constant. To illustrate: When a person walks away from you, the size of her image on your retina gets smaller, but her perceived distance gets larger; these two changes cancel each other out, and the net result is that your perception of the person's size remains relatively constant.

**ILLUSIONS** The size-distance principle seems to be fundamental to understanding a number of size illusions. (An illusion is a percept that is false or distorted; it differs from the state of affairs described by physical science with the aid of measuring instruments.) A good example of a size illusion is the moon illusion. When the moon is near the horizon, it looks as much as 50 percent larger than when it is at its zenith, even though in both locations the moon produces the same size retinal image. One explanation of this illusion is that the perceived distance to the horizon is judged to be greater than that to the zenith; hence, it is the greater perceived distance that leads to the greater perceived size (Holway & Boring, 1941).

Another size illusion is the **Ames room** (named after its inventor, Adelbert Ames). Figure 5-29 shows a view of how the Ames room looks to an observer seeing it through a peephole. When the boy is in the left-hand corner of the room (photograph on the left) he appears much smaller than when he is in the right-hand corner (photograph on the right). Yet it is the same boy in both pictures. Here we have a case in which size constancy has broken down. Why? The reason lies in the construction of the room. Although the room looks like a normal rectangular room to an observer seeing it through

**FIGURE 5-29**
**The Ames Room** *A view of how the Ames room looks to an observer viewing it through the peephole. The size of the boy and dog depends on which one is in the left-hand corner of the room and which one is in the right-hand corner. The room is designed to wreak havoc with our perceptions. Because of the perceived shape of the room, the relative sizes of the boy and the dog seem impossibly different. Yet it is the same boy and dog in both photographs.*

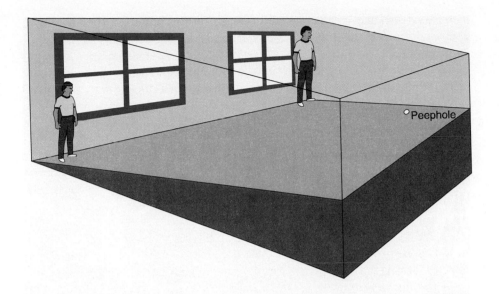

**FIGURE 5-30**
**True Shape of the Ames Room** *This figure shows the true shape of the Ames room. The boy on the left is actually almost twice as far away as the boy on the right; however, this difference in distance is not detected when the room is viewed through the peephole.* (After Goldstein, 1984)

the peephole, it is in fact shaped so that its left corner is almost twice as far from us as its right corner (see the diagram in Figure 5-30). Hence, the boy on the left is in fact much farther away than the one on the right, and consequently projects a smaller retinal image. We do not correct for this difference in distance, though, because we believe we are looking at a normal room and thus assume that both boys are at the same distance. In essence, our assumption that the room is normal blocks our usual application of the size-distance invariance principle, and consequently size constancy breaks down.

Although all of the examples of constancy we have described are visual, constancies occur in the other senses as well. For example, a person will hear the same tune if the frequencies of all its notes double. Whatever the sensory modality, constancies depend on relations between features of the stimulus—between retinal size and distance in the case of size constancy, between the intensity of two adjacent regions in the case of lightness constancy, and so forth. Somehow the perceptual system integrates these features to respond in a constant way, even though the individual features are changing.

## Perceptual Development

An age-old question about perception is whether our abilities to perceive are learned or innate—the familiar nature vs. nurture problem. Its investigation goes back to the philosophers of the seventeenth and eighteenth centuries. One group, the *nativists* (including Descartes and Kant), argued that we are born with the ability to perceive the way we do. In contrast, the *empiricists* (including Berkeley and Locke), maintained that we learn our ways of perceiving through experience with objects in the world. Contemporary psychologists believe that a fruitful integration of the empiricist and nativist viewpoints is possible. No one today doubts that both genetics and experience influence perception; rather, the goal is to pinpoint the contribution of each, and to spell out their interaction.

For the modern researcher, the question "Must we learn to perceive?" has given way to more specific questions: (a) What discriminatory capacity do infants have (which tells us something about inborn capacities), and how

*Testing the visual preferences of an infant*

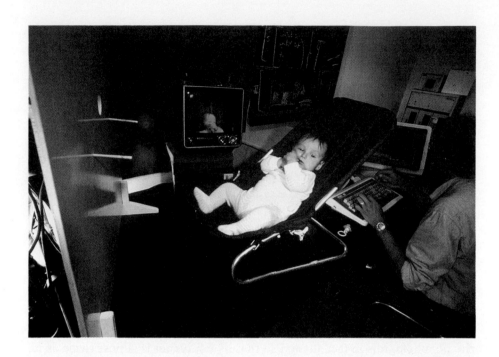

does this capacity change with age under normal rearing conditions? (b) If animals are reared under conditions that restrict what they can learn (referred to as **controlled stimulation**), what effects does this have on their later discriminatory capacity? (c) What effects does rearing under controlled conditions have on perceptual-motor coordination?

## Discrimination by Infants

Perhaps the most direct way to find out what perceptual capacities are inborn is to see what capacities an infant has. At first, you might think that the research should consider only newborns, because if a capacity is inborn it should be present from the first day of life. This idea turns out to be too simple, though. Some inborn capacities, such as form perception, can appear only after other more basic capacities, such as seeing details, have developed. Other inborn capacities may require that there be some kind of environmental input for an appreciable time in order for the capacity to mature. Thus the study of inborn capacities traces perceptual development from the first minute of life through the early years of childhood.

**METHODS OF STUDYING INFANTS** It is hard for us to know what an infant perceives because it cannot talk or follow instructions, and has a fairly limited set of behaviors. To study infant perception, a researcher needs to find a form of behavior through which an infant indicates what it can discriminate. The behavior often used for this purpose is an infant's tendency to look at some objects more than others, and psychologists make use of this behavior in the **preferential looking method.**

This method is illustrated in Figure 5-31. Two stimuli are presented to the infant side by side. The experimenter, who is hidden from the infant's view, looks through a partition behind the stimuli and, by watching the infant's eyes, measures the amount of time that the infant looks at each stimulus. (Usually the experimenter will use a television camera to record the infant's viewing pattern to ensure accuracy.) From time to time, the stimulus positions are switched randomly. If an infant consistently looks at one stimulus more than the other, the experimenter concludes that the infant can tell them apart (discriminate between them).

Psychologists have also used visual **evoked potentials** to study infant perception. To record evoked potentials, electrodes are placed on the back of the baby's head over the visual cortex. The electrodes are not annoying, and the infant quickly adapts to them. To illustrate the method, suppose a pattern consisting of broad stripes is presented to the infant. The electrodes will pick up an electrical response (the evoked potential); when the stripes are made very narrow, the response disappears. The response is thought to be closely related to how well the infant can see the stripes.

Using these techniques, psychologists have studied a variety of perceptual capacities in infants. Some of these capacities are needed to perceive forms, and hence are used in the task of recognition; other capacities studied in infants, particularly depth perception, are involved in the task of localization; and still other capacities are involved in the task of keeping the appearance of perceived objects constant.

**PERCEIVING FORMS** To be able to perceive an object, first one must be able to discriminate one part of it from another, an ability referred to as visual acuity. Related to acuity is contrast sensitivity, roughly the ability to discriminate between dark and light stripes under various conditions. (The dark and light stripes can correspond to different parts of a pattern, hence the relation between contrast sensitivity and acuity.) A large number of studies have focused on acuity and contrast sensitivity in infants.

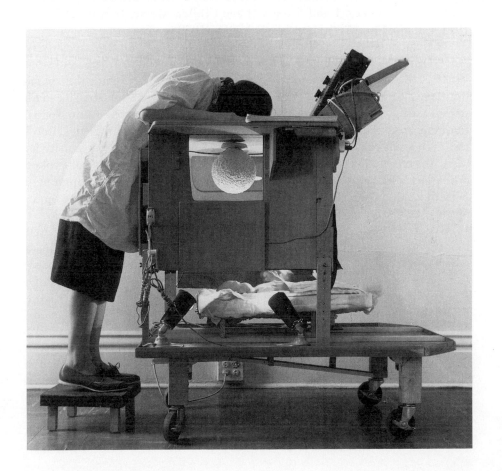

**FIGURE 5-31**
**Preferential Looking Apparatus** *This "looking chamber" has been used to study preferential looking in infants. An infant lies in a crib and looks up at pictures and objects on the ceiling. The experimenter, watching through a peephole, records the infant's looking behavior.* (After Fantz, 1961)

**FIGURE 5-32**
**Spatial Frequency** *The pattern on the right has the higher spatial frequency (smaller distance between successive stripes) and has less apparent contrast.*

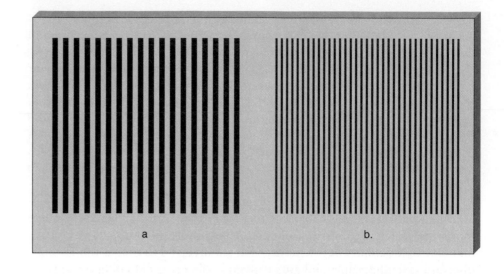

a                                    b.

The method typically used in studying acuity is preferential looking, with a pattern of stripes as one stimulus and a uniform gray field as the other stimulus. Initially, the stripes are relatively wide, and the infant prefers to look at the pattern rather than the uniform field. Then the researcher decreases stripe width until the infant no longer shows a preference. Presumably at this point the infant can no longer discriminate a stripe from its surrounding so that the pattern of stripes no longer has perceptible parts and looks like a uniform field. When first studied at about 1 month of age, infants can see some patterns, but their acuity is very low. Acuity increases rapidly over the first 6 months of life; then it increases more slowly, reaching adult levels between 1 and 5 years of age (Teller, Morse, Borton, & Regal, 1974; Pirchio, Spinelli, Fiorentini, & Maffei, 1978).

Researchers have used the same method to study contrast sensitivity. Now both stimuli are patterns of alternating dark and light stripes, and what varies is the **spatial frequency** of the stripes, where the higher the spatial frequency of a pattern the smaller the distance between successive dark stripes (see Figure 5-32). Infant contrast sensitivity is better at low spatial frequencies (big distances between stripes) than at other frequencies, but is less than adult sensitivity at all frequencies. Like acuity, contrast sensitivity increases rapidly over the first 6 months of life (Banks, 1982). Visual-evoked potentials studies give comparable results. The basis of this development in pattern vision is not completely understood, but we do know that the optics of the eye, the retina, and the cortex continue to develop over this period.

What do these studies tell us about the infant's perceptual world? At 1 month, infants can distinguish no fine details; their vision can discriminate only relatively large objects. Such vision is sufficient, though, to perceive some gross characteristics of an object, including some of the features of a face (which create something like a pattern of dark and light stripes). Figure 5-33 uses the results of acuity and contrast-sensitivity experiments to simulate what a 1-, 2-, and 3-month-old infant sees when viewing a woman's face from a distance of 6 inches. At 1 month, acuity is so poor that it is difficult to perceive facial expressions (and indeed newborns look mostly at the outside contours of a face). By 3 months, acuity has improved to the point where an infant can decipher facial expressions (Goldstein, 1989). No wonder that infants seem so much more socially responsive at 3 months than 1 month.

Being able to discriminate dark from light edges is critical for seeing forms, but what about other aspects of object recognition? Our sensitivity to

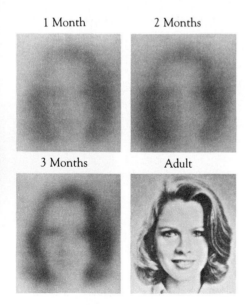

1 Month          2 Months

3 Months          Adult

**FIGURE 5-33**
**Visual Acuity and Contrast Sensitivity** *Simulations of what 1-, 2-, and 3-month-old infants see when they look at a woman's face from a distance of about six inches; the bottom right photograph is what an adult sees. The simulations of infant perception were obtained by first determining an infant's contrast sensitivity, and then applying this contrast-sensitivity function to the photograph on the bottom right.* (After Ginsburg, 1983)

some of the shape features of objects is manifested early. When presented with a triangle, even a 3-day-old infant will direct its eye movements toward the edges and vertices, rather than look randomly over the form (Salapatek, 1975). Also, infants find some shapes more interesting than others. Infants tend to look more at forms that resemble human faces, which appears to be based on a preference for some of the features that comprise a face, like a preference for curved rather than straight contours (Fantz, 1961; 1970). By age 3 months, an infant can recognize something about the mother's face, even in a photograph, as revealed by an infant's preference to look at a photograph of the mother rather than one of an unfamiliar woman (Barrera & Maurer, 1981).

**PERCEIVING DEPTH** Depth perception begins to appear at about 3 months of age but is not fully established until about 6 months. Evidence for this conclusion comes from studies like the following one on binocular disparity. An infant views a random pattern of dots that look like a moving object *only* if the observer is sensitive to binocular-disparity information. Thus, if an infant moves his eyes to follow the object, he is probably sensitive to disparity. In fact, infants younger than 3 months will not follow the moving object, whereas infants between 3 and 6 months do follow it (Fox, Aslin, Shea, & Dumais, 1980).

The use of monocular cues shows a similar developmental course. At $5\frac{1}{2}$ months, but not before, infants will reach for the nearer of two objects, where nearness is signaled by the monocular cue of relative size. Further evidence about the development of monocular depth perception comes from studies of the **visual cliff.** The visual cliff (illustrated in Figure 5-34) consists of a center board placed across a sheet of glass, with a surface of patterned material located directly under the glass on the *shallow side,* and at a distance of a few feet below the glass on the *deep side.* (The appearance of

**FIGURE 5-34**
**Visual Cliff** *The "visual cliff" is an apparatus used to show that infants and young animals are able to see depth by the time they are able to move about. The visual cliff consists of two surfaces, both displaying the same checkerboard pattern and covered by a sheet of thick glass. One surface is directly under the glass; the other is several feet below it. When placed on the center board between the deep and the shallow sides, the kitten refuses to cross to the deep side but will readily move off the board onto the shallow side. (After Gibson & Walk, 1960)*

depth in Figure 5-34—the cliff—is created by an abrupt change in the texture gradient.) An infant old enough to crawl (about 7 months) is placed on the center board; one of her eyes is patched to eliminate binocular depth cues. When the mother calls or beckons from the shallow side, the infant will consistently crawl toward her mother; but when the mother beckons from the deep side, the infant will not cross the "cliff". Thus when old enough to crawl, an infant's depth perception is relatively well developed.

**PERCEIVING CONSTANCIES**   Compared to the perception of form and depth, the perceptual constancies take much longer to fully develop. For example, although there is some degree of size constancy in 6-month-olds, 8-year-old children still show less constancy than adults (Zeigler & Leibowitz, 1957). The constancies are about the way the world looks to us, and of course there is no way for us to be sure what an infant is experiencing. But a number of investigators have been impressed by the fact that infants' natural responses to stimuli often resemble those of adults. They turn toward sounds, defend themselves when an object flies toward them, and do not fall off raised platforms. The similarity of infant and adult responses to the same stimuli suggests that infants and adults may experience these stimuli in a similar way (Bower, 1982).

## Rearing with Controlled Stimulation

We turn now to the question of how specific experiences affect perceptual capacities. To answer this question, researchers have systematically varied the kind of perceptual experiences a young organism has, and then looked at the effects of this experience on subsequent perceptual performance. While the intent of these studies has usually been to study learning, the variations in experiences has sometimes affected innate processes.

**ABSENCE OF STIMULATION**   The earliest experiments on controlled stimulation sought to determine the effects of rearing an animal in the total absence of visual stimulation. The experimenters kept animals in the dark for several months after birth until they were mature enough for visual testing. The idea behind these experiments was that if animals have to *learn* to perceive, they would be unable to perceive when first exposed to the light. The results turned out as expected: chimpanzees reared in darkness for their first 16 months could detect light but could not discriminate patterns (Riesen, 1947). However, subsequent studies showed that prolonged rearing in the dark does more than prevent learning; it causes deterioration of neurons in various parts of the visual system. It turns out that a certain amount of light stimulation is necessary to maintain the visual system. Without any light stimulation, nerve cells in the retina and visual cortex begin to atrophy. Though this fact does not tell us much about the role of learning in perceptual development, it is important in itself.

Single-cell recording studies provided a more thorough account of the devastating effects of no stimulation. Recordings from the visual cortex in newborn cats and monkeys show that they have simple, complex, and hyper-complex cells very similar to those in adult animals (see p. 174) (Hubel & Wiesel, 1963; Wiesel & Hubel, 1974). These cells, however, respond more slowly and are less sharply tuned than adult cells. In kittens, for instance, the cells become adultlike in 4 to 6 weeks if the kittens receive some visual stimulation. If they are reared in darkness, many of their cortical cells do not respond when they are introduced to an illuminated room. Similarly, animals that are raised with one eye patched have few cortical cells that respond to simulation of that eye, and are essentially blind in that eye.

In general, when an animal is deprived of visual stimulation from birth, the longer the time of deprivation, the greater the deficit. Adult cats, on the other hand, can have one eye patched for a long period without losing vision in that eye. These observations led to the idea that a **critical period** exists for the development of inborn visual capacities early in life; lack of stimulation during this period permanently impairs the visual system.

**LIMITED STIMULATION** Because a prolonged, total lack of stimulation can destroy inborn capacities, researchers have shifted strategy. Researchers no longer deprive animals of stimulation for a long period of time; instead they study the effects of rearing animals with stimulation in both eyes, but only of a certain kind. Researchers have raised kittens in an environment in which they see only vertical stripes, or only horizontal stripes (see Figure 5-35). The kittens become blind to stripes in the orientation—vertical or horizontal—that they do not experience. And single-cell recording studies show that many cells in the visual cortex of a "horizontally reared" cat respond to horizontal stimuli and none respond to vertical stimuli, whereas the opposite pattern of results obtains for a "vertically reared" cat (Blakemore & Cooper, 1970; Hirsch & Spinelli, 1970). What happens to the cortical cells that are not stimulated? Do they degenerate or do they become "rewired" to respond to the available stimuli? If degeneration occurs, there should be areas of the visual cortex that are unresponsive. The evidence on this issue is mixed, but it seems to favor the degeneration hypothesis (Movshon & Van Sluyters, 1981).

Of course researchers do not deprive humans of normal visual stimulation, but sometimes this happens naturally or as a consequence of medical treatment. For example, after eye surgery the operated eye is usually patched. If this happens to a child in the first year of life, the acuity of the patched eye is reduced (Awaya et al., 1973). This suggests that there is a critical period early in the development of the human visual system similar to that in animals; if stimulation is restricted during this period, the system will not develop normally. The critical period is much longer in humans than in animals. It may last as long as eight years, but the greatest vulnerability occurs during the first two years of life (Aslin & Banks, 1978).

None of these facts indicate that we have to learn to perceive. Rather, the facts show that certain kinds of stimulation are essential for the *maintenance and development* of perceptual capacities that are present at birth. If there is any learning going on in the situations described above, it is of a very special kind in that it occurs only during an early critical period and involves a partial rewiring of the cortex.

But this does not mean that learning has no effect on perception. For evidence of such effects, we need only consider our ability to recognize common objects, and how this ability is influenced by context and expectation. The fact that we can more readily recognize a familiar object than an unfamiliar one—a dog versus an aardvark, for example—must certainly be due to learning (because had we been reared in an environment rich in aardvarks and sparse in dogs, we could have recognized the aardvark more readily than the dog). Likewise, the fact that certain contexts can facilitate the recognition of particular objects—for example, a farm scene facilitates recognition of a cow—is also almost certainly a consequence of learning.

**FIGURE 5-35**
**Controlled Visual Environment** *In one experiment, kittens were kept in the dark from birth to 2 weeks of age. They were then placed in this tube for five hours a day and spent the rest of the time in the dark. The kitten is on a clear Plexiglass platform, and the striped tube extends above and below it. It is wearing a neck ruff that blocks its view of its own body and prevents head turning. The kittens did not appear to be distressed in this situation. After five months of this exposure, the kittens could see vertical stripes very well but were essentially blind to horizontal stripes. Further, single-cell recording found few cells in their cortices that responded to horizontal stripes.* (After Blakemore & Cooper, 1970)

**PERCEPTUAL-MOTOR COORDINATION**  When it comes to coordinating perceptions with motor responses, learning plays a major role. The evidence for this comes from studies in which subjects receive normal stimulation but are prevented from making normal responses to that stimulation. Under such conditions, perceptual-motor coordination does not develop.

For example, in one study, kittens spent 6 hours a day in a lighted and patterned environment in which they were allowed to move about freely. While they were in this situation, they wore lightweight collars that prevented them from seeing their bodies or paws (see Figure 5-36a). Except for this 6-hour exposure period each day, they stayed in a dark room. After 12 days of this regimen, they were tested for visual-motor coordination. The test consisted of lowering the kitten (with one front paw held and the other free to move) toward a table that had horizontal prongs sticking out of it (see Figure 5-36b). The researcher was interested in determining if the kitten would extend its paw to guide it to a prong. This is a response that a normally reared kitten will make very reliably. All the experimental kittens extended their free paw as they approached the table, indicating that they could see that the table was within reach. But on 50 percent of the trials, the kittens missed the prongs, indicating that they had not learned to guide their limbs to a visual target. After a few hours without the collar in a normally illuminated room, the kittens learned the paw-placing response (Hein & Held, 1967).

Not only is learning required for perceptual motor coordination, but the learning must involve self-produced movements in response to the stimulation. In one experiment, two dark-reared kittens had their first visual experience in the "kitten carousel" illustrated in Figure 5-37. As the active kitten walked, it moved the passive kitten riding in the carousel. Although both kittens received roughly the same visual stimulation, only the active kitten had this stimulation produced by its movement. And only the active kitten successfully learned sensory-motor coordination; for example, only the active kitten learned to put out its paws to ward off a collision.

Very similar results have been obtained with humans. In some experiments people have worn prism goggles that distort the directions of objects. Immediately after putting on these goggles, a person temporarily has trouble reaching for objects and often bumps into things. If a person moves about and attempts to perform motor tasks while wearing the goggles, he or she learns to behave adaptively. On the other hand, if the person is pushed in a wheelchair, he or she does not adapt to the goggles. Apparently, self-produced movement is essential to prism adaption (Held, 1965).

In summary, the evidence indicates that we are born with considerable perceptual capacity. The natural development of some of these capacities may require years of normal input from the environment; hence, environ-

**FIGURE 5-36**
**Learning Perceptual-Motor Coordination** *(a) Kitten wearing a collar that prevented it from seeing its limbs and torso. The collar was lightweight and had little effect on locomotion. Kittens were permitted to move freely 6 hours daily in a lighted and patterned environment while wearing the collar. The rest of the time, they were kept without collars in a dark room. (b) Apparatus for testing visually guided paw placement. The prongs were 2.5 cm. wide and 7.5 cm. apart. During the test trials, the torso, hindlimbs, and one forelimb were supported as shown. The kitten was carried downward toward the pronged edge. The kitten was scored on the basis of whether or not its paw landed on a prong.* (After Hein & Held, 1967)

a.                    b.

**FIGURE 5-37**
**Importance of Self-Produced Movements** *Both kittens received roughly the same visual stimulation, but only the active kitten had this stimulation produced by its own movement.* (After Held & Hein, 1963)

mental effects early in development are often more indicative of innate than learned processes. But there clearly are learning effects on perception as well, which are particularly striking when perception must be coordinated with motor behavior. We have come a long way from asking the global question of whether perception is innate or learned.

*Chapter* **SUMMARY**

1. The study of perception deals with two major functions of the perceptual system: *localization*, or determining where objects are, and *recognition*, or determining what objects are. Localization and recognition are carried out by different regions of the cortex. The study of perception also deals with how the perceptual system keeps the appearance of objects constant, even though their retinal images are changing. Another concern is with how our perceptual capacities develop.

2. To localize objects, first we have to *segregate* objects from one another and then *organize* them into groups. These processes were first studied by *Gestalt* psychologists, who proposed principles of organization. One such principle is that we organize a stimulus into regions corresponding to *figure* and *ground*. Other principles concern the bases that we use to group objects together, including: *proximity, closure, good continuation,* and *similarity*.

3. Localizing an object requires that we know its depth. *Depth perception* is usually thought to be based on *depth cues*. Monocular depth cues include *relative size, superposition, relative height, linear perspective,* and *motion parallax*. Binocular depth cues include *parallax* and *disparity*, with disparity due to the fact that any object provides slightly different images to the two eyes. An alternative to inferring distance on the basis of depth cues is Gibson's notion of *direct perception*, wherein a source of information like a *texture gradient* provides direct information about the depth of an object.

4. Localizing an object requires knowing the motion of moving objects. *Motion perception* can be produced in the absence of an object moving across our retina; one case of this is *stroboscopic motion* in which a series of

rapid, still images induces apparent movement; another case of motion perception without a moving object is *induced motion* in which movement of a large object induces apparent movement of a smaller stationary object. *Real motion* (induced by an object moving across the retina) is partly coded by specific cells in the visual system, as indicated by single-cell recordings and by experiments on *selective adaptation*.

5. Recognizing an object amounts to assigning it to a category and is based mainly on the shape of the object. In *early stages* of recognition, the visual system uses retinal information to describe the object in terms of *features* like lines and angles; cells that detect such features *(feature detectors)* have been found in the visual cortex. In the *later stages* of recognition, the system matches the description of the object to shape descriptions stored in memory to find the best match.

6. Much of the research on the *matching stage* of recognition has used letter patterns. Matching can be explained by a *connectionist model* or network. The bottom level of the network contains features and the next level contains letters; an *exitatory connection* between a feature and a letter means that the feature is part of a letter, while an *inhibitory connection* means the feature is not part of the letter. When a letter is presented, it activates some features in the network, which pass their activation or inhibition up to letters; the letter that receives the most activation is the best match to the input. The network can be expanded to include a level of words and to explain why a letter is easier to recognize when presented in a word than when presented alone.

7. The shape features of natural objects are more complex than lines, being more like simple geometric forms such as cylinders, cones, blocks, and wedges. A limited set of such forms may be sufficient in combination to describe the shapes of all objects that people can recognize. When a pictured object is presented briefly, recognition of the object is good to the extent that its features can be extracted.

8. *Bottom-up* recognition processes are driven solely by the input, while *top-down* recognition processes are driven by a person's knowledge and expectations. Top-down processes lie behind *context* effects in perception, because the context sets up a perceptual expectation, and when this expectation is satisfied less input information than usual is needed for recognition.

9. *Selective attention* is the process by which we select some stimuli for further processing while ignoring others. In vision, the primary means for directing our attention are *eye movements*. Most eye fixations are on the more informative parts of a scene. Selective attention also occurs in audition. Usually, we are able to *selectively listen* by using cues like the direction of the sound and the voice characteristics of the speaker. Our ability to selectively attend is mediated by processes that occur in the early stages of recognition, as well as by processes that occur only after the message's meaning has been determined. In addition to its selective function, attention is also needed to conjoin the features of an object.

10. Another major function of the perceptual system is to keep the appearance of objects the same in spite of large changes in the stimuli received by our sense organs. *Lightness constancy* refers to the fact that an object appears equally light regardless of how much light it reflects, whereas *color constancy* means an object looks roughly the same color regardless of the light source illuminating it. In both cases, constancy depends on relations between object and background elements. Two other well known constancies are *shape* and *location constancy*.

11. The most studied of all constancies is *size constancy*, the fact that any object's size remains relatively constant no matter what its distance from us. The perceived size of an object increases with both the *retinal size* of the object and the *perceived distance* of the object, in accordance with the *size-distance invariance* principle. Thus, as an object moves away from the perceiver, the retinal size decreases but the perceived distance increases, and the two changes cancel each other out, resulting in constancy. This principle can explain certain *illusions*.

12. Research on *perceptual development* is concerned with the extent to which perceptual capacity is inborn and the extent to which it is learned by experience. To determine inborn capacities, researchers study the discrimination capacities of infants using the methods of *preferential looking* and *visual evoked potentials*. *Acuity*, which is critical to recognition, increases rapidly over the first 6 months of life, then increases more slowly until it reaches adult levels between 1 and 5 years of age. *Depth perception* begins to appear at about 3 months of age, but is not fully established until about 6 months. The constancies begin to develop as early as 6 months, but are not fully developed for years.

13. Animals raised in darkness suffer permanent visual impairment, and animals raised with a patch over one eye become blind in that eye. Adult animals do not lose vision even when deprived of stimulation for long periods. These results suggest a *critical period* early in life, during which lack of normal stimulation produces an aberration in an innate perceptual capacity. If stimulation is controlled early in life, so that certain kinds of stimuli are absent, both animals and people become insensitive to the stimuli of which they have been deprived; again, this effect does not have much to do with learning.

14. *Perceptual-motor* coordination must be learned. Animals that cannot see their own limbs do not develop normal coordination. Both animals and people require *self-produced movement* to develop normal coordination.

## *Further* READING

Many of the textbooks listed under Further Reading in Chapter 4 also pertain to the topics considered in this chapter. Several additional sources are appropriate as well.

General treatments of perception are available in Osherson, Kosslyn, and Hollerbach, *Invitation to Cognitive Science (Vol. 2): Visual Cognition and Action* (1990); Coren and Ward, *Sensation and Perception* (3rd ed., 1989); and Rock, *The Logic of Perception* (1983). Gibson's distinctive approach to issues like depth and motion perception in particular, and to perception in general, is presented in *The Ecological Approach to Visual Perception* (1986). Marr's equally distinctive, cognitive-science approach to perception is given in his book *Vision* (1982). A more elementary introduction to some of Marr's work is presented in the early chapters of Johnson-Laird, *The Computer and the Mind* (1988).

Problems of recognition and attention are discussed in Spoehr and Lehmkuhle; *Visual Information Processing* (1982). Studies of brain mechanisms involved in recognition are discussed in Farah, *Visual Agnosia: Disorders of Object Recognition and What They Tell Us About Normal Vision* (1990); and Posner and Marin, (ed.), *Mechanisms of Attention* (1985). The connectionist approach to problems of recognition and localization are contained in an advanced, two-volume set by Rumelhart and McClelland, *Parallel Distributed Processing* (1986); the approach is also discussed in Posner, *Foundations of Cognitive Science* (1989).

# Chapter 6

# Consciousness and Its Altered States

**Aspects of Consciousness 203**
*Consciousness*
*Preconscious Memories*
*The Unconscious*

**Divided Consciousness 207**
*Dissociation*
*Multiple Personality*

**Sleep and Dreams 210**
*Sleep Schedules*
*Depth of Sleep*
*Sleep Disorders*
*Dreams*
*Dream Content*
*Critical Discussion: Theories of Dream Sleep*

**Psychoactive Drugs 219**
*Depressants*
*Opiates*
*Stimulants*
*Hallucinogens*
*Cannabis*
*Critical Discussion: Drug Dependence*

**Meditation 231**
*Traditional Forms of Meditation*
*Meditation for Relaxation*
*Effects of Meditation*

**Hypnosis 235**
*Induction of Hypnosis*
*Hypnotic Suggestions*
*Critical Discussion: The Hidden Observer*

**Psi Phenomena 240**
*Experimental Evidence*
*Debate over the Evidence*
*Anecdotal Evidence*
*Skepticism about Psi*

Detail, *Snowy Hill with Winding Road.*

As you read these words, are you awake or dreaming? Hardly anyone is confused by this question. We all know the difference between an ordinary state of wakefulness and the experience of dreaming. We also recognize other *states of consciousness*, including those induced by drugs such as alcohol and marijuana.

A person's conscious awareness is readily subject to change. At this moment, your attention may be focused on this book; in a few minutes, you may be deep in reverie. To most psychologists, an *altered state of consciousness* exists whenever there is a change from an ordinary pattern of mental functioning to a state that *seems* different to the person experiencing the change. Although this is not a very precise definition, it reflects the fact that states of consciousness are personal and therefore subjective. Altered states of consciousness can vary from the distraction of a vivid daydream to the confusion and perceptual distortion of drug intoxication. In this chapter we will look at some altered states of consciousness that are experienced by everyone (sleep and dreams, for instance), as well as some that result from special circumstances (meditation, hypnosis, and the use of drugs).

## Aspects of Consciousness

Discussions about the nature of conscious experience and the functions of consciousness will occur throughout this book as we consider perception, memory, language, problem solving, and other topics. At this point, it would be helpful to present a general theory of consciousness that would provide a framework for considering these various topics as they are introduced later. Such an approach, however, is not feasible because there is no generally agreed upon theory. Rather, there are almost as many theories of consciousness as there are individuals who have theorized about the topic. This state of affairs may be discouraging for some readers, particularly those whose prior exposure to science has been in areas where the facts are crystal clear and the theories are well established. Yet what can be more exciting or more challenging than venturing into territory that is still uncharted. As important discoveries are being made—in neurophysiology, evolutionary biology, genetics, and various fields of psychology—many observers believe that an explanation of consciousness is tantalizingly close. In the absence of a general theory, our discussion of consciousness can do little more than introduce some terms and concepts that will provide a perspective on the topic as it surfaces in later chapters. An integration of the various speculations that will be offered here awaits future research and insights, some of which may well be provided by students who read these pages.

What is consciousness? The early psychologists equated "consciousness" with "mind." They defined psychology as "the study of mind and consciousness" and used the **introspective method** to study consciousness. As noted in Chapter 1, both introspection as a method for investigation and consciousness as a topic for investigation fell from favor with the rise of **behaviorism** in the early 1900s. John Watson, the founder of behaviorism, and his followers believed that if psychology were to become a science, its data must be objective and measurable. Behavior could be publicly observed and various responses could be objectively measured. In contrast, an individual's private experiences revealed through introspection could not be observed by others or objectively measured. If psychology dealt with actual behavior,

*Reflection is one aspect of consciousness.*

it would be dealing with *public events*, instead of *private events*, which are observable only to the experiencing person.

Behaviorism did not require as radical a change as its pronouncements seemed to imply. The behaviorists themselves dealt with private events when their research required them to. They accepted *verbal responses* as a substitute for introspection when the subject's own experiences were studied. What subjects said was objective, regardless of the uncertainties about the underlying subjective condition. Still, many psychologists continued to believe, regardless of the behaviorists, that when people said they experienced a series of colored afterimages after staring at a bright light, they probably did see colors in succession. That is, their words were not the whole story: the words referred to something of additional psychological interest. While behaviorists could deal with many phenomena in terms of verbal responses, their preoccupation with observable behavior caused them to neglect interesting psychological problems, such as dreaming, meditation, and hypnosis, because the subjective aspects made the topics distasteful to them.

By the 1960s, psychologists began to recognize that the facts of consciousness are too pervasive and important to be neglected. This does not mean that psychology must again be defined exclusively as the study of consciousness; it means only that a complete psychology cannot afford to neglect consciousness. A strict behaviorist's insistence on confining psychology to the study of observable behavior is too limiting. If one can theorize about the nature of consciousness, and that theory leads to testable predictions about behavior, then such theorizing represents a valuable contribution to understanding how the mind works.

## Consciousness

Despite the reemergence of consciousness in psychology, there is still no common agreement on a definition of the term. Many textbooks simply define consciousness as the individual's current awareness of external and internal stimuli—that is, of events in the environment and of bodily sensations, memories, and thoughts. This definition identifies only one aspect of consciousness and ignores the fact that we are conscious also when we try to solve a problem or deliberately select one course of action over others in response to environmental circumstances and personal goals. Thus we are conscious when we monitor the environment (internal and external), but also when we seek to control ourselves and our environment. In short, consciousness involves a) *monitoring* ourselves and our environment so that percepts, memories, and thoughts are represented in awareness; and b) *controlling* ourselves and our environment so that we are able to initiate and terminate behavioral and cognitive activities (Kihlstrom, 1984).

**MONITORING**  Processing information from the environment is the main function of the body's sensory systems, leading to awareness of what is going on in our surroundings as well as within our own bodies. But we could not possibly attend to all of the stimuli that impinge on our senses; there would be an information overload. Our consciousness focuses on some stimuli and ignores others. Often the information selected has to do with changes in our external or internal world. While concentrating on this paragraph, you are probably unaware of numerous background stimuli. But should there be a change—the lights dim, the air begins to smell smoky, or the noise of the air conditioning system ceases—you would suddenly be aware of such stimuli.

Our attention is selective; some events take precedence over others in gaining access to consciousness and in initiating action. Events that are important to survival usually have top priority. If we are hungry, it is difficult for us to concentrate on studying; if we experience a sudden pain, we push all other thoughts out of consciousness until we do something to make it go away.

**CONTROLLING**  Another function of consciousness is to plan, initiate, and guide our actions. Whether the plan is simple and readily completed (such as meeting a friend for lunch) or complex and long-range (such as preparing for a lifetime career), our actions must be guided and arranged to coordinate with events around us. In planning, events that have not yet occurred can be represented in consciousness as future possibilities; we may envision alternative "scenarios," make choices, and initiate appropriate activities.

Not all actions are guided by conscious decisions nor are the solutions to all problems carried out at a conscious level. One of the tenants of modern psychology is that mental events involve both conscious and nonconscious processes and that many decisions and actions are conducted entirely outside of the range of consciousness. The solution to a problem may occur "out of the blue" without our being aware that we have been thinking about it. And once we have the solution, we may be unable to offer an introspective account of how the solution was obtained. One can cite many examples of decision making and problem solving that occur at a nonconscious level, but this does not mean that *all* such behaviors occur without conscious reflection. Consciousness is not only a monitor of ongoing behavior, but plays a role in directing and controlling that behavior.

## Preconscious Memories

From all that is going on around us now and from our store of knowledge and memories of past events, we can focus attention on only a few stimuli at a given moment. We ignore, select, and reject all the time, so that consciousness is continually changing. But objects or events that are not the focus of attention can still have some influences on consciousness. For example, you may not be aware of hearing a clock strike the hour. After a few strokes, you become alert; then you can go back and count the strokes that you did not know you heard. Another example of peripheral attention (or nonconscious monitoring) is the **lunch-line effect** (Farthing, 1992). You are talking with a friend in a cafeteria line, ignoring other voices and general noise, when the sound of your own name in another conversation catches your attention. Clearly, you would not have detected your name in the other conversation if you had not, in some sense, been monitoring that conversation; you were not consciously aware of the other conversation until a special signal drew your attention to it. A considerable body of research indicates that we register and evaluate stimuli that we do not consciously perceive (Kihlstrom, 1987). These stimuli are said to influence us *subconsciously,* or to operate at a nonconscious level of awareness.

Many memories and thoughts that are not part of your consciousness at this moment can be brought to consciousness when needed. At this moment

"Good morning, beheaded—uh, I mean beloved"
*Drawing by Dana Fradon; ©1979 The New Yorker Magazine, Inc.*

you may not be conscious of your vacation last summer, but the memories are accessible if you wish to retrieve them; then they become a vivid part of your consciousness. Memories that are accessible to consciousness are called **preconscious memories.** They include specific memories of personal events, as well as the information accumulated over a lifetime, such as one's knowledge of the meaning of words, the layout of the streets of a city, or the location of a particular country. They also include knowledge about learned skills like the procedures involved in driving a car or the sequence of steps in tying one's shoelace. These procedures, once mastered, generally operate outside conscious awareness, but when our attention is called to them we are capable of describing the steps involved.

## The Unconscious

According to the psychoanalytic theories of Sigmund Freud and his followers, some memories, impulses, and desires are not accessible to consciousness. Psychoanalytic theory assigns these to the **unconscious.** Freud believed that some emotionally painful memories and wishes are *repressed*—that is, diverted to the unconscious, where they may continue to influence our actions even though we are not aware of them. Thoughts and impulses repressed to the unconscious cannot enter our consciousness, but they can affect us in indirect or disguised ways—through dreams, irrational behaviors, mannerisms, and slips of the tongue. The term **"Freudian slip"** is commonly used to refer to unintentional remarks that are assumed to reveal hidden impulses. Saying "I'm sad you're better," when intending to say "I'm glad you're better," would be an example.

Freud believed that unconscious desires and impulses are the cause of most mental illnesses. He developed the method of psychoanalysis, the goal of which is to draw the repressed material to consciousness and, in so doing, cure the individual (see Chapter 17).

Most psychologists accept the idea that there are memories and mental processes that are inaccessible to introspection and accordingly may be described as unconscious. However, many would argue that Freud placed undue emphasis on the emotionally laden aspects of the unconscious and not enough on other aspects. They would include in the unconscious a large array of mental processes that we depend on constantly in our everyday lives but to which we have no conscious access (Kihlstrom, 1987). For example, during perception, the viewer may be aware of two objects in the environment but have no awareness of the mental calculations she performed almost instantaneously to determine that one is closer or larger than the other (see Chapter 5). Although we have conscious access to the outcome of these mental processes—in that we are aware of the size and distance of the object—we have no conscious access to their operations (Velmans, 1991).

In this section we have discussed four concepts—consciousness, nonconscious processes, preconscious memories, and the unconscious—and have tended to treat them as distinct categories. In actuality, however, not all processes and stored memories are so easily categorized. For this reason, some psychologists prefer not to make these types of distinctions, and instead talk about a *nonconscious-conscious continuum* that runs from one extreme of totally unconscious processes (through various gradations) to the other extreme of reflective consciousness (Farthing, 1992). Nevertheless, versions of these concepts are so pervasive that you need to be familiar with them, even though different psychologists talk about them somewhat differently.

# Divided Consciousness

An important function of consciousness is the control of our actions. But some activities are practiced so often that they become habitual, or automatic. Learning to drive a car requires intense concentration at first. We have to concentrate on coordinating the different actions (shifting gears, releasing the clutch, accelerating, steering, and so forth) and can scarcely think about anything else. However, once the movements become automatic, we can carry on a conversation or admire the scenery without being conscious of driving—unless a potential danger appears that quickly draws our attention to the operation of the car.

Skills, like driving a car or riding a bike, once well-learned no longer require our attention. They become automatic, thereby permitting a relatively uncluttered consciousness to focus on other matters. Such *automatic processes* may have negative consequences on occasion, for example, when a driver cannot remember landmarks he passed along the way.

## Dissociation

The more automatic an action becomes, the less it requires conscious control. Another example is the skilled pianist who carries on a conversation with a bystander while performing a familiar piece. The pianist is exercising control over two activities—playing and talking—but does not think about the music unless a wrong key is hit, alerting her attention to it and temporarily disrupting the conversation. You can undoubtedly think of other examples of well-learned, automatic activities that require little conscious control. One way of interpreting this is to say that the control is still there (we can focus on automatic processes if we want to), but it has been *dissociated* from consciousness. (To "dissociate" means to sever the association of one thing from another.)

The French psychiatrist Pierre Janet (1889) originated the concept of **dissociation.** He proposed that under certain conditions some thoughts and actions become split off, or dissociated, from the rest of consciousness and

*Familiarity with a skill makes actions automatic, so that we can perform two tasks simultaneously.*

function outside of awareness. Dissociation differs from Freud's concept of repression because the dissociated memories and thoughts are accessible to consciousness. Repressed memories, in contrast, cannot be brought to consciousness; they have to be inferred from signs or symptoms (such as slips of the tongue).

When faced with a stressful situation, we may temporarily put it out of our minds in order to be able to function effectively; when bored, we may lapse into reverie or daydreams. These are mild examples of dissociation; they involve dissociating one part of consciousness from another. More extreme examples of dissociation are demonstrated by cases of **multiple personality.**

## Multiple Personality

Multiple personality is the existence of two or more integrated and well-developed personalities within the same individual. In most cases, each personality has its own name and age and a specific set of memories and characteristic behaviors; frequently, the different personalities will differ in handwriting, artistic talent, or even in knowledge of foreign languages. Typically, the attitudes and behavior of the alternating personalities are markedly different. For example, if personality A is shy, inhibited, and rigidly moral, personality B may be extraverted, unrestrained, and prone to excessive drinking and sexual promiscuity. In most cases, some of the personalities have no awareness of the experiences of the others. Periods of unexplained amnesia—the loss of memory for hours or days each week—are a clue to the presence of multiple personality.

One of the most famous cases of multiple personality is that of Chris Sizemore, whose alternative personalities—Eve White, Eve Black, and Jane—were portrayed in the movie *The Three Faces of Eve* (Thigpen & Cleckley, 1957) and later elaborated more fully in her autobiography *I'm Eve* (Sizemore & Pittillo, 1977). Another well-studied case of multiple personality is that of Jonah, a 27-year-old man who was admitted to a hospital complaining of severe headaches that were often followed by memory loss. Hospital attendants noticed striking changes in his personality on different days, and the psychiatrist in charge detected three distinct secondary personalities. The relatively stable personality structures that emerged are diagrammed in Figure 6-1 and can be characterized as follows:

■ *Jonah.* The primary personality. Shy, retiring, polite, and highly conventional, he is designated "the square." Sometimes frightened and confused during interviews, Jonah is unaware of the other personalities.

■ *Sammy.* He has the most intact memories. Sammy can coexist with Jonah or set Jonah aside and take over. He claims to be ready when Jonah needs legal advice or is in trouble; he is designated "the mediator." Sammy remembers emerging at age 6, when Jonah's mother stabbed his stepfather and Sammy persuaded the parents never to fight again in front of the children.

■ *King Young.* He emerged when Jonah was 6 or 7 years old to straighten out Jonah's sexual identity after his mother occasionally dressed him in girls' clothing at home and Jonah became confused about boys' and girls' names at school. King Young has looked after Jonah's sexual interests ever since; hence he is designated "the lover." He is only dimly aware of the other personalities.

■ *Usoffa Abdulla.* A cold, belligerent, and angry person. Usoffa is capable of ignoring pain. It is his sworn duty to watch over and protect Jonah;

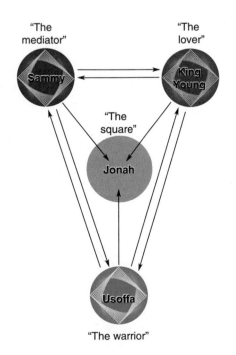

**FIGURE 6-1**
**Jonah's Four Component Personalities** *The three personalities on the periphery have superficial knowledge of each other but are intimately familiar with Jonah, who in turn is totally unaware of them.*
(After Ludwig et al., 1972)

thus he is designated "the warrior." He emerged at age 9 or 10, when a gang of white boys beat up Jonah without provocation. Jonah was helpless, but Usoffa emerged and fought viciously against the attackers. He too is only dimly aware of the other personalities.

The four personalities tested very differently on all measures having to do with emotionally laden topics but scored essentially alike on tests relatively free of emotion or personal conflict, such as intelligence or vocabulary tests.

In cases of multiple personality, consciousness is divided so sharply that several different personalities seem to be living in the same body. Observers note that the switch from one personality to another is often accompanied by subtle changes in body posture and tone of voice. The new personality talks, walks, and gestures differently. There may even be changes in such physiological processes as blood pressure and brain activity (Putnam, 1984).

Although individuals with multiple personalities are relatively rare, enough cases have been studied to uncover some common features that provide us with clues as to how multiple personalities develop in an individual. The initial dissociation seems to occur in response to a traumatic event in childhood (usually between ages 4 and 6). The child copes with a painful problem by creating another personality to bear the brunt of the difficulty (Frischholz, 1985). In Jonah's case, Sammy (the mediator) emerged when Jonah had to deal with his mother's attack on his stepfather. This hypothesis is supported by the fact that most people with multiple personalities were physically or sexually abused as young children.

The gist of the idea is that the child learns to defend himself from the pain of abuse by dissociating the memory from consciousness. In extreme cases in which the child is severely and repeatedly abused, this method of defense over time leads to multiple personalities in which only one or two subpersonalities are conscious of the abuse, while the others have no memory of the pain. It is adaptive for the child to keep the personalities separate, so that he can keep awareness of the abuse from his other selves. That way the feeling and memories of abuse do not continuously flood the child's consciousness when he cannot handle it, for instance while at school or playing with friends (Braun, 1986).

Another factor in the development of multiple personality appears to be an enhanced susceptibility to self-hypnosis, a process by which one is able to put oneself at will into the kind of trance state characteristic of hypnosis (discussed later in this chapter). Multiple-personality patients often make excellent hypnotic subjects, and report that the trance experience is identical to experiences they have had dating back to their childhood. One of the personalities of a patient said, "She creates personalities by blocking everything from her head, mentally relaxes, concentrates very hard, and wishes" (Bliss, 1980, p. 1392). This description sounds very much like self-hypnosis.

Once individuals discover that creating another personality by self-hypnosis relieves them of emotional pain, they are apt to create other personalities in the future when confronted by emotional problems. Thus, when Jonah was beaten by a gang of white boys at age 10, he created another personality, Usoffa Abdulla, to handle the problem. Some multiple-personality patients become so accustomed to defending against problems by means of alternate personalities that they continue the process throughout adulthood, creating new personalities in response to new problems; thus they may end up with a dozen or more different personalities.

# Sleep and Dreams

Sleep seems the opposite of wakefulness, yet the two states have much in common. We think when we sleep, as dreams show, although the type of thinking in dreams departs in various ways from the type we do while awake. We form memories while sleeping, as we know from the fact that we remember dreams. Sleep is not entirely quiescent: some people walk in their sleep. People who are asleep are not entirely insensitive to the environment: parents are awakened immediately by their baby's cry. Nor is sleep entirely planless: some people can decide to wake at a given time and do so.

Many aspects of sleep have interested investigators. Researchers have looked at normal rhythms of waking and sleeping, the depth of sleep at different periods of the night, and individual and environmental factors that affect sleep.

## Sleep Schedules

Newborn babies tend to alternate frequently between sleeping and waking. Much to the relief of parents, a rhythm of two naps a day and longer sleep at night is eventually established. An infant's total sleeping time drops from about 17 hours per day to about 13 hours per day within the first six months of life. Most adults average about 8 hours of sleep per night. However, some people manage on as little as 4 or 5 hours of sleep per night, and there are occasional reports of people who get by on less. Sleep patterns also vary from person to person. We all know "larks" who go to bed early and rise early and "owls" who go to bed late and rise late (Webb, 1975).

Many of our body functions (such as temperature, metabolism, blood and urine composition) have their own inherent tidelike ebb and flow, peaking sometime during the day and slowing down at night in approximate 24-hour cycles. These cyclical patterns form a kind of "internal clock" known as the circadian rhythm (whose name comes from the Latin phrase meaning "about a day"). In conditions in which a person has no way to mark the passing of day and night, the cycle tends to have a natural period of approximately 25 hours. The cause of this departure from a 24-hour cycle is a matter of speculation. In any case, cues from the environment (most importantly the daily cycle of light and dark) are needed to keep our internal clock synchronized with the world around us. In short, we need daily clock resettings, and anything that prevents this or otherwise disturbs our circadian rhythm can disturb our sleep (Kripke, 1985).

In one carefully studied case, a young man, blind since birth, had a circadian rhythm of 24.9 hours. As a consequence, he was completely out of phase with the night-day cycle about every two weeks. The only way he could stay in phase and meet the requirements of his professional life was to take stimulants and sedatives to counteract the rhythmical changes during the different phases of his cycle. Careful efforts to modify his sleep cycle by monitoring and controlling his sleep in a sleep laboratory did not prove successful (Miles, Raynal, & Wilson, 1977).

The jet lag that bothers many people when they travel to a different time zone is caused by disruption of the normal circadian rhythm. Their internal clocks that regulate sleep and metabolism are out of sync with the new light-dark cycle, and it may take several days before they adjust to the new schedule. The fatigue and lack of alertness characteristic of jet lag are

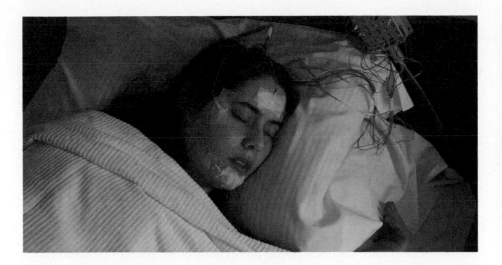

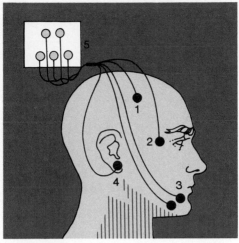

**FIGURE 6-2**
**Arrangement of Electrodes for Recording the Electrophysiology of Sleep** *The diagram shows the way in which electrodes are attached to the subject's head and face in a typical sleep experiment. Electrodes on the scalp (1) record the patterns of brain waves. Electrodes near the subject's eyes (2) record eye movements. Electrodes on the chin (3) record tension and electrical activity in the muscles. A neutral electrode on the ear (4) completes the circuit through amplifiers (5) that produce graphical records of the various patterns.*

not simply the result of the rigors of travel: travel in a north-south direction (with no changes in time zones) does not produce the same symptoms.

## Depth of Sleep

Some people are readily aroused from sleep; others are hard to awaken. Research begun in the 1930s (Loomis, Harvey, & Hobart, 1937) has produced sensitive techniques for measuring the depth of sleep, as well as for determining when dreams are occurring (Dement & Kleitman, 1957). This research uses devices that measure electrical changes on the scalp associated with spontaneous brain activity during sleep, as well as eye movements that occur during dreaming. The graphic recording of the electrical changes, or brain waves, is called an **electroencephalogram,** or EEG (see Figures 6-2 and 6-3).

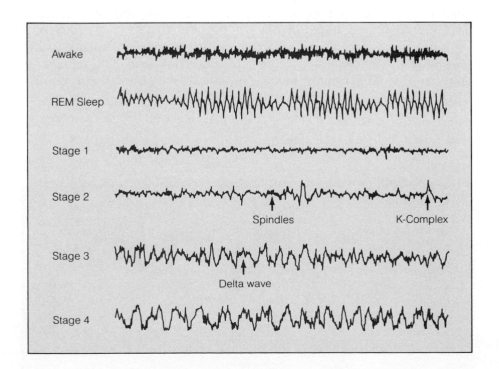

**FIGURE 6-3**
**Electrophysiological Activity During Sleep** *The figure presents EEG recordings during wakefulness and during the various stages of sleep. The Awake Stage is characterized by alpha waves (8–12 hertz). Stage 1 is basically a transition from wakefulness to the deeper stages of sleep. Stage 2 is defined by the presence of sleep spindles (brief bursts of 12–16 hertz waves) and K-complexes (a sharp rise and fall in the brain-wave pattern). Stages 3 and 4 are marked by the presence of delta waves (1–2 hertz), and the only difference between these two stages is the amount of delta wave found. Stage 3 is scored when 20 to 50 percent of the record contains delta waves, and Stage 4 for 50 percent or more.*

**FIVE STAGES OF SLEEP** Analysis of the patterns of brain waves suggests that sleep involves five stages: four depths of sleep and a fifth stage, known as **rapid eye movement** (or REM) sleep. When a person closes her eyes and relaxes, the brain waves characteristically show a regular pattern of 8 to 12 hertz (cycles per second); these are known as **alpha waves.** As the individual drifts into *Stage 1* sleep, the brain waves become less regular and are reduced in amplitude. *Stage 2* is characterized by the appearance of **spindles**—short runs of rhythmical responses of 12 to 16 hertz—and an occasional sharp rise and fall in the amplitude of the whole EEG. The still deeper *Stages 3 and 4* are characterized by slow waves (1 to 2 hertz), which are known as **delta waves.** Generally the sleeper is hard to awaken during Stages 3 and 4, although she can be aroused by something personal, such as a familiar name or a child crying. A more impersonal disturbance, such as a loud sound, may be ignored.

After an adult has been asleep for an hour or so, another change occurs. The EEG becomes very active (even more so than when the subject is awake), but the subject does not wake. The electrodes placed near the subject's eyes detect rapid eye movements; these eye movements are so pronounced that one can even watch the sleeper's eyes move around beneath the closed eyelids. This stage is known as REM sleep; the other four stages are known as non-REM sleep (or NREM).

These various stages of sleep alternate throughout the night. Sleep begins with the NREM stages and consists of several sleep cycles, each containing some REM and some NREM sleep. Figure 6-4 illustrates a typical night's sleep for a young adult. As you can see, the person goes from wakefulness into a deep sleep (Stage 4) very rapidly. After about 70 minutes, Stage 2 reoccurs, immediately followed by the first REM period of the night. Notice that the deeper stages (3 and 4) occurred during the first part of the night, whereas most REM sleep occurred in the last part. This is the typical pattern: the deeper stages tend to disappear in the second half of the night as REM becomes more prominent. There are usually four or five distinct REM periods over the course of an 8-hour night, with an occasional brief awakening as morning arrives.

The pattern of the sleep cycles varies with age. Newborn infants, for instance, spend about half their sleeping time in REM sleep. This proportion drops to 20 to 25 percent of total sleep time by the age of 5 and remains fairly constant until old age, when it drops to 18 percent or less. Older peo-

**FIGURE 6-4**
**Succession of Sleep Stages** *The graph provides an example of the sequence and duration of sleep stages during a typical night. The subject went successively through Stages 1 to 4 during the first hour of sleep. He then moved back through Stages 3 and 2 to REM sleep. Thereafter the subject cycled between NREM and REM periods with two brief awakenings at about 3½ and 6 hours of sleep.*

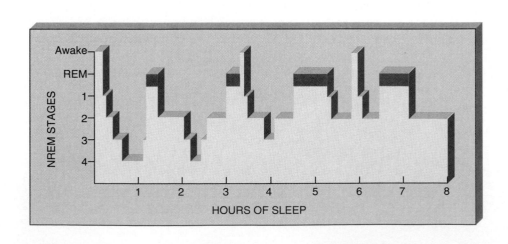

ple tend to experience less Stage 3 and 4 sleep (sometimes these stages disappear completely) and more frequent and longer nighttime awakenings. A natural kind of insomnia seems to set in as people grow older (Gillin, 1985).

The two types of sleep, REM and NREM, are as different from each other as each is from wakefulness. Indeed, some investigators consider REM not to be sleep at all, but rather a third state of existence in addition to wakefulness and NREM sleep.

During NREM sleep, eye movements are virtually absent, heart and breathing rates decrease markedly, there is increased muscle relaxation, and the metabolic rate of the brain decreases 25 to 30 percent compared to wakefulness. In contrast, during REM sleep very rapid eye movements occur in bursts lasting 10 to 20 seconds, heart rate increases, and the brain's metabolic rate increases somewhat compared to wakefulness. Further, during REM sleep we are almost completely paralyzed—only the heart, diaphragm, eye muscles, and smooth muscles (such as the muscles of the intestines and blood vessels) are spared. To summarize, NREM sleep is characterized by an idle brain in a very relaxed body, whereas REM sleep is characterized by a brain that appears to be wide awake in a virtually paralyzed body.

Physiological evidence indicates that in REM sleep the brain is isolated to a large extent from its sensory and motor channels; stimuli from other parts of the body are blocked from entering the brain, and there are no motor outputs. Nevertheless, the brain is still very active in REM sleep, being spontaneously driven by the discharge of giant neurons that originate in the brain stem. These neurons extend into parts of the brain that control eye movements and motor activities. Thus, during REM sleep the brain registers the fact that the neurons normally involved in walking and seeing are activated, even though the body itself is doing neither of these activities (Hobson, 1989).

Sleepers awakened during REM sleep almost always report having a dream, but when awakened during NREM sleep they will report a dream only about 25 percent of the time. The dreams reported when aroused from REM sleep tend to be visually vivid and have emotional and illogical features—they represent the type of experience we typically associate with the word "dream." In contrast, NREM dreams are more like normal thinking, neither as visual nor as emotionally charged as REM dreams, and more related to what is happening in waking life. Thus, mental activity is different in REM and NREM periods, as indicated by the type of dream we report (bizarre and illogical versus thoughtlike) and the frequency of reporting a dream (almost always versus occasionally).

It is important to realize that we become conscious of a dream only if we awaken while dreaming. If we then pay attention and make an effort to remember the dream, some of it will be recalled at a later time. Otherwise, our dream is transient and fades quickly; we may know that we have had a dream but will be unable to remember its contents.

If you are interested in remembering your dreams, keep a notebook and pencil beside your bed. Tell yourself you want to wake up when you have a dream. When you do, immediately try to recall the details and then write them down. As your dream recall improves, look for patterns. Underline anything that strikes you as odd and tell yourself that the next time something similar happens, you are going to recognize it as a sign you are dreaming. The problem, of course, is that you will lose some sleep if you follow this regime.

## Sleep Disorders

About 90 percent of adults sleep 6 to 9 hours per night, with the largest number sleeping 7-½ to 8 hours. While some people sleep only 6 to 7 hours, most of these people have measurable signs of sleepiness during the daytime, even if they do not realize it. It appears that most people require 8 to 9 hours of sleep to be free from daytime sleepiness (Kripke & Gillin, 1985). A *sleep disorder* exists whenever the inability to sleep well produces impaired daytime functioning or excessive sleepiness.

**INSOMNIA** The term **insomnia** is used in reference to complaints about a symptom, namely, dissatisfaction with the amount or quality of one's sleep. Whether or not a person has insomnia is almost always a subjective decision. Many people who complain of insomnia are found to have perfectly normal sleep when studied in a sleep laboratory, whereas others who do not complain of insomnia have detectable sleep disturbances (Trinder, 1988).

A perplexing feature of insomnia is that people seem to overestimate their sleep loss. One study that monitored the sleep of people who identified themselves as insomniacs found that only about half of them were actually awake as much as 30 minutes during the night (Carskadon, Mitler, & Dement, 1974). The problem may be that light or restless sleep sometimes feels like wakefulness or that some people remember only time spent awake and think they have not slept because they have no memory of doing so. Table 6-1 provides some information on how to ensure that you have a restful sleep.

**NARCOLEPSY AND APNEA** Two relatively rare but severe sleep disorders are narcolepsy and apnea. A person with **narcolepsy** may fall asleep while writing a letter, driving a car , or carrying on a conversation. If a student falls asleep while a professor is lecturing, that is perfectly normal; but if a professor falls asleep while lecturing, that may indicate narcolepsy. Individuals with this dysfunction have recurring, irresistible attacks of drowsiness, and simply fall asleep at totally inappropriate times. These episodes can occur several times a day in severe cases, and last from a few seconds to 15–30 minutes. Narcoleptics have difficulty keeping jobs because of their daytime sleepiness and are potentially dangerous if they are driving a car or operating machinery when an attack occurs. Approximately one in a thousand individuals suffers from debilitating narcolepsy, and the incidents of milder, unrecognized cases may be much higher.

Essentially, narcolepsy is the intrusion of REM episodes into daytime hours. During attacks victims go quickly into a REM state, so rapidly in fact that they may lose muscle control and collapse before they can lie down. Moreover, many will report experiencing hallucinations during an attack as reality is replaced by vivid REM dreams. Narcolepsy runs in families, and there is evidence that a specific gene or combination of genes confers susceptibility to the disorder (Hobson, 1988).

In **apnea,** the individual stops breathing while asleep. There are two reasons for apnea attacks. One reason is that the brain fails to send a "breathe" signal to the diaphragm and other breathing muscles, thus causing breathing to stop. The other reason is that muscles at the top of the throat become too relaxed, allowing the windpipe to partially close, thereby forcing the breathing muscles to pull harder on incoming air, which causes the

**REGULAR SLEEP SCHEDULE** Establish a regular schedule of going to bed and getting up. Set your alarm for a specific time every morning, and get up at that time no matter how little you may have slept. Be consistent about naps. Take a nap every afternoon or not at all; when you take a nap only occasionally, you probably will not sleep well that night. Waking up late on weekends can also disrupt your sleep cycle.

**ALCOHOL AND CAFFEINE** Having a stiff drink of alcohol before going to bed may help put you to sleep, but it disturbs the sleep cycle and can cause you to wake up early the next day. In addition, stay away from caffeinated drinks like coffee or cola for several hours before bedtime. Caffeine works as a stimulant even on those people who claim they are not affected by it, and the body needs 4 to 5 hours to halve the amount of caffeine in the bloodstream at any one time. If you must drink something before bedtime, try milk; there is evidence to support the folklore that a glass of warm milk at bedtime induces sleep.

**EATING BEFORE BEDTIME** Don't eat heavily before going to bed, since your digestive system will have to do several hours of work. If you must eat something before bedtime, have a light snack.

**EXERCISE** Regular exercise will help you sleep better, but don't engage in a strenuous workout just before going to bed.

**SLEEPING PILLS** Be careful about using sleeping pills. All of the various kinds tend to disrupt the sleep cycle, and long-term use inevitably leads to insomnia. Even on nights before exams, avoid using a sleeping pill. One bad night of sleep tends not to affect performance the next day, whereas a hangover from a sleeping pill may.

**RELAX** Avoid stressful thoughts before bedtime and engage in soothing activities that help you relax. Try to follow the same routine every night before going to bed; it might involve taking a warm bath or listening to soft music for a few minutes. Find a room temperature at which you are comfortable and maintain it throughout the night.

**WHEN ALL FAILS** If you are in bed and have trouble falling asleep, don't get up. Stay in bed and try to relax. But if that fails and you become tense, then get up for a brief time and do something restful that reduces anxiety. Doing push-ups or some other form of exercise to wear yourself out is not a good idea.

**TABLE 6-1**
**Advice for a Good Night's Sleep**
*There is considerable agreement among researchers and clinicians on how to avoid sleep problems. These recommendations are summarized in the table; some are based on actual research, and others are simply the best judgments of experts in the field.*
(After Pion, 1991)

airway to completely collapse. During an apnea, the oxygen level of the blood drops dramatically, leading to the secretion of emergency hormones. This reaction causes the sleeper to awaken in order to begin breathing again.

Most people have a few apneas a night, but people with severe sleep problems may have several hundred apneas per night. With each apnea they wake up in order to resume breathing, but these arousals are so brief they are generally unaware of doing so. The result is that those who suffer from apnea can spend 12 or more hours in bed each night and still be so sleepy the next day that they cannot function and will fall asleep even in the middle of a conversation (Ancoli-Israel, Kripke, & Mason, 1987).

Sleep apnea is common among older men. Sleeping pills, which make arousal more difficult, lengthen periods of apnea (during which the brain is deprived of oxygen) and may prove fatal. Not waking up is probably one of the main reasons people die in their sleep.

## Dreams

Dreaming is an altered state of consciousness in which remembered images and fantasies are temporarily confused with external reality. Investigators do not yet understand why people dream at all, much less why they dream what they do. However, modern methods of study have answered a great many questions about dreaming.

**DOES EVERYONE DREAM?** Although many people do not recall their dreams in the morning, REM-sleep evidence suggests that nonrecallers do as much dreaming as recallers. If you take people who have sworn that they never dreamed in their life, put them in a dream research laboratory and wake them from REM sleep, you will get dream recall at rates comparable to other people. If someone says "I never dream," what they mean is "I can't recall my dreams."

Researchers have proposed several hypotheses to account for differences in dream recall. One possibility is that nonrecallers simply have more difficulty than recallers in remembering their dreams. Another hypothesis suggests that some people awaken relatively easily in the midst of REM sleep and thus recall more dreams than those who sleep more soundly. The most generally accepted model for dream recall supports the idea that what happens on awakening is the crucial factor. According to this hypothesis, unless a distraction-free waking period occurs shortly after dreaming, the memory of the dream is not consolidated (Koulack & Goodenough, 1976; Hobson, 1988).

**HOW LONG DO DREAMS LAST?** Some dreams seem almost instantaneous. The alarm clock rings and we awaken to complex memories of a fire breaking out and fire engines arriving with their sirens blasting. Because the alarm is still ringing, we assume that the sound must have produced the dream. Research suggests, however, that a ringing alarm clock or other sound merely reinstates a complete scene from earlier memories or dreams. This experience has its parallel during wakefulness when a single cue may tap a rich memory that takes some time to tell. The length of a typical dream can be inferred from a REM study in which subjects were awakened and asked to act out what they had been dreaming (Dement & Wolpert, 1958). The time it took them to pantomime the dream was almost the same

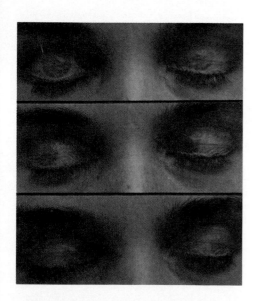

*This multiple-exposure photograph shows the rapid eye movements associated with dreaming.*

as the length of the REM sleep period, suggesting that the incidents in dreams commonly last about as long as they would in real life.

**DO PEOPLE KNOW WHEN THEY ARE DREAMING?** The answer to this question is "sometimes yes." People can be taught to recognize that they are dreaming, and their awareness does not interfere with the dream's spontaneous flow. For example, subjects have been trained to press a switch when they notice that they are dreaming (Salamy, 1970).

Some people have **lucid dreams** in which events seem so normal (lacking the bizarre and illogical character of most dreams) that they feel they are awake and conscious. Only on awakening do they realize it was a dream. Lucid dreamers report doing various "experiments" within their dreams to determine whether they are awake or dreaming. A Dutch physician, van Eeden (1913), was one of the first to give an accurate account of initiating actions within a lucid dream to prove that events were not occurring normally. In a later report, Brown (1936) described a standard experiment in which he jumped and suspended himself in the air. If he did this successfully, he knew he was dreaming. Both Brown and van Eeden report an occasional "false awakening" within a dream. For example, in one of Brown's dreams, he discovered that he was dreaming and decided to call a taxicab as an indication of his control over events. When he reached into his pocket to see if he had some change to pay the driver, he thought that he woke up. He then found the coins scattered about the bed. At this point, he really awoke and found himself lying in a different position and, of course, without any coins.

**CAN PEOPLE CONTROL THE CONTENT OF THEIR DREAMS?** Psychologists have demonstrated that some control of dream content is possible by making suggestions to subjects in the presleep period and then analyzing the content of the dreams that followed. In a carefully designed study of an *implicit predream suggestion,* researchers tested the effect of wearing red goggles for several hours prior to sleep. Although the researchers made no actual suggestion, and the subjects did not understand the purpose of the experiment, many subjects reported that their visual dream worlds were tinted red (Roffwarg, Herman, Bowe-Anders, & Tauber, 1978). In a study of the effect of an *overt predream suggestion,* subjects were asked to try to dream about a personality characteristic that they wished they had. Most of the subjects had at least one dream in which the intended trait could be recognized (Cartwright, 1974).

**Posthypnotic suggestion** is another way of influencing dream content. In one extensive study using this method, detailed dream narratives were suggested to highly responsive hypnotic subjects. After the suggestion, the subject slept until roused from REM sleep. Some of the resulting dreams reflected the thematic aspects of the suggestion without including many of the specific elements, whereas other dreams reflected specific elements of the suggestion (Tart & Dick, 1970).

## Dream Content

Freud's theory that dreams are mental products that can be understood and interpreted was one of the earliest and most comprehensive attempts to explain the content of dreams without reference to the supernatural. In his book, *Interpretation of Dreams* (1900), Freud proposed that dreams provide

*Critical*
# DISCUSSION

## Theories of Dream Sleep

A great deal of research on sleep and dreams has been conducted in recent years, and a number of theories have been proposed. Here we summarize two theories of dream sleep, one proposed by Evans (1984) that takes a cognitive approach and the other by Crick and Mitchison (1983; 1986) that takes a neurobiological approach.

Evans' theory views sleep as a period when the brain disengages from the external world and uses this off-line time to sort through and reorganize the vast array of information that was input during the day. According to the theory, the brain is like a computer with large memory banks and an assortment of control programs. Some of these programs are inherited (instinctive); others

are learned and continually modified by experience. Sleep, particularly REM sleep, is when the brain comes off-line, isolating itself from the sensory and motor neural pathways. In this off-line period the various memory banks and program files are opened and become available for modification and reorganization based on the experiences of the day.

In Evans' theory, we are not consciously aware of the full array of off-line processing that occurs during REM sleep. During dreaming, however, the brain comes back on-line for a brief time and the conscious mind observes a small sample of the programs being run. The brain attempts to interpret this information the same way it would interpret stimuli coming from the outside world, giving rise to the kind of pseudo-event that characterizes dreams. Thus, according to Evans, dreams are nothing more than a small subset of the vast amount of information that is being scanned and sorted during REM sleep, a momentary glimpse by the conscious mind that we remember if we wake. Evans believes that dreams can be useful in inferring the full array of processing that occurs during REM sleep, but they are an extremely small sample on which to base

inferences.

Crick and Mitchison base their theory on the fact that the cortex—unlike other parts of the brain—is made up of richly interconnected *neuronal networks* in which each cell has the capacity to excite its neighbors. They believe that memories are encoded in these networks, with neurons and their many synapses representing different features of a memory. These networks are like spiderwebs, and when one point in the web is excited, perhaps by hearing a few notes of a song, a pulse travels throughout the network, prompting recall of the rest of the song. The problem with such network systems is that they malfunction when there is an overload of incoming information. Too many memories in one network may produce either bizarre associations to a stimulus (fantasies) or the same response whatever the stimulus (obsessions), or associations may be triggered without any stimulus (hallucinations).

To deal with information overload, the brain needs a mechanism to debug and tune the network. Such a debugging mechanism would work best when the system was isolated from external inputs and it would have to have a way of randomly activating the network in order to

the "royal road to a knowledge of the unconscious activities of the mind." He believed that dreams are a disguised attempt at *wish fulfillment*. By this he meant that the dream touches on wishes, needs, or ideas that the individual finds unacceptable and have been repressed to the unconscious (for example, Oedipal longings for the parent of the opposite sex). These wishes and ideas are the **latent content** of the dream. Freud used the metaphor of a censor to explain the conversion of latent content to **manifest content** (the characters and events that make up the actual narrative of the dream). In effect, Freud said, the censor protects the sleeper, enabling him to express repressed impulses symbolically while avoiding the guilt or anxiety that would occur if they were to appear consciously in undisguised form.

The transformation of latent content into manifest content is done by the "dream work," as Freud called it, the function of which is to code and disguise material in the unconscious in such a way that it can reach consciousness. However, sometimes the dream work fails, and anxiety awakens the dreamer. The dream essentially expresses the fulfillment of wishes or needs that are too painful or guilt-inducing to acknowledge consciously (Freud, 1933).

The cognitive side of dreaming—its role in problem solving and thinking—has been increasingly recognized (see the Critical Discussion, "Theo-

eliminate spurious connections. The mechanism Crick and Mitchison propose is REM sleep: the hallucinatory quality of dreams is nothing more than the random neural firing needed for the daily cleanup of the network.

As noted earlier, the brain is very active during REM sleep, barraged with neural signals traveling from the brain stem to the cortex. According to the theory, these signals somehow erase the spurious memory associations formed during the previous day; we awake with the network cleaned up, and the brain ready for new input. Crick and Mitchison also suggest that trying to remember one's dreams—a key aspect of psychoanalysis—may not be a good idea. They believe that such remembering could help to retain patterns of thought that are better forgotten, the very patterns the system is attempting to tune out.

The two theories have some common features, but there are clear differences. Evans views REM sleep as a time when the brain modifies and reorganizes the vast array of information input during the day. Crick and Mitchison, on the other hand, see REM sleep as a time when spurious or useless information is purged from memory. Evans regards conscious dreams as a surface indicator

of the rich reorganizational process taking place during REM sleep, whereas Crick and Mitchison suggest that dreams are little more than random noise with no real content. But both theories assume that REM sleep plays a role in the storage of memories and in preparing the brain from one day to the next to deal with new information inputs. Neither theory assigns to dreams the rich symbolism and concealed meaning that typifies a psychoanalytic approach to the analysis of dream content.

Winson (1990) provides some interesting evidence from animal research that bears on both of these dream theories. The key to this work is a unique brain wave, known as the **theta rhythm.** This six hertz EEG is set in motion by neurons in the brain stem and can be observed in the **hippocampus,** a brain structure known to be involved in forming long-term memories. Winson believes that in an awake animal, theta rhythm "tags" incoming information vital to the animal's survival and this tagged information is meshed into long-term memory at a later time during REM sleep. He points out that theta rhythm is observed in awake animals only when they are engaged in activities

vital to their survival; for example, theta rhythm occurs in cats when they are stalking prey. He discovered that the same brain neurons that were activated when a stimulus was presented to an awake animal while its theta rhythm was pulsing, are reactivated during REM sleep. Theta rhythm is always present during REM sleep and absent during NREM sleep. Monitoring certain brain neurons, Winson showed that only those that fired vigorously during the day while theta rhythm was in progress fired again during the animal's REM sleep. There is some evidence suggesting that a similar mechanism may be at work in humans, and that theta rhythm indeed acts to tag important incoming information for later processing during REM sleep. Thus dreaming would require the meshing of new information with old memories, a process that could explain why dreams often involve a mix of life's current difficulties and childhood experiences.

ries of Dream Sleep"). Although cognitive psychologists reject many of Freud's ideas, they also note that his theory has cognitive aspects. In fact, Freud's emphasis on thought transformations through free association goes far beyond the oversimplified popular notion that all the transformations in dreams can be explained as wish fulfillment.

# Psychoactive Drugs

Since ancient times, people have used drugs to alter their state of consciousness—to stimulate or relax, to bring on sleep or prevent it, to enhance ordinary perceptions, or to produce hallucinations. Drugs that affect behavior, consciousness, and mood are called **psychoactive**. They include not only street drugs such as heroin and marijuana but also tranquilizers, stimulants, and such familiar drugs as alcohol, tobacco, and coffee. Table 6-2 lists and classifies the psychoactive drugs that are commonly used and abused.

It may be difficult for students today to appreciate the major changes in patterns of drug-taking behavior that have occurred over the past 40 years. In the 1950s, very few people used drugs (other than cigarettes and alcohol). Since the 1950s, however, we have moved from a relatively drug-free society to a drug-using society. A number of factors have contributed to this change. For instance, the widespread use of tranquilizers for the treatment of mental illness and emotional problems, which began in the 1950s, and the appearance of oral contraceptives in 1960 did much to change people's attitudes toward drugs. Drugs became an option available to solve problems—problems other than physical illness. In the 1960s and 1970s, Americans also explored new life-styles, following the opportunities provided by easier transportation and expanding job markets. With increased leisure time people looked for new outlets, and the recreational use of drugs became such an outlet.

For these and other reasons, drug use, particularly among young people, increased steadily through the 1960s and 1970s. In the 1980s, however, drug use began a gradual downward trend that has continued in the 1990s (see Figure 6-5). The factors contributing to the decline are many, but certainly one has been a significant increase in the number of young people who believe that using drugs, even experimentally, is dangerous. Another factor appears to be an increased concern for health and physical fitness. Even with this downturn in recent years, the United States still has the highest rates of drug usage among the world's industrialized nations (Johnson, O'Malley, & Bachman, 1992).

All of the drugs listed in Table 6-2 are assumed to affect behavior and consciousness because they act in specific biochemical ways on the brain. With repeated use, an individual can become physically or psychologically dependent on any of these drugs. **Physical dependence,** also called addiction, is characterized by **tolerance** (that is, with continued use, the individual must take more and more of the drug to achieve the same effect) and **withdrawal symptoms** (if use is discontinued, the person experiences unpleasant physical and psychological reactions). **Psychological dependence** refers to a need that develops through learning. People who habitually use a drug to relieve anxiety may become dependent on it, even though no physical need develops. For example, marijuana smokers do not appear to build up tolerance for the drug, and they experience minimal withdrawal symptoms. Nevertheless, a person who learns to use marijuana when faced with stressful situations will find the habit difficult to break. With some drugs, such as alcohol, psychological dependence progresses to physical dependence as more and more of the substance is consumed.

**FIGURE 6-5**
**Illicit Drug Use** *Percentage of American high-school seniors who reported using an illicit drug in the 12-month period prior to graduation. Drugs include marijuana, hallucinogens, cocaine, and heroin, and any nonprescribed use of opiates, stimulants, sedatives, and tranquilizers.* (After Johnson, O'Malley, & Bachman, 1992)

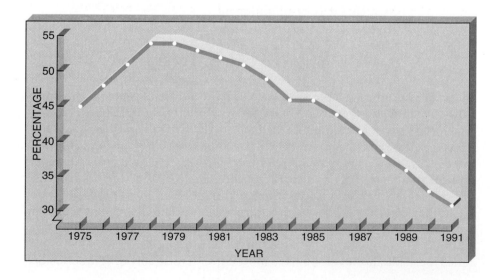

# Depressants

Drugs that depress the central nervous system include the minor tranquilizers, barbiturates (sleeping pills), and ethyl alcohol. Of these, the one most used and abused is alcohol. Almost every society, primitive or industrialized, consumes alcohol. It can be produced by fermenting a wide variety of materials: grains, such as rye, wheat, and corn; fruits, such as grapes, apples, and plums; and vegetables, such as potatoes. Through the process of distillation, the alcoholic content of a fermented beverage can be increased to obtain "hard liquors" such as whiskey or rum.

**EFFECTS OF ALCOHOL** In small quantities, alcohol appears to increase people's energy and make them feel lively and sociable. In reality, it is a central nervous system depressant, not a stimulant. The initial stimulating effect of alcohol is believed to occur because the inhibitory synapses in the brain are suppressed slightly earlier than the excitatory synapses. Since the brain's neurons maintain a close balance between excitation and inhibition, the suppression of inhibitory synapses results in a feeling of excitation, or stimulation. However, the excitatory synapses soon become suppressed, too; the stimulating effects are overridden, causing drowsiness and slowed sensory and motor functions.

Measuring the amount of alcohol in the air we exhale (as in a breath analyzer) gives a reliable index of alcohol in the blood. Consequently, it is easy to determine the relationship between **blood alcohol concentration (BAC)** and behavior. At concentrations of .03 to .05 percent in the blood (30 to 50 milligrams of alcohol per 100 milliliters of blood), alcohol produces light-headedness, relaxation, and release of inhibitions. People say things they might not ordinarily say; they tend to become more sociable and expansive. Self-confidence may increase, whereas motor reactions will begin to slow (a pair of effects that makes it dangerous to drive after drinking).

At a BAC of .10 percent, sensory and motor functions become noticeably impaired. Speech becomes slurred, and people have difficulty coordinating their movements. Some people tend to become angry and aggressive; others grow silent and morose. The drinker is seriously incapacitated at a level of .20 percent, and a level above .40 percent may cause death. The legal definition of intoxication in most states is a BAC of .10 percent (one-tenth of 1 percent).

How much can a person drink without becoming legally intoxicated? The relationship between BAC and alcohol intake is not simple. It depends on a person's sex, body weight, and speed of consumption. Age, individual metabolism, and experience with drinking are also factors. Although the effects of alcohol intake on BAC vary a great deal, the average effects are shown in Figure 6-6. Moreover, it is not true that beer or wine is less likely to make someone drunk than so called hard drinks. A 4-ounce glass of wine, a 12-ounce can of beer, and 1.2 ounces of 80-proof whiskey have about the same alcohol content and will have about the same effect.

**ALCOHOL USAGE** Drinking is viewed as an integral part of social life for many college students. It promotes conviviality, eases tensions, releases inhibitions, and generally adds to the fun. Nevertheless, social drinking can create problems in terms of lost study time, poor performance on an exam because of feeling hung over, and arguments or accidents while intoxicated. Clearly the most serious problem is accidents: alcohol-related automobile

---

## DEPRESSANTS (SEDATIVES)

Alcohol (ethanol)
Barbiturates
  Nembutal
  Seconal
Minor tranquilizers
  Miltown
  Valium

## OPIATES (NARCOTICS)

Opium and its derivatives
  Codeine
  Heroin
  Morphine
Methadone

## STIMULANTS

Amphetamines
  Benzedrine
  Dexedrine
  Methedrine
Cocaine
Nicotine
Caffeine

## HALLUCINOGENS

LSD
Mescaline
Psilocybin
PCP (Phencyclidine)

## CANNABIS

Marijuana
Hashish

**TABLE 6-2**
**Psychoactive Drugs That Are Commonly Abused** *Only a few examples of each class of drug are given. The generic name (for example, psilocybin) or the brand name (Miltown for meprobamate; Seconal for secobarbital) is used, depending on which is more familiar.*

**FIGURE 6-6**
**BAC and Alcohol Intake** *Approximate values of BAC as a function of alcohol consumption in a 2-hour period. For example, if you weigh 180 pounds and had four beers in two hours, your BAC would be between .05 and .09 percent and your driving ability would be seriously impaired. Six beers in the same 2-hour period would give you a BAC of over .10 percent—the level accepted as proof of intoxication.* (After National Highway Traffic Safety Administration)

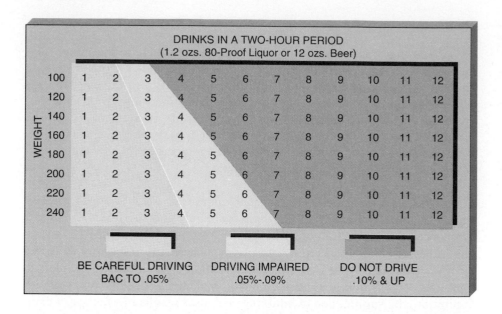

accidents are the leading cause of death among 15- to 24-year-olds. When the legal drinking age was lowered from 21 to 18 years of age in a number of states, traffic fatalities of 18- and 19-year-olds increased 20 to 50 percent. Most states have since raised their minimum drinking age, and a significant decrease in traffic accidents has followed.

About two-thirds of American adults report that they drink alcohol. At least 10 percent of them have social, psychological, or medical problems resulting from alcohol use. Probably half of that 10 percent are physically dependent on alcohol. Heavy or prolonged drinking can lead to serious health problems. High blood pressure, stroke, ulcers, cancers of the mouth, throat, and stomach, cirrhosis of the liver, and depression are some of the conditions associated with the regular use of substantial amounts of alcohol.

The use of alcohol is widespread among those under 21 years of age, although some modest declines have occurred among high-school seniors. The proportion reporting any alcohol use in the prior month fell from a peak of 72 percent in 1980 to 55 percent in 1991. The proportion reporting at least one occasion of "binge drinking" (having five or more drinks in a row) during the prior two weeks also fell from a peak of 41 percent in 1983 to 31 percent in 1991. Since the purchase of alcohol is illegal for high-school seniors, these percentages still represent very high levels of drinking—despite the gradual downward trend (Johnston, O'Malley & Bachman, 1992).

Among college students the drinking rates are even higher, and the proportional decline in them have been smaller. For example, 75 percent of college students in 1991 said they consumed alcohol in the prior month (down from a high of 83 percent in 1982) and 41 percent reported at least one occasion of binge drinking during the prior two weeks (down from a high of 45 percent in 1986). The percentage of college students involved in binge drinking is particularly striking when compared to a much lower percentage for other people of the same age (41 percent for college students and 32 percent for all others, in 1991). Clearly, abusive drinking is a serious problem for college students (Johnston, O'Malley & Bachman, 1992). No single approach has emerged for dealing with the problem, but an increasing number of universities no longer permit alcohol on campus. Others have taken a more aggressive stand. In New Jersey, Rutgers University established spe-

ing for students recovering from alcohol and drug dependency; between classes they can attend counseling sessions without having to leave campus. The efforts of colleges and universities have been intensified by the 1989 Drug Free School and Campuses Act, requiring institutions to make alcohol education programs and services like counseling available to students and employees.

Alcohol can also produce risks for a developing fetus. Mothers who drink heavily are twice as likely to suffer repeated miscarriages and to produce low birth-weight babies. A condition called **fetal alcohol syndrome,** characterized by mental retardation and multiple deformities of the face and mouth, is caused by maternal drinking. The amount of alcohol needed to produce this syndrome is unclear, but it is thought that as little as a few ounces of alcohol a week can be detrimental (Streissguth, Clarren, & Jones, 1985).

**ALCOHOLISM** There are various definitions of alcoholism, but almost all of them include the *inability to abstain* (the feeling that you cannot get through the day without a drink) or a *lack of control* (an inability to stop after one or two drinks). Table 6-3 lists some questions to help people determine whether or not they have a drinking problem.

The peak drinking years for most people are between ages 16 and 25. In the late 20s to early 30s, the average drinker decreases his or her alcohol consumption. The alcoholic, in contrast, maintains or increases his or her drinking pattern and has the first major alcohol-related life problem during this period. The average alcoholic seeks help in the early 40s after a decade of difficulties. If the alcohol problems continue, the person is likely to die 15 years earlier than the life expectancy for the general population (Schuckit, 1989).

*Ages 16 through 25 are peak drinking years for most people.*

The sooner you recognize a drinking problem in yourself, the easier it is to get out from under it. Below are some questions that will help you learn how dependent you are on drinking. This is a time to be absolutely honest with yourself—only you can know how seriously you are being hurt by the role alcohol plays in your life.

1. Has someone close to you sometimes expressed concern about your drinking?
2. When faced with a problem, do you often turn to alcohol for relief?
3. Are you sometimes unable to meet home or work responsibilities because of drinking?
4. Have you ever required medical attention as a result of drinking?
5. Have you ever experienced a blackout—a total loss of memory while still awake—when drinking?
6. Have you ever come in conflict with the law in connection with your drinking?
7. Have you often failed to keep promises you have made to yourself about controlling drinking?

If you have answered yes to any of the above questions, your drinking is probably affecting your life in some major ways and you should do something about it—before it gets worse.

**TABLE 6-3**
**Signs of Alcoholism** *Questions developed by the National Institute on Alcohol Abuse and Alcoholism to help people determine whether or not they have a drinking problem.*

While this scenario describes the *average* alcoholic, heavy drinking can progress to alcoholism at any age. People who become psychologically dependent on alcohol—who habitually use alcohol to handle stress and anxiety—stand a good chance of becoming alcoholics. They are apt to become trapped in a vicious cycle. By resorting to alcohol when confronted with problems, they handle these problems ineffectively. As a consequence, they feel even more anxious and inadequate and consume more alcohol in an attempt to bolster their self-esteem. Prolonged heavy drinking leads to physical dependency: a person's tolerance rises so that more and more alcohol must be consumed to achieve the same effect, and the individual begins to experience withdrawal symptoms when he or she abstains from drinking. Withdrawal symptoms may range from feelings of irritability and general malaise to tremors and intense anxiety. In some instances, they include confusion, hallucinations, and convulsions. This syndrome, called *delirium tremens* (DTs), usually occurs only in chronic alcoholics who stop drinking after a sustained period of heavy consumption (Julien, 1992).

Although our definition of alcoholism includes the inability to abstain from drinking or the lack of control after starting to drink, very few alcoholics stay drunk until they die. They usually alternate periods of abstinence (or light drinking) with periods of serious abuse. Thus, the ability to go for weeks, or even months, without drinking does not mean that an individual is not an alcoholic. Perhaps the most useful criterion for diagnosing alcoholism is whether alcohol is causing problems with job performance, health, or family relationships.

## Opiates

Opium and its derivatives, collectively known as **opiates,** are drugs that diminish physical sensation and the capacity to respond to stimuli by depressing the central nervous system. (These drugs are commonly called "narcotics," but opiates is the more accurate term; the term "narcotics" is not well defined and covers a variety of illegal drugs.) Opiates are medically useful for their painkilling properties, but their ability to alter mood and reduce anxiety has led to widespread illegal consumption. Opium, which is the air-dried juice of the opium poppy, contains a number of chemical substances, including morphine and codeine. Codeine, a common ingredient in prescription painkillers and cough suppressants, is relatively mild in its effects (at least at low doses). Morphine and its derivative, heroin, are much more potent. Most illegal drug use involves heroin because, being more concentrated, it can be concealed and smuggled more easily than morphine.

**HEROIN USAGE** Heroin can be injected, smoked, or inhaled. At first, the drug produces a sense of well-being. Experienced users report a special thrill, or rush, within a minute or two after an intravenous injection. Some describe this sensation as intensely pleasurable, similar to an orgasm. Young people who sniff heroin report that they forget everything that troubles them. Following this, the user feels fixed, or gratified, with no awareness of hunger, pain, or sexual urges. The person may "go on the nod," alternately waking and drowsing while comfortably watching television or reading a book. Unlike the alcoholic, the heroin user can readily produce skilled responses to agility and intellectual tests and seldom becomes aggressive or assaultive.

The changes in consciousness produced by heroin are not very striking; there are no exciting visual experiences or feelings of being transported elsewhere. It is the change in mood—the feeling of euphoria and reduced anxiety—that prompts people to *start* using this drug. However, heroin is very addictive; even a brief period of usage can create physical dependency. After a person has been smoking or "sniffing" (inhaling) heroin for a while, tolerance builds up, and this method no longer produces the desired effect. In an attempt to recreate the original high, the individual may progress to "skin popping" (injecting under the skin) and then to "mainlining" (injecting into a vein). Once the user starts mainlining, stronger and stronger doses are required to produce the high, and the physical discomforts of withdrawal from the drug become intense (chills, sweating, stomach cramps, vomiting, headaches). Thus, the motivation to continue using the drug stems from the need to avoid pain and discomfort.

The hazards of heroin use are many. Death from an overdose is always a possibility because the concentration of street heroin fluctuates widely. Thus, the user can never be sure of the potency of the powder in a newly purchased supply. Death is caused by suffocation resulting from depression of the brain's respiratory center. Heroin use is generally associated with a serious deterioration of personal and social life. Because maintaining the habit is costly, the user often becomes involved in illegal activities.

Additional dangers of heroin use include AIDS (Acquired Immune Deficiency Syndrome), hepatitis, and other infections associated with unsterile injections. Sharing drug needles is an extremely easy way to be infected with the AIDS virus. Blood from an infected person can be trapped in the needle or syringe, and then injected directly into the bloodstream of the next person who uses the needle. The sharing of needles and syringes by those who shoot drugs is the most rapidly increasing way that the AIDS virus is being spread.

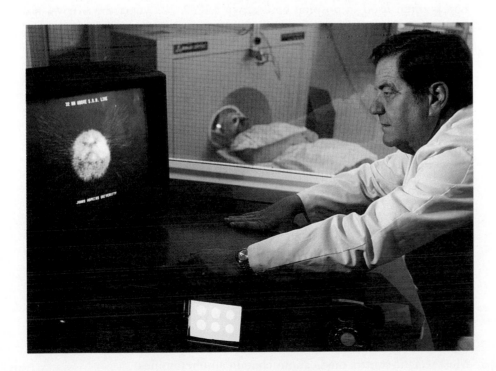

*PET scans show the effects of opiates on the neural activity of different brain areas.*

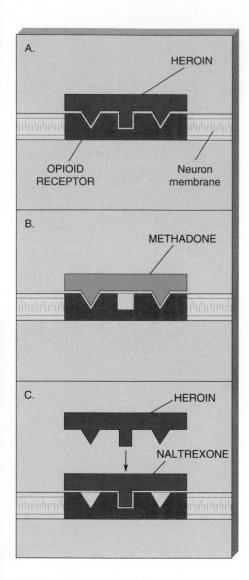

**FIGURE 6-7**
**Drug-Abuse Medications** *(a) Heroin binds to opioid receptors and produces a feeling of pleasure—mimicking the body's naturally occurring endorphins. (b) Methadone, an agonist drug, will also bind to opioid receptors and produce a pleasant sensation. The drug reduces both the craving for heroin and the associated withdrawal symptoms. (c) Naltrexone, an antagonist drug, acts to block the opioid receptors so that heroin cannot gain access to them. The craving for heroin is not satisfied and the drug has not proved generally effective as a treatment method.*

**OPIOID RECEPTORS** In the 1970s, researchers made a major break-through in understanding opiate addiction with the discovery that opiates act on very specific neuroreceptor sites in the brain. Neurotransmitters travel across the synaptic junction between two neurons and bind to neuroreceptors, triggering activity in the receiving neuron (see Chapter 2). In molecular shape, the opiates resemble a group of neurotransmitters called **endorphins.** These endorphins bind to **opioid receptors,** producing sensations of pleasure as well as reducing discomfort (Julien, 1992). Heroin and morphine relieve pain by binding to opioid receptors that are unfilled (see Figure 6-7). Repeated heroin use causes a drop in endorphin production; the body then needs more heroin to fill the unoccupied opioid receptors in order to reduce pain. The person experiences painful withdrawal symptoms when heroin is discontinued because many opioid receptors are left unfilled (since the normal endorphin production has decreased). In essence, the heroin has replaced the body's own natural opiates (Koob and Bloom, 1988).

These research findings have led to the development of new drugs that operate by modulating the opioid receptors. The drug-abuse medications, generally, fall into two classes: *agonists* and *antagonists*. Agonists bind to the opioid receptors to produce a feeling of pleasure thereby reducing the craving for opiates; but they cause less psychological and physiological impairment than the opiates. Antagonists also lock onto the opioid receptors, but in a way that does not activate them; the drug serves to "block" the receptors so that the opiates cannot gain access to them. Thus there is no feeling of pleasure and the craving is not satisfied (see Figure 6-7).

Methadone is the best known agonist drug for treating heroin-dependent individuals. It is addictive in its own right, but it produces less psychological impairment than heroin and has few disruptive physical effects. When taken orally in low doses, it suppresses the craving for heroin and prevents withdrawal symptoms.

Naltrexone, an antagonist drug, blocks the action of heroin because it has a greater affinity for the opioid receptors than does heroin itself. Naltrexone is often used in hospital emergency rooms to reverse the effects of a heroin overdose. But as a treatment for heroin addiction, it has not proved generally effective. It appears to be helpful, however, for those who realize that they have more to gain by being drug free than by being drug dependent. Interestingly, naltrexone does reduce the craving for alcohol. Alcohol causes the release of endorphins, and naltrexone, by blocking opioid receptors, reduces the pleasurable effects of alcohol and consequently the desire for it (Julien, 1992).

## Stimulants

**AMPHETAMINES** In contrast to depressants and opiates, stimulants are drugs that increase arousal. **Amphetamines** are powerful stimulants, sold under such trade names as Methedrine, Dexedrine, and Benzedrine and known colloquially as "speed," "uppers," or "Bennies." The immediate effects of consuming such drugs are an increase in alertness and a decrease in feelings of fatigue and boredom. Strenuous activities that require endurance seem easier when amphetamines are taken. As with other drugs, the ability of amphetamines to alter mood and increase self-confidence is the principal reason for their use. People also use them to stay awake and to lose weight. Most weight-control medications contain amphetamines.

Low doses that are taken for limited periods to overcome fatigue (as during nighttime driving) seem to be relatively safe. However, as the stimulating effects of amphetamines wear off, there is a period of compensatory letdown during which the user feels depressed, irritable, and fatigued. He or she may be tempted to take more of the drug. Tolerance develops quickly, and the user needs increasingly larger doses to produce the desired effect. Since high doses can have dangerous side effects—agitation, confusion, heart palpitations, and elevated blood pressure—medications containing amphetamines should be used with caution.

When tolerance develops to the point at which oral doses are no longer effective, many users inject amphetamines into a vein. Large intravenous doses produce an immediate pleasant experience (a flash or rush); this sensation is followed by irritability and discomfort, which can be overcome only by an additional injection. If this sequence is repeated every few hours over a period of days, it will end in a "crash," a deep sleep followed by a period of lethargy and depression. The amphetamine abuser may seek relief from this discomfort by turning to alcohol or heroin.

Long-term amphetamine use is accompanied by drastic deterioration of physical and mental health. The user, or "speed freak," may develop symptoms that are indistinguishable from those of acute schizophrenia (see Chapter 16). These symptoms include paranoid delusions (the false belief that people are persecuting you or out to get you) and visual or auditory hallucinations. The paranoid delusions may lead to unprovoked violence. For example, in the midst of an amphetamine epidemic in Japan (during the early 1950s when amphetamines were sold without prescription and advertised for "elimination of drowsiness and repletion of the spirit"), 50 percent of the murder cases in a 2-month period were related to amphetamine abuse (Hemmi, 1969).

**COCAINE**  Like other stimulants, **cocaine,** or "coke," a substance obtained from the dried leaves of the coca plant, increases energy and self-confidence; it makes the user feel witty and hyperalert. In the early part of this century, cocaine was widely used and easy to obtain; in fact, it was an ingredient in the early recipe of Coca-Cola. Its use then declined, but recently its popularity has been increasing, even though it is now illegal. Indeed, cocaine is the drug of choice for many conventional and upwardly mobile young adults who consider it safer than heroin or amphetamines.

Cocaine can be inhaled or it can be made into a solution and injected directly into a vein. It can also be converted into a flammable compound known as *crack* and smoked.

One of the earliest studies of the effects of cocaine is reported by Freud (1885). In an account of his own use of cocaine, he was at first highly favorable to the drug and encouraged its use. He noted

> ...the exhilaration and lasting euphoria, which in no way differs from the normal euphoria of the healthy person....You perceive an increase of self-control and possess more vitality and capacity for work....In other words, you are simply normal, and it is so hard to believe that you are under the influence of any drug....Long intensive mental or physical work is performed without any fatigue....This result is enjoyed without any of the unpleasant after-effects that follow exhilaration brought about by alcohol. (1885/1974, p. 9)

Freud soon withdrew this unreserved support, however, after he treated a friend with cocaine and the results were disastrous. The friend developed a

**FIGURE 6-8**

**Molecular Effects of Cocaine** *(a) A nerve impulse causes the release of neurotransmitters that carry the signal across the synapse to a receiving neuron. Some of the neuro-transmitters are then reabsorbed into the originating neuron* (reuptake process), *while the rest are broken up chemically and made inactive* (degradation process). *These processes are discussed in Chapter 2. (b) Several lines of research indicate that cocaine blocks the reuptake process for three neurotransmitters (dopamine, serotonin, and norepinephrine) that are involved in the regulation of mood. With reuptake hampered by cocaine, the normal effects of these neurotransmitters are amplified; in particular, an excess of dopamine is associated with feelings of euphoria. However, prolonged cocaine use produces a shortage of these neurotransmitters since their reuptake for later use is blocked; that is, the body degrades them at a faster rate than it can manufacture them anew. With the normal supply depleted by repeated cocaine use, eurphoria is replaced by anxiety and depression.*

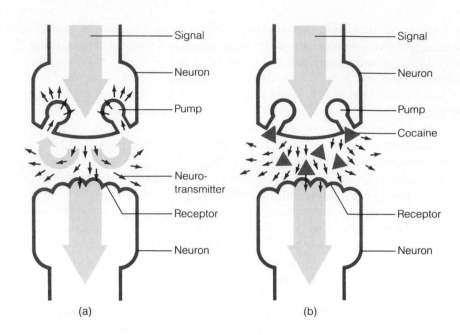

(a)    (b)

severe addiction, demanded larger dosages of the drug, and was debilitated until his death.

Despite earlier reports to the contrary, and as Freud soon discovered, cocaine is highly addictive. In fact, it has become more addictive and dangerous in recent years with the emergence of crack. Tolerance develops with repeated use, and withdrawal effects, while not as dramatic as with the opiates, do occur. The restless irritability that follows the euphoric high becomes, with repeated use, a feeling of depressed anguish. The down is as bad as the up was good and can be alleviated only by more cocaine (see Figure 6-8).

Heavy cocaine users can experience the same abnormal symptoms as high-level amphetamine users. A common visual hallucination is flashes of light ("snow lights") or moving lights. Less common but more disturbing is the feeling that bugs are crawling under the skin—"cocaine bugs." The hallucination may be so strong that the individual will use a knife to cut out the bugs. These experiences occur because cocaine is causing the sensory neurons to fire spontaneously.

Studies of babies exposed to cocaine before birth indicate that the drug is causing an epidemic of damaged infants, some of whom will be impaired for life because the mother used cocaine even briefly during pregnancy. The damaging effects include retarded growth in the womb, neurological abnormalities, malformed genital and urinary organs, and brain-damaging strokes. The research indicates that even a single exposure to cocaine during pregnancy can cause lasting damage. Cocaine readily crosses the placenta and the fetus converts a significant portion into norcocaine—an even more potent drug. Norcocaine does not leave the womb; the fetus excretes it into the amniotic fluid and then swallows it, re-exposing itself repeatedly to the drug. While a single dose of cocaine and its metabolites clear out of an adult body in about 2 days, a fetus is exposed for 5 or 6 days. As a consequence, almost no cocaine-exposed baby escapes its damaging effects (Julien, 1992).

Just as there is a heroin–AIDS connection, injecting cocaine can lead to AIDS and other diseases if drug needles are shared among several people. In some ways AIDS may be more of a problem for cocaine users than for heroin users. One reason is "binge use," with cocaine users sharing a needle for injection many times in a short period, unlike heroin addicts, who fall asleep after injection.

## Hallucinogens

Drugs whose main effect is to change perceptual experience are called **hallucinogens,** or *psychedelics*. Hallucinogens typically change the user's perception of both his or her internal and external worlds. Usual environmental stimuli are experienced as novel events—for example, sounds and colors seem dramatically different. Time perception is so altered that minutes may seem like hours. The user may experience auditory, visual, and tactile hallucinations and will have a decreased ability to differentiate between himself and his surroundings.

Some hallucinogenic drugs are derived from plants—such as mescaline from cactus and psilocybin from mushrooms. Others are synthesized in the laboratory, such as LSD (**lysergic acid diethylamide**) and PCP (**phencyclidine**).

*Drug users who share needles increase their risk of contracting AIDS.*

**LSD** The drug LSD, or "acid," is a colorless, odorless, tasteless substance that is often sold dissolved on sugar cubes or pieces of paper. It is a very potent drug that produces hallucinations at low doses. Some users have vivid hallucinations of colors and sounds, whereas others have mystical or semireligious experiences. Anyone can have an unpleasant, frightening reaction (or "bad trip"), even those who have had many pleasant LSD experiences. Another adverse LSD reaction is the flashback, which may occur days, weeks, or months after the last use of the drug. The individual experiences illusions or hallucinations similar to those experienced when using the drug. Since LSD is almost completely eliminated from the body within 24 hours after it is taken, the flashback is probably a restoration of memories of the prior experience.

More threatening to the LSD user is the loss of reality orientation that can occur with the drug. This alteration in consciousness can lead to an irrational and disoriented behavior and, occasionally, to a panic state in which the victim feels that he cannot control what the body is doing or thinking. People have jumped from high places to their death when in this state. LSD was popular during the 1960s, but its use has declined, probably due to widespread reports of severe drug reactions, as well as reports of genetic damage to users and their offspring.

**PCP** Although it is sold as a hallucinogen (under such street names as "Angel Dust," "Shermans," and "Superacid"), PCP is technically classified as a dissociative anesthetic. It may cause hallucinations, but it also makes the user feel dissociated or apart from the environment.

PCP was first synthesized in 1956 for use as a general anesthetic. It had the advantage of eliminating pain without producing a deep coma. However, its legal manufacture was discontinued when doctors found that the drug produced agitation, hallucinations, and a psychotic-like state resembling schizophrenia among many patients. Because the ingredients are cheap and the drug is relatively easy to manufacture in a kitchen laboratory, PCP is widely used as an adulterant of other, more expensive street drugs. Much of what is sold as THC (the active ingredient of marijuana) is really PCP.

PCP can be taken in liquid or pill form, but more often it is smoked or snorted. In low doses it produces an insensitivity to pain and an experience similar to a moderately drunken state—one of confusion, loss of inhibition, and poor psychomotor coordination. Higher doses produce a disoriented, co-malike condition. Unlike the person who experiences LSD, the PCP user is unable to observe his or her drug-induced state and frequently has no memory of it.

The effects of PCP are not clearly understood. While the drug reduces a person's sensitivity to pain, the user also seems to experience heightened sensory input; the person feels bombarded by an overload of stimuli. Contrary to the popular image, PCP users are seldom violent. When the police or someone else try to help the person because he or she looks drunk or sick, the increased stimulation of being picked up or grabbed increases the PCP user's arousal. In flailing around to get away, the user may injure others and himself, especially since the user is insensitive to pain.

## Cannabis

The **cannabis** plant has been harvested since ancient times for its psychoactive effects. The dried leaves and flowers, or **marijuana,** is the form in which it is most often used in this country, while the solidified resin of the plant, called **hashish** ("hash"), is commonly used in the Middle East. The active ingredient in both substances is THC (tetrahydrocannabinol). Taken orally in small doses (5 to 10 milligrams), THC produces a mild high; larger doses (30 to 70 milligrams) produce severe and longer-lasting reactions that resemble those of hallucinogenic drugs. As with alcohol, the reaction often has two stages: a period of stimulation and euphoria followed by a period of tranquillity and sleep.

Regular users of marijuana report a number of sensory and perceptual changes: a general euphoria and sense of well-being, some distortions of

*Drug use among young people, including marijuana, has declined since the late 1970s.*

space and time, and changes in social perception. Not all marijuana experiences are pleasant. Sixteen percent of regular users report anxiety, fearfulness, and confusion as a "usual occurrence," and about one-third report that they occasionally experience such symptoms as acute panic, hallucinations, and unpleasant distortions in body image (Halikas, Goodwin, & Guze, 1971; Negretc & Kwan, 1972).

Marijuana interferes with performance on complex tasks. Motor coordination is significantly impaired by low to moderate doses; and tracking (the ability to follow a moving stimulus) is especially sensitive to the effects of marijuana (Institute of Medicine, 1982). These findings make it clear that driving while under the drug's influence is dangerous. The number of automobile accidents related to marijuana use is difficult to determine because, unlike alcohol, THC declines rapidly in the blood, quickly going to the fatty tissues and organs of the body. A blood analysis two hours after a heavy dose of marijuana may show no signs of THC, even though an observer would judge the person to be clearly impaired. It is estimated that one-fourth of all drivers involved in accidents are under the influence of marijuana alone or marijuana in combination with alcohol (Jones & Lovinger, 1985).

The effects of marijuana may persist long after the subjective feelings of euphoria or sleepiness have passed. A study of aircraft pilots using a simulated flight-landing task found that performance was significantly impaired as much as 24 hours after smoking one marijuana cigarette containing 19 milligrams of THC—despite the fact that the pilots reported no awareness of any aftereffects on their alertness or performance (Yesavage, Leier, Denari, & Hollister, 1985). These findings have led to concern about marijuana use by those whose jobs involve the public safety.

It is a common subjective experience that marijuana disrupts memory functions, and this observation is well documented by research. Marijuana has two clear effects on memory. (1) It makes short-term memory more susceptible to interference. For example, people may lose the thread of a conversation, or forget what they are saying in the middle of a sentence, due to momentary distractions (Darley et al., 1973a). (2) Marijuana disrupts learning; that is, it interferes with the transfer of new information from short-term to long-term memory (Darley et al., 1973b; Darley et al., 1977). These findings suggest that trying to study while under the influence of marijuana is not a good idea; recall of the material will be poor.

# Meditation

In **meditation,** a person achieves an altered state of consciousness by performing certain rituals and exercises. These exercises include controlling and regulating breathing, sharply restricting one's field of attention, eliminating external stimuli, assuming yogic body positions, and forming mental images of an event or symbol. The result is a pleasant, mildly altered subjective state in which the individual feels mentally and physically relaxed. Some individuals, after extensive meditation practice, may have mystical experiences in which they lose self-awareness and gain a sense of being involved in a wider consciousness, however defined. That such meditative techniques may cause a change in consciousness goes back to ancient times and is represented in every major world religion. Buddhists, Hindus, Sufis, Jews, and Christians all have literature describing rituals that induce meditative states.

## Drug Dependence

All of the drugs we have discussed have profound effects on the central nervous system, and an individual can become psychologically or physically dependent on any of them. The fact that students as young as 11 and 12 years are experimenting with drugs is of concern not only because of possible damage to the still-developing nervous system but because early involvement with drugs predicts a more extensive use of drugs later on.

A longitudinal study of high-school students indicates the following stages in drug usage:

beer and wine→hard liquor→
marijuana→other illegal drugs

This does not mean that the use of a particular drug invariably leads to the use of others in the sequence. Only about one-fourth of the students who drank hard liquor progressed to marijuana, and only one-fourth of the marijuana users went on to try such drugs as LSD, amphetamines, or heroin. The students stopped at different stages of usage, but none of them progressed directly from beer or wine to illegal drugs without drinking liquor first, and very few students progressed

from liquor to hard drugs without trying marijuana first (Kandel, 1975; Kandel et al., 1986).

This stepping-stone theory of drug usage has been criticized because the majority of young people who smoke marijuana do not go on to use other drugs. Nevertheless, heavy use of marijuana does appear to increase the likelihood of using other illegal drugs. A nationwide survey of men 20 to 30 years of age showed that, of those who had smoked marijuana 1,000 times or more (roughly equivalent to daily usage for three years), 73 percent later tried cocaine and 35 percent tried heroin. In contrast, less than 1 percent of the people surveyed who did not smoke marijuana used these harder drugs. Of those who had used marijuana fewer than 100

## Traditional Forms of Meditation

Traditional forms of meditation follow the practices of *yoga*, a system of thought based on the Hindu religion, or *Zen*, which is derived from Chinese and Japanese Buddhism. Two common techniques of meditation are an *opening-up meditation*, in which the subject clears his or her mind for receiving new experiences, and a *concentrative meditation*, in which the benefits are obtained through actively attending to some object, word, or idea. The following is a representative statement of opening-up meditation:

> This approach begins with the resolve to do nothing, to think nothing, to make no effort of one's own, to relax completely and let go of one's mind and body . . . stepping out of the stream of ever-changing ideas and feelings which your mind is in, watch the onrush of the stream. Refuse to be submerged in the current. Changing the metaphor . . . watch your ideas, feelings, and wishes fly across the firmament like a flock of birds. Let them fly freely. Just keep a watch. Don't let the birds carry you off into the clouds. (Chauduri, 1965, pp. 30–31)

Here is a corresponding statement used in an experimental study of concentrative meditation:

> The purpose of these sessions is to learn about concentration. Your aim is to concentrate on the blue vase. By concentration I do not mean analyzing the different parts of the vase, but rather, trying to see the vase as it exists in itself, without any connections to other things. Exclude all other thoughts or feelings or sounds or body sensations. (Deikman, 1963, p. 330)

After a few sessions of concentrative meditation, subjects typically report a number of effects: an altered, more intense perception of the vase; some time shortening, particularly in retrospect; conflicting perceptions, as if the vase fills the visual field and does not fill it; decreasing effectiveness of external stimuli (less distraction and eventually less conscious registration); and an impression of the meditative state as pleasant and rewarding.

times, only 7 percent later tried cocaine and 4 percent tried heroin (O'Donnell & Clayton, 1982).

No single personality type is associated with drug use. People try drugs for a variety of reasons, such as curiosity or the desire to experience a new state of consciousness, escape from physical or mental pain, or as a relief from boredom. However, one trait that is predictive of drug usage is social conformity. People who score high on various tests of social conformity (who see themselves as conforming to the traditional values of American society) are less apt to use drugs than those who score low on such tests. The nonconformist may be either a loner who feels no involvement with other people or a member of a subculture that encourages drug use. (Marlatt,

Baer, Donovan, & Kivlahan, 1988). A study of teenagers identified several additional traits, related to social conformity, that are predictive of drug use. Eighth- and ninth-graders who were rated by their classmates as impulsive, inconsiderate, not trustworthy, lacking in ambition, and having poor work habits were more likely to smoke, drink alcohol, and take other drugs. They were also more likely to start using these drugs early and to be heavy users 12 years later as young adults (Smith, 1986).

Newcomb and Bentler (1988) have conducted a major study of the effects of drug use on young people. They conclude that a life-style that involves regular use of drugs also includes nonconformity to traditional values, involvement

with other deviant or illegal behaviors and involvement with individuals engaged in such behaviors, poor family relations, few educational interests, experiences of emotional turmoil, and feelings of alienation and rebellion.

Experimental studies of meditation, which necessarily are of short duration, provide only limited insight into the alterations of consciousness that a person can achieve when meditative practice and training extend over many years. In his study of the *Matramudra*, a centuries-old Tibetan Buddhist text, Brown (1977) has described the complex training required to master the technique. He has also shown that cognitive changes can be expected at different meditative levels. (In this type of meditation, people proceed through five levels until they reach a thoughtless, perceptionless, selfless state known as concentrative samdhi.)

## Meditation for Relaxation

A somewhat commercialized and secularized form of meditation has been widely promoted in the United States and elsewhere under the name of **Transcendental Meditation** or TM (Forem, 1973). The technique is easily learned from a qualified teacher who gives the novice meditator a **mantra** (a special sound) and instructions on how to repeat it over and over to produce the deep rest and awareness characteristic of TM.

A similar state of relaxation can be produced without the mystical associations of TM. Developed by Benson and his colleagues, the technique includes the following steps:

1. Sit quietly in a comfortable position and close your eyes.
2. Deeply relax all your muscles, beginning at your feet and progressing to your face. Keep them deeply relaxed.
3. Breathe through your nose. Become aware of your breathing. As you breathe out, say the word "one" silently to yourself. For example, breathe in . . . out, "one"; in . . . out, "one"; and so on. Continue for 20 minutes. You may open your eyes to check the time, but do not use an alarm. When you finish, sit quietly for several minutes at first with closed eyes and later with opened eyes.

*Traditional forms of meditation have been practiced for hundreds of years as part of some Eastern religions.*

4. Do not worry about whether you are successful in achieving a deep level of relaxation. Maintain a passive attitude and permit relaxation to occur at its own pace. Expect other thoughts. When these distracting thoughts occur, ignore them by thinking "oh well" and continue repeating "one." With practice, the response should come with little effort.

5. Practice the technique once or twice daily but not within two hours after a meal, since the digestive processes seem to interfere with the subjective changes. (Benson, Kotch, Crassweller, & Greenwood, 1977, p. 442)

During this kind of meditation, a person develops a reduced state of physiological arousal. Subjects report feelings quite similar to those generated by other meditative practices: peace of mind, a feeling of being at peace with the world, and a sense of well-being.

## Effects of Meditation

Meditation is an effective technique for inducing relaxation and reducing physiological arousal. Almost all studies of the phenomenon report a significant lowering of the respiratory rate, a decrease in oxygen consumption, and less elimination of carbon dioxide. The heart rate is lowered, blood flow stabilizes, and the concentration of lactate in the blood is decreased (Dillbeck & Orme-Johnson, 1987). Meditation has also proved effective in helping people deal with chronic feelings of anxiety (Eppley, Abrams & Shear, 1989) and in improving self-esteem (Alexander, Rainforth & Gelderloos, 1991).

A number of people involved in *sports psychology* believe that meditation can be useful in getting maximum performance from an athlete (Syer & Connolly, 1984). Engaging in meditation helps reduce stress before an event, and with experience the athlete can learn to relax different muscle groups and appreciate subtle differences in muscle tension. The meditation may also involve forming mental images of the details of an upcoming event, such as a downhill ski race, until the athlete is in total synchrony with the flow of actions. The skier visualizes the release from the starting platform, speeding down the hill, and moving between the gates, and goes through every action in her mind. By creating visual sensations of a successful performance, the athlete is attempting to program the muscles and body for peak efficiency. Golfing great Jack Nicklaus developed this technique on his own years ago. In describing how he images his performance, Nicklaus wrote:

> I never hit a shot, even in practice, without having a sharp, in-focus picture of it in my head. It's like a color movie. First, I "see" the ball where I want it to finish, nice and white and sitting up high on the bright green grass. Then the scene quickly changes, and I "see" the ball going there: its path, trajectory, and shape, even its behavior on landing. Then there's a sort of fade-out, and the next scene shows me making the kind of swing that will turn the previous images into reality. Only at the end of this short, private, Hollywood spectacular do I select a club and step up to the ball. (1974, p. 79)

The research literature on meditation is of mixed quality and some claims, particularly by those who have a commercial interest in the outcome, are suspect. Nevertheless, on balance, the evidence suggests that meditation may reduce arousal (especially in easily stressed individuals) and may be valuable for those suffering from anxiety and tension. To summarize, we quote from Harré and Lamb:

> The value of meditating for an individual depends on attitude and context. In the spiritual market place many contemporary cults of meditation, with their emphasis on gurus and membership of self-defining elitist institutions, may perhaps be seen as an expression of the disintegration of the family system in the modern West and attendant uncertainty regarding parental and sexual roles and mores. Young people, often desperate for guidance, find parental substitutes in strange places and are liable to become brainwashed practitioners of powerful psychosomatic exercises, access to which is made dependent on cult membership and financial contribution. Only where meditation is used as a means to personal development, insight and above all autonomy can its true potential be realized. (1983, p. 377)

# Hypnosis

Of all altered states of consciousness, none has raised more questions than **hypnosis.** Once associated with the occult, hypnosis has now become the subject of rigorous scientific investigation. As in all fields of psychological investigation, uncertainties remain, but by now many facts have been established. The following definition of hypnosis serves as an introduction to the topic:

> Hypnosis may be defined as a social interaction in which one person (designated the subject) responds to suggestions offered by another person (designated the hypnotist) for experiences involving alterations in perception, memory, and voluntary action. In the classic case, these experiences and their accompanying behaviors are associated with subjective conviction bordering on delusion, and involuntariness bordering on compulsion. (Kihlstrom 1985, pp. 385–86)

## Induction of Hypnosis

In hypnosis, a willing and cooperative subject (the only kind that can be hypnotized under most circumstances) relinquishes some control over his behavior to the hypnotist and accepts some reality distortion. The hypnotist uses a variety of methods to induce this condition. For example, the subject may be asked to concentrate all thoughts on a small target (such as a thumb-tack on the wall) while gradually becoming relaxed. A suggestion of sleepiness may be made because, like sleep, hypnosis is a relaxed state in which a person is out of touch with ordinary environmental demands. But sleep is only a metaphor. The subject is told that he will not really go to sleep but will continue to listen to the hypnotist.

The same state can be induced by methods other than relaxation. A hyperalert hypnotic trance is characterized by increased tension and alertness, and the trance-induction procedure is an active one. For example, in one study, subjects riding a stationary laboratory bicycle while receiving suggestions of strength and alertness were as responsive to hypnotic suggestions as were conventionally relaxed subjects (Banyai & Hilgard, 1976). This result denies the common equation of hypnosis with relaxation, but it is consistent with the trance-induction methods used by the whirling dervishes of some Muslim religious orders.

Modern hypnotists do not use authoritarian commands. Indeed, with a little training, subjects can hypnotize themselves (Ruch, 1975). The subject enters the hypnotic state when the conditions are right; the hypnotist merely helps set the conditions. The following changes are characteristic of the hypnotized state.

■ *Planfulness ceases.* A deeply hypnotized subject does not like to initiate activity and would rather wait for the hypnotist to suggest something to do.

*A therapist induces a hypnotic state.*

HYPNOSIS **237**

- *Attention becomes more selective than usual.* A subject who is told to listen only to the hypnotist's voice will ignore any other voices in the room.
- *Enriched fantasy is readily evoked.* A subject may find herself enjoying experiences at a place distant in time and space.
- *Reality testing is reduced and reality distortion is accepted.* A subject may uncritically accept hallucinated experiences (for example, conversing with an imagined person believed to be sitting in a nearby chair) and will not check to determine whether that person is real.
- *Suggestibility is increased.* A subject must accept suggestions in order to be hypnotized at all, but whether suggestibility is increased under hypnosis is a matter of some dispute. Careful studies have found some increase in suggestibility following hypnotic induction, although less than is commonly supposed (Ruch, Morgan, & Hilgard, 1973).
- *Posthypnotic amnesia is often present.* When instructed to do so, a highly responsive hypnotic subject will forget all or most of what transpired during the hypnotic session. When a prearranged release signal is given, the memories are restored.

Not all individuals are equally responsive to hypnosis, as Figure 6-9 indicates. Roughly 5 to 10 percent of the population cannot be hypnotized even by a skilled hypnotist, and the remainder show varying degrees of susceptibility. However, if a person is hypnotized on one occasion, he probably will be equally susceptible on another (Hilgard, 1961).

One might suspect that individuals who are highly responsive to hypnosis would also be highly suggestible or compliant in other social situations. However, research findings indicate that this is not true; personality tests designed to measure for compliance do not correlate significantly with hypnotic susceptibility. What does appear to be a good predictor of responsiveness to hypnosis is whether or not the individual has a rich imagination, enjoys daydreaming, and has the ability to generate vivid mental images (Hilgard, 1979).

## Hypnotic Suggestions

Suggestions given to a hypnotized subject can result in a variety of behaviors and experiences. The person's motor control may be affected, new memories may be lost or old ones reexperienced, and current perceptions may be radically altered.

**CONTROL OF MOVEMENT**  Many hypnotic subjects respond to direct suggestion with involuntary movement. For example, if a person stands with arms outstretched and hands facing each other and the hypnotist suggests that the subject's hands are attracted to one another, the hands will soon begin to move together, and the subject will feel that they are propelled by some force that she is not generating. Direct suggestion can also inhibit movement. If a suggestible subject is told that an arm is stiff (like a bar of iron or an arm in a splint) and then is asked to bend the arm, it will not bend, or more effort than usual will be needed to make it bend. This response is less common than suggested movement.

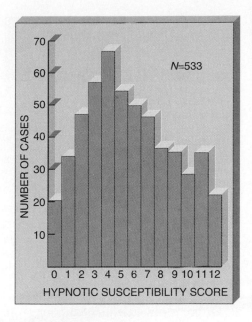

**FIGURE 6-9**
**Individual Differences in Hypnotizability** *After using a standard procedure designed to induce hypnosis, researchers administered 12 test suggestions from the Stanford Hypnotic Susceptibility Scale to 533 subjects. The object of the experiment was to test the appearance of hypnotic responses such as those described in the text (for example, being unable to bend one's arm or separate interlocked fingers when the hypnotist suggests these possibilities). The response was scored as present or absent, and the present responses were totaled for each subject to yield a score ranging from 0 (totally unresponsive) to 12 (most responsive). Most subjects fell in the middle ranges with a few very high and a few very low. (After Hilgard, 1965)*

## The Hidden Observer

The concept of a **hidden observer** originated with Hilgard's (1986) observation that in many hypnotized subjects, a part of the mind that is not within awareness seems to be watching the subject's experience as a whole. His finding has been described as follows:

The circumstances of Hilgard's discovery of a doubled train of thought in hypnosis were suitably dramatic. He was giving a classroom demonstration of hypnosis using an experienced subject who, as it happened, was blind. Hilgard induced deafness, telling him that he would be able to hear when a hand was put on his shoulder. Cut off from what was going on around him, he became bored and began to think of other

things. Hilgard showed the class how unresponsive he was to noise or speech, but then the question arose as to whether he was as unresponsive as he seemed. In a quiet voice, Hilgard asked the subject whether, though he was hypnotically deaf, there might be "some part of him" that could hear; if so, would he raise a forefinger? To the surprise of everyone—including the hypnotized subject—the finger rose.

At this, the subject wanted to know what was going on. Hilgard put a hand on his shoulder so he could hear, promised to explain later, but in the meantime asked the subject what he remembered. What he remembered was that everything had become still, that he was bored and had begun thinking about a problem in statistics. Then he felt his forefinger rise, and he wanted to know why.

Hilgard then asked for a report from "that part of you that listened to me before and made your finger rise," while instructing the hypnotized subject that he would not be able to hear what he himself said. It turned out

that this second part of the subject's awareness had heard all that went on and was able to report it. Hilgard found a suitable metaphor to describe this detached witness—the *hidden observer* (Hebb, 1982, p. 53).

Thus, the hidden-observer metaphor refers to a mental structure that monitors everything that happens, including events that the hypnotized subject is not consciously aware of perceiving.

The presence of the hidden observer has been demonstrated in many experiments (Kihlstrom, 1985; Zamansky & Bartis, 1985). In studies on pain relief, subjects are able to describe how the pain feels, using automatic writing or speaking, at the same time that their conscious system accepts and responds to the hypnotist's suggestion of pain relief. In other studies using automatic writing, hypnotized subjects have written messages of which they were unaware while their attention was directed to another task, such as reading aloud or naming the colors on a display chart (Knox, Crutchfield, & Hilgard, 1975). Hilgard and his colleagues have com-

Subjects who have been roused from hypnosis may respond with movement to a prearranged signal from the hypnotist. This is called a **posthypnotic response.** Even if the suggestion has been forgotten, subjects will feel a compulsion to carry out the behavior. They may try to justify such behavior as rational, even though the urge to perform it is impulsive. For example, a young man searching for a rational explanation of why he opened a window when the hypnotist took off her glasses (the prearranged signal) remarked that the room felt a little stuffy.

**POSTHYPNOTIC AMNESIA**   At the suggestion of the hypnotist, events occurring during hypnosis may be "forgotten" until a signal from the hypnotist enables the subject to recall them. This is called **posthypnotic amnesia.** Subjects differ widely in their susceptibility to posthypnotic amnesia, as Figure 6-10 shows. The items to be recalled in this study were 10 actions the subjects performed while hypnotized. A few subjects forgot none or only one or two items; most subjects forgot four or five items. However, a sizable number of subjects forgot all 10 items. This type of bimodal distribution, showing two distinct groups of subjects, has been found in many studies of posthypnotic amnesia. The group of subjects with the higher recall is larger and presumably represents the average hypnotic responders; the smaller group, the subjects who forgot all 10 items, has been described as hypnotic virtuosos. Differences in recall between the two groups following posthypnotic suggestion do not appear to be related to differences in memory capacity: once the amnesia is cancelled at a prearranged signal from the hypnotist,

pared these phenomena to everyday experiences in which an individual divides attention between two tasks, such as driving a car and conversing at the same time or making a speech and simultaneously evaluating her performance as an orator.

Hidden-observer experiments, although replicated in many laboratories and clinics, have been criticized on methodological grounds. Skeptics argue that implied demands for compliance may have produced the results (see, for example, Spanos & Hewitt, 1980; Spanos, 1986). In an experiment designed to determine the role of compliance, researchers have shown that it is possible to distinguish the responses of the truly hypnotized from those of the merely compliant. They asked subjects of proven low hypnotizability to simulate hypnosis while highly responsive subjects behaved naturally. The experimenter did not know to which group each subject belonged. The simulators did conform to the implied demands in the way they were expected to, but their reports of the subjective experiences

differed significantly from those individuals who were actually hypnotized (Hilgard et al., 1978; Zamansky & Bartis, 1985).

An unresolved problem is why some highly responsive hypnotized subjects do not have access to a hidden observer. One difference between the two groups has been reported. Subjects without a hidden observer are more "compliant" to suggestions of age regression—that is, they report feeling like children again—whereas those with a hidden observer invariably report a persistent duality of awareness. During age regression, they see themselves simultaneously as adult observers and as children. This division between an active participant and an observer is spontaneous and not suggested by the hypnotist (Laurence, 1980).

These are complex matters, not to be simply explained or lightly dismissed. They have implications not only for theories of hypnosis but for our view of consciousness in general. For a further discussion of this topic, see Hilgard (1986).

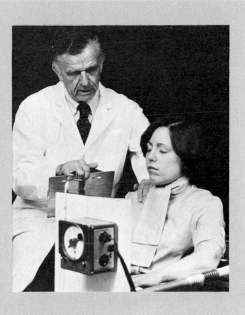

**Pain under Hypnosis** *Previously, when her hand was in the ice water, the subject felt no pain following suggestions of hypnotic anesthesia. By placing a hand on her shoulder, however, Dr. Hilgard can tap a "hidden observer" that reports the pain that the subject had felt at some level.*

highly amnesic subjects remember as many items as those who are less amnesic. Some researchers have suggested that hypnosis temporarily interferes with the person's ability to retrieve a particular item from memory but does not affect actual memory storage (Kihlstrom, 1987).

**AGE REGRESSION** In response to hypnotic suggestion, some individuals are able to relive episodes from earlier periods of life, such as a birthday party at age 10. To some subjects, the episode seems to be pictured as if it were on a television screen; the subjects are conscious of being present and viewing the event but do not feel as if they are producing it. In another type of regression, subjects feel as if they are reexperiencing the events. They may describe the clothing they are wearing, run a hand through their hair and describe its length, or recognize their elementary-school classmates. Occasionally, a childhood language, long forgotten, emerges during regression. For example, an American-born boy whose parents were Japanese and who had spoken Japanese at an early age but had forgotten it began speaking the language again while under hypnosis (Fromm, 1970).

**POSITIVE AND NEGATIVE HALLUCINATIONS** Some hypnotic experiences require a higher level of hypnotic talent than others. The vivid and convincing perceptual distortions of hallucinations, for instance, are relatively rare. Two types of suggested hallucinations have been documented: *positive hallucinations,* in which the subject sees an object or hears a voice that is not actually present; and *negative hallucinations,* in which the subject

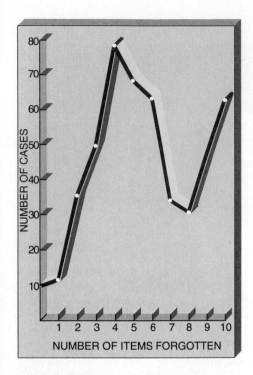

**FIGURE 6-10**

**Distribution of Posthypnotic Amnesia** *Subjects performed 10 actions while hypnotized and were then given posthypnotic amnesia instructions. When asked what occurred during hypnosis, subjects varied in the number of actions they failed to recall: the level of forgetting for a given subject ranged from 0 to 10 items. The experiment involved 491 subjects, and the graph plots the number of subjects at each level of forgetting. The plot shows a bimodal distribution for posthypnotic amnesia with peaks at 4 and 10 items forgotten. (After Cooper, 1979)*

does not perceive something that normally would be perceived. Many hallucinations have both positive and negative components. In order not to see a person sitting in a chair (a negative hallucination), a subject must see the parts of the chair that would ordinarily be blocked from view (a positive hallucination).

Hallucinations can also occur as the result of posthypnotic suggestion. For example, subjects may be told that on arousal from the hypnotic state they will find themselves holding a rabbit that wants to be petted and that the rabbit will ask, "What time is it?" Seeing and petting the rabbit will seem natural to most of the subjects. But when they find themselves giving the correct time of day, they are surprised and try to provide an explanation for the behavior: "Did I hear someone ask the time? It's funny, it seemed to be the rabbit asking, but rabbits can't talk!" is a typical response.

Negative hallucinations can be used effectively to control pain. In many cases, hypnosis completely eliminates pain, even though the source of the pain—a severe burn or a bone fracture, for example—continues. The failure to perceive something (pain) that would normally be perceived qualifies this response as a negative hallucination. The pain reduction need not be complete in order for hypnosis to be useful in giving relief. Reducing the pain by as little as 20 percent can make the patient's life more tolerable. Experimental studies have shown that the amount of pain reduction is closely related to the degree of measured hypnotizability (Hilgard & Hilgard, 1975).

# Psi Phenomena

A discussion of consciousness would not be complete without considering some esoteric and mystical claims about the mind that have attracted widespread public attention. Of particular interest are questions about whether or not human beings can (a) acquire information about the world or other people in ways that do not involve stimulation of the known sense organs, or (b) influence physical events by purely mental means. These questions are the source of controversy over the existence of **psi**, processes of information and/or energy exchange not currently explicable in terms of known science (in other words, known physical mechanisms). The phenomena of psi are the subject matter of **parapsychology** ("beside psychology") and include the following:

1. **Extrasensory perception** (ESP). Response to external stimuli without any known sensory contact.
   a. **Telepathy.** Thought transference from one person to another without the mediation of any known channel of sensory communication (for example, identifying a playing card merely being thought of by another person).
   b. **Clairvoyance.** Perception of objects or events that do not provide a stimulus to the known senses (for example, identifying a concealed playing card whose identity is unknown to anyone).
   c. **Precognition.** Perception of a future event that could not be anticipated through any known inferential process (for example, predicting that a particular number will come up on the next throw of dice).
2. **Psychokinesis** (PK). Mental influence over physical events without the intervention of any known physical force (for example, willing that a particular number will come up on the throw of dice).

## Experimental Evidence

Most parapsychologists consider themselves to be scientists applying the usual rules of scientific inquiry to admittedly unusual phenomena. Yet the claims for psi are so extraordinary and so similar to what are widely regarded as superstitions that some scientists declare psi to be an impossibility and reject the legitimacy of parapsychological inquiry. Such a priori judgments are out of place in science; the real question is whether the empirical evidence is acceptable by scientific standards. Many psychologists who are not yet convinced that psi has been demonstrated are nevertheless open to the possibility that new evidence might emerge that would be more compelling. For their part, many parapsychologists believe that several recent experimental procedures either provide that evidence already or hold the potential for doing so. We shall examine the most promising of these, the *ganzfeld procedure*.

The ganzfeld procedure tests for telepathic communication between a subject acting as the "receiver" and another subject who serves as the "sender." The receiver is sequestered in an acoustically isolated room and placed in a mild form of perceptual isolation: translucent ping-pong ball halves are taped over the eyes and headphones are placed over the ears; diffuse red light illuminates the room, and white noise is played through the headphones. (White noise is a random mixture of sound frequencies similar to the hiss made by a radio tuned between stations.) This homogeneous visual and auditory environment is called the *ganzfeld*, a German word meaning "total field."

The sender sits in a separate acoustically isolated room, and a visual stimulus (picture, slide, or brief videotape sequence) is randomly selected from a large pool of similar stimuli to serve as the "target" for the session. While the sender concentrates on the target, the receiver attempts to describe it by providing a continuous verbal report of his or her ongoing imagery and free associations. Upon completion of the session, the receiver is presented with four stimuli—one of which is the target—and asked to rate the degree to which each matches the imagery and associations experienced during the ganzfeld session. A "direct hit" is scored if the receiver assigns the highest rating to the target stimulus.

More than 50 experiments have been conducted since the procedure was first introduced in 1974; the typical experiment involves about 30 ganzfeld sessions in which a receiver attempts to identify the target transmitted by the sender. An overall analysis of 28 studies (comprising a total of 835 ganzfeld sessions conducted by investigators in 10 different laboratories) reveals that subjects were able to select the correct target stimulus 38 percent of the time. Because a subject must select the target from four alternatives, we would expect a success rate of 25 percent if only chance were operating. Statistically this result is highly significant; the probability that it could have arisen by chance is less than one in a billion (Honorton, 1985).

## Debate over the Evidence

In 1985 and 1986, the *Journal of Parapsychology* published an extended examination of the ganzfeld studies, focusing on a debate between Ray Hyman, a cognitive psychologist and critic of parapsychology, and Charles Honorton, a parapsychologist and major contributor to the ganzfeld database. They agree on the basic quantitative results but disagree on points

*The receiver (top photograph) and the sender (bottom photograph) in a ganzfeld experiment.*

of interpretation (Hyman, 1985; Hyman & Honorton, 1986; Honorton, 1985). We shall use their debate as a vehicle for examining the issues involved in evaluating claims of psi.

**REPLICATION PROBLEM**  In science generally, a phenomenon is not considered established until it has been observed repeatedly by several researchers. Accordingly, the most serious criticism of parapsychology is that it has failed to produce a single reliable demonstration of psi that can be replicated by other investigators. Even the same investigator testing the same individuals over time may obtain statistically significant results on one occasion but not on another. The ganzfeld procedure is no exception; fewer than half (43 percent) of the 28 studies analyzed in the debate yielded statistically significant results.

The parapsychologists' most effective response to this criticism actually comes from within psychology itself. Many statisticians and psychologists are dissatisfied with psychology's focus on the **statistical significance level** as the sole measure of a study's success. As an alternative, they are increasingly adopting the technique of **meta-analysis,** a statistical technique that treats the accumulated studies of a particular phenomenon as a single grand experiment and each study as a single observation. Thus any study that obtains results in the positive direction—even though it may not be statistically significant itself—contributes to the overall strength and reliability of the phenomenon rather than simply being dismissed as a failure to replicate (Glass, McGaw, & Smith, 1981; Rosenthal, 1984).

From this perspective, the ganzfeld studies provide impressive replicability: 23 of the 28 studies obtain positive results (more direct hits than chance would predict), a result whose probability of occurring by chance is less than one in a thousand.

The conventional criterion of replication further requires that any competent investigator be able to reproduce the claimed phenomenon, not just one or two gifted experimenters. This is often a difficult criterion to achieve in new areas of investigation because a number of unsuspected variables might affect the outcome. In psychological experiments, the experimenter is often an important social stimulus for the subject and hence a poorly controlled source of variability. Even in such an established area as classical conditioning, investigators at one university were obtaining positive results 94 percent of the time while other investigators could do so only 62 percent of the time (Rosenthal, 1966; Spence, 1964). Nor is the field of psychology alone here. Similar replication difficulties have been reported in medical studies of placebo efficacy (Moerman, 1981) and in such physical science areas as laser technology (Collins, 1974).

This problem could be even more acute in parapsychology because psi effects may depend on the motivational atmosphere established by the experimenter. Some parapsychologists further believe that the experimenter's own psi abilities and attitudes can have an effect.

Despite these potential difficulties, the replicability of the ganzfeld effect does not appear to rest on the success of one or two investigators. Six of the 10 investigators contributing to the 28 examined studies obtained statistically significant results; and, even if all the studies of the two most successful investigators are discarded from the analysis (half of the studies), the results remain significant (Palmer, Honorton, & Utts, 1989).

The power of a particular experiment to replicate an effect also depends on how strong the effect is and how many observations are made. If an effect is weak, an experiment with too few subjects or observations will fail to detect it at a statistically significant level—even though the effect actually exists.

This is strikingly illustrated by a recent medical experiment designed to determine whether aspirin can prevent heart attacks. The study was discontinued in 1987 because it was already clear the answer was yes. After six years, the aspirin group had already suffered 45 percent fewer heart attacks than a control group that received only placebo medication, a result that would occur by chance less than one time out of a million (The Steering Committee of the Physicians' Health Study Research Group, 1988). With such impressive results, it was considered unethical to keep the control group on placebo medication. This study was widely publicized as a major medical breakthrough.

The pertinent point here is that the study included over 22,000 subjects. If it were to be repeated with 3,000 subjects, a significant aspirin effect would be unlikely to emerge; the experiment would fail to replicate. Despite its undisputed reality and its practical importance, the aspirin effect is actually quite weak.

Now reconsider the ganzfeld effect. If the effect actually exists and has a true direct-hit rate of 38 percent, then statistically we should expect studies with 30 ganzfeld sessions (the average for the 28 studies) to obtain a statistically significant psi effect only about one-third of the time (Utts, 1986). The ganzfeld effect is about three times stronger than the aspirin effect.

In short, it is unrealistic to demand that any real effect be replicable at any time by any competent investigator. The replication issue is more complex than that, and meta-analysis is proving to be a valuable tool for dealing with some of those complexities.

**INADEQUATE CONTROLS**    The second major criticism of parapsychology is that many, if not most, of the experiments have inadequate controls and safeguards. Flawed procedures that would permit a subject to obtain the communicated information in normal sensory fashion either inadvertently, or through deliberate cheating, are particularly fatal. This is called the problem of *sensory leakage*. Inadequate procedures for randomizing (randomly selecting) target stimuli are another common problem.

Methodological inadequacies plague all sciences, but the history of parapsychology is embarrassingly full of promising results that collapsed when the procedures were critically examined (Akers, 1984). One common charge against parapsychology is that preliminary, poorly controlled studies often obtain positive results but that as soon as better controls and safeguards are introduced, the results disappear.

Once a flaw is discovered in a completed experiment, there is no persuasive way of arguing that the flaw did not contribute illegitimately to a positive outcome; the only remedy is to redo the experiment correctly. In a database of several studies, however, meta-analysis can evaluate the criticism empirically by checking to see if, in fact, the more poorly controlled studies obtained more positive results than did the better controlled studies. If there is a correlation between a procedural flaw and positive results across the studies, then there is a problem. In the case of the ganzfeld database, both critic Hyman and parapsychologist Honorton agree that flaws of inadequate security and possible sensory leakage do not correlate with positive results. Hyman claimed to find a correlation between flaws of randomization and positive results, but both Honorton's analysis and two additional analyses by nonparapsychologists dispute his conclusion (Harris & Rosenthal, 1988; Saunders, 1985). Moreover, a series of 11 new studies designed to control for flaws identified in the original database yielded results consistent with the original set of 28 studies (Harris & Rosenthal, 1988; Honorton et al., 1990).

**FILE-DRAWER PROBLEM** Suppose that each of 20 investigators independently decides to conduct a ganzfeld study. Even if there were no genuine ganzfeld effect, there is a reasonable probability that at least one of these investigators would obtain a statistically significant result by pure chance. That lucky investigator would then publish a report of the experiment, but the other 19 investigators—all of whom obtained *null* results—are likely to become discouraged, put their data into a file drawer, and move onto something more promising. As a result, the scientific community would learn about the one successful study but have no knowledge of the 19 null studies buried away in the file drawers. The database of known studies would thus be seriously biased toward positive studies, and any meta-analysis of that database would arrive at similarly biased conclusions. This is called the **file-drawer problem.**

The problem is particularly tricky because it is impossible, by definition, to know how many unknown studies are languishing in file drawers somewhere. Nevertheless, parapsychologists offer two defenses against the charge that the file-drawer problem seriously compromises their database.

First, they point out that the *Journal of Parapsychology* actively solicits and publishes studies that report negative findings. Moreover, the community of parapsychologists is relatively small, and most investigators are cognizant of ongoing work in the various laboratories around the world. When conducting meta-analysis, parapsychologists actively attempt to scout out unpublished negative studies at conventions and through their personal networks.

But their major defense is statistical, and again meta-analysis provides an empirical approach to the problem. By knowing the overall statistical significance of the known database, it is possible to compute the number of studies with null results that would have to exist in file drawers to cancel out that significance. In the case of the ganzfeld database, there would have to be over 400 unreported studies with null results—the equivalent of 12,000 ganzfeld sessions—to cancel out the statistical significance of the 28 studies analyzed in the debate (Honorton, 1985). Not surprisingly, there is consensus that the overall significance of the ganzfeld studies cannot reasonably be explained by the file-drawer effect (Hyman & Honorton, 1986).

Rather than continuing their debate, Hyman and Honorton issued a joint communiqué in which they set forth their areas of agreement and disagreement and made a series of suggestions for the conduct of future ganzfeld studies (Hyman & Honorton, 1986). Their debate and the subsequent discussion provide a valuable model for evaluating disputed domains of scientific inquiry.

*A psychic at work in New Orleans*

## Anecdotal Evidence

In the public's mind, the evidence for psi consists primarily of personal experiences and anecdotes. Such evidence is unpersuasive in science because it suffers fatally from the same problems that jeopardize the experimental evidence—nonreplicability, inadequate controls, and the file-drawer problem.

The replication problem is acute because most such evidence consists of one-time occurrences. A woman announces a premonition that she will win the lottery that day—and she does. You dream about an unlikely event that actually occurs a few days later. A "psychic" correctly predicts the assassination of a public figure. Such incidents may be subjectively compelling, but there is no way to evaluate them because they are not repeatable.

The problem of inadequate controls and safeguards is decisive because such incidents occur under unexpected and ambiguously specified conditions. There is thus no way of ruling out such alternative interpretations as coincidence (chance), faulty memories, and deliberate deception.

And finally, the file-drawer problem is also fatal. The lottery winner who announced ahead of time that she would win is prominently featured in the news. But the thousands of others with similar premonitions who did *not* win are never heard from; they remain in the file drawers. It is true that the probability of this woman's winning the lottery was very low. But the critical criterion in evaluating this case is not the probability that *she* would win but the probability that any *one* of the thousands who thought they would win would do so. That probability is much higher. Moreover, this woman has a personal file drawer that contains all those past instances in which she had similar premonitions and then lost.

The same reasoning applies to *precognitive dreams* (dreams that anticipate an unlikely event that then occurs a few days later). We tend to forget

our dreams unless and until an event happens to remind us of them. We thus have no way of evaluating how often we might have dreamed of similar unlikely events that did *not* occur. We fill our database with positive instances and unknowingly exclude the negative instances.

Perhaps the fullest file drawers belong to the so-called psychics who make annual predictions in the tabloid newspapers. Nobody remembers the predictions that fail, but everybody remembers the occasional direct hits. In fact, these psychics are almost always wrong (Frazier, 1987; Tyler, 1977).

## Skepticism about Psi

If some of the experimental evidence for psi is as impressive as it seems, why hasn't it become part of established science? Why do we continue to be skeptical?

**EXTRAORDINARY CLAIMS** Most scientists believe that extraordinary claims require extraordinary proof. A study reporting that students who study harder get higher grades will be believed even if the study was seriously flawed because the data accord well with our understanding of how the world works. But the claim that two people in a ganzfeld study communicate telepathically is more extraordinary; it violates our a priori beliefs about reality. We thus rightly demand a higher measure of proof from parapsychologists because their claims, if true, would require us to radically revise our model of the world—something we should not undertake lightly. In this way, science is justifiably conservative. Many open-minded nonparapsychologists are genuinely impressed by the ganzfeld studies, for example, but reasonably they can and do ask to see more evidence before committing themselves to the reality of psi.

Extraordinariness is a matter of degree. Telepathy seems less extraordinary to most of us than precognition because we are already familiar with the invisible transmission of information through space. We may not all understand how television pictures get to our living rooms, but we know that they do so. Why should telepathy seem that much more mysterious? Precognition, on the other hand, seems more extraordinary because we have no familiar phenomena in which information flows backward in time.

Extraordinariness also depends on our current model of reality. As our understanding of the world changes, a phenomenon that seemed extraordinary at an earlier time may no longer seem so—even if the quality of the evidence has not changed. Any child who has visited a museum of natural history has seen fragments of a meteorite. But before the nineteenth century, the scientific community did not believe in meteorites. Those who reported seeing them were ridiculed and alternative explanations were advanced to explain away the evidence (Nininger, 1933).

In the twentieth century, quantum mechanics is challenging our everyday model of reality far more radically than most people realize (Herbert, 1987). Some parapsychologists believe that modern physics will provide a model of reality within which psi phenomena will fit comfortably and unremarkably (Stokes, 1987), and many studies of psychokinesis are conducted by physical scientists who explicitly base their theories of psi on quantum mechanics (Jahn & Dunne, 1987). If they are right, the scientific community may come to accept psi not because the data became more convincing but because psi became less extraordinary.

**SKEPTICISM OF PSYCHOLOGISTS** Psychologists are a particularly skeptical group. National polls find that about one-half of all adult Americans believe in ESP, a figure that rises to two-thirds among Americans with college backgrounds. A survey of over 1,000 college professors found that about 66 percent believe that ESP is either an established fact or a likely possibility. Moreover, these favorable views were expressed by a majority of professors in the natural sciences (55 percent), the social sciences excluding psychology (66 percent), and the arts, humanities, and education (77 percent). The comparable figure for psychologists was 34 percent (Wagner & Monnet, 1979).

Psychologists may be more skeptical than others for several reasons. First, claims of psi might seem more extraordinary to psychologists than to others because it is their conceptual world that would require the most radical revisions if psi were shown to exist. Second, they are the most familiar with past instances of extraordinary claims within psychology that turned out to be based on flawed experimental procedures, faulty inference, or even on fraud and deception. Over the history of research on parapsychology, there have been a disturbing number of cases where research claims have later proved to be based on fraudulent data. Those who follow developments in this field have so often encountered charlatans—some very clever—that they have good reason to be skeptical of new claims (Gardner, 1981; Randi, 1982).

Third, psychologists know that popular accounts of psychological findings are frequently exaggerated. For example, the genuinely remarkable findings from research on asymmetries in the human brain (see p. 52) have spawned a host of pop-psychology books and media reports containing unsubstantiated claims about left-brained and right-brained persons. Irresponsible reports about states of consciousness—including hypnosis and psi—appear daily in the media. It is thus pertinent to note that when the college professors in the survey cited above were asked to name the sources for their beliefs about ESP, they most frequently cited reports in newspapers and magazines.

And finally, research in cognitive and social psychology has sensitized psychologists to the biases and shortcomings in our abilities to draw valid inferences from our everyday experiences (see Chapter 18). This makes them particularly skeptical of anecdotal reports of psi where, as we saw above, our judgments are subject to many kinds of errors.

For these several reasons, then, much of the skepticism of psychologists toward psi is well-founded. But some of it is not. The work using the ganzfeld procedure has withstood considerable scrutinizing and warrants consideration.

## *Chapter* SUMMARY

1. A person's perceptions, thoughts, and feelings at any moment in time constitute that person's *consciousness*. An *altered state of consciousness* is said to exist when mental functioning seems changed or out of the ordinary to the person experiencing the state. Some altered states of consciousness, such as sleep and dreams, are experienced by everyone; others result from special circumstances, such as meditation, hypnosis, or the use of drugs.

2. The functions of consciousness are (a) *monitoring* ourselves and our environment so that we are aware of what is happening within our bodies

and in our surroundings; and (b) *controlling* our actions so that they coordinate with events in the outside world. Not all events that influence consciousness are at the center of our awareness at a given moment. Memories of personal events and of the knowledge accumulated during a lifetime that are accessible but are not currently part of one's consciousness are called *preconscious memories.* Events that affect behavior even though we are not aware of perceiving them influence us *subconsciously.*

3. According to psychoanalytic theory, some emotionally painful memories and impulses are *not* available to consciousness because they have been repressed—that is, diverted to the *unconscious.* Unconscious thoughts and impulses influence our behavior even though they reach consciousness only in indirect ways through dreams, irrational behavior, and slips of the tongue.

4. The notion of a divided consciousness assumes that thoughts and memories may sometimes be *dissociated,* or split off, from consciousness, rather than repressed to the unconscious. Extreme examples are cases of *multiple personality,* in which two or more well-developed personalities alternate within the same individual.

5. *Sleep,* an altered state of consciousness, is of interest because of the rhythms evident in sleep schedules and in the depth of sleep. These rhythms are studied with the aid of the *electroencephalogram* (EEG). Patterns of brain waves show four stages (depths) of sleep, plus a fifth stage characterized by *rapid eye movements* (REMs). These stages alternate throughout the night. Dreams occur more often during REM sleep than during the other four stages (NREM sleep).

6. In 1900, Sigmund Freud proposed the most influential theory of dreams. It attributes psychological causes to dreams, distinguishing between the *manifest* and *latent content* of dreams and stating that dreams are wishes in disguise.

7. *Psychoactive drugs* have long been used to alter consciousness and mood. They include *depressants,* such as alcohol and tranquilizers; *opiates,* such as heroin and morphine; *stimulants,* such as amphetamines and cocaine; *hallucinogens,* such as LSD and PCP; and *cannabis,* such as marijuana and hashish.

8. All of these drugs can produce *psychological dependence* (compulsive use to reduce anxiety), and most result in *physical dependence* (increased tolerance and withdrawal symptoms) if used habitually.

9. *Meditation* represents an effort to alter consciousness by following planned rituals or exercises such as those of yoga or Zen. The result is a somewhat mystical state in which the individual is extremely relaxed and feels divorced from the outside world. Simple exercises combining concentration and relaxation can help novices experience meditative states.

10. *Hypnosis* is a responsive state in which subjects focus their attention on the hypnotist and the hypnotist's suggestions. Some people are more readily hypnotized than others, though most people show some susceptibility. Characteristic hypnotic responses include enhanced or diminished *control over movements,* the distortion of memory through *posthypnotic amnesia, age regression,* and positive and negative *hallucinations.* The reduction of pain, as a variety of negative hallucination, is one of the beneficial uses of hypnosis.

11. There is considerable controversy over *psi,* the idea that human beings can acquire information about the world in ways that do not involve

stimulation of known sense organs or can influence physical events by purely mental means. The phenomena of psi includes *extrasensory perception* (ESP) in its various forms (telepathy, clairvoyance, precognition) and *psychokinesis,* movement of objects by the mind.

12. A number of carefully controlled studies (called *ganzfeld experiments*) have been conducted to evaluate ESP via telepathy. These experiments are subject to criticism (replicability, inadequate controls, file-drawer problems). However, a careful analysis of the results does not preclude the possibility of a real ESP effect. Nevertheless, most psychologists remain skeptical about ESP and psi in general, in part because so many past instances of extraordinary claims turned out to be based on flawed experimental procedures, faulty inferences, or even on fraud and deception.

## *Further* READING

Farthing, *The Psychology of Consciousness* (1992) provides a very readable overview of the problems of consciousness and its alterations. See, also, Baars, *Cognitive Theory of Consciousness* (1988); Pope and Singer (eds.), *The Stream of Consciousness* (1978); and Bowers and Meichenbaum (eds.), *The Unconscious Reconsidered* (1984). For philosophical/psychological discussions of consciousness see Lycan, *Consciousness* (1987); Jackendoff, *Consciousness and the Computational Mind* (1990); and Churchland, *Matter and Consciousness* (1988).

Problems of divided consciousness are treated in Hilgard, *Divided Consciousness* (1986); Kluft (ed.), *Childhood Antecedents of Multiple Personality* (1985); and Braun (ed.), *Treatment of Multiple Personality Disorder* (1986).

Useful books on sleep and dreams include Hobson, *Sleep* (1989); Booztin, Kihlstrom, and Schacter (eds.), *Sleep and Cognition* (1990); Anch et al., *Sleep: A Scientific Perspective* (1988); and Hobson, *The Dreaming Brain* (1988).

General textbooks on drugs include Julien, *A Primer of Drug Action* (6th ed., 1992) and Julien, *Drugs and the Body* (1988). *Drug and Alcohol Abuse* (3rd ed., 1989) by Schuckit provides a guide to diagnosis and treatment. For a thoughtful discussion of the legal and social problems of heroin, as well as an evaluation of possible solutions, see Kaplan, *The Hardest Drug; Heroin and Public Policy* (1985).

On meditative practices, see West (ed.), *The Psychology of Meditation* (1987); Goleman, *The Varieties of Meditative Experience* (1977); or Naranjo and Ornstein, *On the Psychology of Meditation* (1977). On meditation for relaxing, see Benson, *The Relaxation Response* (1976). For a discussion of relaxation and mental images in athletics see Syer and Connolly, *Sporting Body Sporting Mind; An Athlete's Guide to Mental Training* (1988) and Butt, *The Psychology of Sport* (2nd ed., 1988).

There are a number of books on hypnosis. Presentations that include methods, theories, and experimental results are E. R. Hilgard, *The Experience of Hypnosis* (1968); Fromm and Shor (eds.), *Hypnosis; Developments in Research and New Perspectives* (2nd ed., 1979); and J. R. Hilgard, *Personality and Hypnosis* (2nd ed., 1979).

For a review of parapsychology, see Wolman, Dale, Schmeidler, and Ullman (eds.), *Handbook of Parapsychology* (1986); Frazier (ed.), *Science Confronts the Paranormal* (1985); Kurtz (ed.), *A Skeptic's Handbook of Parapsychology* (1985); and Gardner, *Science: Good, Bad, and Bogus* (1981).

# Part IV

## Learning, Remembering, and Thinking

7 Learning and Conditioning

8 Memory

9 Thought and Language

*Hollyhocks*, 1914, by Frederick Frieseke (1874–1939), oil on canvas, $25\frac{1}{2}$" × 32".
Courtesy of The National Academy of Design, New York.

# Chapter 7

# Learning and Conditioning

## Perspectives on Learning 253

## Classical Conditioning 254
*Pavlov's Experiments*
*Phenomena and Applications*
*Predictability and Cognitive Factors*
*Biological Constraints*
*Critical Discussion: Neural Basis of Elementary Learning*

## Operant Conditioning 264
*Law of Effect*
*Skinner's Experiments*
*Phenomena and Applications*
*Aversive Conditioning*
*Control and Cognitive Factors*
*Critical Discussion: Economics of Reward*
*Biological Constraints*

## Complex Learning 278
*Cognitive Maps and Abstract Concepts*
*Insight Learning*
*Prior Beliefs*

earning pervades our lives. It is involved not only in mastering a
new skill or academic subject but also in emotional development,
social interaction, and even personality development. We learn
what to fear, what to love, how to be polite, how to be intimate,
and so on. Given the pervasiveness of learning in our lives, it is not surprising that we have already discussed many instances of it—how, for example,
children learn to perceive the world around them, to identify with their own
sex, and to control their behavior according to adult standards. Now, however, we turn to a more systematic analysis of learning.

Learning may be defined as a relatively *permanent* change in behavior
that results from practice; behavior changes that are due to maturation
(rather than practice), or to *temporary* conditions of the organism (such as fatigue or drug-induced states) are not included. All cases of learning are not
the same, though. Four different kinds may be distinguished: (a) *habituation*,
(b) *classical conditioning*, (c) *operant conditioning*, and (d) what we will call
*complex learning*. **Habituation,** the simplest kind of learning, amounts to
learning to ignore a stimulus that has become familiar and has no serious
consequences—for example, learning to ignore the ticking of a new clock.
Classical and operant conditioning both involve forming *associations*—that
is, learning that certain events go together. In **classical conditioning,** an organism learns that one event follows another; for example, a baby learns that
the sight of a breast will be followed by the taste of milk. In **operant conditioning,** an organism learns that a response it makes will be followed by a
particular consequence; for example, a young child learns that striking a
sibling will be followed by disapproval from his or her parents. **Complex
learning** involves something in addition to forming associations; for example, applying a strategy when solving a problem, or constructing a mental
map of one's environment. Our focus will be on the last three kinds of learning (since most interesting cases of human learning go beyond habituation).
Before beginning our discussion of conditioning and learning, though, we
need to consider how the various perspectives on psychology have been applied to the study of learning.

# Perspectives on Learning

Recall from Chapter 1 that there are various perspectives on psychology and
that three of the most important ones are the behavioristic, cognitive, and
biological perspectives. As much as any area in psychology, the study of
learning has involved all three of these perspectives.

Much of the early work on learning, particularly on conditioning, was
done from a behavioristic perspective. Researchers studied how lower organisms learn an association between stimuli or an association between a
stimulus and a response. The focus was on external stimuli and responses, in
keeping with the general behavioristic dictum that behavior is better understood in terms of external causes than mental ones. The behaviorist approach to learning made other key assumptions as well. One was that simple
associations of the classical or operant kind are the building blocks of learning. Thus something as complex as acquiring a language is presumably a
matter of learning many associations (Staats, 1968). Another assumption was
that the same basic laws of learning are in play regardless of what exactly is
being learned or who exactly is doing the learning—be it a rat learning to
run a maze or a child mastering long division (Skinner, 1938; 1971). These
views lead behaviorists to focus on how the behaviors of lower organisms,

*Ivan Pavlov with his assistants*

*UCR response — would happen anyway*

*Stimulus — many temptation*

*conditioned response — happen because of dog taught to respond to certain stimulus*

particularly rats and pigeons, are influenced by rewards and punishments in simple laboratory situations.

This work uncovered a wealth of findings and phenomena that continue to form the basis of much of what we know about associative learning. But, as we will see, the behaviorist assumptions have had to be modified in light of subsequent work. Understanding conditioning, not to mention complex learning, requires us to consider what the organism *knows* about the relations between stimuli and response (even when the organism is a rat or a pigeon), thereby ushering in the cognitive perspective. Also, in cases of complex learning, strategies, rules, and the like must be considered in addition to associations, and again this requires us to adopt a cognitive approach. Furthermore, it now appears that there is *not* a single set of laws that underlies learning in all situations and for all organisms. In particular, different mechanisms of learning seem to be involved in different species, thereby ushering in the biological perspective.

The upshot is that the contemporary study of learning involves an integration of the three perspectives of interest. Accordingly, our treatment of both classical and operant conditioning will consider behaviorist, cognitive, and biological factors (our treatment of complex learning will concern mainly cognitive factors). We begin our discussion with behavioristic work, which introduces the essential phenomena.

## Classical Conditioning

The study of **classical conditioning** began in the early years of this century when Ivan Pavlov, a Russian physiologist who had already won the Nobel prize for research on digestion, turned his attention to learning. While studying digestion, Pavlov noticed that a dog began to salivate at the mere sight of a food dish. While any dog will salivate when food is placed in its mouth, this dog had learned to associate the sight of the dish with the taste of food.

Pavlov had happened upon a case of associative learning, and he decided to see whether a dog could be taught to associate food with other things, such as a light or a tone.

## Pavlov's Experiments

In Pavlov's basic experiment, a researcher first attaches a capsule to the dog's salivary gland to measure salivary flow. Then the dog is placed in front of a pan, in which meat powder can be delivered automatically. A researcher turns a light on in a window in front of the dog. After a few seconds, some meat powder is delivered to the pan, and the light is turned off. The dog is hungry, and the recording device registers copious salivation. This salivation is an **unconditioned response,** or UCR, for no learning is involved; by the same token, the meat powder is an **unconditioned stimulus,** or UCS. The procedure is repeated a number of times—light then food, light then food, and so on. Then, to test if the dog has learned to associate the light with food, the experimenter turns on the light but does not deliver any meat powder. If the dog salivates, it has learned the association. This salivation is a **conditioned response,** or CR, while the light is a **conditioned stimulus,** or CS. The dog has been taught, or conditioned, to associate the light with food and to respond to it by salivating. Pavlov's experiment is diagramed in Figure 7-1.

**EXPERIMENTAL VARIATIONS** Psychologists over the years have devised many variations of Pavlov's experiments, and we will be discussing some of these in what follows. To appreciate these variations, we need to note some critical aspects of the conditioning experiment. Each paired presentation of the conditioned stimulus (CS) and the unconditioned stimulus (UCS) is called a trial. The trials during which the subject is learning the association between the two stimuli is the **acquisition** stage of conditioning. During this stage, repeated pairings of the CS (light) and UCS (meat) are said to strengthen, or **reinforce,** the association between the two, as illustrated in the left-hand curve of Figure 7-2. If the association is not reinforced (the UCS is omitted repeatedly), the response will gradually di-

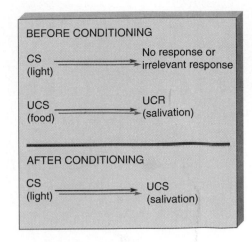

**FIGURE 7-1**
**Diagram of Classical Conditioning**
*The association between the unconditioned stimulus and the unconditioned response exists at the start of the experiment and does not have to be learned. The association between the conditioned stimulus and the unconditioned stimulus is learned. It arises through the pairing of the conditioned and unconditioned stimuli.*

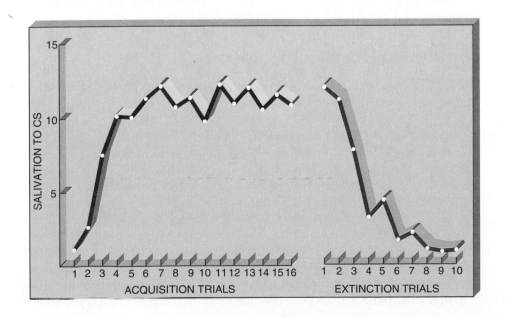

**FIGURE 7-2**
**Acquisition and Extinction of a Conditioned Response** *The curve in the panel on the left depicts the acquisition phase of an experiment. Drops of salivation in response to the conditioned stimulus (prior to the onset of the UCS) are plotted on the vertical axis; the number of trials, on the horizontal axis. After 16 acquisition trials, the experimenter switched to extinction; the results are presented in the panel at the right. (After Pavlov, 1927)*

minish; this is called **extinction** and is illustrated by the right-hand curve in Figure 7-2. Does extinction amount to unlearning the previously acquired association, or to learning to inhibit the CR when the CS is present? Pavlov favored the inhibition answer, and a good deal of recent research indicates he was right—the CS essentially becomes an inhibitory stimulus.

Acquisition and extinction make intuitive sense if we view classical conditioning as learning to predict what will happen next. (This is the heart of the cognitive approach to conditioning that we will later consider.) When the prediction is successful (reinforced), the animal learns to keep making that prediction (acquisition); when things change in the world so that the prediction is outdated (not reinforced), the animal learns to inhibit that prediction (extinction).

**CONDITIONING IN DIFFERENT SPECIES** Classical conditioning is pervasive in the animal kingdom and can occur with organisms as primitive as the flatworm. Flatworms contract their bodies when subjected to mild electric shock, and if they experience sufficient pairings of shock (the UCS) and light (the CS), eventually they will contract to the light alone (Jacobson, Fried, & Horowitz, 1967). At the other end of the spectrum, numerous human responses can be classically conditioned. Many of these are involuntary responses. To illustrate, consider the plight of cancer patients who are undergoing chemotherapy treatments to stop the growth of their tumors. Chemotherapy involves injecting toxic substances into the patients, who as a result often become nauseous and sick to their stomachs. After a number of chemotherapy sessions, patients sometimes become nauseous and sick upon entering the treatment room. The repeated pairing of the chemotherapy (the UCS) and the sight of the treatment room (the CS) has led the patients to associate the room with the chemotherapy, which results in the patients experiencing intestinal upset even before their treatment begins. A related phenomenon arises with young cancer patients who are given ice cream before the chemotherapy session. The ice cream may have been intended to lighten the child's distress about the impending treatment, but alas the ice cream becomes conditioned to the chemotherapy experience (now the ice cream is the CS and the chemotherapy the UCS). The upshot is that the children will be less likely to eat ice cream even outside the chemotherapy setting (Bernstein, 1978).

## Phenomena and Applications

The following discussion considers phenomena that greatly increase the generality of classical conditioning.

**SECOND-ORDER CONDITIONING** Thus far in our discussion of conditioning, the UCS has always been biologically significant, such as food, cold, or shock. However, other stimuli can acquire the power of a UCS by being consistently paired with a biologically significant UCS. Recall the example of a dog exposed to a light (CS) followed by food (UCS), where the light comes to elicit a conditioned response. Once the dog is conditioned, the light acquires the power of a UCS. Thus, if the dog is now put in a situation in which it is exposed to a tone followed by the light (but no food) on each trial, the tone alone will eventually elicit a conditioned response even though it has never been paired with food. (There must also be other trials in which the light is again paired with food; otherwise, the originally conditioned relation between light and food will extinguish.)

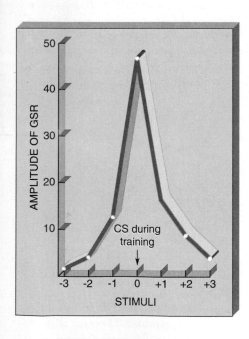

**FIGURE 7-3**
**Gradient of Generalization** *Stimulus 0 denotes the tone to which the galvanic skin response (GSR) was originally conditioned. Stimuli +1, +2, and +3 represent test tones of increasingly higher pitch; stimuli −1, −2, and −3 represent tones of lower pitch. Note that the amount of generalization decreases as the difference between the test tone and the training tone increases.*

The existence of such *second-order* conditioning greatly increases the scope of classical conditioning, especially for humans for whom biologically significant UCs occur relatively frequently. Now, all that is needed for conditioning to occur is the pairing of one stimulus with another, where the latter has previously been paired with a biologically significant event. Consider again our chemotherapy example. Suppose that for a particular patient the sight of the treatment room has become conditioned to the chemotherapy experience (a biologically significant event). If the patient is repeatedly presented a neutral stimulus, say a tone, followed by a picture of the treatment room, the patient may start to experience some unpleasant feeling to the tone alone.

**GENERALIZATION AND DISCRIMINATION** When a conditioned response has been associated with a particular stimulus, other similar stimuli will evoke the same response. Suppose that a person is conditioned to have a mild emotional reaction to the sound of a tuning fork producing a tone of middle C. (The emotional reaction is measured by the **galvanic skin response,** or GSR, which is a change in the electrical activity of the skin that occurs during emotional stress.) The person will also show a GSR to higher or lower tones without further conditioning (see Figure 7-3). The more similar the new stimuli are to the original CS, the more likely they are to evoke the conditioned response. This principle, called **generalization,** accounts in part for an individual's ability to react to novel stimuli that are similar to familiar ones.

A process complementary to generalization is **discrimination.** Whereas generalization is a reaction to similarities, discrimination is a reaction to differences. Conditioned discrimination is brought about through selective reinforcement and extinction, as shown in Figure 7-4. Instead of just one tone, for instance, now there are two. The low-pitched tone, $CS_1$, is always followed by a shock, and the high-pitched tone, $CS_2$, is not. Initially, subjects will show a GSR to both tones. During the course of conditioning, however, the amplitude of the conditioned response to $CS_1$ gradually increases while the amplitude of the response to $CS_2$ decreases. Thus, by the process of **differential reinforcement,** the subjects are conditioned to discriminate between the two tones. The high-pitched tone, $CS_2$, has become a signal to inhibit the learned response.

Generalization and discrimination occur in everyday life. A young child who has learned to associate the sight of her pet dog with playfulness may initially approach all dogs. Eventually, through differential reinforcement, the child may expect playfulness only from dogs that look like hers. The sight of a threatening dog has come to inhibit the child's response of approaching dogs.

**CONDITIONED FEAR** Classical conditioning plays a role in emotional reactions like fear. Suppose a rat is placed in an enclosed compartment in which it is periodically subjected to electric shock (by electrifying the floor). Just before the shock occurs a tone sounds. After repeated pairings of the tone (the CS) and the shock (the UCS), the tone alone will produce reactions in the rat that are indicators of fear, including stopping in its tracks and crouching; in addition, its blood pressure increases. The rat has been conditioned to be fearful when exposed to what was once a neutral stimulus.

Many human fears may be acquired in this way, particularly in early childhood (Jacobs & Nadel, 1985). Perhaps the best evidence that they can be classically conditioned is that some of these fears, especially irrational

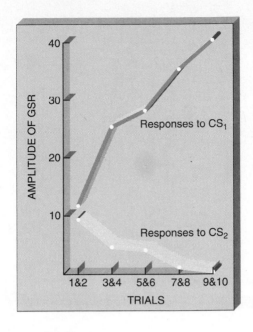

**FIGURE 7-4**
**Conditioned Discrimination** *The discriminative stimuli were two tones of clearly different pitch ($CS_1$ = 700 hertz and $CS_2$ = 3,500 hertz). The unconditioned stimulus, an electric shock applied to the left forefinger, occurred only on trials when $CS_1$ was presented. The strength of the conditioned response, in this case the GSR, gradually increased following $CS_1$ and extinguished following $CS_2$. (After Baer & Fuhrer, 1968)*

ones, can be eliminated by therapeutic techniques based on classical-conditioning principles. A person with an intense fear of cats, for example, may overcome the fear by gradually and repeatedly being exposed to cats. Presumably, a cat was a CS for some noxious UCS a long time ago, and when the person now repeatedly experiences the CS without the UCS, the conditioned fear extinguishes. (See Chapter 16 for a discussion of conditioning and phobias and Chapter 17 for conditioning therapies.)

**CONDITIONING AND DRUG TOLERANCE** In most of our examples thus far the conditioned response resembles the unconditioned response. Pavlov's dogs salivate to the light (the CR) just as they do to the food (the UCR), cancer patients become nauseous at the sight of the treatment room (the CR) just as they do to the chemotherapy treatment (the UCR), and so on. But this is not always the case. There are situations in which the CR is the opposite of the UCR, and some of the most dramatic of these situations involve the use of drugs. Consider, for example, a case where someone regularly takes injections of morphine. Since the sight of the injection is repeatedly followed by the morphine, the injection functions as a CS, morphine as a UCS, and classical conditioning occurs. That is, the sight of the injection will be associated with the intake of morphine. However, while the response to morphine, the UR, is a reduced sensitivity to pain, the response to the sight of the injection, the CR, is an *increase* in sensitivity to pain. The CR is the opposite of the UR.

This phenomenon has implications for the development of *drug tolerance*. It is well-known that as a person continues to use a drug like morphine, a given dose of the drug becomes progressively ineffective; the person must consequently increase the dosage level to get the desired effect. While this development of drug tolerance is partly a matter of physiological adaptation, it appears also to be a matter of classical conditioning. Specifically, with continued use of morphine, conditioning occurs that results in an increase in pain sensitivity, hence increasingly more morphine is needed to obtain the desired level of pain killer. It is not that the pain-killing effect of morphine has decreased, but rather that the background level of pain sensitivity has actually increased. The same process is presumably operative in the use of heroin for nonmedical purposes. After repeated injections, the drug user's conditioned response to the injection is the opposite of the desired effect of a sense of well-being; consequently he must take a higher and higher dosage to produce the desired effect (Siegel, 1979, 1983).

## Predictability and Cognitive Factors

Until now we have analyzed classical conditioning solely in terms of external or environmental events—one stimulus is consistently followed by another, and the organism comes to associate them. Although this behaviorist view was the dominant one for many years, there have long been researchers who argued that the critical factor behind conditioning is what the animal *knows* (Tolman, 1932). In this cognitive view, classical conditioning provides an organism with new knowledge about the relation between two stimuli; given the CS, it has learned to *expect* the UCS. In what follows, we consider the role played by cognitive factors in classical conditioning.

**CONTIGUITY VERSUS PREDICTABILITY** Since Pavlov, researchers have tried to determine the critical factor needed for classical conditioning to occur. Pavlov thought the critical factor was temporal contiguity of the CS

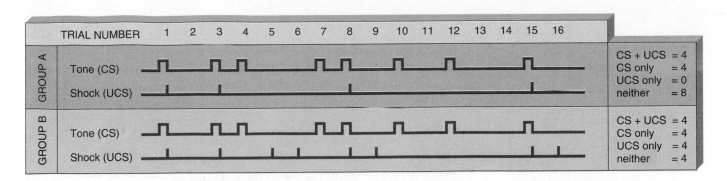

| TRIAL NUMBER | 1 2 3 4 5 6 7 8 9 10 11 12 13 14 15 16 | |
|---|---|---|
| GROUP A Tone (CS) Shock (UCS) | | CS + UCS = 4<br>CS only = 4<br>UCS only = 0<br>neither = 8 |
| GROUP B Tone (CS) Shock (UCS) | | CS + UCS = 4<br>CS only = 4<br>UCS only = 4<br>neither = 4 |

and UCS—that is, the two stimuli must occur close together in time in order for an association to develop. Some evidence supporting this idea comes from experiments that have varied the time interval between the presentation of the CS and the UCS. Typically, conditioning is most effective when the CS precedes the UCS by approximately one-half second, and becomes progressively less effective as the time between CS and UCS increases. There is, however, an alternative to temporal contiguity as the critical factor in classical conditioning, namely that the CS be a *reliable predictor* of the UCS. In other words, for conditioning to occur, perhaps there must be a higher probability that the UCS will occur when the CS has been presented than when it has not. This notion seems quite cognitive.

Rescorla (1967), in an important experiment, contrasted contiguity and predictability. On certain trials of the experiment, Rescorla exposed dogs to shock (the UCS), and on some of these trials he preceded the shock by a tone (the CS). The procedures for two of the groups from the experiment are illustrated in Figure 7-5. The number of temporally contiguous pairings of tone and shock was the same in both groups. The independent variable was that tones preceded all shocks in Group A, whereas in Group B shocks were as likely to be preceded by no tones as tones, so the tone had no real predictive power for Group B. This predictive power of the tone proved critical: Group A became rapidly conditioned, whereas Group B did not (as determined by whether or not the dog responded to the tone in such a way as to avoid the shock). In other groups in the experiment (not shown in Figure 7-5), the strength of the conditioning was directly related to the predictive value of the CS in signaling the occurrence of the UCS. Subsequent experiments support the conclusion that the predictive relation between the CS and UCS is more important than either temporal contiguity or the frequency with which the CS and UCS are paired (Rescorla, 1972).

What a dog is doing in the preceding experiment may be analogized to what a scientist usually does. Confronted with the possibility of an important negative occurrence like a thunderstorm, a scientist—a meteorologist—tries to find something that predicts the event. It cannot be something that merely occurs contiguously with thunderstorms, because many innocuous events will fit this bill (such as clouds and even the presence of trees). Rather, the meteorologist must search for events that are predictive of thunderstorms in that they tend to occur prior to thunderstorms but not at other times. Likewise, when a dog in the preceding experiment has to deal with the important, negative occurrence of shock, it too tries to find some event that can predict it. And like the meteorologist, the dog does not focus on events that merely co-occur with shock (such as the sight of the experimental apparatus, or the tone in Group B of the experiment); rather the dog

## FIGURE 7-5

**Rescorla's Experiment** *The figure presents a schematic representation of two groups from Rescorla's study. For each group, the events for 16 trials are presented. Note that on some trials CS occurs and is followed by UCS (CS + UCS); on other trials CS or UCS occurs alone; and on still other trials, neither CS nor UCS occurs. The boxes to the far right give a count of these trial outcomes for the two groups. The number of CS + UCS trials is identical for both groups, as is the number of trials on which only the CS occurs. But the two groups differ in the number of trials on which UCS occurred alone (never in Group A and as frequently as any other type of trial in Group B). Thus, for Group A, the experimenter established a situation in which the tone was a useful (but not perfect) predictor that shock would follow shortly, whereas for Group B the tone was of no value in predicting subsequent shock. A conditioned response to CS developed readily for Group A but did not develop at all for Group B.*

**TABLE 7-1**
**Experiment on Blocking** *The design of an experiment which shows that a previously learned association can block the learning of a new association.* (After Kamin, 1969)

| | STAGE 1 | STAGE 2 | STAGE 3 |
|---|---|---|---|
| Experimental Group | Light → Shock | Light + Tone → Shock | Tone → No Conditioned Response |
| Control Group | | Light + Tone → Shock | Tone → Conditioned Response |

looks for an event that tends to occur prior to the shock but not at other times (the tone in Group A of the experiment), and hence is truly predictive of the shock.

The importance of predictability is also shown by the phenomenon of **blocking,** discovered by Kamin (1969). Essentially what Kamin showed is that if a CS is *redundant*, providing information that an organism already has, it will not be conditioned to the UCS. Kamin's experiment is outlined in Table 7-1. It involved three stages. In the first stage, an experimental group of animals was repeatedly presented a light, the CS, followed by a shock, the UCS. The experimental animals easily learned the light-shock association. The control group of animals received no training in this first stage. In the second stage, both the experimental and control groups were repeatedly presented a light plus a tone, a compound CS, followed by a shock, the UCS. For the experimental animals, who had already learned to associate the light with shock, the tone was redundant. For the control animals who had no prior learning, the compound CS was informative. In the third and final stage of the experiment, the tone was presented alone to see whether it would produce a conditioned response. The control animals showed conditioned responses, but the experimental animals did not. For the experimental animals, the previously learned light-shock association *blocked* the learning of the new tone-shock association. Why? Presumably because the earlier learning made the shock predictable, and once a UCS is predictable there is little possibility of further conditioning.

**PREDICTABILITY AND EMOTION** Predictability is also important for emotional reactions. If a particular CS reliably predicts that pain is coming, then the absence of that CS predicts that pain is not coming and the organism can relax. The CS is therefore a "danger" signal, and its absence a "safety" signal. When such signals are erratic, the emotional toll on the organism can be devastating. When rats have a reliable predictor that shock is coming, they respond with fear only when the danger signal is present; if they have no reliable predictor, they appear to be continually anxious and may even develop ulcers (Seligman, 1975).

There are clear parallels to human emotionality. If a doctor gives a child a danger signal by telling her that a procedure will hurt, the child will be fearful until the procedure is over. In contrast, if the doctor always tells a child "it won't hurt" when in fact it sometimes does, the child has no danger or safety signals and may become terribly anxious whenever in the doctor's office. As adults, many of us have experienced the anxiety of being in a situation where something disagreeable is likely to happen but no warnings exist for us to predict it. Unpleasant events are, by definition, unpleasant, but unpredictable unpleasant events are downright intolerable.

MODELS OF CLASSICAL CONDITIONING   The findings about predictability have led to a number of models of classical conditioning. The best known of these models was developed by Rescorla and Wagner (1972). Although it has less of a cognitive emphasis than the other models, like them it focuses on the notions of predictability and surprise. According to the **Rescorla-Wagner model,** the amount of conditioning on any trial depends on how *surprising* the UCS is, which in turn depends on how associated the UCS is with possible CSs. The more surprising the UCS, the greater the amount of conditioning on that trial. Early in learning the UCS is very surprising (no CSs yet predict it), and hence a good deal should be learned on each trial. Late in learning, there is at least one CS that predicts the UCS, hence the UCS is not very surprising and rather little is learned on each trial. This pattern—bigger learning gains early rather than later on—in fact characterizes the acquisition of a classically conditioned response (refer back to Figure 7-2).

Another assumption of the Rescorla-Wagner model is that the predictability of the UCS on any trial is determined by all the CSs present on that trial. For example, if there are two CSs present on a trial, say a light and a tone, the amount of conditioning possible for one of the CSs, say the tone, is less the more conditioning that has already occurred to the other CS, the light. This explains the blocking phenomena described above. Essentially, CSs that occur together *compete* with one another for association strength, where the amount to be won in the competition is the amount of unpredictability left in the UCS.

Other models of classical conditioning give greater emphasis to cognitive factors. According to Wagner (1981), just as humans have a short-term memory in which they can rehearse information (see Chapter 8), so do lower animals. And just as humans tend to rehearse in short-term memory primarily information that is unexpected, so lower animals do also. An animal's short-term memory plays a critical role in conditioning. Early in the course of conditioning, a UCS is novel and unpredictable. Consequently, the organism actively rehearses the CS–UCS connection in short-term memory; this rehearsal process is presumably what mediates the acquisition of a classically conditioned response. Once the UCS is no longer surprising, rehearsal decreases and no further learning occurs. This offers another explanation of the blocking phenomenon: once the UCS is completely predictable, there will be no rehearsal of any new association involving that UCS.

Another cognitive model views classical conditioning as the *generation* and *testing* of rules about what events are likely to follow other events (Holyoak, Koh, & Nisbett, 1989). According to this model, an animal is likely to generate a rule whenever two unexpected events occur in close proximity, or whenever an old rule fails. For a rat in a classical conditioning experiment, an unexpected light followed closely by an unexpected shock would lead to the generation of the rule, "If light, then shock." Once a rule is formed, it is strengthened every time it leads to a correct prediction and weakened every time it leads to an incorrect prediction. The "If light, then shock" rule, for example, would be strengthened whenever the light is in fact followed by the shock, and weakened whenever it is not. The rule model clearly predicts that predictability is necessary for conditioning to

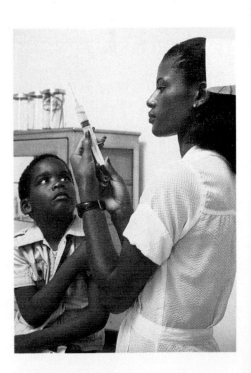

*Knowing when to expect pain lessens anxiety.*

occur, because only correct predictions can strengthen a rule. The model also accounts for the blocking phenomenon: as long as a UCS is predicted by a known rule, no new rule involving that UCS will be generated.

## Biological Constraints

We mentioned earlier in the chapter that different species sometimes learn the same thing by different mechanisms. These phenomena were discovered by *ethologists*, biologists and psychologists who study **ethology**—the study of animal behavior in the natural environment. The phenomena reveal that what an organism can learn by conditioning is constrained by its biology.

ETHOLOGICAL APPROACH   Ethologists like behaviorists are concerned with the behavior of animals, but ethologists place a greater emphasis on evolution and genetics than on learning. This emphasis has led ethologists to study unlearned, innate behaviors. It has also led them to take a distinctive approach to learning, namely to assume that it is rigidly constrained by an animal's genetic endowment and to show that different species will learn different things in different ways. (Early behaviorists, on the other hand, assumed that the laws of learning were the same for different species.) As ethologists put it, when an animal learns it must conform to a genetically determined "behavioral blueprint"; just as an architectural blueprint imposes constraints on the kinds of functions that a building may serve, so a behavioral blueprint imposes genetic constraints on the kinds of associations that an organism may learn. That is, animals are pre-programmed to learn particular things in particular ways.

CONSTRAINTS IN CLASSICAL CONDITIONING   Some of the best evidence for constraints in classical conditioning comes from studies of taste aversion. In a typical study, a rat is permitted to drink a flavored solution, say, vanilla. After drinking it, the rat is mildly poisoned and made ill. When the rat recovers, it is again presented the vanilla solution. Now the rat scrupulously avoids the solution because it has learned to associate the vanilla taste with poison. There is good evidence that such avoidance is an instance of classical conditioning: the initial taste of the solution is the CS, the feeling of being sick is the UCS, and after conditioning the taste signals that sickness is on its way.

According to early behaviorist ideas, a light or a sound might be expected to play the same signaling role as taste. That is, if a light is as effective a stimulus as taste, then an association between a light and feeling sick should be no more difficult to establish than one between a taste and feeling sick. But the facts turn out to be otherwise. This is shown by the experiment that is diagrammed in Table 7-2. In the first stage of the experiment, an experimental group of rats are allowed to lick at a tube that contains a flavored solution; each time the rat licks the tube, a click and a light are presented. Thus the rat experiences three stimuli simultaneously—the taste of the solution, as well as the light and the click. In the second stage of the experiment, rats in the experimental group are mildly poisoned. The question is, What stimuli—the taste or the light-plus-click—will become associated with feeling sick? To answer this, in the third and final stage of the study, rats in the experimental group are again presented the same tube; sometimes the solution in the tube has the same flavor as before but there is no light or click, while other times the solution has no flavor but the light and

**TABLE 7-2**
**Experiment on Constraints and Taste Aversion** *The design of an experiment which shows that taste is a better signal for sickness than shock, while light-plus-sound is a better signal for shock than sickness.* (After Garcia & Koelling, 1966).

|  | STAGE 1 | STAGE 2 | STAGE 3 |
|---|---|---|---|
| Experimental Group | Taste and Light + Click | Sickness | Taste → Avoid |
|  |  |  | Light + Click → Don't Avoid |
| Control Group | Taste and Light + Click | Shock | Taste → Don't Avoid |
|  |  |  | Light + Click → Avoid |

click are presented. The animals avoid the solution when they experience the taste, but not when the light-plus-click is presented; hence, the rats have associated only taste with feeling sick. These results cannot be attributed to taste being a more potent CS than light-plus-click, as shown by the control condition of the experiment that is diagrammed in the bottom of Table 7-2. In the second stage, instead of being mildly poisoned, the rat is shocked. Now, in the final stage of the study, the animal avoids the solution only when the light-plus-click is presented, not when it experiences the taste alone (Garcia & Koelling, 1966).

Thus taste is a better signal for sickness than for shock, while light-plus-click is a better signal for shock than for sickness. Why does this selectivity of association exist? It does not fit with the early behaviorist idea that equally potent stimuli can substitute for one another; since taste and light-plus-click can both be effective CSs, and since being sick and being shocked are both effective UCSs, then either CS should have been associable with either UCS. In contrast, this selectivity of association fits perfectly with the ethological perspective and its emphasis on an animal's evolutionary adaptation to its environment. In their natural habitat, rats (like other mammals) rely on taste to select their food. Consequently, there may be a genetically determined, or "built-in," relation between taste and intestinal reactions, which constrains what association the rat may learn. In particular, the built-in relation fosters an association between taste and sickness but not between light and sickness. Furthermore, in a rat's natural environment, pain resulting from external factors like cold or injury is invariably due to external stimuli. Consequently, there may be a built-in relation between external stimuli and "external pain," which fosters an association between light and shock, but not one between taste and shock.

If rats learn to associate taste with sickness because it fits with their natural means of selecting food, then another species with a different means of selecting food might have trouble learning to associate taste with sickness. This is exactly what happens. Birds naturally select their food on the basis of looks rather than taste, and they readily learn to associate a light with sickness, but not a taste with sickness (Wilcoxin, Dragoin, & Kral, 1971). Here then is a perfect example of different species learning the same thing—what causes sickness—by different means. In short, if we want to know what may be conditioned to what, we cannot consider the CS and UCS in isolation; rather, we must focus on the two in combination and consider how well that combination reflects built-in relations. This conclusion differs considerably from the assumption that the laws of learning are the same for all species and situations.

# Neural Basis of Elementary Learning

Classical and operant conditioning may be the simplest forms of **associative learning,** but as we mentioned at the outset of the chapter, there are more elementary forms of learning. In particular, there is **habituation,** by which an organism learns to ignore a weak stimulus that has no serious consequences—such as tuning out the sound of a loud clock. A related case of learning is **sensitization,** whereby an organism learns to strengthen its reaction to a weak stimulus if a threatening or painful stimulus follows. For instance, we learn to respond more intensely to the sound of a piece of equipment if it is frequently followed by a crash. Researchers have made remarkable progress in determining the biological bases of these two forms of learning.

Consider some of the research of Eric Kandel and his associates, who use snails in their work. The neurons of a snail are similar in structure and function to those of a human, yet its nervous system is simple enough to allow re-searchers to study individual neurons. Indeed, the total number of neurons in a snail is only in the thousands (compared to billions in a human). Also, some of the snail's neurons of interest are among the largest and most accessible in nature. Moreover, the neurons of a snail are collected into discrete groups (or **ganglia**) of 500 to 1,500 neurons, and a single ganglion can control an instance of habituation or sensitization. This makes it possible to give a "cell-by-cell" account of elementary learning.

The *Aplysia*, a large marine animal, is the snail of choice for researchers, and the behavior of particular interest is a withdrawal response. As shown in Figure 1, the *Aplysia's* gill is housed in a cavity that is covered by a protective sheet called the *mantle shelf*; the sheet ends in a fleshy spout called a *siphon*. When the siphon is stimulated by touch, both the siphon and gill contract into the cavity. The withdrawal is controlled by a single ganglion and is subject to habituation and sensitization.

In studies of habituation, the researchers lightly touch the snail's siphon on each trial of the experiment. In the initial trials, the gill-withdrawal reflex is strong, but it gradually weakens after 10 or 15 trials. Essentially, the *Aplysia* has learned to recognize the stimulus as trivial. What cellular events mediate this habituation behavior? The stimulus to the siphon activates 24 sensory neurons, each of which activates the 6 motor neurons in the gill that innervate the con-

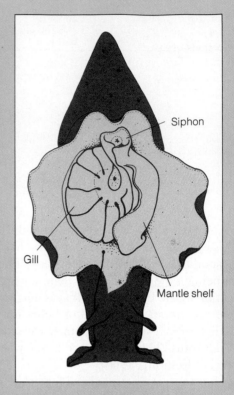

**FIGURE 1**
**Gill Withdrawal in the Aplysia** *When the siphon is stimulated, the animal retracts its gill into the protective sheet of the mantle cavity; this sheet is called the mantle shelf.* (After Kandel, 1979)

tracting muscle. The structure of the system can be understood by looking at the neural connections for a single sensory neuron and a single motor neuron

# Operant Conditioning

In classical conditioning, the conditioned response often resembles the normal response to the unconditioned stimulus: salivation, for example, is a dog's normal response to food. But when you want to teach an organism something novel—such as teaching a dog a new trick—you cannot use classical conditioning. What unconditioned stimulus would make a dog sit up or roll over? To train the dog, you must first persuade it to do the trick and *afterward* reward it with either approval or food. If you keep doing this, eventually the dog will learn the trick.

Much of real-life behavior is like this: responses are learned because they *operate* on, or affect, the environment. Referred to as **operant conditioning,** this kind of learning occurs in our own species, as well as in lower species. Alone in a crib, a baby may kick and twist and coo spontaneously. When left by itself in a room, a dog may pad back and forth; sniff; or perhaps

(see the top of Figure 2). The small triangles in the figure depict *synaptic* connections between neurons, where a synapse involves a space that must be bridged by a chemical *neurotransmitter.* In the *Aplysia,* a neurotransmitter released by the sensory neuron onto the motor neuron causes initial gill withdrawal, and a decrease in the amount of the neurotransmitter is what mediates the habituation of gill withdrawal. That is, after a sufficient number of trials, a touch of the siphon no longer results in the release of enough neurotransmitter to cause the gill motor neuron to fire. Thus, this form of elementary learning is due to chemically induced changes in synaptic connections between neurons (Kandel, 1979).

Sensitization functions in a similar, though more complex, manner. To sensitize gill withdrawal, again the researchers apply a weak tactile stimulus to the siphon, but this time they also apply simultaneously a strong stimulus to the tail. After a number of such trials, gill withdrawal becomes more pronounced. Some of the mediating neural connections are illustrated in the bottom half of Figure 2. Since there are now two stimuli that need to be connected—the siphon touch and the tail stimulus—a bridge must be formed between the two neural pathways. The bridge consists of neural connections from the tail that are added to the circuit from the siphon. The new connections include a synapse between a tail sensory neuron and a *fa-*

*cilitator interneuron* (a neuron that connects other neurons) and a synapse that connects the facilitator interneuron with the circuit that supports gill withdrawal. In essence, the neural activity from the strong stimulus to the tail modifies the neural connection that underlies gill withdrawal. Once more, learning is mediated by changes in the neurotransmitter that bridges the synapse between the siphon's sensory neuron and the gill's motor neuron. But in this case, the change consists of an increase in the amount of the neurotransmitter released by the sensory neuron (Castelluci & Kandel, 1976; Bailey, Chen, Keller, & Kandel, 1992).

Our discussion of sensitization suggests that a cell-by-cell analysis may be possible for classical conditioning. Gill withdrawal in the *Aplysia* can be classically conditioned; and such conditioning, like sensitization, involves modifying the gill withdrawal by a second stimulus. Indeed, researchers have proposed a cellular account of classical conditioning that is remarkably similar to that for sensitization (Hawkins & Kandel, 1984). This proposal has generated some controversy (Gluck & Thompson, 1987), but should the basic ideas of the proposal prove defensible, it would indicate that some forms of conditioning are built on more primitive forms of learning. It would also indicate that, at least for some organisms, the biological basis of simple learning can be localized to the activity of specific neurons.

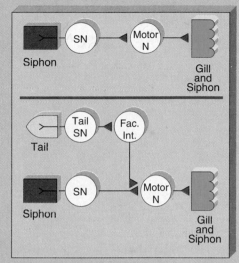

**FIGURE 2**
**Neural Circuits for Habituation and Sensitization** *The top panel illustrates the connection between a single sensory neuron (SN) and a single motor neuron (Motor N) for the gill-withdrawal reflex. Stimulation of the siphon excites the sensory neuron, which in turn excites the motor neuron to innervate the gill. Habituation of gill withdrawal is mediated by a change at the synaptic connection between the sensory and motor neurons. The bottom panel illustrates the connections involved in sensitization of gill withdrawal. Now, stimulation of the tail excites a facilitator interneuron (Fac. int.), which facilitates the impulse being sent from the siphon's sensory neuron.*

pick up a ball, drop it, and play with it. Neither organism is responding to the onset or offset of a specific external stimulus. Rather, they are operating on their environment. Once the organism performs a certain behavior, however, the likelihood that the action will be repeated depends on its consequences. The baby will coo more often if each such occurrence is followed by parental attention, and the dog will pick up the ball more often if this action is followed by petting or a food reward. If we think of the baby as having a goal of parental attention, and the dog as having a goal of food, then operant conditioning amounts to learning that a particular behavior leads to attaining a particular goal (Rescorla, 1987).

## Law of Effect

The study of operant conditioning began at the turn of the century with a series of experiments by E. L. Thorndike (1898). Thorndike, much influenced by Darwin's theory of evolution, was trying to show that learning in

*B. F. Skinner*

**FIGURE 7-6**
**Apparatus for Operant Conditioning**
*The photograph shows a Skinner box with a magazine for delivering food pellets. The computer is used to control the experiment and record the rat's responses.*

animals is continuous with learning in humans. A typical experiment proceeded as follows. A hungry cat is placed in a cage whose door is held fast by a simple latch, and a piece of fish is placed just outside the cage. Initially, the cat tries to reach the food by extending its paws through the bars. When this fails, the cat moves about the cage, engaging in a variety of different behaviors. At some point it inadvertently hits the latch, frees itself, and eats the fish. The researchers then place the cat back in its cage and put a new piece of fish outside. The cat goes through roughly the same set of behaviors until once more it happens to hit the latch. The procedure is repeated again and again. Over trials, the cat eliminates many of its irrelevant behaviors, eventually efficiently opening the latch and freeing itself as soon as it is placed in the cage. The cat has learned to open the latch in order to obtain food.

It may sound as if the cat is acting intelligently, but Thorndike argued that there is little "intelligence" operative here. There is no moment in time at which the cat seems to have an insight about the solution to its problem. Instead, the cat's performance improves gradually over trials. Even if at one point the experimenter places the cat's paw on the latch and pushes it down, thereby demonstrating the solution, the cat's progress continues to be slow. Rather than insight, the cat appears to be engaging in *trial-and-error* behavior, and when a reward immediately follows one of these behaviors, the learning of the action is strengthened. Thorndike referred to this strengthening as the **law of effect**. He argued that in operant learning, the law of effect selects from a set of random responses just those responses that are followed by positive consequences. The process is similar to evolution, in which the law of *survival of the fittest* selects from a set of random species variations just the changes that promote survival of the species. The law of effect, then, promotes the survival of the *fittest responses* (Schwartz, 1989).

## Skinner's Experiments

B. F. Skinner was responsible for a number of changes in how researchers conceptualize and study operant conditioning. His method of studying operant conditioning is simpler than Thorndike's and has been widely accepted.

**EXPERIMENTAL VARIATIONS** In a Skinnerian experiment, a hungry animal—usually a rat or a pigeon—is placed in a box like the one shown in Figure 7-6, which is popularly called a "Skinner box." The inside of the box is bare except for a protruding bar with a food dish beneath it. A small light above the bar can be turned on at the experimenter's discretion. Left alone in the box, the rat moves about, exploring. Occasionally it inspects the bar and presses it. The rate at which the rat first presses the bar is the *baseline* level of bar pressing. After establishing the baseline level, the experimenter activates a food magazine located outside the box. Now, every time the rat presses the bar, a small food pellet is released into the dish. The rat eats the food pellet and soon presses the bar again; the food *reinforces* bar pressing, and the rate of pressing increases dramatically. If the food magazine is disconnected so that pressing the bar no longer delivers food, the rate of bar pressing will diminish. Hence, an operantly conditioned response (or, simply, an *operant*) undergoes *extinction* with nonreinforcement just as a classically conditioned response does. The experimenter can set up a *discrimination* test by presenting food only if the rat presses the bar while the light is on, hence conditioning the rat through selective reinforcement. In this example, the light serves as a **discriminative stimulus** that controls the response.

Thus, operant conditioning increases the likelihood of a response by following the behavior with a reinforcer (often something like food or water). Because the bar is always present in the Skinner box, the rat can respond to it as frequently or infrequently as it chooses. The organism's *rate of response* is therefore a useful measure of the operant's strength; the more frequently the response occurs during a given time interval, the greater its strength.

**IMPLICATIONS FOR CHILD REARING**  Although rats and pigeons have been the favored experimental subjects, operant conditioning applies to many species, including our own. Indeed, operant conditioning has a good deal to tell us about child rearing. A particularly illuminating example of this is illustrated by the following case. A young boy had temper tantrums if he did not get enough attention from his parents, especially at bedtime. Since the parents eventually responded, their attention probably reinforced the tantrums. To eliminate the tantrums, the parents were advised to go through the normal bedtime rituals and then to ignore the child's protests, painful though that might be. By withholding the reinforcer (the attention), the tantrums should extinguish—which is just what happened. The time the child spent crying at bedtime decreased from 45 minutes to not at all over a period of only 7 days (Williams, 1959).

Another application of operant conditioning to child rearing focuses on the temporal relation between a response and its reinforcer. Laboratory experiments have shown that immediate reinforcement is more effective than delayed; the more time between an operant response and a reinforcer, the less the response strength. Many developmental psychologists have noted that the delay of reinforcement is an important factor in dealing with young children. If a child acts kindly to a pet, the act can best be strengthened by praising (rewarding) the child immediately, rather than waiting until later. Similarly, if a child hits someone without provocation, this aggressive behavior will more likely be eliminated if the child is punished immediately, rather than waiting until later.

**SHAPING**  Suppose you want to use operant conditioning to teach your dog a trick—for instance, to press a buzzer with its nose. You cannot wait until the dog does this naturally (and then reinforce it), because you may wait forever. When the desired behavior is truly novel, you have to condition it by taking advantage of natural variations in the animal's actions. To train a dog to press a buzzer with its nose, you can give the animal a food reinforcer each time it approaches the area of the buzzer, requiring it to move closer and closer to the desired spot for each reinforcer until finally the dog's nose is touching the buzzer. This technique of reinforcing only those variations in response that deviate in the direction desired by the experimenter is called **shaping** the animal's behavior.

Animals can be taught elaborate tricks and routines by means of shaping. Two psychologists and their staff have trained thousands of animals of many species for television shows, commercials, and county fairs (Breland & Breland, 1966). One popular show featured "Priscilla, the Fastidious Pig." Priscilla turned on the TV set, ate breakfast at a table, picked up dirty clothes and put them in a hamper, vacuumed the floor, picked out her favorite food (from among foods competing with that of her sponsor!), and

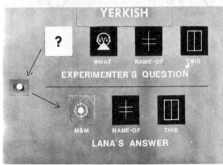

*Animals have been taught very complex responses by means of shaping techniques. At the Yerkes Primate Research Center in Atlanta, a chimpanzee named Lana has learned to answer questions and to make requests by pressing symbols on a computer console. At bottom is an example of how the experiment works. A researcher outside the room asked Lana a question by pressing the symbols on the console for the words "What name of this" and also holding up candy. The chimpanzee answered by pressing the symbols for "M & M name of this."*

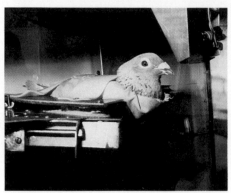
*Pigeon sitting*

*Pigeon pecking key*

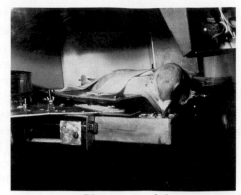
*Pigeon rewarded*

**FIGURE 7-7**
**Search and Rescue by Pigeons** *The Coast Guard has used pigeons to search for people lost at sea. The pigeons are trained, using shaping methods, to spot the color orange—the international color of life jackets. Three pigeons are strapped into a plexiglass chamber attached to the underside of a helicopter. The chamber is divided into thirds so that each bird faces a different direction. When a pigeon spots an orange object, or any other object, it pecks a key that buzzes the pilot. The pilot then heads in the direction indicated by the bird that responded. Pigeons are better suited than people for the task of spotting distant objects at sea. They can stare over the water for a long time without suffering eye fatigue, have excellent color vision, and can focus on a 60- to 80-degree area, whereas a person can only focus on a 2- to 3-degree area.* (After Simmons, 1981)

took part in a quiz program, answering questions from the audience by flashing lights that indicated yes or no. She was not an unusually bright pig; in fact, because pigs grow so fast, a new "Priscilla" was trained every 3 to 5 months. The ingenuity was not the pig's but the experimenters', who used operant conditioning and shaped the behavior to produce the desired result. Pigeons have been trained by shaping of operant responses to locate persons lost at sea (see Figure 7-7), and porpoises have been trained to retrieve underwater equipment.

## Phenomena and Applications

The following phenomena increase the generality of operant conditioning, and show some of its applications to human behavior.

**CONDITIONED REINFORCERS** Most of the reinforcers we have discussed are called *primary* because, like food, they satisfy basic drives. If operant conditioning occurred only with primary reinforcers, it would not be that common in our lives because primary reinforcers are not that common. However, virtually any stimulus can become a *secondary* or **conditioned reinforcer** by being consistently paired with a primary reinforcer; conditioned reinforcers greatly increase the range of operant conditioning (just as second-order conditioning greatly increases the range of classical conditioning).

A minor variation in the typical operant-conditioning experiment illustrates how conditioned reinforcement works. When a rat in a Skinner box presses a lever, a tone sounds momentarily, followed shortly by a delivery of food (the food is a primary reinforcer; the tone will become a conditioned reinforcer). After the animal has been conditioned in this way, the experimenter begins extinction, so that when the rat presses the lever neither the tone nor the food occurs. In time, the animal virtually ceases to press the lever. Then the tone is reconnected but not the food. When the animal discovers that pressing the lever turns on the tone, its rate of pressing markedly increases, overcoming the extinction even though no food follows. The tone has acquired a reinforcing quality of its own through classical conditioning; because the tone was reliably paired with food, it came to signal food.

Our lives abound with conditioned reinforcers. Two of the most prevalent are money and praise. Presumably, money is a powerful reinforcer because it has been paired so frequently with so many primary reinforcers—we can buy food, drink, and comfort, to mention just a few of the obvious things. And mere praise, without even the promise of a primary reinforcer, can sustain many an activity.

**RELATIVITY OF REINFORCEMENT** While it seems natural to think of a reinforcement as a stimulus, it is sometimes more useful to think of it as an *activity;* it is not the food pellet that reinforces lever pressing, but the eating of the pellet. Given this view, we can now ask, What must be the relation between two activities such that one reinforces the other? It appears that any activity that any organism performs frequently can reinforce any other activity that the organism engages in less frequently. For example, in one study, children were offered the choice of operating a pinball machine or eating candy. Children who preferred eating candy would increase their rate of playing the pinball machine if playing the machine led to eating candy; thus, eating candy reinforced playing pinball. For children who preferred playing pinball, however, the reverse was true: they increased their intake of candy only if this increased their chance to play pinball (Premack, 1959).

**GENERALIZATION AND DISCRIMINATION** What was true for classical conditioning holds for operant conditioning as well: organisms generalize what they have learned, and generalization can be curbed by discrimination training. If a young child is reinforced by her parents for petting the family dog, she will soon generalize this petting response to other dogs. Since this can be dangerous (say, the neighbors have a vicious watchdog), the child's parents may provide some discrimination training, so that she is reinforced when she pets the family dog but not the neighbor's.

Discrimination training will be effective to the extent there is a discriminative stimulus (or set of them) that clearly distinguishes cases where the response should be made from those where it should be suppressed. Our young child will have an easier time learning which dog to pet if her parents can point to an aspect of dogs that signal their friendliness (a wagging tail, for example). In general, a discriminative stimulus will be useful to the extent its presence predicts that a response will be followed by reinforcement

*partial reinforcement*
*partial reinforcement effect*
*schedule of reinforcement*
*ratio schedule*

① *fixed ratio*
② *Variable ratio*
③ *Interval schedules*

while its absence predicts that the response will not be followed by reinforcement (or vice versa). Just as in classical conditioning, the predictive power of a stimulus seems critical for conditioning.

**SCHEDULES OF REINFORCEMENT**  In real life, every instance of a behavior is rarely reinforced—sometimes hard work is followed by praise, but often it goes unacknowledged. If operant conditioning occurred only with continuous reinforcement, it might play a limited role in our lives. It turns out, however, that once a behavior is established, it can be maintained when it is reinforced only a fraction of the time. This phenomenon is known as **partial reinforcement,** and it can be illustrated in the laboratory by a pigeon who learns to peck at a key for food. Once this operant is established, the pigeon continues to peck at a high rate even if it receives only occasional reinforcement. In some cases, pigeons who were rewarded with food on the average of once every 5 minutes (12 times an hour) pecked at the key as often as 6,000 times per hour! Furthermore, extinction following the maintenance of a response on partial reinforcement is much slower than extinction following the maintenance of a response on continuous reinforcement. This phenomenon is known as the *partial-reinforcement effect*. It makes intuitive sense because there is less difference between extinction and maintenance when reinforcement during maintenance is only partial.

When reinforcement occurs only some of the time, we need to know exactly how it is scheduled—after every third response? after every five seconds? and so forth. It turns out that the **schedule of reinforcement** determines the pattern of responding. Some schedules are called **ratio schedules,** because with them reinforcement depends on the number of responses the organism makes. It's like being a factory worker who gets paid for piecework. The ratio can be either fixed or variable. On a *fixed ratio* schedule (called an FR schedule), the number of responses that has to be made is fixed at a particular value. If the number is 5 (FR 5), 5 responses are required for reinforcement, if 50 (FR 50), 50 responses are required, and so on. In general, the higher the ratio the higher the rate at which the organism re-

*Praise is a positive reinforcer.*

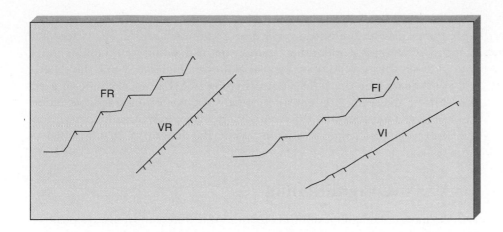

Interval schedule
fixed interval
variable interval

sponds, particularly when the organism is initially trained on a relatively low ratio, say FR 5, and then is continuously shifted to progressively higher ratios, culminating say in FR 100. It is as if our factory worker initially got 5 dollars for every 5 hems sewn, but then times got tough and he needed to do 100 hems to get 5 dollars. But perhaps the most distinctive aspect about behavior under an FR schedule is that there is a pause in responding right after the reinforcement occurs (see the left side of Figure 7-8). It is hard for the factory worker to start on a new set of hems right after he just finished enough for a reward.

On a *variable ratio* schedule (a VR schedule), one still gets reinforced only after making a certain number of responses but that number varies unpredictably. Thus in a VR 5 schedule, the number of responses needed for reinforcement may sometimes be 1, other times 10, with an average of 5. Unlike the behavior with FR schedules, there are no pauses when the organism is operating under a VR schedule (see the left side of Figure 7-8), presumably because the organism has no way of detecting that it is far from a reinforcement. A good example of VR schedule in everyday life is the operation of a slot machine. The number of responses (plays) needed for reinforcement (payoff) keeps varying, and the operator has no way of predicting when reinforcement will occur. VR schedules can generate very high rates of responding (as casino owners appear to have figured out).

Other schedules are called **interval schedules,** because with them reinforcement is available only after a certain time interval has elapsed. Again the schedule can be either fixed or variable. On a *fixed interval* (FI) schedule, the organism is reinforced for its first response after a certain amount of time has passed since its last reinforcement. On an FI 2 (minutes) schedule, for example, reinforcement is available only when 2 minutes have elapsed since the last reinforced response; responses made during that 2 minute interval have no consequence. The distinctive aspects of responding on an FI schedule are a pause that occurs immediately after reinforcement and an increase in the rate of responding as the end of the interval approaches (see the right side of Figure 7-8). A good example of a FI schedule in everyday life is mail delivery, which comes just once a day (FI 24 hours), or in some places twice a day (FI 12 hours). Thus, right after your mail is delivered you would not check it again (this is your pause), but as the end of the mail-delivery interval approaches you will start checking again.

On a *variable interval* schedule (a VI schedule), reinforcement still depends on a certain interval having elapsed, but the interval's duration varies

*The threat of punishment is an effective motivator*

unpredictably. In a VI 10 minute schedule, for example, sometimes the critical interval may be 2 minutes, sometimes 20 minutes, and so on, with an average of 10 minutes. Unlike the variations in responding found under an FI schedule, organisms tend to respond at a uniform high rate when the schedule is a VI one (see the right side of Figure 7-8). For an example of a VI schedule in everyday life, consider redialing a busy number. In order to get reinforced (getting your call through), you have to wait some time interval after your last response (dialing), but the length of that interval is unpredictable.

## Aversive Conditioning

We have talked about reinforcement as if it were almost always positive (food, for example). But negative or aversive events, such as shock or a painful noise, are often used in conditioning. There are different kinds of **aversive conditioning** depending on whether the aversive event is used to weaken an existent response or to learn a new response.

**PUNISHMENT** In **punishment** training, a response is followed by an aversive stimulus or event, which results in the response being weakened or suppressed on subsequent occasions. Suppose a young child who is learning to use crayons starts drawing on the wall (this is the undesirable response); if he is slapped on the hand when he does this (the punishment), he will learn not to do so. Similarly, if a rat learning to run a maze is shocked whenever it chooses a wrong path, it will soon learn to avoid past mistakes. In both cases, punishment is used to decrease the likelihood of an undesirable behavior.*

Although punishment can suppress an unwanted response, it has several significant disadvantages. First, its effects are not as predictable as the results of reward. Reward essentially says, "Repeat what you have done"; punishment says, "Stop it!" but fails to give an alternative. As a result, the organism may substitute an even less desirable response for the punished one. Second, the by-products of punishment may be unfortunate. Punishment often leads to dislike or fear of the punishing person (parent, teacher, or employer) and of the situation (home, school, or office) in which the punishment occurred. Finally, an extreme or painful punishment may elicit aggressive behavior that is more serious than the original undesirable behavior.

These cautions do not mean that punishment should never be employed. It can effectively eliminate an undesirable response if the available alternative responses are rewarded. Rats that have learned to take the shorter of two paths in a maze to reach food will quickly switch to the longer one if they are shocked in the shorter path. The temporary suppression produced by punishment provides the opportunity for the rat to learn to take the longer path. In this case, punishment is an effective means of redirecting behavior because it is informative, and this seems to be the key to the humane and effective use of punishment. A child who gets a shock from an

---

*It is worth noting the relation between the terms *reward* and *punisher* on the one hand, and *positive* and *negative reinforcers* on the other. *Reward* is sometimes used synonymously with *positive reinforcer*—an event whose occurrence following a response increases the probability of that response. But a *punisher* is not the same as a *negative reinforcer*. Negative reinforcement means termination of an aversive event following a response; this increases the probability of that response. Punishment has the opposite effect: it decreases the probability of a response.

electrical appliance may learn which connections are safe and which are hazardous; a teacher's corrections of a student's paper can be regarded as punishing, but they are also informative and can provide an occasion for learning.

**ESCAPE AND AVOIDANCE**  Aversive events can also be used in the learning of new responses. Organisms can learn to make a response to terminate an ongoing aversive event, as when a child learns to turn off a faucet to stop hot water from flowing into his bath. This is called **escape learning**. Organisms can also learn to make a response to prevent an aversive event from even starting, as when we learn to stop at redlights to prevent accidents (and traffic tickets). This is called **avoidance learning**.

Often escape learning precedes avoidance learning. This is illustrated by the following laboratory experiment. A rat is placed in a box consisting of two compartments divided by a barrier. On each trial the animal is placed in one of the compartments. At some point, a warning tone is sounded, and five seconds later the floor of that compartment is electrified; to get away from the shock, the animal must jump the barrier into the other compartment. Initially, the animal jumps the barrier only when the shock starts— this is escape learning. But with practice, the animal learns to jump upon hearing the warning tone, thereby avoiding the shock entirely—this is avoidance learning.

Avoidance learning has generated a great deal of interest, in part because there is something very puzzling about it. What exactly is reinforcing the avoidance response? In the above study, what reinforces the animal for jumping the barrier? Intuitively, it seems to be the absence of shock, but this is a nonevent. How can a nonevent serve as a reinforcer? One solution to this puzzle holds that there are two stages to the learning. The first stage involves classical conditioning. through repeated pairings of the warning (the CS) and the punishing event or shock (the UCS), the animal learns a fear response to the warning. The second stage involves operant conditioning: the animal learns that a particular response (jumping the hurdle) removes an aversive event, namely fear. In short, what first appears to be a nonevent is actually fear, and we can think of avoidance as escape from fear (Mowrer, 1947; Rescorla & Solomon, 1967).

There is an alternative to this two-stage theory that emphasizes cognitive factors (Seligman & Johnston, 1973). According to this cognitive theory, avoidance training leads the animal to certain *expectancies*, namely: (a) if it responds (jumps the barrier, for example), no shock will occur, and (b) if it does not respond, shock will occur. These expectancies are strengthened whenever they are confirmed. The reason why the rat in the preceding study continues to jump the barrier upon hearing the warning tone is that the tone triggers its "respond—no shock" expectancy, and each jump strengthens this expectancy (there is in fact no shock). Moreover, this cognitive theory explains another important fact about avoidance responses— they are difficult to extinguish. Thus, if the shocker in the preceding study were disconnected, the rat would continue to jump the barrier. Why? Because turning off the shocker does nothing to alter the "respond—no shock" expectancy, and hence behavior continues to be controlled by that expectancy. Similarly, if we learned to avoid a once-dangerous situation (a faulty elevator, for example) we may continue to avoid the situation even after the danger is gone (the elevator has been fixed) because nothing has happened to refute our expectancy.

# Control and Cognitive Factors

Our analysis of operant conditioning has tended to emphasize environmental factors—a response is consistently followed by a reinforcing event, and the organism learns to associate the response and the reinforcement. However, the cognitive theory of avoidance that we just discussed suggests that cognitive factors may play an important role in operant conditioning, just as they do in classical conditioning. As we will see, it is often useful to view the organism in an operant conditioning situation as acquiring new *knowledge* about response-reinforcer relations.

**CONTIGUITY VERSUS CONTROL** As was the case in classical conditioning, we want to know what factor is critical for operant conditioning to occur. Again, one of the options is temporal contiguity: an operant is conditioned whenever reinforcement immediately follows the behavior (Skinner, 1948). A more cognitive option, closely related to predictability, is that of control: an operant is conditioned only when the organism interprets the reinforcement as being controlled by its response. Some important experiments by Maier and Seligman (1976) provide more support for the control view than for the temporal contiguity view. (See also the discussion of control and stress in Chapter 15.)

Their basic experiment includes two stages. In the first stage, some dogs learn that whether they receive a shock or not depends on (is controlled by) their behavior, while other dogs learn that they have no control over the shock. Think of the dogs as being tested in pairs. Both members of a pair are in a harness that restricts their movements, and occasionally they receive an electric shock. One member of the pair, the "control" dog, can turn off the shock by pushing a nearby panel with its nose; the other member of the pair, the "yoked" dog, cannot exercise any control over the shock. Whenever the control dog is shocked, so is the yoked dog; and whenever the control dog turns off the shock, the yoked dog's shock is also terminated. The control and yoked dogs therefore receive the same number of shocks.

In the second stage of the study, the experimenter places both dogs in a new apparatus—a box divided into two compartments by a barrier. This is the same avoidance-testing device that we considered a moment ago. As before, on each trial a tone is first sounded, indicating that the compartment that the animal currently occupies is about to be subject to electric shock; to avoid shock, the animal must learn to jump the barrier into the other compartment when they hear the warning tone. Control dogs learn this response rapidly. But the yoked dogs are another story. Initially the yoked dogs make no movement across the barrier, and as trials progress their behavior becomes increasingly passive, lapsing finally into utter helplessness. Why? Because during the first stage the yoked dogs learned that shocks were not under their control, and this belief in noncontrol made conditioning in the second stage impossible. If a belief in noncontrol makes operant conditioning impossible, then a belief in control may be what makes it possible. Many other experiments support the notion that operant conditioning occurs only when the organism perceives reinforcement as being under its control (Seligman, 1975). See Chapter 15 for a detailed discussion of learned helplessness.

**CONTINGENCY LEARNING** We can also talk about the previous results in terms of *contingencies*. We can say that operant conditioning occurs only when the organism perceives a contingency between its responses and reinforcement. In the first stage of the preceding study, the relevant contingency is between pushing a panel and the shock ending; perceiving this contingency amounts to determining that the likelihood of shock ending is greater when the panel is pushed than when it is not. Dogs who do not perceive this contingency in the first stage of the study appear not to look for any contingency in the second stage. This contingency approach makes it clear that the results with operant conditioning fit with the findings about the importance of predictability in classical conditioning: knowing that a CS predicts a UCS can be interpreted as showing that the organism has detected a contingency between the two stimuli. Thus, in both classical and operant conditioning, what the organism seems to learn is a contingency between two events.

Our ability to learn contingencies develops very early, as shown by the following study of three-month-old infants. Every infant in the experiment was lying in his or her crib, with their head on a pillow. Beneath the pillow was a switch that closed whenever the infant turned its head. For subjects in the control group, whenever they turned their heads and closed the switch, a mobile on the opposite side of the crib was activated. For these infants, there was a contingency between head-turning and the mobile moving—the mobile being more likely to move with a head turn than without. These infants quickly learned to turn their head, and they reacted to the moving mobile with signs of enjoyment (they smiled and cooed). The situation is quite different for subjects in the experimental group. For these infants, the mobile was made to move roughly as often as it did for the experimental subjects, but whether it moved or not was not under their control. That is, in the experimental condition, there was no contingency between head-turning and the mobile moving. These infants did not learn to turn their head more frequently. Moreover, after a while they showed no signs of enjoying the mobile moving. With no control over the mobile, it appears to have lost some of its reinforcing character.

## Biological Constraints

As was the case with classical conditioning, biology imposes constraints on what may be learned in operant conditioning.

**MISBEHAVIOR** Some early evidence for biological constraints on operant conditioning came from psychologists who were using operant techniques to teach animals tricks. These trainers reported that instead of learning the desired trick, occasionally the animal would "misbehave" and learn something else that was closer to one of its instinctual (innate) behaviors. In one case, the trainers tried to get a chicken to stand still on a platform, but the chicken insisted on scratching the ground instead. Scratching the ground is related to the chicken's instinctual food-gathering behavior, which successfully competed with the behavior that the trainers were trying to instill. Thus, an instinct sets limits on what could be acquired. In other cases, an animal would succeed initially in learning the desired response only to drift later to a response that was an instinctual food-gathering behavior of its particular species (Breland & Breland, 1961).

**RESPONSE-REINFORCER CONSTRAINTS** Constraints on operant conditioning involve response-reinforcer relations. We can illustrate this point

*Water squirting (a natural behavior for walruses) can be easily conditioned to occur on command.*

# Economics of Reward

The simple operant experiments that we have discussed fail to capture an important aspect of human behavior: many responses that we make represent a *choice* among alternatives. To study choice, operant researchers use experiments in which the animal has at least two responses. The choices that the animal has may differ in their reinforcer or in their schedule of reinforcement, or both. To illustrate, a pigeon may have a choice between two keys, where pecks on one key produce food and pecks on the other, water; alternatively, both keys may lead to food but may have different schedules, so that one key may require five pecks for a reinforcement while the other may require ten (FR 5 versus FR 10).

In analyzing behavior in choice experiments, researchers have found that some concepts and principles of economics are useful (Rachlin, 1980). To see the relation between economic principles and pigeons pecking keys, note that a pigeon in a choice experiment can be thought of as having to choose how to distribute its limited responses—its resources—and that economic theory deals with questions about how to allocate one's limited resources.

We will illustrate the economic approach to operant conditioning by discussing three examples. In each case, we first provide the relevant economic principles and then consider their application to operant experiments.

## DEMAND CURVES

An important concept in economics is that of *demand* for a commodity; this is the amount of the commodity—say, bread or chocolate—that will be purchased at a given price. If we change the price, we generate a *demand curve* like those presented in Figure 1. Note that the curve for chocolate decreases sharply as price is increased; the more it costs, the less chocolate we will buy. The demand for chocolate is therefore said to be *elastic*. In contrast, the curve for bread is barely affected by price; we will purchase roughly the same amount of bread regardless of its cost. Thus, the demand for bread is *inelastic*. All of this conforms to the belief that bread is a necessity and chocolate a luxury.

Consider now the relevance of this to operant conditioning. For rats and pigeons, the equivalent of price is the number of responses that must be made to obtain a reinforcer. This equivalence is illustrated in Figure 2, which includes a rat's demand curve for food. The curve tells us how much food (reinforcement) a rat will "purchase" (work to obtain) at different "prices" (schedules of reinforcement). Rats purchase the same amount of food reinforcements regardless of whether they are rewarded after every two or every eight responses: the demand curve for food is inelastic. The other demand curve in Figure 2 is for brain stimulation (electrical stimulation of certain regions of the brain, which is known to be reinforcing). The demand for brain stimulation is clearly elastic, because the amount purchased decreases sharply with price (the number of responses required for a reinforcement).

The curves in Figure 2 have implications for questions about the nature of reinforcement. It is natural to ask whether one kind of reinforcement is more or less potent than another, say,

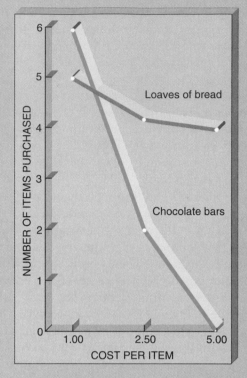

## FIGURE 1
## Hypothetical Demand Curves for Bread and Chocolate
*As the price of a loaf of bread increases from $1.00 to $5.00, the amount of bread purchased decreases hardly at all; the demand for bread is inelastic. In contrast, as the price of a chocolate bar increases from $1.00 to $5.00, the amount purchased decreases sharply; the demand for chocolate is elastic.*

food versus brain stimulation. In the past, researchers interested in this question had devised an experiment in which one response leads to food reinforcement, another leads to brain stimulation, and both are on the same schedule of reinforcement. As Figure 2 makes clear, the results from such an experiment will depend entirely on the choice of the schedule. Specifically when a reinforce-

with pigeons in two different situations; *reward learning*, where the animal acquires a response that is reinforced by food; and *escape learning*, where the animal acquires a response that is reinforced by the termination of shock. In the case of reward, pigeons learn much faster if the response is pecking a key rather than flapping their wings. In the case of escape, the opposite is

ment requires two responses, brain stimulation is the overwhelming choice, but at higher prices (eight responses) food is slightly preferred. The question of which reinforcer is more potent only has a straightforward answer when the demand for both reinforcers is inelastic, or when the demand for both are elastic and their demand curves are the same (Hursh & Natelson, 1981).

## SUBSTITUTABILITY OF COMMODITIES

An economic analysis of choice considers the interactions between the choices. Suppose we are interested in a choice between gasoline and public transportation. Because the demand curves for both commodities are elastic, we expect that when gas prices increase, people more often choose public transportation. This of course is what happens, but it does so because gas and public transportation can *substitute* for one another. In contrast, consider the choice between gas and inexpensive downtown parking, where the two commodities *complement* one another (the more you have of one commodity, the more you want of the other). Now, increases in gas prices will no longer lead to increases in the preference for the other commodity.

Similarly, operant studies of choice must consider whether the two reinforcers substitute for or complement one another. Suppose a pigeon can peck at either of two keys, and both are associated with food reinforcement. The reinforcers, therefore, are substitutes. Consequently, if we give one key a lower price (it requires only 5 responses per reinforcement, for instance, while the other key requires 10), the pigeon will increase its pecks to the lower price key and decrease its pecks to the more expensive one. In contrast, if the reinforcers are food and water, which are complements,

and we lower the price on the key leading to food, the pigeon will peck at both keys more often (the more it eats, the more it wants to drink). The influence of price differences on choice, therefore, depends on the relation between the commodities (Schwartz, 1989).

## OPEN VERSUS CLOSED SYSTEM

The economic principles that we have discussed so far hold only in a *closed system*—that is, in a situation in which there are no alternative sources of the commodities. We can illustrate this concept with a commodity like soda, which has an elastic demand. A decrease in the price of soda should lead you to purchase more, but this is true only if you have no way of obtaining soda other than buying it at market prices. Should you have a benefactor who will supply you for free, there is no reason why your purchases should follow price changes; in this case we are in an *open system*, and the concept of demand does not apply.

There is a parallel to this in operant research. An operant experiment that uses, say, food reinforcement can be performed in two different ways, which correspond to open and closed systems. In the open-system version, if an animal does not obtain enough food reinforcement during an experimental session, it is given a supplement before the next session; the animal has an alternative way of obtaining the desired commodity. In the closed-system version of the experiment, there are no between-session supplements. If the reinforcement schedule is made increasingly demanding (100 rather than 50 responses are required for reinforcement), the resulting behaviors seem to differ for the two versions of the study. In the open-system version, the amount of reinforcement purchased decreases with very demanding schedules; this does not fit with the idea that the demand for food is inelas-

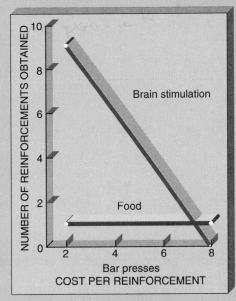

## FIGURE 2
**Demand Curves for Food and Brain Stimulation Reinforcers** *As the "price" of a food pellet increased from two to eight bar presses, the amount of food reinforcement the rats obtained was essentially unchanged; the demand for food is inelastic. In contrast, as the price of brain stimulation increased from two to eight presses, the amount of reinforcement obtained decreased substantially; the demand is elastic.* (After Hirsh & Natelson, 1981)

tic. In the closed-system version, the amount of reinforcement purchased often is the same regardless of the schedule, which is exactly what should happen if the demand for food is inelastic (Schwartz, 1989).

Thus, operant behavior in lower animals can profitably be viewed as a kind of economic decision making. Animals decide how to allocate their limited resources—their responses—in ways that seem similar to the decisions made by humans in economic situations.

---

true; pigeons learn faster if the response is wing flapping rather than pecking (Bolles, 1970).

As was the case in classical conditioning, the results seem inconsistent with the assumption that the same laws of learning apply to all situations, but they make sense from an ethological perspective. The reward case with the pigeons involved eating, and pecking (but not wing flapping) is part of the bird's natural eating activities. Hence, a genetically determined connection between pecking and eating is reasonable. Similarly, the escape case involved a danger situation, and the pigeon's natural reactions to danger include flapping its wings (but not pecking). Birds are known to have a small repertoire of defensive reactions, and they will quickly learn to escape only if the relevant response is one of these natural defensive reactions. In sum, rather than being a means for learning arbitrary associations, operant conditioning also honors the behavioral blueprint.

# Complex Learning

According to the cognitive perspective, the crux of learning—and of intelligence in general—lies in an organism's ability to mentally represent aspects of the world, and then to *operate* on these **mental representations** rather than on the world itself. In many cases, what is mentally represented are associations between stimuli or events; these cases correspond to classical and operant conditioning. In other cases, what is represented seems more complex. It might be a map of one's environment or an abstract concept like *cause*. Also, there are cases where the operations performed on mental repre-

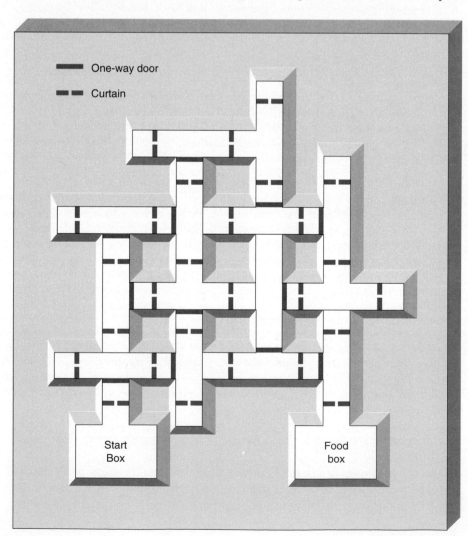

**FIGURE 7-9**
**Diagram of One of Tolman's Mazes**
*A diagram of a maze used by Tolman in his learning experiments with rats. The complexity of the maze (with right and left turns, one-way doors, and curtains limiting the view of the route) tested the rat's ability to form a cognitive map.*

sentations seem more complex than associative processes. The operations may take the form of a mental trial and error, in which the organism tries out different possibilities in its mind. Or the operations may make up a multi-step strategy, in which we take some mental steps only because they enable subsequent ones. The idea of a strategy in particular seems at odds with the assumption that complex learning is built out of simple associations. In what follow, we consider phenomena in learning that directly point to the need to consider non-associative representations and operations. Some of these phenomena involve animals, whereas others involve humans performing tasks that are similar to conditioning.

## Cognitive Maps and Abstract Concepts

An early advocate of the cognitive approach to learning was Edward Tolman, whose research dealt with the problem of rats learning their way through complex mazes (Tolman, 1932). In his view, a rat running through a complex maze was not learning a sequence of right- and left-turning responses but rather was developing a **cognitive map**—a mental representation of the layout of the maze. In a typical experiment of Tolman's, rats in an experimental group were first allowed to explore a maze, like the one in Figure 7-9, in the absence of any reinforcer such as food. A control group had no opportunity to explore the maze. Then food was introduced as a reinforcer, and both experimental and control animals had to find their way through the maze. The experimental group learned to run the maze more quickly than the controls, presumably because they had learned the layout of the maze during their unreinforced exploration, and this cognitive map facilitated their learning of a specific route when the food was introduced.

More recent research provides additional evidence for cognitive maps in rats. To illustrate, consider the maze diagramed in Figure 7-10. The maze consists of a center platform with eight identical arms radiating out. On each trial, the researcher places food at the end of each arm; the rat needs to learn to visit each arm (and obtain the food there) without returning to those it has already visited. Rats learn this remarkably well; after 20 trials, they will virtually never return to an arm they have already visited. (Rats will do this even when the maze has been doused with after-shave lotion to eliminate the odor cues about which arms still have food.) Most important, a rat rarely employs the strategy that would occur to humans—such as always going through the arms in an obvious order, say clockwise. Instead, the rat visits the arms randomly, indicating that it has not learned a rigid sequence of responses. What, then, has it learned? Probably, the rat has developed a representation of the maze, which specifies the spatial relations between arms, and on each trial it makes a mental note of each arm that it has visited (Olton, 1978; 1979).

More recent studies, which involve primates rather than rats, provide even stronger evidence for complex mental representations. Particularly striking are studies showing that chimpanzees can acquire abstract concepts that were once believed to be the sole province of humans. In the typical study, chimpanzees learn to use plastic tokens of different shapes, sizes, and colors as words. For example, they might learn that one token refers to "apples" and another to "paper," where there is no physical resemblance between the token and the object. The fact that chimpanzees can learn these references means they understand concrete concepts like "apple" and

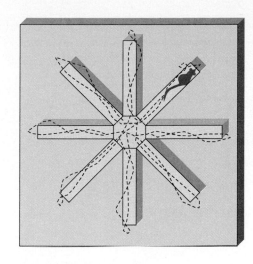

**FIGURE 7-10**
**Maze for Studying Cognitive Maps**
*With food placed at the end of every arm, the rat's problem is to find all the food without retracing its steps. The pattern shown here reflects perfect learning: this rat visited each arm of the maze only once, eating whatever it found there; it did not go back to an empty arm even one time.*

*Using the technique developed by Premack, an experimenter tests a chimpanzee's ability to use language by manipulating plastic chips that represent specific words.*

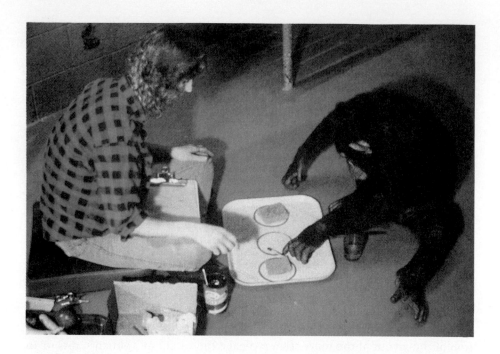

"paper." More impressively, they also have abstract concepts like "same," "different," and "cause." Thus, chimpanzees can learn to use their "same" token when presented either two "apple" tokens or two "orange" ones, and their "different" token when presented one "apple" and one "orange" token. Likewise, chimpanzees seem to understand causal relations. They will apply the token for "cause" when shown some cut paper and scissors, but not when shown some intact paper and scissors (Premack, 1985a; Premack & Premack, 1983).

## Insight Learning

While many early researchers tried to study complex learning with lower species, other early researchers assumed that the best evidence for complex learning would come from higher species, especially primates. Among these researchers, Wolfgang Köhler's work with chimpanzees, carried out in the 1920s, remains particularly important. The problems that Köhler set for his chimpanzees left some room for insight, because no parts of the problem were hidden from view (in contrast, the workings of a food dispenser in a Skinner box are hidden from the animal's view). Typically, Köhler placed a chimpanzee in an enclosed area with a desirable piece of fruit, often a banana, out of reach. To obtain the fruit, the animal had to use a nearby object as a tool. Usually the chimpanzee solved the problem, and did it in a way that suggested he had some insight. The following description from Köhler is typical:

Sultan [Köhler's most intelligent chimpanzee] is squatting at the bars but cannot reach the fruit which lies outside by means of his only available short stick. A longer stick is deposited outside the bars, about two meters on one side of the object and parallel with the grating. It cannot be grasped with the hand, but it can be pulled within reach by means of the small stick. [See Figure 7-11 for an illustration of a similar multiple-stick problem.] Sultan tries to reach the fruit with the smaller of the two sticks. Not succeeding, he tears at a piece of wire that projects from the netting of his cage, but that too is in vain. Then he gazes about him (there are always in the course of these tests some long pauses, during which the animals scrutinize the whole visible area). He suddenly picks up the little stick once more, goes up to the bars directly opposite to the long stick, scratches it towards him with the "auxiliary," seizes it, and goes with it to the point opposite the objective (the fruit), which he secures. From the moment that his eyes fall upon the long stick, his procedure forms one consecutive whole, without hiatus, and although the angling of the bigger stick by means of the smaller is an action that could be complete and distinct in itself, yet observation shows that it follows, quite suddenly, on an interval of hesitation and doubt—staring about—which undoubtedly has a relation to the final objective, and is immediately merged in the final action of the attainment of the end goal. (Köhler, 1925, pp. 174–75.)

Several aspects of the performance of these chimpanzees are unlike those of Thorndike's cats or Skinner's rats and pigeons. For one thing, the solution was sudden, rather than being the result of a gradual trial-and-error process. Another point is that once a chimpanzee solved a problem, thereafter it would solve the problem with few irrelevant moves. This is most unlike a rat in a Skinner box, which continues to make irrelevant responses for many trials. Also, Köhler's chimpanzees could readily transfer what they had learned to a novel situation. For example, in one problem, Sultan was not encaged, but some bananas were placed too high for him to reach, as shown in Figure 7-12. To solve the problem, Sultan stacked some boxes strewn around him, climbed the "platform," and grabbed the bananas. In subsequent problems, if the fruit was again too high to reach, Sultan found other objects to construct a platform; in some cases, Sultan used a table and a small ladder, and in one case Sultan pulled Köhler himself over and used the experimenter as a platform.

There are, therefore, three critical aspects of the chimpanzee's solution: its suddenness, its availability once discovered, and its transferability. These aspects are at odds with the trial-and-error behaviors of the type observed by

**FIGURE 7-11**
**Multiple-Stick Problem** *Using the shorter sticks, the chimpanzee pulls in a stick long enough to reach the piece of fruit. It has learned to solve this problem by understanding the relationship between the sticks and the piece of fruit.*

**FIGURE 7-12**
**Chimpanzee Constructing a Platform** *To reach the bananas hanging from the ceiling, the chimpanzee stacks boxes to form a platform.*

Thorndike, Skinner, and their students. Instead, the chimpanzee's solutions may reflect a *mental* trial and error. That is, the animal forms a mental representation of the problem, manipulates components of the representation until it hits on a solution, and then enacts the solution in the real world. The solution, therefore, appears sudden because the researchers do not have access to the chimpanzee's mental process. The solution is available thereafter because a mental representation persists over time, and the solution is transferable because the representation is either abstract enough to cover more than the original situation or malleable enough to be extended to a novel situation.

Köhler's work suggests that complex learning often involves two phases. In the initial phase, problem solving is used to derive a solution; in the second phase, the solution is stored in memory and retrieved whenever a similar problem situation presents itself. Hence complex learning is intimately related to memory and thinking (the topics of the next two chapters). Moreover, this two-phase structure characterizes not just chimpanzee learning, but also many cases of complex learning in humans. Indeed, it has recently been incorporated into artificial intelligence programs that try to simulate human learning (Rosenbloom, Laird & Newell, 1991).

## Prior Beliefs

Research on animal learning has tended to emphasize the learning of *perfectly predictable* relations. For example, in most studies of classical conditioning, the CS is followed by the UCS 100 percent of the time. But in real life, relations between stimuli or events are usually less than perfectly predictable. The study of associative learning with less than perfect relations has been conducted mainly with humans. In these studies, learning clearly seems to involve processes in addition to those that form associations between the inputs; in particular, subjects in these studies often have *prior beliefs* about the relations to be learned, and these beliefs can determine what is in fact learned.

In the studies of interest, a different pair of stimuli is presented on each trial—say, a picture and a description of a person—and the subject's task is to learn the relation between the members of the pairs—say, that pictures of tall men tend to be associated with brief descriptions. Some striking evidence for the role of prior beliefs comes from cases in which, objectively, there is *no* relation between the stimuli, yet subjects "learn" such a relation. In one experiment, subjects were concerned with the possible relation between the drawings that mental patients made and the symptoms that the patients manifested. On each trial of the experiment, subjects were presented a patient's drawing of a person and one of six symptoms, including the symptoms "suspiciousness of other people" and "concerned with being taken care of." The subject's task was to determine whether any of the signs in the drawing—some aspect of the eyes or mouth, for instance—were associated with any of the symptoms. In fact, the six symptoms had been randomly paired with the drawings so that there was no association between sign (drawing) and symptom. Yet subjects consistently reported there were such relations, and the relations they reported were ones they probably believed *before* participating in the experiment: for example, that large eyes are associated with suspiciousness, or that a large mouth is associated with a desire to be taken care of by others. These nonexistent but plausible relations are referred to as **spurious associations.**

The same spurious associations have been made by some clinical psychologists who tried to use the so-called *Draw-a-Person* test to diagnose psychological problems. Objective assessments of this test have shown it has virtually no correlation with emotional problems. But, in the past, some clinical psychologists insisted that the test had diagnostic value, and in particular that exaggerated eyes in a drawing were associated with suspiciousness of others, and that an exaggerated mouth was associated with a desire to be taken care of (Chapman & Chapman, 1967).

For both the clinical psychologists and the subjects in the experiment described above, prior beliefs about what things generally go together—such as our belief that big eyes go with suspiciousness—influenced the learning of what in fact goes together in the situation at hand. Thus, prior beliefs about the stimuli determined what was "learned." Since prior beliefs are part of one's knowledge, these results attest to the cognitive nature of such learning.

The above research shows the power of prior beliefs on associative learning, but it does not say anything about how learning proceeds when there is in fact an objective association to be learned. Nor does the above work say anything about associative learning when the learner has no relevant prior beliefs. Both of these issues were analyzed in the following study.

On each of a set of trials, subjects were presented a picture of a man with a walking stick, and the heights of both the men and the walking sticks varied from trial to trial. The subjects' task was to estimate the strength of the relation between the two heights by choosing a number between 0 (which indicated no relation) and 100 (a perfect relation). Because the task was novel, subjects presumably had no prior beliefs about the relation of interest; consequently, their learning should be driven by only the input or data (for this reason, it is referred to as **data-driven learning**). Data-driven learning turns out to be conservative, tending to underestimate the objective relations involved. When the objective relation between the two heights was low (as measured by the correlation coefficient between the two heights), often subjects failed to detect any relation; when the objective relation was moderate, subjects generally succeeded in learning there was a relation, but underestimated its strength; only when the objective relation was high and close to perfectly predictive did subjects learn that there was a relation, and estimate it to have a high strength (Jennings, Amabile, & Ross, 1982).

The obvious question is, What would happen to subjects' estimates of low, moderate, and high predictive relations if subjects *did* have prior beliefs about the relations? Given the previous work on spurious associations that shows that people learn even nonexistent relations if they are consistent with their beliefs, we would expect that *belief-driven learning* would tend to over-estimate the objective relations involved. This is exactly what researchers have found. When the task involves estimating the relation between things that people believe ought to be related—for example, on each trial, two different measures of a person's honesty taken from two completely different situations are presented—subjects never fail to detect a relation that exists, and consistently overestimate its predictive strength (Jennings, Amablie, & Ross, 1982).

In the preceding study, the learner's prior beliefs were in agreement with the objective association to be learned. What happens, though, when one's prior beliefs *conflict* with the objective associations? That is, what happens when the beliefs and data are in conflict? In such situations, typically people will go with their prior beliefs. If people believe that two different measures of a person's honesty should be highly related, for example, they may "detect" such a relation even when there is no objective association. However, as the data (the objective association) is made increasingly salient, eventually our prior beliefs will capitulate, and we learn what is in fact there (Alloy & Tabachnik, 1984).

These studies further demonstrate the importance of prior beliefs in human learning, thereby strengthening the case for a cognitive approach to learning. In a way, however, the above studies also have a connection to the ethological approach to learning. Just as rats and pigeons may be constrained to learn only those associations that evolution has prepared them for, so we humans seem to be constrained to learn those associations that our prior beliefs have prepared us for. Without prior constraints of some sort, perhaps there would simply be too many potential associations to consider, and associative learning would be chaotic if not impossible.

*Chapter* **SUMMARY**

1. *Learning* may be defined as a relatively permanent change in behavior that results from practice. Four kinds of learning can be distinguished: (a) *habituation*, in which an organism learns to ignore a familiar and inconsequential stimulus; (b) *classical conditioning*, in which an organism learns that one stimulus follows another; (c) *operant conditioning*, in which an organism learns that a response leads to a particular consequence; and (d) *complex* learning, in which learning involves more than the formation of associations.

2. Early research on learning was done from a behavioristic perspective. It often assumed that: (a) behavior is better understood in terms of external causes than internal ones, (b) simple associations are the building blocks of learning, and (c) the laws of learning are the same for different species and different situations. These assumptions have been modified in light of subsequent work. The contemporary analysis of learning includes cognitive factors and biological constraints as well as behavioristic principles.

3. In Pavlov's experiments, if a *conditioned stimulus* (CS) consistently precedes an *unconditioned stimulus* (UCS), the CS comes to serve as a signal for the UCS and will elicit a *conditioned response* (CR) that often resembles the *unconditioned response* (UCR). Stimuli that are similar to the CS also elicit the CR to some extent, though such *generalization* can be curbed by *discrimination training*. These phenomena occur in organisms as diverse as flatworms and humans. Indeed, there are a number of important human applications of classical conditioning, including *conditioned fear* and *conditioned drug tolerance*. In the latter case, the conditioned response to a stimulus associated with drug use is the opposite of the effect caused by the drug.

4. Cognitive factors also play a role in conditioning. For classical conditioning to occur, the CS must be a reliable predictor of the UCS; that is, there must be a higher probability that the UCS will occur when the CS has been presented than when it has not. The importance of *predictability* is also evident in the phenomenon of *blocking*: if one CS reliably predicts a UCS, and another CS is added, the relation between the added CS and the UCS will not be learned. Models of classical conditioning center on the notions of predictability and surprise.

5. Findings of ethologists challenge the assumption that the laws of learning are the same for all species or for all situations that a given species encounters. According to ethologists, what an animal learns is constrained by its genetically determined "behavioral blueprint." Evidence for such constraints on classical conditioning comes from studies of *taste aversion*. While rats readily learn to associate the feeling of being sick with the taste of a solution, they cannot learn to associate sickness with a light. Conversely, birds can learn to associate light and sickness, but not taste and sickness. These distinctions are the result of innate differences between rats and birds in their food-gathering activities.

6. Operant conditioning deals with situations in which the response operates on the environment rather than being elicited by an unconditioned stimulus. The earliest systematic studies were performed by Thorndike, who showed that animals engage in *trial-and-error* behavior, and that any behavior followed by reinforcement is strengthened (the *law of effect*).

7. In Skinner's experiments, typically a rat or pigeon learns to make a simple response, such as pressing a lever, to obtain reinforcement. The rate of response is a useful measure of *response strength*. *Shaping* is a training procedure used when the desired response is novel; it involves reinforcing only those variations in response that deviate in the direction desired by the experimenter. There are numerous applications of operant conditioning to child rearing.

8. There are a number of phenomena that increase the generality of operant conditioning. One is *conditioned reinforcement*, wherein a stimulus associated with a reinforcer acquires its own reinforcing properties. Other relevant phenomena are *generalization* and *discrimination;* organisms generalize responses to similar situations, though this generalization can be brought under the control of a *discriminative* stimulus. Finally, there are *schedules of reinforcement*. Once a behavior is established, it can be maintained when reinforced only part of the time. Exactly when the reinforcement comes is determined by its schedule; either a *fixed ratio*, a *variable ratio*, a *fixed interval*, or a *variable interval* schedule.

9. The reinforcement in operant conditioning can be an aversive event like shock. There are three different kinds of *aversive conditioning*. In *punishment*, a response is followed by an aversive event, which results in the response being suppressed. In *escape*, an organism learns to make a response to terminate an ongoing aversive event. In *avoidance*, an organism learns to make a response to prevent the aversive event from even starting.

10. Cognitive factors are operative in operant conditioning. For operant conditioning to occur, the organism must believe that reinforcement is at least partly under its *control*; that is, the organism must perceive a *contingency* between its responses and reinforcement. Biological constraints also play a role in operant conditioning. There are constraints on what reinforcers can be associated with what responses. With pigeons: when the reinforcement is food, learning is faster if the response is pecking a key rather than flapping their wings; but when the reinforcement is termination of shock, learning is faster when the response is wing flapping rather than pecking a key.

11. According to the cognitive perspective, the crux of learning is an organism's ability to represent aspects of the world mentally and then to operate on these *mental representations* rather than on the world itself. In complex learning, the mental representations depict more than associations, and the mental operations may constitute a *strategy*. Studies of complex learning in animals indicate that rats can develop a *cognitive map* of their environments, as well as acquire abstract concepts like *cause*. Other studies demonstrate that chimpanzees can solve problems by insight, and then generalize these solutions to similar problems.

12. When learning relations between stimuli that are not perfectly predictive, people often invoke prior beliefs about the relations. This can lead to people detecting relations that are not objectively present (*spurious*

*associations*). When the relation is objectively present, having a prior belief about it can lead to overestimating the relation's predictive strength (*belief-driven learning*), while lacking a prior belief about it can lead to underestimating the relation's predictive strength (*data-driven learning*).

*Further* **READING**

Pavlov's *Conditioned Reflexes* (1927) is the definitive work on classical conditioning. Skinner's *The Behavior of Organisms* (1938) is the corresponding statement on operant conditioning. The major points of view about conditioning and learning, presented in their historical settings, are summarized in Bower and Hilgard, *Theories of Learning* (5th ed., 1981).

For a general introduction to learning, a number of textbooks are recommended. Schwartz's *Psychology of Learning and Behavior* (3rd ed., 1989) is a particularly well-balanced review of conditioning, including discussion of ethology and cognition. Other useful textbooks include Gordon's *Learning and Memory* (1989), Schwartz and Reisberg's *Learning and Memory* (1991), and Domjan and Burkhard's *The Principles of Learning and Behavior* (1985). At the advanced level, the six-volume Estes (ed.), *Handbook of Learning and Cognitive Processes* (1975–1978), covers most aspects of learning and conditioning; and Honig and Staddon (eds.), *Handbook of Operant Behavior* (1977), provides a comprehensive treatment of operant conditioning.

The early cognitive approach is well described in two classics: Tolman's *Purposive Behavior in Animals and Men* (1932; reprint ed. 1967) and Köhler's *The Mentality of Apes* (1925; reprint ed. 1976). For a recent statement of the cognitive approach to animal learning, see Roitblat's *Introduction to Comparative Cognition* (1986).

# Chapter

# 8

# Memory

## Distinctions about Memory 289
*Three Stages of Memory*
*Different Types of Memory*

## Short-Term Memory 291
*Encoding*
*Storage*
*Retrieval*
*Short-Term Memory and Thought*
*Transfer from Short-Term to Long-Term Memory*

## Long-Term Memory 298
*Encoding*
*Retrieval*
*Storage*
*Critical Discussion: Connectionist Models*
*of Memory*
*Encoding-Retrieval Interactions*
*Emotional Factors in Forgetting*

## Implicit Memory 311
*Memory in Amnesia*
*Critical Discussion: Childhood Amnesia*
*Implicit Memory in Normal Subjects*
*Storage versus Retrieval Differences*

## Improving Memory 317
*Chunking and Memory Span*
*Imagery and Encoding*
*Elaboration and Encoding*
*Context and Retrieval*
*Organization*
*Practicing Retrieval*
*PQRST Method*

## Constructive Memory 322
*Simple Inferences*
*Stereotypes*
*Schemata*

Detail, *Hollyhocks.*

It seems, then, that we owe to memory almost all that we either have or are; that our ideas and conceptions are its work, and that our everyday perception, thought, and movement is derived from this source. Memory collects the countless phenomena of our existence into a single whole; and, as our bodies would be scattered into the dust of their component atoms if they were not held together by the attraction of matter, so our consciousness would be broken up into as many fragments as we had lived seconds but for the binding and unifying force of memory. (Hering, 1920)

Hering's words, spoken in his lecture to the Vienna Academy of Sciences many years ago, attest to the importance of memory in mental life. As Hering's comments about consciousness suggest, it is memory that gives us the sense of continuity on which our very notion of a *self* depends. When we think of what it means to be human, we must acknowledge the centrality of memory.

## Distinctions About Memory

Psychologists find it useful to make a few basic distinctions about memory. One distinction concerns three stages of memory: *encoding, storage,* and *retrieval*. Other distinctions deal with different types of memory. Different memories may be used to store information for short and long periods and to store different kinds of information (for example, one memory for facts and another for skills).

### Three Stages of Memory

Suppose one morning you are introduced to a student and told her name is Barbara Cohn. That afternoon you see her again and say something like, "You're Barbara Cohn. We met this morning." Clearly, you have remembered her name. But how exactly did you remember it?

Your minor memory feat can be broken into three stages (see Figure 8-1). First, when you were introduced, you somehow entered Barbara Cohn's name into memory; this is the **encoding stage.** You transformed a physical input (sound waves) that corresponds to her spoken name into the kind of code or representation that memory accepts, and you placed that representation in memory. Second, you retained—or stored—the name during the time between the two meetings; this is the **storage stage.** And, third, you recovered the name from storage at the time of your second meeting; this is the **retrieval stage.**

Memory can fail at any of these three stages. Had you been unable to recall Barbara's name at the second meeting, this could have reflected a failure in encoding, storage, or retrieval. Much of current research on memory attempts to specify the mental operations that occur at each of the three stages of memory and to explain how these operations can go awry and result in memory failure.

**FIGURE 8-1**
**Three Stages of Memory** *Theories of memory attribute forgetting to a failure at one or more of these stages.* (After Melton, 1963)

# Different Types of Memory

**SHORT-TERM VERSUS LONG-TERM MEMORY** The three stages of memory do not operate the same way in all situations. Memory seems to differ between those situations that require us to store material for a matter of seconds and those that require us to store material for longer intervals—from minutes to years. The former situations are said to tap **short-term memory**, whereas the latter reflect **long-term memory**.

We can illustrate this distinction by amending our story about meeting Barbara Cohn. Suppose that during the first meeting, as soon as you had heard her name, a friend came up and you said, "Have you met Barbara Cohn?" In this case, remembering Barbara's name would be an example of short-term memory: you retrieved the name after only a second or two. Remembering her name at the time of your second meeting would be an example of long-term memory, because then retrieval would take place hours after the name was encoded.

When we recall a name immediately after encountering it, retrieval seems effortless, as if the name were still active, still in our consciousness. But when we try to recall the same name hours later, retrieval is often difficult because the name is no longer in our consciousness and, in some sense, has to be brought back. This contrast between short- and long-term memory is similar to the contrast between conscious knowledge and preconscious knowledge—the knowledge we have but are not currently thinking about.

The need to distinguish between short- and long-term memory is further supported by studies of people with **amnesia,** or severe memory loss. In virtually every form of amnesia, people have profound difficulty remembering material for long time intervals but rarely have any trouble remembering material for a few seconds. Thus, a patient with amnesia may be unable to recognize his doctor when she enters the room—even though the patient has seen this doctor every day for years—yet will have no trouble repeating back the physician's full name when she is reintroduced (Milner, Corkin, & Teuber, 1968).

**DIFFERENT MEMORIES FOR DIFFERENT KINDS OF INFORMATION** Until recently, psychologists assumed that the same memory system was used for all contents that had to be stored. For example, the same long-term memory was presumably used to store both one's recollection of a grandmother's funeral and the skill one needs to ride a bike. Recent evidence suggests that this assumption is wrong. In particular, we seem to use a different long-term memory for storing *facts* (such as who the current president is) than we do for retaining *skills* (such as how to ride a bicycle).

Ideally, we should first specify the different memory systems corresponding to different contents, and for each one describe the nature of encoding, storage, and retrieval stages in its short-term and long-term memory. This goal is too ambitious given present knowledge. Most of what we know concerns memory for facts, particularly personal ones about our experiences. The kind of memory situation that we understand best is one in which a person consciously recollects an event in the past, where this recollection is experienced as occurring in a particular time and place. This kind of memory, which is called **explicit memory,** will be the focus of most sections of the chapter. The next two sections consider the nature of encoding, storage, and retrieval in short-term and long-term explicit memory. Then we will examine what is known about another kind of memory, which includes memory for skills, and is referred to as **implicit memory.** After that, we return to our focus on explicit memory, and consider how long-term memory can be improved. In the last section, we discuss situations where we use our general knowledge to embellish what we put into memory, that is, situations where memory is **constructive.**

# Short-Term Memory

Even in those situations in which we must remember information for only a few seconds, memory involves the three stages of encoding, storage, and retrieval.

## Encoding

To encode information into short-term memory, we must attend to it. Since we are selective about what we attend to (see Chapter 5), our short-term memory will contain only what has been selected. This means that much of what we are exposed to never even enters short-term memory and, of course, will not be available for later retrieval. Indeed, many difficulties labeled "memory problems" are really lapses in attention. For example, if you bought some groceries and someone asked you later for the color of the checkout clerk's eyes, you might well be unable to answer because you had not paid attention to them in the first place.

ACOUSTIC CODING  When information is encoded into memory, it is entered in a certain code or representation. For example, when you look up a phone number and retain it until you have dialed it, in what form do you represent the digits? Is the representation visual—a mental picture of the digits? Is it acoustic—the sounds of the names of the digits? Or is it semantic (based on meaning)—some meaningful association that the digits have? Research indicates that we can use any of these possibilities to encode information into short-term memory, although we favor an acoustic code when we are trying to keep the information active by *rehearsing* it—that is, by repeating it over and over to ourselves. **Rehearsal** is a particularly popular strategy when the information consists of verbal items such as digits, letters, or words. So in trying to remember a phone number, we are most likely to encode the number as the sounds of the digit names and to rehearse these sounds to ourselves until we have dialed the number.

In one experiment that provided evidence for an acoustic code, researchers briefly showed subjects a list of six consonants (for example, RLBKSJ); when the letters were removed, the subject had to write all six letters in order. Although the entire procedure took only a second or two, subjects occasionally made errors. When they did, the incorrect letter tended to be similar in sound to the correct one. For the list mentioned, a subject might have written RLTKSJ, replacing the B with the similar-sounding T (Conrad, 1964). This finding supports the idea that the subjects encoded each letter acoustically (for example, "bee" for B), sometimes lost part of this code (only the "ee" part of the sound remained), and then responded with a letter ("tee") that was consistent with the remaining part of the code.

Experiments such as this one have produced another result that points to an acoustic code: it is more difficult to recall the items in order when they are acoustically similar (for example, TBCGVE) than when they are acoustically distinct (RLTKSJ). A striking example of this occurs with Chinese readers. Written Chinese consists of syllable-like units called characters.

*When you look up a telephone number, do you remember it visually, acoustically, or semantically?*

**FIGURE 8-2**
**Testing for Eidetic Images** *This test picture was shown for 30 seconds to elementary school children. After removal of the picture, one boy saw in his eidetic image "about 14" stripes in the cat's tail. The painting, by Marjorie Torrey, appears in Lewis Carroll's* Alice in Wonderland, *abridged by Josette Frank.*

Usually, there are two characters per word, and each character typically shares its name with several others. When Chinese subjects are briefly shown a sequence of characters that they then have to write down in order, they get about six correct if all the characters have different names but only three correct if all have the same name (and hence cannot be coded acoustically). Eliminating the use of an acoustic code thus cuts recall in half (Zhang & Simon, 1985).

**VISUAL CODING** The fact that the Chinese readers in the previous study were able to remember the correct order of three characters with the same name suggests that they also maintained these items in a visual representation. Other experiments indicate that although we can use a visual code for verbal material, the code often fades quickly. To illustrate, after looking at the address 7915 THIRD AVENUE, you may have a visual code of it for a second or two. This representation would preserve visual details, such as the fact that the address is written in all capital letters. After a couple of seconds, however, all that would remain would be the sound of the address (the acoustic code), and this code would not preserve information about the form of the letters (Posner & Keele, 1967).

This dominance of the acoustic code may apply mainly to verbal materials. When a person must store nonverbal items (such as pictures that are difficult to describe and therefore difficult to rehearse acoustically), the visual code may become more important. While most of us can maintain some kind of visual image in short-term memory, a few people are able to maintain images that are almost photographic in clarity. This ability occurs mainly in children. Such children can look briefly at a picture and, when it is removed, still experience the image before their eyes. They can maintain the image for as long as several minutes, and when questioned, provide a wealth of detail, such as the number of stripes on a cat's tail (see Figure 8-2). Such children seem to be reading the details directly from an **eidetic image** (Haber, 1969). Eidetic imagery is very rare, though. Some studies with children indicate that only about 5 percent report visual images that are long-lasting and possess sharp detail. Moreover, when the criteria for possessing true photographic imagery are made more stringent—for example, being able to read an imaged page of text as easily from the bottom up as from the top down—the frequency of eidetic imagery become miniscule, even among children (Haber, 1979). The visual code in short-term memory, then, is something short of a photograph.

The existence of both acoustic and visual codes has led some researchers to argue that short-term memory actually consists of three distinct components. One component is an **acoustic buffer,** which briefly stores information in an acoustic code; a second component is a **visual buffer,** which briefly stores information in a visual code; and the third component is referred to as the **central executive,** and it supervises and coordinates the two buffers (Baddeley, 1986).

## Storage

**LIMITED CAPACITY** Perhaps the most striking fact about short-term memory is that it has a very limited capacity. On the average, the limit is seven items, give or take two ($7 \pm 2$). Some people store as few as five items; others can retain as many as nine. It may seem strange to give such an exact number to cover all people when it is clear that individuals differ greatly in their memory abilities. These differences, however, are primarily due to long-term memory. For short-term memory, most normal adults have a capacity of $7 \pm 2$. This constancy has been known since the earliest days of experimental psychology. Hermann Ebbinghaus, who began the experimental study of memory in 1885, reported results showing that his own limit was seven items. Some 70 years later, George Miller (1956) was so struck by the constancy that he referred to it as the "magic number seven." More recently, the limit has been shown to hold in non-Western cultures (Yu et al., 1985).

Psychologists determined this number by showing subjects various sequences of unrelated items (digits, letters, or words) and asking them to recall the items in order. The items are presented rapidly, and the subject does not have time to relate them to information stored in long-term memory; hence, the number of items recalled reflects only the storage capacity for short-term memory. On the initial trials, subjects have to recall just a few items, say, three or four digits, which they can easily do. Then the number of digits increases over trials until the experimenter determines the maximum number a subject can recall in perfect order. The maximum (almost always between five and nine) is the subject's **memory span.** This task is so simple that you can easily try it yourself. The next time you come across a list of names (a directory in a business or university building, for example), read through the list once and then look away and see how many names you can recall in order. It will probably be between five and nine.

**CHUNKING**  As we just noted, the memory-span procedure discourages subjects from connecting the to-be-remembered items to information in long-term memory. When such connections *are* possible, performance on the memory-span task can change substantially.

To illustrate this change, suppose you were presented the letter string SRUOYYLERECNIS. Because your memory span is $7 \pm 2$, you would probably be unable to repeat the entire letter sequence since it contains 14 letters. Should you notice, however, that these letters spell the phrase SINCERELY YOURS in reverse order, your task would become easier. By using this knowledge, you have decreased the number of items that must be held in short-term memory from 14 to 2. But where did this spelling knowledge come from? From long-term memory, of course, where knowledge about words is stored. Thus, you can use long-term memory to recode new material into larger meaningful units and then store those units in short-term memory. Such units are called **chunks,** and the capacity of short-term memory is best expressed as $7 \pm 2$ chunks (Miller, 1956). Chunking can occur with numbers as well. The string 149-2177-619-93 is beyond our capacity, but 1492-1776-1993 is well within it. The general principle is that we can boost our short-term memory by regrouping sequences of letters and digits into units that can be found in long-term memory (Bower & Springston, 1970).

**FORGETTING**  We may be able to hold on to seven items briefly, but in most cases they will soon be forgotten. Forgetting occurs either because the items are *displaced* by newer ones or because the items *decay* with time.

The notion of **displacement** fits with short-term memory having a fixed capacity. The fixed capacity suggests that we might think of short-term memory as a sort of mental box with roughly seven slots. Each item entering short-term memory goes into its own slot. As long as the number of items does not exceed the number of slots, we can recall the items perfectly, but when all the slots are filled and a new item enters, one of the old ones must go. The new item displaces an old one. To illustrate, suppose your short-term memory is empty (see Figure 8-3). An item enters. Let us say you have been introduced to Barbara Cohn, and the name Cohn enters your short-term memory. Others are introduced soon after, and the list of names in short-term memory grows. Finally, the limit of your memory span is reached. Then each new item that enters short-term memory has a chance to displace Cohn. After one new item, there has been only one chance to displace Cohn; after two new items, there have been two chances; and so on. The likelihood that Cohn will be lost from short-term memory increases steadily with the number of items that have followed it. Eventually, Cohn will be lost from short-term memory. Displacement has been demonstrated experimentally many times. For example, when a list of a dozen words is presented, the chances of recalling a particular item in that list decreases with the number of items that have followed it.

There is another way to think about the fixed capacity of short-term memory and the tendency of new items to displace old ones. Being in short-term memory may correspond to being in a state of activation. The more items we try to keep active, the less activation there is for any one of them. Perhaps only about seven items can be simultaneously maintained at a level of activation that permits all of them to be recalled. Once seven items are active, if a new item is attended to, the activation that it receives will be usurped from items presented earlier; consequently these earlier items may fall below the critical level of activation needed for recall (Anderson, 1983).

The other major cause of forgetting in short-term memory is that information simply decays in time. We may think of the representation of an item as a trace that fades within a matter of seconds. One of the best pieces of evidence for this hypothesis is that our short-term memory span holds fewer words when the words take longer to say; for example, the span is less for long words such as "harpoon" and "cyclone" than for shorter words such as "bishop" and "pewter" (try saying the words to yourself to see the differ-

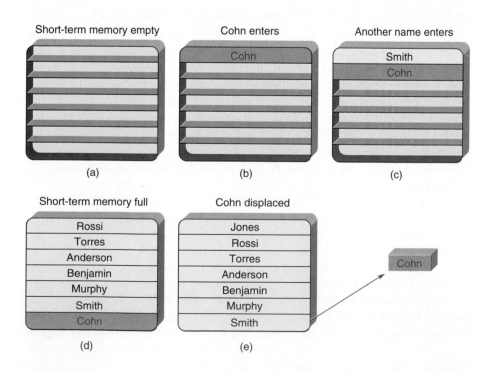

**FIGURE 8-3**
**Forgetting Due to Displacement** *Due to the limited capacity of short-term memory, 7 ± 2 "slots," the addition of a new item can result in the displacement or loss of an old one.*

ence in duration). Presumably this effect arises because as the words are presented we say them to ourselves, and the longer it takes to do this, the more likely it is that some of the words' traces will have faded before they can be recalled (Baddeley, Thompson, & Buchanan, 1975).

It appears, then, that information at the forefront of our memory must soon give way. The one major exception to this involves rehearsal: items that we rehearse are not readily subject to displacement or decay. Rehearsing information may protect it from displacement because we cannot encode new items at the same time we are rehearsing old ones. Rehearsal may offset decay more directly: rehearsing an item that has partly faded may bring it to full strength again.

## Retrieval

Let us think of the contents of short-term memory as being active in consciousness. Intuition suggests that access to this information is immediate. You do not have to dig for it; it is right there. Retrieval, then, should not depend on the number of items in consciousness. But in this case intuition is wrong.

Evidence shows that the more items there are in short-term memory, the slower retrieval becomes. Most of the evidence for such a slowing comes from a type of experiment introduced by Sternberg (1966). On each trial of the experiment, a subject is shown a set of digits, called the *memory list*, that he or she must temporarily hold in short-term memory. It is easy for the subject to maintain the information in short-term memory because each memory list contains between one and six digits. The memory list is then removed from view, and a probe digit is presented. The subject must decide whether the probe was on the memory list. For example, if the memory list is 3 6 1 and the probe is 6, the subject should respond "yes"; given the same memory list and a probe of 2, the subject should respond "no." Subjects rarely make an error on this task; what is of interest, however, is the *decision time*, which is the elapsed time between the onset of the probe and the subject's press of a "yes" or a "no" button. Figure 8-4 presents data from such an experiment, indicating that decision time increases directly with the length of the memory list. What is remarkable about these decision times is that they fall along a straight line. This means that each additional item in short-term memory adds a fixed amount of time to the retrieval process—approximately 40 milliseconds. The same results are found when the items are letters, words, auditory tones, or pictures of people's faces (Sternberg, 1975). Psychologists have obtained similar results with groups as varied as schizophrenic patients, college students under the influence of marijuana, and people from preliterate societies.

These results have led some researchers to hypothesize that retrieval requires a search of short-term memory in which the items are examined one at a time. This **serial search** of short-term memory presumably operates at a rate of 40 milliseconds per item, which is too fast for people to be aware of it (Sternberg, 1966). This interpretation is compatible with thinking of short-term memory as a mental box with a fixed number of slots, for a natural way to find something in a box is to search its compartments in sequence. However, researchers who think of short-term memory as a state of activation are led to a different interpretation of the results. Retrieval of an item in short-term memory may depend on the activation of that item reaching a critical level. That is, one decides a probe is in short-term memory if its representation is above a critical level of activation, and the more items in short-term

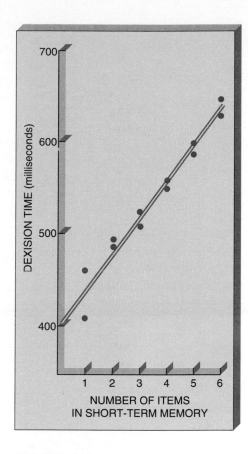

**FIGURE 8-4**
**Retrieval as a Search Process** *Decision times increase in direct proportion to the number of items in short-term memory. Blue circles represent "yes" responses; red circles, "no" responses. The times for both types of decision fall along a straight line. Because the decision times are so fast, they must be measured with equipment that permits accuracy in milliseconds (thousandths of a second).* (After Sternberg, 1966)

"Can we hurry up and get to the test? My short-term memory is better than my long-term memory."
© 1985, reprinted courtesy of Bill Hoest and *Parade* Magazine.

memory the less activation for any one of them (Monsell, 1979). Such **activation models** have been shown to accurately predict many aspects of retrieval from short-term memory (McElree & Doesher, 1989).

## Short-Term Memory and Thought

Short-term memory plays an important role in conscious thought. When consciously trying to solve a problem, we often use short-term memory as a mental work space: we use it to store parts of the problem as well as information accessed from long-term memory that is relevant to the problem. To illustrate, consider what it takes to multiply 35 by 8 in your head. You need short-term memory to store the given numbers (35 and 8), the nature of the operation required (multiplication), and arithmetic facts such as $8 \times 5 = 40$ and $3 \times 8 = 24$. Not surprisingly, performance on mental arithmetic declines substantially if you have to remember simultaneously some words or digits; try doing the above mental multiplication while remembering the phone number 745–1739 (Baddeley & Hitch, 1974). Other research indicates that short-term memory is used not only in numerical problems but also in the whole gamut of complex problems that we routinely confront. For this reason, researchers increasingly refer to short-term memory as "working memory," and conceptualize it as a kind of blackboard in which the mind performs its computations and posts the partial results for later use (Baddeley, 1986; Just & Carpenter, 1987).

The role that short-term memory plays in understanding language is more complicated. The short-term memory system we have described appears not to be involved in understanding relatively simple sentences. The best evidence for this comes from studies of brain-damaged patients with memory disorders. When presented with a list of unrelated words, some patients can correctly repeat only a single word (their memory span is 1), yet when presented with a whole sentence they can repeat and understand the entire thing. In contrast, other brain-damaged patients have a normal memory span, yet are unable to repeat or understand a simple sentence. These findings suggest that we have a special memory system for processing language. A patient who has a defective memory span but normal language understanding has an impaired short-term memory but an intact language memory. On the other hand, a patient who has a normal memory span but defective language understanding has the opposite memory problem (McCarthy & Warrington, 1987a).

The special memory for language seems limited to relatively simple sentences. Once sentences become complex—for example, "The salesman that the doctor met departed"—short-term memory is brought in for help (you can sense yourself using short-term memory to understand the preceding example). Hence short-term memory serves as a back up in sentence understanding (McCarthy & Warrington, 1987b).

When it comes to higher-level language processes like following a conversation or reading a text, short-term memory appears to play a crucial role. When reading for understanding, often we must consciously relate new sentences to some prior material in the text. This relating of new to old seems to occur in short-term memory because people who have more short-term capacity score higher than others on reading comprehension tests (Daneman & Carpenter, 1980). Other work shows that the readability of text depends partly on the likelihood that relevant connecting material is still in short-term memory (Malt, 1985).

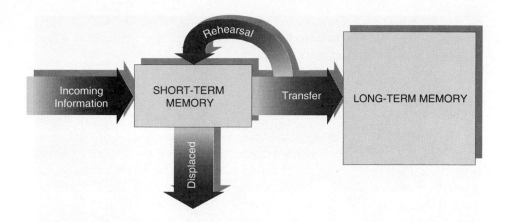

**FIGURE 8-5**
**Dual-Memory Model** *Incoming items
enter the memory system through short-term
memory. Once in short-term memory, an
item can be maintained there by rehearsal.
As an item is rehearsed, information about
it is transferred to long-term memory. Once
rehearsal of an item is terminated, the item
soon will be displaced by a new incoming
item and thus be lost from short-term
memory.*

## Transfer from Short-Term to Long-Term Memory

From what we have seen so far, short-term memory serves two important functions: it stores material that is needed for short time periods, and it serves as a workspace for mental computations. Another possible function is that short-term memory may be a way-station to long-term memory. That is, information may reside in short-term memory while it is being encoded into long-term memory. One theory that deals with this transfer from short- to long-term memory is called the **dual-memory model.** The model was developed a while ago (Atkinson & Shiffrin, 1968, 1971), and variants of it continue to be used to organize and direct research (Raaijmakers, 1992). The model assumes that once information enters short-term memory, it can be either maintained by rehearsal or lost by displacement or decay (see Figure 8-5). In addition, the information can be transferred, or copied, into long-term memory. While there are a number of different ways to implement the transfer, one of the most commonly investigated is rehearsal. As the diagram in Figure 8-5 suggests, rehearsing an item not only maintains it in short-term memory but also causes it to be transferred to long-term memory.

Some of the best support for the dual-memory model comes from experiments on free recall. In a **free-recall experiment,** subjects first see a list of, for example, 40 unrelated words which are presented one at a time. After all the words have been presented, subjects must immediately recall them in any order (hence the designation "free"). The results from such an experiment are shown in Figure 8-6. The chance of correctly recalling a word is graphed as a function of the word's position in the list. The part of the curve to the left in the graph is for the first few words presented, whereas the part to the right is for the last few words presented.

The dual-memory model assumes that at the time of recall the last few words presented are still likely to be in short-term memory, whereas the remaining words are in long-term memory. Hence, we would expect recall of the last few words to be high, because items in short-term memory can easily be retrieved. Figure 8-6 shows this is the case. But recall for the first words presented is also quite good. Why is this? Dual-memory theory has an answer. When the first words were presented, they were entered into short-term memory and rehearsed. Since there was little else in short-term memory, they were rehearsed often and were therefore likely to be transferred to long-term memory. As more items were presented, short-term memory quickly filled up, and the opportunity to rehearse and transfer any given

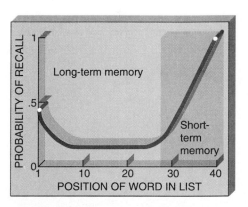

**FIGURE 8-6**
**Results from Free-Recall Experiment** *Probability of recall varies with an
item's position in a list, with the probability
being highest for the last five or so positions,
next highest for the first few positions, and
lowest for the intermediate positions. Recall
of the last few items is based on short-term
memory, whereas recall of the remaining
items is based on long-term memory.*
(After Glanzer, 1972; Murdock, 1962)

*Over time, we tend to remember the meaning of a sentence rather than the exact words.*

item to long-term memory decreased to a low level. So, only the first few items presented enjoyed the extra opportunity of transfer, which is why they were later recalled so well from long-term memory.

While the dual memory model may be right in claiming that information typically needs to reside in short-term memory in order to be transferred to long-term memory, the model may place too much emphasis on rehearsal as a means of transfer. Indeed, psychologists have suspected for a long time that simple rehearsal is not an effective means for transferring information to long-term memory. Three-quarters of a century ago, the psychologist E. C. Sanford noted that his reading a group of five morning prayers aloud almost every day for 25 years (at least 5,000 repetitions) did not succeed in implanting the prayers in permanent memory. When Sanford tested his memory by cueing himself with a word from a prayer to see how much of the litany he could recall, he found that for some of the prayers he could not even recall three words per cue. That is not much memory for two and a half decades of rehearsal (Sanford, 1917; cited in Neisser, 1982).

## Long-Term Memory

Long-term memory involves information that has been retained for intervals as brief as a few minutes (such as a point made earlier in a conversation) or as long as a lifetime (such as an adult's childhood memories). In experiments on long-term memory, psychologists generally have studied forgetting over intervals of minutes, hours, or weeks, but a few studies have involved years or even decades. Experiments that use intervals of years often involve the recall of personal experience (what is called *autobiographical memory*) rather than the recall of laboratory materials. In what follows, studies using both kinds of material are intermixed because they seem to reflect many of the same basic principles.

Our discussion of long-term memory will again distinguish between the three stages of memory—encoding, storage, and retrieval—but this time there are two complications. First, unlike the situation in short-term memory, important interactions between encoding and retrieval occur in long-term memory. In view of these interactions, we will consider some aspects of retrieval in our discussion of encoding, and will present a separate discussion of encoding-retrieval interactions. The other complication is that it is often difficult to know whether forgetting from long-term memory is due to a loss from storage or a failure in retrieval. To deal with this problem, we will delay our discussion of storage until after we have considered retrieval, so that we will have a clearer idea of what constitutes good evidence for a storage loss.

## Encoding

**ENCODING MEANING** For verbal materials, the dominant long-term memory representation is neither acoustic nor visual; instead, it is based on the meanings of the items. Encoding items according to their meanings occurs even when the items are isolated words, but it is more striking when the items are sentences. Several minutes after hearing a sentence, most of what you can recall or recognize is the sentence's meaning. Suppose you heard the sentence, "The author sent the committee a long letter." Two minutes later you could not tell whether you had heard that sentence or one that has the same meaning: "A long letter was sent to the committee by the author" (Sachs, 1967).

Encoding meaning is pervasive in everyday memory situations. When people report on complex social or political situations, they may misremember many of the specifics (who said what to whom, when something was said, who else was there) yet can accurately describe the basic situation that took place. Thus, in the famous Watergate scandal of the early 1970s, the chief government witness (John Dean) was subsequently shown to have made many mistakes about what was said in particular situations, yet his overall testimony accurately described the events that had taken place (Neisser, 1981).

Although meaning may be the dominant way of representing verbal material in long-term memory, we sometimes code other aspects as well. We can, for example, memorize poems and recite them word for word. In such cases, we have coded not only the meaning of the poem but the words themselves. We can also use an acoustic code in long-term memory. When you get a phone call and the other party says "hello," often you recognize the voice. And sometimes when you see someone that you have not encountered for awhile, you may fail to recognize them until they speak. In cases like this, you must have coded the sound of that person's voice in long-term memory. Visual impressions, tastes, and smells are also coded in long-term memory. Thus, long-term memory has a preferred code for verbal material (namely, meaning), but other codes can be used as well.

**ADDING MEANINGFUL CONNECTIONS** Often the items we have to remember are meaningful but the connections between them are not. In such cases, memory can be improved by creating real or artificial links between the items. For example, people learning to read music must remember that the five lines in printed music are referred to as EGBDF; although the symbols themselves are meaningful (they refer to notes on a keyboard), their order seems arbitrary. What many learners do is convert the symbols into the sentence "Every Good Boy Does Fine"; the first letter of each word names each symbol, and the relations between the words in the sentence supply meaningful connections between the symbols. These connections aid memory because they provide retrieval paths between the words: once the word "Good" has been retrieved, for example, there is a path or connection to "Boy," the next word that has to be recalled.

One of the best ways to add connections is to elaborate on the meaning of the material while encoding it. The more deeply or elaborately one encodes the meaning, the better memory will be (Craik & Tulving, 1975). If you have to remember a point made in a textbook, you will recall it better if you concentrate on its meaning rather than on the exact words. And the more deeply and thoroughly you expand on its meaning, the better you will recall it.

An experiment by Bradshaw and Anderson (1982) illustrates some of these points. Subjects read facts about famous people that they would later have to recall, such as "At a critical point in his life, Mozart made a journey from Munich to Paris." Some facts were elaborated by either their causes or consequences, as in "Mozart wanted to leave Munich to avoid a romantic entanglement." Other facts were presented alone. When subjects were later tested for memory, they recalled more facts that were given elaborations than those presented alone. Presumably, in adding the cause (or consequence) to their memory representation, subjects set up a retrieval path from the cause to the target fact in the following manner:

Mozart journeyed from Munich to Paris

cause

Mozart wanted to avoid a romantic entanglement in Munich

At the time of recall, subjects could retrieve the target fact directly, or indirectly, by following the path from its cause. Even if they forgot the target fact entirely, they could infer it if they retrieved the cause.

## Retrieval

Many cases of forgetting from long-term memory result from a loss of access to the information rather than from a loss of the information itself. That is, poor memory often reflects a retrieval failure rather than a storage failure. (Note that this is unlike short-term memory, where forgetting is a result of exceeding the storage capacity, while retrieval is thought to be relatively error-free.) Trying to retrieve an item from long-term memory is like trying to find a book in a large library. Failure to find the book does not necessarily mean it is not there; you may be looking in the wrong place, or it may simply be misfiled and therefore inaccessible.

**EVIDENCE FOR RETRIEVAL FAILURES** Common experience provides much evidence for retrieval failures. Everyone at some point has been unable to recall a fact or an experience, only to have it come to mind later. How many times have you taken an exam and not been able to recall a specific name or date, only to remember it after the exam? Another example is the "tip-of-the-tongue" experience in which a particular word or name lies tantalizingly outside our ability to recall it (Brown & McNeill, 1966). We may feel quite tormented until a search of memory (dredging up and then discarding words that are close but not quite right) finally retrieves the correct word.

A more striking example of retrieval failure is the occasional recovery by a person under hypnosis of a childhood memory that had previously been forgotten. Similar experiences may occur in psychotherapy. Although we lack firm evidence for these observations, they at least suggest that some seemingly forgotten memories are not lost. They are just difficult to get at and require the right kind of **retrieval cue** (anything that can help us retrieve a memory).

For stronger evidence that retrieval failures can cause forgetting, consider the following experiment. Subjects were asked to memorize a long list of words. Some of the words were names of animals, such as dog, cat, horse; some names of fruits, such as apple, orange, pear; some names of furniture, and so on (see Table 8-1). At the time of recall, the subjects were divided into two groups. One group was supplied with retrieval cues such as "animal," "fruit," and so on; the other group, the control group, was not. The group given the retrieval cues recalled more words than the control group. In a subsequent test, when both groups were given the retrieval cues, they recalled the same number of words. Hence, the initial difference in recall between the two groups must have been due to retrieval failures.

Thus, the better the retrieval cues, the better our memory. This principle explains why we usually do better on a recognition test of memory than on a recall test. In a recognition test, we are asked if we have seen a particular item before (for example, "Was Bessie Smith one of the people you met at the party?"). The test item itself is an excellent retrieval cue for our memory of that item. In contrast, in a recall test we have to produce the memorized items with minimal retrieval cues (for example, "Recall the names of everyone you met at the party"). Since the retrieval cues in a recognition test are generally more useful than those in a recall test, recognition tests usually show better memory performance than recall tests (Tulving, 1974).

**INTERFERENCE** Among the factors that can impair retrieval, the most important is interference. If we associate different items with the same cue, when we try to use that cue to retrieve one of the items (the target item), the other items may become active and interfere with our recovery of the target. For example, if your friend, Dan, moves and you finally learn his new phone number, you will find it difficult to retrieve the old number. Why? You are using the cue "Dan's phone number" to retrieve the old number, but instead this cue activates the new number, which interferes with recovery of the old one. Or suppose that your reserved space in a parking garage, which you have used for a year, is changed. You may initially find it difficult to retrieve from memory your new parking location. Why? You are trying to learn to associate your new location with the cue "my parking place," but this cue retrieves the old location, which interferes with the learning of the new one. In both examples, the power of retrieval cues ("Dan's phone number" or "my parking place") to activate particular target items decreases with the number of other items associated with those cues. The more items

## LIST TO BE MEMORIZED

| dog | cotton | oil |
|------|-----------|--------|
| cat | wool | gas |
| horse | silk | coal |
| cow | rayon | wood |
| apple | blue | doctor |
| orange | red | laywer |
| pear | green | teacher |
| banana | yellow | dentist |
| chair | knife | football |
| table | spoon | baseball |
| bed | fork | basketball |
| sofa | pan | tennis |
| knife | hammer | shirt |
| gun | saw | socks |
| rifle | nails | pants |
| bomb | screwdriver | shoes |

## RETRIEVAL CUES

| animals | cloth | fuels |
|-----------|----------|-------------|
| fruit | color | professions |
| furniture | utensils | sports |
| weapons | tools | clothing |

**TABLE 8-1**
**Examples from a Study of Retrieval Failures** *Subjects not given the retrieval cues recalled fewer words from the memorized list than other subjects who did have the cues. This finding shows that problems at the retrieval stage of long-term memory are responsible for some memory failures.*
(After Tulving & Pearlstone, 1966)

associated with a cue, the more overloaded it becomes and the less effectively it can retrieve.

Interference can operate at various levels, including that of whole facts. In one experiment, subjects first learned to associate various facts with the names of professions. For example, they learned that the banker:

(1) was asked to address the crowd,
(2) broke the bottle, and
(3) did not delay the trip.

The lawyer:

(1) realized the seam was split, and
(2) painted an old barn.

The occupational names "banker" and "lawyer" were the retrieval cues here. Since "banker" was associated with three facts, whereas "lawyer" was associated with just two, "banker" should have been less useful in retrieving any one of its associated facts than "lawyer" was ("banker" was the more overloaded cue). When subjects were later given a recognition test, they did take longer to recognize the facts learned about the banker than those learned about the lawyer. In this study, then, interference slowed the speed of retrieval. Many other experiments show that interference can lead to a complete retrieval failure if the target items are very weak or the interference is very strong (Anderson, 1983). Indeed, it has long been thought that interference is a major reason why forgetting increases with time; roughly, the relevant retrieval cues become more and more overloaded with time (see Figure 8-7).

**FIGURE 8-7**
**Forgetting as a Function of Time** *A* forgetting curve *graphs the decline in recall as a function of time. This forgetting curve, the first ever reported, is due to Ebbinghaus (1885). He studied lists of 13 syllables which he repeated until he was able to recall the list without error on two successive trials. Then, after intervals ranging from 20 minutes to 31 days, he tested himself by determining how long it took him to re-learn the list to the original level; the less the forgetting, the fewer trials should be needed to re-learn the list. The figure plots a measure of ease of re-learning (called* savings*) as a function of time; it suggests that one forgets a lot about an event within the first few hours, but after that the rate of forgetting slows down. While this curve is representative of memory for unrelated verbal materials, different kinds of curves are found with different kinds of material (for example, Bahrick and Phelphs, 1987). In all cases, interference is thought to play some role in the changes in forgetting with time.*

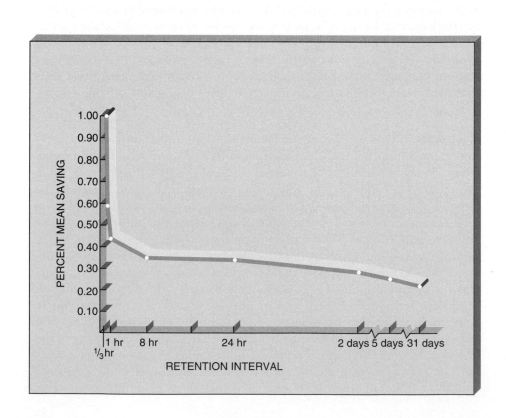

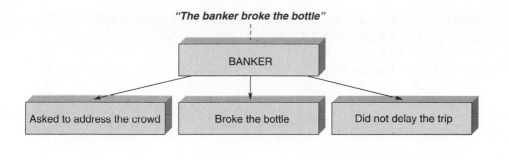

*"The banker broke the bottle"*

BANKER

Asked to address the crowd | Broke the bottle | Did not delay the trip

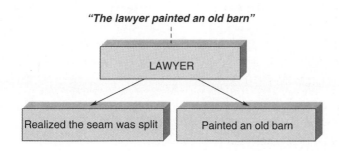

*"The lawyer painted an old barn"*

LAWYER

Realized the seam was split | Painted an old barn

**FIGURE 8-8**
**Retrieval as a Search Process versus an Activation Process** *When presented the sentence, "The banker broke the bottle," the term "banker" accesses the banker representation in long-term memory; once at this representation, there are three paths to be searched. When presented "The lawyer painted an old barn," "lawyer" accesses the lawyer representation, from which there are two paths to be searched. Alternatively, the term "banker" may activate the banker representation, where this activation then spreads simultaneously along the three paths (and similarly for the "lawyer" example).*

**RETRIEVAL MODELS**  In attempting to explain interference effects, researchers have developed a variety of models of retrieval. As was the case when considering retrieval from short-term memory, some models of long-term-memory retrieval are based on a search process whereas others are based on an activation process.

The interference effects in the banker-lawyer experiment fit nicely with the idea that retrieval from long-term memory may be thought of as a search process. To illustrate, consider how a sentence from the preceding study, "The banker broke the bottle," might be recognized (see Figure 8-8). The term "banker" accesses its representation in memory, which localizes the search to the relevant part of long-term memory. Once there, three paths need to be searched to find the fact "broke the bottle." In contrast, if the test sentence was "The lawyer painted an old barn," there are only two paths to be searched (see Figure 8-8). Since the duration of a search increases with the number of paths to be considered, retrieval will be slower for the "banker" sentence than the "lawyer" one. Retrieval generally is more difficult when more facts are associated with a retrieval cue, because each fact adds a path to be searched.

An alternative way to think about the retrieval process is in terms of activation. When trying to recognize "The banker broke the bottle," for example, the subject activates the representation for "banker," and the activation then spreads simultaneously along the three paths emanating from "banker" (see Figure 8-8). When sufficient activation reaches "broke the bottle," the sentence can be recognized. Interference arises because the activation from the banker representation must be subdivided among the paths emanating from it. Hence, the more facts associated with "banker," the thinner the activation on each path, and the longer it will take for sufficient activation to reach any particular fact. So, thinking of retrieval in terms of spreading activation can also account for why interference slows retrieval (Anderson, 1983).

*Critical*
# DISCUSSION

## Connectionist Models of Memory

As noted in Chapter 5, a new way to describe many psychological processes is in terms of **connectionist models.** In such models, knowledge is represented in a network of interconnected units that resemble neurons, and the knowledge is processed by activation and inhibition spreading among the units. One topic that has been a recent focus of connectionist modelling is long-term memory, and in what follows we illustrate some basic aspects of such memory models.

For ease of exposition, let us consider a simple memory task. On each trial of an experiment, a subject is visually presented a different triple of letters, such as RDK, and her task is to learn to verbally recall all three letters when cued with two of them (for example, when cued with RD, the subject should say "RDK"). Figure 1a shows a connectionist network that depicts the subject's memory at the outset of the task. The bottom, or *input*, level of the network contains units that represent the possible stimuli or input—these units represent the visual appearances of individual letters. The top, or *output*, level of the network contains units that represent possible responses or output— these units represent the pronunciations of individual letters. Encoding amounts to forming connections between certain input units and certain output units.

The basic principle assumed to guide encoding is this: When a triple of letters is presented, for each one the subject forms an excitatory connection between its input unit and the output units of all active letters. To illustrate, if RDK is presented, the subject would form excitatory connections between: *(i)* the input unit for R and the output units for "R," "D," and "K" (see Figure 1b); *(ii)* the input unit for D and the output units for "R," "D," and "K" (see Figure 1c); and *(iii)* the input unit for K and the output units for "R," "D," and "K" (see

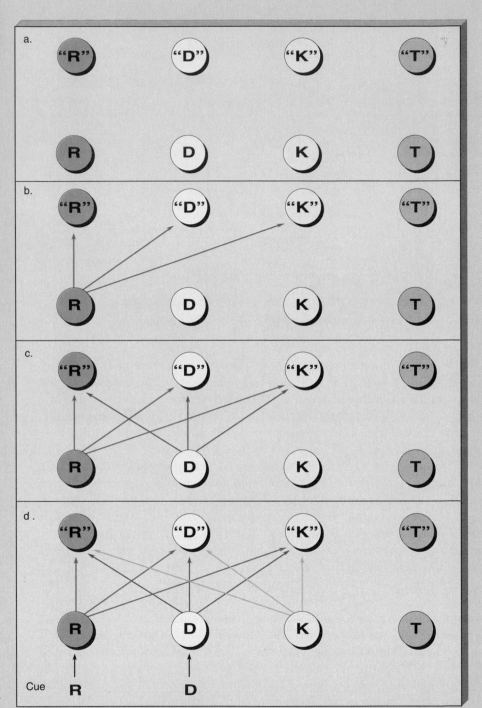

**FIGURE 1**
**A Simple Network for Cued Recall** *This network involves only excitatory connections between units. (a) The bottom level of the network contains input units, which represent the visual appearance of R, D, K, and T, while the top level contains output units that represent the pronunciations of the four letters. Presentation of RDK leads to the formation of: (b) excitatory connections between the input unit for R and the output units for "R," "D," and "K"; (c) excitatory connections between the input unit for D and the output units for "R," "D," and "K"; and (d) excitatory connections between the input unit for K and the output units for "R," "D," and "K". When RD is presented as a cue, the output units for "R," "D," and "K" all become active.*

Figure 1d). (All connections would be formed at the same time.) The fact that these connections are excitatory (as indicated by the arrowheads at their ends) means that if the input units are activated, the excitation will spread to the corresponding output units in a manner analogous to how electrical impulses spread in a network of neurons. If a critical amount of activation reaches an output unit, that unit itself becomes active. Figure 1d, then, represents the resulting network. It explains how a subject can retrieve the names of all three letters in a triple when cued with two of them. Suppose RD is presented as a cue. The cue will activate the input units for R and D, and this activation will spread to the output units for "R," "D," and "K." Assuming that two units of activation is sufficient to make a response unit available, all three letters will be verbally recalled, as the task requires.

The preceding analysis illustrates an important aspect of connectionist models: given part of a memorized pattern, the model will fill in the rest. Such *pattern completion* seems to be a fundamental aspect of human memory. Indeed, our general ability to retrieve full memories given just partial retrieval cues may be viewed as an instance of the pattern-completion nature of memory.

To illustrate a further point about connectionist models of memory, let us change one aspect of our memory task. Instead of the subject having to verbally recall all three letters in the cued-for triple, now she has to respond with just the letter that is not in the cue. For example, cued with RD, she should say "K." How can we alter the network in Figure 1d so that it will accomplish this new task? Since the subject must essentially *inhibit* saying the names of the input letters, let us add inhibitory connections (symbolized by solid circles at their ends) between the input and output unit for each letter (see Figure 2a— it differs from Figure 1d only in the addition of inhibitory connections). Now when RD is presented as a cue, activation will again spread to the output units for "R," "D," and "K"; but inhibition will also be sent to the output units for "R" and "D," which will reduce the activation of these units. As a result, only

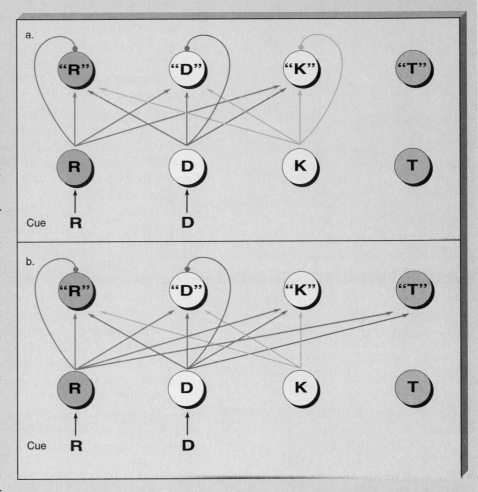

**FIGURE 2**

**A Modified Network** *These networks contain inhibitory as well as excitatory connections. (a) The network after encoding inhibitory connections between each letter and its pronunciation; (b) the network after encoding excitatory connections between the input units for R and D and the output unit for "T."*

the output unit for "K" will have the critical amount of activation needed to become active, and it will be given as a response, as the task requires. Thus, by the subtle interaction of excitatory and inhibitory connections, connectionist models can account for performance in a variety of tasks (Willshaw, 1981).

Such models can also explain interference effects. Suppose that in the preceding task, after memorizing RDK, our subject learns the triple RDT. Now, among other things, excitatory connections will be formed between the inputs unit for R and D and the output unit for "T" (see Figure 2b). These new connections will lead to interference when the subject is cued with RD. Such a cue

will activate the output unit for "T" as well as that for "K" (see Figure 2b), and the two output units will compete with one another, resulting in poorer recall.

Connectionist models of interference are currently being intensively explored (McCloskey & Cohen, 1989; Sloman & Rumelhart, 1991). In some of these models, rather than units representing entire items (such as letters), each unit represents only a feature of an item. That is, the representation of each item is *distributed* over a set of units. Connectionist models with such distributed representation are more powerful than the sort we have illustrated here.

## Storage

Retrieval failures are unlikely to be the only cause of forgetting. The fact that *some* forgetting is due to retrieval failures does not imply that *all* forgetting is. It seems most unlikely that everything we ever learned is still there in memory waiting for the right retrieval cue. Some information is almost certainly lost from storage (Loftus & Loftus, 1980).

Direct evidence of storage loss comes from people who receive **electroconvulsive therapy** to alleviate severe depression (a mild electric current applied to the brain produces a brief epileptic-like seizure and momentary unconsciousness; see Chapter 16). In such cases, the patient loses some memory for events that occurred in the months prior to the shock, but not for earlier events (Squire & Fox, 1980). These memory losses are unlikely to be due to retrieval failures, because if the shock disrupted retrieval then all memories should be affected, not just the recent ones. More likely, the shock disrupts storage processes that *consolidate* new memories over a period of months or longer, and information that is not consolidated is lost from storage.

Psychologists have made substantial progress in determining the physiological bases of consolidation. Several brain structures are involved, including the **hippocampus** and **amygdala,** which are located below the cerebral cortex. The hippocampus' role in consolidation seems to be that of a cross-referencing system, linking together aspects of a particular memory that are stored in separate parts of the brain (Squire, Cohen, & Nadel, 1984). While a global memory loss in humans usually occurs only when the amygdala as well as the hippocampus is impaired, damage to the hippocampus alone can result in severe memory disturbance. This fact was demonstrated by a study that started with an analysis of a particular patient's memory problems (due to complications from coronary bypass surgery), and ended with a detailed autopsy of his brain following the patient's death; the hippocampus was the only brain structure damaged (Zola-Morgan, Squire, & Amaral, 1989).

A recent study with monkeys provides the best evidence we have that the function of the hippocampus is to consolidate relatively new memories. In the study, a group of experimental monkeys learned to discriminate between 100 pairs of objects. For each pair, there was food under one object, which the monkey got only if it picked that object. Since all the objects differed, the monkeys essentially learned 100 different problems. Twenty of these problems were learned 16 weeks before the researchers removed the monkeys' hippocampus; additional sets of 20 problems were learned either 12, 8, 4, or 2 weeks before the hippocampal surgery. Two weeks after surgery, the researchers tested the monkeys' memory with a single trial of each of the 100 pairs. The critical finding was that the experimental monkeys remembered discriminations learned 12, 16, or 20 weeks before surgery as well as normal control monkeys, but remembered the discriminations learned 2 or 4 weeks before surgery less well than the control monkeys. Furthermore, the experimental monkeys actually remember less about the discriminations learned 2 to 4 weeks before surgery than about the discriminations learned earlier. These results suggest that memories stay in the hippocampus for a period of only a few weeks, for it is only during this period that memory is impaired by removal of the hippocampus. Permanent long-term memory storage is almost certainly localized in the cortex, particularly those regions in which sensory information is interpreted (Zola-Morgan & Squire, 1990; Squire, 1992).

## Encoding-Retrieval Interactions

In describing the encoding stage, we noted that operations carried out during encoding (for instance, elaboration) later make retrieval easier. Two other encoding factors also increase the chances of successful retrieval: a) organizing the information at the time of encoding, and b) ensuring that the context in which information is encoded is similar to that in which it will be retrieved.

**ORGANIZATION** The more we organize the material we encode, the easier it is to retrieve. Suppose you were at a conference at which you met various professionals—doctors, lawyers, and journalists. When later you try to recall their names, you will do better if initially you organize the information by profession. Then you can ask yourself, Who were the doctors I met? Who were the lawyers? And so forth. A list of names or words is far easier to recall when we encode the information into categories and then retrieve it on a category-by-category basis.

The following experiment illustrates this principle. The subjects were asked to memorize lists of words. For some subjects, the words in a list were arranged in the form of a hierarchical tree, like the example shown in Figure 8-9. For the other subjects, the words were arranged randomly. When tested later, the subjects presented with the hierarchical organization recalled 65 percent of the words, whereas the subjects presented with random arrangements recalled only 19 percent of the same words. Studies like this leave little doubt that memory is best when the material is highly organized.

Why does hierarchical organization improve memory? Probably because it makes the process underlying retrieval more efficient. To illustrate, suppose that subjects in the preceding experiment used a serial search. Subjects who had seen the words hierarchically organized, as in Figure 8-9, might have proceeded as follows: first they found a high level cluster, such as "metals"; from that high-level cluster, they then searched for a low-level cluster such as "common metals"; and then they searched that low-level cluster for specific words ("aluminum," "copper," "lead," "iron"); and so on. By operating in this way, at no point would subjects have to search a large set. There are only two high-level clusters, never more than three low-level clusters connected to a high-level one, and never more than four specific words in a low-level cluster. Hierarchical organization thus allows us to divide a big search into a sequence of little ones. And with a little search, there is less

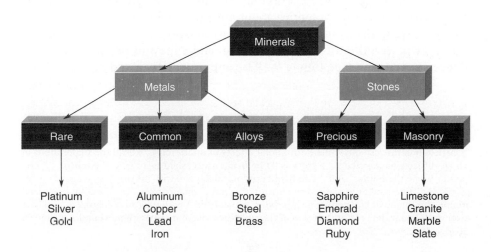

**FIGURE 8-9**
**Hierarchical Organization to Improve Retrieval** *Trees like this are constructed according to the following rule: all items below a node are included in the class labeled by that node. For example, the items "bronze," "steel," and "brass" are included in the class labeled "alloys."* (After Bower, Clark, Winzenz, & Lesgold, 1969)

**FIGURE 8-10**
**Effects of Environmental Context on Retrieval** *In an experiment to demonstrate how context affects retrieval, one group of deep-sea divers learned a list of words while they were on the beach (panel a), whereas another group of divers learned the list while they were beneath 15 feet of water (panel b). Later, each group was divided in half and tried to recall the words in either the same environment they learned in (panels c and f), or in a different environment (panels d and e). There was no overall effect of whether the divers originally learned the words on land or under water. But divers who were tested in an environment different from the one they learned in recalled 40% less than divers who learned and recalled in the same environment (Godden & Baddeley, 1975).*

chance we will bog down by turning up the same words again and again, which is exactly what seems to happen when we search material that is not organized (Raaijmakers & Shiffrin, 1981; Gillund & Shiffrin, 1984).*

**CONTEXT** It is easier to retrieve a particular fact or episode if you are in the same context in which you encoded it (Estes, 1972). For example, it is a good bet that your ability to retrieve the names of your classmates in the first and second grades would improve were you to walk through the corridors of your elementary school. Similarly, your ability to retrieve an emotional moment with your parents would be greater if you were back in the place where the incident occurred. This may explain why we are sometimes overcome with a torrent of memories about our earlier life when we visit a place we once lived. The context in which an event was encoded is itself one of the most powerful retrieval cues possible, and a mass of experimental evidence supports this (see Figure 8-10 for a representative study).

---

*Organization can also offset the detrimental effects of interference. Recall the experiment in which subjects memorized such facts as "The banker was asked to address the crowd," "The banker broke the bottle," and "The banker did not delay the trip." If the first sentence is replaced by "The banker was asked to christen the ship," the "banker" facts will be organized around the theme of christening a ship. Now, subjects take no longer to recognize one of the three facts about the banker than one of the two learned about some other occupation (Smith, Adams, & Schorr, 1978).

Context is not always external to the memorizer—that is, not always a matter of environment. What is happening inside of us when we encode information—our internal state—is also part of context. For example, if we experience an event while under the influence of a particular drug (for instance, alcohol or marijuana), perhaps we can best retrieve it when we are again in that drug-induced state. In such cases, memory would be partly dependent on the internal state during learning; we call this **state-dependent learning.** While the evidence on state-dependent learning is controversial, it suggests that memory does indeed improve when our internal state during retrieval matches that during encoding (Eich, 1980).

## Emotional Factors in Forgetting

So far, we have treated memory as if it were divorced from emotion. But don't we sometimes remember material because of its emotional content? Or forget material because of its emotional content? There has been a great deal of research on these questions. The results suggest that emotion can influence long-term memory in at least five distinct ways.

The simplest idea is that we tend to think about emotionally charged situations, negative as well as positive, more than we think about neutral ones. We rehearse and organize exciting memories more than we do their blander counterparts. For example, you may forget where you saw this or that movie, but if a fire breaks out while you are in a theater, you will describe the setting over and over to friends, as well as think about the setting over and over to yourself, thereby rehearsing and organizing it. Since we know that rehearsal and organization can improve retrieval from long-term memory, it is not surprising that many researchers have found better memory for emotional than for unemotional situations (Rapaport, 1942; Neisser, 1982).

The second way that emotion can affect memory is via **flashbulb memories.** A flashbulb memory is a vivid and relatively permanent record of the circumstances in which you learned of an emotionally charged, significant event, such as the explosion of the space shuttle *Challenger* in 1986. Many people in their 20s remember exactly where they were when they learned of the *Challenger* disaster, and exactly who told them about it, even though these are the kinds of details that we usually forget quickly. Americans 30 years of age or older may have flashbulb memories of the assassination attempt on Ronald Reagan in 1981, while those 40 or older may have such memories of the assassinations of John F. Kennedy and Martin Luther King in the 1960s. Remarkably, there is even a published report indicating that Americans a century ago had flashbulb memories of the assassination of Abraham Lincoln. When Colegrove (1899) interviewed 179 people, 127 of them were able to give full particulars as to where they were and what they were doing when they heard of Lincoln's assassination.

What is responsible for such memories? According to Brown and Kulik (1977), extraordinarily important events trigger a *special memory mechanism,* one that makes a permanent record of everything the person is experiencing at the moment. It is as if we took a picture of the moment, which is why the recollection is dubbed a "flashbulb memory." Other researchers, however, have disputed the idea that a special memory mechanism is involved. They point out that flashbulb memories become less retrievable with time, as do normal long-term memories. In one study, a few days after the *Challenger* explosion, people were asked where they were and what they were doing

*For many people, the explosion of the space shuttle* Challenger *is a flashbulb memory.*

when they heard of the disaster; nine months later, the same people were asked the same questions. Although the people had unusually detailed memories of the event 9 months after it occurred, there was some forgetting during the interval (McCloskey, Wible, & Cohen, 1988). Similarly, people's memories of the assassination attempt on President Reagan show some decrease in recall as the event recedes in time (Pillimer, 1984). Results like these suggest that memory for national tragedies could be an instance of normal memory. The reason we remember the events so vividly is that we keep on hearing and talking about them, the way we do other emotionally charged situations. The issue of whether flashbulb memories involve a special mechanism remains open.

Unlike flashbulb memories, there are cases where negative emotions *hinder* retrieval, which brings us to the third way that emotion can affect memory. An experience that many students have at one time or another illustrates this:

> You are taking an exam about which you are not very confident. You can barely understand the initial question, let alone answer it. Signs of panic appear. Although the second question really isn't hard, the anxiety triggered by the previous question spreads to this one. By the time you look at the third question, it wouldn't matter if it just asked for your phone number. There's no way you can answer it. You're in a complete panic.

What is happening to memory here? Failure to deal with the first question produced anxiety. Anxiety is often accompanied by extraneous thoughts, such as "I'm going to flunk out" or "Everybody will think I am stupid." These thoughts then interfere with any attempt to retrieve the information relevant to the question, and that may be why memory utterly fails. According to this view, anxiety does not directly cause memory failure; rather, it causes, or is associated with, extraneous thoughts, and these thoughts cause memory failure by interfering with retrieval (Holmes, 1974).

Emotion may also affect memory by a kind of *context effect*. As we have noted, memory is best when the context at retrieval matches that at encoding. Since our emotional state during learning is part of the context, if the material we are learning makes us feel sad, then perhaps we can best retrieve that material when we feel sad again. Experimenters have demonstrated such an emotional-context effect in the laboratory. Subjects agreed to keep diaries for a week, recording daily every emotional incident that occurred and noting whether it was pleasant or unpleasant. One week after they handed in their diaries, the subjects returned to the laboratory and were hypnotized (they had been pre-selected to be highly hypnotizable). Half the subjects were put in a pleasant mood, and the other half were put in an unpleasant mood. All were asked to recall the incidents recorded in their diaries. For subjects in a pleasant mood, most of the incidents they recalled had been rated as pleasant when experienced; for subjects in an unpleasant mood at retrieval, most of the incidents recalled had been rated as unpleasant when experienced. As expected, recall was best when the dominant emotion during retrieval matched that during encoding (Bower, 1981).

Thus far, aside from the possibility of a special purpose mechanism for flashbulb memories, all of the means by which emotions can influence memory rely on principles already discussed—namely, rehearsal, interference, and context effects. The fifth view of emotion and memory, Freud's theory of the unconscious, brings up new principles. Freud proposed that some emotional experiences in childhood are so traumatic that allowing them to enter consciousness many years later would cause the individual to be totally overwhelmed by anxiety. (This is different from the example of the exam, where the anxiety was tolerable to consciousness.) Such traumatic experiences are said to be stored in the unconscious, or *repressed;* and they can be retrieved only when some of the emotion associated with them is defused. Repression, therefore, represents the ultimate retrieval failure: access to the target memories is actively blocked. This notion of active blocking makes the **repression hypothesis** qualitatively different from the ideas about forgetting we considered earlier. (For a fuller discussion of Freud's theory, see Chapter 14.)

Repression is such a striking phenomenon that we would of course like to study it in the laboratory, but this has proved difficult to do. To induce true repression in the laboratory, the experimenter must have the subject experience something extremely traumatic; ethical considerations prohibit this. The studies that have been done have exposed subjects to only mildly upsetting experiences. The bulk of the evidence from these studies lends mixed support to the repression hypothesis (Baddeley, 1990; Erdelyi, 1985).

"And then I say to myself, 'If I really wanted to talk to her, why do I keep forgetting to dial 1 first?'"
Drawing by Modell; © 1981 *The New Yorker Magazine,* Inc.

## Implicit Memory

Thus far we have been mainly concerned with situations in which people remember personal facts. In such cases, memory is a matter of consciously recollecting the past, and is said to be expressed *explicitly.* But there seems to be another kind of memory, the kind that is often manifested in skills and that shows up as an improvement on some perceptual, motor, or cognitive task without conscious recollection of the experiences that led to the improvement. For example, with practice we can steadily improve our ability to recognize words in a foreign language, but at the moment we are recognizing a word, and thereby demonstrating our skill, we need not have any conscious recollections of the lessons that led to our improvement. Here, memory is expressed *implicitly* (Schacter, 1989).

## Childhood Amnesia

One of the most striking aspects of human memory is that everyone suffers from a particular kind of amnesia: virtually no person can recall events from the first years of life, though this is the time when experience is at its richest. This curious phenomenon was first discussed by Freud (1905), who called it **childhood amnesia.**

Freud discovered the phenomenon by observing that his patients were generally unable to recall events from their first 3 to 5 years of life. At first you might think there is nothing unusual about this, because memory for events declines with time, and for adults there has been a lot of intervening time since early childhood. But childhood amnesia cannot be reduced to a case of normal forgetting. Most 30-year-olds can recall a good deal about their high school years, but it is a rare 18-year-old that can tell you anything about his or her third year of life; yet the time interval is roughly the same in the two cases (about 15 years). More rigorous evidence along these lines comes from a study in which 18-year-old subjects tried to recall personal memories from all periods of their lives. Memory for an event, of course, declined with the number of years that had passed since that event, but the *rate* of decline was much steeper for events in the first 6 years of life than for events

*This little girl probably will not remember the events surrounding the birth of her baby brother.*

thereafter (Wetzler & Sweeney, cited in Rubin, 1986).

In other studies, people have been asked to recall and date their childhood memories. For most subjects, their first memories are of something that occurred when they were age 3 or older; a few subjects, however, will report memories prior to the age of 1. A problem with these reports, however, is that we

can never be sure that the "remembered" event actually occurred (the person may have reconstructed what he or she thought happened). This problem was overcome in an experiment in which subjects were asked a total of 20 questions about a childhood event that was known to have occurred—the birth of a younger sibling—the details of which could be verified by another per-

## Memory in Amnesia

**AMNESIA**   Much of what we know about implicit memory we have learned from people who suffer **amnesia**. Amnesia refers to a partial loss of memory. It may result from very different causes, including accidental injuries to the brain, strokes, encephalitis, alcoholism, electroconvulsive shock, and surgical procedures (for example, removal of the hippocampus to reduce epilepsy). Whatever its cause, the primary symptom of amnesia is a profound inability to acquire new factual information or to remember day-to-day events; this is referred to as **anterograde amnesia**, and it can be very extensive. There is an intensively studied patient, identified as NA, who is

son. The questions asked of each subject dealt with events that transpired during the mother's leaving for the hospital (for example, "What time of day did she leave?"), when the mother was in the hospital ("Did you visit her?"), and when the mother and infant returned home ("What time of day did they come home?"). The subjects were college students, and their ages at the birth of their siblings varied from 1 to 17 years. The results are shown in the figure. The number of questions answered is plotted as a function of the subject's age when the sibling was born. If the sibling was born before the subject was 3 years old, the person could not recall a thing about it. If the birth occurred after that, recall increased with age at the time of the event. These results suggest an almost total amnesia for the first 3 years of life. (More recent research, however, suggests that such recall may be improved if more cues are given and the cues are more specific, Fivush & Hamond, 1991).

What causes childhood amnesia? Freud (1905) thought that it was due to the repression of sexual and aggressive feelings that a young child experiences toward his parents. But this account predicts amnesia only for events related to sexual and aggressive thoughts, when in fact childhood amnesia extends to all kinds of events. A more accepted explanation is that childhood amnesia is due to a massive difference between how young children encode experience and how adults organize their memories. Adults structure their memories in terms of categories and schemata ("She's that kind of person," "It's that kind of situation"), while young children encode their experiences without embellishing them or connecting them to related events. Once a child begins to form associations between events and to categorize those events, early experiences become lost (Schachtel, 1982).

What causes the shift from early childhood to adult forms of memory? One factor is biological development. The hippocampus, a brain structure involved in consolidating memories, is not mature until roughly a year or two after birth. Therefore, events that take place in the first 2 years of life cannot be sufficiently consolidated and consequently cannot be recalled later. Other causes of the shift to adult memory involve cognitive factors, particularly the development of language and the beginning of schooling. Both language and the kind of thinking emphasized in school provide new ways of organizing experiences, ways that may be incompatible with how the young child encodes experiences. Interestingly, language development reaches an early peak at age 3, while schooling often begins at age 5; and the age span from 3 to 5 is when childhood amnesia seems to end.

Organizational changes may not be the whole story of childhood amnesia. The difference between explicit and implicit memory may also play a role. Much of what we learn in infancy are skills, and they will not be represented in explicit memory, which develops later. There is evidence for this hypothesis in studies with monkeys. Three-month-old monkeys can learn an implicit task as readily as adult monkeys, but they cannot master an explicit task that adults find easy (Mishkin, Malamut, & Bachevalier, 1984).

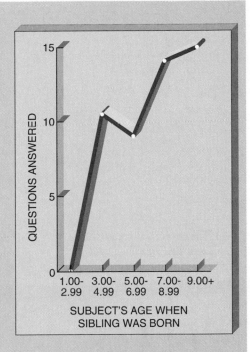

**Recall of an Early Memory** *In an experiment on childhood amnesia, college-age subjects were asked 20 questions about the events surrounding the birth of a younger sibling. The average number of questions answered is plotted as a function of the subject's age when the sibling was born. If the birth occurred before the fourth year of life, no subject could recall a thing about it; if the birth occurred after that, recall increased with age at the time of the event.* (After Sheingold & Tenney, 1982)

unable to participate in a normal conversation because he loses his train of thought with the least distraction. Another patient identified as HM—the most intensively studied of all amnesiacs—reads the same magazines over and over and continually needs to be reintroduced to doctors who have been treating him for more than two decades.

A secondary symptom of amnesia is an inability to remember events that occurred *prior* to the injury or disease. The extent of such **retrograde amnesia** varies from patient to patient. Aside from retrograde and anterograde memory losses, the typical amnesiac appears normal: he or she has a normal vocabulary, the usual knowledge about the world, and in general shows no loss of intelligence.

*Stage 1*
Present list of words for study (example, MOTEL)

*Stage 2*
Present fragments of list words (example, MOT_ _) and non-list words (example, BLA_ _) for completion. Number of list-words completed minus number of non-list words completed = Priming

*Stage 3*
Present original list of words (example, MOTEL) plus new words for recognition (example, STAND)

**TABLE 8-2**
**Procedure of an Experiment to Study Implicit Memory in Amnesia**
(After Warrington & Weiskrantz, 1978)

**SKILLS AND PRIMING**  A striking aspect of amnesia is that not all kinds of memory are disrupted. Thus, while amnesiacs are generally unable to remember old facts about their lives or to learn new ones, they have no difficulty remembering and learning perceptual and motor skills. This suggests that there is a different memory for facts than for skills. More generally, it suggests that explicit and implicit memory (which encode facts and skills, respectively) are different systems.

The skills preserved in amnesia include *motor skills*, such as tying one's shoelaces or riding a bike, and *perceptual skills*, such as normal reading or reading words that are projected into a mirror (and hence reversed). Consider the ability of reading mirror-reversed words. To do this well takes a bit of practice (try holding this book in front of a mirror). Amnesiacs improve with practice at the very same rate as normal subjects, though they may have no memory of having participated in prior practice sessions (Cohen & Squire, 1980). They show normal memory for the skill but virtually no memory for the learning episodes that developed it (the latter being *facts*).

A similar pattern emerges for what might be called *cognitive skills*, like that involved in completing a fragment to form a word (for example, what word is MOT_ _). This pattern is nicely illustrated in the experiment outlined in Table 8-2. In stage 1 of the experiment, amnesiac and normal subjects were presented a list of words to study. In stage 2, fragments of words on the list and fragments of words not on the list were presented, and subjects tried to complete them (see Table 8-2). The normal subjects performed as expected, completing more fragments when they were drawn from words on the list than when they were drawn from words not on the list. This difference is referred to as **priming,** because the words presented in stage 1 facilitated or primed performance on the fragment completion problems of stage 2. Importantly, amnesiacs also completed more fragments in stage 2 when they were drawn from words on the list than when they were drawn from words not on the list. In fact, the degree of priming for amnesiacs was exactly the same as that for normals! This finding indicates that when memory is manifested implicitly, as in priming, amnesiacs perform normally. Lastly, in stage 3 of the experiment, the original words were presented again along with some novel words, and subjects had to recognize which words had appeared on the list. Now amnesiacs remembered far fewer words than normals. Thus, when memory is tested explicitly, as in recognition, amnesiacs perform far below normals.

There is an interesting variation of the preceding study that further strengthens its conclusion. Suppose that in stage 2 subjects are instructed that it will help them in the fragment completion task to try to think of the words presented earlier. This instruction makes fragment completion into an explicit memory task (because conscious recollection is being emphasized). Now amnesiacs show substantially less priming than normal subjects (Graf & Mandler, 1984).

## Implicit Memory in Normal Subjects

Studies that involve only normal subjects also suggest that there are separate stores for explicit and implicit memories. Indeed, these studies suggest that we all have a bit of a split personality, or at least a split memory system.

A number of studies with normals use fragment completion as an implicit memory test, and recall or recognition as an explicit memory test. In

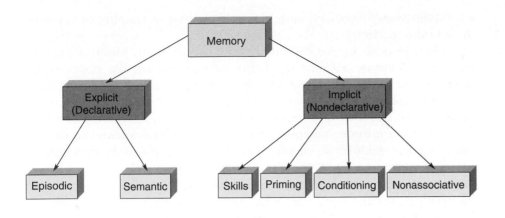

**FIGURE 8-11**
**A Proposed Classification of Different Memory Stores** *Squire et al. (1990) propose several different memory systems. The basic distinction is between explicit and implicit memory (which they refer to as* declarative *and* nondeclarative, *respectively). There are at least four known kinds of implicit memory, corresponding to the memory involved in skills, priming, conditioning, and certain nonassociative phenomenon (such as habituating to a repeated stimulus). There are two kinds of explicit memory, corresponding to semantic and episodic memory.*

one study, normal subjects went through the same three stages that were used in the preceding experiments—(1) original presentation of a list of words, (2) fragment completion of list words and non-list words, and (3) recognition of original words. The critical finding was that there was *no* correlation between the amount of priming a word showed in stage 2 and how easy it was to recognize in stage 3. That is, when the experimenter divided the words into those that were recognized and those that were not, the recognized words showed no more priming than the non-recognized words. Performance on fragment completion seems to be based on a completely different system than that involved in recognition (Tulving, Schacter, & Stark, 1982).

Other studies support the idea of two memory systems by showing that an independent variable that affects explicit memory has no effect on implicit memory, or vice versa. One such variable is whether or not people elaborate an item's meaning. Whereas elaborating a word's meaning boosts its subsequent recall, elaboration has no influence on whether a fragment drawn from that word will be completed (Graff & Mandler, 1984). An independent variable that works the opposite way is whether or not words are presented in the same modality during learning and a subsequent memory test. Subjects who were first presented a list of words auditorally, and subsequently had to recognize them when presented visually, do as well as subjects who were presented the words auditorally during both learning and recognition. So a change in modality of presentation has little effect on explicit memory. Such a change, however, significantly lowers performance on a test of implicit memory (Jacoby & Dallas, 1981).

## Storage versus Retrieval Differences

Some researchers who have argued for two memory systems propose that both explicit and implicit memory come in various forms. One such proposal is presented in Figure 8-11. The basic distinction is between explicit and implicit memory. With regard to implicit memory, a further distinction is made between perceptual-motor skills, such as reading mirror-reversed words, and priming as occurs in fragment completion. The reason for assuming that skills and priming may involve different memory stores is that there are patients with brain damage (those with Alzheimer's disease) who are normal at learning motor skills but show less priming than normal. In contrast, there are other brain-damaged patients (those with Huntington's disease) who show normal priming but are impaired in learning new motor skills (Schacter, 1989).

The theory in Figure 8-11 also posits two different kinds of explicit memory, which are referred to as **episodic** and **semantic**, respectively. Episodic facts refer to personal episodes, while semantic facts refer to general truths. To illustrate, your memory of high-school graduation is an episodic fact, and so is your memory for what you had for dinner last night. In each of these cases, the episode is encoded with respect to you the individual (*your* graduation, *your* dinner, and so on), and often the episode is coded with respect to a specific time and place as well. All of this is in contrast to semantic facts, examples of which include your memory, or knowledge, that the word "bachelor" means an unmarried man, and that September has 30 days. In these cases, the knowledge is encoded in relation to other knowledge rather than in relation to yourself, and there is no coding of time and place. For example, you probably cannot remember much about the context in which you learned that February has 29 days every fourth year (Tulving, 1985).

Are episodic and semantic facts stored in different memories? The very existence of amnesia suggests that they might be. Aside from their severe memory loss, most amnesiacs seem to have normal intelligence. This implies they have a normal vocabulary and normal knowledge about the world, which in turn imply they are relatively normal with respect to semantic knowledge. In most forms of amnesia, then, memory for semantic knowledge is spared while memory for personal episodes is disrupted, suggesting that the two types of facts are indeed stored in different memories.

The idea of different memory stores for different kinds of materials is not without its critics. Roediger (1990), for example, points out that studies with brain damaged patients have already been used to distinguish about 20–25 different memory systems. This proliferation of memory systems seems implausible, and Roediger believes that much of the evidence used to argue for different kinds of memory stores can in fact be interpreted as indicating different retrieval processes operating on a common memory store. The general idea is that an item—for example, the word MOTEL—is represented in memory in terms of both its perceptual appearance and its meaning; implicit-memory situations require retrieval of perceptual information, whereas explicit-memory situations emphasize the retrieval of meaning. This explains some results we presented earlier. Specifically, elaborating the meaning of a word may affect explicit but not implicit memory tests, because a variation in meaning will have an effect only when meaning is what has to be retrieved on the test (an explicit test). Similarly, changing the modality of a word's presentation affects implicit but not explicit tests, because a variation in appearance matters only when perceptual information is what must be retrieved in the test (an implicit test).

A retrieval interpretation of implicit versus explicit memory differences seems plausible when the implicit and explicit tasks both involve words. But in cases where the implicit task involves a perceptual-motor skill and the explicit task involves recall of a fact, the notion of two different stores has intuitive appeal. Skill knowledge is "knowing how"; fact knowledge is "knowing that" (Ryle, 1949), and often the twain never meet. We know how to ride a bike, for example, but it is near impossible to describe it as a set of facts. The knowledge in a skill seems to be represented by the procedures needed to perform the skill, and such knowledge can be retrieved only by executing the procedures (Anderson, 1987).

*Our knowledge of motor skills is implicit; it is very difficult for us to describe a skill as a set of facts.*

# Improving Memory

Having considered the basics of short-term and long-term memory, we are ready to tackle the question of improving memory. We will consider here mainly explicit memory. First, we will consider how to increase the short-term memory span. Then we will turn to a variety of methods for improving long-term memory; these methods work by increasing the efficiency of encoding and retrieval.

## Chunking and Memory Span

For most of us, the capacity of short-term memory cannot be increased beyond 7 ± 2 chunks. However, we can enlarge the size of a chunk and thereby increase the number of items in our memory span. We demonstrated this point earlier: given the string 149-2177-619-93, we can recall all 12 digits if we recode the string into 1492-1776-1993 and then store just these three chunks in short-term memory. Although recoding digits into familiar dates works nicely in this example, it will not work with most digit strings because we have not memorized enough significant dates. But if a recoding system could be developed that worked with virtually *any* string, then short-term memory span could be dramatically improved.

There is a study of a particular subject who discovered such a general-purpose recoding system and used it to increase his memory span from seven to almost 80 random digits (see Figure 8-12). The subject, referred to as SF, had average memory abilities and average intelligence for a college student. For a year and a half, he engaged in a memory-span task for about 3 to 5 hours per week. During this extensive practice, SF, a good long-distance runner, devised the strategy of recoding sets of four digits into running times. For example, SF would recode 3492 as "3:49.2—world class time for the mile," which for him was a single chunk. Since SF was familiar with many running times (that is, had them stored in long-term memory), he could readily chunk most sets of four digits. In those cases in which he could not (1771 cannot be a running time because the second digit is too large), SF tried to recode the four digits into either a familiar date or the age of some person or object.

Use of the above recoding systems enabled SF to increase his memory span from seven to 28 digits (because each of SF's seven chunks contains four digits). SF then built to nearly 80 digits by hierarchically organizing the running times. Thus, one chunk in SF's short-term memory might have pointed to three running times; at the time of recall, SF would go from this chunk to the first running time and produce its four digits, then move to the second running time in the chunk and produce its digits, and so on. One chunk was therefore worth 12 digits. In this way SF achieved his remarkable span of nearly 80 digits. It was due to increasing the *size* of a chunk (by relating the items to information in long-term memory), not to increasing the *number* of chunks that short-term memory can hold. For when SF switched from digits to letters, his memory span went back to seven—that is, seven letters (Ericsson, Chase, & Faloon, 1980).

Lest you think that SF is unique, researchers have used the same procedure—constant practice on a memory-span task—to produce another short-term memory whiz. This subject, referred to as DD, is also a runner and used a similar method of recoding to running times. He was able to increase his memory span to 106 digits (Waldrop, 1987).

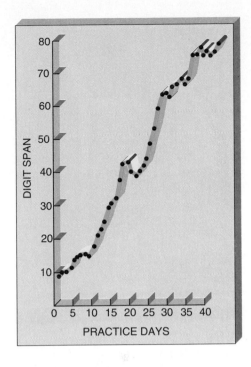

**FIGURE 8-12**
**Number of Digits Recalled by SF**
*This subject greatly increased his memory span for digits by devising a recoding system using chunking and hierarchical organization. Total practice time was about 215 hours.* (After Ericsson, Chase, & Faloon, 1980)

**FIGURE 8-13**
**A Mnemonic System** *The method of loci aids memory by associating items (here, entries on a shopping list) with an ordered sequence of places.*

Caballo → eye → Horse

Pato → pot → Duck

**FIGURE 8-14**
**Foreign Language Learning** *Mental images can be used to associate spoken Spanish words with corresponding English words. Here, possible images for learning the Spanish words for "horse" and "duck" are illustrated.*

This research reflects a relatively recent interest in improving short-term memory. In contrast, there has long been interest in how to improve long-term memory, which is the focus of the rest of this section. We will look first at how material can be encoded to make it easier to retrieve and then consider how the act of retrieval itself can be improved.

## Imagery and Encoding

We mentioned earlier that we can improve the recall of unrelated items by adding meaningful connections between them at the time of encoding, for these connections will later facilitate retrieval. Mental images turn out to be particularly useful for connecting pairs of unrelated items, and for this reason imagery is the major ingredient in many **mnemonic** (memory-*aiding*) systems.

One famous mnemonic system is called the **method of loci** (*loci* is Latin for "places"). The method works especially well with an ordered sequence of arbitrary items, like unrelated words. The first step is to commit to memory an ordered sequence of places, say the locations you would come upon in a slow walk through your house. You enter through the front door into a hallway, move next to the bookcase in the living room, then to the television in the living room, then to the curtains at the window, and so on. Once you can easily take this mental walk, you are ready to memorize as many unrelated words as there are locations on your walk. You form an image that relates the first word to the first location, another image that relates the second word to the second location, and so on. If the words are items on a shopping list—for example, "bread," "eggs," "beer," "milk," and "bacon"—you might imagine a slice of bread nailed to your front door, an egg hanging from the light cord in the hallway, a can of beer in the bookcase, a milk commercial playing on your television, and curtains made from giant strips of bacon (see Figure 8-13). Once you have memorized the items this way, you can easily recall them in order by simply taking your mental walk again. Each location will retrieve an image, and each image will retrieve a word. The method clearly works and is a favorite among those who perform memory feats professionally.

Imagery is also used in the **key-word method** of learning a foreign vocabulary. (See Table 8-3.) Suppose you had to learn that the Spanish word *caballo* means "horse." The key-word method has two steps. The first is to find a part of the foreign word that sounds like an English word. Since *caballo* is pronounced "cob-eye-yo," "eye" could serve as the key word. The next step is to form an image that connects the key word and the English equivalent—for example, a horse kicking a giant eye (see Figure 8-14). This should establish a meaningful connection between the Spanish and English words. To recall the meaning of *caballo*, you would first retrieve the key word "eye" and then the stored image that links it to "horse." Note that the key-word method can also be used to get from English words to Spanish words. If you want to recall the Spanish word for "horse," you would first retrieve the image involving a horse, thereby obtaining the key word "eye" that serves as a retrieval cue for *caballo*. The key-word method may sound complicated, but studies have shown that it greatly facilitates learning the vocabulary of a foreign language (Atkinson, 1975; Pressley, Levin, & Delaney, 1982).

## Elaboration and Encoding

We have seen that the more we elaborate items, the more we can subsequently recall or recognize them. This phenomenon arises because the more connections we establish between items, the larger the number of retrieval possibilities. The practical implications of these findings are straightforward: if you want to remember some fact, expand on its meaning. To illustrate, suppose you read a newspaper article about an epidemic in Brooklyn that health officials are trying to contain. To expand on this, you could ask yourself questions about the causes and consequences of the epidemic: Was the disease carried by a person or an animal? Was the disease transmitted through the water supply? To contain the epidemic, will officials go so far as to stop outsiders from visiting Brooklyn. How long is the epidemic likely to last? Questions about the causes and consequences of an event are particularly effective elaborations because each question sets up a meaningful connection, or retrieval path, to the event.

## Context and Retrieval

Since context is a powerful retrieval cue, we can improve our memory by restoring the context in which the learning took place. If your psychology lecture always meets in one room, your recall of the lecture material may be better when you are in that room than in a different building entirely, because the context of the room is a retrieval cue for the lecture material. Most often, though, when we have to remember something, we cannot physically return to the context in which we learned it. If you are having difficulty remembering the name of a particular high-school classmate, you are not about to go back to your high school just to recall it. In these situations, however, you can try to recreate the context mentally. To retrieve the long forgotten name, you might think of different classes, clubs, and other activities that you were in during high school to see if any of these bring to mind the name you are seeking. When subjects used these techniques in an actual experiment, they were often able to recall the names of high-school classmates that they were sure they had forgotten (Williams & Hollan, 1981).

## Organization

We know that organization during encoding improves subsequent retrieval. This principle can be put to great practical use: we are capable of storing and retrieving a massive amount of information if only we organize it.

Some experiments have investigated organizational devices that can be used to learn many unrelated items. In one study, subjects memorized lists of unrelated words by organizing the words in each list into a story, as illustrated in Figure 8-15. Later, when tested for 12 such lists (a total of 120 words), subjects recalled more than 90 percent of the words. This appears to be a truly remarkable memory feat, but anyone can do it easily.

At this point, you might concede that psychologists have devised some ingenious techniques for organizing lists of unrelated items. But, you argue, what you have to remember are not lists of unrelated items but stories you were told, lectures you have heard, and readings like the present chapter.

| SPANISH | KEY WORD | ENGLISH |
|---------|----------|---------|
| caballo | (eye) | horse |
| charco | (charcoal) | puddle |
| muleta | (mule) | crutch |
| clavo | (claw) | nail |
| lagartija | (log) | lizard |
| payaso | (pie) | clown |
| hiio | (eel) | thread |
| tenaza | (tennis) | pliers |
| jabon | (bone) | soap |
| carpa | (carp) | tent |
| pato | (pot) | duck |

**TABLE 8-3**
**Key-word Method** *Examples of key words used to link Spanish words to their English translation. For example, when the Spanish word muleta is pronounced, part of it sounds like the English word "mule." Thus, "mule" could be used as the key word and linked to the English translation by forming an image of a mule standing erect on a crutch.*

**FIGURE 8-15**
**Organizing Words into a Story** *Three examples of turning a list of 10 unrelated words into a story. The capitalized items are the words on the list.* (After Bower & Clark, 1969)

A LUMBERJACK DARTed out of a forest, SKATEd around a HEDGE past a COLONY of DUCKs. He tripped on some FURNITURE, tearing his STOCKING while hastening toward the PILLOW where his MISTRESS lay.

A VEGETABLE can be a useful INSTRUMENT for a COLLEGE student. A carrot can be a NAIL for your FENCE or BASIN. But a MERCHANT of the QUEEN would SCALE that fence and feed the carrot to a GOAT.

One night at DINNER I had the NERVE to bring my TEACHER. There had been a FLOOD that day, and the rain BARREL was sure to RATTLE. There was, however, a VESSEL in the HARBOR carrying this ARTIST to my CASTLE.

Isn't this kind of material already organized, and doesn't this mean that the previously mentioned techniques are of limited value? Yes and no. Yes, this chapter is more than a list of unrelated sentences, but—and this is the critical point—there is always a problem of organization with any lengthy material, including this chapter. Later you may be able to recall that elaborating meaning aids learning, but this may not bring to mind anything about, say, acoustic coding in short-term memory. The two topics do not seem to be intimately related, but there is a relation between them: both deal with encoding phenomena. The best way to see that relationship is to note the headings and subheadings in the chapter, because these show how the material in the chapter is organized. A most effective way to study is to keep this organization in mind. You might, for example, try to capture part of this chapter's organization by sketching a hierarchical tree like the one shown in Figure 8-16. Then you can use such a hierarchy to guide your memory search whenever you have to retrieve information about this chapter. It may be even more helpful, though, to make your own hierarchical outline of the chapter. Memory seems to benefit most when the organization is done by the rememberers themselves.

**FIGURE 8-16**
**A Hierarchical Tree** *Creating hierarchical trees of chapters in textbooks can help students retrieve information about those chapters. This tree represents the organization of this chapter.*

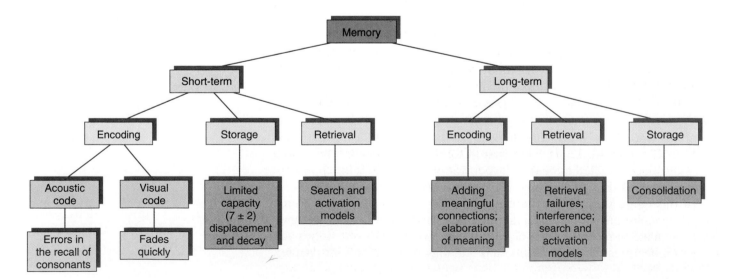

## Practicing Retrieval

Another way to improve retrieval is to practice it—that is, to ask yourself questions about what you are trying to learn. Suppose you have 2 hours in which to study an assignment that can be read in approximately 30 minutes. Reading and rereading the assignment four times is generally much less effective than reading it once and asking yourself questions about it. You can then reread selected parts to clear up points that were difficult to retrieve the first time around, perhaps elaborating these points so they become particularly well connected to each other and to the rest of the assignment. Attempting retrieval is an efficient use of study time. This was demonstrated long ago by experiments using material like that actually learned in courses (see Figure 8-17).

A procedure akin to practicing retrieval may be useful in implicit memory situations. The procedure is referred to as **mental practice,** and it involves the imagined rehearsal of perceptual-motor skill in the absence of any gross body movements. For example, you might imagine yourself swinging at a tennis ball, making mental corrections when the imagined swing seems faulty, without even really moving your arm. Such mental practice can improve performance of the skill, particularly if the mental practice is interspersed with actual physical practice (Swets & Bjork, 1990).

## PQRST Method

Thus far in this section, we have considered particular principles of memory (for example, the principle that organization aids memory search) and then shown their implications for improving memory. In establishing the practical application of memory principles, we can also go in the opposite direction. We can start with a well-known technique for improving memory and show how it is based on principles of memory.

One of the best-known techniques for improving memory, called the **PQRST method,** is intended to improve a student's ability to study and remember material presented in a textbook (Thomas & Robinson, 1982). The method takes its name from the first letters of its five stages: *Preview, Question, Read, Self-Recitation,* and *Test.* We can illustrate the method by showing how it would apply to studying a chapter in this textbook. In the first stage, students preview the material in a chapter to get an idea of its major topics and sections. Previewing involves reading the chapter outline at the beginning of the chapter, skimming the chapter while paying special attention to the headings of main sections and subsections, and carefully reading the summary at the end of the chapter. This kind of preview induces students to organize the chapter, perhaps even leading to the rudiments of a hierarchical organization like that shown above. As we have repeatedly noted, organizing material aids one's ability to retrieve it.

The second, third, and fourth stages (Question, Read, and Self-Recitation) apply to each major section of the chapter as it is encountered. In this book, for example, a chapter typically has five to eight major sections, and students would apply the Question, Read, and Self-Recitation stages to each section before going on to the next one. In the Question stage, students carefully read the section and subsection headings and turn these into questions. In the Read stage, students read the section with an eye toward answering these questions. And in the Self-Recitation stage, the reader tries

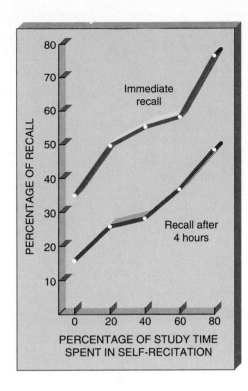

**FIGURE 8-17**
**Practicing Retrieval** *Recall can be improved by spending a large proportion of study time attempting retrieval rather than silently studying. Results are shown for tests given immediately and 4 hours after completing study.* (After Gates, 1917)

*The PQRST method increases understand-ing and retention.*

to recall the main ideas in the section and recites the information (either sub-vocally or, preferably, aloud). For example, if you were applying these stages to the present section of this chapter, you might look at the headings and make up such questions as "How much can the short-term memory span be increased?" or "What exactly is the PQRST method?" Next you would read this section and try to determine answers to your questions (for example, "One person was able to increase his short-term memory span to nearly 80 digits"). Then you would try to recall the main ideas (for example, "You can increase the size of a chunk but not the number of chunks"). The Question and Read stages almost certainly induce students to elaborate the material while encoding it; the Self-Recitation stage induces the student to practice retrieval.

The fifth, or Test, stage occurs after finishing an entire chapter. Students try to recall the main facts from what they have read and to under-stand how the various facts relate to one another. This stage prompts elabo-ration and offers further practice at retrieval. In summary, the PQRST method relies on three basic principles for improving memory: organizing the material, elaborating the material, and practicing retrieval. (For a more in-depth description of the method, see Appendix I.)

## Constructive Memory

In previous chapters, we distinguished between bottom-up and top-down processes, whereby **bottom-up processes** are driven by the input, whereas **top-down processes** are driven by the person's prior knowledge and ex-pectancies. Thus, recall from Chapter 5 that the perception of an object is based partly on the physical characteristics of the input object (bottom-up processes) and partly on the observer's expectations (top-down processes).

The distinction can be applied to memory as well. Bottom-up processes work only on the input information, the actual items that have to be remembered, while top-down processes bring other knowledge to bear on the task. Most of the material we have covered thus far in the chapter deals with bottom-up processes. In the final section, we consider top-down processes, which add information to the input and result in what is called **constructive memory.**

When we hear a sentence or story, we often take it as an incomplete description of a real event, and we use our general knowledge about how the world works to construct a more complete description of the event. How do we do this? By adding to the sentences and stories statements that are likely to follow from them. For example, on hearing "Mike broke the bottle in a barroom brawl," we are likely to infer that it was a beer or whiskey bottle, not a milk or soda bottle. We add this inference to our memory of the sentence itself. Our total memory therefore goes beyond the original information given. We fill in the original information by using our general knowledge about what goes with what (for example, that beer bottles go with bars). We do this because we are trying to explain to ourselves the events we are hearing about. Constructive memory, then, is a by-product of our need to understand the world.

## Simple Inferences

Often when we read a sentence we draw inferences from it and store the inferences along with the sentence. This tendency is particularly strong when reading real text because inferences are often needed to connect different lines. To illustrate, consider the following story, which was presented to subjects in an experiment.

1. Provo is a picturesque kingdom in France.
2. Corman was heir to the throne of Provo.
3. He was so tired of waiting.
4. He thought arsenic would work well.

When reading this story, subjects draw inferences at certain points. At line 3, they infer that Corman wanted to be king, which permits them to connect line 3 to the preceding line. But this is not a necessary inference (Corman could have been waiting for the king to receive him). At line 4, subjects infer that Corman had decided to poison the king, so they can connect this line to what preceded it. Again, the inference is not a necessary one (there are people other than the king to poison, and there are other uses of arsenic). When subjects' memories were later tested for exactly which lines had been presented, they had trouble distinguishing the story lines from the inferences we just described. It is hard to keep separate what was actually presented from what we added to it (Seifert, Robertson, & Black, 1985).

Inferences can also affect memory for visual scenes. This point is strikingly illustrated in the following study. Subjects were shown a film of a traffic accident and then were asked questions about their memory of the accident. One question about the speed of the vehicles was asked in two different ways. Some subjects were asked, "How fast were the cars going when they smashed into each other?" whereas others were asked, "How fast were the cars going when they hit each other?" Subjects asked the "smashed" question might infer that the accident was a very destructive one, perhaps more

**FIGURE 8-18**
**Reconstructing a Memory of an Accident** *The picture at the top represents the subject's original memory for the accident. Then comes the "smashed" question, which leads the subject to draw inferences about the destructiveness of the accident. These inferences may be used to reconstruct the original memory so that it looks more like the picture on the bottom.* (After Loftus & Loftus, 1975)

destructive than they had actually remembered. These subjects were likely to use this inference somehow to alter their memory of the accident to make it more destructive (see Figure 8-18). Subjects asked the "hit" question, however, should be less likely to do this, since "hit" implies a less severe accident than does "smashed."

This line of reasoning was supported by the results of a memory test given 1 week later. In this test, subjects were asked, "Did you see any broken glass?" There was no broken glass in the film of the accident, but subjects who had been asked the "smashed" question were more likely to say mistakenly that there had been glass than were subjects who had been asked the "hit" question. The "smashed" question may have led to reconstruction of the memory for the accident, and the reconstructed memory contained details, such as broken glass, that were never actually part of the accident (Loftus, Schooler, & Wagenaar, 1985). These results have important implications for eyewitness identification: a question phrased in a particular way ("smashed" rather than "hit") can alter the witness's memory structures that an attorney is trying to probe.

## Stereotypes

Another means by which we fill in, or construct, memories is through the use of social **stereotypes**. A stereotype is a packet of inferences about the personality traits or physical attributes of a whole class of people. We may, for example, have a stereotype of the typical German (intelligent, meticulous, serious) or of the typical Italian (artistic, carefree, fun loving). These descriptions rarely apply to many people in the class and can often be misleading guides for social interaction. Our concern here, however, is not with the effects of stereotypes on social interaction (see Chapter 18 for a discussion of this) but with the effects of stereotypes on memory.

When presented with information about a person, we sometimes stereotype that person (for example, "He's your typical Italian") and then combine the information presented with that in our stereotype. Our memory of the person is thus partly constructed from the stereotype. To the extent that our stereotype does not fit the person, our recall can be seriously distorted. Hunter, a British psychologist, provides a firsthand account of such a distortion:

> In the week beginning 23 October, I encountered in the university, a male student of very conspicuously Scandinavian appearance. I recall being very forcibly impressed by the man's nordic, Viking-like appearance—his fair hair, his blue eyes, and long bones. On several occasions, I recalled his appearance in connection with a Scandinavian correspondence I was then conducting and thought of him as the "perfect Viking," visualizing him at the helm of a long-ship crossing the North Sea in quest of adventure. When I again saw the man on 23 November, I did not recognize him, and he had to introduce himself. It was not that I had forgotten what he looked like but that his appearance, as I recalled it, had become grossly distorted. He was very different from my recollection of him. His hair was darker, his eyes less blue, his build less muscular, and he was wearing spectacles (as he always does). (Hunter, 1974, pp. 265–66)

Hunter's stereotype of Scandinavians seems to have so overwhelmed any information he actually encoded about the student's appearance that the result was a highly constructed memory. It bore so little resemblance to the student that it could not even serve as a basis for recognition.

Stereotypes may also work retroactively on memory. We may first hear a relatively neutral description of a person, later find out this person belongs to a particular category, and then use our stereotype of that category to augment our memory of the original description. In a study demonstrating this phenomenon, subjects first read a narrative about events in the life of a woman named Betty K. The narrative followed Betty K's life from birth to early adulthood and contained facts about her social life, such as, "Although she never had a steady boyfriend in high school, she did go out on dates." After reading the story, subjects were given additional facts about Betty K that would lead to stereotyping her. One group of subjects was told that Betty later adopted a lesbian life-style. A second group was told that she later married. Apparently, the first group fit Betty to their stereotype of lesbians, whereas the second group fit her to their stereotype of married women. The stereotyping affected subsequent recognition of the original narrative. Subjects told about Betty's later lesbian activities were more likely to remember that "she never had a steady boyfriend" than that "she did go out on dates." Subjects told about Betty's later marriage did the reverse. Both groups may have reconstructed their memory of the original narrative to make it fit their stereotypes, or they may have used their stereotypes to answer questions when they could not remember the original narrative (Snyder & Uranowitz, 1978; Bellezza & Bower, 1981). Thus, memory for people seems to be particularly susceptible to construction; our memory is a compromise between what is and what we think should be.

*The stereotype of a Scandinavian: blond hair and blue eyes.*

## Schemata

Psychologists use the term **schema** (*schemata* for plural) to refer to a mental representation of a class of people, objects, events, or situations. Stereotypes are thus a kind of schema because they represent classes of people (for example, Italians, women, gays). Similarly, common categories such as *dog* and *table* are another kind of schema because they represent classes of objects. Schemata can also be used to describe our knowledge about how to act in certain situations. For example, most adults have a schema for how to eat in a restaurant (enter the restaurant, find a table, get a menu from the waiter, order food, and so on). Perceiving and thinking in terms of schemata permits us to process large amounts of information swiftly and economically. Instead of having to perceive and remember all the details of each new person, object, or event we encounter, we can simply note that it is like a schema already in memory and encode and remember only its most distinctive features. The price we pay for such "cognitive economy," however, is that an object or event can be distorted if the schema used to encode it does not fit well.

Bartlett (1932) was perhaps the first psychologist to study systematically the effect of schemata on memory. He suggested that memory distortions, much like those that occur when we fit people into stereotypes, can occur when we attempt to fit stories into schemata. Research has confirmed Bartlett's suggestion. For example, after reading a brief story about a character going to a restaurant, subjects are likely to recall statements about the character eating and paying for a meal, even when those actions were never mentioned in the story (Bower, Black, & Turner, 1979).

Schemata seem to affect both the encoding and retrieval stages of long-term memory. If a particular schema is active when we read a story, we tend

*The schema of eating in a restaurant includes knowing that one normally orders an appetizer, a main course, and a dessert, rather than three bowls of soup.*

to encode mainly the facts that are related to the schema. We can illustrate with the following simple story:

1. Steven and Edgar went to a movie.
2. Steven and Edgar talked about business while waiting in line.
3. Steven liked the film, but Edgar thought it was too sentimental.

Assuming that Sentence No. 1 activates our movie schema, we are more likely to encode Sentence No. 3 than No. 2 because Sentence No. 3 is more related to the schema. In later recalling this story, if we could remember that it had to do with going to a movie, we could use our movie schema to search our memory: for example, was there anything in the story about a reaction to the film? Thus, schemata can affect retrieval by guiding search processes (Brewer & Nakamura, 1984).

Situations in which memory is schema-driven and heavily constructive seem a far cry from the simpler situations we covered earlier. Consider, for example, memory for a list of unrelated words: here, memory processes appear more bottom-up; that is, their function is more to *preserve* the input than to *construct* something new. However, there is a constructive aspect even to this simple situation, for techniques such as using imagery add meaning to the input. Similarly, when we read a paragraph about a schema-based activity we must still preserve some of its specifics if we are to recall it correctly in detail. Thus, the two aspects of memory—to preserve and to construct—may always be present, although their relative emphasis may depend on the exact situation.

1. There are three stages of memory: *encoding, storage,* and *retrieval.* Encoding refers to the transformation of information into the kind of code or representation that memory can accept; storage is the retention of the encoded information; and retrieval refers to the process by which information is recovered from memory. The three stages may operate differently in situations that require us to store material for a matter of seconds *(short-term memory)* and in situations that require us to store material for longer intervals *(long-term memory).*

2. Information in short-term memory tends to be encoded *acoustically,* although we can also use a *visual code.* The most striking fact about short-term memory is that its storage capacity is limited to $7 \pm 2$ items, or *chunks.* While we are limited in the number of chunks, we can increase the size of a chunk by using information in long-term memory to *recode* incoming material into larger meaningful units. When the limit of short-term memory is reached, a form of forgetting occurs: a new item can enter short-term memory only by *displacing* an old one. The other major cause of forgetting in short-term memory is that information *decays* with time.

3. Retrieval slows down as the number of items in short-term memory increases. Some have taken this result to indicate that retrieval involves a *search process,* whereas others have interpreted the result in terms of an *activation process.*

4. Short-term memory seems to serve as a mental "work space" in solving certain kinds of problems, such as mental arithmetic and answering questions about text. However, short-term memory does not seem to be involved in the understanding of relatively simple sentences. Short-term memory may also serve the function of being a way-station to permanent memory, in that information may reside in short-term memory while it is being encoded into long-term memory.

5. Information in long-term memory is usually encoded according to its *meaning.* If the items to be remembered are meaningful but the connections between them are not, memory can be improved by adding meaningful connections that provide retrieval paths. The more one *elaborates* the meaning, the better memory will be.

6. Many cases of forgetting in long-term memory are due to *retrieval failures* (the information is there but cannot be found). Retrieval failures are more likely to occur when there is *interference* from items associated with the same retrieval cue. Such interference effects suggest that retrieval from long-term memory may be accomplished by a *sequential search* process or a *spreading activation* process.

7. Some forgetting from long-term memory is due to a loss from storage, particularly when there is a disruption of the processes that *consolidate* new memories. The biological locus of consolidation includes the *hippocampus* and *amygdala,* brain structures located below the cerebral cortex. Recent work suggests that consolidation takes a matter of a few weeks.

8. Retrieval failures in long-term memory are less likely to happen when the items are *organized* during encoding and when the *context* at retrieval is similar to that at encoding. Retrieval processes can also be disrupted by *emotional factors.* In some cases, anxious thoughts interfere with retrieval of the target memory; in others, the target memory may be actively blocked *(repression hypothesis).* In still other cases, emotion can enhance memory, as in *flashbulb memories.*

*Chapter* **SUMMARY**

9. *Explicit memory* refers to the kind of memory manifested in recall or recognition, where we consciously recollect the past. *Implicit memory* refers to the kind of memory that manifests itself as an improvement on some perceptual, motor, or cognitive task with no conscious recollection of the experiences that led to the improvement. While explicit memory—particularly recall and recognition of facts—breaks down in *amnesia*, implicit memory is usually spared. This suggests that there may be separate storage systems for explicit and implicit memory.

10. Research with normal subjects also suggests that there may be separate systems for explicit and implicit memory. Much of this research has relied on a measure of implicit memory called *priming* (for example, the extent to which prior exposure to a list of words later facilitates completing fragments of these words). Some studies reveal that an independent variable that affects explicit memory (amount of elaboration during encoding) has no effect on priming, while other studies show that a variable that affects implicit memory has no effect on explicit memory. While some researchers favor the idea of separate stores for different kinds of explicit and implicit memories, others argue that the apparent differences in memory are really due to different retrieval processes operating on a common store.

11. Although we cannot increase the capacity of short-term memory, we can use *recoding* schemes to enlarge the size of a chunk and thereby increase the memory span. Long-term memory for facts can be improved at the encoding and retrieval stages. One way to improve encoding and retrieval is to use imagery, which is the basic principle underlying mnemonic systems such as the *method of loci* and the *key-word method*.

12. Other ways to improve encoding (and subsequent retrieval) are to elaborate the meaning of the items and to organize the material during encoding (hierarchical organization seems best). The best ways to improve retrieval are to attempt to restore the encoding context at the time of retrieval and to practice retrieving information while learning it. Most of these principles for improving encoding and retrieval are incorporated into the *PQRST method* of studying a textbook, whose five stages are *Preview, Question, Read, Self-Recitation*, and *Test*.

13. Memory for complex materials, such as stories, is often *constructive*. We tend to use our general knowledge of the world to construct a more complete memory of a story or an event. Construction can involve adding simple *inferences* to the material presented; it can also involve fitting the material into *stereotypes* and other kinds of *schemata* (mental representations of classes of people, objects, events, or situations).

*Further* **READING**

There are several introductory books on memory that are readable and up-to-date: Baddeley, *Human Memory* (1990); Ashcraft, *Human Memory and Cognition* (1989); Ellis and Hunt, *Fundamentals of Human Memory and Cognition*, (4th ed., 1989); Anderson, *Cognitive Psychology and Its Implications* (3rd ed., 1990); Glass and Holyoak, *Cognition* (2nd ed., 1986). In addition to these textbooks, Neisser (ed.), *Memory Observed* (1982), provides a survey of remembering in natural contexts.

For an advanced treatment of theoretical issues in memory, see Anderson, *The Architecture of Cognition* (1983); Tulving, *Elements of Episodic Memory*

(1983); the second volume of Atkinson, Herrnstein, Lindzey, and Luce (eds.), *Steven's Handbook of Experimental Psychology* (2nd ed., 1988); and Baddeley, *Working Memory* (1986).

For a review of research on the biological bases of memory and learning, see Squire and Butters (eds.), *The Neuropsychology of Memory* (1984); and Squire, *Memory and Brain* (1987).

# Chapter 9

# Thought and Language

### Concepts and Categories 331
*Functions of Concepts*
*Prototypes*
*Hierarchies of Concepts*
*Acquiring Concepts*
*Critical Discussion: Linguistic Relativity Hypothesis*
*Combining Concepts*

### Reasoning 339
*Deductive Reasoning*
*Inductive Reasoning*

### Language and Communication 344
*Levels of Language*
*Language Units and Processes*
*Effects of Context on Comprehension and Production*

### Development of Language 350
*What is Acquired?*
*Learning Processes*
*Innate Factors*
*Can Another Species Learn Human Language?*
*Critical Discussion: Brain Localization*

### Imaginal Thought 359
*Imagery and Perception*
*Imaginal Operations*
*Visual Creativity*

### Thought in Action: Problem Solving 361
*Problem-Solving Strategies*
*Representing the Problem*
*Experts versus Novices*
*Computer Simulation*

Detail, *Hollyhocks.*

The greatest accomplishments of our species stem from our ability to entertain complex thoughts and to communicate them. Thinking includes a wide range of mental activities. We think when we try to solve a problem that has been presented to us in class; we think when we daydream while waiting for that class to begin. We think when we decide what groceries to buy, plan a vacation, write a letter, or worry about a troubled relationship.

In all cases, thought can be conceived of as a "language of the mind." Introspection suggests that there is more than one language. One *mode of thought* corresponds to the stream of sentences that we seem to "hear in our mind"; this is referred to as *propositional thought* (because it expresses a proposition or claim). Another mode corresponds to images, particularly visual ones, that we can "see" in our mind; this is *imaginal thought*. Finally, there may be a third mode, *motoric thought*, which corresponds to sequences of "mental movements" (Bruner, Olver, Greenfield et al., 1966). While studies of cognitive development have paid some attention to motoric thought in children, research on thinking in adults has emphasized the other two modes, particularly the propositional one; this emphasis is reflected in the current chapter.

The next four sections discuss major topics in propositional thinking. In the first section, we focus on concepts, which are the building blocks of thought, and discuss their use in classifying objects; this is the study of *concepts and categorization*. Then we consider how thoughts are organized in the service of drawing some conclusion; this is the study of *reasoning*. Next, we deal with how thoughts are communicated, which is the study of *language*, and then we consider the development of such communication, or the study of *language acquisition*. We then turn to the imaginal mode of thought. In the final section, we will discuss thought in action—the study of *problem solving*—and consider the uses of both propositional and imaginal thought.

## Concepts and Categories

We can think of a proposition as a statement that expresses a factual claim. "Mothers are hard workers" is one proposition, and "Cats are animals" is another. It is easy to see that such a thought consists of concepts—such as "mothers" and "hard workers" or "cat" and "animal"—combined in a particular way. To understand propositional thought, we first need to understand the concepts that compose it.

### Functions of Concepts

A **concept** represents an entire class—it is the set of properties that we associate with the class. Our concept of "cat" for example, includes, among other things, the properties of having four legs and whiskers. Concepts serve some major functions in mental life. One is that concepts foster *cognitive economy* by dividing the world into manageable units. The world is full of so many different objects that if we treated each one as distinct, we would soon be overwhelmed. For example, if we had to refer to every single object we encountered by a different name, our vocabulary would have to be gigantic—so immense that communication might be impossible. (Think of what it would be like if we had a separate name for each of the seven million colors we can discriminate!) Fortunately, we do not treat each object as unique;

rather, we see it as an instance of a concept or class. Thus, many different objects are seen as instances of the concept "cat," many others as instances of the concept "chair," and so on. By treating different objects as members of the same concept, we reduce the complexity of the world that we have to represent mentally.

Assigning an object to a concept is referred to as **categorization**. When we categorize an object, we treat it as if it has many of the properties associated with the concept, including properties that we have not directly perceived. Hence a second major function of concepts is that they allow us to *predict information* that is not readily perceived. For example, our concept of "apple" is associated with such hard-to-perceive properties as having seeds and being edible, as well as with readily visible properties like being round, having a distinctive color, and being found on trees. We may use the visible properties to categorize some object as an "apple" (the object is red, round, and hangs from a tree), and then infer that the object has the less visible properties as well (it has seeds and is edible). Concepts, then, enable us to go beyond the information given (Bruner, 1957)

We also have concepts of activities, such as "eating"; of states, such as "being old"; and of abstractions, such as "truth," "justice," or even the number "two." In each case we know something about the properties common to members of the concept. Widely used concepts like these generally are associated with a one-word name. This allows us to communicate quickly about experiences that occur frequently. We can also make up concepts on the spot, to serve some specific goal. For example, if you are planning an outing, you might generate the concept "things to take on a camping trip." These kinds of *goal-driven concepts* serve the function of facilitating planning. While such concepts are used relatively infrequently, and accordingly have relatively long names, they still provide us with some cognitive economy and predictive power (Barsalou, 1985).

*The concept of "apple" includes roundness and distinctness of flavor.*

## Prototypes

The properties associated with a concept seem to fall into two sets. One set of properties makes up the **prototype** of the concept, that is, those properties that describe the best examples of the concept. In the concept "bachelor," for example, your prototype might include such properties as a man who is in his 30s, lives alone, and has an active social life. The prototype is what usually comes to mind when we think of the concept. But while the prototype properties may be true of the typical examples of a bachelor, they are clearly not true of all instances (think of an uncle in his 60s who boards with his sister and rarely goes out). This means that a concept must contain something in addition to a prototype; this additional something is a **core** that comprises the properties that are most important for being a member of the concept. Your core of the concept "bachelor" would probably include the properties of being adult, male, and unmarried; these properties are essential for being a member of the concept (Armstrong, Gleitman, & Gleitman, 1983).

As another example, consider the concept "bird." Your prototype likely includes the properties of flying and chirping—which works for the best examples of "bird," such as robins and blue jays, but not for other examples, such as ostriches and penguins. Your core would likely specify something about the biological basis of birdhood—the fact that it involves having certain genes or, at least having parents that are birds.

Note that in both our examples—"bachelor" and "bird"—the prototype properties are salient but not perfect indicators of concept membership, whereas the core properties are diagnostic of concept membership. However, the prototype and core play different roles in concepts like "bachelor" than they do in concepts like "bird." In "bachelor," because the core properties (being adult, for example) are as salient as the prototype properties (being in one's 30s), we primarily use the core in categorizing instances of the concept. In "bird," the core properties (genes) are hidden from view, and consequently we primarily use the prototype in determining membership in the concept. Thus, happening on a small animal, we can hardly inspect its genes or inquire about its parentage. All we can do is check whether it does certain things such as fly and chirp, and use this information to decide whether it is a bird. Concepts like "bachelor" are called **classical concepts,** while concepts like "bird" are called **fuzzy.** Deciding whether an object is a classical concept involves determining whether it has the core properties of the concept; determining whether an object is a fuzzy concept involves determining its similarity to the concept's prototype (Smith, 1989).

Some instances of fuzzy concepts will have more prototype properties than other instances. Among birds, for example, a robin will have the property of flying, whereas an ostrich will not. And the more prototype properties an instance has, the more typical people will consider that instance to be of the concept. Thus, of "bird," most people rate a robin as more typical than an ostrich; of "apple," they rate red apples as more typical than green ones (since red seems to be a property of the concept "apple"); and so on. The *typicality* of an instance has a major effect on its categorization. When people are asked whether or not a pictured animal is a "bird," a robin produces an immediate "yes," whereas a chicken requires a longer decision time. When young children are asked the same question, a robin will almost inevitably be correctly classified, whereas often a chicken will be declared a nonbird (Rosch, 1978).

Categorization is not always a matter of checking whether an object has core properties or of determining the object's similarity to a prototype. Sometimes categorization involves reasoning about the object. To illustrate, suppose that while at a party you were to see a man jump into a pool fully clothed. You would probably categorize him as "being drunk." But jumping into a pool fully clothed is certainly not a core property of "being drunk"; nor it is likely even a prototype property of "being drunk." Rather than checking properties, in this case you seem to be reasoning that: (1) alcohol is often present at parties: (2) drinking alcohol can put one in a state of being drunk; (3) being drunk can lead one to do extreme things; and (4) one example of an extreme thing is jumping into a pool fully clothed. Thus while many categorizations are based on quick checks of an objects' properties, some are based on a slower, deliberative reasoning process (Murphy & Medin, 1985).

## Hierarchies of Concepts

In addition to knowing the properties of concepts, we also know how concepts relate to one another. For example, "apples" are members (or a subset) of a larger concept, "fruit"; "robins" are a subset of "birds," which in turn are a subset of "animals." These two types of knowledge (properties of a concept and relationships between concepts) are represented in Figure 9-1 as a hierarchy. Such a hierarchy allows us to infer that a concept has a particular property even when it is not associated directly with that concept. Suppose you do not have the property of being sweet associated directly with "McIntosh apple." If you were asked, "Is a McIntosh apple sweet?" presumably you would enter your mental hierarchy at "McIntosh apple" (see Figure 9-1), trace a path from "McIntosh apple" to "fruit," find the property of being sweet stored at "fruit," and respond "yes." This idea implies that the time needed to establish a relation between a concept and a property should increase with the distance between them in the hierarchy. This prediction has been confirmed in experiments in which subjects were asked

**FIGURE 9-1**
**Hierarchy of Concepts** *Words in capital letters represent concepts; lowercase words depict properties of these concepts. The blue lines show relationships between concepts, and the red lines connect properties and concepts.*

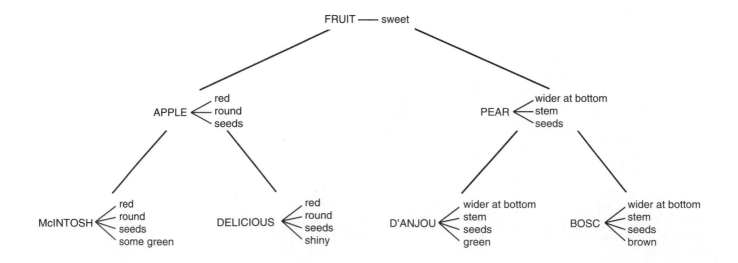

questions such as, "Is an apple sweet?" and "Is a McIntosh apple sweet?" Subjects took longer to answer the McIntosh apple question than the apple question, because the distance in the hierarchy between "McIntosh apple" and "sweet" is greater than that between "apple" and "sweet" (Collins & Loftus, 1975).

As the hierarchy in Figure 9-1 makes clear, an object can be identified at different levels. The same object is at once a "McIntosh apple," an "apple," and a "fruit." However, in any hierarchy, one level is the "basic" or preferred one for classification; this is the level at which we first categorize an object. For the hierarchy in Figure 9-1, the level that contains "apple" and "pear" would be the basic one. Evidence for this claim comes from studies in which people are asked to name pictured objects with the first names that come to mind. People are more likely to call a pictured McIntosh apple an "apple" than either a "McIntosh apple" or a "fruit." It seems then that we first divide the world into basic-level concepts. What determines which level is basic? The answer appears to be that the basic level is the one that has the most *distinctive properties*. In Figure 9-1, "apple" has several properties that are distinctive—they are not shared by other kinds of fruit (for example, red and round are not properties of "pear"). In contrast, "McIntosh apple" has few distinct properties; most of its properties are shared by "Delicious apple," for example (see Figure 9-1). And "fruit," which is at the highest level of Figure 9-1, has few properties of any kind. Thus, we categorize the world first at what turns out to be the most informative level (Mervis & Rosch, 1981).

## Acquiring Concepts

How do we acquire the multitude of concepts that we have? Some concepts may be inborn, such as the concepts of "time" and "space." Other concepts have to be learned.

**LEARNING PROTOTYPES AND CORES**  We can learn about a concept in different ways: either we are explicitly taught something about the concept, or we learn it through experience. Which way we learn depends on *what* we are learning. Explicit teaching is likely to be the means by which we learn cores of concepts, while experience seems to be the standard means by which we acquire prototypes. Thus, someone explicitly tells a child a "robber" is someone who takes another person's possessions with no intention of returning them (the core), while the child's experiences lead him or her to expect robbers to be shiftless, disheveled, and dangerous (the prototype).

Children must also learn that the core is a better indicator of concept membership than the prototype is. It takes a while for them to learn this. In one study, children aged 5 to 10 were presented with descriptions of items and had to decide whether or not they belonged to particular concepts. We can illustrate the study with the concept of "robber." One description given for "robber" depicted a person who matched its prototype but not its core:

A smelly, mean old man with a gun in his pocket who came to your house and takes your TV set because your parents didn't want it anymore and told him he could have it.

Another description used for "robber" was of a person who matched its core but not its prototype:

> A very friendly and cheerful woman who gave you a hug, but then disconnected your toilet bowl and took it away without permission and no intention to return it. (Keil & Batterman, 1984, p. 226)

The younger children often thought the prototypical description was more likely than the core description to be an instance of the concept. Not until age 10 did children show a clear shift from the prototype to the core as the final arbitrator of concept decisions (Keil & Batterman, 1984).

**LEARNING THROUGH EXPERIENCE**   There are at least three different ways in which one can learn a concept through experience with its instances. The simplest way is called the **exemplar strategy**, and we can illustrate it with a child learning the concept of "furniture." When the child encounters a known instance or exemplar—say, a table—she stores a representation of it. Later, when the child has to decide whether or not a new item—say, a desk—is an instance of "furniture," she determines the new object's similarity to stored exemplars of "furniture," including table. This strategy seems to be widely used by children, and it works better with typical instances than atypical ones. Because the first exemplars a child learns tend to be typical ones, new instances are more likely to be correctly classified to the extent they are similar to typical instances. Thus, if a young child's concept of "furniture" consisted of just the most typical instances (say, table and chair), she could correctly classify other instances that looked similar to the learned exemplars, such as "desk" and "sofa," but not instances that looked different from the learned exemplars, such as "lamp" and "bookshelf" (Mervis & Pani, 1981).

Although the exemplar strategy remains part of our repertory for acquiring concepts, as we grow older we start to use another strategy, **hypothesis testing.** We inspect known instances of a concept, searching for properties that are relatively common to them (for example, many pieces of "furniture" are found in living spaces), and we hypothesize that these common properties are what characterize the concept. We then analyze novel objects for these critical properties, maintaining our hypothesis if it leads to a correct categorization about the novel object and revamping it if it leads us astray. The strategy thus focuses on abstractions—on properties that characterize sets of instances rather than just single instances—and is tuned to finding core properties, since they are the ones common to most instances (Bruner, Goodenow & Austin, 1956).

Both the exemplar and hypothesis-testing strategies are driven solely by the input, the known instances, and give little weight to the learner's prior knowledge. In the preceding chapters, we have referred to such strategies as *bottom-up*, and contrasted them with *top-down* strategies, in which people make extensive use of their prior knowledge. In a top-down strategy of concept learning, people use their prior knowledge along with the known instances to determine the critical properties of a concept. An example is provided by the following study.

Two groups of adult subjects were presented the children's drawings shown in Figure 9-2. Their task was to describe the properties that characterized each category. One group of subjects was told that category 1 drawings were done by creative children, while category 2 drawings were done by noncreative children; the other group of subjects was told that category 1

*Category 1*

*Category 2*

**FIGURE 9-2**
**Top-Down Concept Learning** *In an experiment on concept learning, one group of subjects was told that category 1 drawings were done by creative children and category 2 drawings by noncreative children, while another group of subjects was told that category 1 drawings were done by city children and category 2 drawings by farm children. The two groups of subjects offered different kinds of descriptions of the categories. Furthermore, the same feature (for example, the pointed-to-object in the fourth figure of category 1) was sometimes interpreted differently by the two groups.* (After Wisniewski & Medin, 1991)

drawings were done by city children, while category 2 drawings were done by farm children. The two groups of subjects therefore differed in the kind of prior knowledge they would bring to bear, either knowledge about creativity or knowledge about city versus farm living. This difference showed its effect in the descriptions of the categories that the two groups of subjects offered. The creative-noncreative group favored descriptions of the two categories that emphasized the amount of detail in the drawing; for example,

> Creative kids will draw more detail—like eyelashes, teeth, curly hair, shading and coloring. Noncreative kids draw more stick-figurish people.

In contrast, the farm-city group favored descriptions of the two categories that emphasized the clothing in the drawings; for example,

> Farm kids will draw people with overalls, straw or farm hats. City kids will draw people with ties, suits.

Thus learners with different prior knowledge focused on different properties of the instances. Moreover, in some cases, differences in prior knowledge seem to have determined how the learners interpreted the properties in the first place. To illustrate, consider the pointed-to object in the fourth figure of category 1 (see Figure 9-2). Some subjects in the creative-noncreative group interpreted this object as a pocket, and mentioned it as evidence of greater detail. Some subjects in the farm-city group interpreted this same object as a purse, and mentioned it as evidence of an urban background. Prior knowledge therefore may affect every aspect of concept attainment (Wisniewski & Medin, 1991).

# Linguistic Relativity Hypothesis

In our discussion of concepts, we assume that words reflect existing concepts. We assume that language is designed to express propositional thought and, therefore, that the structure of language reflects the structure of thought. However, some have suggested that the relationship between language and thought is the other way around. Rather than thought determining language, it may be that language determines thought. This is the **linguistic relativity hypothesis** proposed by Benjamin Whorf (1956). Whorf argued that the kinds of concepts and perceptions we can have are affected by the particular language we speak. Therefore, people who speak different languages perceive the world in different ways. This provocative idea has caused considerable debate over the years.

Much of the evidence cited in favor of the hypothesis is based on vocabulary differences. For example, English has only one word for snow, whereas Eskimo has four. Consequently, speakers of Eskimo may perceive differences in snow that speakers of English do not. Do such observations constitute strong evidence for the linguistic relativity hypothesis? Critics of the hypothesis argue that they do not (for example, Slobin, 1979; Brown, 1986). According to the critics, language may embody distinctions that are important to a culture, but it does not create those distinctions, nor does it limit its speaker's perceptions to them. English speakers may have the same capacity for perceiving variations in snow as Eskimo speakers, but since such variations are more important in Eskimo cultures than in Anglo cultures one language assigns different words to the variations whereas the other does not. The best evidence for this view is the development of jargons. For example, American skiers talk of "powder" and "corn," not just "snow." This growth in vocabulary may be accompanied by changes in perception: Eskimos and skiers are more likely to notice variations in snow than are Hawaiians. But the critical point is that such changes do not depend on the language spoken. If anything, the language seems to depend on changes in perception.

The linguistic relativity hypothesis has fared no better when it comes to explaining cultural variations in terms describing colors. At one time, many linguists believed that languages differed widely in how they divided the color spectrum and that this led to differences in the perception of colors. Subsequent research showed just the opposite. Berlin and Kay (1969), two anthropologists, studied the *basic color terms* of many languages. Basic color terms are simple, nonmetaphoric words that are used to describe the colors of many different objects. Berlin and Kay found striking commonalities in such terms across languages. For instance, every language takes its basic color terms from a restricted set of 11 names. In English these are "black," "white," "red," "yellow," "green," "blue," "brown," "purple," "pink," "gray," and "orange." No matter what color terms a particular language has, they inevitably correspond to some subset of the colors listed here. In addition, if a language uses fewer than 11 terms, the basic terms chosen are not arbitrary. If a language has only two terms (none has fewer), they correspond to "black" and "white"; if it has three, they correspond to "black," "white," and "red"; if it has six, they correspond to these three plus "yellow," "green," and "blue." Thus, the ordering of basic color terms seems to be universal, rather

## Combining Concepts

We need to understand not only the nature of individual concepts but also how we combine them to form propositional thoughts. One general rule of combination is that we join concepts to produce a proposition that contains a *subject* and a *predicate* (a description). In the proposition "Audrey has curly hair," "Audrey" is the subject, and "has curly hair" is the predicate. In the proposition "The tailor is asleep," "the tailor" is the subject, and "is asleep" is the predicate. And in "Teachers work too hard," "teachers" is the subject, and "work too hard" is the predicate. Note that in some cases the predicate is an attribute ("has curly hair"); in other cases, it is a state ("is asleep"); and in still other cases, it is an activity ("work too hard").

Combining concepts into propositions is the first step toward complex thoughts. The rest of the way is accomplished by combining the propositions themselves. Again, there appear to be only certain ways we can do this. The easiest way to combine propositions into thoughts is by simply joining them—for example, "Anne likes vegetables, but Ed prefers pizza." A more complex way of combining propositions is to attach one proposition to part of another. In "Ben likes the blue blanket," we have two proposi-

than varying from language to language as the linguistic relativity hypothesis might suggest.

In addition, people whose languages use corresponding basic color terms agree on what particular color is most typical of a color term. Suppose two different languages have terms corresponding to "red." When speakers of these languages are asked to pick the best example of red from an array of hues, they make the same choice. Even though the range of hues for what they would call red may differ, their idea of a typical red is the same. Their perceptions are identical, even though their vocabularies are different. Further work by Rosch (1974) suggests that the Dani (a New Guinea people), whose language has only two basic color terms, perceive color variations in exactly the same way as people whose language has all 11. So, the perception of color gives little support to the linguistic relativity hypothesis.

We should not dismiss the hypothesis too quickly, however. Few language domains have been investigated in the same detail as color terms, and perhaps support for the hypothesis will be found in other domains (for example, whether a language codes a particular thing or event by a noun or a verb). Also, the linguistic relativity hypothesis calls attention to an important point. In learning to make fine discriminations in a particular field, it is helpful to have a vocabulary that expresses these discriminations. As we gain expertise in a field (whether skiing, psychology, or something else), we enlarge our vocabulary for distinctions in that field. Jargons help us to think about and communicate these distinctions. Although a distinction must exist in someone's mind before a term can be created to embody it, the importance of that embodiment should not be underestimated.

*Eskimos may perceive differences in snow that we do not.*

tions: "Ben likes the blanket" and "the blanket is blue." The second proposition is attached to part of the predicate of the first. Perhaps the most complex way to combine propositions or thoughts is to insert one into another. For example, "Anne's liking the restaurant was a surprise to everyone" contains two propositions. The first is "Anne liked the restaurant." This proposition then serves as the subject of the second proposition, in which "was a surprise to everyone" is the predicate. Thus, the first proposition has been *embedded* into the second, and such embedding enables us to form very complex thoughts (Clark & Clark, 1977).

## Reasoning

When we think propositionally our sequence of thoughts is organized. Sometimes our thoughts are organized by the structure of long-term memory. A thought about calling your father, for example, leads to a memory of a recent conversation you had with him in your house, which in turn leads to a thought about fixing the house's attic. But memory associations are not the only means we have of organizing thought. The kind of organization of interest to us here manifests itself when we try to *reason*. In such cases, our sequence of thoughts often takes the form of an argument, in which one proposition corresponds to a claim, or *conclusion*, that we are trying to draw. The remaining propositions are reasons for the claim, or *premises* for the conclusion.

## Deductive Reasoning

**LOGICAL RULES**  According to logicians, the strongest arguments are *deductively valid*, which means that it is impossible for the conclusion of the argument to be false if its premises are true (Skyrms, 1986). An example of such an argument is the following:

1.  If it's raining, I'll take an umbrella.
2.  It's raining.
3.  Therefore, I'll take an umbrella.

When asked to decide whether or not an argument is deductively valid, people are reasonably accurate in their assessments of simple arguments. How do we make such judgments? Some theories of **deductive reasoning** assume that we operate like intuitive logicians and use logical rules in trying to prove that the conclusion of an argument follows from the premises. To illustrate, consider the following rule:

> If you have a proposition of the form *If p then q*, and another proposition *p*, then you can infer the proposition *q*.

Presumably, adults know this rule (perhaps unconsciously) and use it to decide that the previous argument is valid. Specifically, they identify the first premise ("If it's raining, I'll take an umbrella") with the *If p then q* part of the rule. They identify the second premise ("It's raining") with the *p* part of the rule, and then they infer the *q* part ("I'll take an umbrella").

Rule-following becomes more conscious if we complicate the argument. Presumably, we apply our sample rule twice when evaluating the following argument:

1.  If it's raining, I'll take an umbrella.
2.  If I take an umbrella, I'll lose it.
3.  It's raining.
4.  Therefore, I'll lose my umbrella.

Applying our rule to Propositions No. 1 and No. 3 allows us to infer "I'll take an umbrella"; and applying our rule again to Proposition No. 2 and the inferred proposition allows us to infer "I'll lose my umbrella," which is the conclusion. One of the best pieces of evidence that people are using rules like this is that the number of rules an argument requires is a good predictor of the argument's difficulty. The more rules that are needed, the more likely it is that people will make an error, and the longer it will take them when they do make a correct decision (Osherson, 1976; Rips, 1983).

**OTHER RULES AND HEURISTICS**  Logical rules do not capture all aspects of deductive reasoning. Such rules are triggered only by the logical *form* of propositions, yet our ability to evaluate a deductive argument often depends on the *content* of the propositions as well. We can illustrate this point by the following experimental problems. Subjects are presented four cards. In one version of the problem, each card has a letter on one side and a digit on the other (see the top half of Figure 9-3). The subject must decide which cards to turn over to determine whether the following claim is correct: "If a card has a vowel on one side, then it has an even number on the other side." While most subjects correctly choose the "E" card, fewer than 10 percent of them also choose the "7" card, which is the other correct choice. (To see that the "7" card is critical, note that if it has a vowel on its other side, the claim is disconfirmed.)

Performance improves drastically, however, in another version of the above problem (see the bottom half of Figure 9-3). Now the claim that subjects must evaluate is "If a person is drinking beer, he or she must be over 19." Each card has a person's age on one side, and what he or she is drinking on the other. This version of the problem is logically equivalent to the preceding version (in particular, "Beer" corresponds to "E," and "16" to "7"); but now most subjects make the correct choices (they turn over the "Beer" and "16" cards). Thus, the content of the propositions affects our reasoning.

Results such as the above imply that we do not always use logical rules when faced with deduction problems. Rather, sometimes we use rules that are less abstract and more relevant to everyday problems, what are called **pragmatic rules.** An example is the *permission rule*, which states that "If a particular action is to be taken, often a precondition must be satisfied." Most people know this rule, and activate it when presented the drinking problem in the bottom half of Figure 9-3; that is, they would think about the problem in terms of permission. Once activated, the rule would lead people to look for failures to meet the relevant precondition (being under 19), which in turn would lead them to choose the "16" card. In contrast, the permission rule would not be triggered by the letter-number problem in the top half of Figure 9-3, so there is no reason for people to choose the "7" card. Thus, the content of a problem affects whether or not a pragmatic rule is activated, which in turn affects the correctness of reasoning (Cheng, Holyoak, Nisbett, & Oliver, 1986).

In addition to rules, we sometimes use **heuristics** in deductive reasoning. Heuristics are shortcut procedures that are relatively easy to apply and that often yield the correct answers, but not inevitably so. Subjects may solve the drinking version of the aforementioned problem by retrieving from long-term memory a relevant fact about drinking (that only young drinkers must be checked to see if the law is being violated) and then applying this fact to the present problem (Rips, 1988). Alternatively, subjects may solve the drinking problem by setting up a concrete representation of the situation, what is called a **mental model.** They may, for example, imagine two people, each with a number on his back and a drink in his hand. They may then inspect this mental model and see what happens, for example, if the drinker with "16" on his back has a beer in his hand. According to this idea, we reason in terms of mental models that are suggested by the content of the problem (Johnson-Laird, 1989).

All of the procedures just described—applying pragmatic rules, retrieving specific facts, and constructing mental models—have one thing in common. They are determined by the content of the problem. This is in contrast to the application of logical rules, which should not be affected by problem content. Hence, our sensitivity to content often prevents us from operating as intuitive logicians.

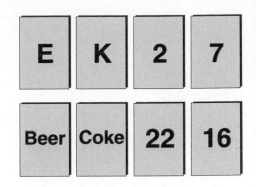

**FIGURE 9-3**
**Content Effects in Deductive Reasoning** *The top row illustrates a version of the problem in which subjects had to decide which two cards should be turned over to test the hypothesis, "If a card has a vowel on one side, it has an even number on the other side." The bottom row illustrates a version of the problem where subjects had to decide which cards to turn over to test the hypothesis, "If a person is drinking beer, he or she must be over 19."* (After Wason & Johnson-Laird, 1972; Griggs & Cox, 1982)

# Inductive Reasoning

**LOGICAL RULES** Logicians have noted that an argument can be good even if it is not deductively valid. Such arguments are *inductively strong*, which means that it is *improbable* that the conclusion is false if the premises are true (Skyrms, 1986). An example of an inductively strong argument is as follows:

1.  Mitch majored in accounting in college.
2.  Mitch now works for an accounting firm.
3.  Therefore, Mitch is an accountant.

This argument is not deductively valid (Mitch may have tired of accounting courses and taken a night-watchman's job in the only place he had contacts). Inductive strength, then, is a matter of probabilities, not certainties, and inductive logic is based on the theory of probability.

We make and evaluate inductive arguments all the time. In doing this, do we rely on the rules of probability theory as a logician or mathematician would? One probability rule that is relevant is the **base-rate rule,** which states that the probability of something being a member of a class (such as Mitch being a member of the class of accountants) is greater the more class members there are (that is, the higher the base rate of the class). Thus, our sample argument about Mitch being an accountant can be strengthened by adding the premise that Mitch joined a club in which 90 percent of the members are accountants. Another relevant probability rule is the **conjunction rule:** the probability of a proposition cannot be less than the probability of that proposition conjoined with another proposition. For example, the probability that "Mitch is an accountant" cannot be less than the probability that "Mitch is an accountant and makes more than $40,000 a year." The base-rate and conjunction rules are rational guides to inductive reasoning, and most people will defer to them when the rules are made explicit. However, in the rough-and-tumble of everyday reasoning, people frequently violate these rules, as we are about to see.

**HEURISTICS** In a series of ingenious experiments, Tversky and Kahneman have shown that people violate some basic rules of probability theory when making inductive judgments. Violations of the base-rate rule are particularly common. In one experiment, one group of subjects was told that a panel of psychologists had interviewed 100 people—30 engineers and 70 lawyers—and had written personality descriptions of them. These subjects were then given five descriptions and for each one were asked to indicate the probability that the person described was an engineer. Some descriptions were prototypical of an engineer (for example, "Jack shows no interest in political issues and spends his free time on home carpentry"); other descriptions were neutral (for example, "Dick is a man of high ability and promises to be quite successful"). Not surprisingly, these subjects rated the prototypical description as more likely to be an engineer than the neutral description. Another group of subjects was given the identical instructions and five descriptions, except they were told that the 100 people were 70 engineers and 30 lawyers (the reverse of the first group). The base rate of engineers therefore differed greatly between the two groups. This difference had virtually no effect: subjects in the second group gave essentially the same ratings as those in the first group. For example, subjects in both groups rated the neutral description as having a 50-50 chance of being an engineer (whereas the rational move would have been to rate the neutral description as more likely to be in the profession with the higher base rate). Subjects completely ignored the information about base rates (Tversky & Kahneman, 1973).

People pay no more heed to the conjunction rule. In one study, subjects were presented the following description:

> Linda is 31 years old, single, outspoken, and very bright. In college, she majored in philosophy . . . and was deeply concerned with issues of discrimination.

Subjects then estimated the probabilities of the following statements:

1. Linda is a bank teller.
2. Linda is a bank teller and is active in the feminist movement.

Statement No. 2 is the conjunction of Statement No. 1 and the proposition "Linda is active in the feminist movement." In flagrant violation of the conjunction rule, most subjects rated No. 2 more probable than No. 1. Note that this is a fallacy because every feminist bank teller is a bank teller, but some female bank tellers are not feminists, and Linda could be one of them (Tversky & Kahneman, 1983).

Subjects in this study based their judgments on the fact that Linda seems more similar to a feminist bank teller than to a bank teller. Though they were asked to estimate *probability*, subjects instead estimated the *similarity* of Linda to the prototype of the concepts "bank teller" and "feminist bank teller." Thus, estimating similarity is used as a heuristic for estimating probability, because similarity often relates to probability yet is easier to calculate. Use of the *similarity heuristic* also explains why people ignore base rates. In the engineer-lawyer study described earlier, subjects may have considered only the similarity of the description to their prototypes of "engineer" and "lawyer." Hence, given a description that matched the prototypes of "engineer" and "lawyer" equally well, subjects judged that engineer and lawyer were equally probable. Reliance on the similarity heuristic can lead to errors even by experts.

Reasoning by similarity shows up in another common reasoning situation, that in which we know some members of a category have a particular property and have to decide whether other category members have the property as well. In one study, subjects had to judge which of the following two arguments seemed stronger

3. All robins have sesamoid bones.
4. Therefore all sparrows have sesamoid bones.
   versus
5. All robins have sesamoid bones.
6. Therefore all ostriches have sesamoid bones.

Not surprisingly, subjects judged the first argument stronger, presumably because robins are more similar to sparrows than they are to ostriches. This use of similarity appears rational, inasmuch as it fits with the idea that things that have many known properties in common are likely to have unknown properties in common as well. But the veneer of rationality fades when we consider subjects' judgments on another pair of arguments:

7. All robins have sesamoid bones.
8. Therefore all birds have sesamoid bones.
   versus
9. All robins have sesamoid bones.
10. Therefore all ostriches have sesamoid bones (the same argument as 5–6).

Subjects judged the first argument stronger, presumably because robins are more similar to the prototype of birds than they are to ostriches. But this judgment is a fallacy: based on the same evidence (that robins have sesamoid bones), it cannot be more likely that *all* birds have some property than that all ostriches do, because ostriches are in fact birds. Again, our similarity-based intuitions can sometimes lead us astray (Osherson, et al., 1990).

Similarity is not our only strong heuristic; another is the *causality heuristic*. People estimate the probability of a situation by the strength of the causal connections between the events in the situation. For example, people judge Statement No. 12 to be more probable than Statement No. 11:

11. Sometime during 1997, there will be a massive flood in North America, in which more than 1,000 people will drown.
12. Sometime during 1997, there will be an earthquake in California, causing a massive flood, in which more than 1,000 people will drown.

Judging No. 12 to be more probable than No. 11 is another violation of the conjunction rule (and hence another fallacy). This time, the violation arises because in Statement No. 12 the flood has a strong causal connection to another event, the earthquake; whereas in Statement No. 11, the flood alone is mentioned and hence has no causal connections.

So our reliance on heuristics often leads us to ignore some basic rational rules, including the base-rate and conjunction rules. But we should not be too pessimistic about our level of rationality. For one thing, the similarity and causality heuristics probably lead to correct decisions in most cases. Another point is that some other rules of probability theory seem more intuitive to us and we use them more. One such rule is the *law of large numbers*, which roughly says that our belief in a claim should increase with the amount of evidence or data mustered in support of that claim. So we should be much more willing to believe that a baseball player is a good hitter if he has a high batting average at the end of the season than if he has the same average at the end of the first month of the season (there are more at-bats, or data, in the first case). People seem to use this rule in everyday reasoning situations as judged by a number of criteria: they report consciously using it, they are as likely to use it with unfamiliar materials as with familiar ones, and they will sometimes overextend the rule to situations that are exceptions to it (Smith, Langston, & Nisbett, 1992).

## Language and Communication

Language is the primary means for communicating thought. Moreover, it is a universal means: every human society has a language, and every human being of normal intelligence acquires his or her native language and uses it effortlessly. The naturalness of language sometimes lulls us into thinking that language use requires no special explanation. Nothing could be further from the truth. Some people can read, and others cannot; some can do arithmetic, and others cannot; some can play chess, and others cannot. But virtually everyone can master and use an enormously complex linguistic system. Why this should be so is among the fundamental puzzles of human psychology.

## Levels of Language

Language use has two aspects: *production* and *comprehension*. In producing language, we start with a propositional thought, somehow translate it into a sentence, and end up with sounds that express the sentence. In comprehending language, we start by hearing sounds, attach meanings to the sounds in the form of words, combine the words to create a sentence, and then somehow extract a proposition from it. Thus, language use seems to involve moving through various levels, and Figure 9-4 makes these levels explicit. At the highest level are sentence units, including sentences and phrases. The next level is that of words and parts of words that carry meaning (the prefix "non" or the suffix "er," for example). The lowest level contains speech sounds. The adjacent levels are closely related to one another: the phrases of a sentence are built from words and prefixes and suffixes, which in turn are constructed from speech sounds. Language is therefore a multilevel system for relating thoughts to speech by word and sentence units (Chomsky, 1965).

There are striking differences in the number of units at each level. All languages have only a limited number of speech sounds; English has about 40 of them. But rules for combining these speech sounds make it possible to produce and understand thousands of words (a vocabulary of 40,000 words is not unusual for an adult). Similarly, rules for combining words make it possible to produce and understand millions of sentences (if not an infinite number of them). Thus, two of the basic properties of language are that it is *structured* at multiple levels and that it is *productive*: rules allow us to combine units at one level into a vastly greater number of units at the next level. Every human language has these two properties.

## Language Units and Processes

With the above as background, let us now consider the units and processes involved at each level of language.

**SPEECH SOUNDS**  In speaking, we use the lips, tongue, mouth, and vocal cords to produce a variety of physical sounds. Not all of these sounds are perceived as distinct, however. In English, we discriminate about 40 **phonemes**, or categories of speech sounds. The sound corresponding to the first letter in "boy" is a phoneme symbolized as /b/. We are good at discriminating different sounds that correspond to different phonemes in our language. But we are poor at discriminating different sounds that correspond to the same phoneme—for example, the sound of the first letter in "pin" and the sound of the second letter in "spin" (Liberman, Cooper, Shankweiler, & Studdert-Kennedy, 1967). They are the same phoneme, /p/, and they sound the same to us even though they have different physical characteristics. The /p/ in "pin" is accompanied by a small puff of air, but the /p/ in "spin" is not (try holding your hand a short distance from your mouth as you say the two words). Thus, our phonemic categories act as filters, in that they convert a continuous stream of speech into a sequence of familiar phonemes.

Every language has a different set of phonemes, which is one reason why we often have difficulty learning to pronounce foreign words. Another language may use speech sounds that never appear in ours. It may take us a while even to hear the new phonemes, let alone produce them. For example, in the Hindi language, the two different /p/ sounds illustrated above

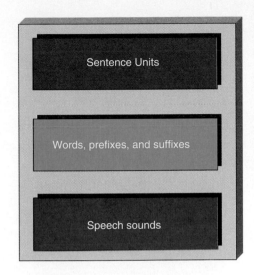

**FIGURE 9-4**
**Levels of Language** *At the highest level are sentence units, including phrases and sentences. The next level is that of words and parts of words that carry meaning. The lowest level contains speech sounds.*

correspond to two different phonemes. Or another language may not make a distinction between two sounds that our language treats as two phonemes. For example, in Japanese the English sounds corresponding to "r" and "l" (/r/ and /l/) are treated as the same phoneme.

When phonemes are combined in the right way, they form words. Each language has its own rules about which phonemes can follow others. In English, for example, /b/ cannot follow /p/ at the beginning of a word (try pronouncing "pbet"). Such rules show their influence when we speak and listen. For example, we have no difficulty pronouncing the plurals of nonsense words we have never heard before. Consider "zuk" and "zug." In accordance with a simple rule, the plural of "zuk" is formed by adding the phoneme /s/, as in "hiss." In English, however, /s/ cannot follow "g" at the end of a word, so to form the plural of "zug" we must use another rule—one that adds the phoneme /z/, as in "fuzz." We may not be aware of these differences in forming plurals, but we have no difficulty producing them. It is as if we "know" the rules for combining phonemes even though we are not consciously aware of the rules: we conform to rules we cannot verbalize.

**WORD UNITS** A **morpheme** is the smallest linguistic unit that carries meaning. Most morphemes are themselves words, such as "time." Others are suffixes, such as "ly," or prefixes, such as "un," which are added onto words to form more complex ones, such as "timely" or "untimely." Most words denote some specific content, such as "house" or "run." A few words, however, primarily serve to make sentences grammatical; such grammatical words, or *grammatical morphemes*, include what are commonly labeled articles and prepositions, such as "a," "the," "in," "of," "on," and "at." Some prefixes and suffixes also play primarily a grammatical role. These grammatical morphemes include the suffixes "ing" and "ed." Grammatical morphemes may be processed in a qualitatively different manner than content words. One piece of evidence for this is that there are forms of brain damage in which the use of grammatical morphemes is impaired more than the use of content words (Zurif, 1990). Also, as we shall see later, grammatical morphemes are acquired in a different manner than are content words.

Every language has rules about how prefixes or suffixes are combined with words. In English, for example, the suffix "er" is regularly added to many verbs to form nouns that refer to people who habitually perform the action described by the verb, as in "speak-speaker" and "paint-painter." Do we actually use these rules, or something like them, in production and comprehension? Our slips of the tongue suggest we do. For example, a speaker who intended to say "Smith favors busting pushers" uttered instead "Smith favors pushing busters" (Garrett, 1975). The morphemes "bust" and "push" were interchanged, whereas the morphemes "ing" and "ers" stayed in their correct positions. This implies that morphemes like "push" and "ers" are treated as separate units (which are usually combined by application of a rule).

The most important aspect of a word is, of course, its meaning. A word can be viewed as the name of a concept; hence, its meaning is the concept it names. Some words are *ambiguous* because they name more than one concept. "Club," for example, names both a social organization and an object used for striking. Sometimes we may be aware of a word's ambiguity, as when hearing the sentence "He was interested in the club." In most cases, however, the sentence context makes the meaning of the word sufficiently clear so we do not consciously experience any ambiguity—for example, "He wanted to join the club." Even in the latter cases, though, there is evidence that we *unconsciously* consider both meanings of the ambiguous word for a brief moment. In one experiment, a subject was presented a sentence like "He wanted to join the club," followed immediately by a test word that the subject had to read aloud as quickly as possible. Subjects read the test word faster if it was related to either meaning of "club" (for example, "group" or "struck") than if it was unrelated to either meaning (for example, "apple"). This suggests that both meanings of "club" were activated during comprehension of the sentence, and that either meaning could prime related words (Tanenhaus, Leiman, & Seidenberg, 1979; Swinney, 1979).

The most striking thing about word units in contrast to speech sounds is that morphemes carry meaning whereas phonemes do not. There is now evidence suggesting that different parts of the brain are involved when a sequence of symbols carries meaning than when it does not. Researchers measured the amount of blood flow in various areas of the brain while subjects decided whether or not letter strings formed words. Thus, subjects responded positively to strings like "blast" but negatively to strings like "floop." Both kinds of strings contained sequences of permissible phonemes, and both led to increased blood flow in a sensory region of the brain. However, only the words also led to increased blood flow in a completely different region in the front of the brain; presumably this region is involved in the assignment of meaning to words (Peterson et al., 1990).

**SENTENCE UNITS** Sentence units include sentences and phrases. An important property of these units is that they can correspond to parts of a proposition. Such correspondences allow speakers to "put" propositions (or thoughts) into sentences and listeners to "extract" propositions (or thoughts) from sentences.

Recall that any proposition can be broken into a subject and predicate. A sentence can be broken into phrases in such a way that each phrase corresponds either to the subject or the predicate of a proposition or to an entire proposition. For example, intuitively we can divide the simple sentence "Irene sells insurance" into two phrases, "Irene" and "sells insurance." The first phrase, which is called a *noun phrase* because it centers on a noun, specifies the subject of an underlying proposition. The second phrase, a *verb phrase*, gives the predicate of the proposition. For a more complex example, consider the sentence "Serious scholars read books." This sentence divides into two phrases, the noun phrase "serious scholars" and the verb phrase "read books." The noun phrase expresses an entire proposition, "scholars are serious"; the verb phrase expresses part (the predicate) of another proposition, "scholars read books" (see Figure 9-5). Again, sentence units correspond closely to proposition units, which provides a link between language and thought.

Thus, when reading or listening to a sentence, people seem to first divide it into noun phrases, verb phrases, and the like, and then extract propositions from these phrases. There is a good deal of evidence for our dividing sentences into phrases and treating the phrases as units. One piece of evidence comes from linguistics: it is easier to insert new words into a sentence if they are placed between phrasal units rather than within such units. Consider the simple sentence "The man left." This sentence remains grammatical if we insert an adverb modifying the sentence between the noun and verb phrases, "The man *obviously* left," but becomes ungrammatical if we insert the adverb within a phrase "The *obviously* man left." (Lasnik, 1990).

**FIGURE 9-5**
**Phrases and Propositions** *The first step in extracting the propositions from a complex sentence is to decompose the sentence into phrases. This decomposition is based on rules like "Any sentence can be divided into a noun phrase and a verb phrase."*

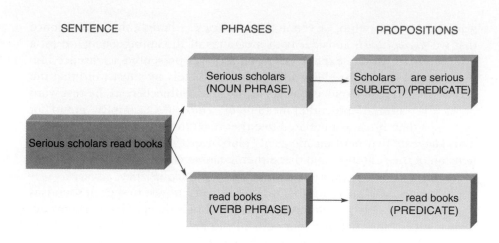

SENTENCE   PHRASES   PROPOSITIONS

Serious scholars read books

Serious scholars (NOUN PHRASE)

read books (VERB PHRASE)

Scholars are serious (SUBJECT) (PREDICATE)

———— read books (PREDICATE)

It's as if the units strive to keep their integrity. Another piece of evidence comes from memory experiments. In one study, subjects listened to sentences such as "The poor girl stole a warm coat." Immediately after each sentence was presented, subjects were given a probe word from the sentence and asked to say the word that came after it. People responded faster when the probe and the response words came from the same phrase ("poor" and "girl") than when they came from different phrases ("girl" and "stole"). Thus, each phrase acts as a unit in memory. When the probe and response are from the same phrase, only one unit needs to be retrieved (Wilkes & Kennedy, 1969).

Analyzing a sentence into noun and verb phrases, and then dividing these phrases into smaller units like nouns, adjectives, and verbs, is called a **syntactic analysis** (*syntax* deals with the relations between words in phrases and sentences). Usually, in the course of understanding a sentence we perform such an analysis effortlessly and unconsciously. Sometimes, however, our syntactic analysis goes awry and we become aware of the process. Consider the sentence, "The horse raced past the barn fell." Many people experience difficulty understanding this sentence. Why? Because on first reading, we assume that "The horse" is the noun phrase and "raced past the barn" the verb phrase, which leaves us with no place for the word "fell." To correctly understand the sentence, we have to repartition it so that the entire phrase "The horse raced past the barn" is the noun phrase, and "fell" is the verb phrase (that is, the sentence is just a shortened version of "The horse who was raced past the barn fell"). In this example people initially run into trouble because they unconsciously commit themselves to one particular syntactic analysis when another one is possible. Other work, however, suggests that in certain cases we are capable of simultaneously considering more than one analysis of a sentence (Garrett, 1990).

## Effects of Context on Comprehension and Production

By way of summary, Figure 9-6 presents an amended version of our levels description of language. The figure suggests that understanding a sentence is the inverse of producing a sentence. To produce a sentence, we start with a propositional thought, translate it into the phrases and morphemes of a sentence, and finally translate these morphemes into phonemes. We work from the highest level down. To understand a sentence, however, we move in the opposite direction—from the lowest level up. We hear phonemes, use them to construct the morphemes and phrases of a sentence, and finally extract the proposition from the sentence unit.

Although this analysis describes some of what occurs in sentence production and understanding, it is oversimplified because it does not consider the *context* in which language processing occurs. Often the context makes what is about to be said predictable. After comprehending just a few words, we jump to conclusions about what we think the entire sentence means (the propositions behind it), and then use our guess about the propositions to help understand the rest of the sentence. In such cases, understanding proceeds from the highest level down as well as from the lowest level up. (Adams & Collins, 1979).

Indeed, there are cases where language understanding is nearly impossible without some context. To illustrate, try reading the following paragraph:

> The procedure is actually quite simple. First you arrange things into different groups. Of course, one pile may be sufficient, depending on how much there is to do. If you have to go somewhere else due to lack of facilities, that is the next step; otherwise you are pretty well set. It is important not to overdo things. That is, it is better to do too few things at once than too many. In the short run this may not seem important but complications can easily arise. A mistake can be expensive as well. At first the whole procedure will seem complicated. Soon, however, it will become just another facet of life. (After Bransford & Johnson, 1973)

In reading the paragraph, you no doubt had difficulty in trying to understand exactly what it was about. But given the context of "washing clothes," you can now use your knowledge about washing clothes to interpret all the cryptic parts of the passage. The "procedure" referred to in the first sentence is that of "washing clothes," the "things" referred to in the first sentence are "clothes," the "different groups" are "groups of clothing of different colors," and so on. Your understanding of the paragraph, if you reread it, should now be excellent.

Perhaps the most salient part of the context, though, is the other person (or persons) we are communicating with. In understanding a sentence, it is not enough to understand its phonemes, morphemes, and phrases; we must also understand the *speaker's intention* in uttering that particular sentence. For example, when someone at dinner asks you, "Can you pass the potatoes," usually you assume that their intention was not to find out if you are physically capable of lifting the potatoes, but rather to induce you to actually pass the potatoes. However, had your arm been in a sling, then given the identical question you might assume that the speaker's intention *was* to determine your physical capability. In both cases, the sentence (and proposition) is the same; what changes is the speaker's goal for uttering that sentence (Grice, 1975). And there is abundant evidence that people extract the speaker's intention as part of the process of comprehension (Clark, 1984).

There are similar effects in the production of language. If someone asks you, "Where is the Empire State Building?" you will say very different things depending on the physical context and the assumptions that you make about the questioner. If the question is asked of you in Cincinnati, for example, you might answer "In New York"; if the question is asked in Brooklyn, you might say "Near Midtown Manhattan"; and if the question is asked in Manhattan, you might say "On 34th Street." In speaking, as in understanding, one must determine how the utterance fits the context.

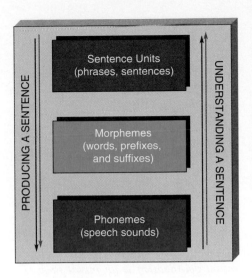

**FIGURE 9-6**
**Levels of Understanding and Producing Sentences** *In producing a sentence, we translate a propositional thought into the phrases and morphemes of a sentence and translate these morphemes into phonemes. In understanding a sentence, we go in the opposite direction—we use phonemes to construct the morphemes and phrases of a sentence and from these units extract the underlying propositions.*

*Infant vocalization is an initial stage of language acquisition.*

# Development of Language

Our discussion of language should indicate the enormity of the task confronting children. They must master all levels of language—not only the proper speech sounds but also how these sounds are combined into thousands of words and how these words can be combined into sentences to express thoughts. It is a wonder that virtually all children in all cultures accomplish so much of this in a mere 4 to 5 years. We will first discuss what is acquired at each level of language and then consider how it is acquired and what roles learning and innate factors play.

## What Is Acquired?

Development occurs at all three levels of language. It starts at the level of phonemes, proceeds to the level of words and other morphemes, and then moves on to the level of sentence units, or syntax.

**PHONEMES AND THEIR COMBINATION**  Recall that adults are good at discriminating different sounds that correspond to different phonemes in their language, but poor at discriminating different sounds that correspond to the same phoneme in their language. Remarkably, children come into the world able to discriminate different sounds that correspond to different phonemes in *any* language. What changes over the first year of life is that infants learn which phonemes are relevant to their language, and lose their ability to discriminate between sounds that correspond to the same phoneme in their language. These remarkable facts were determined by experiments in which infants were presented pairs of sounds in succession while they were sucking on pacifiers. Since infants suck more to a novel stimulus than to a familiar one, their rate of sucking can be used to tell whether they perceive two successive sounds as the same or different. Six-month-old infants increase their rate of sucking when the successive sounds correspond to different phonemes in *any* language, whereas 1-year-olds increase their rate of sucking only when the successive sounds correspond to different phonemes in their own language. Thus, a 6-month-old Japanese child can distinguish /l/ from /r/ but loses this ability by the end of the first year of life (Eimas, 1985).

While children learn which phonemes are relevant in their first year of life, it takes several years for them to learn how phonemes can be combined to form words. When children first begin to talk, they occasionally produce "impossible" words, like "dlumber" for "lumber." They do not yet know that in English /l/ cannot follow /d/ at the beginning of a word. By age 4, children have learned most of what they need to know about phoneme combinations.

**WORDS AND CONCEPTS**  At about 1 year of age, children begin to speak. One-year-olds already have concepts for many things (including family members, household pets, food, toys, and body parts), and when they begin to speak, they are mapping these concepts onto words that adults use. The beginning vocabulary is roughly the same for all children. Children 1 to 2 years old talk mainly about people ("Dada," "Mama," "baby"), animals ("dog," "cat," "duck"), vehicles ("car," "truck," "boat"), toys ("ball," "block," "book"), food ("juice," "milk," "cookie"), body parts ("eye," "nose," "mouth"), and household implements ("hat," "sock," "spoon"). While these words name some of the young child's concepts, by no means

*A child learns to recognize objects as her father reads to her.*

do they name them all. Consequently, young children often have a gap between the concepts they want to communicate and the words they have at their disposal. To bridge this gap, children aged 1 to $2\frac{1}{2}$ years old *overextend* their words to neighboring concepts. For example, a 2-year-old child might use the word "doggie" for cats and cows, as well as dogs (the child is not unsure of the word's meaning—if presented pictures of various animals and asked to pick the "doggie," the child makes the correct choice). At about the age of $2\frac{1}{2}$ years, overextensions begin to disappear, presumably because the child's vocabulary begins to increase markedly, thereby eliminating many of the gaps (Rescorla, 1980; Clark, 1983).

Thereafter, vocabulary development virtually explodes. At $1\frac{1}{2}$ years, a child might have a vocabulary of 25 words; at 6 years, the child's vocabulary is around 15,000 words. To achieve this incredible growth, children have to learn new words at the rate of almost 10 per day (Templin, 1957; Miller & Gildea, 1987). Children seem to be tuned to learning new words. When they hear a word they do not know, they may assume it maps onto one of their concepts that is as yet unlabeled, and they use the context in which the word was spoken to find that concept (Clark, 1983; Markman, 1987).

**FROM PRIMITIVE TO COMPLEX SENTENCES** At about $1\frac{1}{2}$ to $2\frac{1}{2}$ years, the acquisition of phrase and sentence units, or syntax, begins. Children start to combine single words into two-word utterances, such as "There cow" (where the underlying proposition in "There's the cow"), "Jimmy bike" (the proposition is "That's Jimmy's bike"), or "Towel bed" (the proposition is "The towel's on the bed"). There is a **telegraphic** quality about two-word speech. The child leaves out the grammatical words (such as "a," "an," "the," and "is"), as well as other grammatical morphemes (such as the suffixes "ing," "ed," and "s") and puts in only the words that carry the most important content. Despite their brevity, these utterances express most of the basic intentions of speakers, such as locating objects and describing events and actions.

*Children between 18 and 30 months of age learn to combine words into phrases and sentences.*

Children progress rapidly from two-word utterances to more complex sentences that express propositions more precisely. Thus, "Daddy hat" may become "Daddy wear hat" and finally "Daddy is wearing a hat." Such expansions of the verb phrase appear to be the first complex constructions that occur in children's speech. The next step is the use of conjunctions like "and" and "so" to form compound sentences ("You play with the doll *and* I play with the blocks") and the use of grammatical morphemes like the past tense "ed." The sequence of language development is remarkably similar for all children.

## Learning Processes

Now that we have an idea about what children acquire in the language process, we can ask how they acquire it. Learning undoubtedly plays a role; that is why children who are brought up in an English-speaking household learn English and why children raised in a French-speaking household learn French. And innate factors undoubtedly play a role; that is why all children in a household learn language but none of the pets do (Gleitman, 1986). We discuss learning in this section and consider innate factors in the next section. In both discussions, we emphasize sentence units and syntax, for it is at this level of language that the important issues about language acquisition are most clearly illustrated.

**IMITATION AND CONDITIONING** One possibility is that children learn language by *imitating* adults. While **imitation** plays some role in learning words (a parent points to a telephone, says "phone," and the child tries to repeat it), it cannot be the principal means by which children learn to produce and understand sentences. Young children constantly utter sentences they have never heard an adult say, such as "All gone milk." Even when children at the two-word stage try to imitate longer adult sentences (for example, "Mr. Miller will try"), they produce their usual telegraphic utterances

("Miller try"). In addition, the mistakes children make (for instance, "Daddy taked me") suggest that they are trying to apply rules, not simply trying to copy what they have heard adults say (Ervin-Tripp, 1964).

A second possibility is that children acquire language through **conditioning**. Adults may reward children when they produce a grammatical sentence and reprimand them when they make mistakes. For this to work, parents would have to respond to every detail in a child's speech. However, Brown, Cazden, and Bellugi (1969) found that parents do not pay attention to how the child says something as long as the statement is comprehensible. Rare attempts to correct a child (and hence to apply conditioning) are often futile.

CHILD:    Nobody don't like me.
MOTHER: No, say, "nobody likes me."
CHILD:    Nobody don't like me.
MOTHER: No, now listen carefully; say "nobody likes me."
CHILD:    Oh! Nobody don't LIKES me.  (McNeill, 1966, p. 49)

**HYPOTHESIS TESTING** The problem with imitation and conditioning is that they focus on specific utterances (one can only imitate or reinforce something specific). However, children often learn something general, such as a rule; they seem to form a hypothesis about a rule of language, test it, and retain it if it works.

Consider the morpheme "ed." As a general rule in English, "ed" is added to the present tense of verbs to form the past tense (as in "cook–cooked"). Many common verbs, however, are irregular and do not follow this rule (like "go–went" and "break–broke"). Many of these irregular verbs express concepts that children use from the beginning. So at an early point, children use the past tense of some irregular verbs correctly (presumably because they learned them by imitation). They learn the past tense for some regular verbs and discover the hypothesis "add 'ed' to the present tense to form the past tense." This hypothesis leads them to add the "ed" ending to all verbs, including the irregular ones. They say things such as "Annie goed home" and "Jackie breaked the cup," which they have never heard before. Eventually, they learn that some verbs are irregular and stop overgeneralizing their use of "ed."

How do children generate these hypotheses? There are a few *operating principles* that all children use as a guide to forming hypotheses. One is to pay attention to the ends of words. Another is to look for prefixes and suffixes that indicate a change in meaning. A child armed with these two principles is likely to hit the hypothesis that "ed" at the end of verbs signals the past tense, since "ed" is a word ending associated with a change in meaning. A third operating principle is to avoid exceptions, which explains why children initially generalize their "ed"-equals-past-tense hypothesis to irregular verbs. Some of these principles appear in Table 9-1 and they seem to hold for the 40 languages studied by Slobin (1971; 1985).

Recently, there has been a challenge to the idea that learning a language involves learning rules. Some researchers have argued that what looks like an instance of learning a single rule may in fact be a case of learning numerous associations or *connections* (like those in the connectionist models we considered in Chapters 5 and 8). Consider again a child learning the past tense of verbs in English. Instead of learning a rule about adding "ed" to the

1. Look for systematic changes in the form of words.

2. Look for grammatical markers that clearly indicate changes in meaning.

3. Avoid exceptions.

4. Pay attention to the ends of words.

5. Pay attention to the order of words, prefixes, and suffixes.

6. Avoid interruption or rearrangement of constituents (that is, sentence units).

**TABLE 9-1**
**Operating Principles Used by Young Children** *Children from many countries seem to follow these principles in learning to talk and to understand speech.* (After Slobin, 1971)

present tense of a verb, perhaps children are learning associations between the past tense ending "ed" and various *phonetic properties* of verbs that can go with "ed." The phonetic properties of a verb include properties of the sounds that make up the verb, such as whether it contains an "alk" sound at the end. Thus, a child may learn (unconsciously) that verbs containing an "alk" sound at the end—such as "talk," "walk," and "stalk"—are likely to take "ed" as a past tense ending. This proposal has in fact been shown to account for some aspects of learning verb endings, including the finding that at some point in development children add the "ed" ending even to irregular verbs (Rumelhart & McClelland, 1987). However, other aspects of learning verb endings cannot be explained in terms of associations between sounds. For example, the word "break" and the word "brake" (meaning to a stop a car) are identical in sound, but the past tense of the former is "broke" whereas that of the latter is "braked." So a child must learn something in addition to sound connections. This additional knowledge seems best cast in terms of rules (for example, "If a verb is derived from a noun—as in the case of 'brake'—*always* add 'ed' to form the past tense"). Language learning thus seems to involve rules as well as associations (Pinker & Prince, 1988).

## Innate Factors

As noted earlier, some of our knowledge about language is inborn, or innate. There are, however, controversial questions about the extent and nature of this innate knowledge. One question concerns its *richness*. If our innate knowledge is very rich, or specific, then the process of language acquisition should be similar for different languages (because all languages are based on the same knowledge). A second question about innate factors involves *critical periods*. As noted in Chapter 5, a common feature of innate behavior is that it will be acquired more readily if the organism is exposed to the right cues during a critical time period. Are there such critical periods in language acquisition? A third question about the innate contribution to language concerns its possible *uniqueness:* Is the ability to learn a language system unique to the human species? We will consider these three questions in turn.

**RICHNESS OF INNATE KNOWLEDGE** All children, regardless of their culture and language, seem to go through the same sequence of language development. At age 1, the child speaks a few isolated words; at about age 2, the child speaks two- and three-word sentences; at age 3, sentences become more grammatical; and at age 4, the child sounds much like an adult. The fact that this sequence is so consistent across cultures indicates that our innate knowledge about language is very rich.

Indeed, our innate knowledge of language seems to be so rich that children can go through the normal course of language acquisition even when there are no language users around them to serve as models. A group of researchers studied six deaf children of parents who could hear and who had decided not to have their children learn sign language. Before the children received any instruction in lip reading and vocalization—indeed, before they had acquired any knowledge of English—they began to use a system of gestures called **home sign**. Initially, their home sign was a kind of simple pantomime, but eventually it took on the properties of a language. For example, it was organized at both morphemic and syntactic levels, including individual signs and combinations of signs. In addition, these deaf children (who essentially created their own language) went through the same stages of development as normal hearing children. Thus, the deaf children initially gestured one sign at a time, then later put their pantomimes together into two- and three-concept "sentences." These striking results attest to the richness of our innate knowledge (Feldman, Goldin-Meadow, & Gleitman, 1978).

**CRITICAL PERIODS** Like other innate behaviors, language learning has some critical periods. This is particularly evident when it comes to acquiring the sound system of a new language—that is, learning new phonemes and their rules of combination. We have already noted that infants less than 1 year old can discriminate phonemes of any language, but lose this ability by the end of their first year. Hence, the first months of life are a critical period for honing in on the phonemes of one's native language. There also seems to be a critical period in acquiring the sound system of a second language. After a few years of learning a second language, young children are more likely than adults to speak it without an accent, and better able to understand the language when it is spoken in noisy conditions (Lenneberg, 1967; Snow, 1987).

Recent work indicates there is also a critical period in learning syntax. The evidence comes from studies of deaf people who know American Sign Language (abbreviated ASL), which is a full blown language and not a pantomime system. The studies of interest involved adults who had been using ASL for thirty years or more, but who varied in the age at which they first learned the language. Though all subjects were born to hearing parents, some were native signers who were exposed to ASL from birth, others first learned ASL between ages four and six when they enrolled in a special school for the deaf, and still others did not encounter ASL until after they were twelve (their hearing parents had been reluctant to let them learn a sign language rather than a spoken one). If there is a critical period for learning syntax, then the early learners should have shown a greater mastery of some aspects of syntax than the later learners, even thirty years after acquisition. This is exactly what the researchers found. Thus, with respect to understanding and producing words with multiple morphemes—like "untimely" which consists of the morphemes "un," "time," and "ly"—native signers did better than those who learned ASL when entering school, who in turn did better than those who learned ASL after age twelve (Newport, 1990; Meier, 1991).

## Can Another Species Learn Human Language?

Some experts believe that our innate capacity to learn language is unique to our species (Chomsky, 1972). They acknowledge that other species have communication systems but argue that these are qualitatively different from ours. Consider the communication system of the chimpanzee. This species' vocalizations and gestures are limited in number, and the *productivity* of its communication system is very low in comparison to human language, which permits the combination of a relatively small number of phonemes into thousands of words and the combination of these words into an unlimited number of sentences. Another difference is that human language is structured at several levels, whereas chimpanzee communications are not. In particular, in human language, a clear distinction exists between the level of words, or morphemes—at which the elements have meaning—and the level of sounds—at which the elements do not. There is no hint of such a *duality of structure* in chimpanzee communication, because every symbol carries meaning. Still another difference is that chimpanzees do not vary the *order* of their symbols to vary the meaning of their messages, while we

## Brain Localization

Given that innate factors play a large role in language acquisition, it is not surprising that regions of the human brain are specialized for language. In a Critical Discussion in Chapter 2 ("Language and the Brain"), we discussed how damage to certain regions of the left hemisphere results in *aphasia*, or language deficits. There we emphasized the relationship between the site of the brain damage and whether the resulting deficit was primarily one of production or comprehension. In the current discussion, we focus on the relation between the site of the damage and whether the deficit involves syntactic or conceptual knowledge.

Recall from Chapter 2 that there are two regions of the left hemisphere of the cortex that are critical for language: *Broca's area*, which lies in the frontal lobes, and *Wernicke's area*, which lies in the temporal-occipital region (see Figure 2-9). Damage to either of these areas leads to specific kinds of aphasia.

The disrupted language of a patient with *Broca's aphasia* is illustrated by the following interview in which "E" designates the interviewer and "P," the patient:

E:  Were you in the Coast Guard?

P:  No, er, yes, yes . . . ship . . . Massachu . . . chusetts . . . Coast Guard . . . years. [Raises hands twice with fingers indicating "19"]

E:  Oh, you were in the Coast Guard for 19 years.

P:  Oh . . . boy . . . right . . . right.

E:  Why are you in the hospital?

P:  [Points to paralyzed arm] Arm no good. [Points to mouth] Speech . . . can't say . . . talk, you see.

E:  What happened to make you lose your speech?

P:  Head, fall, Jesus Christ, me no good, str, str . . . oh Jesus . . . stroke.

E:  Could you tell me what you've been doing in the hospital?

P:  Yes sure. Me go, er, uh, P. T. nine o'cot, speech . . . two times . . . read . . . wr . . . ripe, er, rike, er, write . . . practice . . . get-ting better.

(Gardner, 1975, p. 61)

The speech is very disfluent. Even in simple sentences, pauses and hesitations are plentiful. This is in contrast to the fluent speech of a patient with *Wernicke's aphasia*:

Boy, I'm sweating, I'm awful nervous, you know, once in a while I get caught up. I can't mention the tarripoi, a month ago, quite a little, I've done a lot well, I impose a lot, while, on the other hand, you know what I mean, I have to run around, look it over, trebin and all that sort of stuff. (Gardner, 1975, p. 68)

In addition to fluency, there are other marked differences between Broca's and Wernicke's aphasias. The speech of a Broca's aphasic consists mainly of content words. It contains few grammatical morphemes and complex sentences and, in general, has a telegraphic quality that is reminiscent of the two-word stage of language acquisition. In contrast, the language of a Wernicke's aphasic preserves syntax but is remarkably devoid of content. There are clear problems in finding the right noun, and occasionally words are invented for the occasion (as in the use of "tarripoi" and "trebbin"). These observations suggest that Broca's aphasia involves a disruption at the syntactic stage, while Wernicke's aphasia involves a disruption at the level of words and concepts.

---

do. For instance, for us, "Jonah ate the whale" means something quite different from "The whale ate Jonah"; there is no evidence for a comparable difference in chimpanzee communications.

The fact that chimpanzee communication is impoverished compared to our own does not prove that chimpanzees lack the capacity for a more productive system. Their system may be adequate for their needs. To determine if chimpanzees have the same innate capacity we do, we must see if they can learn our language.

In one of the best known studies of teaching our language to chimps, Gardner and Gardner (1972) taught a female chimpanzee named Washoe signs adapted from American Sign Language. Sign language was used because chimps lack the vocal equipment to pronounce human sounds. Training began when Washoe was about a year old and continued until she was 5. During this time, Washoe's caretakers communicated with her only by means of sign language. They first taught her signs by shaping procedures, waiting for her to make a gesture that resembled a sign, and then reinforcing her. Later Washoe learned signs simply by observing and imitating. By age

These characterizations of the two aphasias are supported by experiments. In a study that tested for a syntactic deficit, subjects had to listen to a sentence on each trial and show that they understood it by selecting a picture (from a set) that the sentence described. Some sentences could be understood without using much syntactic knowledge. For example, given "The bicycle the boy is holding is broken," one can figure out that it is the bicycle that is broken and not the boy, solely from one's knowledge of the concepts involved. Understanding other sentences requires extensive syntactic analysis. In "The lion that the tiger is chasing is fat," one must rely on syntax (word order) to determine that it is the lion who is fat and not the tiger. On those sentences that did not require much syntactic analysis, Broca's aphasics did almost as well as normals, scoring close to 90 percent correct. But with sentences that required extensive analysis, Broca's aphasics fell to the level of guessing (for example, given the sentence about the lion and tiger, they were as likely to select the picture with a fat tiger as the one with the fat lion). In contrast, the performance of Wernicke's aphasics did not depend on the syntactic demands of the sentence. Thus, Broca's aphasia, but not Wernicke's, seems to be partly a disruption of syntax (Caramazza & Zurif, 1976). The disruption is not total, though, in that Broca's aphasics are capable of handling certain kinds of syntactic analysis (Grodzinski, 1984).

Other work suggests that part of the deficit in Broca's aphasia involves a problem in accessing a word's meaning. Understanding a sentence requires accessing the meaning of each constituent word, and this process appears to be slowed in Broca's aphasia. Support for this claim comes from some recent experiments. These studies take as their starting point the findings that normal subjects access both meanings of an ambiguous word immediately upon hearing the word (see p. 347). In comparable experiments with Broca's aphasics, only the most frequent meaning of an ambiguous word is accessed early on. Thus, immediately after hearing the sentence "He took a walk near the bank of the river," normal subjects read a test word faster if it was related to either meaning of "bank" (for example, "land" or "money") than if it was unrelated to either meaning (for example, "lemon"); this indicates that both meanings of "bank" were accessed, and either meaning could prime the reading of a related word. In contrast, after Broca's aphasics heard the same sentence, they read the test word faster only when it was related to the more frequent or financial meaning of "bank" (for example, they read "money" faster but not "land"). Thus Broca's aphasics may fail to make the appropriate word meanings available at the right time in the processing sequence (Swinney, Zurif, & Nicol, 1989).

Other experiments have tested for a conceptual deficit in Wernicke's aphasia. In one study, subjects were presented three words at a time and were asked to select the two that were most similar in meaning. The words included animal terms, such as "dog" and "crocodile," as well as human terms, such as "mother" and "knight." Normal subjects used the distinction between humans and animals as the major basis for their selections; given "dog," "crocodile," and "knight," for example, they selected the first two. Wernicke's patients, however, ignored this basic distinction. Although Broca's aphasics showed some differences from normals, their selections at least respected the human–animal distinction. A conceptual deficit is thus more pronounced in Wernicke's aphasics than in Broca's aphasics (Zurif, Caramazza, Myerson, & Galvin, 1974).

4, Washoe could produce 130 different signs and understand even more. She could also generalize a sign from one situation to another. For example, she first learned the sign for *more* in connection with *more tickling* and then generalized it to indicate *more milk*.

Other chimpanzees that were studied acquired comparable vocabularies. Some of these studies used methods of manual communication other than sign language. For example, Premack (1971; 1983) taught a chimpanzee named Sarah to use plastic symbols as words and to communicate by manipulating these symbols. In a series of similar studies, Patterson (1978) taught sign language to a gorilla named Koko, starting when Koko was 1 year old. By age 10, Koko had a vocabulary of more than 400 signs (Patterson & Linden, 1981).

Do these studies prove that apes can learn human language? There seems to be little doubt that the apes' signs are equivalent to our words and that the concepts behind some of these signs are equivalent to ours. But there are grave doubts about these studies showing that apes can learn to combine signs in the manner that humans combine words into a sentence.

Thus, not only can people combine the words "snake," "Eve," "killed," and "the" into the sentence "The snake killed Eve," but we can also combine the same words in a different order to produce a sentence with a different meaning, "Eve killed the snake." Although the studies reviewed provide some evidence that apes can combine signs into a sequence resembling a sentence, little evidence exists to show that apes can alter the order of the signs to produce a different sentence (Slobin, 1979; Brown, 1986).

Even the evidence that apes can combine signs into a sentence has come under attack. In early work, researchers reported cases in which an ape produced what seemed to be a meaningful sequence of signs, such as "Gimme flower" and "Washoe sorry" (Gardner & Gardner, 1972). As data accumulated, it became apparent that, unlike human sentences, the utterances of an ape are often highly repetitive. Thus, "You me banana me banana you" is typical of the signing chimps but would be most odd for a human child. In the cases in which an ape utterance is more like a sentence, the ape may have simply been imitating the sequence of signs made by its human teacher. Thus, some of Washoe's most sentence-like utterances occurred when she was answering a question; for example, the teacher signed "Washoe eat?" and then Washoe signed "Washoe eat time." Here, Washoe's combination of signs may have been a partial imitation of her teacher's combination, which is not how human children learn to combine words (Terrace et al., 1979).

The evidence considered thus far supports the conclusion that, although apes can develop a human-like vocabulary, they cannot learn to combine their signs in the systematic way we do. However, a recent study seems to challenge this conclusion (Greenfield & Savage-Rumbaugh, 1990). The researchers worked with a new kind of subject, a pygmy chimpanzee, whose behavior is thought to be more like that of humans than the behavior of the more widely studied common chimpanzee. The subject, a 7-year-old named Kanzi, communicates by manipulating symbols that stand for words. Unlike the case in previous studies, Kanzi learned to manipulate the symbols in a relatively natural way, for example, by listening to his caretakers as they uttered English words while pointing to the symbols. Most importantly, after a

 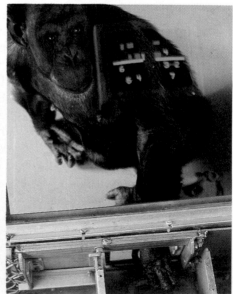

(Left), *5-year-old Panzee goes for a walk after selecting the destination on her keyboard.* (Right), *Lana counts by using a joystick to manipulate numbers on a screen.*

few years of language training, Kanzi demonstrates some ability to vary word order to communicate changes in meaning. For example, if Kanzi were going to bite his half-sister Mulika he would signal "bite Mulika"; but if his sister bit him, he would sign "Mulika bite." Kanzi thus seems to have some syntactic knowledge, roughly that of a 2-year-old human.

These results are tantalizing, but they need to be interpreted with caution. For one thing, so far Kanzi is the only chimpanzee who's shown any syntactic ability; hence, there's a question of how general the results are. Another matter is that, although Kanzi may have the linguistic ability of a 2-year-old, it took him substantially longer to get to that point than it does a human; also, we do not yet know if Kanzi, or any other chimpanzee, can get much beyond that point. But perhaps the main reason to be skeptical about any ape developing comparable linguistic abilities to a human has been voiced by Chomsky (1991):

> If an animal had a capacity as biologically advantageous as language but somehow hadn't used it until now, it would be an evolutionary miracle, like finding an island of humans who could be taught to fly.

# Imaginal Thought

We mentioned at the beginning of the chapter that, in addition to propositional thought, we can also think in an imaginal mode, particularly in terms of visual images. Such visual thinking is the concern of the present section.

## Imagery and Perception

Many of us feel that we do some of our thinking visually. Often it seems that we retrieve past perceptions, or parts of them, and then operate on them in the way we would a real percept. For example, when asked, "What shape are a German shepherd's ears?" most people report that they form a visual image of a German shepherd's head and "look" at the ears to determine their shape. If asked, "What new letter is formed when an upper case *N* is rotated 90 degrees?" people report first forming an image of a capital *N*, then mentally "rotating" it 90 degrees and "looking" at it to determine its identity. And if asked, "How many windows are there in your parents' living room?" people report imagining the room and then "scanning" the image while counting the windows (Shepard & Cooper, 1982; Kosslyn, 1983).

The above examples rest on subjective impressions, but they and other evidence suggest that imagery involves the same representations and processes that are used in perception (Finke, 1985). Our images of objects and places have visual detail: we see the German shepherd, the *N*, or our parents' living room in our "mind's eye." Moreover, the mental operations that we perform on these images seem to be analogous to the operations that we carry out on real visual objects: we scan the image of our parents' room in much the same way we would scan a real room, and we rotate our image of the *N* the way we would rotate the real object.

Imagery may be like perception because it is mediated by the same parts of the brain. Some support for this idea comes from studies of people who have suffered brain damage in a certain region of the right hemisphere. Such patients may develop *visual neglect* of the left side; though not blind, they ignore everything on the left side of their visual field. A male patient, for example, may forget to shave the left side of his face. This visual neglect extends to imagery. When patients are asked to construct a mental image of a familiar location (say, a shopping area) and report all of its contents, they may report only those things on the right side of their image (Bisiach & Luzzatti, 1978). The brain damage has led to the identical problem in perception and imagery.

More recent studies provide further evidence that the parts of the brain involved in perception are also involved in imagery. In one experiment, subjects performed both a mental arithmetic task ("Start at 50, and count down, subtracting by 3s") and a visual imagery task ("Visualize a walk through your neighborhood, making alternating right and left turns starting at your door"). While a subject was doing each task, the amount of blood flow in various areas of his or her cortex was measured. There was more blood flow in the visual cortex when subjects engaged in the imagery task than the mental arithmetic one. Moreover, the pattern of blood flow found during the imagery task was like that normally found in perceptual tasks (Roland & Friberg, 1985). Similar results have been obtained in studies that use other measures of cortical activity, such as EEG techniques that measure brain waves in various regions of the brain. These studies show that there is more electrical activity in the visual cortex when subjects engage in an imagery task than a verbal task. Increasingly, there are detailed studies of imagery that use state-of-the-art *brain-scanning techniques*—such as the measurement of blood flow and electrical activity—and which convincingly demonstrate that the specific brain regions involved in an imagery task are the same as those involved in a comparable perceptual task (Farah, 1988; Kosslyn, 1987).

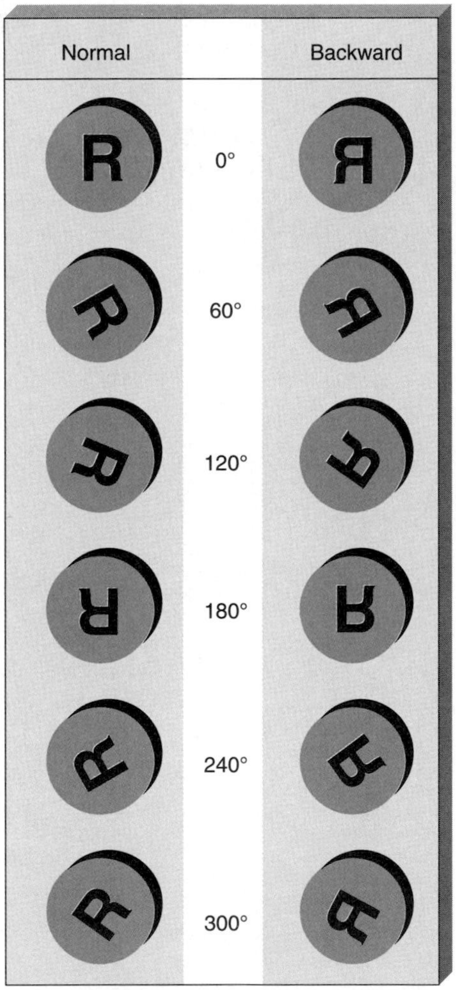

## Imaginal Operations

We have noted that the mental operations performed on images seem to be analogous to those we carry out on real visual objects. Numerous experiments provide objective evidence for these subjective impressions.

One operation that has been studied intensively is mental rotation. In one experiment, subjects saw the capital letter R on each trial. The letter was presented either normally (R) or backward (Я) and in its usual vertical orientation or rotated various degrees (see Figure 9-7). The subjects had to decide if the letter was normal or backward. The more the letter had been rotated from its vertical orientation, the longer it took the subjects to make the decision (see Figure 9-8). This finding suggests that subjects made their decisions by mentally rotating the image of the letter until it was vertical and then checking whether it was normal or backward.

Mental rotation can be used as an aid to perception, particularly the perceptual recognition of rotated objects. When we come across an object that fails to match any stored representation in visual memory (that is, no recognition occurs), we may mentally rotate the object, constantly checking (unconsciously) whether the rotated object matches something in visual memory. Thus imagery and perception may be very tightly linked (Ullman, 1989).

Another operation that is similar in imagery and perception is that of scanning an object or array. In an experiment on scanning an image, subjects first studied the map of a fictional island, which contained seven critical locations. The map was removed, and subjects were asked to form an image of it and fixate on a particular location (for example, the tree in the southern part of the island—see Figure 9-9). Then the experimenter named another

| Normal | | Backward |
|--------|------|----------|
| R | 0° | Я |
| R | 60° | Я |
| R | 120° | Я |
| R | 180° | Я |
| R | 240° | Я |
| R | 300° | Я |

**FIGURE 9-7**
**Study of Mental Rotation** *Shown are examples of the letters presented to subjects in studies of mental rotation. On each presentation, subjects had to decide whether the letter was normal or backward. Numbers indicate deviation from the vertical in degrees.* (After Cooper & Shepard, 1973)

location (for example, the tree at the northern tip of the island). Starting at the fixated location, the subjects were to scan their images until they found the named location and were to push a button on "arrival" there. The greater the distance between the fixated location and the named one, the longer the subjects took to respond. This suggests subjects were scanning their images in much the same way they scan real objects.

Another commonality between imaginal and perceptual processing is that both are limited by *grain size*. On a television screen, for instance, the grain of the picture tube determines how small the details of a picture can be and still remain perceptible. While there is no actual screen in the brain, we can think of our images as occurring in a *mental medium*, the grain of which limits the amount of detail we can detect in an image. If this grain size is fixed, then smaller images should be more difficult to inspect than larger ones. There is a good deal of support for this claim. In one experiment, subjects first formed an image of a familiar animal—say, a cat. Then they were asked to decide whether or not the imaged object had a particular property. Subjects made decisions faster for larger properties, such as the head, than for smaller ones, such as the claws. In another study, subjects were asked to image an animal at different relative sizes—small, medium, or large. Subjects were then asked to decide whether their images had a particular property. Their decisions were faster for larger images than smaller ones. Thus, in imagery as in perception, the larger the image, the more readily we can see the details of an object (Kosslyn, 1980).

## Visual Creativity

There are innumerable stories about scientists and artists producing their most creative work through visual thinking (Shepard & Cooper, 1982). Although not hard evidence, these stories are among the best indicators that we have of the power of visual thinking. It is surprising that visual thinking appears to be quite effective in highly abstract areas like mathematics and physics. Albert Einstein, for example, said he rarely thought in words; rather, he worked out his ideas in terms of "more or less clear images which can be 'voluntarily' reproduced and combined." Perhaps the most celebrated example is in chemistry. Friedrich Kekule von Stradonitz was trying to determine the molecular structure of benzene. One night he dreamed that a writhing, snakelike figure suddenly twisted into a closed loop, biting its own tail. The structure of the snake proved to be the structure of benzene. A dream image had provided the solution to a major scientific problem. Visual images can also be a creative force for writers. Samuel Coleridge's famous poem "Kubla Khan" supposedly came to him in its entirety as a prolonged visual image.

## Thought in Action: Problem Solving

For many people, solving a problem epitomizes thinking itself. In problem solving, we are striving for a goal but have no ready means of obtaining it. We must break the goal into subgoals and perhaps divide these subgoals further into smaller subgoals, until we reach a level that we have the means to obtain (Anderson, 1990).

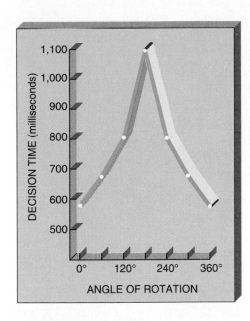

**FIGURE 9-8**
**Decision Times in Mental Rotation Study** *The time taken to decide whether a letter had normal or reversed orientation was greatest when the rotation was 180° so that the letter was upside down.* (After Cooper & Shepard, 1973)

**FIGURE 9-9**
**Scanning Mental Images** *The subject scans the image of the island from south to north, looking for the named location. It appears as though the subject's mental image is like a real map and that it takes longer to scan across the mental image if the distance to be scanned is greater.* (After Kosslyn, Ball, & Reiser, 1978)

We can illustrate these points with a simple problem. Suppose you need to figure out the combination of an unfamiliar lock. You know only that the combination has four numbers and that whenever you come across a correct number, you will hear a click. Your overall goal is to find the combination. Rather than trying four numbers at random, most people decompose the overall goal into four subgoals, each corresponding to finding one of the four numbers in the combination. Your first subgoal is to find the first number, and you have a procedure for accomplishing this—namely, turning the lock slowly while listening for a click. Your second subgoal is to find the second number, and you can use the same procedure, and so on for the remaining subgoals.

The strategies that people use to decompose goals into subgoals is a major issue in the study of problem solving. Another issue is how people mentally represent a problem, because this also affects how readily we can solve the problem. The following discussion considers both of these issues.

## Problem-Solving Strategies

Much of what we know about strategies for decomposing goals derives from the research of Newell and Simon (see, for example, Newell & Simon, 1972). Typically, the researchers ask subjects to think aloud while trying to solve a difficult problem, and they analyze the subjects' verbal responses for clues to the underlying strategy. A number of general-purpose strategies have been identified.

One strategy is to reduce the difference between our *current state* in a problem situation and our *goal state*, wherein a solution is obtained. Consider again the combination lock problem. Initially, our current state includes no knowledge of any of the numbers, while our goal state includes knowledge of all four numbers. We therefore set up the subgoal of reducing the difference between these two states; determining the first number accomplishes this subgoal. Our current state now includes knowledge of the first number. There is still a difference between our current state and our goal state, and we can reduce it by determining the second number, and so on. Thus, the critical idea behind **difference reduction** is that we set up subgoals that, when obtained, put us in a state that is closer to our goal.

A similiar but more sophisticated strategy is **means-ends analysis.** Here, we compare our current state to the goal state in order to find the most important difference between them; eliminating this difference becomes our main subgoal. We then search for a means or a procedure to achieve this subgoal. If we find such a procedure but discover that something in our current state prevents us from applying it, we introduce a new subgoal of eliminating this obstacle. Many commonsense problem-solving situations involve this strategy. Here is an example:

> I want to take my son to nursery school. What's the [most important] difference between what I have and what I want? One of distance. What [procedure] changes distance? My automobile. My automobile won't work. What is needed to make it work? A new battery. What has new batteries? An auto repair shop. (After Newell & Simon, 1972, as cited in Anderson, 1990, p. 232)

Means-ends analysis is more sophisticated than difference reduction because it allows us to take action even if it results in a temporary decrease in similarity between our current state and the goal state. In the above example, the auto repair shop may be in the opposite direction from the nursery school. Going to the shop thus temporarily increases the distance from the goal, yet this step is essential for solving the problem.

Another strategy is to work backward from the goal. This is particularly useful in solving mathematical problems, such as that illustrated in Figure 9-10. The problem is this: given that ABCD is a rectangle, prove that AD and BC are the same length. In **working backwards,** one might proceed as follows:

> What could prove that AD and BC are the same length? I could prove this if I could prove that the triangles ACD and BDC are congruent. I can prove that ACD and BDC are congruent if I could prove that two sides and an included angle are equal. (After Anderson, 1990, p. 238)

We reason from the goal to a subgoal (proving the triangles congruent), from that subgoal to another subgoal (proving the sides and angle equal), and so on, until we reach a subgoal that we have a ready means of obtaining.

The three strategies we have considered—difference reduction, means-ends analysis, and working backwards—are extremely general, and can be applied to virtually any problem. These strategies, which are often referred to as **weak methods,** do not rest on any specific knowledge and may even be innate. People may especially rely on these weak methods when they are first learning about an area and are working on problems with unfamiliar content. We will soon see that when people gain expertise in an area they develop more powerful domain-specific procedures (and representations), which come to dominate the weak methods (Anderson, 1987).

## Representing the Problem

Being able to solve a problem depends not only on our strategy for decomposing it but also on how we represent it. Sometimes a propositional mode, or representation, works best; at other times, a visual image is more effective. To illustrate, consider the following problem:

> One morning, exactly at sunrise, a monk began to climb a mountain. A narrow path, a foot or two wide, spiraled around the mountain to a temple at the summit. The monk ascended at varying rates, stopping many times along the way to rest. He reached the temple shortly before sunset. After several days at the temple, he began his journey back along the same path, starting at sunrise and again walking at variable speeds with many pauses along the way. His average speed descending was, of course, greater than his average climbing speed. Prove that there exists a particular spot along the path that the monk will occupy on both trips at precisely the same time of day. (Adams, 1974, p. 4)

In trying to solve this problem, many people start with a propositional representation. They may even try to write out a set of equations and soon confuse themselves. The problem is far easier to solve when it is represented visually. All you need do is visualize the upward journey of the monk superimposed on the downward journey. Imagine one monk starting at the bottom and the other at the top. No matter what their speed, at some time and at some point along the path the two monks will meet. Thus, there must be a spot along the path the monk occupied on both trips at precisely the same time of day. (Note that the problem did not ask you *where* the spot was.)

Some problems can be readily solved by manipulating either propositions or images. We can illustrate with the following problem: "Ed runs

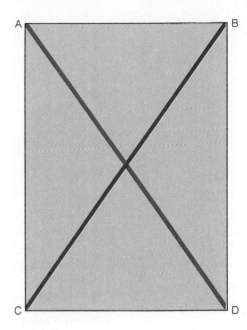

**FIGURE 9-10**
**An Illustrative Geometry Problem**
*Given that ABCD is a rectangle, prove that the line segments AD and BC are the same length.*

*Learning aids help students visualize a math problem.*

**FIGURE 9-11**
**Materials for Candle Problem** *Given the materials depicted (left), how can you support a candle on a door? The solution is shown on page 366.* (After Glucksberg & Weisberg, 1966)

faster than David but slower than Dan; who's the slowest of the three men?" To solve this problem in terms of propositions, note that we can represent the first part of the problem as a proposition that has "David" as subject and "is slower than Ed" as predicate. We can represent the second part of the problem as a proposition with "Ed" as subject and "is slower than Dan" as predicate. We can then deduce that David is slower than Dan, which makes David the slowest. To solve the problem by imagery, we might, for example, imagine the three men's speeds as points on a line, like this:

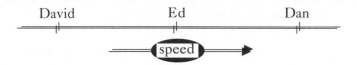

Then we can simply "read" the answer to the question directly from the image. Apparently, some people prefer to represent such problems as propositions, while others tend to represent them visually (Johnson-Laird, 1985).

In addition to the issue of propositions versus images, there are questions about *what* gets represented. Often, we have difficulty with a problem because we fail to include something critical in our representation or because we include something in our representation that is *not* an important part of the problem. We can illustrate with an experiment. One group of subjects was posed the problem of supporting a candle on a door, given only the materials depicted in Figure 9-11. The solution was to tack the box to the door and use the box as a platform for the candle. Most subjects had difficulty with the problem, presumably because they represented the box as a container, not as a platform. Another group of subjects was given the identical problem, except that the contents of the box were removed. These subjects had more success in solving the problem, presumably because they were less likely to include the box's container property in their representation and more likely to include its supporter property.

## Experts versus Novices

In a given content area (physics, geography, or chess, for instance), experts solve problems qualitatively differently than novices. These differences are due to differences in the representations and strategies that experts and novices use. Experts have many more specific representations stored in memory that they can bring to bear on a problem. A master chess player, for example, can look for 5 seconds at a complex board configuration of over 20 pieces and reproduce it perfectly; a novice in this situation can reproduce only the usual $7 \pm 2$ items (see Chapter 8). Experts can accomplish this memory feat because, through years of practice, they have developed representations of many possible board configurations; these representations permit them to encode a complex configuration in just a chunk or two. Further, these representations are presumably what underlies their superior chess game. A master may have stored as many as 50,000 configurations and has learned what to do when each arises. Thus, master chess players can essentially "see" possible moves; they do not have to think them out the way novices do (Chase & Simon, 1973; Simon & Gilmartin, 1973).

Even when confronted with a novel problem, experts represent it differently than novices. This point is nicely illustrated in studies of problem solving in physics. An expert (say, a physics professor) represents a problem in terms of the physical principle that is needed for solution: for example, "this is one of those every-action-has-an-equal-and-opposite-reaction problems." In contrast, a novice (say, a student taking a first course in physics) tends to represent the same problem in terms of its surface features: for example, "this is one of those inclined-plane problems" (Chi, Glaser, & Rees, 1982).

Experts and novices also differ in the strategies they employ. In studies of physics problem solving, experts generally try to formulate a plan for attacking the problem before generating equations, whereas novices typically start writing equations with no general plan in mind (Larkin, McDermott, Simon, & Simon, 1980). Another difference is that experts tend to reason from the givens of a problem toward a solution, while novices tend to work in the reverse direction (the working-backward strategy). This difference in the direction of reasoning has also been obtained in studies of how physicians solve problems. More expert physicians tend to reason in a forward direction—from symptom to possible disease—while the less expert tend to reason in a backward direction—from possible disease to symptom (Patel & Groen, 1986).

The characteristics of expertise we have just discussed—a multitude of representations, representations based on principles, planning before acting, and working-forwards—make up some of the domain-specific procedures that come to dominate the weak methods of problem solving discussed earlier.

## Computer Simulation

To study how people solve problems, researchers often use the method of **computer simulation.** After having people think aloud while solving a complex problem, researchers use their verbal reports as a guide in programming a computer to solve the problem. Then the output of the computer

*A novice player solves chess problems differently from an expert.*

*The solution to the candle problem.*

can be compared to aspects of people's performance on the problem—say, the sequence of moves—to see if they match. If they match, the computer program offers a theory of some aspects of problem solving. Computer simulation has played a major role in the development of the weak methods of problem solving as well as of expert procedures.

Why use computers in this way to learn about people? Perhaps the most interesting answer is Simon's claim: "The reason human beings can think is because they are able to carry out with neurons the simple kinds of processes that computers do with tubes or chips" (1985, p. 3). These simple processes include reading, outputting, storing, and comparing symbols; we do one thing if the symbols match and another if they differ. To the extent that we can closely simulate human problem solving on a digital computer, which uses just these simple processes, we have support for Simon's claim.

Consider what is involved in trying to write a computer program that simulates the way many of us solve simple algebraic equations. When confronted with the equation $3X + 4 = X + 10$, you might have learned to reason as follows:

> The solution of the equation looks like an X followed by an = sign followed by a number—not any number, it has to be one that will fit the equation if I substitute it back in. If I start out with something that has a number on the left side where I don't want it, then I better get rid of it. So given $3X + 4 = X + 10$, I subtract the 4 (I know I have to subtract it from both sides). Then I have a new equation $3X = X + 6$. But I don't want an X on the right side of the equation. So I subtract it and now have $2X = 6$. Now I don't want a 2X, but instead just a plain X on the left side of the equation, so I divide by 2. Then I have $X = 3$. (After Simon, 1985, p. 6)

The above reasoning can be captured by four rules:

1. If there is a number on the left side of the equation, then subtract it from both sides.
2. If there is an X or a multiple of X on the right side of the equation, then subtract it from both sides.
3. If there is a number in front of the X on the left side of the equation, then divide both sides of the equation by it.
4. If you arrive at an equation that looks like "X = Number," quit and check your answer.

Though probably you do not articulate these rules, they may underlie your ability to solve algebraic equations. These rules can readily be translated into a computer program. A program is simply a detailed set of instructions (written in a language designed for a computer) that specifies every step the machine must take. Our rules can be treated as such instructions. Thus, simulation requires that we first be precise about the knowledge involved and then translate it into the language of a computer.

Computer simulation is not without its critics. Some have challenged the basic analogy between computers and people: computers, they say, can only do what they have been programmed to do. However, it is quite possible that humans can also do only what heredity and experience have "programmed" them to do. Another criticism is that the physical basis of human thought, the brain, is very different from the electrical circuitry of computers. Clearly, a brain and a computer differ physically, but they may be similar in how they are organized and how they function. Indeed, such abstract sim-

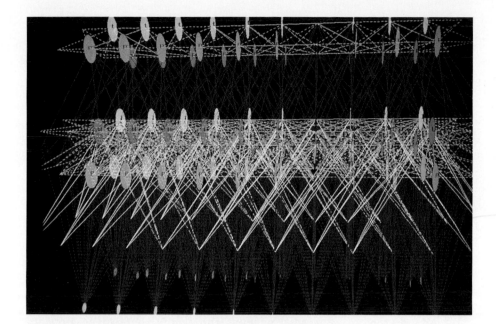

*A computer simulation of mental processes.*

ilarities between brain (or mind) and computers are part of what lies behind the current cognitive perspective on psychology.

At points in this chapter on human thought and language, we have raised questions about these abilities in nonhumans. We have discussed apes that talk or almost talk, and computers that appear to think. These discussions and comparisons suggest that we can improve our understanding of human intelligence by comparing it to nonhuman intelligence, be it natural or of our own making.

## *Chapter* SUMMARY

1. Thought occurs in different modes, including *propositional, imaginal,* and *motoric*. The basic component of a proposition is a *concept,* the set of properties that we associate with a class. Concepts provide us *cognitive economy,* by allowing us to code many different objects as instances of the same concept, and also permit us to *predict information* that is not readily perceptible.

2. A concept includes both a *prototype* (properties that describe the best examples) and a *core* (properties that are most essential for being a member of the concept). Core properties play a major role in *classical* concepts, such as "bachelor"; prototype properties dominate in *fuzzy* concepts such as "bird." Concepts are sometimes organized into hierarchies; in such cases, one level of the hierarchy is the *basic* or preferred level for categorization.

3. Children often learn the prototype of a concept by an *exemplar strategy*. With this technique, a novel item is classified as an instance of a concept if it is sufficiently similar to a known exemplar of the concept. As children grow older, they use *hypothesis testing* as another strategy for learning concepts. In addition, people use *top-down* strategies of concept learning in which they employ their prior knowledge along with the known instances to determine the properties of a concept.

4. In reasoning, we organize our propositions into an argument. Some arguments are *deductively valid:* it is impossible that the conclusion of the argument is false if its premises are true. When evaluating a deductive

argument, we sometimes try to prove that the conclusion follows from the premises by using logical rules. Other times, however, we use *heuristics*—rules of thumb—that operate on the content of propositions rather than on their logical form.

5. Some arguments are *inductively strong:* it is improbable that the conclusion is false if the premises are true. In generating and evaluating such arguments, we often ignore some of the principles of probability theory and rely instead on heuristics that focus on similarity or causality. For example, we may estimate the probability that a person belongs to a category by determining the person's similarity to the category's prototype. Or we may estimate the probability that some member of a category has a particular property by determining the similarity of that member to members known to have the property.

6. Language, our primary means for communicating thoughts, is structured at three levels. At the highest level are *sentence units*, including phrases that can be related to units of propositions. The next level is that of *words* and *parts of words* that carry meaning. The lowest level contains *speech sounds*. The phrases of a sentence are built from words (and other parts of words), whereas the words themselves are constructed from speech sounds.

7. A *phoneme* is a category of speech sounds. Every language has its own set of phonemes and rules for combining them into words. A *morpheme* is the smallest unit that carries meaning. Most morphemes are words: others are prefixes and suffixes that are added onto words. A language also has *syntactic* rules for combining words into phrases and phrases into sentences. Understanding a sentence requires not only analyzing phonemes, morphemes, and phrases, but also using context and understanding the *speaker's intention*.

8. Language development occurs at three different levels. Infants come into the world preset to learn phonemes, but they need several years to learn the rules for combining them. When children begin to speak, they learn words that name familiar concepts. If they want to communicate a concept that is as yet unnamed, they may *overextend* the name of a neighboring concept (for example, they use "doggie" to name cats and cows). In learning to produce sentences, children begin with one-word utterances, progress to two-word telegraphic speech, and then elaborate their noun and verb phrases.

9. Children learn language at least partly by testing hypotheses. Children's hypotheses appear to be guided by a small set of *operating principles*, which call the children's attention to critical characteristics of utterances, such as word endings. Innate factors also play a role in language acquisition. Our innate knowledge of language seems to be very rich, as suggested by the fact that all children seem to go through the same stages in acquiring a language. Like other innate behaviors, some language abilities are learned only during a *critical period*. It is a matter of controversy whether or not our innate capacity to learn language is unique to our species. Many studies suggest that chimpanzees and gorillas can learn signs that are equivalent to our words, but they have difficulty learning to combine these signs in the systematic manner that humans do.

10. Not all thoughts are expressed in propositions; some are manifested as visual images. Such images contain the kind of visual detail found in perceptions. Imagery may be like perception because it is mediated by

the same parts of the brain. Thus, brain damage that results in certain perceptual problems, *visual neglect*, also results in comparable problems in imagery. Also, experiments using *brain scanning techniques* indicate that the specific brain regions involved in an imagery task are the same as those involved in a perceptual task. In addition, the mental operations performed on images (such as scanning and rotation) are like the operations carried out on perceptions.

11. Problem solving requires decomposing a goal into subgoals that are easier to obtain. Strategies for such decomposition include *reducing differences* between the *current state* and the *goal state; means-ends analysis* (eliminating the most important differences between the current and goal states); and *working backward*. Some problems are easier to solve by using a propositional representation; for other problems, a visual representation works best.

12. Expert problem solvers differ from novices in four basic ways: they have more representations to bring to bear on the problem; they represent novel problems in terms of solution principles rather than surface features; they form a plan before acting; and they tend to reason forward rather than working backward. A useful method for studying problem solving is *computer simulation*, in which one tries to write a computer program that solves problems the same way people do. This method requires that we be precise about the knowledge involved in solving the problem.

## Further READING

There are three recent introductions to the psychology of thinking: Osherson and Smith, *Invitation to Cognitive Science (Vol. 3): Thinking* (1990), Sternberg and Smith (Eds.), *The Psychology of Human Thought* (1988), and Baron, *Thinking and Deciding* (1988). The study of concepts is reviewed in Smith and Medin, *Categories and Concepts* (1981). Research on reasoning is reviewed by Kahneman, Slovic, and Tversky, *Judgment Under Uncertainty: Heuristics and Biases* (1982); for more advanced treatments of reasoning, see Holland, Holyoak, Nisbett, and Thagard, *Induction: Processes of Inference, Learning, and Discovery* (1986) and Johnson-Laird and Byrne, *Deduction* (1991). For an introduction to the study of imagery, see Kosslyn, *Ghosts in the Mind's Machine* (1983). For more advanced treatments of imagery, see Kosslyn, *Image and Mind* (1980), and Shepard and Cooper, *Mental Images and Their Transformations* (1982). For an introduction to problem solving, see Anderson, *Cognitive Psychology and Its Implications*, 3rd ed. (1990), Hayes, *The Complete Problem Solver*, 2nd ed. (1989), Mayer, *Thinking, Problem Solving, and Cognition* (1983); for an advanced treatment, see the classic by Newell and Simon, *Human Problem Solving* (1972).

Numerous books deal with the psychology of language. Standard introductions include Clark and Clark, *Psychology and Language: An Introduction to Psycholinguistics* (1977); and Foss and Hakes, *Psycholinguistics: An Introduction to the Psychology of Language* (1978). For more recent surveys, see Osherson and Lasnik, *Invitation to Cognitive Science* (Vol. 1): *Language* (1990); Tartter, *Language Processes* (1986); and Carroll, *Psychology of Language* (1985). For a more advanced treatment, particularly of issues related to Chomsky's theory of language and thought, see Chomsky, *Rules and Representations* (1980); and Fodor, Bever, and Garrett, *The Psychology of Language* (1974). For an account of early language development, see Brown, *A First Language: The Early Stages* (1973); and Pinker, *Language Learnability and Language Development* (1984).

# Part  V

*Motivation and Emotion*

10 Basic Motives

11 Emotion

*Northeaster*, 1895, by Winslow Homer (1836–1910), oil on canvas, $24\frac{3}{8}" \times 50\frac{1}{4}"$, The Metropolitan Museum of Art, Gift of George A. Hearn, 1910.

# Chapter 10

# Basic Motives

## Survival Motives and Homeostasis 373
*Nature of Homeostasis*
*Temperature Regulation as a Homeostatic System*
*Thirst as a Homeostatic System*

## Hunger 377
*Variables of Hunger*
*Satiety Detectors*
*Brain Mechanisms*

## Obesity and Anorexia 382
*Genetic Factors in Obesity*
*Overeating and Obesity*
*Dieting and Weight Control*
*Anorexia*
*Bulimia*

## Adult Sexuality 393
*Hormonal Control*
*Neural Control*
*Early Experiences*
*Cultural Influences*
*Homosexuality*

## Early Sexual Development 404
*Prenatal Hormones*
*Hormones versus Environment*
*Transsexualism*

## Maternal Behavior 407
*Biological Determinants*
*Critical Discussion: Instincts and Maternal-Infant Behavior*
*Environmental Determinants*

## Curiosity Motives 410
*Exploration and Manipulation*
*Sensory Stimulation*

## Common Principles for Different Motives 413

Detail, *Northeaster.*

Having discussed what people can *do*—sense, perceive, learn, remember, think—we will now consider what they *want*. The study of wants and needs goes under the heading of **motivation** and is concerned with factors that energize behavior and give it direction. A hungry organism will direct its behavior toward food and a thirsty organism toward drink. Both will engage in activity more vigorously than an unmotivated organism.

But hunger and thirst are just two among many motives. In this chapter, we deal with *basic* motives—unlearned motives that humans share with other animals. Such basic motives appear to be of several types: one corresponds to *survival* needs of the organism, such as hunger and thirst; a second deals with biologically based *social* needs, such as sex and maternal behavior; and a third involves *curiosity* motives, which are not directly related to the welfare of the organism.

## Survival Motives and Homeostasis

Many survival motives operate partly in accordance with the principle of **homeostasis,** which is the body's tendency to maintain a constant internal environment in the face of a changing external environment. The healthy individual maintains a body temperature that varies only a degree or two, even though the temperature of the environment can vary by more than 100 degrees. Similarly, the healthy person maintains a relatively constant amount of water in his or her body, though the availability of water in the environment may vary drastically. Such internal constancies are essential for survival, since a body temperature that remains substantially above or below normal for hours can result in death, as can a lack of water for 4 to 5 days.

### Nature of Homeostasis

A thermostat is an example of a mechanical homeostatic system. Its purpose is to keep the temperature in your house (the internal environment) relatively constant while the temperature outside your house (the external environment) varies. The operation of a thermostat can tell us a good deal about the principles of homeostasis, as illustrated in the top half of Figure 10-1. The temperature of the room acts as input to the thermostat. The thermostat contains three things: a *sensor* to measure the room temperature, an *ideal value* to represent the desired temperature, and a *comparator* to compare the sensed temperature to the ideal value. If the sensed temperature is less than the ideal value, the mechanism turns the furnace on. This action raises the room temperature until it matches the ideal value, at which point the thermostat turns the furnace off.

We can generalize this description to all homeostatic systems, as shown in the bottom half of Figure 10-1. The core of the system is a particular variable that is being regulated (such as room temperature in the thermostat example). To regulate the variable, the system contains an ideal value of the variable, sensors that measure the variable, a comparator (or central control), and programmed adjustments that the system makes when the variable is at a value above or below the ideal (such as turning the furnace on or off). This framework enables us to understand a number of human motives. In the case of body temperature control, the variable regulated is body temperature; for thirst, the amounts of water in the cells and in the blood are the

**FIGURE 10-1**
**Homeostatic Systems** *The top half of the figure illustrates the workings of a thermostat. The temperature of the room is input to the thermostat; there, a sensor detects the input temperature and compares it to an ideal value. If the sensed temperature is less than the ideal value, the furnace is turned on. The bottom half of the figure illustrates a homeostatic system in general. The system consists of a regulated variable, sensors that detect the variable, and a comparator that gauges the sensed variable against an ideal value. If the sensed variable is less than the ideal value, adjustments are made.*

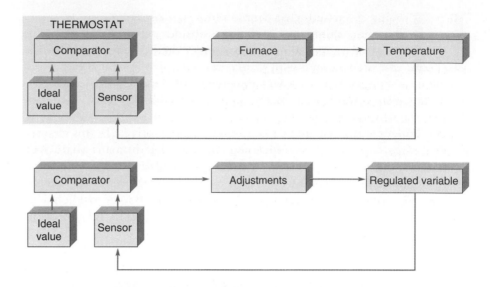

variables that are being regulated; and for hunger, several regulated variables correspond to various sources of energy (blood sugar, fat, and so on). In each case, sensors in the body detect changes from ideal values and activate adjustments that correct the imbalance. In studying these homeostatic systems, researchers seek to determine what variables are being sensed, where the sensors are located, what adjustments are possible, and what region of the brain plays the role of a comparator.

We can use the homeostatic framework to distinguish between two concepts that occur frequently in discussions of motivation, **need** and **drive.** A need is any substantial physiological departure from the ideal value; its psychological counterpart is a drive, an aroused state or urge that results from the need. Using hunger as an example, a need arises when the level of blood sugar drops substantially below an ideal value. This physiological imbalance may be corrected automatically by the liver releasing sugar into the bloodstream. But when these automatic mechanisms cannot maintain a balanced state, a drive is activated and the aroused organism takes action to restore the balance (it seeks foods with a high sugar content).

## Temperature Regulation as a Homeostatic System

Of all human motives, the ability to keep ourselves at a comfortable temperature offers the most straightforward case of a homeostatic system. While temperature regulation may not be our prototype of a motive, it is critical for survival. Our cells cannot function outside certain limits of body temperature: above 45 degrees Centigrade (113 degrees Fahrenheit), most proteins in cells become inactive and cannot carry out their functions; below 0 degrees Centigrade (32 degrees Fahrenheit), the water inside the cells begins to form ice crystals that destroy the cells.

The regulated variable is blood temperature, which is usually an accurate reflection of body temperature. There are sensors of blood temperature in the mouth (we can taste hot and cold foods), the skin (we can feel hot or cold), the spinal cord, and the brain. The chief region of the brain involved is the **hypothalamus,** a small collection of cell nuclei at the base of the brain that is directly linked with the pituitary gland and with other parts of the brain (see Figure 2-7). In addition to sensors, the anterior (front) region of the hypothalamus appears to contain the comparator and the ideal temperature value (really, an ideal temperature *zone*). The anterior hypothalamus therefore functions like a thermostat. If this region is destroyed in a rat, the animal can no longer regulate its temperature. And if the anterior hypothalamus is heated directly (through a wire implanted there), the rat's body temperature drops, even though the body itself is not hot (Barbour, 1912); by heating the hypothalamus, the rat has been "fooled" about the temperature of the rest of its body. (This is analogous to applying a hot burst of air directly to a thermostat: even though room temperature is cool, the thermostat is fooled into dropping the temperature.)

Once the hypothalamic thermostat has determined that the body's temperature is outside of an ideal zone, it can make a variety of adjustments. Some adjustments are automatic, physiological responses. If body temperature is too high, the skin's capillaries may dilate, which increases the amount of warm blood just under the surface of the skin. The additional heat then radiates off the skin, which subsequently lowers the temperature of the blood. Sweating is another physiological means of heat loss for species that have sweat glands all over their bodies (such as humans, horses, and cattle). Species that have sweat glands in their tongues (dogs, cats, and rats) will instead pant to release heat. If body temperature dips too low, the first physiological adjustment is a constriction of the skin's capillaries; this pulls blood away from the cold periphery, which conserves the remaining heat for the vital organs. The body will also generate heat by shivering.

In addition to physiological reactions, we also make behavioral adjustments. The adjustments are obvious. When we feel cool or chilly, we put on extra clothing or seek a warmer place; when we feel too warm, we do the opposite. These behavioral adjustments differ from the physiological ones in several respects. The behavioral adjustments are voluntary acts that we attribute to our "self," while the physiological adjustments are involuntary reactions that we attribute more to our body parts (for example, our sweat glands). Also, physiological adjustments directly affect our internal environment, whereas behavioral adjustments affect our external environment (putting on a sweater protects us from the cool air), which in turn influences our internal environment. These two types of adjustments appear to be localized in different regions of the hypothalamus: the preoptic area regulates our physiological changes, whereas the lateral area regulates our behavior (Satinoff & Rutstein, 1970; Satinoff & Shan, 1971).

## Thirst as a Homeostatic System

The regulation of water intake is another critical ingredient of our survival. Water is a major element of our bodies. It makes up about two thirds of our weight; it is the main component of most tissues and blood; and it is used to carry nutrients and oxygen to our tissues, as well as to carry away wastes. But we are constantly losing water—either by evaporation from the surface of the lungs, or by sweating and urination. We therefore have to continually drink to replace our water losses.

How do we regulate our drinking? What makes us start drinking, and what makes us stop? Again, the system appears to be largely homeostatic. However, the homeostatic system for thirst is more complex than that for temperature because our bodies must regulate two variables: the amount of water inside the body's cells (**intracellular fluid**); and the amount outside the cells, including the blood (**extracellular fluid**). We will examine these two regulated variables in turn.

The typical cause of intracellular fluid loss is a greater concentration of sodium in the water outside the cells than in the water inside the cells. Since sodium cannot permeate the cells' membranes, a pressure to balance the concentrations of sodium on both sides of the membrane leads to water leaving the cells (this is called *osmosis*). The cells then become dehydrated. While all cells may dehydrate, only certain ones play the role of sensors. These are **osmoreceptors** (so named because of their connection to osmosis); they are located in the hypothalamus and in the *preoptic area* that lies in front of the hypothalamus, and they respond to dehydration by becoming slightly deformed or shriveled. In addition to the sensors, the anterior region of the hypothalamus may also contain the comparator and ideal values relevant to intracellular fluid loss (Blass & Epstein, 1971; Peck & Novin, 1971).

Once the hypothalamus detects these changes, it sets homeostatic adjustments in motion. The physiological adjustment involves recovering water from the kidneys before it is excreted as urine. Specifically, activity in the osmoreceptors leads to release of the **antidiuretic hormone** (ADH). ADH regulates the kidneys so they release water back into the bloodstream and form only very concentrated urine. (After a night's sleep, you may notice that your urine is a darker color and has a stronger odor than it does at other times of the day; this is because your body has recovered water from your kidneys to compensate for your not having consumed fluids while asleep.) This physiological mechanism can maintain the body's water balance only to a certain point. When the water deficit is too great, behavioral adjustments are required; you feel thirsty and seek water. All of this makes it clear why a hamburger and fries makes us thirsty. Eating salty food increases the concentration of salt outside the cells and causes water to leave the cells; the shrunken cells are sensors that mediate the thirst drive.

There is more to thirst, though, than a deficit of intracellular fluid. Loss of blood volume, which is part of extracellular fluid, produces thirst even when the cells are not dehydrated. An injured person who has lost a considerable amount of blood feels extremely thirsty, even though the sodium concentration of the remaining blood is unchanged. Likewise, people engaged in vigorous exercise lose salt through perspiration but still have the urge to drink a lot of water, which will only further dilute the salt concentration of their blood. Hence, salt concentration is not critical here. These observations indicate that there is another variable being regulated, namely the total volume of fluid in blood, regardless of its concentration.

The sensors for this variable are located in the kidneys. What they actually detect is a change in blood pressure. The kidneys then secrete a substance called *renin* into the bloodstream. Renin plays a role in two different kinds of homeostatic adjustments to decreased blood volume. It causes the blood vessels to constrict, thereby preventing further blood loss; this reaction is a physiological adjustment. Renin also reacts with a substance circulating in the blood to produce another hormone called **angiotensin;** this induces the feeling of thirst as well as an appetite for salt, which leads to behavioral adjustments (Fitzsimons, 1969; Stricker & Verbalis, 1988).

A homeostatic analysis suggests that a thirsty organism should drink until its intracellular and extracellular elements become rehydrated. But this is not the case. Subjects deprived of water and then allowed to drink will stop before their intracellular and extracellular levels are replenished. Thus, there must be a special mechanism to stop drinking—namely, **satiety sen-**

**sors** that determine when there is sufficient water in the system to replenish the parched cells and the blood. Some of these sensors (osmoreceptors again) are located in the mouth, while others are located in the intestines. In experiments with monkeys, infusion of a small amount of water into the small intestine stops drinking, even if the animal has not had anywhere near enough water to make up its deficit. Thus, our system for regulating water intake is quite complex; it involves a satiety mechanism as well as the regulation of intracellular and extracellular fluid.

# Hunger

Hunger is a powerful motivator, as anyone who has ever experienced starvation can attest to. To survive, we must eat, and do it in such a way that we maintain our body weight. How exactly do we do it? What determines when we begin to eat, and what determines when we stop?

There are a number of obvious answers to these questions, all of which turn out to be unsatisfactory. You might think that the trigger for eating is something external to you; for example you eat because it is mealtime. But this cannot be a major determinant of eating. The number of meals people eat each day differs widely among cultures (as many as five in some European cultures and as few as one in some African cultures), yet as long as food is available, people in different cultures weigh about the same. Other possible external triggers for eating are the sight and smell of food. These cues can sometimes induce people to eat (or overeat); but again they cannot be major determinants of eating. Even when such cues are totally eliminated, people can easily regulate their food intake. We get closer to the right track if we consider internal factors. The most obvious factors have to do with the state of our stomach—stomach contractions signal that it is time to eat, and a

*Social customs influence eating.*

*External influences can arouse hunger.*

distended stomach signals that it is time to stop. Plausible as this may sound, it is again an unsatisfactory answer, since people who have had their stomachs removed (due to cancer or larger ulcers) still regulate their food intake perfectly well.

What, then, are the major determinants of eating? Current research suggests that we automatically monitor the quantities of various nutrients stored in our body (for example, glucose and fats) and are motivated to eat whenever these energy stores fall below critical levels. Again, the system is basically homeostatic; indeed, it is a common observation among researchers that most animals have stable body weights and that if they are given all they want to eat, they somehow eat just enough to maintain their weight. But hunger is too complex for us to give a simple homeostatic analysis. For one thing, several variables have to be regulated. For another, eating is terminated not by the food stores returning to their ideal values but, instead, by satiety sensors detecting that sufficient food has entered the system. Also, clearly not every person is able to maintain homeostasis: just walking down a street, we can see examples of extreme overeating (*obesity*) and extreme undereating (*anorexia*). In trying to understand hunger, we will first consider the variables that are regulated (along with the sensors that gauge them and trigger eating), then we will discuss the satiety detectors that tell us when we have eaten enough, the brain mechanisms that integrate the feeding and satiety cues, and finally the breakdown of homeostasis found in obesity and anorexia.

## Variables of Hunger

The study of hunger is closely tied to the study of metabolism and digestion. In order for our body cells to function, they require certain nutrients. These needed nutrients are the end products of digestion and include glucose (blood sugar), fats, and amino acids. All three appear to be regulated variables in hunger.

Glucose's role is the best documented. Typically, the brain uses only glucose for its energy supply (the rest of the body is more flexible). The brain contains sensors for glucose, which are located in the hypothalamus, and which reflect the extent to which glucose has been absorbed by the cells. (Roughly, the sensors measure the difference in the amount of glucose in the arteries versus that in the veins.) Researchers have implanted microelectrodes in the hypothalami of dogs and cats and recorded neural activity after injections of glucose. They found that cells in the lateral region of the hypothalamus decrease in activity (signaling that glucose levels are sufficient). Researchers have also recorded neural activity after injections of insulin, which lowers glucose levels. They found that cells in the lateral region of the hypothalamus increase their activity (signaling that glucose levels are insufficient). When the sensors indicate too low a glucose level, physiological and behavioral adjustments ensue: either the liver releases stored glucose into the bloodstream or the hungry organism searches for food. There are also glucose sensors outside the brain, specifically in the liver. These detectors are particularly well situated since the liver is among the first organs to receive the products of digestion (Stricker, Rowland, Saller, & Friedman, 1977).

We also regulate the amount of amino acids and fat stored in special fat cells. We would expect amino acids to be regulated, for they are essential in building protein, but it is surprising that a decline in stored fat can trigger feeding. This makes sense, however, when we realize that between meals stored fat is converted into free fatty acids, which are a major source of energy for the body. A lack of fat deposits can therefore lead to a lack of energy. The hypothalamus appears to be able to detect decreases in the size of fat cells. The substance *glycerol*, which is produced during the conversion of fat into free fatty acids, also seems to be a regulated variable. Hunger, then, involves multiple homeostatic systems.

## Satiety Detectors

If we did not stop eating until our stores of nutrients reached their ideal levels, we would routinely eat for the roughly four hours that it takes to digest a meal. Nature has spared us this indignity by providing *satiety sensors*, detectors located in the early parts of the digestive system that signal the brain that the needed nutrients are on their way and that feeding can stop. The termination of feeding is thus handled by a different system—one located earlier in the digestive system—than that responsible for the initiation of feeding. (This is very much like the situation for drinking.)

Where are the satiety sensors for hunger located? One obvious place to look is the mouth and throat. To establish definitively whether the mouth and throat contain satiety sensors, researchers have severed the esophagus of an animal at the point where it connects to the stomach, and brought the cut ends out externally through incisions in the skin. When such an animal eats, the food it swallows cannot make its way to the stomach (hence satiety sensors in the stomach and beyond can have no effect). Such an animal will swallow a somewhat larger than normal meal, then stop eating, which implies that satiety sensors must exist in the mouth and throat. However, the animal soon begins to eat again, which implies that these satiety sensors have only a short-term effect (Janowitz & Grossman, 1949). There must be other satiety sensors farther down the digestive tract.

The next places to look are the stomach and *duodenum* (the part of the small intestine connected directly to the stomach). Both organs do in fact contain satiety sensors. If nutrients are injected directly into the stomach of a hungry animal before it is given access to food, it will eat less than usual. Nutrients injected directly into the duodenum also lead to a decrease in eating. Here, the satiety sensor may be the hormone *cholecystokinin* (CCK). When food enters the duodenum, the upper intestinal mucosa produces CCK, which limits the rate at which food passes from the stomach to the duodenum. Blood levels of CCK may be monitored by the brain as a satiety signal. Consistent with this hypothesis, many studies have found that injections of CCK inhibit eating (Gibbs, Young, & Smith, 1973). (Given this, you might think that CCK would make a wonderful appetite suppressant; it turns out, however, that CCK is *not* effective when ingested orally.)

Another major depository of satiety sensors is the liver. It is the first organ to receive water-soluble nutrients from the digestive system, and hence its receptors provide an accurate gauge of the nutrients being digested. If glucose is injected directly into the liver of a hungry animal, the animal will feed less. Sensors in the liver appear to monitor the level of nutrients that are in the intestines and then pass this information on to the brain (Russek, 1971). In short, we can think of satiety sensors throughout the body as constituting a homeostatic system in which the variable being regulated is the total amount of nutrients in the system; once this variable reaches its ideal value, eating stops.

# Brain Mechanisms

The system for satiety must be integrated with that for feeding. The likely locus of this is the brain, specifically the hypothalamus, which has already been shown to figure centrally in temperature control, fluid regulation, and aspects of feeding. The hypothalamus is particularly well suited for housing a control center for hunger. It contains more blood vessels than any other area of the brain and consequently is readily influenced by the chemical state of the blood. Two regions of the hypothalamus are particularly important: the **lateral hypothalamus** and **ventromedial hypothalamus.**

LH AND VMH SYNDROMES   One way to study the function of a brain area is to destroy cells and nerve fibers in the region and then observe the animal's behavior when the area no longer can serve its normal function. This technique has led to the discovery of two important syndromes. The first, *LH syndrome,* occurs when tissue in the lateral hypothalamus is destroyed. Initially, the animal—typically a rat—refuses to eat or drink and will die unless it is fed intravenously. After several weeks of being intravenously nourished, most of the rats begin to recover: first they eat only palatable wet food but will not drink; eventually they will eat dry food and begin to drink (Teitelbaum & Epstein, 1962). The second syndrome, *VMH syndrome,* occurs when tissue in the ventromedial hypothalamus is destroyed. It has two distinct phases. In the initial or *dynamic phase,* which lasts between 4 and 12 weeks, the animal overeats voraciously, sometimes tripling its body weight within a matter of weeks (see Figure 10-2). In the second or *static phase,* the animal no longer overeats. Rather, it reduces its food intake to slightly more than normal level and maintains its new obese weight. The VMH syndrome has been observed in all animal species studied—from rat to chicken and monkey. For humans, researchers have noted that people with tumors or injuries in the ventromedial hypothalamus may overeat and become extremely obese.

Initially, psychologists interpreted the VMH and LH syndromes as implying the existence of dual hunger centers—a *feeding center* in the lateral hypothalamus and a *satiety center* in the ventromedial hypothalamus (Stellar, 1954). They believed that destruction of the lateral tissue disrupts the feeding center, thereby making it difficult for the animal to eat, while destruction of ventromedial tissue disrupts the satiety center, thereby making it difficult for the animal not to eat. But why, then, do rats nursed through the first few weeks after their lateral-hypothalamic lesions eventually come to regulate their food intake with precision, albeit at a lower weight? Similarly, if destruction of the ventromedial hypothalamus impairs a satiety center, why do the animals actually reduce their food intake during the static phase? These puzzles, and the findings to be presented below, have largely overthrown the dual-center interpretation.

**FIGURE 10-2**
**Hypothalamic Overeating** *Lesions in the ventromedial hypothalamus caused this rat to overeat and gain more than three times its normal weight. Its weight is 1,080 grams, not 80 grams.*

CHANGES IN SET POINT   One newer account holds that the lateral and ventromedial areas are concerned with the regulation of overall body weight. Consider again a fat rat with a ventromedial lesion. We have already noted that eventually it will reach a static phase where it maintains its new obese weight. But suppose the animal's diet is restricted, and its body weight decreases until it reaches its original, normal weight. If the rat is allowed to eat freely again, will it now stay at its original normal weight? The

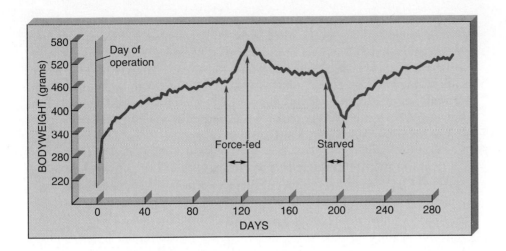

**FIGURE 10-3**
**Effects of Forced Feeding and Starvation on Rats with VMH Lesions**
*Following lesioning of the ventromedial hypothalamus, the rat overeats and gains weight until it stabilizes at a new, obese level. Forced feeding or starvation alters the weight level only temporarily; the rat returns to its stabilized level. (After Hoebel & Teitelbaum, 1966)*

answer is "no"—it will overeat until it returns to its obese state. It is as if the rat is now comfortable only at its heavier weight. That is, damage to the ventromedial area apparently disturbs the animal's long-term weight control system, so that it has to regulate its weight at a higher level. Further, if these obese rats are force-fed until they become extremely obese, they will reduce their food intake until their weight returns to its "normal obese" level (see Figure 10-3).

Similarly, damage to the lateral hypothalamus apparently disturbs weight control so that the animal regulates its weight at a lower level. Recall that after initially refusing all food and water, rats with the LH syndrome resume eating and drinking on their own. But they stabilize at a lower weight level, just as rats with the VMH syndrome stabilize at an obese level (Mitchel & Keesey, 1974). Again, this behavior indicates impairment of a long-term weight control system. Rats that are starved prior to lesioning of the lateral hypothalamus do not refuse to eat after the operation. In fact, many of them overeat, but only until their weight reaches a new level that is lower than their normal weight but higher than their starved, preoperational weight (see Figure 10-4).

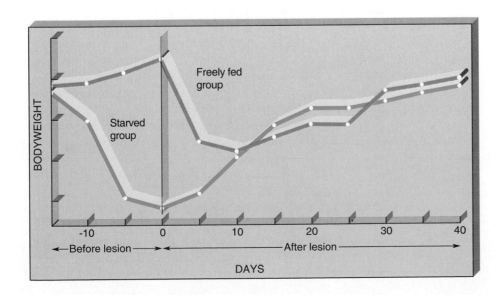

**FIGURE 10-4**
**Body Weight and the Lateral Hypothalamus** *Prior to lesioning the lateral hypothalamus, one group of rats was starved while another group was allowed to feed freely. Following surgery, the starved animals increased their food intake and gained weight while the freely fed group lost weight. Both groups stabilized at the same weight level. (After Powley & Keesey, 1970)*

These findings indicate that the lateral and ventromedial hypothalamus have reciprocal effects on the ideal body weight, that is, the weight at which an individual body functions best. The ideal weight is referred to as the **set point** for body weight. Damage to the ventromedial areas raises the set point; damage to the lateral area lowers it. If *both* areas in a rat are lesioned carefully so that an equivalent amount of tissue is destroyed in each area, the animal does not overeat or undereat; rather, it maintains its presurgery weight level (Keesey & Powley, 1975).

**INTERFERENCE WITH NERVE TRACTS**   Another explanation of the VMH and LH syndromes proposes that the effects reflect not just destruction of hypothalamic nuclei but also interference with some of the 50 different nerve tracts that only pass through these hypothalamic locations. Consider again a fat rat with a lesion in its ventromedial hypothalamus. While the researchers may have been interested in the effects of the lesion on just the hypothalamus per se, such a lesion also affects certain branches of the parasympathetic nervous system that pass through this region. These latter effects alter metabolism so that too many nutrients are converted into fat (for storage) and too few are left as fuel for metabolic processes. As a result, the animal is constantly in need of nutrients, so it constantly overeats. Thus the VMH-lesioned rat may overeat because, in a sense, it is starving.

A lesion in the lateral hypothalamus also may interrupt an important set of nerve fibers called the *nigrostriatal bundle*. These fibers are involved in activating the organism to engage in all kinds of behaviors, not just feeding, and their destruction leads to activation problems and other general deficits (the same fibers are impaired in *Parkinson's disease*, which involves motor inactivation). These deficits in activation may be the reason why a rat with LH syndrome initially will not eat or drink at all. Indeed, when the nigrostriatal bundle is lesioned outside the hypothalamus (the tracts extend beyond the hypothalamus), animals show the same breakdowns in feeding behavior that occur in the early stages of the LH syndrome (Friedman & Stricker, 1976; Stricker, 1983).

Clearly, interpretations of the VMH and LH syndromes are controversial. Since the early 1950s, psychologists trying to explain hunger motivation have gone from hunger centers to set points to extraneous nerve tracts. Perhaps these interpretations are not incompatible: a lesion in the lateral hypothalamus may both lower the set point for body weight and interrupt nerve tracts that activate the organism. Moreover, new interpretations of the role of the hypothalamus in hunger are being developed. Thus, researchers have recently proposed that hunger is caused by the presence in the hypothalamus of a hormone called neuropeptide Y or NPY for short. When rats are hungry, the concentration in the hypothalamus of NPY is higher than normal, and as the rats eat and become full NPY levels drop (Stanley, Anderson, Grayson, and Leibowitz, 1989). Clearly, the brain is an enormously complex organ, and we cannot always expect simple correspondence between its activities and psychological functions.

## Obesity and Anorexia

We have emphasized homeostatic processes in hunger, but our eating behavior shows several departures from homeostasis. Some people's body weights are not as constant as the homeostatic viewpoint suggests. The most frequent deviation from homeostatic regulation of eating—at least for humans—is **obesity.** It is common in our culture. Roughly 25 percent of Americans are obese, a condition often defined as being 30 percent or more in excess of one's appropriate body weight. The prevalence of obesity varies from group to group within society. Obesity is generally more common in women than men. In the United States, obesity is more prevalent in lower-class socioeconomic groups than higher-class ones; however, in developing countries, the reverse is true, as people are more likely to be obese the higher their socioeconomic status (Logue, 1991).

Obesity is a major health hazard. It contributes to a higher incidence of diabetes, high blood pressure, and heart disease. As if this were not bad enough, in our culture obesity can also be a social stigma, as obese people are often perceived as being indulgent and lacking in willpower. This allegation can be most unfair since, as we will see, in many cases a person's obesity is due to genetic factors rather than overeating. Given all of the problems associated with obesity, it is not surprising that each year millions of people spend billions of dollars on special diets and drugs to lose weight.

Most researchers agree that obesity is a complex problem and can involve metabolic, nutritional, psychological, and sociological factors. Obesity probably is not a single disorder but a host of disorders that all have fatness as their major symptom (Rodin, 1981). The question of how one becomes obese is like that of how one gets to Pittsburgh—there are many ways to do it, and which one you "choose" depends on where you are coming from (Offir, 1982). In what follows, we will divide the factors that lead to weight gain into two broad classes: (a) genetics and (b) calorie intake (overeating). Roughly speaking, people may become obese because they are genetically predisposed to be fat, or because they eat too much (for psychological or sociological reasons). Both factors may be involved in some cases of obesity, while in others just genetics or just overeating may be the culprit.

## Genetic Factors in Obesity

It has long been known that obesity runs in families. In families where neither parent is obese, only about 10% of the children will be obese; if one parent is obese, about 40 percent of the children will be too; and if both parents are obese, approximately 70 percent of the children will be too (Gurney, 1936). These statistics suggest a biological basis of obesity, but other interpretations are possible (perhaps the children are simply imitating their parents eating habits). Recent findings, however, strongly support a genetic basis for obesity.

**TWIN STUDIES** One way to get evidence about the role of genetics in obesity is to study identical twins. Since identical twins have the same genes, and since genes supposedly play a role in weight gain, identical twins should be alike in their patterns of weight gain.

In one experiment, twelve pairs of identical twins (all males) were induced to stay in a college dormitory for 100 days. The intent of the experiment was to get the twins to gain weight. Each man ate a diet that contained 1000 extra calories per day. Also, the men's physical activity was restricted; they were not allowed to exercise, and instead spent much of their time reading, playing sedentary games, and watching television. By the end of the 100 days, all of the men had gained weight, but the amount gained varied considerably, from 9 to 30 pounds. However, and this is the critical point,

*To lose weight permanently, overweight individuals must change their eating habits.*

there was hardly any variation in the amount gained within a pair of twins (the variation being between pairs of twins). Identical twins gained almost identical amounts. Moreover, identical twins tended to gain the weight in the same places. If one member of twins gained weight in his middle, so would the other member; if one member of another pair of twins gained the weight on his hips and thighs, so would the other member (Bouchard et al., 1990).

The above results make it clear that both calorie intake and genetics contribute to weight gain. The fact that all the men in the study gained weight shows that increased calories translates into increased weight (hardly surprising). The fact that how much weight the men gained varied from twins to twins but did not vary within a pair of twins shows that genetics determines how much we gain when we increase calorie intake. The above results also make it clear why we should not assume that obese people necessarily eat more than nonobese people. To see this point, suppose that you met two men from the previous study, one of whom had gained 9 pounds (we will refer to him as "plus 9") and the other 30 pounds ("plus 30"). The plus 30 man might appear obese to you while the plus 9 man would probably not. If you assume that obesity is always due to overeating, you would conclude that the plus 30 man had eaten more than the plus 9 man; but we know in fact that the two men ate roughly the same amount. The plus 30 man is heavier not because he ate more, but because of his genetic disposition to weight gain. In short, the fact that some people are very overweight does not necessarily imply that they greatly overeat.

A critic might object to making too much of the preceding twins study. Identical twins not only have identical genes, but also very similar environments, and perhaps environmental factors were responsible for the identical twins being alike in weight gain. To eliminate this potential confounding, we need to study identical twins who have been reared apart and see how similar the members of a pair are in weight gain. Precisely this was done in a recent study conducted in Sweden. The researchers studied the weights of 93 pairs of identical twins reared apart, as well as that of 153 pairs of identical twins reared together. Members of a pair of twins reared apart were found to be remarkably similar in weight; indeed, they were as similar in weight as were pairs of twins reared together! Genes, then, are a major determinant of weight and weight gain.

**FAT CELLS** Given that genetics plays a role in weight gain, we now want to know some details of that role. In particular, what are the digestive and metabolic processes that are affected by genes and that mediate the weight gain? One answer involves fat cells, where all body fat is stored. Organisms—people and animals—vary in how many fat cells they have; this variation is partly due to genetics, and it has major consequences for obesity. In one sample, obese subjects were found to have three times as many fat cells as normal subjects (Knittle & Hirsch, 1968). In other studies, researchers have shown that rats that have double the usual number of fat cells tend to be twice as fat as control rats. And when researchers cut some of the fat cells out of young rats, so that they had only half as many fat cells as their littermates, the operated on rats grew up to be only half as fat as their littermates (Hirsch & Batchelor, 1976; Faust, 1984). Hence, there is a link between genes and the number of fat cells, and another link between the number of fat cells and obesity; by this chain, genes are connected to obesity.

The number of fat cells is not entirely fixed by genes, however. Overeating during the early months of life can increase the number of fat cells. Still, genetics sets important limits on the total number of fat cells. It determines the minimum number of fat cells, since—barring surgery for obesity—an organism can never lose fat cells. In addition, the extent to which overeating produces new fat cells may itself be determined genetically.

The number of fat cells is not the only critical factor; the size of fat cells also matters. While genetics partly determines the size of fat cells, overeating can increase their size while deprivation can decrease it. In most organisms, however, fat cells stay relatively constant in size.

**SET POINTS** We therefore have two genetically based factors—the number and the size of fat cells—that vary from person to person and that are related to obesity. Researchers believe that the combination of these two factors may determine an individual's **set point**, which the hypothalamus tries to maintain. Thus, the set points for obese and nonobese individuals who have the same height and bone structure may be different if the two people differ in the number and size of their fat cells. If this is true, obesity for some individuals is their "normal" weight. Attempts at weight reduction by such individuals would hold them below their biologically determined set point, in a state of chronic deprivation; they would feel hungry all the time—just as a thin person would feel on a starvation diet (Nisbett, 1972).

In pursuing the set-point hypothesis, Stunkard (1982) has argued that appetite-suppressant drugs (such as fenfluramine) act primarily to lower the set point and only secondarily to suppress appetite. His account explains why dieters will lose weight when taking an appetite suppressant, but gain it back once they discontinue the drug. The drug lowers the set point of dieters, thereby facilitating weight loss; but discontinuation of the drug causes the set point to return to its pretreatment level, which causes the dieters to gain weight until they reach their original weight. While this set-point hypothesis may not apply to all cases of obesity, it may account for certain types of problems, particularly the individual who was moderately overweight as a child and remains moderately overweight throughout life.

**METABOLIC RATE** Another metabolic process determined partly by genes is our *metabolic rate*. Two-thirds of a normal person's energy expenditure—which is how we burn up calories—is devoted to metabolic processes (basic bodily functions). Hence, our metabolic rate is a major determinant of weight control: low rates of metabolism expend fewer calories and result in more body weight. One study showed that the risk of gaining 15 pounds in a 2-year period was four times greater for a person with a low metabolic rate than for a person with a high rate (Ravusin et al., 1988). Again, we have a chain linking genes to obesity; this time the intermediate link involves metabolic rate.

In sum, there are various routes by which genes can be responsible for excessive weight gain, including having many and large fat cells, having a high set point, and having a low metabolic rate.

## Overeating and Obesity

While genetics may play a big role in obesity, there is still no doubt that, for many obese people, part of the problem is overeating. Now the question of interest is what factors—other than fat cells, set points, and metabolic rates—induce people to consume too many calories?

**BREAKDOWN OF CONSCIOUS RESTRAINTS** Some people stay obese by binge eating after they diet. An obese man may break his two-day diet and then overeat so much that he eventually consumes more calories than he would have had he not dieted at all. Since the diet was a conscious restraint, the breakdown of control is a factor in increased calorie intake.

To have a more complete understanding of the role of conscious restraints, researchers have developed a questionnaire that asks about diet, weight history, and concern with eating (for example, How often do you diet? Do you eat sensibly in front of others, yet overeat when alone?). The results show that almost everyone—whether thin, average, or overweight—can be classified into one of two categories: people who consciously restrain their eating and people who do not. In addition, regardless of their actual weight, the eating behavior of restrained eaters is closer to that of obese individuals than to that of unrestrained eaters (Herman & Polivy, 1980; Ruderman, 1986). A laboratory study shows what happens when restraints are dropped. Restrained and unrestrained eaters (both of normal weight) were required to drink either two milk shakes, one milk shake, or none; they then sampled several flavors of ice cream and were encouraged to eat as much as they wanted. The more milk shakes the unrestrained eaters were required to drink, the less ice cream they consumed later. In contrast, the restrained eaters who had been preloaded with two milk shakes ate more ice cream than did those who drank one milk shake or none.

**EMOTIONAL AROUSAL** Overweight individuals often report that they tend to eat more when they are tense or anxious, and experiments support this. Obese subjects eat more in a high-anxiety situation than they do in a low-anxiety situation, while normal-weight subjects eat more in situations of low anxiety (McKenna, 1972). Other research indicates that any kind of emotional arousal seems to increase food intake in some obese people. In one study, overweight and normal-weight subjects saw a different film in each of four sessions. Three of the films aroused various emotions: one was

*Binge eating after an attempt to diet.*

distressing; one, amusing; and one, sexually arousing. The fourth film was a boring travelogue. After viewing each of the films, the subjects were asked to taste and evaluate different kinds of crackers. The obese subjects ate significantly more crackers after viewing any of the arousing films than they did after seeing the travelogue. Normal-weight individuals ate the same amount of crackers regardless of which film they had seen (White, 1977).

As for *why* some obese people eat more when emotionally aroused, there are two proposed answers, both of which emphasize early learning. One possibility is that when some people were babies, their caregivers interpreted all of their distress signals as requests for food; consequently, they failed to learn to respond differentially to different needs and feelings (hunger versus anxiety, for example). As adults, such people have difficulty distinguishing hunger from other feelings, including anxiety, and they end up eating whenever they experience emotion (Bruch, 1973). A second possibility is that some obese people may respond to an anxiety-producing situation by doing the one thing they have learned brings them comfort—namely, eating. Such people will eat whenever anxious. The two hypotheses may apply to different kinds of people.

**RESPONSIVENESS TO EXTERNAL CUES** Compared to normal-weight people, obese individuals may be more sensitive to external hunger cues (the sight, aroma, and taste of food) and less sensitive to internal hunger cues (such as satiety signals from the intestines). One study examined the effects of taste on the eating behavior of underweight and overweight subjects. The subjects were allowed to eat as much vanilla ice cream as they wanted and then were asked to rate its quality. Some subjects were given a creamy, expensive brand; the others, a cheap brand with quinine added. Figure 10-5 plots the amount of ice cream subjects ate against their ratings of the ice cream. Overweight subjects ate much more ice cream when they rated it "excellent" than when they rated it "bad," while the ice-cream consumption by underweight subjects was less affected by taste. Other experiments indicate that while people do indeed differ in their *externality* (sensitivity to external cues), by no means are all obese people "externals," nor are all externals obese. Rather, there are externals and internals in every weight category, and only a moderate correlation exists between degree of externality and degree of obesity (Rodin, 1981).

## Dieting and Weight Control

Though genetic factors may limit the amount of weight we can comfortably lose, still, overweight people can generally lose weight by means of a weight control program. For a program to be successful, though, it must involve something other than just extreme dieting.

**LIMITATIONS OF DIETING** Unfortunately, most dieters are not successful, and those who succeed in shedding pounds often regain them. This state of affairs seems to be partly due to two deep-seated human reactions to a temporary deprivation of food (which is what a diet is).

The first reaction is that deprivation per se can lead to subsequent overeating. In some experiments, rats were first deprived of food for four days, then allowed to feed back to their normal weights, and finally allowed to eat as much food as they wanted. These once-deprived rats ate more than

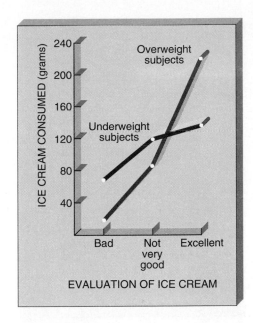

**FIGURE 10-5**
**Taste and Obesity** *The effects of food quality on the amount eaten by overweight and underweight subjects. The subjects rated the quality of ice cream and could eat as much as they desired.* (After Nisbett, 1968)

*Overweight people find exercise difficult, thereby perpetuating their obesity.*

*Exercise is critical in weight loss; it burns calories, but even more important, it helps regulate body metabolism.*

did control rats that had no history of deprivation. Thus, prior deprivation leads to subsequent overeating, even after the weight lost from the deprivation has been regained (Coscina & Dixon, 1983).

The second reaction of interest is that deprivation decreases metabolic rate, and, as you may recall, the lower one's metabolic rate, the fewer calories expended and the greater one's weight. Consequently, the calorie reduction during dieting is partly offset by the lowered metabolic rate, making it difficult for dieters to meet their goal. The reduction in metabolic rate with dieting may also explain why many people find it harder and harder to lose weight with each successive diet: the body responds to each bout of dieting with a reduction in metabolic rate (Brownell, 1988).

Both reactions to dieting—binge eating and lowered metabolic rate—are understandable in terms of an evolutionary approach to psychology. Until very recently in historical time—and indeed, still in underdeveloped countries—whenever human beings experienced deprivation, it was because of scarcity of food in the environment. One adaptive response to such scarcity is to overeat and store in our bodies as much food as possible whenever it is available. Hence evolution may have selected for an ability to overeat following deprivation. This explains the overeating reaction. A second adaptive response to a scarcity of food in the environment is for organisms to decrease the rate at which they expend their limited amount of calories; hence, evolution may have selected for an ability to lower one's metabolic rate during deprivation. This explains the second reaction of interest. These two reactions have served our species well in times of famine, but once famine is not a concern, these reactions keep obese dieters overweight (Polivy & Herman, 1985).

**WEIGHT CONTROL PROGRAMS** To lose weight and keep it off, it seems that overweight individuals need to establish a new set of permanent eating habits (as opposed to temporary dieting) and to engage in a program of exercise. Some support for this conclusion is given by the following study, which compared various methods for treating obesity.

For 6 months, obese individuals followed one of three treatment regimens: (a) behavior modification of eating and exercise habits, (b) drug therapy using an appetite suppressant (fenfluramine), and (c) a combination of behavior modification and drug therapy. Subjects in all three treatment groups were given information on exercise and extensive nutritional counseling, including a diet of no more than 1,200 calories per day. Subjects in the behavior modification groups were taught to become aware of situations that prompted them to overeat, to change the conditions associated with their overeating, to reward themselves for appropriate eating behavior, and to develop a suitable exercise regimen. In addition to the three treatment groups, there were two control groups: one consisted of subjects waiting to take part in the study, and the other comprised subjects who saw a physician for traditional office treatment of weight problems.

Table 10-1 presents the results of the study. The subjects in all three treatment groups lost more weight than the subjects in the two control groups, with the group combining behavior modification and drug therapy losing the most weight and the behavior-modification-only group losing the least. However, during the year after treatment, a striking reversal developed. The behavior-modification-only group regained far less weight than the other two treatment groups; these subjects maintained an average weight loss of 19.8 pounds by the end of the year, whereas the weight losses

| | WEIGHT LOSS AFTER TREATMENT | WEIGHT LOSS ONE YEAR LATER |
|---|---|---|
| Treatment groups | | |
| Behavior modification only | 24.0 | 19.8 |
| Drug therapy only | 31.9 | 13.8 |
| Combined treatment | 33.7 | 10.1 |
| Control groups | | |
| Waiting list | 2.9 (gain) | — |
| Physician office visits | 13.2 | — |

**TABLE 10-1**
**Weight Loss Following Different Treatments** *Weight loss in pounds at the end of 6 months of treatment and on a follow-up 1 year later. Subjects in the two control groups were not available for the 1-year follow-up.* (After Craighead, Stunkard, & O'Brien, 1981)

for the drug-therapy-only group and the combined-treatment group averaged only 13.8 and 10.1 pounds each.

What caused this reversal? An increased sense of self-efficacy may have been a factor. Subjects who received the behavior-modification-only treatment could attribute their weight loss to their own efforts, thereby strengthening their resolve to continue controlling their weight after the treatment ended. Subjects who received an appetite suppressant, on the other hand, probably attributed their weight loss to the medication and so did not develop a sense of self-control. Another possible factor stems from the fact that the medication had decreased the subjects' feelings of hunger, or temporarily lowered their set point, and consequently subjects in the drug-therapy-only group and the combined-treatment group may not have been sufficiently prepared to cope with the increase in hunger that they felt when the medication was stopped.

## Anorexia

While obesity is our most frequent eating problem, the opposite problem has also surfaced in the form of **anorexia nervosa** and **bulimia.** Both of these disorders involve a pathological desire *not* to gain weight. This section treats anorexia, the next one bulimia.

**CHARACTERISTICS** Anorexia is distinguished by an extreme, self-imposed weight loss. Based on standards set by the American Psychiatric Association (1987), individuals should be diagnosed as being anorexic only if they weigh at least 15 percent less than their minimal normal weight. Some anorexics in fact weigh less than 50 percent of their normal weight. For females to be diagnosed as anorexic, in addition to the weight loss they must also have stopped menstruating. The weight loss can lead to a number of dangerous side effects, including emaciation, susceptibility to infection, and other symptoms of undernourishment. In extreme cases, the side effects can lead to death. No wonder that one of the leading investigators of anorexia has described it as, "the relentless pursuit of thinness through self-starvation, even unto death" (Bruch, 1973).

Anorexia is relatively rare; its incidence in the United States is about 1 percent. It is 20 times more likely to occur in women than men, particularly young women between their teens and their thirties. Moreover, most anorexics are white and upper-middle or upper class. Typically, anorexics are entirely focused on food, carefully calculating the amount of calories in anything they might consume. Sometimes this concern reaches the point of obsession, as when one anorexic commented to her therapist, "Of course I had breakfast; I ate my cheerio"; or when another anorexic said, "I won't lick a postage stamp—one never knows about calories" (Bruch, 1973). The obsession with food and possible weight gains leads some anorexics to become compulsive exercisers, sometimes exercising vigorously several hours a day (Logue, 1991).

**DISTORTIONS IN BODY IMAGE** It is a remarkable fact that despite the extreme loss of weight and the problems it leads to, the typical anorexic denies there is any problem and refuses to gain weight. In fact, anorexics frequently think that they look too fat. This suggests that anorexics have a distorted image of their own body, seeing themselves as heavier than they actually are. Indeed, there is experimental evidence for such a distortion. Anorexic and control subjects were given a device that allowed them to adjust someone's photograph to between -20 percent and +20 percent of the photograph's actual width (see Figure 10-6). An anorexic was more likely than a control subject to adjust a picture of herself so that it was larger than actual size; however, she showed no tendency to distort the sizes of other people (Garfinkel & Garner, 1982).

The preceding results suggest that anorexics refusal to eat is mediated by their image of themselves as too fat. To some extent, this kind of distorted image may be held by many college-aged women in our society, which could explain why this group of people is the most likely to become anorexic. Support for this idea is provided by the following experiment. Hundreds of male and female undergraduates were shown drawings of figures of their own sex. The figures of each sex were arranged on a scale running from very thin to very heavy, as shown in Figure 10-7. The subjects

**FIGURE 10-6**
**Distortions in Body Image** *Anorexics and control subjects were allowed to adjust someone's photograph to between −20 percent and +20 percent of the photograph's actual width. An anorexic was more likely than a control subject to adjust a picture of herself so it was larger than actual size.* (After Garfinkel & Garner, 1982).

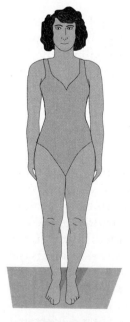

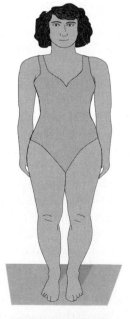

ACTUAL SIZE      CONSTRICTED IMAGE      EXPANDED IMAGE
(-20%)      (+20%)

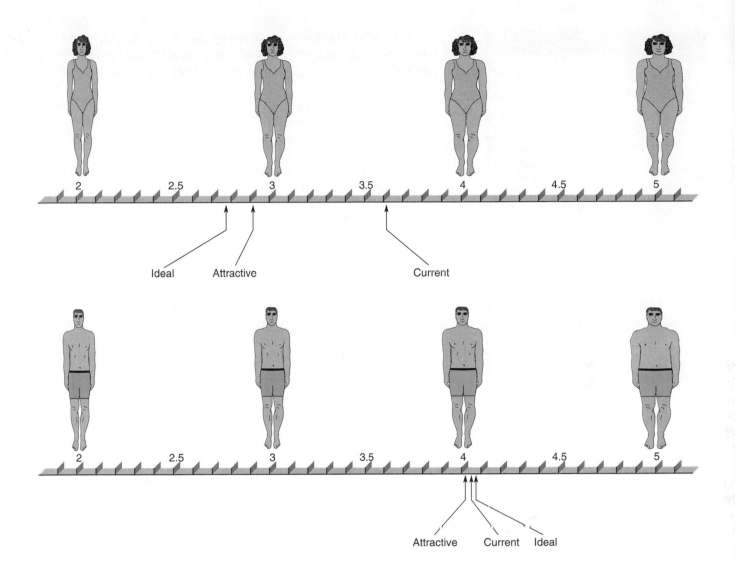

were asked to indicate: (a) the figure that looked most like their current shape; (b) the figure they most wanted to look like, that is, their *ideal;* and (c) the figure they felt would be most attractive to the opposite sex. The results, shown in Figure 10-7, are strikingly different for males and females. The men chose very similar figures for their current figure, their ideal figure, and the figure they thought most attractive to women; that is, men thought that their current weight was close to both their ideal and to what women would find attractive. The women, in contrast, chose very different figures for their current figure and either their ideal figure or the figure that they thought would be most attractive to the opposite sex (the latter two figures being relatively close). Clearly, the women were dissatisfied with their current weight, viewing themselves as too heavy to be attractive to men. But this turns out to be a distorted view. For when the male subjects were asked to choose the female figure to which they would be most attracted, their average choice was substantially heavier than the figures that women had chosen as either their ideal or as being most attractive to the opposite sex. Thus, college women mistakenly think that college men are attracted to very thin women. In short, college women, but not college men, were dissatisfied with their current weight in a way that could lead them to diet and perhaps become anorexic (Fallon & Rozin, 1985).

**FIGURE 10-7**
**Body Images of Male and Female Undergraduates** *Male and female undergraduates were shown figures of their own sex, and asked to indicate: (a) the figure that looked most like their current shape; (b) their ideal figure; and (c) the figure they felt would be most attractive to the opposite sex. Men selected very similar figures for all three choices, but women selected very different figures for their current figure and either their ideal figure or the figure they thought would be most attractive to the opposite sex. (Adapted from Fallon & Roein, 1985).*

**FIGURE 10-8**
*Top, a "perfect" figure for the 1950s: Jayne Mansfield. Bottom, a "perfect" figure for the 1990s: Julia Roberts.*

**POSSIBLE CAUSES**   A number of different kinds of causes of anorexia have been proposed, including personality factors, societal norms, and brain physiology. At this point in time, we lack firm evidence about any of the proposed causes.

That personality factors are involved is suggested by the fact that anorexics tend to be a certain kind of woman—young, white, and from an upwardly mobile family that stresses achievement. This kind of background may lead to stressful family demands and expectations, and in this context a young woman's refusal to eat may seem (unconsciously) like a way of exerting control. Another possibility that has been mentioned is that anorexia represents a denial of sexuality. In addition to not menstruating, girls who are severely underweight will lack other sexual characteristics, such as a truly feminine form (Bruch, 1973).

Many social scientists have suggested that social factors play a major role in anorexia, in particular our society's emphasis on thinness in women. This emphasis has increased markedly in the past 40 years, which fits with the claim that the incidence of anorexia has also increased during that period. An indication of this societal change is the change in what people regard as a "perfect" women's figure. Figure 10-8 contains a photograph of Jayne Mansfield, who was popularly thought to have an ideal figure in the 1950s, next to a photograph of the actress Julia Roberts, one of today's ideals. Roberts is clearly much thinner than Mansfield. Presumably these "perfect" figures greatly influence women's own ideals, which results in women feeling their own figure is much heavier than their ideal (Logue, 1991).

Other researchers have focused on possible biological causes. One hypothesis is that anorexia is caused by malfunctions of the hypothalamus. The critical observation that led to this hypothesis is that sometimes the stop in menstruation in anorexics cannot be attributed to either weight loss or its side effects. Hence, there may be some common factor that is responsible for both irregularities in menstruation and anorexia. The most likely candidate is the hypothalamus, given that it is known to play a role in both eating and hormonal functions (Garfinkle and Garner, 1982).

## Bulimia

**CHARACTERISTICS**   Bulimia is characterized by recurrent episodes of *binge eating* (rapid consumption of a large amount of food in a discrete period of time), followed by attempts to purge the excess eating by means of vomiting and laxatives. The binges can be frequent and extreme. A survey of bulimic women found that most women binged at least once per day (usually in the evening), and that an average binge involved consuming some 4800 calories (often sweet or salty carbohydrate foods). However, because of the purges that follow the binges, a bulimic's weight may stay relatively normal; this allows bulimics to keep their eating disorder hidden. But there can be a large physiological cost for the bulimic's behavior; the vomiting and use of laxatives can disrupt the balance of the electrolyte potassium in the body, which can result in problems like dehydration, cardiac arrhythmias, and urinary infections.

Like anorexia, bulimia primarily afflicts young women. But bulimia is more frequent than anorexia, with an estimated 5 to 10 percent of American women affected to some degree. Rather than being restricted to just the upwardly mobile, bulimia is found in all racial, ethnic, and socioeconomic groups in our society.

**POSSIBLE CAUSES** As was the case with anorexia, researchers have looked for explanations of bulimia in terms of personality, biological, and social factors.

With regard to personality factors, therapists who work with bulimic patients often see them as lacking a sense of identity and self-esteem. In line with this, depression seems to be relatively common in bulimics (Johnson & Larson, 1982). Such people may use food to fulfill their feelings of longing and emptiness. Researchers interested in biological factors in bulimia have also noted the link between bulimia and depression. It has been suggested that the same chemical disorder that underlies some cases of depression may also be the basis of some cases of bulimia; for example, a deficit of the neurotransmitter serotonin could be behind both depression and bulimia (Bruch, 1973).

As for social factors, again the culprit is often thought to be our society's recent over-emphasis on thinner women. Indeed, some bulimic women are quite explicit that their disorder is a way of solving the problem of how to eat lots of high calorie food, yet stay as slim as current cultural norms prescribe. As one bulimic woman put it, "I thought I had the problem licked; I couldn't understand why everyone didn't eat and then vomit" (Garfinkel & Garner, 1982).

In closing our discussion of bulimia and anorexia, it is important to keep in mind three qualifications about the putative causes of these disorders. First and foremost, there is very little hard evidence for any of the possible causes that we have discussed. Most of what we know about anorexia and bulimia comes from clinical reports of patients with these disorders, and not from controlled experiments that can rigorously establish a causal link between some factor and self-starvation. Second, it seems highly unlikely that there is only one cause for anorexia, and one for bulimia. As was the case with obesity, there may be many ways to get to anorexia or bulimia. Third, and finally, despite how little we know about the causes of these eating disorders, treatments for them have been developed. Typically, the treatments involve some form of therapy. Traditional psychotherapies can be useful in dealing with personality issues; behavior modification programs, like that described in our earlier discussion of weight control, seem quite useful in helping anorexics and bulimics bring their eating habits under control.

# Adult Sexuality

Sexual and maternal drives are other powerful motivators. Sexual desire sometimes can be so strong that it becomes an obsession, and a mother's (or father's) desire to protect its young can be so intense as to make her insensitive to pain. Like the survival motives we have considered, sex (and to some extent maternal behavior) is an unlearned motive that humans share with other species, and whose biological basis psychologists are beginning to understand. There are, however, important differences between the motives of sex and maternal behavior, on the one hand, and the motives of temperature, thirst, and hunger on the other. Sex and maternal behavior are *social* motives—their satisfaction typically involves another organism—whereas the survival motives concern only the biological self. In addition, motives such as hunger and thirst stem from tissue needs, while sex and maternal behavior do not involve an internal deficit that needs to be regulated and remedied for the organism to survive. Consequently, social motives do not lend themselves to a homeostatic analysis.

With regard to sex, two critical distinctions should be kept in mind. The first stems from the fact that, although we begin to mature sexually at puberty, the basis for our sexual identity is established in the womb. We therefore distinguish between adult sexuality (that is, beginning with changes at puberty) and early sexual development. The second distinction is between the biological and environmental determinants of sexual behaviors and feelings. For many aspects of sexual development and adult sexuality, a fundamental question is the extent to which the behavior or feeling in question is a product of biology—particularly hormones—or environment and learning—early experiences and cultural norms—or of an interaction between the two. (This distinction between biology and environment is similar to one we drew earlier in our discussion of obesity. There we were concerned with genetic factors, which are of course biological, versus factors that tended to reflect learning and the environment.)

## Hormonal Control

We introduced sexual development in Chapter 3, but it is important here to address the hormonal changes in puberty and how they influence desire and arousal.

**CHANGES AT PUBERTY**   At puberty—roughly ages 11 to 14—hormone changes produce the bodily changes that serve to distinguish males from females. The hormonal system involved is illustrated in Figure 10-9. The general idea is that endocrine glands manufacture hormones (chemical messengers), which travel through the bloodstream to target organs. The process begins in the hypothalamus when it secretes *gonadotropin-releasing factors;* these chemical messengers direct the pituitary gland to produce *gonadotropins,* which are hormones whose targets are the **gonads**—the ovaries

**FIGURE 10-9**
**Hormonal System Involved in Sex**
*By way of hormones, the hypothalamus directs the pituitary, which in turn directs the gonads to secrete the sex hormones.* (After Offir, 1982)

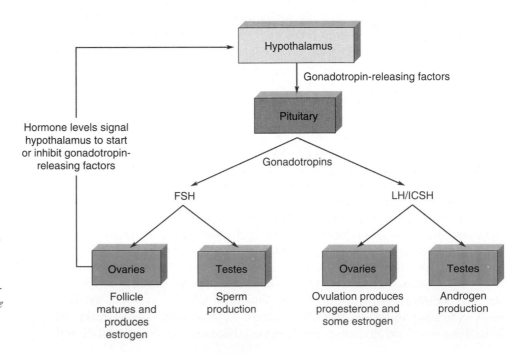

and testes. There are two kinds of gonadotropins. One is called *follicle-stimulating hormone* (FSH). In women, FSH stimulates the growth of *follicles*, clusters of cells in the ovaries that support developing eggs and that secrete the female hormone **estrogen.** In men, FSH stimulates sperm production in the testes. The other gonadotropin produced by the pituitary is called *luteinizing hormone* (LH) in women and *interstitial-cell stimulating hormone* (ICSH) in men. The secretion of LH brings on ovulation—the release of a mature egg from the follicle—and then causes the ruptured follicle to secrete **progesterone,** another female hormone. ICSH, the male equivalent, stimulates the production of the male hormone **androgen.** Although a number of technical terms have been mentioned here, the basic scheme is simple: by way of hormones, the hypothalamus directs the pituitary, which in turn directs the gonads.

The hormones produced by the gonads—estrogen, progesterone, and androgen—are called the *sex hormones* (a bit of a misnomer because all three hormones are produced by males and females, albeit in different amounts). These hormones are responsible for the body changes at puberty. In girls, estrogen causes the development of breasts, the changes in the distribution of body fat that result in a more feminine form, and the maturation of the female genitals. In boys, **testosterone** (a kind of androgen) is responsible for the sudden growth of facial, underarm, and pubic hair; it also causes a deepening of the voice, the development of muscles that lead to a more masculine form, and the growth of the external genitals.

**EFFECTS OF HORMONES ON DESIRE AND AROUSAL** What role do these hormones play in adult sexual desire and arousal? In other species, sexual arousal is closely tied to variations in hormonal levels; in humans, however, hormones play less of a role. One way to assess the contribution of hormones to sexual arousal is to study the effects of **castration.** In males, castration usually involves removal of the testes, which essentially eliminates production of the sex hormones. In experiments with lower species (such as rats and guinea pigs), castration results in the rapid decline and eventual disappearance of sexual activity. For humans, of course, there are no controlled experiments; psychologists rely instead on observations of males with serious illnesses (for example, cancer of the testes) who have undergone *chemical castration* (synthetic hormones administered to suppress or block the use of androgen). These studies typically show that some men lose their interest in sex, while others continue to lead a normal sex life (Money, Wiedeking, Walker, & Gain, 1976; Walker, 1978). Apparently, androgen contributes to sexual desire only in some cases.

Another way to measure the contribution of hormones to sexual desire and arousal in men is to look for a relation between hormonal fluctuation and sexual interest. For example, is a man more likely to feel aroused when his testosterone level is high? It turns out that testosterone level may have no effect on *arousal*—as indicated by the ability to have an erection—but does increase *desire*—as indicated by sexual fantasies (Davidson, 1988). [The major determinants of sexual desire in men, however, seem to be emotional factors; thus, for males (as well as females), the most common cause of low desire in couples seeking sex therapy is marital conflict (Goleman, 1988).]

The lack of hormonal effects on arousal is even more striking in women, particularly in contrast to other species. In all animals, from reptiles to monkeys, castration in a female (removal of the ovaries) results in cessation of sexual activity. The castrated female ceases to be receptive to the male and usually resists sexual advances. The major exception is the human female; following menopause (when the ovaries have ceased to function), sexual desire in most women does not diminish. In fact, some women show an increased interest in sex after menopause, possibly because they are no longer concerned about becoming pregnant.

Studies looking at the relation between hormonal fluctuation and sexual arousal in premenopausal females lead to a similar conclusion: hormones have substantial control of arousal in lower species but not in humans. In female mammals, hormones fluctuate cyclically with accompanying changes in fertility. During the first part of the mammalian cycle (while the egg is being prepared for fertilization), the ovaries secrete estrogen, which prepares the uterus for implantation and also tends to arouse sexual interest. After ovulation occurs, both progesterone and estrogen are secreted. This *fertility* or **estrous cycle** is accompanied by a consequent variation in sexual motivation in most mammalian species. Most female animals are receptive to sexual advances by a male only during the period of ovulation, when the estrogen level is at its highest in the cycle (when they are "in heat"). Among primates, however, sexual activity is less influenced by the fertility cycle; monkey, ape, and chimpanzee females copulate during all phases of the cycle, although ovulation is still the period of most intense sexual activity. In the human female, sexual desire and arousal seems to be barely influenced by the fertility cycle, being affected much more by social and emotional factors.

In sum, the degree of hormonal control over adult sexual behavior decreases from the lower to the higher vertebrates. Still, even for humans there may be some hormonal control, as witnessed by the relation between testosterone and sexual desire in men.

## Neural Control

Hormones are not the only biological factor to consider. The nervous system also is responsible for aspects of sexual arousal and behavior. The mechanisms involved are complex and vary from one species to the next; in humans, some of the neural mechanisms are at the level of the spinal cord. In males, an erection following direct stimulation of the penis is controlled by a spinal reflex, as are pelvic movements and ejaculations. However, all of these actions are still possible in men whose spinal cords have been severed by injury. Similarly, clinical studies of women with spinal cord injuries suggest that lubrication of the vagina may be controlled by a spinal reflex (Offir, 1982).

But the organ most responsible for the regulation of sexual arousal and behavior is the brain. The spinal reflexes are regulated by the brain, and erections can be directly controlled by the brain. Some of our more precise knowledge about the role of the brain in sex comes from experiments with animals. In male rats, electrical stimulation of the posterior hypothalamus produces not only copulation but the entire repertoire of sexual behavior. A male rat stimulated in that area does not mount indiscriminately; instead, he courts the female by nibbling her ears and nipping the back of her neck until she responds. Intromission and ejaculation follow unless the electrical stimulation is terminated. Even a sexually satiated male rat will respond to electrical stimulation by pressing a bar to open a door leading to the female and will court and mate with her (Caggiula & Hoebel, 1966). In humans, of course, the brain's role in sex is far more complex; it involves thoughts and images, thereby leaving room for learning to enter the picture.

# Early Experiences

The environment also has great influence on adult sexuality, one class of determinants being early experience. Experience has little influence on the mating behavior of lower mammals—inexperienced rats will copulate as efficiently as experienced ones—but it is a major determinant of the sexual behavior of higher mammals.

**EXPERIMENTS WITH MONKEYS**   Experience can affect specific sexual responses. For instance, young monkeys exhibit in their play many of the postures required later for copulation. In wrestling with their peers, infant male monkeys display hindquarter grasping and thrusting responses that are components of adult sexual behavior. Infant female monkeys retreat when threatened by an aggressive male infant and stand steadfastly in a posture similar to the stance required to support the weight of the male during copulation. These presexual responses appear as early as 60 days of age and

*Sexual play among snow monkeys.*

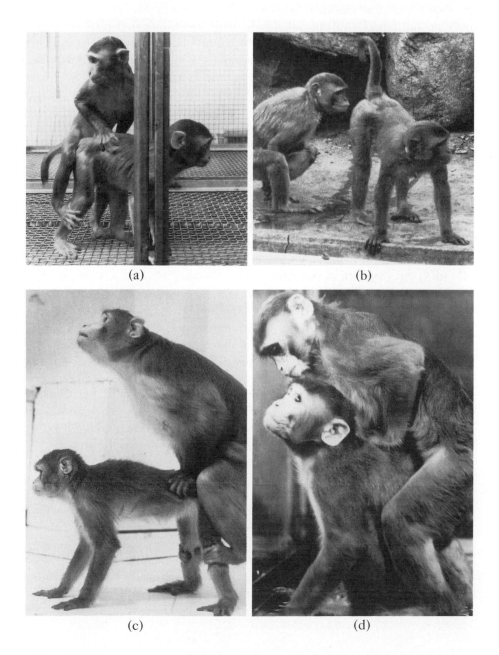

(a)        (b)

(c)        (d)

**FIGURE 10-10**
**Infant Play and Adult Sexual Behavior** *(a) The first presexual step. (b) Inappropriate sexual response: female correct, male incorrect. (c) Basic sexual posture. (d) Inappropriate sexual response: male correct, female incorrect.*

become more frequent and refined as the monkey matures (see Figure 10-10). Their early appearance suggests that they are innate responses to specific stimuli, and the modification and refinement of these responses through experience indicates that learning plays a role in the development of the adult sexual pattern.

Experience also affects the interpersonal aspect of sex. Monkeys raised in partial isolation (in separate wire cages, where they can see other monkeys but cannot have contact with them) are usually unable to copulate at maturity. The male monkeys are able to perform the mechanics of sex: they masturbate to ejaculation at about the same frequency as normal monkeys. But when confronted with a sexually receptive female, they do not seem to know how to assume the correct posture for copulation. They are aroused but aimlessly grope the female or their own bodies. Their problem is not just a deficiency of specific responses. These once-isolated monkeys have social or affectional problems: even in nonsexual situations, they are unable to relate to other monkeys, exhibiting either fear and flight or extreme aggression. Apparently, normal heterosexual behavior in primates depends not only on hormones and the development of specific sexual responses, but also on an affectional bond between two members of the opposite sex. This bond is an outgrowth of earlier interactions with the mother and peers, through which the young monkey learns to trust, to expose its delicate parts without fear of harm, to accept and enjoy physical contact with others, and to be motivated to seek the company of others (Harlow, 1971).

Although we must be cautious about generalizing these findings with monkeys to human sexual development, clinical observations of human infants suggest certain parallels. Human infants develop their first feelings of trust and affection through a warm and loving relationship with the mother or primary caretaker (see Chapter 3). This basic trust is a prerequisite for satisfactory interactions with peers. And affectionate relationships with other youngsters of both sexes lay the groundwork for the intimacy required for sexual relationships among adults.

**SEXUAL PERVERSIONS**  In humans, another kind of sexual problem attributed to early experience is that of sexual perversions, or **paraphilias** as they are technically labeled. Many people have what might be considered minor paraphilias—for example, becoming aroused by a particular odor, or by a particular article of clothing. By and large, sex researchers consider such practices relatively harmless, since they can readily fit in a normal relation between consenting adults. But some people have more serious paraphilias—for example, having sex with young children, or becoming aroused by inflicting intense pain on a partner. Such activities can be devastating, socially, and personally, and people who engage in such activities often say they are simply overcome by an irresistible compulsion to perform the act.

Ethical considerations, of course, preclude doing experiments on the development of paraphilias. So much of what we know about their origin is based on what afflicted adults report to their therapists. Such clinical reports often mention problems in early sexual development. Recently, the sex researchers Money and Lamacz (1989) has been able to trace a few paraphilias as they evolved. Specifically, in the course of treating children who have hormonal abnormalities that affect their sexual development, Money and Lamacz were able to trace the development of paraphilias in seven people. Their findings point to difficulties in early development. Some of the seven people had strict, anti-sexual upbringings, with sex never being mentioned or being actively repressed. Others of the seven suffered traumatic incidents in childhood, such as incest and physical abuse. These painful experiences do not lead to paraphilias in most people—strict upbringings are common, yet serious paraphilias are rare—but they may have such an effect on children who are inherently vulnerable.

## Cultural Influences

Cultural influences constitute another class of environmental determinants. Unlike that of other primates, human sexual behavior is strongly determined by culture.

**SEXUAL ACTIVITY IN DIFFERENT CULTURES**   Every society places some restrictions on sexual behavior. Incest (sexual relations within the family), for example, is prohibited by almost all cultures. Other aspects of sexual behavior—sexual activity among children, homosexuality, masturbation, and premarital sex—are permitted in varying degrees by different societies. Among preliterate cultures studied by anthropologists, acceptable sexual activity varies widely. Some very permissive societies encourage autoerotic activities and sex play among children of both sexes and allow them to observe adult sexual activity. The Chewa of Africa, for example, believe that if children are not allowed to exercise themselves sexually, they will be unable to produce offspring later. The Sambia of New Guinea have institutionalized bisexuality: from pre-puberty until marriage, a boy lives with other males and engages in homosexual practices (Herdt, 1984).

In contrast, very restrictive societies try to control preadolescent sexual behavior and to keep children from learning about sex. The Cuna of South America believe that children should be totally ignorant about sex until they are married; they do not even permit their children to watch animals give birth. And among the Ashanti of Africa, intercourse with a girl who has not undergone the puberty rites is punishable by death for both participants. Similar extreme attitudes are found toward other aspects of sexual behavior: homosexuality, for example, is viewed by some nonliterate societies as an essential part of growing up and by others as an offense punishable by death.

**SEXUAL CHANGES WITHIN THE UNITED STATES**   While the most obvious way to study cultural differences is to investigate practices in different countries, one can also look at culture changes that occur within a country. One such change occurred in the United States and other Western countries between the 1940s and the 1970s. In the 1940s and 1950s, the United States and most other western countries would have been classified as sexually restrictive. Traditionally, the existence of prepubertal sexuality had been ignored or denied. Marital sex was considered the only legitimate sexual outlet, and other forms of sexual expression (homosexual activities, premarital and extramarital sex) were generally condemned and often prohibited by law. Of course, many members of these societies engaged in such activities, but often with feelings of shame.

Over the years, sexual activities became less restricted. Premarital intercourse, for example, became more acceptable and more frequent. Among American college-educated individuals interviewed in the 1940s, 27 percent of the women and 49 percent of the men had engaged in premarital sex by

*A young couple in love.*

**FIGURE 10-11**
**Reported Incidence of Premarital Coitus** *Each data point represents findings from a study of the incidence of premarital sex among college men and women. Note the marked upward trend starting in the 1960s.* (After Hopkins, 1977)

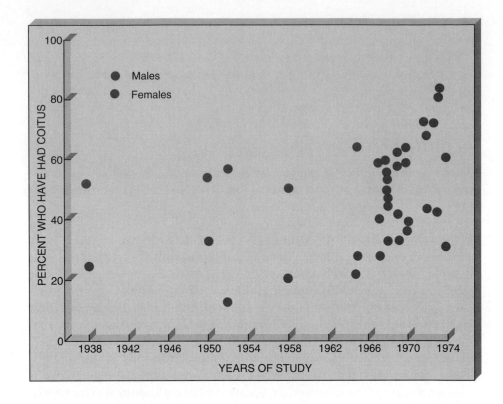

the age of 21 (Kinsey, Pomeroy, & Martin, 1948; Kinsey, Pomeroy, Martin, & Gebhard, 1953). In contrast, several surveys of American college students in the 1970s reported percentages ranging from 40 to over 80 for both males and females (Hunt, 1974; Tavris & Sadd, 1977). Figure 10-11 gives the reported incidence of premarital intercourse in studies conducted over a 35-year span. Note that the change in sexual behavior was greater among women than men and that the biggest changes occurred in the late 1960s. These changes led many observers of the social scene in the 1970s to conclude that there had been a sexual revolution.

Today, it seems that the sexual revolution has been stymied by the fear of sexually transmitted diseases, particularly the Acquired Immunodeficiency Syndrome, or AIDS. Furthermore, the revolution may always have pertained more to behavior than to feelings. In interviews conducted with American college-student couples in the 1970s, only 20 percent thought that sex between casual acquaintances was completely acceptable (Peplau, Rubin, & Hill, 1977). In a similar vein, while women are becoming more like men with regard to sexual behavior, they continue to differ from men in certain critical attitudes toward sex before marriage. The majority of women who engage in premarital sex do so with only one or two partners with whom they are emotionally involved. Men, in contrast, are more likely to seek sex with multiple partners (Hunt, 1974).

### Homosexuality

The term "homosexual" can be applied to either a man or a woman, but female homosexuals are usually called "lesbians." Individuals are considered **homosexual** if they are sexually attracted primarily to members of the same sex. Most experts agree with Kinsey's view that homosexuality is not an either–or matter; sexual behavior falls on a continuum, with exclusively heterosexual and exclusively homosexual individuals at either end of the continuum, and various mixtures of sexual behavior in between. Most young boys engage in erotic play with other boys at some time during their childhood, and many men have one or more homosexual encounters. According to some estimates, only about 4 percent of men become exclusively homosexual. Women are less apt than men to have sexual interactions with each other during childhood or a homosexual episode in later life; and only 1–2 percent of women are exclusively homosexual. Some individuals are *bisexual*, having sexual relations with members of both sexes. And some married individuals may have extramarital homosexual encounters.

**HOMOSEXUALITY AND MENTAL HEALTH**   Until the advent of the sexual revolution in the late 1960s, homosexuality was considered a mental illness or an abnormal perversion. Although some people still view homosexuality as unnatural, most psychologists and psychiatrists consider it to be a variant of sexual expression and not, in itself, an indication or cause of mental illness. In some studies of mental health, homosexuals seemed as well adjusted as heterosexuals in certain areas of life (Bell & Weinberg, 1978). Their job stability and job satisfaction was equal to that of heterosexuals. In other areas of life, homosexuals fared less well. They reported themselves as being more tense and depressed than did a comparable group of heterosexuals. However, this difference between homosexuals and heterosexuals all but disappears if one considers only those homosexuals that are "close-coupled," that is, living in a quasi-marriage. Also, the greater unhappiness of other homosexuals may stem less from their sexual preference than from their treatment as a disapproved-of minority: being attracted to people of the same sex may or may not make you depressed, but being scorned and ostracized because of your sexual preference almost certainly will (Brown, 1986). In any event, these data on homosexuality and mental health were obtained before AIDS had reached epidemic proportions in the homosexual community. No doubt, living (and dying) with AIDS is bad for one's mental health, but this is true of any group at high risk for a deadly disease. In short, there is no evidence that a homosexual orientation, per se, is associated with poor mental health.

**ENVIRONMENTAL AND BIOLOGICAL DETERMINANTS**   Despite considerable research, little of certainty is known about the causes of homosexuality. With regard to environmental causes, common wisdom has it that male homosexuality can result from a young boy identifying with his mother. The most relevant evidence for this "mothering" hypothesis comes from a large study involving extensive interviews with hundreds of homosexuals and heterosexuals about their early development (Bell, Weinberg, & Hammersmith, 1981; Bell & Weinberg, 1978). This study found no difference between homosexual and heterosexual males in the frequency with which they reported that when growing up they wanted to be like their mothers. Thus, there is no evidence for the mothering hypothesis. On the other hand, the two groups of males did differ with regard to identifying with their fathers; many fewer homosexuals reported that while growing up they wanted to be like their fathers. But there is no simple link between a poor relation with a father and male homosexuality, because poor relations

*A homosexual couple.*

**TABLE 10-2**
**Variables Influencing Sexual Preference** *Results are based on interviews conducted in 1969–70 with approximately 1,000 homosexual men and women living in the San Francisco Bay area. The investigators analyzed the respondents' relationships with their parents and siblings while growing up, the degree to which the respondents conformed during childhood to the stereotypical concepts of what it means to be male or female, the respondents' relationships with peers and others outside the home, and the nature of their childhood and sexual experiences. Statistical analyses traced the relationship between such variables and adult sexual preference.* (After Bell, Weinberg, & Hammersmith, 1981)

1. The respondents' identification with their opposite-sex parents while growing up appeared to have had no significant impact on whether they turned out to be homosexual or heterosexual.

2. For both the men and the women in the study, poor relationships with fathers seemed to play a more important role in predisposing them to homosexuality than the quality of their relationships with their mothers.

3. For both men and women, homosexuals were no more likely than heterosexuals to report a first sexual encounter with a member of the same sex.

4. By the time both the boys and the girls reached adolescence, their sexual preference was likely to be determined, even though they might not yet have become very active sexually.

5. Among the respondents, homosexuality was indicated or reinforced by sexual feelings that typically occurred 3 years or so before their first "advanced" homosexual activity. These feelings, more than homosexual activities, appeared to play a crucial role in the development of adult homosexuality.

6. The homosexual men and women in the study were not particularly lacking in heterosexual experiences during their childhood and adolescent years. They were distinguishable from their heterosexual counterparts, however, in that they found such experiences ungratifying.

7. Among both the men and the women in the study, there was a powerful link between gender nonconformity as a child and the development of homosexuality.

8. Insofar as differences can be identified between male and female psychosexual development, gender nonconformity appeared to be somewhat more important for males and family relationships appeared to be more important for females in the development of sexual preference.

with a father were also more prevalent among lesbians than their heterosexual counterparts. (These findings, along with other results from the Bell, Weinberg, and Hammersmith study, are summarized in Table 10-2.)

Some proposals about biological causes of homosexuality seem as tenuous. Thus, there are no reliable differences in body characteristics between homosexuals and heterosexuals. Although some male homosexuals may look quite feminine—and some female homosexuals, quite masculine—this is often not the case. A more plausible locus of biological differences is hormones. With regard to hormone levels in adulthood, the evidence is at best inconsistent. Some studies have found that male homosexuals have lower levels of testosterone than do heterosexual males, while other studies show no difference in overall levels of hormones. Moreover, when male homosexuals are given additional male hormones, their sex drive may increase but their sexual preferences do not change.

A more promising biological hypothesis is that homosexuals and heterosexuals may differ with respect to the hormones they were exposed to while still in the womb. Specifically, during prenatal life male fetuses secrete testosterone (as will be discussed in the section on early sexual development), and this testosterone may masculinize the brain. It is possible that males who get substantially lower than average amounts of testosterone at some critical point in prenatal life are predisposed toward homosexuality in adult life. Similarly, female fetuses exposed to substantially higher than average amounts of testosterone may be predisposed toward lesbianism in adult life. Though the hypothesis may seem far-fetched, there are some data that indirectly support it. Girls who are known to have been exposed to extremely high levels of prenatal testosterone are extremely likely to be "tomboys" in childhood, and more likely than most girls to have lesbian fantasies during early adulthood (Money, 1980; Money, Schwartz, & Lewis, 1984). Also, the prenatal hypothesis seems compatible with the findings listed in Table 10-2, in particular the early emergence of homosexual feelings (Brown, 1986). The hypothesis is also consistent with recent reports of anatomical differences between the hypothalamuses of homosexual men and those of heterosexual men (Le Vay, 1991); the hypothalamus is a region likely to be affected by testosterone levels in the uterus. Still, at this point, the hypothesis remains speculative, and is intended only for those people classified as exclusively homosexual. Even proponents of the hypothesis think that for some people, homosexuality is entirely learned and, if desired, potentially changeable by therapy.

**SEX DIFFERENCES** Studies of heterosexuals have shown that young men and women differ in their attitudes about sex; women are more likely than men to view sex as a part of a loving relationship, and hence to have fewer partners if they engage in premarital sex. This same kind of difference appears between male and female homosexuals. Lesbians are more likely than male homosexuals to have long-term relations with their lovers. Lesbians also have many fewer sexual partners. In the study by Bell and Weinberg (1978), the majority of gay females reported having a total of fewer than 10 sexual partners, while the average gay male reported hundreds of sexual

*Lesbian partners*

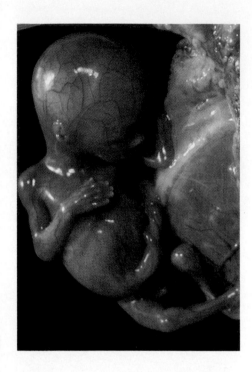

*Prenatal development: 4 months.*

partners. (However, male homosexuals have become far less promiscuous in recent years in a determined effort to reduce the transmission of AIDS.) Also, lesbians place more emphasis on the romantic aspects of their relations than do gay men. The way that people conduct their sexual-romantic lives, therefore, may have less to do with being homosexual or heterosexual than with being male or female.

# Early Sexual Development

For social and sexual experiences to be gratifying in adult life, one needs to develop an appropriate **gender identity**—that is, males need to think of themselves as males, and females as females. This development is quite complex and begins in the womb.

## Prenatal Hormones

For the first couple of months after conception, only the chromosomes of a human embryo indicate whether it will develop into a boy or girl. Up to this stage, both sexes are identical in appearance and have tissues that will eventually develop into testes or ovaries, as well as a genital tubercle that will become either a penis or a clitoris. But between 2 and 3 months, a primitive sex gland, or gonad, develops into testes if the embryo is genetically male (that is, has XY chromosomes—see Chapter 2) or into ovaries if the embryo is genetically female (XX chromosomes). Once testes or ovaries develop, they produce the sex hormones, which then control the development of the internal reproduction structures and the external genitals. The sex hormones are more important for prenatal development than they are for expressions of adult sexuality.

The critical hormone in genital development is androgen (testosterone, which we have previously mentioned, is a kind of androgen). If the embryonic sex glands produce enough androgen, the newborn will have male genitals; if there is insufficient androgen, the newborn will have female genitals, *even* if it is genetically male (XY). The anatomical development of the female embryo does not require female hormones, only the absence of male hormones. In short, nature will produce a female unless androgen intervenes.

The influence of androgen, called *androgenization*, extends far beyond anatomy. After it has molded the genitals, androgen begins to operate on the brain cells. Studies with rats provide direct evidence that prenatal androgen changes the volume and detailed structure of cells in the fetus' hypothalamus, an organ that regulates motivation in humans as well as rats (Money, 1988). These effects of androgen essentially masculinize the brain, and may be responsible for masculine traits and behaviors that appear months or years later.

In a series of experiments, pregnant monkeys were injected with androgen (specifically, testosterone), and their female offspring were observed in detail. These female offspring showed some anatomical changes (penises instead of clitorises) and also acted differently than normal females. They were more aggressive in play, more masculine in sexual play, and less intimidated by approaching peers (Goy, 1968; Phoenix, Goy, & Resko, 1968). These findings indicate that some gender-appropriate behaviors (such as greater aggression for males) may be hormonally determined in monkeys. If the same is true in humans, then some typical aspects of our gender identity are controlled by hormones rather than by the social environment.

## Hormones versus Environment

In humans, much of what is known about the effects of prenatal hormones and early environment has been uncovered by studies of **hermaphrodites.** Hermaphrodites are individuals who are born with both male and female tissue; they may have genitals that appear to be ambiguous (an external organ that could be described as a very large clitoris or a very small penis) or genitals that conflict with internal sex organs (a penis and ovaries). These conditions arise because of prenatal hormonal imbalances, in which a genetically female fetus has too much androgen or a genetically male fetus has too little of it. What, then, will be the eventual gender identity of a hermaphroditic infant who is assigned the wrong sex label at birth—say, an infant with ambiguous external genitalia who is called a boy at birth but is later determined to be genetically female (XX) and to have ovaries?

In most cases such as this, the assigned label and the sex role in which the individual is raised have a much greater influence on gender identity than do the individual's genes and hormones. For example, two genetically female infants had ambiguous external genitals because their fetal sex glands had produced too much androgen (their internal organs were clearly female, though). Both infants had surgery to correct their enlarged clitorises. One infant's genitals were "feminized," and she was raised as a girl; the other infant's genitals were modified to resemble a penis, and he was raised as a boy. Reports indicate that both children grew up secure in their respective sex roles. The girl was somewhat "tomboyish," but feminine in appearance. The boy was accepted as a male by his peers and expressed a romantic interest in girls. Cases such as this suggest that an individual's gender identification is influenced more by the way a person is labeled and raised (that is, by environment) than by his or her hormones (Money, 1980).

But there are also cases that point to the opposite conclusion. The most famous occurred several years ago in remote villages of the Dominican Republic. It involved 18 genetic males who, owing to the fact that their cells were insensitive to the androgen their bodies generated prenatally, were born with internal organs that were clearly male but external genitals that were closer to females, including a clitoris-like sex organ. All 18 were raised as girls, which was at odds with both their genes and their prenatal hormonal environment. When they reached puberty, the surge of male hormones produced the usual bodily changes and turned their clitoris-like sex organs into penis-like organs. The vast majority of these males-reared-as-females rapidly turned into males. They seemed to have little difficulty adjusting to a male gender identity; they went off to work as miners and woodsmen and some found female sexual partners. In this case, biology triumphed over environment (Imperato-McGinley, Peterson, Gautier, & Sturla, 1979). There is controversy, however, about these Dominican hermaphrodites. They do not seem to have been raised as ordinary girls (not surprising since they had ambiguous genitals). Rather, they seemed to have been treated as half-girl, half-boy, which could have made their subsequent transition to males easier (Money, 1987).

Proponents of environmental determination can point to their own incredible case. Identical twin boys had a completely normal prenatal environment. But at the age of 7 months, in a tragic mistake, one of the boys had his penis completely severed in what was supposed to be a routine circumcision. Ten months later, the agonized parents authorized surgery to turn their child into a little girl—the testes were removed and a vagina was given preliminary shape. The child was then given female sex hormones and raised as a girl. Within a few years, the child seemed to have assumed a female gender identity: she preferred more feminine clothes, toys, and activities than her twin brother. What is striking about this case is (a) that environment won out over both genes and a *normal* prenatal environment (in all other cases considered, the prenatal environment has not been entirely normal), and (b) that a comparison can be made between individuals who have identical genes and prenatal hormones but different upbringings. Still, advocates of biological determination are skeptical about basing too much on a single case.

What can we conclude about gender identity? Clearly, prenatal hormones and environment are both major determinants of gender identity that typically work in harmony. When they clash, as they do in certain hermaphrodites, most experts believe that environment will dominate. But this is a controversial area, and expert opinion may change as additional data are gathered.

## Transsexualism

Some people feel that their body is compatible with one sex—say, their internal and external organs are all male—but their gender identity is that of the other sex—they think of themselves as females. Such **transsexuals** (usually males) feel that they were born into the wrong body. They are not homosexuals in the usual sense. Most homosexuals are satisfied with their anatomy and identify themselves as appropriately male or female; they have an appropriate gender identity but are sexually attracted to members of their own sex. Transsexuals, in contrast, think of themselves as members of the *opposite* sex (often from early childhood) and may be so desperately unhappy with their physical appearance that they request hormonal and surgical treatment to change their genitals and secondary sex characteristics.

Doctors have performed several thousand sex-change operations in the United States. For males, hormone treatments can enlarge their breasts, reduce beard growth, and make their bodies more rounded; surgical procedures involve removing the testes and part of the penis and shaping the remaining tissue into a vagina and labia. For women, hormone treatments can increase beard growth, firm their muscles, and deepen their voices; surgical procedures involve removing the ovaries and the uterus, reducing breast tissue, and in some instances constructing a penislike organ. Although a sex-change operation does not make reproduction possible, it can produce a remarkable change in physical appearance. Because the surgery is so drastic, though, it is undertaken only after careful consideration. The individual is usually given counseling and hormone treatments and is required to live as a member of the opposite sex for a year or more prior to the operation. Expert opinion has been divided on whether sex-change surgery genuinely helps transsexual individuals to feel better adjusted to their environment (Hunt & Hampson, 1980).

# Maternal Behavior

In many species, care of the offspring is a more powerful determinant of behavior than is sex, or even hunger and thirst. A mother rat, for example, will more frequently overcome barriers and suffer pain to reach its young than it will to obtain food when hungry or water when thirsty. While humans are not always as dutiful parents as rats are, caring for the young is one of the basic motives in our species, too.

## Biological Determinants

As is the case with sex, hormones play more of a role in the maternal behavior of lower species than in primates. Virgin rats presented with rat pups for several days will begin to build a nest, lick the pups, retrieve them, and finally hover in a nursing posture. If blood plasma from a mother rat that has just given birth is injected into a virgin rat, it will begin to exhibit maternal behavior in less than a day (Terkel & Rosenblatt, 1972). Maternal behavior patterns appear to be innately programmed in the rat's brain, and hormones serve to increase the excitability of these neural mechanisms. The hormonal effects depend on the balance between the female hormones (estrogen and progesterone) and prolactin from the anterior pituitary gland, which stimulates the production of milk.

For humans, hormones have much less influence. If human maternal behavior were chiefly guided by hormones, one would not expect parents to abuse their children as often as they do. Some women abandon their newborn infants or even kill them, and battered children are more commonplace than people realize. In the United States, according to a conservative estimate, approximately 350,000 children each year are physically, sexually, or emotionally abused by their caretakers; a less conservative estimate holds that between 1.4 and 1.9 million children each year are at risk of a serious injury from a family member (Wolfe, 1985). The parents involved in these cases generally received little or no love as children and frequently were beaten by their own parents, indicating the importance of early experience

# Instincts and Maternal-Infant Behavior

The concept of an "instinct" has a long history in the study of behavior. Around the turn of the century, psychologists relied heavily on the concept, attempting to explain all human behavior in terms of instincts (McDougall, 1908). During the 1920s, the concept fell into disrepute, partly because many acts were being cavalierly labeled "instinctive" and partly because the concept did not fit with the emerging theory of behaviorism (Stellar & Stellar, 1985). But later, starting in the 1950s, a group of European ethologists brought the study of instinct under scientific scrutiny and revived interest in the concept. For a behavior to be labeled instinctive, it has to be innately determined and it must be specific to a certain species and appear in the same form in all members of the species. Thus, *innateness, species specificity,* and *fixed-action patterns* are the hallmarks of the ethological approach to instinctive behavior.

One area where the ethological approach has succeeded is in the analysis of maternal behavior. The response patterns that animals display in the care of their young provide a clear example of instinctive behavior. Building nests, removing the amniotic sac so the newborn can breathe, feeding the young, and retrieving them when they stray from the nest are all complex behavior patterns that animals exhibit without having had the opportunity to learn them; hence, they must be innate. A squirrel performs maternal duties in the same manner as all other mothers of its species; therefore, the behavior is species-specific and fixed in its action pattern.

**Imprinting in Ducklings** *The newly hatched duckling follows the model duck around a circular track. The duckling soon becomes imprinted on the model and will follow it in preference to a live duck of its own species. The more effort the duckling has to exert to follow the model (such as climbing a hurdle), the stronger the imprinting.* (After Hess, 1958)

Among the more startling discoveries of ethologists is the phenomenon of **imprinting**. Imprinting refers to a type of early learning in which a newborn forms an attachment with some kind of model (normally, a parent). Imprinting is the basis for the young animal's attachment to its parents. A newly hatched duckling that has been incubated artificially will follow a human being, a wooden decoy, or almost any other moving object that it first sees after birth. Following a wooden decoy for as little as 10 minutes is enough to imprint the duckling on the decoy; the duckling will then remain attached to this object, follow it even under adverse circumstances, and prefer it to a live duck. Imprinting occurs most readily 14 hours after hatching, but can happen any time during the first 2 days of life. After this interval, imprinting is difficult, probably because the duckling has acquired a fear of strange objects.

Ethologists have found imprinting in a number of species—including dogs, sheep, and guinea pigs—but it is most clearly developed in birds that are able to walk or swim immediately after birth. An innate mechanism ensures that the young will follow and will remain close to their mothers (normally the first moving object they see), rather than wander off into a perilous world.

Studies of mallard ducks have identified the stimuli that are important for imprinting in birds and indicate that the phenomenon begins even before birth. Ducklings begin to make sounds in their eggs a week before they break through the shells. Mallard mothers respond to these sounds with clucking signals, which increase in frequency about the

on parental behavior. In primates and humans, experience overrides whatever influence maternal hormones may have.

But we cannot dismiss biology entirely. A number of possible biological determinants of human parental behavior have been suggested by **ethologists** (scientists who study animal behavior in the natural environment). One such possibility is that the distinctive, cute features of a baby (large protruding forehead, large eyes, upturned nose, chubby cheeks, and so forth) serve as *innate releasers* of parental feelings and behavior. That is, our species—and most others—may have evolved so that the characteristic cute features of babies elicit feelings of parenting in adults. Babies that have fewer of these cute features are somewhat more likely to be abused by their

*Austrian ethologist Konrad Lorenz demonstrates how young ducklings follow him instead of their mother because he was the first moving object they saw after they were hatched.*

leasers also play a major role in the sexual behavior of lower animals.)

The higher an animal is on the evolutionary scale, the fewer instinctive behaviors it exhibits and the more that learning determines its actions. But even humans have some instinctual behavior patterns, including the *rooting reflex* of the human infant. Touching a nipple (or a finger) to the cheek of a newborn elicits head turning and simultaneous mouth opening. If the mouth contacts the nipple, it closes on the nipple and begins to suck. This behavior pattern is automatic and can occur even when the infant is sleeping. At about 6 months, the rooting reflex is superseded by voluntary behavior; the typical 6-month-old sees the nipple, reaches for it, and tries to bring it to his or her mouth.

time the ducklings hatch. Auditory stimuli before and after hatching, together with tactile stimulation in the nest after birth, thoroughly imprint the ducklings on the female mallard in the nest. An unhatched duckling that hears a recording of a human voice saying "Come, come, come" instead of its mother's clucking will imprint on a decoy that utters "Come, come, come" as easily as it will imprint on a decoy that utters normal mallard clucks. Ducklings that have been exposed to a mallard female's call prior to hatching are more likely to imprint on decoys that utter mallard clucks (Hess, 1972).

In addition to the concepts of species specificity and fixed-action patterns, ethologists have developed the concept of a **releaser**, a particular environmental stimulus that sets off a species-specific behavior. In some young sea gulls, a red or yellow spot on the mother's beak releases a pecking response by the hatchling, which causes the mother to regurgitate the food that the infant will eat. By varying the color and shape of the spot on cardboard models and by observing whether the young gull pecks at the beak, researchers can determine the characteristics of the releaser to which the bird responds. (Re-

"The Far Side," © 1984 Chronicle Features. Distributed by Universal Press Syndicate.

**When imprinting studies go awry**

parents (see Mook, 1987). In a similar vein, a baby's smile, which appears to be innately determined, seems to be a preprogrammed elicitor of parental behavior. (See the Critical Discussion, "Instincts and Maternal-Infant Behavior," for greater detail.)

## Environmental Determinants

Among primates, maternal behavior is largely influenced by experience and learning. If female monkeys are raised in isolation, they exhibit none of the normal maternal behaviors when they later become mothers (see Chapter 3). They appear to develop little love for their offspring and generally ig-

*Young monkeys "monkeying."*

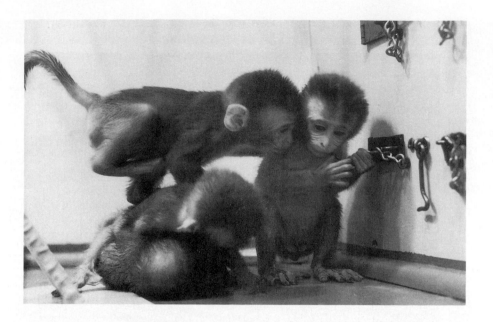

nore them. When they do pay attention to their young, they sometimes abuse them savagely. A mother might try to crush her infant's head or, in extreme cases, even bite the infant to death (Suomi, Harlow, & McKinney, 1972). There is a parallel here between the dreadful parenting of these monkey mothers originally reared in isolation and the child abuse by people who were raised by inadequate parents. Those who are themselves subjected to poor parenting seem strongly inclined to pass it on to their offspring.

## Curiosity Motives

Thus far, all of the motives discussed have been related to the survival of either the individual or the species. An earlier generation of psychologists believed that once an organism has satisfied its motives, it prefers a quiescent state. But this belief has turned out to be wrong. Both people and animals are motivated to *seek* stimulation—to explore actively their environment, even when the activity satisfies no bodily need. Thus, there appears to be a third general class of motives, *curiosity*, which we will briefly survey.

### Exploration and Manipulation

We seem to have inborn drives to manipulate and investigate objects. We give babies rattles, crib gymnasiums, and other toys because we know they like to hold, shake, and pull them. Monkeys enjoy the same sort of activities. If various mechanical devices are placed in a monkey's cage, it will begin to take them apart, becoming more skilled with practice, without receiving any evident reward other than the satisfaction of manipulating them. If the monkey is fed each time it takes a puzzle apart, its behavior changes; it loses interest in manipulation and views the puzzle as a means of acquiring food (Harlow, Harlow, & Meyer, 1950).

While manipulation sometimes is done for its own sake, other times it is for purposes of *investigation*. The monkey—or person—picks up the object, looks at it, tears it apart, and examines the parts, apparently attempting to discover more about it. Piaget made a number of observations bearing on such responses in the early life of the human infant. Within the first few months of life, infants learn to pull a string to activate a hanging rattle—a form of manipulation that might be considered merely entertaining. Between 5 and 7 months, they will remove a cloth from their faces in anticipation of the peekaboo game. At 8 to 10 months, infants look for objects behind or beneath other objects. By 11 months, they begin to experiment with objects, varying the toys' placement or positions; at this point, the behavior seems part of an investigation (Piaget, 1952). This kind of investigative behavior is typical of the growing child, and it seems to develop as a motive apart from any physiological need of the organism.

## Sensory Stimulation

**REDUCED STIMULATION STUDIES** Both exploration and manipulation provide the organism with new and changing sensory input. This change in input may be one reason why humans and animals manipulate and investigate objects: perhaps we have a need for sensory stimulation. Studies in which sensory stimulation is markedly reduced provide some support for this hypothesis. In such experiments, care needs to be taken to alleviate the subjects' anxiety and disorientation about the experimental situation; this is done, in part, by familiarizing subjects with the experimental situation before a session begins. In a typical session, the subject lies on a comfortable bed in a dark, sound-reduced room for 24 hours. Water and food are available through plastic tubes fastened near the pillow, and a chemical toilet is at the foot of the bed (see Figure 10-12). These experiments show decrements in perception: subjects experience some distortions in color and in spatial orientation, and are slower in reacting to visual stimuli than control subjects (Zubek, 1969). Stimulus reduction also produces decrements in problem-solving tasks such as thinking of as many uses as possible for a common object. Thus, people apparently require sensory stimulation for normal perceptual and intellectual functioning (Suedfeld, 1975).

Yet reduced stimulation can make some perceptual processes become more acute and can improve learning. It has helped people change behavior, such as stopping smoking or reducing alcohol intake. A related technique, flotation in a tank, has proved effective in treating stress-related problems such as tension headaches and insomnia (Suedfeld & Coren, 1989). Thus, a decrease in stimulation is sometimes useful, perhaps to allow us to attend more to our own feelings and thoughts ( Suedfeld, 1975).

**INDIVIDUAL DIFFERENCES IN STIMULATION SEEKING** While persons differ in the extent to which they manifest some of the other motives discussed in this chapter, individual differences in curiosity motives seem particularly salient. To try to measure these differences, Zuckerman (1979a) has developed a test called the *Sensation Seeking Scale*, or SSS. The scale includes a range of items designed to assess an individual's desire to engage in adventurous activities, to seek new sensory experiences, to enjoy the excitement of social stimulation, and to avoid boredom. Table 10-3 presents some items on the scale; you may want to answer them before reading further.

Research using the SSS has revealed large differences in stimulation seeking (Carrol, Zuckerman, & Vogel, 1982). Moreover, sensation seeking appears to be a trait that is consistent across a variety of situations; individuals who report enjoying new experiences in one area of life tend to describe themselves as adventurous in other areas. Psychologists have related high scores on the SSS to a number of behavioral characteristics: engaging in risky sports, occupations, or hobbies (parachuting, motorcycle riding, fire fighting, scuba diving); seeking variety in sexual and drug experiences; be-

**FIGURE 10-12**
**Reduced Stimulation Experiment**
*The room is dark and sound-deadened. Food and water stored in the blue box are delivered via the plastic tube. An intercom behind the subject's head permits communication when necessary.*

**TABLE 10-3**
**Sensation Seeking Scale** *A sample of items from the SSS and a scoring procedure. Each item contains two choices. Choose the one that best describes your likes or feelings. If you do not like either choice, mark the choice you dislike the least. Do not leave any items blank.* (Test items courtesy of Marvin Zuckerman)

1.  A. I have no patience with dull or boring persons.
    B. I find something interesting in almost every person I talk to.

2.  A. A good painting should shock or jolt the senses.
    B. A good painting should provide a feeling of peace and security.

3.  A. People who ride motorcycles must have some kind of unconscious need to hurt themselves.
    B. I would like to drive or ride a motorcycle.

4.  A. I would prefer living in an ideal society in which everyone is safe, secure, and happy.
    B. I would have preferred living in the unsettled days of history.

5.  A. I sometimes like to do things that are a little frightening.
    B. A sensible person avoids dangerous activities.

6.  A. I would not like to be hypnotized.
    B. I would like to be hypnotized.

7.  A. The most important goal of life is to live to the fullest and experience as much as possible.
    B. The most important goal in life is to find peace and happiness.

8.  A. I would like to try parachute jumping.
    B. I would never want to try jumping from a plane, with or without a parachute.

9.  A. I enter cold water gradually, giving myself time to get used to it.
    B. I like to dive or jump right into the ocean or a cold pool.

10. A. When I go on a vacation, I prefer the comfort of a good room and bed.
    B. When I go on a vacation, I prefer the change of camping out.

11. A. I prefer people who are emotionally expressive even if they are a bit unstable.
    B. I prefer people who are calm and even-tempered.

12. A. I would prefer a job in one location.
    B. I would like a job that requires traveling.

13. A. I can't wait to get indoors on a cold day.
    B. I am invigorated by a brisk, cold day.

14. A. I get bored seeing the same faces.
    B. I like the comfortable familiarity of everyday friends.

Scoring:

Count one point for each of the following items that you have circled: 1A, 2A, 3B, 4B, 5A, 6B, 7A, 8A, 9B, 10B, 11A, 12B, 13B, 14A. Add your total for sensation seeking and compare it with the norms below:

| 0–3 | Very low | 6–9 | Average | 12–14 | Very high |
|---|---|---|---|---|---|
| 4–5 | Low | 10–11 | High | | |

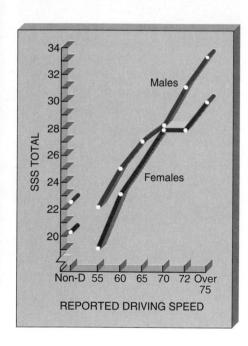

**FIGURE 10-13**
**SSS Scores and Driving Speed** *Subjects were asked at what speed they would usually drive on a highway if conditions were good and the posted speed limit was 55 MPH. Results revealed a significant relationship between reported driving speed and SSS score. Nondrivers (Non-D) and those who drove at or below the speed limit had the lowest SSS scores; scores increased with each increment in driving speed. The sex difference observed in this study is generally the case; males typically score higher on SSS than females.* (After Zuckerman & Neeb, 1980)

having fearlessly in common phobic situations (heights, darkness, snakes); taking risks when gambling; and preferring exotic foods. Even when asked to describe their normal driving habits, high-sensation seekers report driving at faster speeds than low-sensation seekers (see Figure 10-13).

*Sensation-seeking individuals are atracted to dangerous sports.*

# Common Principles for Different Motives

Motives generally can be categorized according to survival needs, social needs, and the need to satisfy curiosity. While the differences between these types are real, we have not addressed some similarities among them.

In the 1940s and 1950s, many psychologists believed that all basic motives operated according to the principle of **drive reduction**: supposedly motives are directed at the reduction of a psychological state that a person experiences as tension, and the person experiences pleasure from this reduction in tension or drive. Drive reduction seems applicable to the survival motives. When deprived of food, we do indeed feel a tension that is reduced by eating, and we experience that reduction as pleasurable. But for such motives as sex, drive reduction sounds less plausible; according to both everyday observation and laboratory experiments, sexual stimulation is rewarding in its own right. Similarly, drive-reduction theory has never been able to come to grips with the curiosity motive. Drive-reduction theory suggests that everyone would avoid extreme tension-producing situations; but some people seek out such situations, like riding roller coasters and sky diving (Geen, Beatty, & Arkin, 1984).

Psychologists today generally reject drive reduction in favor of the principle of **arousal level,** according to which people seek an optimal level of drive or arousal. The optimal level varies from person to person—as demonstrated by individual differences in stimulation seeking. Physiological deprivation, as in hunger and thirst, increases arousal level above the optimum and leads to behavior that brings the level down. In contrast, too little stimulation can sometimes motivate an organism to increase its arousal level. We seek stimulation (including sexual stimulation), novelty, and complexity in our environments, but only up to a point. Though the notion of arousal level is not without its critics, it seems more likely than drive reduction to emerge as a unifying principle of the basic drives.

## Chapter SUMMARY

1. Motives, which give behavior *direction* and *energize* it, are of different types, including *survival*, *social*, and *curiosity*. Survival motives, such as hunger and thirst, operate in part according to *homeostasis*: they maintain a constant internal environment. Homeostasis involves a *regulated*

variable, *sensors* that measure the variable, an *ideal value* of the variable, a *comparator*, and *adjustments* that the system makes when the variable is at a value above or below the ideal value.

2. Our regulation of temperature is an example of homeostasis. The regulated variable is the temperature of the blood, and sensors for this are located in various regions of the body, including the *hypothalamus*. The ideal value and comparator are also located in the hypothalamus. Adjustments are either automatic physiological responses (for example, shivering) or voluntary behavioral ones (such as putting on a sweater).

3. Thirst is another homeostatic motive. There are two regulated variables, *intracellular fluid* and *extracellular fluid*. The loss of intracellular fluid is detected by *osmoreceptors*, cells in the hypothalamus that respond to dehydration; this in turn leads to the release of the *antidiuretic hormone* (ADH), which regulates the kidneys, allowing water to be reabsorbed into the bloodstream. Extracellular fluid is detected by *blood-pressure sensors* in the kidneys.

4. Hunger is a complex, partly homeostatic motive with numerous regulated variables, including *glucose, fats,* and *amino acids*. Glucose sensors have been found in the hypothalamus and liver. In addition to sensors that trigger feeding, there are also *satiety detectors*, which are found in the digestive system (particularly the stomach, duodenum, and liver) and signal the brain that the needed nutrients are on their way.

5. Two regions of the brain are critical for hunger: the *lateral hypothalamus* and the *ventromedial hypothalamus*. Destruction of the lateral hypothalamus leads to undereating; destruction of the ventromedial hypothalamus to overeating. One interpretation of these effects is that the ventromedial and lateral regions have reciprocal effects on the *set point* for body weight: damage to the ventromedial region raises the set point, whereas damage to the lateral region lowers it. Another interpretation proposes that the effects are due to interference with nerve tracts that pass through the hypothalamic locations.

6. People become obese primarily because: (a) they are genetically predisposed to be overweight or (b) they overeat (for psychological reasons). The influence of genes is mediated by their effect on *fat cells, metabolic rate,* and *set points*. As for overeating and obesity, obese people tend to overeat when they break a diet, eat more when emotionally aroused, and are more responsive than normal-weight individuals to external hunger cues. In treating obesity, extreme diets appear ineffective, because the deprivation leads to subsequent overeating and to a lowered metabolic rate. What seems to work best is to establish a new set of permanent eating habits and to engage in a program of exercise.

7. *Anorexia nervosa* is characterized by an extreme, self-imposed weight loss. Anorexia is twenty times more likely to occur in women than men. The weight loss may be mediated by a *distorted body image*, the anorexic erroneously thinking that she looks too fat. Possible causes of anorexia include personality factors (for example, a struggle for autonomy), society's overemphasis on thinness in women, and biological problems (for example, a dysfunctional hypothalamus). *Bulimia* is characterized by recurrent episodes of *binge-eating*, followed by attempts to purge the excess eating by means of vomiting and laxatives. Possible causes again include personality factors (for example, depression), society's emphasis on thinness, and biological factors (for example, a deficit in the neurotransmitter serotonin).

8. The female hormones (*estrogen* and *progesterone*) and male hormones (*androgens*) are responsible for the body changes at puberty but play only a limited role in human sexual arousal. In contrast, there is substantial hormonal control over sex in lower species. Early social experiences with parents and peers have a large influence on adult sexuality in primates and humans. Monkeys raised in isolation have sexual problems as adults. For humans, other environmental determinants of adult sexuality include cultural norms. Although western society became increasingly permissive about premarital sex during the 1960s and 1970s, men and women may still differ in their attitudes toward sex.

9. Sexual interactions with members of the same sex are not uncommon during childhood, but only a small percentage of people become exclusively *homo*sexual as adults. Extensive interviews with homosexuals suggest that they do not differ from heterosexuals with regard to their identifications with parents of the opposite sex. For exclusive homosexuals, there may be a biological predisposition.

10. Prenatal hormones are important for sexual development. If the embryonic sex glands produce enough androgen, the newborn will have male genitals; if there is insufficient androgen, the newborn will have female genitals, even if it is genetically male. In cases in which hormonal imbalances result in *hermaphrodites* (individuals born with both male and female tissue), the assigned label and the sex role in which the individual is raised seem to have greater influence on gender identity than do the individual's genes and hormones.

11. In lower animals, maternal behavior appears to be innately programmed and triggered by hormones. In primates and humans, however, maternal behavior is largely influenced by experience. Monkeys reared in isolation do not exhibit the usual maternal behaviors when they later become mothers.

12. People and animals appear to have inborn curiosity motives to explore and manipulate objects. Manipulation of objects provides the organism with changing sensory input, and studies of *reduced sensory stimulation* show that the absence of changing input can disrupt normal perceptual and intellectual functioning.

13. Psychologists used to believe that all basic motives operate by *drive reduction*, the principle that all motives are directed toward the reduction of tension. But drive reduction does not offer a satisfactory account of sex or the curiosity motives. A more promising principle is that organisms seek an *optimal level of arousal*.

## *Further* **READING**

The biological approach to temperature regulation, thirst, hunger, and sex is surveyed in Carlson, *Physiology of Behavior* (3rd ed., 1986); and Rosenzweig and Leiman, *Physiological Psychology* (2nd ed., 1989). An introduction to human sexuality is provided by Offir, *Human Sexuality* (1982). An explanation of normal and abnormal patterns of eating and drinking is given in Logue, *The Psychology of Eating and Drinking* (2nd ed., 1991); also see Stunkard (ed.), *Obesity* (1980).

For reviews of motivation in general, see Mook, *Motivation: The Organization of Action* (1987); Geen, Beatty, and Arkin, *Human Motivation: Physiological, Behavioral, and Social Approaches* (1984); and Stellar and Stellar, *The Neurobiology of Motivation and Reward* (1985). A review of ethology is presented in Lorenz, *The Foundations of Ethology* (1981); and in McFarland, *Animal Behaviour: Psychobiology, Ethology and Evolution* (1985).

# Chapter 11

# Emotion

## Components of an Emotion 417

## Arousal and Emotion 418
*Physiological Basis*
*Intensity of Emotions*
*Differentiation of Emotions*
*Critical Discussion: Using Arousal to Detect Lies*

## Cognition and Emotion 422
*Intensity and Differentiation of Emotions*
*Dimensions of Emotion*
*Some Clinical Implications*
*Emotion without Cognition*

## Expression and Emotion 429
*Communication of Emotional Expressions*
*Brain Localization*
*Intensity and Differentiation of Emotions*

## General Reactions to Being
## in an Emotional State 435
*Energy and Disruption*
*Attention and Learning: Mood Congruence*
*Evaluation and Estimation: Mood Effects*

## Aggression as an Emotional Reaction 437
*Aggression as a Drive*
*Aggression as a Learned Response*
*Aggressive Expression and Catharsis*

Detail, *Northeaster.*

The most basic feelings that we experience include not only motives such as hunger and sex but also emotions such as joy and anger. Emotions and motives are closely related. Emotions can activate and direct behavior in the same way that basic motives do. Emotions may also accompany motivated behavior: sex, for example, is not only a powerful motive but a potential source of joy, as well.

Despite their similarities, motives and emotions need to be distinguished. One common distinction is that emotions are triggered from the outside, while motives are activated from within. That is, emotions are usually aroused by external events, and emotional reactions are directed toward these events; motives, in contrast, are often aroused by internal events (a homeostatic imbalance, for example) and are naturally directed toward particular objects in the environment (such as food, water, or a mate). Another distinction between motives and emotions is that a motive is usually elicited by a specific need, whereas an emotion can be elicited by a wide variety of stimuli (think of all the different things that can make you angry, for example). These distinctions are not absolute. An external source can sometimes trigger a motive, as when the sight of food triggers hunger. And the discomfort caused by a homeostatic imbalance—severe hunger, for example—can arouse emotions. Nevertheless, emotions and motives are sufficiently different in their sources of activation, subjective experience, and effects on behavior that they merit separate treatment.

## Components of an Emotion

An intense emotion includes several general components. One component is bodily reaction. When angered, for example, you may sometimes tremble or raise your voice, even though you don't want to. Another component is the collection of thoughts and beliefs that accompany the emotion, and that seem to come to mind automatically. Experiencing joy, for example, often involves thinking about the reasons for the joy ("I did it—I'm accepted into college!"). A third component of an emotional experience is facial expression. When you experience disgust, for example, you probably frown, often with your mouth open wide and your eyelids partially closed. Finally, a fourth component concerns your reactions to the experience. These include specific reactions—anger may lead you to aggression, for instance—and more global ones—a negative emotion may darken your outlook on the world.

Thus, our list of the components of an emotion includes:

1. Internal bodily responses, particularly those involving the autonomic nervous system
2. Belief or cognitive appraisal that a particular positive or negative state of affairs is occurring
3. Facial expression
4. Reactions to the emotion

Some of the critical questions in the study of emotion concern the detailed nature of these components. Other critical questions deal with the relations between these components and the subjective experience of an emotion. With regard to the latter, one set of questions concerns how autonomic responses, beliefs and cognitions, and facial expressions contribute to

*Facial expression is a component of emotion.*

the intensity of an experienced emotion. Do you feel angrier, for example, when you experience more autonomic arousal? Indeed, could you even feel angry if you had no autonomic arousal? Similarly, does the intensity of your anger depend on your having a certain kind of thought, or a certain kind of facial expression? In contrast to these questions about the intensity of an emotion, there are also questions about which components of an emotion are responsible for making the different emotions *feel* different. Which components *differentiate* the emotions? To appreciate the difference between questions about intensity and questions about differentiation, note that it is possible that autonomic arousal greatly increases the intensity of our emotions, but that the pattern of arousal is roughly the same for several emotions; if this were the case, autonomic arousal could not differentiate between emotions.

These questions will guide us as we consider in turn autonomic arousal, cognitive appraisal, and facial expression. We will then turn our attention to general reactions of an emotional experience. In the final part of the chapter, we will focus on a specific reaction to an emotion, and consider in detail the topic of aggression. We will be concerned throughout primarily with the more intense affective states—like those involved in happiness, sadness, anger, fear, and disgust—although the ideas and principles that will emerge in our discussion are relevant to a variety of feelings.

# Arousal and Emotion

## Physiological Basis

When we experience an intense emotion, such as fear or anger, we may be aware of a number of bodily changes—including rapid heartbeat and breathing, dryness of the throat and mouth, perspiration, trembling, and a sinking feeling in the stomach (see Table 11-1). Most of the physiological changes that take place during emotional arousal result from activation of the sympathetic division of the autonomic nervous system as it prepares the body for emergency action (see Chapter 2). The **sympathetic system** is responsible for the following changes (all of which need not occur at once):

1. Blood pressure and heart rate increase.
2. Respiration becomes more rapid.
3. The pupils dilate.
4. Perspiration increases while secretion of saliva and mucous decreases.
5. Blood-sugar level increases to provide more energy.
6. The blood clots more quickly in case of wounds.
7. Motility of the gastrointestinal tract decreases; blood is diverted from the stomach and intestines to the brain and skeletal muscles.
8. The hairs on the skin become erect, causing goose pimples.

The sympathetic system gears the organism for energy output. As the emotion subsides, the **parasympathetic system**—the energy-conserving system—takes over and returns the organism to its normal state.

These activities of the autonomic nervous system are themselves triggered by activity in certain critical regions of the brain, including the **hypothalamus** (which, as we saw in the last chapter, plays a major role in many

**TABLE 11-1**
**Symptoms of Fear in Combat Flying**
*Based on reports of combat pilots during
World War II.* (After Shaffer, 1947)

| DURING COMBAT MISSIONS DID YOU FEEL...? | SOMETIMES | OFTEN | TOTAL |
| --- | --- | --- | --- |
| A pounding heart and rapid pulse | 56% | 30% | 86% |
| That your muscles were very tense | 53 | 30 | 83 |
| Easily irritated or angry | 58 | 22 | 80 |
| Dryness of the throat or mouth | 50 | 30 | 80 |
| Nervous perspiration or cold sweat | 53 | 26 | 79 |
| Butterflies in the stomach | 53 | 23 | 76 |
| A sense of unreality—that this could not be happening to you | 49 | 20 | 69 |
| A need to urinate very frequently | 40 | 25 | 65 |
| Trembling | 53 | 11 | 64 |
| Confused or rattled | 50 | 3 | 53 |
| Weak or faint | 37 | 4 | 41 |
| That right after a mission you were unable to remember the details of what had happened | 34 | 5 | 39 |
| Sick to the stomach | 33 | 5 | 38 |
| Unable to concentrate | 32 | 3 | 35 |
| That you had wet or soiled your pants | 4 | 1 | 5 |

biological motives) and parts of the **limbic system.** Impulses from these areas are transmitted to nuclei in the brain stem that control the functioning of the autonomic nervous system. The autonomic nervous system then acts directly on the muscles and internal organs to initiate some of the bodily changes previously described, and acts indirectly by stimulating the adrenal hormones to produce other bodily changes.

Note that the kind of heightened physiological arousal we have described is characteristic of emotional states such as anger and fear, during which the organism must prepare for action—for example, to fight or flee. (The role of this fight-or-flight response in threatening or stressful situations is elaborated in Chapter 15.) Some of the same responses may also occur during joyful excitement or sexual arousal. During emotions such as sorrow or grief, however, some bodily processes may be depressed, or slowed down.

## Intensity of Emotions

What is the relation between heightened physiological arousal and the subjective experience of an emotion? In particular, does our perception of our own arousal make up part of the experience of the emotion? To answer

# Using Arousal to Detect Lies

If autonomic arousal is part of an emotion and if experiencing an emotion is a likely consequence of lying, then we can use the presence of autonomic arousal to infer that a person is lying. This is the theory behind the **lie-detector** test, in which a machine called a **polygraph** (meaning "many writings") simultaneously measures several physiological responses known to be part of autonomic arousal (see Figure 1). The measures most frequently recorded are changes in heart rate, blood pressure, respiration, and the galvanic skin response or **GSR** (a change in the electrical conductivity of the skin that occurs with emotional arousal).

In operating a polygraph, the standard procedure is to make the first recording while the subject is relaxed; this recording serves as a *baseline* for evaluating subsequent responses. The examiner then asks a series of carefully worded questions that the subject has been instructed to answer with a "yes" or "no" response. Some of the questions are "critical," which means that the guilty are likely to lie in response to them (for example, "Did you rob Bert's Cleaners on December 11?"). Other questions are "controls"; even innocent people are somewhat likely to lie in response to these questions (for example, "Have you ever taken something that didn't belong to you?"). Yet other questions are "neutral" (for example, "Do you live in San Diego?"). Critical questions are interspersed among control and neutral ones; sufficient time is allowed between questions for the polygraph measures to return to normal. Presumably, only the guilty should show greater physiological responses to the critical questions than to the others.

**FIGURE 1**

**Polygraph** *The arm cuff measures blood pressure and heart rate, the pneumograph around the rib cage measures rate of breathing, and the finger electrodes measure GSR. The recording on the right shows the physiological responses of a subject as he lies and as he simulates lying. The respiratory trace (top line) shows that he held his breath as he prepared for the first simulation. He was able to produce sizable changes in heart rate and GSR at the second simulation.* (After Kubis, 1962)

However, the use of the polygraph in detecting lies is far from foolproof. A response to a question may show that a subject is aroused but not why he or she is aroused. An innocent subject may be very tense or may react emotionally to certain words in the questions and therefore appear to be lying when telling the truth. On the other hand, a practiced liar may show little arousal when lying. And a knowledgeable subject may be able to "beat" the machine by thinking about something exciting or by tensing muscles during neutral questions, thereby creating a baseline comparable to reactions to the critical questions. The recording in Figure 1 shows the responses to an actual lie and a simulated lie. In this experiment, the subject picked a number and then tried to conceal its identity from the examiner. The number was 27, and a marked change in heart rate and GSR can be seen when the subject denies number 27. The subject simulates lying to number 22 by tensing his toes, producing noticeable reactions in heart rate and GSR.

Because of these and other problems, most state and federal courts will not admit polygraph tests; the courts that do generally require that both sides agree to its introduction. Such tests are frequently used, however, in preliminary criminal investigations and by employers interviewing prospective personnel for trusted positions.

Representatives of the American Polygraph Association have claimed an accuracy rate of 90 percent or better for polygraph tests conducted by a skilled operator. Critics, however, consider the accuracy rate to be much lower. For example, Lykken (1984) claims that in studies involving real-life situations, the lie-detector test is correct only about 65 percent of the time, and an innocent person has a 50-50 chance of failing the test. He argues that the polygraph detects not only the arousal that accompanies lying but also the stress that an

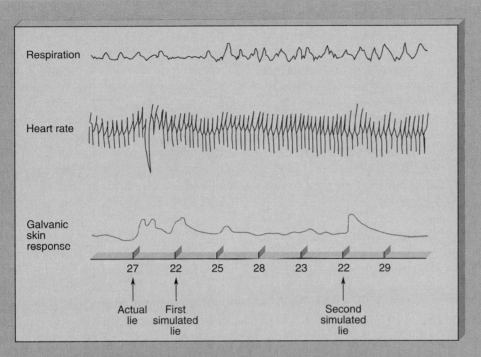

Respiration

Heart rate

Galvanic
skin
response

27    22    25    28    23    22    29

Actual    First              Second
lie    simulated            simulated
lie                 lie

recording of a person's voice is played through a device called a **voice-stress analyzer,** a visual representation of the voice can be produced on a strip of graph paper. The tremors of the vocal cords in the voice of a relaxed speaker resemble a series of waves (see the left-hand graph in Figure 2). When a speaker is under stress, the tremors are suppressed (see the right-hand graph in Figure 2).

The voice-stress analyzer is used in lie detection in essentially the same way as a polygraph; neutral questions are interspersed with critical questions, and recordings of the subject's responses to both are compared. If answers to the critical questions produce the relaxed wave form, the person is probably telling the truth (as far as we know, vocal cord tremors cannot be controlled voluntarily). A stressed wave form, on the other hand, indicates only that the individual is tense or anxious, not necessarily that he or she is lying.

There are, however, two serious problems with the use of the voice-stress analyzer in detecting lies. First, since the analyzer can work over the telephone, from radio or television messages, or from tape recordings, there is potential for the unethical use of this instrument. The second concern is the accuracy of the voice-stress analyzer. Some investigators claim that it is as accurate as the polygraph in distinguishing between the guilty and the innocent; others claim that it is no more accurate than chance. Much more research is required to determine the relationship between voice changes and other physiological measures of emotion (Rice, 1978; Lykken, 1980).

## FIGURE 2
### Effects of Stress on Voice Patterns
*A voice-stress analyzer produces graphic records of speech. The voice printout for a relaxed speaker resembles a series of waves, such as those shown on the left. The waves are produced by tiny tremors of the vocal cords. Under stress, the tremors are suppressed, producing a printout similar to that shown on the right. (After Holden, 1975)*

honest person experiences when strapped to the equipment. Also, guilty people who are less socialized may be less aroused while lying, and consequently harder to detect (Saxe, Dougherty, & Cross, 1985). Nevertheless, many businesses believe that the benefits of these tests outweigh the risks, and polygraph tests are often used in private industry. They are also widely used in law enforcement. The FBI, for example, administers several thousand polygraph tests per year, mostly to follow up leads and to verify specific facts— areas in which, experts agree, the poly-

graph is more useful. In criminal and private cases, anyone has the legal right to refuse a polygraph test. However, this is hardly a safeguard for someone whose refusal, for whatever reason, may endanger a career or job opportunity.

Another type of lie detector measures changes in a person's voice that are undetectable to the human ear. All muscles, including those controlling the vocal cords, vibrate slightly when in use. This tremor, which is transmitted to the vocal cords, is suppressed by activity of the autonomic nervous system when a speaker is under stress. When a tape

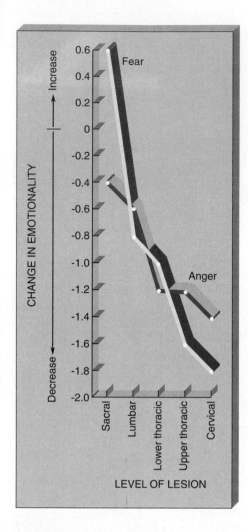

**FIGURE 11-1**
**Relationship Between Spinal Cord Lesions and Emotionality** *Subjects with spinal cord lesions compared the intensity of their emotional experiences before and after injury. Their reports were coded according to the degree of change: 0 indicates no change; a mild change ("I feel it less, I guess") is scored –1 for a decrease or +1 for an increase; and a strong change ("I feel it a helluva lot less") is scored –2 or +2. Note that the higher the lesion, the greater the decrease in emotionality following injury. (After Schachter, 1971; Hohmann, 1962)*

this question, researchers have studied the emotional life of individuals with spinal cord injuries. When the spinal cord is severed or lesioned, sensations below the point of injury cannot reach the brain. Since some of these sensations arise from the sympathetic nervous system, the injuries reduce the contributions of autonomic arousal to felt emotion. In one study, army veterans with spinal cord injuries were divided into five groups, according to the location on the spinal cord at which the lesion occurred. In one group, the lesions were near the neck (at the cervical level), with no innervation of the sympathetic system. In another group, the lesions were near the base of the spine (at the sacral level), with at least partial innervation of the sympathetic nerves. The other three groups fell between these two extremes. The five groups represented a continuum of bodily sensation: the higher the lesion on the spinal cord, the less the feedback of the autonomic nervous system to the brain.

The subjects were interviewed to determine their feelings in situations of fear, anger, grief, and sexual excitement. Each person was asked to recall an emotion-arousing incident prior to the injury and a comparable incident following the injury, and to compare the intensity of emotional experience in each case. The data for states of fear and anger are shown in Figure 11-1. The higher the person's lesion was on the spinal cord (that is, the less the feedback from the autonomic nervous system), the more his emotionality decreased following injury. The same relation was true for states of sexual excitement and grief. A reduction in autonomic arousal resulted in a reduction in the intensity of experienced emotion.

Comments by patients with the highest spinal cord lesions suggested that they could *react* emotionally to arousing situations, but that they did not really *feel* emotional. For example, "It's sort of a cold anger. Sometimes I act angry when I see some injustice. I yell and cuss and raise hell, because if you don't do it sometimes, I've learned people will take advantage of you; but it doesn't have the heat to it that it used to. It's a mental kind of anger." Or,"I say I am afraid, like when I'm going into a real stiff exam at school, but I don't really feel afraid, not all tense and shaky with the hollow feeling in my stomach, like I used to."

The preceding study is important, but it is not entirely objective—the emotional situations varied from person to person, and subjects rated their own experiences. A follow-up study provides a more objective situation: all subjects were exposed to the same situations, and their emotional experiences were rated by independent judges. Male subjects with spinal cord injuries were presented with pictures of clothed and nude females and were told to imagine that they were alone with each woman. Subjects reported their "thoughts and feelings," which then were rated by judges for expressed emotion. Patients who had higher lesions were rated as experiencing less sexual excitement than those whose lesions were lower on their spines (Jasmos & Hakmiller, 1975). Again, the less the feedback of the autonomic system to the brain, the less intense the emotion.

## Differentiation of Emotions

Clearly, autonomic arousal contributes to the intensity of emotional experience. But does it differentiate the emotions? Is there one pattern of physiological activity for joy, another for anger, still another for fear, and so on? This question dates back to a seminal paper that William James wrote over a century ago (James, 1884), in which he proposed that the perception of bodily changes *is* the subjective experience of an emotion: "We are afraid because we run"; "we are angry because we strike." The Danish physiologist Carl Lange arrived at a similar position at about the same time, but for him the bodily changes included autonomic arousal. Their combined position is referred to as the **James-Lange theory,** and it argues as follows: because the perception of autonomic arousal (and perhaps of other bodily changes) constitutes the experience of an emotion, and because different emotions feel different, there must be a distinct pattern of autonomic activity for each emotion. The James-Lange theory therefore holds that autonomic arousal differentiates the emotions.

The theory came under severe attack in the 1920s (particularly that part of the theory dealing with autonomic arousal). The attack was led by the physiologist Walter Cannon (1927), who offered three major criticisms:

1.  Since the internal organs are relatively insensitive structures and not well supplied with nerves, internal changes occur too slowly to be a source of emotional feeling.
2.  Artificially inducing the bodily changes associated with an emotion—for example, injecting a drug such as epinephrine—does not produce the experience of a true emotion.
3.  The pattern of autonomic arousal does not seem to differ much from one emotional state to another; for example, while anger makes our heart beat faster, so does the sight of a loved one.

The third argument, then, explicitly denies that autonomic arousal can differentiate the emotions.

Psychologists have tried to rebut Cannon's third point while developing increasingly more accurate measures of the subcomponents of autonomic arousal. Although a few experiments in the 1950s reported distinct physiological patterns for different emotions (Ax, 1953; Funkenstein, 1955), until the 1980s most studies on this topic had found little evidence for different patterns of arousal being associated with different emotions. A study by Ekman and his collaborators (1983), however, provides strong evidence that there are autonomic patterns distinct to different emotions. Subjects produced emotional expressions for each of six emotions—surprise, disgust, sadness, anger, fear, and happiness—by following instructions about which particular facial muscles to contract (most of the subjects were actors, and they were aided in their task by a mirror and coaching). While they held an emotional expression for 10 seconds, the researchers measured their heart rate, skin temperature, and other indicators of autonomic arousal. A number of these measures revealed differences between the emotions (see Figure 11-2). Heart rate was faster for the negative emotions of anger, fear, and sadness than it was for happiness, surprise, and disgust; and the former three emotions themselves could be partially distinguished by the fact that skin temperature was higher in anger than in fear or sadness. Thus, even though both anger and the sight of a loved one make our heart beat faster, only anger makes it beat *much* faster; and though anger and fear have much in common, anger is hot and fear cold (no wonder people describe their anger as their "blood boiling," and their fear as "bone-chilling" or as "getting cold feet").

Recent work suggests that these distinctive arousal patterns may be universal. Ekman and his colleagues studied members of the Minangkabau culture in Western Samatra, a culture very different from ours. Again, subjects

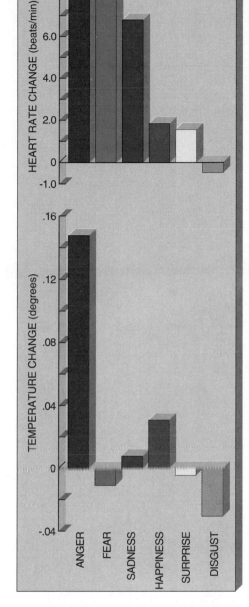

**FIGURE 11-2**
**Arousal Differences for Different Emotions** *Changes in heart rate (upper graph) and right finger temperature (lower graph). For heart rate, the changes associated with anger, fear, and sadness were all significantly greater than those for happiness, surprise, and disgust. For finger temperature, the change associated with anger was significantly different from that for all other emotions. (After Ekman, Levenson, & Frieson, 1983)*

produced facial expressions for various emotions—this time, fear, anger, sadness, and disgust—while measures were taken of their heart rate, skin temperature, and other indicators of arousal. Although the magnitude of the physiological changes were less for the Samatrans than those reported earlier for Americans, the patterns of arousal for the different emotions were the same; again, heart rate was faster for anger, fear, and sadness than for disgust, and skin temperature was highest in anger (Levenson, Ekman, Heider & Friesen, 1992).

These results are important, but by no means do they provide unequivocal evidence for the James-Lange theory or the claim that autonomic arousal is the *only* component that differentiates the emotions. All the above studies demonstrated was that there are *some* physiological differences between emotions, not that these differences are perceived and experienced as *the* qualitative differences between the emotions. Even if autonomic arousal does help differentiate some emotions, it is unlikely that it differentiates *all* emotions; the difference between contentment and pride, for example, is unlikely to be found in visceral reactions. Also, the first two points that Cannon raised against the James-Lange theory still stand: autonomic arousal is too slow to differentiate emotional experiences, and artificial induction of arousal does not yield a true emotion. For these reasons, many psychologists still believe that something other than autonomic arousal must be involved in differentiating the emotions. That something else (or part of it) is usually thought to be one's cognitive appraisal of the situation.

## Cognition and Emotion

When we experience an event or action, we interpret the situation with respect to our personal goals and well-being; the outcome of the appraisal is a belief that is either positive or negative ("I won the match and I feel happy" or "I failed the test and I feel depressed"). This interpretation is known as a **cognitive appraisal,** which has two distinct parts: the appraisal process and the resulting belief.

### Intensity and Differentiation of Emotions

Clearly, our appraisal of a situation can contribute to the intensity of our emotional experience. If we are in a car that starts to roll down a steep incline, we experience fear, if not terror; but if we know the car is part of a roller coaster, the fear is usually much less. If we are told by someone that he or she cannot stand the sight of us, we may feel very angry or hurt if that person is a friend, but feel barely perturbed if the person is a mental patient whom we have never met before. If we watch a film of African tribesmen making an incision in a young boy's body, we may feel outrage if we believe the men are torturing the boy but feel relatively detached if we believe the men are performing a rites-of-passage ritual. In these cases, and countless others, our cognitive appraisal of the situation determines the intensity of our emotional experience (Lazarus, Kanner, & Folkman, 1980; Lazarus, 1991).

Cognitive appraisal may also be heavily responsible for differentiating the emotions. Unlike autonomic arousal, the beliefs resulting from appraisal are rich enough to distinguish among many different kinds of feelings, and the appraisal process itself may be fast enough to account for the speed with which some emotions arise. Also, we often emphasize emotional beliefs when we describe the quality of an emotion. We say, "I felt angry because she was unfair" or "I felt frightened because I was abandoned"; unfairness and abandonment are clearly beliefs that result from a cognitive process.

These observations suggest that cognitive appraisals are often sufficient to determine the quality of emotional experience. This in turn suggests that if people could be induced to be in a neutral state of autonomic arousal, the quality of their emotion would be determined solely by their appraisal of the situation. Schachter and Singer (1962) first tested this claim in an important experiment.

Subjects were given an injection of epinephrine, which typically causes autonomic arousal, such as an increase in heart and respiration rates, muscle tremors, and a jittery feeling. The experimenter then manipulated the information that the subjects were given regarding the effects of epinephrine. Some subjects were correctly informed about the arousal consequences of the drug (heart-rate acceleration, muscle tremors, and so on); other subjects were misinformed about the drug and told it would produce feelings of numbness. The *informed* subjects had an explanation of their arousal; the *misinformed* subjects did not. How the misinformed subjects interpreted their symptoms depended on the situation they were placed in. Subjects were left in a waiting room with another person, ostensibly another subject but actually a confederate of the experimenter; this confederate created either a happy situation (by making paper airplanes, playing basketball with wads of paper, and so on), or an angry situation (by complaining about the experiment, tearing up a questionnaire, and so on). Misinformed subjects who were placed in a happy situation rated their feelings as relatively happy, whereas misinformed subjects placed in an angry situation rated their feelings as relatively angry. Although the autonomic arousal was the same in the two situations (they all experienced rapid heart rate, muscle tremors, and so on), the emotions experienced by misinformed subjects were not; their emotions were determined by their appraisals of the situation. In contrast, the informed subjects' feelings were unaffected by whether they were placed in a happy or angry situation; they already had an explanation of their arousal, and they did not need to rely on an appraisal of the situation.

However, while the autonomic arousal may have been the same in the happy and angry situations, apparently it was not neutral. Follow-up experiments to the Schachter and Singer study have found that subjects rate their experiences more negatively (less happy, or more angry) than the situation warrants, suggesting that the physiological arousal produced by epinephrine is experienced as somewhat unpleasant. Also, these follow-up experiments have sometimes had difficulty reproducing the Schachter and Singer results (Maslach, 1979; Marshall & Zimbardo, 1979). Hence, we need supporting evidence that completely neutral arousal may be misattributed. A subsequent study supplied such evidence. Subjects first engaged in strenuous physical exercise and then participated in a task where they were provoked by a confederate of the experimenter. The exercise induced physiological arousal that was neutral and that persisted until the subject was provoked; this arousal should have combined with any that was elicited by the provocation, thereby resulting in a more intense experience of anger. In fact, subjects who exercised responded more aggressively to the provocation than subjects who did not (Zillman & Bryant, 1974).

**FIGURE 11-3**
**Components of an Emotional Experience: 1** *The beliefs resulting from a cognitive appraisal and the perception of autonomic arousal both contribute to the experience of an emotion.* (After Reisenzein, 1983)

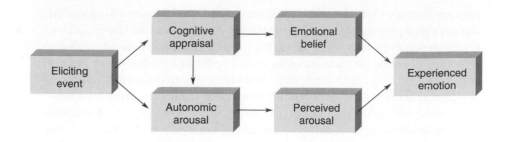

The conclusions that emerge from this line of research are depicted in Figure 11-3. In an emotional situation, an eliciting event typically results in both autonomic arousal and cognitive appraisal; the arousal and appraisal lead, respectively, to *perceived* arousal and an emotional belief, which then determine the experienced emotion. (The perceived arousal and emotional belief are not experienced as independent; rather, the arousal is *attributed* to the belief—"My heart is racing *because* I'm so angry about what Mary said.") Usually, the same eliciting event is responsible for both the arousal and the appraisal. In the studies just reviewed, however, the experimenters arranged the situation so that arousal and appraisal had different sources (for example, injection versus situation), thereby allowing the experimenter to analyze separately the role of each component. These studies indicate that both arousal and appraisal contribute to the intensity of experience—and that sometimes appraisal alone can determine the quality of experience. While research indicates that arousal may aid in differentiating emotions, it seems to play less of a role than does appraisal.

Although the level of analysis portrayed in Figure 11-3 has proved very useful, it oversimplifies things in one important respect. The components, autonomic arousal and cognitive appraisal, are themselves complex events that involve subcomponents, and these subcomponents do not all occur at the same time. For example, suppose an acquaintance says something insulting to you. You may first be aware of the unpleasantness of the remark, then feel a tinge of arousal, next appraise the remark more fully while concurrently experiencing more arousal, and so on. Thus, autonomic arousal and cognitive appraisal are events stretched out in time, and the subcomponents that comprise these events can go on in parallel (Ellsworth, 1991).

## Dimensions of Emotion

We have emphasized that people's appraisal of a situation can determine their emotions, but thus far have had little to say about which aspects or dimensions of a situation determine which emotions occur.

Psychologists have taken different approaches to this problem. One approach assumes that there is a relatively small set of "primary" emotions and associates each emotion with a fundamental life situation. Table 11-2 lists several emotions (such as fear) and their respective triggering situations (threat). These primary emotions can be found in every human culture and throughout the animal kingdom. Their universality provides a reason for singling out these emotions as primary and for describing the situations in terms that are appropriate even for lower species.

Another approach to specifying the determinants of emotion emphasizes cognitive processes and, consequently, may be more appropriate for humans than for lower species. Instead of starting with a primary set of emotions, this approach begins with a primary set of situational dimensions that a person attends to. The theory then associates various combinations of these dimensions with specific emotions. An example is given in Table 11-3. One dimension of a situation is the desirability of an anticipated event, and another is whether or not the event occurs. When we combine these two dimensions, we get four possible situations (the left-hand side of Table 11-3), each of which seems to produce a distinct emotion. (We are using only four emotions in our example just to keep things simple.) When a desired event occurs, we experience *joy*; when a desired event does not occur, we experience *sorrow*; when an undesired event occurs, we experience *distress*; and when an undesired event does not occur, we experience *relief*. To illustrate, suppose a young woman marries an attractive young man who is known to have a drinking problem; she may feel mainly joy (she "got" someone she considers desirable), her rival sorrow (she didn't get someone she considers desirable), her parents distress (they got someone they consider undesirable), and his parents relief (they got rid of an undesirable siutation).

The preceding example invokes only two dimensions, but most theories of cognitive appraisal assume that multiple dimensions are involved. For example, Smith and Ellsworth (1985; 1987) found that at least six dimensions were needed to describe 15 different emotions (including, for example, anger, guilt, and sadness). These dimensions included: (a) the desirability of the situation (pleasant or unpleasant); (b) the effort that one anticipates spending on the situation; (c) the certainty of the situation; (d) the attention that one wants to devote to the situation; (e) the control that one feels over the situation; and (f) the control that one attributes to nonhuman forces in the situation. To illustrate how the last two dimensions operate, anger is associated with an unpleasant situation caused by another person, guilt is associated with an unpleasant situation brought about by one's self, and sadness is associated with an unpleasant situation controlled by circumstances. Thus, if you and your friend miss a concert that you had your heart set on hearing, you will feel anger if you missed it because your friend carelessly misplaced the tickets, guilt if you misplaced them, and sadness if the performance is cancelled due to a performer's illness. The virtue of this kind of approach is that it specifies the appraisal process in detail and accounts for a wide range of emotional experiences.

These two approaches to specifying the dimensions of an emotion—a primary set of emotions versus a primary set of situational dimensions—are not necessarily incompatible. While there may be a fundamental life situation that triggers each emotion (as in the first approach), whether or not we are in such a situation may itself be a matter of interpretation (as in the second approach). Consider fear, which presumably is triggered by a threat (see Table 11-2). What counts as threat often differs from person to person, depending on their prior experiences and personalities; and the process by which a person decides a situation is threatening may involve a consideration of dimensions like desirability and control (Lazarus, 1991).

## Some Clinical Implications

The fact that cognitive appraisals can differentiate emotions helps make sense of a puzzling clinical observation. Clinicians report that sometimes a patient appears to be experiencing an emotion but is not conscious of it.

| EMOTION | SITUATION |
|---------|-----------|
| Grief (Sorrow) | Loss of loved one |
| Fear | Threat |
| Anger | Obstacle |
| Joy | Potential mate |
| Trust | Group member |
| Disgust | Gruesome object |
| Anticipation | New territory |
| Surprise | Sudden novel object |

**TABLE 11-2**
**Primary Emotions and Their Causes**
*Eight primary emotions and their associated situations.* (After Plutchik, 1980)

| SITUATION | EMOTION |
|-----------|---------|
| Desirable and occurs | Joy |
| Desirable and doesn't occur | Sorrow |
| Undesirable and occurs | Distress |
| Undesirable and doesn't occur | Relief |

**TABLE 11-3**
**Primary Situation Aspects and Their Consequences** *Combinations of two situational aspects and their associated emotions.* (After Roseman, 1979; 1984)

*The sensation of joy may be the same whether we are 3 or 30 years of age.*

That is, the patient has no subjective experience of the emotion, yet reacts in a manner consistent with the emotion—for example, though the patient may not feel angry, he acts in a hostile manner. Also, at a later point he may experience the emotion and agree that in some sense he must have been having it earlier. Freud (1915/1976) thought that this phenomenon involved the repression of painful ideas, and modern work on appraisal and emotion is compatible with his hypothesis. Because the belief about a situation usually gives the emotion its quality, preventing that belief from entering consciousness (repression) prevents one from experiencing the quality of the emotion.

Another point of contact between clinical analysis and experimental research concerns emotional development. Clinical work suggests that a person's sensations of pleasure and distress change rather little as he or she develops from child to adult; what does develop, however, are the ideas associated with the sensations (Brenner, 1980). Thus, the sensation of joy may be the same when we are 3 or 30, but what makes us joyous is very different. This developmental pattern fits perfectly with the facts that we have reviewed about emotion. Sensations of pleasure and distress are probably due to feedback from autonomic arousal, and the nature of this arousal may not change much over the life span. In contrast, ideas associated with the sensations are simply emotional beliefs, and they should show the same kind of development as other aspects of cognition.

Finally, the work on appraisal fits with a phenomenon that is familiar not just to clinicians but to all of us: the extent to which a situation elicits an emotion depends on our past experience. When confronted with an overly critical employer, some people will be merely annoyed while others will be enraged. Why the difference? Presumably because of differences in past experience: perhaps those who are enraged suffered a hypercritical authority figure in the past, while those who are only annoyed had no such experience. A possible link between past experience and current emotion is the appraisal process; that is, our past experience affects our beliefs about the current situation, and these beliefs then influence the emotion we experience.

## Emotion without Cognition

Although cognitive appraisal is clearly important for experiencing many emotions, it is worth noting that there are cases of emotion in which no cognitive appraisal seems to be involved. When a rat receives an electric shock for the first time, for example, presumably it has little to think about, and its emotional reaction is devoid of cognitive activity. Similarly, if you are suddenly punched in the face, you may experience an emotion before you interpret the event. In addition to such one-shot experiences, there are recurrent situations in which emotional experience may bypass the cognitive system. In particular, some fear experiences that were acquired in childhood by classical conditioning may not involve any cognitive appraisal. For example, if painful sessions with a doctor were reliably preceded by being in a waiting room, a person may experience substantial fear when in a waiting room as an adult; in this case, the adult experience is not the result of an interpretation of a situation with respect to present goals (Zajonc, 1980; 1984).

The preceding findings suggest there may be two kinds of emotional experiences: those that are based on cognitive appraisal and those that precede cognition. This dichotomy is supported by work on the physiology of emotion, which explores the brain structures involved in emotion. One such structure is the **amygdala,** a small, almond-shaped mass that is located in the lower brain and that is known to register emotional reactions. Until recently, it was thought that the amygdala receives all its inputs from the cortex; since the cortex is the seat of cognition, the amygdala's inputs were thought to always involve cognitive appraisal. But newer research with rats has uncovered connections between sensory channels and the amygdala that do not go through the cortex; these direct connections may be the biological basis of **precognitive emotions** (emotions *not* based on appraisal.) Thus, the amygdala is capable of responding to an alarming situation before the cortex does, which suggests that sometimes we can feel before we can think. To illustrate, if in the corner of your eye you see something that has the shape of a snake, your amygdala will send an alarm signal that makes you jump before your cortex can determine that the object in question is in fact a harmless piece of rope. Though this research is based on rats, there is reason to believe that the neural pathways involved exist in humans as well (Le Doux, 1989).

While we can have emotional experiences without cognitive appraisal, such experiences may be restricted to undifferentiated positive or negative feelings. In more complex emotional experiences, such as pride, disappointment, jealousy, or contempt, cognitive appraisal must play a role. For many subjective feelings, cognitive appraisal is a necessary ingredient, but for others it is not (Zajonc, Murphy, & Inglehart, 1989).

## Expression and Emotion

The facial expression that accompanies an emotion clearly serves to communicate that emotion. Since the publication of Charles Darwin's 1872 classic, *The Expression of Emotion in Man and Animals*, psychologists have regarded the communication of emotion as an important function, one with survival value for the species. Thus, looking frightened may warn others that danger is present, and perceiving that someone is angry tells us that he or she may be about to act aggressively. More recent work goes beyond the Darwinian

*Emotional expression in the mandrill monkey.*

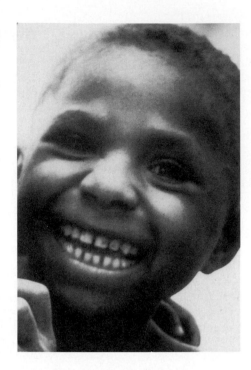
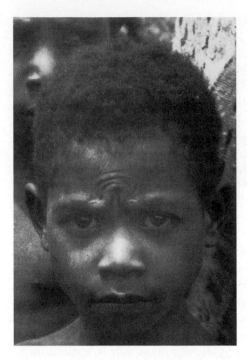

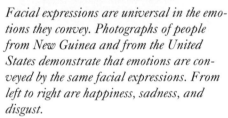

*Facial expressions are universal in the emotions they convey. Photographs of people from New Guinea and from the United States demonstrate that emotions are conveyed by the same facial expressions. From left to right are happiness, sadness, and disgust.*

tradition, suggesting that, in addition to their communicative function, emotional expressions contribute to the subjective experience of emotion, just as arousal and appraisal do.

## Communication of Emotional Expressions

Certain facial expressions seem to have a universal meaning, regardless of the culture in which an individual is raised. The universal expression of anger, for example, involves a flushed face, brows lowered and drawn together, flared nostrils, a clenched jaw, and bared teeth. When people from five different countries (the United States, Brazil, Chile, Argentina, and Japan) viewed photographs showing facial expressions of happiness, anger, sadness, disgust, fear, and surprise, they had little difficulty in identifying the emotion that each expression conveyed. Even members of remote, preliterate tribes that had had virtually no contact with Western cultures (the Fore and Dani tribes in New Guinea) were able to identify the facial expressions correctly. Likewise, American college students who viewed videotapes of emotions expressed by Fore natives identified the emotions accurately, although they sometimes confused fear and surprise (Ekman, 1982).

The universality of certain emotional expressions supports Darwin's claim that they are innate responses with an evolutionary history. According to Darwin, many of the ways in which we express emotion are inherited patterns that originally had some survival value. For example, the expression of disgust or rejection is based on the organism's attempt to rid itself of something unpleasant that it has ingested. To quote Darwin (1872),

> The term "disgust," in its simplest sense, means something offensive to the taste. But as disgust also causes annoyance, it is generally accompanied by a frown, and often by gestures as if to push away or to guard oneself against the offensive object. Extreme disgust is expressed by movements around the mouth identical with those preparatory to the act of vomiting. The mouth is

  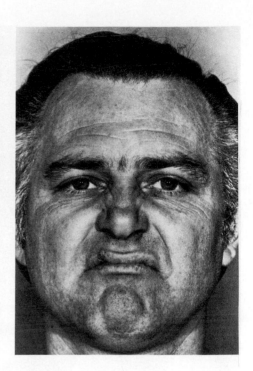

opened widely, with the upper lip strongly retracted. The partial closure of the eyelids, or the turning away of the eyes or of the whole body, are likewise highly expressive of disdain. These actions seem to declare that the despised person is not worth looking at, or is disagreeable to behold. Spitting seems an almost universal sign of contempt or disgust; and spitting obviously represents the rejection of anything offensive from the mouth.

While some facial expressions and gestures seem to be innately associated with particular emotions, others are learned from culture. One psychologist reviewed Chinese novels to determine how Chinese writers portray various human emotions. Many of the bodily changes in emotion (for example, flushing, trembling, goose pimples) represent the same symptoms of emotion in Chinese fiction as they do in western writing. Other bodily expressions, however, convey very different emotions in Chinese fiction than they do in the west. The following quotations from Chinese novels would surely be misinterpreted by an American reader unfamiliar with the culture (Klineberg, 1938).

> "They stretched out their tongues."
> (They showed signs of surprise.)

> "He clapped his hands."
> (He was worried or disappointed.)

> "He scratched his ears and cheeks."
> (He was happy.)

> "Her eyes grew round and opened wide."
> (She became angry.)

Thus, superimposed on the basic expressions of emotion, which appear to be universal, are conventional forms of expressions—a kind of language of emotion recognized by others within a culture.

## Brain Localization

The emotional expressions that are universal (for example, those associated with joy, anger, and disgust) are also highly specific: particular muscles are used to express particular emotions. This combination of universality and specificity suggests that a specialized neurological system may have evolved in humans to interpret the primitive emotional expressions. Recent evidence indicates that there is indeed such a system, and it is localized in the right cerebral hemisphere.

One source of evidence comes from studies in which pictures of emotional expressions are presented to either the left side or the right side of the subject's visual field. Recall from Chapter 2 that a stimulus presented to the left visual field projects to the right hemisphere, and a stimulus presented to the right visual field projects to the left hemisphere. When subjects have to decide which of two emotions the picture manifests, they are faster and more accurate when the picture is projected to their right hemisphere. In addition, when the two halves of the face convey different emotions (one half may be smiling while the other half is frowning), the expression projected to the right hemisphere has the most impact on the subject's decision. Another source of evidence about the localization of emotional expressions comes from studies of patients who have suffered brain damage from strokes or accidents. Patients who have only right-hemisphere damage have more difficulty recognizing facial expressions of emotion than do patients who have only left-hemisphere damage (Etcoff, 1985).

Our system for recognizing emotional expressions seems to be highly specialized. In particular, it is distinct from our ability to recognize faces. Consider a **prosopagnosic,** a person who has such extreme difficulty recognizing familiar faces that he (or she) sometimes fails to recognize his own face! He can, however, recognize emotional expressions: he can tell you that a particular person is happy even when he does not know that the person is his wife (Bruyer et al., 1983). The abilities to recognize faces and to recognize emotions also are differentially affected by electrical stimulation of various regions of the right hemisphere: face recognition is disrupted by stimulation in the region between the parietal and occipital lobes, whereas emotion recognition is disrupted by stimulation of a particular region in the temporal lobe (Fried et al., 1982).

Emotions, in addition to being communicated by facial expressions, are also expressed by variations in voice patterns (particularly variations in pitch, timing, and stress). Some of these variations appear to be universal and specific: a sharp increase in pitch indicates fear, for example. The specialized neurological system for perceiving these emotional clues is again located in the right cerebral hemisphere, and the evidence for this is similar to that for facial expressions. Subjects are more accurate in identifying the emotional tone of a voice presented to the left ear (which projects information primarily to the right hemisphere) than one presented to the right ear (which projects primarily to the left hemisphere). And patients who have solely right-hemisphere damage have more trouble identifying emotions from voice clues than do patients who have solely left-hemisphere damage (Ley & Bryden, 1982).

## Intensity and Differentiation of Emotions

**FACIAL FEEDBACK HYPOTHESIS**   The idea that facial expressions, in addition to their communicative function, also contribute to our experience of emotions is sometimes called the *facial feedback hypothesis* (Tomkins, 1962). According to the hypothesis, just as we receive feedback about (or perceive) our autonomic arousal, so we receive feedback about our facial expression, and this feedback combines with the other components of an emotion to produce a more intense experience. This implies that if you make yourself smile and hold the smile for several seconds, you will begin to feel happier; if you scowl, you will feel tense and angry. (Try it.)

In support of the facial feedback hypothesis, subjects who exaggerate their facial reactions to emotional stimuli report more emotional response than subjects who do not. In one study, subjects judged the pleasantness of various odors while posing either a smile or a frown. Posing a smile resulted in subjects perceiving the odors as more pleasant; posing a frown resulted in them perceiving the odors as less pleasant (Kraut, 1982). It is possible however, that subjects in this experiment "figured out" that when they posed a smile, for example, they were supposed to be happy, and this is why emotional expression affected the judgments. This possibility is ruled out by subsequent studies in which it is most unlikely that subjects noticed any connection between their facial expression and an emotion. In one experiment, subjects rated cartoons for funniness, while they held a pen either in their teeth or in their lips. Holding a pen in one's teeth forces your face into a smile, while holding it in one's lips forces your face into a frown (try it). As expected, the cartoons were rated as funnier when the pen was held in the teeth than when held in the lips (Strack, Martin, & Stepper, 1988). In addition to these studies which show a direct connection between expression

**FIGURE 11-4**
**Components of an Emotional Experience: 2** *Emotional expression, emotional belief, and perceived arousal all contribute to the experience of an emotion.* (After Reisenzein, 1983)

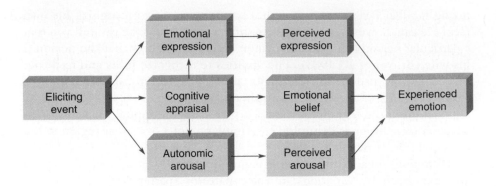

and felt emotion, other experiments indicate that facial expressions may have an indirect effect on emotion by increasing autonomic arousal. Such an indirect influence was demonstrated in an experiment we discussed earlier, where producing particular emotional expressions led to changes in heartbeat and skin temperature. We therefore need to add emotional expression to our list of contributors to emotional experience (see Figure 11-4).

Some researchers also believe that facial expressions can determine the *quality* of emotions. Since the expressions for the primary emotions are distinct and occur rapidly, they are at least plausible candidates for contributing to the differentiation of emotions. Tomkins (1980) has proposed that the feedback from a facial expression is inherently positive or negative, thereby suggesting a means by which facial expressions can distinguish the positive from the negative emotions. Should this suggestion prove true, we are back (in part) to the James-Lange theory mentioned earlier, which holds that emotion is the perception of certain bodily changes; facial expressions are bodily changes—we *are* happy *because* we smirk.

**BLOOD FLOW AND BRAIN TEMPERATURE** Exactly which aspects of a facial expression makes it inherently positive or negative? A possible answer may be found in the fact that the contraction of certain facial muscles can affect the blood flow in neighboring blood vessels. This, in turn, affects cerebral blood flow, which can determine brain temperature, which in turn can facilitate and inhibit the release of various neurotransmitters—and the latter may well be part of the cortical activity that underlies emotion. For example, when smiling, the configuration of facial muscles may lead to a lowering of the temperature in a region of the brain in which the neurotransmitter serotonin is released; this temperature change may block the release of the neurotransmitter, resulting in a positive feeling. The critical path, then, moves from facial expression to blood flow to brain temperature to emotional experience (Zajonc, Murphy, & Inglehart, 1989).

This path from expression to emotion is supported by recent experiments. One study takes advantage of the fact that pronunciation of the German vowel "ü" (as in Für) requires extending a facial muscle that is contracted when smiling. This suggests that the facial expression associated with pronouncing ü can lead to a negative feeling. To test this hypothesis, German subjects read aloud stories that contained either many words with ü or no words with ü; the stories were equated for their content and emotional tone. When asked how much they liked the stories, subjects rated those with ü words as less favorable than those with no ü words. Also, while subjects read the stories, the temperature of their foreheads was measured to provide an estimate of brain temperature. Temperatures rose during stories with ü words but not during stories without such words. Thus, the facial expression needed to produce ü led to both increased brain temperature and negative feeling, which supports the proposed path from facial expression to brain temperature to emotional experience (Zajonc, Murphy, & Inglehart, 1989).

# General Reactions to Being in an Emotional State

At the outset of this chapter we noted that one of the major components of an emotion involves the reactions to being in an emotional state. Although some reactions to being in an emotional state are specific to the emotion experienced—approaching someone when happy or withdrawing when frightened, for example—other reactions seem to apply to emotions in general. In particular, being in an emotional state: a) can energize or disrupt us; b) determine what we attend to and learn; and c) determine what kinds of judgments we make about the world.

## Energy and Disruption

Being in an emotional state sometimes energizes people, but other times disrupts them—depending on the intensity of the experience, the individual who is experiencing it, and the duration of the experience. With regard to intensity, a mild level of emotional arousal tends to produce alertness and interest in the current situation. When emotions become intense, however, whether pleasant or unpleasant, they usually result in some disruption of thought or behavior. The curve in Figure 11-5 represents the relation between a person's level of emotional arousal and his or her effectiveness on a task. At very low levels of emotional arousal (for example, at the point of waking up), we may not attend well to sensory information, and our performance will be relatively poor. Performance is optimal at moderate levels of arousal. At high levels of emotional arousal, our performance begins to decline, probably because we cannot devote enough cognitive resources to the task. The optimum level of arousal and the shape of the curve differ for different tasks. A simple, well-learned routine would be much less susceptible to disruption by emotional arousal than a more complex activity that depends on the integration of several thought processes. During a moment of intense fear, you would probably still be able to spell your name but not be able to play chess well.

Exactly what constitutes an excessive level of emotional arousal depends on the individual, as shown by studies of behavior during crises such as fires or sudden floods. About 15 percent of people show organized, effective behavior, suggesting that their optimum level of emotional arousal has not been exceeded. The majority of people, about 70 percent, show various degrees of disorganization but are still able to function with some effectiveness. The remaining 15 percent are so disorganized that they are unable to function at all; they may panic or exhibit aimless and completely inappropriate behavior, suggesting they are far above their optimal level of emotional arousal (Tyhurst, 1951).

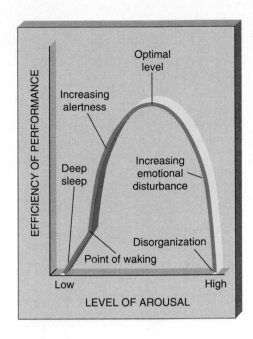

**FIGURE 11-5**
**Emotional Arousal and Performance**
*The curve shows the hypothetical relationship between level of emotional arousal and efficiency of performance. The precise shape of the curve differs for various tasks.* (After Hebb, 1972)

Sometimes intense emotions are not quickly discharged but continue to remain unresolved. Perhaps the situation that makes a person angry (for example, prolonged conflict with a teacher or employer) or fearful (such as worry over the illness of a parent) continues for a long time period. While the physiological changes that accompany anger and fear can have adaptive value (they mobilize us to fight or flee), when maintained too long they can exhaust our resources and even cause tissue damage. A chronic state of heightened arousal can thus take its toll on the individual's health. We will have more to say about the relationship between stress and the body's vulnerability to illness in Chapter 15.

## Attention and Learning: Mood Congruence

When experiencing an emotion, we tend to pay more attention to events that fit our mood than to events that do not. As a consequence, we learn more about the events that are congruent with our mood.

One experiment that demonstrates these phenomena involved three stages. In the first stage, subjects were hypnotized and induced to be in either a happy or sad mood (the subjects had been preselected for being hypnotizeable). In the second stage, the hypnotized subjects read a brief story about an encounter between two men—a happy character and a sad one. The story vividly described the events of the two men's lives and their emotional reactions. After reading the story, subjects were asked who they thought the central character was, and with whom they identified. Subjects who had been induced to be happy identified more with the happy character and thought the story contained more statements about him; subjects who had been induced to be sad identified more with the sad character and estimated that more story statements were about him. These results indicate that subjects paid more attention to the character and events that were congruent with their moods than to those that were not.

Evidence that subjects also *learned* more about mood-congruent events than mood-incongruent ones comes from the third part of the experiment. One day after reading the story, subjects returned to the laboratory, now in a neutral mood. They were asked to recall the story. Subjects recalled more about the character they had identified with: for the previously happy subjects, 55 percent of the facts they recalled were about the happy character; for the previously sad subjects, 80 percent of their recalled facts were about the sad character (Bower, 1981).

Exactly how does the congruence between one's mood and some new material affect the learning of that material? We know that we can learn new material better if we can relate it to information already in memory. One's mood during learning may increase the availability of memories that fit that mood, and such memories will be easier to relate to new material that also fits that mood. Suppose you hear a story about a student flunking out of school. If you are in a bad mood when hearing the story, some of your memories about failure experiences (particularly academic failures) may be easily accessible, and the similarity of these memories to the new fact of someone flunking out of school will make it easy to relate them. In contrast, if you are in a good mood when hearing the story, your most accessible memories may be too dissimilar to a school failure to foster a relation between the old memories and the new fact. So, our mood determines what memories are more accessible, and those memories determine what is easy for us to learn at the moment (Bower, 1981; Isen, 1985).

## Evaluation and Estimation: Mood Effects

Our emotional mood can affect our evaluation of other people. Everyday experiences provide numerous examples of this. For example, when we are in a good mood, a friend's habit of constantly checking his appearance in a mirror may seem just an idiosyncracy; when we are in a bad mood, we may dwell on how vain our friend is. Our mood affects our evaluation of inanimate objects as well. In one experiment, subjects were asked to evaluate their major possessions. Subjects who had just been put in a good mood by receiving a small gift rated their televisions and cars more positively than did control subjects who were in a neutral mood (Isen et al., 1978).

Our mood also affects our judgments about the frequency of various risks in the world. Bad moods lead us to see these risks as more likely; good moods lead us to see the risks as less likely. In an experiment dealing with estimating risks, subjects in the experimental group first read a newspaper story that recounted a tragic death, putting the subjects in a negative mood. Control subjects read a bland newspaper story, putting them in a neutral mood. Then all subjects were asked to estimate the frequencies of various fatalities, including diseases like leukemia and heart disease, and accidents like fires and floods. Subjects who were in a negative mood estimated the frequencies of these fatalities to be almost twice as great as did subjects in a neutral mood. Further, all that mattered for estimating frequencies was the subject's mood, not the content of the story that had put them in that mood. The tragic story that some experimental subjects read involved a case of leukemia, whereas the story that other experimental subjects read involved a death due to fire; both kinds of subjects overestimated the frequencies of leukemia and fire to the same degree. The similarity between the story and the risk had no effect on the estimate of frequency. It is as if the affect was separated from the content of the story, and only the affect guided subsequent estimates. Comparable results were obtained for the effects of being in a good mood. Reading a story about someone's good fortune led subjects to make relatively low estimates about the frequencies of various fatalities, and the extent to which subjects did this did not depend on the similarity between the story and the risk being evaluated (Johnson & Tversky, 1983).

Being in a bad mood, then, makes the world seem a more dangerous place. Such a perception can reinforce the bad mood. Also, as noted earlier, being in a bad mood leads us to selectively attend and learn negative-toned facts; this too can reinforce a bad mood. A similar analysis applies to a good mood. It makes the world seem less risky, and leads us to attend and learn positively toned material. Thus, the general consequences of a mood serve to perpetuate that mood.

## Aggression as an Emotional Reaction

Emotions cause not only general reactions, but specific ones as well. We may laugh when happy, withdraw when frightened, get aggressive when angry, and so forth. Among these typical emotional reactions, psychologists have singled out one in particular for extensive study: aggression.

This special attention is partly due to the social significance of aggression. At the societal level, in an age when nuclear weapons are still widely available, a single aggressive act can spell disaster. At the individual level, many people experience aggressive thoughts and impulses frequently, and how they handle these thoughts will have major effects on their health and interpersonal relations. Another reason why psychologists have focused their research on aggression is because two major theories of social behavior make quite different assumptions about the nature of aggression. Freud's **psychoanalytic theory** views aggression as a drive, and **social-learning theory** views it as a learned response. Research on aggression helps us to evaluate these competing theories.

In the following discussion, we first describe these different views along with related research, and then consider how the views differ with respect to the effects of viewing aggression in the mass media. Keep in mind that what we mean by "aggression" is behavior that is *intended* to injure another person (physically or verbally) or to destroy property. The key concept in this definition is intent. If a person accidentally steps on your foot in a crowded elevator and immediately apologizes, you would not interpret the behavior as aggressive; but if someone walks up to you as you sit at your desk and steps on your foot, you would not hesitate to label the act as aggressive.

## Aggression as a Drive

We will present only those aspects of psychoanalytic theory and social-learning theory that are relevant to aggression. Both theories will be presented in more detail in Chapter 14, where we focus on personality, and Chapters 16 and 17, where we discuss abnormal behavior and its treatment.

According to Freud's early psychoanalytic theory, many of our actions are determined by instincts, particularly the sexual instinct. When expression of these instincts is frustrated, an aggressive drive is induced. Later theorists in the psychoanalytic tradition broadened this **frustration-aggression hypothesis** to the following claim: whenever a person's effort to reach *any* goal is blocked, an aggressive drive is induced that motivates behavior to injure the obstacle (person or object) causing the frustration (Dollard et al.,

*Is aggression a drive or a learned response?*

1939). There are two critical aspects of this proposal: one is that the usual cause of aggression is frustration; the other is that aggression has the properties of a basic drive—being a form of *energy* that *persists* until its goal is satisfied, as well as being an *inborn* reaction (hunger, sex, and other basic drives have these properties). As we will see, it is the drive aspect of the frustration-aggression hypothesis that has proved to be particularly controversial.

**AGGRESSION IN OTHER SPECIES**  If aggression is really a basic drive like hunger, then we would expect other mammalian species to exhibit patterns of aggression that are similar to ours (just as they exhibit patterns of hunger that are similar to ours). The evidence on this issue has changed over the years. In the 1960s, early work in ethology suggested that there was a major difference between humans and other species—namely that animals have evolved mechanisms to control their aggressive instincts whereas humans have not (for example, Ardrey, 1966; Lorenz, 1966). Subsequent work in the 1970s and 1980s, however, suggested that animals may be no less aggressive than we are. The incidence of murder, rape, and infanticide among animals was shown to be much greater than was thought in the 1960s. One kind of murder involves border wars between chimpanzees (Goodall, 1978). In one well-documented case in the Gombe Stream National Park in Tanzania, a gang of five male chimpanzees defended their territory against any strange male that wandered into it. If the gang encountered a group of two or more strangers, their response would be raucous but not deadly; but if there was only one intruder, then one member of the gang might hold his arm, another a leg, while a third member pounded the intruder to death. Or a couple of members of the gang would drag the intruder over the rocks until he died. In another chimpanzee border war observed during the 1970s, a tribe of about 15 chimpanzees destroyed a smaller neighboring group by killing the members off one male at a time. Furthermore, at least for primates, females engage in as many aggressive acts as males, though their encounters are less deadly because their teeth are shorter and less sharp (Smuts, 1986).

While observations like these bring animal aggression more in line with human aggression, there still are many apparent differences. Only humans wage wide-scale wars, for example.

**BIOLOGICAL BASIS OF AGGRESSION IN OTHER SPECIES**  Findings on the biological basis of aggression in animals provide evidence for an aggressive drive in at least some species. Some studies show that mild electrical stimulation of a specific region of the hypothalamus produces aggressive, even deadly, behavior in animals. When a cat's hypothalamus is stimulated via implanted electrodes, the animal hisses, its hair bristles, its pupils dilate, and it will strike at a rat or other objects placed in its cage. Stimulation of a different area of the hypothalamus produces quite different behavior: instead of exhibiting any of these rage responses, the cat coldly stalks and kills a rat.

Similar techniques have produced aggressive behavior in rats. A laboratory-bred rat that has never killed a mouse, nor seen a wild rat kill one, may live quite peacefully in the same cage with a mouse. But if the rat's hypothalamus is stimulated, the animal will pounce on its mouse cage mate and kill it with exactly the same response that is exhibited by a wild rat (a hard bite to the neck that severs the spinal cord). The stimulation seems to trigger an innate killing response that had previously been dormant. Conversely, if a

**FIGURE 11-6**
**Brain Stimulation and Aggression**
*A mild electrical current is delivered to electrodes implanted in the monkey's hypothalamus via remote radio control. The animal's response (attack or flight) depends on its position in the dominance hierarchy of the colony.* (Courtesy Dr. Jose Delgado)

neurochemical blocker is injected into the same brain site in rats that spontaneously kill mice on sight, the rats become temporarily peaceful (Smith, King, & Hoebel, 1970). In these cases, then, aggression has some properties of a drive, since it involves inborn reactions.

In higher mammals, such instinctive patterns of aggression are controlled by the cortex and therefore are influenced more by experience. Monkeys living in groups establish a dominance hierarchy: one or two males become leaders, and the others assume various levels of subordination. When the hypothalamus of a dominant monkey is electrically stimulated, the monkey attacks subordinate males but not females. When a low-ranking monkey is stimulated in the same way, it cowers and behaves submissively (see Figure 11-6). Thus, aggressive behavior in a monkey is not automatically elicited by stimulation of the hypothalamus; rather, the monkey's environment and past experiences also play a role. Humans are similar. Although we are equipped with neurological mechanisms that are tied to aggression, the activation of these mechanisms is usually under cortical control (except in some cases of brain damage). Indeed, in most individuals, the frequency with which aggressive behavior is expressed, the forms it takes, and the situations in which it is displayed are determined largely by experience and social influences.

**BIOLOGICAL BASES OF AGGRESSION IN HUMANS** One biological factor that may be related to aggression in human males is testosterone level. As you may recall from Chapter 10, testosterone is a male sex hormone, which is responsible for many male bodily characteristics and which has been linked to aggression in monkeys. Recent studies suggest that in humans as well, higher levels of testosterone are associated with higher levels of aggression. One large-scale study involved more than 4400 male U.S. veterans. The men were given various psychological tests, some of which tapped aggressiveness; they also had blood samples taken from them so that their testosterone level could be determined. Men who had higher levels of testosterone were more likely to have a history of aggression. Since aggressive behavior in males can sometimes lead to antisocial behavior, we might expect that high testosterone would be an impediment to success in American life. Indeed, men with extremely high testosterone levels were more likely to have low-status than high-status positions (Dabbs & Morris, 1990).

These findings provide some evidence for a biological basis of aggression in humans, and hence for the view that aggression is like a drive. Still, in these studies the link between testosterone and aggression is often tenuous—large numbers of subjects are needed to find the effect—which suggests the need to look elsewhere for determinants of aggression.

## Aggression as a Learned Response

*Social-learning theory* is concerned with human social interaction, but it has its origins in behavioristic studies of animal learning (such as those discussed in Chapter 7). It focuses on the behavior patterns that people develop in response to environmental contingencies. Some social behaviors may be rewarded while others may produce unfavorable results; through the process of differential reinforcement, people eventually select the more successful behavior patterns. Social-learning theory differs from strict behaviorism, however, in that it stresses the importance of cognitive processes. Because people can mentally represent situations, they are able to foresee the likely consequences of their actions and to alter their behavior accordingly.

Social-learning theory further differs from strict behaviorism in that it stresses the importance of **vicarious learning,** or learning by observation. Many behavior patterns are learned by watching the actions of others and observing what consequences it produces for them. A child who observes the pained expressions of an older sibling in the dentist's chair will probably be fearful when the time comes for his or her first dental appointment. Social-learning theory emphasizes the role of **models** in transmitting both specific behaviors and emotional responses. It focuses on such questions as what types of models are most effective and what factors determine whether the modeled behavior that is learned will actually be performed (Bandura, 1973, 1986).

With this emphasis on learning, it is no surprise that social-learning theory rejects the concept of aggression as a frustration-produced drive; the theory proposes instead that aggression is similar to any other learned response. Aggression can be learned through observation or imitation, and the more often it is reinforced, the more likely it is to occur. A person who is frustrated by a blocked goal or disturbed by some stressful event experiences an unpleasant emotion. The response that this emotion elicits will differ, depending on the kinds of responses the individual has learned to use in coping with stressful situations. The frustrated individual may seek help from others, aggress, withdraw, try even harder to surmount the obstacle, or anesthetize himself or herself with drugs or alcohol. The chosen response will be the one that has relieved frustration most successfully in the past. According to this view, frustration provokes aggression mainly in people who have learned to respond to adverse situations with aggressive behavior (Bandura, 1977).

Figure 11-7 shows how social-learning theory differs from psychoanalytic theory (the frustration-aggression hypothesis) in conceptualizing aggression. Social-learning theory assumes that (a) aggression is just one of several reactions to the aversive experience of frustration, and (b) aggression is a response with no drivelike properties, and consequently is influenced by anticipated consequences of behavior.

**FIGURE 11-7**
**Two Views of Aggression** *The diagram schematically represents the determinants of aggression according to psychoanalytic theory (the frustration-aggression hypothesis) and social-learning theory. From the viewpoint of social-learning theory, the emotional arousal caused by unpleasant experiences can lead to any number of different behaviors, depending on the behavior that has been reinforced in the past.*

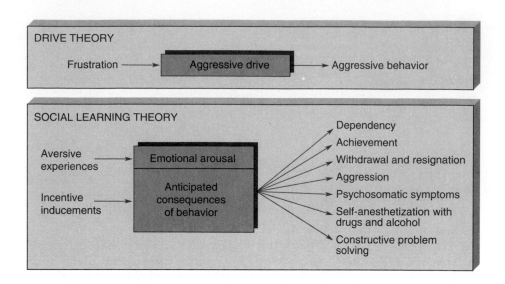

**IMITATION OF AGGRESSION** One source of evidence for social-learning theory is studies showing that aggression, like any other response, can be learned through imitation. Nursery-school children who observed an adult expressing various forms of aggression toward a large, inflated doll subsequently imitated many of the adult's actions, including unusual ones (see Figure 11-8). The experiment was expanded to include two filmed versions of aggressive modeling (one showing an adult behaving aggressively toward the doll, the other showing a cartoon character displaying the same aggressive behavior). The results were equally striking. Children who watched either of the two films behaved as aggressively toward the doll as children who

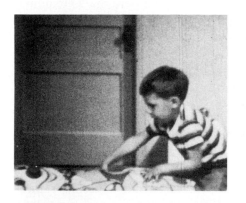

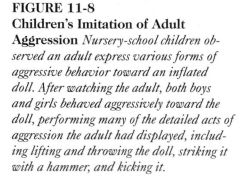
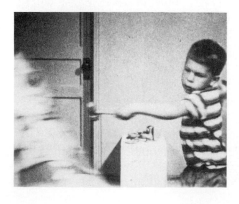

**FIGURE 11-8**
**Children's Imitation of Adult Aggression** *Nursery-school children observed an adult express various forms of aggressive behavior toward an inflated doll. After watching the adult, both boys and girls behaved aggressively toward the doll, performing many of the detailed acts of aggression the adult had displayed, including lifting and throwing the doll, striking it with a hammer, and kicking it.*

had observed a live model displaying aggression. Figure 11-9 shows the measures of aggressive behavior for each of the groups and for two control groups who observed either no model or a nonaggressive model. The conclusion of such studies is that observation of either live or filmed models of aggression increases the likelihood of aggression in the viewer. This may be part of the reason why children whose parents punish them severely are likely to be more aggressive than average; the parents provide the model (Eron, 1987).

**REINFORCEMENT OF AGGRESSION**  Another source of evidence for social-learning theory is that aggression is sensitive to reinforcement contingencies in the same manner that other learned responses are. A number of studies show that children are more likely to express the aggressive responses they learned by watching aggressive models when they are reinforced for such actions or when they observe aggressive models being reinforced. In one study, investigators observed children for 10 weeks, recording instances of interpersonal aggression and the events that immediately followed them, such as positive reinforcers of the aggression (victim winced or cried), punishment of the aggression (victim counterattacked), or neutral reactions (victim ignored the aggressor). For the children who showed the highest overall level of aggression, the most common reaction to their aggressive act was positive reinforcement. For the children who showed the least aggression, punishment was a common reaction. Children who were initially unaggressive, but occasionally succeeded in stopping attacks by counteraggression gradually began to initiate attacks of their own (their aggression was being positively reinforced). Clearly, the consequences of aggression play an important role in shaping behavior (Patterson, Littman, & Bricker, 1967).

## Aggressive Expression and Catharsis

Studies that try to distinguish between aggression as a drive and aggression as a learned response often focus on **catharsis** (purging an emotion by experiencing it intensely). If aggression is a drive, then the expressions of aggression should be cathartic, resulting in a reduction in the intensity of aggressive feelings and actions (analogous to how eating leads to a reduction of hunger-based feelings and actions). On the other hand, if aggression is a learned response, the expression of aggression could result in an increase in such actions (if the aggression is reinforced). Currently, the evidence favors the learned-response view.

**ACTING AGGRESSIVELY**  Psychologists have conducted numerous laboratory studies to determine whether or not aggression decreases once it has been partially expressed. Studies of children indicate that participation in aggressive activities either increases aggressive behavior or maintains it at the same level. Experiments with adults produce similar results. When given repeated opportunities to shock another person (who cannot retaliate), college students become more and more punitive. Subjects who are angry become even more punitive on successive attacks than subjects who are not angry. If aggression were cathartic, the angry subjects should reduce their aggressive drive by acting aggressively and become less punitive the more they aggress (Berkowitz, 1965; Geen & Quanty, 1977).

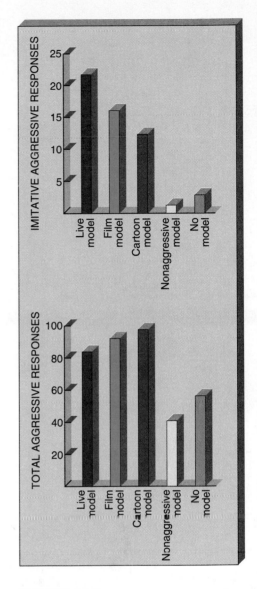

**FIGURE 11-9**
**Imitation of Aggression**
*Observing aggressive models (either live or on film) greatly increases the amount of aggressive behavior that children display, compared to observing a nonaggressive model or no model at all. Note that observation of the live model results in the imitation of more specific aggressive acts, whereas observation of filmed (either real-life or cartoon) models instigates more aggressive responses of all kinds. (After Bandura, 1973)*

Some evidence about catharsis is also taken from real-life situations. In one case, California aerospace workers who had been laid off were first interviewed about how they felt about their companies and supervisors, and subsequently were asked to describe their feelings in writing. If aggression were cathartic, men who expressed a lot of anger in the interviews should have expressed relatively little in the written reports. The results, however, showed otherwise: the men who let out anger in conversation expressed even more in their reports. Fuming in conversation may have kindled the aggression. Another study looked at the relation between the hostility of a country (vis-à-vis its neighboring countries) and the kinds of sports it plays. More belligerent cultures were found to play more combative games. Again, aggression seems to breed aggression rather than dissipate it (Ebbesen, Duncan, & Konečni, 1975).

These results argue against aggression being cathartic. However, there are circumstances in which the expression of aggression may decrease its incidence. For example, behaving aggressively may arouse feelings of anxiety in the aggressors that inhibit further aggression, particularly if they observe their actions have led to injuries. But in these instances, the effect on aggressive behavior can be explained without concluding that an aggressive drive is being reduced. Also, although expressing hostile feelings in action does not usually reduce the aggression, it may make the person feel better. But this may happen because the person feels more powerful and more in control, rather than because the person has reduced an aggressive drive.

**VIEWING VIOLENCE**  Most of the studies we have discussed deal with the consequences of directly expressing aggression. What about the effects of indirectly or vicariously expressing aggression through watching violence on television or in the movies? Is viewing violence cathartic, providing fantasy outlets for an aggressive drive? Or does it elicit aggression by modeling violent behavior? We have already seen that children will imitate live or filmed aggressive behavior in an experimental setting, but how will they react in more natural settings? The amount of media violence to which we are exposed makes this an important question. This is particularly true for children, for whom the amount of violence in certain television programs

*Children often imitate what they see on television*

continues to increase. For example, in 1980 there was an average of 18.6 violent acts per hour in Saturday morning cartoons; by 1990, this number had risen to 26.4 (New York Times, 1990).

Several experimental studies have controlled children's viewing of television: one group watched violent cartoons for a specified amount of time each day; another group watched nonviolent cartoons for the same amount of time. The amount of aggression the children showed in their daily activities was carefully recorded. The children who watched violent cartoons became more aggressive in their interactions with their peers, whereas the children who viewed nonviolent cartoons showed no change in interpersonal aggression (Steuer, Applefield, & Smith, 1971).

The above study involves an experimental group and a control group. However, most studies that deal with children's viewing habits are correlational; they determine the relation between the amount of exposure to televised violence and the degree to which children use aggressive behavior to solve interpersonal conflicts. This correlation is clearly positive (Singer & Singer, 1981), even for children in Finland, which has a limited number of violent programs (Lagerspetz, Viemero, & Akademi, 1986). Correlations, however, do not imply causal relationships. It may be that children who are more aggressive prefer to watch violent television programs—that is, having an aggressive nature causes one to view violence, rather than vice versa.

To evaluate this alternative hypothesis, a study traced television viewing habits over a 10-year period. More than 800 children were studied between the ages of 8 and 9 years. Investigators collected information about each child's viewing preferences and aggressiveness (as rated by schoolmates). Boys who preferred programs that contained a considerable amount of violence were found to be much more aggressive in their interpersonal relationships than boys who preferred programs that contained little violence. So far, the evidence is of the same nature as that in previous studies. But 10 years later, more than half of the original subjects were interviewed concerning their television preferences, given a test that measured delinquency tendencies, and rated by their peers for aggressiveness. Figure 11-10 shows that high exposure to violence on television at age 9 is positively related to aggressiveness in boys at age 19. Most important, the correlation remains significant even when statistical methods are used to control for the degree of childhood aggressiveness, thereby reducing the possibility that the initial level of aggression determines both childhood viewing preferences and adult aggressiveness.

It is interesting that the results showed no consistent relation between the television viewing habits of girls and their aggressive behavior at either age. This agrees with the results of other studies indicating that girls tend to imitate aggressive behavior much less than boys do unless specifically reinforced for doing so. In our society, girls are less likely to be reinforced for behaving aggressively. And since most of the aggressive roles on television are male, females are less likely to find aggressive models to imitate. For boys, however, the majority of studies point to the conclusion that viewing violence does increase interpersonal aggression, particularly in young children. Indeed, this conclusion is supported by a recent review of some 28 studies on this issue (Wood, Wong, & Chachere, 1991). This argues against aggression catharsis and the view that aggression is a drive.

Our survey of aggression has by no means considered all of its possible causes. Common causes of anger and aggression include a loss of self-esteem or a perception that another person has acted unfairly (Averill, 1983);

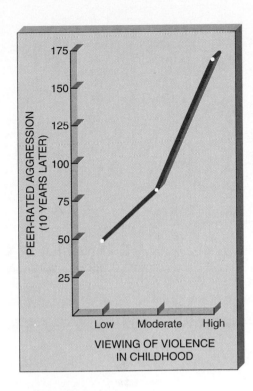

**FIGURE 11-10**
**Relationship Between Childhood Viewing of Violent Television and Adult Aggression** *Preference for viewing violent television programs by boys at age 9 is positively correlated with aggressive behavior at age 19.* (After Eron, Huesmann, Lefkowitz, & Walder, 1972)

neither of these factors has figured centrally in our discussion of aggression as a drive versus aggression as a learned response. Also, many societal factors are involved in the instigation of aggression; conditions of poverty, overcrowding, the actions of authorities such as the police, and the values of one's cultural group are only a few. Some of these social influences will be considered in Chapter 19.

The study of aggression makes it clear that an emotional reaction is a complex event. Similarly, each component of an emotion that we considered—autonomic arousal, cognitive appraisal, and emotional expression—is itself a complex event involving multiple factors. It is no wonder that we still know so little about this side of our lives.

## *Chapter* **SUMMARY**

1. The components of an emotion include *autonomic arousal, cognitive appraisal, emotional expression* and *reactions* to the emotion. One critical question is, What is the nature of these components? Other critical questions are, How do arousal, appraisal, and expression contribute to the intensity of an emotional experience? and Which components *differentiate* the emotions?

2. Intense emotions usually involve physiological arousal caused by activation of the *sympathetic division* of the *autonomic nervous system*. People who have spinal cord injuries, which limit feedback from the autonomic nervous system, report experiencing less intense emotions. Autonomic arousal may also help differentiate the emotions, since the pattern of arousal (for example, heartbeat, skin temperature) differs for different emotions.

3. A *cognitive appraisal* is an analysis of a situation that results in an emotional belief. Such appraisals affect both the intensity and quality of an emotion. When people are induced into a state of undifferentiated arousal (say, by injection of epinephrine), the quality of their emotional experience is determined almost entirely by their appraisal of the situation. There are cases of emotion, however, in which no cognitive appraisal seems to be involved (for example, fear experiences that were acquired in childhood by classical conditioning). These *pre-cognitive emotions* appear to be mediated by distinct neural pathways in the brain.

4. The facial expressions that accompany primary emotions have a universal meaning: people from different cultures agree on what emotion a person in a particular photograph is expressing. The ability to recognize emotional expression is localized in the right cerebral hemisphere and is neurologically distinct from the ability to recognize faces. In addition to their communicative functions, emotional expressions may also contribute to the subjective experience of an emotion (the *facial feedback hypothesis*). In support of this hypothesis, people report more of an emotional experience when they exaggerate their facial reactions to emotional stimuli.

5. Being in an emotional state has some general consequences. One is that emotion can sometimes energize people, but at other times disrupt them. A mild emotion produces alertness whereas an intense emotion can be disruptive. Another general reaction to being in an emotional state is that we tend to pay more attention to and learn more about events that fit our mood than to events that do not. Another consequence is that our emotional mood affects our evaluation of people and

objects, as well as our estimation of what will happen in the future. When in a bad mood, we estimate various risks in life to be relatively frequent; when in a good mood, we estimate these risks to be relatively infrequent.

6. *Aggression* is a typical reaction to anger (though it can occur for other reasons as well). According to early *psychoanalytic theory*, aggression is a *frustration-produced drive;* according to *social-learning theory*, aggression is a *learned response.*

7. The hypothesis that aggression is a basic drive (like hunger) receives some support from studies showing a biological basis of aggression. In lower animals, aggression is controlled by neurological mechanisms in the *hypothalamus.* Stimulation of the hypothalamus of a rat or cat can lead to a rage or killing response. In humans and other higher mammals, aggressive behavior is largely under cortical control, and hence more affected by past experiences and social influences. Even in humans, though, there may be some biological bases of aggression (like *testosterone level* in men).

8. In keeping with the social-learning theory of aggression, aggressive responses can be learned through *imitation* and increased in frequency when positively reinforced. Children are more likely to express aggressive responses when they are reinforced for such actions (for example, their victims wince or cry) than when they are punished for the actions (their victims counterattack).

9. Evidence indicates that aggression either increases subsequent aggressive behavior or maintains it at the same level. Thus, when given repeated opportunities to shock another person (who cannot retaliate), college students become more and more punitive. The indirect or vicarious expression of aggression has similar effects: there is a positive relation between the amount of exposure children have to television violence and the extent to which they act aggressively.

## *Further* **READING**

For an introduction to various views on emotion, some chapters in Mook, *Motivation* (1987) are very useful. For a more technical treatment of emotion, see Lazarus, *Emotion and Adaptation* (1991); Frijda, *The Emotions* (1986); Mandler, *Mind and Emotion* (1982); and Plutchik and Kellerman (eds.), *Emotion: Theory, Research, and Experience* (1980). The role of cognition in emotion is discussed in detail in Ortony, Clore, and Collins, *The Cognitive Structure of Emotions* (1988).

Interesting books on facial expressions and emotion include Ekman's *Emotion in the Human Face* (2nd ed., 1982) and his *Telling Lies: Clues to Deceit in the Marketplace, Politics and Marriage* (1985). For a review and critical analysis of lie detection procedures, see Lykken, *A Tremor in the Blood: Uses and Abuses of the Lie Detector* (1980).

The psychoanalytic theory of emotion is presented in two books by Freud: *Beyond the Pleasure Principle* (1920/1975) and *New Introductory Lectures on Psychoanalysis* (1933/1965). For the social-learning approach, see Bandura, *Social Learning Theory* (1977).

Books on aggression include Bandura, *Aggression: A Social Learning Analysis* (1973); Tavris, *Anger: The Misunderstood Emotion* (1984); Hamburg and Trudeau (eds.), *Biobehavioral Aspects of Aggression* (1981); and Averill, *Anger and Aggression: An Essay on Emotion* (1982).

# Part VI

## *Personality and Individuality*

12 Assessment of Mental Abilities

13 Personality through the Life Course

14 Personality Theory and Assessment

*On the Heights*, 1909, by Charles Courney Curran (1861–1942), oil on canvas, $30\frac{1}{3}$" $\times$ $30\frac{1}{3}$", The Brooklyn Museum of Art, Gift of George D. Pratt.

# Chapter 12

# Assessment of Mental Abilities

**Ability Tests 451**
*Aptitude versus Achievement*
*Generality versus Specificity*

**Characteristics of a Good Test 455**
*Reliability*
*Validity*
*Uniform Procedures*

**Tests of Intellectual Ability 457**
*Historical Background*
*Binet's Method: A Mental-Age Scale*
*Testing Specific Mental Abilities*
*Group Tests*
*Critical Discussion: Coaching and Test Sophistication*

**Predictive Validity 466**
*Test Scores and Academic Performance*
*Group Differences in Test Performance*
*Using Tests to Predict Performance*
*Critical Discussion: Sex Differences in Specific Abilities*

**Nature of Intelligence 470**
*Factorial Approach*
*Information-Processing Approach*
*Critical Discussion: Multiple Intelligences*
*Aspects of Intelligence*

**Genetic and Environmental Influences 478**
*Genetic Relationships and Intelligence*
*Environmental Influences*
*Critical Discussion: Race and Intelligence*

**Ability Tests in Perspective 482**

Detail, *On the Heights.*

P eople vary widely in personality characteristics and mental abilities. In this chapter, we will look at individual differences in ability and at tests designed to assess these differences. Methods of assessing personality differences will be discussed in Chapter 14. The features that make a test useful, however, are the same regardless of the test's purpose; the requirements for a good test apply equally to ability and personality tests.

The use of ability tests to assign schoolchildren to special classes, to admit students to college and professional schools, and to select individuals for jobs is a topic of public debate and controversy. When ability tests were first developed around the turn of the century, they were hailed as an objective and impartial method of identifying talent and ensuring individual opportunity. Testing permitted people to be selected for jobs or advanced schooling on the basis of merit rather than family background, wealth, social class, or political influence. America—a democratic society with a large, heterogeneous population—was particularly enthusiastic about the use of tests to classify students and select employees. To cite one example, the Civil Service Examinations that thousands of people now take annually when applying for government jobs were initiated during the 1880s in an attempt to ensure that such jobs would be given to qualified people instead of to those who had gained favor by supporting newly elected politicians.

Many people still view ability tests as a very useful way of assessing what people can do and for advising them on jobs and professions. Others claim that such tests are narrow and restrictive: they do not measure the characteristics that are most important in determining how well a person will do in college or on the job—motivation, social skills, and qualities of leadership—and they discriminate against minorities. We will look at the evidence on both sides of this controversy.

## Ability Tests

By the time we finish high school, most of us have had some experience with ability tests. Driver's license examinations, grade-school tests of reading and math skills, the competency examinations required for graduation from many high schools, and tests that assess mastery of a particular course (typing, American history, chemistry, and so on) are all ability tests.

A test is essentially a sample of behavior taken at a given point in time. A distinction is often made between *achievement tests* (which are designed to measure accomplished skills and indicate what the person can do at present) and *aptitude tests* (which are designed to predict what a person can accomplish with training). But the distinction between these two types of tests is not clear-cut. All tests assess the individual's current status, whether the purpose of the test is to assess what has been learned or to predict future performance. Both kinds of tests often include similar types of questions and yield results that are highly correlated. Rather than considering aptitude and achievement tests as two distinct categories, it is more useful to think of them as falling along a continuum.

### Aptitude versus Achievement

Tests at either end of the aptitude-achievement continuum are distinguished from each other primarily in terms of purpose. For example, a test of knowledge of mechanical principles might be given on completion of a

**FIGURE 12-1**
**Two Dimensions that Describe Ability Tests** *Any given test falls somewhere along an aptitude-achievement continuum and also along a general-specific continuum. For example, a Spanish vocabulary test or a typing test would fall toward the achievement end of the aptitude-achievement continuum and toward the specific end of the general-specific continuum. The Musical Aptitude Profile, which requires no prior musical knowledge and is designed to predict an individual's capacity to profit from music lessons, also taps a fairly specific area of ability but falls toward the aptitude end of the aptitude-achievement dimension. Most intelligence tests (such as the Stanford-Binet and Wechsler Intelligence Scales) are fairly general in that they sample a range of abilities and are designed to measure aptitude more than achievement of skills. Scholastic achievement tests, such as the SAT and ACT, are also fairly general; they measure achievement in verbal and mathematical reasoning but do not presume the mastery of specific courses.*

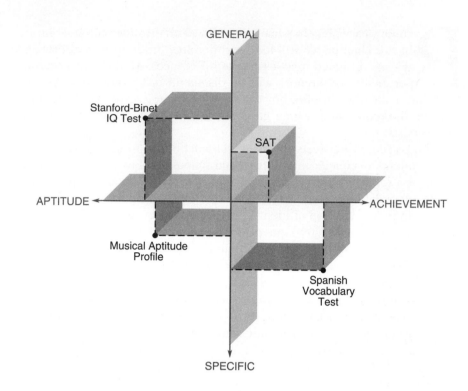

course in mechanics to measure the student's mastery of the course material—to provide a measure of **achievement.** Similar questions might be included in a battery of tests administered to select applicants for pilot training, since knowledge of mechanical principles has been found to be a good predictor of success in flying. The latter test would be considered a measure of **aptitude,** since its results are used to predict a candidate's performance as a student pilot. Thus, whether the test is labeled an aptitude or an achievement test depends more on its purpose than on its content.

Tests at the two ends of the aptitude-achievement continuum can also be distinguished in terms of the *specificity of relevant prior experience.* At one end of the continuum are achievement tests designed to measure mastery of a fairly specific subject matter, such as music theory, European history, or the safe and legal operation of a motor vehicle. At the other extreme are aptitude tests that assume little more in terms of prior experience than the general experience of growing up in the United States. A musical aptitude test, for example, is intended to predict the degree to which a student will benefit from music lessons prior to any instruction. Thus, the Musical Aptitude Profile (Gordon, 1967) does not require any knowledge of musical techniques (see Figure 12-1). It tests a person's ability to identify tones and rhythms that sound similar and to discriminate musical selections that are tastefully performed. Although no specific experience is required, a person's ability to understand instructions given in English and his or her prior experience listening to music would undoubtedly influence the test results.

We will see later that performance on "intelligence" tests (aptitude tests designed to measure a person's general capacity for learning) does depend to some extent on prior experience, even though every attempt is made to devise questions that do not reflect the results of special training.

Somewhere between aptitude tests (which assume little in terms of relevant prior experience) and achievement tests (which measure the mastery of specific subject matter) are tests that measure both aptitude and achieve-

## VERBAL ITEMS

**Antonyms** (tests extent of vocabulary)

1. Choose the word or phrase that is most nearly the *opposite* in meaning to the word in capital letters.

   PARTISAN:  A commoner   D ascetic
              B neutral     E pacifist
              C unifier

**Analogies** (tests ability to see a relationship in a pair of words, to understand the ideas expressed in the relationship, and to recognize a similar or parallel relationship).

2. Select the lettered pair that best expresses a relationship similar to that expressed in the original pair.

   FLURRY: BLIZZARD:   A trickle: deluge   D spray: foam
                       B rapids: rock      E mountain:
                       C lightning:           summit
                         cloudburst

**Sentence completion** (tests ability to recognize the relationships among parts of a sentence)

3. Choose the word or set of words that best fits the meaning of the sentence as a whole.

   Prominent psychologists believe that people act violently because they have been _____ to do so, not because they were born _____ ;

   A forced–gregarious     D taught–aggressive
   B forbidden–complacent  E inclined–belligerent
   C expected–innocent

**Reading passages** (tests ability to comprehend a written passage)

Blocks of questions are presented following passages of roughly 400 to 500 words. Some questions ask about information that is directly stated in the passage; others require applications of the author's principles or opinions; still others ask for judgments (e.g., how well the author supports the claims).

**TABLE 12-1**
**Scholastic Aptitude Test** *A sample of items from the verbal section of the SAT. These items are of middle difficulty and are answered correctly by 50–60 percent of the test takers. The answers are 1: B, 2: A, 3: D .*

ment. An example is the Scholastic Aptitude Test (SAT), which is required for admission to many colleges. The SAT consists of a verbal section (see Table 12-1), which measures vocabulary skills and the ability to understand what is read, and a mathematical section (see Table 12-2), which tests the ability to solve problems requiring arithmetic reasoning, algebra, and geometry. Although the test taps learned material (the verbal and quantitative skills that a person has acquired during 12 years of education), it attempts to avoid questions that depend on knowledge of specific topics and focuses instead on the ability to use acquired skills to solve newly posed problems.

**TABLE 12-2**
**Scholastic Aptitude Test** *A sample of items from the mathematical section of the SAT, also of middle difficulty. The answers are 1: C, 2: C, 3: B, 4: C .*

### MATHEMATICAL ITEMS

1.  If $x^3 = (2x)^2$ and $x \neq 0$, then $x =$

|   |   |   |   |
|---|---|---|---|
| A | 1 | D | 6 |
| B | 2 | E | 8 |
| C | 4 |   |   |

$$l = \frac{x°/y°}{P}$$

Note: Figure is not drawn to scale.

2.  If P is a point on line $l$ in the figure above and x – y = 0, then y =

|   |   |   |   |
|---|---|---|---|
| A | 0  | D | 135 |
| B | 45 | E | 180 |
| C | 90 |   |   |

Each question consists of two quantities, one in Column A and one in Column B. You are to compare the two quantities and on the answer sheet blacken space:

A   if the quantity in Column A is greater;
B   if the quantity in Column B is greater;
C   if the two quantities are equal;
D   if the relationship cannot be determined from the information given.

Note: In certain questions, information concerning one or both of the quantities to be compared is centered above the two columns.

| **Column A** | **Column B** |
|---|---|
| 3. Number of minutes in 1 week | Number of seconds in 7 hours |

$$\frac{5}{x} = \frac{1}{3}$$

| **Column A** | **Column B** |
|---|---|
| 4. $\dfrac{3}{x}$ | $\dfrac{1}{5}$ |

## Generality versus Specificity

Ability tests can also be distinguished along a general-specific continuum, because they vary in the broadness of their content. The Musical Aptitude Profile would be at the specific end of the continuum, as would a typing test or a driver's license examination; these tests measure fairly specific skills. At the general end of the continuum would be high-school competency exams and scholastic aptitude tests (like the SAT), which attempt to measure educational development in a number of areas, as well as most tests that are called *intelligence tests*. An intelligence test is an aptitude test designed to predict performance over a range of abilities. Such tests usually do not contain items that can be answered by the routine application of practiced skills. Instead, they focus on items that require a mixture of the abilities to analyze, to understand abstract concepts, and to solve new problems. Intelligence tests usually include verbal, figurative, and quantitative tasks. Although the attempt to measure general intellectual ability in order to predict what an individual can accomplish with education or training is certainly worthwhile, the label "intelligence test" is unfortunate. The wording implies that people possess an innate capacity, called intelligence, that is fixed in amount and is not influenced by education or experience. Later, we will see that many variables can influence a person's score on an intelligence test. In addition, although some individuals may be more able than others to accomplish a variety of tasks, abilities are not so consistent that a person who is above average at one type of task is above average at all tasks.

## Characteristics of a Good Test

In our society, much depends on test scores. In the elementary-school grades, children are often placed in instructional groups on the basis of their performances on tests. Some high schools require students to pass minimum competency tests in order to graduate. Tests are part of the admissions procedure in many colleges and most professional and graduate schools. Most high-school students who are college-bound must take either the SAT or a similar admission test, the American College Testing Program (ACT). Scores on these tests play an important role in determining who is admitted to college. Applicants to law schools and medical schools must take special admission tests—the Law School Admissions Test (LSAT) and the Medical College Admissions Test (MCAT); many graduate-school departments require students to take the Graduate Record Exam (GRE). People applying to programs to be trained in most professions (dentistry, nursing, pharmacology and accounting, to name a few) must also take special admission tests. And once the training program is completed, more tests must be passed to obtain a license to practice or a certificate of competency. Becoming certified or licensed in almost every trade or profession requires the passage of a standardized examination. In addition, many industries and government agencies select job applicants and place or promote employees on the basis of test scores.

Since tests play such an important role in our lives, it is essential that they measure what they are intended to measure and that the scores accurately reflect the test taker's knowledge and skills. If a test is to be useful, its scores must be both *reliable* and *valid*.

### Reliability

Test scores are *reliable* when they are reproducible and consistent. Tests may be unreliable for a number of reasons. Confusing or ambiguous test items may mean different things to a test taker at different times. Tests may be too short to adequately sample the abilities being tested or scoring may be too subjective. If a test yields different results when it is administered on different occasions or scored by different people, it is unreliable. A simple analogy is a rubber yardstick. If we did not know how much it stretched each time we took a measurement, the results would be unreliable no matter how carefully we marked the measurement. Tests must be reliable if the results are to be used with confidence.

To evaluate **reliability,** two measures must be obtained for the same individual on the same test. This can be done by repeating the test, by giving the test in two different but equivalent forms, or by treating each half of the test separately. If each individual tested achieves roughly the same score on both measures, then the test is reliable. Of course, even for a reliable test, some differences are to be expected between the pair of scores due to chance and errors of measurement. Consequently, a statistical measure of the degree of relationship between the set of paired scores is needed. This degree of relationship is provided by the coefficient of correlation, *r* (discussed in Chapter 1). The coefficient of correlation between paired scores for a group of individuals on a given test is called a *reliability coefficient.* Well-constructed tests usually have a reliability coefficient of *r* = .90 or greater.

## Validity

Tests are *valid* when they measure what they are intended to measure. A college examination in economics that is full of questions containing complex or tricky wording might be a test of a student's verbal ability rather than of the economics learned in the course. Such an examination might be *reliable* (a student would achieve about the same score on a retest), but it would not be a *valid* test of achievement for the course. A test of sense of humor might be made up of jokes that are hard to understand unless the test taker is very bright and well read. This test might be a reliable measure of something (perhaps intelligence or educational achievement), but it would not be a valid test of humor.

To measure **validity,** we must also obtain two scores for each person: the test score and some other measure of the ability in question. This measure is called a *criterion.* Suppose that a test is designed to predict success in learning to type. To determine whether the test is valid, it is given to a group of individuals before they study typing. After completing the course, the students are tested on the number of words per minute that they can type accurately. This is a measure of their success and serves as a criterion. A coefficient of correlation between the early test scores and the scores on the criterion can now be obtained. This correlation coefficient, known as the *validity coefficient,* tells something about the value of a given test for a given purpose. The higher the validity coefficient, the more accurate the prediction that can be made from the test results.

Many tests, however, are intended to predict abilities that are more wide-ranging and difficult to measure than typing skills. Scores on the Medical College Admissions Test (MCAT), for example, are used (along with other information) to select medical students. If the purpose of the test is to predict success in medical school, a person's grade point average could be used as a criterion; correlating MCAT scores with grade point averages would be one way of validating the test. But if the MCAT is intended to predict success as a physician, the problem of validation becomes much more difficult. What criterion should be chosen: annual income, research achievements, contributions to community welfare, evaluation by patients or colleagues, number of malpractice suits? Even if the test administrators could agree on one of these criteria, that criterion would probably be difficult to measure.

The validity of ability tests—how well they predict performance—will be discussed later. The important point to remember here is that the evaluation of a test's validity must take into account the intended uses of the test and the inferences to be made from its scores.

## Uniform Procedure

To a large extent, the reliability and validity of a test depend on the uniformity of the procedures followed in administering and scoring the test. In measuring ability, as in obtaining any scientific measurement, we attempt to control conditions in order to minimize the influence of extraneous variables. Thus, well-accepted ability tests contain clearly specified instructions, time limits (or, in some cases, no time restrictions), and scoring methods. The explanations given by the examiner and the manner in which the examiner presents the test materials must be standard from one test administration to the next.

Of course, not all extraneous variables can be anticipated or controlled. The sex and race of the examiner, for example, will vary. These characteristics could influence a test taker's performance, as could the examiner's general demeanor (facial expression, tone of voice, and so on). Such variables cannot always be controlled and their potential influence should be taken into consideration in evaluating test results.

## Tests of Intellectual Ability

Reliability, validity, and uniform testing procedures are essential requirements for any test—whether the test is designed to measure personality characteristics (to be discussed in Chapter 14), mastery of a specific subject matter, job skills, or the probability of succeeding in college or professional school. This chapter focuses primarily on tests that measure general intellectual ability. Such tests are often called "intelligence tests," but as we noted earlier, many psychologists consider that term inappropriate. There is no general agreement as to what constitutes intelligence, and intelligence cannot be considered apart from an individual's culture and experiences. During this discussion of intelligence tests, these qualifications should be kept in mind.

## Historical Background

The first person to attempt to develop tests of intellectual ability was Sir Francis Galton a century ago. A naturalist and mathematician, Galton developed an interest in individual differences from the evolutionary theory of his cousin, Charles Darwin. Galton believed that certain families are biologically superior—stronger and smarter—than others. Intelligence, he reasoned, is a question of exceptional sensory and perceptual skills, which are passed from one generation to the next. Since all information is acquired

*Alfred Binet with his daughters*

through the senses, the more sensitive and accurate an individual's perceptual apparatus, the more intelligent the person. In 1884, Galton administered a battery of tests (measuring such variables as head size, reaction time, visual acuity, auditory thresholds, and memory for visual forms) to over 9,000 visitors at the London Exhibition. To his disappointment, he discovered that eminent British scientists could not be distinguished from ordinary citizens on the basis of their head size and that measurements such as speed of reaction were not particularly related to other measures of intelligence. Although his tests did not prove very useful, Galton did invent the correlation coefficient, which plays an important role in psychology.

The first tests that approximated contemporary intelligence tests were devised by the French psychologist Alfred Binet. In 1881, the French government passed a law making school attendance compulsory for all children. Previously, slow learners had usually been kept at home; now teachers had to cope with a wide range of individual differences. The government asked Binet to create a test that would detect children who were too slow intellectually to benefit from a regular school curriculum.

Binet assumed that intelligence should be measured by tasks that required reasoning and problem-solving abilities rather than perceptual-motor skills. In collaboration with another French psychologist, Théophile Simon, Binet published a scale in 1905, which he revised in 1908 and again in 1911.

## Binet's Method: A Mental-Age Scale

Binet reasoned that a slow or dull child was like a normal child retarded in mental growth. On tests, the slow child would perform like a normal child of younger age, whereas the mental abilities of a bright child were characteristic of older children. Binet devised a scale of test items of increasing difficulty that measured the kinds of changes in intelligence ordinarily associated with growing older. The higher a child could go on the scale in correctly answering the items, the higher his or her **mental age** (MA). The concept of mental age was critical in Binet's method; using this method, one could compare the MA of a child with his or her **chronological age** (CA) as determined by date of birth.

The scoring system for computing MA was structured so that the *average* MA for a large sample of children of a particular CA, in fact, equalled that CA. For example, the average MA for all 10-year-olds equalled 10 years, but for any particular 10-year-old, his or her MA could be below, equal to, or above 10 years. Thus a bright child's MA is above his or her CA; a slow child's MA is below his or her CA. This type of mental-age scale is easily interpreted by teachers and others who deal with children of differing mental abilities.

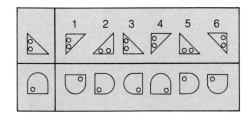

**FIGURE 12-2**
**Novel Items Used in Intelligence Tests** *The following instructions accompany the test: Mark every card to the right that matches the sample card on the left. You can rotate the sample card but not flip it over. (Cards 2, 3, and 6 are correct in the first line; cards 1, 3, and 5 are correct in the second line.)*

**ITEM SELECTION** Since intelligence tests are designed to measure brightness rather than the results of special training (that is, aptitude more than achievement), they should consist of items that do not assume any special training. There are two chief ways to select such items. One way is to choose *novel items*, which provide an uneducated child with just as much chance to succeed as a child who has been taught at home or in school. Figure 12-2 illustrates novel items; in this particular test, the child is asked to choose figures that are alike, on the assumption that the designs are unfamiliar to all children. The other way is to choose *familiar items*, on the assumption that all those for whom the test is designed have had the requisite prior experience to deal with the items. The following problem provides an example of a supposedly familiar item:

> Mark F *if the sentence is foolish; mark S if it is sensible.*
>
> S F  Mrs. Smith has had no children, and I understand that the same was true of her mother.

Of course, this item is fair only for children who know the English language, who can read, and who understand all the words in the sentence. For such children, detection of the fallacy in the statement becomes a valid test of intellectual ability.

Many of the items on intelligence tests assume general knowledge and familiarity with the language of the test. But such assumptions can never be strictly met. The language spoken in one home is never exactly the same as that spoken in another; the available reading material and the stress on cognitive abilities also vary. Even the novel items test perceptual discriminations that may be acquired in one culture and not in another. Despite these difficulties, items can be chosen that work reasonably well. The items included in contemporary intelligence tests have survived in practice after many others have been tried and found defective. It should be remembered, however, that intelligence tests have been validated according to their success in predicting school performance within a particular culture.

**STANFORD-BINET INTELLIGENCE SCALE**  The test items originally developed by Binet were adapted for American schoolchildren by Lewis Terman at Stanford University. He standardized the administration of the

*[handwritten margin notes:]* values roles does not determine the role of another

Western concept that does not justify the of other cultures inconsistent Discriminatory, unfair, can be found to be defective

*Test materials from the 1986 Stanford-Binet Intelligence Scale*

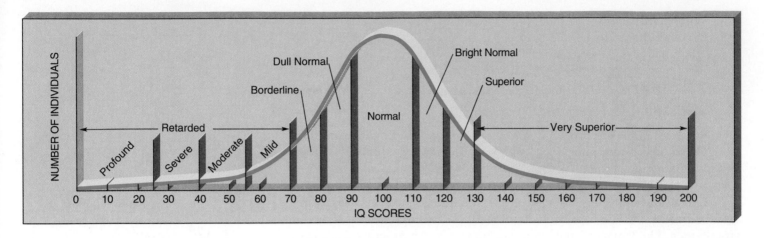

**FIGURE 12-3**

**IQ Distribution** *The distribution of IQ scores expected for a large sample of individuals and the adjectives used to describe various levels of IQ. An IQ between 90 and 110 is judged to be normal; above 130, very superior; and below 70, retarded.*

test and developed age-level norms by giving the test to thousands of children. In 1916, he published the Stanford revision of the Binet tests, now referred to as the Stanford-Binet Intelligence Scale; it was revised in 1937, 1960, 1972, and most recently in 1986.

Terman retained Binet's concept of mental age. Each test item was age-graded at the level at which a substantial majority of the children passed it. A child's mental age could be obtained by summing the number of items passed at each age level. In addition, Terman adopted a convenient index of intelligence suggested by the German psychologist William Stern. This index is the **intelligence quotient,** commonly known as the IQ. It expresses intelligence as a ratio of mental age (MA) to chronological age (CA):

$$IQ = \frac{MA}{CA} \times 100$$

The 100 is used as a multiplier so that the IQ will have a value of 100 when MA is equal to CA. If MA is lower than CA, then the IQ will be less than 100; if MA is higher than CA, then the IQ will be more than 100.

How is the IQ to be interpreted? The distribution of IQs approximates the form of curve found for many differences among individuals, such as differences in height; this bell-shaped **normal distribution curve** is shown in Figure 12-3. Most cases cluster around a midvalue on the normal curve; from there, the number gradually decreases to just a few cases at both extremes. The adjectives commonly used to describe various IQ levels are also shown in the figure.*

## Testing Specific Mental Abilities

The Stanford-Binet uses an assortment of different types of items to test intelligence. Until the 1986 revision, all items contributed equally to the total IQ score. A child might perform very well on a test of vocabulary but poorly on a test requiring drawing geometric forms. These strengths and weaknesses might be noted by the examiner but would not be reflected in

---

*The most recent revision of the Stanford-Binet (Thorndike, Hagen, & Sattler, 1986) uses Standard Age Scores, instead of IQ scores. These can be interpreted in terms of percentiles which show the percent of subjects in the standardization group falling above or below a given score.

*Expectation based on the perception of the researcher or the*

## VERBAL REASONING

**Vocabulary**   Defines words, such as "dollar" and "envelope."

**Comprehension**   Answers questions, such as "Where do people buy food?" and "Why do people comb their hair?"

**Absurdities**   Identifies the "funny" aspect of a picture, such as a girl riding a bicycle on a lake or a bald man combing his head.

**Verbal Relations**   Tells how the first three items in a sequence are alike and how they differ from the fourth: scarf, tie, muffler, shirt.

## QUANTITATIVE REASONING

**Quantitative**   Performs simple arithmetic tasks, such as selecting a die with six spots because the number of spots equals the combination of a two-spot die and a four-spot die.

**Number Series**   Gives the next two numbers in a series, such as

$$20 \quad 16 \quad 12 \quad 8 \quad \underline{\quad} \quad \underline{\quad}.$$

**Equation Building**   Builds an equation from the following array:

$2 \ 3 \ 5 \ + \ =.$ One correct response would be $2 + 3 = 5$.

## ABSTRACT/VISUAL REASONING

**Pattern Analysis**   Copies a simple design with blocks.

**Copying**   Copies a geometrical drawing demonstrated by the examiner, such as a rectangle intersected by two diagonals.

## SHORT-TERM MEMORY

**Bead Memory**   Shown a picture of different-shaped beads stacked on a stick. Reproduces the sequence from memory by placing real beads on a stick.

**Memory for Sentences**   Repeats after the examiner sentences such as "It is time to go to sleep" and "Ken painted a picture for his mother's birthday."

**Memory for Digits**   Repeats after the examiner a series of digits, such as 5-7-8-3, forward and backward.

**Memory for Objects**   Shown pictures of individual objects, such as a clock and an elephant, one at a time. Identifies the objects in the correct order of their appearance in a picture that also includes extraneous objects; for example, a bus, a clown, an *elephant*, eggs, and a *clock*.

**TABLE 12-3**
**Stanford-Binet Items** *Typical examples of items from the 1986 Stanford-Binet Intelligence Scale for a 6- to 8-year-old.*

Some are more alert than others what does not necessarily mean intelligence is the major contributor to the situation. One's perception of how "the pictures" are visualizes add effect to the relative issue at hand.

By performing in the acceptable & appropriate manner then this could only be the reason for the "right" result

Strength & weaknesses as seen by the examiner may/ could not be reflected in the IQ score as a specific answer is required

the IQ score. In line with the current view of intelligence as a composite of different abilities, the 1986 revision groups its tests into four broad areas of intellectual abilities: *verbal reasoning, abstract/visual reasoning, quantitative reasoning,* and *short-term memory* (Sattler, 1988). A separate score is obtained for each area; Table 12-3 gives some examples of items, grouped by area.

**WECHSLER INTELLIGENCE SCALES** One of the first intelligence tests to measure separate abilities was developed by David Wechsler in 1939; it ranks with the Stanford-Binet as one of the best known intelligence

| TEST | DESCRIPTION |
| --- | --- |
| **VERBAL SCALE** | |
| Information | Questions tap a general range of information; for example, "How many nickels make a dime?" |
| Comprehension | Tests practical information and ability to evaluate past experience; for example, "What is the advantage of keeping money in a bank?" |
| Arithmetic | Verbal problems testing arithmetic reasoning. |
| Similarities | Asks in what way certain objects or concepts (for example, *egg* and *seed*) are similar; measures abstract thinking. |
| Digit span | A series of digits presented auditorily (for example, 7-5-6-3-8) is repeated in a forward or backward direction; tests attention and rote memory. |
| Vocabulary | Tests word knowledge. |
| **PERFORMANCE SCALE** | |
| Digit symbol | A timed coding task in which numbers must be associated with marks of various shapes; tests speed of learning and writing. |
| Picture completion | The missing part of an incompletely drawn picture must be discovered and named; tests visual alertness and visual memory. |
| Block design | Pictured designs must be copied with blocks; tests ability to perceive and analyze patterns. |
| Picture arrangement | A series of comic-strip pictures must be arranged in the right sequence to tell a story; tests understanding of social situations. |
| Object assembly | Puzzle pieces must be assembled to form a complete object; tests ability to deal with part - whole relationships. |

**TABLE 12-4**
**Tests Composing the Wechsler Adult Intelligence Scale** *The tests of the Wechsler Intelligence Scale for Children are similar with some modifications.*

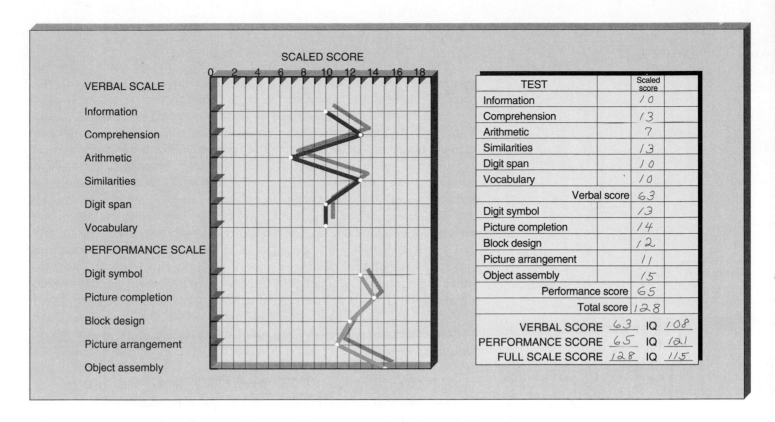

| TEST | | Scaled score |
|---|---|---|
| Information | | 10 |
| Comprehension | | 13 |
| Arithmetic | | 7 |
| Similarities | | 13 |
| Digit span | | 10 |
| Vocabulary | | 10 |
| | Verbal score | 63 |
| Digit symbol | | 13 |
| Picture completion | | 14 |
| Block design | | 12 |
| Picture arrangement | | 11 |
| Object assembly | | 15 |
| | Performance score | 65 |
| | Total score | 128 |

| | | | |
|---|---|---|---|
| VERBAL SCORE | 63 | IQ | 108 |
| PERFORMANCE SCORE | 65 | IQ | 121 |
| FULL SCALE SCORE | 128 | IQ | 115 |

**FIGURE 12-4**
**Profile for Wechsler Adult Intelligence Scale** *The table on the right shows the test scores for a 16-year-old male combined to yield verbal, performance, and full-scale scores. The manual that accompanies the test provides tables (adjusted for age) for use in converting these scores into IQs. Note that the test taker's performance IQ is 13 points above his verbal IQ.*

tests. Wechsler originally developed his test because he felt the Stanford-Binet was not appropriate for adults, and also he felt it depended too heavily on language ability. The Wechsler Adult Intelligence Scale, or WAIS (1939, 1955, 1981), is divided into two parts—a *verbal* scale and a *performance* scale—which yield separate scores as well as a full-scale IQ. The test items are described in Table 12-4. A similar test for children, the Wechsler Intelligence Scale for Children (WISC), was developed later (1958, 1974, 1991).

Items on the performance scale require the manipulation or arrangement of blocks, pictures, or other materials. The Wechsler scales also provide scores for each of the subtests, so the examiner has a clearer picture of the individual's intellectual strengths and weaknesses. For example, separate scores can indicate how well the person performs under pressure (some subtests are timed; others are not) or how verbal skills compare with the ability to manipulate nonverbal material. Figure 12-4 shows a test profile and how scores are summed to yield IQs. The subject who obtained these particular scores tends to do better on performance (nonverbal) tasks. Looking at the profile of scores, this 16-year-old does not appear to be doing as well scholastically as he could be; he has relatively low scores on subtests that tend to be good predictors of school learning (information, arithmetic, and vocabulary). A discrepancy between verbal and performance scores prompts the examiner to look for specific learning problems, such as reading disabilities or language handicaps.

Both the Stanford-Binet and the Wechsler scales meet the requirements for a good test; that is, they show good reliability and validity. The Stanford-Binet scale has a reliability coefficient of about .90 on retest; the WAIS has a retest reliability of .91. Both tests are fairly valid predictors of achievement in school; the correlation between IQ scores on these tests and school grades is approximately .50 (Sattler, 1988).

## Group Tests

The Stanford-Binet and the Wechsler scales are *individual ability tests;* that is, they are administered to a single individual by a specially trained tester. *Group ability tests,* in contrast, can be administered to a large number of people by a single examiner and are usually in pencil-and-paper form (see Figure 12-5). The advantages of an individual test over a group test are many. The tester can be certain the subject understands the questions, can evaluate the person's motivation (is the subject really trying?), and can gain additional clues to intellectual strengths and weaknesses by carefully observing the subject's approaches to different tasks. Group ability tests are useful, however, when large numbers of people have to be evaluated. The armed services, for example, use a number of group tests that measure general intellectual ability and special skills to help select men and women for special jobs, including pilots, navigators, electronic technicians, and computer programmers. Similarly, the Professional and Administrative Career Examination (PACE) was developed by the U.S. Civil Service Commission for use in selecting employees for government jobs.

Other examples of group tests used to measure general ability are the Scholastic Aptitude Test (SAT), developed by the Princeton-based Educational Testing Service, and the American College Test (ACT), developed by the Iowa-based American College Testing Program. Virtually all 4-year colleges require that applicants take either the ACT or SAT as a way of setting a common standard for students from high schools with different curricula and grading standards. The SAT is used mostly by colleges on the East and West coasts, whereas the ACT is dominant in the Midwest, Southeast, and Rocky Mountains.

The SAT has two sections of multiple-choice items, one testing verbal skills and the other mathematical skills (see Table 12-1 and Table 12-2). However, the developers of the SAT will introduce a major revision of their test in the spring of 1994. The revision will involve a new essay section, open-ended (rather than multiple-choice) mathematics questions, and enough additional algebra items to provide two mathematics' subscores. The changes are seen as a way of a) providing students with more detailed feedback on their performance; b) increasing the usefulness of the test for educators and others who use it for student counseling and course placement; and c) comparing the effectiveness of different high schools.

In past years, the ACT consisted of subtests in English, mathematics, social studies, and the natural sciences; students received scores in each of these four areas as well as a composite score. In 1989, the ACT test-developers revised the number of subtests to 12. These include an expanded mathematics section with more than one subscore, a new reading test, an English section that places more emphasis on writing skills, and separate science reasoning tests for biology, chemistry, physics, and the physical sciences. The tests require minimal knowledge of these subjects. Instead, they use graphs, tables, and summaries of research to measure how well students can deal with abstract concepts.

The changes in the SAT and ACT are in response to recent high-school curriculum trends that place a premium on more sophisticated reading, writing, and mathematics skills. Standards are being raised in the nation's high schools, and there is an increased emphasis on abstract thinking and reasoning skills.

## Space Perception

Which of the four patterns would result when the box is unfolded?

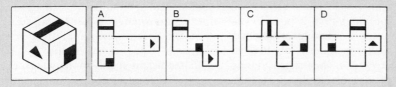

## Mechanical Comprehension

Which bridge is the strongest?

## Word Knowledge

**Stench** most nearly means

A. Puddle of slimy water.
B. Pile of debris.
C. Foul odor.
D. Dead animal.

**Camaraderie** most nearly means

A. Interest in photography.
B. Close friendship.
C. Petty jealousies.
D. Arts and crafts projects.

## General Information

For which of the following taxes was it necessary to amend the U.S. Constitution?

A. Income.
B. Sales.
C. Liquor.
D. Tobacco.

Picasso was a famous

A. poet.
B. painter.
C. philosopher.
D. soldier.

## Arithmetic Reasoning

It cost $0.50 per square yard to waterproof canvas. What will it cost to waterproof a canvas truck cover that is 15′ x 24′?

A. $6.67
B. $18.00
C. $20.00
D. $180.00

The parcel post rate in the local zone is 18 cents for the first pound and 1½ cents for each additional pound. How many pounds can be sent in the local zone for $1.50?

A. 88
B. 89
C. 100
D. 225

**FIGURE 12-5**
**Group Test** *These are sample items from the Armed Services Vocational Aptitude Battery (ASVAB), the basic recruit selection and placement test used by all military services.*

## *Coaching and Test Sophistication*

Courses that claim to improve an applicant's score on such admissions tests as the Scholastic Aptitude Test (SAT), the Law School Admissions Test (LSAT), the Medical College Admissions Test (MCAT), the Graduate Record Examination (GRE), and the Graduate Management Aptitude Test (GMAT) are offered daily in the newspapers. Coaching for such tests has become a profitable business. The degree to which coaching can improve test scores, however, is a controversial issue: if coaching does result in higher scores, applicants who can afford to pay for such courses have an advantage over those who cannot.

Being familiar with testing procedures is clearly helpful. An individual who has had prior experience in taking tests and who knows what to expect will be more confident than a person who has had limited test-taking experience. *Test sophistication* includes being familiar with separate answer sheets, considering *all* the answers in a multiple-choice item rather than picking the first one that seems right, knowing not to spend too much time on puzzling items, and spotting flaws in items that provide additional clues. It also helps to know when to guess. If there is no penalty for incorrect answers, it makes sense to guess when you do not know the correct answer. On tests such as the SAT, where a wrong answer on a four-choice item is scored –1/4 (compared to 1 point for a correct answer and 0 for no response), it pays to guess if the answer can be narrowed to two or three possible alternatives.

Instruction in test-taking strategies and practice with sample test questions are included in most courses that prepare applicants for admissions tests. Commercially published practice booklets, available for the major admissions tests, can be used for a similar kind of self-coaching. Familiarity with the test format, knowledge of test-taking strategies, and practice on sample test items do result in higher test scores, but the gain is substantial only for naive test takers (for example, recent immigrants or students from schools that require little testing). Students who have graduated from American high schools, which provide substantial exposure to objective tests, probably would not benefit from spending more than a day on practice test items.

What about instruction in specific subjects? Admissions tests are designed to measure an individual's aptitude for a particular program of study, and test constructors try to avoid items on which performance can be raised by short-term drill or instruction in specialized topics. However, the verbal section of the SAT (and of the LSAT, MCAT, and GRE) relies heavily on vocabulary, and many of the problems in the quantitative section presume knowledge of high-school alge-

## Predictive Validity

Tests of general ability, such as the Stanford-Binet and Wechsler Intelligence Scales, do predict achievement in school and do provide a measure of what most people think of as brightness. When elementary-school teachers are asked to rank children in their classrooms in terms of brightness, correlations between the teachers' rankings and scores on intelligence tests range from .60 to .80. These correlations would probably be higher except for some interesting biases in judgment. For example, teachers tend to overrate the youngest children in their classrooms and underrate the oldest; apparently, they base their judgments on mental age rather than on IQ, which expresses the relationship between mental age and chronological age. Teachers also tend to overrate girls and underrate boys. In general, children who are sociable, eager, and self-confident—who volunteer for activities and raise their hands to recite—are viewed by their teachers and peers as brighter than children who are withdrawn and quiet, even though their test scores may be the same. In such instances, ability test scores provide a more accurate estimate of ability than the teacher's judgments.

### Test Scores and Academic Performance

Intelligence test scores correlate highly with various measures of academic performance (for example, grades, continuation in school, likelihood of graduating). Youngsters who achieve higher scores on tests like the Stan-

bra and geometry. For individuals who feel deficient in these subjects, a review would be worthwhile. Several studies have shown that coaching in mathematics raises scores on the quantitative section of the SAT for high-school students who are not currently studying math, but it is of little benefit for those enrolled in mathematics courses. Vocabulary flashcards and reading with the aid of a dictionary would be helpful in preparing for the verbal section.

Over the past 30 years, numerous studies have been conducted to determine the effects of coaching on SAT scores. The studies covered a variety of coaching methods and included commercial programs as well as programs offered to students in public and private high schools. The results vary markedly, depending on the length and type of program and the presence or absence of a control group. (Control groups are important because students who enroll in coaching courses are apt to differ from those who do not in a number of ways—especially in level of motivation— and it is difficult to evaluate their test-score gains without referring to a comparable group of students.)

Messick and Jungeblut (1981) have published an analysis of research studies on SAT coaching that include control groups. They conclude that 30 hours of instruction in verbal skills, for instance, can result in average score gains of about 14 points on the verbal section of the SAT. An additional 30 hours of instruction in mathematics skills can result in average score gains of about 26 points on the mathematics section. These gains from 60 hours of instruction represent 40 points on the combined SAT scale. Since SAT scores range from a minimum of 400 to a maximum of 1600, gains of this size are not likely to affect college admission decisions. A subsequent study by Der Simonian and Laird (1983) comes to similar conclusions.

Several studies (without control groups) report much larger gains of 50–80 points on both sections of the SAT (Pallone, 1961; Marron, 1965). However, the subjects in these studies were enrolled in fairly intensive, long-term coaching programs of up to 6 months. The issue here is the difference between *education* and *coaching*. The SAT is designed to assess *developed* abilities. One year of high-school courses in English and algebra does increase SAT scores; it is not surprising that a 6-month coaching course produces a similar effect (Jones, 1984).

What recommendations should be made regarding coaching for admissions tests? For purposes of equity, a brief course in test strategies plus practice on sample test items under examination conditions would help to equalize test sophistication among individuals who have different amounts of experience in taking objective tests. Reviews of vocabulary and of algebra and geometry skills would probably benefit individuals whose background in these areas is deficient. It is probably not worthwhile for people with a normal high-school education to spend a great deal of time or money on coaching courses.

ford-Binet and Wechsler Intelligence Scales get better grades, enjoy school more, stay in school longer, and in later life tend to have greater job success (Barrett & Depinet, 1991). But as students move up the educational ladder—from elementary school to high school to college to graduate school— the correlations between intelligence test scores and measures of academic performance become progressively lower (see Table 12-5). A number of factors contribute to the progressive decrease in the size of validity coefficients as schooling increases. We will see shortly that one of the most important factors is *selection*.

Thus far, we have talked about the relationship between academic performance and tests designed to measure general aptitude for learning (so-called intelligence tests that yield an IQ score). What about scholastic aptitude tests, like the SAT, that measure developed abilities and are designed to predict performance in college? The SAT has been given to millions of college applicants over many years, and numerous studies have correlated SAT scores with freshman grade point averages. The correlations vary from study to study, with a median correlation of about .38 for the verbal section of the SAT and .34 for the mathematics section (Linn, 1982).

These correlations underestimate to some extent the relationship between test scores and college grades, because the criterion data (grade point averages) are collected only for those individuals who actually attend college. If everyone who took the SAT attended college, and the test scores were correlated with his or her freshman grades, the correlations would be much higher. The size of a correlation coefficient is affected by the amount

| EDUCA-TIONAL LEVEL | TYPICAL CORRELA-TIONS |
| --- | --- |
| Elementary School | .60–.70 |
| High School | .50–.60 |
| College | .40–.50 |
| Graduate School | .30–.40 |

**TABLE 12-5**
**Correlation between IQ Scores and Academic Achievement** *Table entries give the correlations typically observed between intelligence test scores obtained at a particular educational level and other measures of academic performance.*

of variability in the measures being correlated; in general, the more select the group, the narrower the range of scores and the lower the correlation. College students are more capable than the population at large. If the entire college-age population were tested and attended college, the correlation between test scores and freshman grades would be higher still.

An example may help to explain why correlations are lower in a selected group. Before there were weight classifications in the sport of boxing, weight was a fairly good predictor of the outcome of a match. A 250-pound boxer could usually defeat a 150-pounder, regardless of differences in training; the correlation between weight and winning was quite high. However, once weight classifications were introduced and boxers fought only boxers of similar weight (heavyweights against heavyweights, lightweights against lightweights, and so on), weight became a poor predictor of outcome.

Although the effects of selection on correlations between SAT scores and grades are less extreme than in the above example, they still can be substantial. For instance, for colleges with freshman classes that show a wide range of scores on the SAT, the correlation between SAT scores and freshman grade point averages is .44. For colleges with less variability, the correlation is .31 (Schrader, 1971). The more select or homogeneous the group is, the lower the correlation.

If correlations between SAT scores and freshman grades are "corrected" statistically to take into account the selective nature of the population, the resulting correlations are around .50. What does correlation of this size mean in terms of predictability? A correlation of .50 indicates that the chances are 44 out of 100 that a student in the top fifth of the distribution of SAT scores will also be in the top fifth of the distribution of freshman grade point averages, whereas the chances that a student in the bottom fifth of the SAT scores will earn such grades are only 4 out of 100. With no knowledge of the test scores, the chances would, of course, be 20 out of 100. Thus, SAT scores improve prediction considerably, but it is also clear that the freshman grades of students with identical SAT scores will vary widely.

## Group Differences in Test Performance

Differences in average performance on ability tests are often found when certain subgroups of the population are studied. For example, children from middle- or upper-income families score higher, on the average, than children from poor families. Mean differences are found in performance on tests of general ability as well as on achievement tests, whether the group of children is defined in terms of parental occupation, education, or income (Speath, 1976). Members of some minority groups—African Americans, Hispanic Americans, American Indians—also tend to score lower on ability tests than Asian Americans or whites (see Table 12-6).

Two points should be emphasized whenever group differences are discussed. First, these are only *average* differences; the size of the differences between subgroups is usually small compared to the variability within groups. Thus, some girls will score higher than most boys on tests of spatial relations; conversely, some boys will score lower than most girls. Similarly, some children from poor families will score higher than most children from higher-income families, and some members of minority groups will score higher than most whites.

Second, group differences in average test scores cannot be viewed as evidence of innate differences in ability. They may reflect differences in home

|  | VERBAL SECTION | MATHEMATICAL SECTION |
|---|---|---|
| Men | 429 | 499 |
| Women | 419 | 455 |
|  |  |  |
| American Indian | 388 | 437 |
| Asian American | 410 | 528 |
| African American | 352 | 385 |
| Mexican American | 380 | 429 |
| Puerto Rican | 359 | 405 |
| Other Hispanic | 383 | 434 |
| White | 442 | 491 |
| Other | 410 | 467 |
|  |  |  |
| All | 424 | 476 |

**TABLE 12-6**
**Group SAT Scores** *Average Scholastic Aptitude Test scores for 1990 by sex and racial and ethnic group. The group averages are based on a total of 1,025,523 high-school seniors who took the SAT. Each section of the SAT is scored on a scale from 200 to 800.* (The College Board)

environment, social expectations, and opportunities to learn. However, to the extent that group differences in average test scores reflect differences in the probability of success in school or on the job, the distinctions need to be understood.

Later we will discuss some possible reasons for differences in test performance among racial, ethnic, and socioeconomic groups. But the existence of group differences does not mean that tests are not useful for predicting performance. Ability tests predict scholastic performance for minority students as well as they do for white students. For example, if African American grade-school children are ranked according to scores on an intelligence test, the rankings predict school performance as well as they do for white children (Barrett and Depinet, 1991). And SAT scores predict college freshman grades for African Americans and Mexican Americans as well as they do for whites (Linn, 1982).

Saying that ability tests are not biased does not deny that society discriminates against minority groups. There is a bias in opportunity against minority groups that results in their lower scores on ability tests and on the criterion measure (grades, class standing, and so forth).

## Using Tests to Predict Performance

Although ability tests are useful in predicting academic performance, they are only one measure and should be used in combination with other information. For example, senior-year high-school grades correlate about as highly with freshman grade point averages as SAT scores do. This fact raises some questions about the usefulness of admissions tests. However, it can be argued that college admission test scores provide an adjustment for the variability in the quality of education among different high schools (grades from one high school may not be equivalent to grades from another). Indeed, a combination of SAT scores and high-school grades does predict college grades better than either of these variables alone.

## Sex Differences in Specific Abilities

Males and females score about the same on intelligence tests (such as the Stanford-Binet and the Wechsler Intelligence Scales). Most intelligence tests have been constructed to minimize sex differences either by deleting items showing large sex differences or by balancing items advantageous to females with those advantageous to males.

Until recently, however, tests of specific abilities have shown some differences between the sexes. Females, *on the average,* have scored higher than males on tests of verbal ability; males, *on the average,* have scored higher than females on tests of mathematical reasoning and visual-spatial skills. Visual-spatial skills are required in tasks such as conceptualizing how an object in space would look from a different perspective and reading maps or blueprints (see figure).

These sex differences in cognitive abilities, which have been observed almost since the beginning of systematic testing, appear to be vanishing. An analysis of more than 3 decades (from 1947 to 1980) of scores on tests of specific abilities given to high-school students nationwide found that differences between boys and girls decreased progressively over that period (Feingold, 1988).

A recent analysis that looked at hundreds of studies of sex differences in ability conducted during the last 20 years reached similar conclusions: male verbal proficiency has been increasing over the years to match that of females, while female ability on tests of mathematical reasoning has been increasing to match that of males (Hyde & Linn, 1988; Linn & Hyde, 1989). The one test that continues to show differences in these abilities is the SAT; males and females score about the same on the verbal section, but males score significantly higher on the mathematical section.

The fact that sex differences in cognitive ability have decreased over the years suggests that earlier differences in test scores reflected differences in training and social expectations: until recently, girls were encouraged to develop interests in poetry and literature; boys were expected to be more concerned with science and mechanical things. Although society has become more egalitarian and parents and teachers are less stereotyped in the abilities they encourage, there are still differences in the way the sexes are treated that may make girls less confident in mathematics. Parents still believe science and mathematics to be less important for girls than for boys; they tend to exaggerate their sons' abilities in these areas and to underestimate the abilities of their daughters. And they are more likely to purchase computers and scientific toys for boys than for girls.

Ability tests can provide a reasonably good indication of whether a person can read and comprehend certain material or solve quantitative problems. But tests cannot assess an individual's social concerns, willingness to work, or interpersonal skills. Tests provide some basis for predicting academic success, but they do not indicate which students will become creative writers, talented teachers, and outstanding physicians.

Scores on admissions tests provide one piece of information. They should be evaluated along with other measures (high-school grades, recommendations, special achievements) to predict an applicant's academic performance.

# Nature of Intelligence

Some psychologists view intelligence as a general capacity for comprehension and reasoning that manifests itself in various ways. This was Binet's assumption. Although his test contained many different kinds of items (testing such abilities as memory span, arithmetic skills, and vocabulary knowledge), Binet noted that bright children tended to score higher than dull children on all of them. He assumed, therefore, that the different tasks sampled a basic ability or faculty.

It seems to us that in intelligence there is a fundamental faculty, the alteration or the lack of which is of the utmost importance for practical life. This faculty is judgment, otherwise called good sense, practical sense, initiative, the faculty of adapting one's self to circumstances. To judge well, to comprehend well, to reason well, these are the essential activities of intelligence. (Binet & Simon, 1905)

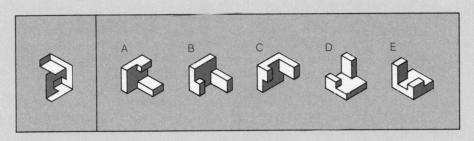

**Visual-Spatial Skills** *An example of the type of problem used to test for visual-spatial abilities. The testee is required to select from the five blocks on the right the one that is the same as the block on the left, except that it has been rotated and presented from a different perspective. The correct answer is B.*

Teachers of science and mathematics also tend to provide more encouragement and reinforcement for boys than for girls (Eccles & Jacobs, 1986).

Thus, differences on the SAT math test may reflect sex differences in self-confidence. It appears too that some of the math questions are biased toward males by subject content. For example, they involve situations taken from sports with which males may be more familiar.

The one area of cognitive ability that continues to show a consistent sex difference is visual-spatial relations. Tests still show a superior performance for males in these skills, particularly when the tasks are timed and require mental rotation of objects (Burnett, 1986). Sex differences in spatial ability may partly account for sex differences in mathematical ability, since spatial visualization is one strategy for solving mathematical problems.

It will be interesting to see whether sex differences in spatial ability diminish in the years ahead as the environment for women changes. Some researchers think that this will be the case. Others believe that sex differences in visual-spatial abilities stem from the effect of sex hormones on the development of the brain during the fetal period. They propose that the ability to visualize objects mentally is related to the rate at which the two cerebral hemispheres develop; the male hormone, testosterone, presumably slows the development of the left hemisphere, resulting in a more highly specialized right hemisphere for males (Benbow, 1988). It remains to be seen whether the biological or the environmental explanation for sex differences in visual-spatial ability will prove to be correct.

Despite the diverse subscales that compose his tests, David Wechsler also believed that "intelligence is the aggregate or global capacity of the individual to act purposefully, to think rationally, and to deal effectively with his environment" (Wechsler, 1958).

## Factorial Approach

Other psychologists question whether there is such a thing as "general intelligence." They believe that intelligence tests sample a number of mental abilities that are relatively *independent of one another.* One method of obtaining more precise information about the kinds of abilities that determine performance on intelligence tests is **factor analysis.** This mathematical technique is used to determine the minimum number of *factors,* or abilities, that are required to explain the observed pattern of correlations for an array of different tests. The basic idea is that two tests that correlate very highly with each other are probably measuring the same underlying ability. The factor analysis of data from an array of tests tells us how many distinguishable factors enter the set of correlations and the weight (or influence) of each factor. Factor analysis is too complicated to describe in detail, but Table 12-7 provides a brief account of the method.

The originator of factor analysis, Charles Spearman (1904), proposed that all individuals possess a general intelligence factor (called $g$) in varying amounts. A person could be described as generally bright or generally dull, depending on the amount of $g$ he or she possessed. According to Spearman, the $g$ factor is the major determinant of performance on intelligence test

**TABLE 12-7**
**Factor Analysis** *An example of the data and major steps involved in factor analysis.*

What are the data that enter into factor analysis, and what are the major steps in the analysis? The data are simply scores on a variety of tests designed to measure various psychological contents or processes. Each of a large number of individuals obtains a score for each of a number of tests. All these scores can then be intercorrelated; that is, we know how the scores of many individuals on Test 1 relate to their scores on Test 2, and so on. These intercorrelations yield a table of correlations known as a *correlation matrix*. An example of such a correlation matrix, based on only nine tests, is given below.

| TESTS | 2 | 3 | 4 | 5 | 6 | 7 | 8 | 9 |
|---|---|---|---|---|---|---|---|---|
| 1 | .38 | .55 | .06 | −.04 | .05 | .07 | .05 | .09 |
| 2 | | .36 | .40 | .28 | .40 | .11 | .15 | .13 |
| 3 | | | .10 | .01 | .18 | .13 | .12 | .10 |
| 4 | | | | .32 | .60 | .04 | .06 | .13 |
| 5 | | | | | .35 | .08 | .13 | .11 |
| 6 | | | | | | .01 | .06 | .07 |
| 7 | | | | | | | .45 | .32 |
| 8 | | | | | | | | .32 |

The three gray boxes of correlations indicate that these are groups of tests with something in common not shared by other tests (that is, they show high correlations). The inadequacy of making such a judgment from a table of correlations of this kind is shown by noting the additional high correlations of Test 2 with Tests 4, 5, and 6, not included in the outlined clusters. We can use factor analysis to tell us more precisely what underlies these correlations. If the correlation matrix contains a number of statistically significant correlations and a number of near-zero correlations, it is apparent that some tests measure similar abilities of one kind and that others measure abilities of other kinds. The purpose of factor analysis is to be more precise about these underlying abilities.

Factor analysis then uses mathematical methods to compute the correlation of each of the tests with each of several possible underlying fac-

items. In addition, special factors, each called *s*, are specific to particular abilities or tests. For example, tests of arithmetic or spatial relationships would each tap a separate *s*. An individual's tested intelligence would reflect the amount of *g* plus the magnitude of the various *s* factors. Performance in mathematics would be a function of a person's general intelligence and mathematical aptitude.

A later investigator, Louis Thurstone (1938), objected to Spearman's emphasis on general intelligence. Thurstone felt that intelligence could be broken down into a number of primary abilities. To determine these abilities, he applied factor analysis to results from a large number of different tests. One set of test items was designed to measure verbal comprehension; another, to measure arithmetical computation; and so on. Thurstone hoped to find a more definitive way of grouping intelligence test items than the rather crude method of item sorting used in the Wechsler verbal and performance scales.

After intercorrelating the scores of all the tests (that is, correlating each test with every other test), Thurstone applied factor analysis to arrive at a set

tors. Such correlations between test scores and factors are known as *factor loadings;* if a test correlates .05 on factor I, .10 on factor II, and .70 on factor III, it is most heavily "loaded" on factor III. For example, the nine tests with the above correlation matrix yield the *factor matrix* below.

| TESTS | FACTORS | | |
|:---:|:---:|:---:|:---:|
| | **I** | **II** | **III** |
| 1 | .75 | −.01 | .08 |
| 2 | .44 | .48 | .16 |
| 3 | .72 | .07 | .15 |
| 4 | .08 | .76 | .08 |
| 5 | −.01 | .49 | −.01 |
| 6 | .16 | .73 | .02 |
| 7 | −.03 | .04 | .64 |
| 8 | .02 | .05 | .66 |
| 9 | −.01 | .10 | .47 |

The gray boxes in the factor matrix show which tests are most highly correlated with each of the underlying factors. The clusters are the same as the clusters in the correlation matrix but are now assigned greater precision. The problem of Test 2 remains because it is loaded almost equally on factor I and factor II; it is obviously not a "factor-pure" test. Having found the three factors that account for the intercorrelations of the nine tests, the factors can be interpreted by studying the content of the tests most highly weighted on each factor. The factor analysis itself is strictly a mathematical process, but the naming and interpretation of the factors depends on psychological considerations.

of basic factors. Test items that best represented each of the discovered factors were used to form new tests; these tests were then given to another group of subjects and the intercorrelations were reanalyzed. After several studies of this kind, Thurstone identified seven factors as the *primary mental abilities* revealed by intelligence tests: verbal comprehension, word fluency, number, space, memory, perceptual speed, and reasoning (see Table 12-8).

Thurstone devised a battery of tests, known as the *Test of Primary Mental Abilities,* to measure each of these abilities. Revised versions of this test are still widely used, but its predictive power is no greater than the predictability of general intelligence tests, such as the Wechsler scales. Thurstone's hope of discovering the basic elements of intelligence through factor analysis was not fully realized for several reasons. His primary abilities are not completely independent; the significant intercorrelations among them provide some support for Spearman's concept of a general intelligence factor. In addition, the number of basic abilities identified by factor analysis depends on the nature of the test items. Other investigators, using different test items and alternative methods of factor analysis, have identified from 20 to

150 factors to represent the range of intellectual abilities (Ekstrom, French, Harman, & Derman, 1976; Ekstrom, French, & Harman, 1979; Guilford, 1982). This lack of consistency in the number and kinds of factors raises doubts about the value of the *factorial approach*. Nevertheless, factor analysis continues to be a principal technique for studying intellectual performance (Carrol, 1988; Comrey & Lee, 1992).

## Information-Processing Approach

Until the 1960s, research on intelligence was dominated by the factorial approach. However, with the development of cognitive psychology and its emphasis on **information-processing models,** a new approach has emerged. This approach is defined somewhat differently by different investigators, but the basic idea is to try to understand intelligence in terms of the cognitive processes that operate when we engage in intellectual activities (Hunt, 1990; Carpenter, Just, & Shell, 1990). The information-processing approach asks:

1. What mental processes are involved in the various tests of intelligence?
2. How rapidly and accurately are these processes carried out?
3. What types of mental representations of information do these processes act upon?

Rather than trying to explain intelligence in terms of factors, this approach

**TABLE 12-8**
**Thurstone's Primary Mental Abilities** *Using factor analysis, Thurstone identified seven factors as the primary abilities revealed by intelligence tests.* (After Thurstone & Thurstone, 1963)

| ABILITY | DESCRIPTION |
| --- | --- |
| Verbal comprehension | The ability to understand the meaning of words; vocabulary tests represent this factor. |
| Word fluency | The ability to think of words rapidly, as in solving anagrams or thinking of words that rhyme. |
| Number | The ability to work with numbers and perform computations. |
| Space | The ability to visualize space-form relationships, as in recognizing the same figure presented in different orientations. |
| Memory | The ability to recall verbal stimuli, such as word pairs or sentences. |
| Perceptual speed | The ability to grasp details quickly and to see similarities and differences between pictured objects. |
| Reasoning | The ability to find a general rule on the basis of presented instances, as in determining how a number series is constructed after being presented with only a portion of that series. |

| COMPONENTS | PROCESSES |
|---|---|
| Metacomponents | Higher-order control processes used for executive planning and decision making in problem solving. |
| Performance components | Processes that execute the plans and implement the decisions selected by metacomponents. |
| Acquisition components | Processes involved in learning new information. |
| Retention components | Processes involved in retrieving information previously stored in memory. |
| Transfer components | Processes involved in carrying over retained information from one situation to another. |

**TABLE 12-9**
**Components of Intelligence** *Sternberg's scheme for classifying the many component processes operative in solving problems.* (After Sternberg, 1985)

attempts to identify the mental processes that underlie intelligent behavior. The information-processing approach assumes that individual differences on a given task depend on the specific processes that different individuals bring into play and the speed and accuracy of these processes. The goal is to use an information-processing model of a particular task to identify appropriate measures of the component processes. These measures may be as simple as the response to a multiple-choice item, or they may include the subject's speed of response, perhaps even eye movements and cortical evoked potentials associated with the response. The idea is to use whatever information is needed to estimate the efficiency of each component process.

The information-processing approach can be illustrated by the work of Sternberg (1985) and his *componential model* of intelligence. He assumes that the test taker possesses a set of mental processes, which he calls *components*, that operate in an organized way to produce the responses observed on an intelligence test. There are many components that fall into the five classes given in Table 12-9. Sternberg selects a specific task from an intelligence test and uses it in a series of experiments to try to identify the components involved in the task. For example, consider analogy tests of the following sort:

lawyer : client :: doctor : (medicine, patient)

A series of experiments with analogy problems led Sternberg to conclude that the critical components were the *encoding process* and the *comparison process*. The subject encodes each of the words in the analogy by forming a mental representation of the word—in this case, a list of attributes of the word that are retrieved from the subject's long-term memory. For example, a mental representation of the word "lawyer" might include the following attributes: college-educated, versed in legal procedures, represents clients in court, and so on. Once the subject has formed a mental representation for each word in the analogy, the comparison process scans the representations looking for matching attributes that solve the analogy.

Other processes are involved in analogy problems, but Sternberg has shown that individual differences on this task are principally determined by the efficiency of the encoding and comparison processes. The experimental

## Multiple Intelligences

Howard Gardner (1983) has proposed an approach to intelligence that is similar in many ways to the factorial and information-processing approaches. Nevertheless, his approach has so many unique features that it deserves special consideration.

According to Gardner, there is no such thing as a singular intelligence; rather, there are at least six distinct kinds of intelligence. These six intelligences are independent of one another, each operating as a separate system (or module) in the brain according to its own rules. The six intelligences are:

1. Linguistic
2. Logical-mathematical
3. Spatial
4. Musical
5. Bodily-kinesthetic
6. Personal

The first three are familiar components of intelligence, and Gardner's description of them is similar to what other theorists have proposed; they are what standard intelligence tests measure. The last three are surprising and may even seem irrelevant in a discussion of intelligence, but Gardner believes that they deserve comparable status to the first three. He argues that musical intelligence, for example, has been more important than logical-mathematical intelligence throughout most of human

history. The development of logical scientific thought occurred late in the evolution of the human species (as an invention of western culture in the aftermath of the Renaissance); in contrast, musical and artistic skills have been with us from the dawn of civilization.

Musical intelligence involves the ability to perceive pitch and rhythm and is the basis for the development of musical competence. Bodily-kinesthetic in-

evidence shows that individuals who score high on analogy problems (skilled performers) spend more time encoding and form more accurate mental representations than do individuals who score low on such problems (less-skilled performers). In contrast, during the comparison stage, the skilled performers are *faster* than the less-skilled performers in matching attributes, but both are *equally accurate*. Thus the better test scores for skilled performers are based on the increased accuracy of their encoding process, but the time they require to solve the problem is a complicated mix of slow encoding speeds and fast comparisons (Pellegrino, 1985; Galotti, 1989).

A factorial approach and an information-processing approach provide complementary interpretations of performance on intelligence tests. Factors such as Thurstone's primary mental abilities are useful in identifying broad areas of strengths and weaknesses. They may indicate that a person is strong in word fluency and verbal comprehension but weak in reasoning. If additional testing is conducted, an information-processing analysis could provide a diagnostic profile of the processes responsible for the observed deficiency. A process analysis may indicate a deficiency at the level of metacomponents

telligence involves the control of one's own body motions and the ability to manipulate and handle objects skillfully: examples are dancers and gymnasts, who develop precise control over movements of their body; or artisans, tennis players, and neurosurgeons, who are able to manipulate objects with finesse.

Personal intelligence has two components that can be regarded as separate—namely, intrapersonal and interpersonal intelligence. *Intra*personal intelligence is the ability to monitor one's own feelings and emotions, to discriminate among them and use the information to guide one's actions. *Inter*personal intelligence, on the other hand, is the ability to notice and understand the needs and intentions of other individuals and to monitor their moods and temperament as a way of predicting how they will behave in new situations.

Gardner analyzes each kind of intelligence from several viewpoints: the cognitive operations involved, the appearance of prodigies and other exceptional individuals, evidence from cases of brain damage, manifestations in different cultures, and the possible course of evolutionary development. Because of heredity or training, some individuals will develop certain intelligences more than others, but every normal person should develop each to some extent. The intelligences interact with, and build on, one another but still operate as

semi-autonomous systems. Each intelligence is an "encapsulated module" within the brain, operating according to its own rules and procedures; certain kinds of brain damage can impair one type of intelligence and have no effect on the others.

In western society, the first three types of intelligence are highly regarded; they are what standard intelligence tests measure. But historical and anthropological evidence suggests that other intelligences have been more highly valued at earlier periods in human history and even today in some non-western cultures. Further, the activities a culture emphasizes will influence how a specific intelligence develops: for example, a boy endowed with unusual bodily-kinesthetic intelligence may become a baseball player in the United States or a ballet dancer in Russia.

Gardner's ideas about personal, musical, and bodily-kinesthetic intelligences are provocative and will undoubtedly lead to new efforts to measure these abilities and to use them as predictors of other variables. As noted earlier, conventional IQ tests are good predictors of college grades, but they are not particularly useful in predicting performance in later life on such indices as job success or career advancement. Measures of other abilities, such as personal intelligence, may help explain why some people with brilliant college records fail miserably in

later life, while lesser students become charismatic leaders (Kornhaber, Krechevsky, & Gardner, 1990).

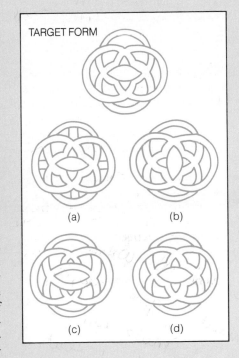

**Spatial Ability** *How quickly patterns can be matched is an indicator of spatial intelligence. From the array of four, choose the pattern that is identical to the target form.*

(such as the choice of strategies used to attack the problem), or retention components (such as slow or inaccurate recall of relevant information), or transfer components (such as poor ability to transfer what has been learned in one situation to another).

## Aspects of Intelligence

Sternberg (1985), in an attempt to generalize his approach, argues that a comprehensive theory of intelligence would involve a much larger set of component processes than have been identified to date by psychologists working in the restricted environment of a laboratory or a typical testing situation. He suggests that this larger set of components would relate not only to "academic intelligence" but also to "practical intelligence"; they would be organized in four clusters that might be labeled roughly as follows:

1.  Ability to learn and profit from experience
2.  Ability to think or reason abstractly

3. Ability to adapt to the vagaries of a changing and uncertain world
4. Ability to motivate oneself to accomplish expeditiously the tasks one needs to accomplish.

Other psychologists—whether working from the perspective of the factorial approach or the information-processing approach—would generally agree with this list. Most intelligence tests in use today are fairly effective in assessing the first two abilities, but they are of minimal value in assessing the last two. Undoubtedly, this is why conventional intelligence tests are effective in predicting academic achievement but are far less predictive of personal achievement outside the academic world. Our ability to measure intelligence with the type of tests in use today probably has reached a ceiling. New methods will have to be developed that assess motivation and practical problem-solving ability in order to improve the predictive power of intelligence tests.

# Genetic and Environmental Influences

People differ in intellectual ability. How much of this difference is due to the particular genes we inherit, and how much is due to the environment in which we are raised? The heredity-environment issue, which has been debated in regard to many aspects of human behavior, has focused primarily on the area of intelligence. Most experts agree that at least some aspects of intelligence are inherited, but opinions differ as to the relative contributions made by heredity and environment.

## Genetic Relationships and Intelligence

Most of the evidence bearing on the inheritance of intelligence is derived from studies correlating IQs between persons of various degrees of genetic relationship. Table 12-10 summarizes the results of over 100 studies of this type. In general, the closer the genetic relationship, the more similar the tested intelligence. The average correlation between the IQs of parents and their natural children is .40; between parents and their adopted children, the correlation is about .31. Identical twins, because they develop from a single egg, share precisely the same heredity; the correlation between their IQs is very high—about .86. The IQs of fraternal twins (who develop from separate eggs and are no more alike genetically than ordinary siblings) have a correlation coefficient of about .60.

Although genetic determinants of intelligence are strong, the results shown in Table 12-10 indicate that environment is also important. Note that when siblings are reared together—in the same home environment—IQ similarity increases. Other studies have shown that the intellectual ability of adopted children is higher than would be predicted on the basis of their natural parents' ability (Scarr & Weinberg, 1976). Environment does make a difference in intelligence.

It is possible to estimate what portion of the variability in test scores is due to environment and what portion is due to heredity from data similar to those given in Table 12-10. Several methods are used to make these estimates; the most common is to compare the variability of fraternal and identical twins on a given trait (Thompson, Detterman, & Plomin, 1991). To do this, two quantities are estimated: (a) the total variability due to both environment and heredity ($V_T$) is estimated from the observed differences between pairs of fraternal twins, and (b) the environmental variability alone ($V_E$) is estimated from the observed differences between pairs of identical twins. The difference between the two quantities ($V_G$) is the variability due to genetic factors (that is, $V_T = V_E + V_G$). The heritability ratio, or simply **heritability** (H), is the ratio between genetic variability and total variability:

$$H = \frac{V_G}{V_T}$$

In other words, heritability is the proportion of a trait's variation within a specified population that can be attributed to genetic differences. Heritability ranges between 0 and 1. When identical twins resemble each other much more than fraternal twins on a given trait, H approaches 1. When the resemblance between identical twins is about the same as the resemblance between fraternal twins on a given trait, H approaches 0.

There are a number of ways to estimate H other than comparing identical and fraternal twins. The theory that permits us to make such estimates is too lengthy to present here, but it is discussed in most genetics textbooks. For our purposes, it is sufficient to say that H measures the fraction of the observed variance in a population that is caused by differences in heredity. It is important to note that H refers to a **population** of individuals, not to a single individual. For example, height has an H of .90, which means that 90 percent of the variance in height observed in a population is due to genetic differences and 10 percent is due to environmental differences. (It does not mean that an individual who is 5 feet 10 inches tall grew to a height of 63 inches due to genetic factors and grew another 7 inches due to environmental factors). In discussing intelligence, H is often misused to designate the fraction of an individual's intelligence that is due to heredity; the use of the term in this way is incorrect.

Heritability estimates for intelligence have ranged widely from one study to another. Some researchers have reported values as high as .87; others, values as low as .10. For the data presented in Table 12-10, the estimate of H is approximately .50 (Chipuer, Rovine, & Plomin, 1989). The fact that heritability estimates vary so widely suggests that the research is plagued by a number of uncontrolled variables that influence the results in ways that cannot be specified. It must be kept in mind that heritability research is based on field studies and not on well-controlled laboratory experiments; individual cases are observed where they can be found. Field studies are always subject to the influence of uncontrolled variables and are particularly suspect when different investigators report quite different conclusions.

Complicating the situation further is the fact that assumptions made in assessing heritability may not always be correct (Plomin and Bergeman, 1991). In research on twins, for example, it is assumed that twins who are reared together experience roughly the same environment, whether they are fraternal or identical twins. But this may not be true. Identical twins look more alike than fraternal twins, and this fact alone may cause parents and others to treat them more alike than fraternal twins (for example, identical twins are more likely to be dressed in identical outfits than fraternal twins).

In the absence of better-controlled studies, a reliable estimate of heritability is not possible. Heredity clearly has an effect on intelligence, but the degree of this effect is uncertain. The findings on heritability do not define or limit what might be possible in a ideal environment. Rather, they indicate

| RELATIONSHIP | CORRELATION |
|---|---|
| Identical twins | |
|    Reared together | .86 |
|    Reared apart | .72 |
| Fraternal twins | |
|    Reared together | .60 |
| Siblings | |
|    Reared together | .47 |
|    Reared apart | .24 |
| Parent/child | .40 |
| Foster parent/child | .31 |
| Cousins | .15 |

**TABLE 12-10**
**Familial Studies of Intelligence** *A summary of more than 100 studies identified in a survey of the world literature on familial resemblances in measured intelligence. The data represent average correlation coefficients for IQ test scores between persons of various relationships. In general, the pattern of correlations indicates that the higher the proportion of genes two family members have in common, the higher the average correlation between their IQs. (After Bouchard, 1990)*

that, in the current societal environment, about one-half of the observed variance of IQ can be traced to genetic variation.*

## Environmental Influences

The environmental conditions that determine how an individual's intellectual potential will develop include nutrition, health, quality of stimulation, emotional climate of the home, and type of feedback elicited by behavior. Given two children with the same genes, the child with the better prenatal and postnatal nutrition, the more intellectually stimulating and emotionally secure home, and the more appropriate rewards for academic accomplishments will attain the higher IQ score when tested in first grade. For example, nutrition in early life can have a long-term influence on intelligence. In one study, the WISC was used to assess IQ at age 8 for a group of 300 children who had been born prematurely. During the initial weeks of life, the diet of these preterm infants was carefully monitored. The type of nutrients consumed during these early weeks had an effect of as much as ten points when IQ was tested eight years later (Lucas et al., 1992).

A review of nearly 200 studies charting IQ development indicates that IQ rises as individuals spend more time in school. Small but consistent decrements in IQ occur during summer vacation, especially among youngsters living in poor areas; children who attend school intermittently experience steadily declining IQs; and children who begin school late or who drop out have lower IQs than their peers. The studies suggest that the magnitude of the effect ranges from losing one-quarter of an IQ point to six IQ points per year of missed school (Ceci, 1991).

HEAD START PROGRAMS   Because children from underprivileged families tend to fall behind in cognitive development even before they enter school, efforts have been made to provide more intellectual stimulation for these children during their early years. In 1965, as part of President Johnson's War on Poverty, Congress authorized funds for a number of programs designed to provide learning experiences for 2- to 5-year-olds from poor homes. These programs, funded by Project Head Start, varied in approach. In some, special teachers visited the children at home several times a week to play with them. They engaged the children in such activities as building with blocks, looking at pictures, and naming colors, and they taught them such concepts as big–little and rough–smooth. In brief, the teachers provided the kind of intellectual stimulation that children in upper-class homes usually receive from their parents. The visiting teachers also taught the parents how to provide the same kinds of activities for their children. In other programs, the children attended special classes in which they inter-

---

*Progress in molecular genetics is occurring at such a fast pace that, by the next edition of this text, the discussion of genetic influences on intelligence may be quite different. Until recently, identifying the genes involved in cognitive ability seemed beyond the scope of modern science because of the number of genes involved and the fact that no single gene is expected to show a major effect. But all of this may change due to new techniques for marking genes and new methods for analyzing the effects of multiple genes on complex traits. Several studies are now in progress relating these new genetic techniques to performance on cognitive tests.

acted with teachers in similar play-learning activities. Some of these programs involved the parents; others did not.

In general, the results of these early education programs have been promising. Children who have participated in such programs score higher on the Stanford-Binet or WISC on entering first grade and tend to be more self-confident and socially competent than children who have not received special attention.

Follow-up studies years later indicate that early education programs produce some lasting benefits. For example, several studies have followed progress through high school of disadvantaged children who participated in special preschool programs when they were 3 years old. By the age of 15, these students were more than a full grade ahead of a matched control group of students who had received no preschool experience. In addition, compared with the control group, the students with preschool experience (a) scored higher on tests of reading, arithmetic, and language usage; (b) were less apt to need special remedial classes; (c) exhibited less antisocial behavior; and (d) were more likely to hold after-school jobs (Hohmann, Banet, & Weikart, 1979; Palmer & Anderson, 1979; Lazar & Darlington, 1982; Zigler & Berman, 1983; Lee, Brooks-Gunn, & Schnur, 1988).

Head Start programs have shown that early intellectual stimulation can have a significant impact on later school performance. But the specific method used appears to be less important than parental involvement. Programs that actively involve the parents, that interest them in their children's development and show them how to provide a more stimulating home environment, tend to produce the greatest gains (Darlington, 1986).

Despite the promise of Head Start efforts, it is clear that such programs alone will not "inoculate" children—particularly inner-city children—from failure in later years. For youngsters growing up in poverty and in neighborhoods devastated by crime and drugs, a year or two of preschool activity will have only a limited effect. To sustain gains from Head Start, many educators now favor transitional programs in the primary grades that would continue to emphasize parental involvement as well as supplementary instruction in subsequent school work.

*Children in an Israeli kibbutz*

*"I'm sorry, but these records are somewhat mixed up. It turns out that 184 is your weight, not your I.Q."*

**KIBBUTZIM** Environmental effects on intellectual performance even more dramatic than Head Start are evidenced by studies of children living in Israeli kibbutzim. Israel has been faced with the problem of large differences in intellectual and educational background among Jews of different cultural ancestry. The average intellectual ability of Jews of European ancestry generally is considerably higher than that of Jews from Arabic countries. The average difference in IQ between the two groups is at least as large as the average difference in IQ between blacks and whites in the United States. The exceptions to this observation are Israeli children who are raised on certain types of kibbutzim, where they do not reside with their parents but live in a children's house under the care of women specially trained in child rearing. Under these special conditions, the children's IQ scores tend to be unrelated to the country of parental origin. Children whose parents came from Arabic countries score as well as children whose parents came from European countries. Although individual differences in IQ scores still exist, the differences are not related to ancestry (Smilansky, 1974). Thus, we have some indication of the contribution an enriched environment can make toward helping children reach their full intellectual potential.

## Ability Tests in Perspective

Despite their limitations, ability tests are one of the most widely used tools that psychology has developed. If these tests are to continue to be useful, however, they must be viewed realistically. They should not be overvalued as providing a fixed, unchangeable measure of what a person can do. Nor should they be discarded because of their obvious shortcomings and replaced by other methods of evaluation that are less valid.

One area of concern has been the use of ability tests to determine class placement for schoolchildren. Children who achieve low scores may be assigned to a slower "track" or placed in a special class for "slow learners"; children who earn high scores may be placed in accelerated or "enriched" programs. Unless schools provide periodic reassessment and unless slow-learner classes emphasize academic skills, a child's initial placement may well determine his or her academic future. Some youngsters who have the potential to succeed in college may be discouraged on the basis of early test scores from taking college preparatory courses. Both parents and teachers must realize that test scores—whether the test is called an intelligence test or an achievement test—can only measure current performance. Questions on an intelligence test are less dependent on schooling, but they do not measure innate capacity; thus, test scores can change with changes in the environment.

The use of tests to classify schoolchildren is a controversial social issue, because a disproportionately large number of minority and underprivileged children have been assigned to special classes for slow learners on the basis of their scores on group intelligence and achievement tests. Legal suits have prompted some states to prohibit the use of group intelligence tests for purposes of classification.

The issue is complicated. Ability tests can be misused in the schools. Teachers often do not know how to interpret test results and may draw sweeping conclusions about a child's ability on the basis of a single test score. More importantly, decisions about placement in special classes should be based on many factors—never on test scores alone. A child's medical and developmental history, social competency, and home environment are some of the variables that should be considered before the child is classified as a slow learner.

Ability tests can serve an important function when properly used. They help the teacher separate a large class of pupils of varying skills into homogeneous learning groups. Ability tests can also be used diagnostically to improve the educational opportunities for disadvantaged children. A child who scores low on a group intelligence test should be given a more intensive evaluation. Individual testing can help to reveal (a) whether the group test scores represent an accurate assessment of the child's current abilities, (b) the child's particular intellectual strengths and weaknesses, and (c) the best instructional program for improving his or her skills. Tests should be used to match instruction with individual needs, not to label a child.

A comparison of intelligence and achievement test scores often yields valuable information. For example, some children whose achievement test scores in reading are low may score quite high on an intelligence test. This discrepancy should alert the teacher to the possibility that the child's reading skills require special attention. This child may do quite well scholastically once his or her specific learning problems are remedied. Without the information from the intelligence test, such a child might be inappropriately placed in a slow-learner group.

Another point of concern is the type of talent measured by ability tests. As noted earlier, the SAT and other admissions tests have proved successful in predicting college grades. But when college admission officials place too much emphasis on test scores, they are apt to overlook students who may have an extraordinary talent in art, drama, or music. They may also overlook students who have aimed all of their energy and enthusiasm toward creative efforts in a specific area (for example, an award-winning science project or an innovative community program). In any selection procedure, scores on

*Elementary-school student taking a standardized test*

## Critical
# DISCUSSION

# Race and Intelligence

The debate over genetic contributions to intelligence has focused on the possibility of inherited racial differences in intelligence—specifically, on the question of whether African Americans are innately less intelligent than white Americans. In view of the heated controversy about this issue, it is important that we examine the available evidence.

On standard intelligence tests, African Americans as a group score 10–15 points lower than white Americans as a group. This fact is not debated; the controversy revolves around the interpretation of this difference. Some behavioral scientists and geneticists believe that the two groups differ in inherited ability (Jensen, 1980; 1985). Others argue that black-white differences in average IQ can be attributed entirely to environmental differences between the two groups (Kamin, 1976). Many believe that genetic and environmental differences are so confounded that the question is unanswerable at present (Loehlin, Lindzey, & Spuhler, 1975; Neisser, 1986). The issues involved are exceedingly complex; the best we can do here is to summarize a few of the main points.

1. Although African Americans and white Americans may differ in physical appearance, they do not represent two distinct biological groups. In fact, differences in gene structures (where known) in most cases are greater *within* the races than between them.

2. Heritability is a population statistic (like infant mortality or birthrate); it depends on the environmental and genetic variation among a given group of people at a given time. Thus, although heritability ratios estimated for white populations indicate that variations in IQ are partly a function of heredity, such estimates do not permit us to make inferences about heritability ratios for African Americans. More importantly, heritability estimates do not tell us anything about differences *between* two populations. The heritability of a characteristic could be the same for two groups, even though the differences between them are caused entirely by environmental factors. For example, suppose the heritability of height is the same for two populations, A and B. If individuals in Population A are raised on a starvation diet, they will be shorter, on the average, than individuals in Population B. Variations in adult height within each group are still influenced by heredity (that is, undernourished individuals with tall parents will be taller than undernourished individuals with short parents), but the differ-

ence in average height between the two groups is clearly the result of environment. To summarize, heritability estimates do not permit us to draw conclusions about differences between population (Mackenzie, 1984; Turkheimer, 1991).

3. Among African Americans, there is some tendency for lightness of skin color (presumably an indication of the degrees of intermixture with whites) to correlate positively with IQ. But such correlations are very low (typically .15) and can be readily explained on the basis of environmental differences—a lighter skin color is associated with less discrimination and greater opportunity.

4. A study of illegitimate children fathered by U.S. servicemen during the occupation of Germany after World War II found no overall difference in average IQ between children whose fathers were African American and those whose fathers were white American. Since these children were all raised by German mothers of similar social status, the results provide strong support for viewing environment as the major determinant of racial IQ differences (Eyferth, Brandt, & Wolfgang, 1960).

5. When African American children are adopted before they are 1-year-old and raised by white American families with above-average in-

intelligence and scholastic aptitude tests should be considered in conjunction with other information.

We must always question the validity of a test score for a particular individual or for a particular purpose, and we must continue to improve methods of assessment. But despite their limitations, ability tests are still the most effective aids we have for judging what job or class or type of training is most appropriate for a given individual (Hartigan & Wigdor, 1989). The alternatives are few. To rely entirely on subjective judgment would introduce the kinds of biases that such tests were designed to eliminate. To assign people at random to jobs or educational programs would benefit neither society nor the individual.

comes and educations, they score more than 15 IQ points higher than underprivileged black children reared by their biological families. The performance of the adopted children on school achievement tests is slightly above the national norms (Scarr & Weinberg, 1976).

6. Ogbu (1986) has theorized that African Americans are in a social position similar to castelike minorities elsewhere in the world, such as the Harijans (untouchables) of India, the Maoris in New Zealand, and the Burakumin of Japan. The average IQ difference between African Americans and white Americans is about the same as between the privileged and deprived groups in each of these other countries. A study of the Burakumin proves interesting in this regard; in 1871 they were emancipated from their pariah status (due to their despised work as tanners) but continue to be treated as outcasts in Japan. Nevertheless, when Burakumin have emigrated to America, their children (treated as any other Japanese in the United States) do as well on IQ tests and in school as other Japanese Americans. Being born into a castelike minority leads one to grow up with the conviction that life will be restricted to a limited set of opportunities. The lower IQ scores of these children become a self-fulfilling prophecy; teachers expect less and so tacitly treat them in ways that make those expectations come true. Fordham

and Ogbu (1986) reported on a study of two groups of equally bright African American high-school students, one group doing well and the other failing in school. Those who did poorly regarded being studious as betraying their racial identity ("acting white," in the students' words). They saw doing well in school and getting a high-status job as selling out to the white persons' values. Similar dynamics occur among Mexican American children: they identify school achievement with betraying their roots.

7. Findings from the National Assessment of Educational Progress and from the College Entrance Examination Board demonstrate a consistent reduction over the last 20 years in the achievement differences between African American and white American students. These reductions occur for reading and mathematics achievement tests in grades 1 through 12 and for the SAT. The consistency of the trend suggests that further reductions will be seen in future years (Jones, 1984). The social changes affecting African Americans have been enormous in the last 30 years; such changes might be expected to elevate aspirations of African American youth and give them evidence that school achievement will enhance their prospects for career success. The improvement of African American achievement levels in recent years is consistent with this supposition.

The authors of this text believe that it is not possible to draw valid conclusions about innate racial differences in intelligence from the available evidence. Cultural and environmental differences between African Americans and white Americans influence the development of cognitive abilities in complex ways, and no study has succeeded in estimating or eliminating these effects. As long as systematic differences remain in the conditions under which African Americans and white Americans are raised (and as long as the effects of these differences cannot be reliably estimated), no valid conclusions can be drawn concerning innate racial differences in intelligence.

## Chapter SUMMARY

1. Ability tests include *aptitude tests* (which are designed to predict what a person can accomplish with training) and *achievement tests* (which measure accomplished skills and indicate what the individual can do at present). Both tests may contain similar types of items, but they differ in their purposes and in the amount of *prior experience* they assume. Some ability tests measure very specific abilities; others cover a range of skills.

2. To be useful, tests must meet certain specifications. Studies of *reliability* tell us whether test scores are consistent over time. Studies of *validity* tell us how well a test measures what it is intended to measure—how well it predicts according to an acceptable criterion. *Uniform testing procedures* are necessary for a test to be reliable and valid.

3. The first successful intelligence tests were developed by the French psychologist Alfred Binet, who proposed the concept of *mental age*. A bright child's mental age is above his or her chronological age; a slow child's mental age is below his or her chronological age. The revision of the Binet scales (the Stanford-Binet) adopts the *intelligence quotient* (IQ) as an index of mental development. The IQ expresses intelligence as a ratio of mental age (MA) to chronological age (CA).

4. Two widely used ability tests, the Wechsler Adult Intelligence Scale (WAIS) and the Wechsler Intelligence Scale for Children (WISC), have both verbal and performance scales so that separate information can be obtained about each type of ability. The Stanford-Binet and the Wechsler scales are *individual tests* that are administered to a single individual by a specially trained tester. *Group ability tests* can be administered to a large number of people at one time.

5. Scores on ability tests correlate quite highly with what we think of as "brightness" and with measures of academic performance. But they do not measure motivation, leadership, and other characteristics that are important for success.

6. Both Binet and Wechsler assumed that intelligence is a *general capacity* for reasoning. Spearman proposed a general factor (*g*) plus specific abilities (each called *s*), which could be identified by the method of *factor analysis*. Thurstone used factor analysis to arrive at seven *primary mental abilities* he considered to be the basic elements of intelligence; variants of his test are still widely used, but their predictive power is no greater than that of tests of general intelligence, such as the Wechsler scales. Factor analysis continues to be an important method for the analysis of test data; this perspective on intelligence is called the *factorial approach*.

7. An alternative perspective on intelligence is the *information-processing approach*. The basic idea of this approach is to try to understand intellectual behavior in terms of the underlying cognitive processes that are brought into play when an individual is confronted with a problem-solving task. The information-processing approach has yielded detailed analyses of the mental processes involved in some tasks used to assess intelligence. A factorial approach and an information-processing approach provide complementary interpretations of performance on intelligence tests. Both approaches have enhanced our understanding of academic intelligence, but their common shortcoming is that they have not proved effective in assessing practical intelligence.

8. Studies correlating IQs between persons with varying degrees of genetic relationship show that heredity plays a role in intelligence. However, such environmental factors as years of schooling, nutrition, intellectual stimulation, and the emotional climate of the home can raise or lower IQ.

9. Despite their limitations, ability tests are still the most objective method available for assessing individual capabilities. But test scores must be considered in conjunction with other information.

*Further* **READING**

For an introduction to individual differences and psychological testing, see Kaplan and Sacuzzo, *Psychological Testing* (2nd ed., 1989); Cronbach, *Essentials of Psychological Testing* (4th ed., 1984); Kail and Pellegrino, *Human Intelligence: Perspectives and Prospects* (1985); Murphy and Davidshofer, *Psychological Testing: Principles and Applications* (2nd ed., 1991); Sattler, *Assess-*

*ment of Children* (1988); Sternberg (ed.), *Human Abilities: An Information-Processing Approach* (1984); and Anastasi, *Psychological Testing* (6th ed., 1988). More advanced treatments of these topics are Fredericksen, Mislevy, and Bejar (Eds.), *Test Theory for a New Generation of Tests* (1992); Sternberg (ed.), *Handbook of Human Intelligence* (1982); Wigdor and Garner (eds.), *Ability Testing: Uses, Consequences, and Controversies* (1982); and Sternberg, *Metaphors of Mind: Conceptions of the Nature of Intelligence* (1990).

For a more general overview of intellectual abilities, see Sternberg, *Intelligence Applied: Understanding and Increasing Your Intellectual Skills* (1986) and Brody, *Intelligence* (2nd ed., 1992). For a historical perspective on intelligence tests and the controversies associated with them, see Fancher, *The Intelligence Men: Makers of the IQ Controversy* (1985). For an introduction to the factorial approach to intelligence, see Comrey and Lee, *A First Course in Factor Analysis* (2nd ed., 1992).

The genetics of intelligence is discussed in Plomin, *Development, Genetics and Psychology* (1986) and in Plomin, DeFries, and McClearn, *Behavioral Genetics: A Primer* (2nd ed., 1989).

# Chapter 13

# Personality through the Life Course

**Childhood: Shaping of Personality 489**
*Genetic Influences*
*Critical Discussion: Minnesota Study of Twins Reared Apart*
*Environmental Influences*
*Critical Discussion: The Debate over Maternal Employment and Daycare*
*Personality–Environment Interactions*
*Cultural Influences*

**Adolescence: Constructing An Identity 508**
*Identity Statuses*
*College versus Family*

**Adulthood: Continuity of Personality 511**
*Evidence for Continuity*
*Critical Discussion: Studying Personality the Long Way*
*Sources of Continuity*
*Sources of Discontinuity*

Detail, *On the Heights.*

The mental abilities that we examined in Chapter 12 are a subset of variables that constitute what we call **personality,** the distinctive and characteristic patterns of thought, emotion, and behavior that define an individual's personal style and influence his or her interactions with the environment. In addition to mental abilities, personality includes variables like sociability, emotional stability, impulsiveness, conscientiousness, and many others.

In this chapter, we examine the interplay of forces that shape an individual's personality through the course of life; that promote, disrupt, or transform the continuity of personality across time; and that enable the individual's personality, in turn, to affect the course of life itself. (We consider formal theories of personality and methods for assessing personality in Chapter 14.)

We also return to two questions first encountered in Chapter 3, the chapter on psychological development. The first is the nature–nurture question: How do biological factors interact with events in an individual's environment to determine the course of development? In Chapter 3, we focused on those biological factors that make us all alike. We saw, for example, that innately determined sequences of growth caused all children to go through the same stages of motor development in the same sequence, irrespective of differences in rearing environments. In this chapter we focus instead on biological factors that individualize us and make us different from one another. The most important of these are our **genotypes,** the characteristics we inherit from our parents' genes.

The second question concerns the continuity of development. In Chapter 3, we considered whether development is best understood as a continuous process of change or as a series of qualitatively distinct stages. In this chapter we consider the degree to which an individual's personality changes or remains the same across the life course.

## Childhood: Shaping of Personality

### Genetic Influences

As we noted in Chapter 3, first-time parents are often surprised that their infant seems to possess a distinctive personality so early in life; when they have a second child, they are often surprised at how different the second is from the first. Research shows that reliable differences can be observed among infants beginning at about 3 months of age in such characteristics as activity level, attention span, adaptability to changes in the environment, and general mood. One infant might be active, easily distracted, and not easily comforted when distressed; another might be predominantly quiet, persistent in concentrating on an activity, and easily comforted. Such mood-related personality characteristics are called **temperaments.**

The early appearance of such characteristics suggests that they are determined in part by genetic factors and are inherited from the parents—despite large differences among children from the same family. As we described in both Chapters 2 and 12, one method of investigating this question is to study pairs of twins. If identical twins (who share all their genes in common) are significantly more alike on a characteristic than fraternal twins

*To what extent is temperament determined by genetics?*

(who, like ordinary siblings, share about half their genes in common) then the characteristic probably has a genetic or heritable component.

In one study of this type, same-sex twins, whose average age was about 5 years, were rated by their parents on the temperaments of sociability, emotionality, and activity. Correlations between identical twins ranged from .5 to .6, whereas correlations between fraternal twins were not significantly different from zero, suggesting that genetic inheritance is an important determinant of these temperaments (Buss & Plomin, 1984). One problem with this and similar studies is that they rely on ratings by parents, who might exaggerate the similarities of identical twins or the differences between fraternal twins (Neale & Stevenson, 1989). Fortunately, studies using more objective methods have confirmed that emotionality, sociability, and activity do have substantial heritable components (Plomin et al., 1988).

Genetic effects on personality are not confined to infant temperament but can also be detected in adult personality traits. A very large Swedish study examined the traits of extraversion (sociability) and neuroticism (emotional instability) in a sample of over 12,000 pairs of adult twins. On both traits, there were correlations of .5 between members of identical-twin pairs and .2 between members of fraternal-twin pairs, implying a substantial genetic influence (Floderus-Myred, Petersen, & Rasmuson, 1980).

As we noted in Chapter 12, however, one difficulty in interpreting the results of twin studies is that identical twin pairs may be treated more alike than fraternal twin pairs, which may account for their greater personality similarities. Ideally one should study a sample of identical twins who had been separated at birth and raised in randomly selected environments. Fortunately, an ongoing research project comes close to fulfilling these conditions: the Minnesota Study of Twins Reared Apart (Bouchard, 1984). As of 1990, over 56 pairs of identical twins had been brought to the laboratory for study. On average, these twin pairs had been separated at 10 weeks of age and had not seen each other again until 34 years later; some had not met until the study brought them together. The Minnesota researchers have now compared these twins with those in an earlier Minnesota study on twins reared together. (Bouchard, et al., 1990; Lykken, 1982; Tellegen, et al., 1988).

These several studies reveal that across a wide range of personality characteristics twins reared apart are just as similar to one another as twins reared together. The median correlations were .49 for identical twins reared apart and .52 for identical twins reared together; the corresponding correlations for fraternal twins were .21 and .23. These results permit us to conclude with greater confidence that identical twins are more similar to one another on personality characteristics than are fraternal twins because they are more similar genetically.

The differences in correlations between identical and fraternal twins found in the Minnesota studies are themselves in accord with results from many other twin studies and imply that about 50 percent of the variability among individuals in many personality traits can be attributed to genetic differences among those individuals. This can be expressed by saying that these traits have heritabilities of about .5 in the populations studied.

It is important to emphasize that this does not mean that 50 percent of a trait within a particular individual is due to his or her genes. The heritability of a trait refers to differences *among* individuals within a population, not to proportions of a trait *within* an individual. If something happens to change the variability of a trait in a population, the heritability of the trait will also change. For example, if everyone in our society were suddenly to be given equal educational opportunities, the variability of intellectual performance in the society would decrease; everybody's scores on standardized measures of intellectual ability would be more similar to one another because the variability caused by differences in education would have been reduced. Surprisingly, this would cause the heritability of intellectual performance—the *proportion* of variability due to inherited differences among individuals—to *increase* because the *proportion* of the variability due to an important environmental factor would have decreased.

In general, the highest heritabilities are found in measures of abilities and intelligence; the next highest heritabilities are typically found in measures of personality—especially those related to sociability and emotional stability; the smallest heritabilities are found for beliefs and attitudes, such as religious beliefs and political attitudes. In the Minnesota study, the correlations on some ability and personality tests between pairs of identical twins reared apart were as high as if the same person took the test twice. (See the Critical Discussion for a further discussion of the Minnesota study.)

Because many adult personality traits can be traced in part to genetic factors, it is reasonable to ask whether such traits might be adult continuations of childhood temperaments. For example, some researchers have suggested that the temperaments of sociability and emotionality might be the childhood versions of extraversion and emotional instability, respectively (Plomin et al., 1988). This question is a version of the continuity question we raised at the beginning of the chapter: To what extent does an individual's personality change or remain the same over the life course?

One pioneering study that has followed the same children over time began in the 1950s with a group of 140 middle- and upper-class infants in the United States. The initial data were gathered through interviews with parents and were later supplemented by interviews with teachers and by tests given directly to the children. The infants were scored on nine traits, which were later combined to define three broad temperament types: infants who were playful, regular in their sleeping and eating patterns, and adapted readily to new situations were classified as *easy* (about 40 percent of the sample); infants who were irritable, irregular in sleeping and eating

## Minnesota Study of Twins Reared Apart

The participants in the Minnesota Study of Twins Reared Apart were assessed on a number of ability and personality measures. In addition, they participated in lengthy interviews, during which they were asked questions about such topics as childhood experiences, fears, hobbies, musical tastes, social attitudes, and sexual interests. A number of startling similarities were found.

The twins with the most dramatically different backgrounds are Oskar Stohr and Jack Yufe. Born in Trinidad of a Jewish father and a German mother, they were separated shortly after birth. The mother took Oskar to Germany, where he was raised by his grandmother as a Catholic and a Nazi. Jack remained with his father, was raised as a Jew, and spent part of his youth on an Israeli kibbutz. The families never corresponded, and the two brothers now lead quite different lives. They were in their late forties when they participated in the study and had met only once before about 20 years earlier. Remarkable similarities were evident when the pair showed up for the study. Both men were wearing blue double-breasted epauletted shirts, mustaches, and wire-rimmed glasses. Their mannerisms and temperaments were similar, and they shared certain idiosyncrasies: both liked spicy foods and sweet liqueurs, were absentminded, flushed the toilet before using it, liked to dip buttered toast in their coffee, and enjoyed surprising people by sneezing in elevators.

Another pair of twins with fairly different backgrounds are now British housewives who were separated during World War II and were raised by families of different socioeconomic statuses. Both twins, who had never met before,

patterns, and responded intensely and negatively to new situations were classified as *difficult* (about 10 percent of the sample); infants who were low inactivity level, tended to withdraw from new situations in a mild way, and required more time than easy infants to adapt to new situations were classified as *slow to warm up* (about 15 percent of the sample). The remaining 35 percent of the infants were not rated high or low on any of the defining dimensions (Thomas et al., 1963). Of the original sample, 133 subjects have now been followed into adult life and have again been assessed on temperament and psychological adjustment.

The results provide mixed evidence for the continuity of temperament. On the one hand, temperament scores across the first five years of these children's lives were significantly correlated with one another, and adult measures of both temperament and adjustment were significantly correlated with measures of childhood temperament obtained at ages 3, 4, and 5. On the other hand, all the correlations were low (about .3) and most of the nine traits considered separately showed little or no continuity across time (Chess & Thomas, 1984; Thomas & Chess, 1986).

The researchers emphasize that the continuity and discontinuity of temperament is a function of the interaction between the child's genotype and the environment. In particular, they believe that the key to healthy development is a *goodness of fit* between the child's temperament and the home environment. For example, they cite the case of Carl, a boy with one of the most difficult temperaments from the first few months of life through 5 years of age. But because Carl's father took delight in his son's "lusty" temperament and allowed for his initial negative reactions to new situations, Carl flourished and became increasingly "easy." At age 23, he was clearly classified into the "easy" temperament group. Nevertheless, Carl's original temperament often emerged briefly whenever life circumstances changed. For example, when he started piano lessons in late childhood, he again showed an intense negative response, followed by slow adaptability and eventual positive, zestful involvement. A similar pattern emerged when he entered college (Thomas & Chess, 1986).

*These twins, separated at birth, showed remarkable similarities in interests and habits when they first met at age 31.*

arrived for their interviews wearing seven rings on their fingers.

There are not, of course, toast-dipping or ring-loving genes; such similarities reflect similarities in the heritable components of more basic personality characteristics. But as we shall see, it is unlikely that genetics alone can account for these extraordinary similarities of twins reared apart. Later in this chapter we will see other surprising findings that emerge from twin studies.

## Environmental Influences

The example of Carl reminds us that even if genetic factors account for as much as 50 percent of the variability in many personality traits, this still leaves 50 percent of the variability to be accounted for primarily by environmental factors and by interactions between those environmental factors and the genetic ones. The interplay among these factors is further illustrated by two areas of research in childhood personality development: differences among children in their patterns of attachment to their parents and differences among parents in their childrearing practices.

ATTACHMENT  As we noted in Chapter 3, an infant's tendency to seek closeness to caregivers and to feel more secure in their presence is called **attachment.** Most of the work on attachment in human infants originated with the psychoanalyst John Bowlby in the 1950s and 1960s. His theory is an integration of concepts from psychoanalytic theory, ethology, and cognitive psychology. According to attachment theory, a child's failure to form a secure attachment to one or more persons in the early years is related to an inability to develop close personal relationships in adulthood (Bowlby, 1973).

ASSESSING ATTACHMENT  Mary Ainsworth, one of Bowlby's associates, made extensive observations of children and their mothers in Uganda and the United States and then developed a laboratory procedure for assessing the security of a child's attachments from about 12–18 months of age (Ainsworth, Blehar, Waters, & Wall, 1978). The procedure is called the Strange Situation and comprises the following sequence of episodes:

1. The mother and the child enter the experimental room. The mother places the baby on the floor surrounded by toys and then goes to sit at the opposite end of the room.
2. A female stranger enters the room, sits quietly for one minute, converses with the mother for a minute, and then attempts to engage the baby in play with a toy.

*The nature of an infant's early attachment to the parents may be related to personal relationships in adulthood.*

3. The mother leaves the room unobtrusively. If the baby is not upset, the stranger returns to sitting quietly. If the baby is upset, the stranger tries to soothe him or her.
4. The mother returns and engages the baby in play while the stranger slips out.
5. The mother leaves again, this time leaving the baby alone in the room.
6. The stranger returns. If the baby is upset, the stranger tries to comfort him or her.
7. The mother returns and the stranger slips out.

Each episode is designed to last 3 minutes but can be shortened if the baby becomes too upset or lengthened if the baby needs additional time to get involved in play. The baby is observed through a one-way mirror during the entire sequence, and several observations are recorded: baby's activity level and play involvement, crying and other distress signs, proximity to and attempts to gain attention of the mother, proximity to and willingness to interact with the stranger, and so on. On the basis of their behaviors, babies are categorized into three main groups. Note that the groups differ from one another primarily in terms of the children's behaviors during the reunion episodes (episodes 4 and 7).

*Securely Attached* Whether or not they are upset at the mother's departures (episodes 3 and 5), babies who are classified as securely attached seek to interact with her when she returns. Some are content simply to acknowledge her return from a distance, while continuing to play with the toys. Others seek physical contact with her. Still others are completely preoccupied with the mother throughout the entire session, showing intense distress when she leaves. In all, about 60–65 percent of American babies are classified into this category.

*Insecurely Attached: Avoidant* These babies show conspicuous avoidance of interaction with the mother in the reunion episodes. Some ignore the mother almost entirely; some display mixed attempts to interact and to avoid interacting.

Avoidant babies may pay little attention to the mother when she is in the room and often do not seem distressed when she leaves. If distressed, they are as easily comforted by the stranger as by the mother. About 20 percent of American babies are classified into this category.

*Insecurely Attached: Ambivalent* Babies are classified as ambivalent if they show resistance to the mother during the reunion episodes. They simultaneously seek and resist physical contact. For example, they may cry to be picked up and then squirm angrily to get down. Some act very passive, crying for the mother when she returns but not crawling toward her and then showing resistance when she approaches. About 10 percent of American babies are classified into this category.

Because some babies did not seem to fit any of these categories, more recent studies have included a fourth category, called *disorganized* (Main & Solomon, 1986). Babies in this category often show contradictory behaviors. For example, they may approach the mother while taking care not to look at her, approach her and then show dazed avoidance, or suddenly cry out after having first settled down. Some seem disoriented, appear emotionless, or look depressed. About 10–15 percent of American babies are now placed into this category, with the percentages being much higher among babies who are maltreated or who come from homes with parents who are in psychiatric treatment.

SENSITIVE RESPONSIVENESS  In attempting to account for differences in attachment among babies, researchers have directed most of their attention to the behavior of the primary caregiver, usually the mother. The main finding has been that it is a caregiver's "sensitive responsiveness" to the baby's needs that produces secure attachment. This is evident as early as the baby's first 3 months of life. For example, mothers of securely attached babies usually respond promptly when the baby cries and behave affectionately when they pick him or her up. They also tailor their responses closely to the baby's needs (Clarke-Stewart, 1973). In feeding, for example, they use an infant's signals to determine when to begin and end feeding, they attend to the baby's food preferences, and they pace their feeding to the baby's speed of eating.

In contrast, mothers of babies who show either type of insecure attachment respond more on the basis of their own wishes or moods than to signals from the baby. For example, they will respond to the baby's cries for attention when they feel like cuddling the baby but will ignore such cries at other times (Stayton, 1973).

Mothers of insecurely attached babies who show the avoidant pattern in the Strange Situation appear to hold their babies as much as mothers of securely attached babies, but they do not seem to enjoy the close bodily contact as much and sometimes act in a rejecting manner. They are especially likely to refuse contact when the baby is distressed and most needs comforting. They also tend to be rigid and compulsive, often giving care "according to the book" rather than responsively to the infant. Researchers propose that the result for the baby is a conflict between approaching and avoiding contact with the mother (Ainsworth, Blehar, Waters, & Wall, 1978; Belsky, Rovine, & Taylor, 1984; Lyons-Ruth, Connell, Zoll, & Stahl, 1987).

Mothers of insecurely attached babies who show the ambivalent pattern in the Strange Situation are inconsistent in their care. Sometimes they respond sensitively to their infants; sometimes they are inaccessible; at yet other times, they are intrusive, interfering with the baby's activity. Like the mothers of avoidant infants, the problem is not that they interact too little or too much, but that the nature and timing of their interaction does not consistently match the infant's needs. The result is that such babies are often frustrated in their attempts to seek contact. This generates the mixture of contact seeking and anger observed in the Strange Situation. Such babies also become much more distressed at little everyday separations than securely attached babies do (Ainsworth, 1989).

INFANT TEMPERAMENT  Not all developmental psychologists agree that the caregiver's responsiveness is the major cause of an infant's attachment behaviors. They call attention to the baby's own inborn temperament (Campos et al., 1983; Kagan, 1984). For example, perhaps the temperaments that make some babies "easy" also make them more securely attached than do the temperaments of "difficult" babies. Moreover, a parent's response to a child is often itself a function of the child's own behavior. Attachment patterns may reflect this interaction between a baby's temperament and the parent's responsiveness.

In reply, attachment theorists point to data that favor the caregiver responsiveness hypothesis. For example, it has been found that an infant's crying changes over the first year much more than the mother's responsiveness to the crying does. Moreover, the mother's responsiveness over a 3-month period predicts the infant's crying over the next 3 months significantly better than the infant's crying predicts the mother's subsequent responsiveness to crying. In short, the mother appears to influence the infant's crying more than the infant influences the mother's responsiveness to crying (Bell & Ainsworth, 1972).

More recent research may provide a resolution to this debate. Recall that the attachment classification in the Strange Situation is not based primarily on the baby's distress when the mother leaves but on how the baby reacts when she returns. It now appears that an infant's temperament predicts the former but not the latter (Frodi & Thompson, 1985; Vaughn, Lefever, Seifer, and Barglow, 1989). For example, babies with "easy" temperaments are not typically distressed when the mother leaves. When she returns, they either tend to greet her happily—thus showing one of the securely attached patterns—or they show the avoidant pattern of insecure attachment. Babies with "difficult" temperaments are typically distressed when the mother leaves. When she returns, they either tend to seek out and cling to her—thus showing one of the securely attached patterns—or they show the ambivalent pattern of insecure attachment (Belsky & Rovine, 1987). Thus the overall reaction of a child to the departure and return of his or her primary caregivers is a function of both their responsiveness to the child and his or her own temperament.

ATTACHMENT TO FATHERS  For many reasons, most of the work on attachment has focused on the mother. The psychoanalytic and ethological theories that underlie Bowlby's attachment theory give a unique place to the mother in the child's early years, and mothers are more likely than fathers to be responsible for early child care—even in industrialized countries like the United States where there have recently been major sex-role changes.

Nevertheless, these same changes have prompted a closer look at babies' attachments to their fathers. Studies of the Strange Situation using the father show that infants react to his presence or absence in ways similar to

*Babies become attached to their fathers more quickly when they regularly spend time together.*

those described for the mother, although attachment to the father seems to develop more slowly (Kotelchuck, 1976). For example, many 1-year-old children cry and stop playing when the mother leaves them alone; similar responses to the father's departure do not appear on the average until the child is about 15 months old. In addition, the 1-year-old child usually protests the mother's departure more vigorously than the father's and clings to her somewhat longer on reunion. These differences lessen with age.

The critical factor in determining when babies become attached to their fathers appears to be the amount of time that they spend together. When fathers are actively involved in their daily care, even young infants react to their father's departure in the Strange Situation in the same way they react to their mother's departure. Moreover, such children tend to be less disturbed when left alone with a stranger than children from families in which the mother provides most of the care (Kotelchuck, 1976).

Babies become attached even to fathers who spend little time with them. Most of the brief interactions between such fathers and their babies tend to be play episodes. Fathers provide fun and excitement, and they tend to engage in more physical, rough-and-tumble play than mothers. If given a choice, 18-month-old children will actually choose to play with their fathers more often than they will with their mothers. But in times of stress, mothers are generally preferred (Clarke-Stewart, 1978).

ATTACHMENT AND LATER DEVELOPMENT  A baby's attachment classification has been found to remain quite stable when retested in the Strange Situation several years later—unless the family experiences major changes in life circumstances (Thompson, Lamb, & Estes, 1982; Main & Cassidy, 1988). Stressful life changes are likely to affect parental responsiveness to the baby that, in turn, affects the baby's feelings of security.

The patterns of early attachment also appear to be related to how children cope with new experiences during the next few years. For example, in

## The Debate over Maternal Employment and Daycare

By the mid-1990s, 75 percent of women in the United States with school-aged children will be in the labor force (compared with 40 percent in 1970); more than 50 percent of mothers with children younger than 1 year of age are already in the labor force (U.S. Bureau of Labor Statistics, 1987).

Working parents provide a variety of arrangements for their children's care. The majority leave their preschoolers at home to be cared for by a sitter or a relative while they work; some leave them at someone else's home to be cared for alone or with other children; and finally, some leave them at daycare centers. Not surprisingly, developmental psychologists—including attachment theorists—have become involved in the debate over the effects on children of maternal employment and daycare.

In terms of intellectual development, children from middle-class families appear to do as well at a good daycare center as they do with parental care at home (Kagan, Kearsley, & Zelazo, 1978; Clarke-Stewart, 1982). Children from homes with poorly educated parents who have low incomes benefit intellectually from their daycare experience. The enrichment programs provided seem to prevent the decline in intellectual performance that often occurs after the age of 2 if such children remain at home (Ramey, 1981).

In the area of social development, it has been found that children who attend daycare centers are more self-sufficient, more cooperative with peers, and more comfortable in new situations than are home-reared children. They are also less polite, less compliant with adults, and more aggressive (Clarke-Stewart & Fein, 1983). Some of these results may depend on the child-rearing attitudes of the parents and the teachers. Children attending daycare centers in the former Soviet Union, Israel, and Sweden also show greater self-sufficiency and ease in social situations, but they do not act as aggressively or rudely as daycare children in the United States. Such behavior is strongly disapproved of by parents and teachers in those countries (Cole & Cole, 1993).

But what about attachment and emotional development? Critics of daycare have voiced concern that the repeated separations of mother and child that are a part of daycare could seriously interfere with the security of young children's attachment to their mothers. Most of the studies on this issue have compared the responses of home-reared children and daycare-reared children under the age of 2 in the Strange Situation. Some of these studies found no significant difference in attachment behavior between the two groups of children; daycare infants were as likely to become distressed as home-reared children when confronting a stranger or being separated from their mothers, and they clearly preferred their mothers to the daycare teachers as a source of comfort (McCartney & Phillips, 1988).

Other studies reported that daycare children did not stay as close to their mothers when playing in the Strange Situation or seek as much physical contact on reunion as did the home-reared children (Hock, 1980; Goossens, 1987). The latter finding has been interpreted by some to indicate that daycare children become more independent as part of their adaptation to daily separation (Clarke-Stewart, 1989). Others, how-

one study, 2-year-olds were given a series of problems requiring the use of tools. Some of the problems were within the child's capacity; others were quite difficult. The toddlers who had been rated as securely attached when they were 12 months of age approached the problems with enthusiasm and persistence. When they encountered difficulties, they seldom cried or became angry; rather, they sought help from the adults who were present. Those who had been rated earlier as insecurely attached behaved quite differently. They became easily frustrated and angry, seldom asked for help, tended to ignore or reject directions from the adults, and quickly gave up trying to solve the problems (Matas, Arend, & Sroufe, 1978).

Another study looked at the social behavior of nursery school children (age 3-1/2 years) whose attachment relationships had been assessed at 15 months of age. The children rated as securely attached earlier tended to be the social leaders: they were active in initiating and participating in activities and were sought out by the other children. Their teachers rated them as self-directed and eager to learn. The insecurely attached children tended to be socially withdrawn and hesitant about participating in activities. Their teachers rated them as less curious about new things and less forceful in pur-

ever, believe that this behavior reflects an underlying doubt about the availability of the mother to meet the child's needs and, thus, an insecure attachment (Belsky & Rovine, 1988). They suggest that an insecure avoidant pattern of attachment (in which the baby refuses to look at or approach the mother when reunited in the Strange Situation) is seen more often in infants who start daycare during the first year of life and/or who experience frequent changes in caregivers (Schwarz, 1983). Most investigators in this area continue to maintain that the findings are inconclusive and that more research on this question should be conducted.

But there is an alternative possibility. Some psychologists have suggested that there is so much variation *within* home-care arrangements and *within* daycare arrangements that meaningful overall differences *between* the two types can never be discovered. They further suggest that it is time to adopt a more radical stance and to question whether public policy would not be better served by asking entirely different questions. They argue—and the statistics cited above demonstrate—that the question of whether mothers should work is essentially irrelevant to modern family life. Mothers do work and, as they point out, "child care is now as essential to family life as the automobile and the refrigerator" (Scarr, Phillips, & McCartney, 1990, p. 26).

Thus, instead of continuing to search for the negative effects of maternal employment and daycare on children—thereby implicitly blaming mothers for abandoning their children by working—these critics argue that we should be putting more effort into investigating the psychological effects on children (and families) of *not* providing adequate, affordable child care to all working parents. A large-scale study of working parents found that most of them had to "package" their child care by juggling several kinds of arrangements. Over one-fourth of the families were forced to use from four to six different kinds of child care during a single work week. Not surprisingly, these families were highly stressed by having to manage such multiple-care arrangements, and most of this stress was experienced by the mothers (Kamerman, 1980).

It is also relevant to note that the traditional two-parent family is no longer the norm: fewer than 7 percent of families now have a father out working and a mother at home with the children (Braverman, 1989). In this decade, the *majority* of children in the United States will experience life in a single-parent household, and 90 percent of these households will be headed by women (Weitzman, 1985). Moreover, these are the families most likely to be in poverty. In this society, the persons most at risk for living in poverty are children (Sidel, 1986; Stipek & McCroskey, 1989). The critics thus argue that when viewed in this context, the question of whether a child in daycare is showing independence or avoidance when mom arrives at the end of the day is hardly the central issue. As one put it,

These stark realities of family life have been reported in the literature for the past decade at least, yet neither mainstream psychological research nor social policy is in synchrony with these facts. To the extent that research on child care and maternal employment continues to focus on the centrality of mothering in the lives of young children, attention is being detracted away from the need for social reforms and a government-sponsored family policy agenda. (Silverstein, 1991, p. 1029)

suing their goals. These differences were not related to intelligence (Waters, Wippman, & Sroufe, 1979).

These studies suggest that children who are securely attached by the time they enter their second year of life are better equipped to cope with new experiences and relationships. However, we cannot be certain that the quality of children's early attachments is directly responsible for their later competence in problem solving and social skills. Parents who are responsive to their children's needs in infancy probably continue to provide effective parenting during early childhood—encouraging autonomy and efforts to cope with new experiences, yet ready with help when needed. Thus, the child's competency and social skills at age 3-1/2 may reflect the current state of the parent-child relationship rather than the relationship that existed two years earlier. Moreover, children's temperaments—which, as we saw earlier, affect their behavior in the Strange Situation—might also be influencing their later competency as preschoolers.

**PARENTAL CHILDREARING PRACTICES** After the first year of a child's life, childrearing becomes more complex as parents take on the tasks

*Children who were securely attached as toddlers are likely to be eager learners and social leaders in preschool.*

of discipline, control, and character building. Parents differ markedly from one another in how they approach these tasks. Some are warm, nurturant, and relaxed; others are cold, aloof, and tense. Some are highly controlling; others tend to be indulgent with their children. Some are child-centered, highly involved in their children's lives; others are parent-centered, more occupied with their own interests and activities. A basic task for psychology is to categorize and summarize these many differences and to determine if and how they help shape the child's personality. One classification that has proven useful for this purpose is displayed in Figure 13-1. It divides parenting practices on two dimensions: the first distinguishes parents who are demanding and controlling from those who are undemanding of their children; the other distinguishes parents who are accepting, responsive, and child-centered from those who are rejecting, unresponsive, and parent-centered. The intersection of these two dimensions produces four kinds of parenting patterns which have been shown empirically to be associated with different outcomes for the children (Baumrind, 1967, 1971; Maccoby & Martin, 1983).

As shown in Figure 13-1, parents who combine control with acceptance and child-centered involvement are called **authoritative.** They exercise high levels of control and require their children to behave at intellectual and social levels consistent with their age and abilities. But authoritative parents combine their control and demands with warmth, nurturance, and two-way communication. They solicit their children's opinions and feelings when family decisions are made, and they offer explanations and reasons for punitive or restrictive measures whenever they feel these must be imposed. Research shows that children of such parents tend to be independent, self-assertive, friendly with peers, and cooperative with parents. They are also likely to be successful both intellectually and socially, they seem to enjoy life, and they have strong motivation to achieve.

In the second category, labeled **authoritarian,** are controlling and demanding parents who simply assert their power without warmth, nurtur-

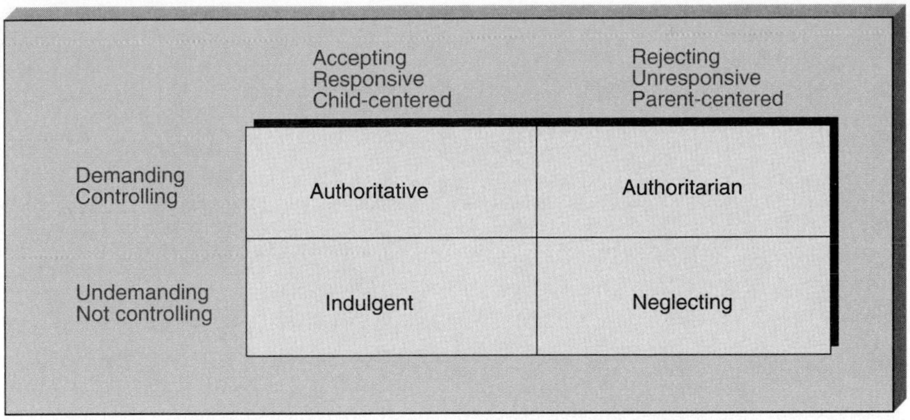

**FIGURE 13-1**
**Childrearing Patterns** *The Demanding-Undemanding and the Accepting-Rejecting dimensions combine to produce four child-rearing patterns.* (After Maccoby & Martin, 1983)

ance, or two-way communication. They attempt to control and evaluate the behavior and attitudes of their children in accordance with an absolute set of standards; they also value obedience, respect for authority, work, tradition, and preservation of order. Children of such parents tend to be moderately competent and responsible, but they also tend to be socially withdrawn and to lack spontaneity. The girls seem to be particularly dependent on their parents and lacking in achievement motivation; the boys tend to be more aggressive than other boys. Some studies also find a link between authoritarian parenting and low self-esteem in boys (Coopersmith, 1967).

**Indulgent** parents, the third category, are accepting, responsive, child-centered parents who place few demands on their children. Such children are more positive in their moods and show more vitality than children of authoritarian families, but their behavior tends to be immature in that they lack impulse control, social responsibility, and self-reliance. There is also evidence that permissiveness for aggression is one factor contributing to children's aggressiveness. It is interesting that even though authoritarian and indulgent parents have almost opposite childrearing styles, both have children who tend to display little self-reliance and may have problems with aggression.

The fourth category contains **neglecting** parents. Most such parents are not neglecting in the extreme ways that would constitute child abuse. Rather, they are concerned with their own activities and uninvolved with those of their children—they are parent-centered rather than child-centered. Interviewers describe them as not knowing their children's whereabouts, activities, and associates when the children are away from home; they are uninterested in events at the children's schools; they have few daily conversations with their children; and they do not consider their children's opinions.

A large-scale longitudinal study conducted in Finland assessed children at ages 8, 14, and 20 years who had parent-centered parents. Compared with children of child-centered parents, children of parent-centered parents at age 14 were impulsive: they lacked concentration, were moody, spent money quickly rather than saving it, and had difficulty controlling aggressive outbursts. They were uninterested in school, likely to be truant, and spent time on the streets and at hangouts. They tended to start drinking, smoking, and dating at earlier ages. At age 20, they were hedonistic and lacked frustration tolerance and emotional control; they also lacked long-term goals, drank to excess, and often had a record of arrests (Pulkkinen, 1982).

*Children raised by parent-centered parents often engage in impulsive behavior, such as experimenting with smoking at an early age.*

More extreme cases of neglecting parents are those who are emotionally unavailable to their children. They are detached, emotionally uninvolved, often depressed, and uninterested in their children. Children of such parents show clear disturbances in their attachment relationships and increasing deficits in all aspects of psychological functioning by age 2; in fact, their deficits are greater than those of children whose parents actually physically abuse them (Egeland & Sroufe, 1981a, 1981b).

This four-fold classification of childrearing patterns helps to summarize the results of many studies conducted over the years, but it should not be interpreted to mean that a particular parent can be easily assigned to a single category. Many parents use different approaches at different times, under different circumstances, and with different children. Some parents may be noncontrolling when their children are young but controlling as they get older. They may be indulgent about toilet training but restrictive about displays of aggression. They may demand more obedience from a daughter than from a son or be more involved with a firstborn than with a laterborn child. And, of course, many two-parent homes contain a mother and father with very different childrearing styles.

The results of studies on childrearing practices and children's personalities are reasonably consistent, but they are fairly weak—much weaker than many researchers had expected. Some psychologists are even coming to believe that, in general, differences between parental childrearing practices have little to do with differences in children's personalities. We will examine this startling conclusion below.

## Personality–Environment Interactions

**GENOTYPE–ENVIRONMENT CORRELATION** In shaping personality, genetic and environmental influences are intertwined from the moment of birth. Parents give their biological offspring both their genes and a home environment, and both are functions of the parents' own genes. As a result, there is a built-in correlation between the child's inherited characteristics (genotype) and the environment in which he or she is raised. For example, because general intelligence is partially heritable, parents with high intelligence are likely to have children with high intelligence. But parents with high intelligence are also likely to provide an intellectually stimulating environment for their children—both through their own interactions with them and through the books, music lessons, trips to museums, and other intellectual experiences that are likely to be a part of their home. Because the child's genotype and environment are positively correlated in this way, he or she will get a double-dose of intellectual advantage. Similarly, children born to parents with low intelligence are likely to encounter a home environment that further exacerbates whatever intellectual disadvantage they may have inherited directly.

Some parents may deliberately construct an environment that is negatively correlated with the child's genotype. For example, introverted parents may encourage social activities in order to counteract the child's own likely introversion: "We make an effort to have people over because we don't want Chris to grow up to be as shy as we are." Parents of a very active child may try to provide more interesting quiet activities. But whether the correlation is positive or negative, the pertinent point is that the child's genotype and environment are not simply independent sources of influence that add together to shape the child's personality.

In addition to being correlated with the environment, a child's genotype also shapes the environment itself (Plomin, DeFries, & Loehlin, 1977; Scarr, 1988; Scarr & McCartney, 1983). In particular, the environment becomes a function of the child's initial personality through three forms of interaction: *reactive, evocative,* and *proactive.*

**REACTIVE INTERACTION** Different individuals exposed to the same environment experience it, interpret it, and react to it differently. An anxious, sensitive child will experience and react to harsh parents differently from a calm, resilient child; the sharp tone of voice that provokes the sensitive child to tears might pass unnoticed by his sister. An extraverted child will attend to people and events around her; her introverted brother will ignore them. A brighter child will get more out of being read to than a less bright child. In other words, each child's personality extracts a subjective psychological environment from the objective surroundings, and it is that subjective environment that shapes subsequent personality development. Even if parents provided exactly the same environment for all their children—which they usually do not—it will not be psychologically equivalent for all of them. **Reactive interaction** occurs throughout life. One person will interpret a hurtful act as the product of deliberate hostility and react to it quite differently from the person who interprets that same act as the product of unintended insensitivity.

**EVOCATIVE INTERACTION** Every individual's personality evokes distinctive responses from others. An infant who squirms and fusses when picked up will evoke less nurturance from a parent than one who likes to be cuddled. Docile children will evoke a less controlling style of childrearing from parents than will aggressive children. For this reason, we cannot simply assume that an observed correlation between the childrearing practices of a child's parents and his or her personality reflects a simple cause-and-effect sequence. Instead, the child's personality can shape the parents' childrearing style which, in turn, further shapes his or her personality. **Evocative interaction** also occurs throughout life: gracious people evoke gracious environments; hostile people evoke hostile environments.

**PROACTIVE INTERACTION** As children get older, they can move beyond the environments imposed by their parents and begin to select and construct environments of their own. These environments, in turn, further shape their personalities. A sociable child will choose to go to the movies with friends rather than to stay home alone and watch television; her sociable personality thus prompts her to select an environment that further reinforces and sustains her sociability. And what she cannot select, she will construct: if nobody invites her to the movies, she will organize the event herself. As the name implies, **proactive interaction** is a process through which individuals become active agents in their own personality development.

The relative importance of these several kinds of personality–environment interaction shifts over the course of development (Scarr, 1988; Scarr & McCartney, 1983). The built-in correlation between a child's genotype and his or her environment is strongest when the child is young and confined almost exclusively to parent-imposed environments. As the child gets older and begins to select and construct his or her own environments, this initial correlation decreases and the influence of proactive interaction increases. As noted, reactive and evocative interactions remain important throughout life.

**SOME UNSOLVED PUZZLES** Studies of twins have produced a number of puzzling patterns that are still not completely understood. One is the greater similarity of identical twins compared with fraternal twins. The problem is that the data are too good. As we saw earlier, the striking similarities of identical twins do not seem to diminish across time or separate rearing environments. In contrast, the similarities of fraternal twins (and non-twin siblings) diminish from childhood through adolescence even when they are reared together; the longer they live together in the same home, the less similar they become (Scarr, 1988; Scarr & McCartney, 1983). And finally, the observed similarities of fraternal twins and non-twin siblings are often lower than they should be if the traits are as heritable as the identical twin correlations imply.

Some of these patterns could emerge if the genes themselves interact

*A sociable child will choose environments that enhance his or her sociability.*

*Because identical twins have identical geno-types, they will evoke similar responses from others and will seek out similar environments.*

with one another so that having all one's genes in common (as identical twins do) is more than twice as effective as having only half one's genes in common (as fraternal twins and non-twin siblings do). There is evidence for this kind of gene-gene interaction for some traits, especially extraversion (Pedersen, Plomin, McClearn, & Friberg, 1988). But personality–environment interactions could also be partially responsible for these patterns.

Consider identical twins. Because they have identical genotypes, they also react to situations in similar ways (reactive interaction); they evoke similar responses from others (evocative interaction); and their similar, genetically guided talents, interests, and motivations lead them to seek out and construct similar environments (proactive interaction). The important point is that these processes all operate whether the twins are reared together or apart. For example, two identical twins separated at birth will still be treated in similar ways by other people because they each independently evoke similar responses from others.

Proactive interaction operates in the same way. Each twin's personality prompts him or her to select friends and environments that happen to be similar to the friends and environments chosen by the other twin. Friends and environments that are similar will treat each twin in similar ways. And so it goes. Because the twins begin with identical genotypic personalities, all the processes of personality–environment interaction act together to promote and sustain their similarity across time—even if they have never been together after birth.

In contrast, the environments of fraternal twins and non-twin siblings increasingly diverge as they get older—even within the same home. They are most alike in early childhood when parents impose a common environment. (Although even here, siblings will react somewhat differently from one another and evoke different responses from the parents.) But as soon as they begin to select and construct environments outside the home, their moderately different talents, interests, and motivations will take them down increasingly divergent paths, thereby producing increasingly divergent personalities.

**SHARED VERSUS NONSHARED ENVIRONMENTS** Twin studies permit researchers to estimate not only how much of the variation among individuals is due to genetic variation, but also how much of the environmentally related variation is due to those aspects of the environment that family members share with one another (for example, the socioeconomic status of the family) as compared with aspects of the environment that family members do not share (for example, friends outside the family). Surprisingly, differences due to the shared aspects of the environment seem to account for almost none of the environmental variation: after their genetic similarities are subtracted out, two children from the same family seem to be no more alike than two children chosen randomly from the population (Plomin & Daniels, 1987). Except for their genetically produced similarities, siblings raised by authoritative parents, for example, are likely to be as different from each other as they are from children raised by indulgent parents. More generally, this conclusion implies that the kinds of variables that psychologists typically study (such as childrearing practices, socioeconomic status of the family) are contributing virtually nothing to individual differences in personality. How can this be so?

One possible explanation might be that the reactive, evocative, and proactive processes act to diminish the differences between environments as long as those environments permit some flexibility of response. A bright child from a neglecting or impoverished home is more likely than a less bright sibling to absorb more information from a television program (reactive interaction), to attract the attention of a sympathetic teacher (evocative interaction), and to go to the library on his or her own (proactive interaction). This child's genotype acts to counteract the potentially debilitating effects of the home environment, and therefore he or she develops differently from a less bright sibling. Only if the environment is severely restrictive will these personality-driven processes be thwarted (Scarr, 1988; Scarr & McCartney, 1983). This explanation is supported by the finding that the most dissimilar pairs of identical twins reared apart are those in which one was reared in a severely restricted environment.

Although this explanation seems plausible, there is no direct evidence that it is correct. In any case, if further research continues to show shared environment effects to be negligible, then research will have to shift from the usual comparisons of children from different families to comparisons of children within the same families—with particular attention paid to the personality–environment interactions within those families.

## Cultural Influences

One reason that differences between families in childrearing practices do not appear to produce systematic differences in children's personalities may be that the studies do not include a large enough range of family environments or children's personalities to detect such differences. For example, families in virtually all twin studies are drawn from a single culture—usually a Western, industrialized culture. Compared with differences between cultures, the families and children within a single culture may be relatively homogeneous.

Most Western, industrialized nations value and attempt to shape citizens who are independent, self-assertive, and motivated to achieve. As a

*Non-Western families emphasize interdependence more than Western families, especially for females.*

member of such a culture, you can confirm this set of values by reviewing your own reactions to the personality types associated with the different parenting patterns summarized in Figure 13-1. In our culture, the authoritative parents and their confident, self-assertive children are clearly the preferred group.

In contrast, most non-Western cultures place much less value on independence and self-assertiveness than our own society. This is especially true for girls and women. Such cultures stress the interdependence of persons with others in the community rather than the independence of persons from one another. Children are encouraged to be part of the functioning community rather than to compete and do better than others (Edwards & Whiting, 1980; Whiting & Edwards, 1988; Whiting & Child, 1953; Whiting & Whiting, 1975).

Parents in many non-Western cultures also differ from parents in our culture in that they punish bad behavior but do not explicitly praise or otherwise reward good behavior. Cross-cultural observations suggest that Western children are not more obedient overall than non-Western children, but they *are* more obedient when their parents are present and they are more likely to seek attention from adults generally (LeVine, 1980). Western parents may sometimes find such attention-seeking annoying, but they willingly put up with it because it expresses the valued trait of self-assertiveness—a trait that is considered disruptive of community functioning in less achievement-oriented cultures.

It appears, then, that each culture manages to shape the kinds of personality characteristics that it values. It also appears that each culture values the kinds of personality characteristics it needs in order to survive and prosper. For example, in agricultural societies

> Carelessness in performance of routine duties leads to a threat of hunger, not for the day of carelessness itself but for many months to come. Individual initiative attempts to improve techniques may be feared because no one can tell immediately whether the changes will lead to a greater harvest or to a disastrous failure. Under those conditions, there might well be a premium on obedience to the older and wiser, and on responsibility in faithful performance to the routine laid down by custom for one's economic role. (Barry, Child, & Bacon, 1959, p. 52)

At the opposite extreme are societies that subsist through hunting or fishing with no means for extended storing of catch. Here individual initiative and development of high skill seem to be at a premium. Where each day's food comes from that day's catch, variations in the energy and skill exerted in food-getting lead to immediate reward or punishment.

To test these speculations, Barry, Child, and Bacon (1959) looked at the relationship between childrearing practices and the degree of food accumulation in six societies. (Food accumulation is high in agricultural societies and low in hunting societies.) As the correlations in Table 13-1 show, high food-accumulation societies stress responsibility and obedience in their childrearing practices; low food-accumulation societies stress achievement, self-reliance, and independence.

To test whether these different kinds of societies do, in fact, tend to produce individuals with the valued attributes, one investigator assessed conformity in samples of individuals from high and low food-accumulating cultures. The participants were given a visual task in which they were required to identify which of several lines matched a standard line. Prior to

| TRAIT STRESSED IN CHILDREARING | CORRELATION WITH FOOD ACCUMULATION | |
|---|---|---|
| | BOYS | GIRLS |
| Responsibility | +.74 | +.62 |
| Obedience | +.50 | +.59 |
| Nurturance | −.01 | +.10 |
| Achievement | −.60 | −.62 |
| Self-Reliance | −.21 | −.46 |
| Independence | −.41 | −.11 |

**TABLE 13-1**
**Childrearing Practices and Food Accumulation** *The table shows the relationship between traits emphasized in childrearing and the degree of food accumulation in six societies. Cultures high in food accumulation stress responsibility and obedience; cultures low in food accumulation stress achievement, self-reliance, and independence. (After Barry, Child, & Bacon, 1959)*

making their own judgment, they were told on each trial which line had been selected most often by other members of their culture. In some cases, these responses were clearly incorrect. The investigator found that individuals from high food-accumulating cultures were significantly more likely than those from low food-accumulating cultures to conform to the alleged responses of others—even when those responses were clearly incorrect (Berry, 1967).

These results are consistent with the hypothesis that different lifestyles put a premium on different personality traits and that cultures shape these traits in their members through different childrearing practices.

# Adolescence: Constructing an Identity

We noted in Chapter 3 that the major developmental task of adolesence is to create an identity, to develop answers to the questions "Who am I?" and "Where am I going?" The psychoanalyst Erik Erikson coined the term **identity crisis** to refer to this active process of self-definition. The word *crisis* is, perhaps, unfortunate because Erikson believed this period of self-doubt to be an integral part of healthy psychosocial development. Similarly, most developmental psychologists believe that adolescence should be a period of "role experimentation" in which young persons can explore alternative behaviors, interests, and ideologies. Many beliefs, roles, and ways of behaving may be "tried on," modified, or discarded in an attempt to shape an integrated concept of the self. Ideally the identity crisis should be resolved by the early or mid-twenties so that the individual can move on to other life tasks.

When this process is successful, the individual is said to have achieved an identity; at a minimum, this usually means having committed oneself to a sexual identity, a vocational direction, and an ideological worldview. Until the identity crisis is resolved, the individual has no consistent sense of self or set of internal standards for evaluating his or her self-worth in the major areas of life. As we noted in Chapter 3, Erikson called this unsuccessful outcome *identity confusion* (Erikson, 1968).

## Identity Statuses

Erikson's ideas were explored empirically by James Marcia (1966, 1980) who designed a semistructured, open-ended interview in which adolescents were asked questions like "Is there any time when you've come to doubt any of your religious beliefs? When? How did it happen? How did you resolve things?" In the occupational area, interviewees were asked what their majors were, what they planned to do after college, how willing they thought they would be to change their occupational plans if something better came along, and so forth.

On the basis of these interviews, Marcia concluded that there are four **identity statuses** or positions on Erikson's identity-formation continuum: *identity achievement, foreclosure, moratorium,* and *identity diffusion.* As shown in Figure 13-2, these four statuses are distinguished by whether the person perceives the domain in question as an identity issue and whether a resolution has been reached. As we describe each of these four statuses, keep in mind that these do not represent enduring personality traits but are snap-

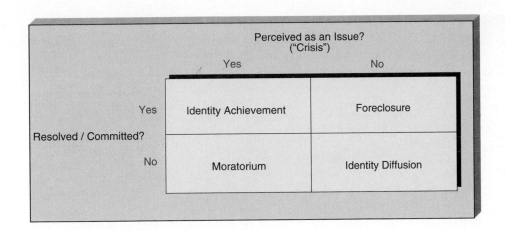

**FIGURE 13-2**
**Identity Statuses** *The individual's identity status in a particular domain is defined in terms of whether the person perceives it as an issue and whether he or she has reached a resolution or committed to a position.*

shots in time of a person's current status. Similarly, it is possible for an individual to be in one status with respect to one domain (for example, religious beliefs) and in another status in another domain (for example, occupational choice).

1. *Identity Achievement*   Those in this status have passed through an identity crisis, a period of active questioning and self-definition. They have committed to ideological positions they have worked out for themselves and decided on an occupation. They have begun to think of themselves as a future doctor, not just a pre-med chemistry major. They have re-examined their family's religious and political beliefs and discarded those that don't seem to fit their identity.

2. *Foreclosure*   Those in this status are also committed to occupational and ideological positions, but they show no signs of ever having gone through an identity crisis. They have accepted the religion of their families without question. When asked about political positions, they often say they have never really given it much thought. Some of them seem committed and cooperative; others simply seem rigid, dogmatic, and conforming. They give the impression that they would be lost if some major event occurred to challenge their unexamined rules and values.

3. *Moratorium*   These are the young people currently in the midst of an identity crisis. They are actively seeking answers but are still finding the conflicts between their parents' plans for them and their own interests unresolved. They may express a set of political or religious beliefs with great intensity for a while only to abandon them after a period of reconsideration. At best, they seem sensitive, ethical, and open-minded; at worst, they appear anxiety-ridden, self-righteous, and vacillating (Scarr, Weinberg, & Levine, 1986).

4. *Identity Diffusion*   This is Marcia's term for Erikson's identity confusion category. Some of those in this category may have experienced an identity crisis in the past; some have not. But in either case, they still have no integrated sense of themselves. They say it might be "interesting" to go to law school or maybe start a business, but they are not taking steps to move in either direction. They say they are not interested in religion or politics. Some seem cynical ("Politics is all just crap"); others just seem shallow and confused. Some, of course, are still too young to have reached the identity development phase of adolescence.

| | IDENTITY STATUS | | | |
| AGE GROUP | IDENTITY ACHIEVEMENT | FORECLOSURE | MORATORIUM | IDENTITY DIFFUSION |
|---|---|---|---|---|
| Pre-high school years | 5 | 37 | 12 | 46 |
| High school underclass years | 9 | 37 | 15 | 39 |
| High school upperclass years | 21 | 36 | 14 | 29 |
| College underclass years | 23 | 26 | 28 | 23 |
| College upperclass years | 40 | 31 | 16 | 14 |

**TABLE 13-2**
**Identity Statuses** *Percent of young people in identity status categories over time in the vocational domain.* (Adapted from Waterman, 1985)

Table 13-2 shows the percent of young people in the four identity statuses over time in the domain of vocational choice. As expected, the percent who have attained identity achievement steadily increases from pre-high school years to college upperclass years, while the percent of those remaining in identity diffusion steadily decreases. Note that the state of identity crisis—moratorium—peaks during the first two years of college. In general, studies show that the level of identity achievement is considerably higher for vocational choice than for political ideology (Waterman, 1985).

## College versus Family

The process of resolving the identity crisis often entails choosing, integrating, or resolving the conflicts between the beliefs and values one has assimilated from one's family and the new beliefs and values one encounters in college. The most intensive study of this process is Theodore Newcomb's classic Bennington Study—an examination of the political attitudes of the entire population of Bennington College, a small, politically liberal, women's college in Vermont. The dates of the study (1935–1939) are a useful reminder that this is not a new phenomenon.

Today Bennington College is coed and tends to attract applicants who are aware of its politically liberal reputation. But in 1935, most of the students came from politically conservative families who could afford to send their daughters to an expensive college in the middle of history's worst economic depression. For example, over two-thirds of the parents of Bennington students were affiliated with the Republican party in the late 1930s.

At Bennington, these women encountered faculty members and older students who held a much more liberal perspective on world affairs (such as the Great Depression and the threat of World War II) than their parents did. And as the women moved through their education at Bennington, they moved progressively further away from their parents' attitudes. For example, in the 1936 presidential campaign, 66 percent of their parents favored the Republican candidate, Landon, over the Democratic candidate, Roosevelt. So did about 62 percent of the Bennington freshmen. But only 43 percent of the sophomores favored Landon, and only 15 percent of the juniors and seniors did.

For most of the women, their increasing liberalism reflected a deliberate choice between college and family. Initially, many of them chose to go along with the college norms for pragmatic or non-intellectual reasons. Here are two examples:

> All my life I've resented the protection of governesses and parents. At college I got away from that, or rather, I guess I should say, I changed it to wanting the intellectual approval of teachers and more advanced students. Then I found that you can't be reactionary and be intellectually respectable.

> Becoming radical meant thinking for myself and, figuratively, thumbing my nose at my family. It also meant intellectual identification with the faculty and students that I most wanted to be like. (Newcomb, 1943, pp. 134, 131)

But as the women continued to mature, their adopted beliefs and attitudes began to become a genuine part of their ideological identities:

> It didn't take me long to see that liberal attitudes had prestige value. . . . I became liberal at first because of its prestige value; I remain so because the problems around which my liberalism centers are important. What I want now is to be effective in solving problems.

> Prestige and recognition have always meant everything to me. . . . But I've sweat blood in trying to be honest with myself, and the result is that I really know what I want my attitudes to be, and I see what their consequences will be in my own life. (Newcomb, 1943, pp. 136–137)

Did these changes in political attitudes become a part of an enduring ideological identity? In general, the answer is yes. A follow-up study of these women 25 years later found that they had remained liberal. For example, in the 1960 presidential election, 60 percent of the Bennington alumnae preferred the Democrat Kennedy over the Republican Nixon, compared with fewer than 30 percent of women with similar socioeconomic backgrounds and educational levels. Moreover, about 60 percent of the Bennington alumnae were politically active, most (66 percent) within the Democratic party (Newcomb, Koening, Flacks, & Warwick, 1967).

*The ideologies that young adults are exposed to in college influence the identities that they will carry the rest of their lives.*

## Adulthood: Continuity of Personality

When you look back over your life, you can probably discern personal patterns and styles that have always seemed a part of your personality. Perhaps you have always been shy or had a problem with procrastination. At the same time, you can probably identify ways in which you have changed; perhaps you are less impulsive than you used to be or better able to relate to others. Sometimes you might be able to identify specific experiences that have changed you. As we have noted, going to college often affects attitudes, values, and personality in far-reaching ways. Understanding the interplay of continuity and change in personality across the life course is a basic task for both personality and developmental psychology.

*Critical*
# DISCUSSION

## Studying Personality the Long Way

Only investigators with a strong ability to delay gratification or an unselfish devotion to science undertake longitudinal studies. For studies designed to span many years, the original investigators may not even be around to reap the final rewards; their studies may outlive them. Other practical reasons also deter most would-be investigators. Longitudinal studies are expensive, and funding can-

not usually be guaranteed over the required time interval. Second, subjects who start out in the study move away, die, decide to discontinue their participation, or cannot otherwise be located for follow-up. In general, the administrative tasks involved in conducting such a study take as much time and effort as collecting the data. For these reasons, many longitudinal studies are conducted under the auspices of research institutes rather than by independent investigators.

In addition to the practical problems, a more substantive problem arises in many long-term longitudinal studies. As the interests of the field change over time, the kinds of data collected in a longitudinal study also change. A study that begins with a focus on academic achievement may fail to gather personality information that later investigators wish to have. Sometimes assessment in-

struments used early in the study become obsolete and are discarded for better instruments as the study progresses. All of these factors make it difficult to compare later observations with earlier ones.

This was the major problem with the two studies discussed in the text that were conducted at the Institute of Human Development (IHD) in Berkeley. Not only were noncomparable measurements made at different points in time, the two studies were themselves not comparable to each other in many ways. These problems were elegantly solved by Jack Block, who used the Q-sort method of personality description to standardize the data (Block, 1961/1978; Block, 1971). (The "Q" in "Q-sort" was arbitrarily chosen and has no particular meaning.)

In the Q-sort technique, a rater or sorter describes an individual's personal-

## Evidence for Continuity

The only effective way to investigate continuity and change in personality over the life course is to conduct longitudinal studies, studies that observe or assess the same persons over time. But because these are very difficult to conduct (see the Critical Discussion, "Studying Personality the Long Way"), there are only a handful of longitudinal studies that cover extensive time periods.

Two of the most ambitious longitudinal studies ever conducted are housed at the Institute of Human Development (IHD) at the University of California in Berkeley. Investigators began the *Berkeley Guidance Study* in 1929 by contacting the parents of every third baby born in Berkeley over an 18-month period and asking them to enroll their newborns in the study; in all, 248 infants and their families were included. The *Oakland Growth Study* began in 1932 with 212 fifth-grade children from elementary schools in Oakland, California. The children from both samples were studied intensively through adolescence and were interviewed again when the Berkeley subjects were about 30, 40, and 50 and the Oakland subjects were about 37, 47, and 57. IHD has generously made its archive available to many investigators around the world.

As described in the Critical Discussion, independent clinical psychologists used a set of personality statements (Q items) to describe the IHD subjects when they were in junior high school (age 13), senior high school (age 16), and as adults (age 30 or 37). The three personality profiles for each subject were then correlated with one another to assess the continuity of the overall personality across these time intervals.

The results show that in general there was strong continuity of personality from early to later adolescence; the mean correlations between the two

*Longitudinal studies enable psychologists to observe the behavior of individuals over decades.*

ity by sorting a set of approximately 100 cards into piles. Each card contains a personality statement (for example, "Has a wide range of interests," "Is self-defeating"). The rater sorts the cards into nine piles, placing those cards that are least descriptive of the individual in pile 1 on the left and those that are most descriptive in pile 9 on the right. The other cards are distributed in the intermediate piles, with those that seem neither characteristic nor uncharacteristic of the individual going into the middle pile (pile 5). Thus each Q item receives a score ranging from 1 to 9, with higher numbers indicating that the item is more characteristic of the person.

Two Q sorts can be compared with each other quantitatively by computing a correlation between them: the 100 scores from the first sort are correlated with the corresponding 100 scores of the other—just as if they were 100 observa-

tions of one variable being correlated with 100 observations of a second variable. Like the more standard correlation between variables, this index of similarity between two Q sorts can range from -1 to +1. Two identical Q sorts will thus have a similarity index of +1. If two Q sorts are descriptions of the same individual at two different times, then this index of similarity will assess the continuity of that individual's overall personality profile over time. The continuity of individual Q items can also be assessed by using the usual method of correlation between variables.

In the IHD studies, all the data on a single subject from the junior high-school years were placed into a single folder. Two to four clinical psychologists independently examined the folder and prepared Q-sort descriptions of the subject. A different set of sorters did the same thing for the data gathered during

the senior high-school period. And finally, the interviewers and independent clinicians prepared Q-sort descriptions of the subjects when they were interviewed as adults in 1960, 1970, and 1980. This total procedure thus converted a bewildering variety of data to a set of independent but standardized personality descriptions on each subject at different ages that could be directly compared with one another.

sets of adolescent Q sorts were .77 and .75 for men and women, respectively. The correlations between the senior high-school and adult Q sorts were lower but still quite impressive: .56 for men and .54 for women.

The strongest continuities are related to intelligence and intellectual interests. For example, the continuities from adolescence to adulthood for the item "Appears to have a high degree of intellectual capacity" were .60 and .61 for men and women, respectively. The corresponding correlations for the item "Genuinely values intellectual and cognitive matters" were .59 and .51. Table 13-3 lists correlations for other personality characteristics that showed substantial continuities.

## Sources of Continuity

Studies of individuals across the life course typically find that measures of intellectual performance show the strongest continuities; personality variables like extraversion, emotional stability, and impulse control are next; and political attitudes and measures of self-opinions (for example, self-esteem, life satisfaction) are last—showing correlations between .2 and .4 over 5–10-year intervals (Conley, 1984; 1985). Interestingly, these results are roughly parallel to those from heritability studies: traits with higher heritabilities generally show stronger continuities, suggesting that the underlying genetic basis of many intellectual and personality characteristics may be contributing to their temporal stability. In general, however, it is not the genotype itself that directly produces continuity, but the interaction of the genotype with the environment—acting through the same processes we discussed earlier when we examined the initial shaping of personality in childhood. In particular, the processes of reactive, evocative, and proactive interaction all

**TABLE 13-3**
**Continuity of Personality** *The table lists some of the personality characteristics that showed the greatest continuity over the years from early adolescence to adulthood.* (After Block, 1971)

| Q ITEMS | CORRELATIONS JUNIOR HIGH TO SENIOR HIGH SCHOOL | CORRELATIONS SENIOR HIGH SCHOOL TO ADULTHOOD |
|---|---|---|
| **Males** | | |
| Is a genuinely dependable and responsible person | .58 | .53 |
| Tends toward undercontrol of needs and impulses; unable to delay gratification | .57 | .59 |
| Is self-defeating | .50 | .42 |
| Enjoys aesthetic impressions; is aesthetically reactive | .35 | .58 |
| **Females** | | |
| Basically submissive | .50 | .46 |
| Emphasizes being with others; gregarious | .39 | .43 |
| Tends to be rebellious and nonconforming | .48 | .49 |
| Is concerned with philosophical problems (for example, religion, values, meaning of life) | .45 | .42 |

act to create environments for the individual that are themselves a function of his or her personality.

For example, in our earlier discussion of proactive interaction, we cited the sociable child who, in selectively choosing to enter and create social situations, creates environments for herself that further reinforce and sustain her sociability. We do the same thing when we choose friends and spouses. Because we are likely to choose companions who share our values and personality traits, they are likely, in turn, to reinforce and sustain those values and traits.

Evidence for this process was obtained in the Bennington Study we discussed earlier. Recall that women who attended Bennington College in the late 1930s became increasingly liberal politically during their college years and had retained their liberal views over the subsequent 25 years. Interviews with these women revealed that they had remained liberal, in part, because they acquired politically liberal friends and married politically liberal husbands who reinforced and sustained their political attitudes (Newcomb, 1943; Newcomb, Koenig, Flacks, & Warwick, 1967).

There is also evidence for this process of proactive interaction in the domain of personality. When the subjects who participated in the Berkeley Guidance Study were interviewed in 1970 and 1980, so were their spouses, thereby providing Q sorts of subjects and spouses that could be directly correlated with each other. Two researchers have recently examined those Q sorts to see whether spouses who were more alike in personality would produce greater personality continuity in each other. To do this, they compared the similarity of each couple's Q sorts from 1970 with the personality continuity of each spouse from 1970 to 1980 (Caspi & Herbener, 1990).

When the researchers divided the 126 couples into three groups of equal size on the basis of the similarity between the spouses' 1970 Q sorts, they found that the least similar spouses showed individual continuities of .4 from 1970 to 1980; moderately similar spouses showed individual continuities of .5; and the most similar spouses showed continuities of .6. Further analyses demonstrated that these findings were not simply due to spouses' similarities in age, social class, or education.

The study also found that spouses who were more similar in personality were also more similar in their enjoyment of daily activities like visiting friends, going out for dinner, and participating in community activities and professional meetings. They also reported less marital conflict and greater closeness, friendliness, and marital satisfaction than less similar spouses. (This last finding exemplifies a well-known phenomenon. We discuss the similarity-produces-liking effect further in Chapter 18.)

**CONTINUITY OF MALADAPTIVE PERSONALITY PATTERNS**  It is easy to appreciate why we might be motivated to create environments for ourselves that sustain those aspects of our personalities that bring us happiness and personal satisfaction. But the same processes of reactive, evocative, and proactive interaction can act in more coercive ways to sustain maladaptive personality patterns as well.

*Couples who enjoy similar activities report greater marital satisfaction.*

For example, consider an adolescent boy who has temper tantrums. His ill-temper may provoke school authorities to expel him (evocative interaction) or cause him to experience school so negatively (reactive interaction) that he chooses to quit as soon as he is legally permitted to do so (proactive interaction). In either case, leaving school cuts short his education, which is likely to lead to lower occupational status. This low occupational status might then lead to an erratic worklife—frequent job changes, bouts of unemployment—which, in turn, might disrupt his marriage and lead to divorce. In this hypothetical scenario, these occupational and marital outcomes are *cumulative* consequences of his childhood personality. Once set in motion by childhood temper tantrums, the chain of events takes over and culminates in the adult outcomes—even if he is no longer ill-tempered as an adult.

Now consider a different scenario that could produce the same outcome. The boy's temper tantrums might coerce his parents into giving in to his demands (evocative interaction), thereby reinforcing his behavior. This reinforcement not only short-circuits the learning of more controlled ways of behaving that might have greater adaptability in the long run, but it also increases the likelihood that he will react in similar ways when similar situations arise in the future (reactive interaction). Thus, he will continue to be ill-tempered as an adult, losing his temper when frustrations arise on the job or when conflicts arise in his marriage. This, in turn, can lead to an erratic worklife, low-level occupational status, and divorce. In this scenario, the same occupational and marital outcomes are *contemporary* consequences of his current personality rather than cumulative consequences of earlier events like quitting school.

Although these scenarios are hypothetical, they are based on actual research findings showing evidence for both cumulative and contemporary consequences of child ill-temperedness. Using the IHD archive from the Berkeley Guidance Study, investigators first identified subjects in the archive who had had severe and frequent temper tantrums in late childhood (8–10 years old). The investigators then traced the continuities and consequences of this ill-temperedness across the subsequent 30 years of the subjects' lives (Caspi, Bem, & Elder, 1989; Caspi, Elder, & Bem, 1987).

**ILL-TEMPERED MALES**  Beginning with male subjects, the investigators first asked the continuity question: Do ill-tempered boys become ill-tempered men? The answer was yes. Correlations between the temper-tantrum scores in late childhood and the Q-sort ratings 20 years later reveal that ill-tempered boys were later described as significantly more undercontrolled, irritable, and moody than their peers.

The investigators then examined the subjects' work histories. The major finding was that ill-tempered boys who came from middle-class homes suffered a progressive deterioration of socioeconomic status as they moved through the life course. They were somewhat more likely than their even-tempered peers to terminate their formal education earlier; the occupational status of their first jobs was significantly lower, and by midlife (age 40), their occupational status was indistinguishable from that of men born into the working class. A majority held jobs of lower occupational status than those held by their fathers at a comparable age. They also had more erratic worklives, changing jobs more frequently and experiencing more unemployment between ages 18 and 40.

*Do ill-tempered children become ill-tempered adults?*

Having established an overall correlation between childhood ill-temperedness and occupational outcomes, the investigators then asked about the path between these two things. Did these subjects become occupationally disadvantaged because their earlier ill-temperedness started them down a particular path (cumulative consequences) or because their current ill-temperedness handicapped them in the world of work (contemporary consequences)? To answer this, the investigators used a correlational procedure called **path analysis,** which divides an overall correlation into separate components of paths. Figure 13-3 shows the results of this analysis; the arrows show the significant path correlations that were found.

As the figure shows, there is a significant path or correlation for males from childhood ill-temperedness to less education and a continuing significant path from less education to low occupational status. In other words, childhood ill-temperedness leads to less education (ill-tempered boys quit

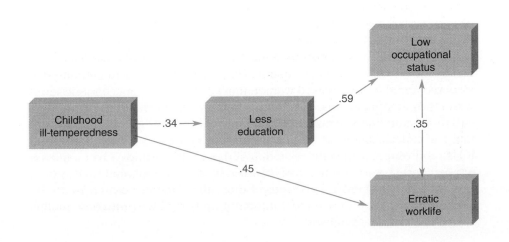

**FIGURE 13-3**
**Path Analysis for Male Ill-Temperedness** *The figure traces the separate paths from childhood ill-temperedness to low occupational status and an erratic worklife at age 40 for middle-class men. Childhood ill-temperedness leads to lower occupational status because ill-tempered children quit school sooner (cumulative consequences). Childhood ill-temperedness leads directly to an erratic worklife because the subjects remain ill-tempered as adults, and this handicaps them in the world of work (contemporary consequences).* (After Caspi, Elder, & Bem, 1987)

school sooner) which, in turn, leads to low occupational status. But at the same time, there is no *direct* path from ill-temperedness to low occupational status. Together, these results imply that low occupational status is a cumulative consequence of earlier childhood ill-temperedness, not a contemporary consequence of current adult ill-temperedness: The reason that ill-tempered males held low occupational status at age 40 is that they had quit school sooner.

The path from childhood ill-temperedness to an erratic worklife shows the opposite pattern. There is no significant path from less education to an erratic worklife, but there is a significant direct path from childhood ill-temperedness to an erratic worklife. This implies that an erratic worklife is a contemporary consequence of adult ill-temperedness, not a cumulative consequence of less education. Ill-tempered males appear to have a more erratic worklife at age 40, in part, because they are still ill-tempered—perhaps exploding on the job when frustrations arise.

Finally, there is a significant correlation between low occupational status and an erratic worklife, but we cannot determine the direction of causality because these two variables are present at the same time. Ill-tempered men may become frustrated with low-status jobs and thus become erratic by quitting or being fired. Alternatively, their erratic worklife may keep them out of better jobs, thus forcing them into lower-status jobs. Both sequences could be in effect.

A person's history of childhood ill-temperedness also affects the domestic sphere. Almost half (46 percent) of men with histories of childhood ill-temperedness had divorced by age 40 compared with only 22 percent of other men.

**ILL-TEMPERED FEMALES**  Like the men, women who had been ill-tempered as young girls also showed personality continuity. Compared with other women, these women were described by both their husbands and their children at the time of the 1970 interviews as less adequate, more ill-tempered mothers.

The Berkeley subjects became adults between 1945 and 1960, a time of quite traditional sex roles in America. As a result, few of the women had occupations outside the home, and the investigators were not able to analyze their occupational status as they had done for the men. But this was also a time when a woman's socioeconomic status was defined by her husband's occupation, and so the investigators looked at the occupational status of these women's husbands. They found that compared with other women, women with a history of childhood ill-temperedness married men who had lower occupational status both at the time of marriage and at midlife. By comparing the jobs held by their husbands at the time of marriage with those held by their fathers at a comparable age, the investigators found that 40 percent of the ill-tempered women moved down in socioeconomic status when they married compared with only 24 percent of other women.

Ill-temperedness in childhood not only consigned these women to marriages at a socioeconomic level lower than that of their childhood homes, but it also contributed to the deterioration of these relationships. Over a quarter (26 percent) of these women had divorced by age 40 compared with only 12 percent of other women. Husbands of those ill-tempered women who were married at the time of the 1970 interviews reported more marital conflict than husbands of other women.

## Sources of Discontinuity

Despite the evidence for the continuity of ill-temperedness discussed above, the correlations themselves are still relatively low, leaving room for many exceptions: ill-tempered children do not inevitably become ill-tempered adults. Often a person will encounter a transforming event or series of events—such as going to college or entering therapy—that starts him or her on a new path and thereby initiates personality change. Individuals whose personalities are at odds with their environments may be directly pressured to change by those who find their patterns of behavior aversive; and finally, many individuals make efforts at one time or another to change their own personality patterns in order to achieve greater happiness. These several sources of change can thus create discontinuities in personality across the life course.

One frequent source of pressure for change arises from society's sex-role norms. For example, one extensive longitudinal study found that boys but not girls showed continuity from childhood to early adulthood on traditionally male-appropriate personality traits like aggression, whereas girls but not boys showed continuity on traditionally female-appropriate traits like dependency (Kagan & Moss, 1962). There was also some evidence that behavior inconsistent with sex-role expectations in childhood may not be entirely suppressed but may be expressed in adulthood in more socially acceptable ways.

This possibility was explored further by the same investigators who had conducted the study of ill-temperedness, again using the IHD archives from the Berkeley Guidance Study (Caspi, Elder, & Bem, 1989). For this study, they selected subjects who had been strongly dependent on adults in late childhood and then traced the continuity of this dependency across the subsequent 30 years of the subjects' lives. Because dependency is discouraged

*Men tend to be more nurturant if they have a history of childhood dependency.*

for boys and men in our society, the investigators were particularly interested in whether this trait would survive the sex-role pressures on the male subjects. Do dependent boys become dependent men?

The answer this time was both more complex and more interesting. Compared with other men, those who had histories of childhood dependency were characterized in adulthood as calm, warm, giving, sympathetic, insightful, undefensive, incisive, and socially poised. Although they sought reassurance from others—a possible echo of their earlier childhood dependency—others felt nurturant toward them and sought them out for advice. It appears that the negative childhood attribute of dependency had been transformed into a related but remarkably positive nurturant personality style in adulthood. We thus see both continuity and discontinuity.

Not unexpectedly, the warm, nurturant adult style of these men conferred its most obvious advantages in the domestic sphere. These men were significantly more likely to have an intact first marriage at midlife than other men (83 percent versus 62 percent); their wives expressed more satisfaction with their marriages than wives of other men; and they and their wives agreed more with one another on such childrearing practices as discipline, affection, and attention. Dependent adolescent boys who worry about being insufficiently assertive should take note—as should adolescent girls who will someday come to appreciate nurturant, lovable men and wonder where to find them.

## *Chapter* SUMMARY

1. Mood-related personality differences that show up in infants as young as 3 months are called *temperaments.* There is some evidence that temperaments are early building blocks for later personality traits. Comparisons of identical and fraternal twins indicate that genetic factors account for about 50 percent of the variability among individuals on many personality characteristics.

2. An infant's tendency to seek closeness to particular people and to feel more secure in their presence is called *attachment.* Attachment can be assessed in a procedure called the *Strange Situation,* a series of episodes in which a child is observed as the primary caregiver leaves and returns to the room. On the basis of the child's reactions, he or she is classified as (a) *Securely Attached;* (b) *Insecurely Attached: Avoidant;* or (c) *Insecurely Attached: Ambivalent.* Securely attached infants tend to have primary caregivers who respond sensitively to their needs. A child's temperament also influences his or her behavior in the Strange Situation. Securely attached children tend to cope with new experiences better than insecurely attached children later in childhood.

3. Parental childrearing practices can be distinguished on two dimensions: the first distinguishes parents who are demanding and controlling of their children from those who are undemanding; the other distinguishes parents who are accepting, responsive, and child-centered from those who are rejecting, unresponsive, and parent-centered. The combination of these two dimensions produces four kinds of parenting patterns: *authoritative, authoritarian, indulgent,* and *neglecting.*

4. *Authoritative* parents combine high control with acceptance and have children who tend to be independent, self-assertive, motivated to achieve, and socially successful. *Authoritarian* parents exercise high control, but have a low level of acceptance. Their children tend to be re-

sponsible but socially withdrawn and lacking in spontaneity and achievement motivation. *Indulgent* parents are accepting but place few demands on their children. Their children show vitality but tend to be immature and lack impulse control, social responsibility, and self-reliance. Finally, *neglecting* parents are more concerned with their own activities and are uninvolved with their children. Their children tend to be impulsive, uninterested in school, and lack long-term goals. Extremely neglecting parents have children who show clear disturbances in their attachment relationships and psychological functioning by age 2. These childrearing practices may not cause the observed differences in children's behaviors so much as they reflect parents' reactions to the children's behavior. Also, the correlations are very low.

5. In shaping personality, genetic and environmental influences do not act independently of one another but are intertwined from the moment of birth. Because parents give a child both their genes and the environment, there is a built-in correlation between the child's *genotype* (inherited personality characteristics) and that environment.

6. Three dynamic processes of personality–environment interaction are (a) *reactive interaction*—different individuals exposed to the same environment experience it, interpret it, and react to it differently; (b) *evocative interaction*—an individual's personality evokes distinctive responses from others; and (c) *proactive interaction*—individuals select or create environments of their own. As a child gets older, the influence of proactive interaction becomes increasingly important.

7. Studies of twins have produced a number of puzzling patterns: the differences between identical twin similarities and fraternal twin similarities are too great to be explained by simple genetic models; identical twins reared apart are as similar to one another as identical twins reared together; and fraternal twins and non-twin siblings become less similar over time, even when they are reared together. These patterns might be due in part to the three processes of personality–environment interaction (reactive, evocative, and proactive).

8. After their genetic similarities are subtracted out, children from the same family seem to be no more alike than children chosen randomly from the population, a surprising finding. If further research confirms this, then the kinds of variables that psychologists typically study (such as childrearing practices, the family's socioeconomic status) are contributing virtually nothing to individual differences in personality. Research will have to begin looking more closely at differences between children within the same family. This finding, too, might be partially accounted for by the three processes of personality–environment interaction.

9. Differences between families drawn from Western industrial societies may be too small for between-family effects to show up. Compared with these societies, most non-Western cultures place less value on independence and self-assertiveness and more on the interdependence of persons with others in the community. In general, agricultural societies stress responsibility and obedience in their childrearing practices; hunting and fishing societies stress achievement, self-reliance, and independence.

10. A major task of adolescence is to arrive at a unique identity, to answer the question "Who am I?" The *identity status* of a young person in a particular domain (for example, religion, vocation, political views) can be classified into four categories on the basis of whether he or she is wrestling with the domain as an identity issue and whether it has been

resolved. The category of *identity achievement* contains those who have passed through an identity crisis and have resolved it. *Foreclosure* contains those who have never tried to work through the identity issue within the domain in question; they have simply accepted the position of their families. *Moratorium* contains those currently in the midst of an identity crisis, actively trying to resolve the issues for themselves. *Identity diffusion* contains those who have not attained an integrated identity. Some may have experienced an *identity crisis* but never resolved it; others may still be too young to have reached this phase of adolescent development. A political identity acquired in college tends to be retained into later adulthood.

11. *Longitudinal studies* observe the same individuals over time and provide the only effective way to assess the continuity of personality through the life course. In general, measures of intellectual performance show the strongest continuities; personality variables like extraversion, emotional stability/instability, and impulse control are next; political attitudes and measures of self-opinions (for example, self-esteem, life satisfaction) are last. Genetic and genotype–environment factors may contribute to the continuity of the intellectual and personality characteristics across time.

12. The three processes of personality–environment interaction influence the continuity of personality. For example, continuity produced by proactive interaction occurs when we choose friends and spouses who are compatible with our personalities, and they, in turn, reinforce and sustain our personalities. One study showed that personalities of spouses who were more alike changed less over a decade than those of spouses who were less alike. More similar spouses also reported more similarities in the activities they enjoyed, less marital conflict, and greater marital satisfaction than less similar spouses.

13. Maladaptive personality patterns can also be sustained over the life course through the processes of personality–environment interaction. These produce *cumulative consequences* when an individual's early personality selects or channels him or her into particular life paths. They produce *contemporary consequences* when the early personality is itself carried forward into adulthood where it evokes distinctive responses from the environment. Both kinds of consequences were demonstrated in a study that followed ill-tempered children across the subsequent 30 years of their lives.

14. Cultural norms are an important environmental influence on personality and its continuity. Individuals who do not conform to the culture's norms are likely to be pressured to change. Sex-role norms provide an example. Aggression shows continuity for males but not for females; dependency shows continuity for females but not for males. Childhood behavior that is inconsistent with sex-role norms may be transformed into more acceptable forms in adulthood. For example, in one study dependent boys became nurturant men with very successful marriages.

*Further* **READING**

A general text on personality development through the life course is Goldhaber, *Life-Span Human Development* (1986). The general textbooks of developmental psychology and the handbooks of infant and child development listed at the end of Chapter 3 also treat the topics discussed in this chapter. Plomin, *Nature and Nurture* (1990) provides an excellent, accessible discussion of behavioral genetics, including the twin method of assessing heritability. For a complete discussion of the differences among children from the same family, see Dunn and Plomin, *Separate Lives: Why Siblings Are so Different* (1990). Research on temperaments is summarized in Plomin and Dunn, *The Study of Temperament: Changes, Continuities and Challenges* (1986).

Cross-cultural studies are reviewed in Munroe, Munroe, and Whiting (eds.), *Handbook of Cross-Cultural Human Development* (1981). The classic studies are Whiting and Child, *Child Training and Personality: A Cross-Cultural Study* (1953); Whiting and Whiting, *Children of Six Cultures: A Psychocultural Analysis* (1975); and more recently, Whiting and Edwards, *Children of Different Worlds: The Formation of Social Behavior* (1988).

The best sources on the longitudinal archives housed at the Institute of Human Development (IHD) in Berkeley are Eichorn, Clausen, Haan, Honzik, and Mussen (eds.), *Present and Past in Middle Life* (1981); and Block, *Lives Through Time* (1971).

# Chapter 14

# Personality Theory and Assessment

## Trait Approach 525
*Personality Types*
*Personality Traits*
*Trait Theories*
*Evaluation of Trait Approach*

## Psychoanalytic Approach 533
*Personality Structure*
*Personality Dynamics*
*Personality Development*
*Modifications of Freud's Theories*
*Psychoanalytic Portrait of Human Personality*
*Evaluation of Psychoanalytic Approach*

## Social-Learning Approach 540
*Social Learning and Conditioning*
*Person Variables*
*Social-Learning Portrait of Human Personality*
*Evaluation of Social-Learning Approach*

## Phenomenological Approach 544
*Humanistic Psychology*
*Personal Construct Psychology*
*Phenomenological Portrait of Human Personality*
*Evaluation of Phenomenological Approach*

## Personality Assessment 551
*General Considerations*
*Critical Discussion: Testimonial Validity and Other Nonsense*
*Trait Assessment*
*Psychoanalytic Assessment*
*Social-Learning Assessment*
*Phenomenological Assessment*

## Consistency Paradox 564
*Critical Discussion: Are Our Intuitions about Consistency Wrong?*
*Person-Centered Solution*
*Aggregation Solution*
*Interactional Solution*

Detail, *On the Heights*.

In Chapter 13, we defined personality as the distinctive and characteristic patterns of thought, emotion, and behavior that define an individual's personal style and influence his or her interactions with the environment. Accordingly, personality psychology seeks (a) to describe and to explain individual differences—the diverse ways in which individuals differ from one another, and (b) to synthesize the many processes that can influence an individual's interactions with his or her environment—biology, development, learning, thinking, emotion, motivation, and social interaction—into an integrated account of the total person. The study of personality is the most ambitious subfield of psychology.

In this chapter, we shall look at the four major approaches to personality and the empirical methods they employ to measure or assess personality. We shall also return to a theme touched on briefly in Chapter 1 by comparing the portraits of the human personality that emerge from their different philosophies of human nature: To what degree are our beliefs, emotions, and actions free and in what ways are they determined by causes beyond our control? Are we basically good, neutral, or evil? Fixed or modifiable? Active or passive in controlling our destinies? What constitutes psychological health or lack of health? These are not empirical questions, and theories of personality do not explicitly attempt to answer them. But each approach does have implicit answers—underlying presumptions about the nature of human personality that give the approach a distinctive flavor. Historically, these more philosophical factors have been as important as the empirical data in provoking controversies and in winning converts for the competing accounts of personality.

It is important to note that many contemporary psychologists are eclectic: they combine elements of the diverse approaches to arrive at their own integrated view of personality; some even claim to subscribe to no theory at all, but simply do empirical research on problems that interest them. In psychology's earlier days, competing schools of thought were much more in evidence, the battle lines more firmly drawn. Nevertheless, we shall see that contemporary controversies over the nature of personality are still quite lively.

## Trait Approach

### Personality Types

The study of personality is not only the most ambitious subfield of psychology, it is also the oldest. In 400 B.C., Hippocrates suggested that there were four basic personality types, associated with the four bodily humors: An excess of black bile produces the melancholic (depressed) type; an excess of yellow bile produces the choleric (irritable) type; blood produces the sanguine (optimistic) type; and phlegm produces the phlegmatic (calm, stolid) type.

A more differentiated typology was published by Theophrastus (372–287 B.C.,), Aristotle's successor as head of the Lyceum in Athens. He proposed a set of 30 personality types, which he presented in a series of character vignettes. Each sketch began with a brief definition of the dominant characteristic of the type and then described several behaviors typical of the type. Among his characters were the Liar, the Tasteless Man, the Flatterer, and the Penurious Man. For example,

Penuriousness is economy carried beyond all measure. A Penurious Man is one who goes to a debtor to ask for his half-obol interest before the end of the month. At a dinner where expenses are shared, he counts the number of cups each person drinks and he makes a smaller libation to Artemis than anyone. . . . If his wife drops a copper, he moves furniture, beds, chests and hunts in the curtains. . . . The coffers of the penurious men are moldy and the keys rust. . . . They have hair cut short and do not put on their shoes until midday; and when they take their cloak to the fuller they urge him to use plenty of earth so that it will not be spotted so soon. (Quoted in Allport, 1937, p. 57)

Body physique has also been a popular basis for personality typologies. The idea that body build and personality characteristics are related is reflected in such popular stereotypes as "fat people are jolly" or "skinny people are intellectuals." Shakespeare's Julius Caesar remarked, "Let me have men about me that are fat; sleek-headed men, and such as sleep o'nights. Yond Cassius has a lean and hungry look; he thinks too much: such men are dangerous. . . . Would he were fatter" (*Julius Caesar,* Act 1, Scene 2).

In the 1940s, the American physician William Sheldon reported correlations between three bodily physiques, called **somatotypes,** and temperament: the endomorphic (soft and round ) somatotype has a relaxed, sociable temperament; the mesomorphic (muscular and athletic) somatotype has an energetic, assertive, courageous temperament; and the ectomorphic (tall and thin ) somatotype has a restrained, fearful, introverted, artistic temperament (Sheldon, 1954). Sheldon's evidence, however was not very strong, and his methods left open the possibility that his temperament ratings simply reflected popular stereotypes. When individuals are rated on specific behaviors rather than on global traits, there are no strong associations between body types and personality (Mischel, 1968). Although most contemporary psychologists do not consider somatotyping useful, some have continued to refine the system and to present confirming data (Carter & Heath, 1971).

The theories discussed above are called **type theories** because they propose that individuals can be categorized into discrete types that are qualitatively different from one another. Typologies have been useful in many sciences. In chemistry, the periodic chart of the elements is a refinement of earlier typologies of physical substances. In biology, the concepts of a species and of sex (male and female) are both type concepts. Nevertheless, type theories of personality are currently not very popular. The very simplicity that makes them appealing also makes them less capable of capturing the complexity and variability of human personality. Even so, some psychologists have called for a revival of typological thinking in personality, arguing that typologies have been rejected for the wrong reasons and that their virtues have been overlooked (Bem, 1983; Gangestad & Snyder, 1985; Kagan, 1989).

## Personality Traits

Whereas typologies comprise discontinuous categories (like male and female), traits are conceived of as continuous dimensions. For example, rather than categorizing body physiques into one of three pure types, Sheldon rated them on three dimensions, using 7-point rating scales. Thus, a 2–7–4 would be low on endomorphy, high on mesomorphy, and moderate on ectomorphy. More generally, trait theories of personality assume that persons vary simultaneously on a number of personality dimensions or scales. We might rate an individual on scales of intelligence, emotional stability, aggressiveness, and so on. To arrive at a global description of personality, we would need to know the individual's rating on a number of scales, and how much of each trait he or she possessed. Actually, we are all trait theorists. When we informally describe ourselves and others with such adjectives as "aggressive," "cautious," "excitable," "intelligent," or "anxious," we are using a layperson's version of trait theory. Our informal theories serve the same purposes as those of the formal trait theorists: they enable us to characterize consistencies in an individual's behavior and thereby to anticipate how he or she will respond to particular situations.

Trait psychologists attempt to go beyond our everyday trait conceptions of personality, however. Specifically, they seek (a) to arrive at a manageably small set of trait descriptors that can encompass the diversity of human personality, (b) to craft ways of measuring personality traits reliably and validly, and (c) to discover the relationships among traits and between traits and specific behaviors. Different trait theorists have approached these tasks in different ways.

## Trait Theories

**GORDON ALLPORT**  One of the most influential trait theorists was Harvard psychologist Gordon Allport, who died in 1967. His major works on personality were *Personality: A Psychological Interpretation* (1937) and *Pattern and Growth in Personality* (1961). Allport regarded traits as the basic building blocks of psychological organization, serving to integrate what would otherwise be dissimilar stimuli and responses. For example, consider a woman for whom the trait of friendliness is central. For her, sitting next to a stranger on an airplane, visiting the family, and working with others at the office are all equivalent situations in that they all evoke what is for her an interrelated set of responses: being interested, personable, helpful, pleasant, outgoing, warm, and attentive. In other words, her trait of friendliness serves as a unifying element, creating an equivalence class of stimuli, an equivalence class of responses, and providing the link between them.

*A trait theorist might describe the individual on the left as bold and adventurous and the individual on the right as quiet and reflective.*

*Mother Theresa's cardinal disposition is altruism.*

Allport distinguished between **common traits** and **personal dispositions.** Common traits are trait dimensions on which individuals can be compared with one another. Personal dispositions refer to the unique patterning or configuration of traits within the individual. Two people may both be honest but may differ in the way that honesty relates to their other traits. One, sensitive to the feelings of others, may tell a "white lie" on occasion; for this person, sensitivity ranks higher than honesty. The other, ranking honesty higher, is scrupulously honest even if it hurts someone. People may also possess the same trait but for different motives. One person may be conscientious because he or she is concerned about the opinion of other people. Another person may be conscientious because it expresses a need to keep life orderly.

Traits also differ in the extent to which they influence the person's behavior. Allport viewed personal dispositions as being organized in a kind of hierarchy, some having a more pervasive influence on a person's behavior than others; he distinguished among cardinal, central, and secondary dispositions. A few people may have one dominant disposition that influences virtually all aspects of their behavior. Allport called these **cardinal dispositions.** A saintly, religious figure such as Mother Theresa might be said to have the cardinal disposition of altruism. Less pervasive but still quite general tendencies to respond are called **central dispositions.** Most of us have 5 to 10 central dispositions that serve to organize and direct many aspects of our lives. For the woman described earlier, friendliness would be a central disposition. Finally, we all have numerous more specific and narrow interests or tendencies to respond that Allport called **secondary dispositions;** a preference for certain kinds of clothes or a tendency to keep a neat desk but a sloppy personal appearance would be examples.

Most trait psychologists focus on what Allport called the common traits, because these lend themselves better to quantitative analysis and the systematic comparison of individuals with one another. In contrast, Allport's notion of personal dispositions lends itself primarily to the in-depth study of individual lives and experiences. While acknowledging the usefulness of quantitative methods and the study of common traits, Allport himself remained convinced that they failed to capture what he considered the essence of personality—individuality. The systematic study of individuality is relatively neglected in contemporary personality psychology, and some psychologists have even questioned whether it is science rather than biography. Later in this chapter, however, we shall see how Allport's more individualized approach offers one solution to a recurring paradox in the study of personality: How can one reconcile the concept of traits with the observation that people are frequently inconsistent in their behavior from one situation to another?

**FACTOR-ANALYTIC THEORIES** The English language contains approximately 18,000 words that refer to characteristics of behavior. As we noted above, one task of trait psychology is to reduce these to a manageable number of traits that can encompass the diversity of human personality. Gordon Allport and a colleague addressed this problem by actually going through the unabridged dictionary and reducing the 18,000 trait-like words to a list of about 4,500 terms by eliminating obscure words and close synonyms. They then organized the list into psychologically meaningful subsets (Allport & Odbert, 1936).

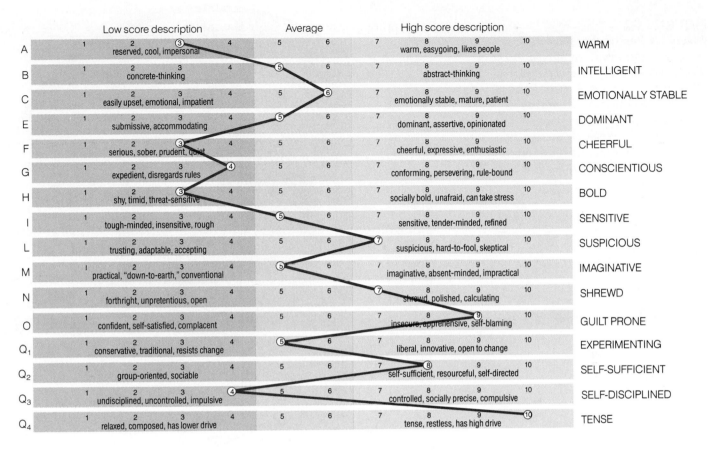

| | Low score description | Average | High score description | |
|---|---|---|---|---|
| A | reserved, cool, impersonal | | warm, easygoing, likes people | WARM |
| B | concrete-thinking | | abstract-thinking | INTELLIGENT |
| C | easily upset, emotional, impatient | | emotionally stable, mature, patient | EMOTIONALLY STABLE |
| E | submissive, accommodating | | dominant, assertive, opinionated | DOMINANT |
| F | serious, sober, prudent, quiet | | cheerful, expressive, enthusiastic | CHEERFUL |
| G | expedient, disregards rules | | conforming, persevering, rule-bound | CONSCIENTIOUS |
| H | shy, timid, threat-sensitive | | socially bold, unafraid, can take stress | BOLD |
| I | tough-minded, insensitive, rough | | sensitive, tender-minded, refined | SENSITIVE |
| L | trusting, adaptable, accepting | | suspicious, hard-to-fool, skeptical | SUSPICIOUS |
| M | practical, "down-to-earth," conventional | | imaginative, absent-minded, impractical | IMAGINATIVE |
| N | forthright, unpretentious, open | | shrewd, polished, calculating | SHREWD |
| O | confident, self-satisfied, complacent | | insecure, apprehensive, self-blaming | GUILT PRONE |
| $Q_1$ | conservative, traditional, resists change | | liberal, innovative, open to change | EXPERIMENTING |
| $Q_2$ | group-oriented, sociable | | self-sufficient, resourceful, self-directed | SELF-SUFFICIENT |
| $Q_3$ | undisciplined, uncontrolled, impulsive | | controlled, socially precise, compulsive | SELF-DISCIPLINED |
| $Q_4$ | relaxed, composed, has lower drive | | tense, restless, has high drive | TENSE |

**FIGURE 14-1**
**Personality Profiles** *The trait names represent the 16 personality factors obtained by factor analysis of a large number of ratings. Factors A–O were obtained from factor analyses of ratings of one person by another; the 4 Q factors were found only in data from self-ratings. A personality test based on the 16 factors measures the level of each factor, and the scores can be graphed as a profile. (From R. B. Cattell, 1986,* The Administrator's Manual for the 16 Personality Factor Questionnaire, *copyright © 1972, 1979, 1986 by the Institute for Personality and Ability Testing, Inc. All rights reserved. Reproduced by permission.)*

The idea of consulting the dictionary to construct a vocabulary for scientific purposes is not as wrongheaded as it may first appear. The motivating assumption is that through linguistic evolution, the lexicon of a natural language will encode most, if not all, of the important distinctions between persons that make a difference in everyday life. The natural language embodies the accumulated wisdom of the ages, and the unabridged dictionary is the written record of that wisdom.

Several subsequent researchers began with the Allport-Odbert list and carried the work further by using the method of **factor analysis**. As we noted in Chapter 12, factor analysis is a statistical technique that examines the intercorrelations among a number of measures and, by grouping those that are most highly correlated, reduces them to a smaller number of independent dimensions, called *factors*.

The most extensive factor-analytic studies of personality have been conducted by Raymond Cattell (1957; 1966). He first condensed the Allport-Odbert list to under 200 terms by further eliminating rare words and near synonyms. He then had people rate their friends on these personality traits and factor analyzed the results. This analysis yielded 12 personality factors, to which he added 4 more obtained by factor analyzing self-ratings. Although Cattell gives his factors strange-sounding technical names (for example, *affectia* versus *sizia*), he also supplies more familiar labels (*outgoing* versus *reserved*). Some of his other factors are *stable–emotional*, *dominant–submissive*, and *imaginative–practical*. As shown in Figure 14-1, a shorthand description of the individual's personality can be obtained by plotting an individual's score for each factor in a single graph.

**FIGURE 14-2**

**Eysenck's Personality Factors** *The figure shows the two major factors that emerge from factor-analytic studies of the intercorrelations between traits by Eysenck and others. The Stable–Unstable axis defines the* neuroticism *factor; the Introverted–Extraverted axis defines the* extraversion *factor. The other terms in the outer ring indicate where other traits are placed with respect to these two factors. The inner ring shows how the "four temperaments" of Hippocrates might correspond to the more contemporary system.* (After Eysenck & Rachman 1965)

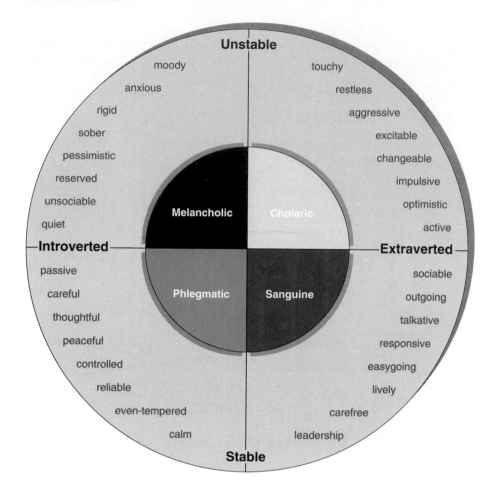

A second major theorist using factor analysis is the British psychologist Hans Eysenck. He and Cattell use the same overall approach, but Eysenck believes that a more useful set of factors can be obtained by using a more restrictive kind of factor analysis (Eysenck, 1953). His major factors are **introversion–extraversion**—a dimension first identified by the psychoanalyst Carl Jung—and emotional instability–stability, which he calls **neuroticism.** (Eysenck has a more recent, third dimension called *psychoticism,* but it is not as well established or researched as the other two (Eysenck & Eysenck, 1976).

Introversion–extraversion refers to the degree to which a person's basic orientation is turned inward toward the self or outward toward the external world. At the introversion end of the scale are individuals who are shy and prefer to work alone; they tend to withdraw into themselves, particularly in times of emotional stress or conflict. At the extraversion end are individuals who are sociable and prefer occupations that permit them to work directly with other people; in times of stress, they seek company. Neuroticism or instability–stability is a dimension of emotionality, with moody, anxious, temperamental, and maladjusted individuals at the neurotic or unstable end, and calm, well-adjusted individuals at the other. Figure 14-2 shows how these two dimensions combine to organize a number of subtraits that are correlated with the factors. For historical purposes, Eysenck has included in this figure the four ancient temperaments of Hippocrates' typology to illustrate how they might relate to his more contemporary system.

How many basic personality factors are there? Even with a rigorous analytic procedure like factor analysis, there is no definitive answer. As we have seen, Cattell arrives at the number 16; Eysenck at 2 (or 3). Other investigators arrive at still different numbers. We encountered a similar situation in Chapter 12, where we saw that the number of factors defining the concept of intelligence could be 1 (Spearman's general intelligence factor, *g*), 7 (Thurstone's primary mental abilities), or as many as 150 (Guilford, 1982).

Some of the discrepancy occurs because different traits are initially put into the analysis; some discrepancy occurs because different types of data are being analyzed (for example, peer-ratings versus self-ratings); and some occurs because different factor analytic methods are employed—it is not as cut and dried a technique as it may first seem. But much of the disagreement is a matter of taste. A researcher who prefers a more differentiated or fine-grained description of personality will stop the factor analysis earlier and accept more factors, arguing that important distinctions would be lost if the factors were further merged. Another researcher, like Eysenck, will prefer to merge several lower-level factors into more general ones, arguing that the resulting factors will be more stable (more likely to reemerge in other analyses). For example, when Cattell's 16 factors are themselves factor analyzed, Eysenck's 2 factors emerge as superfactors.

Despite these disagreements, however, a consensus is emerging among many trait researchers that five trait dimensions may provide the best compromise (John, 1990). Although the five factors were originally identified through a factor analysis of the Allport-Odbert trait list (Norman, 1963), the same five have now emerged from a wide variety of measuring techniques (Digman & Inouye, 1986; McCrae & Costa, 1987). There is still disagreement about how best to name and interpret the factors, but one reasonable way to summarize them is with the acronym NEOAC: Neuroticism, Extraversion, Openness to Experience, Agreeableness, and Conscientiousness. Table 14-1 displays some representative examples of the trait scales that characterize each of the five factors.

| TRAIT FACTOR | REPRESENTATIVE TRAIT SCALES |
|---|---|
| Neuroticism | Calm–Worrying<br>Hardy–Vulnerable<br>Secure–Insecure |
| Extraversion | Retiring–Sociable<br>Quiet–Talkative<br>Inhibited–Spontaneous |
| Openness | Conventional–Original<br>Unadventurous–Daring<br>Conservative–Liberal |
| Agreeableness | Irritable–Good-natured<br>Ruthless–Soft-hearted<br>Selfish–Selfless |
| Conscientiousness | Careless–Careful<br>Undependable–Reliable<br>Negligent–Conscientious |

**TABLE 14-1**
**Five Trait Factors** *The table presents five trait factors that reliably emerge when a wide variety of assessment instruments are factor analyzed. The adjective pairs are examples of trait scales that characterize each of the factors.* (After McCrae & Costa, 1987)

## Evaluation of Trait Approach

The trait approach is not itself a theory of personality but a general orientation and set of methods for assessing stable characteristics of persons. It is the approach typically adopted by researchers who claim no allegiance to a particular theory but who claim to be merely "gathering the facts." For example, the discussion of personality through the life course in Chapter 13 implicitly embodied a trait approach. The approach becomes a theory only when an investigator asserts that a particular set of traits is the most important and attempts to build the structure of personality on it.

At the beginning of this chapter, we noted that personality psychology has two separate tasks. The first involves specifying the variables on which individuals differ from one another. The second involves synthesizing the psychological processes of human functioning into an integrated account of the total person. Trait approaches are directed primarily at the first task, specifying the variables of personality. In contrast, they have little to say about the dynamic processes of personality functioning. Traits are static entities, and trait psychologists who have sought more complete theories of personality have had to look elsewhere for the dynamic aspects of their accounts. For example, when attempting to understand how personality is shaped and modified, Allport adopted a humanistic approach; Eysenck employs a learning theory. We will examine these approaches later in the chapter.

The major criticism of the trait approach is that its basic underlying assumption may be untrue: perhaps individuals are so variable in their behavior across time and situations that it is not valid to think of them as possessing trait-like characteristics. This is a startling charge. The assumption that persons display cross-situational consistencies in their behavior—that they possess traits—seems so obviously true that it is practically synonymous with our intuitive definition of personality. Yet, we are all aware that our own behavior may vary widely from one situation to another. We may assume a dominant role with our friends but not with parents and

*An individual may be withdrawn in some situations and outgoing in others.*

teachers; even with friends, we may be dominant on some occasions and docile on others. For this reason trait measures of personality have not been as successful in predicting behavior across situations as psychologists had hoped or expected. How can we reconcile our intuitions that persons are consistent across situations with the awareness that persons are frequently not consistent? This has been a major topic in contemporary personality psychology and we will devote an entire section to it at the end of the chapter.

## Psychoanalytic Approach

Sigmund Freud, the creator of psychoanalytic theory, is one of the towering intellectual figures of the twentieth century. Whatever its shortcomings as a scientific theory, the psychoanalytic account of personality remains the most comprehensive and influential theory of personality ever created. Its impact extends well beyond psychology, influencing the social sciences, the humanities, the arts, and society generally. Even though psychoanalytic theory plays a less central role in psychology today than it did 40 or 50 years ago, many of its ideas have been absorbed into the mainstream of psychological thinking. Even parents who have done nothing more than raise their children with the occasional guidance of psychiatrist Benjamin Spock's bestselling *Baby and Child Care* are more like Freudian psychologists than they realize.

Freud began his scientific career as a neurologist, treating patients suffering from various "nervous" disorders by using conventional medical procedures. Because these often failed, he tried and then abandoned the technique of hypnosis. Eventually, he discovered the method of **free association,** in which a patient is instructed to say everything that comes to mind, regardless of how trivial or embarrassing it may seem. By listening carefully to these verbal associations, Freud detected consistent themes that were manifestations of unconscious wishes and fears. He found similar themes in the recall of dreams and early childhood memories.

Freud compared the human mind to an iceberg. The small part that shows above the surface of the water represents conscious experience; the much larger mass below water level represents the unconscious, a storehouse of impulses, wishes, and inaccessible memories that affect our thoughts and behavior. Freud was not the first to discover unconscious mental influences—even Shakespeare included them in his plays—but Freud was the first to give them primary importance in the everyday functioning of the normal personality.

Closely allied with Freud's focus on unconscious processes was his determinism about human behavior. **Psychological determinism** is the doctrine that all thoughts, emotions, and actions have causes. Freud maintained not only that all psychological events are caused, but that most of them are caused by unsatisfied drives and unconscious wishes. In one of his earliest publications, *The Psychopathology of Everyday Life* (1901), Freud argued that dreams, humor, forgetting, and slips of the tongue ("Freudian slips") all serve to relieve psychological tension by gratifying forbidden impulses or unfulfilled wishes.

Freud's writings fill 24 volumes. His first major contribution, *The Interpretation of Dreams*, was published in 1900, and his final treatise, *An Outline of Psychoanalysis*, was published in 1940, a year after his death. We can present only the barest outline of Freud's theory of personality here.

*"Very well, I'll introduce you. Ego, meet Id. Now get back to work."*

# Personality Structure

Freud believed that personality is composed of three major systems that interact to govern human behavior: the *id*, the *ego*, and the *superego*.

**THE ID**  The **id** is the most primitive part of the personality, from which the ego and the superego later develop. It is present in the newborn infant and consists of the basic biological impulses (or drives): the need to eat, to drink, to eliminate wastes, to avoid pain, and to gain sexual (sensual) pleasure. Freud believed that aggression is also a basic biological drive (see Chapter 11). In fact, he believed that the sexual and aggressive drives were the most important instinctual determinants of personality throughout life. The id seeks immediate gratification of these impulses. Like a young child, the id operates on the **pleasure principle:** it endeavors to obtain pleasure and to avoid pain, regardless of the external circumstances.

**THE EGO**  Children soon learn that their impulses cannot always be gratified immediately. Hunger must wait until someone provides food. The satisfaction of relieving bladder or bowel pressure must be delayed until the bathroom is reached. Certain impulses—hitting someone or playing with the genitals—may elicit punishment from a parent. A new part of the personality, the **ego,** develops as the young child learns to consider the demands of reality. The ego obeys the **reality principle:** the gratification of impulses must be delayed until the situation is appropriate. It is essentially the executive of the personality: it decides what actions are appropriate and which id impulses will be satisfied and in what manner. The ego mediates among the demands of the id, the realities of the world, and the demands of the superego.

**THE SUPEREGO**  The third part of the personality is the **superego,** which judges whether actions are right or wrong. More generally, the superego is the internalized representation of the values and morals of society and comprises the individual's conscience as well as his or her image of the morally ideal person. The superego develops in response to parental rewards and punishments.

Initially, parents control children's behavior directly by reward and punishment. Through the incorporation of parental standards into the superego, a child brings behavior under his or her own control. Children no longer need anyone to tell them it is wrong to steal; their superego tells them. Violating the superego's standards, or even the impulse to do so, produces anxiety—which was originally the anxiety over the loss of parental love. According to Freud, this anxiety is largely unconscious but may be felt as guilt. If parental standards are overly rigid, the individual may be guilt ridden and inhibit all aggressive or sexual impulses. In contrast, an individual who fails to incorporate any standards for acceptable social behavior will have few behavioral constraints and may engage in excessively self-indulgent or criminal behavior. Such a person is considered to have a weak superego.

The three components of personality are often in opposition: the ego postpones the gratification that the id wants immediately, and the superego battles with both the id and the ego because behavior often falls short of the moral code it represents. In the well-integrated personality, the ego remains in firm but flexible control; the reality principle governs.

## Personality Dynamics

**CONSERVATION OF ENERGY** The science of physics was remarkably successful in the nineteenth century, and Freud was greatly influenced by the German physicist Hermann von Helmholtz, who argued that physiological events could also be explained by the same principles that had been so successful in physics. Freud was particularly impressed by the principle of the conservation of energy—which states that energy may be changed into different forms but is neither created nor destroyed—and he postulated that humans are also closed energy systems. There is a constant amount of psychic energy for any given individual, which Freud called **libido** (Latin for lust), reflecting his view that the sexual drive was primary.

One corollary of the conservation of energy principle is that if a forbidden act or impulse is suppressed, its energy will seek an outlet somewhere else in the system, possibly appearing in disguised form. The desires of the id contain psychic energy that must be expressed in some way, and prohibiting their expression does not abolish them. Aggressive impulses, for example, may be displaced to racing sports cars, playing chess, or to a sarcastic sense of humor. Dreams and neurotic symptoms are also manifestations of psychic energy that has been prevented from direct expression.

**ANXIETY AND DEFENSE** Individuals with an urge to do something forbidden become anxious; expressing the impulse in disguised form can avoid punishment by society or condemnation by the superego, and thereby reduce the anxiety. Freud described several additional strategies the individual can use to prevent or reduce anxiety. These strategies are called the ego's **mechanisms of defense.** The most basic defense mechanism is **repression,** in which the ego pushes a threatening thought or forbidden impulse out of awareness into the unconscious; from the outside it appears that the individual has simply forgotten the thought or impulse. Individuals differ both in their thresholds for anxiety and in the defenses they use to deal with such anxiety. Anxiety and mechanisms of defense are central to Freud's theory of maladaptive behavior and will be examined more fully in Chapter 15.

## Personality Development

Freud believed that during the first 5 years of life, the individual progresses through several developmental stages that affect personality. Applying a broad definition of sexuality, he called these periods **psychosexual stages.** During each stage, the pleasure-seeking impulses of the id focus on a particular area of the body and on activities connected with that area.

Freud called the first year of life the **oral stage** of psychosexual development. During this period, infants derive pleasure from nursing and sucking and begin to put anything they can reach into their mouths. Freud called the second year of life the beginning of the **anal stage** and believed that children find pleasure during this time both in withholding and in expelling feces. These pleasures come into conflict with parents who are attempting toilet training, the child's first experience with imposed control. In the **phallic stage,** from about age 3 to age 6, children begin to derive pleasure from fondling their genitals. They observe the differences between males and females and begin to direct their awakening sexual impulses toward the parent of the opposite sex.

*Toilet training is one of a child's first experiences with imposed control.*

It is during the phallic stage that children must resolve the **Oedipal conflict.** Freud described this conflict most clearly in the case of a boy. Around the age of 5 or 6, the boy's sexual impulses are directed toward the mother. This leads him to perceive his father as a rival for his mother's affection. Freud called this situation the Oedipal conflict, after Sophocles' play in which Oedipus Rex unwittingly kills his father and marries his mother. According to Freud, the boy also fears that his father will retaliate against these sexual impulses by castrating him. Freud labeled this fear *castration anxiety* and considered it to be the prototype of all later anxieties provoked by forbidden internal desires. In a normal case of development, the boy simultaneously reduces this anxiety and settles for vicarious gratification of his feelings toward his mother by *identifying* with his father—internalizing an idealized perception of his father's attitudes and values. The same process in a girl—resulting in her identification with her mother—is analogous but more complicated, and even more controversial.

Resolution of the Oedipal conflict terminates the phallic stage and is succeeded by the **latency period,** which lasts from about age 7 to age 12. During this sexually quiescent time, children become less concerned with their bodies and turn their attention to the skills needed for coping with the environment. Finally, adolescence and puberty usher in the **genital stage,** the mature phase of adult sexuality and functioning.

Freud felt that special problems at any stage could arrest (or *fixate*) development and have lasting effect on the individual's personality. Libido would remain attached to the activities appropriate for that stage. Thus, a person who was weaned very early and who did not have enough sucking pleasure might become fixated at the oral stage. As an adult, this person may be excessively dependent on others and overly fond of such oral pleasures as eating, drinking, and smoking. Such a person is called an *oral personality*. A person fixated at the anal stage of psychosexual development may be abnormally concerned with cleanliness, orderliness, and saving and may tend to resist external pressure—the *anal personality*. Inadequate resolution of the Oedipal conflict can lead to a weak sense of morality, difficulties with authority figures, and many other problems. Note that Freud's theory thus contains a type theory within it—the psychosexual typology.

## Modifications of Freud's Theories

Freud modified his theories throughout his life. Like a good scientist, he remained open to new data, revising earlier positions as new observations accumulated that could not be accommodated by the original theory. For example, one of Freud's major insights was his realization that his patients' reports of childhood seductions were not literally true, but reflected their own early sexual fantasies. (Ironically, the increased sensitivity to child sexual abuse in recent years has led some to argue that Freud's original assumption about the reality of the seductions was probably more correct (Masson, 1984).) Similarly, he revised his theory of anxiety quite late in his career. Freud's theory has been further extended by his daughter Anna, who has played a particularly important role in clarifying the mechanisms of defense (1946/1967) and in applying psychoanalytic theory to the practice of child psychiatry (1958).

But if Freud was open to new data, he was emphatically not open to dissenting opinions. He was particularly adamant that his colleagues and followers not question the libido theory and the centrality of sexual motivation in the functioning of personality. This dogmatism forced a break between Freud and many of his most brilliant associates—some of whom went on to develop rival theories that placed more emphasis on motivational processes other than sexuality. These former associates included Carl Jung and Alfred Adler, as well as later theorists such as Karen Horney, Harry Stack Sullivan, and Erich Fromm.

These dissidents and other, more recent psychoanalytic theorists all place more stress on the role of the ego. They believe that the ego is present at birth, develops independently of the id, and performs functions other than finding realistic ways of satisfying id impulses. These ego functions are learning how to cope with the environment and making sense of experience. Ego satisfactions include exploration, manipulation, and competency in performance. This approach ties the concept of the ego more closely to cognitive processes.

One important part of this new direction is called **object relations theory,** which deals with the child's attachments to people over the course of development. Object relations theorists have not rejected the concept of the id or the importance of biological drives in motivating behavior, but they have an equal interest in such questions as the degree of psychological separateness from parents, the degree of attachment to and involvement with other people versus self-preoccupation, and the strength of the individual's feelings of self-esteem and competency.

Although we did not identify it as such, Erik Erikson's stage theory of development—which we discussed in Chapter 3—is an example of a revised psychoanalytic theory. Erikson himself was trained as a psychoanalyst by Anna Freud, and he perceives his own views as expanding rather than altering Freudian theory. Instead of viewing developmental stages in terms of their psychosexual functions, Erikson sees them as **psychosocial stages** involving primarily ego processes. For Erikson, the important feature of the first year of life is not that it focuses on oral gratification, but that the child is learning to trust (or mistrust) the environment as a satisfier of needs. The important feature of the second year of life is not that it focuses on anal concerns such as toilet training, but that the child is learning autonomy. Toilet training just happens to be a frequent arena of conflict in which the child's striving for autonomy clashes with new obedience demands by parents. Erikson's theory also adds more stages in order to encompass the entire life span.

*According to Freud's psychoanalytic theory, a boy resolves his Oedipal conflict by identifying with his father.*

## Psychoanalytic Portrait of Human Personality

At the beginning of this chapter, we noted that each approach to personality carries with it an intrinsic philosophy of human nature. To what extent are we free or determined? Good, neutral, or evil? Fixed or modifiable? Active or passive? What constitutes psychological health?

Our description of Freud's theory has already implied many of his views on these matters. Freud is often compared with Copernicus and Darwin. Like these two other intellectual pioneers, Freud was accused of undermining the stature and dignity of humanity. The astronomer Copernicus demoted the earth from its position as center of the universe to one of several planets moving around a minor star; Darwin demoted the human species to a descendent of apes. Freud took the next step by emphasizing that human

*Because psychoanalytic theory portrays humans as basically evil, Freud saw the events leading up to World War II as the natural consequence of the human aggressive drive when it is not held in check.*

behavior is determined by forces beyond our control, thereby depriving us of our free will and psychological freedom. By emphasizing the unconscious status of our motivations, he deprived us of our rationality; and, by stressing the sexual and aggressive nature of those motivations, he dealt the final blow to our dignity.

Psychoanalytic theory also draws a dark portrait of human personality as basically evil. Without the restraining forces of society and its internalized representative, the superego, humans would destroy themselves. Freud was a deeply pessimistic man. He was forced to flee from Vienna when the Nazis invaded in 1938 and died in September of 1939, the month that World War II began. He saw these events as the natural consequence of the human aggressive drive when it is not held in check.

Human personality is also relatively fixed. According to psychoanalytic theory, our personalities are basically determined by inborn drives and by environmental events in the first five years of life. Only extensive psychoanalysis can undo some of the negative consequences of early experiences, and it can do so in only limited ways. We also emerge from psychoanalytic theory as relatively passive creatures. Although the ego is in an active struggle with the id and superego, we seem mainly to be impotent, passive pawns of this drama being played out in our unconscious. And finally, for Freud, psychological health consisted of firm but flexible ego control over the impulses of the id. As Freud noted, the goal of psychoanalysis was to ensure that "Where the id was, there shall ego be" (1933).

# Evaluation of Psychoanalytic Approach

Psychoanalytic theory is so broad in scope that it cannot simply be pronounced true or false. But whether it is correct or incorrect in its particulars is virtually irrelevant to its overall impact on our culture and to the value of some of its scientific contributions. For example, Freud's method of free association opened up an entirely new database of observations that had never before been explored systematically. Second, the recognition that our behavior often reflects a compromise between our wishes and our fears accounts for many of the apparent contradictions in human behavior better than any other theory of personality: as a theory of **ambivalence**, psychoanalytic theory has no peer. Third, Freud's recognition that unconscious processes play an important role in much of our behavior is almost universally accepted—although these processes are often reinterpreted in learning-theory or information-processing terms.

Nevertheless, as a scientific theory, the psychoanalytic account has been persistently criticized for its inadequacy (for example, Grünbaum, 1984). One of the main criticisms is that many of its concepts are ambiguous and difficult to define or measure objectively. Also, psychoanalytic theory assumes that very different behaviors may reflect the same underlying motive. For example, a mother who resents her child may be abusive, or she may deny her hostile impulses by becoming overly concerned and protective toward the child—what Freud would call a **reaction formation** (see Chapter 15). When opposite behaviors are claimed to result from the same underlying motive, it is difficult to confirm the presence or absence of the motive or to make predictions that can be empirically verified.

When researchers *have* managed to put the theory to empirical test, it has achieved a mixed record. For example, efforts to link adult personality characteristics to psychosexually relevant events in childhood have generally met with negative outcomes (Sears, Maccoby, & Levin, 1957; Sewell & Mussen, 1952). When relevant character traits *are* identified, they appear to be related to similar character traits in the parents (Beloff, 1957; Hetherington & Brackbill, 1963). Thus, even if a relationship were to be found between toilet-training practices and adult personality traits, it could have arisen because both are linked with a parental emphasis on cleanliness and order. In such a case, a simple learning-theory explanation—parental reinforcement and the child's modeling of the parents—would be a more economical explanation of the adult traits than the psychoanalytic hypothesis.

Psychoanalytic theorists often cite anthropological observations as corroborating evidence for some of Freud's ideas. For example, the cross-cultural taboo against incest is often cited as evidence for the universality of the Oedipal conflict; the taboo is seen as society's attempt to control the Oedipal situation. On the other hand, not all anthropological evidence is supportive of psychoanalytic theory. A particularly instructive example is provided by the anthropologist Bronislaw Malinowski (1927).

Malinowski had read Freud's account of how boys often reveal their Oedipal hostility toward their fathers in dreams in which the father is maimed or killed. According to Freud, such dreams symbolically fulfill the boy's wish to get rid of the rival for his mother's affection. Malinowski collected dream reports from adolescent boys in the Trobriand Islands, where uncles rather than fathers are responsible for disciplining them. He found no instances of dreams in which fathers suffered but several in which uncles met with disaster, implying that it is the discipline not Oedipal rivalry that creates hostility.

Because Freud's own observations were drawn from a culture in which the father was both the mother's lover and the son's disciplinarian, he had no way of determining which function created the son's hostility. The Trobriand Island culture provided Malinowski with a natural laboratory in which the two functions were separated. (Psychoanalytic theorists, however, can counterargue that Malinowski's study is not conclusive because he interviewed older boys, who would have resolved the Oedipal conflict many years earlier in their development, rather than boys 4–6 years of age who would have been in the midst of the conflict. Also see Spiro (1982) for a refutation of Malinowski's conclusion.)

This outcome should also remind us that Freud based his theory on observations of a very narrow range of people—primarily upper-middle-class neurotics in Victorian Vienna. In hindsight, many of Freud's cultural biases are now obvious, particularly in his theories about women. For example, his theory that female psychosexual development is shaped largely by "penis envy"—a girl's feelings of inadequacy because she doesn't have a penis—is almost universally rejected as reflecting the sex bias of Freud and the historical period in which he lived. A little girl's personality development during the Victorian era was surely shaped more decisively by her awareness that she lacked the greater independence, power, and social status of her brother than by her envy for his penis.

Despite these criticisms, however, the remarkable feature of Freud's theory is how well it did manage to transcend its narrow observational base. For example, many experimental studies of the defense mechanisms and reactions to conflict have supported the theory in contexts quite different from those in which Freud developed the theory (for example, Blum, 1953; Erdelyi, 1985; Holmes, 1974; Sears, 1943, 1944; Silverman, 1976).

In general, the structural theory (ego, id, and superego), the psychosexual theory, and the energy concept have not fared well over the years. Even some psychoanalytic writers are prepared to abandon or to modify them substantially (for example, Kline, 1972; Schafer, 1976). On the other hand, Freud's dynamic theory—especially his theory of anxiety and the mechanisms of defense—has withstood the test of time, research, and observation. There is a continuing interest in reformulating psychoanalytic theory in more testable terms and subjecting it to further experimental evaluation (Silverman & Weinberger, 1985).

# Social-Learning Approach

In contrast to both trait and psychodynamic approaches to personality, social-learning approaches emphasize the importance of *environmental*, or *situational*, determinants of behavior. For social-learning theorists, behavior is the result of a continuous interaction between personal and environmental variables. Environmental conditions shape behavior through learning; a person's behavior, in turn, shapes the environment. Persons and situations influence each other reciprocally. To predict behavior, we need to know how the characteristics of the individual interact with the characteristics of the situation. The social-learning approach is the contemporary descendent of behaviorism and its outgrowth, **stimulus-response psychology**, which were dominant in the first half of this century (see Chapter 1 and Appendix II).

# Social Learning and Conditioning

**OPERANT CONDITIONING** The effect of other people—the rewards and punishments they provide—is an important influence on an individual's behavior. Accordingly, social learning is considered to be a special case of **operant conditioning** and the processes related to it that we discussed in Chapter 7. According to social-learning theory, individual differences in behavior result in large part from differences in the kinds of learning experiences a person encounters in the course of growing up. Some behavior patterns are learned through direct experience: the individual is rewarded or punished for behaving in a certain manner. But a person acquires many responses without direct reinforcement—through observational, or vicarious, learning (see Chapter 11). People can learn by observing the actions of others and by noting the consequences of those actions. It would be a slow and inefficient process indeed if all of our behavior had to be learned through the direct reinforcement of our responses. Similarly, the reinforcement that controls the expression of learned behavior may be direct (tangible rewards, social approval or disapproval, or alleviation of aversive conditions), vicarious (observation of someone receiving reward or punishment for behavior similar to one's own), or self-administered (evaluation of one's own performance with self-praise or self-reproach).

The basic tenet of social-learning theory is that people behave in ways that are likely to produce reinforcement. Thus an individual's actions depend on the specific characteristics of the situation, his or her appraisal of the situation (for example, does reinforcement seem likely?), and past reinforcement for behavior in similar situations (or observations of others in similar situations). People behave consistently insofar as the situations they encounter and the roles they are expected to play remain relatively stable.

Because most social behaviors are not uniformly rewarded in all settings, the individual learns to discriminate the contexts in which certain behavior is appropriate and those in which it is not. To the extent that a person is rewarded for the same response in many different situations, **generalization** takes place, ensuring that the same behavior will occur in a variety of settings. Thus, a boy who is reinforced for physical aggression at home, as well

*Children may learn drinking habits by observing their parents.*

as at school and at play, is likely to develop a personality that is pervasively aggressive. More often, aggressive responses are differentially rewarded, and learned discriminations determine the situations in which the individual will display aggression (for example, aggression is acceptable on the football field but not in the classroom). For this reason, social learning theorists challenge the usefulness of characterizing persons with trait terms like "aggressive," arguing that such terms obscure the cross-situational variability of behavior.

CLASSICAL CONDITIONING  Operant conditioning and its related processes apply to **behavior,** the major focus of social-learning approaches. To account for **emotion** or *affect,* social-learning theorists add classical conditioning to their account of personality (see Chapter 7). For example, when a child is punished by a parent for engaging in some forbidden activity, the punishment elicits the physiological responses that we associate with guilt or anxiety. Subsequently, the child's behavior may itself elicit those same responses; he or she will feel guilty when engaging in the forbidden behavior. In the terminology of classical conditioning, we would say that the behavior becomes a **conditioned stimulus** by being paired with the **unconditioned stimulus** of punishment; the anxiety becomes the **conditioned response.** For the social-learning theorist, it is classical conditioning that produces the internalized source of anxiety that Freud labeled the superego. Like operant conditioning, classical conditioning can also operate vicariously and can generalize to stimuli that have not been directly conditioned.

## Person Variables

We noted earlier that personality psychology seeks to specify both the variables on which individuals differ from one another and the general processes of personality functioning. Trait approaches have focused on the first task, describing personality differences in detail while saying virtually nothing about the general dynamic processes of personality functioning. Psychoanalytic theory has attempted to do both.

In contrast, the social-learning approach has focused primarily on process, with little attention devoted to describing individual differences. Because the approach sees every individual's personality as the unique product of an idiosyncratic reinforcement history and emphasizes the degree to which behavior varies across situations, it has not attempted to classify individuals into types or to rate them on traits. However, a few social-learning theorists have begun to consider individual differences in a systematic way, focusing on person variables that seem likely to interact with particular situations to affect behavior. One prominent social-learning theorist, Walter Mischel, has proposed the following variables:

1. *Competencies: What can you do?* Competencies include intellectual abilities, social and physical skills, and other special abilities.
2. *Encoding strategies: How do you see it?* People differ in the way they selectively attend to information, encode (represent) events, and group the information into meaningful categories. An event perceived by one person as threatening may be seen by another as challenging.
3. *Expectancies: What will happen?* Expectations about the consequences of different behaviors will guide the individual's choice of behavior. If you cheat on an examination and are caught, what do you expect the

consequences to be? If you tell your friend what you really think of him or her, what will happen to your relationship? Expectations about our own abilities will also influence behavior: we may anticipate the consequences of a certain behavior but fail to act because we are uncertain of our ability to execute the behavior.

4. *Subjective values: What is it worth?* Individuals who have similar expectancies may choose to behave differently because they assign different values to the outcomes. Two students may expect a certain behavior to please their professors; however, this outcome is important to one student but is not important to the other.

5. *Self-regulatory systems and plans: How can you achieve it?* People differ in the standards and rules they adopt for regulating their behavior (including self-imposed rewards for success or punishments for failure), as well as in their ability to make realistic plans for reaching a goal. (After Mischel, 1973, 1993)

All of these person variables (sometimes referred to as cognitive social-learning person variables) interact with the conditions of a particular situation to determine what an individual will do in that situation.

## Social-Learning Portrait of Human Personality

Like the psychoanalytic approach, the social-learning approach to personality is very deterministic. In contrast to the psychoanalytic approach, however, it pays very little attention to biological determinants of behavior and focuses exclusively on environmental determinants. Like its parent, behaviorism, the social-learning approach has been strongly influenced by the ideas of Darwin. Just as evolution works though natural selection to shape the species to be adaptive to its ecology, so the processes of learning—especially operant conditioning—shape the individual's behavioral repertoire to be adaptive to his or her environment. Inherently, we are neither good nor evil, but extraordinarily modifiable by environmental experiences in our personal histories and contemporary situational circumstances. As we noted in Chapter 3, John Watson, founder of the behaviorist movement in the United States claimed that he could raise an infant to be anything, regardless of the infant's "talents, penchants, tendencies, abilities, vocations, and race of his [or her] ancestors."

Few social-learning theorists would take such an extreme view today. Nevertheless, social-learning theory shares with its predecessor a strong optimism about our ability to change human behavior by changing the environment. Such a view is nicely congruent with American pragmatism and American ideology about equality, so it is not surprising that behaviorism was popular in the United States. Interestingly, the former Soviet Union—whose communist ideology also emphasized equality—has always shared America's view that human personality is quite modifiable by the environment. Thus, it is not accidental that both these societies have embraced a conditioning-based view of human behavior (the Soviet Union was the birthplace of Pavlov and classical conditioning). In contrast, more traditional, class-based societies like England and Germany have produced Charles Darwin, ethologists, trait theorists, and Sigmund Freud—all of whom see human personality as more fixed by biological imperatives.

Even though the human personality that emerges from the social-learning approach is modifiable, it still has a passive quality to it. We still seem to be shaped primarily by forces beyond our control. This portrait is changing, however, as social-learning approaches increasingly emphasize the individual's active role in selecting and modifying the environment, thereby permitting the person to become a causal force in his or her own life. As we shall see, however, this is still not sufficiently active for the humanistic or phenomenological theorists. In particular, they do not believe that it is sufficient to define psychological health merely as optimal adaptation to the environment.

## Evaluation of Social-Learning Approach

Through its emphasis on specifying the environmental variables that evoke specific behaviors, social-learning theory has made a major contribution to both clinical psychology and personality theory. It has led us to see human actions as reactions to specific environments, and it has helped us to focus on the way in which environments control our behavior and how they can be changed to modify behavior. As we will see in Chapter 17, the systematic application of learning principles has proved successful in changing many maladaptive behaviors. Social-learning theorists have also challenged the notion that individuals are cross-situationally consistent, forcing other personality theorists to reexamine the fundamental assumptions of their approaches.

Social-learning theorists have been criticized for overemphasizing the importance of situational influences on behavior and thus losing the person in personality psychology (Carlson, 1971). And, as we shall see later, many personality theorists are unwilling to concede that personality has as little cross-situational consistency as social-learning theory implies.

# Phenomenological Approach

The phenomenological approach to the study of personality focuses on the individual's *subjective experience*—his or her personal view of the world. Phenomenological theories differ from the theories we have discussed so far in that they generally are not concerned with the person's motivational or reinforcement history or with predicting behavior. They focus instead on how the individual perceives and interprets events in his or her current environment; that is, the focus is on the individual's **phenomenology.** Among the subvarieties of the phenomenological approach, the most central is *humanistic psychology.*

## Humanistic Psychology

During the first half of this century, the psychoanalytic and behavioristic approaches were dominant in psychology. In 1962, a group of psychologists founded the Association of Humanistic Psychology. They offered **humanistic psychology** as a "third force," an explicit set of alternative assumptions and concerns to those that characterized the other two approaches. To define its mission, the Association adopted a set of four principles:

1. *The experiencing person is of primary interest.* Humans are not simply objects of study. They must be described and understood in terms of their own subjective views of the world, their perceptions of self, and their feelings of self-worth. The central question each person must face is "Who am I?" In order to learn how the individual attempts to answer

this question, the psychologist must become a partner with the individual in the quest for existential meaning.

2. *Human choice, creativity, and self-actualization are the preferred topics of investigation.* Humanistic psychologists reject the psychoanalytic approach, believing that a psychology based on crippled personalities could only produce a crippled psychology. They also reject behaviorism, a psychology devoid of consciousness derived primarily from the study of lower organisms. People are not simply motivated by basic drives like sex or aggression or physiological needs like hunger and thirst. They have a need to develop their potentials and capabilities. Growth and self-actualization should be the criteria of psychological health, not merely ego control or adjustment to the environment.

3. *Meaningfulness must precede objectivity in the selection of research problems.* The humanistic psychologists believe that too often psychological research is guided by the methods available rather than by the importance of the problems to be investigated. They argue that we should study important human and social problems, even if that sometimes means adopting less rigorous methods. And while psychologists should strive to be objective in collecting and interpreting observations, their choice of research topics can and should be guided by values. In this sense, research is not value-free; values are not something psychologists should pretend not to have or feel they have to apologize for.

4. *Ultimate value is placed on the dignity of the person.* Persons are basically good. The objective of psychology is to understand, not to predict or control people. Even referring to them as "subjects" is considered by many humanistic psychologists to degrade their dignity as full partners in the quest for understanding human personality.

Psychologists who share the values of the Association come from diverse theoretical backgrounds. For example, the trait theorist Gordon Allport was clearly a humanistic psychologist, and we have already pointed out that several psychoanalysts—such as Carl Jung, Alfred Adler, and Erik Erikson—held humanistic views of motivation that diverged from Freud's views. But it is Carl Rogers and Abraham Maslow whose theoretical views lie at the center of the humanistic movement.

**CARL ROGERS** Like Freud, Carl Rogers (1902–1987) developed his theory from his work with patients or clients in the clinic (Rogers, 1951; 1959; 1963; 1970). Rogers was impressed with what he saw as the individual's innate tendency to move in the direction of growth, maturity, and positive change. He came to believe that the basic force motivating the human organism is the actualizing tendency—a tendency toward fulfillment or actualization of all the capacities of the organism. A growing organism seeks to fulfill its potential within the limits of its heredity. A person may not always clearly perceive which actions lead to growth and which actions are regressive. But once the course is clear, the individual chooses to grow rather than to regress. Rogers did not deny that there are other needs, some of them biological, but he saw them as subservient to the organism's motivation to enhance itself.

Rogers's belief in the primacy of actualization forms the basis of his nondirective or **client-centered therapy**. This method of psychotherapy assumes that every individual has the motivation and ability to change and that the individual is the person best qualified to decide on the direction

**Carl Rogers Writing on the Phenomenological Approach** *"The best vantage point for understanding behavior is from the internal frame of reference of the individual himself."*

*"The organism has one basic tendency and striving—to actualize, maintain, and enhance the experiencing organism."*

*"When the individual perceives and accepts into one consistent and integrated system all his sensory and visceral experiences, then he is necessarily more understanding of others and is more accepting of others as separate individuals."* (Rogers, 1951)

that such change should take. The therapist's role is to act as a sounding board while the individual explores and analyzes his or her problems. This approach differs from psychoanalytic therapy, during which the therapist analyzes the patient's history to determine the problem and devise a course of remedial action. (See Chapter 17 for a discussion of various approaches to psychotherapy.)

The central concept in Rogers's theory of personality is the *self*. The self, or **self-concept** (Rogers uses the terms interchangeably), became the cornerstone of his theory. The self consists of all the ideas, perceptions, and values that characterize "I" or "me"; it includes the awareness of "what I am" and "what I can do." This perceived self, in turn, influences both the person's perception of the world and his or her behavior. For example, a woman who perceives herself as strong and competent perceives and acts upon the world quite differently from a woman who considers herself weak and ineffectual. The self-concept does not necessarily reflect reality: a person may be highly successful and respected but still view himself or herself as a failure.

According to Rogers, the individual evaluates every experience in relation to this self-concept. People want to behave in ways that are consistent with their self-image; experiences and feelings that are not consistent are threatening and may be denied admittance to consciousness. This is essentaily Freud's concept of repression, although Rogers felt that such repression is neither necessary nor permanent. (Freud would say that repression is inevitable and that some aspects of the individual's experiences always remain unconscious.)

The more areas of experience that a person denies because they are inconsistent with his or her self-concept, the wider the gulf between the self and reality and the greater the potential for maladjustment. An individual whose self-concept is incongruent with personal feelings and experiences must defend himself or herself against the truth because the truth will result in anxiety. If the incongruence becomes too great, the defenses may break down, resulting in severe anxiety or other forms of emotional disturbance. The well-adjusted person, in contrast, has a self-concept that is consistent with thought, experience, and behavior; the self is not rigid, but flexible, and can change as it assimilates new experiences and ideas.

The other self in Rogers's theory is the *ideal* self. We all have a conception of the kind of person we would like to be. The closer the ideal self is to the real self, the more fulfilled and happy the individual becomes. A large discrepancy between the ideal self and the real self results in an unhappy, dissatisfied person.

Thus, two kinds of incongruence can develop: one, between the self and the experiences of reality; the other, between the self and the ideal self. Rogers had some hypotheses about how these incongruences may develop.

In particular, Rogers believed that people are likely to become more fully functioning if they are brought up with *unconditional positive regard*. This means that they feel themselves valued by parents and others even when their feelings, attitudes, and behaviors are less than ideal. If parents offer only conditional positive regard—valuing the child only when he or she behaves, thinks, or feels correctly—the child is likely to distort his or her self-concept. For example, feelings of competition and hostility toward a younger sibling are natural, but parents disapprove of hitting a baby brother or sister and usually punish such actions. Children must somehow integrate this experience into their self-concept. They may decide that they are bad

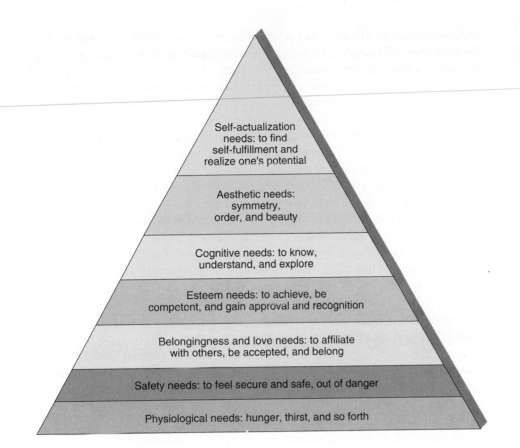

**FIGURE 14-3**
**Maslow's Hierarchy of Needs** *Needs*
*that are low in the hierarchy must be at least*
*partially satisfied before needs that are*
*higher in the hierarchy become important*
*sources of motivation.* (After Maslow,
1970)

and so may feel ashamed. They may decide that their parents do not like them and so may feel rejected. Or they may deny their feelings and decide they do not want to hit the baby. Each of these attitudes contains a distortion of the truth. The third alternative is the easiest for children to accept, but in so doing, they deny their real feelings, which then become unconscious. The more people are forced to deny their own feelings and to accept the values of others, the more uncomfortable they will feel about themselves. Rogers suggested that the best approach is for the parents to recognize the child's feelings as valid while explaining the reasons why hitting is not acceptable.

**ABRAHAM MASLOW** The psychology of Abraham Maslow (1908–1970) overlaps with that of Carl Rogers in many ways. Maslow was first attracted to behaviorism and carried out studies in primate sexuality and dominance. He was already moving away from behaviorism when his first child was born, after which he remarked that anyone who observes a baby cannot be a behaviorist. He was influenced by psychoanalysis, but eventually became critical of its theory of motivation and developed his own. Specifically, he proposed that there is a **hierarchy of needs,** ascending from the basic biological needs to the more complex psychological motivations that become important only after the basic needs have been satisfied (see Figure 14-3). The needs at one level must be at least partially satisfied before those at the next level become important determiners of action. When food and safety are difficult to obtain, the satisfaction of those needs will dominate a person's actions and higher motives are of little significance. Only when basic needs can be satisfied easily will the individual have the time and energy to devote to aesthetic and intellectual interests. Artistic and scientific

*Martin Luther King fulfilled Maslow's criteria for a self-actualizer.*

endeavors do not flourish in societies in which people must struggle for food, shelter, and safety. The highest motive—**self-actualization**—can only be fulfilled after all other needs are fulfilled.

Maslow decided to study *self-actualizers*—men and women who had made extraordinary use of their potential. He began by studying the lives of eminent historical figures such as Spinoza, Thomas Jefferson, Abraham Lincoln, Jane Addams, Albert Einstein, and Eleanor Roosevelt. In this way, he was able to create a composite picture of a self-actualizer. The distinguishing characteristics of such persons are listed in Table 14-2, along with some of the behaviors that Maslow believed could lead to self-actualization.

Maslow extended his study to a population of college students. Selecting students who fit his definition of self-actualizers, Maslow found this group to be in the healthiest 1 percent of the population; these students showed no signs of maladjustment and were making effective use of their talents and capabilities (Maslow, 1970).

Many people experience transient moments of self-actualization, which Maslow called *peak experiences*. A peak experience is an experience of being characterized by happiness and fulfillment—a temporary, nonstriving, non-self-centered state of perfection and goal attainment. Peak experiences may occur in different intensities and in various contexts: creative activities, appreciation of nature, intimate relationships with others, parental experiences, aesthetic perceptions, or athletic participation. After asking a large number of college students to describe any experience that came close to being a peak experience, Maslow attempted to summarize their responses. They spoke of wholeness, perfection, aliveness, uniqueness, effortlessness, self-sufficiency, and the values of beauty, goodness, and truth.

## Personal Construct Theory

Humanistic psychologists are concerned with how individuals feel about and perceive themselves in terms of personal value or worth. **Personal construct theory** takes a more cognitive approach to the individual's phenomenology. According to George Kelly (1905–1966), the originator of personal construct theory, trait psychologists try to characterize a person on personality dimensions that the psychologists themselves have constructed. In contrast, Kelly believed that the psychologist's goal should be to discover the dimensions that individuals themselves use to interpret or to *construe* themselves and their social worlds. These dimensions are the individual's own **personal constructs,** and they constitute the basic units of analysis in Kelly's theory (1955).

More generally, Kelly believed that individuals should be viewed as intuitive scientists. Like formal scientists, they observe the world, formulate and test hypotheses about it, and make up theories about it. Like the psychologists who study them, human subjects also construe or abstract behavior—categorizing, interpreting, labeling, and judging themselves and their world. And, like scientists, individuals can entertain bad theories, beliefs that hinder them in daily life and lead them to bias their interpretations of events and persons, including themselves. (In Chapter 18, we discuss in depth the person-as-scientist view of social information processing.)

In Kelly's view, the purpose of therapy or counseling is to help the person construct more effective interpretations, construals, or theories of the world. If a client claims that he is unable to stand up to authority, the therapist's job is not to determine the truth or falsity of the assertion but to encourage the individual to explore what the implications of viewing himself

*Eleanor Roosevelt was one of Maslow's examples of a self-actualizer.*

## CHARACTERISTICS OF SELF-ACTUALIZERS

Perceive reality efficiently and are able to tolerate uncertainty

Accept themselves and others for what they are

Spontaneous in thought and behavior

Problem-centered rather than self-centered

Have a good sense of humor

Highly creative

Resistant to enculturation, although not purposely unconventional

Concerned for the welfare of humanity

Capable of deep appreciation of the basic experiences of life

Establish deep, satisfying interpersonal relationships with a few, rather than many, people

Able to look at life from an objective viewpoint

## BEHAVIORS LEADING TO SELF-ACTUALIZATION

Experience life as a child does, with full absorption and concentration

Try something new rather than sticking to secure and safe ways

Listen to your own feelings in evaluating experiences rather than to the voice of tradition or authority or the majority

Be honest; avoid pretenses or "game playing"

Be prepared to be unpopular if your views do not coincide with those of most people

Assume responsibility

Work hard at whatever you decide to do

Try to identify your defenses and have the courage to give them up

**TABLE 14-2**
**Self-Actualization** *Listed are the personal qualities that Maslow found to be characteristic of self-actualizers and the behaviors he considered important to the development of self-actualization.* (After Maslow, 1967)

that way are for his daily life and to consider alternative hypotheses about his behaviors. In order to get clients to construe themselves and their social worlds from different perspectives, Kelly used the technique of role playing. For example, the client who claimed he cannot stand up to authority might be asked to role-play his boss, construing the situation as he thinks his boss might. This often helped clients to interpret their own behaviors differently.

Kelly also devised an ingenious measuring instrument for eliciting a person's personal constructs, the **Role Construct Repertory Test** or "Rep Test." (We will discuss this instrument in the section on personality assessment.)

## Phenomenological Portrait of Human Personality

As a matter of principle, phenomenological psychologists—especially humanistic psychologists—have been quite explicit about the values and philosophical presuppositions that underlie their approach to human personality. The four principles set forth by the Association of Humanistic Psychology, which we summarized earlier, draw sharp contrasts between the humanistic portrait of human personality and the portraits drawn by the psychoanalytic and behavioristic approaches.

*Humanistic psychology has provided the psychological rationale for questioning traditional sex roles.*

The phenomenological approach does not dispute that biological and environmental variables can influence behavior, but it emphasizes the individual's own role in defining and creating his or her destiny. Individuals are basically good, striving for growth and self-actualization. They are also modifiable and active. Phenomenological psychologists set a particularly high criterion for psychological health. Mere ego control or adaptation to the environment is not sufficient. Only an individual who is growing toward self-actualization can be said to be psychologically healthy. In other words, psychological health is a process not an end state.

Philosophical positions also have political implications. We pointed out earlier that the philosophical assumptions of behaviorism are quite compatible with American ideology. Its assumption that all humans are created equal and are infinitely modifiable by the environment provides a psychological rationale for politically liberal programs that seek to improve the environments of those who are disadvantaged.

In contrast, the humanistic approach provides support for a much more radical politics. Anything that retards the fulfillment of one's potential—that prevents any human being from becoming all he or she can be—should be challenged. If women in the 1950s were happy and well adjusted to traditional sex roles, the criterion of psychological health defined by behaviorism was satisfied. But from the humanistic perspective, consigning all women to the same role is undesirable—no matter how appropriate that role might be for some women—because it prevents many women from reaching their maximum potential. It is not accidental that the rhetoric of liberation movements—such as women's liberation and gay liberation—echoes the language of humanistic psychology. Betty Friedan's 1963 book, *The Feminine Mystique*, is often credited with initiating the contemporary feminist movement. Friedan criticizes the sexism of Freud and has little good to say about the bland liberalism of behaviorism, but she does have one major hero from the world of psychology: Abraham Maslow.

## Evaluation of Phenomenological Approach

By focusing on the individual's unique perception and interpretation of events, the phenomenological approach brings back the role of private experience to the study of personality. More than any other theory we have discussed, the theories of Rogers and Maslow concentrate on the whole, healthy person and emphasize a positive, optimistic view of human personality. However, a phenomenological theory of personality is incomplete; it does not provide a sufficient analysis of the causes of behavior. A person's self-concept may be an important determinant of behavior, but what determines the particular self-concept he or she holds? Just how does the self-concept affect behavior? These theories do not say.

Phenomenological psychologists emphasize that they study important problems even if they do not always have rigorous methods for investigating them. They have a point; investigating trivial problems just because one has a convenient method for doing so does little to advance the science of psychology. Moreover, the phenomenological psychologists have been increasingly ingenious over the years at devising new methods for assessing self-concepts, personal constructs, and conducting studies that genuinely treat the individual as an equal partner in the research enterprise. Nevertheless, critics can and do question the quality of the evidence in support of the humanistic claims. For example, to what extent are the characteristics of self-actualizers a consequence of a psychological process called self-actualization, and to what extent are they merely reflections of the particular value systems held by Rogers and Maslow? Where, they ask, is the evidence for Maslow's hierarchy of needs?

Phenomenological psychologists are also vulnerable to a criticism that is the mirror image of a criticism they have leveled at Freud. They have criticized Freud for attempting to build a complete theory of personality on observations of neurotic individuals. But critics point out that Rogers and Kelly both built their theories on observations of relatively healthy college students. Accordingly, their theories are best suited to young, well functioning people who have the luxury of worrying about needs at the top of Maslow's hierarchy. The application of these theories to seriously malfunctioning individuals or to socially, culturally, or economically disadvantaged individuals is less apparent.

And finally, some have even criticized the values espoused by the phenomenological theorists. Many observers believe that America already has too obsessive a concern with the individual and too little concern for the welfare of the larger society. A psychology that raises individual self-fulfillment and actualization to the top of the value hierarchy is *too* compatible with American ideology; some critics believe that it even provides a psychological "sanction for selfishness" (Wallach & Wallach, 1983). Although Maslow lists a concern for the welfare of humanity among his characteristics of self-actualizers (see Table 14-2) and some of the self-actualizers identified by Maslow—such as Eleanor Roosevelt—clearly possessed this characteristic, it is conspicuously absent from the hierarchy of needs that is so central to Maslow's formal theory.

# Personality Assessment

The objective assessment of personality serves a number of practical needs in our society. In selecting individuals for high-level positions, employers need to know something about their honesty, their ability to handle stress, and so on. In helping students to make career choices, counselors can offer wiser advice if they know something about a student's personality. Decisions about the kind of treatment that will be most beneficial to an emotionally disturbed person or that will help to rehabilitate a convicted felon require an objective assessment of the individual's personality.

Beyond these practical concerns, methods of assessing personality are essential to the study of personality itself—no matter what theoretical approach one prefers. Although each of the four approaches to personality we have discussed in this chapter can use any of several assessment methods, each tends to favor an assessment strategy tailored to its theoretical concerns. For this reason, we have grouped the assessment methods in this section according to the theoretical approaches.

## General Considerations

In Chapter 12, we introduced some of the requirements of a good test of mental abilities. With some additional complexities, the same criteria apply to tests of personality. Specifically, a good test must have *reliability* and *validity*.

*Like tests of mental ability, personality tests must be reliable and valid.*

**RELIABILITY**   If a test or method of assessment is reliable, it will give reproducible and consistent results. **Reliability** is typically assessed by correlating two sets of scores. For example, when the same test is given to the same group of people on two occasions, their scores on the first occasion should correlate highly with their scores on the second. If they do, then the test is said to have **temporal stability** or **test-retest reliability.** A similar measure of **alternate form reliability** assesses the degree to which two forms of the same test yield equivalent scores. Another common measure of reliability is **internal consistency,** the degree to which the separate questions or items on a test are all measuring the same thing. This can be assessed by correlating the scores obtained by a group of individuals on each item with their total scores. Any item that is not correlated with the total score is an unreliable item; it is failing to contribute to what the test is measuring. Discarding unreliable items "purifies" a test by increasing its internal consistency. As the number of reliable items on a test increases, the reliability of the test's total score also increases.

A special kind of reliability check is required when subjective judgments are involved in an assessment. For example, if two observers independently rate a group of nursery-school children for aggression, we can correlate the ratings of the two observers. This will yield an index of **interscorer agreement** or **interjudge reliability.** This measure of reliability would also be calculated if two or more judges were asked to read presidential inaugural addresses and to rate them for optimism or to count the number of negative references to Iraq.

**VALIDITY**   Reliability assesses the degree to which a test is measuring *something,* but good reliability does not guarantee that the test is measuring what it is intended to measure; it does not guarantee that the test has **validity.** As we noted in Chapter 12, a humor test containing jokes that are hard to understand might well be reliable, but the test might be measuring verbal intelligence or educational achievement rather than sense of humor. In some instances the validity of a test can be assessed by correlating the test score with some external criterion. This correlation is called a **validity coefficient.** For example, the positive correlation between scores on the Scholastic Aptitude Test (SAT) and freshman grades in college indicates that the test has reasonable validity. This kind of validity is called **criterion** or **empirical validity.** Because of sensitivity to race and sex discrimination, the courts are increasingly requiring agencies or companies that use tests for personnel selection to provide evidence that those tests correlate with on-the-job performance—that they have criterion or empirical validity.

A special kind of validity, which applies especially to assessment instruments used in research on personality, is called **construct validity.** If a researcher is designing a test to measure some concept or construct that is part of a theory, it is not always possible to compute a single coefficient that would indicate its criterion validity because it is not clear what the external criterion should be. How, for example, should a researcher assess the validity of a test for achievement motivation? One can think of a number or possibilities. The test could be given to business executives to see if the test correlates with their salaries. Perhaps the test will correlate with teachers' ratings of the ambitiousness of their students. The problem is that there is no single criterion the researcher is willing to accept as the ultimate "true" answer. It would be nice if the test correlated with executive salaries, but if it did not, the researcher would not be willing to judge the test to be invalid. This is known as the **criterion problem** in personality psychology: there is no measure of "truth" against which to validate the measuring instrument. Accordingly, the researcher attempts instead to establish its construct validity.

This is done through the process of research itself. The researcher uses his or her theory both to construct the instrument and to generate predictions from the theory. Studies using the new instrument are then conducted to test those predictions. To the extent that the results of several converging studies are positive, both the theory and the instrument are validated simultaneously. Most often, mixed results suggest ways in which both the theory and the instrument need to be modified.

## Trait Assessment

**PERSONALITY RATINGS**   The most direct way of assessing how much of a particular trait an individual possesses is to ask those who know the person well to rate him or her on a scale of that trait. For example, a rater might be asked to rate the person on the trait of friendliness using a 7-point scale that ranges from "not at all friendly" to "very friendly." Often such scales are labeled at the two ends with opposite traits—for example, "domineering–submissive" or "conscientious–unreliable." Individuals can also be asked to rate themselves on the scales.

As we saw earlier, a number of trait theorists adopted this method as a starting point for their systems by selecting trait terms culled from the unabridged dictionary. For example, Cattell applied factor analysis to trait rating scales of this kind to identify the 16 basic personality factors that form the basis of his system. Twelve of his factors came from peer ratings and four came from self-ratings.

**Q SORT**   One kind of rating method that deserves special mention is the **Q sort,** which we described in detail in Chapter 13. In the Q-sort technique, the rater (sorter) is given a set of cards, each containing a personality statement (for example, "Is cheerful"), and is asked to describe an individual's personality by sorting them into piles. The rater places statements that are least descriptive of the individual in pile 1 on the left and those that are most descriptive in pile 9 on the right. The other statements are distributed in the intermediate piles, thereby assigning each Q item a score ranging from 1 to 9. (Some Q sorts use fewer or more than 9 piles.)

At first glance, this would seem no different from asking raters to rate the individual on a set of traits, using a 9-point rating scale. And, in fact, the item scores can be used in this way if the researcher wishes. But there is an important difference. When filling out rating scales, a rater is implicitly comparing the individual with other individuals (for example, a rating of "very friendly" implies that the individual is very friendly compared with other individuals). When performing a Q sort, however, a rater is explicitly comparing each trait with other traits *within* the same individual (for example, placing the item "friendly" in pile 9 implies that, compared with other traits, friendliness stands out as uniquely descriptive of the individual).

The difference between the two kinds of ratings parallels Allport's distinction between *common traits* and *personal dispositions*. Common traits are those on which individuals can be compared with one another; personal dispositions refer to the unique *patterning* or *configuration* of traits within the individual. It is this unique patterning that is captured by the Q-sort method. The technique thus offers a quantitative way of partially capturing what Allport considered to be the most important feature of personality: individuality.

## Testimonial Validity and Other Nonsense

If you own a personal computer, you can buy an inexpensive program that analyzes handwriting. When it was first introduced, the computer magazines gave it glowing reviews. Some reviewers claimed that it was so embarrassingly accurate that they were reluctant to print the program's descriptions of their own personalities in the review. Testimonials attesting to its accuracy also appeared in advertisements for the handwriting analysis program. Many were similar to the following:

For the first time things that I have been vaguely aware of have been put into concise and constructive statements which I would like to use as a plan for improving myself.

It appears to me that the results . . . are unbelievably close to the truth.

This method of evaluating an assessment instrument by gathering opinions on its accuracy from those who have been assessed establishes what we facetiously suggest should be called its *testimonial validity*. It is a frequently used method—especially by astrologers, fortune-tellers, medical quacks, and other hucksters. In short, it is bunk.

Studies have shown that people tend to view generalized descriptions as accurate summaries of their own personality. In several experiments, college students were given a personality inventory. A few days later, they were handed typed reports in sealed envelopes and asked to rate the accuracy of the evaluations. Unknown to the subjects, all the personality descriptions were identical. Most students in such studies say that the description fits them fairly well (Forer, 1949). The two testimonials quoted above actually came from two subjects in a study of this type (Ulrich, Stachnik & Stainton, 1963). This phenomenon has been dubbed the *Barnum effect*, in reference to the frequently

As we described in Chapter 13, two Q sorts can be compared with each other quantitatively by computing a correlation between them, thereby assessing the degree to which two individuals are similar to one another in their overall personality configurations. If two Q sorts are descriptions of the same individual at two different times, then the correlation assesses the test-retest reliability of the technique or the continuity of that individual's overall personality over time. If two Q sorts are descriptions of a single individual made by two raters, then the correlation assesses interjudge reliability or the degree to which two persons perceive the same individual similarly. (For example, in marital counseling, it could be helpful to assess the degree to which two spouses agree or disagree in their perceptions of each other.) If one of the Q sorts is a description of some hypothetical ideal type (for example, the optimally adjusted personality), then the correlation between an individual's Q sort and the ideal sort assesses the degree to which the person approximates the ideal. A complete description of the Q-sort technique has been written by Block (1961/1978).

**PERSONALITY INVENTORIES** A personality inventory is a questionnaire on which the individual reports his or her reactions or feelings in certain situations. It resembles a structured interview in that it asks the same questions of each person, and the answers are usually given in a form that can be easily scored, often by computer. A personality inventory may be designed to measure a single dimension of personality (such as anxiety level) or several personality traits simultaneously. Again, Cattell provides an example. After he had derived his factors from trait rating scales, he composed questions that best represented each factor and assembled them into a test that yielded a score for each factor—called the Sixteen Personality Factor Questionnaire (16 PF). For example, an individual who answers no to the question "Do you tend to keep in the background on social occasions?" earns a point toward the dominant side of the dominant–submissive factor.

quoted statement by the circus entrepreneur P. T. Barnum, "There's a sucker born every minute."

Check it out for yourself. Here is your personal report:

■ You have a tendency to be critical of yourself. At times, you are extraverted, affable, sociable, while at other times you are introverted, wary, reserved.

■ You pride yourself on being an independent thinker and do not accept others' opinions without satisfactory proof.

■ Some of your aspirations tend to be pretty unrealistic.

■ Under stressful circumstances, you occasionally experience some feelings of self-doubt.

■ Although you have considerable affection for your parents, there have been times when you disagreed with them.

■ Your sexual adjustment has presented problems for you.

In addition to using such general statements, some fortune-tellers and entertainers who claim to "read minds" are quite skilled in picking up cues from the individual's appearance and reactions and then elaborating the statements and tailoring them even more closely to the particular person.

Let the consumer beware. Testimonial validity isn't valid.

Cattell used his theory of the 16 factors as a guide to composing his questions. This is called the **rational method of test construction.** A different method of test construction—the **empirical** or **criterion method**—was used in the development of the Minnesota Multiphasic Personality Inventory (MMPI).

**MINNESOTA MULTIPHASIC PERSONALITY INVENTORY** The MMPI is composed of approximately 550 statements about attitudes, emotional reactions, physical and psychological symptoms, and past experiences. The subject responds to each statement by answering "true," "false," or "cannot say." Some sample test items follow:

■ I have never done anything dangerous for the thrill of it.
■ I daydream very little.
■ My mother or father often made me obey, even when I thought it was unreasonable.
■ At times my thoughts have raced ahead faster than I could speak them.

The responses are scored according to their correspondence to answers given by people with different kinds of psychological problems (see Table 14-3).

The MMPI was developed to aid clinicians in diagnosing personality disturbances. But instead of assuming specific personality traits and formulating questions to measure them, the test designers gave hundreds of test questions to groups of individuals. Each group was known to differ from the norm on a particular criterion. Only the questions that discriminated between groups were retained to form the inventory. For example, to develop a scale of items that distinguish between paranoid and normal individuals, the same questions were given to two groups. The criterion group consisted

**TABLE 14-3**

**MMPI Scales** *The first three scales are "validity" scales, which help to determine whether the person has answered the test items carefully and honestly. For example, the F (Frequency) scale measures the degree to which infrequent or atypical answers are given. A high score on this scale usually indicates that the individual was careless or confused in responding. (However, high F scores often accompany high scores on the Schizophrenia scale, which measures bizarre thinking.) The remaining "clinical" scales were originally named for categories of psychiatric disorders, but interpretation now emphasizes personality attributes rather than diagnostic categories.*

| SCALE NAME | SCALE ABBREVIATION | INTERPRETATION OF HIGH SCORES |
|---|---|---|
| Lie | L | Denial of common frailties |
| Frequency | F | Invalidity of profile |
| Correction | K | Defensive, evasive |
| Hypochondriasis | Hs | Emphasis on physical complaints |
| Depression | D | Unhappy, depressed |
| Hysteria | Hy | Reacts to stress by denying problems |
| Psychopathic deviancy | Pd | Lack of social conformity; often in trouble with the law |
| Masculinity–femininity | Mf | Feminine orientation (males); masculine orientation (females) |
| Paranoia | Pa | Suspicious |
| Psychasthenia | Pt | Worried, anxious |
| Schizophrenia | Sc | Withdrawn, bizarre thinking |
| Hypomania | Ma | Impulsive, excitable |
| Social introversion–extraversion | Si | Introverted, shy |

of individuals who were hospitalized with the diagnosis of paranoid disorder; the control group comprised people who had never been diagnosed as having psychiatric problems but who were similar to the criterion group in age, sex, socioeconomic status, and other important variables. Questions that at face value might seem to distinguish normal from paranoid individuals (for instance, "I think that most people would lie to get ahead") may or may not do so when put to an empirical test. In fact, patients diagnosed as paranoid were significantly less apt to respond "true" to this statement than were normal individuals.

Since the MMPI is derived from differences between criterion and control groups, it does not really matter whether what the person says is true. What is important is the fact that he or she says it. If schizophrenics answer "true" and normal subjects answer "false" to the statement "My mother never loved me," their answers distinguish the two groups regardless of how their mothers actually behaved. This is an advantage of a test based on the method of empirical construction over one based on a test constructor's assumption that certain answers indicate specific personality traits. The disadvantage is that one does not really have a theoretical understanding of the connection between the test responses and the personality characteristics they identify.

In addition to its content scales, the MMPI was the first major inventory to incorporate a number of validity scales within it (see Table 14-3). These are scales that attempt to determine whether the person has answered the test items carefully and honestly. If an individual's scores on any of these scales is too high, then his or her scores on the content scales must be interpreted with particular caution or disregarded altogether. These scales have been helpful but not completely successful at detecting invalid scores.

The MMPI was published in 1943 and is based on research that began in 1939. There are now more than 8,000 published studies on the MMPI, and it has been translated into at least 15 languages. There are even several private companies that provide computer-based scoring and interpretation of the inventory (see Figure 14-4). Increasingly over the years, it became evident that the original inventory was getting out of date and should be revised. But the enormous amount of existing data on the original version discouraged most researchers from every undertaking such a daunting task. Nevertheless, it has now been done. The MMPI-2 was published in 1989 and incorporates a number of significant revisions while maintaining the basic features of the original, including most of the original items. The new standardization involves a much larger and a more diversified sampling that is more representative of the United States population (Graham, 1990). The difficult job of assessing the comparability of scores between the new and original versions is now actively underway. Unfortunately, some of the initial data are not encouraging (Adler, 1990).

Although the MMPI was originally designed to identify people with serious personality disorders, it has been widely used to study normal populations. But because the MMPI does not adequately sample some of the traits

**FIGURE 14-4**
*Computer Printout of an MMPI Profile with Interpretation*

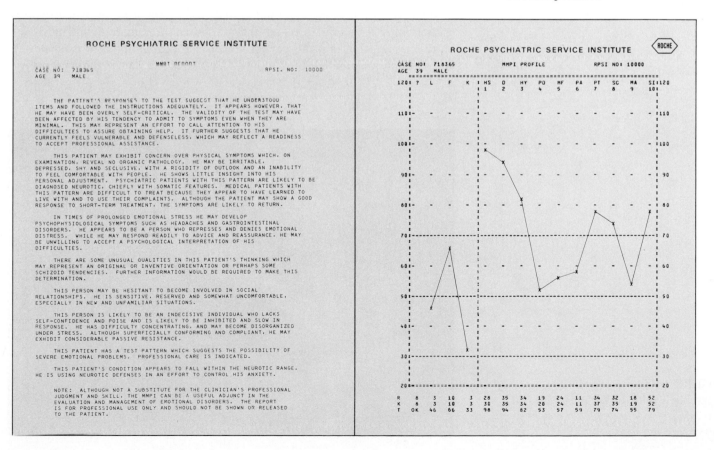

useful in describing the normal personality, the California Psychological Inventory (CPI) was devised, using many of the same items. The CPI scales measure such traits as dominance, sociability, self-acceptance, responsibility, and socialization. The comparison groups for some of the scales were obtained by asking high-school and college students to designate the classmates they would rate high or low on the trait in question. Thus, for the dominance scale, the criterion group consisted of students who were described by their peers as high in dominance (aggressive, confident, self-reliant) and the control group consisted of students who were described by their peers as low in dominance (retiring, lacking in self-confidence, inhibited). Items that revealed a statistically significant difference between the criterion group and the control group formed the dominance scale. The CPI is still one of the most widely validated personality inventories available for use with normal populations (Megargee, 1972).

## Psychoanalytic Assessment

Psychologists who take a psychoanalytic approach to personality are particularly interested in assessing unconscious wishes, motivations, and conflicts. Accordingly, they need assessment methods that reproduce as closely as possible the method of free association, in which the individual is free to say whatever comes to mind. Clearly the fixed structure of personality inventories—specific questions to which the individual must respond by selecting one of the answers presented—is not well-suited to this purpose. For this reason, they have developed **projective tests.** A projective test presents an ambiguous stimulus to which the person may respond as he or she wishes. Theoretically, because the stimulus is ambiguous and does not demand a specific response, the individual *projects* his or her personality onto the stimulus. Projective tests tap the individual's imagination and are based on the assumption that the person reveals something about himself or herself through imaginative productions. Two of the most widely used projec-

**FIGURE 14-5**
**Rorschach Inkblot** *The subject is asked to tell what is seen in the blot; it may be viewed from any angle.*

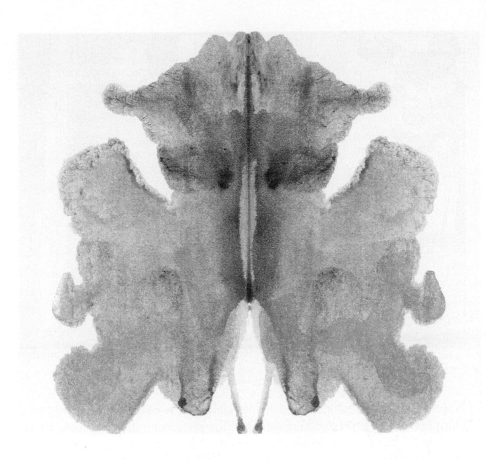

tive techniques are the Rorschach Test and the Thematic Apperception Test.

**RORSCHACH TEST**  The Rorschach Test, developed by the Swiss psychiatrist Hermann Rorschach in the 1920s, consists of a series of 10 cards, each displaying a rather complex inkblot like the one shown in Figure 14-5. Some of the blots are color; some are black and white. The subject is instructed to look at one card at a time and report everything the inkblot resembles. After the subject has finished the 10 cards, the examiner usually goes over each response, asking the subject to clarify some responses and to tell what features of the blot gave a particular impression.

The subject's responses may be scored in various ways. Three main categories are location (whether the response involves the entire inkblot or a part of it), determinants (whether the subject responds to the shape of the blot, its color, or differences in texture and shading), and content (what the response represents). Most testers also score responses according to frequency of occurrence; for example, a response is "popular" if many people assign it to the same inkblot.

Several elaborate scoring systems have been devised based on these categories. But most of these systems proved to have limited predictive value. Consequently, many psychologists base their interpretations on an impressionistic evaluation of the response record, as well as on the subject's general reaction to the test situation (for example, whether the individual is defensive, open, competitive, cooperative, and so on).

In 1974, a new system was introduced that attempted to extract and combine the validated portions of all the scoring systems into one complete

**FIGURE 14-6**
**Thematic Apperception Test** *This picture is similar to the pictures used on the
Thematic Apperception Test. The pictures
usually have elements of ambiguity so that
the subject can "read into" them something
from personal experience or fantasy.*

system. It has undergone extensive revision and is now supplemented by a
computer scoring service and software for microcomputers (Exner, 1986).
Although this system looks more promising than previous efforts, not
enough studies have accumulated to evaluate its validity with any confidence.

**THEMATIC APPERCEPTION TEST**   Another popular projective test, the
Thematic Apperception Test (TAT), was developed at Harvard University
by Henry Murray in the 1930s. The subject is shown as many as 20 ambiguous pictures of persons and scenes, similar to the one in Figure 14-6, and is
asked to make up a story about each. The subject is encouraged to give free
rein to his or her imagination and to tell whatever story comes to mind. The
test is intended to reveal basic themes that recur in a person's imaginative
productions. Apperception is a readiness to perceive in certain ways based
on prior experiences. People interpret ambiguous pictures according to their
apperceptions and elaborate stories in terms of preferred plots or themes
that reflect personal fantasies. If particular problems are bothering the subject, they may become evident in a number of the stories or in striking deviations from the usual theme in one or two stories. When shown a picture
similar to the one in Figure 14-6, a 21-year-old male told the following story:

> She has prepared this room for someone's arrival and is opening the door for a
> last general look over the room. She is probably expecting her son home. She
> tries to place everything as it was when he left. She seems like a very tyrannical
> character. She led her son's life for him and is going to take over again as soon as
> he gets back. This is merely the beginning of her rule, and the son is definitely
> cowed by this overbearing attitude of hers and will slip back into her well-or-
> dered way of life. He will go through life plodding down the tracks she has laid
> down for him. All this represents her complete domination of his life until she
> dies. (Arnold, 1949, p. 100)

Although the original picture shows only a woman standing in an open
doorway looking into a room, the subject's readiness to talk about his rela-

tionship with his mother led to this story of a woman's domination of her son. Facts obtained later confirmed the clinician's interpretation that the story reflected the subject's own problems.

In analyzing responses to the TAT cards, the psychologist looks for recurrent themes that may reveal the individual's needs, motives, or characteristic way of handling interpersonal relationships.

**PROBLEMS WITH PROJECTIVE TESTS** Many other projective tests have been devised. Some ask the subject to draw pictures of people, houses, trees, and so on. Others involve completing sentences that start with "I often wish . . . ," "My mother . . . ," or "I feel like quitting when they . . ." In fact, any stimulus to which a person can respond in an individualistic way could be considered the basis for a projective test. But most projective tests have not been subjected to enough research to establish their usefulness in assessing personality.

The Rorschach Test and the TAT, in contrast, have been intensively researched. The results, however, have not always been encouraging. Reliability of the Rorschach Test has been generally poor because the interpretation of responses is too dependent on the clinician's judgment; the same test protocol may be evaluated quite differently by two trained examiners. And attempts to demonstrate the Rorschach's ability to predict behavior or discriminate between groups have met with limited success. The new comprehensive system, mentioned above, may prove more successful.

The TAT has fared somewhat better. When specific scoring systems are used (for example, to measure achievement motives or aggressive themes), the interscorer reliability is fairly good. But the relationship of TAT scores to overt behavior is complex. Preoccupations are not necessarily acted on. A person who produces a number of stories with aggressive themes may not actually behave aggressively. The individual may be compensating for a need to inhibit aggressive tendencies by expressing such impulses in fantasy. When inhibitions about expressing aggression and strength of aggressive tendencies are estimated from the TAT stories, the relationship to behavior becomes more predictable. Among boys whose tests indicated that they were not very inhibited, the correlation between amount of aggression in the TAT stories and overt aggression was .55. Among boys showing a high degree of inhibition, the correlation between the number of aggressive themes and overt aggression was −.50 (Olweus, 1969).

Defenders of the Rorschach Test and the TAT point out that it is not fair to expect accurate predictions based on test responses alone; story themes or responses to inkblots are meaningful only when considered in light of additional information, such as the person's life history, other test data, and observations of behavior. The skilled clinician uses the results of projective tests to make tentative interpretations about the individual's personality and then verifies or discards them, depending on further information. The tests are helpful in suggesting possible areas of conflict to be explored.

## Social-Learning Assessment

Because of their primary focus on behavior and its situational determinants, psychologists who take a social-learning approach to personality have developed several methods for recording behavior in naturalistic settings. One group of researchers has constructed an elaborate electronic system for

*"Leave us alone! I am a behavior therapist! I am helping my patient overcome a fear of heights!"*

recording the behavior of children in free-play settings. By holding down buttons on a console, a single observer is able to record up to 12 different categories of ongoing behavior simultaneously (for example, "talking," "sitting alone"). The continuous record of behavior is sufficiently precise to enable researchers to relate even small changes in a child's behavior to events and to other children's behavior in the situation (Lovaas, Freitag, Gold, & Kassorla, 1965). Another research program has developed ingenious methods for recording the detailed interactions between highly aggressive children and their family members in everyday settings like the dinner table (Patterson, 1976).

Many behavioral assessments are conducted in conjunction with therapeutic techniques based on social-learning principles (see Chapter 17). In one study of height phobia, fear of heights was assessed by measuring the distance that individuals would climb on a fire escape. After receiving therapy, they were assessed again by having them take an elevator to a roof garden and attempt to count passing cars below for 2 minutes (Lazarus, 1961).

Individuals are often assessed by training them to be self-observers. For example, individuals in behavioral therapy are often asked to keep daily diaries of their activities in order to help the therapist pinpoint sources of anxiety. One study of adolescents provided each subject with an electronic paging device. Whenever they were beeped by the experimenter during the day, they stopped whatever they were doing and filled out a form, recording their current activity and their current level of self-esteem (Savin-Williams & Jaquish, 1981).

As psychologists who take a social-learning approach have become more cognitive in recent years, they have also begun to measure cognitions relevant to behavior, such as expectancies. In one study, patients who had suffered heart attacks were given a list of daily situations that might cause emotional strain (such as complaining to an unsympathetic sales person about poor service) and were asked to indicate whether they thought they could manage the situation and, if so, to rate how confident they felt about doing so (Bandura et al., 1985). And finally, social-learning researchers have occasionally recorded physiological variables in order to assess ongoing emotional reactions to situations.

## Phenomenological Assessment

For phenomenologically oriented psychologists, there is only one valid source for the information they find crucial: the individual himself or herself. Their most common tool is the interview. In early research, investigators would select excerpts from interviews taken during therapy sessions and attempt to discern how the clients' verbalizations reflected changes in their self-concepts during the course of therapy. More recently, they have developed reliable scoring systems for categorizing self-references into theoretically relevant categories, such as approving self-references (Mardsen, 1971; Traux & Mitchell, 1971).

**Q SORT**  The Q-sort technique has already been described in the section on trait assessment. We mention it again here because Carl Rogers pioneered its use as a phenomenological assessment instrument for examining the self-concept. Rogers's Q set contains statements like "I am satisfied with myself"; "I have a warm emotional relationship with others"; and "I don't trust my emotions." In Rogers's procedure, individuals first sort themselves as they actually are—their *real self*—and then sort themselves as they would like to be—their *ideal self.* The correlation between the two sorts indexes the self-ideal discrepancy. A low or negative correlation corresponds to a large *self-ideal discrepancy,* implying feelings of low self-esteem and lack of personal worth—one index of maladjustment.

By repeating this procedure several times during the course of therapy, Rogers could assess the effectiveness of therapy. In one study, correlations between self and ideal Q sorts of individuals seeking therapy averaged –.01 prior to therapy, but increased to +.58 following therapy. The same correlation for a matched control group not receiving therapy did not change (Butler & Haigh, 1954). In other words, the therapy had significantly reduced these individuals' perception of the discrepancy between their real selves and their ideal selves. Note that this could occur even if an individual did not change his or her perception of the real self but instead lowered unrealistic aspirations for the ideal self.

**ROLE CONSTRUCT REPERTORY TEST** The personal construct theory of George Kelly has its own unique assessment device, the *Role Construct Repertory Test,* or "Rep Test." Kelly designed it as a way of eliciting the personal constructs an individual uses to interpret or construe his or her interpersonal world. On this test, subjects or clients fill in a matrix or grid like the one shown in Figure 14-7.

Along the top of the grid is a list of people who are important to the individual. These might be supplied by the assessor or the subject, but they usually include "myself," and sometimes include "my ideal self." On each line of the grid, the assessor circles three of the cells. For example, in the

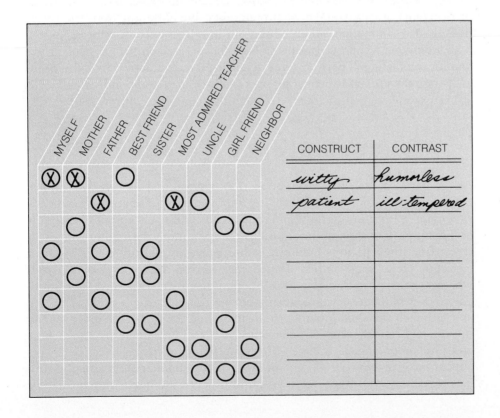

**FIGURE 14-7**
**Role Construct Repertory Test** *In each row, the subject compares three of the persons listed at the top of the grid, placing an "X" under the two who are most alike. He or she then describes how they are alike by writing in the* construct. *Finally, the subject describes how the third person is different from the other two by writing in the* contrast. *This subject indicates that he sees himself and his mother as both being witty and different from his best friend, who is seen as* humorless. *The procedure is repeated for each row in the matrix.*

first row of the figure, the assessor has circled the cells in the columns labeled "myself," "my mother," and "my best friend." The subject is asked to consider these three people and to place an "X" in the cells of the two people who are most similar to each other but different from the third. As shown in the first row, this (male) subject considers himself and his mother to be the most similar pair. He is then asked, "In what way are you and your mother alike but different from your best friend?" In this case, the subject has indicated that he and his mother are both *witty*. This description is called his *construct*. Next, he is asked "In what way is your friend different from you and your mother?" He has responded that his friend is *humorless*. This description is called his *contrast*. For this subject, then, the dimension *witty–humorless* is one of the personal constructs he uses to interpret or construe his interpersonal world.

Note that a construct–contrast pair need not constitute logical opposites. For example, this subject might have labeled himself and his mother as *witty*, but then labeled his best friend as *serious* or *introverted* or *prefers-to-listen-to-humor-rather-than-to-initiate-it*. If that is how he construes the two poles of the dimension, then that is what Kelly wanted to know. The Rep Test is designed to assess the *individual's* constructs, not the psychologist's.

The procedure is repeated with several other triads in the set. By looking at the entire set, the investigator or therapist can explore a number of themes that seem to characterize the individual's construal of the world. For example, some clients will reveal through this procedure that they see the entire world in authoritarian terms; dimensions like *strong—weak, powerful—powerless*, and so forth might appear repeatedly. Or an individual might reveal that she always pairs herself with males on the construct end of dimensions while placing other women on the contrast end.

The Rep Test is a very general procedure and is not restricted to construing persons. For example, an individual may be asked to consider triads of situations or events. (Which two are alike but different from the third? Taking an examination; going out on a blind date; encountering a spider.) The technique has proved valuable both for research on people's constructs and for counseling. There are even specialized mathematical techniques for analyzing the grid and abstracting structural features of the individual's construct system (such as the degree of cognitive complexity it reveals).

## Consistency Paradox

As we noted earlier, the assumption that persons display cross-situational consistencies in their behavior seems so obviously true that it is practically synonymous with our definition of personality. This was certainly the view of Theophrastus when he informed us that penurious men go to collect interest from their debtors before it is due, move the furniture looking for a lost coin, count the number of cups each person drinks at dinner parties where expenses are shared, and postpone putting on their shoes until midday so they will not be worn out so soon.

Although the assumption of cross-situational consistency is most explicit in type and trait theories of personality, it is also present in psychoanalytic and phenomenological theories. For example, even when overt behaviors appear inconsistent—as when a mother who resents her child shows hostility on one day and exaggerated love and concern the next—psychoanalytic theory assumes that a consistent unconscious motivation produces both behaviors. Phenomenological theories assume that the self-concept integrates our behavior and thus provides consistency.

But dissenting voices were heard as long ago as the sixteenth century, when the French essayist Michel de Montaigne wrote an essay entitled "Of the Inconsistency of Our Actions." In it, he sounded very much like a contemporary behaviorist in his insistence that the situation ("neighboring circumstances") determines behavior:

> In view of the natural instability of our conduct, it has often seemed to me that even good authors are wrong to insist on weaving a consistent and solid fabric out of us. . . . He who would judge [us] in detail and distinctly, bit by bit would more often hit upon the truth. . . . The surest thing, in my opinion, would be to trace [our actions] to the neighboring circumstances without getting into any further research and without drawing from them any other conclusions. (1580/1943, pp. 118, 120)

The consistency issue was first addressed empirically 60 years ago, when a series of studies explicitly set out to assess consistency across situations. The best known of these studies was the classic investigation of character by Hartshorne and May in the late 1920s. They gave some 11,000 elementary- and high-school students a large number of behavioral tests designed to measure the traits of altruism, self-control, and honesty in a number of different situations—at home, in the classroom, during athletic competition, and in church. To test honesty, for instance, the children were placed in situations where they had a chance to be dishonest while believing they would not be detected—to keep some of the money they were given to play with, to cheat on a test, to report falsely about the number of push-ups they could do, or the amount of work done at home. The correlations among behaviors in the different situations turned out to be quite low. For example, correlating scores on any two tests used to measure honesty yielded an average correlation of .23. These low correlations led Hartshorne and May to conclude that neither honesty nor dishonesty is a unified character trait; behavior is specific to the situation (Hartshorne & May, 1929).

The debate was reactivated some 40 years later by Walter Mischel (1968). After reviewing additional studies that had accumulated since the Hartshorne-May inquiry, Mischel also concluded that people are quite variable in their behavior across situations. He found that correlations between measures of the same trait in different situations were quite low in most studies—typically less than .30. Similarly, correlations between trait measures on personality tests and actual behavioral observations of the same traits in real situations were also low. (Mischel, 1968).

The paradox that sustains the debate and accounts for its historical durability is this: our intuitions tell us that individuals are consistent; the research tells us that they are not. Intuitions or research? Which one is wrong?

Recent research in social psychology lends some support to those who believe that our intuitions about consistency might be wrong (see the Critical Discussion, "Are Our Intuitions about Consistency Wrong?"). Despite these findings, however, some psychologists continue to maintain that our intuitions capture the reality of personality more faithfully than does the research (Bem & Allen, 1974; Bem, 1983). Their argument is an extension of Gordon Allport's view of personality and provides the first of several proposed solutions to the consistency paradox, the person-centered solution.

*Critical*

**DISCUSSION**

## *Are Our Intuitions About Consistency Wrong?*

Research by social psychologists on the processes of social inference has revealed a number of biases and shortcomings in our abilities to draw valid judgments from the data of everyday experience. (We discuss these in detail in Chapter 18.) This research suggests that there are a number of plausible reasons why our intuitions might be in error about consistency. Here are six:

1. Our preconceived notions of how people behave may lead us to generalize beyond our actual observations. We may fill in the missing data according to our implicit personality theories of which traits and behaviors go together. Moreover, research shows that when we expect two behaviors to be correlated, we tend to see them as correlated even when they are not. Stereotypes of how a "homosexual," a "career woman," or an "athlete" behaves may cause us to attribute greater consistency to a person's actions than actual observations warrant.

2. Many features of an individual remain fairly constant—physical appearance, manner of speaking, expressive gestures, and so on. These constancies help to create an impression that the personality is consistent as well.

3. Our presence can cause people to behave in certain ways. Thus, our acquaintances may appear to behave consistently because we are present as a stimulus during every observation we make. They may behave quite differently when we are not there.

4. Because the actions of another person are such a salient feature of any scene, we tend to overestimate the extent to which behavior is caused by personality characteristics and underestimate the importance of situational forces that may cause the person to act as he or she does. If we observe someone behaving aggressively, we assume that the person has an aggressive disposition and will behave similarly in other settings, even though the situational factors may be quite different. This tendency to underestimate situational influences on behavior has been called the **fundamental attribution error** (see Chapter 18).

## Person-Centered Solution

We saw earlier that Gordon Allport believed that personality psychology should be less concerned with comparing individuals across common traits and more concerned with the unique pattern or configuration of traits within the individual. We shall refer to the first strategy as the *trait-centered approach* and Allport's suggested strategy as the *person-centered approach*. The important difference between the two approaches is illustrated by Allport's response to the findings of Hartshorne and May that the children they observed in their study were not consistently honest or dishonest across situations. He noted that the low correlations "prove only that children are not consistent *in the same way*, not that they are inconsistent with themselves" (1937, p. 250). What did he mean by this?

Consider the two behaviors of lying and stealing, which were relatively uncorrelated in the study. One child may lie in order to avoid hurting the feelings of the teacher, whereas another may steal pennies in order to buy social acceptance from his or her peers. The first child might be consistently empathic and sensitive across situations, the second child consistently insecure about acceptance across situations. But for neither of these two children do the behaviors of lying and stealing belong together in a common category representing an honesty-dishonesty dimension. Honesty and dishonesty are categories in the head of the investigator—a personal construct or way of construing behavior. They are not categories that capture the coherence of either of these children's behaviors. If Hartshorne and May had measured empathy and sensitivity across situations, the first child would

5. The set of situations in which we observe most individuals is usually more limited than we realize. For example, we are so familiar with the warm, sincere personalities of the network news anchors on the national nightly newscasts that we would be shocked if we learned that one of them cheated on a spouse or kicked the family poodle. Because we see them so often, we mistakenly assume that we also see them in a variety of situations. As a result we feel we know them well and readily generalize about their behavior—assuming a consistency that is unwarranted. This example is particularly telling, because the behavior of news anchors is so severely constrained and so situationally determined that it could not possibly convey very much about their personalities. If they deviated even slightly from their prescribed role—if they slouched in their chairs or stood up to stretch, for example—they would be fired.

6. Our language entices us to think about human behavior in trait terms. As we noted earlier, there are about 18,000 trait terms in our language, nearly five percent of the entire lexicon. In contrast, we have an impoverished and awkward vocabulary for labeling situations. But language is not only a cause of how we think, it is also the result of how we think. The fact that our language is so unbalanced in this way probably indicates that we have always found it more important to classify persons rather than situations.

This discussion has presented only the case for the prosecution. The case for the defense appears in the remainder of this section.

*We may feel we know network news anchor Peter Jennings quite well because we see him frequently.*

have shown up as consistent; if they had measured insecurity across situations, the second child would have shown up as consistent. As Allport said, the children are not inconsistent with themselves; they are only inconsistent with the investigator's theory that lying and stealing represent "the same thing." This, according to Allport, is the fallacy of the trait-centered approach to personality.

In contrast, our intuitions appear to follow the person-centered strategy. Consider how we approach the task of describing a friend. We do not invoke a fixed set of trait terms that we apply to everyone. Instead, we first review our friend's behavior and then select a small set of traits that strike us as pertinent *precisely because* they seem to conform to the patterning of our friend's behavior.

If Dick always does his schoolwork early, is meticulous about his personal appearance, and is always punctual, it may well occur to us to describe him as conscientious. In contrast, if Jane is always conscientious about her schoolwork but sloppy about her appearance and never punctual, we may well describe her as a totally dedicated student who has time for little else. The important point is that we are not likely to characterize her as someone who is inconsistently conscientious. That is, we do not first impose a trait term—"conscientious"—on her and then judge her to be inconsistent. Instead, we first attempt to discern a recognizable pattern to her behaviors and only then to put a label on that pattern.

This, then, is the essence of our intuitive approach to personality, and it is the argument of Bem and Allen that in terms of the underlying logic and fidelity to reality, our intuitions about consistency are right, the research wrong (Bem & Allen, 1974; Bem, 1983).

## Aggregation Solution

In our discussion of reliability, we noted that as the number of items on a test increases, the reliability of the entire test increases. For example, the correlation between any two items on the Wechsler Adult Intelligence Scales (WAIS) (see Chapter 12) is only about .16. Clearly it would be absurd to expect an individual's answer to a single item to correlate with his or her intelligence in non-test situations; in other words, a one-item test would have virtually no validity. But because many such items are summed or aggregated on the WAIS, the reliability of the total test score is .96, and its validity—its correlation with many non-test behaviors—is quite impressive.

Now consider the studies that find little cross-situational consistency in behavior. Most are based on only one or two measures of behavior. For example, a typical study may try to relate helpfulness in one situation (giving money to charity) with helpfulness in another (coming to the aid of a person in distress). This is analogous to trying to correlate one item on the WAIS with one of the other items. Low correlations should be expected. Other studies may correlate an individual's score on a scale measuring aggression with an aggressive behavior in a laboratory experiment. Because the aggression scale is an aggregate of many items, it is probably reliable, but the likely unreliability of the single laboratory measure of aggression is rarely considered and almost never actually assessed.

In other words, a more accurate estimate of cross-situational consistency would be obtained if investigators combined several behavioral measures of the same trait to arrive at an **aggregated score**, just as they have always done with their tests. For example, much higher correlations are found in the Hartshorne and May study when aggregated scores are used. When the children's aggregated scores on half of the honesty tests are correlated with those on the other half of the tests, the correlation is .72. This is much higher than the average correlation of a .23 between any two tests for honesty and indicates considerable consistency (Rushton, Jackson, & Paunonen, 1981).

The method of aggregation can also be used to demonstrate the stability of traits over time. In one study, observers followed people for 4 weeks and rated them on variables related to their sociability or their tendency to be impulsive. Although the correlations for any 2 days were quite low, the ratings averaged over the first 14 days correlated .81 with the ratings averaged over the second 14 days (Epstein, 1977). Thus, it appears that we can find considerable consistency in traits, given a large enough sample of behavior.

The aggregation solution also resolves another paradox. In Chapter 13, we reported impressive continuities between childhood personality characteristics (like ill-temperedness and dependency) and adult outcomes thirty years later (like occupational status and marital stability). But how can this be so if simple behaviors are not consistent across situations even when measured within days of each other? The answer, of course, is that the childhood personality characteristics comprised aggregated observations over 3 years and the adult outcomes similarly reflected the consequences of many aggregated behaviors. We cannot predict whether a boy who has a temper tantrum one day when he is ten will have a fight with his wife one day when he is 40. But we can predict from the sum of his temper tantrums over three years in late childhood to a divorce precipitated by several adult years of marital strife.

## Interactional Solution

The interactional solution to the consistency debate reflects the emerging consensus among personality psychologists that an adequate theory of personality must attend to the characteristics of both the person and the situation. Most personality psychologists now recognize the diverse ways in which the person and the situation interact to produce behavior.

We anticipated this resolution in Chapter 13, where we described in detail how the interactions between our genotypes (inherited characteristics) and our environments interact to shape our personalities. The person-situation interactions that produce behavior are directly analogous to the genotype-environment interactions that shape personality in the first place. In particular, situations become a function of our personalities through the same three forms of interaction that cause the environment to become a function of the child's personality: *reactive*, *evocative*, and *proactive*.

**REACTIVE INTERACTION**  Different individuals exposed to the same situation experience it, interpret it, and react to it differently. The person who interprets a hurtful act as the product of hostility will react differently from the person who interprets it as the product of insensitivity.

This kind of interaction—**reactive interaction**—can affect cross-situational consistency because one person might perceive a set of situations to be similar to one another, whereas another person might perceive the same set of situations to be quite different from one another. Dick is motivated to do his homework and to return library books on time because he sees them as similar to one another; both evoke his conscientiousness. In contrast, Jane sees doing homework and returning library books as completely different acts; one is important to her goals, the other trivial. Hence her behavior is "inconsistent" across the two situations.

Because reactive interaction involves the ways in which people construe situations, the phenomenological approach to personality is particularly useful for understanding the complexities and consequences of reactive interaction.

**EVOCATIVE INTERACTION**  Every individual's personality evokes distinctive responses from others. A person who acts in an abrasive manner is apt to evoke more hostile responses from the social environment than one who is tactful and sensitive to the feelings of others.

This kind of interaction—**evocative interaction**—also influences cross-situational consistency. For example, by being abrasive, the individual actually transforms what would otherwise be very different situations into essentially similar ones—unpleasant social situations—in which being abrasive is further provoked and sustained. The social-learning theorists have taken the lead in the study of evocative interaction by providing the necessary conceptual and methodological tools for analyzing reciprocal behavioral interactions.

**PROACTIVE INTERACTION**  Each individual's personality leads him or her to seek out some situations and to avoid others. A person who feels the need to dominate others might seek confrontation, whereas a more submissive individual would try to avoid such situations. The sociable student will choose to take an informal seminar rather than a large class. And once an individual is in a situation, he or she can shape it further: it will be the sociable student who suggests moving the evening seminar to the dormitory lounge.

*A person who acts in an abrasive manner is more likely to evoke hostility than someone who is more tactful.*

**Proactive interaction** creates cross-situational consistencies in behavior because we actively seek out and create situations that are, in fact, similar to one another. Accordingly, we are more consistent in everyday life than the experimental evidence would suggest because we selectively place ourselves into situations that are similar to one another and avoid other situations in which we might behave quite differently. This has implications for the methods psychologists use to study personality.

In particular, the hallmark of the experimental laboratory is the control of conditions: subjects assigned to the same conditions must experience the same treatment if valid inferences are to be drawn. Moreover, subjects should be randomly assigned to conditions. But if individuals differ from one another primarily in their interpretations of situations, in the characteristic responses they evoke from others in situations, in their selection of which situations to enter in the first place, and in their tendencies to reshape the situations they enter, then psychologists who use only the laboratory to study personality will never see its major manifestations.

Clearly, personality psychology needs the contribution of all the approaches discussed in this chapter. In attempting to provide a complete, integrated account of the total person, the study of personality remains the most ambitious subfield of psychology.

## *Chapter* SUMMARY

1. *Personality* refers to the distinctive and characteristic patterns of thought, emotion, and behavior that define an individual's personal style and influence his or her interactions with the environment. Personality psychology seeks (a) to describe and to explain individual differences, and (b) to synthesize the processes that can influence an individual's interactions with the environment into an integrated account of the total person.

2. *Type theories* propose that individuals can be categorized into discrete types that are qualitatively different from one another. Currently, *typologies* are not very popular in psychology. *Trait theories* assume that an individual's personality can be described by its position on a number of continuous dimensions, or scales, each of which represents a trait. A major task of trait theorists is to derive a manageably small set of trait descriptors that can encompass the diversity of human personality. The method of factor analysis has often been used for this purpose. Five factors that are found fairly consistently in factor-analytic studies of personality are *Neuroticism* (maladjustment), *Extraversion, Openness to Experience, Agreeableness,* and *Conscientiousness*. Gordon Allport, Raymond Catell, and Hans Eysenck are three of the most prominent trait theorists.

3. Freud's *psychoanalytic theory* holds that many behaviors, including dreams and slips of the tongue, are caused by unconscious motivations. Personality is primarily determined by the biological drives of sex and aggression and by experiences that occur during the first 5 years of life. Freud's theory of *personality structure* views personality as composed of the *id*, the *ego*, and the *superego*, which are often in conflict. The id operates on the *pleasure principle*, seeking immediate gratification of biological impulses. The ego obeys the *reality principle*, postponing gratification until it can be achieved in socially acceptable ways. The superego (conscience) imposes *moral standards* on the individual. In a well-integrated personality, the ego remains in firm but flexible control over the id and superego; the reality principle governs.

4. Freud's theory of *personality dynamics* proposes that there is a constant amount of psychic energy *(libido)* for each individual. If a forbidden act or impulse is suppressed, its energy will seek an outlet in some other form, such as dreams or neurotic symptoms. The theory assumes that unacceptable id impulses cause anxiety, which can be reduced by *defense mechanisms.*

5. Freud's theory of *personality development* proposes that individuals pass through *psychosexual stages* (such as oral, anal, phallic) and must resolve the *Oedipal conflict*, in which the young child sees the same-sex parent as a rival for the affection of the opposite-sex parent. Freud's theory of anxiety and defense mechanisms has fared better over the years than his structural and developmental theories. Psychoanalytic theory has been modified by others like Jung, Adler, Horney, Sullivan, Fromm, and Erikson—all of whom place more emphasis on functions of the ego and on motives other than sex and aggression.

6. *Social-learning theory* assumes that personality differences result from variations in learning experiences. Responses may be learned through observation, without reinforcement, but reinforcement is important in determining whether the learned responses will be performed. A person's behavior depends on the specific characteristics of the situation in interaction with the individual's appraisal of the situation and reinforcement history. People behave consistently only insofar as the situations they encounter and the roles they are expected to play remain relatively stable.

7. *Phenomenological theories* are concerned with the individual's subjective experience. *Humanistic psychology* was founded as the "third force," an explicit alternative to psychoanalytic and behavioristic approaches. Humanistic psychologists like Carl Rogers and Abraham Maslow emphasize a person's self-concept and striving for growth, or self-actualization. George Kelly's *personal construct theory* focuses on the concepts or constructs individuals use to interpret or *construe* their world.

8. Tests for assessing personality must demonstrate that they yield reproducible and consistent results (*reliability*) and that they measure what they are intended to measure (*validity*). Tests designed to measure a construct that is part of a theory (for example, motivation to achieve) acquire construct validity when predictions from the theory are confirmed in studies using the test.

9. Ratings made on trait dimensions (such as *friendly–unfriendly*) can be made by individuals describing themselves or by people who know them well. The *Q-sort* technique requires the rater to sort statements typed on cards into piles ranging from statements that are least characteristic to statements that are most characteristic of the individual. Whereas rating scales implicitly compare an individual with other individuals across traits, the Q sort explicitly compares each trait with other traits *within* a single individual, thereby describing the *patterning* or *configuration* of traits that compose his or her personality.

10. *Personality inventories* are questionnaires on which individuals report their reactions or feelings in certain situations. Responses to subsets of items are summed to yield scores on separate scales or factors within the inventory. Items on some inventories are composed or selected on the basis of a theory; this is called the *rational* method of test construction. Alternatively, items can be selected because they correlate with some criterion; for example, an item to which schizophrenics answer "true"

significantly more often than do nonschizophrenics would be selected as an item for a schizophrenia scale. This is called the *empirical* or *criterion* method of test construction. The Minnesota Multiphasic Personality Inventory (MMPI) and the California Psychological Inventory (CPI) are examples of empirically constructed tests.

11. Psychologists who take the psychoanalytic approach prefer less structured assessment instruments called *projective* tests, such as the Rorschach Test and the Thematic Apperception Test (TAT). Because the test stimuli are ambiguous, it is assumed that the individual *projects* his or her personality onto the stimulus, thereby revealing unconscious wishes and motives. Psychologists who take the social-learning approach prefer to observe behavior directly in natural settings. Psychologists who take the phenomenological approach focus on the individual's own perceptions and interpretations. These can be assessed by analyzing interviews. The *Role Construct Repertory Test* is specifically designed within the framework of Kelly's *personal construct theory* to elicit the concepts or constructs individuals use to interpret or *construe* their world.

12. There is a long-standing discrepancy between our intuitive assumption—embodied in most theories of personality—that individuals are consistent across situations and studies that seem to demonstrate that they are not. Studies that find low correlations between measures of the same trait in two different situations or between personality test scores and situational measures of the trait support the contention of social-learning theorists that behavior is more dependent on the situation than on enduring traits. In reply, Allport and others have argued that the low correlations only demonstrate that individuals are not consistent in the same way, not that they are inconsistent across situations in their personal dispositions. Others have demonstrated that consistency increases if measures are aggregated across situations or over time.

13. *Interactionism* resolves the debate by recognizing that behavior results from an ongoing reciprocal interaction between personal dispositions and situational variables. In particular, individuals (a) differentially react to situations, (b) evoke different responses from others in situations, and (c) differentially select and shape situations. As a result, situations themselves become a function of the individual's personality through the processes of *reactive*, *evocative*, and *proactive* interaction.

## *Further* READING

General books on personality include Hall, Lindzey, Loehlin, and Manosevitz, *Introduction to Theories of Personality* (1985); Mischel, *Introduction to Personality* (5th ed., 1993); and Feshbach and Weiner, *Personality* (3rd ed., 1991).

For a social-learning approach to personality, see Bandura, *Social Learning Theory* (1977). Freud's theories are presented in their most readable form in his *New Introductory Lectures on Psychoanalysis* (1933; reprint ed., 1965). Other references for psychoanalytic theories of personality include Holzman, *Psychoanalysis and Psychopathology* (1970); and Eagle, *Recent Developments in Psychoanalysis: A Critical Evaluation* (1984).

The phenomenological viewpoint is represented in Maddi and Costa, *Humanism in Personology: Allport, Maslow, and Murray* (1972); and Keen, *A Primer in Phenomenological Psychology* (1982). For Carl Rogers' views, see

Rogers and Stevens, *Person to Person: The Problem of Being Human* (1967); and Rogers, *Carl Rogers on Personal Power* (1977). *Personality and Personal Growth* (2nd ed., 1984) by Frager and Fadiman focuses on the personality theories that are most concerned with understanding human nature and includes a section on such Eastern theories of personality as Yoga, Zen Buddhism, and Sufism.

Aiken, *Assessment of Personality* (1989) is a general text on methods of assessing personality. Cronbach, *Essentials of Psychological Testing* (4th ed., 1984), also contains chapters on personality measurement.

# Part  VII

## Stress, Psychopathology, and Therapy

15      Stress and Coping

16      Abnormal Psychology

17      Methods of Therapy

*Place du Havre*, 1909, by Theodore Earl Butler (1876–1937), $28\frac{1}{8}''\times 19''$, Adelson Gallery, New York.

# Stress and Coping

## Characteristics of Stressful Events 578

*Traumatic Events*
*Controllability*
*Predictability*
*Challenging Our Limits*
*Internal Conflicts*
*Critical Discussion: Sexual Abuse as a Major Stressor*

## Psychological Reactions to Stress 583

*Anxiety*
*Anger and Aggression*
*Apathy and Depression*
*Cognitive Impairment*

## Physiological Reactions to Stress 587

*Physiological Stress Response*
*Stress and Illness*

## How Stress Affects Health 591

*Direct Route*
*Interactive Route*
*Health-Behavior Route*
*Illness-Behavior Route*

## Appraisals and Personality Styles as Mediators of Stress Responses 596

*Psychoanalytic Theory*
*Behavioral Theory*
*Personality Style*

## Coping Skills 602

*Problem-Focused Coping*
*Emotion-Focused Coping*
*Defense Mechanisms as Emotion-Focused Coping*

## Managing Stress 610

*Behavioral Techniques*
*Cognitive Techniques*
*Modifying Type A Behavior*
*Critical Discussion: Can Psychological Interventions Affect the Course of Cancer?*

Detail, *Place du Havre.*

We all experience stress occasionally. Students may be stressed when their relationship with their roommates is not going well, when they must declare a course of study, or when final exams come. Today's rapidly paced society creates stress for many of us. We are constantly pressured to accomplish more and more in less and less time. Air and noise pollution, traffic congestion, crime, and excessive workload are increasingly present in our everyday lives. Finally, we sometimes face major stressful events, such as the death of a parent or a natural disaster. Exposure to stress can lead to painful emotions, for instance anxiety or depression. It can also lead to physical illnesses, both minor and severe. But people's reactions to stressful events differ widely: some people faced with a stressful event develop serious psychological or physical problems, whereas other people faced with the same stressful event develop no problems and may even find the event challenging and interesting. In this chapter we discuss the concept of stress and the effects of stress on the mind and the body. We also look at the differences between people's ways of thinking about and coping with stressful events, and how these differences contribute to adjustment.

Stress has become a popular topic. The media often attribute unusual behavior or illness in people to burn out from stress or a nervous breakdown resulting from stress. For example, when a celebrity attempts suicide, it is often said that he or she was burnt out from the pressures of public life. In their daily lives at school, students often talk about each others' levels of stress. "I'm so stressed out!" is a common claim. But what is stress? In general terms, **stress** occurs when people are faced with events they perceive as endangering their physical or psychological well-being. These events are usually referred to as **stressors,** and people's reactions to them as **stress responses.**

There are some types of events that most people experience as stressful. We will describe the characteristics of such events below. One of the most striking features about the experience of stress, however, is the powerful influence of psychological factors. People show marked individual differences in their reaction to stressors. Even physiological responses to difficult events can be influenced by psychological processes. The last part of this

*The causes of stress vary from one person to the next. What is overwhelming to one person may be exciting and challenging to another.*

chapter focuses on the ways people's appraisals of events, their styles of coping with events, and the social support available to them affect reactions to stressful events. First, though, let us focus on the characteristics of events that cause people to label them as stressful.

# Characteristics of Stressful Events

Countless events create stress. Some are major changes affecting large numbers of people—events such as war, nuclear accidents, and earthquakes. Others are major changes in the life of individuals—for instance, moving to a new area, changing jobs, getting married, losing a friend, suffering a serious illness. Everyday hassles can also be experienced as stressors—losing your wallet, getting stuck in traffic, arguing with your professor, and so on. Finally, the source of stress can be within the individual in the form of conflicting motives or desires. Events that are perceived as stressful usually fall into one or more of the following categories: traumatic events outside the usual range of human experience, uncontrollable events, unpredictable events, events that challenge the limits of our capabilities and self-concept, or internal conflicts.

## Traumatic Events

The most obvious sources of stress are traumatic events—situations of extreme danger that are outside the range of usual human experience. These include natural disasters, such as earthquakes and floods; man-made disasters, such as wars and nuclear accidents; catastrophic accidents, such as car or plane crashes; and physical assaults, such as rape or attempted murder.

While people's reactions to traumatic events vary widely, a common behavior pattern—the disaster syndrome—is observable. At first, survivors are stunned, dazed and appear to be unaware of their injuries or of the danger. They may wander around in a disoriented state, perhaps putting themselves at risk for further injury. For example, an earthquake survivor may wander through buildings that are on the verge of collapse, unaware of the obvious danger. In the next stage, survivors are still passive and unable to initiate even simple tasks, but they may follow orders readily. For example, a rape survivor days after her assault may not even think to fix herself food to eat, but if her close friend calls and insists they go out for food, she will comply. In the third stage survivors become anxious and apprehensive, have difficulty concentrating, and may repeat the story of the catastrophe over and over again. The survivor of a car crash may become extremely nervous when near a car, may be unable to go back to work because he or she cannot concentrate, and may tell friends about the details of the crash repeatedly.

Fortunately, most of us never experience traumatic events. More common events can lead to stress responses, however. Three characteristics of events lead to their being perceived as stressful: their controllability, predictability, and the extent to which they challenge the limits of our capabilities and our self-concept. Of course, the degree to which an event is stressful differs for each individual. That is, people differ in the extent to which they *appraise* the same event as controllable, predictable and a challenge to their capabilities and self-concept, and it is largely these appraisals that influence the perceived stressfulness of the event (Lazarus & Folkman, 1984).

*The disaster syndrome is a common response to highly traumatic events. Victims are stunned and disoriented at first. As time passes they become more responsive but are unable to initiate even simple tasks. Finally they grow anxious and have great difficulty concentrating.*

# Controllability

The more uncontrollable an event seems, the more likely it is perceived as stressful (see Chapter 7). Major uncontrollable events include the death of a loved one, being laid-off from work, or serious illness. Minor uncontrollable events are such things as having a friend refuse to accept your apology for some misdeed or being bumped off a flight because the airline oversold tickets. One obvious reason uncontrollable events are stressful is that if we cannot control them, we cannot stop them from happening.

As we noted, however, it appears that our *perceptions* of the controllability of events are as important to our assessment of their stressfulness as is the actual controllability of those events. Consider this study. Subjects were shown color photographs of victims of violent deaths. The experimental group could terminate the viewing by pressing a button. The control subjects saw the same photographs for the time duration determined by the experimental group, but they could not terminate the exposure. The level of arousal or anxiety in both groups was measured by the galvanic skin response (GSR), a drop in the electrical resistance of the skin that is widely used as an index of autonomic arousal. The experimental group showed much less anxiety in response to the photographs than did the control group, even though the two groups were exposed to the photographs for the same amount of time (Geer & Maisel, 1972).

The belief that we can control events appears to lessen our anxiety about them, even if we never exercise that control. This was demonstrated in a study in which two groups of subjects were exposed to a loud, extremely unpleasant noise. Subjects in one group were told that they could terminate the noise by pressing a button, but they were urged not to do so unless it was absolutely necessary. Subjects in the other group had no control over the noise. None of the subjects who had a control button actually pressed it, so the noise exposure was the same for both groups. Nevertheless, performance on subsequent problem-solving tasks was significantly worse for the group that had no control, indicating that they were more disturbed by the noise than was the group that had the potential for control (Glass & Singer, 1972).

# Predictability

Being able to predict the occurrence of a stressful event—even if the individual cannot control it—usually reduces the severity of the stress. As discussed in Chapter 7, laboratory experiments show that both humans and animals prefer predictable aversive events to unpredictable ones. In one study, rats were given a choice between a signaled shock and an unsignaled shock. If the rat pressed a bar at the start of a series of shock trials, each shock was preceded by a warning tone. If the rat failed to press the bar, no warning tones sounded during that series of trials. All of the rats quickly learned to press the bar, showing a marked preference for predictable shock (Abbott, Schoen, & Badia, 1984). Humans generally choose predictable over unpredictable shocks, too. They also show less emotional arousal and report less distress while waiting for predictable shocks to occur, and they perceive predictable shocks as less aversive than unpredictable ones of the same intensity (Katz & Wykes, 1985).

How do we explain these results? One possibility is that a warning signal

| LIFE EVENT | VALUE |
| --- | --- |
| Death of spouse | 100 |
| Divorce | 73 |
| Marital separation | 65 |
| Jail term | 63 |
| Death of close family member | 63 |
| Personal injury or illness | 53 |
| Marriage | 50 |
| Fired from job | 47 |
| Marital reconciliation | 45 |
| Retirement | 45 |
| Change in health of family member | 44 |
| Pregnancy | 40 |
| Sex difficulties | 39 |
| Gain of new family member | 39 |
| Business readjustment | 39 |
| Change in financial state | 38 |
| Death of close friend | 37 |
| Change to different line of work | 36 |
| Foreclosure of mortgage | 30 |
| Change in responsibilities at work | 29 |
| Son or daughter leaving home | 29 |
| Trouble with in-laws | 29 |
| Outstanding personal achievement | 28 |
| Wife begins or stops work | 26 |
| Begin or end school | 26 |
| Change in living conditions | 25 |
| Revision of personal habits | 24 |
| Trouble with boss | 23 |
| Change in residence | 20 |
| Change in school | 20 |
| Change in recreation | 19 |
| Change in church activities | 19 |
| Change in social activities | 18 |
| Change in sleeping habits | 16 |
| Change in eating habits | 15 |
| Vacation | 13 |
| Christmas | 12 |
| Minor legal violations | 11 |

**TABLE 15-1**
**Life Events Scale** *This scale, also known as the Holmes and Rahe Social Readjustment Rating Scale, measures stress in terms of life changes.* (After Holmes & Rahe, 1967)

before an aversive event allows the person or animal to initiate some sort of preparatory process that acts to lessen the effects of a noxious stimulus. An animal receiving the signal that a shock is about to happen may shift its feet in such a way as to reduce the experience of the shock. A man who knows he is about to receive a shot in the doctor's office can try to distract himself to lessen the pain. A woman who hears warnings of an impending hurricane can board up her windows in an attempt to prevent damage to her house. Another possibility is that with unpredictable shock, there is no safe period; with predictable shock, the subject (human or animal) can relax to some extent until the signal warns that shock is about to occur. Recall from Chapter 7 that this has been called the *safety signal hypothesis* (Seligman & Binik, 1977). A real-life example of the presence of a safety signal is when an employee's boss, who tends to criticize the employee in front of others, is out of town on a business trip. The boss's absence is a signal to the employee that he is safe to relax. An employee whose boss never goes out of town, and who criticizes him unpredictably throughout the day, has no safety signals, however, and may chronically feel stressed. An earthquake is one type of natural event for which there is no safety signal.

Some jobs are filled with unpredictability and are considered very stressful, such as fire fighting and emergency-room medicine. Serious illnesses often are very unpredictable. One of the major problems faced by cancer patients who receive treatment is that they cannot be sure whether or not they have been cured until many years have passed. Every day they must confront the uncertainty of a potentially disastrous future.

Another example of chronic unpredictability is women whose husbands were reported missing in action in Vietnam. Not knowing whether their husbands were alive or dead made it difficult for them to resolve their grief and proceed with their lives. Compared with wives of men who were killed in action and with wives of men who were prisoners, women married to MIAs showed the poorest physical and emotional health (Hunter, 1979).

## Challenging Our Limits

Some situations are largely controllable and predictable, but are still experienced as stressful because they push us to the limits of our capabilities and challenge our views of ourselves. Final exam week is a good example. Most students work much longer hours during final exam week than they do during the rest of the year. This physical and intellectual exertion is experienced as stressful by some people. Some students also find the limits of their knowledge and intellectual capabilities tested by exams. Even among students who are capable of doing well on exams, the possibility that they may fail important exams may challenge their view of themselves as competent and their decision to pursue a particular profession. A study of West Point Military Academy cadets found that those who were high on motivation to pursue a military career but who were performing poorly in examinations were at increased risk to develop an illness, specifically mononucleosis (Kasl, Evans, & Niederman, 1979).

Although we enter some pressure situations enthusiastically and joyfully, they still may be stressful. Marriage is a good example; it entails many, many new adjustments. Individuals are often challenged to the limits of their patience and tolerance as they become accustomed to the idiosyncrasies of their new spouses (for example, his or her habit of leaving clothes lying around everywhere). When minor irritations or major disagreements over important matters (for instance, financial decisions) lead to arguments

*A stressor can be positive or negative. If an event is predictable and controllable, such as a wedding, we can perceive it as challenging and exciting. If an event is unpredictable and uncontrollable, such as the press, noise, and possible danger of a crowded city sidewalk, we can perceive it as threatening.*

between newlyweds, they may find their beliefs that they married the right persons challenged.

Researchers Holmes and Rahe (1967) argued that any change in life that requires numerous readjustments can be perceived as stressful. In an attempt to measure the impact of life changes, they developed the *Life Events Scale*, shown in Table 15-1. The life events are ranked in order of the most stressful (death of a spouse) to the least stressful (minor violations of the law). To arrive at this scale, the investigators examined thousands of interviews and medical histories to identify the kinds of events that people found stressful. Because marriage appeared to be a critical event for most people, it was placed in the middle of the scale and was assigned an arbitrary value of 50. The investigators then asked approximately 400 men and women of varying ages, backgrounds, and marital status to compare marriage with a number of life events. They were asked such questions as, "Does the event call for more or less readjustment than marriage?" Those interviewed were then asked to assign a point value to each event on the basis of their evaluation of its severity and the time required for adjustment. These ratings were used to construct the scale in Table 15-1.

You may not agree with the exact ordering of these events. Studies have found some cultural and age differences (Masuda & Holmes, 1978; Ruch & Holmes, 1971). In addition, it is important to note that some people do not find major changes or pressure situations such as exam week stressful. They experience such situations as challenging and are invigorated by them. Later we will discuss characteristics of individuals that affect whether situations are viewed as stressors or challenges.

## Internal Conflicts

So far, we have discussed only external events in which something or someone in the environment challenges our well-being. Stress can also be brought about by internal processes—unresolved conflicts that may be conscious or unconscious. Conflict occurs when a person must choose between

## Sexual Abuse As a Major Stressor

One type of stress that is tragically common in our society is sexual abuse. Estimates of the incidence of sexual abuse vary, depending on the methods of individual studies (see Cutler & Nolen-Hoeksema, 1991). In one of the largest studies of sexual abuse, 3,132 randomly selected adults living in Los Angeles were interviewed in person (Burnam et al., 1988; Stein et al., 1988). Seventeen percent of the women and 9 percent of the men reported having had some type of experience of sexual assault at some time in their lives. Over 80 percent of the assaults occurred before the victims were 25 years old; 6.8 percent of the women and 3.8 percent of the men reported experiencing some type of sexual abuse involving physical contact before the age of 16. Kilpatrick and colleagues (1985) conducted telephone interviews with 2,004 randomly selected women in South Carolina and found that 14.5 percent reported one or more experiences of attempted or completed sexual assault, 5 percent reported they had been raped, and 4 percent reported they had been victims of attempted rape. Russell and Howell (1983) found a higher rate of rape experiences in a study using in-person interviews to gather information from a random sample of 930 adult women in San Francisco. Rather than simply asking women if they had ever been raped, the interviewers asked these women if they had ever had an experience of forced intercourse, intercourse obtained by threat of force, intercourse completed when they were drugged, unconscious, asleep, or otherwise totally helpless and thus unable to consent (this is the legal definition of rape in California). Twenty-four percent of the women interviewed reported having had at least one such experience.

The impact of rape and other types of sexual violence on the victim's emotional health appears to be great. Several studies have found that in the first six months after a rape or other assault, women and men show high levels of depression, anxiety, dismay, and many other indicators of emotional distress (Burgess & Holmstrom, 1974; Kilpatrick, Veronen & Resick, 1979; Wirtz & Harrell, 1987). For some people, this emotional distress declines over time.

*Most young adults experience conflict and frustration when they wish for independence but must wait to achieve it.*

incompatible, or mutually exclusive, goals or courses of action. Many of the things people desire prove to be incompatible. You want to play on your college volleyball team but cannot devote the time required and still earn the grades necessary to apply to graduate school. You want to join your friends for a pizza party but are afraid you will fail tomorrow's exam if you don't stay home and study. You don't want to go to your uncle's for dinner but you don't want to listen to your parents' complaints if you reject the invitation. The goals in these instances are incompatible because the action needed to achieve one automatically prevents you from reaching the other.

Even if two goals are equally attractive—for example, you receive two good job offers—you may agonize over the decision and experience regrets after making a choice. This stress would not have occurred if you had been offered only one job.

Conflict may also arise when two inner needs or motives are in opposition. In our society, the conflicts that are the most pervasive and difficult to resolve generally occur between the following motives:

- *Independence versus dependence*   Particularly when faced with a difficult situation, we may want someone to take care of us and solve our problems. But we are taught that we must stand on our own and assume responsibilities. At other times, we may wish for independence, but circumstances or other people force us to remain dependent.
- *Intimacy versus isolation*   The desire to be close to another person and to share our innermost thoughts and emotions may conflict with the fear of being hurt or rejected if we expose too much of ourselves.

For others, however, emotional distress is long-lasting. The following letter describes one rape survivor's lingering distress and fear:

> No one except someone who has experienced rape can know the late night, quiet playback and the thousands of stirring memories ready to rear up their ugly heads at the slightest incitement. Even almost a year later, as the "anniversary" draws near, I can feel all of my original reactions once again full force, and they are something which will not recede in time. Only women who have spent lonely nights such as this one trying to exorcise the ghosts can truly comprehend the insolence and hideousness of rape. And our number is growing, faster all the time. (J. Pilgrim, letter quoted by Thom, 1987, p. 222).

In their study, Burnam and colleagues (1988) found that assault victims were twice as likely as people who had not been assaulted to have a diagnosable depressive disorder, anxiety disorder, or substance abuse disorder at some time after the assault. They were most likely to develop these disorders if they had been assaulted as a child. In fact, people who had been assaulted as children remained at higher risk than the non-assaulted people for developing a psychological disorder throughout their lives.

The stressfulness of sexual abuse comes not only from the abuse itself, but also from the blame society often lays upon survivors for having been abused. Particularly with regard to women and rape, cultural myths and stereotypes can lead survivors to conceal their experiences, in guilt and fear of being ridiculed for having "let themselves" be abused. Examples of these myths include "only bad girls get raped," "any women can resist rape if she really wants to," "women ask for it," "when a woman says 'no' she really means 'yes'," and "women cry rape to hurt men" (Burt, 1980).

As society's awareness of the high incidence of rape and sexual abuse increases, we can hope that more measures will be taken to stop abuse and that attitudes toward survivors will change for the better. In the meantime, abuse survivors can be helped through psychotherapy and through participation in support groups of other people who have shared their experiences.

■ *Cooperation versus competition*   Our society places much emphasis on competition and success. Competition begins in early childhood among siblings, continues through school, and culminates in business and professional rivalry. At the same time, we are urged to cooperate and to help others.

■ *Impulse expression versus moral standards*   Impulses must be regulated to some degree in all societies. We noted in Chapter 3 that much of childhood learning involves internalizing cultural restrictions placed on impulses. Sex and aggression are two areas in which our impulses frequently conflict with moral standards, and violation of these standards can generate feelings of guilt.

These four areas present the greatest potential for serious conflict. Trying to find a workable compromise between opposing motives can create considerable stress.

## Psychological Reactions to Stress

Stressful situations produce emotional reactions ranging from exhilaration (when the event is demanding but manageable) to the common emotions of anxiety, anger, discouragement, and depression. If the stressful situation continues, our emotions may switch back and forth among any of these, depending on the success of our coping efforts.

## Anxiety

The most common response to a stressor is **anxiety.** By anxiety, we mean the unpleasant emotion characterized by such terms as "worry," "apprehension," "tension," and "fear" that we all experience at times in varying degrees.

People who live through events that are beyond the normal range of human suffering (for example, natural disasters, rape, kidnapping) sometimes develop a severe set of anxiety-related symptoms known as **post-traumatic stress disorder.** The major symptoms include (a) feeling *numb* to the world, with a lack of interest in former activities and a sense of estrangement from others; (b) reliving the trauma repeatedly in memories and dreams; and (c) sleep disturbances, difficulty concentrating, and over-alertness. Some individuals also feel guilty about surviving when others did not.

Post-traumatic stress disorder may develop immediately after the disaster, or it may be brought on by some minor stress weeks, months, or even years later. And it may last a long time. A study of survivors of Nazi concentration camps found that 97 percent were still troubled with anxiety 20 years after they were freed from the camps. Many still relived the traumas of persecution in their dreams and were fearful that something terrible would happen to their spouses or their children whenever they were out of sight (Krystal, 1968).

Post-traumatic stress disorder became widely accepted as a diagnostic category because of difficulties experienced by Vietnam veterans. Although stress reactions to the horrors of battle had been noted in earlier wars (in World War I it was called "shell shock" and in World War II "combat fa-

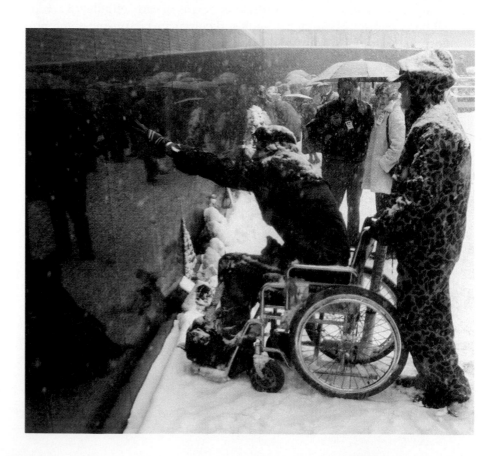

*Post-traumatic stress disorder affects about one-sixth of the Vietnam War veterans, and almost half of the vets still have memories about the war that they are trying to forget.*

tigue"), veterans of Vietnam seemed especially prone to develop the long-term symptoms we have described. A survey estimated that 15 percent of Vietnam veterans have suffered from post-traumatic stress disorder since their discharge (Centers for Disease Control, 1988). Substance abuse, violence and interpersonal problems are common correlates of post-traumatic stress disorder. In a study of 713 men who served in Vietnam, 16 percent reported having problems resulting from drinking heavily, such as trouble at school or work, problems with friends, and passing out. Sixteen percent had been arrested at least once; and 44 percent said that they had memories from the war that they were still trying to forget (Yager, Laufer, & Gallops, 1984).

The soldiers who fought in Vietnam were young (average age 19), and the conditions of warfare were unusual: absence of clear front lines, unpredictable attacks in dense jungle conditions, difficulty in distinguishing between Vietnamese allies and enemies, and the lack of support for the war on the home front. To this day, some Vietnam veterans still re-experience in memories or in dreams the traumatic events that happened to them. As one veteran wrote: "The war is over in history. But it never ended for me" (Marbly, 1987, p. 193).

## Anger and Aggression

Another common reaction to a stressful situation is anger, which may lead to aggression. Laboratory studies have shown that some animals behave aggressively in response to a variety of stressors, including overcrowding, electric shock, and the failure to receive an expected food reward. If a pair of animals is shocked in a cage from which they cannot escape, they begin fighting when the shock starts and stop fighting when it ends.

Children often become angry and exhibit aggressive behavior when they experience **frustration.** As we noted in Chapter 11, the **frustration-aggression hypothesis** assumes that whenever a person's effort to reach a goal is blocked, an aggresive drive is induced that motivates behavior to injure the object—or the person—causing the frustration. While research has shown that aggression is not an inevitable response to frustration, it certainly is one of them. When one child takes a toy from another, the second is likely to attack the first in an attempt to regain the toy. In the late 1980s, some adults frustrated by interminable traffic jams on hot Los Angeles freeways began shooting at each other. Fortunately, adults usually express their aggression verbally rather than physically; they are more apt to exchange insults than blows.

Direct aggression toward the source of frustration is not always possible or wise. Sometimes the source is vague and intangible. The person does not know what to attack but feels angry and seeks an object on which to vent these feelings. Sometimes the individual responsible for the frustration is so powerful that an attack would be dangerous. When circumstances block direct attack on the cause of frustration, aggression may be *displaced:* the aggressive action may be directed toward an innocent person or object rather than toward the actual cause of the frustration. A man who is reprimanded at work may take out unexpressed resentment on his family. A student, angry at her professor for an unfair grade, may blow up at her roommate. A child frustrated by experiences at school may resort to vandalism of school property. (See discussion of displacement on page 609.)

*Prisoners in a Nazi concentration camp show expressions of learned helplessness and disbelief at the moment of liberation (Buchenwald, Germany, 1945).*

## Apathy and Depression

Although a common response to frustration is active aggression, the opposite response of withdrawal and apathy is also common. If the stressful conditions continue and the individual is not successful in coping with them, apathy may deepen into depression.

The theory of **learned helplessness** (Seligman, 1975) explains how experience with aversive, uncontrollable events can lead to apathy and depression (see also Chapter 7). A series of experiments showed that dogs placed in a shuttle box (an apparatus with two compartments separated by a barrier) quickly learn to jump to the opposite compartment to escape a mild electric shock delivered to their feet through a grid on the floor. If a light is turned on a few seconds before the grid is electrified, the dogs can learn to avoid the shock entirely by jumping to the safe compartment when signaled by the light. However, if the dog has had a previous history of being in another enclosure in which shocks were unavoidable and inescapable—in which nothing the animal did terminated the shock—then it is very difficult for the dog to learn the avoidance response in a new situation when it is appropriate. The animal simply sits and endures the shock in the shuttle box, even though an easy jump to the opposite compartment would eliminate discomfort. Some dogs never learn, even if the experimenter demonstrates the proper procedure by carrying them over the barrier. The experimenters concluded that the animals had learned through prior experience that they were helpless to avoid the shock and so gave up trying to do so, even in a new situation. This learned helplessness was difficult to overcome (Overmeier & Seligman, 1967).

Some humans also appear to develop learned helplessness, characterized by apathy, withdrawal, and inaction, in response to uncontrollable events. Not all do, however. The original learned helplessness theory has had to be modified to take into account the fact that some people become helpless following uncontrollable events, but other people are invigorated by the challenge that such events pose (Wortman & Brehm, 1975). This modified theory will be discussed in the section on personality style.

The original learned helplessness theory is useful, however, in helping us to understand why some people seem to give up and take it when exposed to difficult events. For example, the theory has been used to explain why prisoners in Nazi concentration camps did not revolt against their captors more often: they had come to believe that they were helpless to do anything about their captivity and thus did not try to escape. Women caught in marriages with a battering husband frequently do not try to escape. These women often say that they feel helpless to do anything about their situations because they fear what their husbands would do if they tried to leave, or because they do not have the economic resources to support themselves and their children.

## Cognitive Impairment

In addition to the emotional reactions to stress we have just discussed, people often show substantial cognitive impairment when faced with serious stressors. They find it hard to concentrate and to organize their thoughts logically. They may be easily distracted. As a result, their performace on tasks, particularly complex tasks, tends to deteriorate.

This cognitive impairment may come from two sources. High levels of emotional arousal can interfere with a mind's processing of information (recall Figure 11-5, page 435). So the more anxious, angry, or depressed we are following a stressor, the more likely we are to experience cognitive impairment. Cognitive impairment may also result from the distracting thoughts that go through our heads when faced with a stressor. We contemplate possible sources of action, we worry about the consequences of our actions, and we may berate ourselves for not being able to handle the situation better. For instance, students who have a condition called *test anxiety* tend to worry while trying to work on a test about possible failures and about their inadequacies. They can become so distracted by these negative thoughts that they fail to follow instructions and neglect or misinterpret obvious information provided by questions. As anxiety mounts, they have difficulty retrieving facts they had learned well. (See the discussion of emotion and memory in Chapter 8.)

Cognitive impairment during stressful periods often leads people to adhere rigidly to behavior patterns because they cannot consider alternative patterns. People have been trapped in flaming buildings because they persisted in pushing against exit doors that opened inward; in their panic, they failed to consider the possibility of an alternate action. Some people resort to old, childlike behavior patterns that are not appropriate to the situation. The cautious person may become even more cautious and withdraw entirely, whereas the aggressive person may lose control and strike out heedlessly in all directions.

## Physiological Reactions to Stress

The body reacts to stressors by initiating a complex sequence of innate responses to a perceived threat. If the threat is resolved quickly, these emergency responses subside, and our physiological state returns to normal. If the stressful situation continues, a different set of internal responses occurs as we attempt to adapt to a chronic stressor.

# Physiological Stress Response

Whether you fall into an icy river, encounter a knife-wielding assailant, or are terrified by your first parachute jump, your body responds in similar ways. Regardless of the stressor, your body automatically prepares to handle the emergency. Recall from Chapter 11 that this has been called the **fight-or-flight response**. Quick energy is needed, so the liver releases extra sugar (glucose) to fuel the muscles, and hormones are released that stimulate the conversion of fats and proteins to sugar. The body's metabolism increases in preparation for expending energy on physical action. Heart rate, blood pressure, and breathing rate increase, and the muscles tense. At the same time, certain unessential activities, such as digestion, are curtailed. Saliva and mucus dry up, thereby increasing the size of air passages to the lungs. Thus, an early sign of stress is a dry mouth. The body's natural pain killers, *endorphins*, are secreted and the surface blood vessels constrict to reduce bleeding in case of injury. The spleen releases more red blood cells to help carry oxygen, and the bone marrow produces more white corpuscles to fight infection.

Most of these physiological changes result from activation of two neuroendocrine systems controlled by the hypothalamus: the **sympathetic system** and the **adrenal-cortical system.** The hypothalamus has been called the brain's stress center because of its dual function in emergencies. Its first function is to activate the sympathetic division of the autonomic nervous system (see Chapter 2). The hypothalamus transmits nerve impulses to nuclei in the brain stem that control the functioning of the autonomic nervous system. The sympathetic division of the autonomic system acts directly on the smooth muscles and internal organs to produce some of the bodily changes described above—for example, increased heart rate, elevated blood pressure, dilated pupils. The sympathetic system also stimulates the inner core of the adrenal glands (the adrenal medulla) to release the hormones **epinephrine** (adrenaline) and **norepinephrine** into the blood stream. Epinephrine has the same effect on the muscles and organs as the sympathetic nervous system does (for example, it increases heart rate and blood pressure) and thus serves to perpetuate a state of arousal. Norepinephrine, through its action on the pituitary gland, is indirectly responsible for the release of extra sugar from the liver (see Figure 15-1).

The above events describe only the first function of the hypothalamus: activation of the sympathetic system. The hypothalamus carries out its second function (activation of the adrenal-cortical system) by signaling the **pituitary gland**, which lies just below it (recall Figure 2-7, page 45), to secrete **adrenocorticotrophic hormone (ACTH)**, the body's "major stress hormone" (see Chapter 2). ACTH stimulates the outer layer of the adrenal glands (the adrenal cortex) resulting in the release of a group of hormones (the major one is cortisol) that regulate the blood levels of glucose and of certain minerals. The amount of cortisol in blood or urine samples is often used as a measure of stress. ACTH also signals other endocrine glands to release about 30 hormones, each of which plays a role in the body's adjustment to emergency situations.

A wide variety of physical and psychological stressors triggers this response pattern. While the physiological components of the fight-or-flight response are valuable in helping an individual deal with physical threat requiring immediate action, they are not very adaptive for dealing with many modern-day sources of stress. In situations in which action is impossible or

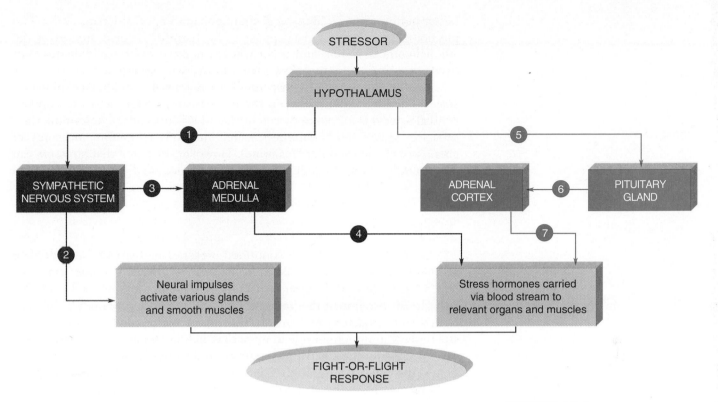

**FIGURE 15-1**
**Fight-or-Flight Response** *A stressful situation activates the hypothalamus which, in turn, controls two neuroendocrine systems: the sympathetic system (shown in red) and the adrenal-cortical system (shown in green). The sympathetic nervous system, responding to neural impulses from the hypothalamus (1), activates various organs and smooth muscles under its control (2). For example, it increases heart rate and dilates the pupils. The sympathetic nervous system also signals the adrenal medulla (3) to release epinephrine and norepinephrine into the bloodstream (4). The adrenal-cortical system is activated when the hypothalamus secretes CRF, a chemical that acts on the pituitary gland lying just below the hypothalamus (5). The pituitary gland, in turn, secretes the hormone ACTH, which is carried via the bloodstream to the adrenal cortex (6) where it stimulates the release of a group of hormones, including cortisol, that regulate blood glucose levels (7). ACTH also signals the other endocrine glands to release some 30 hormones. The combined effect of the various stress hormones carried via the bloodstream plus the neural activity of the sympathetic division of the autonomic nervous system constitute the fight-or-flight response.*

in which the threat continues and must be dealt with over an extended period of time, such intense physiological arousal can be harmful.

Laboratory studies with animals have shown that prolonged exposure to a stressor produces a number of bodily changes: enlarged adrenal glands, shrunken lymph nodes, and stomach ulcers (Selye, 1979). These changes decrease the organism's ability to resist other stressors, including infectious and disease-producing agents. As we will see later, chronic arousal can make both animals and people susceptible to illness.

We have focused on the negative aspects of the physiological arousal elicited by stressors. Studies have shown, however, that exposure to intermittent stressors can have later benefits in the form of physiological toughness. In essence, intermittent stress (occasional exposure but with recovery periods) leads to stress tolerance later on (Dienstbier, 1989). For example, young rats who are removed from their cages and handled daily (a stressor for them) are less fearful when exposed to other stressors as adults and show a quicker return to their normal levels of the stress hormones (Levine, 1960; Meaney et al., 1987). Similarly, rats that were toughened by having to swim in cold water for a period of 14 consecutive days performed better on a later swim test and showed less depletion of epinephrine and norepinephrine than rats who had received no prior exposure to cold water (Weiss et al., 1975).

The physiological responses that appear to be beneficial involve arousal of the sympathetic system and occur when a person makes active efforts to cope with the stressful situation (Frankenhauser, 1983). Increases in epinephrine and norepinephrine correlate positively with performance on a variety of tasks (from students taking tests to paratroopers engaged in training jumps): high levels of these hormones in blood and urine were related to better performance (Johansson & Frankenhaeuser, 1973; Ursin, 1978). The physiological responses that appear to be harmful involve arousal of the adrenal-cortical system and occur when a person experiences distress but does not actively attempt to cope with the stressful situation.

Research on the positive aspects of stress arousal is still in an exploratory stage. The interaction between the sympathetic system and the adrenal-cortical system is exceedingly complex, and it is difficult to determine their separate effects using current research methods (primarily measures of chemistry of the blood and/or urine). However, the idea that stressors can have beneficial effects under certain circumstances has generated increased interest among researchers.

## Stress and Illness

Attempts to adapt to the continued presence of a stressor may deplete the body's resources and make it vulnerable to illness. Chronic stress can lead to such physical disorders as ulcers, high blood pressure, and heart disease. It can also impair the immune system, decreasing the body's ability to fight invading bacteria and viruses. Indeed, doctors estimate that emotional stress plays an important role in more than half of all medical problems.

**Psychosomatic disorders** are physical disorders in which emotions are believed to play a central role. The term "psychosomatic" is derived from the Greek words *psyche* ("mind") and *soma* ("body"). A common misconception is that people with psychosomatic disorders are not really sick and do not need medical attention. On the contrary, the symptoms of psychosomatic illness reflect physiological disturbances associated with tissue damage and pain; a peptic ulcer caused by stress is indistinguishable from an ulcer caused by a factor unrelated to stress, such as long-term heavy usage of aspirin.

Traditionally, research in psychosomatic medicine focused on such illnesses as asthma, hypertension (high blood pressure), ulcers, colitis, and

*People who have little control over their high-stress jobs become at risk for coronary heart disease.*

rheumatoid arthritis (see Taylor, 1986, for a review). Researchers looked for relationships between specific illnesses and characteristic attitudes toward, or ways of coping with, stressful life events. For example, individuals with hypertension were said to feel that life was threatening and, consequently, they must be on guard at all times. Those suffering from colitis were believed to be angry but unable to express their anger. However, most studies that reported characteristic attitudes to be related to specific illnesses have not been replicated. Thus, the hypothesis that people who share the same ways of reacting to stress will be vulnerable to the same illnesses has generally not been confirmed. An important exception is the research on coronary heart disease and Type A behavior patterns, as we will see shortly.

Today the focus of psychosomatic research is much broader, and the term "psychosomatic medicine" is being replaced by **behavioral medicine.** Behavioral medicine is an interdisciplinary field that attracts specialists from psychology and medicine. It seeks to learn how social, psychological, and biological variables combine to cause illness, and how behavior and environments can be changed to promote health.

## How Stress Affects Health

We have seen that exposure to stressful events can cause a variety of physical and psychological problems. Just how does stress affect health? Taylor (1986) has described four different routes: the direct route, the interactive route, the health behavior route, and the illness behavior route.

### Direct Route

The physiological response the body undergoes in the face of a stressor may have a direct, negative effect on physical health if this response is chronically maintained. Long-term overarousal of the sympathetic system or the adrenal-cortical system can cause damage to arteries and organ systems. Stress may also have a direct effect on the immune system's ability to fight off disease.

**CHRONIC OVERAROUSAL** The chronic overarousal caused by chronic stressors may contribute to coronary heart disease. Coronary heart disease (CHD) occurs when the blood vessels that supply the heart muscles are narrowed or closed (by the gradual build-up of a hard, fatty substance called plaque), blocking the flow of oxygen and nutrients to the heart. This can lead to pain, called angina pectoris, that radiates across the chest and arm. When oxygen to the heart is completely blocked, it can cause a myocardial infarction—a heart attack.

Coronary heart disease is a leading cause of death and chronic illness in the United States. Nearly half of the deaths in the U.S. every year are caused by coronary heart disease, many before the age of 65 years. There seems to be a genetic contribution to coronary heart disease: people with family histories of CHD are at increased risk for CHD. CHD is also linked to high blood pressure, high serum cholesterol, diabetes, smoking, and obesity.

People in high stress jobs are at increased risk for CHD, particularly jobs that are highly demanding (in terms of workload, responsibilities, and role conflicts) but which provide little control (the worker has little control over the speed, nature, and conditions of work). An example of such a high stress job is an assembly line in which rapid, high-quality production is expected and the work is machine-paced rather than self-paced.

In one study, some 900 middle-aged men and women were followed over a 10-year period and examined for the development of heart disease. Two independent methods—occupational titles and the subjects' self-reports of their own feelings about their jobs—were used to classify workers along the dimensions of job demand and job control. The results showed that both men and women in occupations classified as "high strain" (high demand combined with low control) had a risk of coronary heart disease $1\frac{1}{2}$ times greater than those in other occupations (Karasek et al., 1981; Karasek et al., 1982).

High family demands in addition to a stressful job can adversely affect a woman's cardiovascular health. Employed women in general are not at a higher risk of coronary heart disease than homemakers. However, employed mothers are more likely to develop heart disease. The likelihood of disease increases with the number of children for working women but not for home-makers (Haynes & Feinleib, 1980). The researchers did not examine the effects of children in the home on men's health.

Experimental studies with animals have shown that disruption of the social environment can induce pathology that resembles coronary artery disease (Manuck, Kaplan, & Matthews, 1986; Sapolsky, 1990). Some of the key experiments have been conducted with a type of macaque monkey whose social organization involves the establishment of stable hierarchies of social dominance: dominant and submissive animals can be identified within a given group based on the animals' social behavior. The introduction of unfamiliar monkeys into an established social group is a stressor that leads to increased aggressive behavior as group members attempt to re-establish a social dominance hierarchy (Manuck, Kaplan, & Matthews, 1986).

In these studies, some monkey groups remained stable with fixed memberships; other groups were stressed by the repeated introduction of new members. After about two years under these conditions, the high ranking or dominant males in the unstable social condition showed more extensive atherosclerosis (the build-up of plaque on the artery walls) than the subordinate males (Sapolsky, 1990).

**THE IMMUNE SYSTEM** One relatively new area of research in behavioral medicine is **psychoimmunology**, the study of how the body's immune system is affected by stress and other psychological variables. The immune system, by means of specialized cells called lymphocytes, protects the body from disease-causing microorganisms. It affects our susceptibility to infectious diseases, allergies, cancers, and autoimmune disorders (that is, diseases such as rheumatoid arthritis, in which the immune cells attack the normal tissue of the body).

There is no single index of the quality of an individual's immune functioning, or *immunocompetence*. It is a complex system with many interacting components, and different investigators have chosen to focus on the different components of the system. Evidence from a number of areas suggests that stress affects the ability of the immune system to defend the body. Let us look at a few examples. One recent study indicates that the common belief that we are more likely to catch a cold when we are under stress is probably correct (Cohen, Tyrel, & Smith, 1991). Researchers exposed some 400 healthy volunteers to a nasal wash containing one of five cold viruses or an innocuous salt solution. Each participant answered questions about the number of stressful events experienced in the past year, the degree to which they felt able to cope with daily demands, and the frequency of negative emotions such as anger and depression. Based on these data, each subject was assigned a stress index ranging from 3 (lowest stress) to 12 (highest stress). The volunteers were examined daily for cold symptoms and for the presence of cold viruses or virus-specific antibodies in their upper respiratory secretions.

The majority of the virus-exposed volunteers showed signs of infection, but only about a third actually developed colds. The rates of viral infection and of actual cold symptoms increased in accordance with the reported stress levels. Compared with the lowest stress group, volunteers who reported the highest stress were significantly more likely to become infected with the cold virus and almost twice as likely to develop a cold (see Figure 15-2). These results held even after controlling statistically for a number of variables that might influence immune functioning, such as age, allergies, cigarette and alcohol use, exercise, and diet. The two indicators of immunocompetence that were measured in this study did not show any specific change as a result of stress, so exactly how stress lowered the body's resistance to the cold virus remains to be determined.

This study is unusual in that the subjects were exposed to a virus, lived in special quarters near the laboratory for a number of days both before and after exposure, and were carefully monitored. Such controlled conditions for studying the effects of stress on health are seldom feasible. Most studies look at individuals undergoing a particular stressful event—such as academic pressures, bereavement, or marital disruption—and evaluate their immunocompetence, using various indices. For example, one study found that during examination periods college students have lower levels of an antibody in their blood that defends against respiratory infections (Jemmott et al., 1985), and another found that medical students show lowered immune functioning on a number of blood-sample measures (Glaser et al., 1985; Glaser et al., 1986). A study of men whose wives had died from breast cancer demonstrated that the responsiveness of the men's immune system functioning declined significantly within the month following their wives' deaths, and in some cases remained low for a year thereafter (Schleifer et al., 1979). Similarly, a series of studies revealed that individuals of both sexes who have recently been separated or divorced show poorer immune functioning than matched control subjects who are still married, even though no significant differences were found between the two groups in health-related behaviors such as smoking and diet (Kiecolt-Glaser et al., 1987, 1988).

Psychological factors that reduce stress can attenuate these adverse immunological changes. For example, Kiecolt-Glaser and colleagues (1985) trained older adults to use relaxation techniques to reduce stress. These adults showed improvement on a number of indices of immunological functioning, whereas a control group of older adults who received no relaxation training showed no improvement in immunocompetence over the same period of time.

One factor that appears to be important is the extent to which an individual can control the stress. Recall that controllability is one of the variables that determines the severity of stress. A series of animal studies demonstrates that uncontrollable shock has a much greater effect on the immune system than controllable shock (Laudenslager et al., 1983; Visintainer, Volpicelli, & Seligman, 1982). In these experiments, rats are subjected to electric

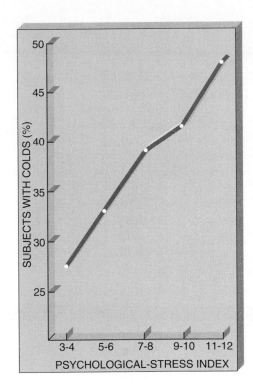

**FIGURE 15-2**
**Stress and Colds** *The graph shows the percentage of virus-exposed subjects who developed colds as a function of the degree of stress reported.* (After Cohen, Tyrel, & Smith, 1991)

**FIGURE 15-3**
**Yoked Controls in a Stress Experiment** *A series of electrical shocks are preprogrammed to be delivered simultaneously to the tails of the two animals. The rat on the left can terminate a shock when it occurs by pressing the lever in front of him. The rat on the right has no control in the situation (his lever is inoperative) but he is yoked to the first rat. That is, when the first rat receives a shock, the yoked rat simultaneously receives the same shock and it remains on until the first rat presses his lever. The lever presses of the yoked rat have no effect on the shock sequence for either animal.*

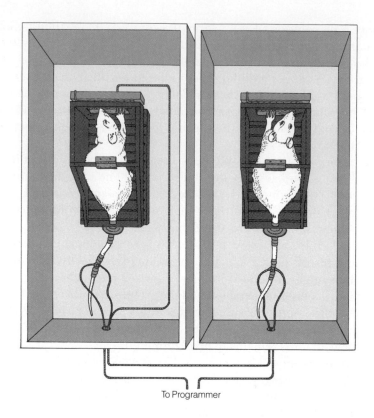

To Programmer

shock. One group can press a lever to turn off the shock. The other animals, the yoked controls, receive an identical sequence of shocks but their levers are ineffective (see Figure 15-3).

In one study using this procedure, the investigator looked at how readily the rats' T-cells multiplied when challenged by an invader. T-cells are lymphocytes that secrete chemicals that kill harmful cells, such as cancer cells. They found that the T-cells from rats who could control the shock multiplied as readily as did those from rats who were not stressed at all. T-cells from rats exposed to uncontrollable shock, on the other hand, multiplied only weakly. Thus, shock (stress) interfered with the immune response only in rats who could not control them (Laudenslager et al., 1983).

In another study, the investigators implanted tumor cells into rats, gave them shocks, and recorded whether the rats' natural defenses rejected the cells or whether they developed into tumors. Only 27 percent of the rats given uncontrollable shocks rejected the tumors, whereas 63 percent of the rats who could turn the shocks off rejected the tumors—even though the rats received identical amounts of shock (Visintainer, Volpicelli, & Seligman, 1982).

Perceptions of control also appear to mediate the influence of stress on the immune system in humans. In one study on the effects of marital separation or divorce on immune functioning, the partner who had initiated the separation (the one more in control of the situation) was less distressed, reported better health, and showed better immune system functioning than the non-initiator (Kiecolt-Glaser et al., 1988). Similarly, a study of women with breast cancer found that those with a pessimistic perspective—that is, who felt they had little control over events on the world—were the most likely to develop new tumors over a five-year period, even after the physical severity of their diseases were taken into account (Levy & Heiden, 1991).

The immune system is incredibly complicated, employing a number of different weapons that interact to defend the body. Much remains to be discovered about the immune system and even more about its relationship to the nervous system. Scientists once believed that the immune system operated quite independently, isolated from other physiological systems. But current studies are making it increasingly evident that the immune system and the nervous system have numerous anatomical and physiological connections. For example, researchers are discovering that lymphocytes have receptors for a number of different neurotransmitters. Thus, these immune system cells are equipped to receive messages from the nervous system that may alter the way they behave. One of the reasons a link between neurotransmitters and the immune system is important is that negative emotional states (for example, anxiety or depression) can affect neurotransmitter levels. Thus, stressful situations may affect immune system functioning only if these situations arouse negative emotional states.

As research on psychoimmunology yields additional information about the links between the nervous and immune systems, we will gain a clearer understanding of how mental attitudes affect health.

## Interactive Route

As we have noted several times already, not everyone exposed to stressful circumstances becomes ill. Also, not everyone with a maladaptive personality trait, such as the inability to express anger, develops physical or psychological illness (see page 601). There is substantial evidence that it is only when stressful circumstances and personality interact with each other, or with a pre-existing biological vulnerability to a disorder, that illness develops (Cohen & Williamson, 1991). This type of interactive model is often referred to as a **vulnerability-stress model**, or a diathesis-stress model. (A diathesis is a vulnerability, or predisposition to a disorder.) The vulnerability makes the individual susceptible to a particular disorder, but it is only when he or she encounters the stress that the disorder actually develops.

A biological vulnerability to a disorder may involve a genetic predisposition to the disorder or a structural abnormality in the body that predisposes the individual to the disorder. For example, vulnerability to hypertension or to diabetes is, in part, genetically determined. But for some people, this genetic predisposition may only lead to the development of the disease when the individual is confronted with chronic stressful circumstances. Similarly, stress may not actually cause cancer to develop initially, but the study of tumors in rats suggests that stress can contribute to the progression of an existing cancer. Finally, mental illness following stressors may be more likely to happen when an individual has a pre-existing vulnerability to the disorder. Women who develop severe, long-lasting depressions after giving birth (known as *post-partum depressions*) tend to have a history of previous depressions occurring at times other than the post-partum period (O'Hara, Neunaber, & Zekowski, 1984).

This vulnerability-stress model, as it relates to mental disorders, will be discussed further in Chapter 16. Currently, a great deal of research is focused on the interactions among vulnerabilities, stress, and health.

*Health behaviors—that is, what we eat, how much we exercise, and how much sleep we get—influence our bodies' abilities to fight disease.*

## Health-Behavior Route

When we are feeling stressed, we often do not take proper care of ourselves. Students taking exams stay up all night, often for several nights in a row. They may skip meals, snacking only on junk food. Many men whose wives have died do not know how to cook for themselves, and thus may eat poorly or hardly at all. In their grief, some bereaved men increase alcohol consumption and smoking. People under stress cease normal exercise routines and become sedentary. Each of these *health behaviors* influences the body's ability to fight disease and its general functioning, and may contribute to the development of illness. Thus, stress may indirectly affect health by reducing positive health behaviors and increasing negative behaviors.

## Illness-Behavior Route

The final model of the stress-illness relationship is the *illness-behavior model.* Stressors lead to a number of unpleasant symptoms: nervousness, depression, fatigue, sleep problems, upset stomach. Some people interpret these symptoms as signs of illness and seek medical help for them. In turn, the caring and attention they receive from medical professionals may *reinforce* these illness behaviors—that is, make it more likely that they will seek medical attention for stress symptoms again in the future. Also, by interpreting stress symptoms as illness, the person may have an excuse for avoiding the stressor (staying home in bed). Studies indicate that people under stress are more likely to use health services than people who are not under stress, even though they may not be any more ill (Cohen & Williamson, 1991; Gortmaker, Eckenrode, & Gore, 1982; Watson & Pennebaker, 1989).

An important implication of the illness-behavior model is that people's reports of their illnesses may not provide accurate information about their actual level of illness. People who are gaining reinforcement for their illness behaviors may report more illnesses than they actually have. This possible biasing of people's self-reports of their illnesses makes it important for studies of stress and health to include objective measures of health.

# Appraisals and Personality Styles as Mediators of Stress Responses

As we have noted, events that are uncontrollable or unpredictable, or that challenge our views of ourselves, tend to be experienced as stressful. Some people appear more likely than others to appraise events in these ways, and thus to experience stress responses to the events. There are three basic theories about why some people are prone to appraise events as stressful: psychoanalytic theory, behavioral theory, and personality theory.

## Psychoanalytic Theory

Psychoanalysts make a distinction between **objective anxiety,** which is a reasonable response to a harmful situation, and **neurotic anxiety,** which is anxiety out of proportion to the actual danger. Freud believed that neurotic anxiety stems from unconscious conflicts within an individual between unacceptable **id** impulses (mainly sexual and aggressive) and the constraints imposed by the **ego** and **superego** (see Chapter 14). Many id impulses pose a threat to the individual because they are contradictory to personal or social values. A woman may not consciously acknowledge that she has strong hostile feelings toward her mother because these feelings conflict with her belief that a child should love her parents. If she acknowledged her true feelings, she would destroy her self-concept as a loving daughter and would risk the loss of her mother's love and support. When she begins to feel angry toward her mother, the aroused anxiety serves as a signal of potential danger. Thus, this woman may experience even a minor conflict with her mother, such as a disagreement about where the family should go for vacation, as a major stressor. A woman who is not so conflicted in her feelings about her mother would experience this as a less severe stressor.

According to psychoanalytic theory, we all have some unconscious conflicts. For some people, however, these conflicts are more severe and greater in number, and these people see more events in life as stressful.

## Behavioral Theory

While Freud saw unconscious conflicts as the internal source of stress responses, behaviorists have focused on ways in which individuals learn to associate stress responses with certain situations. We discussed the learned helplessness theory, which in its original form was a behavioral theory. Through repeated experiences with uncontrollable events, people become convinced that nothing they do can control events, and thus show passivity and lowered motivation; in other words, they give up. The other key component of learned helplessness is that people, and animals, do not seem to be able to learn how to control new situations that truly are controllable. Thus, the child born and raised in an impoverished neighborhood, who is constantly told directly and indirectly that he will never be able to escape, may eventually stop trying to escape. He may not see opportunities to increase his education or to get a good job because he has learned that he cannot control such things, so why bother to even try.

People may also react to specific situations with fear and anxiety because those situations caused them harm or were stressful in the past. Some phobias develop through such **classical conditioning** (see Chapter 7). For example, a person whose car nearly slid off the road on the side of a steep mountain may experience anxiety now every time she is in a high place. Or a student who failed a final exam in a particular classroom may feel anxious the next year when he re-enters the room to take another class.

Sometimes fears are difficult to extinguish. If your first reaction is to avoid or escape the anxiety-producing situation, you may not be able to determine when the situation is no longer dangerous. The little girl who has been punished for assertive behavior in the past may never learn that it is acceptable for her to express her wishes in new situations because she never tries to. Thus, people can continue to have fears about particular situations because they chronically avoid the situation and therefore never challenge their fears.

## Personality Style

A modification of the learned helplessness theory proposed by Abramson and her colleagues (1978) focuses on one type of personality style that relates to the attributions or causal explanations people give for important events. These researchers argued that when people attribute negative events to causes that are internal to them ("it's my fault"), that are stable in time ("it's going to last forever"), and that affect many areas of their lives ("it will impact everything I do"), they are most likely to show a helpless, depressed response to negative events. For example, if a person whose spouse left him attributed the break-up of his marriage to his "bad" personality (an internal, stable, and global attribution), he would tend to lose self-esteem and expect future relationships to fail as well. In turn, he would show lowered motivation, passivity, and sadness. In contrast, if he made a less pessimistic attribution, such as attributing the failure of his marriage to simple incompatibility between himself and his wife, he would tend to maintain his self-esteem and motivation for the future (for similar arguments, see Weiner, 1972).

Abramson and colleagues propose that people have consistent styles of making attributions for the events in their lives, which they called **attributional styles,** and that these styles influence the degree to which people view events as stressful and have helpless, depressive reactions to difficult events. A number of studies support this theory (Peterson & Seligman, 1984). In one study, researchers assessed the attributional styles of students a few weeks before they were to take a midterm exam. Just before the exam, they also asked the students what grade they would consider a failure and what grade they would be happy with. Then, after the students received their grades from the exam, they measured the students' levels of sadness and depression. Among students who received a grade below their standards, those who had a pessimistic style of attributing events were significantly more depressed than those who had a more optimistic attributional style (Metalsky, Halberstadt, & Abramson, 1987).

A pessimistic attributional style is also linked to physical illness (Peterson & Seligman, 1987; Peterson, Seligman, & Vaillant, 1988). Students with more pessimistic attributional styles report more illness and make more visits to the health center than students with a more optimistic attributional style. In a 35-year-long study of men in the Harvard classes of 1939–1940, researchers found that men who had a pessimistic attributional style at age 25 were more likely to develop physical illness over the subsequent years than men with a more optimistic attributional style. How does attributional style affect health? We do not know for sure yet. People with a pessimistic attributional style tend to feel they have little control over their lives and, as noted earlier, perceptions of uncontrollability have been linked to lowered immune system functioning. People with a pessimistic attributional style also may not take good care of themselves, and their negative health behaviors may contribute to illness. A good deal of work is necessary before we understand the links between attributional style and health.

**HARDINESS** Another line of research has focused on people who are *most* resistant to stress—who do not become physically or emotionally impaired even in the face of major stressful events (Kobasa, 1979; Kobasa, Maddi, & Kahn, 1982). In one study, more than 600 men who were executives or managers in the same company were given checklists and were asked to describe all of the stressful events and illnesses they had experienced over the previous three years. Two groups were selected for comparison: the first group scored above average on both stressful events and illness; the second group scored equally high on stress but *below average* on illness. Members of both groups then filled out detailed personality questionnaires. Analysis of the results indicated that the high-stress/low-illness men dif-

*Hardy individuals—that is, those who do not become ill when stressed—are more actively involved in their work, are more oriented to challenge and change, and feel more in control of their lives than those who are vulnerable to the effects of stress.*

fered from the men who became ill under stress on three major dimensions: they were more actively involved in their work and social lives, they were more oriented toward challenge and change, and they felt more in control of events in their lives (Kobasa, 1979).

Arguably, these personality differences could be the *result* rather than the *cause* of illness. For example, it is hard for people to be involved in work or in social activity when they are ill. The investigators therefore conducted a longitudinal study that considered the personality characteristics of business executives before they became ill, and then monitored their life stress and the extent of their illnesses for a period of two years. The results showed that the executives whose attitudes toward life could be rated high on involvement, feeling of control, and positive responses to change remained healthier over time than men who scored low on these dimensions (Kobasa, Maddi, & Kahn, 1982). The most important factor appears to be attitude toward change. Men who view change as a challenge—for example, regarding the loss of a job as an opportunity to pursue a new career rather than as a setback—are apt to experience less stress and to turn the situation to their advantage. Although this study was conducted with men only, similar results have been found in a study of women (Wiebe & McCallum, 1986).

The personality characteristics of stress-resistant or hardy individuals are summarized by the terms "commitment," "control," and "challenge." These characteristics are interrelated with the factors we have discussed as influencing the perceived severity of stressors. For example, the sense of being in control of life events reflects feelings of competency and also influences the appraisal of stressful events. Challenge also involves cognitive evaluation, the belief that change is normal in life and should be viewed as an opportunity for growth rather than as a threat to security.

**TYPE A PATTERN** One behavior pattern or personality style that has received a great deal of attention is the **Type A pattern.** Physicians noted over the years that heart attack victims tend to be hostile, aggressive, impatient persons who were overinvolved in their work. In the 1950s two cardiologists defined a constellation of behaviors (the Type A pattern) that seemed to characterize patients with coronary heart disease (Friedman & Rosenman, 1974). People who exhibit this Type A behavior pattern are extremely competitive and achievement oriented; they have a sense of time urgency, find it difficult to relax, and become impatient and angry when confronted with delays or with people they view as incompetent. Although outwardly self-confident, they are prey to constant feelings of self-doubt; they push themselves to accomplish more and more in less and less time. Some common Type A behaviors are listed in Table 15-2. Type B people are those who do not exhibit the characteristics listed for Type A. Type B people are able to relax without feeling guilty and to work without becoming agitated; they lack a sense of urgency, with its accompanying impatience, and are not easily roused to anger.

To examine the relationship between Type A behavior and coronary heart disease, more than 3,000 healthy, middle-age men were evaluated by means of a structured interview. The interview was designed to be irritating. The interviewer kept the subject waiting without explanation and then asked a series of questions about being competitive, hostile, and pressed for time. Examples are Do you ever feel rushed or under pressure? Do you eat quickly? Would you describe yourself as ambitious and hard driving or relaxed and easy-going? Do you resent it if someone is late? The interviewer

Thinking of or doing two things at once

Scheduling more and more activities into less and less time

Failing to notice or be interested in the environment or things of beauty

Hurrying the speech of others

Becoming unduly irritated when forced to wait in line or when driving behind a car you think is moving too slowly

Believing that if you want something done well, you have to do it yourself

Gesticulating when you talk

Frequent knee jiggling or rapid tapping of your fingers

Explosive speech patterns or frequent use of obscenities

Making a fetish of always being on time

Having difficulty sitting and doing nothing

Playing nearly every game to win, even when playing with children

Measuring your own and others' success in terms of numbers (number of patients seen, articles written, and so on )

Lip clicking, head nodding, fist clenching, table pounding, or sucking in of air when speaking

Becoming impatient while watching others do things you think you can do better of faster

Rapid eye blinking or tic-like eyebrow lifting

**TABLE 15-2**
**Type A Behaviors** *Some behaviors that characterize people prone to coronary heart disease.* (After Friedman & Rosenman, 1974)

interrupted, asked questions in a challenging manner, and threw in nonsequiturs. The interview was scored more on the way the person behaved in answering the questions than on the answers themselves. For example, extreme Type A men spoke loudly in an explosive manner, talked over the interviewer so as not to be interrupted, appeared tense and tight-lipped, and described hostile incidents with great emotional intensity. Classic Type B men sat in a relaxed manner, spoke slowly and softly, were easily interrupted, and smiled often.

After the subjects were classified as Type A or Type B, they were studied for $8\frac{1}{2}$ years. During that period, Type A men had twice as many heart attacks or other forms of coronary heart disease than Type B men. These results held up even after diet, age, smoking, and other variables were taken into account (Rosenman et al., 1975). Other studies confirmed this two-fold risk and linked Type A behavior to heart disease in both men and women (Haynes, Feinleib, & Kannel, 1980; Kornitzer et al., 1982). In addition, Type A behavior correlates with severity of coronary artery blockage as determined at autopsy or in X-ray studies of the inside of coronary blood vessels (Friedman et al., 1968; Williams et al., 1988).

After reviewing the evidence, in 1981 the American Heart Association decided that Type A behavior should be classified as a risk factor for coronary heart disease. However, two more recent studies failed to find a link between Type A behavior and heart disease (Case, Heller, Case & Moss, 1985; Shekelle et al., 1983). While some researchers attribute this failure to the way Type A individuals were assessed in these studies, others believe that the definition of Type A behavior, as originally formulated, is too diffuse. They argue that time urgency and competitiveness are *not* the most important components; the crucial variable may be hostility.

Several studies have found that a person's level of hostility is a better predictor of heart disease than is his or her overall level of Type A behavior (Booth Kewley & Friedman, 1987; Thoresen, Telch, & Eagleston, 1981; Dembroski et al., 1985). To examine further the anger component of Type A behavior, several studies have used personality tests rather than interviews to measure hostility. For example, a 25-year study of 118 male lawyers found that those who scored high on hostility traits on a personality inventory taken in law school were five times as likely to die before age 50 as classmates who were not hostile (Barefoot et al., 1989). In a similar follow-up study of physicians, hostility scores obtained in medical school predicted the incidence of coronary heart disease as well as mortality from all causes (Barefoot, Williams, & Dahlstrom, 1983). In both studies, this relationship is independent of the effects of smoking, age, and high blood pressure. There is some evidence that when anger is repressed, or held in, it may be even more destructive to the heart than anger that is overtly expressed (Spielberger et al., 1985; Wright, 1988).

How does Type A behavior or its component trait of hostility lead to coronary heart disease? One plausible biological mechanism is the way the individual's sympathetic nervous system responds to stress. When exposed to stressful experimental situations (for example, when faced with threat of failure, harassment, or competitive task demands), most subjects report feeling angry, irritated, and tense. However, subjects who score high on hostility as a trait show much larger increases in blood pressure, heart rate, and the secretion of stress-related hormones than subjects with low hostility scores (Suarez & Williams, 1989). The same results are found when Type A subjects are compared with Type B subjects (Manuck & Kranz, 1986). The

*Type A individuals are hurried, tense, and hostile, and are twice as likely to suffer coronary heart disease as Type B individuals.*

sympathetic nervous systems of hostile and/or Type A individuals appear to be hyper-responsive to stressful situations. All of these physiological changes can damage the heart and blood vessels.

Hostile and non-hostile people may have fundamentally different nervous systems. When non-hostile individuals are aroused and upset, their parasympathetic nervous systems act like a stop switch to calm them down. In contrast, hostile individuals may have a weak parasympathetic nervous system. When they are angered, their adrenalin fires off and they stay unpleasantly aroused. As a consequence, they interact differently with the world (Williams, 1989).

The good news about the Type A behavior pattern is that it can be modified through well-established therapy programs, and people who are able to reduce their Type A behavior show lowered risk of coronary heart disease. We will discuss this therapy later in the chapter.

# Coping Skills

The emotions and physiological arousal created by stressful situations are highly uncomfortable, and this discomfort motivates the individual to do something to alleviate it. The process by which a person attempts to manage stressful demands is called *coping*, and it takes two major forms. A person can focus on the specific problem or situation that has arisen, trying to find some way of changing it or avoiding it in the future. This is called **problem-focused coping.** A person can also focus on alleviating the emotions associated with the stressful situation, even if the situation itself cannot be changed. This second process is called **emotion-focused coping** (Lazarus & Folkman, 1984). When dealing with a stressful situation, most people use both problem-focused coping and emotion-focused coping.

## Problem-Focused Coping

Strategies for solving problems include defining the problem, generating alternative solutions, weighing the alternatives in terms of costs and benefits, choosing among them, and implementing the selected alternative. Problem-focused strategies can also be directed inward: the person can change something about himself or herself instead of changing the environment. Changing levels of aspiration, finding alternative sources of gratification, and learning new skills are examples. How skillfully the individual employs these strategies depends on his or her range of experiences and capacity for self-control.

Suppose you receive a warning that your are about to fail a course required for graduation You might confer with the professor, devise a work schedule to fulfill the requirements, and then follow it; or you might decide that you cannot fulfill the requirements in the time remaining and so sign up to retake the course in summer school. Both of these actions are problem-focused methods of coping.

People who tend to use problem-focused coping in stressful situations show lower levels of depression both during and after the stressful situation (Billings & Moos, 1984). Of course, people who are less depressed may find it easier to use problem-focused coping. But longitudinal studies show that problem-focused coping leads to shorter periods of depression, even taking into account people's initial levels of depression. In addition, therapies that

*How do you cope with disappointments: in a problem-focused or an emotion-focused manner?*

teach depressed people to use problem-focused coping can be effective in helping them to overcome their depressions and react more adaptively to stressors (Nezu, Nezu, & Perri, 1989).

## Emotion-Focused Coping

People engage in emotion-focused coping to prevent their negative emotions from overwhelming them and preventing them from engaging in actions to solve their problems. They also use emotion-focused coping when a problem is uncontrollable.

There are many ways we try to cope with our negative emotions. Some researchers have divided these into behavioral strategies and cognitive strategies (Moos, 1988). *Behavioral strategies* include engaging in physical exercise to get our minds off a problem, using alcohol or other drugs, venting anger, seeking emotional support from friends. *Cognitive strategies* include temporarily setting aside thoughts about the problem (for example, "I decided it wasn't worth worrying about") and reducing the threat by changing the meaning of the situation (for instance, "I decided that her friendship wasn't that important to me"). Cognitive strategies often involve reappraising the situations. Obviously, some behavioral and cognitive strategies we would expect to be adaptive, but other strategies we would expect to only cause the person more stress (such as drinking heavily). Various studies have found that poor adjustment to stress is associated with confrontative coping (aggression or risk taking), wishful thinking, denial, and dangerous escapism (see Lazarus & Folkman, 1984).

Other researchers have classified emotion-focused coping strategies differently, into ruminative strategies, distraction strategies, and negative avoidant strategies (Nolen-Hoeksema, 1991). *Ruminative strategies* include isolating ourselves to think about how badly we feel, worrying about the consequences of the stressful event or our emotional state, or repetitively talking about how bad things are without taking any action to change them.

*Distraction strategies* include engaging in pleasant activities that are reinforcing and tend to increase our sense of control, such as engaging in sports, going to movies with friends, or playing with our children. The point of distraction strategies is to take a breather from our negative feelings and regain a sense of mastery. *Negative avoidant strategies* are activities that may distract us from our moods, but they differ from distraction strategies in that avoidant strategies are potentially dangerous activities that may only exacerbate our moods. Examples include heavy drinking, reckless behaviors (for example, driving fast on mountain roads), berating other people in an aggressive way.

Both ruminative strategies and avoidant strategies tend to increase and prolong depressed moods, whereas distraction strategies tend to decrease and shorten depressed moods. In a laboratory study, researchers had depressed subjects engage either in a ruminative task or a distracting task for ten minutes (for ethical reasons, researchers could not have subjects engage in avoidant tasks such as drinking). The ruminative task had them focus on their current physical sensations ("focus on your current level of energy," "focus on how your body feels right now") and their personal characteristics ("focus on your most dominant traits"). The distracting task had them focus on geographical locations and the shape of objects ("focus on the shape of the Golden Gate Bridge," "focus on the face of the Mona Lisa"). Subjects who engaged in the distracting task showed complete relief from their depressed mood, but subjects who engaged in the ruminative task showed increased depressed mood (Morrow & Nolen-Hoeksema, 1990; Nolen-Hoeksema & Morrow, 1991b).

More naturalistic, longitudinal studies have also shown that ruminative and avoidant strategies prolong depression, whereas distraction strategies help to reduce it. For example, one longitudinal study of recently bereaved people found that those who used ruminative and avoidant strategies to deal

*When we use emotion-focused coping, we may isolate ourselves and ruminate over the problem; we may try to distract ourselves from the problem by, say, exercising or going to the movies; or we may try to avoid the problem by engaging in harmful behaviors, such as drinking. How effective is each of these three types of behaviors in solving problems?*

with their grief showed longer depressions (Nolen-Hoeksema, Parker, & Larson, 1992). Another longitudinal study was conducted quite by accident. A group of researchers at Stanford University just happened to have taken measures of emotion-focused coping tendencies and levels of depression in a large group of students two weeks before the major earthquake that hit the San Francisco Bay Area in 1989. They remeasured students' levels of depression again both 10 days and 7 weeks following the earthquake. They also estimated how much environmental stress the students experienced as a result of the earthquake (that is, injury to themselves, to their friends or family, and to their homes). The results showed that students who evidenced a ruminative style of coping with emotions before the earthquake were more likely to be depressed 10 days and still 7 weeks following the earthquake. This was true even after the students' levels of depression before the earthquake were taken into account (Nolen-Hoeksema & Morrow, 1991a).

You might ask whether people who engage in ruminative coping are more sensitive to their own feelings and thus more likely to solve their problems, whereas people who engage in distraction coping are denying their emotions and problems, and thus will fare worse in the end. The evidence to date suggests that the answer is no. People who engage in ruminative coping are *less* likely also to engage in active problem-solving following stressors. In contrast, people who use pleasant activities to take a breather from their moods for a while are *more* likely to turn to active problem-solving to deal with their stressors (Nolen-Hoeksema & Morrow, 1991a; Nolen-Hoeksema, Parker, & Larson, 1992). In addition, people who use ruminative coping may actually do a *poorer* job of problem-solving when they do try. Two laboratory studies have shown that depressed people who have spent ten minutes ruminating and then go on to do a problem-solving task show poorer performance at problem-solving than depressed people who have

spent ten minutes engaging in distraction before attempting the problem-solving task (Nolen-Hoeksema & Lyubomirsky, 1992; Nolen-Hoeksema & Morrow, 1991b). Ruminating may get in the way of good problem-solving.

# Defense Mechanisms as Emotion-Focused Coping

The coping strategies we have discussed thus far have been the focus of relatively recent research. There is a long history of thought on emotion-focused coping in the psychoanalytic literature, however (A. Freud, 1946/1967). Freud used the term **defense mechanisms** to refer to unconscious strategies that people use to deal with negative emotions. These emotion-focused strategies do not alter the stressful situation; they simply change the way the person perceives or thinks about it. Thus, all defense mechanisms involve an element of *self-deception*.

We all use defense mechanisms at times. They help us over the rough spots until we can deal more directly with the stressful situation. Defense mechanisms indicate personality maladjustment only when they become the dominant mode of responding to problems. One difference between the defense mechanisms and the coping strategies we discussed earlier is that the defense mechanisms are unconscious processes, whereas the coping strategies are often engaged in consciously. As we describe below, however, some of the unconscious defense mechanisms, when taken to the extreme, may lead an individual to show some of the maladaptive conscious coping strategies described earlier.

**REPRESSION**  Freud considered **repression** to be the basic, and most important, defense mechanism. In repression, impulses or memories that are too frightening or painful are excluded from conscious awareness. Memories that evoke shame, guilt, or self-deprecation are often repressed. Freud believed that repression of certain childhood impulses is universal. He maintained that all young boys have feelings of sexual attraction toward the mother and feelings of rivalry and hostility toward the father (the **Oedipal conflict**); these impulses are repressed to avoid the painful consequences of acting on them. In later life, individuals may repress feelings and memories that could cause anxiety because they are inconsistent with their self-concepts. Feelings of hostility toward a loved one and experiences of failure may be banished from conscious memory.

Repression is different from **suppression.** Suppression is the process of deliberate self-control, keeping impulses and desires in check (perhaps holding them in privately while denying them publicly) or temporarily pushing aside painful memories. Individuals are aware of suppressed thoughts but are largely unaware of repressed impulses or memories.

Freud believed that repression is seldom completely successful. The repressed impulses threaten to break through into consciousness; the individual becomes anxious (although unaware of the reason) and employs several other defense mechanisms to keep the partially repressed impulses from awareness, as we will see below.

Interest in people who habitually repress or suppress painful thoughts and emotions has resurged in recent years. People with a repressive style appear to have a heightened vulnerability to illness in general, including more coronary heart disease and a more rapid course of cancer (Bonnano & Singer, 1990). Another line of research has shown that people who confide in others about traumatic events and the emotions they feel in reaction to those events tend to show better health than people who do not confide in others (Pennebaker & Beall, 1986). For example, wives of men who died by suicide were more likely to be physically ill over the years following their husbands' deaths if they never confided to others that their husbands committed suicide (Pennebaker & O'Heeron, 1984).

How may repression or suppression contribute to poor physical health? First, as Freud suggested, suppression and repression seldom are completely satisfactory. People who try to suppress thoughts may actually ruminate more about the unwanted thoughts and emotions than people who express them to other people. Several studies have shown that trying to suppress thoughts actually leads us to think those thoughts more frequently than when we stop trying to suppress them (Wegner, Schneider, Carter, & White, 1987). In other words, there is a *rebound effect* whereby suppressed unwanted thoughts come back with greater force once the person's guard is down. In the study of widows of suicide victims, the researchers found that women who had not told anyone about their husbands' suicides actually ruminated more about it than women who had confided in others about the suicide (Pennebaker & O'Heeron, 1984). Thus, people who habitually try to push unwanted thoughts out of their minds might find these thoughts coming back with great force, causing them much distress. In turn, this heightened level of distress and the physiological arousal accompanying it could have negative effects on the body.

Second, the act of suppressing or repressing thoughts in itself may be physically taxing and thus have negative effects on the body. That is, constantly pushing thoughts out of our minds, and monitoring whether or not the thoughts are returning, may require physical energy and may lead to chronic arousal, which damages the body.

Pennebaker (1990) has shown that having people recount traumas and the emotions associated with them, whether in conversations with other people or simply by writing about them in diaries, reduces the people's tendencies to ruminate about the traumas, and may lead to improvements in their health. Expressing traumas and emotions about traumas may reduce ruminations and help a person's health in a number of ways. Verbally expressing fears and emotions may help to make them more concrete and thus somehow easier to deal with. When we tell others about our traumas and emotions, the listeners provide social support and validation for our feelings. Finally, talking about a trauma may help us to *habituate* to the trauma—to get used to the trauma so it does not create the same level of negative emotion every time we think about it.

**RATIONALIZATION** When the fox in Aesop's fable rejected the grapes he could not reach because they were sour, he illustrated a defense mechanism known as **rationalization**. Rationalization does not mean "to act rationally," as we might assume; it is the assignment of logical or socially desirable motives to what we do so that we seem to have acted rationally. Rationalization serves two purposes: it eases our disappointment when we fail to reach a goal ("I didn't want it anyway"), and it provides us with acceptable motives for our behavior. If we act impulsively or on the basis of motives we do not wish to acknowledge even to ourselves, we rationalize what we have done to place our behavior in a more favorable light.

In the search for the good reason rather than the true reason, individuals make a number of excuses. These excuses are usually plausible; they simply do not tell the whole story. For example, "My roommate failed to wake me"

or "I had too many other things to do" may be true, but they are perhaps not the real reasons for the individual's failure to perform the behavior in question. Individuals who are really concerned set an alarm clock or find the time.

An experiment involving posthypnotic suggestion (see Chapter 6) demonstrates the process of rationalization. A hypnotist instructs a subject under hypnosis that when he wakes from the trance he will watch the hypnotist, and when the hypnotist takes off her glasses, the subject will raise the window, but he will not remember that the hypnotist told him to do this. Aroused from the trance, the subject feels a little drowsy but soon circulates among the people in the room and carries on a normal conversation, furtively watching the hypnotist. When the hypnotist casually removes her glasses, the subject feels an impulse to open the window. He takes a step in that direction but hesitates. Unconsciously, he mobilizes his wishes to be a reasonable person; seeking a reason for his impulse to open the window, he says "Isn't it a little stuffy in here?" Having found the needed excuse, he opens the window and feels more comfortable (Hilgard, 1965).

**REACTION FORMATION**   Sometimes individuals can conceal a motive from themselves by giving strong expression to the opposite motive. Such a tendency is called **reaction formation.** A mother who feels guilty about not wanting her child may become overindulgent and overprotective to assure the child of her love and to assure herself that she is a good mother. In one case, a mother who wished to do everything for her daughter could not understand why the child was so unappreciative. At great sacrifice, she had the daughter take expensive piano lessons and assisted her in the daily practice sessions. Although the mother thought she was being extremely kind, she was actually being very demanding—in fact, hostile. She was unaware of her own hostility, but when confronted with it, the mother admitted that she had hated piano lessons as a child. Under the conscious guise of being kind, she was unconsciously being cruel to her daughter. The daughter vaguely sensed what was going on and developed symptoms that required psychological treatment.

Some people who crusade with fanatical zeal against loose morals, alcohol, and gambling may be manifesting reaction formation. Some of these individuals may have a background of earlier difficulties with these problems, and their zealous crusading may be a means of defending themselves against the possibility of backsliding.

**PROJECTION**  All of us have undesirable traits that we do not acknowledge, even to ourselves. One unconscious mechanism, **projection,** protects us from recognizing our own undesirable qualities by assigning them in exaggerated amounts to other people. Suppose you have a tendency to be critical of or unkind to other people, but you would dislike yourself if you admitted this tendency. If you are convinced that the people around you are cruel or unkind, your harsh treatment of them is not based on *your* bad qualities—you are simply "giving them what they deserve." If you can assure yourself that everybody else cheats on college examinations, your unacknowledged tendency to take some academic shortcuts seems not so bad. Projection is really a form of rationalization, but it is so pervasive in our culture that it merits discussion in its own right.

**INTELLECTUALIZATION**  **Intellectualization** is an attempt to gain detachment from a stressful situation by dealing with it in abstract, intellectual terms. This kind of defense is frequently a necessity for people who must deal with life-and-death matters in their daily jobs. The doctor who is continually confronted with human suffering cannot afford to become emotionally involved with each patient. In fact, a certain amount of detachment may be essential for the doctor to function competently. This kind of intellectualization is a problem only when it becomes such a pervasive life-style that individuals cut themselves off from all emotional experiences.

**DENIAL**  When an external reality is too unpleasant to face, an individual may deny that it exists. The parents of a fatally ill child may refuse to admit that anything is seriously wrong, even though they are fully informed of the diagnosis and the expected outcome. Because they cannot tolerate the pain that acknowledging reality would produce, they resort to the defense mechanism of **denial.** Less extreme forms of denial may be seen in individuals who consistently ignore criticism, fail to perceive that others are angry with them, or disregard all kinds of clues suggesting that a marriage partner is having an affair.

Sometimes, denying facts may be better than facing them. In a severe crisis, denial may give the person time to face the grim facts at a more gradual pace. For example, victims of a stroke or a spinal cord injury might give up altogether if they were fully aware of the seriousness of their conditions. Hope gives them the incentive to keep trying. Servicemen who have faced combat or imprisonment report that denying the possibility of death helped them to function. In these situations, denial clearly has an adaptive value. On the other hand, the negative aspects of denial are evident when people postpone seeking medical help: for example, a woman may deny that a lump in her breast may be cancerous and so may delay going to a physician.

**DISPLACEMENT**  The last defense mechanism we consider fulfills its function (reduces anxiety) while partially gratifying the unacceptable motive. Through the mechanism of **displacement,** a motive that cannot be gratified in one form is directed into a new channel. An example of displacement was provided in our discussion of anger that could not be expressed toward the source of frustration and was redirected toward a less threatening object.

Freud felt that displacement was the most satisfactory way of handling aggressive and sexual impulses. The basic drives cannot be changed, but we can change the object toward which a drive is directed. For example, sexual impulses toward the parents cannot be safely gratified, but such impulses can be displaced toward a more suitable love object. Erotic impulses that cannot be expressed directly may be expressed indirectly in creative activities such as art, poetry, and music. Hostile impulses may find socially acceptable expression through participation in contact sports.

It seems unlikely that displacement actually eliminates the frustrated impulses, but substitute activities do help to reduce tension when a basic drive is thwarted. For example, the activities of taking care of others or seeking companionship may help reduce the tension associated with unsatisfied sexual needs.

# Managing Stress

Thus far we have primarily focused on factors within individuals that influence their perceptions and the impact of stressful events on them. The emotional support and concern of other people also can make stress more bearable. Divorce, the death of a loved one, or a serious illness is usually more devastating if an individual must face it alone. A study of Israeli parents who had lost a son (either through accidents or in the Yom Kippur War) found that bereavement exacted a heavier toll for those who were already widowed or divorced. Their mortality rate in the 10-year period following their loss was higher than the mortality rate for parents who could share their grief with each other (Levav, Friedlander, Kark & Peritz, 1988).

Numerous studies indicate that people who have many social ties (spouse, friends, relatives, and group memberships) live longer and are less apt to succumb to stress-related illnesses than are people who have few supportive social contacts (Cohen & Wills, 1985). Friends and family can provide support in many ways. They can bolster self-esteem by loving us despite our problems. They can provide information and advice, companionship to distract us from our worries, and financial or material aid. All of these tend to reduce feelings of helplessness and to increase our confidence in our ability to cope.

Stress is easier to tolerate when the cause of the stress is shared by others. Community disasters (floods, earthquakes, tornadoes, wars) often seem to bring out the best in people (Nilson et al., 1981). Individual anxieties and conflicts tend to be forgotten when people are working together against a common enemy or toward a common goal. For example, during the intensive bombing of London in World War II there was a marked decline in the number of people seeking help for emotional problems.

Sometimes, however, family and friends can increase the stress. Minimizing the seriousness of the problem or giving blind assurance that everything will be all right may produce more anxiety than failing to offer support at all. A study of graduate students facing crucial examination suggests that spouses who are realistically supportive ("I'm worried, but I know you'll do the best you can") are more helpful than spouses who deny any possibility of failure ("I'm not worried; I'm sure you'll pass). In the latter case, the student has to worry not only about failing the exam but also about losing respect in the eyes of the spouse (Mechanic, 1962). Other people can also make demands and create burdens on an individual at the very time he or she is dealing with other stressors (Rook, 1984). For example, a person who is caring for a terminally ill parent is more likely to suffer from depression if

*Disasters tend to rally individuals to work toward a common goal.*

she is also being criticized and harassed by siblings for how she is caring for the parent (Nolen-Hoeksema, Parker, & Larson, 1992).

In addition to seeking positive social support in times of stress, people can learn other techniques to reduce the negative effects of stress on the body and the mind. Below we discuss some behavioral and cognitive techniques shown to help people reduce the effects of stress, then discuss in detail how these techniques are applied to reduce Type A behavior and coronary heart disease.

## Behavioral Techniques

Among the behavioral techniques that have been used to help people control their physiological responses to stressful situations are *biofeedback, relaxation training,* and *aerobic exercise.*

In **biofeedback training**, individuals receive information (feedback) about an aspect of their physiological state and then attempt to alter that state. For example, in a procedure for learning to control tension headaches, electrodes are attached to the participant's forehead so that any movement in the forehead muscle can be electronically detected, amplified, and fed back to the person as an auditory signal. The signal, or tone, increases in pitch when the muscle contracts and decreases when it relaxes. By learning to control the pitch of the tone, the individual learns to keep the muscle relaxed. (Relaxation of the forehead muscle usually ensures relaxation of scalp and neck muscles also.) After 4 to 8 weeks of biofeedback training, the participant learns to recognize the onset of tension and to reduce it without feedback from the machine (Tarler-Benlolo, 1978).

Physiological processes that are controlled by the autonomic nervous system, such as heart rate and blood pressure, have traditionally been assumed to be automatic and not under voluntary control. However, laboratory studies have demonstrated that people can learn to modify heart rate and blood pressure (see Figure 15-4). The results of these studies have led to new procedures for treating patients with high blood pressure (hypertension). One procedure is to show patients a graph of their blood pressure while it is being monitored and to teach them techniques for relaxing different muscle groups. The patients are instructed to tense their muscles (for example, to clench a fist or to tighten the abdomen), release the tension, and notice the difference in sensation. By starting with the feet and ankle muscles and progressing through the body to the muscles that control the neck and face, the patients learn to modify muscular tension. This combination of biofeedback with **relaxation training** had proved effective in lowering blood pressure for some individuals (Tarler-Benlolo, 1978).

Reviews of numerous studies using biofeedback and relaxation training to control headaches and hypertension conclude that the most important variable is *learning how to relax* (Runck, 1980). Some people may learn to relax faster when they receive biofeedback. Others may learn to relax equally well when they receive training in muscle relaxation without any specific biofeedback. The usefulness or relaxation training seems to depend on the individual. Some people who are not conscientious about taking drugs to relieve high blood pressure are more responsive to relaxation training, whereas others who have learned to control their blood pressure through relaxation may eventually drop the procedure because they find it too time-consuming.

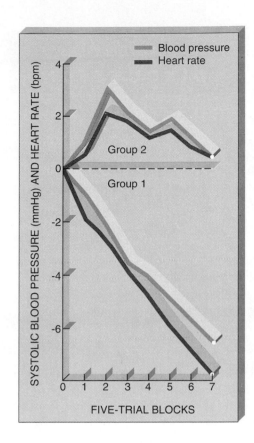

**FIGURE 15-4**
**Operant Conditioning of Blood Pressure and Heart Rate** *One group of subjects received biofeedback (a light and a tone) whenever their blood pressure and heart rate decreased simultaneously (Group 1); the other group received the same feedback whenever their blood pressure and heart rate increased simultaneously (Group 2). The subjects achieved significant simultaneous control of blood pressure and heart rate during a single conditioning session. The group reinforced for lowering both functions achieved increasingly more control over trials; the group reinforced for raising both functions was less consistent.* (After Schwartz, 1975)

## Can Psychological Interventions Affect the Course of Cancer?

Many scientists are skeptical that psychological interventions can significantly affect the course of major disease processes, such as cancer. They argue that suggestions that cancer patients can control their disease through the power of their will have done more harm than good, because cancer patients are made to feel they are to blame if they cannot cure themselves. However, evidence increasingly suggests that at least some types of supportive psychological interventions can slow the progress of cancer. David Spiegel and his colleagues (Spiegel, Bloom, Kraemer, & Gottheil, 1989) produced some of the best evidence, unintentionally. Several years ago, these researchers began a study in which they randomly assigned women with metastatic breast cancer either to a series of weekly support groups or to no support groups (all women were receiving standard medical care for their cancer). The focus of the groups was on facing death and learning to live one's remaining days to the fullest. Spiegel and colleagues had no intention of affecting the course of the cancer—they did not believe this was possible. They only wanted to improve the quality of life for these women.

The researchers were quite surprised when, 48 months after the study began, all of the women who had not been in the support groups had died of their cancer, whereas a third of the women in the support groups were still alive. The average survival (from the time the study began) for the women in the support groups was about 40 months, compared to about 19 months for the women who were not in the support groups.

There were no differences between the groups, other than their participation

Another factor important in controlling stress is physical fitness. Individuals who regularly engage in **aerobic exercise** (any sustained activity that increases heart rate and oxygen consumption, such as jogging, swimming, or cycling) show significantly lower heart rates and blood pressure in response to stressful situations than individuals who do not exercise regularly (Blumenthal et al., 1990; Holmes & McGilley, 1987; Holmes & Roth, 1985). In turn, Brown (1991) found that physically fit people were much less likely to become physically ill following stressful events than people who were not fit. Because of these findings, many stress management programs also emphasize physical fitness.

## Cognitive Techniques

People who are able to control their physiological or emotional responses through biofeedback and relaxation training in the laboratory will have more difficulty doing so in actual stressful situations, particularly if they continue to interact in ways that make them tense. Consequently, an additional approach to stress management focuses on changing the individual's cognitive responses to stressful situations. **Cognitive behavior therapy** attempts to help people identify the kinds of stressful situations that produce their physiological or emotional symptoms and to alter the way they cope with these situations. For example, a man who suffers from tension headaches would be asked to begin by keeping a record of their occurrence and rating the severity of each headache and the circumstances in which it occurred. Next he is taught how to monitor his responses to these stressful events and is asked to record his feelings, thoughts, and behavior prior to, during, and following the event. After a period of self-monitoring, certain relationships often become evident among situational variables (for example, criticism by a supervisor or co-worker); thoughts ("I can't do anything right"); and emotional, behavioral, and physiological responses (depression, withdrawal, and headache).

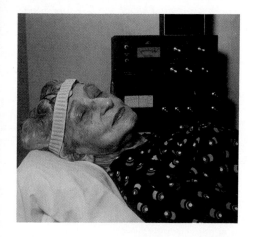

*In this biofeedback procedure for treating headaches, the sensors measure forehead muscle contractions and finger temperature. Cold fingers are often a sign of tension.*

in the weekly support meetings, that could explain the differences in average survival time. That is, the two groups did not differ in the initial seriousness of their cancers, the type of therapy received, or other variables that might have affected their survival time. Spiegel and colleagues were forced to believe that their intervention actually increased the number of months that the women in the support group lived (for similar results, see Richardson, Shelton, Krailo, & Levine, 1990).

How did the intervention affect the progress of these women's cancer? The researchers attributed the effect to the social support the women received from the other women in the group:

The support groups were intensely emotional and supportive. Members discussed their deepest fears of dying and death, visited other members in the hospital, grieved when they died, attended their funerals, and mourned the loss of abilities and friendships. In addition to sharing grief, the women in these groups derived tremendous strength from one another. They came to feel like experts in living, a wisdom that grew from their confrontation with death. They chose new life projects, ranging from imparting life values to their children to writing books of poetry (Spiegel, 1991, p. 62)

In addition, support group members showed lower levels of emotional distress and learned how to control their physical pain better than women who did not participate in the support groups.

Further studies are under way to determine exactly how psychological interventions can affect the course of disease. It may be that reducing distress leads to improved immune system functioning, which slows the course of disease. Studies such as this one are intriguing, however, and hold promise for new ways of helping people facing serious illness.

The next step is trying to identify the expectations or beliefs that might explain the headache reactions (for example, "I expect to do everything perfectly, so the slightest criticism upsets me" or "I judge myself harshly, become depressed, and end up with a headache"). The final and most difficult step is trying to change something about the stressful situation, the individual's way of thinking about it, or the individual's behavior. The options might include finding a less stressful job, recognizing that the need to perform perfectly leads to unnecessary anguish over errors, or learning to behave more assertively in interactions instead of withdrawing.

This summary of cognitive therapy for coping with stressful situations does not do justice to the procedures involved. Chapter 17 provides a more detailed description. Biofeedback, relaxation training, and cognitive therapy have all proved useful in helping people control their physiological and emotional responses to stress. Some research suggests that the improvements gained is more likely to be maintained over time with a combination of cognitive and behavior therapy. (Holroyd, Appel, & Andrasik, 1983). This is not surprising, since the complex demands of everyday life often require flexible coping skills; being able to relax may not be an effective method of coping with some of life's stresses. Programs for stress management frequently employ a combination of biofeedback, relaxation training, and cognitive modification techniques.

## Modifying Type A Behavior

A combination of cognitive and behavioral techniques effectively reduces Type A behavior (Friedman et al., 1985). The subjects were more than 1,000 individuals who had experienced at least one heart attack. Subjects in the treatment group were helped to reduce their sense of time urgency by practicing standing in line (a situation Type A individuals find extremely irritating) and using the opportunity to reflect on things that they do not normally have time to think about, or to watch people, or to strike up a conversation with a stranger. Treatment also included learning to express themselves without exploding at people and to alter certain specific behaviors (such as interrupting the speech of others or talking or eating hurriedly). Therapists helped the subjects re-evaluate basic beliefs (such as the notion that success depends on the quantity of work produced) that might drive much of a Type A person's urgent and hostile behavior. Finally, subjects found ways to make the home and work environment less stressful (such as reducing the number of unnecessary social engagements).

The critical dependent variable in this study was the occurrence of another heart attack. By the end of the study, $4\frac{1}{2}$ years later, the experimental group had a cardiac recurrence rate almost half that of control subjects who were not taught how to alter their life-styles. Clearly, learning to modify Type A behavior was beneficial to these subjects' health (Friedman et al., 1985).

The more we understand about how stress, and our ways of thinking about and coping with stress, affect physical and emotional health, the more we can develop techniques to improve our lives. Research on stress and coping, and more generally on behavioral medicine or health psychology, is rapidly expanding and holds much promise for the future.

## *Chapter* **SUMMARY**

1. Events are often considered stressful when they are *traumas* outside the range of normal human experience, are perceived as *uncontrollable* or *unpredictable*, when they *challenge* the limits of our capabilities, and when they cause *internal conflicts* between competing goals.

2. Common psychological reactions to stress include anxiety, anger and aggression, apathy and depression, and cognitive impairment (for example, problems in concentration and performance).

3. The body reacts to stress with the *fight-or-flight response*. The *sympathetic nervous system* causes increased heart rate, elevated blood pressure, dilated pupils, and the release of extra sugar from the liver. The *adrenal-cortical system* causes the release of adrenocorticotropic hormone (ACTH), which stimulates the release of cortisol in the blood. These reactions prepare the body to fight the stressor or to flee from it. When chronically aroused, however, these physiological responses can cause wear-and-tear on the body.

4. Stress may affect health directly by creating chronic overarousal of the sympathetic system or the adrenal cortical system or by impairing the immune system. Alternately, the *vulnerability-stress model* states that stress only leads to illness when an individual has a psychological or physical vulnerability to a specific disorder. People under stress often do not engage in positive health behaviors, and this may lead to illness. Finally, some people may over-interpret the symptoms brought about by stress and seek sympathy and concern from others for these symptoms, leading them to exaggerate their experiences of illness.

5. The ways humans *appraise* events may influence their vulnerability to illness following events. For example, people who tend to explain bad events by internal, stable, and global causes are more likely to develop *learned helplessness* following bad events and to become ill.

6. People with the *Type A behavior pattern* tend to be hostile, aggressive, impatient persons who are overinvolved in their work. Studies of men and women show that people with this style are at increased risk for coronary heart disease.

7. Coping strategies are divided into *problem-focused strategies* and *emotion-focused strategies*. People who take active steps to solve problems are less likely to show depression and illness following negative life events. People who use rumination or avoidance strategies to cope with negative emotions show longer and more severe distress following events. Psychoanalytic theory describes a number of unconscious strategies *(defense mechanisms)* people use to cope with negative emotions; repression, reaction formation, denial, and projection are examples.
8. Behavioral techniques, such as relaxation training, and cognitive techniques, such as challenging negative thoughts, can help people react more adaptively to stress. Type A behavior can be changed through behavioral and cognitive techniques, resulting in a reduction of people's risk for coronary heart disease.

*Further* **READING**

*Stress and Stress Management: Research and Applications* (1984) by Hamberger and Lohr discusses the different models of stress, some relevant research findings, and various methods for controlling stress. *Stress, Appraisal, and Coping* (1984) by Lazarus and Folkman emphasizes the role of cognitive appraisal in determining stress. For a cognitive behavior approach to stress prevention and management, see Meichenbaum and Jaremko (eds.), *Stress Reduction and Prevention* (1983); and a paperback, *Stress Inoculation Training* (1985), by Meichenbaum.

The developing field of health psychology is described in *The Psychology of Health, Illness, and Medical Care* (1991) by DiMatteo. See also *Behavioral Medicine: The Biopsychological Approach* (1985), edited by Schneiderman and Tapp, and *Mechanisms of Psychological Influence on Physical Health* (1989), edited by Carstensen and Neale. For a review of research on stress and heart disease see *Handbook of Stress, Reactivity, and Cardiovascular Disease* (1986), edited by Matthews. For a comprehensive review of the literature on psychology and health, see Taylor's *Health Psychology* (1986).

A classic account of defense mechanisms is given by Anna Freud in *The Ego and the Mechanisms of Defense* (rev. ed., 1967).

# Chapter 16

# Abnormal Psychology

**Abnormal Behavior 617**
*Defining Abnormality*
*What Is Normality?*
*Classifying Abnormal Behavior*

**Anxiety Disorders 624**
*Generalized Anxiety and Panic Disorders*
*Phobias*
*Obsessive-Compulsive Disorders*
*Understanding Anxiety Disorders*

**Mood Disorders 635**
*Depression*
*Bipolar Disorders*
*Critical Discussion: Depression and Suicide*
*Understanding Mood Disorders*
*Critical Discussion: Illusion and Well-Being*

**Schizophrenia 645**
*Characteristics of Schizophrenia*
*Understanding Schizophrenia*

**Personality Disorders 658**
*Antisocial Personality*
*Understanding Antisocial Personalities*
*Critical Discussion: Insanity as a Legal Defense*

Detail, *Place du Havre.*

Most of us have periods when we feel anxious, depressed, unreasonably angry, or inadequate in dealing with life's complexities. Trying to lead a satisfying and meaningful life is not easy in an era of rapid social and technological change. Many of our traditional assumptions about work, religion, sex, marriage, and family are being questioned, and the social values that gave our grandparents a sense of security no longer provide clear guidelines for behavior. It is an unusual person who manages to get through life without periods of loneliness, self-doubt, and despair. In fact, about a third of Americans will experience a severe enough mental or emotional problem at least once during their lifetime that, if diagnosed, would be classified as a mental disorder (Regier et al., 1988).

## Abnormal Behavior

In this chapter, we will look at some individuals who have serious mental disorders and some who have developed self-destructive life-styles. The behaviors we discuss are classified as "abnormal," but as we will see, the dividing line between "normal" and "abnormal" behavior is far from clear.

### Defining Abnormality

What do we mean by "abnormal" behavior? By what criteria do we distinguish it from "normal" behavior? There is no general agreement, but most attempts to describe abnormality are based on one or more of the following definitions.

**DEVIATION FROM STATISTICAL NORMS** The word *abnormal* means "away from the norm." Many characteristics, such as height, weight, and intelligence, cover a range of values when measured over a population. Most people fall within the middle range of height, while a few individuals are abnormally tall or abnormally short. One definition of abnormality is based on *statistical frequency:* abnormal behavior is statistically infrequent or deviant from the norm. But according to this definition, the person who is extremely intelligent or extremely happy would be classified as abnormal. Thus, in defining abnormal behavior, we must consider more than statistical frequency.

**DEVIATION FROM SOCIAL NORMS** Every society has certain standards, or norms, for acceptable behavior; behavior that deviates markedly from these norms is considered abnormal. Usually, but not always, such behavior is also statistically infrequent in that society. However, several problems arise when deviation from social norms is used as a criterion for defining abnormality.

Behavior that is considered normal by one society may be considered abnormal by another. For example, members of some African tribes do not consider it unusual to hear voices when no one is actually talking or to see visions when nothing is actually there, but such behaviors are considered abnormal in most societies. Another problem is that the concept of abnormality changes over time within the same society. Most Americans would have considered smoking marijuana or appearing nearly nude at the beach abnormal behaviors 30 years ago. Today, such behaviors tend to be viewed as differences in life-style rather than as signs of abnormality.

*According to some social scientists, behavior is abnormal if it is maladaptive—that is, if it interferes with the welfare of the individual or is harmful to society.*

Thus, ideas of normality and abnormality differ from one society to another and over time within the same society. Any definition of abnormality must include more than social compliance.

**MALADAPTIVENESS OF BEHAVIOR**  Rather than defining abnormal behavior in terms of deviance from either statistical or societal norms, many social scientists believe that the most important criterion is how the behavior affects the well-being of the individual or of the social group. According to this criterion, behavior is abnormal if it is *maladaptive*, if it has adverse effects on the individual or on society. Some kinds of deviant behavior interfere with the welfare of the individual (a man who is so fearful of crowds that he cannot ride the bus to work; an alcoholic who drinks so heavily that he or she cannot keep a job; a woman who attempts suicide). Other forms of deviant behavior are harmful to society (an adolescent who has violent aggressive outbursts; a paranoid individual who plots to assassinate national leaders). If we use the criterion of maladaptiveness, all of these behaviors would be considered abnormal.

**PERSONAL DISTRESS**  A fourth criterion considers abnormality in terms of the individual's subjective feelings of distress rather than the individual's behavior. Most people diagnosed as mentally ill feel acutely miserable. They are anxious, depressed, or agitated and many suffer from insomnia, loss of appetite, or numerous aches and pains. Sometimes personal distress may be the only symptom of abnormality; the individual's behavior may appear normal to the casual observer.

None of these definitions provides a completely satisfactory description of abnormal behavior. In most instances, all four criteria—statistical frequency, social deviation, maladaptive behavior, and personal distress—are considered in diagnosing abnormality.

## What Is Normality?

Normality is even more difficult to define than abnormality, but most psychologists would agree that the following qualities indicate emotional well-being. These characteristics do not make sharp distinctions between the mentally healthy and the mentally ill; rather, they represent traits that the normal person possesses to a *greater degree* than the individual who is diagnosed as abnormal.

1. *Efficient perception of reality*  Normal individuals are fairly realistic in appraising their reactions and capabilities and in interpreting what is going on in the world around them. They do not consistently misperceive what others say and do, and they do not consistently overevaluate their abilities and tackle more than they can accomplish, nor do they underestimate their abilities and shy away from difficult tasks.
2. *Self-knowledge*  Well-adjusted people have some awareness of their own motives and feelings. Although none of us can fully understand our feelings or behavior, normal people have more self-awareness than individuals who are diagnosed as mentally ill.
3. *An ability to exercise voluntary control over behavior*  Normal individuals feel fairly confident about their ability to control their behavior. Occasionally, they may act impulsively, but they are able to restrain sexual

and aggressive urges when necessary. They may fail to conform to social norms, but their decision to act as such is voluntary rather than the result of uncontrollable impulses.

4. *Self-esteem and acceptance*  Well-adjusted people have some appreciation of their own self-worth and feel accepted by those around them. They are comfortable with other people and are able to react spontaneously in social situations. At the same time, they do not feel obligated to subjugate their opinions to those of the group. Feelings of worthlessness, alienation, and lack of acceptance are prevalent among individuals who are diagnosed as abnormal.

5. *An ability to form affectionate relationships*  Normal individuals are able to form close and satisfying relationships with other people. They are sensitive to the feelings of others and do not make excessive demands on others to gratify their own needs. Often, mentally disturbed people are so concerned with protecting their own security that they become extremely self-centered. Preoccupied with their own feelings and strivings, they seek affection but are unable to reciprocate. Sometimes they fear intimacy because their past relationships have been destructive.

6. *Productivity*  Well-adjusted people are able to channel their abilities into productive activity. They are enthusiastic about life and do not need to drive themselves to meet the demands of the day. A chronic lack of energy and excessive susceptibility to fatigue are often symptoms of psychological tension resulting from unsolved problems.

A word of warning may be appropriate before proceeding further. It is common for students studying abnormal psychology for the first time to see signs of mental disorders in themselves, just as medical students diagnose themselves as suffering from every new disease they read about. Most of us at one time or another have had some of the symptoms we will be describing, and that is no cause for alarm. However, if you have been bothered by distressing feelings for quite a while, it never hurts to talk to someone about them—perhaps someone in your school's counseling service or student health service.

## Classifying Abnormal Behavior

A broad range of behaviors has been classified as abnormal. Some abnormal behaviors are acute and transitory, resulting from particularly stressful events, whereas others are chronic and lifelong. Some abnormal behaviors result from disease or damage to the nervous system. Others are the products of undesirable social environments or faulty learning experiences. Often these factors overlap and interact. Each person's behavior and emotional problems are unique; no two individuals behave in exactly the same manner or share the same life experiences. However, enough similarities exist for mental health professionals to classify cases into categories.

A classification system has advantages and disadvantages. If the various types of abnormal behavior have different causes, we can hope to uncover them by grouping individuals according to similarities in behavior and then looking for other ways in which the persons may be similar. A diagnostic label also enables those who work with disturbed individuals to communicate information more quickly and concisely. The diagnosis of **schizophrenia** indicates quite a bit about a person's behavior. Knowing

**TABLE 16-1**
**Categories of Mental Disorders** *Listed are the main diagnostic categories of DSM-III-R. Each category includes numerous subclassifications. Personality disorders and developmental disorders (such as mental retardation and delayed language) are coded on Axis II.* (After American Psychiatric Association, 1987)

1. **Disorders usually first evident in infancy, childhood, or adolescence**
   Includes mental retardation, hyperactivity, childhood anxieties, eating disorders (for example, anorexia and bulimia), speech disorders, and other deviations from normal development.

2. **Organic mental disorders**
   Disorders in which the functioning of the brain is known to be impaired, either permanently or transiently; may be the result of aging, degenerative diseases of the nervous system (for example, syphilis or Alzheimer's disease), or the ingestion of toxic substances (for example, lead poisoning or drugs).

3. **Psychoactive substance use disorders**
   Includes excessive use of alcohol, barbiturates, amphetamines, cocaine, and other drugs that alter behavior. Marijuana and tobacco are also included in this category, which is controversial.

4. **Schizophrenia**
   A group of disorders characterized by loss of contact with reality, marked disturbances of thought and perception, and bizarre behavior. At some phase delusions or hallucinations almost always occur.

5. **Delusional (paranoid) disorders**
   Disorders characterized by excessive suspicions and hostility accompanied by feelings of being persecuted; reality contact in other areas is satisfactory.

6. **Mood disorders**
   Disturbances of normal mood; the person may be extremely depressed, abnormally elated, or may alternate between periods of elation and depression.

7. **Anxiety disorders**
   Includes disorders in which anxiety is the main symptom (generalized anxiety or panic disorders) or anxiety is experienced unless the individual avoids feared situations (phobic disorders) or tries to resist performing certain rituals or thinking persistent thoughts (obsessive-compulsive disorders). Also includes post-traumatic stress disorder.

8. **Somatoform disorders**
   The symptoms are physical, but no organic basis can be found and psychological factors appear to play the major role. Included are conversion disorders (for example, a woman who resents having to care for her invalid mother suddenly develops a paralyzed arm) and hypochondriasis (excessive preoccupation with health and fear of disease when there is no basis for concern.) Does *not* include psychosomatic disorders that have an organic basis. (See Chapter 15.)

that an individual's symptoms are similar to those of other patients (whose progress followed a particular course or who benefited from a certain kind of treatment) is also helpful in deciding how to treat the patient.

Disadvantages arise, however, if we allow a diagnostic label to carry too much weight. Labeling induces us to overlook the unique features of each case and to expect the person to conform to the classification. We may also forget that a label for maladaptive behavior is not an explanation of that behavior; the classification does not tell us how the behavior originated or what maintains the behavior.

9. **Dissociative disorders**
Temporary alterations in the functions of consciousness, memory, or identity due to emotional problems. Included are amnesia (the individual cannot recall anything about his or her history following a traumatic experience) and multiple personality (two or more independent personality systems existing within the same individual).

10. **Sexual disorders**
Includes problems of sexual identity (for example, transsexualism), sexual performance (for example, impotence, premature ejaculation, and frigidity), and sexual aim (for example, sexual interest in children, sadism, and masochism).

11. **Sleep disorders**
Includes chronic insomnia, excessive sleepiness, sleep apnea, sleepwalking, and narcolepsy.

12. **Factitious disorders**
Physical or psychological symptoms that are intentionally produced or feigned. Differs from malingering in that there is no obvious goal, such as disability payments or the avoidance of military service. The best-studied form of this disorder is called Münchausen syndrome: the individual's plausible presentation of factitious physical symptoms results in frequent hospitalizations.

13. **Impulse control disorder**
Includes kleptomania (compulsive stealing of objects not needed for personal use or their monetary value), pathological gambling and pyromania (setting fires for the pleasure or relief of tension derived thereby).

14. **Personality disorders**
Long-standing patterns of maladaptive behavior that constitute immature and inappropriate ways of coping with stress or solving problems. Antisocial personality disorder and narcissistic personality disorder are two examples.

15. **Conditions not attributable to a mental disorder**
This category includes many of the problems for which people seek help, such as marital problems, parent-child difficulties, and academic or occupational problems.

The classification of mental disorders used by most mental health professionals in this country is the *Diagnostic and Statistical Manual of Mental Disorders,* 3rd edition, revised (DSM-III-R, for short), which corresponds generally to the international system formulated by the World Health Organization. The major categories of mental disorders classified by DSM-III-R are listed in Table 16-1. Some of these disorders will be discussed in more detail later in the chapter.

DSM-III-R provides an extensive list of subcategories under each of these headings, as well as a description of the symptoms that must be present for the diagnosis to be applicable. The complete diagnosis for an individual is fairly comprehensive. Each person is evaluated on five separate dimensions or axes. Axis I includes the categories listed in Table 16-1, except for personality disorders and developmental disorders (such as mental retardation or language problems) that make up Axis II. Axes I and II were separated to ensure that the presence of long-term disturbances would be considered when attending to the present disturbance. For example, a person who is now a heroin addict would be diagnosed on Axes I as having a psychoactive substance use disorder; he might also have a long-standing antisocial personality disorder, which would be listed on Axis II.

The remaining three axes are not needed to make the actual diagnosis but are included to ensure that factors other than a person's symptoms are considered in the overall assessment. The five axes are listed below.

I: The diagnostic category listed in Table 16-1 with the appropriate sub-classification. For example, "schizophrenia, paranoid type."

II: Personality and developmental disorders are listed here, if present.

III: A list of any current physical disorders that may be relevant to understanding and treating the person.

IV: Documentation of stressful events that may have precipitated the disorder (such as divorce, death of a loved one).

V: An evaluation of how well the individual has functioned socially and occupationally during the previous year.

All of these variables are helpful in determining treatment and prognosis.

You have probably heard the terms "neurosis" and "psychosis" and may be wondering where they fit into the categories of mental disorders listed in Table 16-1. Traditionally, these terms denoted major diagnostic categories. **Neuroses** (plural of *neurosis*) included a group of disorders characterized by anxiety, personal unhappiness, and maladaptive behavior that were seldom serious enough to require hospitalization. The individual could usually function in society, although not at full capacity. **Psychoses** (plural of *psychosis)* included more serious mental disorders. The individual's behavior and thought processes were so disturbed that he or she was out of touch with reality, could not cope with the demands of daily life, and usually had to be hospitalized.

Neither neuroses nor psychoses appear as major categories in DSM-III-R. There are several reasons for this departure from earlier classification systems, but the main one concerns precision of diagnosis. Both categories were fairly broad and included a number of mental disorders with quite dissimilar symptoms. Consequently, mental health professionals did not always agree on the diagnosis for a particular case. DSM-III-R attempts to achieve greater consensus by grouping disorders according to very specific behavioral symptoms, without implying anything about their origins or treatment. The intention is to describe what clinical workers *observe* about individuals who have psychological problems in a way that ensures accurate communication among mental health professionals. Consequently, DSM-III-R includes many more categories than previous editions of the manual. Disorders that were formerly categorized as neuroses (because they were assumed to be ways of coping with internal conflicts) are listed in DMS-III-R under three separate categories: anxiety disorders, somatoform disorders, and dissociative disorders.

Although psychosis is no longer a major category, DSM-III-R recognizes that people diagnosed as having schizophrenia, delusional disorders, some mood disorders, and certain organic mental disorders exhibit **psychotic behavior** at some point during their illness. Their thinking and perception of reality are severely disturbed and they may have **hallucinations** (false sensory experiences, such as hearing voices or seeing strange visions) and/or **delusions** (false beliefs, such as the conviction that all thoughts are controlled by a powerful being from another planet).

These issues will become clearer as we look more closely at some of the mental disorders listed in Table 16-1. In the remainder of this chapter, we will examine anxiety disorders, mood disorders, schizophrenia, and one type of personality disorder. Alcoholism and drug dependence (both classified as psychoactive substance use disorders) are covered in Chapter 6. Multiple personality, a dissociative disorder, is also discussed in Chapter 6.

Table 16-2 gives the likelihood of the major mental disorders during one's lifetime. The study on which this table is based found that mental disorders are more common among people under age 45 and more common in women than in men. However, men were twice as likely as women to abuse drugs and five times as likely to abuse alcohol. Antisocial personality disorders affected four times as many men as women, but more women suffered from mood and anxiety disorders.

**PERSPECTIVES ON MENTAL DISORDERS** Attempts to understand the causes of mental disorders and proposals for treating them generally fall under one of the approaches to psychology described in Chapter 1. The **biological perspective,** also called the medical or disease model, emphasizes the idea that bodily disturbances cause disordered behavior. Researchers using this approach look for genetic irregularities that may predispose a person to develop a particular mental disorder. They also look for abnormalities in specific parts of the brain, defects in neurotransmission, and problems in the functioning of the autonomic nervous system. By implication, a drug able to alter the physiological malfunction may be effective in treating, or even preventing, the mental disorder.

The **psychoanalytic perspective** on mental disorders emphasizes the importance of unconscious conflicts, usually originating in early childhood, and the use of defense mechanisms to handle the anxiety generated by the repressed impulses and emotions. Bringing the unconscious conflicts and emotions into awareness presumably eliminates the need for the defense mechanisms and alleviates the disorder.

The **behavioral perspective** looks at mental disorders from the standpoint of learning theory and assumes that maladaptive behaviors are learned ways of coping with stress. This approach investigates how fears become conditioned to specific situations and the role that reinforcement plays in the origin and maintenance of inappropriate behaviors.

The **cognitive perspective,** like the psychoanalytic perspective, is concerned with internal processes. Rather than stressing hidden motivations, emotions, and conflicts, however, it emphasizes conscious mental processes. The way we think about ourselves (our **self-schema**), the way we appraise stressful situations, and our strategies for coping with them are all interrelated. From the cognitive viewpoint, some mental disorders stem from disordered cognitive processes and can be alleviated by changing these faulty cognitions.

| DISORDER | RATE |
| --- | --- |
| Anxiety disorders | 14.6% |
| Mood disorders | 8.3% |
| Schizophrenia | 1.3% |
| Antisocial personality | 2.5% |
| Substance use disorders | 16.4% |

**TABLE 16-2**
**Lifetime Prevalence Rates of Selected Disorders.** *Listed are the percentage of individuals in the United States population who have experienced one of these mental disorders during their lifetime. These percentages are based on interviews with a sample of 18,571 individuals, age 18 and over, in five major United States cities.* (After Regier et al., 1988)

*Disorders can be understood or explained in many ways: genetic, chemical, or neurological causes; unconscious conflicts; learned, inappropriate behaviors; and faulty cognitions.*

The ideas embodied in these summaries will become clearer as we discuss them in relation to specific mental disorders. Each of these approaches has something important to say about mental disorders, but none has the complete answer. Some disorders, such as schizophrenia, have a stronger biological component than others. But psychological and environmental factors also play a role. One way of integrating these factors is the **vulnerability-stress model** which considers the interaction between a *predisposition* that makes a person vulnerable for developing an illness and stressful environmental conditions the individual encounters. (This is also called the *diathesis-stress model;* recall from Chapter 15 that "diathesis" refers to a constitutional predisposition toward an illness, but the term can be extended to include any characteristic of a person that increases his or her chance of developing a disorder.) On a biological level, vulnerability might be genetic. For some of the disorders we will discuss, having a close relative with the disorder increases the person's risk of developing it. On a psychological level, a chronic feeling of hopelessness and inadequacy might make an individual vulnerable for the development of depression.

Being vulnerable for a disorder does not, by any means, guarantee that the person will develop the disorder. Whether or not the predisposition leads to an actual disorder depends on the kinds of stressors the individual encounters. These would include poverty, malnutrition, frustration, conflicts, and traumatic life events.

The key point of the vulnerability-stress model is that both vulnerability and stress are necessary. It helps explain why some people become mentally ill when confronted with a minimum of stress, while others remain healthy regardless of how difficult their lives may be.

# Anxiety Disorders

Most of us feel anxious and tense in the face of threatening or stressful situations. Such feelings are normal reactions to stress. Anxiety is considered abnormal only when it occurs in situations that most people can handle with little difficulty. *Anxiety disorders* include a group of disorders in which anxiety either is the main symptom (*generalized anxiety* and *panic disorders*) or is experienced when the individual attempts to control certain maladaptive behaviors (*phobic* and *obsessive-compulsive disorders*). (Post-traumatic stress disorder, which involves anxiety following a traumatic event, was discussed in Chapter 15.)

## Generalized Anxiety and Panic Disorders

A person who suffers from a **generalized anxiety disorder** lives each day in a state of high tension. She or he feels vaguely uneasy or apprehensive much of the time and tends to overreact even to mild stresses. An inability to relax, disturbed sleep, fatigue, headaches, dizziness, and rapid heart rate are the most common physical complaints. In addition, the individual continually worries about potential problems and has difficulty concentrating or making decisions. When the individual finally makes a decision, it becomes the source of further worry ("Did I foresee all possible consequences?" or "Will disaster result?"). Some self-descriptions provided by people with chronically high levels of anxiety appear in Table 16-3.

*Anxiety becomes disruptive when a person experiences it from events that most others do not consider stressful.*

People who suffer generalized anxiety may also experience panic attacks—episodes of acute and overwhelming apprehension or terror. During panic attacks, the individual feels certain that something dreadful is about to happen. This feeling is usually accompanied by such symptoms as heart palpitations, shortness of breath, perspiration, muscle tremors, faintness, and nausea. The symptoms result from excitation of the sympathetic division of the autonomic nervous system (see Chapter 2) and are the same reactions an individual experiences when extremely frightened. During severe panic attacks, the person fears that he or she will die. The following personal account describes how terrifying such experiences can be:

> I remember walking up the street, the moon was shining and suddenly everything around me seemed unfamiliar, as it would be in a dream. I felt panic rising inside me, but managed to push it away and carry on. I walked a quarter of a mile or so, with the panic getting worse every minute. . . . By now, I was sweating, yet trembling; my heart was pounding and my legs felt like jelly. . . . Terrified, I stood, not knowing what to do. The only bit of sanity left in me told me to get home. Somehow this I did very slowly, holding onto the fence in the road. I cannot remember the actual journey back, until I was going into the house, then I broke down and cried helplessly. . . . I did not go out again for a few days. When I did, it was with my mother and baby to my grandmother's a few miles away. I felt panicky there and couldn't cope with the baby. My cousin suggested we go to my Aunt's house, but I had another attack there. I was sure I was going to die. Following this, I was totally unable to go out alone, and even with someone else I had great difficulty. Not only did I get the panicky fainting spells, but I lived in constant fear of getting them. (Melville, 1977, pp. 1, 14)

People who experience generalized anxiety and **panic disorders** may have no clear idea of why they are frightened. This kind of anxiety is sometimes called "free-floating" because it is not triggered by a particular event; rather, it occurs in a variety of situations.

## Phobias

In contrast to the vague apprehension of generalized anxiety disorders, the fears in phobic disorders are more specific. Someone who responds with intense fear to a stimulus or situation that most people do not consider particularly dangerous is said to have a **phobia.** The individual usually realizes that his or her fear is irrational but still feels anxiety (ranging from strong uneasiness to panic) that can be alleviated only by avoiding the feared object or situation.

Many of us have an irrational fear or two—snakes, insects, and heights are common ones. However, a fear is usually not diagnosed as a phobic disorder unless it interferes considerably with the person's daily life. Examples of phobic disorders would be a woman whose fear of enclosed places prevents her from entering elevators or a man whose fear of crowds prevents him from attending the theater or walking along congested sidewalks.

DSM-III-R divides phobic disorders into three broad categories: simple phobias, social phobias, and agoraphobia. A **simple phobia** is a fear of a specific object, animal, or situation. Irrational fears of snakes, germs, enclosed places, and darkness are examples. Some people may develop a simple phobia but be normal in other respects. In more serious cases, the individual has a number of phobias that interfere with many aspects of life and may be intertwined with obsessive or compulsive behavior.

I am often bothered by the thumping of my heart.

Little annoyances get on my nerves and irritate me.

I often become suddenly scared for no good reason.

I worry continuously and that gets me down.

I frequently get spells of complete exhaustion and fatigue.

It is always hard for me to make up my mind.

I always seem to be dreading something.

I feel nervous and high-strung all the time.

I often feel I cannot overcome my difficulties.

I feel constantly under strain.

**TABLE 16-3**
**Generalized Anxiety** *The statements listed in the table are self-descriptions by individuals who have chronically high levels of anxiety.* (After Sarason & Sarason, 1989)

People with **social phobias** feel extremely insecure in social situations and have an exaggerated fear of embarrassing themselves. Often they are fearful that they will betray their anxiety by such signs as hand tremors, blushing, or a quavering voice. These fears are usually unrealistic: individuals who fear they might shake do not do so; those who fear they will stutter or quaver actually speak quite normally. Fear of public speaking or of eating in public are the most common complaints of socially phobic individuals.

**Agoraphobia** is the most common phobia among people seeking professional help. It is also the most disabling. The word is Greek for "fear of the marketplace." Individuals suffering from agoraphobia are afraid of entering unfamiliar settings. They avoid open spaces, crowds, and traveling. In extreme cases, the individual may be afraid to leave the familiar setting of home. The following incident in the life of a woman suffering from agoraphobia shows how distressing such fears can be.

> The woman who lives next door is a very nice person and I like her. One day she asked me if I would drive over to a big shopping center that had recently opened about five miles from where we live. I didn't know how to tell her that there isn't a chance in the world that I'd go to that shopping center or any other place outside our neighborhood. She must have seen how upset I got, but I was shaking like a leaf even more inside. I imagined myself in the crowd, getting lost, or passing out. I was terrified by the openness of the shopping center and the crowds. I made an excuse this time, but I don't know what I'll say next time. Maybe I'll just have to let her in on my little bit of craziness. (Sarason & Sarason, 1989, p. 155)

Agoraphobics usually have a history of panic attacks. They become fearful of being incapacitated by an attack away from the security of home and where no one may be available to help them. Crowded enclosed places where escape to safety would be difficult (such as a bus or a theater) are especially terrifying. But agoraphobics also fear open spaces (large bodies of water, bare landscapes, an empty street) and feel more comfortable when the space is circumscribed by trees, or when an enclosed space (perhaps symbolic of home) is easily reached. Agoraphobics are usually very dependent. A large percentage of them exhibited separation anxiety (fear of being away from mother) in childhood, long before developing agoraphobia (Gittelman & Klein, 1985). While simple phobias and social phobias are fairly easy to treat, agoraphobia is much more difficult.

## Obsessive-Compulsive Disorders

A man gets out of bed several times each night and checks all the doors to make sure they are locked. On returning to bed he is tormented by the thought that he may have missed one. Another man takes three or four showers in succession, scrubbing his body thoroughly with a special disinfectant each time, fearful that he may be contaminated by germs. A woman has recurrent thoughts about stabbing her infant and feels panic-stricken whenever she has to handle scissors or knives. A teenage girl is always late to school because she feels compelled to repeat many of her actions (replacing her brush on the dresser, arranging the school supplies in her bookbag, crossing the threshold to her bedroom) a set number of times, usually some multiple of the number four.

All of these people have symptoms of an **obsessive-compulsive disorder,** their lives are dominated by repetitive acts or thoughts. **Obsessions** are persistent intrusions of unwelcome thoughts, images, or impulses that elicit anxiety. **Compulsions** are irresistible urges to carry out certain acts or rituals that reduce anxiety. Obsessive thoughts are often linked with compulsive acts (for example, thoughts of lurking germs which lead to the compulsion to wash eating utensils many times before using them). Regardless of whether the repetitive element is a thought (obsession) or an act (compulsion), the central feature of the disorder is the subjective experience of loss of volition. The victims struggle mightily to rid themselves of the troublesome thoughts or to resist performing the repetitive acts but are unable to do so.

At times, all of us have persistently recurring thoughts ("Did I leave the gas on?") and urges to perform ritualistic behavior (arranging the materials on a desk in a precise order before starting an assignment). But for people with obsessive-compulsive disorders, such thoughts and acts occupy so much time that they seriously interfere with daily life. The individuals recognize their thoughts as irrational and repugnant but are unable to ignore or suppress them. They realize the senselessness of their compulsive behavior but become anxious when they try to resist their compulsions, and feel a release of tension once the acts are carried out.

Obsessive thoughts cover a variety of topics, but most often they are concerned with causing harm to oneself or others, fear of contamination, and doubt that a completed task has been accomplished satisfactorily (Rachman & Hodgson, 1980; Stern & Cobb, 1978). Interestingly enough, the content of obsessions changes with the times. In earlier days obsessive thoughts about religion and sex were common—for example, blasphemous thoughts or impulses to shout obscenities in church or expose one's genitals in public. They are less frequent today. While obsessions about contamination used to focus on syphilis, AIDS has now become the object of many contamination fears (Rapoport, 1989).

Some people with an obsessive-compulsive disorder have intrusive thoughts without overt repetitious actions. However, the majority of patients with obsessive thoughts also exhibit compulsive behavior (Akhtar et al., 1975). Compulsions take a variety of forms, of which the two most common are *washing* and *checking* (Foa & Steketee, 1989). "Washers" are individuals who feel contaminated when exposed to certain objects or thoughts and

*An obsessive-compulsive person who fears contamination may spend hours every day performing cleaning rituals.*

*Box 1*

# Obsessive-Compulsive Disorder

Mike, a 32-year-old patient, engaged in checking rituals that were triggered by a fear of harming others. When driving he felt compelled to stop the car often to check whether he had run over people, particularly babies. Before flushing the toilet, Mike inspected the commode to be sure that a live insect had not fallen into the toilet—he did not want to be responsible

for killing any living creature. In addition, he repeatedly checked the doors, stoves, lights, and windows, making sure that all were shut or turned off so that no harm, such as fire or burglary, would befall his family as a result of his "irresponsible" behavior. In particular he worried about the safety of his 15-month-old daughter, repeatedly checking the gate to the basement to be sure that it was locked. He did not carry his daughter while walking on concrete floors in order to avoid killing her by accidentally dropping her. Mike performed these and many other checking rituals for an average of four hours a day. Checking behavior started several months after his marriage, 6 years before treatment. It increased 2 years later, when Mike's wife was pregnant with their first child, and continued to worsen over the years.

Treatment for Mike included a form of systematic desensitization (see p. 678) in which he imagined scenes of his fears. For example, he was asked to imagine that he forgot to check the windows and doors; a burglar entered and stole his wife's jewelry; she blames him for the theft. Or to imagine that he dropped his baby daughter on the concrete floor because he wasn't holding her properly and she suffered serious injuries. His homework involved actual exposure to the feared situation—for example, walking his daughter on a concrete floor until his anxiety subsides or closing doors and windows and checking only once.

At a 3-year follow-up, Mike reported 10 minutes of checking per day in contrast to 4 hours before treatment (Foa & Steketee, 1989, pp. 185, 200).

spend hours performing washing and cleaning rituals. "Checkers" are people who check doors, lights, ovens, the accuracy of a completed task—ten, twenty, or one hundred times—or who repeat ritualistic acts over and over again. They believe that their actions will prevent future "disaster" or punishments. Sometimes these rituals are related to the anxiety-evoking obsessions in a direct way (for example, repeatedly checking to see if the stove is off to avoid possible fire); other rituals are not rationally related to the obsessions (for example, dressing and undressing to prevent one's husband from having an accident). The common theme behind all of these repetition behaviors is doubt. Obsessive-compulsive individuals cannot trust their senses or their judgment; they can't trust their eyes that see no dirt or really believe that the door is locked. The case described in Box 1 shows how time consuming and extensive checking rituals can be.

Obsessive-compulsive disorders are related to phobic disorders in that both involve severe anxiety and both may appear in the same patient. However, there are important differences. Phobic patients seldom ruminate constantly about their fears nor do they show ritualistic compulsive behavior. And the two disorders have different evoking stimuli. Dirt, germs, and harm to others—which are common obsessive-compulsive preoccupations—seldom cause major problems for phobic individuals.

Is there a specific type of personality that is vulnerable to an obsessive-compulsive disorder?

We sometimes label a person who is exceedingly neat, meticulous, and exasperatingly attentive to details a compulsive personality—or sometimes an obsessive-compulsive personality. Such people also tend to be rigid in their thinking and behavior and highly moralistic. It is tempting to suppose that when an obsessive-compulsive personality is under stress, he or she reacts by developing an obsessive-compulsive disorder. However, this hypothesis is not supported by evidence. The results of personality tests indicate that people with *obsessive-compulsive disorders* do not have the characteristics of an *obsessive-compulsive personality* (Rachman & Hodgson, 1980). We should note, in addition, that people with obsessive-compulsive personalities tend to be proud of their meticulousness and attention to detail. Individuals with obsessive-compulsive disorders, in contrast, abhor their symptoms and wish to be rid of them.

## Understanding Anxiety Disorders

We do not know why some people become chronically anxious, but their reactions seem to reflect feelings of inadequacy in situations that they perceive as threatening. Following the approaches to understanding mental disorders described earlier, theories of anxiety disorders have focused on internal conflicts, learned responses to external events, maladaptive cognitions, and biological factors.

**PSYCHOANALYTIC PERSPECTIVE** Psychoanalytic theory assumes that the major determinants of anxiety disorders are internal conflicts and unconscious motives. As we noted in Chapter 15, Freud distinguished between **objective anxiety**, which is a reasonable response to a harmful situation, and **neurotic anxiety**, which is out of proportion to the actual danger. He believed that neurotic anxiety stems from unconscious conflicts within the individual between unacceptable **id** impulses (mainly sexual and aggressive) and the constraints imposed by the **ego** and **superego**. When these impulses come close to consciousness, anxiety is aroused and serves as a signal of potential danger. Because the source of anxiety is unconscious, the person does not know why he or she feels apprehensive.

Later psychoanalysts expanded the causes of neurotic anxiety to include the perception of oneself as helpless and unable to cope, fear of separation or being abandoned, and anticipation of disapproval and withdrawal of love. These feelings are assumed to be largely unconscious.

*To what extent is chronic anxiety a result of internal conflict, learned response, unrealistic appraisal, or genetic predisposition?*

From a psychoanalytic viewpoint, phobias are ways of coping with anxiety by displacing it onto an object or situation that can be avoided. The classic example is the case of Little Hans, a 5-year-old who developed an intense fear of horses. Freud interpreted the boy's phobia in terms of Oedipal fears (see p. 536 in Chapter 14) by the following analysis. Hans was in love with his mother, jealously hated his father, and wanted to replace him (the **Oedipal Conflict**); he feared that his father would retaliate by castrating him; the anxiety produced by this conflict was enormous because the wishes were unacceptable to the child's conscious mind; the anxiety was displaced onto an innocent object (a large horse that Hans had seen fall down and thrash about violently in the street).

According to psychoanalytic theory, bringing the unconscious conflict to light and gaining insight into the fears that are being displaced onto the phobic object should cure the phobia. However, as we will see in Chapter 17, psychoanalysis has not proved very successful in treating phobias.

Obsessions and compulsions also serve to protect the individual from recognizing the true source of his or her anxiety. Obsessive thoughts are unacceptable impulses (hostility, destructiveness, inappropriate sexual urges) that have been repressed and somehow reappear in a disguised form. The individual feels that they are not a part of herself or himself and may commit compulsive acts to undo or atone for forbidden impulses. A mother who is obsessed with thoughts of murdering her infant may feel compelled to check many times during the night to assure herself that the child is well. Compulsive rituals also serve to keep threatening impulses out of the individual's conscious awareness: a person who is continually busy has little opportunity to think improper thoughts or commit improper actions.

**BEHAVIORAL PERSPECTIVE** Psychologists who work within the framework of learning theory view anxiety as triggered more by specific external events than by internal conflicts. Generalized anxiety occurs when a person feels unable to cope with many everyday situations and consequently feels apprehensive much of the time. Phobias are viewed as avoidance responses that may be learned either directly from frightening experiences (developing a fear of dogs after being attacked by one) or vicariously by observing fearful responses in others.

The classical conditioning paradigm (see Chapter 7) provides an explanation of how innocuous objects or situations can become the focus of a phobia: a neutral object (the conditioned stimulus) paired with a traumatic event (the unconditioned stimulus) produces fear of the neutral object (the conditioned response). Learning theorists would explain the case of Little Hans according to this paradigm. The horse (the CS, previously a neutral object) paired with a traumatic event (the US, sight of the horse falling down and thrashing violently) produced a fear of horses (the CR, or phobia).

The precipitating trauma, when it can be identified in phobic cases, is well described by classical conditioning. And considerable evidence from laboratory experiments with animals and humans shows that pairing a neutral object with a frightening situation produces fear of the neutral object. However, there are problems with this explanation of phobias. Simple phobias almost always are restricted to a certain set of objects, rather than to any object that happens to be present at the same time as the traumatic event. Why, for example, are phobias of the dark common, but phobias of pajamas nonexistent, although both are paired with nighttime trauma? Why do we have phobias of snakes and insects but not phobias of kittens or lambs? And

why are phobias of knives and guns rare, even though both objects are often paired with injury?

The notion of **prepared conditioning** has been proposed as an explanation. Humans are biologically predisposed, or prepared, to react with fear only to certain classes of dangerous objects or situations. When these objects or situations are paired with trauma, fear conditioning occurs rapidly and is very resistant to extinction (Seligman, 1971; Rosenhan & Seligman, 1989). The majority of common phobias were once actually dangerous to our early ancestors. Natural selection may have favored those ancestors who learned quickly (with only minimal exposure to trauma) that strangers, heights, snakes, large animals, and the dark were dangerous. Thus, there may be a select group of objects, all dangerous in an earlier time, that are readily conditionable to trauma. We are less likely to become conditioned to fear other objects (such as lambs, guns, and electric outlets) either because they were never dangerous or because their origin is too recent to have been subject to natural selection. Thus, phobias are instances not of ordinary classical conditioning but of prepared classical conditioning.

A series of laboratory experiments lends support to the idea that people are more prepared to learn to be afraid of certain objects than they are of others. Fear was conditioned in student volunteers using a variety of prepared conditioned stimuli (pictures of snakes or spiders) and unprepared stimuli (pictures of houses, faces, or flowers). The pictures were followed by a brief, painful electric shock. Fear conditioning, as measured by galvanic skin response (see Chapter 7), occurred much more rapidly to prepared stimuli than to unprepared ones. In fact, conditioning occurred in one pairing of electric shock with pictures of snakes and spiders, but it took four or five pairings for subjects' fear to be conditioned to faces, houses, or flowers. A subsequent experiment found the conditioning properties of guns to be similar to those for flowers, not snakes and spiders (Ohman, Fredrikson, Hugdahl, & Rimmo, 1976). Presumably, guns have not been around long enough for us to have become biologically prepared to develop phobias of them.

Viewing phobias as a form of prepared learning helps explain their irrationality and their resistance to extinction. With normal fear conditioning, once the unconditioned stimulus (for instance, the electric shock) is no longer paired with the conditioned stimulus, fear extinguishes rapidly. This does not appear to be the case for prepared fear conditioning. In one study, students were conditioned to fear either snakes and spiders or houses and faces by pairing each with shock. At the end of the conditioning (when the electrodes were removed), fear extinguished immediately to houses and faces but remained intense to snakes and spiders (Hugdahl & Ohman, 1977).

While some phobias appear to result from actual frightening experiences, others may be learned vicariously, through observation. Fearful parents tend to produce children who share their fears. A child who observes his or her parents react with fear to a variety of situations may accept such reactions as normal. Indeed, studies find a high correlation between the fears of a mother and those of her child.

As we will see in the next chapter, the treatment of phobias within the framework of learning theory uses various techniques to extinguish fear responses to the phobic object or situation.

**COGNITIVE PERSPECTIVE**  A cognitive analysis of anxiety disorders focuses on the way that anxious people think about situations and potential dangers. Individuals who suffer from generalized anxiety tend to make unrealistic appraisals of certain situations, primarily those in which the possibility of danger is remote. They consistently overestimate both the *degree* of harm and the *likelihood* of harm. This kind of mental set makes a person hypervigilant, always on the lookout for signs of danger. For example, a sudden noise in the house is interpreted as burglars; the screech of brakes in the street means one's child is in danger. This hypervigilance and expectation of harm result in continual bodily mobilization for danger. Thus, the physiological responses characteristic of the **fight-or-flight response** (tremors, rapid heart rate, clammy hands, muscle tension) are present much of the time.

The cognitive theory of obsessions assumes that we all have unwanted and repetitive thoughts on occasion. For example, song lyrics or advertising jingles often intrude unbidden into consciousness. But we are able to dismiss them, as well as the more abhorrent thoughts that occasionally run through our heads. The more anxiety-provoking the content of the obsession, the more difficult it is for anyone—obsessive or nonobsessive—to dismiss the thought. And the more stressed we are, the more frequent and intense are these thoughts. If a person is anxious to begin with, obsessive thoughts will be more disturbing and more difficult to dismiss.

If an event triggers a disturbing thought in a nonobsessive person, he or she may find the thought unacceptable but will not become anxious and will easily dismiss it. In contrast, the obsessive person will be made anxious by the thought, and the anxiety will reduce his or her ability to dismiss it. The thought will persist, and the obsessive's inability to disregard it will lead to further anxiety, which will increase his or her susceptibility to the intrusive thought.

Studies of obsessive-compulsive individuals have revealed that those persons hold unreasonable beliefs and assumptions. They believe that they (1) should be perfectly competent, (2) must avoid criticism or disapproval, and (3) will be severely punished for their mistakes and imperfections. At some level they also seem to believe that thinking certain thoughts or performing certain rituals will help them avoid the disastrous consequences that they imagine are just around the corner (Sarason & Sarason, 1989). Repetitive checking behaviors may be attempts to ensure that the task was done properly so that disaster is forestalled. Compulsive washing rituals may assure safety for the person obsessed with thoughts of disease and germs. These behaviors are reinforced by the relief from anxiety. But the relief is temporary. The obsessive thoughts return with increased frequency and intensity, and the individual must perform the ritual each time the thought recurs.

As we will see in the next chapter, the cognitive approach to treating obsessive disorders uses the technique of thought stopping to help the individual terminate obsessive thoughts. The treatment for generalized anxiety and phobias focuses on helping individuals develop more realistic and rational appraisals of themselves and the situations they encounter.

**BIOLOGICAL PERSPECTIVE**   Anxiety disorders tend to run in families. About 15 percent of parents and siblings of people who have anxiety disorders are similarly affected (Carey & Gottesman, 1981). This finding does not, of course, prove a hereditary basis for such disorders, since these individuals usually live together and thus experience similar environments. However, the results of twin studies provide firmer evidence for an inherited predisposition for panic attacks. Identical twins, as you recall, develop from the same egg and share the same heredity; fraternal twins develop from different eggs and are no more alike genetically than ordinary siblings. An identical twin is three times more likely to suffer from panic attacks if the other twin does than are fraternal twins (Torgersen, 1983).

Evidence for a biochemical basis for panic disorders comes from laboratory studies showing that a number of substances (including caffeine, sodium lactate, and the inhalation of a mixture of carbon dioxide and oxygen) can trigger panic attacks in individuals who suffer from spontaneous panic attacks. These same substances usually have no effect on normal individuals or on phobics who experience anxiety in response to an external stimulus (see McNally, 1990, for a review). In addition, scientists have identified a brain chemical (cholecystokinin) that will produce an attack in patients with panic disorders. Drugs that are capable of preventing panic attacks appear to block the effect of this chemical on neurons (Bradwejn, Koszycki, & Meterissian, 1990).

These and other data have convinced biological theorists that panic disorder is a disease of the body rather than a mental disorder. However, cognitive theorists are not so sure. They claim that panic disorder results from "catastrophic misinterpretation" of bodily sensations (Clark, 1988; Clark & Beck, 1988). For example, panic may arise when a person misinterprets rapid heartbeat and breathlessness as a sign of an impending heart attack or dizziness as a sign of a stroke. Catastrophic misinterpretation may also underlie panic attacks produced in the laboratory by the administration of sodium lactate or inhalation of an oxygen/carbon-dioxide mixture. These agents produce similar physiological effects in both panic patients and control subjects, yet only panic patients consistently respond with a panic attack (Yerazani, Balon, & Pohl, 1989).

What determines whether someone will panic in response to unusual bodily sensations? One possibility is that pre-existing beliefs about the harmfulness of such sensations may predispose individuals to interpret them catastrophically and thereby panic. If catastrophic misinterpretation is the cause of panic disorder, then teaching patients to correctly interpret their bodily sensations should cure the disorder. And apparently it does. In these treatment studies, patients brought to the clinic overbreathe (hyperventilate) into a bag. At first this will usually induce an immediate panic attack by producing shortness of breath. The patients are then taught to recognize that shortness of breath is simply the result of hyperventilating when they are under stress and not a sign of an impending heart attack or other catastrophe. Investigators using these treatment methods have reported complete reduction in panic attacks in almost all patients, with no relapse (Beck, 1988; Clark, 1988).

The debate about a specific biochemical cause for panic disorders remains to be resolved by further research. It is clear, however, that both biological and psychological factors play a role. Genetic research suggests that individuals may inherit a general anxiety proneness that manifests itself in various anxiety disorders, including panic disorders.

The chemical systems in the brain that regulate feelings of anxiety undoubtedly involve the complex interaction of a number of neurotransmitters acting on different brain areas. In 1960, a group of drugs called **benzodiazepines** were developed and marketed under such trade names as Valium and Librium. These drugs proved effective in reducing anxiety (see Chapter 17 for a discussion of their merits and disadvantages). Researchers subsequently discovered that the drugs were effective because they bind to specific receptor molecules in certain neurons of the brain, thereby influencing neural transmission (see Chapter 2). The discovery of receptor sites for antianxiety drugs set off a search for a natural body substance that might act in the same way to keep anxiety in proper balance. So far, a natural Val-

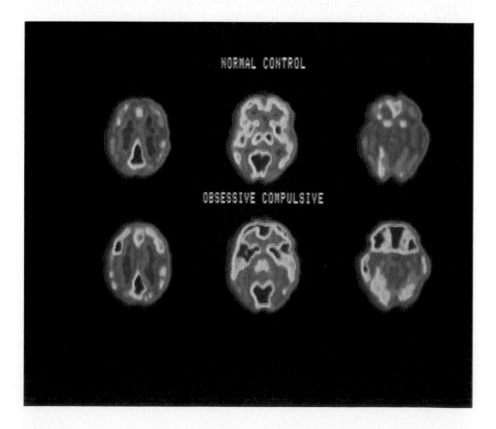

*PET scans reveal metabolic differences between the brain of an obsessive-compulsive patient and that of a normal subject. In the photos (three different cross-sections) red corresponds to the highest level of metabolic activity and blue to the lowest level. The obsessive-compulsive individual has elevated levels in several areas, including the basal ganglia.*

ium has not been found, but investigators have learned a great deal about the benzodiazepine receptors and how certain chemicals operate to increase or decrease anxiety (Costa, 1985).

There appear to be three specific docking areas on the benzodiazepine receptor site: one for the benzodiazepine molecule with its antianxiety effects, another for compounds that cause anxiety (the effects of which are blocked by administration of the benzodiazepines), and the third for a group of substances that block the effects of both the benzodiazepines and the anxiety-provoking compounds. The identification of these three receptor sites suggests that some substances secreted in the brain produce the subjective experience of fear and anxiety and other substances block this effect. The ratio of these substances may lead either to an emotionally stable or to an anxious individual (Agras, 1985).

The fact that head injuries, tumors, and encephalitis have all been associated with the development of obsessive-compulsive disorders has prompted the search for brain abnormalities that may make an individual vulnerable to repetitive thoughts and behaviors. PET scan studies (see Chapter 2) of obsessive-compulsive individuals have shown that the metabolic activity in a specific region of their brains (a circuit that runs between the frontal lobes and the basal ganglia) differs from that of normal individuals (Baxter et al., 1988). This region is believed to be involved in the brain's strategy for coping with repeated stimuli and in the control of repetitive movements. In essence, this part of the brain may play a role in telling the rest of the brain to stop worrying about contamination once the hands have been washed or about fire once the stove has been turned off. The exact nature of the brain chemistry abnormality is unknown, and such abnormalities may not be found in all cases of obsessive-compulsive disorders. Nevertheless, treatment with drugs that block the uptake of a neurotransmitter for which the basal ganglia have particularly dense receptors relieves obsessive-compulsive symptoms in about 60 percent of cases (Rapoport, 1989).

# Mood Disorders

In **mood disorders** the person may be severely depressed or manic (wildly elated), or may experience periods of depression as well as periods of mania. Mood disorders are divided into *depressive disorders*, in which the individual has one or more periods of depression without a history of manic episodes, and *bipolar disorders*, in which the individual alternates between periods of depression and periods of elation, usually with a return to normal mood in between the two extremes. Manic episodes without some history of depression are very uncommon.

## Depression

Almost everyone gets depressed at times. Most of us have periods when we feel sad, lethargic, and not interested in any activities—even pleasurable ones. **Depression** is a normal response to many of life's stresses. Among the situations that most often precipitate depression are failure at school or at work, the loss of a loved one, and the realization that illness or aging is depleting one's resources. Depression is considered abnormal only when it is out of proportion to the event and continues past the point at which most people begin to recover.

Although depression is characterized as a disorder of mood, there are actually four sets of symptoms. In addition to emotional (mood) symptoms, there are cognitive, motivational, and physical symptoms. An individual need not have all of these to be diagnosed as depressed, but the more symptoms he or she has, and the more intense they are, the more certain we can be that the individual is suffering from depression.

Sadness and dejection are the most salient emotional symptoms in depression. The individual feels hopeless and unhappy, often has crying spells, and may contemplate suicide. Equally pervasive in depression is the loss of gratification or pleasure in life. Activities that used to bring satisfaction seem dull and joyless. The depressed person gradually loses interest in hobbies, recreation, and family activities. Most depressed patients report that they no longer derive gratification from what had been major interests in life, and many report losing interest in and affection for other people.

The cognitive symptoms consist primarily of negative thoughts. Depressed individuals tend to have low self-esteem, feel inadequate, and blame themselves for their failures. They feel hopeless about the future and are pessimistic that they can do anything to improve their life.

Motivation is at a low ebb in depression. The depressed person tends to be passive and has difficulty initiating activities. The following conversation between a patient and his therapist illustrates this passivity. The man, who had been hospitalized after a suicide attempt, spent his days sitting motionless in the lounge. His therapist decided to try to engage him in some activities:

THERAPIST: I understand that you spend most of your day in the lounge. Is that true?

PATIENT: Yes, being quiet gives me the peace of mind I need.

THERAPIST: When you sit here, how's your mood?

PATIENT: I feel awful all the time. I just wish I could fall in a hole somewhere and die.

THERAPIST: Do you feel better after sitting for 2 or 3 hours?

PATIENT: No, the same.

THERAPIST: So you're sitting in the hope that you'll find peace of mind, but it doesn't sound like your depression improves.

PATIENT I get so bored.

THERAPIST: Would you consider being more active? There are a number of reasons why I think increasing your activity level might help.

PATIENT: There's nothing to do around here.

THERAPIST: Would you consider trying some activities if I could come up with a list?

PATIENT: If you think it will help, but I think you're wasting your time. I don't have any interests.

(Beck, Rush, Shaw, & Emery, 1979, p. 200)

The physical symptoms of depression include loss of appetite, sleep disturbances, fatigue, and loss of energy. Since a depressed person's thoughts are focused inward, rather than toward external events, he or she may magnify aches and pains and worry about health.

As we see from this description of its many symptoms, depression can be a debilitating disorder. Fortunately, most depressive episodes are of relatively short duration. Depressed people gradually recover, with or without treatment. About one-quarter of depressive episodes last less than a month, half last less than 3 months, and one-quarter last a year or longer. Only about 10 percent of the latter group do not recover and remain chronically depressed (Lewinsohn, Fenn, & Franklin, 1982). Unfortunately, depressive episodes tend to recur. About half the individuals who have a depressive episode will experience another one. Generally, the more stable a person is before the first episode, the less likely that depression will recur.

## Bipolar Disorders

The majority of depressions occur without episodes of mania. But between 5 and 10 percent of mood disorders involve both poles of the mood continuum and are classified as **bipolar disorders,** also known as **manic-depression.** The individual alternates between depression and normal mood and between extreme elation and normal mood. In some cases the cycle between depressive episodes and manic episodes is swift with only a brief return to normality in between.

People experiencing manic episodes behave in a way that appears, on the surface, to be the opposite of depression. During mild manic episodes, the individual is energetic, enthusiastic, and full of self-confidence. He or she talks continually, rushes from one activity to another with little need of sleep, and makes grandiose plans, paying little attention to their practicality. Unlike the kind if joyful exuberance that characterizes normal elation, manic behavior has a driven quality and often expresses hostility more than it does elation.

People experiencing severe manic episodes behave somewhat like the popular concept of a "raving maniac." They are extremely excited and constantly active. They may pace about, sing, shout, or pound the walls for hours. They are angered by attempts to interfere with their activities and

# Depression and Suicide

The most disastrous consequence of depression is suicide. Of the reported 25,000 people who end their lives by suicide in the United States every year, the majority are suffering from depression. However, since suicide deaths are underreported (due to the stigma attached and the fact that many accidental deaths are probably suicides), the number of actual suicides per year may well be closer to 50,000. The number of people who attempt suicide but fail has been estimated at anywhere from two to eight times the number of suicides (Shneidman, 1985).

Women attempt to commit suicide about three times more often than men do, but men succeed in killing themselves more often than women. The greater number of suicide attempts by women is probably related to the greater incidence of depression among women. The fact that men are more successful in their attempts is related to the choice of method. Until recently, women have tended to use less-lethal means, such as cutting their wrists or overdosing on sleeping pills; men are more apt to use firearms or carbon monoxide fumes or to hang themselves. However, with the marked increase in the number of women owning guns, suicide by firearms has now become the woman's method of first choice (Wintemute, Teret, Kraus, & Wright, 1988). Consequently, the fatality rate for women is changing. (Attempted suicides are successful 80 percent of the time when firearms are involved, while only 10 percent of drug or poison ingestions are fatal—a powerful argument for not keeping firearms in the home.)

Among the reasons most frequently cited by those who have attempted suicide are depression, loneliness, ill health, marital problems, and financial or job difficulties (Farberow & Shneidman, 1965; Shneidman, 1985).

While elderly people have traditionally had the highest rate of suicide, and still do, their rate has been decreasing. In contrast, the suicide rate among adolescents and young adults (traditionally low) has been increasing. In fact, the incidence of suicide among 15- to 24-year-olds in the United States has quadrupled over the last four decades. In a recent national survey of high school seniors, 27 percent reported they had "thought seriously" about killing themselves, and one in 12 said they had actually tried (Centers for Disease Control, 1991).

College students are twice as likely to kill themselves as are nonstudents of the same age (Murphy & Wetzel, 1980). The increased suicide rate among college students is found not only in the United States but in European countries, India, and Japan, as well. There are a number of possible reasons for the greater despair among college students: living away from home for the first time and having to cope with new problems; trying to stay at the top academically when the competition is much fiercer than it had been in high school; indecision about a career choice; loneliness caused by the absence of long-time friends and anxiety about new ones.

A study of the lives and academic records of college students who committed suicide found that they were moodier, drove themselves harder, and were depressed more frequently than their nonsuicidal classmates. They had also given recurrent warnings of their suicidal intent to others. The major precipitating events appear to have been worry about academic work and physical health and difficulties in their relationships with others (Seiden, 1966). However, we cannot be sure whether these factors caused the suicides or whether academic difficulties and interpersonal

may become abusive. Impulses (including sexual ones) are immediately expressed in actions or words. These individuals are confused and disoriented and may experience delusions of great wealth, accomplishment, or power.

Manic episodes can occur without depression, but this is very rare. Usually a depressive episode will occur eventually, once a person has experienced a manic episode. The depression is similar to what we have already described.

Bipolar disorders are relatively uncommon. Whereas about 6 percent of adult females and 3 percent of adult males in the United States have experienced a major depression at some time, less than 1 percent of the adult population has had a bipolar disorder, which appears to be equally common in men and women. Manic-depression differs from other mood disorders in that it tends to occur at an earlier age, is more likely to run in families, responds to different therapeutic medications, and is apt to recur unless treated. These facts suggest that biological variables play a more important role than psychological variables in bipolar disorders.

problems were secondary to a severe depression.

It may be that college students who contemplate suicide never learned how to deal with personal problems and emotions before going to college. One study, for example, found that students with suicidal thoughts were not faced with more stressful situations than other students but had fewer resources for dealing with problems and intense emotions (Carson & Johnson, 1985).

Suicidal college students, on the average, have higher records of academic achievement than their nonsuicidal classmates, whereas most adolescents who commit suicide have exceptionally poor high-school records. Suicidal teenagers tend to be dropouts or to have behavior problems in school, although a few are academically gifted students who feel pressure to be perfect and to stay at the top of the class (Leroux, 1986).

The outstanding characteristic of adolescents who attempt suicide is social isolation: they describe themselves as loners, most have parents who were divorced or separated, a large number have alcoholic parents, and they report little parental affection (Berman & Jobes, 1991; Rohn et al., 1977).

A major factor contributing to suicide, in addition to depression, is drug abuse. For example, one study of 283 suicides found that nearly 60 percent were drug abusers and 84 percent abused both alcohol and other drugs (Rich, Fowler, Fogarty, & Young, 1988). It is not clear if the drug abuse caused these people to become depressed and kill themselves or if they turned to drugs as a way of coping with depression and killed themselves when the drugs did not help. But in many of the cases drug abuse appears to have preceded the psychological problems.

Young drug abusers (under age 30) who committed suicide had a greater than expected frequency of intense interpersonal conflict or the loss of a spouse or romantic partner in the weeks prior to killing themselves. They may have felt that they had lost their only source of support. And they might have been able to handle the stress without resorting to suicide had their personal resources not been depleted by drug use.

Some individuals commit suicide because they find their emotional distress intolerable and see no solution to their problems other than death. Their sole motivation is to end their life. In other cases, the person does not really wish to die but seeks to impress others with the seriousness of his or her dilemma. The suicide attempt is motivated by a desire to communicate feelings of despair and to change the behavior of other people. Examples would be a woman who takes an overdose of sleeping pills when her lover threatens to leave or a student who does the same when pressured by his parents to achieve beyond his abilities. The suicide attempt is a cry for help.

Some experts use the term *parasuicide* for nonfatal acts in which a person deliberately causes self-injury or ingests a substance in excess of any prescribed or generally recognized therapeutic dosage (Kreitman, 1977). The term "parasuicide" is preferred to "suicide attempt" because it does not necessarily imply a wish to die. As noted earlier, there are many more parasuicides than suicides. However, most people who commit suicidal acts are experiencing such turmoil and stress that their thinking is far from clear. They are not sure whether they want to live or die; they want to do both at the same time, usually one more than the other. Since the best predictor of a future suicide is a prior attempt, all parasuicides should be taken seriously. Few people commit suicide without signaling their intentions to someone. Thus, a person who talks about suicide may actually attempt it. Many communities have established suicide-prevention centers where troubled individuals can seek help, either through telephone contact or in person.

## Understanding Mood Disorders

Depression is one of the most prevalent emotional disorders. Because depression is so common and can be so debilitating, much effort has been devoted to determining its causes. We will look briefly at several approaches to understanding affective disorders.

**PSYCHOANALYTIC PERSPECTIVE** Psychoanalytic theories interpret depression as a *reaction to loss*. Whatever the nature of the loss (rejection by a loved one, loss of status, loss of moral support provided by a group of friends), the depressed person reacts to it intensely because the current situation brings back all the fears of an earlier loss that occurred in childhood—that being the loss of parental affection. For some reason, the individual's needs for affection and care were not satisfied in childhood. A loss in later life causes the individual to regress to his or her helpless, dependent state when the original loss occurred. Part of the depressed person's behavior, therefore, represents a cry for love—a display of helplessness and an appeal for affection and security (White & Watt, 1981).

Reaction to loss is complicated by angry feelings toward the deserting person. An underlying assumption of psychoanalytic theories is that people who are prone to depression have learned to repress their hostile feelings because they are afraid of alienating those on whom they depend for support. When things go wrong, they turn their anger inward and blame themselves. For example, a woman may feel extremely hostile toward the employer who fired her. But because her anger arouses anxiety, she uses the defense mechanism of projection to internalize her feelings: she is not angry; rather, others are angry at her. She assumes the employer had a good reason for rejecting her: she is incompetent and worthless.

Psychoanalytic theories suggest that the depressed person's low self-esteem and feelings of worthlessness stem from a childlike need for parental approval. A small child's self-esteem depends on the approval and affection of the parents. But as a person matures, feelings of worth also should be derived from the individual's sense of his or her own accomplishments and effectiveness. The self-esteem of a person prone to depression depends primarily on external sources: the approval and support of others. When these supports fail, the individual may be thrown into a state of depression.

Psychoanalytic theories of depression, therefore, focus on loss, overdependence on external approval, and internalization of anger. They seem to provide a reasonable explanation for some of the behaviors exhibited by depressed individuals, but they are difficult to prove or to refute. Some studies indicate that people who are prone to depression are more likely than the average person to have lost a parent in early life (Roy, 1981; Barnes & Prosen, 1985). But parental loss (through death or separation) is also found in the case histories of people who suffer from other types of mental disorders, and most people who suffer such a loss do not develop emotional problems in adulthood (Tennant, Smith, Bebbington, & Hurry, 1981).

**BEHAVIORAL PERSPECTIVE** Learning theorists assume that lack of reinforcement plays a major role in depression. The inactivity of the depressed person and the feelings of sadness are due to a low rate of positive reinforcement and/or a high rate of unpleasant experiences (Lewinsohn, Hoberman, Teri, & Hautziner, 1985; Lewinsohn, Mischel, Chaplin, & Barton, 1980). Many of the events that precipitate depression (such as the death of a loved one, loss of a job, or impaired health) reduce accustomed reinforcement. In addition, people prone to depression may lack the social skills either to attract positive reinforcement or to cope effectively with aversive events.

Once people become depressed and inactive, their main source of reinforcement is the sympathy and attention they receive from relatives and friends. This attention may initially reinforce the very behaviors that are maladaptive (weeping, complaining, criticizing themselves, talking about suicide). But because it is tiresome to be around someone who refuses to cheer up, the depressed person's behavior eventually alienates even close associates, producing a further reduction in reinforcement and increasing the individual's social isolation and unhappiness. A low rate of positive reinforcement further reduces the individual's activities and the expression of behaviors that might be rewarded. Both activities and rewards decrease in a vicious cycle.

**COGNITIVE PERSPECTIVE** Cognitive theories of depression focus not on what people *do* but on how they view themselves and the world. One of the most influential cognitive theories, developed by Aaron Beck, is derived from extensive therapeutic experience with depressed patients (Beck, 1976; Beck, 1991; Beck, Rush, Shaw, & Emery, 1979). Beck was struck by how consistently these patients appraise events from a negative and self-critical viewpoint. They expect to fail rather than to succeed, and they tend to magnify failures and minimize successes in evaluating their performance. When things go wrong, they tend to blame themselves rather than the circumstances.

As we noted in Chapter 11, people's appraisals of a situation can determine their emotions (see p. 424). We all constantly appraise and evaluate what happens to us and what we do. Sometimes we are aware of our appraisals, but other times we are not. It seemed to Beck that the negative thoughts of depressed individuals tended to arise quickly and automatically, as though by reflex, and were not subject to conscious control. Such thoughts were usually followed by unpleasant emotions (sadness, despair) of which the patients were very much aware, even though they were unaware of, or barely aware of, the preceding automatic thoughts. Later, in working with more severely depressed patients, Beck noted that the negative thoughts were no longer peripheral but occupied a dominant place in consciousness and were repetitive (Beck, 1991).

Beck grouped the negative thoughts of depressed individuals into three categories, which he called the **cognitive triad**: negative thoughts about the self, about present experiences, and about the future. Negative thoughts about the self (a negative self-schema) consist of the depressed person's belief that he is worthless and inadequate. Any present misfortune is blamed on these personal inadequacies or defects. Even in ambiguous situations, where there are more plausible explanations for why things went wrong, the depressed person will blame himself. The depressed person's negative view of the future is one of hopelessness. He believes that his inadequacies and defects will prevent him from ever improving his situation.

Beck proposes that the depressed person's negative self-schema ("I am worthless," "I can't do anything right," "I am unlovable") is formed during childhood or adolescence through such experiences as loss of a parent, social rejection by peers, criticism by parents or teachers, or a series of tragedies. These negative beliefs are activated whenever a new situation resembles in some way, perhaps only remotely, the conditions in which the beliefs were learned, and depression may result. Moreover, according to Beck, depressed individuals make some systematic errors in thinking (cognitive distortions) that lead them to misperceive reality in a way that contributes to their negative self-schema. These cognitive distortions are listed in Table 16-4. Note that the same distortions could be used by a person who has a positive self-schema to *enhance* his view of himself. But for the depressed person, these errors in thinking, confirm his view that he is unworthy and responsible for calamities. As we will see in Chapter 17, cognitive therapy for depression attempts to identify and correct the individual's distorted thinking.

Another cognitive approach to depression, which focuses on the kinds of attributions, or causal explanations, that people make when bad things happen, was discussed in Chapter 15 (p. 598). This theory proposes that people who characteristically attribute negative events to causes that are internal ("it's my fault") are stable over time ("it's going to last forever"), and affect many areas of their lives ("it will impact everything I do") are more prone to

**OVERGENERALIZATION** Drawing a sweeping conclusion on the basis of a single event. For example, a student concludes from his poor performance in one class on a particular day that he is inept and stupid.

**SELECTIVE ABSTRACTION** Focusing on an insignificant detail while ignoring the more important features of a situation. For example, from a conversation in which her boss praises her overall job performance, a secretary remembers the only comment that could be construed as mildly critical.

**MAGNIFICATION AND MINIMIZATION** Magnifying small bad events and minimizing major good events in evaluating performance. For example, a woman gets a small dent in her car fender and views it as a catastrophe (magnification) while the fact that she gave an excellent presentation in class does nothing to raise her self-esteem (minimization).

**PERSONALIZATION** Incorrectly assuming responsibility for bad events in the world. For example, when rain dampens spirits at an outdoor buffet, the host blames himself rather than the weather.

**ARBITRARY INFERENCE** Drawing a conclusion when there is little evidence to support it. For example, a man concludes from his wife's sad expression that she is disappointed in him; if he had checked out the situation, he would have discovered she was distressed by her friend's illness.

**TABLE 16-4**
**Cognitive Distortions in Depression**
*According to Beck's theory, these are the principle errors in thinking that characterize depressed individuals.*

depression than individuals who have a less pessimistic attributional style (Abramson et al., 1978; Peterson and Seligman, 1984). The theory does not claim that attributional style alone is enough to cause depression. A pessimistic attributional style is important only when a person encounters intense or frequent negative events in his or her life (Abramson, Metalsky, and Alloy, 1989).

Cognitive theories of depression have stimulated a great deal of research. The results of some studies have been supportive, while others raise questions (see Haaga, Dyck, & Ernst, 1991 for a review). Depressed individuals score consistently higher on scales designed to measure negative thinking than do nondepressed people (both normal subjects and those suffering from mental disorders other than depression). And their negative thinking does encompass the three aspects of Beck's cognitive triad—the self, the present, and the future. However, evidence that depressive thinking is especially inaccurate or illogical is weak. It is not clear that only those who are depressed distort information and evaluate themselves in illogical ways. Although depressed individuals are consistently pessimistic, in some instances they seem to perceive reality more accurately than normals (see the Critical Discussion on Illusion and Well-Being). In addition, the extent to which self-critical attitudes and/or a pessimistic attributional style *precede* rather than *accompany* a depressed episode is also unclear. A number of studies using mildly depressed individuals as subjects (mostly college students) have found a relationship between a pessimistic explanatory style and the degree of depression experienced when faced with bad events (Peterson and Seligman, 1984). However, studies of severely depressed, hospitalized patients found that depressive cognitions accompany depression but are *not* apparent after a depressive episode. Once the patient's depression had lifted, they did not differ from control subjects (who had never been depressed) in the way they interpreted bad events (Fennell and Campbell, 1984; Hamilton and Abramson, 1983). Thus a pessimistic attributional style may be a *symptom* rather than a *cause* of depression. It is an important symptom, however, because the intensity of a patient's negative beliefs does predict the speed of recovery from a period of depression (Brewin, 1985).

The way a person interprets bad events may be less important for the development of depression than is the belief that one has control over one's life. We noted in Chapter 15 that stressful situations are less disturbing if the individual believes that he or she can exert some control over them. Confidence in one's ability to cope with bad events may increase resistance to depression (Abramson, Metalsky, & Alloy, 1989).

**BIOLOGICAL PERSPECTIVE** A tendency to develop mood disorders, particularly bipolar disorders, appears to be inherited. Evidence from twin studies shows that if one identical twin is diagnosed as manic-depressive, there is a 72 percent chance that the other twin will suffer from the same disorder. The corresponding figure for fraternal twins is only 14 percent. These figures, called *concordance rates*, represent the likelihood that both twins will have a specific characteristic, given that one of the twins has the characteristic. The concordance rate for identical twins suffering from depression (40 percent) also exceeds the rate for fraternal twins (11 percent), but the difference between these two rates is much less than is the difference between the rates for manic-depressive twins (Allen, 1976). This comparison indicates that bipolar disorders are more closely related to genetic factors than are depressive disorders.

The specific role that genetic factors play in mood disorders is far from clear. However, it seems likely that a biochemical abnormality is involved. Mounting evidence indicates that our moods are regulated by the **neurotransmitters** that transmit nerve impulses from one neuron to another (see Chapter 2). A number of chemicals serve as neurotransmitters in different parts of the nervous system, and normal behavior requires a careful balance among them. Two neurotransmitters believed to play an important role in mood disorders are **norepinephrine** and **serotonin.** Both of these neurotransmitters, which belong to a class of compounds called *biogenic amines*, are localized in areas of the brain that regulate emotional behavior (the limbic system and the hypothalamus). A widely accepted hypothesis is that depression is associated with a deficiency of one or both of these neurotransmitters and that mania is associated with an excess of one or both of them. However, the evidence is indirect, based largely on the effects that certain drugs have on behavior and on neurotransmitter activity. For example, the drug reserpine, which is used to treat high blood pressure, sometimes produces severe depression as a side effect. Animal research has shown that the drug causes a decrease in the brain levels of serotonin and norepinephrine. In contrast, amphetamines (or "speed"), which produce an emotional high, facilitate the release of both of these neurotransmitters. (However, amphetamines are *not* useful in treating depression, for several reasons.)

Drugs that are effective in relieving depression increase the availability of both norepinephrine and serotonin in the nervous system. Two major classes of antidepressant drugs act in different ways to increase neurotransmitter levels. The **monoamine oxidase** (MAO) **inhibitors** block the activity of an enzyme that can destroy both norepinephrine and serotonin, thereby increasing the concentration of these two neurotransmitters in the brain. The **tricyclic antidepressants** prevent *reuptake* (the process by which neurotransmitters are taken back by the nerve terminals from which they were released) of serotonin and norepinephrine, thereby prolonging the duration of their activity. Since these drugs affect both serotonin and norepinephrine, it is difficult to distinguish between the roles of these two neurotransmitters in depressive disorders. Some studies indicate that serotonin plays the major role; others imply that norepinephrine does. It is possible that each neurotransmitter may be involved but in different subtypes of depression.

Research using new techniques is studying the long-term effects of antidepressants on the neuron's postsynaptic receptors. Antidepressant drugs require time to be effective: both tricyclics and MAO inhibitors take from 1 to 3 weeks before they begin to relieve the symptoms of depression. These observations do not fit with the discovery that the drugs, when they are first taken, increase norepinephrine and serotonin levels only temporarily; after several days, the neurotransmitters return to their previous levels. Thus, an increase in norepinephrine or serotonin per se cannot be the mechanism that relieves depression. Preliminary evidence indicates that these antidepressants increase the sensitivity of both norepinephrine and serotonin postsynaptic receptors. The time frame within which this occurs corresponds well with the course of drug action on symptoms (Charney & Heninger, 1983; Charney, Heninger, & Sternberg, 1984). Thus, even though the patient's levels of norepinephrine or serotonin are low once again, they may be able to use these neurotransmitters more effectively because the receptors receiving them have become more sensitive.

The neurotransmitter systems that regulate mood and emotion are

## Illusion and Well-Being

In discussing cognitive theories of depression, we noted that depressed individuals appraise themselves and the world from a negative viewpoint. They are self-critical, expect to fail rather than succeed, magnify failures and minimize successes in evaluating their performance, and are pessimistic about the future. An ironic possibility is that their appraisals may be closer to reality than those of nondepressed individuals. Those of us who are not depressed may suffer from illusions: we may look at ourselves and the world through rose-colored glasses.

Numerous studies indicate that most people have (a) unrealistically positive views of themselves, (b) exaggerated perceptions of how much control they have over events, and (c) unrealistic optimism about the future (Taylor & Brown, 1988). For example, when asked to indicate how accurately positive and negative personality adjectives describe themselves, normal subjects judged positive traits to be overwhelmingly more characteristic of themselves than negative attributes (Brown, 1986). In addition, most people recall positive information about themselves more readily than negative information (Kuiper, Olinger, MacDonald & Shaw, 1985); recall successes more often than failures (Silverman, 1964); tend to recall their performance on a task as better than it actually was (Crary, 1966); and attribute positive outcomes to their own ability and negative outcomes to chance factors (Zuckerman, 1979b). When college students, who were interacting on a group task, rated themselves along a number of personality dimensions (for example, friendly, assertive), their ratings were significantly more positive than the ratings of observers who had watched the group interaction (Lewinsohn, Mischel, Chaplin, & Barton, 1980).

Moreover, there seems to be a pervasive tendency to see oneself as better than others. Individuals judge positive personality traits to be *more* descriptive of themselves than of the average person, but see negative personality attributes as *less* descriptive of themselves than of the average person (Brown, 1986). This effect has been documented for a wide range of traits; individuals even believe that their driving ability is superior to others (Svenson, 1981). Because it is logically impossible for most people to be better than the average, these positive views of the self are unrealistic and illusory.

---

incredibly complex, and we are only beginning to understand them. The fact that some of the newest drugs that have proved successful in relieving depression do not appear to influence serotonin and norepinephrine levels suggests that other neurotransmitter systems are also involved. Several neurotransmitter systems, acting alone or in combination, may be responsible for depressive symptoms (McNeal & Cimbolic, 1986). And bipolar disorders may involve the malfunctioning of yet a different neurotransmitter system (Depue & Iacono, 1989).

There is no doubt that mood disorders involve biochemical changes in the nervous system. The unresolved question is whether the physiological changes are the cause or the result of the psychological changes. For example, people who deliberately behave as if they were experiencing a manic episode exhibit changes in neurotransmitter levels similar to those found among actual manic patients (Post, Kotin, Goodwin, & Gordon, 1973). The depletion of norepinephrine may cause certain kinds of depression, but an earlier link in the causal chain leading to depression may be feelings of helplessness or loss of emotional support.

**VULNERABILITY AND STRESS** All of the theories we have discussed make important points about the nature of depression. Inherited physiological characteristics may predispose an individual to extreme mood changes. Early experiences (the loss of parental affection or the inability to gain gratification through one's own efforts) may also make a person vulnerable to depression in later life. The kinds of stressful events that depressed patients report precipitated their disorder are usually within the range of normal life experiences; they are experiences most people can handle without becom-

*Being poor or having young children increases one's vulnerability to depression.*

Similarly, studies have shown that most people believe they have more control over situations than they actually do. For example, people believe that they have greater control if they personally throw the dice than if someone else does it for them (Fleming & Darley, 1986). People overestimate their degree of control over events that are largely determined by chance: when an expected outcome occurs, they often overestimate the degree to which they were instrumental in bringing it about (Miller & Ross, 1975).

Most people are more optimistic about the future than reality warrants. When college students were asked what was possible for them in the future, they reported four times as many positive as negative possibilities (Markus & Nurius, 1986). People estimated the likelihood that they would experience a variety of pleasant events (such as getting a high-salaried job or having a gifted child) as higher than those of their peers (Weinstein, 1980). Conversely, when asked about their chances of experiencing negative events (a car accident, becoming ill), most people believed they are *less* likely than their peers to do so (Kuiper, MacDonald, & Deery, 1983).

To summarize, most of us have unrealistically positive views of ourselves, an exaggerated belief in our ability to control our environment, and a belief that our future will be better than that of the average person. These positive illusions enable us to cope with an uncertain, and sometimes frightening, world. They provide the motivation to persist in the face of obstacles, and they help us avoid depression.

Traditional views of mental health assert that well-adjusted individuals possess accurate perceptions of themselves and of their ability to control events in their lives. Indeed, the description of normality presented earlier in this chapter includes *efficient perception of reality* as one of the criteria that distinguishes between a normal person and one who is diagnosed as abnormal. The evidence presented here indicates that this criterion should be modified.

Clearly, we need to perceive what is going on in the world and what other people say and do with some degree of accuracy. Nevertheless, positive illusions about our personal qualities and about our ability to control events appear to make us happier, more optimistic, and more willing to undertake challenges. Such illusions may be especially adaptive under circumstances that tend to produce depression. The belief in ourselves as competent and effective, facing a future that is generally positive helps in overcoming setbacks and blows to our self-esteem (Taylor & Brown, 1988).

ing abnormally depressed. Thus, the concept of vulnerability is helpful in understanding why some people develop depression but others do not when confronted with a particular stressful experience.

Some additional factors that have been found to increase vulnerability to depression include having few social skills, being poor, being very dependent on others, having children under the age of 7, and not having a close and intimate confidant. The last of these appears to be the most important, at least for women, since it has been the most consistently identified over various studies (Bebbington, Sturt, Tennant, & Hurry, 1984; Brown & Harris, 1978; Campbell, Cope, & Teasdale, 1983). Having an intimate, confiding relationship with a husband or friend decreased the risk of a woman's becoming depressed when confronted with a stressful life situation. This is consistent with the research (discussed in Chapter 15) indicating that social supports help to buffer the severity of stressful events.

Depression has many causes, which may range from being determined almost entirely by an inherited biochemical abnormality to being exclusively the result of psychological or environmental factors. Most cases fall in between the two extremes and involve a mixture of genetic, early developmental, and environmental factors.

# Schizophrenia

**Schizophrenia** is the label applied to a group of disorders characterized by severe personality disorganization, distortion of reality, and an inability to function in daily life. It occurs in all cultures, even those that are remote from the stresses of industrialized civilization, and appears to have plagued humanity for at least 200 years. The

## Box 2
## *Schizophrenia*

WG, a handsome, athletic-looking youth of 19, was admitted to the psychiatric service on the referral of his family physician. The boy's parents said, on his admission, that their son's behavior during the previous several months had changed drastically. He had been an adequate student in high school, but he had had to leave college recently because he was failing all his subjects. He had excelled in a variety of nonteam sports—swimming, weight-lifting, track—winning several letters, but now he did not exercise at all. Although he had always been careful about his health and had hardly ever mentioned any physical problems, within the past several weeks he had repeatedly expressed vague complaints about his head and chest, which, he said, indicated that he was

"in very bad shape." During the past several days, the patient had spent most of his time sitting in his room, staring vacantly out of his window. He had become (quite uncharacteristically) careless about his personal appearance and habits.

Although there was no doubt that the patient had exhibited serious recent changes in behavior, further conversation with the parents indicated that the patient's childhood and adolescent adjustment had not been healthy. He had always been painfully shy, except in highly structured situations, and had spent much of his free time alone (often working out with weights). He had no really close friends. . . .

The personnel of the psychiatric service found it difficult to converse with the patient; an ordinary diagnostic interview was impossible. For the most part, the boy volunteered no information. He would usually answer direct questions, but often in a flat, toneless way devoid of emotional coloring. Frequently, his answers were

not logically connected to the questions. Observers often found it taxing to record their conversations with the patient. After speaking to him for a while, they would find themselves wondering just what the conversation had been about.

At times, the disharmony between the content of the patient's words and his emotional expression was striking. For example, while speaking sympathetically of an acute illness that had rendered his mother bedridden during a portion of the previous fall, the boy giggled constantly.

At times, WG became agitated and spoke with a curious intensity. On one occasion, he spoke of "electrical sensations" and "an electrical current" in his brain. On another, he revealed that when lying awake at night, he often heard a voice repeating the command, "You'll have to do it." The patient felt that he was somehow being influenced by a force outside himself to commit an act of violence—as yet undefined—directed at his parents (Hofling, 1975, pp. 372–373).

disorder affects about 1 percent of the population, occurs equally in men and women, and usually appears in late adolescence or early adulthood (most cases have their onset between the ages of 15 and 35). Those labeled schizophrenic usually require hospitalization, sometimes for months or years. At any given time, this diagnostic group occupies about half of the beds in mental hospitals and constitutes a large proportion of outpatients. Sometimes schizophrenia develops slowly as a gradual process of increasing seclusiveness and inappropriate behavior. Sometimes the onset of schizophrenia is sudden, marked by intense confusion and emotional turmoil; such acute cases are usually precipitated by a period of stress in individuals whose lives have tended toward isolation, self-preoccupation, and feelings of insecurity. The case described in Box 2 seems to fall into the latter category, although it lacks the intensity of onset that sometimes occurs.

## Characteristics of Schizophrenia

Whether schizophrenia develops slowly or suddenly, the symptoms are many and varied. The primary characteristics of schizophrenia can be summarized under the following headings, although not every person diagnosed as suffering from the disorder will exhibit all of these symptoms.

**DISTURBANCES OF THOUGHT AND ATTENTION** Whereas affective disorders are characterized by disturbances of mood, schizophrenia is characterized by disturbances of *thought*. Both the *process* of thinking and the *content* of thought may be disordered. The following excerpt from a patient's writings illustrates how difficult it is to understand schizophrenic thinking.

> If things turn by rotation of agriculture or levels in regards and timed to everything; I am referring to a previous document when I made some remarks that were facts also tested and there is another that concerns my daughter she has a lobed bottom right ear, her name being Mary Lou. Much of abstraction has been left unsaid and undone in these productmilk syrup, and others, due to economics, differentials, subsidies, bankruptcy, tools, buildings, bonds, national stocks, foundation craps, weather, trades, government in levels of breakages and fuses in electronics too all formerly states not necessarily factuated. (Maher, 1966, p. 395)

By themselves, the words and phrases make sense, but they are meaningless in relation to each other. The juxtaposition of unrelated words and phrases and the idiosyncratic word associations (sometimes called a "word salad") are characteristic of schizophrenic writing and speech. They reflect a *loosening of associations* in which the individual's ideas shift from one topic to another in ways that appear unrelated. Moreover, a schizophrenic's train of thought often seems influenced by the *sound* of words rather than by their meaning. The following account by a schizophrenic patient of her thoughts in response to her doctor's questions illustrates this tendency to form associations by rhyming words.

| | |
|---|---|
| DOCTOR: | How about the medication? Are you still taking the Haldol? (an antipsychotic drug) |
| PATIENT THINKS: | *Foul Wall.* She nods but does not reply. |
| DOCTOR: | What about the vitamins? |
| PATIENT THINKS: | *Seven sins. Has-beens.* She nods. |
| DOCTOR: | I don't think you're taking all your meds. |
| PATIENT THINKS: | *Pencil leads.* |

(North, 1987, p. 261)

The confused thought processes that are the hallmark of schizophrenia seem to stem from a general difficulty in focusing attention and filtering out irrelevant stimuli. Most of us are able to focus our attention selectively. From a mass of incoming sensory information, we are able to select the stimuli that are relevant to the task at hand and to ignore the rest. A person who suffers from schizophrenia is perceptually receptive to many stimuli at the same time and has trouble making sense of the profusion of inputs, as the following statement by a schizophrenic patient illustrates.

> I can't concentrate. It's diversions of attention that trouble me. I am picking up different conversations. It's like being a transmitter. The sounds are coming through to me, but I feel my mind cannot cope with everything. It's difficult to concentrate on any one sound. (McGhie & Chapman, 1961, p. 104)

A sense of being unable to control one's attention and to focus one's thoughts is central to the experience of schizophrenia.

In addition to the disorganized thought processes that make it difficult to understand what a schizophrenic is trying to say are disturbances in the *content* of thought. Most individuals suffering from schizophrenia show a *lack of insight.* When asked what is wrong or why they are hospitalized, they seem to have no appreciation of their condition and little realization that their behavior is unusual. They are also subject to **delusions,** holding beliefs that most people would disagree with or view as misinterpretations of reality. The most common delusions are beliefs that external forces are trying to control the individual's thoughts and actions. These *delusions of influence* include the belief that one's thoughts are being broadcast to the world so that others can hear them, that strange thoughts (not one's own) are being inserted into the individual's mind, or that feelings and actions are being imposed on the person by some external force. Also frequent are beliefs that certain people or certain groups are threatening or plotting against the individual (*delusions of persecution*). Less common are beliefs that the person is powerful and important (*delusions of grandeur*).

A person who has persecutory delusions is called **paranoid.** He or she may become suspicious of friends and relatives, may fear being poisoned, or may complain of being watched, followed, and talked about. So-called motiveless crimes, when an individual attacks or kills someone for no apparent cause, are sometimes committed by people who are later diagnosed as suffering from paranoid schizophrenia.

**DISTURBANCES OF PERCEPTION** During acute schizophrenic episodes, people often report that the world appears *different* to them (noises seem louder; colors, more intense). Their own bodies may no longer appear the same (their hands may seem to be too large or too small; their legs, overly extended; their eyes, dislocated in the face). Some patients fail to recognize themselves in a mirror or see their reflection as a triple image. The most dramatic disturbances of perception are called **hallucinations,** sensory experiences in the absence of relevant or adequate external stimulation. Auditory hallucinations (usually voices telling the person what to do or commenting on his or her actions) are the most common. Visual hallucinations

*German psychiatrist Hans Prinzhorn is responsible for the most extensive collection of artwork by mental patients available. This painting from the collection, by August Neter, illustrates the hallucinations and paranoid fantasies from which many schizophrenic patients suffer.*

(such as seeing strange creatures or heavenly beings) are somewhat less frequent. Other sensory hallucinations (a bad odor emanating from the individual's body, the taste of poison in food, the feeling of being pricked by needles) occur infrequently. Hallucinations may occur independently or as part of a delusional belief. An example would be a patient who hears voices threatening to kill him and believes they are part of a plot to eliminate him because of his supernatural powers.

In one sense, hallucinations are not that far removed from ordinary experiences. We all know what visual hallucinations are like because we have them in dreams. But for most people dreams only occur during REM sleep (see Chapter 6), not while awake. It is possible that some sort of neurotransmitter-mediated process inhibits dreams during the waking state and that this process has failed in schizophrenics who hallucinate (Assad and Shapiro, 1986).

Auditory hallucinations may have their origin in ordinary thought. We often carry on internal dialogues, for example, commenting on our actions or having an imaginary conversation with another person. We may even on occasion talk to ourselves aloud. The voices that schizophrenic patients hear, calling them bad names or telling them what to do, are similar to internal dialogues. But the patient experiencing an auditory hallucination does not believe that the voices originate within the self or that they can be controlled. "The inability to distinguish between external and internal, real and imagined, controllable and imposed, is central to the schizophrenic experience" (Rosenhan & Seligman, 1989).

**DISTURBANCES OF AFFECT** Schizophrenic individuals usually fail to exhibit normal emotional responses. They often are withdrawn and unresponsive in situations that should make them sad or happy. For example, a man may show no emotional response when informed that his daughter has cancer. However, this blunting of emotional expression can conceal inner turmoil, and the person may erupt with angry outbursts.

Sometimes the schizophrenic individual expresses emotions that are inappropriately linked to the situation or to the thought being expressed. For instance, a patient may smile while speaking of tragic events. Since our emotions are influenced by cognitive processes, it is not surprising that disorganized thoughts and perceptions are accompanied by changes in emotional responses. This point is illustrated by the following comment of a schizophrenic patient.

> Half the time I am talking about one thing and thinking about half a dozen other things at the same time. It must look queer to people when I laugh about something that has got nothing to do with what I am talking about, but they don't know what's going on inside and how much of it is running around in my head. You see I might be talking about something quite serious to you and other things come into my head at the same time that are funny and this makes me laugh. If I could only concentrate on one thing at the one time I wouldn't look half so silly. (McGhie & Chapman, 1961, p. 104)

**MOTOR SYMPTOMS AND WITHDRAWAL FROM REALITY** Schizophrenic patients often show bizarre motor activity. They may grimace or adopt strange facial expressions. They may gesture repeatedly using peculiar sequences of finger, hand, and arm movements. Some may become very agitated and move about in continual activity, as in a manic state. Some, at the other extreme, may become totally unresponsive and immobile, adopting an

Box 3

# Psychotic Episode

This account is by a schizophrenic patient who recovered and later became a psychiatrist. Her descriptions of her thoughts and emotions, drawn from memory and a diary, are interspersed with excerpts from her medical records (North, 1987, pp. 282–284).

*The helicopters. Oh no, not the helicopters. Have come to tear the feathers out of my frontal lobes. Help me, nurse, help me, can't you hear them? Gotta get back into my body to save it. Am so far away. Out of reach of the neural connections. The doctor is thinking I would make good glue. He is a witch doctor. He is sending radio messages to the helicopters to help them find me.*

Dr. Kopetti observed:

. . . still catatonic at this time. Totally unresponsive. . . . I would wonder if she'll be able to cope with the pressures of school again. . . . she apparently does not respond to antipsychotic agents and has a low threshold for extrapyramidal symptoms [muscular side effects].

*Big pieces are cracking off the edge of my consciousness. I will never be back. The universe disappears with one slight wave of my hand.*

A nurse observed in my chart:

Data: patient acting out in response to voices, i.e., posturing, crying out. States she's frightened, refused to undress for sleep for fear of needing to get out of room quickly. . . . was found standing in one place for long periods of time, eyes wide open, staring. . . . patient standing in room facing wall, arms outstretched to wall. . . . was not responsive to verbalization, responded with blank stare. . . . frequently pacing around room suspiciously, jumps when others approach her. Several times said, "Am I dead?" Seemed out of touch with her body at times, holding her hands in angular positions.

*The pendulum has swung to the far side where everything dissipates into everything. It can't swing back. I am scared of the change. I am scared to move.*
*"Would you like to be made into hotdog meat?" Ah, the voices. Where have they been? I must be on track again.*
*"Hotdogs for lunch!"*
*My head splits down the middle, brains falling out all over the floor, and I put out an awkward hand to catch them. They slip right through my metal fingers. Do they put brain meat in hotdogs?*
*"You can put down your hand, Carol. You don't have to hold it there." Had the nurse said that or had I said it? Or had the voices said it? Or was it a slice from another Dimension?*
*Hand back to my side. Try to think straight. There is a logical way out of this maze. Just don't forget your thoughts. Don't forget.*

. . . Patient talked about having difficulty telling "where the voices ended and her thoughts begin." Thought that her skull was split in half and asked me to examine it—was reassured that I didn't see or feel a split. Also said she feels like she's going to "fall out of her body," but didn't know where she'd fall to. At one time, patient put her hands over her ears and said, "I don't want hotdogs for lunch" when it had nothing to do with the conversation.

unusual posture and maintaining it for long periods of time. For example, a patient may stand like a statue with one foot extended and one arm raised toward the ceiling and maintain this state of *catatonic immobility* for hours. Such an individual, who appears completely withdrawn from reality, may be responding to inner thoughts and fantasies. The episode described in Box 3 gives a feeling for the kind of inner turmoil and distress that may underlie a schizophrenic patient's outward unresponsiveness and bizarre behavior.

**DECREASED ABILITY TO FUNCTION** Besides the specific symptoms we have described, schizophrenics have many impairments in their ability to carry out the daily routines of living. If the disorder occurs in adolescence, the individual shows a decreasing ability to cope with school, has limited social skills, and few friends. The adult schizophrenic is usually unsuccessful in obtaining or holding a job. Personal hygiene and grooming deteriorate. The individual becomes more and more seclusive and avoids the company of other people. The signs of schizophrenia are many and varied. Trying to make sense of the variety of symptoms is complicated by the fact that some may result directly from the disorder, while others may be a reaction to life in a mental hospital or to the effects of medication.

## Understanding Schizophrenia

Although more research has been devoted to trying to understand the nature of schizophrenia than to any other mental disorder, the causes are still not understood. New evidence indicates that both the structure and activity of schizophrenic brains are abnormal. However, environmental factors also play a role in the development of the disorder. We will examine the biological evidence first and then consider social and psychological variables.

**BIOLOGICAL PERSPECTIVE** Family studies show that there is a hereditary predisposition toward developing schizophrenia; relatives of schizophrenics are more likely to develop the disorder than are people from families free of schizophrenia. Figure 16-1 gives the lifetime risk of developing schizophrenia as a function of how closely an individual is genetically related to a person diagnosed as schizophrenic. Note that an identical twin of a schizophrenic is 3 times as likely as a fraternal twin to develop schizophrenia and 46 times as likely as an unrelated person to develop the disorder. However, fewer than half of the identical twins of schizophrenics develop schizophrenia themselves, even though they share the same genes. This fact demonstrates the importance of environmental variables.

We say that a pair of twins is *concordant* for schizophrenia if both members have the disorder; the pair is *discordant* if only one member is afflicted. The offspring of identical twins discordant for schizophrenia have approximately the same risk of developing schizophrenia as the offspring of concordant twins, and this risk is much greater than that of the general population. That is, the children of the normal twin are as likely as the children of the schizophrenic twin to develop the disorder (Gottesman & Bertelsen, 1989). Thus, the normal twin must carry the schizophrenia genes which he or she transmits to his or her children.

Studies of the children of schizophrenic mothers and/or fathers who were adopted in early infancy and reared in foster homes provide further evidence for the heritability of schizophrenia. Compared with matched control

**FIGURE 16-1**
**Genetic Relationships and**
**Schizophrenia.** *The lifetime risk of developing schizophrenia is largely a function of how closely an individual is genetically related to a schizophrenic and not a function of how much their environment is shared. In the case of an individual with two schizophrenic parents, genetic relatedness cannot be expressed in terms of percentage, but the regression of the individual's "genetic value" on that of the parents is 1, the same as it is for identical twins.* (After Gottesman, 1991; Gottesman & Shields, 1982)

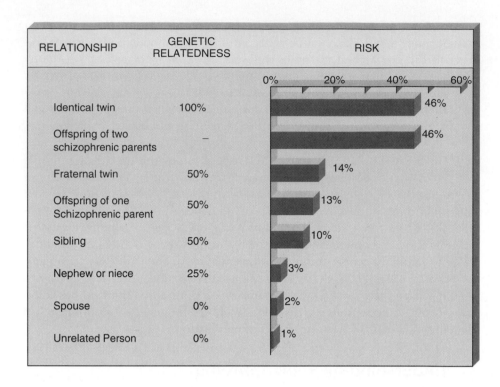

| RELATIONSHIP | GENETIC RELATEDNESS | RISK |
|---|---|---|
| Identical twin | 100% | 46% |
| Offspring of two schizophrenic parents | — | 46% |
| Fraternal twin | 50% | 14% |
| Offspring of one Schizophrenic parent | 50% | 13% |
| Sibling | 50% | 10% |
| Nephew or niece | 25% | 3% |
| Spouse | 0% | 2% |
| Unrelated Person | 0% | 1% |

groups of normal adopted children, the children with a biological parent diagnosed as schizophrenic were much more likely to develop schizophrenia and to have siblings who developed the disorder (Heston, 1966; Kety et al., 1978, 1988).

Although the tendency for schizophrenia to run in families has been recognized for many years, a search for the specific genes involved has become possible only recently with the development of new molecular biology techniques for genetic mapping. To locate the relevant genes, researchers find a family with a high incidence of schizophrenia over several generations. They examine the DNA of family members and search for a short sequence of DNA that is different in schizophrenic and in normal family members. If family members with a particular DNA sequence at a particular location on a chromosome frequently have schizophrenia, but family members with a different sequence on that location never have the disease, then that DNA sequence is either part of the disease-causing gene or very close to it on the chromosome (Byerly et al., 1989). Several studies of DNA samples from families with an unusually high incidence of schizophrenia found evidence of a defective gene, or cluster of genes, located on chromosome 5 (Bassett, 1989; Sherrington et al., 1988). However, other researchers studying a different group of high-incidence families found no evidence linking chromosome 5 with the disorder (Kennedy et al., 1988; McGuffin et al., 1990).

It may be that different genes are involved for different variants of the disorder. This idea is compatible with the view that schizophrenia is a group of disorders that produce similar symptoms but have different biological causes. Or, it may be that schizophrenia is a polygenic disorder, involving the accumulation of several defective genes. Whatever the means of genetic transmission, the familial data (in Figure 16-1) make it clear that we are not dealing with a genetic disorder that has a clear inheritance pattern such as Huntington's Disease or Phenylketonuria (PKU). As you may recall from

Chapter 2 (see p. 63), Huntington's Disease is caused by a single dominant gene passed from parent to child; on the average, half of the offspring will develop the disease. PKU is associated with a recessive gene; on the average, a quarter of the offspring will be affected. The genetic component in the transmission of schizophrenia is probably similar to that associated with diabetes or coronary heart disease: a number of genes acting together may make an individual susceptible to the disorder, and environmental factors will determine whether the disorder develops and the degree of its severity.

How do the genetic abnormalities that predispose an individual to schizophrenia affect the brain? Current research focuses on two main areas: irregularities in neurochemistry and differences in brain structure between schizophrenics and normals. While neurochemical theories of mood disorders center on norepinephrine and serotonin, the culprit in schizophrenia is believed to be **dopamine,** a neurotransmitter active in an area of the brain that is involved in the regulation of emotion (the limbic system). The **dopamine hypothesis** proposes that schizophrenia is caused by too much dopamine at certain synapses in the brain. This excess may be due to over-production of the neurotransmitter or to faulty regulation of the reuptake mechanism by which dopamine returns to and is stored by vesicles in the presynaptic neurons. It might also be due to oversensitive dopamine receptors or to too many dopamine receptors.

Evidence for the importance of dopamine comes from two sources. First, drugs that are effective in relieving the symptoms of schizophrenia, called **antipsychotic drugs,** reduce the amount of usable dopamine in the brain. Researchers believe that they do so by blocking the dopamine receptors. These drugs do not cure schizophrenia, but they do reduce hallucinations and delusions, improve concentration, and make schizophrenic symptoms less bizarre. Moreover, the therapeutic effectiveness of a particular drug has been found to parallel its potency in blocking dopamine receptors (Creese, Burt, & Snyder, 1978).

*The odds of all four identical quadruplets being diagnosed as schizophrenic are 1 in 2 billion—yet these quadruplets, the Genains, were. They have been in and out of hospitals since high school.*

Further evidence that an abnormality in dopamine metabolism may be the underlying cause of schizophrenia comes from observations of the effects of amphetamines, which increase the release of dopamine. Drug users who overdose on amphetamines exhibit psychotic behavior that closely resembles schizophrenia, and their symptoms can be relieved by the same antipsychotic drugs used to treat schizophrenia. When low doses of amphetamines are given to schizophrenic patients, their symptoms become much worse. In these cases, the drug does not produce a psychosis of its own; rather, it exacerbates whatever symptoms the patient may be experiencing (Snyder, 1980). For example, one patient entered the hospital claiming that spirits rose out of people's heads and spoke to him. After treatment with antipsychotics, he admitted that his talk about spirits had been "crazy talk," but within one minute of an amphetamine injection he again claimed that spirits were rising out of the interviewer's head (Janowsky, El-Yousef, Davis, & Sererke, 1973).

Thus, enhancing the action of dopamine aggravates schizophrenic symptoms, and blocking dopamine receptors alleviates them. Studies using positron emission tomography (PET), one of the techniques for obtaining detailed pictures of the living brain described in Chapter 2, have found the density of a certain class of dopamine receptors (called D2 receptors) to be significantly greater in a group of schizophrenics who had never been treated with drugs than in either a group of drug-treated schizophrenics or normals (Wong et al., 1986; 1989). This, along with other findings, indicates that an excess of cells that are sensitive to dopamine may be the important neurochemical defect in schizophrenia.

As for structural abnormalities in the brain, studies using computer axial tomography (CAT) and magnetic resonance imagery (MRI) have found that some schizophrenics have significantly larger cerebral ventricles (the cavities that contain the cerebrospinal fluid) than nonschizophrenics. In several studies, patients with schizophrenia had larger ventricles than their brothers and sisters, including identical twins of the patients (Andreasen, 1988). By inference, if the ventricles are larger than normal, the brain tissue must be smaller than normal; ventricular enlargement suggests a process of deterio-

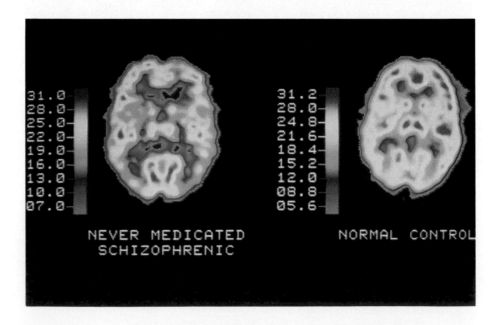

*This PET scan shows the metabolic differences between areas of the brain of a schizophrenic patient and that of a normal patient.*

ration or atrophy of brain tissue. The frontal lobes, the temporal lobes, and the hippocampus are brain areas that studies thus far have indicated may be smaller than normal in schizophrenics (Suddathg et al., 1990).

The evidence from studies of brain structure and brain biochemistry has lead some investigators to postulate that there may be two forms of schizophrenia. Type I schizophrenia is characterized by *positive symptoms* or behavioral excesses which include hallucinations, delusions, bizarre behavior, and confused thinking. Patients with positive symptoms usually functioned well before their schizophrenic symptoms first appeared; their disturbed behaviors tend to come and go so that at times their social behavior is reasonably effective; they usually respond well to antipsychotic drugs that block the transmission of the neurotransmitter dopamine; and their brain scans generally do not show structural abnormalities. Type II schizophrenia is characterized by *negative symptoms* or behavioral deficits such as poverty of speech, emotional unresponsiveness, seclusiveness, and impaired attention. Patients with negative symptoms usually have a history of poor social and educational functioning prior to their initial psychotic episode and continue to function poorly afterward (Fenton & McGlashan, 1992). They show little, if any, improvement with antipsychotic drugs, and their brain scans are likely to show structural abnormalities (Fenton & McGlashan, 1992).

Type I schizophrenia is assumed to result from difficulties in neurotransmission, and Type II from abnormalities in brain structure. One possible cause of the structural abnormality is damage to the brain by viral infection. Some data suggest that such an infection could occur during fetal development. In 1957 a major influenza epidemic occurred in Helsinki, Finland. Rates of schizophrenia were examined in adults who had been exposed during their mothers' pregnancies. Those exposed during the second trimester of pregnancy (which is a critical period of growth for cortical development) had much higher rates than those exposed during either of the other trimesters or in nonexposed controls (Mednick et al., 1988).

However, not all of the data support the distinctions between Type I and Type II schizophrenia. Some schizophrenic patients have both positive and negative symptoms, and the symptoms may change over the course of the illness. Nevertheless, investigators may be on the verge of isolating a subgroup of schizophrenic patients who have signs of brain pathology and suffer negative symptoms.

**SOCIAL AND PSYCHOLOGICAL PERSPECTIVE** Numerous studies in the United States and other countries have revealed that the incidence of schizophrenia is significantly higher among the lower classes than among the middle and upper classes (Dohrenwend, 1973; Strauss, 1982). The highest rates of schizophrenia are found in central city areas inhabited by the lowest socioeconomic class. The relationship does not show a continuous progression of higher rates of schizophrenia as the social class becomes lower. Instead, there is a marked difference between the number of schizophrenics in the lowest social class and those in the others. No one knows why social class is related to schizophrenia. Two quite different types of explanation have been proposed: social selection and social causation.

1. *Social selection—downward mobility.* Because their coping skills are poor, individuals who suffer from schizophrenia have difficulty completing their education and getting a decent job. They gradually drift downward in society and become part of the lower classes.

2. *Social causation—adversity and stress.* Living under conditions of poverty in areas with high crime rates, run-down housing, and inadequate schools creates enough additional stress to precipitate schizophrenic disorders, particularly in individuals who are genetically predisposed to schizophrenia.

Evidence indicates that both explanations are true (Brenner, 1982; Fried, 1982; Kosa & Zola, 1975), with social selection probably playing the greater role (Dohrenwend et al., 1992).

Research on the role of psychological factors in the development of schizophrenia has focused on relationships within the family. During the 1950s and 1960s numerous investigators recorded detailed observations of families in which one member was diagnosed as schizophrenic in an attempt to determine the kinds of parental attitudes and behaviors that contributed to the disorder. They came to various conclusions, most of which proved difficult to replicate. A major problem was that the families were studied *after* a mental disorder in one family member had affected the entire family. While some of the atypical family interactions may have preceded the onset of the disorder, others may represent reactions to the stresses of living with a mentally ill person. For example, unclear or conflicting communications between parent and offspring has been identified as a factor that distinguishes between schizophrenic and normal families. The parents are described as communicating in ways that create confusion and uncertainty (Wynne, Singer, Bartko, & Toohey, 1977). However, the results of a related study suggest that the parents' communication problems may be a response to unclear communication from their schizophrenic children. In this study the experimenter asked parents and sons, independently, to describe specific objects so that someone listening to their descriptions could identify the objects without seeing them. The descriptions were tape-recorded and played for others in the experiment, including normal and schizophrenic sons and their parents. The investigator found that the parents of schizophrenic sons did not differ from parents of normals sons in their ability to communicate ideas. The poorest communicators were the schizophrenic sons. To quote the investigator, "The communication disorder of the schizophrenic sons had an immediate negative effect not only on the parents of schizophrenic sons but on all parents who heard and attempted to respond to them" (Liem, 1974, p. 445).

*A stressful childhood may contribute to the severity of schizophrenia.*

A longitudinal study attempted to eliminated the problem inherent in earlier studies by observing family relationships *before* a family member was diagnosed as schizophrenic. The study began with 64 families that contained at least one teenager referred to a psychology clinic for help with mild to moderately severe emotional problems. The adolescents and their families were studied intensively and then followed up for the next 15 years with periodic assessments. The highest incidence of schizophrenia occurred among families in which the parents (a) dealt with the adolescent in a critical and hostile manner, and (b) were confusing in their communications. The combination of negative parental attitudes and confused communication was more predictive of future schizophrenia than either variable alone (Goldstein, 1987). However, the causal relationship is still not clear. It is possible that communication problems and critical parental attitudes were a consequence of the parents' attempts to cope with a child whose behavior was disturbed or unusual even before he or she was diagnosed as schizophrenic. In other words, is the parents' deviance a cause of the child's maladaptive behavior, or are the child's atypical characteristics a cause of the parents' behavior? This question remains unanswered. But whatever their role in causing the initial schizophrenic behavior, family disorganization and parental rejection are important in determining the severity of the illness and the prognosis for recovery (Anderson, Reiss, & Hogarty, 1986; Roff & Knight, 1981).

In addition to disturbed family relationships, other traumatic events (such as the early death of one or both parents) are found with greater than average frequency in the backgrounds of people who develop schizophrenia. Stressful childhoods of various kinds may contribute to the disorder. In general, the more stressful the childhood, the more severe the schizophrenic disorder.

**VULNERABILITY AND STRESS**  Most individuals who live in poverty or who experience a disturbing and stressful childhood do *not* develop schizophrenia. While earlier theories of schizophrenia emphasized environmental factors, the explanation that currently has the greatest support views schizophrenia as an inherited brain disorder that makes the individual vulnerable to stresses of life. It remains to be seen whether the same brain abnormality is characteristic of all persons diagnosed as schizophrenic, whether there are different brain defects for different types of schizophrenia, or whether some cases of schizophrenia are due solely to environmental causes.

Currently, some 50 longitudinal studies are being conducted with children who have been identified as having a high risk of developing schizophrenia. The studies follow the children from their early years to adulthood in an attempt to pinpoint some of the factors that determine whether or not the disorder will develop. In most of these studies, the children are considered to have a high risk because they have at least one schizophrenic parent (John, Mednick, & Schulsinger, 1982; Steffy et al., 1984; Marcus et al., 1987; Tienari et al., 1987; Mednick, Cannon, Parnas, & Schulsinger, 1989; Moldin et al., 1990). Other investigators have selected their high-risk group on the basis of psychophysiological measures or behavioral characteristics that they believe to be precursors of schizophrenia (Garmezy, 1974; Garmezy & Devine, 1984).

The high-risk subjects are usually matched with a control group of children who have no family background of mental illness and who show no early signs of psychopathology. The development of both groups is carefully monitored through periodic testing and interviews with parents, teachers, and peers. Once a high-risk subject has a schizophrenic breakdown, he or she is matched both with a subject from the high-risk group who has remained well and with a well member of the control group. Thus, the background of the individual who develops schizophrenia can be compared with that of a nonschizophrenic high-risk subject and a normal, low-risk subject.

Most of these studies, started in the 1960s and 1970s, are still in progress, and the subjects are now young adults. Some have already become schizophrenic, and many more are expected to do so within the next decade. Consequently, the data available at present consist mainly of comparisons between high-risk and low-risk groups. These data indicate that the high-risk child is similar to an adult schizophrenic in many ways. For example, high-risk children are rated low in social competence and tend to perform poorly on tasks that require sustained attention or abstract thinking.

Preliminary data on high-risk subjects who later developed schizophrenia indicate that they differ from the high-risk subjects who have remained well in the following ways. The subjects who developed the disorder

1.  Were more apt to have experienced birth complications that may have affected the functioning of their nervous system.
2.  Were more likely to have been separated from their mothers at an early age.
3.  Had fathers who were more likely to have been hospitalized, with diagnoses ranging from alcoholism to schizophrenia.
4.  Were more likely to show inappropriate behavior in school. The boys were described by their teachers as anxious, lonely, and causing disciplinary problems; the girls, as withdrawn, isolated, and poorly controlled.

When more data from these ongoing high-risk studies become available, we should have a better understanding of how innate and environmental factors interact to produce schizophrenia. Recently, investigators have identified an atypical pattern of infant development (involving certain lags and spurts in the maturation of motor and visual abilities) that may prove useful as a screening test to identify children with a high risk of schizophrenia (Fish et al., 1992).

## Personality Disorders

**Personality disorders** are long-standing patterns of maladaptive behavior. In Chapter 14, we described *personality traits* as enduring ways of perceiving or relating to the environment and thinking about oneself. When personality traits become so inflexible and maladaptive that they significantly impair the individual's ability to function, they are called personality disorders. Personality disorders constitute immature and inappropriate ways of coping with stress or solving problems. They are usually evident by early adolescence and may continue throughout adult life.

Unlike people with mood or anxiety disorders, which also involve maladaptive behavior, people who have personality disorders usually do not feel upset or anxious and are not motivated to change their behavior. They do not lose contact with reality or display marked disorganization of behavior, unlike individuals suffering from schizophrenia.

DSM-III-R lists 11 personality disorders. For example, someone who has a *narcissistic personality disorder* is described as having an inflated sense of self-importance, being preoccupied with fantasies of success, constantly seeking admiration and attention, and being insensitive to the needs of others and often exploiting them. *Dependent personality disorders* are characterized by a passive orientation to life, an inability to make decisions or accept responsibility, a tendency to be self-deprecating, and a need for continual support from others.

Most of the personality disorders listed in DSM-III-R have not been the subject of much research. Moreover, the characteristics of the various personality disorders overlap, so that agreement in classifying individuals is poor. The personality disorder that has been studied the most and is the most reliably diagnosed is the antisocial personality (formerly called psychopathic personality).

## Antisocial Personality

People who have **antisocial personalities** seem to have little sense of responsibility, morality, or concern for others. Their behavior is determined almost entirely by their own needs. In other words, they lack a *conscience*. Whereas the average person realizes at an early age that some restrictions are placed on behavior and that pleasures must sometimes be postponed in consideration of the needs of others, individuals who have antisocial personalities seldom consider any desires except their own. They behave impulsively, seek immediate gratification of their needs, and cannot tolerate frustration.

The term "antisocial personality" is somewhat misleading, because these characteristics do not describe most people who commit antisocial acts. Antisocial *behavior* results from a number of causes, including membership in a delinquent gang or a criminal subculture, the need for attention and status, loss of contact with reality, and an inability to control impulses. Most juvenile delinquents and adult criminals do have some concern for others (for family or gang members) and some code of moral conduct (you don't betray a friend). In contrast, antisocial *personalities* have little feeling for anyone except themselves and seem to experience little guilt or remorse, regardless of how much suffering their behavior may cause others. Other characteristics of the antisocial personality (sociopath, for short) include a great facility for lying, a need for thrills and excitement with little concern for possible injury, and an inability to alter behavior as a consequence of punishment. Such individuals are often attractive, intelligent, charming people who are quite facile in manipulating others—in other words, good con artists. Their façade of competence and sincerity wins them promising jobs, but they have little staying power. Their restlessness and impulsiveness soon lead them into an escapade that reveals their true nature; they accumulate debts, desert their families, squander company money, or commit crimes. When caught, their declaration of repentance are so convincing that they often escape punishment and are given another chance. But antisocial personalities seldom live up to these declarations; what they say has little relation to what they feel or do (see Box 4).

The two characteristics considered most indicative of an antisocial personality disorder are: (a) lack of empathy and concern for others, and (b) lack of shame or guilt—the inability to feel remorse for one's actions, regardless of how reprehensible they may be (Hare, 1980).

## Box 4
# *Antisocial Personality*

A 40-year-old man was convicted of check forgery and embezzlement. He was arrested with a young woman, age 18, whom he had married bigamously some months before. She was unaware of the existence of any previous marriage. The subject in this case had already been convicted for two previous bigamous marriages and for 40 other cases of passing fraudulent checks.

The circumstances of his arrest illustrate the impulsivity and lack of insight characteristic of many antisocial personalities. He had gotten a job managing a small restaurant; the absentee owner, who lived in a neighboring town, had arranged to stop by at the end of each week to check on progress and to collect the income. The subject was provided with living quarters over the restaurant, a small salary, and a percentage of the cash register receipts. At the end of the first week, the subject took all the money (he had failed to bank it nightly as he had been instructed) and departed shortly before the employer arrived; he left a series of vulgar messages scribbled on the walls saying he had taken the money because the salary

was "too low." He found lodgings with his wife a few blocks from the restaurant and made no effort to escape detection. He was arrested a few days later.

During the inquiry, it emerged that the subject had spent the past few months cashing checks in department stores in various cities. He would make out the check and send his wife in to cash it; he commented that her genuine innocence of the fact that he had no bank account made her very effective in not arousing suspicion. He had not bothered to use a false name when he signed the checks or the bigamous marriage contract, but he seemed surprised that the police discovered him so quickly.

Inquiry into the subject's past history revealed that he had been educated mostly in private schools and that his parents were financially well-to-do. They had planned for him to go to college, but his academic record was not good enough (although on examination he proved to have superior intelligence). Failing to get into college, he started work as an insurance salesman trainee and did very well. He was a distinguished-looking young man and an exceptionally fluent speaker.

Just as it appeared that he could anticipate a successful career in the insurance business, he ran into trouble because he failed to turn in the checks that customers had given him to pay their initial premiums. He admitted to

having cashed these checks and to spending the money (mostly on clothes and liquor). It apparently did not occur to him that the company's accounting system would quickly discern this type of embezzlement. In fact, he expressed amused indignation at the company's failure to realize that he intended to pay back the money from his salary. No legal action was taken, but he was requested to resign. His parents reimbursed the company for the missing money.

At this point, the subject enlisted in the army and was sent to Officer Candidate School, from which he graduated as a second lieutenant. He was assigned to an infantry unit, where he soon got into trouble that progressed from minor infractions (drunk on duty, smuggling women into his quarters) to cashing fraudulent checks. He was court-martialed and given a dishonorable discharge. From then on, his life followed a pattern of finding a woman to support him (with or without marriage) and then running off with her money to the next woman when life became too tedious.

At his trial, where he was sentenced to five years in prison, he gave a long and articulate speech, pleading clemency for the young woman who was being tried with him, expressing repentance for having ruined her life, and stating that he was glad to have the opportunity to repay society for his crimes (Maher, 1966, pp. 214-215).

## Understanding Antisocial Personalities

What factors contribute to the development of the antisocial personality? We might expect individuals with such personalities to have been raised by parents who provided no discipline or moral training, but the answer is not that simple. Although some sociopaths come from environments in which antisocial behavior is reinforced and adult criminals serve as models for personality development, many come from good homes and were raised by parents who are prominent and respected members of the community.

As yet, there is no well-supported theory to explain why antisocial personalities develop. Many factors are probably involved and vary from case to case. Current research focuses on biological determinants and on the quality of the parent-child relationship.

**BIOLOGICAL FACTORS** The clinical impression that sociopaths experience little anxiety about future discomforts or punishments has been supported by experimental studies. One study compared two groups of adolescent male delinquents selected from the detention unit of a juvenile court. One group had been diagnosed as having antisocial personality disorders; the other, adjustment reactions of adolescence. The experimenters tested galvanic skin response, GSR, (see Chapter 11) under stress. Dummy electrodes were attached to each subject's leg, and he was told that in 10 minutes he would be given a very strong but not harmful shock. (A large clock was visible so that the subject knew precisely when the shock was supposed to occur—no shock was actually administered.) The two groups showed no difference in GSR measures during periods of rest or in response to auditory or visual stimulation. However, during the 10 minutes of shock anticipation, the maladjusted group showed significantly more tension than the antisocial group. At the moment when the clock indicated the shock was due, most of the maladjusted subjects exhibited an abrupt drop in skin resistance (indicating a sharp increase in anxiety). *None* of the sociopathic subjects showed this reaction (Lippert & Senter, 1966).

Studies in prisons have shown that, compared with other prisoners, antisocial personalities do not learn to avoid shocks as quickly and do not exhibit as much autonomic nervous system activity under a variety of conditions (Hare, 1970; Lykken, 1957). These findings have led to the hypothesis that sociopaths may have been born with an *underreactive autonomic nervous system*, which would explain why they fail to respond normally to threats of danger that deter most people from antisocial acts. Interpretations must be made with caution, however. It is possible that antisocial personalities may view an experimental situation as a game and may try to play it extra cool by attempting to control their responses.

Subsequent studies using measures of arousal other than the GSR have concluded that sociopaths' arousal levels are low because they are able to ignore or tune out aversive stimuli (Hare, 1988; Jutai & Hare, 1983). In addition, tests of mental functioning indicate that antisocial personalities are deficient in the ability to plan, to change strategies, and to inhibit impulsive actions (Gorenstein, 1982). The above findings provide an explanation for sociopathic behavior. Because his arousal level is low, the sociopath seeks thrills and excitement. Since he has almost no anxiety, it provides little deterrence. Because the sociopath is deficient in planning and in inhibition, he behaves impulsively. These are possible reasons for the sociopath's misconduct without remorse and for his thrill-seeking without regard for society's rules.

**PARENTAL INFLUENCES** According to psychoanalytic theory, the development of a conscience, or superego, depends on an affectionate relationship with an adult during early childhood. Normal children internalize their parents' values (which generally reflect the values of society) because they want to be like their parents and fear the loss of their parents' love if they do not behave in accordance with these values. A child who receives no love from either parent does not fear its loss; he or she does not identify with the rejecting parents and does not internalize their rules. Reasonable as this theory seems, it does not conform to all of the data. Many rejected children do

## Insanity as a Legal Defense

How should the law treat a mentally disturbed person who commits a criminal offense? Should individuals whose mental faculties are impaired be held responsible for their actions? These questions are of concern to behavioral and social scientists, to members of the legal profession, and to individuals who work with criminal offenders.

Over the centuries, an important part of Western law has been the concept that a civilized society should not punish a person who is mentally incapable of controlling his or her conduct. In 1724, an English court maintained that a man was not responsible for an act if "he doth not know what he is doing, no more than . . . a wild beast." Modern standards of legal responsibility, however, have been based on the M'Naghten decision of 1843.

M'Naghten, a Scotsman, suffered the paranoid delusion that he was being persecuted by the English prime minister, Sir Robert Peel. In an attempt to kill

Peel, he mistakenly shot Peel's secretary. Everyone involved in the trial was convinced by M'Naghten's senseless ramblings that he was insane. He was judged not responsible by reason of insanity and sent to a mental hospital, where he remained until his death. But Queen Victoria was not pleased with the verdict—apparently she felt that political assassinations should not be taken lightly—and called on the House of Lords to review the decision. The decision was upheld, and rules for the legal definition of insanity were put into writing. The M'Naghten Rule states that a defendant may be found not guilty by reason of insanity only if he were so severely disturbed at the time of his act that he did not know what he was doing, or if he did know what he was doing, did not know that it was wrong.

The M'Naghten Rule was adopted in the United States, and the distinction of knowing right from wrong remained the basis of most decisions of legal insanity for over a century. Some states added to their statutes the doctrine of "irresistible impulse," which recognizes that some mentally ill individuals may respond correctly when asked if a particular act is morally right or wrong but may be unable to control their behavior.

During the 1970s, a number of state and federal courts adopted a broader legal definition of insanity proposed by the American Law Institute, which states: "A person is not responsible for

criminal conduct if at the time of such conduct, as a result of mental disease or defect, he lacks substantial capacity either to appreciate the wrongfulness of his conduct or to conform his conduct to the requirements of the law." The word *substantial* suggests that any incapacity is not enough to avoid criminal responsibility but that total incapacity is not required either. The use of the word *appreciate* rather than *know* implies that intellectual awareness of right or wrong is not enough; individuals must have some understanding of the moral or legal consequences of their behavior before they can be held criminally responsible.

The problem of legal responsibility in the case of mentally disordered individuals became a topic of increased debate in the wake of John Hinckley, Jr.'s, acquittal, by reason of insanity, for the attempted assassination of President Reagan in 1981. Many Americans were outraged by the verdict and felt that the insanity defense was a legal loophole that allowed too many guilty people to go free. In response, Congress enacted the Insanity Defense Reform Act (1984), which contains a number of provisions designed to make it more difficult to absolve a defendant of legal responsibility. For example, the act changes the American Law Institute's "lacks substantial capacity . . . to appreciate" to "unable to appreciate"; it stipulates that the mental disease or defect be "severe" (the intent being to exclude

not develop antisocial personalities, and some people who do were indulged in childhood.

According to learning theory, antisocial behavior is influenced by the kind of models the parents provide and the kind of behavior they reward. A child may develop an antisocial personality if he or she learns that punishment can be avoided by being charming, lovable, and repentant. A child who is consistently able to avoid punishment by claiming to be sorry and promising never to do it again may learn that it is not the deed that counts but charm and ability to act repentant. If the same child is indulged in other respects and never has to wait or work for a reward, he or she does not learn to tolerate frustration. Two characteristics of sociopaths are a lack of frustration tolerance and the conviction that being charming and appearing contrite excuses wrongdoing. In addition, a child who is always protected from frustration or distress may have no ability to empathize with the distress of others (Maher, 1966).

nonpsychotic disorders such as antisocial personality); and it shifts the burden of proof from the prosecution to the defense (instead of the prosecution having to prove that the person was sane beyond a reasonable doubt at the time of the crime, the defense must prove he or she was not sane, and must do so with "clear and convincing evidence"). This law applies to all cases tried in federal courts and about half the state courts. It is still too early to evaluate its impact.

Another attempt to clarify the legal defense of insanity is the verdict "guilty but mentally ill." Initially proposed by Michigan, it has been adopted by eleven states. (In some of these states this verdict replaces the not guilty by reason of insanity verdict; in other states it is an additional option.) Generally, the laws permit a finding of guilty but mentally ill when a defendant is found to have a substantial disorder of thought or mood that afflicted him at the time of the crime and that significantly impaired his judgment, behavior, capacity to recognize reality, or ability to cope with the ordinary demands of life. The effect of this mental illness, however, falls short of legal insanity. The guilty but mentally ill verdict allows jurors to convict a person they perceive as dangerous while attempting also to ensure that he or she receives psychotherapeutic treatment. The individual could be given treatment in prison or be treated in a mental hospital and returned to prison when deemed fit to complete the sentence. The problem remains as to whether treatment in either place would be sufficient to rehabilitate the person.

Public concern that the insanity defense may be a major loophole in the criminal law is largely groundless. The defense is rarely used, and actual cases of acquittal by reason of insanity are even rarer. Jurors seem reluctant to believe that people are not morally responsible for their acts, and lawyers, knowing that an insanity plea is apt to fail, tend to use it only as a last resort. Fewer than 1 percent of defendants charged with serious crimes are found not guilty by reason of insanity.

The question of mental disorder exerts its greatest impact earlier in the legal process. Many accused people who are mentally ill never come to trial. In the United States, the law requires that the defendant be *competent to stand trial*. An individual is judged competent to stand trial if he or she is able (a) to understand the charges, and (b) to cooperate with a lawyer in preparing a defense. The competency issue is basic to the American ideal of a fair trial and is quite separate from the question of whether the person was "insane" at the time the crime was committed. In a preliminary hearing, the judge receives evidence about the accused's mental competency. The judge may drop the charges and commit the individual to a psychiatric facility (if the crime is not serious) or commit the accused and file the charges until he or she is deemed competent to stand trial. Because court calendars are congested and trials are expensive, judges often prefer to deal with mentally disturbed defendants in this way, particularly if they believe that the mental hospital will provide adequate treatment and secure confinement.

Many more persons are confined to mental institutions because they are found incompetent to stand trial than because they are found not guilty by reason of insanity. These people, many of whom are not dangerous, often are confined longer than they would have been if they had been convicted of the crime in question. Indeed, before the widespread use of antipsychotic drugs, individuals deemed incompetent to stand trial were often committed to mental institutions for life. However, in 1972, the Supreme Court ruled that defendants found incompetent to stand trial due to mental illness could not be held indefinitely. Judges now attempt to bring such individuals to trial or to release them within 18 months. In deciding on release, the seriousness of the crime and the potential for future dangerous behavior are important considerations. Unfortunately, at present our data for predicting whether an individual is likely to commit a dangerous act are not very reliable.

Undoubtedly, a number of family interaction patterns foster the development of an antisocial personality. In some cases, children who have been subjected to parental neglect and abuse may develop a vindictive cast to their personalities and seek revenge against a society that has neglected and hurt them.

A longitudinal study that followed up in adulthood a group of individuals who were seen at a child guidance clinic provides evidence of some factors that predict antisocial personality disorders. Ninety percent of an initial sample of 584 cases were located 30 years after their referral to the clinic. An additional 100 control subjects, who lived in the same area but who had not been referred to the clinic, were also followed up in adulthood. The adult subjects were interviewed intensively, and any current maladjustments were diagnosed. The most likely candidate for a later diagnosis of antisocial personality disorder was described as a boy who was referred to the guidance clinic for theft or aggression, who had shown a variety of antisocial behaviors, who had a history of truancy, and who showed little guilt over behavior. His childhood involved either inconsistent discipline or no discipline at all. And his father showed antisocial behavior (Robins, 1966). The last two findings support the learning theory emphasis on the kinds of models parents provide and the way they handle rewards and punishments in the development of sociopathic behavior.

## *Chapter* SUMMARY

1. The diagnosis of abnormal behavior is based on *statistical frequency, social norms, adaptiveness of behavior,* and *personal distress.* Characteristics indicative of good mental health include an *efficient perception of reality, self-knowledge, control of behavior, self-esteem,* an *ability to form affectionate relationships,* and *productivity.*

2. DSM-III-R classifies mental disorders according to specific behavioral symptoms. Such a classification system helps to communicate information and provides a basis for research. However, each case is unique, and diagnostic labels should not be used to pigeonhole individuals.

3. Theories about the causes of mental disorders and proposals for treating them can be grouped under one of the following perspectives: *biological, psychoanalytic, behavioral,* and *cognitive.* The *vulnerability-stress model* emphasizes the interaction between a predisposition (biological and/or psychological) that makes a person vulnerable for developing a disorder and stressful environmental conditions the individual encounters.

4. Anxiety disorders include *generalized anxiety* (constant worry and tension), *panic disorders* (sudden attacks of overwhelming apprehension), *phobias* (irrational fears of specific objects or situations), and *obsessive-compulsive disorders* (persistent unwanted thoughts, or *obsessions,* combined with urges, or *compulsions,* to perform certain acts).

5. Psychoanalytic theories attribute anxiety disorders to unresolved, *unconscious conflicts.* Behavioral theories focus on anxiety as a *learned response* to external events and invoke the concept of *prepared conditioning* to explain some phobias. Cognitive theories emphasize the way anxious people think about potential dangers: their overestimation of the likelihood and degree of harm makes them tense and physiologically prepared for danger; they are unable to dismiss obsessive thoughts and believe that compulsive rituals will prevent disaster. Biological theories focus on the interaction of a number of *neurotransmitters* that regulate feelings of anxiety. Biochemical abnormalities have been identified for panic attacks and obsessive-compulsive disorders.

6. Mood disorders are divided into *depressive disorders* (the individual has one or more periods of depression) and *bipolar disorders* (the individual alternates between periods of depression and periods of elation, or mania). Sadness, loss of gratification in life, negative thoughts, and lack of motivation are the main symptoms of depression. Psychoanalytic theories view depression as a *reactivation of the loss of parental affection* in a person who is *dependent on external approval* and tends *to turn anger inward.* Learning theories focus on *reduced positive reinforcement.*

7. Beck's theory views depression as a *cognitive triad* of negative thoughts about the self, present experiences, and the future. The depressed person's *negative self-schema* is fueled by systematic errors in thinking that distort reality. The *attributional theory* of Seligman and Abramson proposes that a pessimistic explanatory style that invokes *internal, stable,* and *global causes for bad events* leads to depression. Negative cognitions

and pessimistic attributions accompany depression but may not be a primary cause.

8.  Some mood disorders may be influenced by inherited abnormalities in the metabolism of certain *neurotransmitters* (such as *norepinephrine* and *serotonin*). Inherited predispositions and early experiences may make people *vulnerable* to depression when under stress.

9.  *Schizophrenia* is characterized by disturbances in the *form of thought* (disorganized thought processes that stem from difficulty in filtering out irrelevant stimuli) and in the *content of thought* (delusions and lack of insight). Other symptoms include perceptual disturbances (such as *hallucinations*), inappropriate affect, bizarre motor activity, withdrawal, and impaired functioning. Research on the causes of schizophrenia has focused on evidence for a hereditary disposition to the disorder, defects in the metabolism of neurotransmitters (the *dopamine hypothesis*), social factors, and deviant family relationships. Studies of high-risk children point to some predictors of schizophrenia.

10. *Personality disorders* are long-standing patterns of maladaptive behavior that constitute immature and inappropriate ways of coping with stress or solving problems. Individuals classified as having *antisocial personalities* are impulsive, show little guilt, are concerned only with their own needs, and are frequently in trouble with the law. An underreactive nervous system, parental modeling of antisocial behavior, and lack of (or inconsistent) discipline are possible explanations for this disorder.

*Further* **READING**

General textbooks on abnormal psychology include Davison and Neale, *Abnormal Psychology* (5th ed., 1990); Sarason and Sarason, *Abnormal Psychology: The Problem of Maladaptive Behavior* (6th ed., 1989) Rosenhan and Seligman, *Abnormal Psychology* (2nd ed., 1989); Carson & Butcher, *Abnormal Psychology and Modern Life* (9th ed., 1992). *Mending Minds* (1992), a paperback by Heston, provides a briefer description of the major mental disorders, with case histories and descriptions of treatment options.

The hereditary aspects of mental illness are reviewed in Plomin DeFries, and McClearn, *Behavioral Genetics: A Primer* (2nd ed., 1989). *Schizophrenia Genesis: The Origins of Madness* (1991), a paperback by Gottesman, presents the latest research findings on the genetics of this disorder, a discussion of social and psychological factors, and personal accounts by schizophrenic patients and their families.

*Panic: Facing Fears, Phobias, and Anxiety* (1985) by Agras provides an interesting discussion of the way fears develop into phobias. *The Boy Who Couldn't Stop Washing: The Experience and Treatment of Obsessive-Compulsive Disorder* (1989) by Rapoport provides a fascinating account of this disorder, including descriptions of clinical cases and research findings on treatment.

The world of psychosis from the patient's viewpoint is graphically described in Green, *I Never Promised You a Rose Garden* (1971); and in North, *Welcome Silence* (1987). In *Holiday of Darkness* (1982) by Endler, a well-known psychologist provides an account of his personal battle with depression and discusses the effects of various treatments.

Chapter

17

# Methods of Therapy

### Historical Background 667
*Early Asylums*
*Modern Treatment Facilities*
*Professions Involved in Psychotherapy*

### Techniques of Psychotherapy 673
*Psychoanalysis*
*Psychoanalytic Therapies*
*Behavior Therapies*
*Cognitive Behavior Therapies*
*Humanistic Therapies*
*An Eclectic Approach*
*Group and Family Therapy*

### Effectiveness of Psychotherapy 693
*Evaluating Psychotherapy*
*Comparing Psychotherapies*
*Common Factors in Psychotherapies*
*Critical Discussion: The Placebo Response*

### Biological Therapies 698
*Psychotherapeutic Drugs*
*Electroconvulsive Therapy*

### Enhancing Mental Health 703
*Community Resources and Paraprofessionals*
*Promoting Your Own Emotional Well-Being*

Detail, *Place du Havre.*

In this chapter, we will look at methods for treating abnormal behavior. Some of these methods focus on helping individuals gain an understanding of the causes of their problems, some attempt to modify thoughts and behavior directly, some involve biological interventions, and some specify ways in which the community can help. The treatment of mental disorders is closely linked to theories about the causes of such disorders. A brief history of the treatment of the mentally ill will illustrate how methods change as theories about human nature and the causes of its disorders change.

# Historical Background

According to one of the earliest beliefs (espoused by the ancient Chinese, Egyptians, and Hebrews), a person with a mental disorder was possessed by evil spirits. These demons were exorcised by such techniques as prayer, incantation, magic, and the use of purgatives concocted from herbs. If these treatments were unsuccessful, more extreme measures were taken to ensure that the body would be an unpleasant dwelling place for the evil spirit. Flogging, starving, burning, and even stoning to death were not infrequent forms of treatment.

The first progress in understanding mental disorders was made by the Greek physician Hippocrates (circa 460–377 B.C.), who rejected demonology and maintained that mental disorders were the result of a disturbance in the balance of body fluids. Hippocrates, and the Greek and Roman physicians who followed him, argued for a more humane treatment of the mentally ill. They stressed the importance of pleasant surroundings, exercise, proper diet, massage, and soothing baths, as well as some less desirable treatments, such as bleeding, purging, and mechanical restraints. Although there were no institutions for the mentally ill during this period, many individuals were cared for with great kindness by physicians in temples dedicated to the Greek and Roman gods.

This progressive view of mental illness did not continue, however. Primitive superstitions and a belief in demonology were revived during the Middle Ages. The mentally ill were considered to be in league with Satan and to possess supernatural powers with which they could cause floods, pestilence, and injuries to others. Seriously disturbed individuals were treated cruelly: people believed that by beating, starving, and torturing the mentally ill, they were punishing the devil. This type of cruelty culminated in the witchcraft trials that sentenced to death thousands of people (many of them mentally ill) during the fifteenth, sixteenth, and seventeenth centuries.

## Early Asylums

In the latter part of the Middle Ages, cities created asylums to cope with the mentally ill. These asylums were simply prisons; the inmates were chained in dark, filthy cells and were treated more as animals than as human beings. It was not until 1792, when Philippe Pinel was placed in charge of an asylum in Paris, that some improvements were made. As an experiment, Pinel was allowed to remove the chains that restrained the inmates. Much to the amazement of skeptics who thought Pinel was mad to unchain such "animals," the experiment was a success. When released from their restraints,

*Philippe Pinel in the courtyard of the hospital of Salpêtrière.*

*As late as the early nineteenth century, English asylums used rotating devices in which patients were whirled around at high speeds.*

placed in clean, sunny rooms, and treated kindly, many people who for years had been considered hopelessly insane improved enough to leave the asylum.

By the beginning of the twentieth century, the fields of medicine and psychology were making great advances. In 1905, a mental disorder known as *general paresis* was shown to have a physical cause: a syphilis infection acquired many years before the symptoms of the disorder appeared. General paresis is characterized by a gradual decline in mental and physical functions, marked personality changes, and delusions and hallucinations. Without treatment, death occurs within a few years. The syphilis spirochete remains in the body after the initial genital infection disappears, and it gradually destroys the nervous system. At one time, general paresis accounted for more than 10 percent of all admissions to mental hospitals, but today few cases are reported, due to the effectiveness of penicillin in treating syphilis (Dale, 1975).

The discovery that general paresis was the result of a disease encouraged those who believed that mental illness was biological in origin. At about the same time, Sigmund Freud and his followers laid the groundwork for understanding mental illness in terms of psychological factors; likewise Pavlov's laboratory experiments demonstrated that animals could become emotionally disturbed if forced to make decisions beyond their capacities.

Despite these scientific advances, in the early 1900s the public still did not understand mental illness and viewed mental hospitals and their inmates with fear and horror. Clifford Beers undertook the task of educating the public about mental health. As a young man, Beers developed a bipolar disorder and was confined for 3 years in several private and state hospitals. Although chains and other methods of torture had been abandoned long before, the straitjacket was still widely used to restrain excited patients. Lack of funds made the average state mental hospital—with its overcrowded wards, poor food, and unsympathetic attendants—a far from pleasant place to live. After his recovery, Beers wrote about his experiences in the now-famous book *A Mind That Found Itself* (1908), which aroused considerable public interest. Beers worked ceaselessly to educate the public about mental illness and helped to organize the National Committee for Mental Hygiene. In 1950, this organization joined with two related groups to form the National Association for Mental Health. The mental hygiene movement played an invaluable role in stimulating the organization of child-guidance clinics and community mental health centers to aid in the prevention and treatment of mental disorders.

## Modern Treatment Facilities

Mental hospitals have been upgraded markedly since the time of Beers, but there is still much room for improvement. Most people who require hospitalization for mental disorders are first admitted to the psychiatric ward of a general hospital, where their condition is evaluated. If more than a brief period of hospitalization is indicated, they may be transferred to a public or private mental hospital. The best of these hospitals are comfortable and well-kept places that provide a number of therapeutic activities: individual and group psychotherapy, recreation, occupational therapy (designed to teach skills, as well as to provide relaxation), and educational courses to help patients prepare for a job upon release from the hospital. The worst are primarily custodial institutions where inmates lead a boring existence in run-down, overcrowded wards and receive little treatment except for medication. Most mental hospitals fall somewhere in between these two extremes.

Beginning in the early 1960s emphasis shifted from treating mentally disturbed individuals in hospitals to treating them in their own communities. This movement toward *deinstitutionalization* was motivated partly by the recognition that hospitalization has some inherent disadvantages, regardless of how good the facilities may be. Hospitals remove people from the social support of family and friends and from their patterns of daily life; they tend to make people feel "sick" and unable to cope with the world; and they encourage dependency. They are also very expensive.

During the 1950s psychotherapeutic drugs (discussed later in this chapter) were discovered that could relieve depression and anxiety and reduce psychotic behavior. When these drugs became widely available in the 1960s, it was possible for many hospitalized patients to be discharged and returned home to be treated as outpatients. The Community Mental Health Centers Act of 1963 made federal funds available for the establishment of community treatment centers. These community mental health centers were designed to provide outpatient treatment and a number of other services, including short-term hospitalization and partial hospitalization. Partial

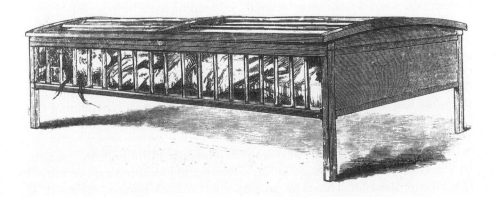

*The "crib"—a restraining device used in a New York mental institution in 1882.*

**FIGURE 17-1**
**Patients in Mental Hospitals** *The number of patients cared for in United States state and county mental hospitals has decreased dramatically over the past 35 years.*

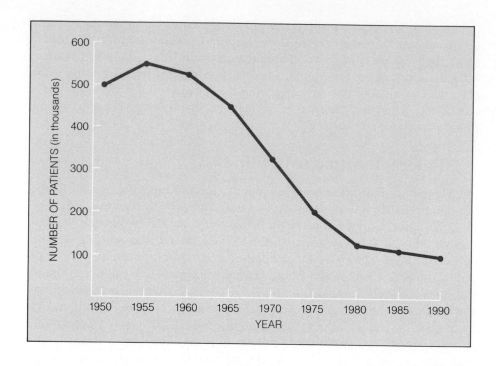

hospitalization is more flexible than traditional hospitalization: individuals may receive treatment at the center during the day and return home in the evening or may work during the day and spend nights at the center. Unfortunately, most centers are currently so overcrowded that they cannot begin to provide beds and services for the many mentally ill people who need them.

As Figure 17-1 shows, the number of patients treated in state and county mental hospitals has decreased dramatically over the past 35 years. For some patients the policy of deinstitutionalization has worked. The services of the mental health centers, along with help from their families and the use of psychotherapeutic drugs, have enabled them to resume a satisfactory life. For others, however, deinstitutionalization has had unfortunate consequences, largely because the facilities in most communities are far from adequate.

Many individuals who improve with hospitalization and could manage on their own with assistance do not receive adequate follow-up care in terms of outpatient therapy or help in finding friends, housing, and jobs. As a consequence, they lead a revolving door existence, going in and out of institutions between unsuccessful attempts to cope on their own. About half of all patients discharged from state hospitals are readmitted within a year.

Some discharged patients are too incapacitated to even attempt to support themselves or to function without custodial care; they may live in dirty, overcrowded housing or roam the streets. The disheveled man standing on the corner talking to himself and shouting gibberish may be one victim of deinstitutionalization. The woman with all of her worldly possessions in a shopping bag who spends one night in the doorway of an office building and the next in a subway station, may be another. A large proportion of street people suffer from some sort of mental disorder.

The increasing visibility of homeless mentally-ill individuals, particularly in large cities, has aroused public concern and prompted a move toward reinstitutionalization. However, an important ethical issue is involved. If such people are not readjusting to society, should they be involuntarily committed to a mental hospital? One of the most cherished civil rights in a democratic society is the right to liberty. It is essential that any commitment proceedings safeguard this right.

Some experts believe that legal action is warranted only if a person is potentially dangerous to others. The rare, but highly publicized, occasions when a mentally ill person experiencing a psychotic episode attacks an innocent bystander have generated fears for public safety. But dangerousness is difficult to predict. Studies have shown that mental health professionals are poor at predicting whether a person will commit a dangerous act (Monahan, 1976). Moreover, our legal system is designed to protect people from preventative detention. A person is assumed innocent until proven guilty by the courts, and prisoners are released from penitentiaries even though statistics show that most will commit additional crimes. Should mentally ill individuals not have the same rights? And what about the person who appears self-destructive, more dangerous to himself than to others? Should he or she be committed? These complex issues have yet to be resolved.

Aside from the legal issues, the problem of providing care for the mentally ill remains. Funds need to be directed toward two areas. One is the improvement of outpatient services to help those who can make it on their own with adequate assistance. The other is the development of alternative residential facilities (such as small-group homes) for patients who are unable to function outside of a sheltered environment, as well as for those who need help in the transition from hospital to independent living. Evidence indicates that residential treatment centers cost less to operate and are more effective for many patients than are traditional hospitals (Kiesler, 1982).

## Professions Involved in Psychotherapy

Whether a person receives therapy in a hospital, a community mental health center, a private clinic, or an office, several different types of professionals may be involved.

*A child psychiatrist works with a young patient.*

A **psychiatrist** has an M.D. degree and has completed a three-year residency in a mental health facility, during which he or she received supervision in the diagnosis of abnormal behavior, drug therapy, and psychotherapy. Subsequently, many but not all psychiatrists take an examination in psychiatry and become board-certified. As a physician, the psychiatrist is the only mental health professional who can prescribe medication and, in most states, hospitalization.

The term **psychoanalyst** is reserved for individuals who have received specialized training at a psychoanalytic institute learning the methods and theories derived from Freud. The program usually takes several years, during which the trainees must undergo their own personal psychoanalysis as well as treat several clients psychoanalytically while under supervision. Until recently, most psychoanalytic institutes required their graduates to have an M.D. degree. Thus, most psychoanalysts are psychiatrists. However, the vast majority of psychiatrists are not psychoanalysts.

Psychologists who work as therapists have obtained graduate training in clinical, counseling, or school psychology. Usually, they hold a Ph.D. (Doctor of Philosophy) or Psy.D. (Doctor of Psychology) degree. The Ph.D. emphasizes training in research as well as diagnosis and therapy. The Psy.D. is a more applied degree, focusing mainly on diagnosis and therapy. Both degrees require four or five years of postgraduate study plus a year or more of internship. In addition, most states require psychologists to pass a licensing or certification examination.

**Clinical psychologists** work with people suffering from a broad range of mental disorders. **Counseling psychologists** focus more on problems of adjustment and often concentrate on specific areas such as student, marriage, or family counseling. **School psychologists** are concerned with young people who have academic difficulties.

**Psychiatric social workers** have completed a two-year master's degree program (M.S.W.) which includes training in interviewing, therapy, and in extending treatment procedures to the home and community. The psychiatric social worker is often called on to collect information about a patient's

*A clinical psychologist talking with a client.*

home situation and to assist the patient in getting help from community resources (such as hospitals, clinics, and social agencies).

Sometimes, these professionals work as a team. The psychiatrist prescribes psychotherapeutic medications and monitors their effectiveness; the psychologist sees the same client in individual or group psychotherapy; the social worker monitors the home environment. In mental hospitals a fourth professional is available: the **psychiatric nurse**. Psychiatric nursing is a field within the nursing profession that requires special training in the understanding and treatment of mental disorders. In our discussion of psychotherapeutic techniques, we will not specify the profession of the psychotherapists; we will assume that they are trained and competent members of any one of these professions.

# Techniques of Psychotherapy

**Psychotherapy** refers to the treatment of mental disorders by psychological (rather than physical or biological) means. The term embraces a variety of techniques, all of which are intended to help emotionally disturbed individuals modify their behavior, thoughts, and emotions so that they can develop more useful ways of dealing with stress and with other people. Some psychotherapists believe that modification of behavior is dependent on the individual's understanding of his or her unconscious motives and conflicts (psychoanalysts, for example). Others feel that people can learn to cope with their problems without necessarily exploring the factors that have led to their development (behavior therapists and cognitive behavior therapists, for example). Despite differences in techniques, most methods of psychotherapy have certain basic features in common. They involve a helping relationship between two people: the client (patient) and the therapist. The client is encouraged to discuss intimate concerns, emotions, and experiences freely without fear of being judged by the therapist or having confidences betrayed. The therapist, in turn, offers sympathy and understanding, engenders trust, and tries to help the client develop more effective ways of handling his or her problems.

## Psychoanalysis

Psychoanalytic theories of personality (see Chapter 14) assume that within each individual are opposing forces (the **id**, the **ego**, and the **superego**) that make internal conflicts inevitable. These conflicts, of which the person may or may not be aware, have a powerful influence on personality development and on the ability to handle life stresses. Freud believed that psychological disorders are the result of conflicts, usually originating in early childhood, of which the individual is *not* aware; the impulses and emotions involved have been repressed to the unconscious.

Unconscious conflicts between the aggressive and sexual impulses of the id and the constraints imposed by the ego and superego were considered by Freud to be the most crucial for later maladjustment. For example, a young boy may naturally feel hostile toward the new baby brother who usurps some of the parental love that was once exclusively his. If the parents refuse to acknowledge the boy's feelings and severely punish any expression of anger toward the baby, the boy must deny these impulses in order to retain his parents' love. The unwanted impulse to hurt the baby (and any

*Freud's office in Vienna offered the comfort of his famous couch, as well as a collection of Egyptian, Greek, and Roman antiquities.*

emotions or memories associated with this impulse) may be pushed out of consciousness. These unconscious feelings of sibling rivalry may influence relationships in later life, perhaps taking the form of intense jealousy of and competition with friends and co-workers. Because the original conflict was repressed, the individual will have no awareness of the source of these emotions.

A key assumption of psychoanalysis is that a person's current problems cannot be successfully resolved without a thorough understanding of their unconscious basis in the early relationships with parents and siblings. The goal of psychoanalysis is to bring conflicts (repressed emotions and motives) into awareness so that they can be dealt with in a more rational and realistic way.

**FREE ASSOCIATION AND DREAM ANALYSIS** One of the main techniques psychoanalysts use to facilitate the recovery of unconscious conflicts is **free association**. The client is encouraged to give free rein to thoughts and feelings and to say whatever comes to mind without editing or censoring. This is not easy to do, however. In conversation, we usually try to keep a connecting thread running through our remarks and to exclude irrelevant ideas. In addition, most of us have spent a lifetime learning to be cautious and to think before speaking; thoughts that strike us as inappropriate, stupid, or shameful usually remain unspoken.

With practice, however, and with encouragement from the analyst, free association becomes easier. But even individuals who conscientiously try to give free rein to their thoughts will occasionally find themselves blocked. When a patient remains silent, abruptly changes the subject, or is unable to recall the details of an event, the analyst assumes that the person is resisting the recall of certain thoughts or feelings. Freud believed that blocking, or *resistance*, results from the individual's unconscious control over sensitive areas and that these are precisely the areas that should be explored.

Another technique often used with free association is *dream analysis*. Freud believed that dreams were "the royal road to the unconscious"; they represented an unconscious wish or fear in disguised form. He distinguished between the *manifest* (obvious, conscious) *content* and the *latent* (hidden, unconscious) *content* of dreams (see Chapter 6). By talking about the manifest content of a dream and then free associating to that content, the analyst and client attempt to discern the unconscious meaning.

**TRANSFERENCE**  In psychoanalysis, the patient's attitudes toward the analyst are considered to be an important part of treatment. Sooner or later, the client develops strong emotional responses to the psychoanalyst. Sometimes the responses are positive and friendly; sometimes, negative and hostile. Often these reactions are inappropriate to what is taking place in the therapy sessions. The tendency for the client to make the therapist the object of emotional responses is known as **transference**: the client expresses attitudes toward the analyst that the client actually feels toward other people who are, or were, important in his or her life. Freud assumed that transference represents relics of childhood reactions to parents, and he utilized this transference of attitudes as a means of explaining to patients the childhood origin of many of their concerns and fears. By pointing out how their clients are reacting to them, analysts help their patients achieve a better understanding of how they react to others. The following excerpt shows an analyst's use of transference, followed by the use of free association.

PATIENT:  I don't understand why you're holding back on telling me if this step is the right one for me at this time in my life.

ANALYST:  This has come up before. You want my approval before taking some action. What seems to be happening here is that one of the conflicts you have with your wife is trying to get her approval of what you have decided you want to do, and that conflict is occurring now between us.

PATIENT:  I suppose so. Other people's approval has always been very important to me.

ANALYST:  Let's stay with that for a few minutes. Would you free associate to that idea of getting approval from others. Just let the associations come spontaneously—don't force them.

(Woody & Robertson, 1988, p. 129)

**INTERPRETATION**  The analyst helps the client gain **insight** into the nature of the unconscious conflicts that are the source of his or her difficulties through **interpretation**. An interpretation is a hypothesis that summarizes a segment of the client's behavior and offers an explanation of its motivation. In the previous excerpt, the analyst offers an interpretation by comparing the patient's behavior in the therapy situation (seeking approval for a proposed action) to the kind of approval-seeking behavior that causes conflict with his wife. The client appears to tentatively accept the interpretation.

Interpretation may also take the form of calling attention to the patient's resistances—a sudden blocking of free association, changing the subject, or forgetting an appointment. All of these behaviors may indicate that the client is trying to avoid uncomfortable topics. Interpretations must be skillfully timed; that is, made at a point when unconscious material is close to awareness and the patient is ready to accept painful insights. An interpretation offered before a client is ready to accept it may only arouse anxiety and defensiveness.

**WORKING THROUGH** As an analysis progresses, the patient goes through a lengthy process of reeducation known as **working through**. By examining the same conflicts over and over as they have appeared in a variety of situations, the client comes to understand them and to see how pervasive certain of his attitudes and behaviors are. By working through painful childhood emotions during therapy, the person becomes strong enough to face these emotions with less anxiety and to deal with them in a more realistic manner.

Psychoanalysis is a lengthy, intensive, and expensive process. Client and analyst usually meet for 50-minute sessions several times a week for at least a year, and often several years. Psychoanalysis is most successful with individuals who are highly motivated to solve their problems, who can verbalize their feelings with some ease, and who can afford it.

## Psychoanalytic Therapies

Since Freud's time, numerous forms of psychotherapy based on Freudian concepts have developed. They share in common the premise that mental disorders stem from unconscious conflicts and fears, but they differ from classical psychoanalysis in a number of ways and are usually called **psychoanalytic therapies**. (The term *psychodynamic therapies* is also used.) As noted in Chapter 14, the ego analysts (such as Karen Horney and Heinz Hartman) placed greater emphasis on the role of the rational, problem-solving ego in directing behavior and correspondingly less emphasis on the role of unconscious sexual and aggressive drives. They sought to strengthen the functions of the ego, in particular self-esteem and feelings of competency, so that the individual could deal more constructively with current anxieties and interpersonal relationships. Their general strategy was (a) to give the client insight into how the past continues to influence the present and (b) to develop the client's awareness of what can be done in the present to correct the harmful effects of the past.

The techniques of psychoanalysis have been modified too. Contemporary psychoanalytic therapy is usually briefer, more flexible, and less intense. Sessions are scheduled less frequently, usually once a week. There is less emphasis on a complete reconstruction of childhood experiences and more attention to problems arising from the way the individual is currently interacting with others. Free association is often replaced with a direct discussion of critical issues, and the psychoanalytic therapist may be more direct, raising pertinent topics when it seems appropriate rather than waiting for the client to bring them up. While transference is still considered an important part of the therapeutic process, the therapist may try to limit the intensity of the transference feelings.

Still central, however, is the psychoanalytic therapist's conviction that unconscious motives and fears are at the core of most emotional problems and that insight and the working-through process are essential to a cure (Auld and Hyman, 1991). As we will see in the next section, behavior therapists do not agree with these views.

## Behavior Therapies

The term **behavior therapy** includes a number of different therapeutic methods based on the principles of learning and conditioning discussed in Chapter 7. Behavior therapists assume that maladaptive behaviors are learned ways of coping with stress and that some of the techniques developed in experimental work on learning can be used to substitute more appropriate responses for maladaptive ones. Whereas psychoanalysis is concerned with understanding how the individual's past conflicts influence behavior, behavior therapy focuses more directly on the behavior itself.

Behavior therapists point out that, although the achievement of insight is a worthwhile goal, it does not ensure behavior change. Often we understand why we behave the way we do in a certain situation but are not able to change our behavior. If you are unusually timid about speaking in class, you may be able to trace this fear to past events (your father criticized your opinions whenever you expressed them, your mother made a point of correcting your grammar, you had little experience in public speaking during high school because you were afraid to compete with your older brother who was captain of the debate team). Understanding the reasons behind your fear probably will not make it easier for you to contribute to class discussions.

In contrast to psychoanalysis, which attempts to change certain aspects of the individual's personality, behavior therapies tend to focus on fairly circumscribed goals: the modification of maladaptive behaviors in specific situations. Behavior therapists are also more concerned than psychoanalysts with obtaining experimental evaluations of their techniques.

In the initial therapy session a behavior therapist listens carefully to the client's statement of the problem. What exactly does the client want to change? Is it a fear of flying or of speaking in public? A problem with uncontrolled eating or drinking? Feelings of inadequacy and helplessness? An inability to concentrate and get work done? The first step is to define the problem clearly and to break it down into a set of specific therapeutic goals. If, for example, the client complains of general feelings of inadequacy, the therapist will try to get the client to describe these feelings more specifically: to pinpoint the kinds of situations in which they occur and the kinds of behaviors associated with them. Inadequate to do what? To speak up in class or in social situations? To get assignments completed on time? To control eating? Once the behaviors that need changing are specified, the therapist and client work out a treatment program employing some of the procedures

*Individuals in an agoraphobia workshop discuss their fear of appearing in public places.*

we will describe. The therapist chooses the treatment method that is appropriate for the particular problem.

**SYSTEMATIC DESENSITIZATION AND EXPOSURE** Systematic de-sensitization can be viewed as a *deconditioning* or **counterconditioning** process. This procedure is highly effective in eliminating fears or phobias. The principle of the treatment is to substitute a response that is incompatible with anxiety—namely, relaxation. It is difficult to be both relaxed and anxious at the same time. The client is first trained to relax deeply. One way is to progressively relax various muscles, starting, for example, with the feet and ankles and proceeding up the body to neck and facial muscles. The person learns what muscles feel like when they are truly relaxed and how to discriminate various degrees of tension. Sometimes drugs and hypnosis are used to help people who cannot relax otherwise.

The next step is to make up a hierarchy of the anxiety-producing situations. The situations are ranked in order from the one that produces the least anxiety to the one that is most fearful. The client is then asked to relax and experience or imagine each situation in the hierarchy, starting with the one that is least anxiety-producing. (Experiencing the actual situation works best, but an alternative method is to visualize or imagine it.)

An example will make the procedure clearer. Suppose the client is a woman who suffers from agoraphobia (see Chapter 16) and experiences intense anxiety whenever she leaves the security of her home. The anxiety hierarchy might begin with a walk to the corner mailbox. Somewhere around the middle of the list might be a drive to the supermarket, and at the top, a plane trip alone to a distant city. After the woman has learned to relax and has constructed the hierarchy, desensitization begins. She sits with her eyes closed in a comfortable chair while the therapist describes the least anxiety-producing situation to her. If she can imagine herself in the situation without any increase in muscle tension, the therapist proceeds to the next item on the list. If the woman reports any anxiety while visualizing a scene, she concentrates on relaxing; the same scene is visualized until all anxiety is neutralized. This process continues through a series of sessions until the situation that originally provoked the most anxiety now elicits only relaxation. At this point, the woman has been systematically desensitized to anxiety-provoking situations through the strengthening of an incompatible response—relaxation.

Although desensitization through visually imagined scenes has been effective in reducing fears or phobias, it is less effective than desensitization through actual encounters with the feared stimuli. The woman in our hypothetical case would probably lose her fears more readily if she actually exposed herself to the anxiety-producing situations in a sequence of graduated steps and managed to tolerate each situation until her anxiety subsided (Sherman, 1972). Whenever possible, a behavior therapist tries to combine real-life and symbolic desensitization.

Some behavioral researchers believe that the specific learning process underlying the success of systematic desensitization is **extinction,** rather than counterconditioning. They suggest that *exposure* to the feared situation per se is the important factor; relaxation is merely a useful way to encourage a person to confront what he or she fears. Exposing oneself to a fear-arousing stimulus and discovering that nothing bad happens extinguishes the conditioned fear response (see p. 257). And, indeed, if phobic individuals can force themselves to stay in the feared situation for a long period (for example, a claustrophobic sits in a closet for hours or someone who fears contamination goes for days without washing), the initial terror gradually subsides. This procedure, exposing a phobic individual to the most feared situation or object for an extended length of time without the opportunity to escape, is called **flooding.** It has proved particularly effective in treating agoraphobia (which sometimes resists desensitization) and obsessive-compulsive disorders (Emmelkamp & Kuipus, 1979; Steketee & White, 1990).

**SYSTEMATIC REINFORCEMENT** Whether the underlying learning process is counterconditioning or extinction, systematic desensitization and exposure are based on principles of classical conditioning. **Systematic reinforcement,** based on the principles of operant conditioning (see Chapter 7), has also proved to be an effective method of modifying behavior, especially with children.

The procedure can be illustrated by the case of a third-grade student who was inattentive in school, refused to complete assignments or to participate in class, and spent most of her time daydreaming. In addition, her social skills were poor and she had few friends. The behavior to be reinforced was defined as "on task" behavior, which included paying attention to schoolwork or instructions from the teacher, completing reading assignments, and taking part in class discussions. The reinforcement consisted of beans that were used as tokens to be exchanged for special privileges that the girl valued, such as standing first in line (three beans) or being allowed to stay after school to help the teacher with special projects (nine beans). Anytime the teacher observed the student performing on-task behaviors, she placed one bean in a jar.

During the first 3 months of treatment, the girl completed 12 units of work, compared to 0 units during the 3 months before the reinforcement regime started. In the final 3 months, she completed 36 units and was performing at the same level as the rest of the class. A follow-up the next year showed that the girl was maintaining her academic performance. She also showed a marked improvement in social skills and was accepted more by the other children (Walker, Hedberg, Clement, & Wright, 1981). This is a common finding: improving behavior in one area of life often produces added benefits (Kazdin, 1982).

Reinforcement of desirable responses can be accompanied by extinction of undesirable ones. For example, a young boy who habitually shouts to get his mother's attention could be ignored whenever he does so and reinforced by her attention only when he comes to where she is and speaks in a conversational tone.

Operant conditioning procedures involving rewards for desirable responses and no rewards for undesirable ones have been used successfully in dealing with a broad range of childhood problems, including bed-wetting, aggression, tantrums, disruptive classroom behavior, poor school performance, and social withdrawal. Similar procedures have been used with retarded adults and severely disordered mental patients.

A number of mental hospitals have instituted "token economies" on wards with very regressed, chronic patients to induce socially appropriate behavior. Tokens (which can later be exchanged for food and privileges such as watching television) are given for dressing properly, interacting with other patients, eliminating "psychotic talk," helping on the wards, and so on. Such programs have proved successful in improving both the patients' behavior and the general functioning of the ward (Paul and Lentz, 1977).

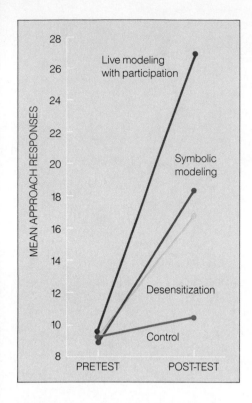

**FIGURE 17-2**
**Treatment of Snake Phobia** *The mean number of snake-approach responses by subjects before and after they received different behavior therapy treatments.* (After Bandura, Blanchard, & Ritter, 1969)

**MODELING** Another effective means of changing behavior is **modeling**, which makes use of observational learning. Since observing other models is a principle way in which humans learn, watching people who are displaying adaptive behavior should teach people with maladaptive responses better coping strategies. Observing the behavior of a model (either live or videotaped) has proved effective in reducing fears and teaching new skills. Figure 17-2 shows the results of a study in which modeling was combined with gradual practice in the treatment of snake phobia.

Modeling is effective in overcoming fears and anxieties because it gives the person a chance to observe someone else go through the anxiety-provoking situation without getting hurt. Watching videotapes of models enjoying a visit to the dentist or going through various hospital procedures has proved successful in helping both children and adults overcome their fears of such experiences (Shaw & Thoresen, 1974; Melamed & Siegel, 1975).

**BEHAVIOR REHEARSAL** In a therapy session modeling is often combined with role-playing, or **behavioral rehearsal**. The therapist helps the individual rehearse or practice more adaptive behaviors. In the following excerpt, a therapist helps a young man overcome his anxieties about asking girls for dates. The young man has been pretending to talk to a girl over the phone and finishes by asking for a date.

CLIENT: By the way (pause), I don't suppose you want to go out Saturday night?

THERAPIST: Up to actually asking for the date, you were very good. However, if I were the girl, I think I might have been a bit offended when you said, "By the way." It's like your asking her out is pretty casual. Also, the way you phrased the question, you are kind of suggesting to her that she doesn't want to go out with you. Pretend for the moment I'm you. Now, how does this sound: "There is a movie at the Varsity Theater this Saturday that I want to see. If you don't have other plans, I'd like very much to take you."

CLIENT: That sounded good. Like you were sure of yourself and liked the girl, too.

THERAPIST: Why don't you try it.

CLIENT: You know that movie at the Varsity? Well, I'd like to go, and I'd like to take you Saturday, if you don't have anything better to do.

THERAPIST: Well, that certainly was better. Your tone of voice was especially good. But the last line "if you don't have anything better to do" sounds like you don't think you have too much to offer. Why not run through it one more time.

CLIENT: I'd like to see the show at the Varsity Saturday, and if you haven't made other plans, I'd like to take you.

THERAPIST: Much better. Excellent, in fact. You were confident, forceful, and sincere.

(Rimm & Masters, 1979, p. 74)

Another area in which behavioral rehearsal has been used to develop social skills is **assertiveness training**. Some people feel anxious in social situations because they do not know how to speak up for what they feel is right or to say no when others take advantage of them. By practicing *assertive responses* (first in role-playing with the therapist and then in real-life situations), the individual not only reduces anxiety but also develops more effective coping techniques. The therapist determines the kinds of situations in which the person is passive and then helps him or her to think of and to practice some assertive responses that might be effective. The following situations might be worked through during a sequence of therapy sessions:

■ Someone steps in front of you in line.

■ A friend asks you to do something you do not want to do.

■ Your boss criticizes you unjustly.

■ You return defective merchandise to a store.

■ You are annoyed by the conversation of people behind you in the movies.

■ The mechanic did an unsatisfactory job of repairing your car.

Most people do not enjoy dealing with such situations, but some individuals are so fearful of asserting themselves that they say nothing and instead build up feelings of resentment and inadequacy. In assertiveness training, the client rehearses with the therapist effective responses that could be made in such situations and gradually tries them in real life. The therapist tries to teach the client to express his needs in a way that is straightforward and forceful, but not seen by others as hostile or threatening.

**SELF-REGULATION** Because client and therapist seldom meet more than once per week, the client must learn to control or regulate his or her own behavior so that progress can be made outside the therapy hour. Moreover, if people feel they are responsible for their own improvement, they are more likely to maintain such gains. **Self-regulation** involves monitoring, or observing, one's own behavior and using various techniques—*self-reinforcement, self-punishment, control of stimulus conditions, development of incompatible responses*—to change the maladaptive behavior. An individual monitors his or her behavior by keeping a careful record of the kinds of situations that elicit the maladaptive behavior and the kinds of responses that are incompatible with it. A person concerned with alcohol dependency would note the kinds of situations in which he or she is most tempted to drink and would try to control such situations or to devise a response that is incompatible with drinking. A man who finds it hard not to join his coworkers in a noontime cocktail might plan to eat lunch at his desk, thereby avoiding the situation. If he is tempted to relax with a drink on arriving home from work, he might substitute a game of tennis or a jog around the block as a means of relieving tension. Both of these activities would be incompatible with drinking.

Self-reinforcement is rewarding yourself immediately for achieving a specific goal; the reward could be praising yourself, watching a favorite television program, telephoning a friend, eating a favorite food. Self-punishment is arranging some aversive consequence for failing to achieve a goal, such as depriving yourself of something you enjoy (*not* watching a favorite television program, for instance) or making yourself do an unpleasant

**TABLE 17-1**
**Self-Regulation of Eating** *The program illustrates the use of learning principles to help control food intake.* (After Stuart & Davis, 1972; O'Leary & Wilson, 1975)

## SELF-MONITORING

*Daily Log*    Keep a detailed record of everything you eat. Note amount eaten, type of food and caloric value, time of day, and the circumstances of eating. This record will establish the caloric intake that is maintaining your present weight. It will also help to identify the stimuli that elicit and reinforce your eating behavior.

*Weight Chart*    Decide how much you want to lose and set a weekly goal for weight loss. Your weekly goal should be realistic (between 1 and 2 pounds). Record your weight each day on graph paper. In addition to showing how your weight varies with food intake, this visual record will reinforce your dieting efforts as you observe progress toward your goal.

## CONTROLLING STIMULUS CONDITIONS

Use these procedures to narrow the range of stimuli associated with eating:

1. Eat only at predetermined times, at a specific table, using a special place mat, napkin, dishes, and so forth. Do *not* eat at other times or in other places (for example, while standing in the kitchen).
2. Do *not* combine eating with other activities, such as reading or watching television.
3. Keep in the house only those foods that are permitted on your diet.
4. Shop for food only after having had a full meal; buy only those items that are on a previously prepared list.

## MODIFYING ACTUAL EATING BEHAVIOR

Use these procedures to break the chain of responses that makes eating automatic:

1. Eat very slowly, paying close attention to the food.
2. Finish chewing and swallowing before putting more food on the fork.
3. Put your utensils down for periodic short breaks before continuing to eat.

## DEVELOPING INCOMPATIBLE RESPONSES

When tempted to eat at times other than those specified, find a substitute activity that is incompatible with eating. For example, exercise to music, go for a walk, talk with a friend (preferably one who knows you are dieting), study your diet plan and weight graph, noting how much weight you have lost.

## SELF-REINFORCEMENT

Arrange to reward yourself with an activity you enjoy (watching television, reading, planning a new wardrobe, visiting a friend) when you have maintained appropriate eating behavior for a day. Plan larger rewards (for example, buying something you want) for a specified amount of weight loss. Self-punishment (other than foregoing a reward) is probably less effective because dieting is a fairly depressing business anyway. But you might decrease the frequency of binge eating by immediately reciting to yourself the aversive consequences or by looking at an unattractive picture of yourself in a bathing suit.

task (such as cleaning your room). Depending on the kind of behavior the individual wants to change, various combinations of self-reinforcement, self-punishment, or control of stimuli and responses may be used. Table 17-1 outlines a program for self-regulation of eating.

## Cognitive Behavior Therapies

The behavior therapy procedures we have discussed thus far have focused on modifying behavior directly with little attention paid to the individual's thinking and reasoning processes. Initially, behavior therapists discounted the importance of cognition, preferring a strict stimulus-response approach. They regarded any consideration of beliefs and attitudes as a return to the kind of unscientific introspection that Watson objected to at the beginning of this century (see Chapter 1). However, in recent years behavior therapists have paid increased attention to the role of cognitive factors—the individual's thoughts, expectations, and interpretation of events—in determining behavior and in mediating behavior change.

**Cognitive behavior therapy** is a general term for treatment methods that use behavior modification techniques but also incorporate procedures designed to change maladaptive beliefs. The therapist attempts to help people control disturbing emotional reactions, such as anxiety and depression, by teaching them more effective ways of interpreting and thinking about their experiences. For example, as we noted in discussing Beck's cognitive theory of depression (see Chapter 16), depressed individuals tend to appraise events from a negative and self-critical viewpoint. They expect to fail rather than to succeed, and they tend to magnify failures and to minimize successes in evaluating their performance. In treating depression, cognitive behavior therapists try to help their clients recognize the distortions in their thinking and make changes that are more in line with reality. The following dialogue illustrates how a therapist, by carefully directed questioning, makes a client aware of the unrealistic nature of her beliefs.

THERAPIST: Why do you want to end your life?

CLIENT: Without Raymond, I am nothing. . . . I can't be happy without Raymond. . . . But I can't save our marriage.

THERAPIST: What has your marriage been like?

CLIENT: It has been miserable from the very beginning. . . . Raymond has always been unfaithful. . . . I have hardly seen him in the past five years.

THERAPIST: You say that you can't be happy without Raymond. . . . Have you found yourself happy when you are with Raymond?

CLIENT: No, we fight all the time and I feel worse.

THERAPIST: You say you are nothing without Raymond. Before you met Raymond, did you feel you were nothing?

CLIENT: No, I felt I was somebody.

THERAPIST: If you were somebody before you knew Raymond, why do you need him [in order] to be somebody now?

CLIENT: (puzzled) Hmmm. . . .

THERAPIST: If you were free of the marriage, do you think that men might be interested in you—knowing that you were available?

CLIENT: I guess that maybe they would be.

| | |
|---|---|
| THERAPIST: | Is it possible that you might find a man who would be more constant than Raymond? |
| CLIENT: | I don't know. . . . I guess it's possible. . . . |
| THERAPIST: | Then what have you actually lost if you break up the marriage? |
| CLIENT: | I don't know. |
| THERAPIST: | Is it possible that you'll get along better if you end the marriage? |
| CLIENT: | There is no guarantee of that. |
| THERAPIST: | Do you have a *real* marriage? |
| CLIENT: | I guess not. |
| THERAPIST: | If you don't have a real marriage, what do you actually lose if you decide to end the marriage? |
| CLIENT: | (long pause) Nothing, I guess. |

(Beck, 1976, pp. 280–291)

The behavioral component of the treatment comes into play when the therapist encourages the client to formulate alternative ways of viewing her situation and then test the implications. For example, the woman in this dialogue might be asked to record her moods at regular intervals and then to note how her depression and feelings of self-esteem fluctuate as a function of what she is doing. If she finds she feels worse after interacting with her husband than when she is alone or is interacting with someone else, this information could serve to challenge her belief that she "can't be happy without Raymond."

Cognitive behavior therapists often combine behavior modification techniques with specific instructions for handling negative thoughts. In treating a person with an obsessive-compulsive disorder, for example, a procedure called *thought stopping* might be used. The client signals the therapist when an obsessive thought enters consciousness and the therapist shouts "Stop!". The client is startled and realizes that the interruption has driven away the unwanted thought. The client is then trained to utter "stop" subvocally whenever an upsetting thought or image begins to intrude.

A program to help someone overcome agoraphobia might include training in positive thinking, along with systematic desensitization (accompanied excursions that take the individual progressively further from home). The therapist teaches the client to replace self-defeating internal dialogues ("I'm so nervous, I know I'll faint as soon as I leave the house") with positive self-instructions ("Be calm; I'm not alone; even if I have a panic attack there is someone to help me"). Table 17-2 describes a program for the treatment of depression that includes techniques for modifying behavior and for changing attitudes.

Cognitive behavior therapists agree that it is important to alter a person's beliefs in order to bring about an enduring change in behavior. Nevertheless, most maintain that behavioral procedures are more powerful than strictly verbal ones in affecting cognitive processes. For example, to overcome anxiety about giving a speech in class, it is helpful to think positively: "I know the material well, and I'm sure I can present my ideas effectively"; "The topic is interesting, and the other students will enjoy what I have to say." But successfully presenting the speech to a roommate and again before a group of friends will probably do more to reduce anxiety. Suc-

### INSTRUCTION IN SELF-CHANGE SKILLS

Pinpointing the target behavior and recording its baseline rate of occurrence; discovering the events or situations that precede the target behavior and the consequences (either positive or negative) that follow it; setting goals for change and choosing reinforcers

### RELAXATION TRAINING

Learning progressive muscle relaxation to handle the anxiety that often accompanies depression; monitoring tension in daily situations and applying relaxation techniques

### INCREASING PLEASANT EVENTS

Monitoring the frequency of enjoyable activities and planning weekly schedules so that each day contains a balance between negative/neutral activities and pleasant ones

### COGNITIVE STRATEGIES

Learning methods for increasing positive thoughts and decreasing negative thoughts; for identifying irrational thoughts and challenging them; and for using self-instructions to help handle problem situations

### ASSERTIVENESS TRAINING

Identifying situations in which being nonassertive adds to feelings of depression; learning to handle social interactions more assertively via modeling and role-playing

### INCREASING SOCIAL INTERACTION

Identifying the factors that are contributing to low social interaction (such as getting in the habit of doing things alone, feeling uncomfortable due to few social skills); deciding on activities that need to be increased (such as calling friends to suggest getting together) or decreased (such as watching television) in order to improve the level of pleasant social interaction

**TABLE 17-2**
**Coping With Depression** *A program for the treatment of depression that combines behavioral and cognitive techniques. This is a condensed description of a 12-session course used successfully to treat depressed individuals in small groups.* (After Lewinsohn, Antonuccio, Steinmetz, & Teri, 1984)

cessful performance increases our feeling of mastery. In fact, it has been suggested that all therapeutic procedures that are effective give the person a sense of mastery or *self-efficacy.* Observing others cope and succeed, being verbally persuaded that we can handle a difficult situation, and judging from internal cues that we are relaxed and in control contribute to our feelings of self-efficacy. But the greatest sense of efficacy comes from actual performance, from personal mastery experiences. In essence, nothing succeeds like success (Bandura, 1984).

## Humanistic Therapies

**Humanistic therapies** are based on the phenomenological approach to personality discussed in Chapter 14. While there are different varieties of humanistic therapies, they all emphasize the individual's natural tendency toward growth and self-actualization. Psychological disorders are assumed to arise when the process of reaching one's potential is blocked by circumstances or by other people (parents, teachers, spouses) who try to channel the person's development along lines they find acceptable. When this occurs, the person begins to deny his true feelings. The person's awareness of his uniqueness becomes narrowed and the potential for growth is reduced. Humanistic therapies seek to help people get in touch with their real selves and to make deliberate choices regarding their lives and behavior, rather than letting external events determine their behavior. The goal of humanistic therapy is to help the client to become more fully the person he or she is capable of becoming.

Like the psychoanalyst, the humanistic therapist attempts to increase the person's awareness of underlying emotions and motives. But the emphasis is on what the individual is experiencing in the here and now, rather than in the past. The humanistic therapist does not interpret the person's behavior (as a psychoanalyst might) or try to modify it (as a behavior therapist would) because such actions would impose the therapist's own views on the patient. The goal of the humanistic therapist is to facilitate exploration of the individual's own thoughts and feelings and to assist the individual in arriving at his or her own solutions. This approach will become clearer as we look at **client-centered therapy** (also called **nondirective therapy**), one of the first humanistic therapies.

Client-centered therapy, developed in the 1940s by the late Carl Rogers, is based on the assumption that the individual is the best expert on himself or herself and that people are capable of working out solutions to their own problems. The task of the therapist is to facilitate this progress—not to ask probing questions, to make interpretations, or to suggest courses of action. In fact, Rogers preferred the term "facilitator" to "therapist," and he called the people he worked with "clients" rather than "patients" because he did not view emotional difficulties as an indication of an illness to be cured.

*Carl Rogers (top right) facilitating discussion in a therapy group.*

Client-centered therapy can be described rather simply, but in practice it requires great skill and is much more subtle than it first appears. The therapist begins by explaining the nature of the interviews. The responsibility for working out problems is the client's. He or she is free to leave at any time and to choose whether to return. The relationship is private and confidential; the person is free to speak of intimate matters without fear of reproof or of the information being revealed to others. Once the situation is structured, the client does most of the talking. Usually, the client has much to say. The therapist is an interested and alert listener. When the client stops, as though expecting the therapist to say something, the therapist usually acknowledges and accepts the feelings the person has expressed. For example, if a man has been talking about his nagging mother, the therapist may say, "You feel that your mother tries to control you." The object is to *clarify* the feelings that the person has been expressing, not to judge them or to elaborate on them.

Generally, individuals begin therapy with rather low evaluations of themselves, but in the course of facing their problems and of trying to arrive at solutions, they begin to view themselves more positively. For instance, one client began the initial session with the following statements:

> Everything is wrong with me. I feel abnormal. I don't do even the ordinary things of life. I'm sure I will fail on anything I undertake. I'm inferior. When I try to imitate successful people, I'm only acting. I can't go on like this.

By the final interview, the client expressed attitudes that contrasted strikingly with the statements in the first interview:

> I am taking a new course of my own choosing. I am really changing. I have always tried to live up to others' standards that were beyond my abilities. I've come to realize that I'm not so bright, but I can get along anyway. I no longer think so much about myself. I'm much more comfortable with people. I'm getting a feeling of success out of my job. I don't feel quite steady yet and would like to feel that I can come for more help if I need it. (Snyder et al., 1947)

To determine whether this kind of progress is typical, researchers have analyzed recorded interviews. When clients' statements are classified and plotted, the course of therapy turns out to be fairly predictable. In the early interviews, people spend a good deal of time talking about their problems and describing symptoms. During the course of therapy, they make more and more statements that indicate they are achieving an *understanding* of their particular problems. By classifying all clients' remarks as either "problem restatements" or "statements of understanding and insight," the progressive increase in insight as therapy proceeds becomes evident (see Figure 17-3).

What do client-centered therapists do to bring about these changes? Rogers believed that the most important qualities for a therapist are empathy, warmth, and genuineness. *Empathy* refers to the ability to understand the feelings the client is trying to express *and* the ability to communicate this understanding to the client. The therapist must adopt the client's frame of reference and must strive to see the problems as the client sees them. By *warmth*, Rogers meant a deep acceptance of the individual as he or she is, including the conviction that this person has the capacity to deal constructively with his or her problems. A therapist who is *genuine* is open and honest and does not play a role or operate behind a professional façade. People are reluctant to reveal themselves to those they perceive as phony. Rogers

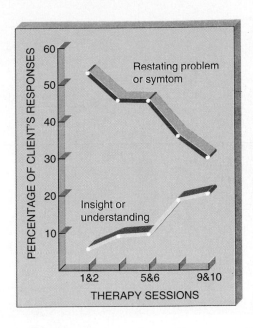

**FIGURE 17-3**
**Changes During Client-Centered Therapy** *Description and restatement of the problem on the part of the client gradually gives way during the course of therapy to increased frequency of statements that indicate understanding.* (After Seeman, 1949)

believed that a therapist who possesses these attributes will facilitate the client's growth and self-exploration (Rogers, 1970; Truax & Mitchell, 1971).

Rogers was the first to make tape recordings of therapy sessions and to permit them to be studied and analyzed. He and his colleagues have contributed much to the field of psychotherapy research. Client-centered therapy has some limitations, however. Like psychoanalysis, it appears to be successful only with individuals who are fairly verbal and who are motivated to discuss their problems. For people who do not voluntarily seek help or who are seriously disturbed and are unable to discuss their feelings, more directive methods are usually necessary. In addition, by using the client's self-reports as the only measure of psychotherapeutic effectiveness, the client-centered therapist ignores behavior outside of the therapy session. Individuals who feel insecure and ineffective in their interpersonal relationships often need help in modifying their behavior.

## An Eclectic Approach

There are many variations of psychotherapy in addition to the ones we have discussed here. Several other approaches to psychotherapy are listed in Table 17-3. Most psychotherapists do not adhere strictly to any *single* method. Instead, they take an *eclectic approach*, selecting from the different techniques the ones they feel are most appropriate for the individual client. Although their theoretical orientation may be toward a particular method or school (for example, more psychoanalytic than behaviorist), eclectic psychotherapists feel free to discard the concepts they view as not especially helpful and to select techniques from other schools. In short, they are flexible in their approach to therapy.*

In dealing with a highly anxious individual, for instance, an eclectic psychotherapist might first prescribe tranquilizers or relaxation training to help reduce the person's level of anxiety. (Most psychoanalysts would not take this approach, however, because they believe that anxiety is necessary to motivate the client to explore his or her conflicts.) To help the client understand the origins of his or her problems, the eclectic therapist might discuss certain aspects of the patient's history but might feel it unnecessary to explore childhood experiences to the extent that a psychoanalyst would. The therapist might use educational techniques, such as providing information about sex and reproduction to help relieve the anxieties of an adolescent boy who feels guilty about his sexual impulses or explaining the functioning of the autonomic nervous system to reassure an anxious woman that some of her symptoms, such as heart palpitations and hand tremors, are not indications of a disease.

Recognizing that often no single therapeutic approach deals successfully with all aspects of a problem, more and more therapists are specializing in specific problems. For example, some clinicians specialize in problems of sexual dysfunction. They learn all they can about the physiological processes that lead to orgasm; the effect of drugs (such as alcohol, tranquilizers, and other medications) on sexual performance; and the way in which such factors as anxiety, sexual traumas, and poor communication between partners contribute to sexual dysfunction. Once sex therapists have learned all

---

*The term *integrative psychotherapy* is sometimes used instead of eclectic pschochotherapy.

**TABLE 17-3**
Other Approaches to Psychotherapy
Listed are several psychotherapies not discussed in the text.

| NAME | FOCUS | METHODS |
| --- | --- | --- |
| **Gestalt therapy** | To become aware of the whole personality by working through unresolved conflicts and discovering those aspects of the individual's being that are blocked from awareness. Emphasis is on becoming intensely aware of how one is feeling and behaving at the moment. | Therapy in a group setting, but therapist works with one individual at a time. Acting out fantasies, dreams or the two sides to a conflict are methods used to increase awareness. Combines psychoanalytic emphasis on resolving internal conflicts with behaviorist emphasis on awareness of one's behavior and humanistic concern for self-actualization. |
| **Reality therapy** | To clarify the individual's values and to evaluate current behavior and future plans in relation to these values. To force the individual to accept responsibility. | Therapist helps the individual perceive the consequences of possible courses of action and decide on a realistic solution or goal. Once a plan of action is chosen, a contract may be signed in which the client agrees to follow through. |
| **Rational-Emotive therapy** | To replace certain irrational ideas (It is essential to be loved and admired by everyone all the time; I should be competent in all respects; People have little control over their sorrow and unhappiness) with more realistic ones. Assumes that cognitive change will produce emotional changes. | Therapist attacks and contradicts the individual's ideas (sometimes subtly, sometimes directly) in an attempt to persuade her or him to take a more rational view of the situation. Similar to Beck's cognitive therapy but therapist is more direct and confrontive. |
| **Transactional analysis** | To become aware of the intent behind the individual's communications; to eliminate subterfuge and deceit so that the individual can interpret his or her behavior accurately. | Therapy in a group setting. Communications between married couples or group members are analyzed in terms of the part of the personality that is speaking —"parent," or "child," or "adult" (similar to Freud's supergo, id, and ego)—and the intent of the message. Destructive social interactions or games are exposed for what they are. |
| **Hypnotherapy** | To relieve the symptoms and strengthen ego processes by helping the individual set reality aside and make constructive use of imagery. | Therapist uses various hypnotic procedures in an attempt to reduce conflict and doubt by focusing the individual's attention, to modify symptoms through direct suggestion or displacement, and to strengthen the individual's ability to cope. |

there is to know about the variables involved in normal and abnormal sexual functioning, they examine the various therapeutic systems to see what techniques can be applied to specific problems. Although sex therapists may draw on all of the approaches we have discussed, biological and cognitive behavioral methods are most often used in treating sexual dysfunctions.

Other therapists specialize in anxiety, depression, alcoholism, and marital problems. Some concentrate on certain age groups, seeking to learn all they can about the problems of children, adolescents, or the aged. Within their special areas, therapists generally use an eclectic, or integrative, approach.

## Group and Family Therapy

Many emotional problems involve an individual's difficulties in relating to others, including feelings of isolation, rejection, and loneliness and the inability to form meaningful relationships. Although the therapist can help the individual to work out some of these problems, the final test lies in how well the person can apply the attitudes and responses learned in therapy to relationships in everyday life. **Group therapy** permits clients to work out their problems in the presence of others, to observe how other people react to their behavior, and to try out new methods of responding when old ones prove unsatisfactory. It is often used as a supplement to individual psychotherapy.

Therapists of various orientations (psychoanalytic, humanistic, and cognitive behaviorist) have modified their techniques to be applicable to therapy groups. Group therapy has been used in a variety of settings: in hospital wards and outpatient psychiatric clinics, with parents of disturbed children, and with teenagers in correctional institutions, to name a few. Typically, the groups consist of a small number of individuals (6 to 12 is considered optimal) who have similar problems. The therapist usually remains in the background, allowing the members to exchange experiences, to comment on one another's behavior, and to discuss their own problems as well as those of the other members. However, in some groups the therapist is quite active. For

*Alcoholics Anonymous is an example of a self-help group.*

| | |
|---|---|
| AIDS Counseling Program | Loss Support (grief recovery) |
| AIRS (teenage chemical dependency) | Make Today Count (breast cancer support) |
| Adult Children of Alcoholics | Narcotics Anonymous |
| Adults Molested as Children | PMS Association (Pre-Menstrual Syndrome) |
| Affective Disorders Group (mood disorders) | Parent Aid (parents at risk for child abuse) |
| Al-Anon (families of alcoholics) | Parents United (sexual abuse) |
| Ala-Teen (teenage alcohol abuse) | Parkinson's Disease Support Group |
| Alcoholics Anonymous | Pre Ala-Teen (child alcohol dependency) |
| Alzheimer's Disease Family Support Group | Project Return (recovering mental patients) |
| Arthritis Support Group | Recovery Inc. |
| Battered Women's Support Group | Phobia Foundation |
| Bi-Polar Support Group (manic-depression) | Single Parent Support Group |
| CREATE (college students recovering from mental illness) | Sudden Infant Death Syndrome |
| Emotional Health Anonymous | Survivors of Suicide |
| Epilepsy Support Group | Teen Mothers Support Group |
| Gay Men's Coming Out Group | Victims of Homicide (family and loved ones) |
| Grandmother's Support Group (mothers of teenage mothers) | Voices (schizophrenic support group) |
| Lesbian Support Group | |

**TABLE 17-4**
**Examples of Self-Help Groups** *Listed are some of the self-help groups available in one large community.* (After San Diego Mental Health Association, 1989)

example, in a group desensitization session, people who share the same phobias (such as fear of flying or anxieties about tests) may be led together through a systematic desensitization hierarchy. Or in a session for training social skills, a group of shy and unassertive individuals may be coached by the therapist in a series of role-playing scenes. Group therapy has several advantages over individual therapy. It saves therapist time because one therapist can help several people at once. An individual can derive comfort and support from observing that others have similar, perhaps more severe problems. A person can learn vicariously by watching how others behave and can explore attitudes and reactions by interacting with a variety of people, not just with the therapist. Groups are particularly effective when they provide the participants with opportunities to acquire new social skills through modeling and to practice these skills in the group.

Most groups are led by a trained therapist. However, the number and variety of self-help groups—groups that are conducted without a professional therapist—are increasing. Self-help groups are voluntary organizations of people who meet regularly to exchange information and to support each other's efforts to overcome a common problem. *Alcoholics Anonymous* is the best known of the self-help groups. Another is *Recovery, Inc.*, an organization open to former mental patients. Other groups help people cope with specific stressful situations such as bereavement, divorce, and single parenthood. Table 17-4 lists a variety of self-help groups.

*Family therapy (left) and marriage counseling (right).*

**MARITAL AND FAMILY THERAPY** Problems in communicating feelings, satisfying one's needs, and responding appropriately to the needs and demands of others become intensified in the intimate context of marriage and family life. To the extent that they involve more than one client and focus on interpersonal relationships, **marital therapy** and **family therapy** can be considered specialized forms of group therapy.

The high divorce rate and the number of couples seeking help for difficulties centering around their relationship have made marital, or couple, therapy a growing field. Studies show that joint therapy for both partners is more effective in solving marital problems than is individual therapy for only one partner (Gurman & Kniskern, 1981).

There are many approaches to marital therapy, but most focus on helping the partners communicate their feelings, develop greater understanding and sensitivity to each other's needs, and work on more effective ways of handling their conflicts. Some couples enter marriage with very different, and often unrealistic, expectations about the roles of husband and wife, which can wreak havoc with their relationship. The therapist can help them clarify their expectations and work out a mutually agreeable compromise. Sometimes the couple negotiates *behavioral contracts*, agreeing on the behavior changes each person is willing to make in order to create a more satisfying relationship and specifying the rewards and penalties they can use with each other to ensure the changes.

Family therapy overlaps with marital therapy but has a somewhat different origin. It developed in response to the discovery that many people who improved in individual therapy while away from their family—often in institutional settings—relapsed when they returned home. It became apparent that many of these people came from a disturbed family setting that required modification itself if the individual's gains were to be maintained. The basic premise of family therapy is that the problem shown by the identified patient is a sign that something is wrong with the entire family; the *family system* is not operating properly. The difficulty may lie in poor communication among family members or in an alliance between some family members that excludes others. For example, a mother whose relationship with her husband is unsatisfactory may focus all her attention on her son. As a result, the husband and daughter feel neglected and the son, upset by his mother's smothering and the resentment directed toward him by his father and sister, develops problems in school. While the boy's school difficulties may be the reason for seeking treatment, it is clear that they are only a symptom of a more basic family problem.

In family therapy, the family meets regularly with one or two therapists (usually a male and a female). The therapist, while observing the interactions among family members, tries to help each member become aware of the way he or she relates to the others and how his or her actions may be contributing to the family's problems. Sometimes videotape recordings are played back to make the family members aware of how they interact with each other. Other times, the therapist may visit the family in the home to observe conflicts and verbal exchanges as they occur in their natural setting. It often becomes apparent that problem behaviors are being reinforced by the responses of family members. For example, a young child's temper tantrums or a teenager's eating problems may be inadvertently reinforced by the attention they elicit from the parents. The therapist can teach the parents to monitor their own and their children's behavior, to determine how their reactions may be reinforcing the problem behavior, and then to alter the reinforcement contingencies.

# Effectiveness of Psychotherapy

How effective is psychotherapy? Which methods work best? These questions are not easy to answer. Research into the effectiveness of psychotherapy is hampered by several major difficulties. How do we decide whether an individual has improved? What measures of improvement are valid? How do we know what caused the change?

## Evaluating Psychotherapy

Evaluating the effectiveness of psychotherapy is a very difficult task because so many variables must be considered. For instance, a large percentage of people with psychological problems get better without any professional treatment. This phenomenon is called **spontaneous remission,** a term borrowed from medicine. Many physical illnesses run a certain course, and barring complications, the individual will recover without specific treatment. However, the word "spontaneous" is not really appropriate in describing recovery from psychological disorders without professional help. Some mental disorders do improve by themselves, simply with the passage of time—much like the common cold. This is particularly true of depression. But more often, improvement that occurs in the absence of treatment is not spontaneous; rather, it is the result of external events—usually changes in the individual's life situation or the help of another person.

Many emotionally disturbed people who do not seek professional assistance are able to improve with the help of a nonprofessional, such as a friend, teacher, or religious adviser. We cannot consider these recoveries to be spontaneous; but since they are not due to psychotherapy, they are included in the rate of spontaneous remission, which ranges from about 30 to

60 percent, depending on the particular disorder being studied (Bergin & Lambert, 1978). To allow for those who would have improved without treatment, any evaluation of psychotherapy must compare a treated group with an untreated control group. Psychotherapy is judged to be effective if the client's improvement after therapy is greater than any improvement that occurs without therapy over the same period. The ethical problem of allowing someone to go without treatment is usually resolved by composing the control group of individuals on a waiting list. Members of the waiting-list control group are interviewed at the start of the study to gather baseline information but receive no treatment until after the study. Unfortunately, the longer the study (and time is needed to measure improvement, especially with insight therapies), the harder it is to keep people on a waiting list.

A second major problem in evaluating psychotherapy is measuring the outcome. How do we decide whether a person has been helped by therapy? We cannot always rely on the individual's own assessment. Some people report that they are feeling better simply to please the therapist or to convince themselves that their money was well spent. The *hello–goodbye effect* has long been recognized by therapists. At the beginning of therapy (the "hello"), people tend to exaggerate their unhappiness and their problems to convince the therapist that they really need help. At the end of therapy (the "goodbye"), they tend to exaggerate their well-being to express appreciation to the therapist for his or her efforts or to convince themselves that their time and money were not wasted. These phenomena must be considered when evaluating the client's view of his or her progress.

The therapist's evaluation of the treatment as successful cannot always be considered an objective criterion, either. The therapist has a vested interest in proclaiming that the client is better. And sometimes the changes that the therapist observes during the therapy session do not carry over into real-life situations. Assessment of improvement, therefore, should include at least three independent measures: the client's evaluation of progress; the therapist's evaluation; and the judgment of a third party, such as family members and friends or a clinician not involved in the treatment.

Other outcome measures that may be used in evaluating the effectiveness of psychotherapy include scores on tests (such as the Minnesota Multiphasic Personality Inventory or the Beck Depression Inventory) and, in the case of behavior therapy, changes in the target behavior (such as a decrease in compulsive acts). Measures of improvement in a person's life outside of the therapy situation—performing more effectively at work or school, drinking less, a decrease in antisocial activities—are more meaningful but are often difficult to obtain in long-term studies of psychotherapeutic effectiveness.

Despite these problems, researchers have been able to conduct many psychotherapy evaluation studies. Rather than discuss individual studies, we will look at a major evaluation that attempted to answer the question of whether psychotherapy works. The investigators located 475 published studies that compared at least one therapy group with an untreated control group. Using a complicated statistical procedure called meta-analysis (see Chapter 6), they determined the magnitude of effect for each study by comparing the average change produced in treatment (on measures such as self-esteem, anxiety, and achievement in work and school) with that of the control group. They concluded that individuals receiving therapy were better off than those who had received no treatment. The average psychotherapy patient showed greater improvement than 80 percent of the untreated control-group patients (Smith, Glass, & Miller, 1980).

A subsequent review that analyzed a new sample of studies yielded comparable results (Shapiro & Shapiro, 1982). When we look at improvement rates as a function of the number of therapy sessions (see Figure 17-4), it is clear that treated groups show a rate of change that is above and beyond spontaneous remission estimates. By the eighth therapy session approximately 50 percent of patients are measurably improved, and 75 percent have shown improvement by the end of 6 months of weekly psychotherapy.

## Comparing Psychotherapies

Psychotherapy produces greater improvement than no treatment, but are the different therapeutic approaches equally effective? A number of reviews have analyzed studies in which the results of different psychotherapies were compared (for example, Bergin & Lambert, 1978; Smith, Glass, & Miller, 1980; Rachman & Wilson, 1980). The conclusion of most of these reviews is that there is little difference in effectiveness between therapies. This conclusion, disturbing to some therapists, has been called the "Dodo bird verdict," in reference to the Dodo bird in *Alice in Wonderland* who said "Everyone has won and all must have prizes." How can therapies that espouse such different methods produce such similar results? Numerous possible explanations have been suggested (see Stiles, Shapiro, & Elliott, 1986). We will mention only two.

Perhaps certain therapies are effective for certain problems or disorders but are relatively ineffective for others. When specific therapies are used to treat a wide range of disorders, they may help some cases but not others. Thus, averaging results over cases may conceal the special strengths of a particular therapy. We need to know which treatment is effective for which problem.

There are some clues. We know, for example, that systematic desensitization and exposure are effective for eliminating specific fears or phobias, whereas psychoanalytic and client-centered therapies are not. In treating depression, the nondirective approach of client-centered therapy may bring temporary relief but usually fails to change the self-defeating thoughts and behavior patterns that underlie the disorder. When we want to change specific behaviors, cognitive behavior therapies generally work better than insight therapies. But if the goal is self-understanding, then more global therapies such as psychoanalytic and client-centered therapy are appropriate.

We know, too, that none of the psychotherapies are very successful in treating schizophrenia or bipolar disorders. However, psychotherapy can be beneficial (when used in combination with some of the biological therapies described in the next section) in helping the patient deal with the problems of daily living. The task for future evaluators is to determine the disorder for which each therapy is particularly effective. Matching the right therapy and therapist with the right patient will improve the overall effectiveness of treatment.

Another reason why different psychotherapies may be equally effective in helping clients is because they all share certain factors. It may be these common factors, rather than the specific therapeutic techniques employed, that promote positive change.

## Common Factors in Psychotherapies

One school of therapy emphasizes insight; another, modeling and reinforcement; and yet another, empathy and warmth. But perhaps these variables are not the crucial ones. Other factors that are common to most psychotherapies, but which receive little emphasis when therapists write

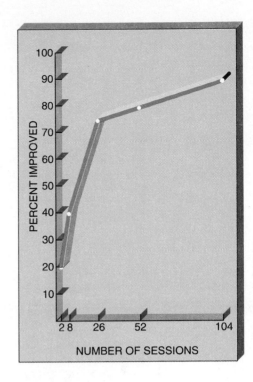

**FIGURE 17-4**
**Improvement with Psychotherapy** *The figure shows the relationship between the number of sessions of individual psychotherapy and the percentage of patients improved. Improvement was rated by indpendent researchers following the termination of treatment.* (After Howard, Kopta, Krause, & Orlinsky, 1986)

*A relationship of mutual respect and trust is important to successful psychotherapy.*

about what they do, may be more important (Garfield, 1980; Orlinsky & Howard, 1987).

**AN INTERPERSONAL RELATIONSHIP OF WARMTH AND TRUST**  Regardless of the type of therapy provided, in a good therapeutic relationship, client and therapist have mutual respect and regard for one another. The client must believe that the therapist understands and is concerned with his or her problems. Although behavior therapy may sound like a rather impersonal procedure when it is described in a textbook, studies indicate that experienced behavior therapists show as much empathy and depth of interpersonal involvement as experienced psychoanalytically oriented therapists (Sloane et al., 1975). A therapist who understands our problems and believes we can solve them earns our trust, which increases our sense of competence and our confidence that we can succeed.

**REASSURANCE AND SUPPORT**  Our problems often seem insurmountable and unique to us. Discussing them with an expert who accepts our difficulties as not unusual and indicates that they can be resolved is reassuring. Having someone help us with problems we have not been able to solve alone also provides a sense of support and a feeling of hope. In fact, the most successful therapists, regardless of their method of psychotherapy, are those who form a helpful, supportive relationship with their clients (Luborsky et al., 1985).

**DESENSITIZATION**  We have already talked about systematic desensitization, the specific techniques of behavior therapy aimed at helping individuals to lose their fear of certain objects or situations. But many types of psychotherapy can encourage a broader kind of desensitization. When we discuss events and emotions that have been troubling us in the accepting atmosphere of a therapy session, they gradually lose their threatening quality. Problems that we brood about alone can become magnified beyond proportion; sharing problems with someone else often makes them seem less serious. Several other hypotheses can also explain how desensitization occurs in psychotherapy. For example, putting events that are disturbing into words may help us reappraise the situation in a more realistic manner. From the viewpoint of learning theory, repeatedly discussing distressing experiences in the security of a therapeutic setting (where punishment is not forthcoming) may gradually extinguish the anxiety associated with them. Whatever the process, desensitization does appear to be a factor common to many kinds of psychotherapy.

**REINFORCEMENT OF ADAPTIVE RESPONSES** Behavior therapists use reinforcement as a technique to increase positive attitudes and actions. But any therapist in whom a client places trust and confidence functions as a reinforcing agent; that is, the therapist tends to express approval of the behaviors or attitudes deemed conducive to better adjustment and to ignore or express disapproval of maladaptive attitudes or responses. Which responses are reinforced depends on the therapist's orientation and therapeutic goals. The use of reinforcement may be intentional or unintentional; in some instances, the therapist may be unaware that he or she is reinforcing or failing to reinforce a particular client behavior. For example, client-centered therapists believe in letting the client determine what is discussed during the therapy sessions and do not wish to influence the trend of the client's conversation. However, reinforcement can be subtle; a smile, a nod of the head, or a simple "um hmm" following certain client statements may increase the likelihood of their recurrence.

Since the goal of all psychotherapies is to bring about a change in the client's attitudes and behaviors, some type of learning must take place in therapy. The therapist needs to be aware of his or her role in influencing the client by means of reinforcement and should use this knowledge consciously to facilitate desired changes.

**UNDERSTANDING OR INSIGHT** All of the psychotherapies we have been discussing provide the client with an *explanation* of his or her difficulties—how they arose, why they persist, and how they can be changed. For the individual in psychoanalysis, this explanation may take the form of a gradual understanding of repressed childhood fears and the ways in which these unconscious feelings have contributed to current problems. A behavior therapist might inform the client that current fears are the result of previous conditioning and can be conquered by learning responses that are incompatible with the current ones. A client seeing a cognitive behavior therapist might be told that his or her difficulties stem from the irrational belief that one must be perfect or must be loved by everyone.

How can such different explanations all produce positive results? Perhaps the precise nature of the insights and understanding provided by the therapist is relatively unimportant. It may be more important to provide the client with an explanation for the behavior or feelings that he or she finds so distressing and to present a set of activities (such as free association or relaxation training) that both therapist and client believe will alleviate the distress. When a person is experiencing disturbing symptoms and is unsure of their cause or how serious they might be, he or she will feel reassured contacting a professional who seems to know what the problem is and offers ways of relieving it. The knowledge that change is possible gives the individual hope, and hope is an important variable in facilitating change. (See the Critical Discussion, "The Placebo Response.")

## The Placebo Response

**Placebos** are commonly used in research on the effectiveness of drugs. A placebo is an inert substance (known to have no pharmacological effect) that is made to look like an active drug—in essence, a sugar pill. Placebos are used in drug research as controls (a) for the patients' expectations that the medicine will make them feel better, (b) for the researcher's belief that the medicine is effective, and (c) for the beneficial effects of extra attention from nurses and other personnel that stem from being a research subject. A **double-blind** procedure is usually employed: one group of patients is given the drug and a comparable group is given the placebo, but neither the patients nor the researchers (or whoever judges the results) knows until the end of the study which pills contain the active medication and which

are the placebos. Since both the patients and the researchers are blind to the nature of the pills, the method is termed double-blind. If the rate of improvement is greater in those who received the drug, then the drug is considered to be therapeutically effective. If both groups of patients show similar improvement, then whatever positive response occurs with the drug is considered to be a placebo effect and the drug is judged to be ineffective.

All responses that cannot be explained on the basis of actual drug effects are considered to be placebo responses—that is, due to unknown and nonpharmacological causes. Such unknown causes are generally assumed to be psychological in nature.

Placebo responses can be very powerful. For example, 40 percent of patients who were suffering from a painful heart disease (angina pectoris) reported marked relief from their symptoms after undergoing a diagnostic procedure that they believed was an operation to cure the problem (Beecher, 1961). In treating psychological disorders, placebos are often as effective as medication. A review of studies in which patients were given either an antianxiety drug or a placebo found that improvement rates for patients receiving placebos were usually as good as, and often better than,

the rates for those receiving drugs (Lowinger & Dobie, 1969).

Until the beginning of modern scientific medicine, almost all medications were placebos. Patients were given every conceivable substance—crocodile dung, lozenges of dried vipers, spermatic fluid of frogs, spiders, worms, and human excrement—prepared in every possible manner to treat their symptoms. Throughout medical history, patients have been purged, poisoned, leached, bled, heated, frozen, sweated, and shocked (Shapiro & Morris, 1978). Since physicians and healers traditionally have held positions of honor and respect, their "treatments" must have helped at least some of their patients. We assume their effectiveness was due to the placebo response. Scientists also attribute documented cases of faith healing and various forms of miraculous cures to placebo effects.

Some clinicians have suggested that the placebo response may be one of the reasons why psychotherapy works (Lieberman & Dunlap, 1979; Wilkins, 1984). According to this view, almost any method of psychotherapy should show positive results if the client believes it will be effective. If this is true, it becomes important for the therapist to convey to the client his or her conviction that the method of treatment will

Our discussion of common factors among psychotherapies is not intended to deny the value of some specific treatment methods. Perhaps the most effective therapist is one who recognizes the importance of the common factors and utilizes them in a planned manner for all patients, but who also selects the specific procedures most appropriate for each individual case. This suggests that the training of future therapists should be more eclectic, less committed to a particular school of psychotherapy, and more open to a variety of procedures. It should encourage a systematic search for the procedures that are most effective and efficient for specific problems.

## Biological Therapies

The biological approach to abnormal behavior assumes that mental disorders, like physical illnesses, are caused by biochemical or physiological dysfunctions of the brain. Several biological theories were mentioned in discussing the etiology of schizophrenia and the mood disorders in Chapter 16. Biological therapies include the use of drugs and electroconvulsive shock.

be successful.

The idea that placebo responses play a central role in psychotherapy is disturbing to some clinicians. They feel that it links psychotherapy with quackery or charlatanism and implies that the process is one of self-deception. This is not the case. Physicians and psychotherapists have known for a long time that a patient's attitudes and beliefs are very important in determining the effectiveness of treatment. Any treatment will be more effective if the patient believes in it and is motivated to use it in the proper manner. Rather than deny the importance of the placebo effect, it would be better to continue investigating the variables that contribute to it.

In addition, researchers who wish to demonstrate the effectiveness of a specific therapeutic technique should control for the placebo response. Sophisticated studies do this by including a placebo control group, as well as an untreated control group. For example, an experiment designed to test the efficacy of systematic desensitization in reducing anxiety about public speaking included the following groups: systematic desensitization, insight therapy, attention-placebo, and untreated control. The subjects in the attention-placebo group met with a sympathetic therapist who led them to believe that a pill would re-duce their overall sensitivity to stress. To convince them, the therapist had them listen to a "stress tape" (presumably one used in training astronauts to function under stress) for several sessions after ingesting the "tranquilizer." In reality, the pill was a placebo and the tape contained nonverbal sounds that had been found in other research to be boring rather than stressful. In this way, the researcher raised the subjects' expectations that their speech anxiety would be lessened by taking a pill. The results of this study revealed that the systematic desensitization group improved (they reduced their speech anxiety) much more than the no-treatment group and more than the attention-placebo and insight therapy groups, who reacted about the same to their forms of therapy. The latter two groups, however, did show significant improvement (Paul, 1967). By including the attention-placebo group, the experimenter was able to conclude that the success of the systematic desensitization procedure was not due solely to the placebo effect.

The mechanism that causes placebo responses is unknown. Numerous hypotheses have been proposed, but so far there is little empirical verification for any of them. One group of explanations focuses on social influence (see Chapter 19). Because patients tend to view physicians and therapists as socially powerful individuals, they may be very suggestible to the influence of such authorities and may be easily persuaded that beneficial results will occur. In addition, the role of patient entails certain prescribed behaviors. A good patient is one who gets better; getting better justifies the therapists' initial concern and subsequent interest.

Other explanations focus on the individual's expectations. The person who administers the treatment may communicate, by intended or unintended means, expectations about the effects of the treatment. The patients also arrive with certain expectations, based on their previous experiences. Expectations that one will get better and a strong desire that it happen are the essential ingredients of hope. And hope can have a powerful influence on our emotions and bodily processes. Some researchers speculate that this influence may be mediated by the endorphin group of neurotransmitters. We noted in Chapter 2 how endorphins, the "brain's natural opiates," affect mood and the subjective experience of pain. Endorphins may turn out to play an important role in the placebo response.

## Psychotherapeutic Drugs

By far the most successful biological therapy is the use of drugs to modify mood and behavior. The discovery in the early 1950s of drugs that relieved some of the symptoms of schizophrenia represented a major breakthrough in the treatment of severely disturbed individuals. Intensely agitated patients no longer had to be physically restrained by straitjackets, and patients who had been spending most of their time hallucinating and exhibiting bizarre behavior became more responsive and functional. As a result, psychiatric wards became more manageable, and patients could be discharged more quickly. A few years later, the discovery of drugs that could relieve severe depression had a similar beneficial effect on hospital management and population. We saw in Figure 17-1 the reduction in the number of mental-hospital residents that occurred following the introduction of antipsychotic and antidepressant drugs. About the same time, a group of drugs were being developed to relieve anxiety.

**ANTIANXIETY DRUGS**  Drugs that reduce anxiety belong to the family called benzodiazepines. They are commonly known as **tranquilizers** and are marketed under such trade names as Valium (diazepam), Librium (chlordiazepoxide), and Xanax (alprazolam). **Antianxiety drugs** reduce tension and cause drowsiness. Like alcohol and the barbiturates, they depress the action of the central nervous system. Family physicians often prescribe tranquilizers to help people cope during difficult periods in their lives. The drugs are also used to treat anxiety disorders, withdrawal from alcohol, and physical disorders related to stress. For example, antianxiety drugs may be combined with systematic desensitization in the treatment of a phobia to help the individual relax when confronting the feared situation.

Although tranquilizers may be useful on a short-term basis, the overall benefits are debatable, and such drugs clearly are overprescribed and misused. Until quite recently (before some of the dangers became apparent), Valium and Librium were the two most widely prescribed drugs in this country (Julien, 1992). The dangers of tranquilizer overuse are several. Depending on a pill to relieve anxiety may prevent a person from exploring the *cause* of the anxiety and from learning more effective ways of coping with tension. More importantly, long-term use of tranquilizers can lead to physical dependency, or addiction (see Chapter 6). Although tranquilizers are not as addictive as barbiturates, tolerance does develop with repeated use and the individual experiences severe withdrawal symptoms if the drug is discontinued. In addition, tranquilizers impair concentration, including driving performance, and can cause death if combined with alcohol.

**ANTIPSYCHOTIC DRUGS** Most of the **antipsychotic drugs** that relieve the symptoms of schizophrenia belong to the family called **phenothiazines**. Examples are Thorazine (chlorpromazine) and Prolixin (fluphenazine). These drugs have been called "major tranquilizers," but the term is not really appropriate, because they do not act on the nervous system in the same way as barbiturates or antianxiety drugs. They may cause some drowsiness and lethargy, but they do not induce deep sleep even in massive doses (the person can be easily aroused). They also seldom create the pleasant, slightly euphoric feeling associated with low doses of antianxiety drugs. In fact, the psychological effects of the antipsychotic drugs when administered to normal individuals are usually unpleasant. Hence, these drugs are seldom abused.

In Chapter 16, we discussed the theory that schizophrenia is caused by excessive activity of the neurotransmitter dopamine. Antipsychotic drugs block dopamine receptors. Because the drug's molecules are structurally similar to dopamine molecules, they bind to the postsynaptic receptors of dopamine neurons, thereby blocking the access of dopamine to its receptors. (The drug itself does not activate the receptors.) A single synapse has many receptor molecules. If all of them are blocked, transmission across the synapse will fail. If only some of them are blocked, transmission will be weakened. The clinical potency of an antipsychotic drug is directly related to its ability to compete for dopamine receptors.

Neurons that have receptors for dopamine are concentrated in the reticular system, the limbic system, and the hypothalamus. The reticular system selectively filters the flow of messages from the sense organs to the cerebral cortex and controls the individual's state of arousal. The limbic system and the hypothalamus are important in the regulation of emotion. Alteration of neural activity in these areas may account for the calming effects of antipsychotic drugs, although we have no idea as yet of the processes involved.

Whatever their method of action, antipsychotic drugs are effective in alleviating the hallucinations and confusion of an acute schizophrenic episode and in restoring rational thought processes. These drugs do not cure schizophrenia; most patients must continue to receive a maintenance dosage in order to function outside of a hospital. Many of the characteristic symptoms of schizophrenia—emotional blunting, seclusiveness, difficulties in sustaining attention—remain. Nevertheless, antipsychotic drugs shorten the length of time patients must be hospitalized, and they prevent relapse. Studies of schizophrenics living in the community find that the relapse rate for those taking one of the phenothiazines is typically half the relapse rate of those receiving a placebo (Hogarty et al., 1979).

Unfortunately, antipsychotic drugs do not help all schizophrenic patients. In addition, the drugs have unpleasant side effects—dryness of the mouth, blurred vision, difficulty concentrating, and sometimes neurological symptoms—that prompt many patients to discontinue their medication. With long-term usage, more serious side effects may also occur (for example, low blood pressure and a muscular disorder in which there are involuntary movements of the mouth and chin). Researchers continue to search for drugs that will relieve the symptoms of schizophrenia with fewer side effects.

**ANTIDEPRESSANT DRUGS** **Antidepressant drugs** help to elevate the mood of depressed individuals. These drugs energize rather than tranquilize, apparently by increasing the availability of two neurotransmitters (norepinephrine and serotonin) that are deficient in some cases of depression (see Chapter 16). The two major classes of antidepressant drugs act in different ways to increase neurotransmitter levels. The **monoamine oxidase (MAO) inhibitors** (examples are Nardil and Parnate) block the activity of an enzyme that can destroy both norepinephrine and serotonin, thereby increasing the concentration of these two neurotransmitters in the brain. The **tricyclic antidepressants** (examples are Tofranil and Elavil) prevent the **reuptake** of serotonin and norepinephrine, thereby prolonging the duration of the neurotransmitters' actions. (Recall that *reuptake* is the process by which neurotransmitters are drawn back into the nerve terminals that released them.) Both classes of drugs have proved effective in relieving certain types of depression, presumably those caused more by biological factors than environmental ones. However, like the antipsychotic drugs, the antidepressants can produce some undesirable side effects.

Antidepressants are not stimulants, as amphetamines are (see Chapter 6); they do not produce feelings of euphoria and increased energy. In fact, a patient may undergo several weeks of medication before a change in mood is observed. This is one reason why electroconvulsive therapy, which acts more quickly, is sometimes the preferred treatment for severely depressed, suicidal individuals. We will discuss electroconvulsive therapy in the next section.

The search for drugs that are more effective, have fewer side effects, and act more quickly than the tricyclic antidepressants and MAO inhibiters has intensified in the past few years. As a result, new drugs appear on the market almost daily. Among these newer drugs (called *second-generation antidepressants*) are several that selectively increase serotonin levels, by blocking its reuptake, without affecting norepinephrine. Examples are fluoxetine (Prozac) and clomipramine (Anafranil). In addition to relieving depression, these two drugs have also proved helpful in treating both obsessive-compulsive disorders and panic disorders (see Lickey & Gordon, 1991).

Antidepressants are not effective in treating the depression that occurs with bipolar disorders. However, another drug, lithium, has proved very successful. Lithium reduces extreme mood swings and returns the individual to a more normal state of emotional equilibrium. Although the effectiveness of this drug has been known for more than 40 years, researchers have only recently discovered how its complex action on certain neurotransmitters achieves this normalizing effect (Worley, Heller, Snyder, & Baraban, 1988).

Drug therapy has successfully reduced the severity of some types of mental disorders. Many individuals who would require hospitalization otherwise can function within the community with the help of these drugs. On the other hand, there are limitations to the application of drug therapy. All therapeutic drugs can produce undesirable side effects. In addition, many psychologists feel that these drugs alleviate symptoms without requiring the individual to face the personal problems that may be contributing to the disorder. Biochemical abnormalities undoubtedly play a role in schizophrenia and in the more severe mood disorders, but psychological factors are also important. Attitudes and methods of coping with problems that have developed gradually over a lifetime cannot be changed by the administration of a drug. When therapeutic drugs are prescribed, psychotherapeutic help is usually also required.

## Electroconvulsive Therapy

In **electroconvulsive therapy** (ECT), also known as **electroshock therapy,** a mild electric current is applied to the brain to produce a seizure similar to an epileptic convulsion. ECT was a popular treatment from about 1940 to 1960, before antipsychotic and antidepressant drugs became readily available. Today, ECT is used only in cases of severe depression when patients fail to respond to drug therapy.

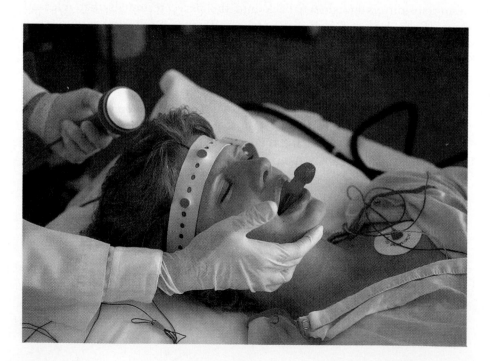

*A patient being prepared for electroconvulsive therapy.*

ECT has been the subject of much controversy and public apprehension for several reasons. At one time, it was used indiscriminately in mental hospitals to treat such disorders as alcoholism and schizophrenia, for which it produced no beneficial results. Before more refined procedures were developed, ECT was a frightening experience for the patient, who was often awake until the electric current triggered the seizure and produced momentary unconsciousness. The patient frequently suffered confusion and memory loss afterward. Occasionally, the intensity of the muscle spasms accompanying the brain seizure resulted in physical injuries.

Today, ECT involves little discomfort. The patient is given a short-acting anesthesia and then is injected with a muscle relaxant. A brief, very weak electric current is delivered to the brain either across both temples or to the temple on the side of the nondominant cerebral hemisphere. The minimum current required to produce a brain seizure is administered, since the seizure itself—*not* the electricity—is therapeutic. The muscle relaxant prevents the convulsive spasm of body muscles and possible injury. The individual awakens within a few minutes and remembers nothing about the treatment. Four to six treatments are usually administered over a period of several weeks.

The most troublesome side effect of ECT is memory loss. Some patients report a gap in memory for events that occurred up to 6 months before ECT, as well as an impaired ability to retain new information for a month or two following treatment. However, if very low dosages of electricity are used (the amount is carefully calibrated for each patient to be just sufficient to produce a seizure), memory problems are minimal (Sackeim & Malitz, 1985).

No one knows how the electrically induced seizures relieve depression. Brain seizures do cause the massive release of a number of neurotransmitters, including norepinephrine and serotonin; deficiencies of these two neurotransmitters may be an important factor in some cases of depression (see Chapter 16). Currently researchers are trying to determine the similarities and dissimilarities between ECT and antidepressant drugs in terms of the way each affects neurotransmitters. However it works, ECT is effective in bringing people out of severe, immobilizing depression and does so faster than drug therapy (Janicak et al., 1985).

## Enhancing Mental Health

The prevention and treatment of mental disorders is a problem of tremendous concern for both the community and the nation. Early in this chapter, we noted that the Community Mental Health Centers Act, passed by Congress in 1963, provided funds for the establishment of community mental health centers so that people could be treated close to family and friends rather than in large state psychiatric hospitals. These community centers provide short-term hospitalization, outpatient treatment, and a 24-hour emergency service. They are also concerned with preventing emotional problems and so consult with schools, juvenile courts, and other community agencies.

Federal funding for community mental health centers has been cut drastically in recent years, greatly diminishing services for the poor. Increased efforts by states, communities, and volunteer organizations are essential to help fill the void.

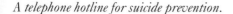

*A telephone hotline for suicide prevention.*

## Community Resources and Paraprofessionals

A variety of community resources have been developed in response to the psychological needs of different groups. One such resource is the *halfway house*, where patients who have been hospitalized can live while making the transition back to an independent life in the community. Residential centers are also available to people recovering from alcohol and drug problems, to delinquent or runaway youths, and to battered wives. *Rap centers*, where troubled teenagers can discuss their problems with each other and with sympathetic counselors, play an important role in many communities; *youth centers* provide job counseling, remedial education, and help with family and personal problems.

CRISIS INTERVENTION   *Crisis intervention* provides immediate help for individuals and families undergoing intense stress. During periods of acute emotional turmoil, people often feel overwhelmed and incapable of dealing with the situation. They may not be able to wait for a therapy appointment, or they may not know where to turn. One form of crisis intervention is provided by 24-hour, walk-in services, often in a community mental health center, where the individual receives immediate attention. There, a therapist helps to clarify the problem, provides reassurance, suggests a plan of action, and mobilizes the support of other agencies or family members. This kind of therapy is usually short-term (five or six sessions) and provides the support the person requires to handle the crisis at hand. Such short-term intervention often prevents the need for hospitalization.

Another form of crisis intervention is the *telephone hot line*. Telephone crisis centers are usually staffed by volunteers under the direction of mental health professionals. Some focus specifically on suicide prevention; others are more general and help distressed callers find the particular kind of assistance they need. The volunteers usually receive training that emphasizes listening with care, evaluating the potential for suicide, conveying empathy and understanding, providing information about community resources, giving hope and reassurance, and recording the caller's name and phone number before he or she hangs up so that a professional can follow up on the problem. Most major cities in the United States have developed some form of telephone hot line to help people who are undergoing periods of severe stress, as well as specialized hot lines to deal with child abuse, rape victims, battered wives, and runaways. The phone numbers are widely publicized in the hope of reaching those who need help.

**PARAPROFESSIONALS AS THERAPISTS**  Most of the community programs we have discussed could not function without the help of paraprofessionals. Because the need for psychological services outstrips the supply of available therapists, concerned citizens can play a valuable role. People of all ages and backgrounds have been trained to work in the area of community mental health. College students have served as companions for hospitalized patients. Older individuals who have successfully raised families have been trained as mental health counselors to work with adolescents in community clinics, to counsel parents of youngsters who have behavior problems, and to work with schizophrenic children. Former mental patients, recovered drug addicts, and exconvicts have been trained to help those faced with problems similar to the ones they have experienced.

Many residential mental health programs are run by nonprofessionals in consultation with trained therapists. An outstanding example is Achievement Place, which is a home-style facility in Kansas where couples act as surrogate parents for a group of youngsters referred by the courts because of their delinquent behavior (see Figure 17-5). Behavior therapy methods are used to extinguish aggressive behavior and to reward social skills. Follow-up data show that youths who graduate from Achievement Place have fewer contacts with courts and police and achieve slightly higher grades than do individuals who are placed on probation or in a traditional institution for delinquents (Fixsen, Phillips, Phillips, & Wolf, 1976). At present, there are 80 Achievement Places throughout the United States modeled after the original Kansas facility.

## Promoting Your Own Emotional Well-Being

Aside from seeking professional help, there are many ways that each of us can positively influence our own psychological well-being. By monitoring our feelings and behavior we can determine the kinds of actions and situations that cause us pain or get us into difficulty, and, conversely, the kinds

**FIGURE 17-5**
**Residential Program for Delinquent Youths** *A family conference at Achievement Place—a group home for youngsters with behavior problems who are referred by the courts. The youngsters and their professional teacher-parents meet daily to discuss rules of conduct, decide on consequences for violations of the rules, criticize aspects of the program, and evaluate a peer manager who oversees many of the activities.*

that benefit us the most. By trying to analyze our motives and abilities, we can enhance our capacity to make active choices in our lives, instead of passively accepting what comes.

The problems that people face vary greatly, and there are no universal guidelines for staying psychologically healthy. However, a few general suggestions have emerged from the experiences of therapists.

**ACCEPT YOUR FEELINGS** Anger, sorrow, fear, and a feeling of having fallen short of ideals or goals are all unpleasant emotions, and we may try to escape anxiety by denying these feelings. Sometimes we try to avoid anxiety by facing situations unemotionally, which leads to a false kind of detachment or cool that may be destructive. We may try to suppress all emotions, thereby losing the ability to accept as normal the joys and sorrows that are a part of our involvement with other people.

Unpleasant emotions are a normal reaction to many situations. There is no reason to be ashamed of feeling homesick, of being afraid when learning to ski, or of becoming angry at someone who has disappointed us. These emotions are natural, and it is better to recognize them than to deny them. When emotions cannot be expressed directly (for example, it may not be wise to tell off your boss), it helps to find another outlet for releasing tension. Taking a long walk, pounding a tennis ball, or discussing the situation with a friend can help to dissipate anger. As long as you accept your right to feel emotion, you can express it in indirect or substitute ways when direct channels of expression are blocked.

**KNOW YOUR VULNERABILITIES** Discovering the kinds of situations that upset you or cause you to overreact may help to guard against stress. Perhaps certain people annoy you. You could avoid them, or you could try to understand just what it is about them that disturbs you. Maybe they seem so poised and confident that they make you feel insecure. Trying to pinpoint the cause of your discomfort may help you to see the situation in a new light. Perhaps you become very anxious when you have to speak in class or present a paper. Again, you could try to avoid such situations, or you could gain confidence by taking a course in public speaking. (Many colleges offer courses specifically aimed at learning to control speech anxiety.) You could also reinterpret the situation. Instead of thinking "Everyone is waiting to criticize me as soon as I open my mouth," you could tell yourself "The class will be interested in what I have to say, and I'm not going to let it worry me if I make a few mistakes."

Many people feel especially anxious when they are under pressure. Careful planning and spacing of work can help you avoid feeling overwhelmed at the last minute. The strategy of purposely allowing more time than you think you need to get to classes or to appointments can eliminate one source of stress.

**DEVELOP YOUR TALENTS AND INTERESTS** People who are bored and unhappy seldom have many interests. Today's college and community programs offer almost unlimited opportunities for people of all ages to explore their talents in many areas, including sports, academic interests, music, art, drama, and crafts. Often, the more you know about a subject, the more interesting it (and life) becomes. In addition, the feeling of competency gained from developing skills can do a great deal to bolster self-esteem.

**BECOME INVOLVED WITH OTHER PEOPLE** Feelings of isolation and loneliness form the core of most emotional disorders. We are social beings, and we need the support, comfort, and reassurance provided by other people. Focusing all of your attention on your own problems can lead to an unhealthy preoccupation with yourself. Sharing your concerns with others often helps you to view your troubles in a clearer perspective. Also, being concerned for the welfare of other people can reinforce your feelings of self-worth.

**KNOW WHEN TO SEEK HELP** Although these suggestions can help to promote emotional well-being, there are limits to self-understanding and self-help. Some problems are difficult to solve alone. Our tendency toward self-deception makes it hard to view problems objectively, and we may not know all of the possible solutions. When you feel that you are making little headway in gaining control over a problem, it is time to seek professional help from a counseling or clinical psychologist, a psychiatrist, or some other trained therapist. The willingness to seek help is a sign of emotional maturity, not a sign of weakness; do not wait until you feel overwhelmed. Obtaining psychological help when it is needed should be as accepted a practice as going to a physician for medical problems.

*Chapter* **SUMMARY**

1. Treatment of the mentally ill has progressed from the ancient notion that abnormal behavior resulted from the possession of evil spirits that needed to be punished, to custodial care in ill-kept and isolated asylums, to modern mental hospitals and community mental health centers. The policy of *deinstitutionalization* (despite its good intentions) has created the problem of homeless mentally ill, causing concern about civil rights and adequate care.

2. *Psychotherapy* is the treatment of mental disorders by psychological means. One type of psychotherapy is *psychoanalysis*, which was developed by Freud. He believed that unconscious conflicts between the aggressive and sexual impulses of the id and the constraints imposed by the ego and superego were the cause of most mental disorders. Through the methods of *free association* and *dream analysis*, repressed thoughts and feelings are brought to the patient's awareness. By *interpreting* these dreams and associations, the analyst helps the individual gain *insight* into his or her problems. *Transference*, the tendency to express feelings toward the analyst that the client has for important people in his or her life, provides another source of interpretation. Through the processes of *working through*, the individual becomes able to cope with problems more realistically.

3. *Psychoanalytic therapies*, based on Freudian concepts, are briefer than psychoanalysis and place more emphasis on the problem-solving functions of the ego (as opposed to the id's sexual and aggressive impulses) and the individual's current interpersonal problems (as opposed to a complete reconstruction of childhood experiences).

4. *Behavior therapies* apply methods based on learning principles to *modify* the individual's behavior. These methods include *systematic desensitization* (the individual learns to relax in situations that previously produced anxiety), *flooding*, *reinforcement* of adaptive behaviors, *modeling* and *rehearsal* of appropriate behavior, and techniques for *self-regulation* of behavior.

5. *Cognitive behavior therapies* use behavior modification techniques but also incorporate procedures for changing maladaptive beliefs. The therapist helps the individual to replace irrational interpretations of events with more realistic ones.

6. *Humanistic therapies* help individuals to become aware of their real selves and to solve their problems with a minimum of therapist intervention. Carl Rogers, who developed *client-centered psychotherapy,* believed that the therapist's characteristics necessary for the client's growth and self-exploration are *empathy, warmth,* and *genuineness.*

7. Rather than adhering strictly to any single method, most therapists take an *eclectic* approach, selecting from the different techniques the ones most appropriate for a given client. Some therapists specialize in treating specific problems, such as alcoholism, sexual dysfunction, or depression.

8. *Group therapy* provides an opportunity for the individual to explore his or her attitudes and behavior in interaction with others who have similar problems. *Marital therapy* and *family therapy* are specialized forms of group therapy that help couples, or parents and children, to learn more effective ways of relating to one another and of handling their problems.

9. The effectiveness of psychotherapy is hard to evaluate because of the difficulty of defining a *successful outcome* and of controlling for *spontaneous remission.* Research indicates that psychotherapy does help but that different approaches do not differ greatly in effectiveness. Factors common to the various psychotherapies—a *warm and trustful interpersonal relationship, reassurance and support, desensitization, insight,* and *reinforcement of adaptive responses*—may be more important in producing positive change than are specific therapeutic methods.

10. *Biological therapies* include *electroconvulsive therapy* (ECT), and the use of *psychotherapeutic drugs.* Of the two, drug therapy is by far the most widely used. *Antianxiety drugs* are used to reduce severe anxiety and to help individuals cope with life crises. *Antipsychotic drugs* have proved effective in the treatment of schizophrenia, *antidepressants* help to elevate the mood of depressed patients, and *lithium* has been successful in treating bipolar disorders.

11. The prevention and treatment of mental disorders is of great concern in our society. Community resources that offer help include *halfway houses, residential centers* for people who have special problems, and various forms of *crisis intervention.* We can promote our own emotional health by accepting our feelings as natural, discovering our vulnerabilities, developing talents and interests, becoming involved with others, and recognizing when to seek professional help.

## *Further* **READING**

Interesting material on the historical treatment of the mentally ill can be found in Veith, *Hysteria: The History of a Disease* (1970); and Bell, *Treating the Mentally Ill: From Colonial Times to the Present* (1980).

A review of the various methods of psychotherapy is provided by Woody and Robertson, *Becoming a Clinical Psychologist* (1988); and Corsini, *Current Psychotherapies* (1984). *Psychotherapy: An Eclectic Approach* (1980) by Garfield describes the process of psychotherapy, the features common to most psychotherapies, and psychotherapy research.

For an introduction to psychoanalytic methods, see Luborsky, *Principles of Psychoanalytic Psychotherapy* (1984) and Auld and Hyman, *Resolution of*

*Inner Conflict: An Introduction to Psychoanalytic Therapy* (1991). For client-centered therapy, see *On Becoming a Person: A Therapist's View of Psychotherapy* (1970) and *Carl Rogers on Personal Power* (1977), both by Rogers. The principles of behavior therapy are presented in Bellack, Hersen, and Kazdin (Eds.), *International Handbook of Behavior Modification and Therapy*, (2nd ed., 1990); and Suinn, *Anxiety Management Training: A Behavior Therapy* (1990). The application of cognitive-behavior therapy to a variety of mental disorders is described in *Cognitive Psychotherapy: Theory and Practice* (1988), edited by Perris, Blackburn, and Perris. *Panic: Facing Fears, Phobias, and Anxiety* (1985) by Agras describes behavior therapy methods for overcoming fears.

An overview of group therapy is presented in Yalom, *The Theory and Practice of Group Psychotherapy* (3rd ed., 1985). For a cognitive-behavioral approach to marital and couple therapy see Beck, *Love Is Never Enough* (1988).

*Medicine and Mental Illness* (1991), a paperback by Lickey and Gordon, presents a very readable summary of biological research on the major mental disorders. It describes symptoms and DSM-III-R diagnostic criteria, evidence of drug effectiveness, and how psychotherapeutic drugs affect the brain.

For ways to modify your own behavior, see Watson and Tharp, *Self-Directed Behavior: Self-Modification for Personal Adjustment* (5th ed., 1989). *Feeling Good* (1981), a paperback by Burns, provides a step-by-step program for using cognitive therapy techniques to understand and to change feelings of depression, anxiety, and anger. *Necessary Losses* (1986) by Viorst, written from a psychoanalytic viewpoint, is a sensitive and wise analysis of how we grow and change through the losses that are an inevitable part of life.

# Part VIII

## *Social Behavior*

18 Social Beliefs and Attitudes

19 Social Interaction and Influence

# Chapter 18

# Social Beliefs and Attitudes

## Intuitive Science of Social Beliefs 713
*Collecting Data*
*Detecting Covariation*
*Inferring Causality*
*Critical Discussion: Information Processing Biases: Cognitive or Motivational?*

## Attitudes 725
*Consistency of Attitudes*
*Functions of Attitudes*
*Attitudes and Behavior*

## Interpersonal Attraction 736
*Liking*
*Love*
*Critical Discussion: Passion through Misattribution?*

Detail, *Street Scene*.

Social psychology is the study of how people perceive, think, and feel about their social world and how they interact and influence one another. How do we form impressions of other people, interpret their behaviors, or infer their motives? How are our social beliefs and attitudes formed and changed? What determines whom we like and dislike? How do we respond to different kinds of social influence? How do groups of individuals make decisions? How can prejudice and intergroup conflict be reduced?

In seeking answers to such questions, social psychologists begin with the general premise that human behavior is a function of both the person and the situation. As we noted in our earlier discussion of personality (Chapters 13 and 14), each individual brings a unique set of personal attributes to a situation (leading different persons to act in different ways in the same situation) and each situation brings a unique set of forces to bear on the individual (leading him or her to act in different ways in different situations).

Social psychologists emphasize two points within this general premise. The first is the *power of a situation* to determine a person's social behavior. As we shall see, research in social psychology has repeatedly demonstrated situations to be more powerful determinants of behavior than our intuitions would lead us to believe. The second point is the importance of the person's *interpretation of a situation* in determining his or her response to it. Persons do not react simply to the objective features of a situation but to their own subjective interpretations of it. The person who interprets a hurtful act as the product of hostility reacts differently from the person who interprets that same act as the product of insensitivity.

For this reason, an understanding of social behavior requires a particularly detailed understanding of the ways in which we perceive and interpret our social world. Accordingly, this chapter deals entirely with social beliefs and attitudes. Chapter 19 deals with social interaction and influence.

## Intuitive Science of Social Beliefs

We are all psychologists. In attempting to understand other people and ourselves, we are informal scientists who construct our own intuitive theories of human behavior. In doing so, we face the same basic tasks as the formal scientist (Nisbett & Ross, 1980). First, we *observe* or *collect* data ("My friend Chris asserts that women should have the right to obtain abortions"; "Lee Yamuri achieved the highest score on the math test"). Second, we try to *detect covariation* or *correlation*, to discern what goes with what ("Do most people who also oppose the death penalty support the right to abortion?" "On the average, do Asians seem to do better in math and science than non-Asians?"). And third, we attempt to *infer cause and effect*, to evaluate what causes what ("Does Chris support the right to abortion out of genuine conviction or because of peer pressure to express liberal attitudes?" "Do Asian students excel in math and science because they are inherently smarter or because their families stress the value of education?").

Our intuitive attempts to apply scientific reasoning to everyday life work surprisingly well. Social interaction would be chaos if our informal theories of human behavior did not possess substantial validity. But we also make a number of systematic errors in arriving at social judgments, and, ironically, our theories themselves often interfere with making accurate

*Unlike our intuitions, a survey researcher takes great care to ensure that a representative sample is polled before making predictions.*

judgments. As we shall see, our theories can actually shape our perceptions of the data, distort our estimates of covariation, and bias our evaluations of cause and effect.

## Collecting Data

The first difficulty we face as informal scientists is collecting data in a systematic and unbiased way. When a survey researcher wants to estimate how many Americans support a woman's right to abortion, he or she takes great care to ensure that a random or representative sample of people are contacted so that the numbers of Catholics, Protestants, men, women, and so forth are interviewed in proportion to their percentage of the total population. But when we, as informal survey researchers, try to make this estimate intuitively, our major source of data is likely to be the people we know personally. Obviously this is not a representative sample of the population.

Another major source of data for us is the mass media, which also provide a nonrandom and nonrepresentative sample of data. For example, the media necessarily give more attention to a small number of antiabortion protesters publicly demonstrating at a medical clinic than they do to a larger number of people who silently support the clinic's abortion service. The media are not being biased here in the usual sense; they are simply reporting the news. But the data they give us are still not a reliable sample from which to estimate public opinion.

A survey researcher also keeps accurate records of the data. But in everyday life, we constantly accumulate information in our heads and then attempt to recall it from memory when we are later called upon to make some judgment. Thus, not only are the data we collect a biased sample in the first place, but the data we actually bring to bear on our social judgments are further biased by problems of selective recall.

**VIVIDNESS**   One of the factors that influences the information we notice and remember is its *vividness*. Research has shown that when both vivid and nonvivid information compete for our attention, our estimates and judgments are more influenced by the vivid information—even when the nonvivid information is more reliable and potentially more informative (Nisbett & Ross, 1980; Taylor & Thompson, 1982).

In one study, introductory psychology students who planned to major in psychology were given information about upper-level psychology courses and then asked to indicate which courses they planned to take. The subjects either heard two or three students make some informal remarks about each course in a face-to-face session or they saw a statistical summary of course evaluations made by past students in the courses. The subjects were more influenced in their choices by the face-to-face remarks than by the statistical summary—even when the summary was accompanied by written quotations of those same remarks. The vivid face-to-face information was more influential than the nonvivid written information even though it was based on less complete and representative data (Borgida & Nisbett, 1977).

The vividness effect is a particular problem with information from the mass media. Even if reporters scrupulously gave equal coverage to both the vivid and nonvivid sides of an issue, our own information processing tendencies would supply the bias. Thus, even if a television newscast reports the results of a survey showing that a national majority supports abortion rights, we are still more likely to store and later recall the vivid pictures of the antiabortion protest when we intuitively try to estimate public opinion.

**SCHEMATA** Even if we could collect data in a systematic and unbiased way, our perceptions of the data can still be biased by our existing expectations and preconceptions—our theories—of what the data *should* look like. Whenever we perceive any object or event, we compare the incoming information with our memories of previous encounters with similar objects and events. In earlier chapters, we saw that often our memories of objects and events are not photograph-like reproductions of the original stimuli, but simplified reconstructions of our original perceptions. As noted in Chapter

*Vivid events both influence our judgments more and are more memorable than nonvivid events.*

8, such representations or memory structures are called *schemata* (or the singular, **schema**) and are the result of perceiving and thinking in terms of mental representations of classes of people, objects, events, or situations.

The process of searching for the schema in memory that is most consistent with the incoming data is called **schematic processing**. Schemata and schematic processing permit us to organize and process an enormous amount of information with great efficiency. Instead of having to perceive and remember all the details of each new object or event, we can simply note that it is like one of our preexisting schemata and encode or remember only its most prominent features. Schematic processing typically occurs rapidly and automatically; usually we are not even aware that any processing of information is taking place at all.

For example, we have schemata for different kinds of people. When someone tells you that you are about to meet an extravert, you retrieve your extravert schema in anticipation of the coming encounter. The extravert schema consists of a set of interrelated traits such as sociability, warmth, and possibly loudness and impulsiveness. As we shall discuss later, general person-schemata like these are sometimes called **stereotypes**. We also have schemata of particular persons, such as the president of the United States or our parents. We even have a schema about ourselves—a set of organized self-concepts stored in memory (Markus, 1977). When you see a job advertisement for a peer counselor, you can evaluate the match between your counselor schema and your **self-schema** to decide whether you should apply.

Research confirms that schemata help us to process information. For example, if people are explicitly instructed to remember as much information as they can about a person, they actually remember less than if they are simply told to try to form an impression of him or her (Hamilton, 1979). The instruction to form an impression induces the subjects to search for various person-relevant schemata that help them organize and recall material better. The self-schema also permits us to organize and process information efficiently. For example, people can recall a list of words better if they are told to decide whether each word describes themselves as they go through the list (Ganellen & Carver, 1985; Rogers, Kuiper, & Kirker, 1977).

Without schemata and schematic processing, we would simply be overwhelmed by the information that inundates us. We would be very poor information processors. But the price we pay for such efficiency is a bias in our perception of the data. Consider, for example, the impression you form of Jim from the following observations of his behavior.

> Jim left the house to get some stationery. He walked out into the sun-filled street with two of his friends, basking in the sun as he walked. Jim entered the stationery store, which was full of people. Jim talked with an acquaintance while he waited to catch the clerk's eye. On his way out, he stopped to chat with a school friend who was just coming into the store. Leaving the store, he walked toward the school. On his way he met the girl to whom he had been introduced the night before. They talked for a short while, and then Jim left for school. After school Jim left the classroom alone. Leaving the school, he started on his long walk home. The street was brilliantly filled with sunshine. Jim walked down the street on the shady side. Coming down the street toward him, he saw the pretty girl whom he had met on the previous evening. Jim crossed the street and entered a candy store. The store was crowded with students, and he noticed a few familiar faces. Jim waited quietly until he caught the counterman's eye and then gave his order. Taking his drink, he sat down at a side table. When he had finished his drink he went home. (Luchins, 1957, pp. 34-35)

| CONDITIONS | PERCENTAGE RATING JIM AS FRIENDLY |
|---|---|
| Friendly description only | 95 |
| Friendly first—unfriendly last | 78 |
| Unfriendly first—friendly last | 18 |
| Unfriendly description only | 3 |

What impression do you have of Jim? Do you think of him as friendly and outgoing or shy and introverted? If you think of him as friendly, you agree with 78 percent of people who read this description. But examine the description closely; it is actually composed of two very different portraits. Up to the sentence that begins "After school, Jim left . . . ," Jim is portrayed in several situations as fairly friendly. After that point, however, a nearly identical set of situations shows him to be much more of a loner. Whereas 95 percent of the people who are shown only the first half of the description rate Jim as friendly, only 3 percent of the people who are shown only the second half do so. Thus, in the combined description that you read, Jim's friendliness dominates the overall impression. But when individuals read the same description with the unfriendly half of the paragraph appearing first, only 18 percent rate Jim as friendly; his nonfriendliness leaves the major impression (see Table 18-1). In general, the first information we receive has the greater impact on our overall impressions. This is known as the **primacy effect.**

The primacy effect has been found repeatedly in several different kinds of impression formation studies, including studies using real rather than hypothetical persons. For example, subjects who watched a male student attempt to solve a series of difficult multiple-choice problems were asked to assess his general ability (Jones et al., 1968). Although the student always solved exactly 15 of the 30 problems correctly, he was judged more capable if the successes came mostly at the beginning of the series than if they came near the end. Moreover, when asked to recall how many problems the student had solved, subjects who had seen the 15 successes bunched at the beginning estimated an average of 21, whereas subjects who had seen the successes at the end estimated an average of 13.

Although several factors contribute to the primacy effect, it appears to be primarily a consequence of schematic processing. When we are first attempting to form our impressions of a person, we actively search in memory for the person schema or schemata that best match the incoming data. At some point we make a preliminary decision: this person is friendly (or some such judgment). We then assimilate any further information to that judgment and dismiss any discrepant information as not representative of the real person we have come to know. For example, when explicitly asked to reconcile the apparent contradictions in Jim's behavior, subjects sometimes say that Jim is really friendly but was probably tired by the end of the day (Luchins, 1957). Our theory of Jim, which has already been established, shapes our perception of all subsequent data about him. More generally, our subsequent perceptions become schema-driven and therefore relatively impervious to new data. There is truth to the conventional warning that first impressions are important.

**THEORIES** Schemata are actually minitheories of everyday objects and events. But more elaborate theories also affect our perception of data. In an elegant demonstration of this, students who held strongly divergent beliefs about whether or not capital punishment (the death penalty) acts as a deterrent against homicide read a summary of two purportedly authentic studies. One of the studies appeared to show that capital punishment was a deterrent, and the other appeared to show that it was not. The students also read a critique of each study that criticized its methodology. The results showed that students on each side of the issue found the study supporting their own position to be significantly more convincing and better conducted than the other study. The more unsettling result, however, was that after reading all the evidence on both sides, students were actually more convinced about the correctness of their initial position than they were at the beginning of the study (Lord, Ross, & Lepper, 1979). This implies that evidence introduced into public debate in the hope of resolving an issue—or at least moderating extreme views—will tend instead to polarize public opinion even further. Proponents of each side will pick and choose from the evidence so as to bolster their initial opinions (Nisbett & Ross, 1980).

## Detecting Covariation

Detecting covariation, or correlation—discovering what goes with what—is a fundamental task in every science. Discovering that symptoms of an illness covary with the amount of environmental pollution or correlate with the presence of a virus is the first step toward a cure. And as intuitive scientists of human behavior, we perceive—or think we perceive—such correlations all the time ("People who are against capital punishment seem more likely to hold a pro-choice position on abortion"; "Asians seem to do better in math and science than non-Asians"). Our schemata of classes of persons—stereotypes—are actually minitheories of covariation: The stereotype of an extravert, a gay person, or a college professor is a theory of what particular traits or behaviors go with certain other traits or behaviors.

Research shows that we are not very accurate at detecting covariations. Once again, our theories mislead us. When our schemata or theories lead us to expect two things to covary, we overestimate the correlation between them, even seeing illusory correlations that do not exist. But when we do not have a theory that leads us to expect them to covary, we underestimate the correlation, even failing to detect a correlation that is strongly present in the data.

This was demonstrated by two researchers who were intrigued by the fact that clinical psychologists routinely report correlations between their clients' responses to projective tests (see Chapter 14) and their personality characteristics, whereas research studies fail to find such correlations. For example, experienced clinicians have often reported that gay men are more likely than heterosexual men to see anal images, feminine clothing, and three other, similar kinds of images in Rorschach inkblots. Controlled studies, however, have not found any of these images to be correlated with a homosexual orientation (Chapman & Chapman, 1969). The researchers hypothesized that psychologists see these correlations because the reported images fit a popular stereotype, or schema, of male homosexuality. Several experiments have now confirmed this hypothesis.

In one, college students were asked to study a set of Rorschach cards. Each card contained the inkblot, a description of the image a client had reported seeing in it, and a statement of two personal characteristics that the client possessed. The images described included the five stereotyped images reported by clinical psychologists to be correlated with male homosexuality plus a number of other unrelated images (for example, images of food). The characteristics reported were either homosexuality ("has sexual feelings toward other men") or unrelated characteristics (for example, "feels sad and depressed much of the time"). The cards were carefully constructed so that no image was systematically associated with homosexuality.

After studying all the cards, subjects were asked to report if they had noticed "any general kind of thing that was seen most often by men" with the different characteristics. The results revealed that the students in this study—like experienced clinical psychologists—erroneously reported a correlation between the stereotyped images and homosexuality. They did not report any correlations between the nonstereotyped images and homosexuality.

The researchers then repeated the study, modifying the cards so that two of the nonstereotyped images (a monster image in one inkblot and an animal-human image in another) *always* appeared with the characteristic of homosexuality—a perfect correlation. Despite this, subjects still reported seeing the nonexistent correlation with the stereotyped images more than twice as often as the perfect correlation with the nonstereotyped images.

As intuitive scientists, we are schema- or theory-driven. We see covariations our theories have prepared us to see and fail to see covariations our theories have not prepared us to see.

**PERSISTENCE OF STEREOTYPES**   Perhaps it is not surprising that the inexperienced students in the study just described are misled by their stereotypes to see nonexistent correlations in the data. But why should this be true of experienced clinical psychologists? Why doesn't their daily contact with real data correct their mistaken perceptions of covariation? More generally, why do our stereotypes persist in the face of nonconfirming data?

We can illustrate some of the factors involved by representing the covariation task in a 2 × 2 table, as shown in Figure 18-1. It displays some hypothetical data relevant to a popular stereotype similar to that explored in

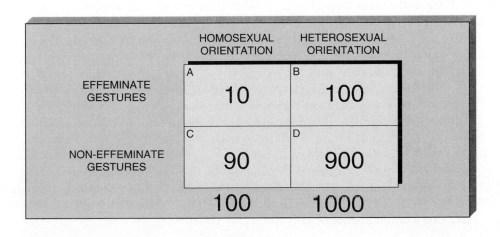

|  | HOMOSEXUAL ORIENTATION | HETEROSEXUAL ORIENTATION |
|---|---|---|
| EFFEMINATE GESTURES | A  10 | B  100 |
| NON-EFFEMINATE GESTURES | C  90 | D  900 |
|  | 100 | 1000 |

**FIGURE 18-1**
**Stereotypes as Covariations** *To determine whether there is a correlation between sexual orientation and effeminate gestures, we need to know whether the* proportion *of men with effeminate gestures differs as a function of sexual orientation. This requires taking all four cells into account so that the column totals can be computed. Invalid stereotypes often persist because we attend only to cell A and neglect the other cells. There is, in fact, no correlation between the two factors in these hypothetical data.*

the Rorschach inkblot study: the stereotype that gay men display effeminate gestures. The table classifies a hypothetical sample of 1,100 men into the 4 cells of the table according to whether they have a homosexual or a heterosexual orientation and whether they do or do not display effeminate gestures.

The correct way to assess whether the two factors are correlated is to examine whether the *proportion* of homosexual men who display effeminate gestures (the left-hand column) is different from the *proportion* of heterosexual men who display effeminate gestures (the right-hand column). To do this, we must first add up the two cells in each column to find how many men with each kind of orientation there are in the sample. When we do this, we see that 10 out of 100, or 10 percent of the gay men display effeminate gestures and 100 out of 1,000, or 10 percent of the heterosexual men do so. In other words, there is *no* correlation in these data between sexual orientation and effeminate gestures. It is important to note that to assess the correlation, we had to take into account all four cells of the table. Now consider what our intuitions would tell us if we encountered these data in daily life—where we do not have the data neatly laid out in front of us.

In our society, men with a homosexual orientation are in a minority (about 10 percent of the population), as are men who display effeminate gestures. When the two occur together (as in cell A, gay men with effeminate gestures), it is a particularly distinctive occurrence. This has two consequences. First, research has shown that people *overestimate* the frequency with which they have actually encountered such distinctive combinations (Hamilton & Gifford, 1976; Hamilton & Sherman, 1989). Second, even if we did not overestimate their frequency, we are still most likely to notice and to remember instances that fall into cell A and to remain oblivious to the instances that fall into the other cells of the table.

Part of the reason for this is that the relevant information is almost never available to us. In particular, we almost never have the opportunity to assess the frequency of cell C, the number of gay men who do *not* display effeminate gestures. Cell B also provides an inferential trap for some people. When they observe a man with effeminate gestures, they may simply *assume* he is gay even though they have no knowledge of his actual sexual orientation. He might belong to either cell A or cell B. But through circular reasoning, they illegitimately convert cell B disconfirmations of their stereotype into cell A confirmations. Note that it is the stereotype itself that leads them to make this inferential error—another instance of how our information processing is schema- or theory-driven.

But even if the data from cells other than cell A were available to us, it would not typically occur to us that we need to know this other information. We find it particularly difficult to take into account—or to understand why we *need* to take into account—cell D, the frequency of *non*-gay men who do *not* display effeminate gestures. Why is this difficult?

We noted earlier in this chapter that we are more likely to notice and to remember vivid rather than nonvivid information. This is why cell A is noticed, remembered, and overestimated: gay men with effeminate gestures are distinctive and, hence, vivid. In contrast, there are not many events that are less vivid—and hence, less noticeable and less memorable—than events that do *not* occur. But this is precisely what cell D events are: nonevents. The *non*-gay man who does *not* display effeminate gestures does not constitute a psychological event for us. It is difficult to notice or to appreciate the relevance of nonevents in daily life.

This difficulty was cleverly employed by Arthur Conan Doyle in his Sherlock Holmes story, "The Adventure of Silver Blaze," in which the famous detective is asked to discover who had stolen a prize race horse from its private stable during the night. Holmes draws the police inspector's attention to "the curious incident of the dog in the night-time." Puzzled, the inspector says, "The dog did nothing in the night-time." To which Holmes replies: "That was the curious incident." Holmes then deduces correctly that the horse was stolen by its own trainer—because the dog had *not* barked and, hence, must have known the intruder (Doyle, 1892/1981, p. 197).

The nonvividness of nonevents also leads the news media to promote and sustain stereotypes. When a gay man commits a murder—especially one with sexual overtones—both the sexual orientation and the murder are featured in the news story; when a heterosexual man commits a murder—even one with sexual overtones—sexual orientation is not mentioned. Thus cell A events are widely publicized—thereby fueling the stereotype—whereas cell B events are not seen as relevant to sexual orientation. And, of course, cell C and D events—men of any sexual orientation who do *not* commit murder—are not news. They are nonevents.

**SELF-FULFILLING STEREOTYPES**    Our schemata influence not only our perceptions and inferential processes, but also our behavior and social interactions. And this, too, can sustain our stereotypes. In particular, our stereotypes can lead us to interact with those we stereotype in ways that cause them to fulfill our expectations. Thus, our stereotypes can become both self-perpetuating and self-fulfilling. Two studies illustrate this process.

In one, the investigators first noted that white job interviewers employed a less friendly manner when interviewing African-American applicants than when interviewing white applicants. They hypothesized that this could cause African-American applicants to come off less well in the interviews. To test this hypothesis, they trained interviewers how to reproduce both the less friendly and the more friendly interviewing styles. Applicants (all white) were then videotaped while being interviewed by an interviewer using one of these two styles. Judges who later viewed the tapes rated applicants who had been interviewed in a less friendly manner significantly lower on their interview performance than those who had been interviewed in the more friendly manner (Word, Zanna, & Cooper, 1974). The study thus confirmed the hypothesis that prejudiced individuals can interact in ways that actually evoke the stereotyped behaviors that sustain their prejudice.

A commonly held stereotype is that physically attractive people are more sociable, poised, and outgoing (Dion, Berscheid, & Walster, 1972). To find out if this stereotype could be self-fulfilling, researchers had unacquainted male and female college students talk to each other over the telephone for about 10 minutes. Before each conversation, the man was shown a photograph of either an attractive or an unattractive woman and told (falsely) that it was a photograph of his phone partner.

The conversations were recorded on two-track tapes, and analyses of the men's side of the conversations showed that those who believed they were talking to an attractive woman were friendlier, more outgoing, and more sociable than were men who believed they were talking to a less attractive woman. More interestingly, judges who listened to the woman's half of each conversation without hearing the male partner or knowing his belief about the woman's attractiveness rated women whose partners believed they were attractive as more sociable, poised, and humorous than women

*An interviewer's prejudice can evoke stereotyped behavior in the interviewee that sustains the prejudice.*

"*Folks, I endorse Scrunchies because I eat Scrunchies. As God is my witness, I don't just say I eat them, I really and truly do eat them. In fact, folks, I never eat anything but. And if you don't believe me, I can supply documentation from my personal physician.*"
Drawing by Ross; © 1976 *The New Yorker Magazine*, Inc.

whose partners believed they were unattractive. The men's stereotype of physically attractive women became self-fulfilling in a 10-minute telephone conversation (Snyder, Tanke, & Berscheid, 1977).

## Inferring Causality

The heart of most sciences is the discovery of causes and effects. Similarly, as intuitive scientists, we feel we truly understand some instance of human behavior when we know why it occurred or what caused it. Suppose, for example, a famous athlete endorses a breakfast cereal on television. Why does she do it? Does she really like the cereal or is she doing it for the money? You give a five-dollar donation to Planned Parenthood. Why? Are you altruistic? Were you being pressured? Do you need a tax writeoff? Do you believe in the work of the organization?

Each of these cases creates an attribution problem. We see some behavior—perhaps our own—and must decide to which of many possible causes the action should be attributed. Our intuitive attempts to infer the causes of behavior is a central topic in social psychology (Heider, 1958; Kelley, 1967).

**FUNDAMENTAL ATTRIBUTION ERROR** As the two examples above illustrate, one of the major attribution tasks we face daily is deciding whether an observed behavior reflects something unique about the *person* (his or her attitudes, personality characteristics, and so forth) or something about the *situation* in which we observe the person. If we infer that something about the person is primarily responsible for the behavior (for instance, the athlete really loves the cereal), then our inference is called an *internal* or **dispositional attribution** ("disposition" here refers to a person's beliefs, attitudes, and personality characteristics). If, however, we conclude that some external cause is primarily responsible for the behavior (for instance, money, social norms, threats), it is called an *external* or **situational attribution.**

Fritz Heider, the founder of modern attribution theory, first noted that an individual's behavior is so compelling to us that we take it at face value and give insufficient weight to the circumstances surrounding it (1958). Recent research has confirmed Heider's observation. We underestimate the situational causes of behavior, jumping too easily to conclusions about the dispositions of the person. Another way of stating it is that we (in Western society, at any rate) have a schema of cause and effect for human behavior that gives too much weight to the person and too little to the situation. One psychologist has termed this bias toward dispositional attributions rather than situational attributions the **fundamental attribution error** (Ross, 1977).

In one of the first studies to reveal this bias, subjects read a debater's speech that either supported or attacked Cuba's leader Fidel Castro. The subjects were explicitly told that the debater had been assigned which side of the issue to argue by the debate coach; the debater had no choice. Despite this knowledge, when asked to estimate the debater's actual attitude toward Castro, subjects inferred that he or she held a position close to the one argued in the debate. In other words, the subjects made a dispositional attribution even though situational forces were fully sufficient to account for the behavior (Jones & Harris, 1967). This effect is quite powerful. Even when the subjects themselves get to choose which side of the issue that a speaker is to argue, they still tend to see him or her as actually holding that opinion (Gilbert & Jones, 1986). The effect occurs even if the presentations are deliberately designed to be drab and unenthusiastic and the speaker simply reads a transcribed version of the speech in a monotone and uses no gestures (Schneider & Miller, 1975).

**SELF-ATTRIBUTIONS**  As informal scientists of human behavior, one of our major tasks is understanding ourselves. As we shall see, the judgments we make about our own thoughts, emotions, behaviors, motives, and personalities are governed by many of the same processes that govern our judgments of others.

We saw in Chapter 11 that we often judge what emotion we are experiencing through a process of cognitive appraisal. Although the physiological arousal of our autonomic nervous system provides us with the information that we are experiencing an emotion, the more subtle judgment of *which* emotion we are experiencing often depends on our perceptions—our cognitive appraisals—of the surrounding circumstances. This suggests the more general possibility that we may rely on cues external to ourselves in order to make judgments about many of our inner states.

This possibility is the basis for **self-perception theory** by Daryl Bem (1972), who proposes that we make judgments about ourselves using the same inferential processes—and making the same kinds of errors—that we use for making judgments about others. Specifically, the theory proposes that individuals come to know their own attitudes, emotions, and other internal states partially by inferring them from observations of their own behavior and the circumstances in which the behavior occurs. Thus to the extent that internal cues are weak, ambiguous, or uninterpretable, the individual is like any outside observer who must rely on external cues to infer the individual's inner states.

These propositions are illustrated by the common remark, "This is my second sandwich; I guess I was hungrier than I thought." Here the speaker has decided on the basis of a self-observation that he or she had originally misjudged an internal state. Similarly, the self-observation "I've been biting my nails all day; something must be bugging me" is based on the same external evidence that might lead a friend to remark, "You've been biting your nails all day; something must be bugging you."

A more formal and surprising illustration of self-perception theory is provided by an *induced-compliance* experiment originally conducted in order to test Festinger's theory of *cognitive dissonance* (1957) (which will be discussed later in the chapter). Male college students participated one at a time in an experiment in which they worked for an hour on dull, repetitive tasks. After completing the tasks, some subjects were offered $1 to tell the next subject that the tasks had been fun and interesting. Others were offered $20 to do this. All subjects complied with the request. Later they were asked how much they had enjoyed the tasks. As shown in Figure 18-2, subjects who had been paid only $1 stated that they had, in fact, enjoyed the tasks. But subjects who had been paid $20 did not find them significantly more enjoyable than control subjects who never spoke to another subject (Festinger & Carlsmith, 1959). The small incentive for complying with the experimenter's request—but not the large incentive—led individuals to *believe* what they had heard themselves say. Why should this be so?

Just as we try to decide whether an athlete on television really loves the cereal she endorses or whether she is just saying so for the money, so too, self-perception theory proposes that subjects in this experiment looked at

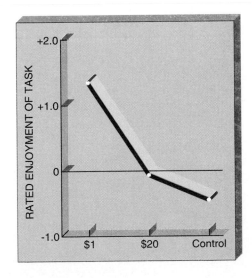

**FIGURE 18-2**
**Induced-Compliance Experiment** *The smaller incentive for agreeing to say the tasks were interesting led subjects to infer that they had actually enjoyed the tasks. The larger incentive did not.* (After Festinger & Carlsmith, 1959)

their own behavior (telling another subject that the tasks were interesting) and implicitly asked themselves, "Why did I do this?" It further proposes that they sought an answer the same way an outside observer would, by trying to decide whether to make a dispositional attribution (he did it because he really did enjoy the tasks) or a situational attribution (he did it for the money). When the individual is paid only $1, the observer is more likely to make a dispositional attribution: "He wouldn't be willing to say it for only $1, so he must have actually enjoyed the tasks." But if the individual is paid $20, the observer is more likely to make a situational attribution: "Anyone would have done it for $20, so I can't judge his attitude toward the tasks on the basis of his statement." If the individual follows the same inferential process as this hypothetical outside observer, then subjects paid $1 make a dispositional attribution about their own behavior: "I must think the tasks were enjoyable; otherwise, I would not have said so." But subjects paid $20 attribute their behavior to the money and thus express the same attitudes toward the tasks as the control subjects who made no statements to another subject.

**FUNDAMENTAL ATTRIBUTION ERROR IN SELF-PERCEPTION** There is a subtle point about the findings in this experiment. We know that all the subjects were willing to tell the next subject that the tasks were enjoyable—even subjects who were offered only $1 to do so. But the subjects themselves do not know this. Thus, when subjects paid $1 infer that they must think the tasks are enjoyable because otherwise they would not have said so, they are wrong. They should be inferring that they talked to the next subject because they were paid $1 to do so. In other words, the subjects are making a dispositional attribution about their own behavior when they should be making a situational attribution. They are committing the fundamental attribution error.

An experiment designed as a quiz game illustrates how both individuals and observers make the same fundamental error in the same setting. Pairs of male or female subjects were recruited to participate in a question-and-answer game of general knowledge. One member of the pair was randomly assigned to be the questioner and to make up 10 difficult questions to which he or she knew the answers (for example, "What is the world's largest glacier?"). The other subject served as the contestant and attempted to answer the questions. When the contestant failed a question, the questioner would give the answer. In a reenactment of the study, observers also watched the contest. After the game was completed, both participants and observers were asked to rate the level of general knowledge possessed by the questioner and the contestant, relative to the "average student." It is important to note that participants and observers all knew that the roles of questioner and contestant had been assigned randomly.

As Figure 18-3 shows, questioners judged both themselves and the contestant to be about average in level of general knowledge. But contestants rated the questioner as superior and themselves as inferior to the average student. They attributed the outcome of the game to their (and the questioner's) level of knowledge rather than taking into account the overwhelming situational advantage enjoyed by the questioner—who gets to decide which questions to ask and gets to omit any questions to which he or she does not know the answer. Observers, aware that the questioner could ask questions which neither they nor the contestant could answer, rated the questioner's level of knowledge even higher. In other words, both contes-

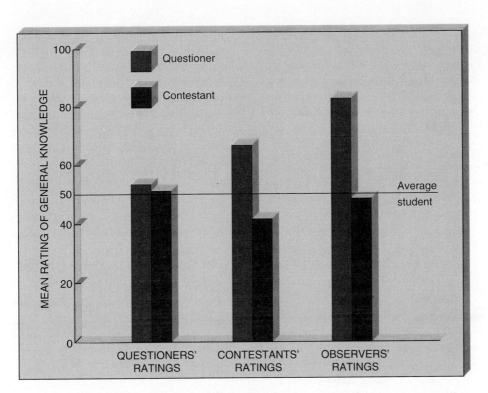

**FIGURE 18-3**
**Fundamental Attribution Error** *Ratings of questioners and contestants after they had participated in a quiz game. The questioner is rated as superior by both the contestant and observers even though the questioner had an overwhelming situational advantage. Both contestants and observers gave too much weight to dispositional causes and too little to situational causes.* (After Ross, Amabile, & Steinmetz, 1977)

tants and observers gave too much weight to dispositional causes and too little to situational causes—the fundamental attribution error (Ross, Amabile, & Steinmetz, 1977).

One implication of this study is that people who select the topics discussed in a conversation will be seen as more knowledgeable than those who passively let others set the agenda—even if everyone is aware of the differential roles being played. This, in turn, has implications for contemporary sex roles. Research has shown that men talk more than women in mixed-sex interactions (Henley, Hamilton, & Thorne, 1985); they interrupt more (West & Zimmerman, 1983); and they are more likely to raise the topics discussed (Fishman, 1983). The questioner-contestant study implies that one consequence of these sex-role patterns is that women leave most mixed-sex interactions thinking themselves less knowledgeable than the men, with bystanders of both sexes sharing this illusion. The moral is clear: the fundamental attribution error can work for or against you. If you want to appear knowledgeable both to yourself and to others, learn how to structure the situation so that you control the choice of topics discussed. Be the questioner, not the contestant.

# Attitudes

Except for the consideration of possible motivational biases in self-attributions, our discussion of social information processing has focused exclusively on cognitive functioning, the processes of perceiving and thinking. With the concept of **attitude**, one of social psychology's most central concepts, we can begin to incorporate affective functioning—emotions and feelings—into our model of the person as a processor of social information.

Attitudes are likes and dislikes—favorable or unfavorable evaluations of and reactions to objects, people, situations, or any other aspects of the world, including abstract ideas and social policies. We often express our attitudes in

## Information Processing Biases: Cognitive or Motivational?

So far, we have implied that information processing biases are rooted in cognitive or perceptual factors. But when dealing with an individual's interpretation of his or her own behavior, we must also consider the possibility that the biases are motivational—that the individual distorts self-judgments in order to enhance or defend his or her self-image. The Freudian defense mechanisms, discussed in Chapter 15, are examples of

such motivational processes. A question currently under debate within social psychology is whether the biases of the kind we have been discussing in this chapter can all be explained by cognitive factors or whether some of them require motivational explanations. For example, we have interpreted the findings of the $1–$20 experiment (in which the smaller incentive led subjects to believe their own statement that they had enjoyed the tasks) as a purely cognitive phenomenon of self-perception, a set of self-attributions biased by the fundamental attribution error. But as we shall see later, these same results can also be interpreted motivationally.

Even judgments that appear to be obviously self-serving can stem from purely cognitive factors. When college students are asked to explain examination grades they have received, they tend to attribute A and B grades to personal internal factors like ability and effort and C, D, and F grades to external factors like test difficulty and bad luck (Bernstein, Stephan, & Davis, 1979). In one study, subjects played a competitive

game that was rigged so that winners and losers were randomly determined. Winners attributed their wins to skill and effort, whereas losers blamed their losses on luck (Snyder, Stephan, & Rosenfeld, 1976). Similarly, gamblers tend to attribute wins to their gambling skills or strategies, whereas they interpret their losses as near misses due to "flukes" (Gilovich, 1983). But even though these judgments are self-serving, they are not necessarily the product of motivational processes. Because we usually try to succeed and rarely try to fail, it makes some sense to attribute our successes to internal factors and failures to external factors: We fail *despite* our abilities and efforts, not because of them. And if we have often succeeded in the past, then it is quite rational to attribute an unexpected failure to external rather than to enduring internal causes. Thus, these apparently self-serving attributions may not only derive from purely cognitive factors, but may well be correct! On the other hand, one well-designed study controlled for the subjects' expectancies of success

opinion statements: "I love oranges"; "I can't abide Republicans." But even though attitudes express feelings, they are often linked to cognitions, specifically to beliefs about the attitude objects ("Oranges contain lots of vitamins"; "Republicans have no compassion for the poor"). Moreover, attitudes are sometimes linked to actions we take with respect to the attitude objects ("I eat an orange every morning"; "I never vote for Republicans").

Accordingly, social psychologists usually conceive of attitudes as comprising a *cognitive* component, an *affective* component, and a *behavioral* component. For example, in studying negative attitudes toward minority groups, social psychologists distinguish between negative **stereotypes** (negative beliefs and perceptions about a group—the cognitive component), **prejudice** (negative feelings toward the group—the affective component), and **discrimination** (negative actions against members of the group—the behavioral component). Some theorists prefer to define an attitude as comprising only the cognitive and affective components; others include only the affective component. But despite differing definitions, all share a concern with the interrelationships among the pertinent beliefs, feelings, and behaviors.

## Consistency of Attitudes

Certain attitudes seem to go together. For example, people who support affirmative action seem likely to advocate stronger gun control, to oppose capital punishment, and to hold a pro-choice position on abortion. On the surface these diverse attitudes do not seem to follow one another logically.

and failure and still found self-serving bias (Ross & Sicoly, 1979).

The same interpretive problem arises in another pervasive self-enhancement phenomenon that is sometimes called the Lake Wobegon effect—after Garrison Keillor's fictional community in which "all the children are above average." In 1976–1977, the College Entrance Examination Board surveyed the nearly one million high-school seniors who took the Scholastic Aptitude Test, asking them to compare themselves with their peers. Seventy percent of the seniors described themselves as above average in leadership ability; only 2 percent rated themselves as below average. When asked about their ability to get along with others, all the seniors rated themselves as at least average, 60 percent rated themselves in the top 10 percent, and 25 percent rated themselves in the top 1 percent (Myers, 1990, p. 84). Most business people see themselves as more ethical than the average business person (Brenner & Molander, 1977); most drivers—including drivers who have been hospitalized for acci-

dents—describe themselves as safer and more skillful than the average driver (Svenson, 1981); and 94 percent of all college professors say they do above-average work (Cross, 1977).

Research suggests that both cognitive and motivational factors might play a role in the Lake Wobegon effect. One cognitive factor derives from the ambiguity of the rating task itself: Does leadership ability mean the ability to get the task done or to resolve conflicts within the group? Does the above-average professor excel at giving lectures, conducting small seminars, doing research, serving on committees, designing curricula, or advising students? Because the criteria are usually left unspecified when we make such judgments, we are free to select the dimension on which we do best. When asked how she compares with other professors, the superb lecturer is likely to think primarily of her lecturing ability and rate herself as above average. She is not likely to think of her mediocre committee work as relevant to the judgment. Through this selective cognitive process, virtually all professors can

claim—honestly and correctly—that they do above-average work. Research supports this explanation, showing, for example, that the more criteria that can be used to define "doing well," the stronger the Lake Wobegon effect becomes (Dunning, Meycrowitz, & Holzberg, 1989). On the other hand, motivational factors also appear to play a role. Students who had been told that extraversion was important to success in life rated themselves as more extraverted on an extraversion–introversion scale than did students who had been told that introversion was important (Kunda & Sanitioso, 1989).

These examples illustrate how difficult it is to resolve the debate over cognitive versus motivational explanations of self-enhancing biases in self-judgments. Some authors have argued that the opposing positions are formulated in ways that do not even permit the debate to be resolved on empirical grounds (Tetlock & Levi, 1982).

Yet knowing that a person holds one of the attitudes often permits us to guess the others with fair accuracy, and there does seem to be a kind of logic involved. The attitudes all appear to follow more or less from a common set of underlying values that we might label as "liberal."

The same kind of logic can be discerned among "conservative" attitudes. Many people who oppose affirmative action and gun control laws cite their belief in the value of individual freedom as the basis for their opinions. Even those who disagree with such opinions can appreciate the logic involved. But many such freedom-loving individuals also feel that women belong in the home, that marijuana use should be more heavily penalized, and that homosexual behavior should be illegal. Here the logic is less than clear, yet these attitudes, too, seem strangely predictable.

In short, people's attitudes often appear to have a kind of internal logic to them, but it is not usually a strict kind of formal logic. Instead, it is a kind of psycho-logic, and it is this psycho-logic that social psychologists have studied under the label of cognitive consistency. The basic premise of *cognitive consistency* theories is that we all strive to be consistent in our beliefs, attitudes, and behaviors, and that inconsistency acts as an irritant or a stimulus that motivates us to modify or change them until they form a coherent, if not logical, package. Throughout the years, the consistency theorists have amassed a great deal of evidence for this basic premise (Abelson et al., 1968).

But most of the research on consistency has been conducted with college students in laboratory studies. Psychologists and political scientists who have analyzed the public mind outside the social psychology laboratory are divided in their views about the ideological coherence of public opinion on social and political issues (Kinder & Sears, 1985). One of those who believes the public to be ideologically innocent has said

> As intellectuals and students of politics we are disposed by training and sensibility to take political ideas seriously. . . . We are therefore prone to forget that most people take them less seriously than we do, that they pay little attention to issues, rarely worry about the consistency of their opinions, and spend little or no time thinking about the values, presuppositions and implications that distinguish one political orientation from another. (McClosky, quoted by Abelson, 1968)

An example of such nonconsistency was revealed in a national survey taken by the *New York Times* and CBS News in the late 1970s. The survey showed that a majority of Americans said they disapprove of "most government-sponsored welfare programs." Yet over 80 percent said they supported: the government's "program providing financial assistance for children raised in low-income homes where one parent is missing" (Aid to Families with Dependent Children, a major welfare program); the government's program for "helping poor people buy food for their families at cheaper prices" (the essence of the federal food-stamp program); and the government's program for paying for health care for poor people (the Medicaid program). The strong support for these major welfare programs was similar among all types of people—rich and poor, liberal and conservative, Democrat and Republican.

An earlier national survey, designed specifically to probe this kind of inconsistency, found a similar contradiction between an *ideological* conservatism and an *operational* liberalism in attitudes toward welfare. One out of four Americans was conservative on questions concerning the general concept of welfare but simultaneously liberal on questions concerning specific welfare programs (Free & Cantril, 1967).

Despite these findings, we need to be cautious about accusing someone of being inconsistent, because his or her attitudes may simply be inconsistent with our own ideological framework; inconsistency may be in the eye of the beholder. For example, opposition to capital punishment is usually characterized as a liberal position, whereas opposition to legalized abortion is usually thought of as a conservative position. Yet there is a quite logical coherence to the views of a person who, being against all taking of life, opposes both capital punishment and legalized abortion. (Catholic clergy often hold this set of views, for example.) Another example is provided by libertarians, who are opposed to any government interference in our lives. They are conservative on economic issues—the free market, not the government, should control the economic system—and in their opposition to government enforced civil rights laws and affirmative-action programs. But they are liberal on personal social issues, believing, for example, that the government should not criminalize the use of marijuana or concern itself with our private sexual behavior. To libertarians, both conservatives and liberals are inconsistent.

Nevertheless, the evidence suggests that most citizens do not organize their beliefs and attitudes according to any kind of overall ideology; nonconsistency, if not inconsistency, seems more prevalent than consistency. This has led one psychologist to propose that many of our attitudes come packaged as **opinion molecules.** Each molecule is made up of (a) a belief, (b) an attitude, and (c) a perception of social support for the opinion. In other

words, each opinion molecule contains a fact, a feeling, and a following (Abelson, 1968): "It's a fact that when my Uncle Charlie had back trouble, he was cured by a chiropractor [*fact*]"; "You know, I feel that chiropractors have been sneered at too much [*feeling*], and I'm not ashamed to say so because I know a lot of people who feel the same way [*following*]." Or, "Americans don't really want universal health insurance [*following*], and neither do I [*feeling*]. It would lead to socialized medicine [*fact*]."

Opinion molecules serve important social functions. First, they act as conversational units, giving us something coherent to say when a particular topic comes up in conversation. They also give a rational appearance to our unexamined agreement with friends and neighbors on social issues. But most important, they serve as badges of identification with our important social groups, reinforcing our sense of belonging to a social community. Thus, the fact and the feeling are less important ingredients of an opinion molecule than the following.

## Functions of Attitudes

Attitudes serve a number of different psychological functions for us. Different people might hold the same attitude for different reasons, and a person might hold a particular attitude for more than one reason. The functions that an attitude serves for the person also influence how consistent it is with his or her other attitudes and how easily it can be changed. Over the years attitude theorists have identified and discussed a number of the functions that attitudes might serve (for example, Katz, 1960; Smith, Bruner, & White, 1956; Herek, 1986). We discuss five of them here.

**INSTRUMENTAL FUNCTION** Attitudes that we hold for practical or utilitarian reasons are said to serve an *instrumental* function. They simply express specific instances of our general desire to obtain benefits or rewards and avoid punishment. For example, most Americans favor more government services but oppose higher taxes. As this example indicates, such attitudes are not necessarily consistent with one another. To change such attitudes, the person needs only to be convinced that some alternative would bring more benefits.

**KNOWLEDGE FUNCTION** Attitudes that help us to make sense of the world, that bring order to the diverse information we must assimilate in our daily lives, are said to serve a *knowledge* function. Such attitudes are essentially *schemata* that permit us to organize and process diverse information efficiently without having to attend to its details. For example, until its recent demise, negative attitudes toward the Soviet Union helped many Americans to organize and interpret world events in terms of the cold war. The attitude that Democrats just want to "tax and spend" or that Republicans care only for the wealthy provides a quick schematic way of interpreting and evaluating the proposals and candidates offered by the two parties. Like other schemata, such attitudes often oversimplify reality and bias our perception of events.

**VALUE-EXPRESSIVE FUNCTION** Attitudes that express our values or reflect our self-concepts are said to serve a *value-expressive* function. For example, a person might have positive attitudes toward gay people because of deeply held values about diversity, personal freedom, and tolerance; another person might have negative attitudes because of deeply held religious convictions that condemn homosexuality. Because value-expressive attitudes derive from a person's underlying values or self-concept, they tend to be consistent with one another. As we noted earlier, broad political values, such as liberalism or conservatism, can serve as a basis for value-expressive attitudes. Such attitudes do not change easily; the individual has to be convinced that an alternative attitude would be more consistent with his or her underlying values or self-concept.

**EGO-DEFENSIVE FUNCTION** Attitudes that protect us from anxiety or from threats to our self-esteem are said to serve an *ego-defensive* function. The concept of ego defensiveness comes from Sigmund Freud's psychoanalytic theory (see Chapter 14). One of the mechanisms of ego defense Freud describes is **projection**: the individual represses his or her own unacceptable impulses and then expresses hostile attitudes toward others who are perceived to possess those same impulses. For example, a person who is fearful of his or her own possible homosexual feelings is likely to deny and repress such feelings and then to display hostility toward gay people. (The term "homophobia" accurately describes anti-gay prejudice that serves such an ego-defensive function; it is less accurate when used more broadly to refer to all anti-gay attitudes.) In one study, students at a liberal California university were asked to write essays describing their attitudes toward lesbians and gay men. A content analysis of the essays revealed negative attitudes serving an ego-defensive function in about 35 percent of the essays (Herek, 1987).

The notion that negative attitudes toward minority groups can serve an ego-defensive function is called the **scapegoat theory of prejudice**, because the person's hostility often takes the form of blaming the groups for both personal and societal problems. The theory was tested in the late 1940s by a group of psychologists at the University of California at Berkeley. The research sought to discover whether psychoanalytic theory could explain the kind of anti-Semitism and fascist ideology that had emerged in Nazi Germany and whether one could identify individuals who would be particularly susceptible to such an ideology. The research, described in the book *The Authoritarian Personality*, has become a classic in social psychology (Adorno, Frenkel-Brunswick, Levinson, & Sanford, 1950).

Using attitude questionnaires, the investigators first confirmed their hypothesis that individuals who were anti-Semitic were also likely to be prejudiced against many groups other than their own—called "outgroups." In interviews, such individuals recalled rigidly moralistic parental discipline, a hierarchical family structure, and an anxious concern about the family's socioeconomic status.

According to the investigators, such home environments produce individuals with "authoritarian personalities"—individuals who are submissive and obedient to those they consider their superiors (including authority figures), but contemptuous of and aggressive toward those they consider inferior. As the psychoanalytic theory of prejudice predicts, authoritarian individuals repress knowledge of their own undesirable characteristics, projecting them instead onto members of "inferior" outgroups.

Although the authoritarian personality study has been criticized for a number of shortcomings (Christie & Jahoda, 1954), many of its original conclusions have withstood the test of continued research. In particular, there does appear to be an authoritarian personality type who seems particularly susceptible to a fascist ideology that has hostility toward outgroups at its core. More recent research does suggest, however, that prejudice and authoritarian attitudes may be acquired more directly in the home environment through the usual learning processes rather than through the more involved psychoanalytic processes described in the original research (Altemeyer, 1988).

**SOCIAL ADJUSTMENT FUNCTION** Attitudes that help us feel a part of a social community are said to serve a *social adjustment* function. The opinion molecules we discussed earlier provide one example. Another example is

*Authoritarian individuals—who are submissive to those they consider to be their superiors but contemptuous of those they consider to be their inferiors—are more likely to join fascist groups that are openly hostile to outgroups.*

provided by people who hold the prescribed beliefs and attitudes of a particular church or political party because their friends, families, and neighbors do; the actual content of the beliefs and attitudes is less important than the social bonds they provide. To the extent that attitudes serve primarily a social adjustment function, they are likely to change if the social norms change.

This was strikingly shown in the American South during the 1950s, when legalized racial segregation was being dismantled. Surveys showed that Americans in the South were generally opposed to desegregation and were more likely than Americans in the North to express negative attitudes toward African Americans. Some psychologists suggested that Southern Americans might be more authoritarian than Northern Americans—that racial attitudes in the South were serving an ego-defensive function. But Thomas Pettigrew, a social psychologist who specializes in race relations, argued that racial attitudes in the South were being sustained primarily by simple conformity to the prevailing social norms of the region—a social adjustment function (Pettigrew, 1959).

Using the questionnaire developed for measuring authoritarianism, Pettigrew found that Southerners were no more authoritarian than Northerners (although authoritarian individuals in both regions were more prejudiced against African Americans than nonauthoritarian individuals). Moreover, Southerners who were prejudiced against African Americans were not necessarily prejudiced against other outgroups—which is contrary to what the theory of authoritarianism predicts. In fact, the South has historically been one of the least anti-Semitic regions in the United States, and one survey at the time showed Southern whites to be unfavorable toward African Americans but quite favorable toward Jews (Prothro, 1952). Also, veterans from the South—whose army experience had exposed them to different social norms—were considerably less prejudiced than nonveterans, even though veterans from both South and North were more authoritarian than nonveterans.

The subsequent history of desegregation confirmed Pettigrew's analysis. As desegregation progressed, surveys showed that attitudes toward a particular desegregation step tended to be unfavorable just before the change had been implemented but then became favorable soon afterwards (Pettigrew, 1959). Thus some communities had accepted the desegregation of public accommodations but were still opposed to school desegregation; other communities showed just the reverse pattern. In one study, it was estimated that about 40 percent of the sample had firm opinions favoring or opposing desegregation, but that the remaining 60 percent favored whatever the social norms happened to be at the time (Minard, 1952).

It is often said that one cannot legislate attitudes. In the literal sense this is obviously true. But legislation and judicial decrees change public policies and practices, and these, in turn, frequently lead to changes in the social norms. To the extent that a citizen's attitudes are serving a social adjustment function, they, too, will change. Under these conditions, the quickest path to changing "hearts and minds" is to change behavior first by changing the social norms.

## Attitudes and Behavior

A major reason for studying attitudes is the expectation that they will enable us to predict a person's future behavior. A political candidate is only interested in a survey of voter attitudes if the attitudes expressed relate to voting behavior. The assumption that a person's attitudes determine his or her behavior is deeply ingrained in Western thinking, and in many instances the assumption holds. For example, a survey of presidential campaigns from 1952 to 1964 reveals that 85 percent of the voters surveyed showed a correspondence between their attitudes 2 months before the election and their actual vote in the election (Kelley & Mirer, 1974).

But in other cases, the assumption of attitude-behavior consistency appears to be violated. The classic study usually cited in this connection was conducted during the 1930s. A white professor traveled across the United States with a young Chinese couple. At that time, there was quite strong prejudice against Asians and there were no laws against racial discrimination in public accommodations. The three travelers stopped at over 200 hotels, motels, and restaurants and were served at all the restaurants and all but one of the hotels and motels without problem. Later, a letter was sent to all of the establishments visited asking them whether or not they would accept a Chinese couple as guests. Of the 128 replies received, 92 percent said they would not. In other words, these proprietors expressed attitudes that were much more prejudiced than their behavior (LaPiere, 1934).

This study illustrates that behavior is determined by many factors other than attitudes, and these other factors affect attitude-behavior consistency. One obvious factor is the degree of constraint in the situation: we must often act in ways that are not consistent with what we feel or believe. As children, we ate asparagus that we detested, and as adults we attend lectures and dinner parties that we would compare unfavorably to our experience with asparagus. In the racial discrimination study, the prejudiced proprietors may have found it difficult to act on their prejudices when actually faced with an Asian couple seeking service. Public accommodation laws against discrimination now make it even more difficult to display such prejudices than it was in 1934. Peer pressure can exert similar influences on behavior. For example, a teenager's attitude toward marijuana is moderately correlated with his or her actual use of marijuana, but the number of marijuana-using friends the teenager has is an even better predictor of his or her marijuana use (Andrews & Kandel, 1979).

In general, attitudes tend to predict behavior best when they are (a) strong and consistent; (b) based on the person's direct experience; and (c) specifically related to the behavior being predicted. We shall look briefly at each of these.

Strong and consistent attitudes predict behavior better than weak or ambivalent attitudes. This is illustrated by the surveys of presidential voting, mentioned earlier. Most of the attitude-vote inconsistencies came from voters with weak or ambivalent attitudes. Many such voters experience ambivalence because they are cross-pressured by friends and associates who do not agree with one another. For example, a Jewish businessperson belongs to an ethnic group that generally holds liberal political positions, but she also belongs to a business community that frequently holds conservative political positions, particularly on economic issues. When it comes time to vote, such a person is subjected to conflicting pressures. Ambivalence and conflict can arise from within the person as well. When the affective and cognitive components of an attitude are not consistent with one another—for example, when we like something we know is bad for us—then it is often difficult to predict the behavior (Norman, 1975).

Attitudes based on direct experience predict behavior better than do attitudes formed from just reading or hearing about an issue. For example, during a housing shortage at a university, many freshmen had to spend the first few weeks of the term in crowded temporary housing. Researchers measured attitudes of students toward the housing crisis and their willingness to sign and distribute petitions or to join committees to study it. For students who actually had to live in the temporary housing, there was a high correlation between their attitude toward the crisis and their willingness to take action to solve it. But for students who had not directly experienced the temporary housing, no such correlation existed (Regan & Fazio, 1977). There are many more examples of a strong relationship between behaviors and attitudes based on direct experiences, and these have been interpreted as evidence for the self-perception process, described earlier, in which individuals infer their attitudes from observations of their own behaviors (Fazio & Zanna, 1981).

And finally, attitudes specifically related to the behavior being assessed tend to predict better than attitudes only generally related. For example, general environmental attitudes in one study were not related to a willingness to take action on behalf of the Sierra Club, but attitudes specifically toward the Sierra Club were strongly related (Weigel, Vernon, & Tognacci, 1974). Similarly, attitudes toward birth control correlated only .08 with a woman's use of oral contraceptives over a 2-year span, but attitudes toward the pill in particular correlated .7 with that behavior (Davidson & Jaccard, 1979).

**COGNITIVE DISSONANCE THEORY** Our discussion of attitude-behavior consistency has covered only half the topic so far. We have examined how attitudes might lead to behavior, but it is also possible for behavior to lead to attitudes. The most influential theory of this sequence of events has been Leon Festinger's theory of cognitive dissonance. Like cognitive consistency theories in general, cognitive dissonance theory assumes that

*Behavior is more predictable for individuals whose attitudes toward AIDS stem from direct experience.*

there is a drive toward cognitive consistency; two cognitions that are inconsistent with one another will produce discomfort that motivates the person to remove the inconsistency and bring the cognitions into harmony. This inconsistency-produced discomfort is called **cognitive dissonance** (Festinger, 1957).

Although cognitive dissonance theory addresses several kinds of inconsistency, it has been the most provocative in predicting that engaging in behavior that is counter to one's attitudes creates dissonance pressure to change the attitudes so they are consistent with the behavior. The theory further states that engaging in counterattitudinal behavior produces the most dissonance, and hence the most attitude change, when there are no compensating consonant (that is, consistent) reasons for engaging in the behavior. This was illustrated in an experiment that we have already discussed in the context of self-perception theory, the $1–$20 induced-compliance experiment by Festinger and Carlsmith (1959).

Recall that subjects in this study were induced to tell a waiting subject that a series of dull tasks had been fun and interesting. Subjects who had been paid $20 to do this did not change their attitudes, but subjects who had been paid only $1 came to believe that the tasks had, in fact, been enjoyable. According to cognitive dissonance theory, being paid $20 provides a very consonant reason for complying with the experimenter's request to talk to the waiting subject, and hence the person experiences little or no dissonance. The inconsistency between the person's behavior and his or her attitude toward the tasks is outweighed by the far greater consistency between the compliance and the incentive for complying. Accordingly, the subjects who were paid $20 did not change their attitudes; the subjects who were paid $1, however, had no consonant reason for complying. Accordingly, they experienced dissonance, which they reduced by coming to believe that they really did enjoy the tasks. The general conclusion is that dissonance-causing behavior will lead to attitude change in induced-compliance situations when the behavior can be induced with a *minimum* amount of pressure, whether in the form of reward or punishment.

Experiments with children have confirmed the prediction about minimal punishment. If children obey a very mild request not to play with an attractive toy, they come to believe that the toy is not as attractive as they first thought—a belief that is consistent with their observation that they are not playing with it. But if the children refrain from playing with the toy under a strong threat of punishment, they do not change their liking for the toy (Aronson & Carlsmith, 1963; Freedman, 1965).

Cognitive dissonance theory successfully predicts a number of other attitude change phenomena as well, and it has inspired extensive research and intensive debate. In fact, we have seen that both cognitive dissonance theory and self-perception theory claim to explain the results of induced-compliance studies. There is even a third theory, *impression management theory*, that predicts the results of induced-compliance studies (Tedeschi & Rosenfeld, 1981).

Each of these theories has been supported by several studies, and each theory has also generated data that the other theories cannot explain. Several investigators have now concluded that all the theories may be correct—each under slightly different circumstances—and that the focus of research should be on specifying when and where each theory applies (Baumeister & Tice, 1984; Fazio, Zanna, & Cooper, 1977; Paulhus, 1982).

# Interpersonal Attraction

Of all our attitudes, the most important are undoubtedly our attitudes toward other people. The questions that often concern us most whenever we meet new people are whether or not they like us and we like them. Beyond the initial encounter, our concerns often center on how to nurture and guide the relationship from an initial liking or attraction to a deeper friendship or possibly even to intimacy and love. Accordingly, social psychologists have long been interested in the factors that promote liking or interpersonal attraction, and they have shown a willingness to study love and intimacy as well. Some of the findings have confirmed commonly held notions about liking and loving, but others have produced surprises. We begin with liking—namely, friendship and the early stages of more intimate relationships.

## Liking

When Great Britain's Prince Charles married Lady Diana Spencer, social psychologists were not surprised that he married "the girl next door," a very attractive woman whom he had known for years and who shared many of his social background characteristics and attitudes. As we shall see, these are precisely the determinants of interpersonal attraction: physical attractiveness, proximity, familiarity, and similarity.

**PHYSICAL ATTRACTIVENESS**   To most of us there is something mildly undemocratic about the possibility that a person's physical appearance is a determinant of how well others like him or her. Unlike character and personality, physical appearance is a factor over which we have little control, and hence it seems unfair to use it as a criterion for liking someone. In fact, surveys taken over a span of several decades have shown that people do not rank physical attractiveness as very important in their liking of other people (Perrin, 1921; Tesser & Brodie, 1971).

But research on actual behavior shows otherwise (see Brehm, 1992, for a review). One group of psychologists set up a "computer dance" in which college men and women were randomly paired with one another. At intermission everyone filled out an anonymous questionnaire evaluating his or her date. In addition, the experimenters obtained several personality test scores for each person, as well as an independent estimate of his or her physical attractiveness. The results showed that only physical attractiveness played a role in how much the person was liked by his or her partner. None of the measures of intelligence, social skills, or personality were related to the partners' liking for one another (Walster, Aronson, Abrahams, & Rottmann, 1966). Moreover, the importance of physical attractiveness continues to operate not only on first dates but on subsequent ones as well (Mathes, 1975).

The importance of physical attractiveness is not confined just to dating and mating patterns. For example, physically attractive boys and girls (5 and 6 years of age) are more popular with their peers than are less attractive children (Dion & Berscheid, 1972). Even adults are affected by a child's physical attractiveness. One investigator had women read a description of an aggressive act committed by a 7-year-old child. The description was accompanied by a photograph of either an attractive or an unattractive child. The women believed that the attractive child was less likely than the unattractive child to commit a similar aggressive act in the future (Dion, 1972).

Why is physical attractiveness so important? Part of the reason is that our own social standing and self-esteem are enhanced when we are seen with physically attractive companions. Both men and women are rated more favorably when they are with an attractive romantic partner or friend than when they are with an unattractive companion (Sheposh, Deming, & Young, 1977; Sigall & Landy, 1973). But there is an interesting twist to this: both men and women are rated less favorably when they are seen with a *stranger* who is physically more attractive than they (Kernis & Wheeler, 1981). Apparently they suffer by comparison when compared with the other person. This effect has been found in other studies. For example, male college students who had just watched a television show starring beautiful young women gave lower attractiveness ratings to a photograph of a more typical-looking woman—as did both men and women who were first shown a photograph of a highly attractive woman (Kenrick & Gutierres, 1980).

Fortunately, there is hope for the unbeautiful among us. First of all, physical attractiveness appears to decline in importance when a permanent partner is being chosen (Stroebe, Insko, Thompson, & Layton, 1971). And, as we shall see, several other factors can work in our favor.

**PROXIMITY**  An examination of 5,000 marriage license applications in Philadelphia in the 1930s found that one-third of the couples lived within five blocks of each other (Rubin, 1973). Research shows that the best single predictor of whether two people are friends is how far apart they live. In a study of friendship patterns in apartment houses, residents were asked to name the three people they saw socially most often. Residents mentioned 41 percent of neighbors who lived in the apartment next door, 22 percent of those who lived two doors away (about 30 feet) and only 10 percent of those who lived at the other end of the hall (Festinger, Schachter, & Back, 1950).

Studies of college dormitories show the same effect. After a full academic year, roommates were twice as likely as floormates to be friends, and floormates were more than twice as likely as dormitory residents in general to be friends (Priest & Sawyer, 1967). A study of male trainees at the Training Academy of the Maryland State Police is even more striking. The academy assigns trainees to dormitory rooms and classroom seats by name in alphabetical order. Thus the closer two trainees' last names are alphabetically, the more likely they are to spend time in close proximity to one another. The researchers asked trainees who had been at the academy for 6 months to name their three closest friends there. Despite an intensive training course in which all trainees get to know one another quite well, there was a strong alphabetical proximity effect. On the average, each person chosen as a best friend was only 4.5 letters away from the person who chose him—an alphabetical proximity significantly closer than the 15.3 letters expected by chance (Segal, 1974).

There are cases, of course, in which neighbors and roommates hate one another, and the major exception to the friendship-promoting effect of proximity seems to occur when there are initial antagonisms. In a test of this, a subject waited in a laboratory with a female confederate who treated the subject pleasantly or unpleasantly. When she was pleasant, the closer she sat to the subject the better she was liked; when she was unpleasant, the closer she sat to the subject, the less she was liked. Proximity simply increased the

*Certainly, unbeknownst to William Evans, the perfect woman for him is a waitress in Caracas named Ramona. Good luck, Bill.* © 1989, Los Angeles Times Syndicate. Reprinted with permission.

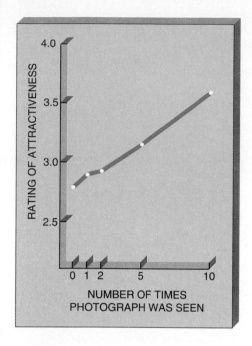

**FIGURE 18-4**
**Familiarity Breeds Liking** *Subjects were asked to rate photographs of unknown faces according to how much they thought they would like the person. The lowest ratings of liking were made by subjects who had never seen the photograph before; the highest ratings of liking were made by subjects who had seen the photograph most often. (After Zajonc, 1968)*

intensity of the initial reaction (Schiffenbauer & Schiavo, 1976). But because most initial encounters probably range from neutral to pleasant, the most frequent result of sustained proximity is friendship.

Those who believe in miracles when it comes to matters of the heart may believe that there is a perfect mate chosen for each of us waiting to be discovered somewhere in the world. But if this is true, the far greater miracle is the frequency with which Fate conspires to place this person within walking distance.

**FAMILIARITY** One of the major reasons that proximity creates liking is that it increases *familiarity,* and there is now abundant research that familiarity all by itself—sheer exposure—increases liking (Zajonc, 1968). This *familiarity-breeds-liking* effect is a very general phenomenon. For example, rats repeatedly exposed to either the music of Mozart or Schoenberg come to prefer the composer they have heard, and humans repeatedly exposed to selected nonsense syllables or Chinese characters come to prefer those they have seen most often. The effect even occurs when individuals are unaware that they have been previously exposed to the stimuli (Moreland & Zajonc, 1979; Wilson, 1979). More germane to the present discussion is a study in which subjects were exposed to pictures of faces and then asked how much they thought they would like the person shown. The more frequently they had seen a particular face, the more they said they liked it and thought they would like the person (Zajonc, 1968)—(see Figure 18-4). Similar results are obtained when individuals are exposed to one another in actual interaction.

In one clever demonstration of the familiarity-breeds-liking effect, the investigators took photographs of college women and then prepared prints of both the original face and its mirror image. These prints were then shown to the women themselves, their female friends, and their lovers. The women themselves preferred the mirror-image prints by a margin of 68 percent to 32 percent, but the friends and lovers preferred the nonreversed prints by a margin of 61 percent to 39 percent (Mita, Dermer, & Knight, 1977). Can you guess why?

The moral is clear. If you are not beautiful or you find your admiration of someone unreciprocated, be persistent and hang around. Proximity and familiarity are your most powerful weapons.

**SIMILARITY** An old saying declares that opposites attract, and lovers are fond of recounting how different they are from each other: "I love boating, but she prefers mountain climbing." "I'm in engineering, but he's a history major." What such lovers overlook is that they both like outdoor activities; they are both preprofessionals; they are both Democrats; they are both the same nationality; the same religion; the same social class; the same educational level; and they are probably within 3 years of each other in age and within 5 IQ points of each other in intelligence. In short, the old saying is mostly false.

Research all the way back to 1870 supports this conclusion. Over 99 percent of the married couples in the United States are of the same race, and most are of the same religion. Moreover, statistical surveys show that husbands and wives are significantly similar to each other not only in sociological characteristics—such as age, race, religion, education, and socioeconomic class—but also with respect to psychological characteristics like intelligence and physical characteristics such as height and eye color (Rubin, 1973). A study of dating couples finds the same patterns, in addition to finding that

*The saying "opposites attract" is a myth: couples tend to have many common attributes.*

couples were also similar in their attitudes about sexual behavior and sex roles. Moreover, couples who were most similar in background at the beginning of the study were most likely to be together 1 year later (Hill, Rubin, & Peplau, 1976). Of particular pertinence to our earlier discussion is the finding that couples are closely matched on physical attractiveness as well (Berscheid & Walster, 1978).

For example, in one study, judges rated photographs of each partner of 99 couples for physical attractiveness without knowing who was paired with whom. The physical attractiveness ratings of the couples matched each other significantly more closely than did the ratings of photographs that were randomly paired into couples (Murstein, 1972). Similar results were obtained in a real-life field study in which separate observers rated the physical attractiveness of members of couples in bars and theater lobbies and at social events (Silverman, 1971).

This matching of couples on physical attractiveness appears to come about because we weigh a potential partner's attractiveness against the probability that the person would be willing to pair up with us. Put bluntly, less attractive people seek less attractive partners because they expect to be rejected by someone more attractive than themselves. A study of a video dating service found that both men and women were most likely to pursue a relationship with someone who matched them in physical attractiveness. Only the most attractive people sought dates with the most attractive partners (Folkes, 1982). The overall result of this chilling marketplace process is attractiveness similarity: most of us end up with partners who are about as attractive as we are.

But similarities on dimensions other than physical attractiveness are probably even more important over the long-term course of a relationship. A longitudinal study of 135 married couples, discussed in Chapter 13, found that spouses who were more similar to each other in personality also resembled each other more in terms of how much they enjoyed similar daily activities like visiting friends, going out for dinner, and participating in community activities and professional meetings. These couples also reported less marital conflict and greater closeness, friendliness, and marital satisfaction than less similar spouses (Caspi & Herbener, 1990).

In an ambitious study of similarity and friendship, male students received free room for the year in a large house at the University of Michigan in exchange for their participation. On the basis of information from tests and questionnaires, some men were assigned roommates who were quite similar to them and others were assigned roommates who were quite dissimilar. The investigator observed the friendship patterns that developed over the course of the year, obtaining more questionnaire and attitude data from the participants at regular intervals. In all other respects the men lived as they would in any dormitory.

Roommates who were initially similar generally liked each other and ended up as better friends than those who were dissimilar. When the study was repeated with a new group of men the next year, however, the familiarity-breeds-liking effect turned out to be even more powerful than similarity. Regardless of whether low or high similarity had been the basis for room assignments, roommates came to like each other (Newcomb, 1961).

One reason that similarity produces liking is probably that people value their own opinions and preferences and enjoy being with others who validate their choices, possibly boosting their self-esteem in the process. But perhaps the major reason that similarity produces liking is just a repeat of factors we have seen before—proximity and familiarity. Both social norms and situational circumstances throw us together with people who are like us. Most religious groups prefer (or insist) that their members date and mate within the religion, and cultural norms regulate what is considered acceptable in terms of race and age matches—a couple comprising an older woman and a younger man is still viewed as inappropriate. Situational circumstances also play an important role. Many couples meet in college or graduate school, thus assuring that they will be similar in educational level, general intelligence, professional aspirations, and probably in age and socioeconomic status. Moreover, tennis players will have met on the tennis courts, political liberals at a pro-choice rally, and gay people at a meeting of the Gay People's Union.

Despite all this, it is often suggested that the saying that opposites attract may still apply to certain complementary personality traits (Winch, Ktsanes, & Ktsanes, 1954). To take the most obvious example, one partner may be quite dominant and thus require someone who is relatively more submissive. A person with strong preferences may do best with someone who is very flexible or even wishy-washy. But despite the plausibility of this complementarity hypothesis, there is not much evidence for it (Levinger, Senn, & Jorgensen, 1970). In one study, marital adjustment among couples married for up to 5 years was found to depend more on similarity than on complementarity (Meyer & Pepper, 1977). Attempts to identify the pairs of personality traits that bring about complementarity have not been very successful (Strong et al., 1988). When all is said and done, it is similarity that wins the day.

## Love

**LIKING AND LOVING**   Love is more than just intense liking. Most of us know people we like very much but do not love, and some of us have experienced even passionate love for someone we do not particularly like. Research confirms these everyday observations. One of the first researchers to study romantic love compiled a number of statements that people thought reflected liking and loving and constructed separate scales to measure each (Rubin, 1973). Items on the liking scale tap the degree to which the other person is regarded as likable, respected, admired, and having maturity and good judgment. Items on the love scale tap three main themes: a sense of attachment ("It would be hard for me to get along without _____"), a sense of caring for the other person ("I would do almost anything for _____"), and a sense of trust ("I feel that I can confide in _____ about virtually everything"). The two scales are only moderately correlated with each other: .56 for men and .36 for women.

**LOVE AND MARRIAGE** The concept of romantic love is an old one, but the belief that it has much to do with marriage is more recent and far from universal. In some non-Western cultures, marriage is still considered to be a contractual or financial arrangement that has nothing whatever to do with love. In our own society, the link between love and marriage has actually become stronger over the past 25 years. Over the years, college students have been asked "if a man (woman) had all the other qualities you desired, would you marry this person if you were not in love with him (her)?" In 1967, about 65 percent of the men but only 24 percent of college women said that they would refuse to marry such a person (the majority of women were undecided; only 4 percent actually said yes) (Kephart, 1967). The modern feminist movement had just begun at that time, and it may be that women were then more likely than now to consider marriage a necessary condition for their own financial security. When the survey was repeated in 1984, 85 percent of both men and women said that they would refuse to marry without being in love (Simpson, Campbell, & Berscheid, 1986).

**PASSIONATE AND COMPANIONATE LOVE** Several social scientists have attempted to distinguish different kinds of love. One of the most widely accepted distinctions is between *passionate* love and *companionate* love (Hatfield, 1988; Peele, 1988).

*The passionate component of romantic love becomes less important than the companionate component in later life.*

*Critical*

# DISCUSSION

## Passion through Misattribution?

In his first-century Roman handbook *The Art of Love*, Ovid offered advice on romantic conquest to both men and women. Among his more intriguing suggestions to a man was that he take a woman in whom he is interested to the gladiator contests, where she could be easily aroused to passion. He did not say why this should be so, however. It was not until 1887 that a psychological explanation for this bit of wisdom was offered:

Love can only be excited by strong and vivid emotion, and it is almost immaterial whether these emotions are agreeable or disagreeable. The Cid wooed the proud heart of Donna Ximene, whose father he had slain, by shooting one after another of her pet pigeons (Adolf Horwicz, quoted in Finck, 1887, p. 240)

These romantic tactics should strike a familiar chord. As discussed both in

Chapter 11 and earlier in this chapter in the discussion of self-perception, we often judge what emotion we are experiencing through a process of cognitive appraisal. Although the physiological arousal of our autonomic nervous system provides us with the information that we are experiencing an emotion, the more subtle judgment of *which* emotion we are experiencing often depends on our cognitive appraisals of the surrounding circumstances. As we also noted in Chapter 11, arousal from one source (for example, the gladiator contest) can carry over to intensify the arousal experienced from a different source (for example, the beloved) (Zillmann & Bryant, 1974; Zillmann, 1978, 1984).

Ovid and Horwicz are thus suggesting that a person who is physiologically aroused (by whatever means) might attribute that arousal to love or sexual passion—to the advantage of any would-be lover who happens to be at hand.

There is now solid experimental evidence for this phenomenon, but disagreement about the process underlying it. In a study conducted in a natural setting, an attractive female experimenter approached men who were alone and were crossing a rickety, swaying bridge suspended over 200 feet above rocks and rapids. The assumption was that crossing the bridge produced high physiological arousal due to fear. She asked

each man to help her with a psychological study by writing an imaginative story to a picture (see the discussion of the Thematic Apperception Test in Chapter 14). After he had finished writing, the woman offered him her telephone number in case he was interested in knowing more about the study. In control conditions, a male experimenter was used or the experimenter approached men who were crossing a low, non-arousing, stable bridge. The stories were scored for sexual imagery and a record was kept of which men later telephoned the experimenter.

The results showed that men who encountered the female experimenter on the high bridge put more sexual imagery in their stories than did men in the control conditions. They were also more likely to telephone later (Dutton & Aron, 1974).

Perhaps you can detect flaws in this study. Maybe only macho men cross the high bridge and only wimps cross the low bridge, and it is this difference in subject populations that produces the differential results. Or perhaps the woman herself acted differently or appeared more attractive on the high bridge than on the low bridge. Some researchers have also suggested that the presence of the woman on the bridge reduces the man's fear and that this would enhance her attractiveness (Kenrick &

**Passionate love** is defined as an intensely emotional state in which "tender and sexual feelings, elation and pain, anxiety and relief, altruism and jealousy coexist in a confusion of feelings" (Berscheid & Walster, 1978, p. 177). It has been proposed that the experience of passionate love combines physiological arousal with the perception that the arousal is evoked by the beloved (Berscheid & Walster, 1974). (See the Critical Discussion, "Passion through Misattribution?")

In contrast, **companionate love** is defined as "the affection we feel for those with whom our lives are deeply intertwined" (Berscheid & Walster, 1978, p. 177). The characteristics of companionate love are trust, caring, tolerance of the partner's flaws and idiosyncrasies, and an emotional tone of warmth and affection rather than high-pitched emotional passion.

Many of the young men and women in the 1984 survey, cited above, stated that if love disappears from a marriage, that is sufficient reason to end it. Those young people who equate love with only its passionate variant are likely to be disappointed: most successful, long-term couples emphasize companionate elements of their relationship. One investigator suggests that

Cialdini, 1977; Riordan & Tedeschi, 1983).

To control for these several possibilities, several additional studies have now been conducted. In one, male subjects were physiologically aroused in one of three ways: by running in place, by watching a videotape of a comedy routine, or by watching a videotape of a grisly killing. They then watched a tape of a woman who was dressed and made up to look either attractive or unattractive. Finally, all subjects rated the woman on several scales, including her general attractiveness and the degree to which they would be interested in dating her and kissing her.

The results showed that no matter how the arousal had been obtained, subjects liked the attractive woman more and the unattractive woman less than did control subjects who had not been aroused. The high arousal intensified both positive and negative reactions to the woman (White, Fishbein, & Rutstein, 1981).

Because arousal in this study was elicited in several ways, the fear-reduction hypothesis cannot explain the results, but the misattribution hypothesis can. Another set of investigators, however, has offered yet another possible interpretation: *response facilitation*, a well known phenomenon in psychology. When an organism is aroused, whatever response it is most likely to make in the situation—called the dominant response—will be facilitated or intensified. (We discuss response facilitation in a quite different context in Chapter 19.) If the subject's dominant response in these studies is attraction to the woman, then this will be intensified by the additional arousal. Note, too, that if the subject's dominant response in the situation is to *not* be attracted to the woman, then the arousal would intensify this negative response, exactly what was found in the study described above (Allen, Kenrick, Linder, & McCall, 1989).

There is an empirical way to distinguish between the two explanations. The misattribution explanation implies that the effect will only occur if the person is unaware of the true source of arousal—so that he or she can plausibly misattribute it to the targeted person. The response facilitation explanation, however, implies that the effect will occur whether or not the person is aware of the true source of arousal.

Accordingly, another study was conducted in which male subjects were aroused by exercise. Some subjects were made aware of their arousal and its cause just before seeing a videotape of the attractive woman; others were not. The results showed that aroused subjects were more attracted to the woman than unaroused subjects even when they were aware of the arousal and its cause (Allen, Kenrick, Linder, & McCall, 1989). This finding supports the response facilitation explanation. The verdict is not final, however: an earlier study found that aroused subjects were more likely to be attracted to the woman when they were distracted from the true source of their arousal than when they were not (White & Kight, 1984).

But whatever the specific mechanism, the phenomenon itself appears to be genuine. Readers of both sexes should feel encouraged to buy a pair of tickets to the hockey game.

as a relationship continues over time, interdependence grows and the potential for strong emotion actually increases. This can be seen when longtime partners experience intense feelings of loneliness and desire when temporarily separated from each other or in the emotional devastation typically experienced by someone who loses a longtime partner. But, paradoxically, because companionate couples become so compatible and coordinated in their daily routines, the actual frequency of strong emotions is usually fairly low (Berscheid, 1983).

The importance of companionate love is illustrated in a study that compared long-term marriages in the United States—where couples claim to marry for love—with marriages in Japan that had been arranged by the couples' parents. As expected, the American marriages started out with a higher level of expressed love and sexual interest than did the Japanese arranged marriages. But the amount of love expressed decreased in both groups until there were no differences between the two groups after 10 years (Blood, 1967). As the sixteenth Century writer Giraldi put it: "The history of a love affair is in some sense the drama of its fight against time."

But the decline of expressed love did not necessarily spell marital failure. Many couples in this study reported quite gratifying marriages, marriages that had evolved into a deep companionate love characterized by communication between the partners, an equitable division of labor, and equality of decision-making power. The moral would appear to be that passionate love might be terrific for starters, but the sustaining forces of a good long-term relationship are less exciting, undoubtedly require more work, and have more to do with equality than with passion. A disappointment for romantics, perhaps, but heartening news for advocates of sexual equality.

**TRIANGULAR THEORY OF LOVE** A similar but more differentiated classification of love divides it into three components: *intimacy, passion*, and *commitment* (Sternberg, 1986). Intimacy is the emotional component and involves closeness and sharing of feelings. Passion is the motivational component that captures sexual attraction and the romantic feeling of being "in love." Commitment is the cognitive component that reflects the person's intention to remain in the relationship. Combining these components in different ways yields the eight kinds of relationships shown in Table 18-2. As can be seen, passionate love is split in this scheme into two types: *infatuated* love and *romantic* love. Both are characterized by high passion and low commitment, but infatuated love is low on intimacy, whereas romantic love is high on intimacy. Companionate love is characterized by high intimacy and commitment but low passion.

Still other classifications of love have been proposed. One is based on the notion of adult *attachment styles*, analogous to attachment styles in infancy (see Chapters 3 and 13) (Hazan & Shaver, 1987; Shaver, Hazan, & Bradshaw, 1988). Another draws an analogy with colors, proposing three primary and three secondary "colors" of love (Lee, 1973, 1977, 1988; Hendrick & Hendrick, 1986). Recent attempts to integrate these several classification systems, however, have produced inconsistent results (Hendrick & Hendrick, 1989; Levy & Davis, 1988). At the moment, the distinction between passionate and companionate love may be the most useful (Brehm, 1992).

|  | INTIMACY | PASSION | COMMITMENT |
|---|---|---|---|
| Nonlove | Low | Low | Low |
| Liking | High | Low | Low |
| Infatuated love | Low | High | Low |
| Romantic love | High | High | Low |
| Empty love | Low | Low | High |
| Companionate love | High | Low | High |
| Fatuous love | Low | High | High |
| Consummate love | High | High | High |

**TABLE 18-2**
**Triangular Theory of Love** *The three dimensions of love combine to produce eight different types of love relationships.* (After Sternberg, 1986)

1. *Social psychology* is the study of how people perceive, think, and feel about their social world and how they interact and influence one another. Beginning with the premise that human behavior is a function of both the person and the situation, social psychologists emphasize the *power of a situation* and the importance of the person's *interpretation of a situation* in determining social behavior.

2. In attempting to understand others and ourselves, we construct intuitive theories of human behavior by performing the same tasks as a formal scientist: *collecting data, detecting covariation,* and *inferring causality.* Our theories themselves, however, can shape our perceptions of the data, distort our estimates of covariation, and bias our evaluations of cause and effect. For example, we tend to notice and recall vivid information more than nonvivid information, and this biases our social judgments.

3. *Schematic processing* is the perceiving and interpreting of incoming information in terms of simplified memory structures called *schemata.* Schemata constitute minitheories of everyday objects and events. They allow us to process social information efficiently by permitting us to encode and to remember only the unique or most prominent features of a new object or event.

4. Because schemata constitute simplifications of reality, schematic processing produces biases and errors in our processing of social information. In forming impressions of other people, for example, we are prone to the *primacy effect;* the first information we receive evokes an initial schema and, hence, becomes more powerful in determining our impression than does later information. In general, schematic processing produces perceptions that are resistant to change and relatively impervious to new data.

5. We are not very accurate at detecting covariations or correlations between events in everyday life. When our schemata or theories lead us to expect two things to covary, we overestimate their actual correlation; but when we do not have a theory, we underestimate their correlation.

6. *Stereotypes* can be thought of as theories or schemata of covariation. Like other schemata, they are resistant to change. In particular, they lead us to overlook the very data that would disconfirm them. Moreover, they can be self-perpetuating and self-fulfilling, because they influence those who hold them to behave in ways that actually evoke the stereotyped behavior.

7. *Attribution* is the process by which we attempt to interpret and to explain the behavior of other people—that is, to discern the causes of their actions. One major attribution task is to decide whether someone's action should be attributed to *dispositional* causes (the person's personality or attitudes) or to *situational* causes (social forces or other external circumstances). We tend to give too much weight to dispositional factors and too little to situational factors. This bias has been called the *fundamental attribution error.*

8. *Self-perception theory* proposes that we make judgments about ourselves using the same inferential processes—and making the same kinds of errors—that we use for making judgments about others. For example, we often commit the fundamental attribution error when interpreting our own behavior.

9. *Attitudes* are likes and dislikes—favorable or unfavorable evaluations of and reactions to objects, people, events, or ideas. Attitudes comprise a

*cognitive* component, an *affective* component, and a *behavioral* component. A major issue in attitude research is the degree of consistency among a person's attitudes. Despite evidence for attitude consistency in laboratory studies, social scientists are divided in their views about the degree to which citizens hold coherent opinions about social and political issues.

10. Attitudes serve many different functions: Attitudes that we hold for practical reasons serve an *instrumental* function; those that help us make sense of the world serve a *knowledge* function; those that express our values or reflect our self-concepts serve a *value-expressive* function; those that protect us from anxiety or threats to our self-esteem serve an *ego-defensive* function; those that help us feel a part of a social community serve a *social adjustment* function.

11. The *scapegoat theory of prejudice* holds that negative attitudes toward minority groups sometimes serve an ego-defensive function, leading individuals to *repress* their own undesirable characteristics and to *project* those same characteristics onto minority groups. The *Authoritarian Personality* is a classic study in social psychology that tested this theory and described the kind of person who would be particularly likely to hold this kind of prejudice. Negative attitudes toward desegregation and African Americans in the American South in the 1950s served primarily a social adjustment function and, hence, changed relatively easily as the social norms changed.

12. Attitudes tend to predict behavior best when they are (a) strong and consistent, (b) based on the person's direct experience, and (c) specifically related to the behavior being predicted. *Cognitive dissonance theory* proposes that when a person's behaviors are inconsistent with his or her attitudes, the discomfort produced by this dissonance leads the person to change the attitudes to be consistent with the behavior. *Self-perception theory* and *impression management theory* offer alternative explanations for the same phenomenon. All three theories may be partially correct under different circumstances.

13. Many factors influence whether we will be attracted to someone. The most important are *physical attractiveness, proximity, familiarity,* and *similarity.* The old saying that "opposites attract" has not been upheld by research.

14. The link between love and marriage is historically recent and far from universal. In our own society the link has become closer over the past 25 years, with more women and men today refusing to marry someone they do not love. There have been several attempts to classify different types of love. *Passionate* love is characterized by intense and often conflicting emotions, whereas *companionate* love is characterized by trust, caring, tolerance of the partner's flaws, and an emotional tone of warmth and affection. Even though passionate love decreases over time in long-term relationships, the potential for strong emotion actually increases. But because companionate couples become so compatible in their daily routines, the actual frequency of strong emotions is fairly low.

*F u r t h e r* **READING**

Three comprehensive textbooks in social psychology are Lippa, *Introduction to Social Psychology* (1990); Myers, *Social Psychology* (3rd ed., 1990); and Sears, Peplau, and Taylor, *Social Psychology* (7th ed., 1991). More advanced treatments are available in Lindzey and Aronson (eds.), *The Handbook of Social Psychology* (3rd ed., 1985).

A major theme of this chapter—that persons act as informal scientists in arriving at social judgments—is treated in detail in Nisbett and Ross, *Human Inference: Strategies and Shortcomings of Social Judgment* (1980). A delightful extension of this basic theme is presented by Gilovich, *How We Know What Isn't So: The Fallibility of Human Reason in Everyday Life* (1991).

A number of books deal in more depth with the other topics discussed. Recommended are Aronson, *The Social Animal* (6th ed., 1991); Bem, *Beliefs, Attitudes, and Human Affairs* (1970); Brehm, *Intimate Relationships* (2nd ed., 1992); and Ross and Nisbett, *The Person and the Situation: Perspectives of Social Psychology* (1991).

# Chapter 19

# Social Interaction and Influence

## Presence of Others 749

*Social Facilitation*
*Deindividuation*
*Bystander Intervention*
*Critical Discussion: Social Impact Theory*

## Interpersonal Influence 759

*Conformity to a Majority*
*Obedience to Authority*
*Critical Discussion: Ethical Issues in Milgram's Obedience Experiments*
*Power of Situations*
*Rebellion*
*Persuasive Influence of Minorities*
*Cognitive Response Theory of Persuasion*

## Group Decision Making 778

*Group Polarization*
*Groupthink*

Detail, *Street Scene.*

In Chapter 18, we discussed the part of social psychology that deals with how people perceive, think, and feel about their social world—their social beliefs and attitudes. In this chapter we examine how people interact and influence one another.

For most of us, the term *social influence* connotes direct and deliberate attempts to change our beliefs, attitudes, or behaviors. But many forms of social influence are indirect or unintentional. For example, the mere physical presence of other persons can affect us in a number of subtle ways. We are also influenced by **social norms**—implicit rules and expectations that dictate what we ought to think and how we ought to behave; these range from the trivial to the profound. Social norms tell us to face forward when riding in an elevator, and they govern how long we can gaze at a stranger before being considered rude. More profoundly, social norms can create and maintain racism or sexism in a society. As we shall see, the success of direct and deliberate social influence itself often depends on our unwitting and automatic allegiance to social norms.

Social interaction and influence are central to communal life. Cooperation, altruism, and love all involve social interaction and influence. But pressing social problems over the years have frequently prompted social psychologists to focus their concern on interactions and influences that cause our society grief. Accordingly, just as the chapter on psychopathology dwells on the dark side of individual behavior, this chapter focuses disproportionately on the dark side of social behavior. Some of the findings are disturbing, even depressing. But just as the study of psychopathology has led to effective therapies, so, too, the study of problematic social interactions has led us to more effective ways of dealing with them. By understanding the principles underlying many of our social problems, we simultaneously understand the principles underlying their solutions.

# Presence of Others

## Social Facilitation

In 1898, the psychologist Norman Triplett was examining the speed records of bicycle racers and he noticed that many cyclists achieved higher speeds when they raced against each other than when they raced against the clock. This led him to perform one of social psychology's earliest laboratory experiments. He instructed children to turn a fishing reel as fast as possible for a fixed period of time. Sometimes two children worked at the same time in the same room, each with his or her own reel. Other times they worked alone. Although his published data are difficult to evaluate, Triplett reported that many children worked faster in *coaction*—that is, when another child doing the same task was present—than when they worked alone.

Since this experiment, many studies have demonstrated the facilitating effects of coaction with both human and animal subjects. For example, worker ants in groups will dig more than three times as much sand per ant than when alone (Chen, 1937), many animals will eat more food if other members of their species are present (Platt, Yaksh, & Darby, 1967), and college students will complete more multiplication problems in coaction than when alone (F. H. Allport, 1920, 1924). Soon after Triplett's experiment on coaction, psychologists discovered that the presence of a passive spectator— an audience rather than a coactor—also facilitates performance. For example, the presence of an audience had the same facilitating effect on students'

**FIGURE 19-1**
**Social Facilitation Experiment**
*Diagrams of runways and mazes used in Zajonc's social facilitation experiment with cockroaches.* (After Zajonc et al., 1969)

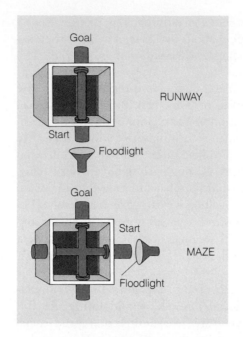
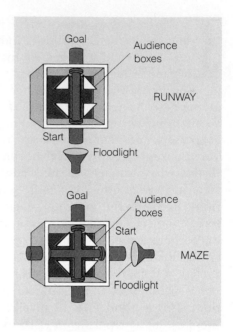

multiplication performance as did that of the coactors in the earlier study (Dashiell, 1930). These coaction and audience effects have been called **social facilitation.**

But even this simple case of social influence turned out to be more complicated than social psychologists first thought. For example, researchers found that subjects made more errors on the multiplication problems when in coaction or in the presence of an audience than when they performed alone (Dashiell, 1930). In other words, the quality of performance declined even though quantity increased. In other studies, however, the quality of performance improved when coactors or audiences were present (for example, Dashiell, 1935; Cottrell, 1972). How can these contradictions be reconciled?

In examining the findings, psychologist Robert Zajonc (1965, 1980) noted that simple responses, highly practiced responses, or instinctive responses (such as eating) were typically facilitated, whereas complex or newly learned responses were typically impaired in the presence of coactors or audiences. He proposed that a long-known principle of motivation could account for the findings: a high level of drive or arousal tends to energize the dominant responses of an organism. If the mere presence of another member of the species raises the general arousal or drive level of an organism, then the dominant response will be facilitated. For simple or well-learned behaviors, the dominant response is most likely to be the correct response, and performance should be facilitated. For complex behaviors or behaviors just being learned, the dominant or most probable response is likely to be incorrect. On a multiplication problem, for example, there are many wrong responses but only one correct one. Performance should therefore be impaired.

A number of experiments with both human and animal subjects tested this theory of social facilitation. In one particularly clever study, cockroaches could run down a straight runway into a darkened goal box to escape a bright floodlight (see Figure 19-1). The researchers found that the roaches reached the goal box faster if they ran in pairs than if they ran alone. But when the escape response was made more complicated by requiring the roaches to make a right-angle turn to find the goal box, pairs of roaches took longer to reach the box than did single roaches. In other words, the presence of coactors facilitated performance in the simple runway but impaired performance in the complex runway (Zajonc, Heingartner, & Herman, 1969). This experiment was repeated by having all of the roaches run alone, but with an audience of roaches that watched from small plexiglass boxes set alongside the runways. Again, the presence of other roaches—even if they were just spectators—facilitated performance when the dominant response (running down the straight runway) was correct and impaired performance when the dominant response was incorrect.

A direct analog of the cockroach study found that human subjects learn a simple maze faster but a complex maze more slowly when an audience is present than when it is not (Hunt & Hillery, 1973). Other studies have shown that people memorize easy word lists faster but difficult word lists more slowly in the presence of an audience than when alone (Cottrell, Rittle, & Wack, 1967).

Because social facilitation occurs in nonhuman species, it would not seem to require complex cognitive processes. But one theory suggests that social facilitation in humans is due not to the mere presence of others but to feelings of competition or to concerns about being evaluated, and it is these cognitive concerns that raise the drive level. Even the early studies of coaction found that, if all elements of rivalry and competition were removed, social facilitation effects were reduced or eliminated (Dashiell, 1930). Other studies show that audience effects vary depending on how much the person feels that he or she is being evaluated. For example, social facilitation effects are enhanced if an expert watches but diminished if the audience consists only of "undergraduates who want to watch a psychology experiment" (Henchy & Glass, 1968; Paulus & Murdock, 1971). In one study, when the audience wore blindfolds and hence could not watch or evaluate the individual's performance, no social facilitation effects were found (Cottrell, Wack, Sekerak, & Rittle, 1968).

One problem with most of these studies, however, is that subjects may still experience concern about being evaluated, even when alone or in the mere presence of others, because they know that their performances are being recorded and evaluated by the experimenter. Thus, these studies still leave open the question of whether or not social facilitation effects in humans ever arise purely from the mere presence of others.

In a study designed to eliminate subjects' concerns about being evaluated in both the alone and mere presence conditions, each subject was shown to a waiting room, seated in front of a computer, and asked to provide some "background information before the experiment begins." The computer first prompted the subject to enter his or her name (such as "Joan Smith") and then to construct a code name by typing his or her name backwards and alternating each letter with ascending digits (for example, "h1t2i3m4S5n6a7o8J"). That was the entire experiment, and it was over before the subject realized that it had even begun. The computer automatically recorded both how long it took the subject to type his or her name (the easy task) and to type the code name (the difficult task). One group of subjects typed while alone in the room (alone condition). Another group of subjects typed while the experimenter looked over their shoulders (evaluation condition). A third group typed in the presence of a blindfolded person who wore headphones, faced away from the subject, and was said to be waiting to be in a sensory deprivation experiment (mere presence condition).

| CONDITION | TIME TO COMPLETE TASK | |
| --- | --- | --- |
| | EASY TASK | DIFFICULT TASK |
| Alone (Baseline) | 15 | 52 |
| Evaluation | 7 | 63 |
| Mere Presence | 10 | 73 |

**TABLE 19-1**
**Social Facilitation in the Presence of Another Individual**
*When subjects either are being evaluated or are merely in the presence of another individual, they perform an easy task more quickly but a difficult task more slowly than they would if alone. The dependent variable is the mean time (in seconds) required to complete a typing task.* (After Schmitt, Gilovich, Goore, & Joseph, 1986)

The results revealed that social facilitation effects were produced by the mere presence of another individual (see Table 19-1). Compared with subjects in the alone condition, subjects in both the evaluation and mere presence conditions performed the easy task more quickly but the difficult task more slowly—the characteristic pattern of social facilitation (Schmitt, Gilovich, Goore, & Joseph, 1986).

Two additional theories have been proposed to account for social facilitation effects. *Distraction-conflict theory* suggests that the presence of others distracts the person, causing a conflict over how to allocate attention between the others and the task to be performed. It is this attentional conflict—rather than the mere presence of another person or a concern over being evaluated—that raises the drive level and causes social facilitation effects (Sanders & Baron, 1975; Baron, 1986). *Self-presentation theory* proposes that the presence of others enhances the individual's desire to present a favorable image. On easy tasks this leads to more effort and concentration and thus to improved performance. On difficult tasks, however, this desire magnifies the frustrations imposed by the tasks and leads to embarrassment, withdrawal, or excessive anxiety, all of which lead to poorer performance (Bond, 1982). There are research results that support each of these theories, and it seems likely that all of the proposed processes—mere presence, concern over evaluation, distraction-conflict, and desire to present a favorable image—contribute to social facilitation effects (Sanders, 1984).

## Deindividuation

At about the same time that Triplett was performing his laboratory experiment on social facilitation, another observer of human behavior, Gustave LeBon, was taking a less dispassionate view of group coaction. In his book *The Crowd* (1895), he complained that "the crowd is always intellectually inferior to the isolated individual. . . . The mob man is fickle, credulous, and intolerant, showing the violence and ferocity of primitive beings . . . women, children, savages, and lower classes . . . operating under the influence of the spinal cord." LeBon believed that the aggressive and immoral behaviors shown by lynch mobs (and, in his view, French Revolutionists) spread by contagion through a mob or crowd like a disease, breaking down a man's moral sense and self-control. This caused crowds to commit destructive acts that no lone individuals—except, of course, women, children, savages, and lower classes—would commit.

Despite his obvious prejudices, LeBon's observations have some validity. The modern counterpart to his theory is built on the concept of **deindividuation,** a concept first proposed by Festinger, Pepitone, and Newcomb (1952) and extended by Zimbardo (1970) and Diener (1979, 1980). Their theories propose that certain conditions that are sometimes present in groups can lead individuals to experience a psychological state of deindividuation, a feeling that they have lost their personal identities and merged anonymously into the group. This produces diminished restraints against impulsive behavior and the other cognitive and emotional conditions associated with unruly mob behavior. The several antecedents and consequences of deindividuation proposed by Diener are illustrated in Figure 19-2. Note that antecedent conditions lead to deindividuation by producing a state of reduced self-awareness in the individual.

In one study of deindividuation, college women, participating in groups of four, were required to deliver electric shocks to another woman who was

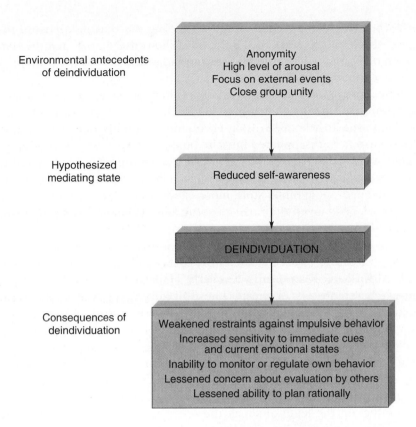

**FIGURE 19-2**
**Antecedents and Consequences of Deindividuation** *One explanation of crowd behavior traces it to a loss of personal identity in certain group situations.* (After Diener, 1979)

supposedly in a learning experiment. Half of the women were deindividuated by making them feel anonymous. They were dressed in bulky laboratory coats and hoods that hid their faces, and the experimenter spoke to them only as a group, never referring to any of them by name (see Figure 19-3). The remaining women were individuated by having them remain in their own clothes and wear large identification tags. In addition, the women in the second group were introduced to each other by name. During the experiment, each woman had a shock button in front of her that she was to

**FIGURE 19-3**
**Anonymity Produces Deindividuation** *When women were disguised so that they felt anonymous, they delivered more shock to an innocent victim than did nondisguised subjects.*

push when the learner made an error. Pushing the button appeared to deliver a shock to the learner. The results showed that the deindividuated women delivered twice as much shock to the learner as did the individuated groups (Zimbardo, 1970).

One clever study was conducted simultaneously at several homes in a community on Halloween. Children out trick-or-treating were greeted at the door by a woman who asked that each child take only one piece of candy. The woman then disappeared into the house briefly, giving the children the opportunity to take more candy. Some of the children had been asked their names while others remained anonymous. Children who came in groups or who remained anonymous stole more candy than did children who came alone or who had given their names to the adult (Diener, Fraser, Beaman, & Kelem, 1976).

These experiments are not definitive, however. For example, you can see from Figure 19-3 that the laboratory coats and hoods in the first study resembled Ku Klux Klan outfits. Similarly, Halloween costumes often represent witches, monsters, or ghosts. These all carry aggressive or negative connotations. It may be that the roles suggested by the costumes rather than the anonymity they provided produced the behavior. To test this possibility, the shock experiment was repeated, but this time each subject wore one of three outfits: a Ku Klux Klan-type costume, a nurse's uniform, or the subject's own clothes. The results of the revised experiment did not replicate those of the original study: wearing a Ku Klux Klan-type costume had only a small effect on the level of shock the subjects administered. More significantly, those wearing nurses' uniforms actually gave fewer shocks than did the control group who wore their own clothes, suggesting that a uniform encourages the person to play the kind of role it connotes. This study shows that anonymity does not inevitably lead to enhanced aggression (Johnson & Downing, 1979).

A second qualification also has emerged from the research: being in a group is not itself a critical variable in producing deindividuation. Being in a group produces deindividuation only when it provides the other antecedent conditions listed in Figure 19-2, especially anonymity and a reduction of self-awareness (Diener, 1980). Most of the initial studies of deindividuation included both a group context and anonymity, so that it was not possible to identify which was the critical variable.

## Bystander Intervention

In earlier chapters, we noted that people do not react simply to the objective features of a situation but to their own subjective interpretations of it. In this chapter we have seen that even social facilitation, a primitive kind of social influence, depends in part on the individual's interpretation of what others are doing or thinking. But as we shall now see, defining or interpreting the situation is often the very mechanism through which individuals influence one another.

In 1964, Kitty Genovese was murdered outside her home in New York City late at night. She fought back, and the murder took over half an hour. At least 38 neighbors heard her screams for help, but nobody came to her aid. No one even called the police.

The American public was horrified by this incident, and social psychologists began to investigate the causes of what at first was termed "bystander apathy." Their work showed that "apathy" was not a very accurate term, however. It is not simple indifference that prevents bystanders from intervening in emergencies. First, there are realistic deterrents such as physical danger. Second, getting involved may mean lengthy court appearances or other entanglements. Third, emergencies are unpredictable and require quick, unplanned action; few of us are prepared for such situations. Finally, one risks making a fool of oneself by misinterpreting a situation as an emergency when it is not. Researchers concluded that "the bystander to an emergency situation is in an unenviable position. It is perhaps surprising that anyone should intervene at all" (Latané & Darley, 1970, p. 247).

Although we might suppose that the presence of other bystanders would embolden an individual to act despite the risks, research demonstrates the reverse. Often it is the very presence of other people that prevents us from intervening. Specifically, the presence of others serves (a) to define the situation as a nonemergency, and (b) to diffuse the responsibility for acting.

**DEFINING THE SITUATION**   Many emergencies begin ambiguously. Is the man who is staggering about ill or simply drunk? Is the woman being threatened by a stranger, or is she arguing with her husband? Is that smoke from a fire or just steam pouring out the window? One common way to deal with such dilemmas is to postpone action, to act as if nothing is wrong, and to look around to see how others are reacting. What you are likely to see, of course, are other people who, for the same reasons, are also acting as if nothing is wrong. A state of **pluralistic ignorance** develops—that is, everybody in the group misleads everybody else by defining the situation as a nonemergency. We have all heard about crowds panicking because each person leads everybody else to overreact. The reverse situation—in which a crowd lulls its members into inaction—may be even more common. Several experiments demonstrate this effect.

In one experiment, male college students were invited to an interview. As they sat in a small waiting room, a stream of smoke began to pour through a wall vent. Some subjects were alone in the waiting room when this occurred; others were in groups of three. The experimenters observed them

*Although many passers-by have noticed the man lying on the sidewalk, no one has stopped to help—to find out if he is asleep, sick, drunk, or dead. If others were not present, someone would be more likely to come to his aid.*

through a one-way window and waited 6 minutes to see if anyone would take action or report the situation. Of the subjects tested alone, 75 percent reported the smoke within about 2 minutes. In contrast, fewer than 13 percent of the people tested in groups reported the smoke within the entire 6-minute period, even though the room was filled with smoke. Those who did not report the smoke subsequently reported that they decided that it must have been steam, air conditioning vapors, or smog—practically anything but a real fire or an emergency. This experiment thus showed that bystanders can define situations as nonemergencies for one another (Latané & Darley, 1968).

But perhaps these subjects were simply afraid to appear cowardly. To check this out, a similar study was designed in which the "emergency" did not involve personal danger. Subjects in the testing room heard a female experimenter in the next office climb up on a chair to reach a bookcase, fall to the floor, and yell "Oh my god—my foot. . . . I can't move it. Oh . . . my ankle. . . . I can't get this thing off me." She continued to moan for about a minute longer. The entire incident lasted about 2 minutes. Only a curtain separated the woman's office from the testing room in which subjects waited, either alone or in pairs. The results confirmed the findings of the smoke study. Of the subjects who were alone, 70 percent came to the woman's aid, whereas only 40 percent of those in two-person groups offered help. Again, those who had not intervened claimed later that they were unsure of what had happened but had decided that it was not serious (Latané & Rodin, 1969). The presence of others in these experiments produced pluralistic ignorance; each person, observing the calmness of the others, resolved the ambiguity of the situation by deciding no emergency existed.

**DIFFUSION OF RESPONSIBILITY** Pluralistic ignorance can lead individuals to define a situation as a nonemergency, but this process does not explain such incidents as the Genovese murder in which the emergency is abundantly clear. Moreover, Kitty Genovese's neighbors could not observe one another behind their curtained windows and hence could not tell whether others were calm or panicked. The crucial process here was **diffusion of responsibility.** When each individual knows that many others are present, the burden of responsibility does not fall solely on him or her. Each can think, "Someone else must have done something by now; someone else will intervene."

To test this hypothesis, experimenters placed subjects in individual booths and told them that they would participate in a group discussion about personal problems faced by college students. To avoid embarrassment, the discussion would be held through an intercom. Each person would speak for 2 minutes. The microphone would be turned on only in the booth of the person speaking, and the experimenter would not be listening. Actually, the voices of all participants except the subject's were tape recordings. On the first round, one of the taped participants mentioned that he had problems with seizures. On the second round, this individual sounded as if he were actually starting to have a seizure and begged for help. The experimenters waited to see if the subject would leave the booth to report the emergency and how long it would take. Note that (a) the emergency is not at all ambiguous, (b) the subject could not tell how the bystanders in the other booths were reacting, and (c) the subject knew the experimenter could not hear the emergency. Some subjects were led to believe that the discussion group consisted only of themselves and the seizure victim. Others were told that they were part of a three-person group; and still others, that they were part of a six-person group.

Of the subjects who thought that they alone knew of the victim's seizure, 85 percent reported it; of those who thought they were in a three-person group, 62 percent reported the seizure; and, of those who thought they were part of a six-person group only 31 percent reported it (see Figure 19-4). Interviews showed that all the subjects perceived the situation to be a real emergency. Most were very upset by the conflict between letting the victim suffer and rushing for help—perhaps foolishly and unnecessarily. In fact, subjects who did not report the seizure appeared more upset than those who did. Clearly we cannot interpret their nonintervention as apathy or indifference. Instead, the presence of others diffused the responsibility for acting (Darley & Latané, 1968; Latané & Darley, 1968).

If pluralistic ignorance and diffusion of responsibility are minimized, will people help one another? To find out, three psychologists used the New York City subway system as their laboratory (Piliavin, Rodin, & Piliavin, 1969). Two male and two female experimenters boarded a subway train separately. The female experimenters took seats and recorded the results, while the two men remained standing. As the train moved along, one of the men staggered forward and collapsed, remaining prone and staring at the ceiling until he received help. If no help came, the other man finally helped him to his feet. Several variations of the study were tried: the victim either carried a cane (so he would appear ill) or smelled of alcohol (so he would appear drunk). Sometimes the victim was caucasian; other times, African American. There was no ambiguity; clearly the victim needed help. Diffusion of responsibility was minimized because each bystander could not continue to assume that someone else was intervening. Therefore, people should help.

The results supported this optimistic expectation. The victim with the cane received spontaneous help on over 95 percent of the trials, within an average of 5 seconds. The drunk victim received help in half of the trials, on the average within 2 minutes. Both African American and caucasian cane victims were aided by African American and caucasian bystanders. There was no relationship between the number of bystanders and the speed of help, suggesting that diffusion of responsibility had indeed been minimized. And all of this occurred on the New York City subway system. This not only tends to support the proposed explanations of bystander nonintervention but may disconfirm some of our stereotypes about New York City subway riders.

**ROLE OF HELPING MODELS** In the subway study, as soon as one person moved to help, many others followed. This suggests that just as individuals use other people as models to define a situation as a nonemergency (pluralistic ignorance), they also use other people as models to indicate when to be helpful. This possibility was tested in a study by counting the number of drivers who stopped to help a woman whose car had a flat tire (the test car). During some test periods, another car with a flat tire (the model car) was parked alongside the highway, one-quarter mile before the test car. The model car was raised on a jack and a woman was watching a man change the flat tire. Of 4,000 passing cars, 58 stopped to help the woman when the model car was present, but only 35 stopped when there was no model car—a statistically significant difference. This experiment indicates that others not only help us decide when *not* to act in an

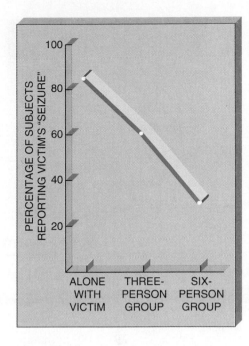

**FIGURE 19-4**
**Diffusion of Responsibility** *The percentage of subjects who reported a victim's apparent seizure declined as the number of other people the subject believed were in his or her discussion group increased.* (After Darley & Latané, 1968)

## Social Impact Theory

Each of the social influence phenomena discussed in this chapter has one or more theories that attempt to explain it. One of the investigators who initiated the research on bystander intervention has attempted to construct a more abstract theory that would summarize, if not exactly explain, all of these phenomena. He has called this a theory of **social impact** (Latané, 1981). The purpose of such a theory is not to replace the individual theories, but to incorporate them into a more general framework as special cases.

Two propositions of the theory are of interest here. The first proposition is illustrated in Figure 1 and states that the social impact of any source of influence on a target individual increases with the number, immediacy, and strength or importance of the sources. For example, this proposition predicts that social facilitation effects will increase with the number of coactors or audience members present, with their immediacy or salience to the individual, and with their importance to the individual. Thus we

have seen that social facilitation effects are weaker if an audience is blindfolded (less immediacy), and they are stronger if the audience consists of an expert rather than of undergraduates (greater importance).

A number of studies outside the arena of social facilitation are also consistent with this proposition. For example, when reciting a poem before an audience, individuals rate themselves as increasingly nervous as the number and the status of audience members increase (Latané & Harkins, 1976). Stutterers reading aloud in front of an audience stutter more as the audience increases in size (Porter, 1939). We will see additional illustrations of this proposition later when we discuss conformity and obedience.

The second proposition is illustrated in Figure 2 and states that the social impact of a source *decreases* as the number, immediacy, and importance of *targets* increases. Thus, the first proposition deals with the multiplication of impact due to multiple sources of influence; the second, with the diffusion of impact over multiple targets. For example, the second proposition describes the diffusion of responsibility in emergency situations: the more bystanders present in an emergency situation, the less pressure there is on any particular bystander to intervene.

A number of other studies also support this diffusion-of-impact proposi-

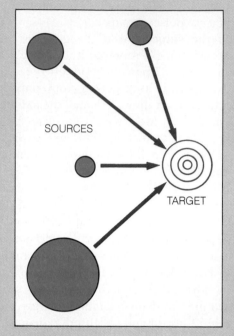

**FIGURE 1**
**Multiplication of Social Impact**
*The social impact of a source of influence on a target individual increases with the number of sources (the number of circles), the immediacy of the sources (the nearness of the circles), and the strength or importance of the sources (the size of the circles).* (After Latané, 1981)

tion. For example, we illustrated the multiplication-of-impact proposition by noting that performers become increasingly nervous as the size of the audience

emergency but also serve as models to show us how and when to be good Samaritans (Bryan & Test, 1967).

**ROLE OF INFORMATION** Now that you have read about the factors that deter bystanders from intervening in an emergency, would you be more likely to act in such a situation? An experiment at the University of Montana suggests that you would. Undergraduates were either given a lecture or shown a film based on the material discussed in this section. Two weeks later, each undergraduate was confronted with a simulated emergency while walking with one other person (a confederate of the experimenters). A male victim was sprawled on the floor of a hallway. The confederate did not react as if the situation were an emergency. Of those who had heard the lecture or seen the film, 43 percent offered help, compared with only 25 percent of those who had not—a statistically significant difference (Beaman, Barnes, Klentz, & McQuirk, 1978). For society's sake, perhaps you should reread this section!

increases—as the number of sources impinging on a single target increases. The diffusion-of-impact proposition is illustrated by a study of performers in a talent show. Solo performers were about six times more nervous than those who performed in a 10-person act (Jackson & Latané, 1981). The impact of the source (the audience) was diffused over several targets (the performers).

In another study of impact diffusion, records were kept of how much diners in a restaurant tipped the waiter or waitress. The researchers reasoned that one motive for leaving a tip is a feeling of obligation and that this feeling of obligation should be diffused or divided when several diners share the check. In the restaurant they studied, the average tip was about 15 percent. An individual dining alone tipped an average of nearly 19 percent, whereas parties of five to six people tipped less than 13 percent (Freeman, Walker, Borden, & Latané, 1975). A study of Billy Graham's evangelical rallies varying in size from 2,000 to 143,000 persons revealed that the percentage of people present who were willing to come forward and inquire into Christianity declined as the size of the rally increased (Latané, 1981).

One of the major phenomena predicted by the diffusion-of-impact proposition is *social loafing*. In 1913, a German researcher named Ringelmann conducted a study on how collective action influenced individual effort. Male sub-

jects were asked to pull as hard as they could on a rope, either pulling alone or in groups of varying sizes. He found that as the number of pullers increased, the average force contributed by each worker decreased (Ringelmann, 1913; also see Kravitz & Martin, 1986). More recent studies have replicated this finding using different kinds of tasks (Petty, Harkins, Williams, & Latané, 1977; Latané, Williams, & Harkins, 1979).

Perhaps you have noticed an apparent contradiction here. The presence of coactors is supposed to produce social facilitation—increased drive and effort —not social loafing. According to social impact theory, the critical difference lies in the role played by the "others" in the situation. When each person performs a task independently, the others put competitive or evaluative pressure on each other. There are many sources acting on each individual target; thus, multiplication of impact occurs (Figure 1). When a group of individuals work on a shared task, the boss or experimenter serves as a single source and his or her influence is diffused over many targets; hence, Figure 2 applies. Cognitive processes may also contribute to social loafing. Each person may believe that others in the group are not contributing their fair share and thus be less motivated to work to capacity. Or each individual may feel that his or her own contribution will be less recognizable when working in a group, leading to a diffu-

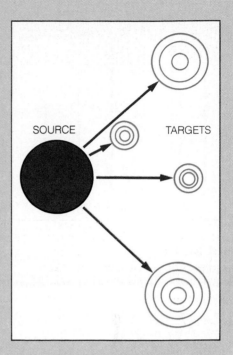

**FIGURE 2**
**Diffusion of Social Impact** *The impact of a source decreases as the number, immediacy, and importance of targets increase.* (After Latané, 1981)

sion of responsibility. A more recent study found that social loafing decreases when the task is made more challenging and when individuals believe they can make a unique contribution to the group effort (Harkins & Petty, 1982).

# Interpersonal Influence

## Conformity to a Majority

When we are in a group, we may find ourselves in the minority on some issue. This is a fact of life to which most of us have become accustomed. If we decide that the majority is a more valid source of information than our own experience, we may change our minds and conform to the majority opinion. But imagine yourself in a situation in which you are sure that your own opinion is correct and that the group is wrong. Would you yield to social pressure under those circumstances? This is the kind of conformity that social psychologist Solomon Asch decided to investigate in a series of classic studies (1952, 1955, 1958).

In Asch's standard procedure, a single subject was seated at a table with a group of seven to nine others (all confederates of the experimenter). The group was shown a display of three vertical lines of different lengths, and

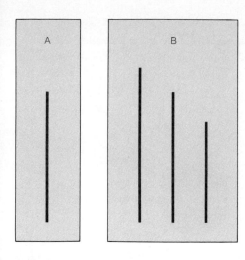

**FIGURE 19-5**
**Representative Stimulus in Asch's Study** *After viewing display A, the subjects were told to pick the matching line from display B. The displays shown here are typical in that the correct decision is obvious.* (After Asch, 1958)

members of the group were asked to judge which line was the same length as a standard drawn in another display (see Figure 19-5). Each individual announced his or her decision in turn, and the subject sat in the next to the last seat. The correct judgments were obvious, and on most trials everyone gave the same response. But on several predetermined critical trials, the confederates had been instructed to give the wrong answer. Asch then observed the amount of conformity this procedure would elicit from his subjects.

The results were striking. Even though the correct answer was always obvious, the average subject conformed to the group consensus on 32 percent of the critical trials; 74 percent of the subjects conformed at least once. Moreover, the group did not have to be large to obtain such conformity. When Asch varied the size of the group from 2 to 16, he found that a group of 3 or 4 confederates was just as effective at producing conformity as were larger groups (Asch, 1958).

Why didn't the obviousness of the correct answer provide support for the individual's independence from the majority? Why isn't a person's confidence in his or her ability to make simple sensory judgments a strong force against conformity?

According to one line of argument, it is precisely the obviousness of the correct answer in the Asch experiment that produces the strong forces toward conformity (Ross, Bierbrauer, & Hoffman, 1976). Disagreements in real life typically involve difficult or subjective judgments such as which economic policy will best reduce inflation or which of two paintings is more aesthetically pleasing. In these cases, we expect to disagree with others oc-

**Resistance of Majority Opinion** *(top)*
*All of the group members except the man sixth from the left are confederates previously instructed to give uniformly wrong answers on 12 of the 18 trials. Number 6, who has been told he is participating in an experiment in visual judgment, therefore finds himself a lone dissenter when he gives the correct answers. (bottom left) The subject, showing the strain of repeated disagreement with the majority, leans forward anxiously to look at the exhibit in question. (bottom right) This particular subject persists in his opinion, saying that "he has to call them as he sees them." (After Asch, 1958)*

casionally; we even know that being a minority of one in an otherwise unanimous group is a plausible, if uncomfortable, possibility.

The Asch situation is much more extreme. Here the individual is confronted with unanimous disagreement about a simple physical fact, a bizarre and unprecedented occurrence that appears to have no rational explanation. Subjects are clearly puzzled and tense. They rub their eyes in disbelief and jump up to look more closely at the lines. They squirm, mumble, giggle in embarrassment, and look searchingly at others in the group for some clue to the mystery. After the experiment, they offer halfhearted hypotheses about optical illusions or suggest—quite aptly—that perhaps the first person occasionally made a mistake, and each successive person followed suit because of conformity pressures (Asch, 1952).

Consider what it means to dissent from the majority under these circumstances. Just as the judgments of the group seem incomprehensible to the subject, so the subject believes that his or her dissent will be incomprehensible to the group. Group members will surely judge him or her to be incompetent, even out of touch with reality. Similarly, if the subject dissents repeatedly, this will seem to constitute a direct challenge to the group's competence, a challenge that requires enormous courage when one's own perceptual abilities are suddenly and inexplicably called into question. Such a challenge violates a strong social norm against insulting others. This fear of "What will they think of me?" and "What will they think I think of them?" inhibits dissent and generates the strong pressures to conform in the Asch situation.

Conformity pressures are far less strong when the group is not unanimous. If even one confederate breaks with the majority, the amount of conformity drops from 32 percent of the trials to about 6 percent. In fact, a group of eight containing only one dissenter produces less conformity than a unanimous majority of three (Asch, 1958). Surprisingly, the dissenter does not even have to give the correct answer. Even when the dissenter's answers are more incorrect than the majority's, their influence is broken and subjects are more inclined to give their own, correct, judgments (Asch, 1955; Allen & Levine, 1969). Nor does it matter who the dissenter is. An African-American dissenter reduces the conformity rate among racially prejudiced white subjects just as effectively as a white dissenter (Malof & Lott, 1962). In a variation that approaches the absurd, conformity was significantly reduced even though the subjects thought the dissenter was so visually handicapped that he could not see the stimuli (Allen & Levine, 1971). It seems clear that the presence of but one other deviant to share the potential disapproval or ridicule of the group permits the subject to dissent without feeling totally isolated. Social impact theory (see the previous Critical Discussion) would describe this as a result of diffusing the social forces over a large number of targets.

If Asch's conformity situation is unlike most situations in real life, why did Asch use a task in which the correct answer was obvious? The reason is that he wanted to study pure public conformity, uncontaminated by the possibility that subjects were actually changing their minds about the correct answers. (Although Asch reports that a few subjects actually did decide that the group was correct on some of the critical trials.) Several variations of Asch's study have utilized more difficult or subjective judgments, and although they may reflect life more faithfully, they do not permit us to assess the effects of pure pressure to conform to a majority when we are certain that our own minority judgment is correct (Ross, Bierbrauer, & Hoffman, 1976).

## Obedience to Authority

In Nazi Germany from 1933 to 1945, millions of innocent people were systematically put to death in concentration camps. The mastermind of this horror, Adolph Hitler, may well have been a psychopathic monster. But he could not have done it alone. What about all those who ran the day-to-day operations, who built the ovens and gas chambers, filled them with human beings, counted bodies, and did the necessary paperwork? Were they all monsters, too?

Not according to social philosopher Hannah Arendt (1963), who covered the trial of Adolph Eichmann, a Nazi war criminal who was found guilty and was executed for causing the murder of millions of Jews. She described him as a dull, ordinary, unaggressive bureaucrat who saw himself as a little cog in a big machine. The recent publication of a partial transcript of Eichmann's pretrial interrogation supports Arendt's view. Several psychiatrists found Eichmann to be quite sane, and his personal relationships were quite normal. He sincerely believed that the Jews should have been allowed to emigrate to a separate territory and had argued that position within Hitler's security service. Moreover, he had a Jewish mistress in secret—a crime for an SS officer—and a Jewish half cousin whom he arranged to have protected during the war (Von Lang & Sibyll, 1983).

Arendt subtitled her book about Eichmann *A Report on the Banality of Evil* and concluded that most of the "evil men" of the Third Reich were just ordinary people following orders from superiors. This suggests that all of us might be capable of such evil and that Nazi Germany was an event less wildly alien from the normal human condition than we might like to think. As Arendt put it, "in certain circumstances the most ordinary decent person can become a criminal." This is not an easy conclusion to accept because it is more comforting to believe that monstrous evil is done only by monstrous persons. In fact, our emotional attachment to this explanation of evil was vividly shown by the intensity of the attacks on Arendt and her conclusions.

The problem of obedience to authority arose again in 1969, when a group of American soldiers serving in Vietnam killed a number of civilians in the community of My Lai, claiming that they were simply following orders. Again the public was forced to ponder the possibility that ordinary citizens are willing to obey authority in violation of their own moral consciences.

This issue was explored empirically in a series of important and controversial studies conducted by Stanley Milgram (1963, 1974) at Yale University. Ordinary men and women were recruited through a newspaper ad that offered four dollars for one hour's participation in a "study of memory." On arriving at the laboratory, the subject was told that he or she would be playing the role of teacher in the study. The subject was to read a series of word pairs to another subject and then test that learner's memory by reading the first word of each pair and asking him to select the correct second word from four alternatives. Each time the learner made an error, the subject was to press a lever that delivered an electric shock to him.

The subject watched while the learner was strapped into a chair and an electrode was attached to his wrist. The subject was then seated in an adjoining room in front of a shock generator whose front panel contained 30 lever switches set in a horizontal line. Each switch was labeled with a voltage rating, ranging in sequence from 15 to 450 volts, and groups of adjacent switches were labeled descriptively, ranging from "Slight Shock" up to "Danger: Severe Shock." When a switch was depressed, an electric buzz

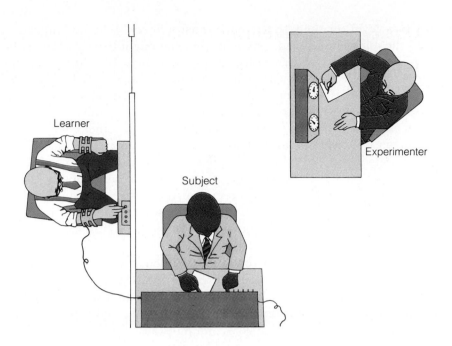

**FIGURE 19-6**
**Milgram Obedience Experiment** *The subject was told to give the learner a more intense shock after each error. If the subject objected, the experimenter insisted it was necessary to go on.* (After Milgram, 1974)

sounded, lights flashed, and the needle on a voltage meter deflected to the right. To illustrate how it worked, the subject was given a sample shock of 45 volts from the generator. As the procedure began, the experimenter instructed the subject to move one level higher on the shock generator after each successive error (see Figure 19-6).

The learner did not actually receive any shocks. He was a 47-year-old, mild-mannered man who had been specially trained for his role. As he began to make errors and the shock levels escalated, he could be heard protesting through the adjoining wall. As the shocks became stronger, he began to shout and curse. At 300 volts he began to kick the wall, and at the

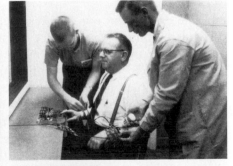

**Milgram Experiment** *(top left) The "shock generator" used in Milgram's experiment on obedience. (top right) The victim is strapped into the "electric chair." (bottom left) A subject receives the sample shock before starting the "teaching session." (bottom right) A subject refuses to go on with the experiment. Most subjects became deeply disturbed by the role they were asked to play, whether they continued in the experiment to the end or refused at some point to go on.* (From the film *Obedience,* distributed by New York University Film Library; copyright © 1965 by Stanley Milgram)

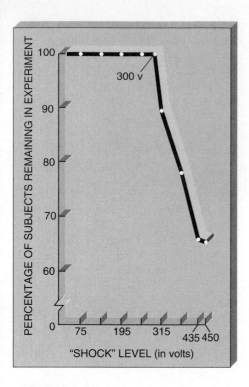

**FIGURE 19-7**
**Obedience to Authority** *The percentage of subjects willing to administer a punishing shock did not begin to decline until the intensity level of the shock reached 300 volts (the danger level).* (After Milgram, 1963)

next shock level (marked "Extreme Intensity Shock"), he no longer answered the questions or made any noise. As you might expect, many subjects began to object to this excruciating procedure, pleading with the experimenter to call a halt. But the experimenter responded with a sequence of prods, using as many as necessary to get the subject to go on: "Please continue"; "The experiment requires that you continue"; "It is absolutely essential that you continue"; and "You have no other choice—you must go on." Obedience to authority was measured by the maximum amount of shock the subject would administer before refusing to continue.

Milgram found that 65 percent of the subjects continued to obey throughout, going all the way to the end of the shock series (450 volts). Not one subject stopped prior to administering 300 volts—the point at which the learner began to kick the wall (see Figure 19-7). What produces such obedience?

Milgram suggests that the potential for obedience to authority is such a necessary requirement for communal life that it has probably been built into our species by evolution. The division of labor in a society requires that individuals be willing at times to subordinate and coordinate their own independent actions to serve the goals and purposes of the larger social organization. Parents, school systems, and businesses all nurture this willingness further by reminding the individual about the importance of following the directives of others who "know the larger picture." To understand obedience in a particular situation, then, we need to understand the factors that persuade individuals to relinquish their autonomy and become voluntary agents of the system. Four such factors—social norms, surveillance, buffers, and ideological justification—are well illustrated in the Milgram experiments.

**SOCIAL NORMS** By replying to the advertisement and agreeing to be in the study, subjects in Milgram's experiments had voluntarily assented to an implicit contract to cooperate with the experimenter, to follow the directions of the person in charge, and to see the job through to completion. This is a very strong social norm, and we tend to underestimate how difficult it is to break such an agreement and to go back on our implied word to cooperate.

The experiment was also designed to reinforce this norm by making it particularly difficult to stop once it had begun. The procedure starts rather innocently as an experiment in memory and then gradually escalates. Once subjects begin to give shocks and to raise the shock levels, there is no longer a natural stopping point. By the time they want to quit, they are trapped. The experimenter makes no new demands, only that they continue to do what they are already doing. In order to break off, they must suffer the guilt and embarrassment of acknowledging that they were wrong to begin at all. And the longer they put off quitting, the harder it is to admit their misjudgment in going as far as they have. It is easier to continue. Imagine how much less obedience there would be if subjects had to begin by giving the strongest shock first.

Finally, the potential quitter faces a dilemma over violating a social norm of etiquette (being polite) similar to the one confronting a subject in the Asch situation. Dissenting in that case implied that the subject thought the group was incompetent. Dissenting in the Milgram situation is equivalent to accusing the experimenter of being immoral—an even more compelling force that pushes the subject to stay in line and go along with the experiment.

INTERPERSONAL INFLUENCE    **765**

If social norms like these can produce so much obedience in Milgram's studies, then it is easy to imagine how much more powerful the penalties for quitting would be in Nazi Germany or in military service once one has already "signed on."

**SURVEILLANCE**    An obvious factor in the Milgram experiment is the constant presence or surveillance of the experimenter. When the experimenter left the room and issued his orders by telephone, obedience dropped from 65 percent to 21 percent (Milgram, 1974). Moreover, several of the subjects who continued under these conditions cheated by administering shocks of lower intensity than they were supposed to.

**BUFFERS**    Milgram's subjects believed that they were committing acts of violence, but there were several buffers that obscured this fact or diluted the immediacy of the experience. For example, the learner was in the next room, out of sight and unable to communicate. Milgram reports that obedience drops from 65 percent to 40 percent if the learner is in the same room as the subject. If the subject must personally ensure that the learner holds his hand on a shock plate, obedience declines to 30 percent. The more direct the person's experience with the victim—the fewer buffers between the person and the consequences of his or her act—the less the person will obey.

The most common buffer found in warlike situations is the remoteness of the person from the final act of violence. Thus, Adolph Eichmann argued that he was not directly responsible for killing Jews; he merely arranged for their deaths indirectly. Milgram conducted an analog to this "link-in-the-chain" role by requiring a subject only to pull a switch that enabled another teacher (a confederate) to deliver the shocks to the learner. Under these conditions, obedience soared: a full 93 percent of the subjects continued to the end of the shock series. In this situation, the subject can shift responsibility to the person who actually delivers the shock.

The shock generator itself served as a buffer—an impersonal mechanical agent that actually delivered the shock. Imagine how obedience would have declined if subjects were required to hit the learner with their fists. In real life, we have analogous technologies that permit us to destroy distant

*Those who make the decisions about war are remote from the final act of violence: Chairman of the Joint Chiefs of Staff Colin Powell.*

*Technology is removing individual button pushers further and further from the destruction that they unleash.*

fellow humans by remote control, thereby removing us from the sight of their suffering. Although we probably all agree that it is worse to kill thousands of people by pushing a button that releases a guided missile than it is to beat one individual to death with a rock, it is still psychologically easier to push the button. Such are the effects of buffers.

**IDEOLOGICAL JUSTIFICATION**   The fourth and most important factor producing voluntary obedience is the individual's acceptance of an *ideology*—a set of beliefs and attitudes—that legitimates the authority of the person in charge and justifies following his or her directives. Nazi officers such as Eichmann believed in the primacy of the German state and hence in the legitimacy of orders issued in its name. Similarly, the American soldiers who followed orders to shoot enemy civilians in Vietnam had already committed themselves to the premise that national security requires strict obedience to military commands.

In the Milgram experiments, the "importance of science" is the ideology that legitimates even quite extraordinary demands. Some critics of the Milgram experiments have argued that they were artificial, that the prestige of a scientific experiment led people to obey without questioning the dubious procedures in which they participated, and that people in real life would never do such a thing (for example, see Baumrind, 1964). Indeed, when Milgram repeated his experiment in a rundown set of offices and removed any association with Yale University from the setting, obedience dropped from 65 percent to 48 percent (Milgram, 1974).

But this criticism misses the major point. The prestige of science is not an irrelevant artificiality but an integral part of Milgram's demonstration. Science serves the same legitimating role in the experiment that the German state served in Nazi Germany and that national security serves in wartime killing. It is precisely their belief in the importance of scientific research that prompts individuals to subordinate their personal moral autonomy and independence to those who claim to act on science's behalf.

**OBEDIENCE IN EVERYDAY LIFE**   Because the Milgram experiments have been criticized for being artificial (for example, Orne & Holland, 1968), it is instructive to look at an example of obedience to authority under more ordinary conditions. Researchers investigated whether nurses in public and private hospitals would obey an order that violated hospital rules and professional practice (Hofling et al., 1966). While on regular duty, the subject (a nurse) received a phone call from a doctor she knew to be on the staff but had not met: "This is Dr. Smith from Psychiatry calling. I was asked to see Mr. Jones this morning, and I'm going to have to see him again tonight. I'd like him to have had some medication by the time I get to the ward. Will you please check your medicine cabinet and see if you have some Astroten? That's ASTROTEN." When the nurse checked the medicine cabinet, she saw a pillbox labeled:

**ASTROTEN**

5 mg. capsules

Usual dose: 5 mg.

Maximum daily dose:

10mg.

After she reported that she had found it, the doctor continued, "Now will you please give Mr. Jones a dose of 20 milligrams of Astroten. I'll be up within 10 minutes; I'll sign the order then, but I'd like the drug to have started taking effect." A staff psychiatrist, posted unobtrusively nearby, terminated each trial by disclosing its true nature when the nurse either poured the medication (actually a harmless placebo), refused to accept the order, or tried to contact another professional.

This order violated several rules: The dose was clearly excessive. Medication orders are not permitted to be given by telephone. The medication was unauthorized—that is, it was not on the ward stock list clearing it for use. Finally, the order was given by an unfamiliar person. Despite all this, 95 percent of the nurses started to give the medication. Moreover, the telephone calls were all brief, and the nurses put up little or no resistance. None of them insisted on a written order, although several sought reassurance that the doctor would arrive promptly. In interviews after the experiment, all the nurses stated that such orders had been received in the past and that doctors became annoyed if the nurses balked.

## Power of Situations

In Chapter 18, we saw that people typically overestimate the role of personal dispositional factors and underestimate the role of situational factors in controlling behavior—the **fundamental attribution error.** Studies on conformity and obedience illustrate this point—not through their results, but through our surprise at their results. We simply do not expect the situational forces to be as effective as they are. When college students are told about Milgram's procedures (but not given the results) and are asked whether they would continue to administer the shocks in the Milgram situation after the learner begins to pound on the wall, about 99 percent of the students say they would not (Aronson, 1991). Milgram himself surveyed psychiatrists at a leading medical school. They predicted that most subjects would refuse to go on after reaching 150 volts, that only about 4 percent would go beyond 300 volts, and that fewer than 1 percent would go all the way to 450 volts. In one study, subjects were asked to estimate obedience rates after they had reenacted the entire Milgram procedure, complete with shock apparatus and a tape recording of the protesting learner. Whether they played the role of the actual subject or the role of an observer, all subjects continued to vastly underestimate the compliance rates actually obtained by Milgram, as shown in Figure 19-8 (Bierbrauer, 1973).

The nursing study on administering medication yields comparable results. When nurses who had not been subjects were given a complete description of the situation and asked how they themselves would respond, 83 percent reported that they would not have given the medication, and most of them thought a majority of nurses would also refuse. Of 21 nursing students asked the same question, all of them reported that they would not have given the medication as ordered.

There is an amusing footnote to the nursing study. The study was conducted and reported by psychiatrists, and they offer a psychoanalytic explanation for the nurses' compliance—complete with references to Oedipal feelings that female nurses are likely to have for male doctors. Most contemporary social psychologists are likely to regard such a dispositional explanation as superfluous—even silly—and to believe that the situational forces in this study were quite sufficient to account for the 95 percent compliance

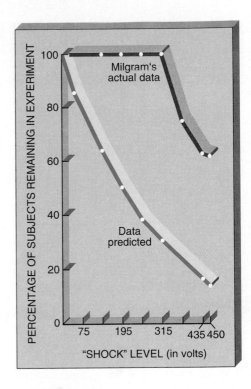

**FIGURE 19-8**
**Predicted and Actual Compliance**
*The upper curve presents the Milgram data and shows the percentage of subjects who remained obedient in the situation, continuing to administer shocks as the voltage increased. The lower curve is from a study in which role-playing subjects participated in a reenactment of the Milgram experiment and attempted to predict what percentage of the actual subjects would continue to be obedient as shock increased. The role-playing subjects vastly underestimated the magnitude of the situational forces and the likelihood of obedience in the Milgram situation. (After Bierbrauer, 1973)*

## Ethical Issues in Milgram's Obedience Experiments

Over the years, Milgram's obedience experiments have become as well known for the ethical questions they raise about the conduct of psychological research as they have for their results. The first published criticism appeared soon after Milgram published his early findings (Baumrind, 1964), and an entire book has now been written about the controversy itself (Miller, 1986). The criticisms primarily concern the welfare of those who served as subjects.

First, critics argue that Milgram's procedures created an unacceptable level of stress in the subjects during the experiment itself. In support of this claim, they quote Milgram's own description:

In a large number of cases, the degree of tension reached extremes that are rarely seen in sociopsychological laboratory studies. Subjects were observed to sweat, tremble, stutter, bite their lips, groan, and dig their fingernails into their flesh. These were characteristic rather than exceptional responses to the experiment.

One sight of tension was the regular occurrence of nervous laughing fits. Fourteen of the 40 subjects showed definite signs of nervous laughing and smiling. The laughter seemed entirely out of place, even bizarre. Full-blown, uncontrollable seizures were observed for 3 subjects. On one occasion we observed a seizure so violently convulsive that it was necessary to call a halt to the experiment. . . . (Milgram, 1963, p. 375)

Second, critics express concern about the long-term psychological effects on subjects and their self-esteem of having learned that they would be willing to give potentially lethal shocks to a fellow human being. And finally, critics argue that subjects are likely to feel foolish and "used" when told the true nature of the experiment, thereby making them less trusting of psychologists in particular and of authority in general.

Milgram has replied to these and other criticisms of his experiments. His major defense is that in general, the subjects themselves do not agree with the critics. After each session, Milgram conducted a careful "debriefing," explaining the reasons for the procedures and re-establishing positive rapport with the

rate observed. In short, they are likely to believe that the authors of the nursing study are themselves committing the fundamental attribution error.

In sum, our reactions to conformity and obedience experiments dramatically illustrate a major lesson of social psychology: we seriously underestimate the extent and power of social and situational forces on human behavior.

## Rebellion

One reason the experiments on conformity and obedience obtain such high compliance is that the social pressures in these studies are directed toward a lone individual. According to social impact theory, social influence will be less powerful if it is diffused over many target individuals, suggesting that a group of individuals might be less susceptible to it—perhaps even showing a bit of rebellion. We have already seen some data to support this suggestion: a subject in the Asch conformity situation is less likely to go along with the group's incorrect judgments if there is at least one other dissenter.

A similar phenomenon occurs in the Milgram obedience situation. In one variation of the procedure, two additional confederates were employed. They were introduced as subjects who would also play teacher roles. Teacher 1 would read the list of word pairs; Teacher 2 would tell the learner if he was right or wrong; and Teacher 3 (the subject) would deliver the shocks. The confederates complied with the instructions through the 150-

subject. This included a reassuring chat with the "victim" whom the subject had thought was receiving the shocks. After the completion of an experimental series, subjects were sent a detailed report of the results and purposes of the experimental project. Milgram then conducted a survey of the subjects, asking them how they felt about their participation "now that [you] have read the report, and all things considered."

Milgram found that 83.7 percent of the subjects indicated that they were glad to have taken part in the study; 15.1 percent reported neutral feelings; and 1.3 percent stated that they were sorry to have participated. These percentages were about the same for those who had obeyed and those who had defied the experimenter during the experiment itself. In addition, 80 percent felt that more experiments of this sort should be carried out, and 74 percent indicated that they had learned something of personal importance as a result of being in

the study. Milgram also hired a psychiatrist to interview 40 of the subjects in person to determine whether the study had any possible injurious effects. This follow-up revealed no indications of long-term distress or traumatic reactions among subjects; typically they felt that their participation was instructive and enriching (Milgram, 1964).

With respect to the concern that subjects might be less trusting of authority in the future, Milgram noted that "the experimenter is not just any authority: he is an authority who tells the subject to act harshly and inhumanely against another man. I would consider it of the highest value if participation in the experiment could . . . inculcate a skepticism of this kind of authority" (1964, p. 852).

In Chapter 1 we noted that research guidelines set forth by the United States government and the American Psychological Association emphasize two major principles. The principle of

*minimal risk* specifies that the risks anticipated in a research study should be no greater than those ordinarily encountered in daily life. The principle of *informed consent* specifies that subjects must enter a study voluntarily and be permitted to withdraw from it at any time without penalty if they so desire. They must also be told ahead of time about any aspects of the study that could be expected to influence their willingness to cooperate. When this requirement cannot be strictly met, a thorough "debriefing" must adequately eliminate any negative feelings the subject might have experienced.

Milgram's studies were conducted in the early 1960s, before these guidelines were in effect. Despite the importance of the research and the precautions that Milgram took, it seems likely that most of the review boards that must now approve federally funded research projects would not permit these experiments to be conducted today.

volt shock, at which point Teacher 1 informed the experimenter that he was quitting. Despite the experimenter's insistence that he continue, Teacher 1 got up from his chair and sat in another part of the room. After the 210-volt shock, Teacher 2 also quit. The experimenter then turned to the subject and ordered him to continue alone. Only 10 percent of the subjects were willing to complete the series in this situation. In a second variation, there were two experimenters rather than two additional teachers. After a few shocks, they began to argue—one of them saying that they should stop the experiment; the other saying they should continue. Under these circumstances, not a single subject would continue despite the orders to do so by the second experimenter (Milgram, 1974).

A more recent experiment examined more directly the possibility that *groups* of subjects might be moved to rebel against unjust authority. Citizens from a nonuniversity community were recruited by phone for 10 dollars to spend 2 hours at a local motel assisting in research on "group standards" sponsored by a fictitious company, the Manufacturer's Human Relations Consultants, or MHRC (Gamson, Fireman, & Rytina, 1982). Nine subjects, both male and female, were recruited for each group session. When they arrived, they were given a letter explaining that legal cases sometimes hinge on the notion of community standards and that MHRC collects evidence on such standards by bringing together concerned citizens for group discussion. The subjects were then seated in front of video cameras and microphones at a U-shaped table, where they filled out a background questionnaire and signed a "participation agreement" giving MHRC permission to videotape them as they engaged in group discussion. The man in charge, who intro-duced himself as the coordinator, then read the background of a pending court case. The basic facts were as follows:

> A service station manager was suing an oil company because it had canceled the franchise on his service station. The oil company had conducted an investiga-tion of the man and discovered that he was living with a woman to whom he was not married. The company claimed that his lifestyle violated the moral standards of the local community and that he would therefore not be able to maintain good relations with customers; accordingly, they decided to revoke his franchise license. The man sued for breach of contract and invasion of privacy, arguing that the company was out to get him because he had publicly criticized the company's gas pricing policies in a local television interview.

After presenting the case, the coordinator asked the group to discuss it while being videotaped. After a general discussion, the cameras were turned off and the group was given a short break. Before resuming the videotaping, the coordinator requested three of the group members to argue as if they were personally offended by the station manager's lifestyle. This second dis-cussion was taped, there was another break, and three additional individuals were designated to argue in the same way in the next discussion. Finally, the coordinator asked each individual to go on camera alone and voice objec-tions to the station manager's affair, stating an intention to boycott the station, and arguing that the manager should lose his franchise. Group mem-bers were also told that they would be asked to sign notarized affidavits giving MHRC the right to introduce the tapes as evidence in court after editing them as it saw fit.

As MHRC's motives began to dawn on them, all but one of the 33 groups in this experiment began to dissent: "Can you assure us that the court is going to know these aren't our real opinions?"; "Would you mind leaving the tape on while you give us these instructions, so that it doesn't appear . . . "; "Do these professional people know what you're doing in fact is suborning perjury?" (Gamson, Fireman, & Rytina, 1982, pp. 62, 65). One group even decided to take direct action by gathering up materials from the table and taking them to the local newspaper.

Overall, 16 of the 33 groups rebelled completely—all members refused to sign the final affidavit—and a majority refused to do so in 9 additional groups. Only a minority refused in the remaining 8 groups, although a num-ber of dissenting comments were voiced. Compared to the Milgram situa-tion, then, obedience to authority had clearly been undermined in this study. But why?

The two studies differ in several respects, so we cannot be certain that the important difference was having a group rather than a lone individual as the target. Nevertheless, this seems to be the most likely factor. In fact, the circumstances producing rebellion in the MHRC study appear to be the same ones we have seen operating in other group contexts: defining the situation and conformity.

In the bystander intervention studies, we noted that individuals in a group define an ambiguous situation for one another. Subjects in the MHRC study were given ample opportunity during the breaks to define and clarify the situation for one another by sharing their suspicions of MHRC's motives. Some of the comments were "How are people going to know that these aren't our opinions?"; "We don't want to be faced with the situation where you read in the *New York Times* one day that thanks to a new method of litigation [group laughter] that this poor schnook [group laughter] lost his license" (Gamson, Fireman, & Rytina, 1982, pp. 101, 102).

The preliminary questionnaires also indicated that 80 to 90 percent of the subjects initially disagreed with the position they were asked to take: they were quite tolerant of an unmarried man and woman living together; they were critical of large oil companies; and they believed that an employee's private life was none of a company's business. The group members could also share these opinions with one another. The researchers compared the 23 groups in which a majority of subjects initially held dissenting opinions with the 10 groups that initially held fewer dissenting opinions. They found that 65 percent of the former groups produced complete rebellion—nobody signed the affidavits—whereas only 10 percent of the latter groups rebelled completely. A majority of the groups also contained some individuals who had been active in past protests and strikes, and these groups were also more likely to rebel than groups without such role models. Lone subjects in the Milgram obedience studies obviously had none of these opportunities for sharing information, receiving social support for dissent, or seeing role models for disobedience.

But before we congratulate the human species for bold independence and autonomy in the face of social pressure, we should consider the implication of these findings more closely. They suggest that many of the individuals in the groups were not choosing between obedience and autonomy but between obedience and conformity: obey the coordinator or conform to the group's norm to disobey. As the researchers observed, "Many were uncertain at this point, waiting to see what others would do, delaying decision as long as possible. Ultimately, they were faced with an unavoidable choice—to sign or not to sign—and loyalty to the group became one major factor in their decision." Some who had already signed the affidavit crossed out their names or tore up the form. As one subject told the coordinator, "I didn't personally say anything I didn't believe, but I'm not going to sign this either, if the rest of the group isn't signing" (Gamson, Fireman, & Rytina, 1982, p. 99).

Obeying or conforming may not strike you as a very heroic choice. But these are among the processes that provide the social glue for the human species. Several years before this study was conducted, a social historian noted that "disobedience when it is not criminally but morally, religiously or politically motivated is always a collective act and it is justified by the values of the collectivity and the mutual engagements of its members" (Walzer, 1970, p. 4).

## Persuasive Influence of Minorities

A number of European scholars have been critical of social psychological research in North America because of its preoccupation with conformity and the influence of the majority on the minority. As they correctly point out, intellectual innovation, social change, and political revolution often occur because an informed and articulate minority—sometimes a minority of one—begins to convert others to its point of view (Moscovici, 1976). Why not study innovation and the influence that minorities can have on the majority?

To make their point, these European investigators deliberately began their experimental work by setting up a laboratory situation virtually identical to Asch's conformity situation. Subjects were asked to make a series of simple perceptual judgments in the face of confederates who consistently gave the incorrect answer. But instead of placing a single subject in the midst of several confederates, these investigators planted two confederates, who consistently gave incorrect responses, in the midst of four real subjects. The experimenters found that the minority was able to influence about 32 percent of the subjects to make at least one incorrect judgment. For this to occur, however, the minority had to remain consistent throughout the experiment. If they wavered or showed any inconsistency in their judgments, they were unable to influence the majority (Moscovici, Lage, & Naffrechoux, 1969).

Since this initial demonstration of minority influence, many additional studies have been conducted in both Europe and North America, including several that required groups to debate social and political issues rather than to make simple perceptual judgments. The general finding is that minorities can move majorities toward their point of view if they present a consistent position without appearing rigid, dogmatic, or arrogant. Such minorities are perceived to be more confident and, occasionally, more competent than the majority (Maass & Clark, 1984). Minorities are also more effective if they argue a position that is consistent with the developing social norms of the larger society. For example, in two experiments in which feminist issues were discussed, subjects were moved significantly more by a minority position that was in line with recent social norms (feminist) than by one opposed to these new norms (antifeminist) (Paicheler, 1976, 1977).

But the most interesting finding from this research is that the majority members in these studies show a change of private attitudes, not just the public conformity that was found in the Asch conformity experiments. In fact, minorities sometimes obtain private attitude change from majority members even when they fail to obtain public conformity. In one study, groups of subjects read a purported summary of a group discussion of gay rights held by five undergraduates like themselves. In all cases four discussants had favored one position and a minority of one had consistently favored the opposite position. In some discussions, the majority had been for gay rights and the minority against; in other discussions, the majority and

*Persuasion by a minority can change the attitude of the majority if the minority is not perceived as rigid, dogmatic, or arrogant.*

minority positions were reversed. After reading the summary, subjects voiced considerable public agreement with the majority view—regardless of whether it had been for or against gay rights—but written ratings revealed that opinions had shifted toward the minority position (Maass & Clark, 1983).

These findings serve to remind us that the majorities of the world typically have the social power to approve and disapprove, to accept or reject, and it is this power that can obtain public conformity. In contrast, minorities rarely have such social power. But if they have credibility, then they have the power to produce genuine attitude change and, hence, innovation, social change, and revolution.

## Cognitive Response Theory of Persuasion

Just as the practices of Nazi Germany under Hitler prompted social psychologists to be interested in obedience to authority, so propaganda efforts on both sides in World War II prompted them to study persuasion. Intensive research began in the late 1940s at Yale University, where investigators sought to determine the characteristics of successful persuasive communicators, successful communications, and the kinds of persons who are most easily persuaded (Hovland, Janis, & Kelley, 1953). As research on these topics continued over the years, a number of interesting phenomena were discovered but few general principles emerged. The results became increasingly complex and difficult to summarize, and every conclusion seemed to require several "it-depends" qualifications. Recently, however, the situation has improved markedly. Social psychology's contemporary interest in information processing (see Chapter 18) has stimulated new thinking about persuasion and has given rise to theories that provide a more unified framework for understanding its many complexities.

Among the new approaches to persuasion are several variations of **cognitive response theory.** This theory proposes that persuasion induced by a communication is actually self-persuasion produced by the thoughts that the person generates while reading, listening to, or even just anticipating the communication. These thoughts can be about the content of the communication itself or about other aspects of the situation, such as the credibility of the communicator. If the communication evokes thoughts supportive of the position being advocated, the individual will move toward that position; if the communication evokes unsupportive thoughts (such as counterarguments or disparaging thoughts about the communicator), the individual will remain unconvinced or even *boomerang*—shift away from the position being advocated (Greenwald, 1968; Petty, Ostrom, & Brock, 1981).

A number of studies support this theory. In one, each subject read a communication containing arguments on a controversial issue and wrote a one-sentence reaction (cognitive response) to each argument. One week later the subjects were unexpectedly given a memory test asking them to recall both the arguments in the communication and their written reactions to those arguments. Subjects' opinions on the issue were assessed both before receiving the communication and then, again, at the time of the memory test one week later. The results showed that the amount of opinion change produced by the communication was significantly correlated with both the supportiveness of subjects' reactions to the communication and to subjects' later recall of those reactions, but it was *not* significantly correlated with subjects' recall of the arguments themselves (Love & Greenwald, 1978). This experiment not only supports the theory, but also explains what had previously been a puzzling observation—that the persistence of opinion change is often unrelated to an individual's memory for the arguments that produced that change.

Cognitive response theory also proposes that a persuasive communication will be *unsuccessful* to the extent that the target individual is both motivated to generate counterarguments against the position being advocated and has the ability and opportunity to do so. As we shall now see, the theory provides a unified explanation for several long-standing phenomena of persuasion.

**ONE-SIDED VERSUS TWO-SIDED COMMUNICATION**   A tactical decision facing any persuasive communicator is whether to present only the side of the issue favorable to his or her conclusions or to present both sides of the issue and to argue explicitly against the opposing side. This was explored empirically as early as 1945 by psychologists in the United States Army's Information and Education Division. After the Allies had defeated Germany in World War II, the Army did not want soldiers to be overconfident about the ease of defeating the Japanese, with whom the United States was still at war. The psychologists designed two radio broadcasts that argued that the war would last at least 2 more years. One broadcast presented only arguments in favor of that conclusion. The other broadcast presented arguments on both sides; for example, it raised and responded to the counterargument that the United States now had the advantage of fighting the war on only one front.

The researchers found that for soldiers who already agreed that the war would last a long time, the one-sided broadcast was more effective than the two-sided broadcast. The two-sided broadcast apparently alerted them to counterarguments they would not have thought of otherwise and thus weakened the effect of the broadcast. But for soldiers who initially disagreed with the communication's conclusion, the one-sided broadcast was less effective (Hovland, Lumsdaine, & Sheffield, 1949). These soldiers already possessed a set of counterarguments that they could generate while hearing the broadcast. Moreover, they were more likely to perceive the one-sided broadcast as biased and hence to generate unfavorable thoughts about its credibility. Later research has shown that just being aware that opposing arguments exist renders a one-sided communication less persuasive than a two-sided one (Jones & Brehm, 1970).

There is an additional advantage to two-sided communications. Regardless of whether they agree or disagree with the position advocated, individuals exposed to two-sided communications are more resistant to later counterarguments than are individuals exposed to one-sided communications (Lumsdaine & Janis, 1953). Two-sided communications not only expose individuals to counterarguments but to the refutations of those counterarguments as well, giving those individuals a new set of contrary cognitive responses to generate when later exposed to communications from the opposing side.

**INOCULATION AGAINST PERSUASION**   As we have just seen, two-sided communications can serve to immunize an individual's newly acquired opinions against counterattack. Psychologist William McGuire decided to pursue this biological analogy by asking whether it was possible to inoculate people against persuasion as we inoculate them against a virus.

Would a weak attack on an individual's beliefs stimulate him or her to marshal counterarguments against a full-blown attack the same way a vaccination containing a weakened form of a virus stimulates the body to produce antibodies against it?

To perform this feat, McGuire needed "germ free" beliefs—beliefs that had not previously been exposed to attack. For this purpose, he selected *cultural truisms,* beliefs that are so widely believed that nobody thinks of questioning them (for example, "It's a good idea to brush your teeth after every meal if at all possible"). First, he confirmed that attacking such beliefs with strong arguments could markedly diminish an individual's belief in them. (Did you know that the American Dental Association has warned that too much toothbrushing can damage your gums?) He then showed that subjects who first received a mild attack on their belief in a truism and then read or wrote an essay refuting this attack were better able to resist a subsequent strong attack. Moreover, this inoculation defense was more effective than a supportive defense in which subjects simply read paragraphs presenting arguments in favor of the truism—analogous to giving a person vitamins to bolster the body's general resistance (Papageorgis & McGuire, 1961; McGuire & Papageorgis, 1961; McGuire, 1964).

**FOREWARNING** Mildly attacking individuals' beliefs is not the only way to stimulate them to marshal counterarguments against persuasion. A simple *forewarning* that they are about to receive a communication with which they will disagree is also sufficient. Even a warning issued only 2 minutes before receiving the communication is sufficient to produce resistance to it (Freedman & Sears, 1965; Hass & Grady, 1975), and research shows that forewarned subjects do, in fact, utilize this time to construct counterarguments (Petty & Cacioppo, 1977). Unwarned subjects will also show resistance to a communication if they are simply instructed to list their thoughts on the topic beforehand. This demonstrates that it is not forewarning per se that induces resistance to a communication but the anticipatory thinking about the topic.

**PRACTICAL APPLICATIONS** As we noted earlier, social psychologists initiated research on persuasion in response to practical problems involved in the prosecution of World War II. Although much of the subsequent research has been conducted in laboratories, exposing college students to communications on relatively unimportant issues, there has always been an interest in the practical applications of the findings. Cognitive response theory is no exception.

For example, one education program has been designed to inoculate junior high-school students against peer pressure to smoke. High-school students conducted sessions in which they taught seventh-graders how to generate counterarguments. For example, in role-playing sessions they were taught to respond to being called "chicken" for not taking a cigarette by saying things like "I'd be a real chicken if I smoked just to impress you." They were also taught to respond to advertisements implying that liberated women smoke by saying, "She's not really liberated if she is hooked on tobacco." Several inoculation sessions were held during seventh and eighth grades, and records were kept of how many of the students smoked from the beginning of the study through the ninth grade. The results show that inoculated students were half as likely to smoke as students at a matched junior high school that used a more typical smoking education program (McAlister

*Learning how to generate counterarguments can inoculate young people against peer pressure to use drugs.*

et al., 1980). Similar programs have been designed to inoculate elementary-school children against being taken in by deceptive television commercials (Cohen, 1980; Feshbach, 1980).

**CENTRAL VERSUS PERIPHERAL ROUTES OF PERSUASION** Although research on cognitive response theory has focused primarily on the individual's thoughts about the substantive arguments in a communication, the individual can also respond to other features of the situation—such as cues about the communicator's credibility. Richard Petty and John Cacioppo, two major contributors to cognitive response theory, have recently clarified the persuasion domain even further by demonstrating the importance of distinguishing between two routes that persuasion can take in producing belief and attitude change (Petty & Cacioppo, 1981; 1986).

Persuasion is said to follow the *central route* when the individual responds to substantive information about the issue under consideration. This can be information contained in the persuasive communication itself or information that is part of the individual's preexisting knowledge. Most of the research on cognitive response theory explores this route. Persuasion is said to follow the *peripheral route* when the individual responds instead to non-content cues in a communication (such as the sheer number of arguments it contains) or to the context of the communication (such as the credibility of the communicator or the pleasantness of the surroundings).

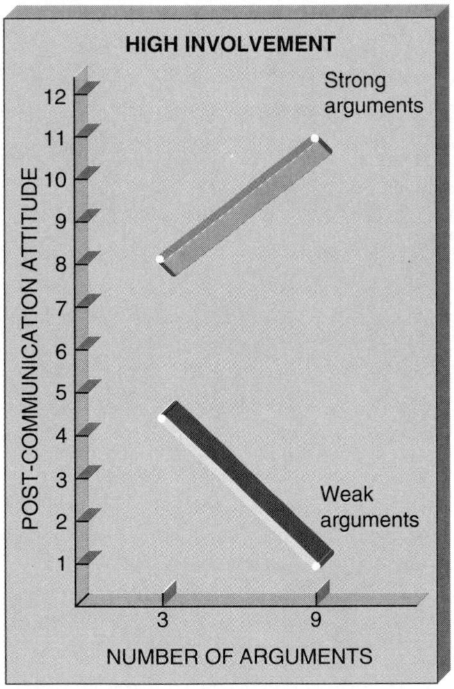

As we have seen, the central route to persuasion is taken only when the individual is both motivated to generate thoughts in response to the substantive contents of a communication and has the ability and opportunity to do so. The peripheral route is taken when the individual is unable or unwilling to put in the cognitive work required to carefully evaluate the content of the communication. Several factors can influence which route will be taken. One such factor is personal involvement. If a communication addresses an issue in which the individual has a personal stake, he or she is more likely to attend carefully to the arguments. In such a case, the individual is also likely to have a rich store of prior information and opinion on the issue—which can provide many cognitive responses to the communication. On the other hand, if an issue has no personal relevance for the individual, he or she is not likely to make much of an effort either to support or to refute arguments about it. What happens then?

According to one recent theory, when we are unwilling or unable to process the content of a communication, we may utilize simple rules of thumb—called *heuristics*—to infer the validity of its arguments. Examples of such rules might include "Messages with many arguments are more likely to be valid than messages with few arguments"; "Politicians always lie"; or "College professors know what they are talking about." This special case of cognitive response theory is called the **heuristic theory of persuasion** (Chaiken, 1980; Eagly & Chaiken, 1984).

This line of reasoning about the two routes of persuasion has been tested in several studies. In one rather complex study, college undergraduates read an essay allegedly written by the chairperson of a university committee charged with advising the chancellor on changes in academic policy. The essay advocated that the university institute a comprehensive examination that every undergraduate would have to pass in his or her major field before being permitted to graduate. In order to manipulate the personal involvement of the students in the issue, half of them were told that any pol-

**FIGURE 19-9**
**Post-Communication Attitudes** *When subjects have high involvement in the issue, nine strong arguments produce more agreement with the essay than three strong arguments but nine weak arguments produce less agreement than three weak arguments.* (After Petty & Cacioppo, 1984)

icy changes adopted by the chancellor would be instituted the following year (high involvement), whereas the other half were told that any changes would take effect in 10 years (low involvement). Different forms of the essay were also used. Some contained strong arguments; others contained weak arguments. Some contained only three arguments; others contained nine.

The post-communication attitudes of students in the high-involvement conditions are shown in Figure 19-9. It can be seen that strong arguments produced more favorable attitudes overall than did weak arguments. But more importantly, nine strong arguments produced greater agreement with the essay than did three strong arguments, whereas nine weak arguments produced less agreement with the essay than did three weak arguments. How do the theories account for these patterns?

The theory about routes of persuasion predicts that students in the high-involvement conditions will be motivated to process the essay's substantive arguments and thus generate topic-relevant cognitive responses. This is the central route of persuasion, and cognitive response theory predicts that strong arguments will evoke more supportive cognitive responses and fewer counterarguments than will weak arguments and will thus produce more agreement with the essay—as, indeed, they did. Moreover, nine strong arguments should be more persuasive than three strong arguments because the more strong arguments the individual encounters, the more supportive cognitive responses he or she will generate. In contrast, nine weak arguments should be less persuasive than three weak arguments because the more weak arguments the individual encounters, the more counterarguments he or she will generate. These predictions accord with the findings displayed in Figure 19-9.

As shown in Figure 19-10, a very different pattern emerges for students in the low-involvement conditions. Here the theory about routes of persuasion predicts that students in the low-involvement conditions will not be motivated to scrutinize the essay's arguments closely and will instead rely on simple heuristics to evaluate its merits and form their attitudes. This is the peripheral route, and the heuristic theory of persuasion predicts that an individual in this setting will not even bother to determine whether the arguments are strong or weak but will simply invoke the heuristic rule: "Messages with many arguments are more likely to be valid than messages with few arguments." Thus, strong arguments will be no more effective than weak arguments, and nine arguments will be more persuasive than three arguments—regardless of whether they are strong or weak. This is precisely the pattern shown in Figure 19-10: overall, there were no significant differences between strong and weak arguments, but nine arguments were more effective than three arguments in both conditions (Petty & Cacioppo, 1984).

An experiment that varied the expertise of the communicator rather than the number of arguments found similar results: subjects in the high-involvement conditions were more influenced by the strength of the arguments, but subjects in the low-involvement conditions relied more on the heuristic "Arguments made by an expert are more valid than arguments made by a nonexpert" (Petty, Cacioppo, & Goldman, 1981).

The complexity of the results in these studies should give you some idea of how chaotic the findings from persuasion research must have appeared before the recent theories imposed some order on them. The findings remain complex, but at least they now fall into some sensible patterns.

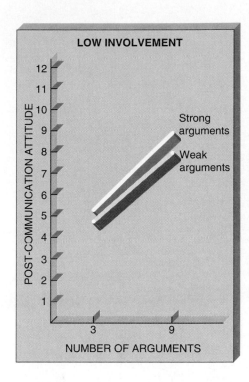

**FIGURE 19-10**
**Post-Communication Attitudes** *When subjects have low involvement in the issue, nine arguments produce more agreement than three arguments, regardless of whether the arguments are strong or weak.*

# Group Decision Making

Many decisions in everyday life are made not by individuals but by groups. Members of a family jointly decide where to spend their vacation; a jury judges a defendant to be guilty; a city council votes to raise property taxes; or the president and the Joint Chiefs of Staff decide to commit troops to an area of international conflict. How do such decisions compare with those that might have been made by individual decision makers? Are group decisions more risky or cautious, more prudent or reckless? These are the questions that concern us in this section.

## Group Polarization

In the 1950s, the conventional wisdom was that decisions made by groups were typically cautious and conservative. For example, it was argued that because business decisions were increasingly being made by committees, the bold, innovative risk-taking of entrepreneurs such as Andrew Carnegie was a thing of the past (for example, Whyte, 1956). James Stoner, then a graduate business student at M.I.T., decided to test this assumption (1961).

In his study, subjects were asked to consider a number of hypothetical dilemmas. In one, an electrical engineer must decide whether to stick with his present job at a modest but adequate salary or to take a job with a new firm offering more money and a possible partnership in the new venture if it succeeds, but no long-term security. In another, a man with a severe heart ailment must seriously curtail his customary way of life or he can choose to undergo a medical operation that would either cure him completely or prove fatal. Subjects were asked to decide how good the odds of success would have to be before they would advise the person to try the riskier course of action. For example, they could recommend that the engineer go for the riskier job if the chances that the new venture would succeed were 5 in 10, or 3 in 10, or only 1 in 10. By using numerical odds like these, Stoner was able to compare the riskiness of different decisions quantitatively.

In the study, subjects first made their decisions alone, as individuals. They then met in groups and arrived at a group decision for each dilemma. After the group discussion, they again considered the dilemmas privately as individuals. When Stoner compared the group's decisions with the average of the individuals' pre-group decisions, he found that the group's decisions were *riskier* than the individual's initial decisions. Moreover, this shift reflected genuine opinion change on the part of group members, not just public conformity to the group decision: the private individual decisions after the group discussion were significantly riskier than the initial decisions. These findings were subsequently replicated by other researchers, even in situations that presented subjects with real rather than hypothetical risks (Bem, Wallach, & Kogan, 1965; Wallach, Kogan, & Bem, 1962, 1964). The phenomenon was initially called the "risky shift" effect.

This turned out not to be an accurate characterization. Even in the early studies, group decisions tended to shift slightly but consistently in the cautious direction on one or two of the hypothetical dilemmas (Wallach, Kogan, & Bem, 1962). After many more studies, it became clear that group discussion leads to decisions that are not necessarily more risky but are *more ex-*

*treme* than the individual decisions: if group members are initially inclined to be risky on a particular dilemma, then the group will become more risky; if group members are initially inclined to be cautious, the group will be even more cautious. Accordingly, the phenomenon is now called the **group polarization** effect (Myers & Lamm, 1976). There are now more than 300 studies of this effect (Myers, 1990).

Group polarization extends beyond issues of risk and caution. For example, group discussion caused French students' initially positive attitudes toward Premier Charles de Gaulle to become even more positive and their initially negative attitudes toward Americans to become even more negative (Moscovici & Zavalloni, 1969). Jury decisions can be similarly affected, leading to more extreme verdicts (Isozaki, 1984). Polarization in juries is more likely to occur on judgments concerning values and opinions (for example, What would an appropriate punishment be for a guilty defendant?) than on judgments concerning matters of fact (Is the defendant guilty?), and they are most likely to show polarization when they are required to reach unanimous decisions—as juries often are (Kaplan & Miller, 1987).

Many explanations for the group polarization effect have been offered over the years, but the two that have best survived intensive testing are *informational influence* and *normative influence* (Isenberg, 1986). *Informational influence* occurs when people learn new information and hear novel arguments relevant to the decision under discussion. For example, in discussing whether the electrical engineer should go with the new venture, it is quite common for someone in the group to argue that riskiness is warranted because electrical engineers can always find good jobs. The more arguments raised in the discussion in favor of a position, the more likely it is that the group will move toward that position. And this is where the bias enters: members of a group are most likely to present points in favor of the position they initially favor and to discuss repeatedly information they already share (Stasser, Taylor, & Hanna, 1989; Stasser & Titus, 1985). Accordingly, the discussion will be biased in favor of the group's initial position, and the group will polarize as more of the group members become convinced.

*Normative influence* occurs when people compare their own views with the norms of the group. During discussion, they may learn that others have similar attitudes or even more extreme views than they themselves do. If they are motivated to be seen positively by the group, they may conform to the group's position or even express a position that is more extreme than the group's. As one researcher noted, "To be virtuous . . . is to be different from the mean—in the right direction and to the right degree" (Brown, 1974, p. 469).

But normative influence is not simply pressure to conform. Often the group provides a frame of reference for its members, a context within which they can re-evaluate their initial positions. This is illustrated by a common and amusing event that frequently occurs in group polarization experiments. For example, in one group, a subject began the discussion of the dilemma facing the electrical engineer by confidently announcing "I feel this guy should really be willing to take a risk here. He should go with the new job even if it has only a 5 in 10 chance of succeeding." Other group members were incredulous: "You think that 5 in 10 is being risky? If he has any guts, he should give it a shot even if there is only 1 chance in 100 of success. I mean, what has he really got to lose?" Eager to re-establish his reputation as a risk-taker, the original individual quickly shifted his position further in the risky direction. By redefining the meaning of "risky," the group thus moves

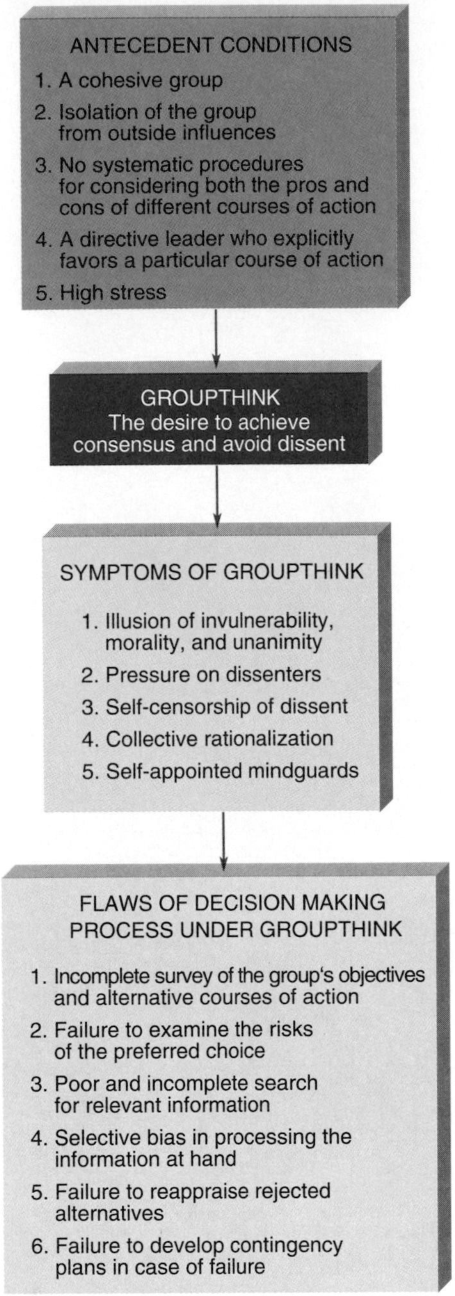

ANTECEDENT CONDITIONS

1. A cohesive group
2. Isolation of the group from outside influences
3. No systematic procedures for considering both the pros and cons of different courses of action
4. A directive leader who explicitly favors a particular course of action
5. High stress

GROUPTHINK
The desire to achieve consensus and avoid dissent

SYMPTOMS OF GROUPTHINK

1. Illusion of invulnerability, morality, and unanimity
2. Pressure on dissenters
3. Self-censorship of dissent
4. Collective rationalization
5. Self-appointed mindguards

FLAWS OF DECISION MAKING PROCESS UNDER GROUPTHINK

1. Incomplete survey of the group's objectives and alternative courses of action
2. Failure to examine the risks of the preferred choice
3. Poor and incomplete search for relevant information
4. Selective bias in processing the information at hand
5. Failure to reappraise rejected alternatives
6. Failure to develop contingency plans in case of failure

**FIGURE 19-11**
**The Causes and Consequences of Groupthink (After Jaris, 1982)**

both its own decision and its members' post-discussion attitudes further toward the risky extreme of the scale (Wallach, Kogan, & Bem, 1962; from the authors' private notes).

As this example illustrates, both informational and normative influence occur simultaneously in group discussions, and several studies have attempted to untangle them. Some studies have shown that the polarization effect occurs if subjects simply hear the arguments of the group, without knowing the actual positions of other members of the group (Burnstein & Vinokur, 1973, 1977). This demonstrates that informational influence by itself is sufficient to produce polarization. Other studies have shown that the polarization effect also occurs when people learn others' positions but do not hear any supporting arguments, demonstrating that normative influence by itself is sufficient (Sanders & Baron, 1977; Goethals & Zanna, 1979). Typically, the normative effect is smaller than the informational effect (Isenberg, 1986).

## Groupthink

"How could we have been so stupid?" This was President John Kennedy's reaction to the disastrous failure of his administration's attempt to invade Cuba at the Bay of Pigs in 1961 and overthrow the government of Fidel Castro. The plan was badly conceived at many levels. For example, if the initial landing were unsuccessful, the invaders were supposed to retreat into the mountains. But no one in the planning group had studied the map closely enough to realize that no army could have gotten through the 80 miles of swamp that separated the mountains from the landing area. As it turned out, this didn't matter because other miscalculations caused the invading force to be wiped out long before the retreat would have taken place.

The invasion had been conceived and planned by the president and a small group of his advisors. Writing four years later, one of these advisors, the historian Arthur Schlesinger, Jr., blamed himself

for having kept so silent during those crucial discussions in the Cabinet Room, though my feelings of guilt were tempered by the knowledge that a course of objection would have accomplished little save to gain me a name as a nuisance. I can only explain my failure to do more than raise a few timid questions by reporting that one's impulse to blow the whistle on this nonsense was simply undone by the circumstances of the discussion. (1965, p. 255)

What were these "circumstances of the discussion" that led the group to pursue such a disastrous course of action? After reading Schlesinger's account, social psychologist Irving Janis proposed a theory of **groupthink**, a phenomenon in which members of a group are led to suppress their own dissent in the interests of group consensus (Janis, 1982). After analyzing several other foreign-policy decisions, Janis set forth the antecedent conditions and symptoms of groupthink as well as the symptoms of defective decision making that result from it. These are outlined in Figure 19-11.

As shown in the figure, the stage for groupthink is set when a cohesive group of decision makers assembles in isolation from outside influences and without systematic procedures for considering both the pros and cons of different courses of action. It is further fostered by a directive leader who explicitly favors a particular course of action and by high stress—often due to an external threat, recent failures, moral dilemmas, and an apparent lack of viable alternatives. Recent research has confirmed that groupthink is particularly likely to develop in situations that involve external threats to the group (McCauley, 1989). All these conditions foster a strong desire to achieve and maintain group consensus and to avoid "rocking the boat" with dissent.

The symptoms of groupthink include group-shared illusions of invulnerability, morality, and unanimity. These are achieved by direct pressure on dissenters or—as Schlesinger's account notes—self-censorship. As a result, the group members spend more time rationalizing their decision rather than realistically examining its strengths and weaknesses. Moreover, there are often self-appointed *mindguards*, group members who actively attempt to prevent the group from considering information that would challenge the effectiveness or morality of its decisions. For example, the Attorney General (President Kennedy's brother Robert) privately warned Schlesinger that "The President has made his mind up. Don't push it any further." The Secretary of State actually withheld information from the group that had been provided by intelligence experts who warned against an invasion of Cuba (Janis, 1982). Finally, Figure 19-11 lists the flaws of decision making that follow from groupthink and lead ultimately to poor decisions.

Janis has also analyzed two successful group decisions: the Truman administration's decision to implement the Marshall Plan (which helped Europe recover from World War II) and the Kennedy administration's handling of the Soviet Union's attempts to install missiles in Cuba. In later publications, Janis spelled out some of the safeguards groups could use to avoid the hazards of groupthink.

First, of course, he thinks that group members should be told about groupthink, its causes and its consequences. Among his more specific suggestions are that the group leader foster an atmosphere of open debate and not openly endorse any position before the discussion begins; that one or more members be assigned explicitly to play the role of "devil's advocate," actively questioning the group's decisions throughout; that outside experts be brought in to challenge the group and give it fresh perspectives; and finally—once the group has arrived at a consensus—that there be a "second chance" meeting in which members can rediscuss any lingering doubts or reservations (Janis, 1982, 1985).

There has also been criticism of Janis's theory. First, it is based on historical analysis more than on laboratory experimentation. Experiments that have been done have yielded mixed results (for example, Callaway, Marriott, & Esser, 1985; Courtright, 1978; Flowers, 1977; Longley & Pruitt, 1980; McCauley, 1989). The processes that Janis calls groupthink are clearly quite complex, and his theory will undoubtedly prove to be incorrect in some of its particulars. Nevertheless, the very existence of the theory should help diminish the kind of flawed group decision making that has so frequently proved disastrous in the past.

*Chapter* **SUMMARY**

1. Although the term *social influence* often connotes direct and deliberate attempts to change our beliefs, attitudes, or behaviors, many forms of social influence are indirect or unintentional. Even the mere physical presence of other persons can affect us. We are also influenced by *social norms*, implicit rules and expectations of how we ought to think and behave. The success of direct and deliberate social influence often depends on our allegiance to social norms.

2. Both humans and animals respond more quickly when in the presence of other members of their species. This *social facilitation* occurs whether the others are performing the same task (coactors) or are simply watching (an audience). The presence of others appears to raise the organism's drive level. This facilitates the correct performance of simple response but hinders the performance of complex responses. For humans, cognitive factors, such as a concern with evaluation, also play a role.

3. The uninhibited aggressive behavior sometimes shown by mobs and crowds may be the result of a state of *deindividuation*, in which individuals feel that they have lost their personal identities and have merged into the group. Anonymity reduces self-awareness and contributes to deindividuation. Some of the consequences of deindividuation are weakened restraints against impulsive behavior, increased sensitivity to immediate cues and current emotional states, and a lessened concern about the evaluation by others. Being in a group and feeling anonymous do not inevitably lead to increased aggressiveness, however.

4. A bystander to an emergency is less likely to intervene or help if in a group than if alone. Two major factors that deter intervention are *defining the situation* and *diffusion of responsibility*. By attempting to appear calm, bystanders may define the situation for each other as a nonemergency, thereby producing a state of *pluralistic ignorance*. The presence of other people also diffuses responsibility so that no one person feels the necessity to act. Bystanders are more likely to intervene when these factors are minimized, particularly if at least one person begins to help.

5. *Social impact theory* summarizes many phenomena of social influence by proposing that (a) the social impact or effectiveness of influence on a target individual *increases* with the number, immediacy, and importance of the *sources* of influence; and (b) the social impact of a source of influence *decreases* as the number, immediacy, and importance of *targets* increase.

6. In a series of classic studies on *conformity*, Solomon Asch found that a unanimous group exerts strong pressure on an individual to conform to the group's judgments—even when those judgments are clearly wrong. Much less conformity is observed if even one person dissents from the group.

7. In a series of classic studies on *obedience*, Stanley Milgram demonstrated that ordinary people would obey an experimenter's order to deliver strong electric shocks to an innocent victim. Factors conspiring to produce the high obedience rates include *social norms* (for example, the implied contract to continue the experiment until completed); the *surveillance* of the experimenter; *buffers* that distance the person from the consequences of his or her acts; and the *legitimating role of science*, which leads people to abandon their autonomy to the experimenter. There has also been controversy about the ethics of the experiments themselves.

8. Obedience to authority can be undermined—and rebellion provoked—if the individual is with a group whose members have the opportunity to share their opinions, can give each other social support for dissenting, and can provide role models for disobedience. But the individual may then have to choose between obedience to the authority and conformity to the group that has decided to rebel.

9. Studies of conformity and obedience reveal that situational factors exert more influence over behavior than most of us realize. We tend to underestimate situational forces on behavior.

10. A minority of persons within a larger group can move the majority to

ward its point of view if it maintains a consistent dissenting position without appearing rigid, dogmatic, or arrogant. Minorities sometimes obtain private attitude change from majority members even when they fail to obtain public conformity.

11. *Cognitive response theory* proposes that persuasion induced by a communication is actually self-persuasion produced by the thoughts that the person generates while reading or hearing the communication. If the communication evokes thoughts supportive of the position being advocated, the individual will move toward that position; if the communication evokes unsupportive thoughts—such as counterarguments or disparaging thoughts about the communicator—the individual will remain unpersuaded. The theory provides a unified explanation for several previously discovered phenomena of persuasion.

12. Persuasion can take two routes in producing belief and attitude change: the *central route*, in which the individual responds to the substantive arguments of a communication, and the *peripheral route*, in which the individual responds to noncontent cues in a communication (such as the number of arguments) or to context cues (such as the credibility of the communicator or the pleasantness of the surroundings). A communication about an issue of personal relevance is more likely to generate thoughts in response to the communication's substantive arguments. When an issue is of little personal relevance or when people are unwilling or unable to respond to the substantive content of a communication, they tend to use simple *heuristics*—rules of thumb—to judge the merits of the communication.

13. When groups make decisions, they often display *group polarization:* the group decision is in the same direction but is more extreme than the average of the group members' initial positions. This is not just public conformity; group members' private attitudes typically shift in response to the group discussion as well. The effect is due, in part, to *Informational influence* in which group members learn new information and hear novel arguments relevant to the decision under discussion. Group members tend to raise more arguments in favor of their initial position than against it, thus biasing the discussion and pushing the final decision further in the direction of the initial positions. Group polarization is also produced by *normative influence* in which people compare their own initial views with the norms of the group. They may then adjust their position to conform to the group's majority position. In addition, the group can provide a frame of reference that causes them to perceive their initial position as too weak or too moderate as an expression of their actual attitude.

14. An analysis of disastrous foreign policy decisions reveals that a cohesive group of decision makers with a directive leader can fall into the trap of *groupthink*, in which members of the group suppress their own dissenting opinions in the interest of group consensus. This gives rise to a group-shared illusion of invulnerability, morality, and unanimity. This, in turn, produces a flawed decision-making process and bad decisions. It has been suggested that groupthink can be avoided if: the leader fosters an atmosphere of open debate and does not endorse any position before discussion begins; some group members are assigned to be "devil's advocates"; outside experts are brought in; and there is a "second chance" meeting at which members can reconsider any lingering doubts or reservations about their decision.

*Further* **READING**

The three comprehensive textbooks in social psychology listed at the end of Chapter 18 also cover the topics discussed in this chapter. They are: Lippa, *Introduction to Social Psychology* (1990); Myers, *Social Psychology* (3rd ed., 1990); and Sears, Peplau, and Taylor, *Social Psychology* (7th ed., 1991). Aronson, *The Social Animal* (6th ed., 1991) covers several topics in social influence. More advanced treatments are available in Lindzey and Aronson (eds.), *The Handbook of Social Psychology* (3rd ed., 1985).

Many of the topics in this chapter are covered in paperback books written for general audiences, often by the original investigators. Milgram, *Obedience to Authority* (1974) is well worth reading, especially before forming an opinion about this controversial series of studies. Latané and Darley, *The Unresponsive Bystander: Why Doesn't He Help?* (1970) is a report by two of the original researchers in that area. Petty and Cacioppo, *Attitudes and Persuasion: Classic and Contemporary Approaches* (1981) is a good summary of both earlier and current work on persuasion written by two major contributors to this area. Janis, *Groupthink: Psychological Studies of Policy Decisions and Fiascoes* (2nd ed., 1982) is the major source for the groupthink phenomenon. And finally, LeBon's classic book, *The Crowd* (1895), is available in several editions.

*Appendix*

# I

# How to Read a Textbook: The PQRST Method

A central topic in psychology is the analysis of learning and memory. Almost every chapter of this book refers to these phenomena; Chapter 7 ("Learning and Conditioning") and Chapter 8 ("Memory") are devoted exclusively to learning and memory. In this appendix we review a method for reading and studying information presented in textbook form. The theoretical ideas underlying this method are discussed in Chapter 8; the method is described here in greater detail for readers who wish to apply it in studying this textbook.

This approach for reading textbook chapters, called the PQRST method, has been shown to be very effective in improving a reader's understanding of and memory for key ideas and information. The method takes its name from the first letter of the five steps one follows in reading a chapter—*P*review, *Q*uestion, *R*ead, *S*elf-recitation, *T*est. The steps or stages are diagramed in the figure on the next page. The first and last stages (Preview and Test) apply to the chapter as a whole; the middle three stages (Question, Read, Self-recitation) apply to each major section of the chapter as it is encountered.*

**STAGE P (PREVIEW)** In the first step, you preview the entire chapter by skimming through it to get an idea of major topics. This is done by reading the chapter outline and then skimming the chapter, paying special attention to the headings of main sections and subsections and glancing at pictures and illustrations. The most important aspect of the preview stage is to read carefully the summary at the end of the chapter once you have skimmed through the chapter. Take time to consider each point in the summary; questions will come to mind that should be answered later as you read the full text. The preview stage will give you an overview of the topics covered in the chapter and how they are organized.

**STAGE Q (QUESTION)** As noted earlier, you should apply Stages Q, R, and S to each major section of the chapter as it is encountered. The typical chapter in this textbook has about five to eight major sections, each section beginning with a heading set in large, dark green letters. Work through the

---

*The PQRST method as described here is based on the work of Thomas and H. A. Robinson (1982) and Spache and Berg (1978); their work, in turn, is based on the earlier contributions of R. P. Robinson (1970). In some sources, the name SQ3R is used instead of PQRST. The S, the Q, and the three Rs stand for the same five steps, but are relabeled as Survey, Question, Read, Recite, and Review. We find PQRST to be easier to remember than SQ3R.

**PQRST Method** *The first and last stages apply to the chapter as a whole, whereas the middle three stages apply to each section of the chapter as it is encountered.*

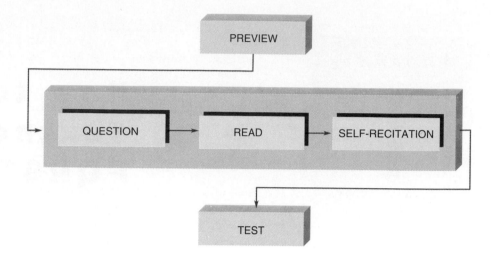

chapter one section at a time, applying Stages Q, R, and S to each section before going on to the next section. Before reading a section, read the heading of the section and the headings of the subsections. Then turn the topic headings into one or more questions that you should expect to answer while reading the section. Ask yourself: "What are the main ideas the author is trying to convey in this section?" This is the Question Stage.

**STAGE R (READ)**   Next, read the section carefully for meaning. As you read, try to answer the questions you asked in Stage Q. Reflect on what you are reading, and try to make connections to other things you know. You may choose to mark or underline key words or phrases in the text. Try, however, not to mark more than 10 to 15 percent of the text. Too much underlining defeats the intended purpose, which is to make key words and ideas stand out for later review. It is probably best to delay taking notes until you have read the entire section and encountered all the key ideas, so you can judge their relative importance.

**STAGE S (SELF-RECITATION)**   After you have finished reading the section, try to recall the main ideas and recite the information. Self-recitation is a powerful means of fixing the material in your memory. Put the ideas into your own words and recite the information (preferably aloud or, if you are not alone, to yourself). Check against the text to be sure that you have recited the material correctly and completely. Self-recitation will reveal blanks in your knowledge and help you organize the information in your mind. After you have completed one section of the chapter in this way, turn to the next section and again apply Stages Q, R, and S. Continue in this manner until you have finished all sections of the chapter.

**STAGE T (TEST)**   When you have finished reading the chapter, you should test and review all of the material. Look over your notes and test your recall for the main ideas. Try to understand how the various facts relate to each other and how they were organized in the chapter. The test stage may require that you thumb back through the chapter to check key facts and ideas. You should also reread the chapter summary at this time; as you are doing so, you should be able to add details to each entry in the summary. Don't put off the test stage until the night before an examination. The best time for a first review of the chapter is immediately after you have read it.

Research indicates that the PQRST method is very helpful and definitely preferable to simply reading straight through a chapter (Thomas & Robinson, 1982). Self-recitation is particularly important; it is better to spend a significant percentage of study time in an active attempt to recite than it is to devote the entire time to reading and rereading the material (Gates, 1917). Studies also show that a careful reading of the summary of the chapter before reading the chapter itself is especially productive (Reder & Anderson, 1980). Reading the summary first provides an overview of the chapter that helps organize the material as you read through the chapter. Even if you choose not to follow every step of the PQRST method, special attention should be directed to the value of self-recitation and reading the chapter summary as an introduction to the material.

The PQRST method and various other study skills, including taking lecture notes and preparing for and taking examinations, are discussed in an excellent book entitled *Building Better Study Skills: Practical Methods for Succeeding in College*, published by the American College Testing Program, Iowa City, Iowa. As its subtitle indicates, this book focuses on practical methods for achieving personal and academic success in college.

*Appendix*

# II

# Brief History of Psychology

Although psychology is a young science, people throughout history have been concerned with psychological issues. Books on the history of psychology discuss the views of early Greek philosophers, especially those of Plato and Aristotle. After the Greeks, Saint Augustine (A.D. 354 – 430) is considered the next great precursor of modern psychology because of his interest in introspection and his curiosity about psychological phenomena, including the behavior of infants and of crowds at chariot races. Descartes (1596 – 1650) left his mark on psychology by theorizing that animals are machines that can be studied much as other machines are studied. He also introduced the concept of reflex action, which has occupied a significant place in psychology. Many prominent philosophers of the seventeenth and eighteenth centuries—Leibnitz, Hobbes, Locke, Kant, and Hume, to name five—grappled with psychological questions.

## Roots of Contemporary Psychology

### Two Early Approaches

In the nineteenth century, two theories of the mind competed for support. One, known as *faculty psychology*, was a doctrine of inherited mental powers. According to this theory, the mind has a few distinct and independent "faculties" or mental agencies—such as thinking, feeling, and willing—that account for its activities. These faculties were further broken into subfaculties: we remember through the subfaculty of memory, imagine through the subfaculty of imagination, and so on. Faculty psychology encouraged early nineteenth-century *phrenologists*, such as Gall, to try to localize special faculties in different parts of the brain.

The *association psychologists* held an opposing view. They denied inborn faculties of the mind; instead, they limited the mind's content to ideas that enter by way of the senses and then become associated through such principles as similarity, contrast, and contiguity. They explained all mental activity through the *association of ideas*—a concept principally developed by British philosophers.

Both faculty psychology and association psychology have present-day counterparts. The search for mental abilities as factors in psychological tests is related to faculty psychology. Current research on memory and learning is related to earlier association theory. Faculty psychology took note of the inherited aspects of behavior, whereas associationism emphasized the environment as the determiner of behavior. The environment versus heredity issue runs throughout the history of psychology.

*Wilhelm Wundt*

# Wundt's Laboratory

Wilhelm Wundt is given credit for founding psychology as an academic discipline. The founding date is usually cited as 1879, the year that Wundt established the first formal psychological laboratory at the University of Leipzig in Germany. Wundt's research was primarily concerned with the senses, especially vision; but he and his coworkers also studied attention, emotion, and memory.

Wundt's psychology relied on *introspection* as a method of studying mental processes. The introspective method was inherited from philosophy, but Wundt added a new dimension to the concept. Pure self-observation was not sufficient; it had to be supplemented by experiments. His experiments systematically varied some physical dimension of a stimulus, and the introspective method was used to determine how these physical changes modified consciousness.

Wundt's approach to research can be illustrated by one of his experiments on *reaction time*. In this experiment, the subject was required to press a key as quickly as possible after the onset of a light, and the subject's reaction time was carefully measured. Wundt found that the response time was longer when a subject paid careful attention to detecting the onset of light than it was when the subject's attention was directed to making a quick finger movement to press the key. The subject reacted very quickly in both cases, but there was a difference in reaction time of about .1 second. To explain this strange finding, Wundt distinguished between *perception* and *apperception*. When attention was focused on the finger movement, simple perception occurred and the light triggered the response promptly. But when attention was focused on the stimulus, an additional activity of apperception occurred, which involved a "richer" perception of the light. Wundt decided that this apperception required about .1 second. His interpretation is no longer accepted, for we now know that the processes intervening between stimulus and response are organized in more complex ways; but such studies helped to launch psychology as an experimental science.

Until his death in 1920, Wundt's personal influence on psychology was singularly important. Many pioneers in American psychology were trained in Wundt's laboratory. The first formal psychology laboratory in the United States was established in 1883 at Johns Hopkins University by G. Stanley Hall (who had studied with Wundt), although William James had set up a small demonstration laboratory at Harvard by 1875. The first person to be called "professor of psychology" in the United States was J. McKeen Cattell, another Wundt student, who acquired that title at the University of Pennsylvania in 1888. Before the end of the 1890s, Wundt's students were to be found in many American universities.

# Other Roots of Contemporary Psychology

Although the impetus for establishing psychological laboratories came largely from Germany, there were other influences. In England, Sir Francis Galton was a pioneer in the study of individual differences and exerted an important influence on the development of intelligence tests. Galton invented the statistical technique of correlation and developed the index that later became known as the *coefficient of correlation*.

The influence of the theory of evolution through natural selection, propounded by Charles Darwin, also came from England. Darwin's theory es-

*Sir Francis Galton*

tablished the continuity between animals and human beings and thus led to comparative studies in psychology.

Another area of influence on psychology came from medicine, especially from the treatment of the mentally ill. Hypnotism, for example, has a long history as a form of therapy, dating from the work of Anton Mesmer in the late 1700s. Another Viennese physician, Sigmund Freud, founded psychoanalysis early in the present century.

# Schools of Psychology

## Structuralism and Functionalism

*William James*

When scientific psychology emerged in the latter part of the nineteenth century, researchers were making great advances in chemistry and physics by analyzing complex compounds (molecules) into their elements (atoms). These successes encouraged psychologists to look for the mental elements of which more complex experiences were composed. If the chemist made headway by analyzing water into hydrogen and oxygen, perhaps the psychologist could make progress by considering the taste of lemonade (perception) as a molecule of conscious experience to be analyzed into elements (sensations)—such as sweet, bitter, cold, and whatever—that could be identified by introspection. This was the approach taken by Wundt and his students; its major proponent in the United States was E. B. Titchener, a Wundt-trained psychologist at Cornell University. Since the goal was to specify mental structures, Titchener introduced the term *structuralism* to describe this brand of psychology.

But there was vigorous opposition to the purely analytical character of structuralism. William James—a distinguished psychologist at Harvard University—was impatient with the restrictions on psychology as it was developing under the structuralists. James felt that less emphasis should be placed on analyzing the elements of consciousness and more emphasis should be placed on understanding its fluid, streaming, personal character. His principal interest was in studying how the mind worked so that an organism could adapt to its environment. Because James asked how consciousness functions (particularly in the adaptive process), his approach to psychology was named *functionalism*. James' writing on *habits* as a mode of adaptation helped set the stage for a psychology that included the learning process as a central topic of study.

Interest in adaptation was influenced by Darwin's theory of natural selection. Consciousness evolved, so the argument ran, only because it served some purpose in guiding the activities of the individual. With this emphasis on the functional role of consciousness came a recognition that the introspetive method of structuralism was too restrictive. To find out how the organism adapts to its environment, the functionalists argued that data derived from introspection had to be supplemented by observations of actual behavior, including the study of animal behavior and the development of behavior (developmental psychology). Thus, functionalism broadened the scope of psychology to include behavior as a dependent variable. But along with the structuralists, functionalists still regarded psychology as the science of conscious experience and the principal investigative method as introspection.

Structuralism and functionalism played important roles in the early development of psychology. Because each viewpoint provided a systematic

**Important Dates in the History of Psychology**

| | |
|---|---|
| B.C. 400 | Hippocrates relates personality characteristics to body types and proposes a physiological (as opposed to demonological) theory of mental illness. |
| B.C. 350 | Aristotle stresses the objective observation of man's behavior and proposes three principles to account for the association of ideas. |
| A.D. 400 | Saint Augustine, influenced by Platonic ideas, makes careful introspections in his *Confessions*. |
| 1650 | René Descartes characterizes the mind–body relationship as one of interaction. |
| 1651 | Thomas Hobbes foreshadows associationism by declaring that all ideas come from sensory experience. |
| 1690 | John Locke carries Hobbes' notion a step further by declaring that at birth the mind is a blank slate (*tabula rasa*). |
| 1749 | David Hartley formalizes a doctrine of associationism and suggests a neurological basis for memory. |
| 1781 | Immanuel Kant's *Critique of Pure Reason* attacks associationism and the nativistic approach; it stongly influences later philosophers and psychologists. |
| 1809 | Franz Gall and Johann Spurzheim give prominence through phrenology to the study of mental faculties and brain function. |
| 1821 | Pierre Flourens performs the first significant experiments in localization of brain functions. |
| 1822 | Friedrich Bessel measures individual differences in reaction time for astronomical observations. |
| 1838 | Johannes Müller formulates the doctrine of specific nerve energies. |
| 1846 | Ernst Weber derives the first quantitative law in psychology. |
| 1850 | Hermann von Helmholtz measures the rates of conduction of nerve impulses. |
| 1859 | Charles Darwin publishes *The Origin of Species*, propounding the theory of evolution through natural selection. |
| 1860 | Gustav Fechner publishes *Elements of Psychophysics*, in which he presents various methods for measuring the relationship between physical stimuli and sensations. |
| 1869 | Sir Francis Galton studies individual differences and applies Darwin's concept of selective adaptation to the evolution of races. |
| 1879 | Wilhelm Wundt opens the first formal psychological laboratory at the University of Leipzig. |
| 1883 | G. Stanley Hall establishes the first psychological laboratory in America at Johns Hopkins University. |
| 1885 | Hermann Ebbinghaus publishes the first experimental studies of memory. |
| 1890 | William James' *Principles of Psychology* is published in the United States. |

1892   Edward Titchener at Cornell University establishes "structuralism" as a major influence in American psychology.

1898   Edward Thorndike performs some of the first controlled experiments on animal learning.

1900   Sigmund Freud publishes *The Interpretation of Dreams*, which presents many of his ideas on psychoanalysis.

1905   Alfred Binet and Theodore Simon devise the first intelligence test.

1906   Ivan Pavlov publishes the results of his studies on classical conditioning.

1908   William McDougall's publication of *An Introduction to Social Psychology* marks the formal inauguration of the field of social psychology.

1912   Max Wertheimer publishes the first formulation of Gestalt psychology.

1913   John B. Watson exerts a major impact on the course of psychology with his behaviorist manifesto.

1917   Wolfgang Köhler publishes the results of his studies on problem solving in primates.

1922   Edward Tolman presents his initial ideas on purposive behaviorism.

1929   Karl Lashley publishes *Brain Mechanisms and Intelligence*.

1935   Louis Thurstone develops factor analysis.

1938   B. F. Skinner publishes *The Behavior of Organisms*, which summarizes early research on operant conditioning.

1949   Donald Hebb, in *Organization of Behavior*, presents a theory that bridges the gap between neurophysiology and psychology.

1950   William Estes lays the foundation for a mathematical approach to theories of learning.

1954   The Swiss psychologist Jean Piaget publishes *The Construction of Reality in the Child*, which focuses attention on cognitive development.

1957   Noam Chomsky publishes *Syntactic Structures*, a book that presents a cognitive approach to language behavior.

1958   Herbert Simon and colleagues publish *Elements of a Theory of Human Problem Solving*, which reformulates classical psychological problems in terms of information-processing models.

1962   David Hubel and Torsten Weisel discover the relationship between the activity of individual neurons in the visual cortex to specific features of a visual stimulus.

1979   The journal *Cognitive Science* and a society by the same name are founded, serving to catalyze research on the representational and computational capacities of the mind.

Events since 1980 are not listed because not enough time has elapsed to judge their long-term impact on the field.

*John B. Watson*

approach to the field, the two were considered competing *schools of psychology*. As psychology developed, other schools evolved and vied for leadership. By 1920, structuralism and functionalism were being displaced by three newer schools: behaviorism, Gestalt psychology, and psychoanalysis.

## Behaviorism

Of the three new schools, behaviorism had the greatest influence on scientific psychology. Its founder, John B. Watson, reacted against the tradition of his time—that conscious experience was the province of psychology—and boldly proclaimed a psychology *without* introspection. Watson made no assertions about consciousness when he studied the behavior of animals and infants. He decided not only that the results of animal psychology and child psychology could stand on their own as a science, but also that they set a pattern that adult psychology might well follow.

In order to make psychology a science, Watson said, psychological data must be open to public inspection like the data of any other science. Behavior is public; consciousness is private. Science should deal with public facts. Because psychologists were growing impatient with introspection, the new behaviorism caught on rapidly, particularly in the 1920s; for a time, most of the younger psychologists in the United States called themselves "behaviorists." In Russia, the work of Ivan Pavlov on the conditioned response was regarded as an important area of research by the behaviorists. The conditioned response was being investigated in the United States in a limited way before the advent of behaviorism, but Watson was responsible for its subsequent widespread influence on psychology.

Watson argued that nearly all behavior is the result of conditioning, and that the environment shapes our behavior by reinforcing specific habits. The conditioned response was viewed as the smallest indivisible unit of behavior, an "atom of behavior" from which more complicated behaviors could be built. All types of complex behavioral repertoires arising from special training or education were regarded as nothing more than an interlinked fabric of conditioned responses.

Behaviorists found it congenial to discuss psychological phenomena as beginning with a stimulus and ending with a response—giving rise to the term *stimulus-response (S-R) psychology*. S-R psychologists went beyond the earlier behaviorists in their willingness to infer hypothetical processes between the stimulus input and the response output, processes that were called *intervening variables*.

If broad definitions are used, so that "stimulus" refers to a whole class of antecedent conditions and "response" refers to a whole class of outcomes (actual behavior and products of behavior), S-R psychology becomes merely a psychology of independent and dependent variables. Viewed in this way, S-R psychology is not a particular theory but a *language* that can be used to make psychological information explicit and communicable. As such, the S-R outlook is widely prevalent in psychology today.

## Gestalt Psychology

At about the same time that Watson announced behaviorism in America, Gestalt psychology was appearing in Germany. The word *Gestalt* translates from the German as "form" or "configuration," and the psychology announced by Max Wertheimer in 1912 was a psychology concerned with the

*Wolfgang Köhler*

organization of mental processes. The position came to be identified most closely with Wertheimer and his colleagues Kurt Koffka and Wolfgang Köhler, all of whom migrated to the United States.

The earliest Gestalt experiments dealt with perceived motion, particularly the *phi phenomenon*. When two separated lights are flashed in succession (provided the timing and spatial locations are proper), the subject sees a single light moving from the position of the first light to that of the second. The phenomenon of apparent motion was familiar, but the Gestalt psychologists sensed the theoretical importance of the patterning of stimuli in producing the effect. Our experiences depend on the *patterns* formed by stimuli and on the *organization* of experience, they decided. What we see is relative to background, to other aspects of the whole. The whole is different from the sum of its parts; the whole consists of parts in relationship.

Although the Gestalt psychologists did not subscribe to the introspective psychology of their day any more than Watson did, they were vigorous opponents of behaviorism. They did not want to give up a kind of free introspection that goes by the name of *phenomenology*. They wanted to be able to ask a person what something looked like, what it meant. They were interested in the perception of motion, in how people judged sizes, and in the appearance of colors under changes in illumination.

The importance of perception in all psychological events has led those influenced by Gestalt psychology to a number of perception-centered interpretations of learning, memory, and problem solving. These interpretations, spoken of as forms of cognitive theory, were instrumental in laying the groundwork for current developments in cognitive psychology.

*Sigmund Freud*

## Psychoanalysis

Sigmund Freud introduced psychoanalytic psychology to the United States in a series of lectures given at Clark University in 1909 on the invitation of psychologist G. Stanley Hall. Thus, the first scholarly recognition of Freud's work in the United States came from psychologists. Freud's influence became so pervasive that those who know nothing else about psychology have at least a nodding acquaintance with psychoanalysis.

If one of Freud's theories is to be singled out for consideration along with behaviorism and Gestalt psychology, it is his interpretation of the *unconscious*. Basic to Freud's theory of the unconscious is the conception that the unacceptable (forbidden, punished) wishes of childhood are driven out of awareness and become part of the unconscious, where they remain influential. The unconscious presses to find expression, which it does in numerous ways, including dreams, slips of speech, and unconscious mannerisms. The method of psychoanalysis—free association under the guidance of the analyst—is itself a way of helping unconscious wishes find verbal expression. In classical Freudian theory, these unconscious wishes were almost exclusively sexual. This emphasis on childhood sexuality was one of the barriers to the acceptance of Freud's theories when they were first announced.

## Recent Developments

Despite the important contribution of Gestalt psychology and psychoanalysis, psychology was dominated by behaviorism until World War II,

*Herbert Simon*

particularly in the United States. With the end of the war, interest in psychology increased and many people were attracted to careers in the field. Sophisticated instruments and electronic equipment became available, and a wider range of problems could be examined. This expanded program of research made it evident that earlier theoretical approaches were too restrictive.

This viewpoint was strengthened by the development of computers in the 1950s. Computers, properly programmed, were able to perform tasks—such as playing chess and proving mathematical theorems—that previously could only be done by human beings. It became apparent that the computer offered psychologists a powerful tool with which to theorize about psychological processes. A series of brilliant papers, published in the late 1950s by Herbert Simon (who was later awarded the Nobel prize) and his colleagues, indicated how psychological phenomena could be *simulated* using the computer. Many old psychological issues were recast in terms of *information-processing systems*. The human being could now be viewed as a processor of information. The senses provide an input channel for information; mental operations are applied to the input; the transformed input creates a mental structure that is stored in memory; that structure interacts with others in memory to generate a response. The power of the computer permitted psychologists to theorize about complex mental processes and investigate the implications of the theory by simulating it on a computer. If the response (output) stage of the computer simulation agreed with the observed behavior of actual people, the psychologist could have some confidence in the theory.

The information-processing approach provided a richer and more dynamic approach to psychology than S-R theory with its intervening variables. Similarly, the information-processing approach permitted some of the speculations of Gestalt psychology and psychoanalysis to be formulated in a precise fashion as programs in a computer; in this way, earlier ideas about the nature of the mind could be made concrete and checked against actual data.

Another factor that led to a changing viewpoint in psychology in the 1950s was the development of modern linguistics. Prior to that time, linguists were primarily concerned with a description of a language; now they began to theorize about the mental structures required to comprehend and to speak a language. Work in this area was pioneered by Noam Chomsky, whose book *Syntactic Structures*, published in 1957, provided the basis for an active collaboration between psychologists and linguists. A rapid development of the field of *psycholinguistics* followed, providing the first significant psychological analyses of language.

At the same time, important advances were occurring in neuropsychology. A number of discoveries about the brain and the nervous system established clear relationships between neurobiological events and mental processes. It became increasingly difficult to assert, as some of the early behaviorists had, that a science of psychology could be established without links to neurophysiology.

The development of information-processing models, psycholinguistics, and neuropsychology has produced a psychology that is highly cognitive in orientation. There is no agreed-on definition of *cognitive psychology*, but its principal concern is the scientific analysis of mental processes and mental structures. Cognitive psychology is not exclusively concerned with thought and knowledge. Its early concerns with the representation of knowledge and human thought led to the label "cognitive psychology," but the approach has been expanded to all areas of psychology, including motivation, perception, psychopathology, and social psychology.

During this century, the focus of psychology has come full circle. After rejecting conscious experience as ill-suited to scientific investigation and turning to the study of behavior, psychologists are once again theorizing about the mind, but this time with new and more powerful tools. The gain from behaviorism has been an emphasis on the objectivity and reproducibility of findings—an emphasis that has found a place in cognitive psychology.

From a historical perspective, it is too early to judge the long-term significance of recent developments in psychology. What is evident, however, is that there is great excitement in the field today, and many psychologists believe that it is in a period of revolutionary change and progress. Understanding how the mind works is a challenge that deserves the best intellectual effort we can put forth.

## *Further* **READING**

For a general survey of the history of psychology, see Hilgard, *Psychology in America: A Historical Survey* (1987); Watson, *The Great Psychologists: From Aristotle to Freud* (4th ed., 1978); Wertheimer, *A Brief History of Psychology* (rev. ed., 1979); and Schultz, *A History of Modern Psychology* (4th ed., 1987). See also Boring, *A History of Experimental Psychology* (2nd ed., 1950); and Herrnstein and Boring, *A Source Book in the History of Psychology* (1965).

# *Appendix* III

# Statistical Methods and Measurement

M uch of the work of psychologists calls for making measurements—either in the laboratory or under field conditions. This work may involve measuring the eye movements of infants when first exposed to a novel stimulus, recording the galvanic skin response of people under stress, counting the number of trials required to condition a monkey that has a prefrontal lobotomy, determining achievement test scores for students using computer-assisted learning, or counting the number of patients who show improvement following a particular type of psychotherapy. In all these examples, the *measurement operation* yields numbers; the psychologist's problem is to interpret them and to arrive at some general conclusions. Basic to this task is *statistics*—the discipline that deals with collecting numerical data and with making inferences from such data. The purpose of this appendix is to review certain statistical methods that play an important role in psychology.

This appendix is written on the assumption that the problems students have with statistics are essentially problems of clear thinking about data. An introductory acquaintance with statistics is *not* beyond the scope of anyone who understands enough algebra to use plus and minus signs and to substitute numbers for letters in equations.

## Descriptive Statistics

Statistics serves, first of all, to provide a shorthand description of large amounts of data. Suppose that we want to study the college entrance examination scores of 5,000 students recorded on cards in the registrar's office. These scores are the raw data. Thumbing through the cards will give us some impressions of the students' scores, but it will be impossible for us to keep all of them in mind. So we make some kind of summary of the data, possibly averaging all the scores or finding the highest and lowest scores. These statistical summaries make it easier to remember and to think about the data. Such summarizing statements are called *descriptive statistics*.

### Frequency Distributions

Items of raw data become comprehensible when they are grouped in a *frequency distribution*. To group data, we must first divide the scale along which they are measured into intervals and then count the number of items that fall into each interval. An interval in which scores are grouped is called a *class interval*. The decision of how many class intervals the data are to be

**TABLE 1**

**Raw Scores** *College entrance examination scores for 15 students, listed in the order in which they were tested.*

| | | |
|---|---|---|
| 84 | 75 | 91 |
| 61 | 75 | 67 |
| 72 | 87 | 79 |
| 75 | 79 | 83 |
| 77 | 51 | 69 |

**TABLE 2**

**Frequency Distribution** *Scores from Table 1 accumulated with class intervals of*

| CLASS INTERVAL | NUMBER OF PERSONS IN CLASS |
|---|---|
| 50–59 | 1 |
| 60–69 | 3 |
| 70–79 | 7 |
| 80–89 | 3 |
| 90–99 | 1 |

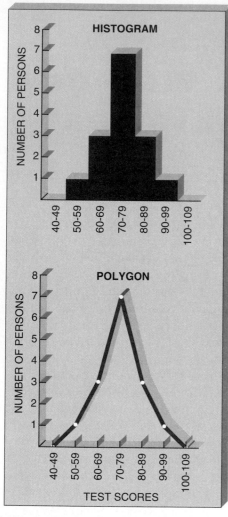

**FIGURE 1**
**Frequency Diagrams** *The data from Table 2 are plotted here. A frequency histogram is on the top; a frequency polygon, on the bottom.*

grouped into is not fixed by any rules but is based on the judgment of the investigator.

Table 1 provides a sample of raw data representing college entrance examination scores for 15 students. The scores are listed in the order in which the students were tested (the first student tested had a score of 84; the second, 61; and so on). Table 2 shows these data arranged in a frequency distribution for which the class interval has been set at 10. One score falls in the interval from 50 to 59, three scores fall in the interval from 60 to 69, and so on. Note that most scores fall in the interval from 70 to 79 and that no scores fall below the 50 to 59 interval or above the 90 to 99 interval.

A frequency distribution is often easier to understand if it is presented graphically. The most widely used graph form is the *frequency histogram*; an example is shown in the top panel of Figure 1. Histograms are constructed by drawing bars, the bases of which are given by the class intervals and the heights of which are determined by the corresponding class frequencies. An alternative way of presenting frequency distributions in graph form is to use a *frequency polygon*, an example of which is shown in the bottom panel of Figure 1. Frequency polygons are constructed by plotting the class frequencies at the center of the class interval and connecting the points obtained by straight lines. To complete the picture, one extra class is added at each end of the distribution; since these classes have zero frequencies, both ends of the figure will touch the horizontal axis. The frequency polygon gives the same information as the frequency histogram but by means of a set of connected lines rather than bars.

In practice, we would obtain a much greater number of items than those plotted in Figure 1, but a minimum amount of data is shown in all of the illustrations in this appendix so that you can easily check the steps in tabulating and plotting.

## Measures of Central Tendency

A *measure of central tendency* is simply a representative point on our scale—a central point with scores scattered on either side. Three such measures are commonly used: the *mean*, the *median*, and the *mode*.

The mean is the familiar arithmetic average obtained by adding the scores and dividing by the number of scores. The sum of the raw scores in Table 1 is 1125. If we divide this by 15 (the number of students' scores), the mean turns out to be 75.

The median is the score of the middle item, which is obtained by arranging the scores in order and then counting into the middle from either end. When the 15 scores in Table 1 are placed in order from highest to lowest, the eighth score from either end turns out to be 75. If the number of cases is even, we simply average the two cases on either side of the middle. For instance, the median of 10 items is the arithmetic average of the fifth and sixth cases.

The mode is the most frequent score in a given distribution. In Table 1, the most frequent score is 75; hence, the mode of the distribution is 75.

In a *symmetrical distribution*, in which the scores are distributed evenly on either side of the middle (as in Figure 1), the mean, median, and mode all fall together. This is not true for distributions that are *skewed*, or unbalanced. Suppose we want to analyze the departure times of a morning train. The train usually leaves on time; occasionally it leaves late, but it never leaves early. For a train with a scheduled departure time of 8:00 A.M., one week's record might be as follows:

|       |      |        |   |      |
|-------|------|--------|---|------|
| M     | 8:00 | Mean   | = | 8:07 |
| Tu    | 8:04 | Median | = | 8:02 |
| W     | 8:02 | Mode   | = | 8:00 |
| Th    | 8:19 |        |   |      |
| F     | 8:22 |        |   |      |
| Sat   | 8:00 |        |   |      |
| Sun   | 8:00 |        |   |      |

The distribution of departure times in this example is skewed because of the two late departures; they raise the mean departure time but do not have much effect on the median or the mode.

Skewness is important because, unless it is understood, the differences between the median and the mean may sometimes be misleading (see Figure 2). If, for example, two political parties are arguing about the prosperity of the country, it is possible for the mean and median incomes to move in opposite directions. Suppose that a round of wage increases has been combined with a reduction in extremely high incomes. The median income might have gone up while the mean went down. The party wanting to show that incomes were getting higher would choose the median, whereas the party wishing to show that incomes were getting lower would choose the mean.

The mean is the most widely used measure of central tendency, but there are times when the mode or the median is a more meaningful measure.

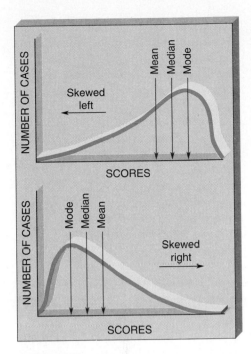

**FIGURE 2**
**Skewed Distribution Curves** *Note that skewed distributions are designated by the direction in which the tail falls. Also note that the mean, median, and mode are not identical for a skewed distribution; the median commonly falls between the mode and the mean.*

## Measures of Variation

Usually more information is needed about a distribution than can be obtained from a measure of central tendency. For example, we need a measure to tell us whether scores cluster closely around their average or whether they scatter widely. A measure of the spread of scores around the average is called a *measure of variation*.

Measures of variation are useful in at least two ways. First, they tell us how representative the average is. If the variation is small, we know that individual scores are close to it. If the variation is large, we cannot use the mean as a representative value with as much assurance. Suppose that clothing is being designed for a group of people without the benefit of precise measurements. Knowing their average size would be helpful, but it also would be important to know the spread of sizes. The second measure provides a yardstick that we can use to measure the amount of variability among the sizes.

To illustrate, consider the data in Figure 3, which show frequency distributions of entrance examination scores for two classes of 30 students. Both classes have the same mean of 75, but they exhibit clearly different degrees of variation. The scores of all the students in Class I are clustered close to the mean, whereas the scores of the students in Class II are spread over a wide range. Some measure is required to specify more exactly how these

**FIGURE 3**
**Distributions Differing in Variation**
*It is easy to see that the scores for Class I cluster closer to the mean than the scores for Class II, even though the means of the two classes are identical (75). For Class I, all the scores fall between 60 and 89, with most of the scores falling in the interval from 70 through 79. For Class II, the scores are distributed fairly uniformly over a wide range from 40 through 109. This difference in variability between the two distributions can be measured using the standard deviation, which is smaller for Class I than for Class II.*

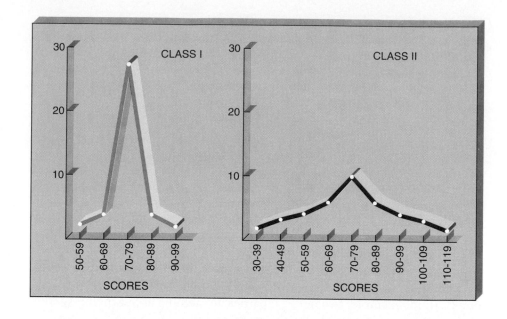

**TABLE 3**
**Computation of the Standard Deviation**

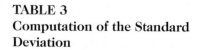

| CLASS I SCORES (MEAN = 75) | | |
|---|---|---|
| | $d$ | $d^2$ |
| 77 − 75 = | 2 | 4 |
| 76 − 75 = | 1 | 1 |
| 75 − 75 = | 0 | 0 |
| 74 − 75 = | −1 | 1 |
| 73 − 75 = | −2 | 4 |
| | | 10 |

Sum of $d^2$ = 10

Mean of $d^2 = \frac{10}{5} = 2.0$

Standard deviation $(\sigma) = \sqrt{2.0} = 1.4$

| CLASS II SCORES (MEAN = 75) | | |
|---|---|---|
| | $d$ | $d^2$ |
| 90 − 75 = | 15 | 225 |
| 85 − 75 = | 10 | 100 |
| 75 − 75 = | 0 | 0 |
| 65 − 75 = | −10 | 100 |
| 60 − 75 = | −15 | 225 |
| | | 650 |

Sum of $d^2$ = 650

Mean of $d^2 = \frac{650}{5} = 130$

Standard deviation $(\sigma) = \sqrt{130} = 11.4$

two distributions differ. Two measures of variation frequently used by psychologists are the *range* and the *standard deviation.*

To simplify arithmetic computation, we will suppose that five students from each class seek entrance to college and that their entrance examination scores are as follows:

> Student scores from Class I:
> 73, 74, 75, 76, 77 (mean = 75)

> Student scores from Class II:
> 60, 65, 75, 85, 90 (mean = 75)

We will now compute the measures of variation for these two samples.

The *range* is the spread between the highest score and the lowest score. The range of scores for the five students from Class I is 4 (from 73 to 77); the range of scores from Class II is 30 (from 60 to 90).

The range is easy to compute, but the standard deviation is more frequently used because it has certain properties that make it the preferred measure. One such property is that it is an extremely sensitive measure of variation because it accounts for every score, not just extreme values as the range does. The standard deviation, denoted by the lowercase Greek letter *sigma* ($\sigma$), measures how far the scores making up a distribution depart from that distribution's mean. The deviation *d* of each score from the mean is computed and squared; then the average of these squared values is obtained. The standard deviation is the square root of this average. Written as a formula,

$$\sigma = \sqrt{\frac{\text{sum of } d^2}{N}}$$

*Specimen Computation of the Standard Deviation* The scores for the samples from the two classes are arranged in Table 3 for easy computation of the standard deviation. The first step involves subtracting the mean from each score (the mean is 75 for both classes). This operation yields positive *d* values for scores above the mean and negative *d* values for scores below the mean. The minus signs disappear when the *d* values are squared in the next column. The squared deviations are added and then divided by *N*, the number of cases in the sample; in our example, $N = 5$. Taking the square root yields the standard deviation. In this example, the two standard deviations give us much the same information as the ranges.*

# Statistical Inference

Now that we have become familiar with statistics as a way of describing data, we are ready to turn to the processes of interpretation—to the making of inferences from data.

## Populations and Samples

First, it is necessary to distinguish between a *population* and a *sample* drawn from that population. The United States Census Bureau attempts to describe the whole population by obtaining descriptive material on age, marital status, and so on from everyone in the country. The word *population* is appropriate to the census because it represents *all* the people living in the United States.

In statistics, the word "population" is not limited to people or animals or things. The population may be all of the temperatures registered on a thermometer during the last decade, all of the words in the English language, or all of any other specified supply of data. Often we do not have access to the total population, and so we try to represent it by a sample drawn in a *random* (unbiased) fashion. We may ask some questions of a random fraction of the people, as the United States Census Bureau has done as part of recent censuses; we may derive average temperatures by reading the thermometer at specified times, without taking a continuous record; we may estimate the number of words in the encyclopedia by counting the words on a random number of pages. These illustrations all involve the selection of a *sample* from the population. If any of these processes are repeated, we will obtain slightly different results due to the fact that a sample does not fully represent the whole population and therefore contains *errors of sampling*. This is where statistical inference enters.

A sample of data is collected from a population in order to make inferences about that population. A sample of census data may be examined to see whether the population is getting older, for example, or whether there is a trend of migration to the suburbs. Similarly, experimental results are studied to determine what effects experimental manipulations have had on behavior—whether the threshold for pitch is affected by loudness, whether child-rearing practices have detectable effects later in life. To make *statistical inferences*, we have to evaluate the relationships revealed by the sample data. These inferences are always made under some degree of uncertainty

---

*For this introductory treatment, we will use *sigma* ($\sigma$) throughout. However, in the scientific literature, the lowercase letter $s$ is used to denote the standard deviation of a *sample* and $\sigma$ is used to denote the standard deviation of the *population*. Moreover, in computing the standard deviation of a sample $s$, the sum of $d^2$ is divided by $N-1$ rather than by $N$. For reasonably large samples, however, the actual value of the standard deviation is only slightly affected whether we divide by $N-1$ or $N$. To simplify this presentation, we will not distinguish between the standard deviation of a sample and that of a population; instead, we will use the same formula to compute both. For a discussion of this point, see Phillips (1992).

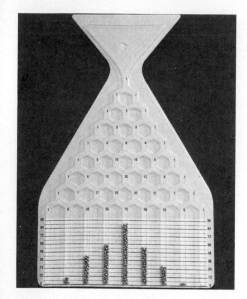

**FIGURE 4**
**Device to Demonstrate a Chance Distribution** *The board is held upside down until all the steel balls fall into the reservoir. Then the board is turned over and held vertically until the balls fall into the nine columns. The precise number of balls falling into each column will vary from one demonstration to the next. On the average, however, the heights of the columns of balls will approximate a normal distribution, with the greatest height in the center column and gradually decreasing heights in the outer columns.*

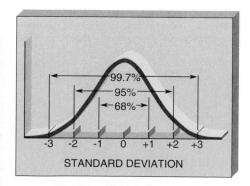

**FIGURE 5**
**Normal Distribution** *The normal distribution curve can be constructed using the mean and the standard deviation. The area under the curve below −3σ and above +3σ is negligible.*

due to sampling errors. If the statistical tests indicate that the magnitude of the effect found in the sample is fairly large (relative to the estimate of the sampling error), then we can be confident that the effect observed in the sample holds for the population at large.

Thus, statistical inference deals with the problem of making an inference or judgment about a feature of a population based solely on information obtained from a sample of that population. As an introduction to statistical inference, we will consider the normal distribution and its use in interpreting standard deviations.

## Normal Distribution

When large amounts of data are collected, tabulated, and plotted as a histogram or polygon, they often fall into a roughly bell-shaped symmetrical distribution known as the *normal distribution*. Most items fall near the mean (the high point of the bell), and the bell tapers off sharply at very high and very low scores. This form of curve is of special interest because it also arises when the outcome of a process is based on a large number of *chance* events all occurring independently. The demonstration device displayed in Figure 4 illustrates how a sequence of chance events gives rise to a normal distribution. The chance factor of whether a steel ball will fall to the left or right each time it encounters a point where the channel branches results in a symmetrical distribution: more balls fall straight down the middle, but occasionally one reaches one of the end compartments. This is a useful way of visualizing what is meant by a chance distribution closely approximating the normal distribution.

The normal distribution (Figure 5) is the mathematical representation of the idealized distribution approximated by the device shown in Figure 4. The normal distribution represents the likelihood that items within a normally distributed population will depart from the mean by any stated amount. The percentages shown in Figure 5 represent the *percentage of the area* lying under the curve between the indicated scale values; the total area under the curve represents the whole population. Roughly two-thirds of the cases (68 percent) will fall between plus and minus one standard deviation from the mean (±1σ); 95 percent of the cases within ±2σ; and virtually all cases (99.7 percent) within ±3σ. A more detailed listing of areas under portions of the normal curve is given in Table 4.

Using Table 4, let us trace how the 68 percent and 95 percent values in Figure 5 are derived. We find from Column 3 of Table 4 that between −1σ and the mean lies .341 of the total area and between +1σ and the mean also lies .341 of the area. Adding these values gives us .682, which is expressed in Figure 5 as 68 percent. Similarly, the area between −2σ and +2σ is 2 × .477 = .954, which is expressed as 95 percent.

These percentages have several uses. One is in connection with the interpretation of standard scores, to which we turn next. Another is in connection with tests of significance.

## Scaling of Data

In order to interpret a score, we often need to know whether it is high or low in relation to other scores. If a person taking a driver's test requires .500 seconds to brake after a danger signal, how can we tell whether the performance is fast or slow? Does a student who scores 60 on a physics examination pass the course? To answer questions of this kind, we have to derive a *scale* against which the scores can be compared.

**RANKED DATA**  By placing scores in rank order from high to low, we derive one kind of scale. An individual score is interpreted on the basis of where it ranks among the group of scores. For example, the graduates of West Point know where they stand in their class—perhaps 35th or 125th in a class of 400.

**STANDARD SCORES**  The standard deviation is a convenient unit to use in scaling because we can interpret how far away $1\sigma$ or $2\sigma$ is from the mean (see Table 4). A score based on a multiple of the standard deviation is known as a *standard score*. Many scales used in psychological measurement are based on the principle of standard scores.

*Specimen Computations of Standard Scores*  Table 1 presented college entrance scores for 15 students. Without more information, we do not know whether these scores are representative of the population of all college applicants. On this examination, however, we will assume that the population mean is 75 and the standard deviation is 10.

What, then, is the *standard score* for a student who had 90 on the examination? We must express how far this score lies above the mean in multiples of the standard deviation.

Standard score for grade of 90:

$$\frac{90 - 75}{10} = \frac{15}{10} = 1.5\sigma$$

As a second example, consider a student with a score of 53.

Standard score for grade of 53:

$$\frac{53 - 75}{10} = \frac{-22}{10} = -2.2\sigma$$

In this case, the minus sign tells us that the student's score is below the mean by 2.2 standard deviations. Thus, the sign of the standard score (+ or–) indicates whether the score is above or below the mean, and its value indicates how far from the mean the score lies in standard deviations.

**TABLE 4**
**Area of the Normal Distribution as Proportion of Total Area**

| STANDARD DEVIATION | (1) AREA TO THE LEFT OF THIS VALUE | (2) AREA TO THE RIGHT OF THIS VALUE | (3) AREA BETWEEN THIS VALUE AND MEAN |
|---|---|---|---|
| $-3.0\sigma$ | .001 | .999 | .499 |
| $-2.5\sigma$ | .006 | .994 | .494 |
| $-2.0\sigma$ | .023 | .977 | .477 |
| $-1.5\sigma$ | .067 | .933 | .433 |
| $-1.0\sigma$ | .159 | .841 | .341 |
| $-0.5\sigma$ | .309 | .691 | .191 |
| $0.0\sigma$ | .500 | .500 | .000 |
| $+0.5\sigma$ | .691 | .309 | .191 |
| $+1.0\sigma$ | .841 | .159 | .341 |
| $+1.5\sigma$ | .933 | .067 | .433 |
| $+2.0\sigma$ | .977 | .023 | .477 |
| $+2.5\sigma$ | .994 | .006 | .494 |
| $+3.0\sigma$ | .999 | .001 | .499 |

## How Representative Is a Mean?

How useful is the mean of a sample in estimating the population mean? If we measure the height of a random sample of 100 college students, how well does the sample mean predict the true population mean (that is, the mean height of *all* college students)? These questions raise the issue of making an *inference* about a population based on information from a sample.

The accuracy of such inferences depends on *errors of sampling*. Suppose we were to select two random samples from the same population and compute the mean for each sample. What differences between the first and the second mean could be expected to occur by chance?

Successive random samples drawn from the same population will have different means, forming a distribution of *sample means* around the *true mean* of the population. These sample means are themselves numbers for which the standard deviation can be computed. We call this standard deviation the *standard error of the mean*, or $\sigma_M$, and can estimate it on the basis of the following formula:

$$\sigma_M = \frac{\sigma}{\sqrt{N}}$$

where $\sigma$ is the standard deviation of the sample and $N$ is the number of cases from which each sample mean is computed.

According to the formula, the size of the standard error of the mean decreases as the sample size increases; thus, a mean based on a large sample is more trustworthy (more likely to be close to the actual population mean) than a mean based on a smaller sample. Common sense would lead us to expect this. Computations of the standard error of the mean permit us to make clear assertions about the degree of uncertainty in our computed mean. The more cases in the sample, the more uncertainty has been reduced.

## Significance of a Difference

In many psychological experiments, data are collected on two groups of subjects; one group is exposed to certain specified experimental conditions, and the other serves as a control group. The question is whether there is a difference in the mean performance of the two groups, and if such a difference is observed, whether it holds for the population from which these groups of subjects have been sampled. Basically, we are asking whether a difference between two sample means reflects a true difference or whether this difference is simply the result of sampling error.

As an example, we will compare the scores on a reading test for a sample of first-grade boys with the scores for a sample of first-grade girls. The boys score lower than the girls as far as mean performances are concerned, but there is a great deal of overlap; some boys do extremely well, and some girls do very poorly. Thus, we cannot accept the obtained difference in means without making a test of its *statistical significance*. Only then can we decide whether the observed differences in sample means reflect true differences in the population or are due to sampling error. If some of the brighter girls and some of the duller boys are sampled by sheer luck, the difference could be due to sampling error.

As another example, suppose that we have set up an experiment to compare the grip strength of right-handed and left-handed men. The top panel of Table 5 presents hypothetical data from such an experiment. A sample of five right-handed men averaged 8 kilograms stronger than a sample of five left-handed men. In general, what can we infer from these data about left-handed and right-handed men? Can we argue that right-handed men are stronger than left-handed men? Obviously not, because the averages derived from most of the right-handed men would not differ from those from the left-handed men; the one markedly deviant score of 100 tells us we are dealing with an uncertain situation.

Now suppose that the results of the experiment were those shown in the bottom panel of Table 5. Again, we find the same mean difference of 8 kilograms, but we are now inclined to have greater confidence in the results, because the left-handed men scored consistently lower than the right-handed men. Statistics provides a precise way of taking into account the reliability of the mean differences so that we do not have to depend solely on intuition to determine that one difference is more reliable than another.

These examples suggest that the significance of a difference will depend on both the size of the obtained difference and the variability of the means being compared. From the standard error of the means, we can compute the *standard error of the difference between two means* $\sigma_{D_M}$. We can then evaluate the obtained difference by using a *critical ratio*—the ratio of the obtained difference between the means $D_M$ to the standard error of the difference between the means:

$$\text{Critical ratio} = \frac{D_M}{\sigma_{D_M}}$$

This ratio helps us to evaluate the significance of the difference between the two means. As a rule of thumb, a critical ratio should be 2.0 or larger for the difference between means to be accepted as significant. Throughout this book, statements that the difference between means is "statistically significant" indicate that the critical ratio is at least that large.

Why is a critical ratio of 2.0 selected as statistically significant? Simply because a value this large or larger can occur by chance only 5 out of 100 times. Where do we get the 5 out of 100? We can treat the critical ratio as a standard score because it is merely the difference between two means, expressed as a multiple of its standard error. Referring to Column 2 in Table 4, we note that the likelihood is .023 that a standard deviation as high as or higher than +2.0 will occur by chance. Because the chance of deviating in the opposite direction is also .023, the total probability is .046. This means that 46 times out of 1,000, or about 5 times out of 100, a critical ratio as large as 2.0 would be found by chance if the population means were identical.

The rule of thumb that says a critical ratio should be at least 2.0 is just that—an arbitrary but convenient rule that defines the "5 percent level of significance." Following this rule, we will make fewer than 5 errors in 100 decisions by concluding on the basis of sample data that a difference in means exists when in fact there is none. The 5 percent level need not always be used; a higher level of significance may be appropriate in certain experiments, depending on how willing we are to make an occasional error in inference.

*Specimen Computation of the Critical Ratio* The computation of the critical ratio calls for finding the *standard error of the difference between two means*, which is given by the following formula:

$$\sigma_{D_M} = \sqrt{(\sigma_{M_1})^2 + (\sigma_{M_2})^2}$$

**TABLE 5**
**Significance of a Difference** *Two examples that compare the difference between means are shown below. The difference between means is the same (8 kilograms) in both the top and the bottom panel. However, the data in the bottom panel indicate a more reliable difference between means than do the data in the top panel.*

| STRENGTH OF GRIP IN KILOGRAMS, RIGHT-HANDED MEN | STRENGTH OF GRIP IN KILOGRAMS, LEFT-HANDED MEN |
|---|---|
| 40 | 40 |
| 45 | 45 |
| 50 | 50 |
| 55 | 55 |
| 100 | 60 |
| Sum 290 | Sum 250 |
| Mean 58 | Mean 50 |

| STRENGTH OF GRIP IN KILOGRAMS, RIGHT-HANDED MEN | STRENGTH OF GRIP IN KILOGRAMS, LEFT-HANDED MEN |
|---|---|
| 56 | 48 |
| 57 | 49 |
| 58 | 50 |
| 59 | 51 |
| 60 | 52 |
| Sum 290 | Sum 250 |
| Mean 58 | Mean 50 |

In this formula, $\sigma_{M_1}$ and $\sigma_{M_2}$ are the standard errors of the two means being compared.

As an illustration, suppose we wanted to compare reading achievement test scores for first-grade boys and girls in the United States. A random sample of boys and girls would be identified and given the test. We will assume that the mean score for the boys was 70 with a standard error of .40 and that the mean score for the girls was 72 with a standard error of .30. On the basis of these samples, we want to decide whether there is a real difference between the reading achievement of boys and girls in the population as a whole. The sample data suggest that girls do achieve better reading scores than boys, but can we infer that this would have been the case if we had tested all the girls and all the boys in the United States? The critical ratio helps us make this decision.

$$\sigma_{D_M} = \sqrt{(\sigma_{M_1})^2 + (\sigma_{M_2})^2}$$

$$= \sqrt{.16 + .09} = \sqrt{.25}$$

$$= .5$$

$$\text{Critical ratio} = \frac{D_M}{\sigma_{D_M}} = \frac{72-70}{.5} = \frac{2.0}{.5} = 4.0$$

Because the critical ratio is well above 2.0, we may assert that the observed mean difference is statistically significant at the 5 percent level. Thus, we can conclude that there is a reliable difference in performance on the reading test between boys and girls. Note that the sign of the critical ratio could be positive or negative, depending on which mean is subtracted from which; when the critical ratio is interpreted, only its magnitude (not its sign) is considered.

# Coefficient of Correlation

Correlation refers to the concomitant variation of paired measures. Suppose that a test is designed to predict success in college. If it is a good test, high scores on it will be related to high performance in college and low scores will be related to poor performance. The *coefficient of correlation* gives us a way of stating the degree of relationship more precisely. (This topic was discussed on pp. 17–19. You may find it helpful to review that material.)

**TABLE 6**
**Computation of a Product-Moment Correlation**

| STUDENT | ENTRANCE TEST (*x*-score) | FRESHMAN GRADES (*y*-score) | (*dx*) | (*dy*) | (*dx*)(*dy*) |
|---|---|---|---|---|---|
| Adam | 71 | 39 | 6 | 9 | +54 |
| Bill | 67 | 27 | 2 | –3 | –6 |
| Charles | 65 | 33 | 0 | 3 | 0 |
| David | 63 | 30 | –2 | 0 | 0 |
| Edward | 59 | 21 | –6 | –9 | +54 |
| Sum | 325 | 150 | 0 | 0 | +102 |
| Mean | 65 | 30 | | | |

$\sigma_x = 4$
$\sigma_y = 6$

$$r = \frac{\text{Sum }(dx)(dy)}{N\sigma_x\sigma_y} = \frac{+102}{5 \times 4 \times 6} = +.85$$

## Product-Moment Correlation

The most frequently used method of determining the coefficient of correlation is the *product-moment method,* which yields the index conventionally designated by the lower-case letter *r.* The product-moment coefficient *r* varies between perfect positive correlation ($r = +1.00$) and perfect negative correlation ($r = -1.00$). Lack of any relationship yields $r = .00$.

The formula for computing the product-moment correlation is

$$r = \frac{\text{Sum } (dx)(dy)}{N\sigma_x\sigma_y}$$

Here, one of the paired measures has been labeled the *x*-score; the other, the *y*-score. The *dx* and *dy* refer to the deviations of each score from its mean, *N* is the number of paired measures, and $\sigma_x$ and $\sigma_y$ are the standard deviations of the *x*-scores and the *y*-scores.

The computation of the coefficient of correlation requires the determination of the sum of the (*dx*)(*dy*) products. This sum, in addition to the computed standard deviations for the *x*-scores and *y*-scores, can then be entered into the formula.

*Specimen Computation of Product-Moment Correlation* Suppose that we have collected the data shown in Table 6. For each subject, we have obtained two scores—the first being a score on a college entrance test (to be labeled arbitrarily the *x*-score) and the second being freshman grades (the *y*-score).

Figure 6 is a *scatter diagram* of these data. Each point represents the *x*-score and *y*-score for a given subject; for example, the uppermost right-hand point is for Adam (labeled A). Looking at these data, we can easily detect that there is some positive correlation between the *x*-scores and the *y*-scores. Adam attained the highest score on the entrance test and also earned the highest freshman grades; Edward received the lowest scores on both. The other students' test scores and grades are a little irregular, so we know that the correlation is not perfect; hence, *r* is less than 1.00.

We will compute the correlation to illustrate the method, although no researcher would consent, in practice, to determining a correlation for so few cases. The details are given in Table 6. Following the procedure outlined in Table 3, we compute the standard deviation of the *x*-scores and then the standard deviation of the *y*-scores. Next, we compute the (*dx*)(*dy*) products for each subject and total the five cases. Entering these results in our equation yields an *r* of +.85.

## Interpreting a Correlation Coefficient

We can use correlations in making predictions. For example, if we know from past experience that a certain entrance test correlates with freshman grades, we can predict the freshman grades for beginning college students who have taken the test. If the correlation were perfect, we could predict their grades without error. But *r* is usually less than 1.00, and some errors in prediction will be made; the closer *r* is to 0, the greater the sizes of the errors in prediction.

Although we cannot go into the technical problems of predicting freshman grades from entrance examinations or of making other similar predictions, we can consider the meanings of correlation coefficients of different sizes. It is evident that with a correlation of 0 between *x* and *y*, knowledge of *x* will not help to predict *y*. If weight is unrelated to intelligence, it does us no good to know a subject's weight when we are trying to predict his or her

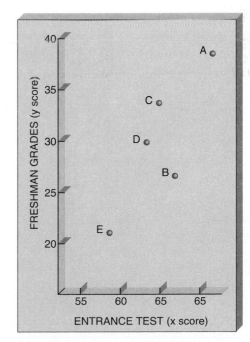

**FIGURE 6**
**Scatter Design** *Each point represents the x- and y-scores for a particular student. The letters next to the points identify the students in the data table (A = Adam, B = Bill, and so on).*

**FIGURE 7**
**Scatter Diagrams Illustrating Correlations of Various Sizes** *Each dot represents one individual's score on two tests, x and y. In A, all cases fall on the diagonal and the correlation is perfect (r = +1.00); if we know a subject's score on x, we know that it will be the same on y. In B, the correlation is 0; knowing a subject's score on x, we cannot predict whether it will be at, above, or below the mean on y. For example, of the four subjects who score at the mean of x (dx=0), one makes a very high score on y (dy=+2), one a very low score (dy=−2), and two remain average. In both C and D, there is a diagonal trend to the scores, so that a high score on x is associated with a high score on y and a low score on x with a low score on y, but the relationship is imperfect. It is possible to check the value of the correlations by using the formulas given in the text for the coefficient of correlation. The computation has been greatly simplified by presenting the scores in the deviation form that permits entering them directly into the formulas. The fact that the axes do not have conventional scales does not change the interpretation. For example, if we assigned the values 1 through 5 to the x and y coordinates and then computed r for these new values, the correlation coefficients would be the same.*

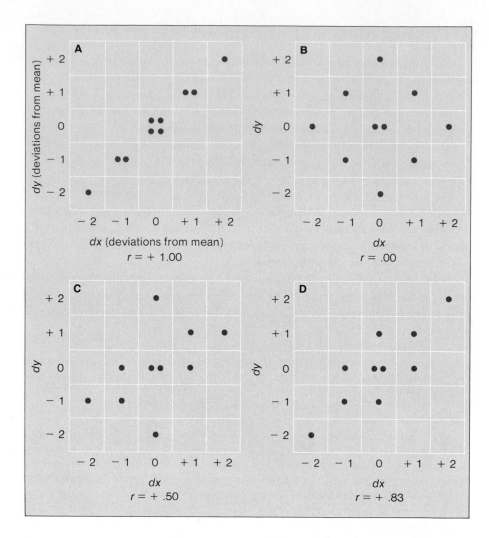

intelligence. At the other extreme, a perfect correlation would mean 100 percent predictive efficiency—knowing *x*, we can predict *y* perfectly. What about intermediate values of *r*? Some appreciation of the meaning of correlations of intermediate sizes can be gained by examining the scatter diagrams in Figure 7.

In the preceding discussion, we did not emphasize the sign of the correlation coefficient, since this has no bearing on the strength of a relationship. The only distinction between a correlation of *r* = + .70 and *r* = − .70 is that increases in *x* are accompanied by increases in *y* for the former, and increases in *x* are accompanied by decreases in *y* for the latter.

Although the correlation coefficient is one of the most widely used statistics in psychology, it is also one of the most widely misused procedures. Those who use it sometimes overlook the fact that *r* does not imply a cause-and-effect relationship between *x* and *y*. When two sets of scores are correlated, we may suspect that they have some causal factors in common, but we cannot conclude that one of them causes the other (see p. 19).

Correlations sometimes appear paradoxical. For example, the correlation between study time and college grades has been found to be slightly negative (about − .10). If a causal interpretation were assumed, we might conclude that the best way to raise grades would be to stop studying. The negative correlation arises because some students have advantages over others in grade making (possibly due to better college preparation), so that often those who study the hardest are those who have difficulty earning the best grades.

This example provides sufficient warning against assigning a causal interpretation to a coefficient of correlation. It is possible, however, that when two variables are correlated, one may be the cause of the other. The search for causes is a logical one, and correlations can help us by providing leads to experiments that can verify cause-and-effect relationships.

## Further READING

There are a number of textbooks on statistics written from the viewpoint of psychological research. Examples are McCall, *Fundamental Statistics for Behavioral Sciences* (5th ed., 1990); Welkowitz, Ewen, and Cohen, *Introductory Statistics for the Behavioral Sciences* (3rd ed., 1982); Hinkle, Wiersma, and Jurs, *Applied Statistics for the Behavioral Sciences* (2nd ed., 1988); and Phillips, *How to Think About Statistics* (revised edition, 1992).

The role of statistics in the design of psychological experiments is discussed in Keppel, Saufley, and Tokunaga *Introduction to Design and Analysis* (2nd ed., 1992).

# Glossary

The glossary defines the technical words that appear in the text and some common words that have special meanings when used in psychology. No attempt is made to give the range of meanings beyond those used in the text. For fuller definitions and other shades of meaning, consult any standard dictionary of psychology.

## A

**ability.** Demonstrable knowledge or skill. Ability includes aptitude and achievement. See also *achievement, aptitude.*

**abreaction.** In psychoanalysis, the process of reducing emotional tension by reliving (in speech or action or both) the experience that caused the tension.

**absolute threshold.** The intensity or frequency at which a stimulus becomes effective or ceases to become effective, as measured under experimental conditions. See also *difference threshold, threshold.*

**accommodation.** (1) The process by which the lens of the eye varies its focus. (2) In Piaget's theory of cognitive development, the process by which an infant modifies a pre-existing schema in order to include a novel object or event. See also *assimilation, schema.*

**acetylcholine.** The most common of the neurotransmitters. It is found in many synapses in the brain and spinal cord, and is particularly prevalent in an area of the brain called the hippocampus, which plays a key role in the formation of new memories. See also *neurotransmitter.*

**achievement.** Acquired ability, such as school attainment in spelling. See also *aptitude.*

**achromatic colors.** Black, white, and gray. See also *chromatic colors.*

**acoustic buffer.** In short-term memory, a hypothesized component of the encoding process which briefly stores information in an acoustic code (i.e., the sound of the digit, letter, or word). See also *central executive, encoding, short-term memory, visual buffer.*

**acquisition.** The stage during which a new response is learned and gradually strengthened. See also *classical conditioning.*

**ACTH.** See *adrenocorticotropic hormone.*

**action potential.** Synonymous with *nerve impulse.* The wave of electrical activity that is transmitted down the axon of the neuron when the cell membrane becomes depolarized. See also *depolarization, graded potentials, resting potential.*

**activation model.** In short-term memory, the proposal that retrieval of an item depends on the activation of that item reaching a critical level; the more items in short-term memory the less activation for any one of them. An alternative to the hypothesis that retrieval depends on a serial search. See also *serial memory search, short-term memory.*

**acupuncture.** A healing procedure developed in China in which needles are inserted in the skin at critical points and twirled, eliminating pain. See also *gate control theory of pain.*

**addiction.** See *physical dependence.*

**additive mixture.** The mixture of colored lights; two spotlights of different colors focused on the same spot yield an additive color mixture. See also *subtractive mixture.*

**ADH.** See *antidiuretic hormone.*

**adipocytes.** Special fat cells in the body. Obese individuals have many more of them and thus, perhaps, a higher body fat base line.

**adolescence.** The period of transition from childhood to adulthood during which the individual develops to sexual maturity. See also *puberty.*

**adolescent growth spurt.** A period of rapid physical growth that accompanies the onset of puberty.

**adrenal gland.** One of a pair of endocrine glands located above the kidneys. The medulla of the gland secretes the hor-mones epinephrine and norepinephrine. The cortex of the gland secretes a number of hormones, collectively called the *adrenocortical hormones,* which include cortisol. See also *endocrine gland.*

**adrenalin.** See *epinephrine.*

**adrenal-cortical-system.** A neuro-endocrine system activated in response to stress. On a signal from the hypothalamus, the pituitary gland secretes a number of hormones. One stimulates the thyroid gland to make more energy available; the other (adrenocorticotropic hormone, ACTH) triggers the outer layer of the adrenal gland (the adrenal cortex) to release some 30 hormones (including cortisol) which play a role in the body's adjustment to emergencies. See also *adrenocorticotropic hormone, cortisol.*

**adrenocorticotropic hormone (ACTH).** A hormone released by the pituitary gland in response to stress; known as the body's major "stress" hormone. It is carried by the bloodstream to the adrenal glands and various other organs of the body, causing the release of some 30 hormones, each of which plays a role in the body's adjustment to emergency situations. See also *corticotropin-release factor.*

**aerobic exercise.** Any sustained activity that increases oxygen consumption, such as jogging, swimming, cycling, or fast walking.

**affect.** Emotion.

**affective experience.** An emotional experience, whether pleasant or unpleasant, mild or intense. See also *emotion.*

**afferent neuron.** See *sensory neuron.*

**afterimage.** The sensory experience that remains when a stimulus is withdrawn. Usually refers to visual experience—for example, the negative afterimage of a picture or the train of colored images that results after staring at the sun.

**age regression.** In hypnosis, the reliving through fantasy of experiences that are based on early memories or that are appropriate to a younger age. See also *hypnosis*.

**aggregated score.** A combination of several measures of the same behavior or characteristic.

**aggression.** Behavior intended to harm another person.

**agnosia.** A perceptual disturbance, resulting from damage to the cerebral cortex, in which the individual has difficulty identifying familiar objects or placing them in space even though visual acuity is normal. People suffering from agnosia appear to perceive but are not capable of understanding the information presented to them. See also *associative agnosia, prosopagnosia*.

**agoraphobia.** Fear of being alone or being in a public place where escape might be difficult or help unavailable should the individual be incapacitated by a panic attack. See also *panic disorder, phobia*.

**AI.** See *artificial intelligence*.

**all-or-none principle.** The rule that the nerve impulse in a single neuron is independent of the strength of stimulation; the neuron either responds completely (fires its action potential) or not at all.

**alpha waves.** See *electroencephalogram*.

**alternate form reliability.** The consistency between two or more versions of the same test when given to the same person. See also *reliability*.

**ambivalence.** Simultaneous liking and disliking of an object or person; the conflict caused by an incentive that is at once positive and negative. See also *conflict*.

**Ames room.** A perceptual illusion; specifically, a room that when viewed through a peephole leads to distortions in size judgments. See also *size constancy*.

**amnesia.** A partial or complete loss of memory. May be due to psychological factors (for example, emotional trauma) or physiological factors (some form of brain damage) and may involve loss of memory for events occurring prior to or subsequent to the amnesia-causing trauma. See also *anterograde amnesia, retrograde amnesia*.

**amphetamines.** Central nervous system stimulants that produce restlessness, irritability, anxiety, and rapid heart rate. Dexedrine sulfate ("speed") and methamphetamine ("meth") are two types of amphetamines. See also *depressants, stimulants*.

**amygdala.** A brain structure located below the cerebral cortex that is involved in consolidation of new memories. See also *diencephalon, hippocampus*.

**anal stage.** The second stage in Freud's psychoanalytic theory of psychosexual development, following the oral stage. The sources of gratification and conflict have to do with the expulsion and retention of feces. See also *psychosexual development*.

**androgens.** The collective name for male sex hormones, of which testosterone, secreted by the testes, is best known. See also *gonads*.

**angiotensin.** A hormone critical in the regulation of thirst. When produced, it induces a feeling of thirst as well as an appetite for salt.

**anorexia nervosa.** An eating disorder which mainly afflicts young women and is characterized by an extreme, self-imposed weight loss. See also *bulimia*.

**anterograde amnesia.** Loss of memory for events and experiences occurring subsequent to an amnesia-causing trauma; the patient is unable to acquire new information, although recall of information learned prior to the onset may be largely unaffected. See also *amnesia, retrograde amnesia*.

**anthropology.** The science that studies chiefly preliterate ("primitive") societies. Its main divisions are archaeology (the study of the physical monuments and remains from earlier civilizations), physical anthropology (concerned with the anatomical differences among men and their evolutionary origins), linguistic anthropology, and social anthropology (concerned with social institutions and behavior). See also *behavioral sciences*.

**antianxiety drug.** Central nervous system depressant (belonging to the family of drugs called benzodiazapines) that reduces anxiety and tension. Causes some drowsiness but less than barbituates. Diazepam (Valium) and alprazolam (Xanax) are examples (syn. *tranquilizer*).

**antidepressant.** Drug used to elevate the mood of depressed individuals, presumably by increasing the availability of the neurotransmitters norepinephrine and/or serotonin. Examples are imipramine (Tofranil), isocarboxazid (Marplan), and tranylcypromine (Parnate).

**antidiuretic hormone (ADH).** Hormone secreted by the pituitary gland that signals the kidney to reabsorb water into the bloodstream instead of excreting it as urine.

**antipsychotic drug.** A drug that reduces psychotic symptoms, used more frequently in the treatment of schizophrenia. The phenothiazines, such as chlorpromazine (Thorazin) and fluphenazine (Prolixin), are examples (syn. *neuroleptic drug*). See also *phenothiazines, psychotic behavior*.

**antisocial personality.** A type of personality disorder marked by impulsivity, inability to abide by the customs and laws of society, and lack of anxiety or guilt regarding behavior (syn. *sociopathic personality, psychopathic personality*).

**anxiety.** A state of apprehension, tension, and worry. Synonymous with fear for some theorists, although others view the object of anxiety (such as a vague danger or foreboding) as less specific than the object of a fear (such as a vicious animal). See also *neurotic anxiety, objective anxiety*.

**anxiety disorders.** A group of mental disorders characterized by intense anxiety or by maladaptive behavior designed to relieve anxiety. Includes generalized anxiety and panic disorders, phobic and obsessive-compulsive disorders. Major category of DSM-III-R covering most of the disorders formerly called neuroses. See also *generalized anxiety disorder, neurosis, obsessive-compulsive disorder, panic disorder, phobic disorder, post-traumatic stress disorder*.

**anxiety hierarchy.** A list of situations or stimuli to which a person responds with anxiety ranked in order from the least anxiety-producing to the most fearful. Used by behavior therapists in systematically desensitizing patients to feared stimuli by associating deep relaxation with the situations rather than anxiety. See also *behavior therapy, systematic desensitization*.

**apathy.** Listlessness, indifference; one of the consequences of frustration. See also *frustration*.

**aphagia.** Inability to eat. See also *hyperphagia*.

**aphasia.** Impairment or loss of ability to articulate words or comprehend speech.

**apnea.** A sleep disturbance characterized by inhibited breathing during sleep.

**apparent motion.** See *phi phenomenon, stroboscopic motion*.

**appetitive behavior.** Seeking behavior. See also *aversive behavior*.

**aptitude.** The capacity to learn—for instance, a person's typing aptitude prior to practice on a typewriter. Aptitude tests are designed to predict the outcome of training, hence to predict future ability on the basis of present ability. See also *achievement*.

**arousal level.** The principle according to which people seek an optimal level of drive or arousal.

**artificial intelligence (AI).** A field of research combining computer science and cognitive psychology; it is concerned with (a) using computers to stimulate human thought processes and (b) devising computer programs that act "intelligently" and can adapt to changing circumstances. In essence, it is the science of making machines (computers) do things that are normally done by the human mind. See also *cognitive psychology, cognitive science, computer simulation.*

**assertiveness training.** The use of behavioral rehearsal to help an individual learn to express his or her needs in an effective, nonhostile manner. See also *behavioral rehearsal.*

**assimilation.** In Piaget's theory of cognitive development, the process by which an infant comprehends a novel object or event in terms of a pre-existing schema. See also *accommodation, schema.*

**association areas.** Areas of the cerebral cortex that are not directly concerned with sensory or motor processes; they integrate inputs from various sensory channels and presumably function in learning, memory, and thinking.

**associative agnosia.** A perceptual disturbance, resulting from damage to specific areas of the cerebral cortex, in which the individual has difficulty recognizing familiar objects presented visually, although he or she can readily name the objects if allowed to touch or hear them. See also *agnosia, prosopagnosia.*

**associative learning.** Learning that certain contingencies (or relations) exist between events; learning that one event is associated with another.

**astigmatism.** In vision, an optical defect that prevents horizontal and vertical contours from being in focus simultaneously. See also *strabismus.*

**attachment.** The tendency of the young organism to seek closeness to particular individuals and to feel more secure in their presence.

**attention.** The focusing of perception leading to heightened awareness of a limited range of stimuli. It has both overt behavioral components and internal components. See also *orienting reflex.*

**attitude.** A like or dislike; a favorable or unfavorable evaluation of and reaction to an object, person, event, or idea. An attitude comprises a *cognitive* component, an *affective* component, and a *behavioral* component.

**attribution.** The process by which we attempt to explain the behavior of other people. Attribution theory deals with the rules people use to infer the causes of observed behavior. See also *dispositional attribution, situational attribution.*

**attributional style.** A person's characteristic way of giving causal explanations (attributions) for important events. People with a pessimistic attributional style, who attribute negative events to causes

that are internal, stable over time, and global are presumably more prone to depression than people with a more optimistic style who attribute such events to external, temporary, and specific causes. See also *attribution.*

**auditory area.** A brain region located at the top of the temporal lobe of each cerebral hemisphere where auditory signals carried by the acoustic nerve are analyzed. Because nerve fibers from each side of the head cross over at the brain stem before reaching the auditory area, signals from each ear reach both temporal lobes. Thus, damage to one lobe does not produce deafness in one ear.

**authoritarian parents.** Parents who exercise a high level of control over their children's behavior without warmth, nurturance, or two-way communications. See also *authoritative parents.*

**authoritarian personality.** A personality type who is submissive and obedient to superiors but contemptuous of and aggressive toward those he or she considers inferior. Shows prejudice against minority groups. The *Authoritarian Personality* is a classic social psychological study, based in psychoanalytic theory, which examined this personality type. See also *scapegoat theory of prejudice.*

**authoritative parents.** Parents who combine a high level of control over their children's behavior with warmth, nurturance, and two-way communication. See also *authoritarian parents.*

**autism.** Absorption in fantasy to the exclusion of interest in reality; a symptom of schizophrenia. See also *schizophrenia.*

**autistic thinking.** A form of associative thinking, controlled more by the thinker's needs or desires than by reality; wishful thinking.

**automatic writing.** Writing that the writer is unaware of (does not know that he or she is producing); familiar in hypnosis. See also *hypnosis.*

**autonomic nervous system.** The division of the peripheral nervous system that regulates smooth muscle (organ and glandular) activities. It is divided into the sympathetic and parasympathetic divisions. See also *parasympathetic division, peripheral nervous system, sympathetic system.*

**autoshaping.** A shaping procedure that involves aspects of both operant and classical conditioning and does not require the presence of an experimenter. See also *shaping of behavior.*

**average.** See *measure of central tendency.*

**aversive behavior.** Avoidance behavior. See also *appetitive behavior.*

**aversive conditioning.** A form of conditioning in which an undesirable response

is extinguished through association with punishment; has been used in behavior therapy to treat alcoholism, smoking, and sexual problems. See also *behavior therapy, counterconditioning.*

**avoidance learning.** Learning to make a response to a warning signal in order to avoid an aversive event. See also *escape learning.*

**awareness.** See *consciousness.*

**axon.** That portion of a neuron that transmits impulses to other neurons. See also *dendrite, neuron.*

## B

**BAC.** See *blood alcohol concentration.*

**Barnum effect.** Refers to the readiness of people to believe that general descriptions, as given in astrological characterizations, refer to them personally.

**basal mental age.** In individual tests of the Binet type, the highest age level at which, and below which, all tests are passed. See also *mental age.*

**base-rate rule.** A rule in probability theory, which states that the probability of something (e.g., a person or object) being a member of a class is greater the more class members there are. People frequently violate this rule when reasoning about real-world situations.

**basic level.** In a hierarchy of concepts, the level at which one first categorizes an object.

**basilar membrane.** A membrane of the ear within the coils of the cochlea supporting the organ of Corti. Movements of the basilar membrane stimulate the hair cells of the organ of Corti, producing the neural effects of auditory stimulation. See also *cochlea.*

**behavior.** Those activities of an organism that can be observed by another organism or by an experimenter's instruments. Included within behavior are verbal reports made about subjective, conscious experiences. See also *conscious processes.*

**behavior genetics.** The study of the inheritance of behavioral characteristics.

**behavior modification.** See *behavior therapy.*

**behavior therapy.** A method of psychotherapy based on learning principles. It uses such techniques as counterconditioning, reinforcement, and shaping to modify behavior (syn. *behavior modification*). See also *cognitive behavior therapy.*

**behavioral assessment.** Personality appraisal through direct observations of behavior, often in controlled or contrived social situations. See also *personality assessment.*

**behavioral medicine.** An interdisciplinary field that focuses on how social, psychological, and biological variables contribute to illness and how behavior and environments can be changed to promote health. An outgrowth of earlier research on psychosomatic aspects of illness. See also *psychosomatic disorder*.

**behavioral perspective.** An approach to psychology that focuses only on observable behavior, and tries to explain it in terms of its relation to environmental events. See also *behaviorism*.

**behavioral rehearsal.** A technique used by behavior therapists in which the therapist helps the individual rehearse, or role-play, more adaptive behaviors. Practicing assertive response in situations where a person tends to be timid is an example. See also *assertiveness training*.

**behavioral sciences.** The sciences concerned in one way or another with the behavior of humans and lower organisms (especially social anthropology, psychology, and sociology but including some aspects of biology, economics, political science, history, philosophy, and other fields of study.)

**behaviorism.** A school or system of psychology associated with the name of John B. Watson; it defined psychology as the study of behavior and limited the data of psychology to observable activities. In its classical form it was more restrictive than the contemporary behavioral viewpoint in psychology.

**belief-driven learning.** A kind of associative learning in which people have prior beliefs about the relation that has to be learned; learning is driven by the beliefs as well as by the input. See also *data-driven learning*.

**benzodiazepines.** A class of drugs with similar chemical structures that are effective in reducing anxiety. Examples are diazepam (Valium) and alprozolam (Xanax). See *antianxiety drug*.

**binocular cues.** See *distance cues*.

**binocular disparity.** The fact that an object projects slightly different images on the two retinas due to the different positions of the right and left eyes.

**binocular parallax.** A cue for depth perception that arises because any visible point will differ slightly in its direction to the two eyes. See also *binocular disparity*.

**biofeedback.** A procedure that permits individuals to monitor their own physiological processes (such as heart rate, blood pressure) which they are normally unaware of, to learn to control them.

**biological perspective.** An approach to psychology that tries to explain behavior in terms of electrical and chemical events taking place inside the body, particularly within the brain and nervous system.

**biological psychologist.** A psychologist concerned with the relationship between biological processes and behavior. Same as *physiological psychologist*.

**biological therapy.** Treatment of emotional problems or mental disorders by drugs, electric shock, or other methods directly affecting bodily processes. See also *psychotherapy*.

**bipolar cells.** Cells in the retina that transmit electrical impulses from photoreceptors to ganglion cells. See also *ganglia, photoreceptors, retina*.

**bipolar disorder.** A mood disorder in which people experience episodes of depression and mania (exaggerated excitement) or of mania alone. Typically the individual alternates between the two extremes, often with periods of normal mood in between (syn. *manic-depression*). See also *depression, mood disorder*.

**blind spot.** An insensitive area of the retina where the nerve fibers from the ganglion cells join to form the optic nerve.

**blocking.** A phenomenon in classical conditioning: if one conditioned stimulus reliably predicts an unconditioned stimulus, and another conditioned stimulus is added, the relation between the added conditioned stimulus and the unconditioned stimulus will not be learned.

**blood alcohol concentration (BAC).** The concentration, in milligrams, of alcohol per 100 milliliters of blood. The legal definition of intoxication in most states is a blood alcohol concentration of .10 percent (100 milligrams of alcohol per 100 milliliters of blood).

**blood pressure.** The pressure of the blood against the walls of the blood vessels. Changes in blood pressure following stimulation serve as one indicator of emotion.

**bottom-up processes.** Processes in perception, memory, and comprehension that are driven solely by the information input, and that do not involve the organism's prior knowledge and expectations. See also *top-down processes*.

**brain stem.** The structures lying near the core of the brain; essentially all of the brain with the exception of the cerebrum and the cerebellum and their dependent parts.

**brightness.** The dimension of color that describes its nearness in brilliance to white (as contrasted to black). A bright color reflects more light than a dark one. See also *hue, saturation*.

**Broca's area.** A portion of the left cerebral hemisphere involved in the control of speech. Individuals with damage in this area have difficulty enunciating words correctly and speak in a slow and labored way; their speech often makes sense, but it includes only key words.

**bulimia.** An eating disorder which mainly afflicts young women and is characterized by episodes of binge eating, followed by attempts to purge the excess by means of vomiting and laxatives. See also *anorexia nervosa*.

### C

**cannabis.** The hemp plant from which marijuana is obtained. See also *marijuana*.

**Cannon-Bard theory.** A classical theory of emotion proposed by Cannon and Bard. The theory states that an emotion-producing stimulus activates the cortex and bodily responses at the same time; bodily changes and the experience of emotion occur simultaneously. See also *cognitive-appraisal theory, James-Lange theory*.

**cardiac muscle.** A special kind of muscle found only in the heart. See also *smooth muscle, striate muscle*.

**cardinal disposition.** In Gordon Allport's personality theory, a personality trait that influences virutally all aspects of an individual's behavior. See also *central disposition, common trait, personal disposition, secondary disposition*.

**case history.** A biography obtained for scientific purposes; the material is sometimes supplied by interview, sometimes collected over the years. See also *longitudinal study*.

**castration.** Surgical removal of the gonads; in the male, removal of the testes; in the female, removal of the ovaries.

**catatonic immobility.** A fixity of posture maintained for long periods with accompanying muscular rigidity and a trance-like state of consciousness. A symptom in some cases of schizophrenia. See also *schizophrenia*.

**categorization.** Assigning an object to a concept. See also *concept*.

**catharsis.** Reduction of an impulse or emotion through direct or indirect expression, particularly verbal and fantasy expression.

**central core.** The most central and the evolutionarily oldest portion of the brain. It includes structures that regulate basic life processes, including most of the brain stem. See also *brain stem, cerebellum, hypothalamus, reticular system*.

**central disposition.** In Gordon Allport's personality theory, a personality trait that influences many aspects of an individual's behavior. Most people have a small number of *central dispositions* and a much larger number of *secondary dispositions*. See also *cardinal disposition, common trait, personal disposition, secondary disposition*.

**central executive.** In short-term memory, a hypothesized component of the encoding process that coordinates the acoustic and visual buffers. See also *acoustic buffer, encoding, short-term memory, visual buffer*.

**central fissure.** A fissure of each cerebral hemisphere that separates the frontal and parietal lobes (syn. *fissure of Rolando*).

**central nervous system.** In vertebrates, the brain and spinal cord, as distinct from the nerve trunks and their peripheral connections. See also *autonomic nervous system, peripheral nervous system*.

**cerebellum.** Lobed structure attached to the rear of the brain stem that regulates muscle tone and coordination of intricate movements.

**cerebral cortex.** The surface layer of the cerebral hemispheres in higher animals, including humans. It is commonly called gray matter because its many cell bodies give it a gray appearance in cross section, in contrast with the myelinated nerve fibers that make up the white matter in the center.

**cerebral hemisphere.** Two large masses of nerve cells and fibers constituting the bulk of the brain in humans and other higher animals. The hemispheres are separated by a deep fissure, but connected by a broad band of fibers, the corpus callosum (syn. *cerebrum*). See also *cerebral cortex, left hemisphere, right hemisphere, split-brain subject*.

**cerebrum.** See *cerebral hemispheres*.

**childhood amnesia.** The inability to recall events from the first years of one's life.

**chlorpromazine.** See *antipsychotic drug*.

**chromatic colors.** All colors other than black, white, and gray; for instance, red, yellow, blue. See also *achromatic colors*.

**chromosome.** Rodlike structures found in pairs in all the cells of the body, carrying the genetic determiners (genes) that are transmitted from parent to offspring. A human cell has 46 chromosomes, arranged in 23 pairs, one member of each pair deriving from the mother, one from the father. See also *gene*.

**chronological age (CA).** Age from birth; calendar age. See also *mental age*.

**chunk.** The largest meaningful unit of information that can be stored in short-term memory; short-term memory holds 7±2 chunks. See also *short-term memory*.

**cilia.** Hairlike structures that are sometimes parts of receptors.

**circadian rhythm.** A cycle or rhythm that is roughly 24 hours long. Sleep-wakefulness, body temperature, and water excretion follow a circadian rhythm, as do a number of behavioral and psychological variables.

**clairvoyance.** Perception of objects or events that do not provide a stimulus to the known senses (for example, identifying a concealed playing card, the identity of which is unknown). See also *extrasensory perception, parapsychology, precognition, psi, psychokinesis, telepathy*.

**classical concept.** A concept where every instance must have every property mentioned in the concept. An example is the concept of *bachelor*; every instance must have the properties of being adult, male, and unmarried. See also *fuzzy concept*.

**classical conditioning.** Conditioned response experiments conforming to the pattern of Pavlov's experiment. The main feature is that the originally neutral conditioned stimulus, through repeated pairing with the unconditioned one, acquires the response originally given to the unconditioned stimulus. See also *operant conditioning*.

**claustrophobia.** Fear of closed places. See also *phobia*.

**client-centered therapy.** A method of psychotherapy developed by Carl Rogers in which the therapist is nondirective and reflective and does not interpret or advise. The operating assumption is that the client is the best expert on his or her problems and can work them out in a nonjudgmental, accepting atmosphere. (syn. *nondirective counseling*). See also *humanistic therapies*.

**clinical psychologist.** A psychologist, usually with a Ph.D. or Psy.D. degree, trained in the diagnosis and treatment of emotional or behavioral problems and mental disorders. See also *counseling psychologist, psychiatrist*.

**cocaine.** A central nervous system stimulant derived from leaves of the coca plant. Increases energy, produces euphoria, and in large doses causes paranoia.

**cochlea.** The portion of the inner ear containing the receptors for hearing. See also *basilar membrane, organ of Corti*.

**coding.** See *encoding*.

**coding by pattern.** Coding the quality of a sensation in terms of the pattern of neural firing. See also *coding by specificity*.

**coding by specificity.** Coding the quality of a sensation in terms of the specific neurons involved. See also *coding by pattern, specific nerve energies*.

**coefficient of correlation.** A numerical index used to indicate the degree of correspondence between two sets of paired measurements. The most common kind is the product-moment coefficient designated by *r*.

**cognition.** An individual's thoughts, knowledge, interpretations, understandings, or ideas. See also *cognitive processes*.

**cognitive appraisal.** The interpretation of an event or situation with respect to one's goals and well-being. The cognitive appraisal of an event influences both the quality and intensity of the emotion experienced and the degree of perceived threat.

**cognitive behavior therapy.** A psychotherapy approach that emphasizes the influence of a person's beliefs, thoughts, and self-statements on behavior. Combines behavior therapy methods with techniques designed to change the way the individual thinks about self and events. See also *behavior therapy*.

**cognitive dissonance.** The condition in which one has beliefs or attitudes that disagree with each other or with behavioral tendencies; when such cognitive dissonance arises, the subject is motivated to reduce the dissonance through changes in behavior or cognition.

**cognitive map.** A hypothetical structure in memory that preserves and organizes information about the various events that occur in a learning situation; a mental picture of the learning situation. See also *schema*.

**cognitive perspective.** An approach to psychology that focuses on mental processes such as perceiving, remembering, reasoning, deciding, and problem solving, and tries to explain behavior in terms of these mental processes. See also *cognitive psychology, cognitive science*.

**cognitive processes.** Mental processes of perception, memory, and information processing by which the individual acquires information, makes plans, and solves problems.

**cognitive psychology.** A general approach to psychology that stresses the role of mental processes in understanding behavior. The cognitive psychologist explains behavior at the level of mental representations and the mental processes that operate on these representations to produce products (including responses). The approach is not restricted to the study of thought and knowledge; its early concerns with these topics led to the label "cognitive psychology," but in recent years the approach has been generalized to all areas of psychology. See also *artificial intelligence, cognitive science, information-processing model, mental representation*.

**cognitive response theory.** A theory that proposes that persuasion induced by a communication is actually self-persuasion produced by the thoughts that the individual generates while receiving or even just anticipating the communication.

**cognitive science.** A term introduced in the 1970s to focus attention on how humans acquire and organize knowledge; a "new" science dedicated to understanding cognition. In addition to psychology, the disciplines relevant to cognitive science are neuroscience, linguistics, philosophy, mathematics, and computer science (particularly that branch of computer science known as artificial intelligence). See also *artificial intelligence, cognitive psychology.*

**cognitive-appraisal theory.** A theory of emotion that proposes that the subjective emotional state is a function of the individual's appraisal, or analysis, of the emotion-arousing situation. A state of physiological arousal can produce different emotions (even antithetical ones) depending on how the person appraises the situation. See also *Cannon-Bard theory, James-Lange theory.*

**cognitive distortions.** In Beck's theory of depression, systematic errors in thinking that lead depressed individuals to misperceive reality in a way that contributes to their negative self-schema. Examples are overgeneralization (drawing a sweeping conclusion on the basis of a single negative event) and selective abstraction (focusing on an insignificant negative detail while ignoring the more important positive features of a situation). See also *depression, self-schema.*

**cognitive triad.** In Beck's theory, the major concommitant, and possibly cause, of depression. Consists of negative thoughts about the self, the present situation, and the future. See also *depression.*

**color blindness.** Defective discrimination of chromatic colors. See also *dichromatism, monochromatism, red-green color blindness, trichromatism.*

**color circle.** An arrangement of chromatic colors on the circumference of a circle in the order in which they appear in the spectrum but with the addition of nonspectral reds and purples. The colors are so arranged that those opposite each other are complementaries in addictive mixture. See also *color solid.*

**color constancy.** The tendency to see a familiar object as of the same color, regardless of changes in illumination on it that alter its stimulus properties. See also *perceptual constancy.*

**color solid.** A three-dimensional representation of the psychological dimensions of color, with hue around the circumference, saturation along each radius, and brightness from top to bottom. See also *color circle.*

**color-opponent cells.** In color vision, cells that respond only to their two opponent colors. See also *opponent-color theory.*

**common trait.** In Gordon Allport's personality theory, a trait on which different individuals can be compared with one another. Contrasted with *personal disposition,* which refers to the unique patterning or configuration of traits within the individual. See also *cardinal disposition, central disposition, personal disposition, secondary disposition.*

**companionate love.** An affection people feel for those with whom their lives are deeply intertwined. Characterized by trust, caring, tolerance of the partner's flaws and idiosyncrasies, and an emotional tone of warmth and affection. Contrasted with *passionate love.* See also *passionate love.*

**complementary colors.** Two colors that in additive mixture yield either a gray or an unsaturated color of the hue of the stronger component.

**complex cell.** A cell in the visual cortex that responds to a bar of light or straight edge of a particular orientation located anywhere in the visual field. See also *simple cell.*

**complex learning.** Learning that involves more than forming associations; for example, using a strategy to solve a problem or forming a mental map of one's surroundings. Contrasted with habituation and conditioning which are simpler types of learning. See also *habituation, classical conditioning, operant conditioning.*

**compulsion.** A repetitive action that a person feels driven to make and is unable to resist; ritualistic behavior. See also *obsession, obsessive-compulsive disorder.*

**computer program.** See *program.*

**computer simulation.** The use of a computer to simulate a phenomenon or system in order to study its properties. In psychology, the simulation usually involves an attempt to program a computer to mimic how the mind processes information and solves problems. In this sense, the computer program is literally a theory of how the mind functions See also *artificial intelligence, cognitive psychology, information-processing model.*

**computerized axial tomography (CT).** A computer-based procedure that analyzes data obtained by a scanning beam of X rays to provide a picture of a cross-sectional slice through the body or brain.

**concept.** The properties or relationships common to a class of objects or ideas. Concepts may be of concrete things (such as the concept *poodle* referring to a given variety of dog) or of abstract ideas (such as *equality, justice, number*), implying relationships common to many different kinds of objects or ideas. See also *classical concept, fuzzy concept.*

**concrete operational stage.** Piaget's third stage of cognitive development (ages 7 to 11 years) during which a child becomes capable of logical thought and achieves conservation concepts. See also *conservation.*

**conditioned emotion.** An emotional response acquired by conditioning: one aroused by a stimulus that did not originally evoke it. See also *conditioning.*

**conditioned fear.** A fear acquired by classical conditioning. The object that the organism comes to fear was originally neutral, but when it is repeatedly paired with an aversive stimulus it becomes an object of fear.

**conditioned reinforcer.** A stimulus that has become reinforcing through prior association with a reinforcing stimulus (syn. *secondary reinforcer*). See also *reinforcing stimulus.*

**conditioned response (CR).** In classical conditioning, the learned or acquired response to a conditioned stimulus; in other words, to a stimulus that did not evoke the response originally. See also *conditioned stimulus, unconditioned response, unconditioned stimulus.*

**conditioned stimulus (CS).** In classical conditioning, a stimulus previously neutral that comes to elicit a conditioned response through association with an unconditioned stimulus. See also *conditioned response, unconditioned response, unconditioned stimulus.*

**conditioning.** The process by which conditioned responses are learned. See also *classical conditioning, operant conditioning.*

**conduction loss.** A hearing deficit in which threshold elevation (loss of sensitivity) occurs equally at all frequencies as the result of poor conduction in the middle ear. See also *sensory-neural loss.*

**cone.** In the eye, a specialized cell of the retina found predominantly in the fovea and more sparsely throughout the retina. The cones mediate both chromatic and achromatic sensations. See also *fovea, retina, rod.*

**conflict.** The simultaneous presence of opposing or mutually exclusive impulses, desires, or tendencies. See also *ambivalence.*

**conjunction rule.** A rule in probability theory, which states that the probability of a proposition cannot be less than the probability of that proposition conjoined with another proposition. People frequently violate the rule when reasoning about real-world situations.

**connectionist models.** Models of cognitive processes (like perception) that incorporate a network of nodes, with excitatory and inhibitory connections between them.

**connotative meaning.** The suggestive and emotional meanings of a word or symbol, beyond its denotative meaning. Thus, *naked* and *nude* both refer to an unclothed body (denotative meaning), but they have somewhat different connotations. See also *denotative meaning*.

**conscience.** An internal recognition of standards of right and wrong by which the individual judges his or her conduct. See also *superego*.

**conscious processes.** Events such as perceptions, private thoughts, and dreams, of which only the person is aware. They are accessible to others through verbal report or by way of inference from other behavior (syn. *experience, awareness*).

**consciousness.** We are conscious when we are aware of external events, reflect on past experiences, engage in problem solving, are selective in attending to some stimuli rather than others, and deliberately choose an action in response to environmental conditions and personal goals. In short, consciousness has to do with a) *monitoring* ourselves and our environment so that percepts, memories, and thoughts are accurately represented in awareness; and b) *controlling* ourselves and our environment so that we are able to initiate and terminate behavioral and cognitive activities. In some contexts, the term is used as a synonym for *awareness*.

**conservation.** Piaget's term for the ability of the child to recognize that certain properties of objects (such as mass, volume, number) do not change despite transformations in the appearance of the objects. See also *preoperational stage*.

**construct validity.** The ability of a test or assessment instrument to confirm predictions of the theory underlying some theoretical concept or construct. Confirming results validate both the concept and the assessment instrument simultaneously. See also *criterion problem, validity*.

**constructive memory.** Using general knowledge stored in memory to construct and elaborate a more complete and detailed account of some event.

**contemporary consequences.** Outcomes in an individual's life that result from a childhood personality disposition that he or she has carried into adulthood from childhood. See also *cumulative consequences, path analysis*.

**contrast sensitivity.** In visual perception, the ability to discriminate between dark and light stripes under various conditions.

**control group.** In an experimental design

contrasting two groups, that group not given the treatment whose effect is under study. See also *experimental group*.

**control processes.** Regulatory processes that serve to establish equilibrium or monitor goal-directed activities. See also *homeostasis*.

**controlled stimulation.** Conditions in which the perceptual experiences of an organism are systematically varied in order to determine the effect on subsequent performance. For example, rearing kittens in an environment where they see only vertical stripes for the first few months of life or having humans wear prism goggles that distort the directions of objects.

**core.** The part of a concept that contains the properties that are more essential for determining membership in the concept. See also *prototype*.

**cornea.** The transparent surface of the eye through which light enters and rays are bent inward to begin image formation. See also *lens, pupil, retina*.

**corpus callosum.** A large band of nerve fibers connecting the two cerebral hemispheres.

**correlation.** See *coefficient of correlation*.

**correlational method.** A research method used to determine whether some difference that is not under the researcher's control is associated, or correlated, with another difference of interest. See also *coefficient of correlation*.

**corticotropin-release factor (CRF).** A substance secreted by neurons in the hypothalamus in response to stress. It, in turn, is carried through a channel-like structure to the pituitary gland, causing ACTH (the body's major "stress" hormone) to be released. See also *adrenocorticotropic hormone*.

**cortisol.** One of the steroid hormones produced by the adrenal glands. It has many effects on the body, including the formation of glucose, the reduction of inflammation, and the retention of water. Its level in the blood is used as a measure of stress. See also *adrenal glands, adrenocortical system*.

**counseling psychologist.** A trained psychologist, usually with a Ph.D. or Psy.D. degree, who deals with personal problems not classified as illness, such as academic, social, or vocational problems of students. He or she has skills similar to those of the clinical psychologist but usually works in a nonmedical setting. See also *clinical psychologist, psychiatrist*.

**counterconditioning.** In behavior therapy, the replacement of a particular response to a stimulus by the establishment of another (usually incompatible) response.

**CRF.** See *corticotropin-release factor*.

**criterion.** (a) A set of scores or other records against which the success of a predictive test is verified. (b) A standard selected as the goal to be achieved in a learning task; for example, the number of runs through a maze to be made without error as an indication that the maze has been mastered.

**criterion method of test construction.** See *empirical method of test construction*.

**criterion problem.** The difficulty that arises in validating a test or assessment instrument when there is no criterion behavior the investigator is willing to accept as the "true" measure of the concept being evaluated. See also *construct validity, validity*.

**criterion validity.** The ability of a test or assessment instrument to predict the behavior it is designed to predict (syn. *empirical validity*). See also *criterion, validity*.

**critical period.** A stage in development during which the organism is optimally ready to learn certain response patterns. There is some evidence for a critical period in language learning; a child not exposed to language prior to adolescence has great difficulty acquiring language thereafter (syn. *sensitive period*). See also *ethology, imprinting*.

**cross-pressure.** Conflicting social influences on an individual's beliefs, attitudes, or behaviors. Usually arises when a person identifies with more than one reference group.

**cues to distance.** See *distance cues*.

**culture-fair test.** A type of intelligence test that has been constructed to minimize bias due to the differing experiences of children raised in a rural rather than an urban culture or in a lower-class rather than in a middle-class or upper-class culture (syn. *culture-free test*).

**cumulative consequences.** Outcomes in an individual's life that result from the cumulative effects of some childhood personality disposition. The childhood disposition initiates a chain of events that culminates in the later outcomes—even if the individual no longer carries the disposition as an adult. See also *contemporary consequences, path analysis*.

**cumulative curve.** A graphic record of the responses emitted during an operant conditioning session. The slope of the cumulative curve indicates the rate of response.

**D**

**dark adaptation.** The increased sensitivity to light when the subject has been continuously in the dark or under conditions of reduced illumination. See also *light adaptation.*

**data-driven learning.** A kind of associative learning in which people have no prior beliefs about the relation that has to be learned; learning is driven only by the input or data. See also *belief-driven learning.*

**db.** See *decibel.*

**decibel (db).** A measure of sound intensity. A change of 10 decibels corresponds to a change in sound power of 10 times; 20 decibels, a change of 100 times; and so forth.

**deductive reasoning.** Reasoning about arguments in which the conclusion cannot be false if the premises are true. See also *inductive reasoning.*

**defense mechanisms.** In Freud's psychoanalytic theory, the strategies used by the ego to ward off or to reduce anxiety. These consist of adjustments made unconsciously, either through action or the avoidance of action, to keep from recognizing personal motives that might threaten self-esteem or heighten anxiety. Repression, denial, and projection are examples.

**degradation.** The process in which enzymes in the membrane of a receiving neuron react with a neurotransmitter to break it up chemically and make it inactive; one method (in addition to reuptake) of terminating a neurotransmitter's action. See also *neurotransmitter, reuptake.*

**deindividuation.** A psychological state in which persons feel that they have lost their personal identities and have merged anonymously into a group. Hypothesized to be the basis for the impulsive, aggressive behaviors sometimes shown by mobs and crowds.

**delayed conditioning.** A classical conditioning procedure in which the CS begins several seconds or more before the onset of the UCS and continues with it until the response occurs. See also *simultaneous conditioning, trace conditioning.*

**delta waves.** See *electroencephalogram.*

**delusion.** False beliefs characteristic of some forms of psychotic disorder. They often take the form of delusions of grandeur or delusions of persecution. See also *hallucination, illusion, paranoid schizophrenia.*

**dendrite.** The specialized portion of the neuron that (together with the cell body) receives impulses from other neurons. See also *axon, neuron.*

**denial.** A defense mechanism by which unacceptable impulses or ideas are not perceived or allowed into full awareness. See also *defense mechanisms.*

**denotative meaning.** The primary meaning of a symbol, something specific to which the symbol refers or points (for example, my street address is denotative; whether I live in a desirable neighborhood is a connotative meaning secondary to the address itself). See also *connotative meaning.*

**deoxyribonucleic acid (DNA).** The basic hereditary material of all organisms; a nucleic acid polymer incorporating the sugar deoxyribose. In higher organisms, the great bulk of DNA is located within the chromosomes.

**dependent variable.** The variable whose measured changes are attributed to (or correspond to) changes in the independent variable. In psychological experiments, the dependent variable is often a response to a measured stimulus. See also *independent variable.*

**depolarization.** Change in the resting potential of the nerve cell membrane in the direction of the action potential; the inside of the membrane becomes more positive. See also *action potential, resting potential.*

**depressants.** Psychoactive drugs that tend to reduce arousal. Alcohol, barbiturates, and opiates are examples.

**depression.** A mood disorder characterized by sadness and dejection, decreased motivation and interest in life, negative thoughts (for example, feelings of helplessness, inadequacy, and low self-esteem) and such physical symptoms as sleep disturbances, loss of appetite, and fatigue. See also *mood disorder.*

**depth perception.** The perception of the distance of an object from the observer or the distance from front to back of a solid object. See also *distance cues.*

**determinism.** See *psychological determinism.*

**developmental psychologist.** A psychologist whose research interest lies in studying the changes that occur as a function of the growth and development of the organism, in particular the relationship between early and later behavior.

**deviation IQ.** An intelligence quotient (IQ) computed as a standard score with a mean of 100 and a standard deviation of 15 (Wechsler) or 16 (Stanford-Binet), to correspond approximately to traditional intelligence quotients. See also *intelligence quotient.*

**diathesis-stress model.** See *vulnerability-stress model.*

**dichromatism.** Color blindness in which either the red-green or the blue-yellow system is lacking. The red-green form is relatively common; the blue-yellow form is the rarest of all forms of color blindness. See also *monochromatism, red-green color blindness, trichromatism.*

**diencephalon.** A cluster of nuclei, located below the cerebral cortex, that is involved in the consolidation of new memories. See also *amygdala, hippocampus.*

**difference reduction.** A problem-solving strategy in which one sets up subgoals that, when obtained, put one in a state closer to the goal. See also *means-ends analysis, working backwards.*

**difference threshold.** The minimum difference between a pair of stimuli that can be perceived under experimental conditions. See also *absolute threshold, just noticeable difference, threshold, Weber's law.*

**differential reinforcement.** A procedure in conditioning in which reinforcement is given only in the presence of a certain stimulus. The outcome of this procedure is a conditioned discrimination.

**diffusion of responsibility.** The tendency for persons in a group situation to fail to take action (as in an emergency) because others are present, thus diffusing the responsibility for acting. A major factor in inhibiting bystanders from intervening in emergencies.

**disaster syndrome.** A three-stage behavior pattern that is a common reaction to a traumatic event. The person is at first dazed and disoriented, then passive but able to respond to instructions, and finally anxious, apprehensive, and unable to concentrate.

**discrimination.** (a) In perception, the detection of differences between two stimuli. (b) In conditioning, the differential response to the positive (reinforced) stimulus and to the negative (nonreinforced) stimulus. See also *generalization.* (c) In social psychology, prejudicial treatment, as in racial discrimination. See also *prejudice.*

**discriminative stimulus.** A stimulus that becomes an occasion for an operant response; for example, a knock that leads one to open the door. The stimulus does not elicit the operant response in the same sense that a stimulus elicits respondent behavior. See also *operant behavior.*

**dishabituation.** A return in strength of a response following habituation to a repeated stimulus. Indicates renewed attention on the part of the organism to a change in the stimulus situation. See also *habituation.*

**displaced aggression.** Aggression against a person or object other than that which was (or is) the source of frustration. See also *scapegoat.*

**displacement.** a) A defense mechanism whereby a motive that may not be directly expressed (such as sex or aggression) appears in a more acceptable form. See also *defense mechanism.* b) The principle of loss of items from short-term memory as too many new items are added. See also *chunk, short-term memory.*

**dispositional attribution.** Attributing a person's actions to internal dispositions (attitudes, traits, motives), as opposed to situational factors. See also *situational attribution.*

**dissociation.** The process whereby some ideas, feelings, or activities lose relationship to other aspects of consciousness and personality and operate automatically or independently.

**dissonance.** (a) In music, an inharmonious combination of sounds; contrasted with consonance. (b) In social psychology, Festinger's term for discomfort arising from a perceived inconsistency between one's attitudes and one's behavior. See also *cognitive dissonance.*

**distance cues.** (a) In vision, the monocular cues according to which the distance of objects is perceived—such as superposition of objects, perspective, light and shadow, and relative movement—and the binocular cues used in stereoscopic vision. See also *stereoscopic vision.* (b) In audition, the corresponding cues governing perception of distance and direction, such as intensity and time differences of sound reaching the two ears.

**dizygotic (DZ) twins.** Twins developed from separate eggs. They are no more alike genetically than ordinary brothers and sisters and can be of the same or different sexes (syn. *fraternal twins*). See also *monozygotic twins.*

**DNA.** See *deoxyribonucleic acid.*

**dominance.** The higher status position when social rank is organized according to a dominance–submission hierarchy; commonly found in human societies and in certain animal groups.

**dominant gene.** A member of a gene pair which, if present, determines that the individual will show the trait controlled by the gene, regardless of whether the other member of the pair is the same or different (that is, recessive). See also *recessive gene.*

**dopamine.** A neurotransmitter of the central nervous system believed to play a role in schizophrenia. It is synthesized from an amino acid by the action of certain body enzymes and, in turn, is converted into norepinephrine. See also *neurotransmitter, norepinephrine.*

**dopamine hypothesis.** The hypothesis that schizophrenia is related to an excess of the neurotransmitter dopamine; either schizophrenics produce too much dopamine or have an abnormally large number of dopamine receptors. See also *dopamine, schizophrenia.*

**double blind.** An experimental design, often used in drug research, in which neither the investigator not the patients know which subjects are in the treatment and which in the nontreatment condition until the experiment has been completed.

**Down's syndrome.** A form of mental deficiency produced by a genetic abnormality (an extra chromosome on pair 21). Characteristics include a thick tongue, extra eyelid folds, and short, stubby fingers (syn. *mongolism*).

**drive.** (a) An aroused condition of the organism based on deprivation or noxious stimulation, including tissue needs, drug or hormonal conditions, and specified internal or external stimuli, as in pain. (b) Loosely, any motive. See also *motive, need.*

**drive-reduction theory.** The theory that a motivated sequence of behavior can be best explained as moving from an aversive state of heightened tension (or drive) to a goal state in which the drive is reduced. The goal of the sequence, in other words, is drive reduction. See also *drive, incentive theory, motive, need.*

**DSM-III-R.** The third edition of the *Diagnostic and Statistical Manual of the American Psychiatric Association*, revised.

**dual-memory theory.** A theory that distinguishes between a short-term memory of limited capacity and a virtually unlimited long-term memory. Information can only be encoded into long-term memory via short-term memory. See also *long-term memory, short-term memory.*

**DZ twins.** See *dizygotic twins.*

### E

**eardrum.** The membrane at the inner end of the auditory canal, leading to the middle ear. See also *middle ear.*

**early selection.** Selective attention that occurs in the early stages of recognition, when the organism is constructing a description of the input and before the meaning of the input has been determined. See also *late selection, selective attention.*

**educational psychologist.** A psychologist whose research interest lies in the application of psychological principles to the education of children and adults in schools. See also *school psychologist.*

**EEG.** See *electroencephalogram.*

**efferent neuron.** See *motor neuron.*

**ego.** In Freud's tripartite division of the personality, the rational part or controlling self. Operates on the *reality principle*, holding back the impulses of the id until they can be satisfied in socially approved ways. See also *id, reality principle, su-*

*perego.*

**ego analyst.** A psychoanalyst, who focuses on the integrative, positive functions of the ego (for example, coping with the environment) rather than the functions of the id (for example, gratifying sexual impulses). Heinz Hartman and David Rapaport are considered ego analysts. See also *ego, id, psychoanalyst.*

**eidetic imagery.** The ability to retain visual images of pictures that are almost photographic in clarity. Such images can be described in far greater detail than would be possible from memory alone. See also *mental imagery.*

**elaboration.** A memory process wherein one expands verbal material so as to increase the number of ways to retrieve the material.

**electroconvulsive therapy (ECT).** A treatment for severe depression in which a mild electric current is applied to the brain, producing a seizure similar to an epileptic convulsion. Also known as *electroshock therapy.*

**electroencephalogram (EEG).** A record obtained by attaching electrodes to the scalp (or occasionally to the exposed brain). Among the brain waves observed are alpha waves (8-13 Hz), characteristic of relaxed wakefulness; delta waves (1-3 Hz), a slower wave of high amplitude that occurs during deep sleep; and theta waves (4-7 Hz), a pattern characteristic of the EEG of the hippocampus and indicative of behavioral arousal.

**electroshock therapy.** See *electroconvulsive therapy.*

**emotion.** The condition of the organism during affectively toned experience, whether mild or intense. See also *affective experience.*

**emotion-focused coping.** Ways of reducing anxiety or stress that do not deal directly with the anxiety-producing situation; defense mechanisms are a form of emotion-focused coping. See also *problem-focused coping.*

**empirical method of test construction.** Selecting items for a test or assessment instrument by comparing the responses of some criterion group (for example, paranoid individuals) with a control group and retaining only those that discriminate between the two groups. Also called the criterion method of test construction. See also *rational method of test construction.*

**empirical validity.** See *criterion validity.*

**empiricism.** The view that behavior is learned as a result of experience. See also *nativism.*

**encoding.** Transforming a sensory input into a form (code) that can be processed by the memory system.

**endocrine system.** A system of ductless glands that discharge their secretions (hormones) into the extracellular fluid around capillaries and hence into the bloodstream. The hormones secreted by the endocrine glands are important integrators of bodily functions. See also *hormone.*

**endorphins.** A group of neurotransmitters in the brain released in response to stress that have the effect of blocking pain. Opiates, a class of drugs that includes heroin and morphine, are similar in molecular shape to endorphins and mimic this naturally occurring substance.

**engineering psychologist.** A psychologist who specializes in the relationship between people and machines, seeking, for example, to design machines that minimize human error.

**epinephrine.** The principal hormone secreted by the adrenal medulla in response to stressful situations. Its effects are similar to those brought about by stimulation of the sympathetic division of the autonomic nervous system (for example, arousal, increased heart rate and blood pressure). It is also an excitatory neurotransmitter in the central nervous system (syn. *adrenalin*). See also *adrenal gland, norepinephrine.*

**episodic memory.** A type of memory that stores facts about personal episodes. The fact or episode is encoded with respect to the memorizer, and often with respect to the specific time and place as well. See also *semantic memory.*

**equilibratory senses.** The senses that give discrimination of the position of the body in space and of the movement of the body as a whole. See also *kinesthesis, semicircular canals, vestibular sacs.*

**escape learning.** Learning to make a response in order to terminate an aversive event. See also *avoidance learning.*

**ESP.** See *extrasensory perception.*

**estrogens.** A group of female sex hormones produced principally by the ovaries. They are responsible for the development of female body characteristics and hair distribution, and for preparing the reproductive system for pregnancy. See also *androgens.*

**estrous cycle.** Recurring episodes of sexual receptivity that precede ovulation in most female mammals. They are characterized by rising and falling levels of estrogens and progesterone in the bloodstream. See also *estrogens, progesterone.*

**ethology.** An interdisciplinary science combining zoology, biology, and psychology to study animal behavior, primarily in the natural environment of the species

being observed. Most of the work has been on insects, birds, and fish, but in recent years the approach has been applied to human behavior. Naturalistic observation characterizes the approach, and the theoretical ideas tend to focus on the interplay of genetic and environmental factors in understanding behavior. See also *imprinting, instinct.*

**evocative interaction.** The interaction between individuals and their environments that arises because the behavior of different individuals evokes different responses from others. See also *proactive interaction, reactive interaction.*

**evoked potential.** An electric discharge in some part of the nervous system produced by stimulation elsewhere. The measured potential is commonly based on response averaging by a computer.

**evolutionary psychology.** An area of research that studies how psychological processes have evolved by means of natural selection; those behaviors that aided survival or increased the chance of reproduction have tended to persist through the course of evolutionary history.

**exemplar strategy.** A categorization strategy in which (a) old instances of a concept are memorized and (b) a new item is declared a member of that concept if it is sufficiently similar to the memorized instances.

**excitatory synapse.** A synapse at which the neurotransmitter changes the membrane permeability of the receiving cell in the direction of depolarization. See also *depolarization, inhibitory synapse, synapse.*

**expectation.** An anticipation or prediction of future events based on past experience and present stimuli.

**experimental design.** A plan for collecting and treating the data of a proposed experiment. The design is evolved after preliminary exploration, with the aims of economy, precision, and control, so that appropriate inferences and decisions can be made from the data.

**experimental group.** In an experimental design contrasting two groups, that group of subjects given the treatment whose effect is under investigation. See also *control group.*

**experimental method.** The method of investigation of natural events that seeks to control the variables involved so as to more precisely define cause-and-effect relationships. Most frequently done in a laboratory, but need not be. See also *observational method, variable.*

**experimental psychologist.** A behaviorist or cognitive psychologist who uses experimental methods to study how peo-

ple (and other animals) react to sensory stimuli, perceive the world, learn and remember, reason and respond emotionally.

**explicit memory.** The kind of memory that underlies a conscious recollection of something in the past. See also *implicit memory.*

**extinction.** (a) The experimental procedure, following classical or operant conditioning, of presenting the conditioned stimulus without the usual reinforcement. (b) The reduction in response that results from this procedure. See also *reinforcement.*

**extracellular fluid.** Fluid, including the blood, outside the cells; one of the critical variables monitored in the control of thirst.

**extrasensory perception (ESP).** Response to external stimuli without any known sensory contact. See also *clairvoyance, parapsychology, precognition, psi, psychokinesis, telepathy.*

**extraversion.** See *introversion–extraversion.*

**F**

**fact memory.** The kind of memory that presumably stores factual information. See also *skill memory.*

**factor analysis.** A statistical method used in test construction and in interpreting scores from batteries of tests. The method enables the investigator to compute the minimum number of determiners (factors) required to account for the intercorrelations among the scores on the tests making up the battery. See also *general factor, special factor.*

**family therapy.** Psychotherapy with the family members as a group rather than treatment of the patient alone. See also *group therapy.*

**feature detector.** A general term for any perceptual mechanism that detects distinctive features in a complex display. An example is a line (or edge) detector in vision. Since anything we see can be approximated by a series of line segments at angles to each other, feature detectors have been postulated to be the building blocks for recognizing more complex forms.

**Fechner's law.** The assertion that the perceived magnitude of a stimulus increases in proportion to the logarithm of its physical intensity.

**fetal alcohol syndrome.** Abnormal development of the fetus and infant caused by maternal alcohol consumption during pregnancy. Features of the syndrome include retarded growth, small head circumference, a flat nasal bridge, a small midface, shortened eyelids, and mental retardation.

**fight-or-flight response.** A pattern of bodily responses that prepares the organism for an emergency. Most of these physiological changes result from activation of the sympathetic system and the adrenal-cortical system. Includes increases in pupil size, heart rate, blood pressure, respiration, muscle tension, and the secretion of epinephrine, norepinephrine, ACTH and other hormones; decreases in saliva, mucous, digestive activity, and the size of blood vessels. See also *ACTH, adrenal-cortical system, epinephrine, norepinephrine, sympathetic system.*

**figure-ground organization.** Perceiving a pattern as foreground against a background. Patterns are commonly perceived this way even when the stimuli are ambiguous and the foreground–background relationships are reversible.

**file-drawer problem.** A problem that arises because studies that fail to obtain positive results are less likely to be published than studies that do obtain positive results. (Failed studies are thus said to "go into the file drawer" rather than being published.) The file-drawer effect causes the database of known studies to be biased toward confirming studies.

**filter.** Any device that allows some things to pass through it and not others; for example, an electronic device that allows only particular sound frequencies to pass or an optical lens that transmits only certain wavelengths of light. Various types of filters are embedded in the sensory system (optical, mechanical, chemical, neural) that pass some signals and not others. A neuron in the sensory system that is preceded by a filter will respond only to signals that pass through the filter; such a neuron is said to be "tuned" to those signals. See also *specific neuron code hypothesis.*

**fixation.** In Freud's psychoanalytic theory, arrested development through failure to pass beyond one of the earlier stages of psychosexual development or to change the objects of attachment (such as fixation at the oral stage or fixation on the mother).

**flashbulb memory.** A vivid and relatively permanent record of the circumstances in which one learned of an emotionally charged, significant event.

**flooding.** A behavior therapy procedure in which a fearful person exposes himself or herself to what is frightening, in reality or in imagination, for extended periods of time without opportunity to escape. See also *behavior therapy.*

**flow chart.** A diagramatic representation of the sequence of choices and actions in an activity.

**formal operational stage.** Piaget's fourth stage of cognitive development (age 11 and up) in which the child becomes able to use abstract rules.

**fovea.** In the eye, a small area in the central part of the retina, packed with cones; the most sensitive part of the retina for detail vision and color vision in daylight. See also *cone, retina.*

**fraternal twins.** See *dizygotic twins.*

**free association.** (a) The form of word-association experiment in which the subject gives any word he or she thinks of in response to the stimulus word. (b) In psychoanalysis, the effort to report without modification everything that comes into awareness.

**free recall.** A memory task in which a subject is given a list of items (usually one at a time) and is later asked to recall them in any order.

**frequency theory of pitch.** Same as *temporal theory of pitch.*

**Freudian slip.** In psychoanalytic theory, a mistake or substitution of words in speaking or writing that is contrary to the speaker's conscious intention and presumably expresses wishes or thoughts repressed to the unconscious.

**frontal lobe.** A portion of each cerebral hemisphere, in front of the central fissure. See also *occipital lobe, parietal lobe, temporal lobe.*

**frustration.** (a) As an event, the thwarting circumstances that block or interfere with goal-directed activity. (b) As a state, the annoyance, confusion, or anger engendered by being thwarted, disappointed, defeated.

**frustration-aggression hypothesis.** The hypothesis that frustration (thwarting a person's goal-directed efforts) induces an aggressive drive, which, in turn, motivates aggressive behavior.

**fundamental.** The frequency being played in a musical note.

**fundamental attribution error.** The tendency to underestimate situational influences on behavior and assume that some personal characteristic of the individual is responsible; the bias toward dispositional rather than situational attributions. See also *attribution, dispositional attribution, situational attribution.*

**fuzzy concept.** A concept in which one primarily relies on prototype properties in determining membership, and hence cannot always be sure of one's decisions. See also *prototype.*

## G

**GABA.** See *gamma-aminobutyric acid.*

**galvanic skin response (GRS).** Changes in electrical conductivity of, or activity in, the skin, detected by a sensitive galvanometer. The reactions are commonly used as an emotional indicator.

**gamma-aminobutyric acid (GABA).** An important inhibitory neurotransmitter.

**ganglia** (sing. *ganglion*). A collection of nerve cell bodies and synapses, constituting a center lying outside the brain and spinal cord, as in the sympathetic ganglia. See also *nuclei.*

**gate control theory of pain.** According to this theory, the sensation of pain requires not only that pain receptors be activated, but also that a neural gate in the spinal cord allow these signals to continue to the brain. Pressure stimulation tends to close the gate; this is why rubbing a hurt area can relieve pain. Attitudes, suggestions, and drugs may act to close the gate.

**gender constancy.** A child's realization that a person's sex does not change with age or appearance (e.g., wearing opposite-sex clothes). A direct analogue to Piaget's concept of *conservation* in the child's understanding of the physical world.

**gender identity.** The degree to which one regards oneself as male or female. See also *sex role, sex typing.*

**gender schema.** A mental structure that organizes the person's perceptual and conceptual world into gender categories (male-female, masculine-feminine). *Gender schema theory* holds that society produces gender identity and sex typing by teaching individuals to use the gender schema as a set of "lenses" through which to view reality. See also *gender identity, schema, sex typing.*

**gene.** The basic unit of hereditary transmission, localized within the chromosomes. Each chromosome contains many genes. Genes are typically in pairs, one member of the pair being found in the chromosome from the father, the other in the corresponding chromosome from the mother. See also *chromosome, dominant gene, recessive gene.*

**general factor (g).** (a) A general ability underlying test scores, especially in tests of intelligence, as distinct from special abilities unique to each test. (b) A general ability with which each of the primary factors correlates. See also *factor analysis, special factor.*

**General Problem Solver (GPS).** A computer program to simulate human problem solving by setting up subgoals and reducing the discrepancies to each subsequent subgoal. See also *simulation.*

**generalization.** (a) In concept formation, problem solving, and transfer of learning, the detection by the learner of a characteristic or principle common to a class of objects, events, or problems. (b) In conditioning, the principle that once a conditioned response has been established to a given stimulus, similar stimuli will also evoke that response. See also *discrimination*.

**generalized anxiety disorder.** An anxiety disorder characterized by persistent tension and apprehension. May be accompanied by such physical symptoms as rapid heart rate, fatigue, disturbed sleep, and dizziness. See also *anxiety disorders*.

**genetics.** That branch of biology concerned with heredity and the means by which hereditary characteristics are transmitted.

**genital stage.** In Freud's psychoanalytic theory, the final stage of psychosexual development, beginning at puberty and culminating in mature adult sexuality. See also *psychosexual development*.

**genotype.** In genetics, the characteristics that an individual has inherited and will transmit to his or her descendants, whether or not the individual manifests these characteristics. See also *phenotype*.

**geon.** In perception, geometric forms (such as cylinders, cones, blocks, and wedges) that comprise the features of objects. Recognition of an object is good to the extent that the geons of the object can be recovered.

**Gestalt psychology.** A system of psychological theory concerned primarily with perception that emphasizes pattern, organization, wholes, and field properties.

**glia cells.** Supporting cells (not neurons) composing a substantial portion of brain tissue; recent speculation suggests that they may play a role in neural conduction.

**glutamate.** An amino acid that serves as an important excitatory neurotransmitter. See also *neurotransmitter*.

**gonads.** Testes in the male, ovaries in the female. As duct glands, the sex glands are active in mating behavior, but as endocrine glands their hormones affect secondary sex characteristics as well as maintaining functional sexual activity. The male hormones are known as androgens, the female hormones as estrogen and progesterone (syn. *sex glands*). See also *androgens, endocrine gland, estrogens, progesterone*.

**graded potentials.** Potential changes of varying size induced in a neuron's dendrites or cell body by stimulation from synapses from other neurons. When the graded potentials reach a threshold of depolarization, an action potential occurs. See also *action potential, depolarization*.

**gradient of texture.** If a surface is perceived visually as having substantial tex-

ture (hard, soft, smooth, rough, and so on) and if the texture has a noticeable grain, it becomes fine as the surface recedes from the viewing person, producing a gradient of texture that is important in judgments of slant and distance. See also *distance cues*.

**group polarization.** The tendency of groups to arrive at decisions that are in the same direction but are more extreme than the mean of the pre-discussion decisions of the individuals in the group.

**group test.** A test administered to several people at once by a single tester. A college exam is usually a group test.

**group therapy.** A group discussion or other group activity with a therapeutic purpose participated in by more than one client or patient at a time. See also *psychotherapy*.

**groupthink.** The tendency of members of some decision-making groups to suppress their own dissenting opinions in the interests of group consensus, thereby producing an inadequate decision-making process and poor decisions.

**GSR.** See *galvanic skin response*.

**gustation.** The sense of taste.

## H

**habit.** A learned stimulus-response sequence. See also *conditioned response*.

**habituation.** The reduction in the strength of a response to a repeated stimulus. In general, almost any stimulus will produce habituation; for example, a pure tone sounded for a half-hour may decrease as much as 20 db in perceived loudness. See also *dishabituation*.

**hair cells.** In audition, hairlike receptors in the cochlea that bend due to vibration of the basilar membrane and then send electrical impulses to the brain. See also *basilar membrane, cochlea*.

**hallucination.** A sense experience in the absence of appropriate external stimuli; a misinterpretation of imaginary experiences as actual perceptions. See also *delusion, illusion, schizophrenia*.

**hallucinogens.** Drugs whose main effect is to change perceptual experience and "expand consciousness." LSD and marijuana are examples (syn. *psychedelic drugs*).

**halo effect.** The tendency to bias our perception of another person in the direction of one particular characteristic that we like or dislike.

**hashish.** See *marijuana*.

**heritability.** The proportion of the total variability of a trait in a given population that is attributable to genetic differences among individuals within the population.

**hermaphrodite.** An individual born with

genitals that are ambiguous in appearance or that are in conflict with the internal sex glands. See also *transsexual*.

**heroin.** An extremely addictive central nervous system depressant derived from opium. See also *opiates*.

**hertz (Hz).** The unit used to measure the frequency of a sound wave, specifically the number of cycles per second.

**heterosexual.** A person who is attracted to and seeks sexual relations with members of the opposite sex.

**heuristic.** In problem solving, a strategy that can be applied to a variety of problems and that usually, but not always, yields a correct solution.

**heuristic theory of persuasion.** A theory that proposes that when we are unwilling or unable to process the content of a persuasive communication, we evaluate its validity by utilizing simple rules of thumb (*heuristics*). One such rule might be "messages with many arguments are more likely to be valid than messages with few arguments."

**hidden observer.** A metaphor to describe the concealed consciousness in hypnosis, inferred to have experiences differing from, but parallel to, the hypnotic consciousness.

**hierarchies of concepts.** The relationships among individual concepts. See also *concept*.

**hierarchy of needs.** Maslow's way of classifying needs and motives, ascending from basic biological needs to a peak of self-actualization, supposedly the highest human motive.

**hippocampus.** A brain structure located below the cerebral cortex, that is involved in the consolidation of new memories; its role seems to be that of a cross-referencing system, linking together aspects of a particular memory that are stored in separate parts of the brain. See also *amygdala*.

**home sign.** A system of gestures used by deaf children that initially functions as a kind of simple pantomime but eventually takes on the properties of a language.

**homeostasis.** An optimal level of organic function, maintained by regulatory mechanisms known as homeostatic mechanisms; for example, the mechanisms maintaining a uniform body temperature.

**homosexual.** A person who prefers to have sexual relations with others of the same sex. Can be male or female, but female homosexuals are often termed *lesbians*. Not to be confused with transsexual. See also *transsexual*.

**hormone.** A chemical messenger produced by an organ in one part of the body and transported through the bloodstream to other parts of the body where it has a specific effect on cells that recognize its message. See also *endocrine system*.

**hue.** The dimension of color from which the major color names are derived (red, yellow, green, and so on), corresponding to wavelength of light. See also *brightness, saturation*.

**humanistic psychology.** A psychological approach that emphasizes the uniqueness of human beings; it is concerned with subjective experience and human values. Often referred to as a third force in psychology in contrast to behaviorism and psychoanalysis. See also *phenomenology*.

**humanistic therapies.** A general term for approaches to psychotherapy that emphasize the individual's subjective experiences, free will, and ability to solve his or her own problems. Client-centered therapy and Gestalt therapy are examples. See also *client-centered therapy*.

**hunger drive.** A drive based on food deprivation. See also *drive, specific hunger*.

**hypercomplex cell.** A cell in the visual cortex that responds to a particular orientation and length. See also *complex cell, feature detector, simple cell*.

**hyperphagia.** Pathological overeating. See also *aphagia*.

**hypnosis.** The responsive state achieved following a hypnotic induction or its equivalent. In this state, one person (the subject) responds to suggestions offered by another person (the hypnotist) and experiences alterations in perception, memory, and voluntary action.

**hypnotic induction.** The procedure used in establishing hypnosis in a responsive person. It usually involves relaxation and stimulated imagination. See also *hypnosis*.

**hypnotic trance.** The dreamlike state of heightened suggestibility induced in a subject by a hypnotist. See also *posthypnotic suggestion*.

**hypothalamus.** A small but very important structure located just above the brain stem and just below the thalamus. Considered a part of the central core of the brain, it includes centers that govern motivated behavior such as eating, drinking, sex, and emotions; it also regulates endocrine activity and maintains body homeostasis. See also *lateral hypothalamus, ventromedial hypothalamus*.

**hypothesis testing.** Gathering information and testing alternative explanations of some phenomenon.

**hypothetical construct.** One form of inferred intermediate mechanism. The construct is conceived of as having properties of its own, other than those specifically required for the explanation; for example, drive that is inferred from the behavior of a deprived organism and is used in the explanation of later behavior.

**Hz.** See *hertz*.

**I**

**id.** In Freud's tripartite division of the personality, the most primitive part, consisting of the basic biological impulses (or drives). The source of psychic energy or *libido*. Operates on the *pleasure principle*, endeavoring to obtain pleasure and to avoid pain, regardless of external circumstances. See also *ego, libido, pleasure principle, superego*.

**ideal self.** In Carl Roger's theory, the conception of the kind of person one would like to be. A large discrepancy between the ideal self and the real self creates unhappiness and dissatisfaction. See also *self-concept*.

**identical twins.** See *monozygotic twins*.

**identification.** (a) The normal process of acquiring appropriate social roles in childhood through copying, in part unconsciously, the behavior of significant adults; for example, the child's identification with his or her like-sexed parent. See also *imitation*. (b) Close affiliation with others of like interest, such as identifying with a group.

**identification figures.** Adult models (especially parents) copied, partly unconsciously, by the child. See also *identification*.

**identity crisis.** In Erikson's theory of psychosocial development, a period of self-doubt and active questioning about one's definition of self ("Who am I?" "Where am I going?") which typically takes place during adolescence. See also *identity formation, identity status, psychosocial stages*.

**identity formation.** The process of achieving adult personality integration, as an outgrowth of earlier identifications and other influences. See also *identification, identity crisis, identity status, psychosocial stages*.

**identity status.** An individual's position on Erikson's identity-formation continuum, which includes *identity achievement, foreclosure, moratorium*, and *identity diffusion (or confusion)*. See also *identity crisis, identity formation*.

**illusion.** In perception, a misinterpretation of the relationships among presented stimuli so that what is perceived does not correspond to physical reality; especially, but not exclusively, an optical or visual illusion. See also *delusion, hallucination*.

**illusory conjunctions.** In perception, an incorrect pairing of features from two different objects.

**imitation.** Behavior that is modeled on or copies that of another. See also *identification*.

**implicit memory.** The kind of memory that underlies perceptual and cognitive skills. It is often expressed as an improvement on some perceptual or cognitive task without any conscious recollection of the experiences that led to the improvement. See also *explicit memory*.

**impossible figures.** A figure in which recognition is normal when attending to each part, but the parts do not fuse into a single coherent picture.

**imprinting.** A term used by ethologists for a species-specific type of learning that occurs within a limited period early in the life of the organism and is relatively unmodifiable thereafter, such as young ducklings learning to follow one adult female (usually the mother) within 11-18 hours after birth. But whatever object they are given to follow at this time, they will thereafter continue to follow. See also *critical period, ethology*.

**incentive.** (a) A tangible goal object that provides the stimuli that lead to goal activity. (b) Loosely, any goal. See also *negative incentive, positive incentive*.

**incentive theory.** A theory of motivation that emphasizes the importance of negative and positive incentives in determining behavior; internal drives are not the sole instigators of activity. See also *drive-reduction theory*.

**independent variable.** The variable under experimental control with which the changes studied in the experiment are correlated. In psychological experiments, the independent variable is often a stimulus, responses to which are dependent variables under investigation. See also *dependent variable*.

**individual differences.** Relatively persistent dissimilarities in structure of behavior among persons or members of the same species.

**induced motion.** The perception of motion caused when a larger object surrounding a smaller object moves; the smaller object may appear to be the one that is moving even if it is stationary. See also *stroboscopic motion*.

**inductive reasoning.** Reasoning about arguments in which it is improbable that the conclusion is false if the premises are true. See also *deductive reasoning*.

**indulgent parents.** Responsive, child-centered parents who exercise low levels of control over their children's behavior and place few demands on them. See also *authoritarian parents, authoritative parents, neglecting parents*.

**industrial psychologist.** A psychologist who is concerned with such problems as selecting people most suitable for particular jobs, developing job training programs, and figuring out the determinants of consumer behavior.

**infancy.** The period of helplessness and dependency in humans and other organisms; in humans, roughly the first 2 years.

**information-processing model.** In general, a model based on assumptions regarding the flow of information through a system; usually best realized in the form of a computer program. In cognitive psychology, theories of how the mind functions are often represented in the form of an information-processing model. By simulating the model on a computer, one can study the properties and implications of the theory. See also *cognitive psychology, computer simulation, model.*

**inhibitory synapse.** A synapse at which the neurotransmitter changes the membrane permeability of the receiving cell in the direction of the resting potential; in other words, keeps it from firing. See also *excitatory synapse, synapse.*

**inner ear.** The internal portion of the ear containing, in addition to the cochlea, the vestibular sacs and the semicircular canals. See also *cochlea, semicircular canals, vestibular sacs.*

**insight.** (a) In problem-solving experiments the perception of relationships leading to solution. Such a solution can be repeated promptly when the problem is again confronted. (b) In psychotherapy, the discovery by the individuals of dynamic connections between earlier and later events so that they come to recognize the roots of their conflicts.

**insomnia.** Dissatisfaction with the amount or quality of one's sleep. The diagnosis is subjective because many people who complain of insomnia are found to have normal sleep when studied in the laboratory, whereas others who do not complain of insomnia are found to have detectable sleep disturbances. See also *apnea.*

**instinct.** The name given to unlearned, patterned, goal-directed behavior, which is species-specific, as illustrated by nest building in birds or by the migration of salmon (syn. *species-specific behavior*). See also *ethology.*

**insulin.** The hormone secreted by the pancreas. See also *hormone.*

**intellectualization.** A defense mechanism whereby a person tries to gain detachment from an emotionally threatening situation by dealing with it in abstract, intellectual terms. See also *defense mechanisms.*

**intelligence.** (a) That which a properly standardized intelligence test measures. (b) The ability to learn from experience, think in abstract terms, and deal effectively with one's environment. See also *intelligence quotient, mental age.*

**intelligence quotient (IQ).** A scale unit used in reporting intelligence test scores, based on the ratio between mental age and chronological age. The decimal point is omitted so that the average IQ for children of any one chronological age is set at 100. See also *chronological age, deviation IQ, mental age.*

**interactionism.** (a) Within personality-development theory, a framework in which personality is seen as resulting from the interaction between the child's genotype (inherited characteristics) and the environment in which he or she is raised. (b) In personality theory, a framework in which behavior is seen as resulting from the interaction between consistent personality dispositions or traits and the situations in which people find themselves. See also *evocative interaction, proactive interaction, reactive interaction.*

**interaural intensity.** The difference in intensity of sounds reaching the two ears; it aids in the localization of sounds at high frequencies. See also *interaural time difference.*

**interaural time difference.** The difference in time between the arrival of sound waves at the two ears; it aids in the localization of sounds at low frequencies. See also *interaural intensity.*

**interference.** A factor that can impair retrieval from long-term memory. It arises when different items are associated with the same retrieval cue; attempted retrieval of one of these items can be blocked by the inadvertent retrieval of the other item. See also *long-term memory, retrieval cue.*

**interjudge reliability.** The consistency achieved by two or more observers when assessing or rating some behavior (for example, in rating the aggressiveness of nursery-school children). Also called interscorer agreement. See also *reliability.*

**intermittent reinforcement.** See *partial reinforcement.*

**internal consistency.** A form of test reliability. Specifically, the homogeneity of a set of items on a test, the degree to which they are all measuring the same variable. See also *reliability.*

**interneurons.** Neurons in the central nervous system that receive messages from sensory neurons and send them to other interneurons or to motor neurons. See also *motor neuron, sensory neuron.*

**interpretation.** In psychoanalysis, the analyst's calling attention to the patient's resistances in order to facilitate the flow of associations; also the explanation of symbols, as in dream interpretation. See also *resistance.*

**interscorer agreement.** See *interjudge reliability.*

**interval schedules.** In operant conditioning, reinforcement schedules in which reinforcement occurs only after a certain time interval has elapsed. On a fixed interval (FI) schedule, the organism is reinforced for its first response only after a certain amount of time has passed since its last response. On a variable interval (VI) schedule, reinforcement still depends on time since last response, but the interval's duration varies unpredictably. See also *ratio schedules.*

**intervening variable.** A process inferred to occur between stimulus and response, thus accounting for one response rather than another to the same stimulus. The intervening variable may be inferred without further specification, or it may be given concrete properties and become an object of investigation.

**interview.** A conversation between an investigator (the interviewer) and a subject (the respondent) used for gathering pertinent data for the subject's benefit (as in the psychotherapeutic interview) or for information-gathering (as in a sample survey).

**intracellular fluid.** Water contained within the body's cells; one of the critical variables monitored in the control of thirst.

**introspection.** (a) A form of trained self-observation, in which individuals describe the content of their consciousness without the intrusion of meanings or interpretations. (b) Any form of reporting on subjective (conscious) events or experiences. See also *phenomenology.*

**introspective method.** See *introspection.*

**introversion–extraversion.** The personality dimension first identified by Carl Jung that refers to the degree to which a person's basic orientation is turned inward toward the self or outward toward the external world. At the introversion end are shy individuals who tend to withdraw into themselves; at the extraversion end are sociable individuals who prefer to be with others.

**ion channel.** A specialized protein molecule that permits specific ions to enter or leave cells. Some ion channels open or close in response to appropriate neurotransmitter molecules; others open or close in response to voltage changes across the cell membrane. This process regulates depolarization and the firing of nerve impulses.

**ion pump.** A protein molecule that helps to maintain an uneven distribution of electrically charged ions across the cell membrane of a neuron by pumping them into or out of the cell. Ion pumps work with ion channels to regulate depolarization and firing of nerve impulses. See also *depolarization, ion channel*.

**J**

**James–Lange theory.** A classical theory of emotion, named for the two men who independently proposed it. The theory states that the stimulus first leads to bodily responses, and then the awareness of these responses constitutes the experience of emotion. See also *Cannon–Bard theory, cognitive-appraisal*.

**jnd.** See *just noticeable difference*.

**just noticeable difference (jnd).** A barely perceptible physical change in a stimulus; a measure of the difference threshold. The term is used also as a unit for scaling the steps of sensation corresponding to increases in the magnitude of stimulation. See also *difference threshold, Weber's law*.

**K**

**key-word method.** A technique for learning vocabulary of a foreign language via an intermediate key word related to the sound of the foreign word and the meaning of the English equivalent. See also *mnemonics*.

**kinesthesis.** The muscle, tendon, and joint senses, yielding discrimination of position and movement of parts of the body. See also *equilibratory senses*.

**L**

**late selection.** Selective attention that occurs in the later stages of recognition, after the organism has determined the meaning of the input. See also *early selection*.

**latency.** (a) A temporal measure of response, referring to the time delay between the occurrence of the stimulus and the onset of the response. (b) In Freud's psychoanalytic theory, a period in middle childhood, roughly the years 6–12, when both sexual and aggressive impulses are said to be in a somewhat subdued state, so that the child's attention is directed outward, and curiosity about the environment makes him or her ready to learn. See also *psychosexual development*.

**latent content.** The underlying significance of a dream (such as the motives or wishes being expressed by it) as interpreted from the manifest content. See also *manifest content*.

**latent learning.** Learning that is not demonstrated by behavior at the time of learning but can be shown to have occurred by increasing the reinforcement for such behavior.

**lateral fissure.** A deep fissure at the side of each cerebral hemisphere, below which lies the temporal lobe (syn. *fissure of Sylvius*).

**lateral hypothalamus (LH).** An area of the hypothalamus important to the regulation of food intake. Electrical stimulation of this area will make an experimental animal start to eat; destruction of brain tissue here causes an animal to stop eating. See also *hypothalamus, ventromedial hypothalamus*.

**law of effect.** The phenomenon that any behavior that is followed by reinforcement is strengthened; from the infinite pool of possible responses, those that lead to reinforcement are repeated, whereas those that do not are extinguished. Some argue that the law of effect is comparable to the principle of natural selection: adaptive responses are selected from the pool of possible responses and their occurrence is made more likely by reinforcement, whereas nonadaptive responses are allowed to become extinct. See also *reinforcement*.

**learned helplessness.** A condition of apathy or helplessness created experimentally by subjecting an organism to unavoidable trauma (such as shock, heat, or cold). Being unable to avoid or escape an aversive situation produces a feeling of helplessness that generalizes to subsequent situations.

**learning.** A relatively permanent change in behavior that occurs as the result of practice. Behavior changes due to maturation or temporary conditions of the organism (such as fatigue, the influence of drugs, adaptation) are not included.

**learning curve.** A graph plotting the course of learning, in which the vertical axis (ordinate) plots a measure of proficiency (amount per unit time, time per unit amount, errors made, and so on), while the horizontal axis (abscissa) represents some measure of practice (trials, time, and so on.)

**left hemisphere.** The left cerebral hemisphere. Controls the right side of the body and, for most people, speech and other logical, sequential activities (syn. *major hemisphere*). See also *cerebral hemispheres, corpus callosum, right hemisphere, split-brain subject*.

**lens.** The part of the eye that helps focus light rays on a single point of the retina. See also *cornea, pupil, retina*.

**lesbian.** See *homosexual*.

**LH.** See *lateral hypothalamus*.

**libido.** (Latin for lust). In Freud's psychoanalytic theory, the psychic energy of the id. See also *id*.

**lie detector.** See *polygraph, voice stress analyzer*.

**light adaptation.** The decreased sensitivity of the eye to light when the subject has been continuously exposed to high levels of illumination. See also *dark adaptation*.

**lightness constancy.** The tendency to see a familiar object as of the same brightness, regardless of light and shadow that change its stimulus properties. See also *perceptual constancy*.

**limbic system.** A set of structures in and around the midbrain, forming a functional unit regulating motivational and emotional types of behavior, such as waking and sleeping, excitement and quiescence, feeding, and mating.

**linear perspective.** In perspective, a monocular cue for depth. When parallel lines appear to converge, they are perceived as vanishing in the distance. See also *relative height, relative size, superposition*.

**linguistic relativity hypothesis.** The proposition that one's thought processes, the way one perceives the world, are related to one's language.

**lithium carbonate.** A compound based on lithium, an element related to sodium. Has been successful in treating bipolar disorders. See also *bipolar disorder*.

**localized functions.** Behavior controlled by known areas of the brain; for example, vision is localized in the occipital lobes.

**location constancy.** The tendency to perceive the place at which a resting object is located as remaining the same even though the relationship to the observer has changed. See also *perceptual constancy*.

**long-term memory (LTM).** The relatively permanent component of the memory system, as opposed to short-term memory. See also *short-term memory*.

**long-term potentiation (LTP).** An increase in synaptic efficiency (lasting hours to days) following a particular pattern of excitatory stimulation (brief, high-frequency currents). First described in the hippocampus, but found in many brain areas. This strengthening of the synaptic connection is achieved by the activity of the NMDA receptors embedded in the dendrites of the receiving neuron. LTP appears to be one of the chief means by which new memories are stored. See also *NMDA*.

**longitudinal study.** A research method that studies an individual through time, taking measurements at periodic intervals. See also *case history.*

**loudness.** An intensity dimension of hearing correlated with the amplitude of the sound waves that constitute the stimulus. Greater amplitudes yield greater loudnesses. See also *pitch, timbre.*

**LSD.** See *lysergic acid diethylamide.*

**LTP.** See *long-term potentiation.*

**lucid dream.** A dream in which events seem so normal (lacking the bizarre and illogical character of most dreams) that the dreamer believes he or she is awake and conscious.

**lunch-line effect.** An example of peripheral attention. Even though you may be absorbed in conversation in a room full of people, the sound of your name in another conversation will usually attract your attention; this phenomenon suggests a nonconscious monitoring of that conversation.

**lysergic acid diethylamide.** A powerful psychoactive drug capable of producing extreme alterations in consciousness, hallucinations, distortions in perception, and unpredictable mood swings.

**M**

**magnetic resonance imaging (MRI).** A computer-based scanning procedure that uses strong magnetic fields and radio-frequency pulses to generate a picture of a cross section of the brain or body. Provides greater precision than the CT scanner.

**major hemisphere.** See *left hemisphere.*

**manic-depression.** See *bipolar disorder.*

**manifest content.** The remembered content of a dream, the characters, and their actions, as distinguished from the inferred latent content. See also *latent content.*

**mantra.** See *transcendental meditation.*

**MAO.** See *monoamine oxidase.*

**MAOI.** See *monoamine oxidase inhibitor.*

**marijuana.** The dried leaves of the hemp plant (canabis); also known as hashish, "pot," or "grass." Hashish is actually an extract of the plant material and, hence, is usually stronger than marijuana. Intake may enhance sensory experiences and produce a state of euphoria.

**marital therapy.** Psychotherapy with both members of a couple aimed at resolving problems in their relationship (syn. *couples therapy*). See also *psychotherapy.*

**masochism.** A pathological desire to inflict pain on oneself or to suffer pain at the hands of others. See also *sadism.*

**maternal drive.** The drive, particularly in animals, induced in the female through bearing and nursing young, leading to nestbuilding, retrieving, and other forms of care. See also *drive.*

**maturation.** Growth processes in the individual that result in orderly changes in behavior, whose timing and patterning are relatively independent of exercise or experience though they may require a normal environment.

**maze.** A device use in the study of animal and human learning, consisting of a correct path and blind alleys.

**mean.** The arithmetical average; the sum of all scores divided by their number. See also *measure of central tendency.*

**means-ends analysis.** A problem-solving strategy in which one compares one's current state to the goal state in order to find the most important difference between them; eliminating this difference then becomes the main subgoal. See also *difference reduction, working backwards.*

**measurement.** Assigning numbers to different levels, amounts, or sizes of a variable.

**measure of central tendency.** A value representative of a frequency distribution, around which other values are dispersed; for example, the mean, the median, or mode of a distribution of scores. See also *mean, median, mode.*

**measure of variation.** A measure of the dispersion or spread of scores in a frequency distribution, such as the range or the standard deviation. See also *standard deviation.*

**mechanisms of defense.** See *defense mechanisms.*

**median.** The score of the middle case when cases are arranged in order of size of score. See also *measure of central tendency.*

**meditation.** An altered state of consciousness in which the individual is extremely relaxed and feels divorced from the outside world; the individual loses self-awareness and gains a sense of being involved in a wider consciousness. This meditative state is achieved by performing certain rituals, including regulating breathing, sharply restricting one's field of attention, and assuming yogic body positions. A commercialized form of meditation has been widely promoted under the name of *transcendental meditation or TM.*

**medulla.** The lowest section of the brainstem, a slight enlargement of the spinal cord as it enters the skull; the point at which the major nerve tracts cross over so that the right cerebral hemisphere controls the left side of the body, and the left cerebral hemisphere controls the right side.

**memory decay.** A major cause of forgetting in short-term memory in which information simply fades with time.

**memory span.** The number of items (digits, letters, words) that can be reproduced in order after a single presentation; usually 7±2. See also *chunk, short-term memory.*

**memory trace.** The inferred change in the nervous system that persists between the time something is learned and the time it is recalled.

**menarche.** The first menstrual period, indicative of sexual maturation in a girl.

**mental age (MA).** A scale unit proposed by Binet for use in intelligence testing. If an intelligence test is properly standardized, a representative group of children of age 6 should earn an average mental age of 6, those of age 7, a mental age of 7, and so on. A child whose MA is above his or her chronological age (CA) is advanced; one whose MA lags behind is retarded. See also *chronological age, intelligence quotient.*

**mental imagery.** Mental pictures used as an aid to memory. Not the same as eidetic imagery. See also *eidetic imagery.*

**mental model.** A concrete mental representation of a problem situation that may be useful in solving the problem. See also *mental representation.*

**mental practice.** The imagined rehearsal of a perceptual-motor skill in the absence of gross body movements. For example, picturing yourself serving a tennis ball and making mental corrections when the movement seems faulty, without actually moving your arm.

**mental representation.** A hypothesized "inner representation" of objects and events in human memory. Some theorists endow mental representations with the very properties they are alleged to represent (a "picture of the mind"); others argue that they involve an abstract characterization much like the propositional logic used by mathematicians (the way information is represented in a digital computer); and yet others believe that they are best thought of as a kind of private symbol system that may vary from person to person. The general concept is pervasive in cognitive psychology. See also *mental imagery.*

**mental retardation.** Subnormal intellectual functioning with impairment in social adjustment.

**mental rotation.** The notion that a mental image of an object can be rotated in the mind in a fashion analogous to rotating the real object.

**meta-analysis.** A statistical technique that treats the accumulated studies of a particular phenomenon as a single grand experiment and each study as a single observation.

**method of constant stimuli.** A psychophysical method for determining sensory thresholds. Stimuli with magnitudes varying around the threshold are presented to a subject many times to see what percentage of the time the subject detects them. See also *psychophysical methods*.

**method of loci.** An aid to serial memory. Verbal material is transformed into mental images, which are then located at successive positions along a visualized route, such as an imaged walk through the house or down a familiar street.

**middle ear.** The part of the ear that transmits sound waves from the eardrum to the oval window of the inner ear by means of three tiny connecting bones (malleus, incus, and stapes). See also *cochlea, eardrum, inner ear, oval window*.

**minor hemisphere.** See *right hemisphere*.

**mnemonics.** A system for improving memory often involving a set of symbols that can substitute for the material to be remembered; for example, in attempting to remember a number sequence, one may translate the sequence into letters of the alphabet that in turn approximate words that are easily remembered.

**mode.** The most frequent score in a distribution, or the class interval in which the greatest number or cases fall. See also *measure of central tendency*.

**model.** (a) Miniature systems are often constructed according to a logical, mathematical, or physical model. That is, the principles according to which data are organized and made understandable parallel those of the model; for instance, the piano keyboard is a model for understanding the basilar membrane; the thermostat is a model for the feedback principle of homeostasis. (b) In behavior therapy, one who *models* or performs behaviors that the therapist wishes the patient to imitate.

**modeling.** In social learning theory, the process by which a person learns social and cognitive behaviors by observing and imitating others.

**mongolism.** See *Down's syndrome*.

**monoamine oxidase (MAO).** One of the enzymes responsible for the breakdown of a group of neurotransmitters called biogenic amines (norepinephrine, dopamine, and serotonin are examples); believed to be important in the regulation of emotion. Drugs that inhibit the action of this enzyme (MAO inhibitors) are used in treating depression. See also *antidepressant, monamine oxidase inhibitor,*

*neurotransmitter.*

**monoamine oxidase inhibitor (MAOI).** A class of drugs used to treat depression; the drug inhibits the action of an enzyme (monoamine oxidase) that breaks down certain neurotransmitters (such as dopamine, norepinephrine, and serotonin), thereby prolonging the action of these neurotransmitters. See also *antidepressant, monoamine oxidase, neurotransmitter.*

**monochromatism.** Total color blindness, the visual system being achromatic. A rare disorder. See also *dichromatism, trichromatism.*

**monocular cues.** See *distance cues.*

**monozygotic (MZ) twins.** Twins developed from a single egg. They are always of the same sex and commonly much alike in appearance, although some characteristics may be in mirror image; for example one right-handed, the other left-handed (syn. *identical twins*). See also *dizygotic twins.*

**mood disorder.** A mental disorder characterized by disturbances of mood. Depression, mania (exaggerated excitement), and bipolar disorders in which the individual experiences both extremes of mood are examples. See also *bipolar disorder, depression.*

**moon illusion.** A perceptual illlusion that makes the moon appear as much as 50 percent larger when it is near the horizon than when it is at its zenith, even though at both locations the moon produces the same retinal image.

**moral realism.** In Piaget's theory of cognitive development, the preoperational child's treatment of social rules as absolute and unchangeable. Also see *preoperational stage.*

**morpheme.** The smallest meaningful unit in the structure of a language, whether a word, base, or affix; such as *man, strange, ing, pro*. See also *phoneme.*

**motion aftereffect.** The illusion of movement in a static object that occurs after viewing motion for an extended period of time; the aftereffect occurs in the opposite direction of the viewed motion.

**motion parallax.** A monocular cue to depth perception. When you are moving rapidly, nearby objects appear to move more quickly in the opposite direction than distant objects do. This difference in apparent speed provides a cue to the respective depths of the objects.

**motivation.** A general term referring to the regulation of need-satisfying and goal-seeking behavior. See also *motive.*

**motive.** Any condition of the organism that affects its readiness to start on or continue in a sequence of behavior.

**motor area.** A projection area in the brain lying in front of the central fissure. Elec-

trical stimulation commonly results in movement, or motor, responses. See also *somatosensory area.*

**motor neuron.** A neuron, or nerve cell, that conveys messages from the brain or spinal cord to the muscles and glands (syn. *efferent neuron*). See also *sensory neuron.*

**MRI.** See *magnetic resonance imaging.*

**multiple personality.** The existence of two or more integrated and well-developed personalities within the same individual. Each personality has its own set of memories and characteristic behaviors. Typically, the attitudes and behavior of the alternating personalities are markedly different.

**multivariate experiment.** A type of experiment that involves the simultaneous manipulation of several independent variables. See also *independent variable.*

**myelin sheath.** The fatty sheath surrounding certain nerve fibers known as myelinated fibers. Impulses travel faster and with less energy expenditure in myelinated fibers than in unmyelinated fibers.

**MZ twins.** See *monozygotic twins.*

## N

**nanometer (nm).** A billionth of a meter. Wavelength of light is measured in nanometers.

**narcissism.** Self-love; in Freud's psychoanalytic theory, the normal expression of pregenital development.

**narcolepsy.** A sleep disturbance characterized by an uncontrollable tendency to fall asleep for brief periods at inopportune times.

**narcotics.** See *opiates.*

**nativism.** The view that behavior is innately determined. See also *empiricism.*

**nature-nurture issue.** The problem of determining the relative importance of heredity (nature) and the result of upbringing in a particular environment (nurture) on mature ability.

**need.** A physical state involving any lack or deficit within the organism. See also *drive, motive.*

**negative incentive.** An object or circumstance away from which behavior is directed when the object or circumstance is perceived or anticipated. See also *positive incentive.*

**negative reinforcement.** Reinforcing a response by the removal of an aversive stimulus. See also *negative reinforcer.*

**negative reinforcer.** Any stimulus that, when removed following a response, increases the probability of the response. Loud noises, electric shock, and extreme heat or cold classify as negative reinforcers. See also *punishment*.

**negative symptoms.** In schizophrenia, behavioral deficits such as flattened affect, apathy, and poverty of speech. Presumed to result from abnormalities in brain structure. See also *positive symptoms, schizophrenia*.

**neglecting parents.** Parents who exercise low levels of control over their children's behavior and are more occupied with their own interests and activities than those of their children. Extreme neglecting parents are emotionally unavailabe to their children, being detached, emotionally uninvolved and uninterested in them. See also *authoritarian parents, authoritative parents, indulgent parents*.

**nerve.** A bundle of elongated axons belonging to hundreds or thousands of neurons, possibly both afferent and efferent neurons. Connects portions of the nervous system to other portions and to receptors and effectors. See also *axon, neuron*.

**nerve cell.** See *neuron*.

**neuron.** The nerve cell; the basic unit of a synaptic nervous system.

**neuroreceptor molecule.** A protein molecule in a cell membrane that is sensitive to a particular chemical, such as a neurotransmitter. When the appropriate chemical activates a neuroreceptor molecule, changes occur in the cell membrane that either increase or decrease its permeability. Some neurotransmitters have an excitatory effect when locked to their neuroreceptors; others have an inhibitory effect. See also *neurotransmitter*.

**neurosis** (pl. *neuroses*). A mental disorder in which the individual is unable to cope with anxieties and conflicts and develops symptoms that he or she finds distressing, such as obsessions, compulsions, phobias, or anxiety attacks. In Freud's psychoanalytic theory, neurosis results from the use of defense mechanisms to ward off anxiety caused by unconscious conflicts. No longer a diagnostic category of DSM-III-R. See also *anxiety disorders, obsessive-compulsive disorder, phobia*.

**neurotic anxiety.** Fear that is out of proportion to the actual danger posed (such as stage fright). See also *anxiety, objective anxiety*.

**neuroticism.** The name of the emotional instability–stability dimension in Eysenck's factor-analytic theory of personality. Moody, anxious, and maladjusted individuals are at the neurotic or unstable end; calm, well-adjusted individuals are at the other. See also *introversion–extraversion*.

**neurotransmitter.** A chemical involved in the transmission of nerve impulses across the synapse from one neuron to another. Usually released from small vesicles in the synaptic terminals of the axon in response to the action potential; diffuses across synapse to influence electrical activity in another neuron. See also *dopamine, epinephrine, norepinephrine, serotonin*.

**NMDA.** See *N-methyl D-aspartate receptor*.

**N-methyl D-aspartate receptor (NMDA receptor).** A receptor molecule that requires two successive chemical signals to activate it; the first signal makes the receptor more responsive (a phenomenon known as long-term potentiation) so that when a second chemical signal occurs (the neurotransmitter glutanate), the receptor is activated. NMDA receptors are particularly dense in the hippocampus and may explain how memories are stored by linking neurons to form new neural circuits. See also *hippocampus, neurotransmitter, neuroreceptor molecule*.

**nonconscious processes.** A considerable body of research indicates that we register and evaluate stimuli that we are not consciously aware of. The stimuli are said to influence us unconsciously or to operate at an unconscious (or subconscious) level of awareness. See also *consciousness*.

**noncontingent reinforcement.** Reinforcement not contingent on a specific response.

**noradrenalin.** See *norepinephrine*.

**norepinephrine.** One of the hormones secreted by the adrenal medulla; its action in emotional excitement is similar in some, but not all, respects to that of epinephrine. It is also a neurotransmitter of the central nervous system. Norepinephrine synapses can be either excitatory or inhibitory. Believed to play a role in depression and bipolar disorders (syn. *noradrenaline*) See also *adrenal gland, epinephrine*.

**norm.** An average, common, or standard performance under specified conditions; for example, the average achievement test score of 9-year-old children or the average birth weight of male children. See also *social norms, test standardization*.

**normal curve.** The plotted form of the normal distribution.

**normal distribution.** The standard symmetrical bell-shaped frequency distribution, whose properties are commonly used in making statistical inferences from measures derived from samples. See also *normal curve*.

**nuclei** (sing. *nucleus*). A collection of nerve cell bodies grouped in the brain or spinal cord. See also *ganglia*.

**null hypothesis.** A statistical hypothesis that any difference observed among treatment conditions occurs by chance and does not reflect a true difference. Rejection of the null hypothesis means that we believe the treatment conditions are actually having an effect.

**O**

**object constancy.** See *perceptual constancy*.

**object permanence.** Piaget's term for the child's realization that an object continues to exist even though it is hidden from view. See also *sensorimotor stage*.

**object relations theory.** An outgrowth of psychoanalytic theory that deals with the person's attachments to others over the course of development. Emphasizes ego functioning more than did classical psychoanalytic theory.

**object size.** The size of an object as determined from measurement at its surface. When size constancy holds, the observer perceives a distant object as being near its object size. See also *retinal size*.

**objective anxiety.** Fear that is proportionate to the danger posed.

**observational method.** Studying events as they occur in nature, without experimental control of variables; for instance, studying the nest-building of birds or observing children's behavior in a play situation. See also *experimental method*.

**obsession.** A persistent, unwelcome, intrusive thought, often suggesting an aggressive or sexual act. See also *compulsion, obsessive-compulsive disorder*.

**obsessive-compulsive disorder.** An anxiety disorder taking one of three forms: (a) recurrent thoughts, often disturbing and unwelcome (obsessions); (b) irresistible urges to repeat stereotyped or ritualistic acts (compulsions); (c) both of these in combination. See also *anxiety disorders*.

**occipital lobe.** A portion of the cerebral hemisphere, behind the parietal and temporal lobes. See also *frontal lobe, parietal lobe, temporal lobe*.

**Oedipal conflict.** In Freud's psychoanalytic theory, the conflict that arises during the phallic stage of psychosexual development in which the individual is sexually attracted to the parent of the opposite sex and perceives the same-sex parent as a rival. See also *phallic stage, psychosexual development*.

**olfaction.** The sense of smell.

**olfactory bulb.** A region of the brain involved in olfaction (smell); it is a way station between the receptors in the nasal passage and the olfactory cortex.

**olfactory epithelium.** The specialized skin within the nasal cavity that contains the receptors for the sense of smell.

**operant behavior.** Behavior defined by the stimulus to which it leads rather than by the stimulus that elicits it; such as behavior leading to reward (syn. *instrumental behavior*). See also *respondent behavior*.

**operant conditioning.** The strengthening of an operant response by presenting a reinforcing stimulus if, and only if, the response occurs (syn. *instrumental conditioning, reward learning*). See also *classical conditioning*.

**opiates.** Opium or one of its chemical derivatives: codeine, morphine, or heroin. Central nervous system depressants that relieve pain and produce euphoria, all highly addictive (syn. *narcotics*). See also *heroin*.

**opinion molecule.** A cognitive unit comprising a belief, an attitude, and a perception of social support for the individual's view on the matter. For example, "I believe that Democrats are compassionate toward the poor" (*belief*); "I prefer having Democrats in office" (*attitude*); "And I think the American people agree with me" (*perception of social support*).

**opioid receptors.** Neuroreceptor molecules in specific areas of the brain and spinal cord to which a group of neurotransmitters, called endorphins, bind. These molecules also have an affinity for opiates. There are several distinct types of opioid receptors; each has a different affinity for binding with various opiates. See also *neurotransmitter, neuroreceptor molecule*.

**opponent-color theory.** A theory of color perception that postulates two types of color-sensitive units that respond in opposite ways to the two colors of an opponent pair. One type of unit responds to red or green, the other to blue or yellow. Since a unit cannot respond in two ways at once, reddish-greens and yellowish-blues cannot occur. See also *trichromatic theory, two-stage color theory*.

**opponent-process theory.** In emotion, the theory that assumes the brain is organized to oppose or suppress emotional responses, whether they are pleasurable or aversive.

**optic chiasma.** A cross-over junction of the optic nerves, located near the base of the brain, where nerve fibers from the inner half of each retina (nearest the nose) cross to the opposite side of the brain. The resulting left optic tract carries data about objects seen in the right-hand side of the field of vision, and the right optic tract carries signals from objects seen on the left.

**optic nerve.** In vision, a nerve formed out of axons of the ganglion cells, which leads to the brain. See also *bipolar cells, ganglia, photoreceptors, retina*.

**oral behavior.** Behavior deriving from the infant's need to suck or, more generally, to be fed through the mouth.

**oral stage.** In Freud's psychoanalytic theory, the first stage of psychosexual development; pleasure derives from the lips and mouth, as in sucking at the mother's breast. See also *psychosexual development*.

**organizational psychologist.** See *industrial psychologist*.

**orienting reflex.** (a) A nonspecific response to change in stimulation involving depression of cortical alpha rhythm, galvanic skin response, pupillary dilation, and complex vasomotor responses (a term introduced by Russian psychologists). (b) Head or body movements that orient the organism's receptors to those parts of the environment in which stimulus changes are occurring.

**osmoreceptors.** Hypothesized cells in the hypothalamus that respond to dehydration by stimulating the release of ADH by the pituitary gland, which, in turn, signals the kidneys to reabsorb water into the bloodstream. See also *antidiuretic hormone, volumetric receptors*.

**otoliths.** "Ear stones." See *vestibular sacs*.

**outer ear.** The external ear and auditory canal, whose purpose is to funnel sound waves towards the inner ear. See also *inner ear, middle ear*.

**oval window.** A membrane on the cochlea of the inner ear that receives vibrations from the ear drum via three connecting bones (malleus, incus, and stapes). Vibrations at the oval window set up similar vibrations in the internal fluid of the cochlea, ultimately activating the hair cells that serve as auditory receptors. See also *cochlea, hair cells*.

**ovarian hormones.** See *estrogen, progesterone*.

**overextension.** The tendency of a child, in learning a language, to apply a new word too widely; for example, to call all animals "doggie."

**overtone.** A higher frequency tone, a multiple of the fundamental frequency, that occurs when a tone is sounded by a musical instrument. See also *timbre*.

## P

**paired-associate learning.** The learning of stimulus-response pairs, as in the acquisition of a foreign language vocabulary. When the first member of a pair (the stimulus) is presented, the subject's task is to give the second member (the response).

**pancreas.** A bodily organ situated near the stomach. As a duct gland, it secretes pancreatic juice into the intestines, but some specialized cells function as an endocrine gland, secreting the hormone insulin into the bloodstream. See also *endocrine gland*.

**pandemonium theory.** An early effort in the field of artificial intelligence to build a computer-based machine that could stimulate the process of pattern recognition. The system was designed for the recognition of hand-printed letters, and many psychologists argue that it has important resemblances to human recognition. See also *artificial intelligence, simulation*.

**panic disorder.** An anxiety disorder in which the individual has sudden and inexplicable episodes of terror and feelings of impending doom accompanied by physiological symptoms of fear (such as heart palpitations, shortness of breath, muscle tremors, faintness). See also *anxiety, anxiety disorders*.

**parallel processing.** A theoretical interpretation of information processing in which several sources of information are all processed simultaneously. See also *serial processing*.

**paranoid schizophrenia.** A schizophrenic reaction in which the patient has delusions of persecution. See also *schizophrenia*.

**paraphilias.** Same as sexual perversions. Sexual attraction to unusual objects as well as sexual activities that are unusual in nature. Examples are fetishism (sexual attractions to an inanimate object or some specific nongenital part of a person), exhibitionism (obtaining sexual gratification by exposing one's genitals to an unwilling observer), and pedophilia (a preference for obtaining sexual gratification through contact with youngsters who are legally underage).

**parapsychology** ("beside psychology"). A subfield of psychology that studies psi phenomena (extrasensory perception and psychokinesis). See also *clairvoyance, extrasensory perception, precognition, psi, psychokinesis, telepathy*.

**parasympathetic system.** A division of the autonomic nervous system, the nerve fibers of which originate in the cranial and sacral portions of the spinal cord. Active in relaxed or quiescent states of the body and to some extent antagonistic to the sympathetic division, or system. See also *sympathetic system*.

**parathyroid glands.** Endocrine glands adjacent to the thyroid gland in the neck, whose hormones regulate calcium metabolism, thus maintaining the normal excitability of the nervous system. Parathyroid inadequancy leads to tetany.

See also *endocrine system*.

**parietal lobe.** A portion of the cerebral hemisphere, behind the central fissure and between the frontal and occipital lobes. See also *frontal lobe, occipital lobe, temporal lobe*.

**partial reinforcement.** Reinforcing a given response only some proportion of the times it occurs (syn. *intermittent reinforcement*). See also *reinforcement, reinforcement schedule*.

**passionate love.** An intensely emotional state in which tender and sexual feelings, elation and pain, anxiety and relief, altruism and jealousy coexist in a confusion of feelings. Combines physiological arousal with perception that the arousal is evoked by the beloved. Contrasted with companionate love. See also *companionate love*.

**path analysis.** A correlational procedure that divides an overall correlation between two variables into separate components or paths. For example, path analysis can help to determine whether a link between childhood temper tantrums and later occupational problems is direct or is due to some intervening link like dropping out of school. See also *contemporary consequences, cumulative consequences*.

**pattern recognition.** The perceptual process of determining what an object is.

**PCP.** See *phencyclidine*.

**percept.** The result of the perceptual process; that which the individual perceives.

**perception.** A general term to describe the whole process of how we come to know what is going on around us; the entire sequence of events from the presentation of a physical stimulus to the phenomenological experiencing of it. Perception is viewed as a set of subprocesses that occur in a multilevel, interactive system. The lower levels in this system, the parts closely associated with the sense organs, are called sensory processes. See also *sensory processes*.

**perceptual constancy.** The tendency to see objects as relatively unchanged under widely altered conditions of illumination, distance, and position. See also *color constancy, lightness constancy, location constancy, shape constancy, size constancy*.

**perceptual defense.** The supposed prevention of an individual's conscious perceptual system from recognizing an anxiety-producing situation perceived by the individual's unconscious perceptual system.

**perceptual patterning.** The tendency to perceive stimuli according to principles such as proximity, similarity, continuity, and closure. Emphasized by Gestalt psychologists. See also *figure-ground organization, gestalt psychology*.

**performance.** Overt behavior, as distinguished from knowledge or information not translated into action. The distinction is important in theories of learning.

**peripheral nervous system.** That part of the nervous system outside the brain and spinal cord; it includes the autonomic nervous system and the somatic nervous system. See also *autonomic nervous system, somatic nervous system*.

**personal construct.** In George Kelly's theory of personality, a dimension used by an individual to interpret or "construe" his or her environment. Considered by Kelly to be the basic unit of personality organization. See also *Role Construct Repertory Test*.

**personal construct theory.** A phenomenological theory of personality proposed by George Kelly that characterizes an individual in terms of his or her own personal constructs (or interpretation of the world) rather than on the basis of trait dimensions proposed by psychologists. The Role Construct Repertory Test assesses these personal constructs. See also *personal construct, Role Construct Repertory Test*.

**personal disposition.** In Gordon Allport's personality theory, the unique patterning or configuration of traits within an individual. See also *cardinal disposition, central disposition, common trait, secondary disposition*.

**personality.** The distinctive and characteristic patterns of thought, emotion, and behavior that define an individual's personal style and influence his or her interactions with the environment.

**personality assessment.** The measurement or appraisal of personality. See also *behavioral assessment*.

**personality disorders.** Ingrained, habitual, and rigid patterns of behavior or character that severely limit the individual's adaptive potential; often society sees the behavior as maladaptive whereas the individual does not.

**personality inventory.** An inventory for self-appraisal, consisting of many statements or questions about personal characteristics and behavior that the person judges to apply or not to apply to him or her. See also *projective test*.

**personality profile.** A chart plotting the ratings of a number of traits of the same individual on a common scale in parallel rows so that the pattern of traits can be visually perceived. See also *trait*.

**personality psychologist.** A psychologist whose area of interest focuses on classifying individuals and studying the differences between them. This specialty overlaps both developmental and social psychologists to some extent. See also *developmental psychologist, social psychologist*.

**person-centered therapy.** See *client-centered therapy*.

**PET scan.** See *positron emission tomography*.

**phallic stage.** In Freud's psychoanalytic theory, the third stage of psychosexual development in which gratification is associated with stimulation of the sex organs and sexual attachment is to the parent of the opposite sex. See also *Oedipal conflict, psychosexual development*.

**phasic pain.** The kind of sharp pain experienced immediately upon suffering an injury; usually brief with a rapid increase in intensity followed by a decrease. See also *tonic pain*.

**phencyclidine (PCP).** Originally developed as an anesthetic but discontinued because of the bizarre reactions it produced, this drug causes an insensitivity to pain and makes the users feel dissociated from themselves and from their environments. Overdoses result in prolonged periods of stupor or coma.

**phenomenological perspective.** An approach to psychology that focuses on subjective experience and tries to describe it from each individual's unique perspective. See also *humanistic psychology*.

**phenomenology.** The study of an individual's subjective experience or unique perception of the world. Emphasis is on understanding events from the subject's point of view rather than focusing on behavior. See also *humanistic psychology, introspection*.

**phenothiazines.** A group of antipsychotic drugs that relieve the symptoms of schizophrenia by blocking the access of the neurotransmitter dopamine to its receptors. Chlorpromazine (Thorazine) and fluphenazine (Prolixin) are examples. See also *antipsychotic drug, dopamine, neurotransmitter*.

**phenotype.** In genetics, the characteristics that are displayed by the individual organism—such as eye color or intelligence —as distinct from those traits that one may carry genetically but not display. See also *genotype*.

**pheromones.** Special chemicals secreted by many animals that float through the air to attract other members of the same species. They represent a primitive form of communication.

**phi phenomenon.** Stroboscopic motion is its simpler form. Commonly produced by successively turning on and off two separated stationary light sources; as the first is turned off and the second turned on, the subject perceives a spot of light moving from the position of the first to that of the second. See also *stroboscopic motion.*

**phobia.** Excessive fear in the absence of real danger. See also *agoraphobia, claustrophobia.*

**phobic disorder.** An anxiety disorder in which phobias are severe or pervasive enough to interfere seriously with the individual's daily life. See also *anxiety disorders, phobia.*

**phoneme.** The smallest unit in the sound system of a language; it serves to distinguish utterances from one another. See also *morpheme.*

**photoreceptors.** The chemicals in rods and cones responsible for tranducing light into electrical impulses. See also *cones, rods, transduction.*

**physical dependence.** With repeated use of a drug, an individual can become dependent on that drug. Physical dependence is characterized by tolerance (with continued use, the individual must take more and more of the drug to achieve the same effect) and withdrawal (if use is discontinued, the person experiences unpleasant physical symptoms) (syn. *addiction*).

**physiological motive.** A motive based on an evident bodily need, such as the need for food or water.

**physiological psychologist.** See *biological psychologist.*

**pitch.** A qualitative dimension of hearing correlated with the frequency of the sound waves that constitute the stimulus. Higher frequencies yield higher pitches. See also *loudness, timbre.*

**pituitary gland.** An endocrine gland joined to the brain just below the hypothalamus. It consists of two parts, the anterior pituitary and the posterior pituitary. The anterior pituitary is the more important part because of its regulation of growth and of other endocrine glands (syn. *hypophysis.*). See also *endocrine system.*

**place theory of pitch.** A theory of hearing that associates pitch with the place on the basilar membrane where activation occurs. See also *temporal theory of pitch.*

**placebo.** An inert substance used in place of an active drug; given to the control group in an experimental test.

**pleasure principle.** In Freud's psychoanalytic theory, the strategy followed by the *id,* seeking to obtain pleasure and to avoid pain regardless of external circumstances. See also *id, reality principle.*

**pluralistic ignorance.** The tendency for persons in a group to mislead each other about a situation; for example, to define an emergency as a nonemergency because others are remaining calm and are not taking action.

**polygenic traits.** Characteristics—intelligence, height, emotional stability—determined by many sets of genes.

**polygraph.** A device that measures simutaneously several physiological responses that accompany emotion; for instance, heart and respiration rate, blood pressure, and GSR. Commonly known as a "lie detector" because of its use in determining the guilt of a subject through responses while he or she answers questions. See also *GSR, voice stress analyzer.*

**pop-out effect.** A phenomenon in perception, wherein when searching for a primitive feature in a large array, the target feature seems to "pop out."

**population.** The total universe of all possible cases from which a sample is selected. The usual statistical formulas for making inferences from samples apply when the population is appreciably larger than the sample—for instance, 5 to 10 times larger than the sample. See also *sample.*

**positive incentive.** An object or circumstance toward which behavior is directed when the object or circumstance is perceived or anticipated. See also *negative incentive.*

**positive reinforcement.** Reinforcing a response by the presentation of a positive stimulus. See also *positive reinforcer.*

**positive reinforcer.** Any stimulus that, when applied following a response, increases the probability of the response (syn. *reward*). See also *negative reinforcer.*

**positive symptoms.** In schizophrenia, behavioral excesses such as hallucinations and bizarre behavior. Contrasted with negative symptoms and presumed to be caused by irregularities in neural transmission. See also *negative symptoms, schizophrenia.*

**positron emission tomography (PET).** A computer-based scanning procedure that measures the radioactivity of glucose molecules to map the metabolic activities of the living brain.

**posthypnotic amnesia.** A particular form of posthypnotic suggestion in which the hypnotized person forgets what has happened during the hypnosis until signaled to remember. See also *posthypnotic suggestion.*

**posthypnotic response.** See *posthypnotic suggestion.*

**posthypnotic suggestion.** A suggestion made to a hypnotized person that he or she will perform in a prescribed way (commonly to a prearranged signal) when no longer hypnotized. The activity, the posthypnotic response, is usually carried out without the subject's awareness of its origin. See also *hypnosis.*

**post-traumatic stress disorder.** An anxiety disorder in which a stressful event that is outside the range of usual human experience, such as military combat or a natural disaster, brings in its aftermath such symptoms as a re-experiencing of the trauma and avoidance of stimuli associated with it, a feeling of estrangement, a tendency to be easily startled, nightmares, recurrent dreams, and disturbed sleep. See also *anxiety disorder.*

**PQRST method.** A technique for reading and studying information presented in textbook form. The method takes its name from the first letter of the five steps one follows in reading a textbook chapter: *Preview, Question, Read, Self-recitation, Test.*

**pragmatic rules.** Rules used in deductive reasoning that are less abstract than logical rules, but still applicable to many different domains of life. An example is the *permission* rule.

**precognition.** Perception of a future event that could not be anticipated through any known inferential process (for example, predicting that a particular number will come up on the next throw of dice). See also *clairvoyance, extrasensory perception, parapsychology, psi, psychokinesis, telepathy.*

**preconscious memories.** Memories and thoughts that are not part of your consciousness at this moment, but which can be brought to consciousness when needed. They include specific memories of personal events as well as information accumulated over a lifetime. See also *consciousness.*

**preferential looking method.** A method of examining infants' perceptual preferences by presenting them two stimuli simultaneously and noting the amount of time the infants gaze at each object.

**prejudice.** Negative feelings toward a group. Derived from "pre-judgment," usually implies negative feelings not based on adequate or valid data about the group. See also *attitude, discrimination, stereotype.*

**preoperational stage.** Piaget's second stage of cognitive development (ages 2–7 years). The child can think in terms of symbols but does not yet comprehend certain rules or operations, such as the principle of conservation. See also *conservation.*

**prepared conditioning.** The proposal that humans are biologically predisposed, or prepared, by evolutionary selection to associate fear with objects or situations that were dangerous in earlier times. Explains why people develop phobias (conditioned fears) of snakes and heights but not of lambs or guns. See also *classical conditioning.*

**primacy effect.** (a) In memory experiments, the tendency for initial words in a list to be recalled more readily than later words. (b) In studies of impression formation, the tendency for initial information to carry more weight than information received later.

**primary abilities.** The abilities, discovered by factor analysis, that underlie intelligence test performance. See also *factor analysis.*

**primary sex characteristics.** The structural or physiological characteristics that make possible sexual union and reproduction. See also *secondary sex characteristics.*

**priming.** The increased accessibility or retrievability of information stored in memory produced by the prior presentation of relevant cues.

**proactive interaction.** The interaction between individuals and their environments that arises because different individuals choose to enter different situations and to shape those situations differently after entering them. See also *evocative interaction, reactive interaction.*

**proactive interference.** The interference of earlier learning with the learning and recall of new material. See also *retroactive interference.*

**probe.** In studies of memory, a digit or other item from a list to be remembered that is presented as a cue to the subject; for example, the subject could be asked to give the next digit in the list.

**problem-focused coping.** Reducing anxiety or stress by dealing in some way with the anxiety-producing situation. Escaping the situation or finding a way to alter it are examples. See also *emotion-focused coping.*

**problem-solving strategies.** The various strategies that can be employed in solving a problem. Of special interest are a class of strategies that involve breaking the solution to a problem into a series of subgoals. The subgoals are to be accomplished as intermediate steps toward ultimately reaching the final goal.

**product-moment correlation.** See *coefficient of correlation.*

**progesterone.** A female sex hormone produced by the ovaries; it helps prepare the uterus for pregnancy and the breasts for lactation.

**program.** (a) A plan for the solution of a problem; often used interchangeably with "routine" to specify the precise sequence of instructions enabling a computer to solve a problem. (b) In teaching, a set of materials arranged so as to maximize the learning process.

**projection.** A defense mechanism by which people protect themselves from awareness of their own undesirable traits by attributing those traits excessively to others. See also *defense mechanisms.*

**projective test.** A personality test in which subjects reveal ("project") themselves through imaginative productions. The projective test gives much freer possibilities of response than the fixed-alternative personality inventory. Examples of projective tests are the Rorschach Test (ink blots to be interpreted) and the Thematic Apperception Test (pictures that elicit stories). See also *personality inventory.*

**prolactin.** Pituitary hormone prompting the secretion of milk. See also *hormones.*

**proposition.** A sentence or component of a sentence that asserts something, the predicate, about somebody (or something), the subject. All sentences can be broken into propositions.

**prosopagnosia.** The inability to recognize familiar faces; in severe cases, the person may be unable to recognize his or her own face. See also *agnosia, associative agnosia.*

**prototype.** The part of a concept that contains the properties that describe the best examples of the concept. See also *core.*

**psi.** Processes of information and/or energy exchange not currently explicable in terms of known physical mechanisms. See also *clairvoyance, extrasensory perception, parapsychology, precognition, psychokinesis, telepathy.*

**psychedelic drugs.** See *hallucinogens.*

**psychiatric nurse.** A nurse specially trained to deal with patients suffering from mental disorders.

**psychiatric social worker.** A social worker trained to work with patients and their families on problems of mental health and illness, usually in close relationship with psychiatrists and clinical psychologists. See also *clinical psychologist, psychiatrist.*

**psychiatrist.** A medical doctor specializing in the treatment and prevention of mental disorders both mild and severe. Se also *clinical psychologist, psychoanalyst.*

**psychiatry.** A branch of medicine concerned with mental health and mental illness. See also *psychiatrist, psychoanalyst.*

**psychoactive drugs.** Drugs that affect one's behavior and thought processes. See also *depressants, hallucinogens, stimulants.*

**psychoanalysis.** (a) The method developed by Freud and extended by his followers for treating mental disorders. (b) The theory of personality which grew out of experiences with the psychoanalytic method of treatment. The theory emphasizes the role of unconscious processes in personality development and in motivation.

**psychoanalyst.** A psychotherapist, usually trained as a psychiatrist, who uses methods related to those originally proposed by Freud for treating neuroses and other mental disorders. See also *clinical psychologist, psychiatrist.*

**psychoanalytic perspective.** An approach to psychology that tries to explain certain kinds of behaviors in terms of unconscious beliefs, fears, and desires. See also *psychoanalysis.*

**psychoanalytic psychotherapy.** A method of treating mental disorders based on the theories of Freud but briefer and less intense than psychoanalysis. Less emphasis on exploration of childhood experiences and more attention to the client's current interpersonal problems. See also *psychoanalysis.*

**psychoanalytic theory.** See *psychoanalysis.*

**psychoimmunology.** An area of research in behavioral medicine that studies how the body's immune system is affected by psychological variables. See also *behavioral medicine.*

**psychokinesis (PK).** Mental influence over physical events without the intervention of any known physical force (for example, willing that a particular number will come up on the throw of dice). See also *clairvoyance, extrasensory perception, parapsychology, precognition, psi, telepathy.*

**psycholinguistics.** The study of the psychological aspects of language and its acquisition.

**psychological dependence.** Habitual use of a drug to relieve anxiety even though no physical dependence (addiction) has developed. See also *physical dependence.*

**psychological determinism.** The doctrine that all thoughts, emotions, and actions have causes.

**psychological motive.** A motive that is primarily learned rather than based on biological needs.

**psychology.** The science that studies behavior and mental processes.

**psychometric function.** A curve plotting the percentage of times the subject reports detecting a stimulus against a measure of the physical energy of the stimulus.

**psychopathic personality.** See *antisocial personality.*

**psychopharmacology.** The study of the effects of drugs on behavior.

**psychophysical methods.** Procedures used to determine thresholds of sensory modalities.

**psychophysics.** A name used by Fechner for the science of the relationship between mental processes and the physical world. Now usually restricted to the study of the sensory consequences of controlled physical stimulation.

**psychosexual development.** In Freud's psychoanalytic theory, the idea that development takes place through stages (oral, anal, phallic, latent, genital), each stage characterized by a zone of pleasurable stimulation and appropriate objects of sexual attachment, culminating in adult sexuality. See also *anal stage, genital stage, latency, oral stage, psychosocial stages.*

**psychosexual stages.** See *psychosexual development.*

**psychosis.** (pl. *psychoses*). A severe mental disorder in which thinking and emotion are so impaired that the individual is seriously out of contact with reality. No longer a major diagnostic category in DSM-III-R. See also *psychotic behavior.*

**psychosocial stages.** A modification by Erikson of the psychoanalytic theory of psychosexual development, giving more attention to the social and environmental problems associated with the various stages of development and adding some adult stages beyond genital maturing. See also *psychosexual development.*

**psychosomatic disorder.** Physical illness that has psychological causes (syn. *psychophysiological disorder*).

**psychotherapy.** Treatment of personality maladjustment or mental disorders by psychological means, usually, but not exclusively, through personal consultation. See also *biological therapy.*

**psychotic behavior.** Behavior indicating gross impairment in reality contact as evidenced by delusions and/or hallucinations. May result from damage to the brain or from a mental disorder such as schizophrenia or a bipolar disorder. See also *psychosis.*

**puberty.** The period during which the reproductive organs become functionally mature. The development of the secondary sex characteristics (particularly the growth and pigmentation of underarm and pubic hair) marks the onset of puberty and the capacity for reproduction, the culmination. See also *adolescent growth spurt, secondary sex characteristics.*

**punishment.** A procedure used to decrease the strength of a response by presenting an aversive stimulus whenever the response occurs. Note that such a stimulus when applied would be a punisher; when removed, it would act as a negative reinforcer, reinforcing whatever led to its removal. See also *negative reinforcer.*

**pupil.** In the eye, a circular opening in the iris (the colored part of the eye) that expands and contracts, varying according to the intensity of light present. See also *cornea, lens, retina.*

### Q

**Q-sort technique.** An assessment technique by which a rater provides a systematic description of an individual's personality by sorting a set of personality statements (for example, "Has a wide range of interests") into groups, ranging from those that are least descriptive to those that are most descriptive of the individual.

### R

**rapid eye movements (REMS).** Eye movements that usually occur during dreaming and that can be measured by attaching small electrodes laterally to and above the subject's eye. These register changes in electrical activity associated with movements of the eyeball in its socket.

**rapport.** (a) A comfortable relationship between the subject and the tester, ensuring cooperation in replying to test questions. (b) A similar relationship between therapist and patient. (c) A special relationship of hypnotic subject to hypnotist.

**rating scale.** A device by which raters can record their judgments of others (or of themselves) on the traits defined by the scale.

**ratio schedules.** In operant conditioning, reinforcement schedules where reinforcement depends on the number of responses the organism makes. On a fixed ratio (FR) schedule, the number of responses required is fixed at a particular value (for example, five responses for a reinforcement). On a variable ratio (VR) schedule, reinforcement occurs only after a certain number of responses, but that number varies unpredictably (for example, sometimes one response, other times ten, but with an average of five). VR schedules generate very high rates of responding. See also *interval schedules.*

**rational method of test construction.** The procedure of generating or selecting items for a test or assessment instrument by using an underlying theory. See also *empirical method of test construction.*

**rationalization.** A defense mechanism in which self-esteem is maintained by assigning plausible and acceptable reasons for conduct entered on impulsively or for less acceptable reasons. See also *defense mechanisms.*

**reaction formation.** A defense mechanism in which a person denies a disapproved motive through giving strong expressions to its opposite. See also *defense mechanisms.*

**reaction time.** The time between the presentation of a stimulus and the occurrence of a response. See also *latency.*

**reactive interaction.** The interaction between individuals and their environments that arises because different individuals interpret, experience, and react to situations in different ways. See also *evocative interaction, proactive interaction.*

**reality principle.** In Freud's psychoanalytic theory, the strategy followed by the ego, holding back the impulses of the id until they can be satisfied in socially approved ways. See also *ego, pleasure principle.*

**receiver-operating-characteristic curve (ROC curve).** The function relating the probablity of hits and false alarms for a fixed signal level in a detection task. Factors influencing response bias may cause hits and false alarms to vary, but their variation is constrained to the ROC curve. See also *signal detection task.*

**recency effect.** In memory experiments, the tendency for the last words in a list to be recalled more readily than other list words.

**receptive field.** In vision, a region of the retina that is associated with a specific cortical neuron; when a stimulus appears anywhere in the field, the associated neuron fires. See also *feature detector.*

**receptor.** A specialized portion of the body sensitive to particular kinds of stimuli and connected to nerves composed of afferent neurons (such as the retina of the eye). Used more loosely, the organ containing these sensitive portions (such as the eye or the ear).

**recessive gene.** A member of a gene pair that determines the characteristic trait or appearance of the individual only if the other member of the pair is recessive. If the other member of the pair is dominant, the effect of the recessive gene is masked. See also *dominant gene.*

**recoding.** A process for improving short-term memory by grouping items into a familiar unit or chunk.

**recognition.** To recognize something is to associate it correctly with a category, such as "chair," or with a specific name, such as "John Jones." It is a high-level process that requires learning and remembering.

**recurrent inhibition.** A process whereby some receptors in the visual system when stimulated by nerve impulses inhibit the firing of other visual receptors, thus making the visual system responsive to changes in illumination.

**red-green color blindness.** The commonest form of color blindness, a variety of dichromatism. In the two subvarieties, red-blindness and green-blindness, both red and green vision are lacking, but achromatic bands are seen at different parts of the spectrum. See also *color blindness, dichromatism.*

**reduced stimulation study.** An experimental situation in which sensory stimulation is markedly reduced (syn. *sensory deprivation study*).

**reductionism.** In psychology, a kind of explanation that tries to explain (or reduce) psychological notions to biological ones.

**refractory phase.** The period of temporary inactivity in a neuron after it has fired once.

**registration.** A term to describe receptive processing in which information is processed but not perceived. See also *perception.*

**regression.** A return to more primitive or infantile modes of response.

**rehearsal.** The conscious repetition of information in short-term memory, usually involving speech. The process facilitates the short-term recall of information and its transfer to long-term memory. See also *dual-memory theory.*

**reincarnation.** The belief in rebirth; in other words, that a person has lived before.

**reinforcement.** (a) In classical conditioning, the experimental procedure of following the conditioned stimulus by the unconditioned stimulus. (b) In operant conditioning, the analogous procedure of following the occurrence of the operant response by the reinforcing stimulus. (c) The process that increases the strength of conditioning as a result of these arrangements. See also *negative reinforcement, partial reinforcement, positive reinforcement.*

**reinforcement schedule.** A well-defined procedure for reinforcing a given response only some proportion of the time it occurs. See also *interval schedules, partial reinforcement, ratio schedules.*

**reinforcing stimulus.** (a) In classical conditioning, the unconditioned stimulus. (b) In operant conditioning, the stimulus that reinforces the operant (typically, a reward) (syn. *reinforcer*). See also *negative reinforcer, positive reinforcer.*

**relative height.** In perception, a monocular cue for depth. Among identical objects, those that are higher in an image are perceived as being farther away. See also *distance cues, linear perspective, relative height, superposition.*

**relative size.** In perception, a monocular cue for depth. If an image contains an array of objects of similar shape, the smaller objects are perceived as being farther away. See also *distance cues, linear perspective, relative height, superposition.*

**relaxation training.** Training in various techniques for relaxing muscle tension. The procedure is based on Jacobson's progressive relaxation method, in which the person learns how to relax muscle groups one at a time, the assumption being that muscular relaxation is effective in bringing about emotional relaxation.

**releaser.** A term used by ethologists for a stimulus that sets off a cycle of instinctive behavior. See also *ethology, instinct.*

**reliability.** The self-consistency of a test as a measuring instrument. Reliability is measured by a coefficient of correlation between scores on two halves of a test, alternate forms of the test, or retests with the same test; a high correlation signifies high consistency of scores for the population tested. See also *validity.*

**REMs.** See *rapid eye movements.*

**repression.** (a) A defense mechanism in which an impulse or memory that is distressing or might provoke feelings of guilt is excluded from conscious awareness. See also *defense mechanisms, suppression.* (b) A theory of forgetting.

**Rescorla–Wagner model.** A model of classical conditioning. It assumes that the amount of conditioning between a conditioned stimulus and an unconditioned stimulus on any trial depends on the predictability of the unconditioned stimulus; the less predictable the unconditioned stimulus, the greater the amount of conditioning.

**reserpine.** See *antipsychotic drugs.*

**resistance.** In psychoanalysis, a blocking of free association; a psychological barrier against bringing unconscious impulses to the level of awareness. Resistance is part of the process of maintaining repression. See also *interpretation, repression.*

**respondent behavior.** A type of behavior corresponding to reflex action, in that it is largely under the control of and predictable from the stimulus (syn. *elicited behavior*). See also *operant behavior.*

**response.** (a) The behavioral result of stimulation in the form of a movement or glandular secretion. (b) Sometimes, any activity of the organism, including central responses (such as an image or fantasy) regardless of whether the stimulus is identified and whether identifiable movements occur. (c) Products of the organism's activity, such as words typed per minute.

**resting potential.** The electrical potential across the nerve cell membrane when it is in its resting state (in other words, not responding to other neurons); the inside of the cell membrane is slightly more negative than the outside. See also *action potential.*

**reticular system.** A system of ill-defined nerve paths and connections within the brain stem, lying outside the well-defined nerve pathways, and important as an arousal mechanism.

**retina.** The portion of the eye sensitive to light, containing the rods and the cones. See also *cone, rod.*

**retinal image.** The image projected onto the retina by an object in the visual field.

**retinal size.** The size of the retinal image of an object; retinal size decreases in direct proportion to the object's distance. See also *object size.*

**retrieval.** Locating information in memory.

**retrieval cue.** Anything that can help you retrieve information from memory.

**retroactive interference.** The interference in recall of something earlier learned by something subsequently learned. See also *proactive interference.*

**retrograde amnesia.** Loss of memory for events and experiences occurring in a period of time prior to the amnesia-causing trauma; usually considered to be a failure of the ability to retrieve the information rather than a true loss of that information. See also *amnesia, anterograde amnesia.*

**reuptake.** The process by which a neurotransmitter is "taken up" again (reabsorbed) by the synaptic terminals from which it had been released. See also *neurotransmitter, synaptic terminals.*

**reward.** A synonym for *positive reinforcement.* See also *positive reinforcement.*

**right hemisphere.** The right cerebral hemisphere. Controls the left side of the body and, for most people, spatial and patterned activities (syn. *minor hemisphere*). See also *cerebral hemispheres, corpus callosum, left hemisphere, split-brain subject.*

**ROC curve.** See *receiver-operating-characteristic curve.*

**rod.** In the eye, an element of the retina mediating achromatic sensation only; particularly important in peripheral vision and night vision. See also *cone, retina.*

**Role Construct Repertory Test.** A measuring instrument devised by George Kelly for eliciting a person's constructs. Also called the *Rep Test.* See also *personal construct, personal construct theory.*

**role-playing.** A method for teaching attitudes and behaviors important to interpersonal relations by having the subject assume a part in a spontaneous play, whether in psychotherapy or in leadership training.

**Rorschach Test.** See *projective test.*

# S

**saccade.** The quick, almost instantaneous movement of the eyes between eye fixations.

**sadism.** A pathological motive that leads to inflicting pain on another person. See also *masochism.*

**safety signal hypothesis.** The suggestion that the reason organisms prefer predictable to unpredictable aversive events is because predictability provides a safe period.

**sample.** A selection of scores from a total set of scores known as the "population." If selection is random, an unbiased sample results; if selection is nonrandom, the sample is biased and unrepresentative. See also *population.*

**satiety sensors.** Detectors located in different parts of the digestive or thirst systems that signal that the needed nutrients or fluids are on their way and that feeding or drinking can stop.

**saturation.** The dimension of color that describes its purity; if highly saturated, it appears to be pure hue and free of gray, but if of low saturation, it appears to have a great deal of gray mixed with it. See also *brightness, hue.*

**scaling.** Converting raw data into types of scores more readily interpreted, such as ranks, centiles, standard scores.

**scapegoat.** A form of displaced aggression in which an innocent but helpless victim is blamed or punished as the source of the scapegoater's frustration. See also *displaced aggression, scapegoat theory of prejudice.*

**scapegoat theory of prejudice.** The theory that some hostility toward minority groups arises because prejudiced individuals repress their own unacceptable impulses and then express hostile attitudes toward others who are perceived to possess those same impulses. The hostility often takes the form of blaming the group for both personal and societal problems.

**schedule of reinforcement.** The frequency and/or timing with which reinforcement occurs. See also *ratio schedules, interval schedules.*

**schema.** (pl. *schemata*). Some psychologists use the term to designate specific theoretical ideas about mental events; others use it in a very broad and vaguely defined sense. However used, the term refers to cognitive structures stored in memory that are abstract representations

of events, objects, and relationships in the real world. It is a key ingredient of cognitive theories of psychological phenomena. See also *cognitive map, schematic processing.*

**schematic processing.** The cognitive process of searching for the schema in memory that is most consistent with the incoming information. See also *schema.*

**schizoid.** Having some characteristics that resemble schizophrenia but are less severe. Occurs with higher frequency in families of schizophrenics and thus tends to support a genetic basis for schizophrenia. See also *schizophrenia.*

**schizophrenia.** A group of mental disorders characterized by major disturbances in thought, perception, emotion, and behavior. Thinking is illogical and usually includes delusional beliefs; distorted perceptions may take the form of hallucinations; emotions are flat or inappropriate; bizarre behavior includes unusual postures, stereotyped movements, and "crazy talk." The individual withdraws from other people and from reality. Inherited brain or biochemical abnormalities are implicated.

**school psychologist.** A professional psychologist employed by a school or school system, with responsibility for testing, guidance, research, and so on. See also *educational psychologist.*

**script.** A schema or abstract cognitive representation of events and social interactions (for example, a birthday party). See also *schema.*

**second order conditioning.** Conditioning in which the UCS is *not* biologically significant (such as food, water, or shock) but gains power as a UCS by being consistently paired with a biologically significant UCS. For example, a dog conditioned to salivate at the sound of a tone paired with food will learn to salivate to a light that is followed by the tone. The tone (not a biologically significant event) has become a UCS because of its prior association with food. See also *classical conditioning, unconditioned stimulus.*

**secondary disposition.** In Gordon Allport's personality theory, one of an individual's many narrow and specific personality traits. Contrasted with a cardinal or a central disposition. See also *cardinal disposition, central disposition, common trait, personal disposition.*

**secondary sex characteristics.** The physical features distinguishing the mature male from the mature female, apart from the reproductive organs. In humans, the deeper voice of the male and the growth of the beard are illustrative. See also *primary sex characteristics.*

**selective adaptation.** In perception, a loss of sensitivity to motion that occurs when we view motion. The adaptation is selective because we lose sensitivity to the motion viewed, and to similar motions, but not to motion that differs significantly in direction or speed. Presumably the result of fatigued neurons in the cerebral cortex.

**selective attention.** The perceptual processes by which we select certain input, but not others, for recognition.

**selective breeding.** A method of studying genetic influences by mating animals that display certain traits and selecting for breeding from among their offspring those that express the trait. If the trait is primarily determined by heredity, continued selection for a number of generations will produce a strain that breeds true for that trait.

**self-actualization.** A person's fundamental tendency toward maximal realization of his or her potentials; a basic concept in humanistic theories of personality such as those developed by Maslow and Rogers.

**self-concept.** The composite of ideas, feelings, and attitudes people have about themselves. For some theorists, self-concept is synonymous with the *self.*

**self-consciousness.** A state of heightened self-awareness; the disposition to be self-attentive.

**self-perception.** The individual's awareness of himself or herself; differs from self-consciousness because it may take the form of objective self-appraisal. See also *self-consciousness.*

**self-perception theory.** The theory that attitudes and beliefs are influenced by observations of one's own behavior; sometimes we judge how we feel by observing how we act.

**self-regulation.** In behavior therapy, monitoring one's own behavior and using techniques such as self-reinforcement or controlling stimulus conditions to modify maladaptive behavior. See also *behavior therapy.*

**self-schema.** (pl. *self-schemata*). A generalization or theory about oneself derived from past experience. Self-schemata are assumed to influence the way we selectively attend to, process, and recall personally relevant information (syn. *self-concept*). See also *schema.*

**semantic conditioning.** A form of classical conditioning in which semantic concepts are used as the conditioned stimuli and generalization occurs through semantic similarities.

**semantic memory.** A type of memory that stores general knowledge, such as the meanings of words. Knowledge is encoded in relation to other knowledge rather than in relation to the memorizer. See also *episodic memory.*

**semicircular canals.** Three curved tubular canals, in three planes, which form part of the labyrinth of the inner ear and are concerned with equilibrium and motion. See also *equilibratory senses.*

**sensation.** The conscious experience associated with a very simple stimulus like the onset of a tone or light. At one time, the distinction between sensation and perception had great theoretical importance with perception viewed as a combination of sensations. Today, the dividing line between sensation and perception is much less clear, and it seems best to view such experiences as lying along a continuum.

**sensitive period.** See *critical period.*

**sensitization.** A simple form of learning in which an organism learns to strengthen its reaction to a weak stimulus if a threatening or painful stimulus follows.

**sensorimotor stage.** Piaget's first stage of cognitive development (birth–2 years) during which the infant discovers relationships between sensations and motor behavior. See also *object permanence.*

**sensory adaptation.** The reduction in sensitivity that occurs with prolonged stimulation and the increase in sensitivity that occurs with lack of stimulation; most noted in vision, smell, taste, and temperature sensitivity. See also *dark adaptation, light adaptation.*

**sensory modalities.** The individual senses.

**sensory-neural loss.** A hearing deficit in which threshold elevation (loss of sensitivity) is greater at high rather than low frequencies. See also *conduction loss.*

**sensory neuron.** A neuron, or nerve cell, that conveys messages to the brain or spinal cord from the sense receptors informing the organism about events in the environment or within the body (syn. *afferent neuron*). See also *motor neuron, receptor.*

**sensory processes.** The subprocesses of the perceptual system that are closely associated with the sense organs. Sensory processes provide selectively filtered information about the stimuli that impinge on us; higher-level processes use this information to form a mental representation of the scene. See also *filter, perception.*

**septal area.** A portion of the brain deep in the central part, between the lateral ventricles, that appears to yield a state akin to pleasure when stimulated electrically (in a rat, at least).

**serial memory search.** Comparing a test stimulus in sequence to each item in short-term memory. See also *short-term memory.*

**serial processing.** A theoretical interpretation of information processing in which several sources of information are processed in a serial order; only one source being attended to at a time. See also *parallel processing.*

**serotonin.** A neurotransmitter in both the peripheral and central nervous systems. It is an inhibitory transmitter whose actions have been implicated in various processes including sleep, the perception of pain, and mood disorders (depression and manic-depression). See also *neurotransmitter.*

**set point.** In an analysis of feeding and hunger, the weight at which an individual body functions best.

**sex role.** The full complement of attitudes and behaviors that a society considers appropriate for the individual because of his or her sex. See also *sex typing.*

**sex typing.** The acquisition of attitudes and behaviors that a society considers appropriate for the individual because of his or her sex. Distinguished from *gender identity,* which is the degree to which one regards oneself as male or female. See also *sex role.*

**sex-linked trait.** A trait determined by a gene transmitted on the same chromosomes that determine sex, such as red-green color blindness. See also *X, Y chromosome.*

**shape constancy.** The tendency to see a familiar object as of the same shape regardless of the viewing angle. See also *perceptual constancy.*

**shaping of behavior.** Modifying operant behavior by reinforcing only those variations in response that deviate in the direction desired by the experimenter.

**shock therapy.** See *electroconvulsive therapy.*

**short-term memory (STM).** The assumption that certain components of the memory system have limited capacity and will maintain information for only a brief time. The definition varies somewhat from theory to theory. See also *long-term memory.*

**sibling.** A brother or sister.

**sibling rivalry.** Jealousy between siblings, often based on their competition for parental affection.

**signal detection theory.** A theory of the sensory and decision processes involved in psychophysical judgments, with special reference to the problem of detecting weak signals in noise. See also *signal detection task.*

**signal detection task.** A procedure whereby the subject must judge on each trial whether a weak signal was embed-ded in a noise background. Saying "yes" when the signal was presented is called a "hit" and saying "yes" when the signal was not presented is called a *false alarm.* See also *receiver-operating-characteristic curve.*

**simple cell.** A cell in the visual cortex that responds to a bar of light or straight edge of a particular orientation and location in the visual field. See also *complex cell.*

**simple phobia.** Excessive fear of a specific object, animal, or situation in the absence of real danger. See also *phobia, phobic disorder.*

**simulation.** See *computer simulation.*

**simultaneous conditioning.** A classical conditioning procedure in which the CS begins a fraction of a second before the onset of the UCS and continues with it until the response occurs. See also *delayed conditioning, trace conditioning.*

**sine wave.** A cyclical wave that when plotted corresponds to the plot of the trigonometric sine function. The sound waves of pure tones yield this function when plotted.

**situational attribution.** Attributing a person's actions to factors in the situation or environment, as opposed to internal attitudes and motives. See also *dispositional attribution.*

**size constancy.** The tendency to see a familiar object as of its actual size regardless of its distance. See also *perceptual constancy.*

**size-distance invariance principle.** The proposal that the perceived size of an object is equal to the product of the retinal size of the object and the perceived distance of the object.

**skill memory.** The kind of memory that presumably stores perceptual and motor skills, such as the ability to ride a bicycle. See also *fact memory.*

**smooth muscle.** The type of muscle found in the digestive organs, blood vessels, and other internal organs. Controlled via the autonomic nervous system. See also *cardiac muscle, striate muscle.*

**social facilitation.** The phenomenon in which an organism performs responses more rapidly when other members of its species are present.

**social impact theory.** A general theory of social influence that proposes that the impact of any source of influence on a target individual increases as the number, immediacy, and importance of sources increases, but decreases as the number, immediacy, and importance of targets decreases.

**social learning theory.** The application of learning theory to the problems of personal and social behavior (syn. *social* *behavior theory).*

**social loafing.** The phenomenon in which individuals put in less effort when working in concert with others than when working alone.

**social norms.** A group or community's unwritten rules that govern its members' behavior, attitudes, and beliefs.

**social phobia.** Extreme insecurity in social situations accompanied by an exaggerated fear of embarrassing oneself. See also *phobia, phobic disorder.*

**social psychologist.** A psychologist who studies social interaction and the ways in which individuals influence one another.

**socialization.** The shaping of individual characteristics and behavior through the training that the social environment provides.

**sociology.** The science dealing with group life and social organization in literate societies. See also *behavioral sciences.*

**sociopathic personality.** See *antisocial personality.*

**somatic nervous system.** A division of the peripheral nervous system consisting of nerves that connect the brain and spinal cord with the sense receptors, muscles, and body surface. See also *autonomic nervous system, peripheral nervous system.*

**somatosensory area.** Area in the parietal lobe of the brain that registers sensory experiences, such as heat, cold, touch, and pain (syn. *body-sense area*). See also *motor area.*

**somatotypes.** Types of bodily physiques postulated by Sheldon's type theory to be associated with personality temperaments. See also *type theory.*

**spatial frequency.** In perception, the distance between successive dark bars in a grating consisting of alternating dark and light bars. Spatial frequency is a determinant of visual resolution. See also *contrast sensitivity.*

**spatial localization.** The perceptual process of determining where in the visual field an object is. See also *pattern recognition.*

**spatial resolution.** The ability to see spatial patterns. Visual acuity and the contrast threshold are measures of spatial resolution.

**speaker's intention.** The speaker's goal in uttering a particular sentence, which is distinct from the actual content of the sentence.

**special factor(s).** A specialized ability underlying test scores, especially in tests of intelligence; for example, a special ability in mathematics, as distinct from general intelligence. See also *factor analysis, general factor.*

**species-specific behavior.** See *instinct.*

**specific hunger.** Hunger for a specific food incentive, such as a craving for sweets. See also *hunger drive.*

**specific nerve energies.** Johannes Müller's proposal that the brain codes qualitative differences between sensory modalities by the specific neural pathways involved.

**spindle.** An EEG characteristic of Stage 2 sleep, consisting of short bursts of rhythmical responses of 13–16 Hz; slightly higher than alpha. See also *electroencephalogram.*

**split-brain subject.** A person who has had an operation that severed the corpus callosum, thus separating the functions of the two cerebral hemispheres. See also *cerebral hemispheres, corpus callosum.*

**spontaneous remission.** Recovery from an illness or improvement without treatment.

**sports psychology.** The study of human behavior in sport. The goal of much of the work is to help athletes develop psychological skills that maximize performance and enhance the sport experience. For example, hypnosis and biofeedback have been used to control an athlete's anxiety level during competition and mental imagery has been employed to help perfect the synchrony and flow of certain body movements.

**spreading activation.** A proposed model of retrieval from long-term memory in which activation subdivides among paths emanating from an activated mental representation.

**spurious association.** A plausible but nonexistent relation between two stimuli. Human learners frequently report such relations when trying to learn less-than-perfect relations.

**S-R psychology.** See *stimulus-response psychology.*

**stabilized retinal image.** The image of an object on the retina when special techniques are used to counteract the minute movements of the eyeball that occur in normal vision. When an image is thus stabilized it quickly disappears, suggesting that the changes in stimulation of retinal cells provided by the eye movements are necessary for vision.

**stages of development.** Developmental periods, usually following a progressive sequence, that appear to represent qualitative changes in either the structure or the function of the organism (such as Freud's psychosexual stages, Piaget's cognitive stages).

**standard deviation.** The square root of the mean of the squares of the amount by which each case departs from the mean of all the cases (syn. *root mean square deviation*).

**state-dependent learning.** Learning that occurs during a particular biological state—such as when drugged—so that it can only be demonstrated or is most effective when the person is put in the same state again.

**statistical significance.** The trustworthiness of an obtained statistical measure as a statement about reality; for example, the probability that the population mean falls within the limits determined from a sample. The expression refers to the reliability of the statistical finding and not to its importance.

**statistics.** The discipline that deals with sampling data from a population of individuals, and then drawing inferences about the population from the sample. See also *statistical significance.*

**stereoscopic vision.** (a) The binocular perception of depth and distance of an object owing to the overlapping fields of the two eyes. (b) The equivalent effect when slightly unlike pictures are presented individually to each eye in a stereoscope. See also *distance cues.*

**stereotype.** A schema, or abstract cognitive representation, of the personality traits or physical attributes of a class or group of people. The schema is usually an overgeneralization, leading us to assume that every member of the group possesses the particular characteristic; for instance the false stereotype that all male homosexuals are effeminate. See also *schema.*

**steroids.** Complex chemical substances, some of which are prominent in the secretions of the adrenal cortex and may be related to some forms of mental illness. See also *adrenal gland.*

**stimulants.** Psychoactive drugs that increase arousal. Amphetamines, cocaine, and caffeine are examples.

**stimulation-produced analgesia.** An analgesic effect produced by the stimulation of a region of the midbrain. See also *gate control theory of pain.*

**stimulus** (pl. *stimuli*). (a) Some specific physical energy impinging on a receptor sensitive to that kind of energy. (b) Any objectively describable situation or event (whether outside or inside the organism) that is the occasion for an organism's response. See also *response.*

**stimulus-response (S-R) psychology.** A psychological view that all behavior is in response to stimuli and that the appropriate tasks of psychological science are those identifying stimuli, the responses correlated with them, and the processes intervening between stimulus and response.

**STM.** See *short-term memory*.

**strabismus.** In vision, a lack of binocular depth perception caused by a person's eyes not pointing in the same direction early in life. See also *astigmatism*.

**stress.** A state that occurs when people encounter events that they perceive as endangering their physical or psychological well-being.

**stress responses.** Reactions to events an individual perceives as endangering his or her well-being. These may include bodily changes that prepare for emergency (the fight-or-flight response) as well as such psychological reactions as anxiety, anger and agression, apathy and depression, and cognitive impairment. See also *fight-or-flight response*.

**stressors.** Events that an individual perceives as endangering his or her physical or psychological well-being.

**striate muscle.** Striped muscle; the characteristic muscles controlling the skeleton, as in the arms and legs. Activated by the somatic, as opposed to the autonomic, nervous system. See also *cardiac muscle, smooth muscle*.

**stroboscopic motion.** An illusion of motion resulting from the successive presentation of discrete stimulus patterns arranged in a progression corresponding to movement, such as motion pictures. See also *phi phenomenon*.

**subtractive mixture.** Color mixture in which absorption occurs so that results differ from additive mixture obtained by mixing projected lights. Subtractive mixture occurs when transparent colored filters are placed one in front of the other and when pigments are mixed. See also *additive mixture*.

**superego.** In Freud's tripartite division of the personality, the part that represents the internalization of the values and morals of society; the conscience that controls the expression of the id's impulses through moral scruples. See also *conscience, ego, id*.

**superposition.** In perception, a monocular cue for depth. If an object has contours that cut through those of another, obstructing the other object's view, the overlapping object is perceived as being nearer. See also *distance cues, linear perspective, relative height, relative size*.

**suppression.** A process of self-control in which impulses, tendencies to action, and wishes to perform disapproved acts are in awareness but not overtly revealed. See also *repression*.

**survey method.** A method of obtaining information by questioning a large sample of people.

**symbol.** Anything that stands for or refers to something other than itself.

**sympathetic system.** A division of the autonomic nervous system, characterized by a chain of ganglia on either side of the spinal cord, with nerve fibers originating in the thoracic and lumbar portions of the spinal cord. Active in emotional excitement and to some extent antagonistic to the parasympathetic division. See also *parasympathetic system*.

**synapse.** The close functional connection between the axon of one neuron and the dendrites or cell body of another neuron. See also *excitatory synapse, inhibitory synapse*.

**synaptic gap.** The space between the presynaptic cell membrane and the postsynaptic cell membrane; the space across a synapse. See also *synapse*.

**synaptic terminals.** Small swellings at the end of axon branches that enclose synaptic vesicles containing neurotransmitters. See also *neurotransmitter, synapse, synaptic vesicles*.

**synaptic vesicles.** Small spherical or irregularly shaped structures within a synaptic terminal that contain neurotransmitters; when stimulated, they discharge the neurotransmitters. See also *neurotransmitter, synapse, synaptic terminals*.

**syntactic analysis.** In language, an analysis that divides a sentence into noun phrases and verb phrases, and then divides these phrases into smaller units like nouns, adjectives, and verbs.

**systematic desensitization.** A behavior therapy technique in which hierarchies of anxiety-producing situations are imagined (or sometimes confronted in reality) while the person is in a state of deep relaxation. Gradually the situations become dissociated from the anxiety response. See also *anxiety hierarchy, behavior therapy, counterconditioning*.

**systematic reinforcement.** A method for modifying behavior by reinforcing desirable responses (with praise or tangible rewards) and ignoring undesirable ones. Used in behavior therapy. See also *behavior therapy*.

## T

**tabula rasa.** Latin, meaning *blank slate*. The term refers to the view that human beings are born without any innate knowledge or ideas; all knowledge is acquired through learning and experience. Proposed by the 17th- and 18th-century British empiricists (Locke, Hume, Berkeley, Hartley).

**tachistoscope.** An instrument for the brief exposure of words, symbols, pictures, or other visually presented material; sometimes called a T-scope.

**taste buds.** Receptors for taste located in clusters on the tongue and around the mouth.

**T-cell (thymus-dependent cell).** A type of lymphocyte that recognizes and destroys foreign antigens (enzymes, toxins, or other substances) and thus plays an important role in the body's immune response.

**telegraphic speech.** A stage in the development of speech in which the child preserves only the most meaningful and perceptually salient elements of adult speech. The child tends to omit prepositions, articles, prefixes, suffixes, and auxiliary words.

**telepathy.** Thought transference from one person to another without the mediation of any known channel of sensory communication (for example, identifying a playing card merely being thought of by another person). See also *clairvoyance, extrasensory perception, parapsychology, precognition, psi, psychokinesis*.

**temperament.** An individual's characteristic mood, sensitivity to stimulation, and energy level. Temperament is usually conceptualized as a genetic predisposition because striking differences in reactivity to stimulation, general mood, and activity level can be observed in newborns.

**temperature regulation.** The process by which an organism keeps its body temperature relatively constant.

**temporal lobe.** A portion of the cerebral hemisphere, at the side below the lateral fissure and in front of the occipital lobe. See also *frontal lobe, occipital lobe, parietal lobe*.

**temporal theory of pitch.** A theory of pitch perception which assumes that the neural impulses traveling up the auditory nerve correspond to a tone's vibrations. If the neural response follows the waveform of the sound, then the auditory system could pick out and respond to this overall frequency. See also *place theory of pitch*.

**temporal stability.** See *test-retest reliability*.

**test battery.** A collection of tests whose composite scores are used to appraise individual differences.

**test method.** A method of psychological investigation. Its advantages are that it allows the psychologist to collect large quantities of useful data from many people, with a minimum of disturbance of their routines of existence and with a minimum of laboratory equipment.

**test profile.** A chart plotting scores from a number of tests given to the same individual (or group of individuals) in parallel rows on a common scale, with the scores connected by lines, so that high and low scores can be readily perceived. See also *personality profile*.

**test standardization.** The establishment of norms for interpreting scores by giving a test to a representative population and by making appropriate studies of its reliability and validity. See also *norm, reliability, validity*.

**test-retest reliability.** The consistency of a test when given over successive occasions to the same person (syn. *temporal stability*). See also *reliability*.

**testosterone.** The primary male sex hormone produced by the testes; it is important for the growth of the male sex organs and the development of the secondary male sex characteristics. It influences the sex drive. See also *androgens, secondary sex characteristics*.

**texture gradient.** A cue for perceiving depth directly. When viewing a surface in perspective, the elements that make up the featured surface appear to be packed closer and closer together, giving an impression of depth. See also *distance cues*.

**thalamus.** Two groups of nerve cell nuclei located just above the brain stem and inside the cerebral hemispheres. Considered a part of the central core of the brain. One area acts as a sensory relay station, the other plays a role in sleep and waking; this portion is considered part of the limbic system. See also *hypothalamus*.

**Thematic Apperception Test (TAT).** See *projective test*.

**theory.** A set of assumptions (axioms) advanced to explain existing data and predict new events; usually applicable to a wide array of phenomena.

**theta rhythm.** See *electroencephalogram*.

**thinking.** The ability to imagine or represent objects or events in memory and to operate on these representations. Ideational problem solving as distinguished from solution through overt manipulation.

**threshold.** The transitional point at which an increasing stimulus or an increasing difference not previously perceived becomes perceptible (or at which a decreasing stimulus or previously perceived difference becomes imperceptible). The value obtained depends in part on the methods used in determining it. See also *absolute threshold, difference threshold*.

**thyroid gland.** An endocrine gland located in the neck, whose hormone thyroxin is important in determining metabolic rate. See also *endocrine gland*.

**timbre.** The quality distinguishing a tone of a given pitch sounded by one instrument from that sounded by another. The differences are due to overtones and other impurities. See also *overtone*.

**tip-of-the-tongue phenomenon.** The experience of failing to recall a word or a name when we are quite certain we know it.

**TM.** See *meditation*.

**T-maze.** An apparatus in which an animal is presented with two alternative paths, one of which leads to a goal box. It is usually used with rats and lower organisms. See also *maze*.

**tolerance.** The need to take more and more of a drug to achieve the same effect. An important factor in physical dependency on drugs.

**tonic pain.** The kind of steady, long-lasting pain experienced after an injury has occurred; usually produced by swelling and tissue damage. In contrast to phasic pain. See also *phasic pain*.

**top-down processes.** Processes in perception, memory, and comprehension that are driven by the organism's prior knowledge and expectations, rather than by the input. See also *bottom-down processes*.

**trace conditioning.** A classical conditioning procedure in which the CS terminates before the onset of the UCS. See also *delayed conditioning, simultaneous conditioning*.

**trait.** A persisting characteristic or dimension of personality according to which individuals can be rated or measured. See also *personality profile*.

**trait theory.** The theory that human personality is most profitably characterized by the scores that an individual makes on a number of scales, each of which represents a trait or dimension of his or her personality.

**tranquilizer.** A drug that reduces anxiety and agitation. See *antianxiety drug*.

**transcendental meditation (TM).** See *meditation*.

**transducer.** A device such as an electrode or gauge that, in psychophysiology, converts physiological indicators into other forms of energy that can be recorded and measured.

**transduction.** The translation of a physical energy into electrical signals by specialized receptor cells. See also *receptor cells*.

**transference.** In psychoanalysis, the patient's unconsciously making the therapist the object of emotional response, transferring to the therapist responses appropriate to other persons important in the patient's life history.

**transsexual.** An individual who is physically one sex but psychologically the other. Transsexuals sometimes resort to surgery and hormonal treatment to change their physical appearance. They do not, however, consider themselves to be homosexual. See also *homosexual*.

**trichromatic theory.** A theory of color perception that postulates three basic color receptors (cones), a "red" receptor, a "green" receptor, and a "blue" receptor. The theory explains color blindness by the absence of one or more receptor types (syn. *Young-Helmholtz theory*). See also *opponent-color theory, two-stage color theory*.

**trichromatism.** Normal color vision, based on the classification of color vision according to three color systems: black-white, blue-yellow, and red-green. The normal eye sees all three; the colorblind eye is defective in one or two of the three systems. See also *dichromatism, monochromatism*.

**tricyclic antidepressant.** A class of antidepressants that relieve the symptoms of depression by preventing the reuptake of the neurotransmitters serotonin and norepinephrine, thereby prolonging their action. Imipramine (brand names, Tofranil and Elavil) is the drug most commonly prescribed. See also *antidepressant*.

**two-point threshold.** A kind of pressure threshold; it is the minimum distance by which two thin rods touching the skin must be separated before they are felt as two points rather than one.

**two-stage color theory.** A theory of color vision that postulates three types of cones (in agreement with trichromatic theory) followed by red-green and yellow-blue opponent processes (in agreement with opponent-color theory). This theory accounts for much of what is known about color vision, and serves as a prototype for the analysis of other sensory systems. See also *opponent-color theory, trichromatic theory*.

**type A and type B.** Two contrasting behavior patterns found in studies of coronary heart disease. Type A people are rushed, competitive, aggressive, and overcommitted to achieving; type Bs are more relaxed and feel less pressure. Type As are at risk for heart disease.

**type theory.** The theory that human subjects can profitably be classified into a small number of classes or types, each class or type having characteristics in common that set its members apart from other classes or types. See also *trait theory*.

**U**

**unconditioned response (UCR).** In classical conditioning, the response given originally to the unconditioned stimulus used as the basis for establishing a conditioned response to a previously neutral stimulus. See also *conditioned response, conditioned stimulus, unconditioned stimulus.*

**unconditioned stimulus (UCS).** In classical conditioning, a stimulus that automatically elicits a response, typically via a reflex, without prior conditioning. See also *conditioned response, conditioned stimulus, unconditioned response.*

**unconscious.** See *unconscious processes.*

**unconscious inference.** A term used by the German scientist Hermann von Helmholtz to describe the process by which the perceiver progresses from experiencing sensations evoked by an object to recognizing the properties of the object. We make this inference automatically and unconsciously, and eventually we do not even notice the sensations on which it is based. Helmholtz argued that unconscious inference is the basis of many perceptual phenomena, including distance and object perception.

**unconscious motive.** A motive of which the subject is unaware or aware of in distorted form. Because there is no sharp dividing line between conscious and unconscious, many motives have both conscious and unconscious aspects.

**unconscious processes.** Memories, impulses, and desires that are not available to consciousness. According to the psychoanalytic theories of Sigmund Freud, painful memories and wishes are sometimes repressed—that is, diverted to the unconscious where they continue to influence our actions even though we are not aware of them. See also *consciousness.*

## V

**validity.** The predictive significance of a test for its intended purposes. Validity can be measured by a coefficient of correlation between scores on the test and the scores that the test seeks to predict; in other words, scores on some criterion. See also *criterion, reliability.*

**validity coefficient.** The correlation between a test score and some criterion to which the test is supposed to predict.

See also *criterion, validity.*

**variable.** One of the conditions measured or controlled in an experiment. See also *dependent variable, independent variable.*

**variance.** The square of a standard deviation.

**ventromedial hypothalamus (VMH).** Area of the hypothalamus important to the regulation of food intake. Electrical stimulation of this area will make an experimental animal stop eating; destruction of brain tissue here produces voracious eating, eventually leading to obesity. See also *hypothalamus, lateral hypothalamus.*

**vestibular apparatus.** An organ in the inner ear that contains receptors for body movement and kinesthesis.

**vestibular sacs.** Two sacs in the labyrinth of the inner ear, called the *saccule* and *utricle,* which contain the otoliths ("ear stones"). Pressure of the otoliths on the hair cells in the gelatinous material of the utricle and saccule gives us the sense of body tilt or linear acceleration. See also *equilibratory senses.*

**vicarious learning.** Learning by observing the behavior of others and noting the consequences of that behavior (syn. *observational learning*).

**visual acuity.** The threshold for the minimum size of detail that a person can visually detect.

**visual area.** A projection area lying in the occipital lobe. In humans, damage to this area produces blindness in portions of the visual field corresponding to the amount and location of the damage.

**visual buffer.** In short-term memory, a hypothesized component of the encoding process that briefly stores information in a visual code (i.e., a visual representation of verbal and nonverbal items). See also *acoustic buffer, central executive, encoding, short-term memory.*

**visual cliff.** An experimental apparatus with glass over a patterned surface, one half of which is just below the glass and the other half, several feet below. Used to test the depth perception of animals and human infants.

**visual field.** The total visual array acting on the eye when it is directed toward a fixation point.

**visual-evoked potentials.** A method of studying perception using electrodes

placed on the back of the head over the visual cortex. The electrodes record electrical responses related to how well the observer can discriminate a presented stimulus.

**VMH.** See *ventromedial hypothalamus.*

**voice stress analyzer.** A device that graphically represents changes in a person's voice associated with emotion. Used in lie detection. See also *polygraph.*

**volumetric receptors.** Hypothesized receptors that regulate water intake by responding to the volume of blood and body fluids. Renin, a substance secreted by the kidneys into the bloodstream, may be one volumetric receptor; it constricts the blood vessels and stimulates the release of the hormone, angiotensin, which acts on cells in the hypothalamus to produce thirst. See also *osmoreceptors.*

**voluntary processes.** Activities selected by choice and controlled or monitored according to intention or plan. See also *control processes.*

**vulnerability-stress model.** An interactive model of physical or mental disorders that proposes that an individual will develop a disorder only when he or she has both some constitutional vulnerability (predisposition) and experiences stressful circumstances. Same as *diathesis-stress model.*

## W

**weak methods.** General problem-solving strategies that do not depend on specific knowledge of a problem. Examples are difference reduction, means-ends analysis, and working backwards. See also *difference reduction, means-ends analysis,* and *working backwards.*

**Weber's constant.** See *Weber's law.*

**Weber's law.** The observation that the difference threshold is a fixed proportion of the stimulus magnitude at which it is measured. The proportion is constant over a wide range of stimulus magnitudes, and is called Weber's constant. The value of Weber's constant depends on the sensory modality; the smaller the constant, the more sensitive the modality. See also *difference threshold.*

**Wernicke's area.** A portion of the left

cerebral hemisphere involved in language understanding. Individuals with damage in this area are not able to comprehend words; they can hear words, but they do not know their meanings.

**withdrawal symptoms.** Unpleasant physiological and psychological reactions that occur when a person suddenly stops taking an addictive drug; these range from nausea, anxiety, mild tremors, and difficulty sleeping at low levels of dependence to vomiting, cramps, hallucinations, agitation, and severe tremors or seizures at higher levels. See also *physical dependence.*

**working backwards.** A problem-solving strategy in which one works backwards from the goal towards the current state. See also *difference reduction, means-ends analysis.*

**working through.** In psychoanalytic therapy, the process of reeducation by having patients face the same conflicts over and over in the consultation room, until they can independently face and master the conflicts in ordinary life.

## X

**X chromosome.** A chromosome that, if paired with another X chromosome, determines that the individual will be a female. If it is combined with a Y chromosome, the individual will be a male. The X chromosome transmits sex-linked traits. See also *chromosome, sex-linked trait, Y chromosome.*

**XYY syndrome.** An abnormal condition in which a male has an extra Y sex chromosome; reputedly associated with unusual aggressiveness, although the evidence is not conclusive. See also *Y chromosome.*

## Y

**Y chromosome.** The chromosome that, combined with an X chromosome, determines maleness. See also *chromosome, sex-linked trait, X chromosome.*

**Young-Helmholtz theory.** See *trichromatic theory.*

## Z

**zygote.** A fertilized ovum or egg. See also *dizygotic twins, monozygotic twins.*

# Copyrights and Acknowledgments and Illustration Credits

Darley, J. M. and Latane, B. (1968) "Bystander intervention in emergencies: Diffusion of responsibility," *Journal of Personality and Social Psychology*, 8:377–83. Copyright © 1968 by the APA. Adapted by permission of the publisher and author. **19-5b** Adapted from *Readings in Social Psychology* by Alfred R. Lindesmith, copyright © 1969 by Holt, Rinehart and Winston, Inc., reproduced by permission of the publisher. **19-6a** From OBEDIENCE TO AUTHORITY: AN EXPERIMENTAL VIEW, copyright © 1974 by Stanley Milgram. Harper & Row, Publishers, Inc. Reprinted by permission of Alexandra Milgram. **19-8, 19-9** Petty, R. E. and Gaioppo, J. T. (1984) "The effects of involvement on responses to argument quantity and quality: Central and peripheral routes to persuasion," *Journal of Personality and Social Psychology*, 46:69–81. Copyright © 1984 by the APA. Adapted by permission of the publisher and author. **pp. 732, 733** Latane, B. (1981) "The psychology of social impact," *American Psychologist*, 36:343–56. Copyright © 1981 by the APA. Adapted by permission of the publisher and author. **pg. 742** Beirbrauer, G. (1979) "Why did he do it? Attribution of obedience and the phenomenon bias," *European Journal of Social Psychology*, 9:67–84. Copyright © 1979 John Wiley & Sons, Ltd. Reprinted by permission of the publisher.

## PHOTOS

### Chapter 1

**Page 8** Fritz Goro, LIFE Magazine, © 1971 Time Inc.; **10** Superstock Four by Five; **11** The Bettmann Archive; **14** © 1988 L. Manna; **20** Courtesy, Dr. Shirley Strum, University of California, San Diego. Photo by Bob Campbell; **25** B. Daemmrich/Stock Boston.

### Chapter 2

**39** CNRI/Science Photo Library/Photo Researchers; **46** © M. Kezar/TSW-Click, Chicago; **47** (left) M. Minton, Mallinckrodt Institute of Radiology/(c) 1989; Discover Publications; **47** (right) © D. McCoy/Rainbow; **49** © Martin Rotker/Phototake, NYC; **62** © NYC Cytogenics Lab/Peter Arnold, Inc.; **64** R. Langridge, UCSF/(c) D. McCoy/Rainbow; **66** M. Bates/Stock Boston.

### Chapter 3

**72** E. Crews; **74** E. Crews; **77** E. Crews; **78–79** E. Crews; **81** (top) Courtesy, Professor C. K. Rovee-Colier; **81** (bottom) © George Murrell; **84** Anderson/Monkmeyer; **86** Doug Goodman/Monkmeyer Press; **87** (top) © Marcia Weinstein; **87** (bottom) © Marcia Weinstein; **88** (left) E. Crews; **88** (right) Superstock Four By Five; **95** Courtesy of Frank Keil, Cornell University; **97** E. Crews; **100** © 1984 Martin Rogers/Stock Boston; **101** Superstock Four By Five; **103** (top) Skjold; **103** (bottom) Daemmrich/Stock Boston; **106, 107** Courtesy of Daryl Bem; **110** E. Crews; **112** Daemmrich/Stock Boston; **114** Superstock Four By Five; **116** Reproduced with the permission of the Children's Defense Fund; **115** (top) **115** (bottom) Stock Boston; **119** (top) Spencer Grant/Stock Boston; **119** (bottom) Superstock Four By Five; **121** Superstock Four By Five.

### Chapter 4

**139** Courtesy, Inmont Corporation; **139** Courtesy, Munsell Color, Baltimore, Maryland; **141** Fritz Goro, LIFE Magazine © 1944 Time Inc.; **142** Courtesy, Inmont Corporation; **143** Courtesy, The American Optical Corporation; **150** Superstock Four By Five; **151** © Boroff/TexaStock; **156** M. Weinstein; **166** Kaiser Porcelain, Ltd., London, England; **166** Salvador Dali, *Slave Market with Disappearing Bust of Voltaire*, 1940. The Salvador Dali Museum, St. Petersburg, Florida.

### Chapter 5

**170** California Museum of Photography, University of California, Riverside; **171** (left) © B. Hrynewych/Stock Boston; **171** (right) © M. Winter/Stock Boston; **184** Yarbus, D. L. (1967) "Eye Movements and Vision", Plenum Publishing Corporation. Reproduced by permission of the publisher; **190** © Norm Snyder, New York; **192** © P. Plailly/Science Photo Library/Photo Researchers; **193** Photo by David Linton; © 1989 Ann Linton; **194** Ginsberg, A. (1983) "Contrast perception in the human infant", unpublished manuscript, reproduced in SENSATION AND PERCEPTION, 2e, by E. Bruce Goldstein, copyright © 1984 by Wadsworth, Inc. Reprinted by permission of the publisher. Photo courtesy, Wadsworth, Inc.; **195** © William Vandivert, *Scientific American*, April 1960, cover photo.

### Chapter 6

**204** © B. Ullmann/Taurus Photos; **207** © James Newberry; **211** © 1988 L. Manna; **216** Dreamstage Scientific Catalog, © 1977 J. A. Hobson and Hoffmann-La Roche, Inc; **223** B. Daemmrich, **224** M. Forsyth/Monkmeyer Press; **225** © 1985 H. Morgan/Rainbow; **227** © C. Fitch/Taurus Photos; **229** © 1991 Custom Medical Stock Photos; **230** Superstock Four By Five, Inc.; **234** C. Wolinsky/Stock Boston; **235** B. Daemmrich; **236** © 1986 B. Bartholomew/Black Star; **239** © E. Arneson; **241** Courtesy, C. Honorton, Psychophysical Research Laboratories, Princeton, New Jersey; **246** © 1987 J. Mejuto; all rights reserved.

### Chapter 7

**254** The Bettmann Archive; **261** E. Lettau/FPG International; **266** (bottom) © Richard Wood The Picture Cube; **266** (top) Courtesy, Dr. B. F. Skinner; **267** Yerkes Regional Primate Research Center of Emory University; **268** Courtesy, Naval Oceans System Center; **270** Stock Boston; **272** Stock Boston; **275** © Sea World; **279** © R. Malmares; **280** Yerkes Regional Primate Research Center of Emory University.

### Chapter 8

**292** From ALICE IN WONDERLAND by Lewis Carroll, illustrated by Marjorie Torrey. Abridged under the supervision of Josette Frank. Copyright © 1955 by Random House, Inc. Reprinted by permission of the publisher; **298** Bill Binzen/Rainbow Stock; **310** © A/P Wide World Photos; **312** Bob Pizaro/Comstock; **316** © C. Kuhn/TexaStock; **322** Superstock Four By Five; **325** P. Markow/FPG International; **326** B. Daemmrich.

### Chapter 9

**332** Monkmeyer Press; **339** Superstock Four By Five; **350** Comstock; **351** Camilla Smith/Rainbow Stock; **352** Custom Medical Stock; **355** Photo Edit; **358** Magnum Photos; **363** B. Seitz/Photo Researchers; **364, 366** Susan Holtz; **365** E. Crews; **371** Courtesy, UCSD Public Information Office; photo by Alan Decker.

### Chapter 10

**377** Dollarhide/Monkmeyer; **378** B. Gallery/Stock Boston; **380** Courtesy, Dr. Neal E. Miller, Emeritus Professor, Rockefeller University; Research Affiliate, Yale University; **384** Photo Works/Monkmeyer; **386** Arlene Collins/Monkmeyer; **388** (top) Kinne/Comstock; **388** (bottom) Comstock; **392** (top) The Bettmann Archive; **392** (bottom) © Myles Aronowitz/Shooting Star; **397** (top) © D. Fritts/Animals, Animals; **397** (bottom) Harlow Primate Laboratory, University of Wisconsin; **399** Superstock Four By Five; **401** Skjold; **403** © 1973 Camera M. D. Studios; all rights reserved; **404** Comstock; **409** © Nina Leen, LIFE Magazine, © Time Inc.; **410** Harlow Primate Laboratory/ University of Wisconsin; **411** Photo courtesy Peter Suedfeld and Elizabeth J. Ballard; **413** Superstock Four By Five.

# References

The numbers in boldface following each reference give the text pages on which the article or book is cited. Citations in the text are made by author and date of publication.

ABBOTT, B. B., SCHOEN, L. S., & BADIA, P. (1984). Predictable and unpredictable shock: Behavioral measures of aversion and physiological measures of stress. PSYCHOLOGICAL BULLETIN, *96*, 45–71. **579**

ABELSON, R. P. (1968). Computers, polls, and public opinion—Some puzzles and paradoxes. TRANSACTION, *5*, 20–27. **728, 729**

ABELSON, R. P., ARONSON, E., MCGUIRE, W. J., NEWCOMB, T. M., ROSENBERG, M. J., & TANNENBAUM, P. H. (Eds.). (1968). THEORIES OF COGNITIVE CONSISTENCY: A SOURCEBOOK (pp. 112–39) Chicago: Rand McNally. **727**

ABRAMSON, L. Y., GARBER, J., EDWARDS, N., & SELIGMAN, M. E. P. (1978). Expectancy change in depression and schizophrenia. JOURNAL OF ABNORMAL PSYCHOLOGY, *87*, 165–179. **597**

ABRAMSON, L. Y., METALSKY, G. I., & ALLOY, L. B. (1989). Hopelessness depression: A theory-based subtype of depression. PSYCHOLOGICAL REVIEW, *96*, 358–372. **642**

ABRAMSON, L. Y., SELIGMAN, M. E. P., & TEASDALE, J. (1978). Learned helplessness in humans: critique and reformulation. JOURNAL OF ABNORMAL PSYCHOLOGY, *87*, 49–74. **642**

ABRAVANEL, E., & SIGAFOOS, A. D. (1984). Exploring the presence of imitation during early infancy. CHILD DEVELOPMENT, *55*, 381–392. **78**

ADAMS, J. L. (1974). CONCEPTUAL BLOCKBUSTING. Stanford, CA: Stanford Alumni Association. **363**

ADAMS, M., & COLLINS, A. (1979). A schema-theoretic view of reading. In R. O. Freedle (Ed.), NEW DIRECTIONS IN DISCOURSE PROCESSING, Vol. 12. Norwood, NJ: Ablex. **349**

ADLER, T. (1990, April). Docs the "new" MMPI beat the "classic?" APA MONITOR, pp. 18–19. **557**

ADORNO, T. W., FRENKEL-BRUNSWIK, E., LEVINSON, D. J., & SANFORD, R. N. (1950). THE AUTHORITARIAN PERSONALITY. New York: Harper. **731**

AGRAS, W. S. (1985). PANIC: FACING FEARS, PHOBIAS, AND ANXIETY. New York: Freeman. **635, 665, 709**

AIKEN, L. R. (1989). ASSESSMENT OF PERSONALITY. Boston: Allyn and Bacon. **573**

AINSWORTH, M. D. S. (1989). Attachments beyond infancy. AMERICAN PSYCHOLOGIST, *44*, 709–716. **496**

AINSWORTH, M. D. S., BLEHAR, M. C., WALTERS, E., & WALL, S. (1978). PATTERNS OF ATTACHMENT: A PSYCHOLOGICAL STUDY OF THE STRANGE SITUATION. Hillsdale, NJ: Erlbaum. **493, 495**

AKERS, C. (1984). Methodological criticisms of parapsychology. In S. Krippner (Ed.), ADVANCES IN PARAPSYCHOLOGICAL RESEARCH (Vol. 4). Jefferson, NC: McFarland. **243**

AKHTAR, S., WIG, N. N., VARMA, V. K., PERSHARD, D., & VERMA, S. K. (1975). A phenomenological analysis of symptoms in the obsessive-compulsive neurosis. BRITISH JOURNAL OF PSYCHIATRY, *127*, 342–348. **627**

ALBERTS, B., BRAY, D., LEWIS, J., RAFF, M., ROBERTS, K., & WATSON, J. D. (1989). MOLECULAR BIOLOGY OF THE CELL. New York: Garland. **69**

ALEXANDER, C. N., RAINFORTH, M. V., & GELDERLOOS, P. (1991). Transcendental meditation, self-actualization, and psychological health: A conceptual overview and statistical meta-analysis. JOURNAL OF SOCIAL BEHAVIOR AND PERSONALITY, *6(5)*, 189–247. **234**

ALLEN, J. B., KENRICK, D. T., LINDER, D. E., & MCCALL, A. M. (1989). Arousal and attraction: A response-facilitation alternative to misattribution and negative-reinforcement models. JOURNAL OF PERSONALITY AND SOCIAL PSYCHOLOGY, *57*, 261–270. **743**

ALLEN, M. G. (1976). Twin studies of affective illness. ARCHIVES OF GENERAL PSYCHIATRY, *35*, 1476–1478. **642**

ALLEN, V. L., & LEVINE, J. M. (1969). Consensus and conformity. JOURNAL OF EXPERIMENTAL SOCIAL PSYCHOLOGY, *5* (No. 4), 389–399. **761**

ALLEN, V. L., & LEVINE, J. M. (1971). Social support and conformity: The role of independent assessment of reality. JOURNAL OF EXPERIMENTAL SOCIAL PSYCHOLOGY, *7*, 48–58. **761**

ALLOY, L. B., & TABACHNIK, N. (1984). Assessment of covariation by animals and humans: Influence of prior expectations and current situational information. PSYCHOLOGICAL REVIEW, *91*, 112–149. **284**

ALLPORT, F. H. (1920). The influence of the group upon association and thought. JOURNAL OF EXPERIMENTAL PSYCHOLOGY, *3*, 159–182. **749**

ALLPORT, F. H. (1924). SOCIAL PSYCHOLOGY. Boston: Houghton Mifflin. **749**

ALLPORT, G. W., & ODBERT, H. S. (1936). Trait-names: A psycholexical study. PSYCHOLOGICAL MONOGRAPHS, *47*, (1, Whole No. 211.). **528**

ALLPORT, G. W. (1937). PERSONALITY: A PSYCHOLOGICAL INTERPRETATION. New York: Henry Holt. **526, 527, 566**

ALLPORT, G. W. (1961). PATTERNS AND GROWTH IN PERSONALITY. New York: Holt, Rinehart & Winston. **527**

ALTEMEYER, B. (1988). ENEMIES OF FREEDOM: UNDERSTANDING RIGHT-WING AUTHORITARIANISM. San Francisco: Jossey-Bass. **731**

AMERICAN PSYCHIATRIC ASSOCIATION. (1987). DIAGNOSTIC AND STATISTICAL MANUAL OF MENTAL DISORDERS (3rd ed., rev.). Washington, DC: American Psychiatric Association. **389, 620**

AMERICAN PSYCHOLOGICAL ASSOCIATION. (1990). Ethical principles of psychologists. AMERICAN PSYCHOLOGIST, *45*, 390–395. **20**

ANASTASI, A. (1988). PSYCHOLOGICAL TESTING (5th ed.). New York: Macmillan. **487**

ANCH, M. A., BROWMAN, C. P., MITLER, M. M., & WALSH, J. K. (1988). SLEEP: A SCIENTIFIC PERSPECTIVE. Englewood Cliffs, NJ: Prentice-Hall. **249**

ANCOLI-ISRAEL, S., KRIPKE, D. F., & MASON, W. (1987). Characteristics of obstructive and central sleep apnea in the elderly: An interim report. BIOLOGICAL PSYCHIATRY, *22*, 741–750. **216**

ANDERSON, C. M., REISS, D. J., & HOGARTY, G. E. (1986). SCHIZOPHRENIA AND THE FAMILY. New York: Guilford Press. **657**

ANDERSON, J. R. (1983). THE ARCHITECTURE OF COGNITION. Cambridge, MA: Harvard University Press. **294, 302, 303, 328**

ANDERSON, J. R. (1987). Skill acquisition: Compilation of weak-method problem solutions. PSYCHOLOGICAL REVIEW, *94*, 192–210. **316, 363**

ANDERSON, J. R. (1990). COGNITIVE PSYCHOLOGY AND ITS IMPLICATIONS (3rd ed.). New York: Freeman. **30, 328, 361, 362, 363, 369**

ANDREASEN, N. C. (1988). Brain imaging: Applications in psychiatry. SCIENCE, *239*, 1381–1388. **47, 654**

ANDREWS, K. H., & KANDEL, D. B. (1979). Attitude and behavior. AMERICAN SOCIOLOGICAL REVIEW, *44*, 298–310. **733**

ARDREY, R. (1966) THE TERRITORIAL IMPERATIVE. New York: Dell. **439**

ARENDT, H. (1963). EICHMANN IN JERUSALEM: A REPORT ON THE BANALITY OF EVIL. New York: Viking Press. **762**

ARMSTRONG S. L., GLEITMAN, L. R., & GLEITMAN, H. (1983). What some concepts might not be. COGNITION, *13*, 263–308. **333**

ARNOLD, M. (1949). A demonstrational analysis of the TAT in a clinical setting. JOURNAL OF ABNORMAL AND SOCIAL PSYCHOLOGY, *44*, 97–111. **560**

ARONSON, E. (1991). THE SOCIAL ANIMAL (6th ed.). New York: Freeman. **747, 767, 784**

ARONSON, E., & CARLSMITH, J. M. (1963). The effect of the severity of threat on the devaluation of forbidden behavior. JOURNAL OF ABNORMAL AND SOCIAL PSYCHOLOGY, *66*, 584–588. **735**

ASCH, S. E. (1952). SOCIAL PSYCHOLOGY. Englewood Cliffs, NJ: Prentice-Hall. **759, 761**

ASCH, S. E. (1955). Opinions and social pressures. SCIENTIFIC AMERICAN, *193*, 31–35. **759, 761**

ASCH, S. E. (1958). Effects of group pressure upon modification and distortion of judgments. In E. E. Maccoby, T. M. Newcomb, & E. L. Hartley (Eds.), READINGS IN SOCIAL PSYCHOLOGY (3rd ed.). New York: Holt, Rinehart & Winston. **759, 760, 761**

ASHCRAFT, M. H. (1989). HUMAN MEMORY AND COGNITION. Glenview, IL: Scott, Foresman & Co. **328**

ASLIN, R. N. (1987). Visual and auditory development in infancy. In J. D. Osofsky (Ed.), HANDBOOK OF INFANT DEVELOPMENT (2nd ed.). New York: Wiley. **80**

ASLIN, R. N., & BANKS, M. S. (1978). Early visual experience in humans: Evidence for a critical period in the development of binocular vision. In S. Schneider, H. Liebowitz, H. Pick, & H. Stevenson (Eds.), PSYCHOLOGY: FROM BASIC RESEARCH TO PRACTICE. New York: Plenum. **197**

ASSAD, G., & SHAPIRO, B. (1986). Hallucinations: Theoretical and clinical overview. AMERICAN JOURNAL OF PSYCHIATRY, *143*, (9), 1088–1097. **649**

ATKINSON, R. C. (1975). Mnemotechnics in second-language learning. AMERICAN PSYCHOLOGIST, *30*, 821–828. **318**

ATKINSON, R. C. (1974). Teaching children to read using a computer. AMERICAN PSYCHOLOGIST, *29*, 169–178. **16**

ATKINSON, R. C., HERRNSTEIN, R. J., LINDZEY, G., & LUCE, R. D. (Eds.). (1988). STEVENS' HANDBOOK OF EXPERIMENTAL PSYCHOLOGY (Vols. 1 and 2). New York: Wiley. **163, 329**

ATKINSON, R. C., & SHIFFRIN, R. M. (1968). Human memory: A proposed system and its control processes. In K. W. Spence (Ed.), THE PSYCHOLOGY OF LEARNING AND MOTIVATION: ADVANCES IN RESEARCH AND THEORY, 2, (89–195). **297**

ATKINSON, R. C., & SHIFFRIN, R. M. (1971). The control of short-term memory. SCIENTIFIC AMERICAN, *224*, 82–90. **297**

AULD, F., & HYMAN, M. (1991). RESOLUTION OF INNER CONFLICT: AN INTRODUCTION TO PSYCHOANALYTIC THERAPY. Washington, DC: American Psychological Association. 708–709. **676**

AVERILL, J. R. (1982). ANGER AND AGGRESSION: AN ESSAY ON EMOTION. New York: Springer-Verlag. **447**

AVERILL, J. R. (1983) Studies on anger and aggression: Implications for theories of emotion. AMERICAN PSYCHOLOGIST, *38*, 1145–1160. **445**

AWAYA, S. MIYAKE Y., IMAYUMI, Y., SHIOSE, Y., KNADA, T., & KOMURO, K. (1973). Amblyopia. JAPANESE JOURNAL OF OPTHALMOLOGY, *17*, 69–82. **197**

AX, A. (1953). The physiological differentiation between fear and anger in humans. PSYCHOSOMATIC MEDICINE, *15*, 433–442. **421**

BAARS, B. J. (1988). COGNITIVE THEORY OF CONSCIOUSNESS. New York: Cambridge University Press. **249**

BADDELEY, A. D. (1986) WORKING MEMORY. New York: Oxford University Press. **292, 296, 329**

BADDELEY, A. D. (1990). HUMAN MEMORY: THEORY AND PRACTICE. Boston: Allyn and Bacon. **311, 328**

BADDELEY, A. D., & HITCH, G. J. (1974). Working memory. In G. H. Bower (Ed.), THE PSYCHOLOGY OF LEARNING AND MOTIVATION (Vol. 8). New York: Academic Press. **296**

BADDELEY, A. D., THOMPSON, N., & BUCHANAN, M. (1975). Word length and the structure of short-term memory. JOURNAL OF VERBAL LEARNING AND VERBAL BEHAVIOR, *14*, 575–589. **295**

BAER, P. E., & FUHRER, M. J. (1968). Cognitive processes during differential trace and delayed conditioning of the G. S. R. JOURNAL OF EXPERIMENTAL PSYCHOLOGY, *78*, 81–88. **257**

BAHRICK, H. P., & PHELPHS, E. (1987). Retention of Spanish vocabulary over eight years. JOURNAL OF EXPERIMENTAL PSYCHOLOGY: LEARNING, MEMORY AND COGNITION, *13*, 344–349. **302**

BAILLARGEON, R. (1987). Object permanence in 3-1/2- and 4-1/2-month-old infants. DEVELOPMENTAL PSYCHOLOGY, *23*, 655–664. **91, 92**

BAILLARGEON, R., SPELKE, E. S., & WASSERMAN, S. (1985) Object permanence in five-month-old infants. COGNITION, *20*, 191–208. **91**

BAILEY, C. H., CHEN, M., KELLER,

F., & KANDEL, E. R. (1992). Serotonin-mediated endocytosis of apCAM: an early step of learning-related synaptic growth in aplysia. SCIENCE, *256*, 645–649. **265**

BANDURA, A. (1973). AGGRESSION: A SOCIAL LEARNING ANALYSIS. Englewood Cliffs, NJ: Prentice-Hall. **441, 443, 447**

BANDURA, A. (1977). SOCIAL LEARNING THEORY. Englewood Cliffs, N.J: Prentice-Hall. **441, 447, 572**

BANDURA, A. (1984). Recycling misconceptions of perceived self-efficacy. COGNITIVE THERAPY AND RESEARCH, *8*, 231–255. **685**

BANDURA, A. (1986). SOCIAL FOUNDATIONS OF THOUGHT AND ACTION: A SOCIAL COGNITIVE THEORY. Englewood Cliffs, NJ: Prentice-Hall. **102, 441**

BANDURA, A., BLANCHARD, E. B., & RITTER, B. (1969). The relative efficacy of desensitization and modeling approaches for inducing behavioral, affective, and attitudinal changes. JOURNAL OF PERSONALITY AND SOCIAL PSYCHOLOGY, *13*, 173–199. **680**

BANDURA, A., TAYLOR, C. B., EWART, C. K., MILLER, N. M., & DEBUSK, R. F. (1985). Exercise testing to enhance wives' confidence in their husbands' cardiac capability soon after clinically uncomplicated acute myocardial infarction. AMERICAN JOURNAL OF CARDIOLOGY, *55*, 635–638. **562**

BANKS, M. S. (1982). The development of spatial and temporal contrast sensitivity. CURRENT EYE RESEARCH, *2*, 191–198. **194**

BANKS, W. P., & PRINTZMETAL, W. (1976). Configurational effects in visual information processing. PERCEPTION AND PSYCHOPHYSICS, *19*, 361–367. **167**

BANKS, W. P., & SALAPATEK, P. (1983). Infant visual perception. In P. H. Mussen (Ed.), HANDBOOK OF CHILD PSYCHOLOGY (Vol. 2). New York: Wiley. **80**

BANYAI, E. I., & HILGARD, E. R. (1976). A comparison of active-alert hypnotic induction with traditional relaxation induction. JOURNAL OF ABNORMAL PSYCHOLOGY, *85*, 218–224. **236**

BARBOUR, H. G. (1912). Die wirkung unmittelbarer erwarmung und abkuhlung der warmenzentrum auf die korpertemperatur. ACHIV FUR EXPERIMENTALLE PATHALOGIE UND PHARMAKOLOGIE, *70*, 1–26. **375**

BAREFOOT, J. C., DODGE, K. A., PETERSON, B. L., DAHLSTROM, W. G., & WILLIAMS, R. B., JR. (1989) The Cook-Medley hostility scale: Item content and ability to predict survival. PSYCHOSOMATIC MEDICINE, *51*, 46–57. **601**

BAREFOOT, J. C., WILLIAMS, R. B., & DAHLSTROM, W. G. (1983). Hostility, CHD incidence and total mortality: A 25-year follow-up study of 255 physicians. PSYCHOSOMATIC MEDICINE, *45*, 59–63. **601**

BARKOW, J., COSMIDES, L., & TOOBY, J. (1990). THE ADAPTED MIND: EVOLUTIONARY PSYCHOLOGY AND THE GENERATION OF CULTURE. Oxford University Press. **31**

BARLOW, H. B., & MOLLON, J. D. (1982). THE SENSES. Cambridge: Cambridge University Press. **163**

BARNES, G. E., & PROSEN, H. (1985). Parental death and depression. JOURNAL OF ABNORMAL PSYCHOLOGY, *94*, 64–69. **640**

BARON, J. (1988). THINKING AND DECIDING. Cambridge: Cambridge University Press. **369**

BARON, R. S. (1986). Distraction-conflict theory: Progress and problems. In L. Berkowitz (Ed.), ADVANCES IN EXPERIMENTAL SOCIAL PSYCHOLOGY (Vol. 19). New York: Academic Press. **754**

BARRERA, M. E., & MAURER, D. (1981). Recognition of mother's photographed face by the three-month-old infant. CHILD DEVELOPMENT, *52*, 714–716. **195**

BARRETT, G. V., & DEPINET, R. L. (1991). A reconsideration of testing for competence rather than for intelligence. AMERICAN PSYCHOLOGIST, *46*, (10), 1012–1024. **467, 469**

BARRY, H., CHILD, I., & BACON, M. (1959). Relation of child training to subsistence economy. AMERICAN ANTHROPOLOGIST, *61*, 51–63. **507**

BARSALOU, L. W. (1985). Ideals, central tendency, and frequency of instantiation as determinants of graded structure in categories. JOURNAL OF EXPERIMENTAL PSYCHOLOGY: LEARNING, MEMORY, AND COGNITION, *11*, 629–654. **332**

BARTLETT, F. C. (1932). REMEMBERING: A STUDY IN EXPERIMENTAL AND SOCIAL PSYCHOLOGY. Cambridge: Cambridge University Press. **325**

BARTOSHUK, L. M. (1979). Bitter taste of saccharin: Related to the genetic ability to taste the bitter substance propylthiourial (PROP). SCIENCE, *205*, 934–935. **155**

BASSETT, A. S. (1989). Chromosome 5 and schizophrenia: Implications for genetic linkage studies, current and future. SCHIZOPHRENIA BULLETIN, *15*, 393–402. **652**

BAUM, A., GATCHEL, R. J., FLEMING, R., & LAKE, C. R. (1981). CHRONIC AND ACUTE STRESS ASSOCIATED WITH THE THREE MILE ISLAND ACCIDENT AND DECONTAMINATION: PRELIMINARY FINDINGS OF A LONGITUDINAL STUDY. Technical report submitted to the U.S. Nuclear Regulatory Commission.

BAUMEISTER, R. F., & TICE, D. M. (1984). Role of self-presentation and choice in cognitive dissonance under forced compliance: Necessary or sufficient causes? JOURNAL OF PERSONALITY AND SOCIAL PSYCHOLOGY, *43*, 838–852. **735**

BAUMRIND, D. (1967). Childcare practices anteceding three patterns of preschool behavior. GENETIC PSYCHOLOGY MONOGRAPHS, *75*, 43–88. **500**

BAUMRIND, D. (1971). Current patterns of parental authority. DEVELOPMENTAL PSYCHOLOGY MONOGRAPHS, *1*, 1–103. **500**

BAXTER, L. R., JR., SCHWARTZ, J. M., MAZZIOTTA, J. C., PHELPS, M. E., PAHL, J. J., GUZE, M. D., & FAIRBANKS, L. (1988) Cerebral glucose matabolic rates in nondepressed patients with obsessive-compulsive disorder. AMERICAN JOURNAL OF PSYCHIATRY, *145*, 1560–1563. **635**

BEAMAN, A. L., BARNES, P. J., KLENTZ, B., & MCQUIRK, B. (1978). Increasing helping rates through information dissemination: Teaching pays. PERSONALITY AND SOCIAL PSYCHOLOGY BULLETIN, *4*, 406–411. **758**

BEATON, A. (1986). LEFT SIDE/RIGHT SIDE: A REVIEW OF LATERALITY RESEARCH. New Haven: Yale University Press. **69**

BEBBINGTON, P., STURT, E., TENNANT, C., & HURRY, J. (1984). Misfortune and resilience: A community study of women. PSYCHOLOGICAL MEDICINE, *14*, 347–363. **645**

BECK, A. T. (1976). COGNITIVE THERAPY AND THE EMOTIONAL DISORDER. New York: International Universities Press. **641, 684**

BECK, A. T. (1988a). LOVE IS NEVER ENOUGH. New York: Harper & Row. **634**

BECK, A. T. (1988b). Cognitive approaches to panic disorder: Theory and therapy. In S. Rachman & J. D. Maser (Eds.), PANIC: PSYCHOLOGICAL PERSPECTIVES. Hillsdale, NJ: Erlbaum. **709**

BECK, A. T. (1991). Cognitive therapy. AMERICAN PSYCHOLOGIST, *46* (4), 368–375. **641**

BECK, A. T., RUSH, A. J., SHAW, B. F., & EMERY, G. (1979). COGNITIVE THERAPY OF DEPRESSION. New York: Guilford Press. **636, 641**

BEECHER, H. K. (1961). Surgery as placebo. JOURNAL OF AMERICAN MEDICAL ASSOCIATION, *176*, 1102–1107. **698**

BEERS, C. W. (1908) A MIND THAT FOUND ITSELF. New York: Doubleday. **668**

BÉKÉSY, G. VON (1960). EXPERIMENTS IN HEARING, (E. G. Weaver, Trans). New York: McGraw-Hill. **151**

BELL, A. P., & WEINBERG M. S. (1978). HOMOSEXUALITIES: A STUDY OF DIVERSITY AMONG MEN AND WOMEN. New York: Simon & Schuster. **401, 403**

BELL, A. P., WEINBERG, M. S., & HAMMERSMITH, S. K. (1981). SEXUAL PREFERENCE: ITS DEVELOPMENT IN MEN AND WOMEN. Bloomington: Indiana University Press. **401, 402**

BELL, L. V. (1980). TREATING THE MENTALLY ILL: FROM COLONIAL TIMES TO THE PRESENT. New York: Praeger. **708**

BELL, S. M., & AINSWORTH, M. D. (1972). Infant crying and maternal responsiveness. CHILD DEVELOPMENT, *43*, 1171–1190. **496**

BELLACK, A. S., HERSEN, M., & KAZDIN, A. E. (Eds.) (1990). INTERNATIONAL HANDBOOK OF BEHAVIOR MODIFICATION AND THERAPY. New York: Plenum Press. **709**

BELLEZZA, F. S., & BOWER, G. H. (1981). Person stereotypes and memory for people. JOURNAL OF PERSONALITY AND SOCIAL PSYCHOLOGY, *41* (No. 5), 856–865. **325**

BELOFF, H. (1957). The structure and origin of the anal character. GENETIC PSYCHOLOGY MONOGRAPHS, *55*, 141–172. **539**

BELSKY, J., & ROVINE, M. J. (1987). Temperament and attachment security in the strange situation: An empirical rapprochement. CHILD DEVELOPMENT, *58*, 787–795. **496**

BELSKY, J., & ROVINE, M. (1988). Nonmaternal care in the first year of life and security of infant–parent attachment. CHILD DEVELOPMENT, *59*, 157–167. **499**

BELSKY, J., ROVINE, M., & TAYLOR, D. G. (1984). The Pennsylvania infant and family development project III: The origins of individual differences in infant-mother attachment: Maternal and infant contributions. CHILD DEVELOPMENT, *55*, 718–728. **495**

BEM, D. J. (1970). BELIEFS, ATTITUDES, AND HUMAN AFFAIRS. Belmont, CA: Brooks/Cole. **747**

BEM, D. J. (1972) Self-perception theory. In L. Berkowitz (Ed.), ADVANCES IN EXPERIMENTAL SOCIAL PSYCHOLOGY (Vol. 6). New York: Academic Press. **723**

BEM, D. J. (1983) Toward a response style theory of persons in situations. In R. A. Dienstbier & M. M. Page (Eds.), NEBRASKA SYMPOSIUM ON MOTIVATION 1982: PERSONALITY—CURRENT THEORY AND RESEARCH (Vol. 30, pp. 201–231). Lincoln: University of Nebraska Press. **526, 565, 567**

BEM, D. J., & ALLEN, A. (1974). On predicting some of the people some of the time: The search for cross-situational consistencies in behavior. PSYCHOLOGICAL REVIEW, *81*, 506–520. **565, 567**

BEM, D. J., WALLACH, M. A., & KOGAN, N. (1965). Group decision-making under risk of aversive consequences. JOURNAL OF PERSONALITY AND SOCIAL PSYCHOLOGY, *1*, 453–460. **778**

BEM, S. L. (1981). Gender schema theory: A cognitive account of sex typing. PSYCHOLOGICAL REVIEW, *88*, 354–364. **110**

BEM, S. L. (1985). Androgyny and gender schema theory: A conceptual and empirical integration. In T. B. Sonderegger (Ed.), NEBRASKA SYMPOSIUM ON MOTIVATION 1984: PSYCHOLOGY AND GENDER (pp. 179–226). Lincoln, NE: University of Nebraska Press. **109, 110**

BEM, S. L. (1987). Gender schema theory and the romantic tradition. In P. Shaver, & C. Hendrick (Eds.), REVIEW OF PERSONALITY AND SOCIAL PSYCHOLOGY (Vol. 7, pp. 251–271). Newbury Park, CA: Sage. **97**

BEM, S. L. (1989). Genital knowledge and gender constancy in preschool children. CHILD DEVELOPMENT, *60*, 649–662. **105, 106, 107**

BEM, S. L. (1993). THE LENSES OF GENDER: TRANSFORMING THE DEBATE ON SEXUAL INEQUALITY. New Haven, CT: Yale University Press. **97, 110, 123**

BEM, S. L., MARTYNA, W., & WATSON, C. (1976). Sex typing and androgyny: Further explorations of the expressive domain. JOURNAL OF PERSONALITY AND SOCIAL PSYCHOLOGY, *34*, 1016–1023. **103**

BENBOW, C. P. (1988). Sex differences in mathematical reasoning ability in intellectually talented preadolescents: Their nature, effects, and possible causes. BEHAVIORAL AND BRAIN SCIENCES, *11*, 169–232. **471**

BENSON, H. (1976) THE RELAXATION RESPONSE. New York: Morrow. **249**

BENSON, H., KOTCH, J. B., CRASSWELLER, K. D., & GREENWOOD, M. M. (1977). Historical and clinical considerations of the relaxation response. AMERICAN SCIENTIST, *65*, 441–443. **234**

BERGIN, A. E., & LAMBERT, M. J. (1978). The evaluation of therapeutic outcomes. In S. L. Garfield & A. E. Bergin (Eds.), HANDBOOK OF PSYCHOTHERAPY AND BEHAVIOR CHANGE (2nd ed.). New York: Wiley. **694, 695**

BERKOWITZ, L. (1965). The concept of aggressive drive. In L. Berkowitz (Ed.), ADVANCES IN EXPERIMENTAL SOCIAL PSYCHOLOGY (Vol. 2). New York: Academic Press. **443**

BERLIN, B., & KAY, P. (1969). BASIC COLOR TERMS: THEIR UNIVERSALITY AND EVOLUTION. Los Angeles: University of California Press. **338**

BERMAN, A. L. & JOBES, D. A. (1991). ADOLESCENT SUICIDE ASSESSMENT AND INTERVENTION. Washington, DC: American Psychological Association. **639**

BERNSTEIN, W. M., STEPHAN, W. G., & DAVIS, M. H. (1979). Explaining attributions for achievement: A path analytic approach. JOURNAL OF PERSONALITY AND SOCIAL PSYCHOLOGY, *37*, 1810–1821. **726**

BERRY, J. W. (1967). Independence and conformity in subsistence-level societies. JOURNAL OF PERSONALITY AND SOCIAL PSYCHOLOGY, *7*, 415–418. **508**

BERSCHEID, E. (1983). Emotion. In H. H. Kelley, E. Berscheid, A. Christensen, J. H. Harvey, T. L. Huston, G. Levinger, E. McClintock, L. A. Peplau, & D. R. Peterson (Eds.), CLOSE RELATIONSHIPS (pp. 110–168). New York: Freeman. **743**

BERSCHEID, E., & WALSTER, E. H. (1974). A little bit about love. In T. Huston (Ed.), FOUNDATION OF INTERPERSONAL ATTRACTION. New York: Academic Press. **742**

BERSCHEID, E., & WALSTER, E. H. (1978). INTERPERSONAL ATTRACTION (2nd ed.). Menlo Park, CA: Addison-Wesley. **739, 742**

BEIDERMAN, I. (1987). Recognition by components: A theory of human image understanding. PSYCHOLOGICAL REVIEW, *94*, 115–1947. **179, 180, 181**

BIEDERMAN, I. (1990). Higher-level vision. In D. N. Osherson, S. M. Kossyln, & J. M. Hollerbach (Eds.). AN INVITATION TO COGNITIVE SCIENCE: VI-

SUAL COGNITION AND ACTION (Vol. 2). Cambridge, MA: MIT Press. **179**

BIEDERMAN, I., & JU, G. (1988). Surface versus edge-based determinants of visual recognition. COGNITIVE PSYCHOLOGY, *20*, 38–64. **173**

BIERBRAUER, G. (1973). ATTRIBUTION AND PERSPECTIVE: EFFECTS OF TIME, SET, AND ROLE ON INTERPERSONAL INFERENCE. Unpublished Ph.D. dissertation, Stanford University. **767**

BILLINGS, A. G., & MOOS, R. H. (1984). Coping, stress, and social resources among adults with unipolar depression. JOURNAL OF PERSONALITY AND SOCIAL PSYCHOLOGY, *46*, 887–891. **602**

BINET, A., & SIMON, T. (1905). New methods for the diagnosis of the intellectual level of subnormals. ANNALS OF PSYCHOLOGY, *11*, 191. **470**

BIRNHOLZ, J. C., & BENACERRAF, B. R. (1983). The development of human fetal hearing. SCIENCE, *222*, 516–518. **81**

BISIACH, E., & LUZZATI, C. (1978). Unilateral neglect of representational space. CORTEX, *14*, 129–133. **360**

BLAKEMORE, C., & COOPER, G. F. (1970). Development of the brain depends on the visual environment. NATURE, *228*, 477–478. **197**

BLASS, E. M., & EPSTEIN, A. N. (1971). A lateral preoptic osmosensitive zone for thirst in the rat. JOURNAL OF COMPARATIVE AND PHYSIOLOGICAL PSYCHOLOGY, *76*, 378–394. **376**

BLISS, E. L. (1980). Multiple personalities: Report of fourteen cases with implications for schizophrenia and hysteria. ARCHIVES OF GENERAL PSYCHIATRY, *37*, 1388–1397. **209**

BLOCK, J. (1961/1978). THE Q-SORT METHOD IN PERSONALITY ASSESSMENT AND PSYCHIATRIC RESEARCH. Palo Alto: Consulting Psychologists Press. **512, 554**

BLOCK, J. (1971). LIVES THROUGH TIME. Berkeley: Bancroft. **512, 514, 523**

BLOOD, R. O. (1967). LOVE MATCH AND ARRANGED MARRIAGE. New York: Free Press. **743**

BLUM, G. S. (1953). PSYCHOANALYTIC THEORIES OF PERSONALITY. New York: McGraw-Hill. **540**

BLUMENTHAL, J. A., FREDRIKSON, M., KUHN, C. M., ULMER, R. L., WALSH-RIDDLE, M., & APPELBAUM, M. (1990). Aerobic exercise reduces levels of cardiovascular and sympathoadrenal responses to mental stress in subjects without prior evidence of myocardial ischemia. AMERICAN JOURNAL OF CARDIOLOGY, *65*, 93–98. **612**

BOFF, K. R., KAUFMAN, L., & THOMAS, J. P. (Eds.) (1986). HANDBOOK OF PERCEPTION AND HUMAN PERFORMANCE (Vol. 1). New York: Wiley. **163**

BOLLES, R. C. (1970). Species-specific defense reactions and avoidance learning. PSYCHOLOGICAL REVIEW, *77*, 32–48. **277**

BONANNO, G. A., & SINGER, J. L. (1990). Repressive personality style: Theoretical and methodological implications for health and pathology. In J. L. Singer (Ed.), REPRESSION AND DISSOCIATION (pp. 435–465). Chicago: University of Chicago Press. **606**

BOND, C. F. (1982). Social facilitation: A self-presentational view. JOURNAL OF PERSONALITY AND SOCIAL PSYCHOLOGY, *42*, 1042–1050. **754**

BOOTH-KEWLEY, S., & FRIEDMAN, H. S. (1987). Psychological predictors of heart disease: A quantitative review. PSYCHOLOGICAL BULLETIN, *101*, 343–362. **601**

BOOTZIN, R. R., KIHLSTROM, J. F., & SCHACTER, D. L. (Eds.) (1990). Sleep and Cognition. Washington, DC: American Psychological Assoc. **249**

BORGIDA, E., & NISBETT, R. E. (1977). The differential impact of abstract vs. concrete information on decisions. JOURNAL OF APPLIED SOCIAL PSYCHOLOGY, *7*, 258–271. **715**

BORING, E. G. (1930). A new ambiguous figure. AMERICAN JOURNAL OF PSYCHOLOGY, *42*, 444–445. **182**

BOUCHARD, C. et al (1990). The response to long-term overeating in identical twins. NEW ENGLAND JOURNAL OF MEDICINE, *322*, 1477–1482. **384, 478, 490**

BOUCHARD, T. J., JR. (1984). Twins reared apart and together: What they tell us about human diversity. In S. Fox (Ed.), THE CHEMICAL AND BIOLOGICAL BASES OF INDIVIDUALITY. New York: Plenum. **490**

BOUCHARD, T. J., & MCGUE, M. (1981). Familial studies of intelligence: A review. SCIENCE, *212*, 1055–1059. **479**

BOWER, G. H. (1981). Mood and memory. AMERICAN PSYCHOLOGIST, *6*, 129–148. **311, 436**

BOWER, G. H., BLACK, J. B., & TURNER, T. R. (1979). Scripts in memory for text. COGNITIVE PSYCHOLOGY, *11*, 177–220. **325**

BOWER, G. H., & CLARK, M. C. (1969). Narrative stories as mediators for serial learning. PSYCHONOMIC SCIENCE, *14*, 181,–182. **320**

BOWER, G. H., CLARK, M. C., WINZENZ, D., & LESGOLD, A. (1969) Hierarchical retrieval schemes in recall of categorized word lists. JOURNAL OF VERBAL LEARNING AND VERBAL BEHAVIOR, *8*, 323–343. **307**

BOWER, G. H., & HILGARD, E. R. (1981). THEORIES OF LEARNING (5th ed.). Englewood Cliffs, NJ: Prentice-Hall. **30, 287**

BOWER, G. H., & SPRINGSTON, F. (1970). Pauses as recoding points in letter series. JOURNAL OF EXPERIMENTAL PSYCHOLOGY, *83*, 421–430. **293**

BOWER, T. G. R. (1982). DEVELOPMENT IN INFANCY (2nd ed.). San Francisco: Freeman. **196**

BOWERS, K. S., & MEICHENBAUM, D. H. (Eds.) (1984). THE UNCONSCIOUS RECONSIDERED. New York: Wiley. **249**

BOWLBY, J. (1973). ATTACHMENT AND LOSS: SEPARATION, ANXIETY AND ANGER (Vol. 2). London: Hogarth Press. **97, 100, 493**

BOYNTON, R. M. (1979). HUMAN COLOR VISION. New York: Holt, Rinehart & Winston. **163**

BOYNTON, R. M. (1988). Color vision. ANNUAL REVIEW OF PSYCHOLOGY, *39*, 69–100.

BRADSHAW, G. L., & ANDERSON, J. R. (1982). Elaborative encoding as an explanation of levels of processing. JOURNAL OF VERBAL LEARNING AND VERBAL BEHAVIOR, *21*, 165–174. **300**

BRADWEJN, J., KOSZYCKI, D., & METERISSIAN, G. (1990). Cholecystokinin tetrapeptide induces panic attacks identical to spontaneous panic attacks in patients suffering from panic disorder. CANADIAN JOURNAL OF PSYCHIATRY, *35*, 83–85. **633**

BRANSFORD, J. D., & JOHNSON, M. K. (1973). Considerations of some problems of comprehension. In W. G. Chase (Ed.), VISUAL INFORMATION PROCESSING. New York: Academic Press. **349**

BRAUN, B. G. (1986). TREATMENT OF MULTIPLE PERSONALITY DISORDER. Washington, DC: American Psychiatric Press. **209, 249**

BRAVERMAN, L. B. (1989). Beyond the myth of motherhood. In M. McGoldrick, C. M. Anderson, & F. Walsh (Eds.), WOMEN AND FAMILIES (pp. 227–243). New York: Free Press. **499**

BRAZELTON, T. B. (1978). The remarkable talents of the newborn. BIRTH & FAMILY JOURNAL, *5*, 4–10. **81**

BREGMAN, A. S., & REIDNICKY, A. I.

(1975). Auditory segregation: Stream of streams? JOURNAL OF EXPERIMENTAL PSYCHOLOGY: HUMAN PERCEPTION AND PERFORMANCE, *1*, 263–267. **168**

BREHM, S. S. (1992). INTIMATE RELATIONSHIPS (2nd ed.). New York: McGraw-Hill. **736, 744, 747**

BRELAND, K., & BRELAND, M. (1961). The misbehavior of organisms. AMERICAN PSYCHOLOGIST, *16*, 681–684. **275**

BRELAND, K., & BRELAND, M. (1966). ANIMAL BEHAVIOR. New York: Macmillan. **267**

BRENNER, C. (1980). A psychoanalytic theory of affects. In R. Plutchik & H. Kellerman (Eds.), EMOTION: THEORY, RESEARCH, AND EXPERIENCE (Vol. 1). New York: Academic Press. **428**

BRENNER, M. H. (1982). Mental illness and the economy. In D. L. Parron, F. Solomon, & C. D. Jenkins (Eds.), BEHAVIOR, HEALTH RISKS, AND SOCIAL DISADVANTAGE. Washington, DC: National Academy Press. **656**

BRENNER, S. N., & MOLANDER, E. A. (1977, January–February). Is the ethics of business changing? HARVARD BUSINESS REVIEW, 57–71. **727**

BREWER, W. F., & NAKAMURA, G. V. (1984). The nature and functions of schemas. In R. S. Wyer & T. K. Srull (Eds.), HANDBOOK OF SOCIAL COGNITION (Vol. 1). Hillsdale, NJ: Erlbaum. **326**

BREWIN, C. R. (1985). Depression and causal attributions: What is their relation? PSYCHOLOGICAL BULLETIN, *98*, 297–300. **642**

BRIDGER, W. H. (1961). Sensory habituation and discrimination in the human neonate. AMERICAN JOURNAL OF PSYCHIATRY, *117*, 991–996. **77**

BROADBENT, D. E. (1958). PERCEPTION AND COMMUNICATION. London: Pergamon Press. **185**

BRODY, N. (1992). INTELLIGENCE (2nd ed.). San Diego: Academic Press. **487**

BROOKS-GUNN, J., & RUBLE, D. N. (1983). The experience of menarche from a developmental perspective. In J. Brooks-Gunn & A. C. Petersen (Eds.), GIRLS AT PUBERTY: BIOLOGICAL AND PSYCHOLOGICAL PERSPECTIVES. New York: Plenum. **112**

BROWN, A. E. (1936). Dreams in which the dreamer knows he is asleep. JOURNAL OF ABNORMAL PSYCHOLOGY, *31*, 59–66. **217**

BROWN, D. P. (1977). A model for the levels of concentrative meditation. INTERNATIONAL JOURNAL OF CLINICAL AND EXPERIMENTAL HYPNOSIS,

*25*, 236–273. **233**

BROWN, E. L., & DEFFENBACHER, K. (1979). PERCEPTION AND THE SENSES. Oxford: Oxford University Press. **158**

BROWN, G. W., & HARRIS, T. (1978). SOCIAL ORIGINS OF DEPRESSION: A STUDY OF PSYCHIATRIC DISORDER IN WOMEN. London: Tavistock. **645**

BROWN, J. (1991). Staying fit and staying well: Physical fitness as a moderator of life stress. JOURNAL OF PERSONALITY AND SOCIAL PSYCHOLOGY, *60*, 555–561. **612**

BROWN, J. D. (1986). Evaluations of self and others: Self-enhancement biases in social judgments. SOCIAL COGNITION, *4*, 353–376. **644**

BROWN, R. (1973). A FIRST LANGUAGE: THE EARLY STAGES. Cambridge, MA: Harvard University Press. **369**

BROWN, R. (1974). Further comment on the risky shift. AMERICAN PSYCHOLOGIST, *29*, 468–470. **779**

BROWN, R. (1986). SOCIAL PSYCHOLOGY: THE SECOND EDITION. New York: Free Press. **338, 358, 406**

BROWN, R., CAZDEN, C. B., & BELLUGI, U. (1969). The child's grammar from 1 to 3. In J. P. Hill (Ed.), MINNESOTA SYMPOSIUM ON CHILD PSYCHOLOGY (Vol. 2). Minneapolis: University of Minnesota Press. **353**

BROWN, R., & KULIK, J. (1977). Flashbulb memories. COGNITION, *5*, 73–99. **309**

BROWN, R. W., & McNEILL, D. (1966). The "tip-of-the-tongue" phenomenon. JOURNAL OF VERBAL LEARNING AND VERBAL BEHAVIOR, *5*, 325–337. **301**

BROWNELL, K. (1988). Yo-yo dieting. PSYCHOLOGY TODAY, *22*,(Jan), 20–23. **388**

BROZAN, N. (1985 March 13). U.S. leads industrialized nations in teen-age births and abortions. NEW YORK TIMES, p. 1. **117**

BRUCH, H. (1973). EATING DISORDERS: OBESITY, ANOREXIA NERVOSA, AND THE PERSON WITHIN. New York: Basic Books. **387, 389, 390, 392, 393**

BRUNER, J. S. (1957). Going beyond the information given. In CONTEMPORARY APPROACHES TO COGNITION: A SYMPOSIUM HELD AT THE UNIVERSITY OF COLORADO. Cambridge, MA: Harvard University Press. **332**

BRUNER, J. S., GOODNOW, J. J., & AUSTIN, G. A. (1956). A STUDY OF THINKING. New York: Wiley. **336**

BRUNER, J. S., OLVER, R. R., GREENFIELD, P. M., & collaborators (1966). STUDIES IN COGNITIVE GROWTH.

New York: Wiley. **331**

BRUYER, R., LATERRE, C., SERON, X., & collaborators (1983). A case of prosopagnosia with some preserved covert remembrance of familiar faces. BRAIN AND COGNITION, *2*, 257–284. **433**

BRYAN, J. H., & TEST, M. A. (1967). Models and helping: Naturalistic studies in aiding behavior. JOURNAL OF PERSONALITY AND SOCIAL PSYCHOLOGY, *6*, 400–407. **758**

BUCK, L., & AXEL, R. (1991). A novel multigene family may encode odorant receptors: A molecular basis for odor recognition. CELL, *65*, 175–187. **155**

BURGESS, A. W., & HOLMSTROM, L. (1974). Rape trauma syndrome. AMERICAN JOURNAL OF PSYCHIATRY, *131*, 981–986. **582**

BURNAM, M. A., STEIN, J. A., GOLDING, J. M., SIEGEL, J. M., SORENSON, S. B., FORSYTHE, A. B., & TELLES, C. A. (1988). Sexual assault and mental disorders in a community population. JOURNAL OF CONSULTING AND CLINICAL PSYCHOLOGY, *56*, 843–850. **582**

BURNS, D.D. (1981). FEELING GOOD: THE NEW MOOD THERAPY. New York: Penguin Books. **709**

BURNSTEIN, E., & VINOKUR, A. (1973). Testing two classes of theories about group-induced shifts in individual choice. JOURNAL OF EXPERIMENTAL SOCIAL PSYCHOLOGY, *9*, 123–137. **780**

BURNSTEIN, E., & VINOKUR, A. (1977). Persuasive arguments and social comparison as determinants of attitude polarization. JOURNAL OF EXPERIMENTAL SOCIAL PSYCHOLOGY, *13*, 315–332. **780**

BURT, M. R. (1980). Cultural myths and supports for rape. JOURNAL OF PERSONALITY AND SOCIAL PSYCHOLOGY, *38*, 217–230. **583**

BUSS, A. H., & PLOMIN, R. (1984). TEMPERAMENT: EARLY DEVELOPING PERSONALITY TRAITS. Hillsdale, NJ: Erlbaum. **490**

BUSS, D. M. (1991). Evolutionary personality psychology. ANNUAL REVIEW OF PSYCHOLOGY, *42*, 459–491. **27**

BUTLER, J. M., & HAIGH, G. V. (1954). Changes in the relation between self-concepts and ideal concepts consequent upon client-centered counseling. In C. R. Rogers & R. F. Dymond (Eds.), PSYCHOTHERAPY AND PERSONALITY CHANGE: CO-ORDINATED STUDIES IN THE CLIENT-CENTERED APPROACH, 55–76. Chicago: University of Chicago Press. **563**

BUTT, D. S. (1988). THE PSYCHOLOGY

OF SPORT: THE BEHAVIOR, MOTIVATION, PERSONALITY AND PERFORMANCE OF ATHLETES (2nd ed.). New York: Van Nostrand Reinhold. **249**

BUTTERFIELD, E. L., & SIPERSTEIN, G. N. (1972). Influence of contingent auditory stimulation on nonnutritional sucking. In J. Bosma (Ed.), ORAL SENSATION AND PERCEPTION: THE MOUTH OF THE INFANT. Springfield, IL: Charles B. Thomas. **81**

BYERLY, W. B. et al. (1989). Mapping genes for manic-depression and schizophrenia with DNA markers. TRENDS IN NEUROSCIENCES, *12*, 46–48. **652**

CAGGIULA, A. R., & HOEBEL, B. G. (1966). A "copulation-reward site" in the posterior hypothalamus. SCIENCE, *153*, 1284–1285. **396**

CAIN, W. S. (1988). Olfaction. In R. C. Atkinson, R. J. Herrnstein, G. Lindzey, & R. D. Luce (Eds.), STEVENS' HANDBOOK OF EXPERIMENTAL PSYCHOLOGY (Vol. 1). New York: Wiley, 409–459. **155**

CALLAWAY, M. R., MARRIOTT, R. G., & ESSER, J. K. (1985). Effects of dominance on group decision making: Toward a stress-reduction explanation of groupthink. JOURNAL OF PERSONALITY AND SOCIAL PSYCHOLOGY, *49*, 949–952. **781**

CAMPBELL, E. A., COPE, S. J., & TEASDALE, J. D. (1983). Social factors and affective disorder: An investigation of Brown and Harris's model. BRITISH JOURNAL OF PSYCHIATRY, *143*, 548–553. **645**

CAMPOS, J. J., BARRETT, K. C., LAMB, M. E., GOLDSMITH, H. H., & STENBERG, C. (1983). Socioemotional development. In P. Mussen (Ed.), HANDBOOK OF CHILD PSYCHOLOGY (Vol. 1, 1–101). New York: Wiley. **496**

CANNON, K., & LONG, R. (1971). Premarital sexual behavior in the sixties. JOURNAL OF MARRIAGE AND FAMILY, *33*, 36–39. **113**

CANNON, W. B. (1927). The James-Lange theory of emotions: A critical examination and an alternative theory. AMERICAN JOURNAL OF PSYCHOLOGY, *39*, 106–124. **421**

CARAMAZZA, A., & ZURIF, E. B. (1976) Dissociation of algorithmic and heuristic processes in language comprehension: Evidence from aphasia. BRAIN AND LANGUAGE, *3*, 572–582. **357**

CAREY, G., & GOTTESMAN, I. I. (1981). Twin and family studies of anxiety, phobic, and obsessive disorders. In D. F. Klein & J. Rabkin (Eds.), ANXIETY: NEW RESEARCH AND CHANGING CONCEPTS. New York: Haven Press. **633**

CARLSON, N. R. (1988). FOUNDATIONS OF PHYSIOLOGICAL PSYCHOLOGY. Boston: Allyn & Bacon. **69**

CARLSON, R. (1971). Where is the person in personality research? PSYCHOLOGICAL BULLETIN, *75*, 203–219. **544**

CARLSON W. R. (1986). PHYSIOLOGY OF BEHAVIOR (3rd ed.). Boston: Allyn & Bacon. **415**

CARPENTER, P. A., JUST, M. A., & SHELL, P. (1990). What one intelligence test measures: A theoretical account of the processing in the Raven Progressive Matrices Test. PSYCHOLOGICAL REVIEW, *97*, 404–431. **474**

CARROL, E. N., ZUCKERMAN, M., & VOGEL, W. H. (1982). A test of the optimal level of arousal theory of sensation seeking. JOURNAL OF PERSONALITY AND SOCIAL PSYCHOLOGY, *42*, 572–575. **411**

CARROLL, D. W. (1985). PSYCHOLOGY OF LANGUAGE. Monterey, CA: Brooks/Cole. **369**

CARROLL, J. B. (1988). Individual differences in cognitive functioning. In R. C. Atkinson, R. J. Herrnstein, G. Lindzey, & R. D. Luce (Eds.), STEVENS' HANDBOOK OF EXPERIMENTAL PSYCHOLOGY (Vol. 2). New York: Wiley. **474**

CARSKADON, M. A., MITLER, M. M., & DEMENT, W. C. (1974). A comparison of insomniacs and normals: Total sleep time and sleep latency. SLEEP RESEARCH, *3*, 130. **214**

CARSON, N. D., & JOHNSON, R. E. (1985). Suicidal thoughts and problem-solving preparations among college students. JUNIOR COLLEGE STUDENT PERSONNEL, *26* (6), 484–487. **639**

CARSON, R. C. & BUTCHER, J. N. (1992). ABNORMAL PSYCHOLOGY AND MODERN LIFE. Glenview, IL: Scott, Foresman & Co. **665**

CARSTENSEN, L. L., & NEALE, J. M. (1989). MECHANISMS OF PSYCHOLOGICAL INFLUENCE ON PHYSICAL HEALTH. New York: Plenum. **615**

CARTER, J. E., & HEATH, B. (1971). Somatotype methodology and kinesiology research. KINESIOLOGY REVIEW, *2*, 10. **526**

CARTERETTE, E. C., & FRIEDMAN, M. P. (Eds.) (1974–1978) HANDBOOK OF PERCEPTION, Vols. 1–11. New York: Academic Press. **163**

CARTWRIGHT, R. D. (1974). The influence of a conscious wish on dreams: A methodological study of dream meaning and function. JOURNAL OF ABNORMAL PSYCHOLOGY, *83*, 387–393. **217**

CASE, R. (1985). INTELLECTUAL DEVELOPMENT: A SYSTEMATIC REINTERPRETATION. New York: Academic Press. **94**

CASE, R. B., HELLER, S. S., CASE, N. B., & MOSS, A. J. (1985) Type A behavior and survival after acute myocardial infarction. NEW ENGLAND JOURNAL OF MEDICINE, *312*, 737. **601**

CASPI, A., BEM, D. J., & ELDER, G. H., JR. (1989). Continuities and consequences of interactional styles across the life course. JOURNAL OF PERSONALITY, *56*, 375–406. **516**

CASPI, A., ELDER, G. H., JR., & BEM, D. J. (1987). Moving against the world: Life-course patterns of explosive children. DEVELOPMENTAL PSYCHOLOGY, *22*, 303–308. **516, 517**

CASPI, A., ELDER, G. H., JR., & BEM, D. J. (1989) Moving toward the world: Life-course patterns of dependent children. Unpublished manuscript, Harvard University. **519**

CASPI, A., & HERBENER, E. S. (1990). Continuity and change: Assortative marriage and the consistency of personality in adulthood. JOURNAL OF PERSONALITY AND SOCIAL PSYCHOLOGY, *58*, 250–258. **515, 740**

CASTELLUCI, V. & KANDEL, E. R. (1976). Presynaptic facilitation as a mechanism for behavioral sensitization in Aplysia. SCIENCE, *194*, 1176–1178. **265**

CATTELL, R. B. (1957). PERSONALITY AND MOTIVATION STRUCTURE AND MEASUREMENT. Yonkers-on-Hudson, N.Y.: World Publishers. **529**

CATTELL, R. B. (1966). THE SCIENTIFIC ANALYSIS OF PERSONALITY. Chicago: Aldine. **529**

CATTELL, R. B. (1986). THE HANDBOOK FOR THE 16 PERSONALITY FACTOR QUESTIONNAIRE. Champaign, IL: Institute for Personality and Ability Testing. **529**

CAVE, K. R. & WOLFE, J. M. (1989). Modeling the role of parallel processing in visual search. COGNITIVE PSYCHOLOGY, *22*, 225–271. **176**

CECI, S. J. (1991). How much does schooling influence general intelligence and its cognitive components? A reassessment of the evidence. DEVELOPMENTAL PSYCHOLOGY, *27* (3), 703–722. **480**

CENTERS FOR DISEASE CONTROL (1988) Health status of Vietnam veterans: Psychosocial characteristics. JOURNAL OF THE AMERICAN MEDICAL ASSOCIATION, *259*, 2701–2707. **585**

CENTERS FOR DISEASE CONTROL (1991, January 4). Premarital sexual experiences among adolescent women—

United States, 1970-1988. MORBIDITY AND MORTALITY WEEKLY REPORT, *39*, 929–932. **113**

CENTERS FOR DISEASE CONTROL (1991, September 20) Attempted suicide among high school students—U.S. 1990. MORBIDITY AND MORTALITY WEEKLY REPORT, *40*, 633-635. **638**

CENTERS FOR DISEASE CONTROL (1992, January 3). Sexual behavior among high school students—United States, 1990. MORBIDITY AND MORTALITY WEEKLY REPORT, *40*, 885–888. **113, 117**

CERELLA, J. (1985). Information processing rates in the elderly. PSYCHOLOGICAL BULLETIN, *98*, 67–83. **120**

CHAIKEN, S. (1980). Heuristic versus systematic information processing and the use of source versus message cues in persuasion. JOURNAL OF PERSONALITY AND SOCIAL PSYCHOLOGY, *39*, 752–766. **776**

CHAPMAN, L. J., & CHAPMAN, J. P. (1969). Illusory correlation as an obstacle to the use of valid psychodiagnostic signs. JOURNAL OF ABNORMAL PSYCHOLOGY, *74*, 271–280. **718**

CHARNEY, D. S., & HENINGER, G. R. (1983). Monoamine receptor sensitivity and depression: Clinical studies of antidepressant effects on serotonin and noradrenergic function. PSYCHOPHARMACOLOGY BULLETIN, *20*, 213–223. **643**

CHARNEY, D. S., HENINGER, G. R., & STERNBERG, D. E. (1984). Serotonin function and mechanism of action of antidepressant treatment: Effects of amitriptyline and desipramine. ARCHIVES OF GENERAL PSYCHIATRY, *41*, 359–365. **643**

CHASE, W. G., & SIMON, H. A. (1973a). The mind's eye in chess. In W. G. Chase (Ed.), VISUAL INFORMATION PROCESSING. New York: Academic Press. **364**

CHASE, W. G., SIMON, H. A. (1973b). Perception in Chess. COGNITIVE PSYCHOLOGY, *4*, 55–81. **95**

CHAUDURI, H. (1965). PHILOSOPHY OF MEDITATION. New York: Philosophical Library. **232**

CHEN, S. C. (1937). Social modification of the activity of ants in nest-building. PHYSIOLOGICAL ZOOLOGY, *10*, 420–436. **749**

CHENG, P. W., HOLYOAK, K. J., NISBETT, R. E., & OLIVER, L. (1986). Pragmatic versus syntactic approaches to training deductive reasoning. COGNITIVE PSYCHOLOGY, *18*, 293–328. **341**

CHESS, S., & THOMAS, A. (1984). ORIGINS AND EVOLUTION OF BEHAVIOR DISORDERS: INFANCY TO EARLY ADULT LIFE. New York: Brunner/Mazel. **492**

CHI, M. (1978). Knowledge structures and memory development. In R. S. Siegler (Ed.), CHILDREN'S THINKING: WHAT DEVELOPS? Hillsdale, NJ: Erlbaum. **94**

CHI, M., GLASER, R., & REES, E. (1982). Expertise in problem solving. In R. Sternberg (Ed.), ADVANCES IN THE PSYCHOLOGY OF HUMAN INTELLIGENCE (Vol. 1). Hillsdale, NJ: Erlbaum. **365**

CHIPEUR, H. M., ROVINE, M. J., & PLOMIN, R. (1989, June) LISREL modeling: Genetic and environmental influences on IQ revisited. Presented at the Annual Meeting of the Behavior Genetics Association at Charlottesville, VA. **479**

CHOMSKY, N. (1965). ASPECTS OF THE THEORY OF SYNTAX. Cambridge, MA: MIT Press. **345**

CHOMSKY, N. (1972). LANGUAGE AND MIND (2nd ed.). New York: Harcourt Brace Jovanovich. **355**

CHOMSKY, N. (1980). RULES AND REPRESENTATIONS. New York: Columbia University Press. **369**

CHOMSKY, N. (1991, March). Quoted in DISCOVER. **359**

CHRISTIE, R., & JOHODA, M. (Eds.). (1954). STUDIES IN THE SCOPE AND METHOD OF "THE AUTHORITARIAN PERSONALITY." New York: Free Press. **731**

CHURCHLAND, P. M. (1988). MATTER AND CONSCIOUSNESS. Cambridge: MIT Press. **249**

CHURCHLAND, P. M. (1990). Cognitive activity in artificial neural networks. In Osherson & Smith (Eds.), INVITATION TO COGNITIVE SCIENCE: THINKING (Vol. 3). Cambridge, MA: MIT Press. **26**

CHURCHLAND, P. S., & SEJNOWSKI, T. J. (1988). Perspectives on cognitive neuroscience. SCIENCE, *242*, 741–745. **13**

CLARK, D. M. (1988). A cognitive model of panic attacks. In S. Rachman & J. D. Maser (Eds), PANIC: PSYCHOLOGICAL PERSPECTIVES. Hillsdale, NJ: Erlbaum. **633, 634**

CLARK, D. M., & BECK, A. T. (1988). Cognitive approaches. In C. G. Last & M. Hersen (Eds.), HANDBOOK OF ANXIETY DISORDERS. Elmsford, NY: Pergamon Press. **633**

CLARK, E. V. (1983). Meanings and concepts. In P. H. Mussen (Ed.), HANDBOOK OF CHILD PSYCHOLOGY (Vol. 3). New York: Wiley. **351**

CLARK, H. H. (1984). Language use and language users. In G. Lindzey & E. Aronson (Eds.), THE HANDBOOK OF SOCIAL PSYCHOLOGY (Vol. 2, 3rd. ed.). New York: Harper & Row. **349**

CLARK, H. H., & CLARK, E. V. (1977). PSYCHOLOGY AND LANGUAGE: AN INTRODUCTION TO PSYCHOLINGUISTICS. New York: Harcourt Brace Jovanovich. **339, 369**

CLARKE-STEWART, K. A. (1973). Interactions between mothers and their young children: Characteristics and consequences. MONOGRAPHS OF THE SOCIETY FOR RESEARCH IN CHILD DEVELOPMENT, *38* (6 & 7, Serial No. 153). **495**

CLARKE-STEWART, K. A. (1978). Popular primers for parents. AMERICAN PSYCHOLOGIST, *35*, 359–369. **497**

CLARKE-STEWART, K. A. (1982). DAYCARE. Cambridge, MA: Harvard University Press. **498**

CLARKE-STEWART, K. A. (1982). Infant day care: Maligned or malignant? AMERICAN PSYCHOLOGIST, *44*, 266–273. **498**

CLARKE-STEWART, K. A., & FEIN, G. G. (1983). Early childhood programs. In P. H. Mussen (Ed.), HANDBOOK OF CHILD PSYCHOLOGY (Vol. 2). New York: Wiley. **498**

COHEN, N. J., & SQUIRE, L. R. (1980). Preserved learning and retention of pattern analyzing skill in amnesia: Dissociation of knowing how and knowing that. SCIENCE, *210*, 207–209. **314**

COHEN, S. (1980, September). Training to understand TV advertising: Effects and some policy implications. Paper presented at the American Psychological Association convention, Montreal. **776**

COHEN, S., TYRRELL, D. A. J., & SMITH, A. P. (1991). Psychological stress and susceptibility to the common cold. THE NEW ENGLAND JOURNAL OF MEDICINE, *325*, 606–612. **592, 593**

COHEN, S., & WILLIAMSON, G. M. (1991). Stress and infectious disease in humans. PSYCHOLOGICAL BULLETIN, *109*, 5–24. **595, 596**

COHEN, S., & WILLS, T. A. (1985). Stress, social support, and the buffering hypothesis. PSYCHOLOGICAL BULLETIN, *98*, 310–357. **610**

COLBY, A., KOHLBERG, L., GIBBS, J., & LIEBERMAN, M. A. (1983). A longitudinal study of moral judgment. MONOGRAPHS OF THE SOCIETY FOR RESEARCH IN CHILD DEVELOPMENT, *48* (No. 200), 1–2. **91**

COLE, M., & COLE, S. R. (1993). THE DEVELOPMENT OF CHILDREN. (2nd ed.) New York: Scientific American Books. **123, 498**

COLEGROVE, F. W. (1899). Individual Memories. AMERICAN JOURNAL OF PSYCHOLOGY, 10, 228–255. **309**

COLLINS, A. M., & LOFTUS, E. G. (1975). A spreading-activation theory of semantic processing. PSYCHOLOGICAL REVIEW, 82, 407–428. **335**

COLLINS, H. M. (1974). The TEA set: Tacit knowledge and scientific networks. SCIENCE STUDIES, 4, 165–186. **242**

COMREY, A. L., & LEE, H. B. (1992). A FIRST COURSE IN FACTOR ANALYSIS (2nd ed.). Hillsdale, NJ: Erlbaum **474, 487**

CONDRY, J., & CONDRY, S. (1976). Sex differences: A study in the eye of the beholder. CHILD DEVELOPMENT, 47, 812–819. **103**

CONRAD, R. (1964). Acoustic confusions in immediate memory. BRITISH JOURNAL OF PSYCHOLOGY, 55, 75–84. **291**

COOPER, L. A., & SHEPARD, R. N. (1973). Chronometric studies of the rotation of mental images. In W. G. Chase (Ed.), VISUAL INFORMATION PROCESSING. New York: Academic Press. **360**

COOPER, L. M. (1979). Hypnotic amnesia. In. E. Fromm & R. E. Shor (Eds.), HYPNOSIS: DEVELOPMENTS IN RESEARCH AND NEW PERSPECTIVES (rcv. ed.). New York: Aldine. **240**

COOPERSMITH, S. (1967). THE ANTECEDENTS OF SELF-ESTEEM. San Francisco: Freeman. **501**

CORDUA, G. D., MCGRAW, K. O., & DRABMAN, R. S. (1979). Doctor or nurse: Children's perception of sex-typed occupations. CHILD DEVELOPMENT, 50, 590–593. **104**

COREN, S., & WARD, L. M. (1989). SENSATION & PERCEPTION (3rd ed.). San Diego: Harcourt Brace Jovanovich. **163, 201**

CORNELL, E. H., & MCDONNELL, P. M. (1986). Infants' acuity at twenty feet. INVESTIGATIVE OPTHALMOLOGY AND VISUAL SCIENCE, 27, 1417–1420. **78**

CORSINI, R. J. (1984). CURRENT PSYCHOTHERAPIES (3rd ed.). Itasca, IL: Peacock. **708**

COSCINA, D. V., & DIXON. L. M. (1983). Body weight regulation in anorexia nervosa: Insights from an animal model. In. F. L. Darby, P. E. Garfinkel, D. M. Garner, & D. V. Coscina, (Eds.), ANOREXIA NERVOSA: RECENT DEVELOPMENTS. New York: Allan R. Liss. **388**

COSTA, E. (1985). Benzodiazepine/GABA interactions: A model to investigate the neurobiology of anxiety. In A. H. Tuma & J. D. Maser (Eds.), ANXIETY AND THE ANXIETY DISORDERS. Hillsdale, NJ: Erlbaum. **635**

COSTA, P. T., & MCCRAE, R. R. (1980) Still stable after all these years: Personality as a key to some issues in aging. In P. B. Bolles & O. G. Brim (Eds.), LIFE-SPAN DEVELOPMENT AND BEHAVIOR (Vol. 3). New York: Academic Press. **120**

COTTRELL, N. B. (1972). Social facilitation. In C. G. McClintock (Ed.), EXPERIMENTAL SOCIAL PSYCHOLOGY. New York: Holt, Rinehart & Winston. **750**

COTTRELL, N. B., RITTLE, R. H., & WACK, D. L. (1967). Presence of an audience and list type (competitional or noncompetitional) as joint determinants of performance in paired-associates learning. JOURNAL OF PERSONALITY, 35, 425–434. **751**

COTTRELL, N. B., WACK, D. L., SEKERAK, G. J., & RITTLE, R. H. (1968) Social facilitation of dominant responses by the presence of an audience and the mere presence of others. JOURNAL OF PERSONALITY AND SOCIAL PSYCHOLOGY, 9, 245–250. **751**

COURTRIGHT, J. A. (1978). A laboratory investigation of groupthink. COMMUNICATIONS MONGRAPHS, 43, 229–246. **781**

CRAIGHEAD, L. W., STUNKARD, A. J., & O'BRIEN, R. M. (1981). Behavior therapy and pharmacotherapy for obesity. ARCHIVES OF GENERAL PSYCHIATRY, 38, 763–768. **389**

CRAIK, F. I. M., & TULVING, E. (1975). Depth of processing and the retention of words in episodic memory. JOURNAL OF EXPERIMENTAL PSYCHOLOGY: GENERAL, 104, 268–294. **300**

CRARY, W. G. (1966). Reactions to incongruent self-experiences. JOURNAL OF CONSULTING PSYCHOLOGY, 30, 246–252. **644**

CREESE, I., BURT, D. R., & SNYDER, S. H. (1978). Biochemical actions of neuroleptic drugs. In L. L. Iversen, S. D. Iversen, & S. H. Snyder (Eds.), HANDBOOK OF PSYCHOPHARMACOLOGY (Vol. 10). New York: Plenum. **653**

CRICK, F., & MITCHISON, G. (1983). The function of dream sleep. NATURE, 304, 111–114. **218**

CRICK, F., & MITCHISON, G. (1986) REM sleep and neural nets. JOURNAL OF MIND AND BEHAVIOR, 7, 229–250. **218**

CRONBACH, L. J. (1984). ESSENTIALS OF PSYCHOLOGICAL TESTING (4th ed.). New York: Harper & Row. **486, 573**

CROSS, P. (1977). Not can but will college teaching be improved? NEW DIRECTIONS FOR HIGHER EDUCATION, 17, 1–15. **727**

CUTLER, S. E., & NOLEN-HOEKSEMA, S. (1991). Accounting for sex differences in depression through female victimization: Childhood sexual abuse. SEX ROLES, 24, 425–438. **582**

DABBS, J. M., & MORRIS, R., JR. (1990). Testosterone, social class, and antisocial behavior in a sample of 4,462 men. PSYCHOLOGICAL SCIENCE, 1, 209–211. **441**

DALE, A. J. D. (1975.) Organic brain syndromes associated with infections. In A. M., Freedman, H. I. Kaplan, & B. J. Sadock (Eds.), COMPREHENSIVE TEXTBOOK OF PSYCHIATRY (Vol. 2). 1, 1121–1130. Baltimore, MD: Williams Wilkins. **668**

DAMASIO, A. R. (1985). Disorders of complex visual processing: Agnosia, achromatopsia, Balint's syndrome, and related difficulties of orientation and construction. In M. M. Mesulam (Ed.). PRINCIPLES OF BEHAVIORAL NEUROLOGY, 259–288. Philadelphia, PA: F. A. Davis Company. **186, 187**

DAMON, W. (1977). THE SOCIAL WORLD OF THE CHILD. San Francisco: Jossey-Bass. **104**

DAMON, W. (1983). SOCIAL AND PERSONALITY DEVELOPMENT. New York: Norton & Company. **123**

DANEMAN, M., & CARPENTER, P. A. (1980). Individual differences in working memory and reading. JOURNAL OF VERBAL LEARNING AND VERBAL BEHAVIOR, 19, 450–466. **296**

DARIAN-SMITH, I. (Ed.) (1984). HANDBOOK OF PHYSIOLOGY: THE NERVOUS SYSTEM: SECTION 1, VOL. 3. SENSORY PROCESSES. Bethesda, MD: American Physiological Society. **163**

DARLEY, C. F., TINKLENBERG, J. R., ROTH, W. T., HOLLISTER, L. E., & ATKINSON, R. C. (1973a). Influence of marijuana on storage and retrieval processes in memory. MEMORY AND COGNITION, 1, 196–200. **15, 231**

DARLEY, C. F., TINKLENBERG, J. R., HOLLISTER, L. E., & ATKINSON, R. C. (1973b). Marijuana and retrieval from short-term memory. PSYCHOPHARMACOLOGIA, 29, 231–238. **231**

DARLEY, C. F., TINKLENBERG, J. R., ROTH, W. T., VERNON, S., & KOPELL, B. S. (1977). Marijuana effects on long-term memory assessment and retrieval. PSYCHOPHARMACOLOGY, 52, 239–241. **231**

DARLEY, J. M., & LATANÉ, B. (1968). Bystander intervention in emergencies: Diffusion of responsibility. JOURNAL OF PERSONALITY AND SOCIAL PSYCHOL-

OGY, 8, 377–383. **757**

DARLINGTON, R. B. (1986). Long-term effects of preschool programs. In U. Neisser (Ed.), THE SCHOOL ACHIEVEMENT OF MINORITY CHILDREN. Hillsdale, NJ: Erlbaum. **481**

DARWIN, C. (1859) ON THE ORIGIN OF THE SPECIES. London: Murray. **72**

DARWIN, C. (1872). THE EXPRESSION OF EMOTION IN MAN AND ANIMALS. New York: Philosophical Library. **430**

DASHIELL, J. F. (1930). An experimental analysis of some group effects. JOURNAL OF ABNORMAL AND SOCIAL PSYCHOLOGY, 25, 190–199. **750, 751**

DASHIELL, J. F. (1935). Experimental studies of the influence of social situations on the behavior of individual human adults. In C. Murchison (Ed.), HANDBOOK OF SOCIAL PSYCHOLOGY. Worcester, MA: Clark University. **750**

DAVIDSON, A. R., & JACCARD, J. J. (1979). Variables that moderate the attitude-behavior relations: Results of a longitudinal survey. JOURNAL OF PERSONALITY AND SOCIAL PSYCHOLOGY, 37, 1364–1376. **734**

DAVIDSON, E. S., YASUNA, A., & TOWER, A. (1979). The effects of television cartoons on sex-role stereotyping in young girls. CHILD DEVELOPMENT, 50, 597–600. **104**

DAVISON, G. C. & NEALE, J. M. (1990). ABNORMAL PSYCHOLOGY (5th ed.). New York: John Wiley & Sons. **665**

DECASPER, A. J., & FIFER, W. P. (1980). Of human bonding: Newborns prefer their mothers' voices. SCIENCE, 208, 1174–1176. **81**

DECASPER, A. J., & PRESCOTT, P. A. (1984). Human newborns' perception of male voices: Preference, discrimination and reinforcing value. DEVELOPMENTAL PSYCHOBIOLOGY, 17, 481–491. **81**

DECASPER, A. J., & SIGAFOOS, A. D. (1983). The intrauterine heartbeat: A potent reinforcer for newborns. INFANT BEHAVIOR AND DEVELOPMENT, 6, 19–25. **82**

DECASPER, A. J., & SPENCE, M. J. (1986). Prenatal maternal speech influences newborns' perception of speech sounds. INFANT BEHAVIOR AND DEVELOPMENT, 9, 133–150. **82.**

DEIKMAN, A. J. (1963). Experimental meditation. JOURNAL OF NERVOUS AND MENTAL DISEASE, 136, 329–373. **232**

DEMBROSKI, T. M., MACDOUGALL, J. M., WILLIAMS, B., & HANEY, T. L. (1985). Components of Type A hostility and anger: Relationship to angiographic findings. PSYCHOSOMATIC MEDICINE, 47, 219–233. **601**

DEMENT, W. C., & KLEITMAN, N. (1957). The relation of eye movements during sleep to dream activity: An objective method for the study of dreaming. JOURNAL OF EXPERIMENTAL PSYCHOLOGY, 53, 339–346. **211**

DEMENT, W. C., & WOLPERT, E. (1958). The relation of eye movements, bodily motility, and external stimuli to dream content. JOURNAL OF EXPERIMENTAL PSYCHOLOGY, 55, 543–553. **216**

DENNIS, W., & DENNIS, M. (1940). The effects of cradling practices upon the onset of walking in Hopi children. JOURNAL OF GENETIC PSYCHOLOGY, 56, 77–86. **74**

DENNY, N. W. (1980). Task demands and problem-solving strategies in middle-age and older adults. JOURNAL OF GERONTOLOGY, 35, 559–564. **120**

DEPUE, R. A., & IACONO, W. G. (1989). Neurobehavioral aspects of affective disorders. In M. R. Rosenzweig & L. W. Porter (Eds.), ANNUAL REVIEW OF PSYCHOLOGY (Vol. 40). Palo Alto, CA: Annual Reviews, Inc. **644**

DER SIMONIAN, R., & LAIRD, N. M. (1983). Evaluating the effect of coaching on SAT scores: A meta-analysis. HARVARD EDUCATIONAL REVIEW, 53, 1–15. **467**

DEVALOIS, R. L., & DEVALOIS, K. K. (1980). Spatial vision. ANNUAL REVIEW OF PSYCHOLOGY, 31, 309–341. **175**

DEVALOIS, R. L., & JACOBS, G. H. (1984). Neural mechanisms of color vision. In I. Darian-Smith (Ed.), HANDBOOK OF PHYSIOLOGY (Vol. 3). Bethesda, MD: American Physiological Society. **144**

DIENER, E. (1979). Deindividuation, self-awareness, and disinhibition. JOURNAL OF PERSONALITY AND SOCIAL PSYCHOLOGY, 37, 1160–1171. **754, 755**

DIENER, E. (1980). Deindividuation: The absence of self-awareness and self-regulation in group members. In P. B. Paulus (Ed.), THE PSYCHOLOGY OF GROUP INFLUENCE. Hillsdale, NJ: Erlbaum. **752, 754**

DIENER, E., FRASER, S. C., BEAMAN, A. L., & KELEM, R. T. (1976). Effects of deindividuation variables on stealing among Halloween trick-or-treaters. JOURNAL OF PERSONALITY AND SOCIAL PSYCHOLOGY, 33, 178–183. **752**

DIENSTBIER, R. A. (1989). Arousal and physiological toughness: Implications for mental and physical health. PSYCHOLOGICAL REVIEW, 96, 84–100. **589**

DIGMAN, J. M., & INOUYE, J. (1986). Further specification of the five robust factors of personality. JOURNAL OF PER-

SONALITY AND SOCIAL PSYCHOLOGY, 50, 116–123. **531**

DILLBECK, M. C., & ORME-JOHNSON, D. W. (1987). Physiological differences between transcendental meditation and rest. AMERICAN PSYCHOLOGIST, 42 (9), 879–881. **234**

DIMATTEO, M. R. (1991). THE PSYCHOLOGY OF HEALTH, ILLNESS, AND MEDICAL CARE—AN INDIVIDUAL PERSPECTIVE. Pacific Grove, CA: Brooks/Cole. **615**

DION, K. K. (1972). Physical attractiveness and evaluations of children's transgressions. JOURNAL OF PERSONALITY AND SOCIAL PSYCHOLOGY, 24, 207–213. **737**

DION, K. K., & BERSCHEID, E. (1972). Physical attractiveness and social perception of peers in preschool children. Unpublished manuscript, University of Minnesota, Minneapolis. **736**

DION, K. K., BERSCHEID, E., & WALSTER, E. (1972). What is beautiful is good. JOURNAL OF PERSONALITY AND SOCIAL PSYCHOLOGY, 24, 285–290. **721**

DOBELLE, W. H., MEADEJOVSKY, M. G., & GIRVIN, J. P. (1974). Artificial vision for the blind: Electrical stimulation of visual cortex offers hope for a functional prosthesis. SCIENCE, 183, 440–444. **153**

DOHRENWEND, B. P., LEVAV, I., SHROUT, P. E., SCHWARTZ, S., NAVEH, G., LINK, B. G., SKODOL, A. E., & STUEVE, A. (1992). Socioeconomic status and psychiatric disorders: the causation-selection issue. SCIENCE, 255, 946–952. **656**

DOHRENWEND, B. S. (1973). Social status and stressful life events. JOURNAL OF PERSONALITY AND SOCIAL PSYCHOLOGY, 28, 225–235. **655**

DOLLARD, J., DOOB, L. W., MILLER, N. E., MOWRER, O. H., & SEARS, R. R. (1939). FRUSTRATION AND AGGRESSION. New Haven: Yale University Press. **438, 439**

DOMJAN, M., & BURKHARD, B. (1986). THE PRINCIPLES OF LEARNING AND BEHAVIOR. Monterey, CA: Brooks/Cole. **287**

DOWLING, J. E., & BOYCOTT, B. B. (1966). Organization of the primate retina. PROCEEDINGS OF THE ROYAL SOCIETY OF LONDON, SERIES B, 166, 80–111. **136**

DOYLE, A. C. (1892/1981). THE ORIGINAL ILLUSTRATED SHERLOCK HOLMES. Secaucus, NJ: Castle Books. (Originally published in America by Harper & Bros. in *McClure's Magazine*, 1893). **721**

DUCLAUX, R., & KENSHALO, D. R. (1980). Response characteristics of cutaneous warm fibers in the monkey. JOURNAL OF NEUROPHYSIOLOGY, *43*, 1–15. **158**

DUNN, J., & PLOMIN, R. (1990). SEPARATE LIVES: WHY SIBLINGS ARE SO DIFFERENT. New York: Basic Books. **523**

DUNNING, D., MEYEROWITZ, J. A., & HOLZBERG, A. (1989). Ambiguity and self-evaluation: The role of idiosyncratic trait definitions in self-serving assessments of ability. JOURNAL OF PERSONALITY AND SOCIAL PSYCHOLOGY, *57*, 1082–1090. **727**

DUTTON, D. G., & ARON, A. P. (1974). Some evidence for heightened sexual attraction under conditions of high anxiety. JOURNAL OF PERSONALITY AND SOCIAL PSYCHOLOGY, *30*, 510–517. **742**

EAGLE, M. N. (1984). RECENT DEVELOPMENTS IN PSYCHOANALYSIS: A CRITICAL EVALUATION. New York: McGraw-Hill. **572**

EAGLY, A. H., & CHAIKEN, S. (1984). Cognitive theories of persuasion. In L. Berkowitz (Ed.), ADVANCES IN EXPERIMENTAL SOCIAL PSYCHOLOGY (Vol. 17, pp. 267–359). New York: Academic Press. **776**

EBBESEN, E., DUNCAN, B., & KONECNI, V. (1975). Effects of content of verbal aggression on future verbal aggression: A field experiment. JOURNAL OF EXPERIMENTAL PSYCHOLOGY, *11*, 192–204. **444**

EBBINGHANS, H. (1885). Uber das Gedachthis. Leipzig: Dunckes and Humblot. **302**

ECCLES, J. S., & JACOBS, J. E. (1986). Social forces shape math attitudes and performance. SIGNS, *11*, 367–380. **471**

EDWARDS, C. P., & WHITING, B. B. (1980). Differential socialization of girls and boys in light of cross-cultural research. In C. Super & S. Harkness (Eds.), ANTHROPOLOGICAL PERSPECTIVES ON CHILD DEVELOPMENT (pp. 45–58). San Francisco: Jossey-Bass. **507**

EGAN, J. P. (1975). SIGNAL DETECTION THEORY AND ROC ANALYSIS. New York: Academic Press. **133**

EGELAND, B., & SROUFE L. A. (1981a). Attachment and early maltreatment. CHILD DEVELOPMENT, *52*, 44–52. **502**

EGELAND, B., & SROUFE, L. A. (1981b). Developmental sequelae of maltreatment in infancy. NEW DIRECTIONS FOR CHILD DEVELOPMENT, *11*, 77–92. **502**

EIBL-EIBESFELDT, I. (1970). ETHOLOGY: THE BIOLOGY OF BEHAVIOR, (E. Klinghammer, Trans.). New York: Holt, Rinehart & Winston. **98**

EICH, J. E. (1980). The cue-dependent nature of state-dependent retrieval. MEMORY AND COGNITION, *8*, 157–173. **309**

EICHORN, D. H., CLAUSEN, J. A., HAAN, N., HONZIK, M. P., & MUSSEN, P. H. (Eds.) (1981). PRESENT AND PAST IN MIDDLE LIFE. New York: Academic Press. **523**

EIMAS, P. D. (1975). Speech perception in early infancy. In L. B. Cohen & P. Salapatek (Eds.), INFANT PERCEPTION: FROM SENSATION TO COGNITION (Vol. 2). New York: Academic Press. **77**

EIMAS, P. D. (1985). The perception of speech in early infancy. SCIENTIFIC AMERICAN, *252*, 46–52. **350**

EKMAN, P. (1982). EMOTION IN THE HUMAN FACE (2nd ed.). New York: Cambridge University Press. **430, 447**

EKMAN, P. (1985). TELLING LIES: CLUES TO DECEIT IN THE MARKETPLACE, POLITICS, AND MARRIAGE. New York: Norton. **447**

EKMAN, P., LEVENSON, R. W., & FRIESON, W. V. (1983). Autonomic nervous system activity distinguishes among emotions. SCIENCE, *221*, 1208–1210. **421**

EKSTROM, R. B., FRENCH, J. W., HARMAN, H. H., & DERMAN, D. (1976). MANUAL FOR KIT OF FACTOR-REFERENCED COGNITIVE TESTS, 1976. Princeton, NJ: Educational Testing Service. **474**

EKSTROM, R. B., FRENCH, J. W., & HARMAN, H. H. (1979). Cognitive factors: Their identification and replication. MULTIVARIATE BEHAVIORAL RESEARCH MONOGRAPHS. Ft. Worth, TX: Society for Multivariate Experimental Psychology. **474**

ELLIS, H. C., & HUNT, R. R. (1989). FUNDAMENTALS OF HUMAN MEMORY AND COGNITION (4th ed.). Dubuque, Iowa: Wm. C. Brown. **328**

ELLSWORTH, P. (1991). Some implications of cognitive appraisals on theories of emotion. In K. T. Strongman (Ed.), INTERNATIONAL REVIEW OF STUDIES ON EMOTION (Vol. 1). New York: Wiley. **426**

ELMES, D. G., KANTOWITZ, B. H., & ROEDIGER, H. L. (1989). RESEARCH METHODS IN PSYCHOLOGY (3rd ed.). St. Paul, MN: West. **30**

EMMELKAMP, P., & KUIPERS, A. (1979). Agoraphobia: a follow-up study four years after treatment. BRITISH JOURNAL OF PSYCHIATRY, *134*, 352–355. **679**

ENDLER, N. S. (1982). HOLIDAY OF DARKNESS. New York: Wiley. **665**

ENGEN, T. (1982). THE PERCEPTION OF ODORS. New York: Academic Press. **163**

EPPLEY, K. R., ABRAMS, A. I., & SHEAR, J. (1987). Differential effects of relaxation techniques on trait anxiety: a meta-analysis. JOURNAL OF CLINICAL PSYCHOLOGY, *45*, 957–974. **234**

EPSTEIN, S. (1977). Traits are alive and well. In D. Magnusson & N. S. Endler (Eds.), PERSONALITY AT THE CROSSROADS: CURRENT ISSUES IN INTERACTIONAL PSYCHOLOGY. Hillsdale, NJ: Erlbaum. **568**

ERDELYI, M. H. (1985). PSYCHOANALYSIS: FREUD'S COGNITIVE PSYCHOLOGY. New York: Freeman. **311, 540**

ERICSSON, K. A., CHASE, W. G., & FALOON, S. (1980). Acquisition of a memory skill. SCIENCE, *208*, 1181–1182. **317**

ERIKSON, E. H. (1963). CHILDHOOD AND SOCIETY (2nd ed.). New York: Norton. **97, 118**

ERIKSON, E. H. (1968). IDENTITY: YOUTH AND CRISIS. New York: Norton. **508**

ERIKSON, E. H. (1976). Reflections on Dr. Borg's lifestyle. DAEDALUS, *105*, 1–28. **47**

ERON, L. D. (1987). The development of aggressive behavior from the perspective of a developing behaviorism. AMERICAN PSYCHOLOGIST, *42*, 435–442. **443**

ERON, L. D., HUESMANN, L. R., LEFKOWITZ, M. M., & WALDER, L. O. (1972). Does television violence cause aggression? AMERICAN PSYCHOLOGIST, *27*, 253–263. **6, 445**

ERVIN-TRIPP, S. (1964). Imitation and structural change in children's language. In E. H. Lenneberg (Ed.), NEW DIRECTIONS IN THE STUDY OF LANGUAGE. Cambridge, MA: MIT Press. **353**

ESTES, W. K. (1972). An associative basis for coding and organization in memory. In A. W. Melton & E. Martin (Eds.), CODING PROCESSES IN HUMAN MEMORY. Washington, DC: Winston. **308**

ESTES, W. K. (Ed.). (1975–1979) HANDBOOK OF LEARNING AND COGNITIVE PROCESSES (Vols. 1–6). Hillsdale, NJ: Erlbaum. **287**

ETCOFF, N. L. (1985). The neuropsychology of emotional expression. In G. Goldstein & R. E. Tarter, (Eds.), ADVANCES IN CLINICAL NEUROPSYCHOLOGY (Vol. 3). New York: Plenum. **432**

EVANS, C. (1984). LANDSCAPES OF THE NIGHT: HOW AND WHY WE DREAM. New York: Viking. **218**

EXNER, J. (1986). THE RORSCHACH: A COMPREHENSIVE SYSTEM (2nd ed., Vol. 1). New York: Wiley. **560**

EYFERTH, K., BRANDT, U., & WOLFGANG, H. (1960). FARBIGE KINDER IN DEUTSCHLAND. Munich: Juventa. **484**

EYSENCK, H. J. (1953). THE STRUCTURE OF HUMAN PERSONALITY. New York: Wiley. **530**

EYSENCK, H. J., & EYSENCK, S. B. G. (1976). PSYCHOTICISM AS A DIMENSION OF PERSONALITY. London: Hodder & Stroughton. **530**

EYSENCK, H. J., & RACHMAN, S. (1965). THE CAUSES AND CURES OF NEUROSIS: AN INTRODUCTION TO MODERN BEHAVIOR THERAPY BASED ON LEARNING THEORY AND THE PRINCIPLES OF CONDITIONING. San Diego: Knapp. **530**

FAGOT, B. I. (1978). The influence of sex of child on parental reactions to toddler children. CHILD DEVELOPMENT, *49*, 459–465. **103**

FAGOT, B. I., & LEINBACH, M. D. (1989). The young child's gender schema: Environmental input, internal organization. CHILD DEVELOPMENT, *60*, 663–672. **109**

FALLON, A. E., & ROZIN, P. (1985). Sex differences in perceptions of desirable body shape. JOURNAL OF ABNORMAL PSYCHOLOGY, *94*, 102–105. **391**

FANCHER, R. E. (1985). THE INTELLIGENCE MEN: MAKERS OF THE IQ CONTROVERSY. New York: Norton. **487**

FANTZ, R. L. (1961). The origin of form perception. SCIENCE, *204*, 66–72. **80, 193, 195**

FANTZ, R. L. (1970). Visual perception and experience in infancy: Issues and approaches. In NATIONAL ACADEMY OF SCIENCE, EARLY EXPERIENCE AND VISUAL INFORMATION PROCESSING IN PERCEPTUAL AND READING DISORDERS, 351–381. New York: National Academy of Science. **195**

FARAH, M. J. (1988). Is visual imagery really visual? Overlooked evidence from neuropsychology. PSYCHOLOGICAL REVIEW, *95*, 307–317. **360**

FARAH, M. J. (1990). VISUAL AGNOSIA: DISORDERS OF OBJECT RECOGNITION AND WHAT THEY TELL US ABOUT NORMAL VISION. Cambridge, MA: MIT Press. **186, 201**

FARBEROW, N. L., & SCHNEIDMAN, E. S. (1965). THE CRY FOR HELP. New York: McGraw-Hill. **638**

FARTHING, G. W. (1992). THE PSYCHOLOGY OF CONSCIOUSNESS. Englewood Cliffs, NJ: Prentice-Hall. **205, 206, 249**

FAUST, I. M. (1984). Role of the fat cell in energy balance physiology. In A. T. Stunkard & E. Stellar (Eds.), EATING AND ITS DISORDERS. New York: Raven Press. **385**

FAZIO, R., & ZANNA, M. P. (1981). Direct experience and attitude-behavior consistency. In L. Berkowitz (Ed.), ADVANCES IN AN EXPERIMENTAL SOCIAL PSYCHOLOGY (Vol. 14). New York: Academic Press. **734**

FAZIO, R., ZANNA, M. P., & COOPER, J. (1977). Dissonance and self-perception: An integrative view of each theory's proper domain of application. JOURNAL OF EXPERIMENTAL SOCIAL PSYCHOLOGY, *13*, 464–479. **735**

FECHNER, G. T. (1860/1966). ELEMENTS OF PSYCHOPHYSICS (H. E. Adler, Trans.). New York: Holt, Rinehart & Winston. **130**

FEINGOLD, A. (1988). Cognitive gender differences are disappearing. AMERICAN PSYCHOLOGIST, *43*, 95–103. **470**

FELDMAN, H., GOLDIN-MEADOW, S., & GLEITMAN, L. R. (1978). Beyond Herodotus: The creation of language by linguistically deprived children. In A. Lock (Ed.), ACTION, GESTURE, AND SYMBOL: THE EMERGENCE OF LANGUAGE. London: Academic Press. **355**

FENNELL, M. J. V., & CAMPBELL, E. H. (1984). The cognitions questionnaire: Specific thinking errors in depression. BRITISH JOURNAL OF CLINICAL PSYCHOLOGY, *23*, 81–92. **642**

FENTON, W. S., & MCGLASHAN, T. H. (1992). TESTING SYSTEMS FOR ASSESSMENT OF NEGATIVE SYMPTOMS IN SCHIZOPHRENIA. ARCHIVES OF GENERAL PSYCHIATRY, *49*, 179–184. **655**

FESHBACH, N. D. (1980, September). The child as psychologist and economist: Two curricula. Paper presented at the American Psychological Association convention. Montreal. **776**

FESHBACH, S., & WEINER, B. (1991). PERSONALITY (3rd ed.). Lexington, MA: Heath. **572**

FESTINGER, L. (1957) A THEORY OF COGNITIVE DISSONANCE. Stanford: Stanford University Press. **723, 735**

FESTINGER, L., & CARLSMITH, J. M. (1959). Cognitive consequences of forced compliance. JOURNAL OF ABNORMAL AND SOCIAL PSYCHOLOGY, *58*, 203–210. **723, 735**

FESTINGER, L., PEPITONE, A., & NEWCOMB, T. M. (1952). Some consequences of deindividuation in a group. JOURNAL OF ABNORMAL AND SOCIAL PSYCHOLOGY, *47*, 383–389. **754**

FESTINGER, L., SCHACHTER, S., & BACK, K. (1950). SOCIAL PRESSURES IN INFORMAL GROUPS: A STUDY OF HUMAN FACTORS IN HOUSING. New York: Harper & Row. **737**

FIELD, J. (1987). The development of auditory-visual localization in infancy. In B. E. McKenzie & R. H. Day (Eds.), PERCEPTUAL DEVELOPMENT IN EARLY INFANCY. Hillsdale, NJ: Erlbaum. **77**

FIELD, T. M., WOODSON, R., GREENBERG, R., & COHEN, D. (1982). Discrimination and imitation of facial expressions by neonates. SCIENCE, *218*, 179–181. **79**

FINCK, H. T. (1887). ROMANTIC LOVE AND PERSONAL BEAUTY: THEIR DEVELOPMENT, CAUSAL RELATIONS, HISTORIC AND NATIONAL PECULIARITIES. London: Macmillan. **742**

FINKE, R. A. (1985). Theories relating mental imagery to perception. PSYCHOLOGICAL BULLETIN, *98*, 236–259. **359**

FISH, B., MARCUS, J., HANS, S. L., AUERBACH, J. G., & PERDUE, S. (1992). Infants at risk for schizophrenia: sequelae of a genetic neurointegrative defect. ARCHIVES OF GENERAL PSYCHIATRY, *49*, 221–235. **658**

FISHER, G. H. (1967) Preparation of ambiguous stimulus materials. PERCEPTION AND PSYCHOPHYSICS, *2*, 421–422. **182**

FISHMAN, P. (1983). Interaction: The work women do. In B. Thorne, C. Kramarae & N. Henley (Eds.), LANGUAGE, GENDER, AND SOCIETY. Rowley, MA: Newbury House. **725**

FITZSIMONS, J. T. (1969). The role of a renal thirst factor in drinking induced by extra cellular stimuli. JOURNAL OF PHYSIOLOGY, London, *201*, 349–368. **376**

FIVUSH, R. & HAMOND, N. R. (1991). Autobiographical memory across the preschool years: Toward reconceptualizing childhood memory. In R. Fivush & N. R. Hamond (Eds.). KNOWING AND REMEMBERING IN YOUNG CHILDREN. New York: Cambridge University Press. **313**

FIXSEN, D. L., PHILLIPS, E. L., PHILLIPS, E. A., & WOLF, M. M. (1976). The teaching-family model of group home treatment. In W. E. Craighead, A. E. Kazdin, & M. J. Mahoney (Eds.), BEHAVIOR MODIFICATION: PRINCIPLES, ISSUES, AND APPLICATIONS. Boston: Houghton Mifflin. **705**

FLAVELL, J. H. (1985). COGNITIVE DEVELOPMENT (2nd ed.). Englewood Cliffs, NJ: Prentice-Hall. **123**

FLEMING, J., & DARLEY, J. M. (1986).

Perceiving Intention in Constrained Behavior: The Role of Purposeful and Constrained Action Cues in Correspondence Bias Effects. Unpublished manuscript, Princeton University, Princeton, NJ. **645**

FLODERUS-MYRED, B., PETERSEN, N., & RASMUSON, I. (1980). Assessment of heritability for personality based on a short form of the Eysenck Personality Inventory. BEHAVIOR GENETICS, *10*, 153–161. **490**

FLOWERS, M. L. (1977). A laboratory test of some implications of Janis's groupthink hypothesis. JOURNAL OF PERSONALITY AND SOCIAL PSYCHOLOGY, *35*, 888–896. **781**

FOA, E., & STEKETEE, G. (1989). Obsessive-compulsive disorder. In C. Lindemann (Ed.) HANDBOOK OF PHOBIA THERAPY. Northvale, NJ: Jason Aronson Inc. **627, 628**

FODOR, J. A. (1981). REPRESENTATIONS: PHILOSOPHICAL ESSAYS ON THE FOUNDATIONS OF COGNITIVE SCIENCE. Cambridge, MA: MIT Press. **13**

FODOR, J. A., BEVER, T. G., & GARRETT, M. F. (1974). THE PSYCHOLOGY OF LANGUAGE: AN INTRODUCTION TO PSYCHOLINGUISTICS AND GENERATIVE GRAMMAR. New York: McGraw-Hill. **369**

FODOR, J. A., & PYLYSHYN, Z. W. (1981). How direct is visual perception? Some reflections of Gibson's "ecological approach." COGNITION, *9*, 139–196. **170**

FOLKES, V. S. (1982). Forming relationships and the matching hypothesis. PERSONALITY AND SOCIAL PSYCHOLOGY BULLETIN, *8*, 631–636. **739**

FORDHAM, S., & OGBU, J. U. (1986). Black students' school success: Coping with the "burden of 'acting white'." THE URBAN REVIEW, *18*, 176–206. **485**

FOREM, J. (1973). TRANSCENDENTAL MEDITATION: MAHARISHI MAHESH YOGI AND THE SCIENCE OF CREATIVE INTELLIGENCE. New York: Dutton. **233**

FORER, B. R. (1949). The fallacy of personal validation: A classroom demonstration of gullibility. JOURNAL OF ABNORMAL AND SOCIAL PSYCHOLOGY, *44*, 118–123. **554**

FOSS, D. J., & HAKES, D. T. (1978). PSYCHOLINGUISTICS: AN INTRODUCTION TO THE PSYCHOLOGY OF LANGUAGE. Englewood Cliffs, NJ: Prentice-Hall. **369**

FOX, R., ASLIN, R. N., SHEA, S. L., & DUMAIS, S. T. (1980). Stereopsis in human infants. SCIENCE, *207*, 323–324. **195**

FRAGER, R., & FADIMAN, J. (1984). PERSONALITY AND PERSONAL GROWTH (2nd ed.). New York: Harper & Row. **573**

FRANKENBURG, W. K., & DODDS, J. B. (1967). The Denver developmental screening test. JOURNAL OF PEDIATRICS, *71*, 181–191. **73**

FRANKENHAEUSER, M. (1983). The sympathetic-adrenal and pituitary-adrenal response to challenge: Comparison between the sexes. In T. M. Dembroski, T. H. Schmidt, & G. Blumchen (Eds.), BIOBEHAVIORAL BASES OF CORONARY HEART DISEASE. Basel: Karger. **589**

FRANKLIN, J. (1987). MOLECULES OF THE MIND. New York: Atheneum. **41**

FRAZIER, K. (Ed.). (1985). SCIENCE CONFRONTS THE PARANORMAL. Buffalo: Prometheus Books. **249**

FRAZIER, K. (1987). Psychic's imagined year fizzles (again). SKEPTICAL INQUIRER, *11*, 335–336. **246**

FREDERIKSEN, N., MISLEVY, R. J., & BEJAR, I. (Eds.) (1992). TEST THEORY FOR A NEW GENERATION OF TESTS. Hillsdale, NJ: Erlbaum **487**

FREE, L. A., & CANTRIL, H. (1967). THE POLITICAL BELIEFS OF AMERICANS. New Brunswick, NJ: Rutgers University Press. **728**

FREEDMAN, J. L. (1965). Long-term behavioral effects of cognitive dissonance. JOURNAL OF EXPERIMENTAL SOCIAL PSYCHOLOGY, *1*, 145–155. **735**

FREEDMAN, J. L., & SEARS, D. O. (1965). Warning, distraction, and resistance to influence. JOURNAL OF PERSONALITY AND SOCIAL PSYCHOLOGY, *1*, 262–266. **775**

FREEMAN, S., WALKER, M. R., BORDEN, R., & LATANÉ, B. (1975). Diffusion of responsibility and restaurant tipping: Cheaper by the bunch, PERSONALITY AND SOCIAL PSYCHOLOGY BULLETIN, *1*, 584–587. **759**

FRENCH, G. M., & HARLOW, H. F. (1962). Variability of delayed-reaction performance in normal and brain-damaged rhesus monkeys. JOURNAL OF NEUROPHYSIOLOGY, *25*, 585–599. **52**

FREUD, A. (1958). Adolescence. THE PSYCHOANALYTIC STUDY OF THE CHILD, *13*, 255–278. **536**

FREUD, A. (1946/1967). THE EGO AND THE MECHANISMS OF DEFENSE (rev. ed.). New York: International Universities Press. **536**

FREUD, S. (1885). UEBER COCA. Vienna: Moritz Perles. (Translated in Freud, 1974.) **227**

FREUD, S. (1885/1974). COCAINE PAPERS (edited and introduction by R. Byck; notes by A. Freud). New York: Stonehill. **227**

FREUD, S. (1900/1953). THE INTERPRETATION OF DREAMS (Reprint ed., Vol. 4, 5). London: Hogarth Press. **217, 533**

FREUD, S. (1901/1960). PSYCHOPATHOLOGY OF EVERYDAY LIFE (Standard ed., Vol. 6). London: Hogarth Press. **533**

FREUD, S. (1905/1948). THREE CONTRIBUTIONS TO THEORY OF SEX (4th ed.; A. A. Brill, Trans.). New York: Nervous and Mental Disease Monograph. **11, 312, 313**

FREUD, S. (1915/1976). Repression. In J. Strachey (Ed. and Trans.), THE COMPLETE PSYCHOLOGICAL WORKS: STANDARD EDITION (Vol. 14). London: Hogarth Press **428**

FREUD, S. (1920/1975). BEYOND THE PLEASURE PRINCIPLE. New York: Norton. **447**

FREUD, S. (1925/1961). Some psychical consequences of the anatomical distinctions between the sexes. In J. Strachey (Ed. and Trans.) THE COMPLETE PSYCHOLOGICAL WORKS: STANDARD EDITION (Vol. 18) London: Hogarth Press. **102**

FREUD, S. (1933/1964). NEW INTRODUCTORY LECTURES ON PSYCHOANALYSIS (J. Strachey, Ed. and Trans.). New York: Norton. **101**

FREUD, S. (1933/1965). Revision of the theory of dreams. In J. Strachey (Ed. and Trans.), NEW INTRODUCTORY LECTURES ON PSYCHOANALYSIS, (Vol. 22, Lect. 29). New York: Norton. **447, 572**

FREUD, S. (1940) An outline of psychoanalysis. INTERNATIONAL JOURNAL OF PSYCHOANALYSIS, *21*, 27–84. **533**

FRIED, I., MATEER, C., OJEMANN, G., WHONS, R., & FEDIO, P. (1982). Organization of visuospatial functions in human cortex. BRAIN, *105*, 349–371. **433**

FRIED, M. (1982). Disadvantage, vulnerability, and mental illness. In D. L. Parron, F. Solomon, & C. D. Jenkins (Eds.), BEHAVIOR, HEALTH RISKS, AND SOCIAL DISADVANTAGE. Washington, DC: National Academy Press. **656**

FRIEDAN, B. (1963). THE FEMININE MYSTIQUE. New York: Dell Publishing. **550**

FRIEDMAN, M., & ROSENMAN, R. H. (1974). Type A Behavior. New York: Knopf. **600**

FRIEDMAN, M., ROSENMAN, R. H., STRAUS, R., WURM, M., & KOSITCHECK, R. (1968). The relationship of behavior pattern A to the state of coronary vasculature. AMERI-

CAN JOURNAL OF MEDICINE, 44, 525–537. **601**

FREIDMAN, M., THORESEN, C. E., GILL, J. J., & collaborators (1985, March), Alteration of Type A behavior and its effect upon cardiac recurrences in post-myocardial infarction subjects: Summary results of the recurrent coronary prevention project. Paper presented at meetings of the Society of Behavioral Medicine, New Orleans. **613, 614**

FREIDMAN, M. I., & STRICKER, E. M. (1976). The physiological psychology of hunger: A physiological perspective. PSYCHOLOGICAL REVIEW, 83, 401–431. **382**

FRIJDA, N. (1986). THE EMOTIONS. Cambridge, England: Cambridge University Press. **447**

FRISCHHOLZ, E. J. (1985). The relationship among dissociation, hypnosis, and child abuse in the development of multiple personality disorder. In R. P. Kluft (Ed.), CHILDHOOD ANTECEDENTS OF MULTIPLE PERSONALITY. Washington, DC: American Psychiatric Press. **209**

FRODI, A., & THOMPSON, R. (1985). Infants' affective responses in the strange situation: Effects of prematurity and of quality of attachment. CHILD DEVELOPMENT, 56, 1280–1290. **496**

FROMM, E. (1970). Age regression with unexpected reappearance of a repressed childhood language. INTERNATIONAL JOURNAL OF CLINICAL AND EXPERIMENTAL HYPNOSIS, 18, 79–88. **239**

FROMM, E., & SHOR, R. E. (Eds.) (1979). HYPNOSIS: DEVELOPMENTS IN RESEARCH AND NEW PERSPECTIVES (2nd. ed.). Chicago: Aldine. **249**

FUNKENSTEIN, D. (1955). The physiology of fear and anger. SCIENTIFIC AMERICAN, 192, 74–80. **421**

FURSTENBERG, F. F., JR., BROOKS-GUNN, J., & MORGAN, S. P. (1987). ADOLESCENT MOTHERS IN LATER LIFE. New York: Cambridge Press. **116**

GALANTER, E. (1962) Contemporary psychophysics. In R. Brown & collaborators (Eds.), NEW DIRECTIONS IN PSYCHOLOGY (Vol. 1). New York: Holt, Rinehart & Winston. **128**

GALOTTI, K. M. (1989). Approaches to studying formal and everyday reasoning. PSYCHOLOGICAL BULLETIN, 105, 331–351. **476**

GAMSON, W. B., FIREMAN, B., & RYTINA, S. (1982). ENCOUNTERS WITH UNJUST AUTHORITY. Homewood, IL: Dorsey Press. **769, 770, 771**

GANELLEN, R. J., & CARVER, C. S. (1985). Why does self-reference promote incidental encoding? JOURNAL OF PER-SONALITY AND SOCIAL PSYCHOLOGY, 21, 284–300. **716**

GANGESTAD, S., & SNYDER, M. (1985). To carve nature at its joints: On the existence of discrete classes in personality. PSYCHOLOGICAL REVIEW, 92, 317–349. **526**

GARCIA, J., & KOELLING, R. A. (1966). The relation of cue to consequence in avoidance learning. PSYCHONOMIC SCIENCE, 4, 123–124. **263**

GARDNER, B. T., & GARDNER, R. A. (1972). Two-way communication with an infant chimpanzee. In A. M. Schrier & F. Stollnitz (Eds.), BEHAVIOR OF NONHUMAN PRIMATES (Vol. 4). New York: Academic Press. **356, 358**

GARDNER, H. (1975). THE SHATTERED MIND. New York: Knopf. **356**

GARDNER, H. (1983). FRAMES OF MIND: THE THEORY OF MULTIPLE INTELLIGENCE. New York: Basic Books. **476**

GARDNER, H. (1985). THE MIND'S NEW SCIENCE: A HISTORY OF THE COGNITIVE REVOLUTION. New York: Basic Books. **31**

GARDNER, M. (1981). SCIENCE: GOOD, BAD, AND BOGUS. New York: Prometheus. **247, 249**

GARFIELD, S. L. (1980). PSYCHOTHERAPY: AN ECLECTIC APPROACH. New York: Wiley-Interscience. **696, 708**

GARFINKEL, P. E., & GARNER, D. M. (1982). ANOREXIA NERVOSA: A MULTIDISCIPLINARY PERSPECTIVE. New York: Brunner/Mazel. **390, 392, 393**

GARMEZY, N. (1974). Children at risk: The search for the antecedents of schizophrenia: Pt. 2. Ongoing research programs, issues and intervention. SCHIZOPHRENIA BULLETIN, 1, 55–125. **657**

GARMEZY, N., & DEVINE, E. (1984). Project competence: The Minnesota studies of children vulnerable to psychopathology. In N. F. Watt, E. J. Anthony, N. F. Wynne, & J. E. Rolf (Eds.), CHILDREN AT RISK FOR SCHIZOPHRENIA: A LONGITUDINAL PERSPECTIVE. Cambridge: Cambridge University Press. **657**

GARRETT, M. F. (1975). The analysis of sentence production. In Bower, G. H. (Ed.), THE PSYCHOLOGY OF LEARNING AND MOTIVATION (Vol. 9). New York: Academic Press. **346**

GARRETT, M. F. (1990). Sentence processing. In D. N. Osherson & H. Lasnik, AN INVITATION TO COGNITIVE SCIENCE: LANGUAGE (Vol. 1). Cambridge, MA: MIT Press. **348**

GATES, A. I. (1917). Recitation as a factor in memorizing. ARCHIVES OF PSY-CHOLOGY, No. 40. **321**

GEEN, R. G., & QUANTY, M. B. (1977). The catharsis of aggression. In L. Berkowitz (Ed.), ADVANCES IN EXPERIMENTAL SOCIAL PSYCHOLOGY, (Vol. 10). New York: Academic Press. **443**

GEEN, R. G., BEATTY, W. W., & ARKIN, R. M. (1984). HUMAN MOTIVATION: PHYSIOLOGICAL, BEHAVIORAL, AND SOCIAL APPROACHES. Boston: Allyn & Bacon. **413, 415**

GEER, J., & MAISEL, E. (1973). Evaluating the effects of the prediction-control confound. JOURNAL OF PERSONALITY AND SOCIAL PSYCHOLOGY, 23, 314–319. **579**

GEISLER, W. S. (1978). Adaptation, afterimages and cone saturation. VISION RESEARCH, 18, 279–289. **128**

GELMAN, R., & GALLISTEL, C. R. (1978). THE YOUNG CHILD'S UNDERSTANDING OF NUMBER: A WINDOW ON EARLY COGNITIVE DEVELOPMENT. Cambridge, MA: Harvard University Press. **92**

GESCHWIND, N. (1979). Specializations of the human brain. SCIENTIFIC AMERICAN, 241, 180–199. **56**

GESCHWIND, N., & GALABURDA, A. M. (1987). CEREBRAL LATERALIZATION. Cambridge: MIT Press. **52, 57**

GESELL, A., & THOMPSON, H. (1929) Learning and growth in identical twins: An experimental study by the method of co-twin control. GENETIC PSYCHOLOGY MONOGRAPHS, 6, 1–123. **74**

GIBBS, J., YOUNG, R. C., & SMITH, G. P. (1973). Cholecystokinin decreases food intake in rats. JOURNAL OF COMPARATIVE AND PHYSIOLOGICAL PSYCHOLOGY, 84, 484–495. **37**

GIBSON, E. J., & WALK, R. D. (1960). The "visual cliff." SCIENTIFIC AMERICAN, 202, 64–71. **195**

GIBSON, J. J. (1950). THE PERCEPTION OF THE VISUAL WORLD. Boston: Houghton Mifflin. **170**

GIBSON, J. J. (1966). THE SENSES CONSIDERED AS PERCEPTUAL SYSTEMS. Boston: Houghton Mifflin. **170, 172**

GIBSON, J. J. (1979). THE ECOLOGICAL APPROACH TO VISUAL PERCEPTION. Boston: Houghton Mifflin. **170, 172, 201**

GILBERT, D. T., & JONES, E. E. (1986). Perceiver-induced constraint: Interpretations of self-generated reality. JOURNAL OF PERSONALITY AND SOCIAL PSYCHOLOGY, 50, 269–280. **723**

GILLIGAN, C. (1982). IN A DIFFERENT VOICE. Cambridge, MA: Harvard University Press. **91**

GILLIN, J. C. (1985). Sleep and Dreams. In G. L. Klerman, M. M. Weissman, P. S.

Applebaum & L. H. Roth (Eds.), PSY-CHIATRY (Vol. 3). Philadelphia: Lippincott. **213**

GILLUND, G., & SHIFFRIN, R. M. (1984). A retrieval model for both recognition and recall. PSYCHOLOGICAL REVIEW, *91*, 1–61. **308**

GILOVICH, T. (1983). Biased evaluation and persistence in gambling. JOURNAL OF PERSONALITY AND SOCIAL PSYCHOLOGY, *40*, 797–808. **726**

GILOVICH, T. (1991). HOW WE KNOW WHAT ISN'T SO: THE FALLIBILITY OF HUMAN REASON IN EVERYDAY LIFE. New York: Free Press. **747**

GINSBERG, A. (1983). Contrast perception in the human infant. Unpublished manuscript. **194**

GITTELMAN, R., & KLEIN, D. F. (1985). Childhood separation anxiety and adult agoraphobia. In A. H. Tuma & J. D. Maser (Eds.), ANXIETY AND THE ANXIETY DISORDERS. Hillsdale, NJ: Erlbaum. **626**

GLANZER, M. (1972). Storage mechanisms in recall. In G. H. Bower & J. T. Spence (Eds.), THE PSYCHOLOGY OF LEARNING AND MOTIVATION (Vol. 5). New York: Academic Press. **297**

GLASER, R., RICE, J., SPEICHER, C. E., STOUT, J. C., & KIECOLT-GLASER, J. K. (1986). Stress depresses interferon production by leukocytes concomitant with a decrease in natural killer cell activity. BEHAVIORAL NEUROSCIENCE, *100*, 675–678. **593**

GLASS, A. L., & HOLYOAK, K. J. (1986). COGNITION (2nd ed.). New York: Random House. **328**

GLASS, D. C., & SINGER, J. E. (1972). URBAN STRESS: EXPERIMENTS ON NOISE AND SOCIAL STRESSORS. New York: Academic Press. **579**

GLASS, G. V., MCGAW, B., & SMITH, M. L. (1981). Meta-analysis in Social Research. Beverly Hills, CA: Sage. **242**

GLEITMAN, H. (1986). PSYCHOLOGY (2nd ed.). New York: Norton. **352**

GLEITMAN, L. R. (1986). Biological predispositions to learn language. In P. Marler & H. S. Terrace (Eds.), THE BIOLOGY OF LEARNING. New York: Springer-Verlag. **352**

GLUCK, M. A., & THOMPSON, R. F. (1987). Modeling the neural substrates of associative learning and memory: A computational approach. PSYCHOLOGICAL REVIEW, *94*, 176–191. **265**

GODDEN, D., & BADDELEY, A. D. (1975). Context-dependent memory in two natural environments: On land and under water. BRITISH JOURNAL OF PSYCHOLOGY, *66*, 325–331. **308**

GOETHALS, G. P., & ZANNA, M. P.

(1979). The role of social comparison in choice shifts. JOURNAL OF PERSONALITY AND SOCIAL PSYCHOLOGY, *37*, 1469–1476. **780**

GOLDHABER, D. (1986). LIFE-SPAN HUMAN DEVELOPMENT. San Diego: Harcourt Brace Jovanovich. **123, 522**

GOLDIN-MEADOW, S. (1982). The resilience of recursion: A structure within a conventional model. In E. Wanner & L. R. Gleitman (Eds.), LANGUAGE ACQUISITION: THE STATE OF THE ART. Cambridge: Cambridge University Press. **76**

GOLDSTEIN, E. B. (1989). SENSATION AND PERCEPTION (3rd ed.). Belmont, CA: Wadsworth. **134, 140, 151, 156, 163, 170, 173, 194**

GOLDSTEIN, M. J. (1987). The UCLA high risk project. SCHIZOPHRENIA BULLETIN, *13*, 505–514. **657**

GOLEMAN, D. J. (1977). THE VARIETIES OF MEDITATIVE EXPERIENCE. New York: Dutton. **249**

GOLEMAN, D. J. (1988, October 18). Chemistry of sexual desire yields its elusive secret. NEW YORK TIMES. **395**

GOODALL, J. (1978). Chimp killings: Is it the man in them? SCIENCE NEWS, *113*, 276. **439**

GOODGLASS, H., & BUTTERS, N. (1988). Psychobiology of cognitive processes. In R. C. Atkinson, R. J. Herrnstein, G. Lindzey, & R. D. Luce (Eds.), STEVENS' HANDBOOK OF EXPERIMENTAL PSYCHOLOGY (Vol. 2). New York: Wiley. **52**

GOOSSENS, F. A. (1987). Maternal employment and day care: Effects on attachment. In L. W. C. Tavecchio, & M. H. Van Ijzendoorn (Eds.), ATTACHMENT IN SOCIAL NETWORKS Amsterdam: North-Holland. **498**

GORDON, E. (1967). A three-year longitudinal predictive validity study of the musical aptitude profile. STUDIES IN THE PSYCHOLOGY OF MUSIC (Vol. 5). Iowa City: University of Iowa Press. **452**

GORDON, W. (1989). LEARNING & MEMORY. Pacific Grove, CA: Brooks/Cole. **287**

GORENSTEIN, E. E. (1982). Frontal lobe functions in psychopaths. JOURNAL OF ABNORMAL PSYCHOLOGY, *91*, 368–379. **661**

GORTMAKER, S. L., ECKENRODE, J., & GORE, S. (1982). Stress and the utilization of health services: A time series and cross-sectional analysis. JOURNAL OF HEALTH AND SOCIAL BEHAVIOR, *23*, 25–38. **596**

GOTTESMAN, I. I., (1991). SCHIZOPHRENIA GENESIS: THE ORIGINS OF MADNESS. New York: W. H. Freeman.

**652, 665**

GOTTESMAN I. I., & BERTELSEN, A. (1989). Confirming unexpressed genotypes for schizophrenia. ARCHIVES OF GENERAL PSYCHIATRY, *46*, 867–872. **651**

GOTTESMAN, I. I., & SHIELDS, J. (1982). SCHIZOPHRENIA: THE EPIGENETIC PUZZLE. New York: Cambridge University Press. **652**

GOY, R. W. (1968). Organizing effect of androgen on the behavior of rhesus monkeys. In R. F. Michael (Ed.), ENDOCRINOLOGY OF HUMAN BEHAVIOUR. London: Oxford University Press. **404**

GRAF, P., & MANDLER, G. (1984). Activation makes words more accessible, but not necessarily more retrievable. JOURNAL OF VERBAL LEARNING AND VERBAL BEHAVIOR, *23*, 553–568. **314, 315**

GRAHAM, J. R. (1990). THE MMPI-2: ASSESSING PERSONALITY AND PSYCHOPATHOLOGY. New York: Oxford University Press. **557**

GREEN, D. M., & SWETS, J. A. (1966). SIGNAL DETECTION THEORY AND PSYCHOPHYSICS. New York: Wiley. **132**

GREEN, D. M., & WIER, C. C. (1984). Auditory perception. In I. Darian-Smith (Ed.), HANDBOOK OF PHYSIOLOGY (Vol. 3). Bethesda, MD: American Physiological Society. **150**

GREEN, H. (1971). I NEVER PROMISED YOU A ROSE GARDEN. New York: New American Library. **665**

GREENFIELD, P. M., & SAVAGE-RUMBAUGH, S. (1990). Grammatical combination in Pan *Paniscus:* Processes of learning and invention in the evolution and development of language. In S. Parker & K. Gibson (Eds.), "LANGUAGE" AND INTELLIGENCE IN MONKEYS AND APES: COMPARATIVE DEVELOPMENTAL PERSPECTIVES. New York: Cambridge University Press. **358**

GREENWALD, A. G. (1968). Cognitive learning, cognitive response to persuasion, and attitude change. In A. G. Greenwald, T. C. Brock, & T. M. Ostrom (Eds.), PSYCHOLOGICAL FOUNDATIONS OF ATTITUDES. New York: Academic Press. **773**

GRICE, H. P. (1975). Logic and conversation. In G. Harman, & D. Davidson (Eds.), THE LOGIC OF GRAMMAR. Encino, CA: Dickinson. **349**

GRIGGS, R. A., & COX, J. R. (1982). The elusive thematic-materials effect in Watson's selection task. BRITISH JOURNAL OF PSYCHOLOGY, *73*, 407–420. **341**

GRODZINSK, Y. (1984). The syntactic characterization of agrammatism. COG-

NITION, *16*, 99–120. **357**

GROVES, P. M., & REBEC, G. V. (1992). INTRODUCTION TO BIOLOGICAL PSYCHOLOGY (4th ed.). Dubuque, IA: Brown. **37, 41, 69**

GRÜNBAUM, A. (1984). THE FOUNDATIONS OF PSYCHOANALYSIS. Berkeley, CA: University of California Press. **539**

GUILFORD, J. P. (1982). Cognitive psychology's ambiguities: Some suggested remedies. PSYCHOLOGICAL REVIEW, *89*, 48–49. **474, 531**

GURMAN, A. S., & KNISKERN, D. P. (1981). HANDBOOK OF FAMILY THERAPY. New York: Brunner/Mazel. **692**

GURNEY, R. (1936). The hereditary factor in obesity. ARCHIVES OF INTERNAL MEDICINE, *57*, 557–561. **383**

HAAGA, D. A. F., DYCK, M. J., & ERNST, D. (1991). Empirical status of cognitive theory of depression. PSYCHOLOGICAL BULLETIN, *110*, 215–236. **642**

HABER, R. N. (1969). Eidetic images. SCIENTIFIC AMERICAN, *220*, 36–55. **292**

HABER, R. N. (1979). Twenty years of haunting eidetic imagery: Where's the ghost? BEHAVIORAL AND BRAIN SCIENCES, *24*, 583–629. **292**

HAITH, M. M., BERGMAN, T., & MOORE, M. J. (1977). Eye contact and face scanning in early infancy. SCIENCE, *198*, 853–855. **80**

HALIKAS, J. A., GOODWIN, D. W., & GUZE, S. B. (1971). Marijuana effects: A survey of regular users. JOURNAL OF AMERICAN MEDICAL ASSOCIATION, *217*, 692–694. **231**

HALL, C. S., LINDZEY, G., LOEHLIN, J. C., & MANOSEVITZ, M. (1985). INTRODUCTION TO THEORIES OF PERSONALITY. New York: Wiley. **572**

HAMBERGER, L. K., & LOHR, J. M. (1984). STRESS AND STRESS MANAGEMENT: RESEARCH AND APPLICATIONS. New York: Springer. **615**

HAMBURG, D., & TRUDEAU, M. B. (Eds.). (1981). BIOBEHAVIORAL ASPECTS OF AGGRESSION. New York: Alan Liss. **447**

HAMILTON, D. L. (1979). A cognitive-attributional analysis of stereotyping. In L. Berkowitz (Ed.), ADVANCES IN EXPERIMENTAL SOCIAL PSYCHOLOGY (Vol. 12). New York: Academic Press. **716**

HAMILTON, D. L., & GIFFORD, R. K. (1976). Illusory correlation in interpersonal perception: A cognitive basis of stereotypic judgments. JOURNAL OF EXPERIMENTAL SOCIAL PSYCHOLOGY, *12*, 392–407. **720**

HAMILTON, D. L., & SHERMAN, S. J.

(1989). Illusory correlations: Implications for stereotype theory and research. In D. Bar-Tal, C. F. Gravmann, A. W. Kruglanski, & W. Stroebe (Eds.), STEREOTYPES AND PREJUDICE: CHANGING CONCEPTIONS. New York: Springer-Verlag. **720**

HAMILTON, E. W., & ABRAMSON, L. Y. (1983). Cognitive patterns and major depressive disorder: A longitudinal study in a hospital setting. JOURNAL OF ABNORMAL PSYCHOLOGY, *92*, 173–184, **642**

HARE, R. D. (1970). PSYCHOPATHY: THEORY AND RESEARCH. New York: Wiley. **661**

HARE, R. D. (1980). A research scale for the assessment of psychopathy in criminal populations. PERSONALITY AND INDIVIDUAL DIFFERENCES, *1*, 111–119. **659**

HARE, R. D. (1988). Male psychopaths and their criminal careers. JOURNAL OF CONSULTING AND CLINICAL PSYCHOLOGY, *56*, 710–714. **661**

HARKINS, S. G., & PETTY, R. E. (1982). Effects of task difficulty and task uniqueness on social loafing. JOURNAL OF PERSONALITY AND SOCIAL PSYCHOLOGY, *43*, 1214–1229. **759**

HARLOW, H. F. (1971). LEARNING TO LOVE. San Francisco: Albion. **398**

HARLOW, H. F., & HARLOW, M. K. (1969). Effects of various mother-infant relationships on rhesus monkey behaviors. In B. M. Foss (Ed.), DETERMINANTS OF INFANT BEHAVIOR (Vol. 4). London: Methuen. **99**

HARLOW, H. F., HARLOW, M. K., & MEYER, D. R. (1950). Learning motivated by a manipulation drive. JOURNAL OF EXPERIMENTAL PSYCHOLOGY, *40*, 228–234. **410**

HARRÉ, R., & LAMB, R. (Eds.) (1983). THE ENCYCLOPEDIC DICTIONARY OF PSYCHOLOGY. Cambridge, MA: MIT Press. **235**

HARRIS, M. J., & ROSENTHAL, R. (1988). INTERPERSONAL EXPECTANCY EFFECTS AND HUMAN PERFORMANCE RESEARCH. Washington, DC: National Academy Press. **244**

HARTIGAN, J. A., & WIGDOR, A. K. (Eds.) (1989). FAIRNESS IN EMPLOYMENT TESTING. Washington, DC: National Academy Press. **484**

HARTSHORNE, H., & MAY, M. A. (1929). STUDIES IN THE NATURE OF CHARACTER II: STUDIES IN SERVICE AND SELF-CONTROL. New York: Macmillan. **565**

HARTUP, W. W., & MOORE, S. G. (1963). Avoidance of inappropriate sex-typing by young children. JOURNAL

OF CONSULTING PSYCHOLOGY, *27*, 467–473. **104**

HASS, R. G., & GRADY, K. (1975). Temporal delay, type of forewarning and resistance to influence. JOURNAL OF EXPERIMENTAL SOCIAL PSYCHOLOGY, *11*, 459–469. **775**

HATFIELD, E. (1988). Passionate and companionate love. In R. J. Sternberg, & M. L. Barnes (Eds.), THE PSYCHOLOGY OF LOVE (pp. 191–217). New Haven, CT: Yale University Press. **741**

HAWKINS, R. D., & KANDEL, E. R. (1984). Is there a cell-biological alphabet for simple forms of learning? PSYCHOLOGICAL REVIEW, *91*, 375–391. **265**

HAXBY, J. V., GRADY, C. L., HORWIZ, B., UNGERLEIDER, L. G., MISHKIN, M., CARSON, R. E., HERSCOVITCH, P., SCHAPIRO, M. B., & RAPOPORT, S. I. (1991). Dissociation of object and spatial visual processing pathways in human extrastriate cortex. NEUROBIOLOGY, *88*, 1621–1625. **165**

HAYES, C. E. (Ed.) (1987). RISKING THE FUTURE: ADOLESCENT SEXUALITY, PREGNANCY, AND CHILDBEARING (Vol. 1). Washington, DC: National Academy Press. **116**

HAYES, J. R. (1989). THE COMPLETE PROBLEM SOLVER (2nd edition). Hillsdale, NJ: Erlbaum. **369**

HAYES, L. A., & WATSON, J. S. (1981). Neonatal imitation: Fact or artifact. DEVELOPMENTAL PSYCHOLOGY, *17*, 655–660. **78**

HAYNES, S. G., & FEINLEIB, M. (1980). Women, work, and coronary heart disease: Prospective findings from the Framingham heart study. AMERICAN JOURNAL OF PUBLIC HEALTH, *70*, 133–141. **592**

HAYNES, S. G., FEINLEIB, M., & KANNEL, W. B. (1980). The relationship of psychosocial factors to coronary heart disease in the Framingham Study: Pt. 3. Eight-year incidence of coronary heart disease. AMERICAN JOURNAL OF EPIDEMIOLOGY, *111*(No. 1), 37–58. **601**

HAZAN, C., & SHAVER, P. (1987). Romantic love conceptualized as an attachment process. JOURNAL OF PERSONALITY AND SOCIAL PSYCHOLOGY, *52*, 511–524. **744**

HEBB, D. O. (1972). TEXTBOOK OF PSYCHOLOGY (3rd ed.). Philadelphia: Saunders. **435**

HEBB, D. O. (1982). Understanding psychological man: A state-of-the-science report. PSYCHOLOGY TODAY, *16*, 52–53. **238**

HECHT, S., & HSIA, Y. (1945). Dark adaptation following light adaptation to red and white lights. JOURNAL OF THE OPTICAL SOCIETY OF AMERICA, *35*, 261–267. **137**

HECHT, S., SHLAER, S., & PIREENE, M. H. (1942). Energy, quanta, and vision. JOURNAL OF GENERAL PHYSIOLOGY, *25*, 819–840. **128**

HEIDER, F. (1958). THE PSYCHOLOGY OF INTERPERSONAL RELATIONS. New York: Wiley. **722**

HEIN, A., & HELD, R. (1967). Dissociation of the visual placing response into elicited and guided components. SCIENCE, *158*, 390–392. **198**

HELD, R. (1965). Plasticity in sensory motor systems. SCIENTIFIC AMERICAN, *21*(No. 5), 84–94. **198**

HELD, R., & HEIN, A. (1963) Movement produced stimulation in the development of visually guided behavior. JOURNAL OF COMPARATIVE AND PHYSIOLOGICAL PSYCHOLOGY, *56*, 872–876. **199**

HEMMI, T. (1969). How we have handled the problem of drug abuse in Japan. In F. Sjoqvist & M. Tottie (Eds.), ABUSE OF CENTRAL STIMULANTS. New York: Raven Press. **227**

HENCHY, T., & GLASS, D. C. (1968). Evaluation apprehension and social facilitation of dominant and subordinate responses. JOURNAL OF PERSONALITY AND SOCIAL PSYCHOLOGY, *10*, 446–454. **751**

HENDRICK, C., & HENDRICK, S. S. (1986). A theory and method of love. JOURNAL OF PERSONALITY AND SOCIAL PSYCHOLOGY, *50*, 392–402. **744**

HENDRICK, C., & HENDRICK, S. S. (1989). Research on love: Does it measure up? JOURNAL OF PERSONALITY AND SOCIAL PSYCHOLOGY, *56*, 784–794. **744**

HENLEY, N., HAMILTON, M., & THORNE, B. (1985). Womanspeak and manspeak: Sex differences and sexism in communication, verbal and nonverbal. In A. G. Sargent (Ed.), BEYOND SEX ROLES. St. Paul, MN: West. **725**

HENSEL, H. (1973). Cutaneous thermoreceptors. In A. Iggo (Ed.), HANDBOOK OF SENSORY PHYSIOLOGY (Vol. 2). Berlin: Springer-Verlag. **158**

HERBERT, N. (1987). QUANTUM REALITY: BEYOND THE NEW PHYSICS. Garden City, NY: Anchor. **246**

HERDT, G. H. (Ed.) (1984). RITUALIZED HOMOSEXUALITY IN MELANESIA. Berkeley: University of California Press. **399**

HEREK, G. M. (1986). The instrumentality of attitudes: Toward a neofunctional theory. JOURNAL OF SOCIAL ISSUES, *42*, 99–114. **729**

HEREK, G. M. (1987). Can functions be measured? A new perspective on the functional approach to attitudes. SOCIAL PSYCHOLOGY QUARTERLY, *50*, 285–303. **730**

HERING E. (1878). OUTLINES OF A THEORY OF THE LIGHT SENSE (L. M. Hurvich & D. Jameson, Trans.). Cambridge, MA: Harvard University Press. **143**

HERING, E. (1920). Memory as a universal function of organized matter. In S. Butler (Ed.) UNCONSCIOUS MEMORY. London: Jonathan Cape. **289**

HERMAN, C. P., & POLIVY, J. (1980). Retrained eating. In A. J. Stunkard (Ed.), OBESITY. Philadelphia: Saunders. **386**

HESS, E. H. (1958). "Imprinting" in animals. SCIENTIFIC AMERICAN, *198*, 81–90. **408**

HESS, E. H. (1972). "Imprinting" in a natural laboratory. SCIENTIFIC AMERICAN, *227*, 24–31. **409**

HESTON, L. L. (1966). Psychiatric disorders in foster home reared children of schizophrenic mothers. BRITISH JOURNAL OF PSYCHIATRY, *112*, 819–825. **652**

HESTON, L. L. (1992). Mending Minds, A Guide to the New Psychiatry of Depression, Anxiety, and Other Serious Mental Disorders. New York: W. H. Freeman. **665**

HETHERINGTON, E. M., & BRACKBILL, Y. (1963). Etiology and covariation of obstinacy, orderliness, and parsimony in young children. CHILD DEVELOPMENT, *34*, 919–943. **539**

HILGARD, E. R. (1961). Hypnosis and experimental psychodynamics. In H. Brosin (Ed.), LECTURES ON EXPERIMENTAL PSYCHIATRY. Pittsburgh: Pittsburgh University Press. *18*, **327**

HILGARD, E. R. (1965). HYPNOTIC SUSCEPTIBILITY. New York: Harcourt Brace Jovanovich. **237, 608**

HILGARD, E. R. (1968). THE EXPERIENCE OF HYPNOSIS. New York: Harcourt Brace Jovanovich. **249**

HILGARD, E. R. (1986). DIVIDED CONSCIOUSNESS: MULTIPLE CONTROLS IN HUMAN THOUGHT AND ACTION. New York: Wiley-Interience. **238, 239, 249**

HILGARD, E. R. (1987). PSYCHOLOGY IN AMERICA: A HISTORICAL SURVEY. San Diego: Harcourt Brace Jovanovich. **30**

HILGARD, E. R., & HILGARD, J. R. (1975). HYPNOSIS IN THE RELIEF OF PAIN. Los Altos, CA: Kaufmann. **240**

HILGARD, E. R., HILGARD, J. R., MACDONALD, H., MORGAN, A. H., & JOHNSON, L. S. (1978). Covert pain in hypnotic analgesia: Its reality as tested by the real-simulator design. JOURNAL OF ABNORMAL PSYCHOLOGY, *87*, 655–663. **239**

HILGARD, J. R. (1979). PERSONALITY AND HYPNOSIS: A STUDY OF IMAGINATIVE INVOLVEMENT (2nd ed.). Chicago: University of Chicago Press. **237, 249**

HILL, C., RUBIN, Z., & PEPLAU, L. A. (1976). Breakups before marriage: The end of 103 affairs. JOURNAL OF SOCIAL ISSUES, *32*, 147–168. **739**

HILLYARD, S. A. (1985). Electrophysiology of human selective attention. TRENDS IN NEUROSCIENCE, *8*, 400–406. **185**

HIRSCH, J., & BATCHELOR, B. R. (1976). Adipose tissue cellularity and human obesity. CLINICAL ENDOCRINOLOGY AND METABOLISM, *5*, 299–311. **385**

HIRSCH, H. V. B., & SPINELLI, D. N. (1970). Visual experience modifies distribution of horizontally and vertically oriented receptive fields in cats. SCIENCE, *168*, 869–871. **197**

HIRSH, S. R., & NATELSON, B. J. (1981). Electrical brain stimulation and food reinforcement dissociated by demand elasticity. PHYSIOLOGY AND BEHAVIOR, *18*, 141–150. **277**

HOBSON, J. A. (1988). THE DREAMING BRAIN. New York: Basic Books. **214, 216**

HOBSON, J. A. (1989). SLEEP. New York: Freeman. **213, 249**

HOCHBERG, J. (1978). PERCEPTION (2nd ed.). Englewood Cliffs, NJ: Prentice-Hall. **184**

HOCK, E. (1980). Working and nonworking mothers and their infants: A comparative study of maternal caregiving characteristics and infant social behavior. MERRILL PALMER QUARTERLY, *26*, 79–102. **498**

HOEBEL, B. G., & TEITELBAUM, P. (1966). Effects of force-feeding and starvation on food intake and body weight on a rat with ventromedial hypothalamic lesions. JOURNAL OF COMPARATIVE AND PHYSIOLOGICAL PSYCHOLOGY, *61*, 189–193. **381**

HOFLING, C. K. (1975). TEXTBOOK OF PSYCHIATRY FOR MEDICAL PRACTICE (3rd ed.). Philadelphia: Lippincott. **646**

HOFLING, C. K., BROTZMAN, E., DALRYMPLE, S., GRAVES, N., & PIERCE, C. M. (1966). An experimental study in nurse–physician relationships. JOURNAL OF NERVOUS AND MENTAL DISEASE, *143*, 171–180. **766**

HOGARTY, G. E., SCHOOLER, N. R., ULRICH, R., MUSSARE, F., FERRO,

P., & HERRON, E. (1979). Fluphenazine and social therapy in the after care of schizophrenic patients. ARCHIVES OF GENERAL PSYCHIATRY, 36, 1283–1294. **701**

HOHMANN, G. W. (1962). Some effects of spinal cord lesions on experienced emotional feelings. PSYCHOPHYSIOLOGY, 3, 143–156. **420**

HOHMANN, M., BANET, B., & WEIKART, D. (1979). YOUNG CHILDREN IN ACTION. Ypsilanti, MI: High Scope Press. **481**

HOLDEN, C. (1975). Lie detectors: PSE gains audience despite critic's doubt. SCIENCE, 190, 359–362. **425**

HOLLAND, J. H., HOLYOAK, K. J., NISBETT, R. E., & THAGARD, P. R. (1986). INDUCTION: PROCESSES OF INFERENCE, LEARNING, AND DISCOVERY. Cambridge, MA: MIT Press. **369**

HOLMES, D. S. (1974). Investigations of repression: Differential recall of material experimentally or naturally associated with ego threat. PSYCHOLOGICAL BULLETIN, 81, 632–653. **310, 540**

HOLMES, D. S., & MCGILLEY, B. M. (1987). Influence of a brief aerobic training program on heart rate and subjective response to stress. PSYCHOSOMATIC MEDICINE, 49, 366–374. **612**

HOLMES, D. S., & ROTH, D. L. (1985). Association of aerobic fitness with pulse rate and subjective responses to psychological stress. PSYCHOPHYSIOLOGY, 22, 525–529. **612**

HOLMES, T. H. (1979). Development and application of a quantitative measure of life change magnitude. In J. E. Barrett(Ed.), STRESSFUL LIFE EVENTS: THEIR NATURE AND EFFECTS. New York: Wiley. **581**

HOLMES, T. H., & RAHE, R. H. (1967). The social readjustment rating scale. JOURNAL OF PSYCHOSOMATIC RESEARCH, 11, 213–218. **580, 581**

HOLROYD, K. A., APPEL, M. A., & ANDRASIK, F. (1983). A cognitive-behavioral approach to psychophysiological disorders. In D. Meichenbaum & M. E. Jaremko (Eds.), STRESS REDUCTION AND PREVENTION. New York: Plenum. **613**

HOLWAY, A. H., & BORING, E. G. (1941). Determinants of apparent visual size with distance variant. AMERICAN JOURNAL OF PSYCHOLOGY, 54, 21–37. **190**

HOLYOAK, K., KOH, K., & NISBETT, R. E. (1989). A theory of conditioning: Inductive learning within rule-based default hierarchies. PSYCHOLOGICAL REVIEW, 96, 315–340. **261**

HOLZMAN, P. S. (1970). PSYCHOANALYSIS AND PSYCHOPATHOLOGY. New York: McGraw-Hill. **572**

HONIG, W. K., & STADDON, J. E. R. (Eds.) (1977). HANDBOOK OF OPERANT BEHAVIOR. Englewood Cliffs, NJ: Prentice-Hall. **287**

HONORTON, C. (1985). Meta-analysis of psi ganzfeld research: A response to Hyman. JOURNAL OF PARAPSYCHOLOGY, 49, 51–91. **241, 242, 244**

HONORTON, C., BERGER, R. E., VARVOGLIS, M. P., QUANT, M., DERR, P., SCHECHTER, E., & FERRARI, D. C. (1990). Psi communication in the ganzfeld: Experiments with an automated testing system and a comparison with a meta-analysis of earlier studies. JOURNAL OF PARAPSYCHOLOGY, 54, 99–139. **244**

HOPKINS, J. R. (1977). Sexual behavior in adolescence. JOURNAL OF SOCIAL ISSUES, 33, 67–85. **400**

HOVLAND, C., JANIS, I., & KELLEY, H. H. (1953). COMMUNICATION AND PERSUASION. New Haven: Yale University Press. **773**

HOVLAND, C. I., LUMSDAINE, A. A., & SHEFFIELD, F. D. (1949). Experiments on mass communication. STUDIES IN SOCIAL PSYCHOLOGY IN WORLD WAR II (Vol. III). Princeton, NJ: Princeton University Press. **774**

HOWARD, K. I., KOPTA, S. M., KRAUSE, M. S., & ORLINSKY, D. E. (1986). The dose-effect relationship in psychotherapy. AMERICAN PSYCHOLOGIST, 41, 159–164. **705**

HUBEL, D. H., & WIESEL, T. N. (1963). Receptive fields of cells in striate cortex of very young visually inexperienced kittens. JOURNAL OF NEUROPHYSIOLOGY, 26, 994–1002. **196**

HUGDAHL, K., & OHMAN, A. (1977). Effects of instruction on acquisition and extinction of electrodermal response to fear-relevant stimuli. JOURNAL OF EXPERIMENTAL PSYCHOLOGY: HUMAN LEARNING AND MEMORY, 3, 608–618. **632**

HUMMEL, J. E. & BIEDERMAN, I. (1992). Dynamic binding in a neural network for shape recognition. PSYCHOLOGICAL REVIEW, 99, 480–517. **180**

HUNT, D. D., & HAMPSON, J. L. (1980). Follow up of 17 biologic male transsexuals after sex reassignment surgery. AMERICAN JOURNAL OF PSYCHIATRY, 137, 432–438. **406**

HUNT, E. (1990). A modern arsenal for mental assessment. EDUCATIONAL PSYCHOLOGIST, 25, 223–241. **474**

HUNT, M. (1974). SEXUAL BEHAVIOR IN THE 1970's. Chicago: Playboy Press. **400**

HUNT, P. J., & HILLERY, J. M. (1973) Social facilitation at different stages in learning. Paper presented at the Midwestern Psychological Association Meetings, Cleveland. **751**

HUNTER, E. J. (1979, May). Combat casualities who remain at home. Paper presented at Western Regional Conference of the Interuniversity Seminar, "Technology in Combat." Navy Postgraduate School, Monterey, CA. **580**

HUNTER, I. M. L. (1974). MEMORY. Baltimore: Penguin. **324**

HURVICH, L., & JAMESON, D. (1957). An opponent-process theory of color vision. PSYCHOLOGICAL REVIEW, 64, 384–404. **144**

HURVICH, L. M. (1981). COLOR VISION. Sunderland, MA: Sinauer Associates. **144, 163**

HYDE, J. S., & LINN, M. C. (1988). Gender differences in verbal ability: A meta-analysis. PSYCHOLOGICAL BULLETIN, 104, 53-69. **470**

HYMAN, R. (1985). The ganzfeld psi experiment: A critical appraisal. JOURNAL OF PARAPSYCHOLOGY, 49, 3–49. **242**

HYMAN, R., & HONORTON, C. (1986). A joint communique: The psi ganzfeld controversy. JOURNAL OF PARAPSYCHOLOGY, 50, 351–364. **242, 244**

IMPERATO-MCGINLEY, J., PETERSON, R. E., GAUTIER, T., & STURLA, E. (1979). Androgens and the evolution of male gender identity among male pseudohermaphrodites with 5 alpha reductase deficiency. NEW ENGLAND JOURNAL OF MEDICINE, 300, 1233–1237. **405**

INSTITUTE OF MEDICINE (1982). MARIJUANA AND HEALTH. Washington, DC: National Academy Press. **231**

ISEN, P. M. (1985). The assymetry of happiness and sadness in effects on memory in normal college students. JOURNAL OF EXPERIMENTAL PSYCHOLOGY: GENERAL, 114, 388–391. **436**

ISEN, P. M., SHALKER, T. E., CLARK, M., & KARP, L. (1978). Affect, accessibility of material in memory, and behavior: A cognitive loop? JOURNAL OF PERSONALITY AND SOCIAL PSYCHOLOGY, 36, 1–12. **437**

ISENBERG, D. J. (1986). Group polarization: A critical review and meta-analysis. JOURNAL OF PERSONALITY AND SOCIAL PSYCHOLOGY, 50, 1141–1151. **779, 780**

ISOZAKI, M. (1984). The effect of discussion on polarization of judgments. JAPANESE PSYCHOLOGICAL RESEARCH, 26, 187–193. **779**

JACKENDOFF, R. (1990). CONSCIOUS-NESS AND THE COMPUTATIONAL MIND. Cambridge: MIT Press. **249**

JACKLIN, C. N., & MACCOBY, E. E. (1978). Social behavior at 33 months in same-sex and mixed-sex dyads. CHILD DEVELOPMENT, *49*, 557–569. **105**

JACKSON, J. M., & LATANÉ, B. (1975). All alone in front of all those people: Stage fright as a function of number and type of coperformers and audience. JOURNAL OF PERSONALITY AND SOCIAL PSYCHOLOGY, *40*, 73–85. **759**

JACOBS, W. J., & NADEL, W. (1985). Stress-induced recovery of fears and phobias. PSYCHOLOGICAL REVIEW, *92*, 512–531. **257**

JACOBSON, A. L., FRIED, C., & HOROWITZ, S. D. (1967). Classical conditioning, pseudoconditioning, or sensitization in the planarian. JOURNAL OF COMPARATIVE AND PHYSIOLOGICAL PSYCHOLOGY, *64*, 73–79. **256**

JACOBSON, S. W. (1979). Matching behavior in the young infant. CHILD DEVELOPMENT, *50*, 425–430. **78**

JACOBY, L. L., & DALLAS, M. (1981). On the relationship between biographical memory and perceptual learning. JOURNAL OF EXPERIMENTAL PSYCHOLOGY: GENERAL, *110*, 306–340. **315**

JAHN, R. G., & DUNNE, B, J, (1987). MARGINS OF REALITY. San Diego: Harcourt Brace & Jovanovich. **246**

JAMES, W. (1884). What is an emotion? MIND, *9*, 188–205. **420**

JANET, P. (1889). L'AUTOMISMEPSY-CHOLOGIGUE. Paris: Felix Alcan. **207**

JANICAK, P. C., DAVIS, J. M., GIBBONS, R. D., ERICKSEN, S., CHANG, S., & GALLAGHER, P. (1985). Efficacy of ECT: A meta-analysis. AMERICAN JOURNAL OF PSYCHIATRY, *142*, 297–302. **703**

JANIS, I. L. (1982). GROUPTHINK: PSYCHOLOGICAL STUDIES OF POLICY DECISIONS AND FIASCOES (2nd ed.). Boston: Houghton Mifflin. **780, 781, 784**

JANIS, I. L. (1985). Sources of error in strategic decision making. In J. M. Pennings (Ed.), ORGANIZATIONAL STRATEGY AND CHANGE. San Francisco: Jossey-Bass. **781**

JANOWITZ, H. D., & GROSSMAN, M. I. (1949). Some factors affecting the food intake of normal dogs and dogs esophagostomy and gastric fistula. AMERICAN JOURNAL OF PHYSIOLOGY, *159*, 143–148. **379**

JANOWSKY, D. S., EL-YOUSEF, M. F., DAVIS, J. M., & SERERKE, H. S. (1973). Provocation of schizophrenic symptoms by intravenous injection of methylphenidate. ARCHIVES OF GENERAL PSYCHIATRY, *28*, 185–191. **654**

JASMOS, T. M., & HAKMILLER, K. L. (1975). Some effects of lesion level, and emotional cues on affective expression in spinal cord patients. PSYCHOLOGICAL REPORTS, *37*, 859–870. **420**

JEMMOTT, J. B., III, BORYSENKO, M., MCCLELLAND, D. C., CHAPMAN, R., MEYER, D., & BENSON, H. (1985). Academic stress, power motivation, and decrease in salivary secretory immunoglubulin: A secretion rate. LANCET, *1*, 1400–1402. **593**

JENNINGS, D., AMABILE, T. M., & ROSS, L. (1982). Informal covariation assessment: Data-based vs. theory-based judgments. In A. Tversky, D. Kahneman, & P. Slovic (Eds.), JUDGMENT UNDER UNCERTAINTY: HEURISTICS AND BIASES. New York: Cambridge University Press. **284**

JENSEN, A. R. (1980). BIAS IN MENTAL TESTING. New York: Free Press. **484**

JENSEN, A. R. (1985). The nature of the black–white difference on various psychometric tests: Spearman's hypothesis. THE BEHAVIORAL AND BRAIN SCIENCES, *8*, 193–263. **484**

JOHANSSON, G., & FRANKEN-HAEUSER, J. (1973). Temporal factors in sympatho-adrenomedullary activity following acute behavioral activation. BIOLOGICAL PSYCHOLOGY, *1*, 63–73. **590**

JOHN, O. P. (1990). The "Big Five" factor taxonomy: Dimension of personality in the natural language and in questionnaires. In L. A. Pervin (Ed.), HANDBOOK OF PERSONALITY: THEORY AND RESEARCH (pp. 66–100). New York: Guilford Press. **531**

JOHN, R. S., MEDNICK, S. A., & SCHULSINGER, F. (1982). Teacher reports as a predictor of schizophrenia and borderline schizophrenia: A Bayesian decision analysis. JOURNAL OF ABNORMAL PSYCHOLOGY, *91*, 399–413. **657**

JOHNSON, C. & LARSON, R. (1982). Bulimia: An analysis of moods and behavior. PSYCHOSEMATIC MEDICINE, *44*, 341–351. **393**

JOHNSON, E. J., & TVERSKY, A. (1983). Affect, generalization, and the perception of risk. JOURNAL OF PERSONALITY AND SOCIAL PSYCHOLOGY, *45*, 20–31. **437**

JOHNSON, R. D., & DOWNING, L. L. (1979). Deindividuation and valence of cues: Effects on prosocial and antisocial behavior. JOURNAL OF PERSONALITY AND SOCIAL PSYCHOLOGY, *37*, 1532–1538. **752**

JOHNSON-LAIRD, P. N. (1985). The deductive reasoning ability. In R. J. Sternberg (Ed.), HUMAN ABILITIES: AN INFORMATION PROCESSING APPROACH. New York: Freeman. **364**

JOHNSON-LAIRD, P. N. (1988). THE COMPUTER AND THE MIND: AN INTRODUCTION TO COGNITIVE SCIENCE. Cambridge: Harvard University Press. **201**

JOHNSON-LAIRD, P. N. (1989). Mental models. In M. I. Posner (Ed.), FOUNDATIONS OF COGNITIVE SCIENCE. Cambridge, MA: MIT Press. **341**

JOHNSON-LAIRD, P. N. & BYRNE, R. M. J. (1991). DEDUCTION. Hillsdale, NJ: Erlbaum. **369**

JOHNSTON, L. D., O'MALLEY, P. M., & BACHMAN, J. G. (1992). ILLICIT DRUG USE, SMOKING, AND DRINKING BY AMERICA'S HIGH SCHOOL STUDENTS, COLLEGE STUDENTS, AND YOUNG ADULTS, 1975–1991. Rockville, MD: National Institute on Drug Abuse DHHS publication nos. (ADM) 92–1920 & (ADM) 92–1940, in press. **220, 222**

JONES, E. E., & HARRIS, V. A. (1967). The attribution of attitudes. JOURNAL OF EXPERIMENTAL SOCIAL PSYCHOLOGY, *3*, 1–24. **722**

JONES, E. E., ROCK, L., SHAVER, K. G., GOETHALS, G. R., & WARD, L. M. (1968). Pattern of performance and ability attribution: An unexpected primacy effect. JOURNAL OF PERSONALITY AND SOCIAL PSYCHOLOGY, *9*, 317–340. **717**

JONES, H. C., & LOVINGER, P. W. (1985). THE MARIJUANA QUESTION AND SCIENCE'S SEARCH FOR AN ANSWER. New York: Dodd, Mead. **231**

JONES, L. V. (1984). White–Black Achievement Differences: The Narrowing Gap. AMERICAN PSYCHOLOGIST, *39*, 1207–1213. **467, 485**

JONES, R. A., & BREHM, J. W. (1970). Persuasiveness of one- and two-sided communications as a function of awareness there are two sides. JOURNAL OF EXPERIMENTAL SOCIAL PSYCHOLOGY, *6*, 47–56. **774**

JULESZ, B. (1971). FOUNDATIONS OF CYCLOPEAN PERCEPTION. Chicago: University of Chicago Press. **169**

JULIEN, R. M. (1988). DRUGS AND THE BODY. New York: Freeman. **69, 249**

JULIEN, R. M. (1992). A PRIMER OF DRUG ACTION: A CONCISE, NONTECHNICAL GUIDE TO THE ACTIONS, USES, AND SIDE EFFECTS OF PSYCHOACTIVE DRUGS (6th ed.). New York: Freeman. **69, 224, 226, 228, 249, 700**

JUST, M. A., & CARPENTER, P. A.

(1980). A theory of reading: From eye fixations to comprehension. PSYCHOLOGICAL REVIEW, 87, 329–354. **183**

JUST, M. A., & CARPENTER, P. A. (1987). THE PSYCHOLOGY OF READING AND LANGUAGE COMPREHENSION. Boston: Allyn and Bacon. **296**

JUTAI, J. W., & HARE, R. D. (1983). Psychopathy and selective attention during performance of a complex perceptual-motor task. PSYCHOPHYSIOLOGY, 20, 140–151. **661**

KAGAN, J. (1979). Overview: Perspectives on human infancy. In J. D. Osofsky (Ed.), HANDBOOK OF INFANT DEVELOPMENT. New York: Wiley-Interscience. **75**

KAGAN, J. (1989). Temperamental contributions to social behavior. AMERICAN PSYCHOLOGIST, 44, 668–674. **526**

KAGAN, J., KEARSLEY, R. B., & ZELAZO, P. (1978). INFANCY: ITS PLACE IN HUMAN DEVELOPMENT. Cambridge, MA: Harvard University Press. **98, 99, 498**

KAGAN, N. (1984). THE NATURE OF THE CHILD. New York: Basic Books. **496**

KAGAN, N., & MOSS, H. A. (1962). BIRTH TO MATURITY. New York: Wiley. **519**

KAHNEMAN, D., SLOVIC, P., & TVERSKY, A. (Eds.) (1982). JUDGMENT UNDER UNCERTAINTY: HEURISTICS AND BIASES. New York: Cambridge University Press. **369**

KAIL, R. (1989). THE DEVELOPMENT OF MEMORY IN CHILDREN (3rd ed.). New York: Freeman. **123**

KAIL, R., & PELLEGRINO, J. W. (1985). HUMAN INTELLIGENCE: PERSPECTIVES AND PROSPECTS. New York: Freeman. **486**

KAMERMAN, S. B. (1980). PARENTING IN AN UNRESPONSIVE SOCIETY. New York: Free Press. **499**

KAMIN, L. J. (1969). Predictability, surprise, attention, and conditioning. In B. A. Campbell & R. M. Church (Eds.), PUNISHMENT AND AVERSIVE BEHAVIOR. New York: Appleton-Century-Crofts. **260**

KAMIN, L. J. (1976). Heredity, intelligence, politics, and psychology. In N. J. Block & G. Dworkin (Eds.), THE IQ CONTROVERSY. New York: Pantheon. **484**

KANDEL, D. B. (1975). Stages in adolescent involvement in drug use. SCIENCE, 190, 912–914. **232**

KANDEL, D. B., DAVIES, M., KARUS, D. K., & YAMAGUCHI, K. (1986). The consequences in young adulthood of adolescent drug involvement. ARCHIVES

GENERAL PSYCHIATRY, 43, 746–754. **232**

KANDEL, E. R. (1979). Small systems of neurons. In R. Thompson (Ed.), THE BRAIN. San Francisco: Freeman. **264, 265**

KAPLAN, J. (1985). THE HARDEST DRUG: HEROIN AND PUBLIC POLICY. Chicago: University of Chicago Press. **249**

KAPLAN, M. R., & MILLER, C. E. (1987). Group decision making and normative versus informational influence: Effects of type of issue and assigned decision rule. JOURNAL OF PERSONALITY AND SOCIAL PSYCHOLOGY, 53, 306–313. **779**

KAPLAN, R. M., & SACCUZZO, D. (1989). PSYCHOLOGICAL TESTING: PRINCIPLES AND ISSUES. Pacific Grove: Brooks/Cole. **486**

KARASEK, R., BAKER, D., MARXER, F., AHLBOM, A., & THEORELL, T. (1981). Job decision latitude, job demands, and cardiovascular disease: A prospective study of Swedish men. AMERICAN JOURNAL OF PUBLIC HEALTH, 71, 694–705. **592**

KARASEK, R. A., THEORELL, T. G., SCHWARTZ, J., PIEPER, C., & ALFREDSSON, L. (1982). Job, psychological factors and coronary heart disease: Swedish prospective findings and U.S. prevalence findings using a new occupational inference method. ADVANCES IN CARDIOLOGY, 29, 62–67. **592**

KASL, S. V., EVANS, A. S., & NIEDERMAN, J. C. (1979). Psychosocial risk factors in the development of infectious mononucleosis. PSYCHOSOMATIC MEDICINE, 41, 445–466. **580**

KATZ, D. (1960). The functional approach to the study of attitudes. PUBLIC OPINION QUARTERLY, 24, 163–204. **729**

KATZ, R., & WYKES, T. (1985). The psychological difference between temporally predictable and unpredictable stressful events: Evidence for information control theories. JOURNAL OF PERSONALITY AND SOCIAL PSYCHOLOGY, 48, 781–790. **579**

KAZDIN, A. E. (1982). Symptom substitution, generalization, and response covariation: Implications for psychotherapy outcome. PSYCHOLOGICAL BULLETIN, 91, 349–365. **679**

KEEN, E. (1982). A PRIMER IN PHENOMENOLOGICAL PSYCHOLOGY. New York: Holt, Rinehart & Winston. **572**

KEESEY, R. E., & POWLEY, T. L. (1975). Hypothalamic regulation of body weight. AMERICAN SCIENTIST, 63, 558–565. **382**

KEIL, F. C. (1986). The acquisition of

natural kind and artifact terms. In W. Demopoulos, & A. Marras (Eds.), LANGUAGE LEARNING AND CONCEPT ACQUISITION (pp. 133–153). Norwood, NJ: Ablex. **96**

KEIL, F. C. (1989). CONCEPTS, KINDS, AND COGNITIVE DEVELOPMENT. Cambridge, MA: MIT Press. **95, 96**

KEIL, F. C., & BATTERMAN, N. A. (1984) Characteristic-to-defining shift in the development of word meaning. JOURNAL OF VERBAL LEARNING AND VERBAL BEHAVIOR, 23, 221–236. **336**

KELLEY, H. H. (1967). Attribution theory in social psychology. In D. Levine (Ed.), NEBRASKA SYMPOSIUM ON MOTIVATION (Vol. 15). Lincoln: University of Nebraska Press. **722**

KELLEY, S. JR., & MIRE, T. W. (1974). The simple act of voting. AMERICAN POLITICAL SCIENCE REVIEW, 68, 572–591. **733**

KELLY, G. A. (1955). THE PSYCHOLOGY OF PERSONAL CONSTRUCTS. New York: Norton. **548**

KENNEDY, J. L., GIUFFRA, L. A., & collaborators (1988). Evidence against linkage of schizophrenia to markers on chromosome 5 in northern Swedish pedigree. NATURE, 336, 167–170. **652**

KENRICK, D. T., & CIALDINI, R. B. (1977). Romantic attraction: Misattribution versus reinforcement explanations. JOURNAL OF PERSONALITY AND SOCIAL PSYCHOLOGY, 35, 381–391. **742, 743**

KENRICK, D. T., & GUTIERRES, S. E. (1980). Contrast effects and judgments of physical attractiveness: When beauty becomes a social problem. JOURNAL OF PERSONALITY AND SOCIAL PSYCHOLOGY, 38, 131–140. **737**

KENSHALO, D. R., NAFE, J. P., & BROOKS, B. (1961). Variations in thermal sensitivity. SCIENCE, 134, 104–105. **158**

KEPHART, W. M. (1967). Some correlates of romantic love. JOURNAL OF MARRIAGE AND THE FAMILY, 29, 470–474. **741**

KERNIS, M. H., & WHEELER, L. (1981). Beautiful friends and ugly strangers: Radiation and contrast effects in perception of same-sex pairs. JOURNAL OF PERSONALITY AND SOCIAL PSYCHOLOGY, 7, 617–620. **737**

KETY, S. S. (1988). Schizophrenic illness in the families of schizophrenic adoptees: findings from the Danish national sample. SCHIZOPHRENIA BULLETIN, 14, 217–222. **652**

KETY, S. S., ROSENTHAL, D., WENDER, P. H., SCHULSINGER, F., & JACOBSEN, B. (1978). The biological and adoptive families of adopted individuals who become schizophrenic. In L. C. Wynne, R. L. Cromwell, & S. Matthysse (Eds.), THE NATURE OF SCHIZOPHRENIA. New York: Wiley. **652**

KIECOLT-GLASER, J. K., FISHER, B. S., OGROCKI, P., STOUT, J. C., SPEICHER, C. E., & GLASER, R. (1987). Marital quality, marital disruption, and immune function. PSYCHOSOMATIC MEDICINE, *49*, 13–33. **593**

KIECOLT-GLASER, J. K., KENNEDY, S., MALKOFF, S., FISHER, L., SPEICHER, C. E., & GLASER, R. (1988). Marital discord and immunity in males. PSYCHOSOMATIC MEDICINE, *50*, 213–229. **593, 594**

KIESLER, C. A. (1982) Mental hospitals and alternative care: Noninstitutionalization as potential policy for mental patients. AMERICAN PSYCHOLOGIST, *34*, 349–360. **671**

KIHLSTROM, J. F. (1984). Conscious, subconscious, unconscious: A cognitive view. In K. S. Bowers & D. Meichenbaum, (Eds.). THE UNCONSCIOUS: RECONSIDERED. New York: Wiley. **204**

KIHLSTROM, J. F. (1985). Hypnosis. ANNUAL REVIEW OF PSYCHOLOGY, *36*, 385–418. **235, 238**

KIHLSTROM, J. F. (1987). The Cognitive Unconscious. SCIENCE, *237*, 1445–1452. **205, 206, 239**

KILPATRICK, D., VERONEN, L., & RESICK, P. (1979). The aftermath of rape: recent empirical findings. AMERICAN JOURNAL OF ORTHOPSYCHIATRY, *49*, 658–669. **582**

KILPATRICK, D., RESICK, P., & VERONEN, L. (1981). Effects of a rape experience: A longitudinal study. JOURNAL OF SOCIAL ISSUES, *37*, 105–122. **582**

KIMMEL, D. C., & WEINER, I. B. (1985). ADOLESCENCE: A DEVELOPMENTAL TRANSITION. Hillsdale, NJ: Erlbaum. **123**

KINDER, D. R., & SEARS, D. O. (1985). Public opinion and political action. In G. Lindzey & E. Aronson, (Eds.), THE HANDBOOK OF SOCIAL PSYCHOLOGY (3rd ed., Vol. 2). New York: Random House. **728**

KINSEY, A. C., POMEROY, W. B., & MARTIN, C. E. (1948). SEXUAL BEHAVIOR IN THE HUMAN MALE. Philadelphia: Saunders. **21, 113, 400**

KINSEY, A. C., POMEROY, W. B., MARTIN, C. E., & GEBHARD, P. H. (1953). SEXUAL BEHAVIOR IN THE HUMAN FEMALE. Philadelphia: Saunders. **21, 113, 400**

KLAHR, D. (1982). Nonmonotone assessment of monotone development: An in-

formation processing analysis. In S. Strauss (Ed.), U-SHAPED BEHAVIORAL GROWTH. New York: Academic Press. **94**

KLATZKY, R. L., LEDERMAN, S. J., & METZGER, V. A. (1985). Identifying objects by touch: An expert system. PERCEPTION AND PSYCHOPHYSICS, *37*, 299–302. **158**

KLINE, P. (1972). FACT AND FANCY IN FREUDIAN THEORY. London: Methuen. **540**

KLINEBERG, O. (1938). Emotional expression in Chinese literature. JOURNAL OF ABNORMAL AND SOCIAL PSYCHOLOGY, *33*, 517–520. **431**

KLUFT, R. P. (Ed.) (1985). CHILDHOOD ANTECEDENTS OF MULTIPLE PERSONALITY. Washington, DC: American Psychiatric Press. **249**

KNITTLE, J. L., & HIRSCH, J. (1968). Effect of early nutrition on the development of rat epididymal fat pads: Cellularity and metabolism. JOURNAL OF CLINICAL INVESTIGATION, *47*, 2091. **385**

KNOX, V. J., CRUTCHHELD, L., & HILGARD, E. R. (1975). The nature of task interference in hypnotic dissociation: An investigation of hypnotic behavior. INTERNATIONAL JOURNAL OF CLINICAL AND EXPERIMENTAL HYPNOSIS, *23*, 305–323. **238**

KOBASA, S. C. (1979). Stressful life events, personality, and health: An inquiry into hardiness. JOURNAL OF PERSONALITY AND SOCIAL PSYCHOLOGY, *37*, 1–11. **598, 599**

KOBASA, S. C., MADDI, S. R., & KAHN, S. (1982). Hardiness and health: A prospective study. JOURNAL OF PERSONALITY AND SOCIAL PSYCHOLOGY, *42*, 168–177. **598, 599**

KOBASIGAWA, A., ARAKAKI, K., & AWIGUNI, A. (1966). Avoidance of feminine toys by kindergarten boys: The effects of adult presence or absence, and an adult's attitudes toward sextyping. JAPANESE JOURNAL OF PSYCHOLOGY, *37*, 96–103. **104**

KOHLBERG, L. (1966). A cognitive-developmental analysis of children's sex-role concepts and attitudes. In E. E. Maccoby (Ed.), THE DEVELOPMENT OF SEX DIFFERENCES (pp. 82–173). Stanford, CA: Stanford University Press. **102, 104, 105**

KOHLBERG, L. (1969) Stage and sequence: The cognitive-developmental approach to socialization. In D. A. Goslin (Ed.), HANDBOOK OF SOCIALIZATION THEORY AND RESEARCH. Chicago: Rand McNally. **90**

KOHLBERG, L. (1976). Moral stages and

moralization: The cognitive-developmental approach. In T. Lickong (Ed.), MORAL DEVELOPMENT AND BEHAVIOR. New York: Holt, Rinehart & Winston. **90**

KOHLER, W. (1925). THE MENTALITY OF APES. New York: Harcourt Brace. (Reprint ed., 1976. New York: Liveright.) **281, 287)**

KOHOUT, J. (1991). CHANGES IN SUPPLY: WOMEN IN PSYCHOLOGY. Paper presented at the meeting of the American Psychological Association, San Francisco, California. Data compiled by Office of Demographic, Employment and Educational Research, Education Directorate American Psychological Association 8/91. **24**

KOLB, B., & WHISHAW, I. Q. (1985). FUNDAMENTALS OF HUMAN NEUROPSYCHOLOGY (2nd ed.). San Francisco: Freeman. **69**

KOOB, G. F., & BLOOM, F. E. (1988). Cellular and molecular mechanisms of drug dependence. SCIENCE, *242*, 715–723. **226**

KORNER, A. F. (1973). Individual differences at birth: Implications for early experience and later development. In J. C. Westman (Ed.), INDIVIDUAL DIFFERENCES IN CHILDREN. New York: Wiley. **83**

KORNHABER, M., KRECHEVSKY, M., & GARDNER, H. (1990). Engaging intelligence. EDUCATIONAL PSYCHOLOGIST, *25* (3 & 4), 177–199. **477**

KORNITZER, M., MAGOTTEAU, V., & collaborators. (1982). Angiographic findings and the Type A pattern assessed by means of the Bortner scale. JOURNAL OF BEHAVIORAL MEDICINE, *5*, 313–320. **601**

KOSA, J., & ZOLA, I. K. (Eds.) (1975). POVERTY AND HEALTH: A SOCIOLOGICAL ANALYSIS. Cambridge, MA: Harvard University Press. **656**

KOSAMBI, D. D. (1967). Living prehistory in India. SCIENTIFIC AMERICAN, *215*, 105. **159**

KOSSLYN, S. M. (1980). IMAGE AND MIND. Cambridge, MA: Harvard University Press. **361, 369**

KOSSLYN, S. M. (1983). GHOSTS IN THE MIND'S MACHINE. New York: Norton. **359, 369**

KOSSLYN, S. M. (1987). Seeing and imagining in the cerebral hemispheres: A computational approach. PSYCHOLOGICAL REVIEW, *94*, 148–175. **360**

KOSSLYN, S. M. (1988). Aspects of a cognitive neuroscience of mental imagery: SCIENCE, *240*, 1621–1626. **57**

KOSSLYN, S. M., BALL, T. M., & REISER, B. J. (1978). Visual images preserve metric spatial information: Evidence from studies of image scanning. JOURNAL OF EXPERIMENTAL PSYCHOLOGY: HUMAN PERCEPTION AND PERFORMANCE, *4*, 47–60. **361**

KOTELCHUCK, M. (1976). The infant's relationship to the father: Experimental evidence. In M. Lamb, (Ed.), THE ROLE OF THE FATHER IN CHILD DEVELOPMENT. New York: Wiley. **497**

KOULACK, D., & GOODENOUGH, D. R. (1976). Dream recall and dream recall failure: An arousal-retrieval model. PSYCHOLOGICAL BULLETIN, *83*, 975–984. **216**

KRAUT, (1982). Social presence, facial feedback, and emotion. JOURNAL OF PERSONALITY AND SOCIAL PSYCHOLOGY, *42*, 853–863. **433**

KRAVITZ, D. A. & MARTIN, B. (1986). Ringelmann rediscovered: The original article. JOURNAL OF PERSONALITY AND SOCIAL PSYCHOLOGY, *50*, 936–941. **759**

KREITMAN, N. (1977). PARASUICIDE. London: Wiley. **639**

KRIPKE, D. F. (1985) Biological Rythms. In G. L. Klerman, M. M. Weissman, P. S. Applebaum, & L. H. Roth, (Eds.), PSYCHIATRY (Vol. 3). Philadelphia: Lippincott. **210**

KRIPKE, D. F., & GILLIN, J. C. (1985). Sleep disorders. In G. L. Klerman, M. M. Weissman, P. S. Applebaum, & L. N. Roth (Eds.), PSYCHIATRY (Vol. 3). Philadelphia: Lippincott. **214**

KRYSTAL, H. (1968). MASSIVE PSYCHIC TRAUMA. New York: International University Press. **584**

KUBIS, J. F. (1962). Cited in B. M. Smith (1967), The polygraph. SCIENTIFIC AMERICAN, *216*, 21, 25–31, 146, **424**

KUIPER, N. A., MACDONALD, M. R., & DERRY, P. A. (1983). Parameters of a depressive self-schema. In J. Suls, & A. G. Greenwald (Eds.), PSYCHOLOGICAL PERSPECTIVES ON THE SELF (Vol. 2). Hillsdale, NJ: Erlbaum. **645**

KUIPER, N. A., OLINGER, L. J., MACDONALD, M. R., & SHAW, B. F. (1985). Self-schema processing of depressed and nondepressed content: The effects of vulnerability on depression. SOCIAL COGNITION, *3*, 77–93. **644**

KUMAN, I. G., FEDROV, C. N., & NOVIKOVA, L. A. (1983). Investigation of the sensitive period in the development of the human visual system. ZH. VYSHP. NERV. DEYAT (JOURNAL OF HIGHER NERVOUS ACTIVITY), *33*, 434–441. **76**

KUNDA, Z., & SANITIOSO, R. (1989). Motivated changes in the self-concept. JOURNAL OF EXPERIMENTAL SOCIAL

PSYCHOLOGY, *25*, 272–285. **727**

KURTINES, W., & GREIF, E. B. (1974). The development of moral thought: Review and evaluation of Kohlberg's approach. PSYCHOLOGICAL BULLETIN, *81*, 453–470.

KURTZ, P. (Ed.). (1985). A SKEPTIC'S HANDBOOK OF PARAPSYCHOLOGY. Buffalo: Prometheus Books. **249**

LACKNER, J., & GARRETT, M. (1973). Resolving ambiguity: Effects of biasing context in the unattended ear. COGNITION, *1*, 359–372. **186**

LAGERSPETZ, K., VIEMERO, V., & AKADEMI, A. (1986). Television and aggressive behavior among Finnish children. In L. R. Huesmann & L. D. Eron (Eds.), TELEVISION AND THE AGGRESSIVE CHILD. New York: Erlbaum. **445**

LAMB, M. E., & BORNSTEIN, M. H. (1987). DEVELOPMENT IN INFANCY: AN INTRODUCTION (2nd ed.). New York: Random House. **123**

LAND, E. H. (1977). The retinex theory of color vision. SCIENTIFIC AMERICAN, *237*, 108–128. **188**

LANGLOIS, J. H., & DOWNS, A. C. (1980). Mothers, fathers, and peers as socialization agents of sex-typed play behaviors in young children. CHILD DEVELOPMENT, *51*, 1237–1247. **103**

LAPIERE, R. (1934). Attitudes versus actions. SOCIAL FORCES, *13*, 230–237. **733**

LARKIN, J. H., MCDERMOTT, J., SIMON, D. P., & SIMON, H. A. (1980). Expert and novice performance in solving physics problems. SCIENCE, *208*, 1335–1342. **365**

LASNIK, H. (1990). Syntax. In D. N. Osherson & H. Lasnik, AN INVITATION TO COGNITIVE SCIENCE (Vol. 1). Cambridge, MA: MIT Press. **347**

LATANÉ, B. (1981) The psychology of social impact. AMERICAN PSYCHOLOGIST, *36*, 343–356. **758, 759**

LATANÉ, B., & DARLEY, J. M. (1968). Group inhibition of bystander intervention in emergencies. JOURNAL OF PERSONALITY AND SOCIAL PSYCHOLOGY, *10*, 215–221. **756, 757**

LATANÉ, B., & DARLEY, J. M. (1970). THE UNRESPONSIVE BYSTANDER: WHY DOESN'T HE HELP? New York: Appleton-Century-Crofts. **753, 784**

LATANÉ, B., & HARKINS, S. G. (1976). Crossmodality matches suggest anticipated stage fright, a multiplicative power function of audience size and status. PERCEPTION AND PSYCHOPHYSICS, *20*, 482–488. **758**

LATANÉ, B., & RODIN, J. (1969). A lady in distress: Inhibiting effects of friends

and strangers on bystander intervention. JOURNAL OF EXPERIMENTAL AND SOCIAL PSYCHOLOGY, *5*, 189–202. **756**

LATANÉ, B., WILLIAMS, K. D., & HARKINS, S. G. (1979). Many hands make light work: The causes and consequences of social loafing. JOURNAL OF PERSONALITY AND SOCIAL PSYCHOLOGY, *37*, 822–832. **759**

LAUDENSLAGER, M. L., RYAN, S. M., DRUGAN, R. C., HYSON, R. L., & MAIER, S. F. (1983). Coping and immunosuppression: Inescapable but not escapable shock suppresses lymphocyte proliferation. SCIENCE, *221*, 568–570. **593, 594**

LAURENCE, J. R. (1980). DUALITY AND DISSOCIATION IN HYPNOSIS. Unpublished M. A. thesis, Concordia University, Montreal. **239**

LAWLER, R. W., & YAZDANI, M. (Eds.) (1987). ARTIFICIAL INTELLIGENCE AND EDUCATION (Vol. 1). Norwood, NJ: Ablex.

LAZAR, I., & DARLINGTON, R. (1982). Lasting effects of early education: A report from the Consortium for Longitudinal Studies. MONOGRAPHS OF THE SOCIETY FOR RESEARCH IN CHILD DEVELOPMENT, *47*, 2–3. **481**

LAZARUS, R. S. (1961). Group therapy of phobic disorders by systematic desensitization. JOURNAL OF ABNORMAL AND SOCIAL PSYCHOLOGY, *63*, 504–510. **562**

LAZARUS, R. S. (1991 a). Cognition and motivation in emotion. AMERICAN PSYCHOLOGIST, *46*, 352–367. **422, 427, 447**

LAZARUS, R. S. (1991 b). EMOTION AND ADAPTATION. New York: Oxford University Press.

LAZARUS, R. S., & FOLKMAN, S. (1984). STRESS, APPRAISAL, AND COPING. New York: Springer. **578, 602, 603, 615**

LAZARUS, R. S., KANNER, A. D., & FOLKMAN, S. (1980). Emotions: A cognitive-phenomenological analysis. In R. Plutchik & H. Kellerman (Eds.), EMOTION: THEORY, RESEARCH, AND EXPERIENCE (Vol. 1). New York: Academic Press. **422**

LE BON, G. (1895). THE CROWD. London: Ernest Benn. **754, 784**

LE DEOX, J. E. (1989). Cognitive-emotional interactions in the brain. COGNITION AND EMOTION, *3*. 267–289. **429**

LEE, J. A. (1973). THE COLORS OF LOVE: AN EXPLORATION OF THE WAYS OF LOVING. Don Mills, Ontario: New Press. **744**

LEE, J. A. (1977). A typology of styles of

loving. PERSONALITY AND SOCIAL PSYCHOLOGY BULLETIN, 3, 173–182. **744**

LEE, J. A. (1988). Love-styles. In R. J. Sternberg, & M. L. Barnes (Eds.), THE PSYCHOLOGY OF LOVE (pp. 38–67). New Haven, CT: Yale University Press. **744**

LEE, V. E., BROOKS-GUNN, J., & SCHNUR, E. (1988). Does head start work? A 1-year follow-up comparison of disadvantaged children attending head start, no preschool, and other preschool programs. DEVELOPMENTAL PSYCHOLOGY, 24, 210–222. **481**

LENNEBERG, E. H. (1967). BIOLOGICAL FOUNDATIONS OF LANGUAGE. New York: Wiley. **355**

LERNER, R., KARSON, M., MEISELS, M., & KNAPP, J. R. (1975). Actual and perceived attitudes of late adolescents: The phenomenon of the generation gaps. JOURNAL OF GENETIC PSYCHOLOGY, 126, 197–207. **114**

LEROUX, J. A. (1986). Suicidal behavior and gifted adolescents. Roeper Rev., 9 (2), 77–79. **639**

LEVAV, I., FRIEDLANDER, Y., KARK, J. D., & PERITZ, E. (1988). An epidemiologic study of mortality among bereaved parents. THE NEW ENGLAND JOURNAL OF MEDICINE, 319, 457–461. **610**

LEVAY, S. (1991). A difference in hypothalmic structure between heterosexual and homosexual men. SCIENCE, 253, 1034–1037. **403**

LEVENSON, R. W., EKMAN, P., HEIDER, K., & FRIESIN, W. V. (1992). Emotion and autonic nervous system activity in an Indonesian culture. JOURNAL OF PERSONALITY AND SOCIAL PSYCHOLOGY, 62, 972–988. **422**

LEVINE, R. A. (1980). Anthropology and child development. NEW DIRECTIONS FOR CHILD DEVELOPMENT, 8, 71–86. **507**

LEVINE, S. (1960). Stimulation in infancy. SCIENTIFIC AMERICAN, 202, 80–86. **589**

LEVINGER, G., SENN, D. J., & JORGENSEN, B. W. (1970). Progress toward permanence in courtship: A test of the Kerckhoff-Davis hypotheses. SOCIOMETRY, 33, 427–443. **740**

LEVINSON, D. J., DARROW, C., KLEIN, E. B., LEVINSON, M. H., & McKEE, B. (1978). THE SEASONS OF A MAN'S LIFE. New York: Knopf. **120**

LEVY, J. (1985). Right brain, left brain: Facts and fiction. PSYCHOLOGY TODAY, 19, 38–44. **58**

LEVY, M. B., & DAVIS, K. E. (1988). Love styles and attachment styles compared: Their relation to each other and to various relationship characteristics. JOURNAL OF SOCIAL AND PERSONAL RELATIONSHIPS, I, 439–471. **744**

LEVY, S. M., & HEIDEN, I., (1991). Depression, distress and immunity: Risk factors for infectious disease. STRESS MEDICINE, 7, 45–51. **595**

LEWINSOHN, P. M., ANTONUCCIO, D. O., STEINMETZ, J. L., & TERI, L. (1984). THE COPING WITH DEPRESSION COURSE: PSYCHOEDUCATIONAL INTERVENTION FOR UNIPOLAR DEPRESSION. Eugene, OR: Castalia. **685**

LEWINSOHN, P. M., FENN, D., & FRANKLIN, J. (1982). The relationship of age of onset to duration of episode in unipolar depression. Unpublished manuscript, University of Oregon. **637**

LEWINSOHN, P. M., HOBERMAN, H., TERI, L., HAUTZINER, M. (1985). An integrative theory of depression. In S. Reiss & R. Bootsin, (Eds.), THEORETICAL ISSUES IN BEHAVIOR THERAPY. New York: Academic Press. **640**

LEWINSOHN, P. M., MISCHEL, W., CHAPLIN, W., & BARTON, R. (1980). Social competence and depression: The role of illusory self-perceptions. JOURNAL OF ABNORMAL PSYCHOLOGY, 89, 203–212. **640, 644**

LEY, R. G., & BRYDEN, M. P. (1982). A dissociation of right and left hemispheric effects for recognizing emotional tone and verbal content. BRAIN AND COGNITION, 1, 3–9, **433**

LIBERMAN, A. M., COOPER, F., SHANKWEILER, D., & STUDERT-KENNEDY, M. (1967). Perception of the speech code. PSYCHOLOGICAL REVIEW, 74, 431–459. **345**

LICKEY, M. E. & GORDON, B. (1991). MEDICINE AND MENTAL ILLNESS. New York: Freeman. **702, 709**

LIEBERMAN, L. R., & DUNLAP, J. T. (1979). O'Leary and Borkovec's conceptualization of placebo: The placebo paradox. AMERICAN PSYCHOLOGIST, 34, 553–554. **698**

LIEM, J. H. (1974). Effects of verbal communications of parents and children: A comparison of normal and schizophrenic families. JOURNAL OF CONSULTING AND CLINICAL PSYCHOLOGY, 42, 438–450. **656**

LINDZEY, G., & ARONSON, E. (Eds.) (1985). THE HANDBOOK OF SOCIAL PSYCHOLOGY (3rd ed.). Hillsdale, NJ: Erlbaum. **746, 784**

LINN, M. C., & HYDE, J. S. (1989, February). GENDER, MATHEMATICS, AND SCIENCE. Paper presented at the annual meeting of the American Association for the Advancement of Science, San Francisco. **470**

LINN, R. L. (1982). Ability Testing: Individual differences, prediction, and differential prediction. In A. Wigdor & W. Gardner, (Eds.), ABILITY TESTING: USES, CONSEQUENCES, AND CONTROVERSIES. Washington, DC: National Academy Press. **467, 469**

LIPPA, R. A. (1990). INTRODUCTION TO SOCIAL PSYCHOLOGY. Belmont, CA: Wadsworth. **746, 784**

LIPPERT, W. W., & SENTER, R. J. (1966). Electrodermal responses in the sociopath. PSYCHONOMIC SCIENCE, 4, 25–26. **661**

LIVINGSTONE, M., & HUBEL, D. (1988). Segregation of form, color, movement, and depth: Anatomy, physiology, and perception. SCIENCE, 240, 740–750. **166**

LOEB, G. (1985). The functional replacement of the ear. SCIENTIFIC AMERICAN, 252, 104–111. **152, 153**

LOEHLIN, J. C., LINDZEY, G., & SPUHLER, J. N. (1975). RACE DIFFERENCES IN INTELLIGENCE. San Francisco: Freeman. **484**

LOFTUS, E. F., & LOFTUS, G. R. (1980). On the permanence of stored information in the human brain. AMERICAN PSYCHOLOGIST, 35, 409–420. **306**

LOFTUS, E. F., SCHOOLER, J. W., & WAGENAAR, W. A. (1985). The fate of memory: Comment on McCloskey and Zaragoza. JOURNAL OF EXPERIMENTAL PSYCHOLOGY: GENERAL, 114, 375–380. **324**

LOFTUS, G. R., & LOFTUS, E. F. (1975). HUMAN MEMOS: THE PROCESSING OF INFORMATION. New York: Halstead Press. **324**

LOGUE, A. W. (1991). THE PSYCHOLOGY OF EATING AND DRINKING: AN INTRODUCTION (2nd edition). New York: Freeman. **383, 390, 392, 415**

LONGLEY, J., & PRUITT, D. G. (1980). Groupthink: A critique of Janis's theory. In L. Wheeler (Ed.), REVIEW OF PERSONALITY AND SOCIAL PSYCHOLOGY (Vol. 1). Beverly Hills, CA: Sage. **781**

LOOMIS, A. L., HARVEY, E. N., & HOBART, G. A. (1937). Cerebral states during sleep as studied by human potentials. JOURNAL OF EXPERIMENTAL PSYCHOLOGY, 21, 127–144. **211**

LORD, C. G., ROSS, L., & LEPPER, M. R. (1979). Biased assimilation and attitude polarzation: The effects of prior theories on subsequently considered evidence. JOURNAL OF PERSONALITY AND SOCIAL PSYCHOLOGY, 37, 2098–2109. **718**

LORENZ, K. (1966). ON AGGRESSION. New York: Harcourt Brace Jovanovich.

**439**
LORENZ, K. (1981). THE FOUNDATIONS OF ETHOLOGY. New York: Springer-Verlag. **415**

LOVAAS, O. I., FREITAG, G., GOLD, V. J., & KASSORLA, I. C. (1965). Recording apparatus for observation of behaviors of children in free play settings. JOURNAL OF EXPERIMENTAL CHILD PSYCHOLOGY, *2*, 108–120. **562**

LOVE, R. E., & GREENWALD, A. C. (1978). Cognitive responses to persuasion as mediators of opinion change. JOURNAL OF SOCIAL PSYCHOLOGY, *104*, 231–241. **773**

LOWINGER, P., & DOBIE, S. (1969). What makes the placebo work? A study of placebo response rate. ARCHIVES OF GENERAL PSYCHIATRY, *20*, 84–88. **698**

LUBORSKY, L. (1984). PRINCIPLES OF PSYCHOANALYTIC PSYCHOTHERAPY: A MANUAL FOR SUPPORTIVE-EXPRESSIVE TREATMENT. New York: Basic Books. **708**

LUBORSKY, L. L., MCLELLAN, A. T., WOODY, G. E., O'BRIEN, E. P., & AUERBACH, A. (1985). Therapist success and its determinants. ARCHIVES OF GENERAL PSYCHIATRY, *42*, 602–611. **696**

LUCAS, A., MORLEY, R., COLE, T. J., LISTER, G., & LEESON-PAYNE, C. (1992). Breast milk and subsequent intelligence quotient in children born preterm. THE LANCET, *339*, 261–264. **480**

LUCHINS, A. (1957). Primacy-recency in impression formation. In C. I. Hovland, (Ed.), THE ORDER OF PRESENTATION IN PERSUASION. New Haven: Yale University Press. **716, 717**

LUDWIG, A. M., BRANDSMA, J. M., WILBUR, C. B., BENDFELDT, F., & JAMESON, D. H. (1972). The objective study of a multiple personality. ARCHIVES OF GENERAL PSYCHIATRY, *26*, 298–310. **208**

LUMSDAINE, A. A., & JANIS, I. L. (1953). Resistance to "counter-propaganda" produced by one-sided and "two-sided propaganda" presentations. PUBLIC OPINION QUARTERLY, *17*, 311–318. **774**

LUNDIN, R. W. (1985). THEORIES AND SYSTEMS OF PSYCHOLOGY, (3rd ed.). Lexington, MA: Heath. **30**

LURIA, Z., & RUBIN, J. Z. (1974). The eye of the beholder: Parents' views on sex of newborns. AMERICAN JOURNAL OF ORTHOPSYCHIATRY, *44*, 512–519. **103**

LYCAN, W. G. (1987). CONSCIOUSNESS. Cambridge: MIT Press. **249**

LYKKEN, D. T. (1957). A study of anxiety in the sociopathic personality. JOURNAL OF ABNORMAL AND SOCIAL PSYCHOLOGY, *55*, 6–10. **661**

LYKKEN, D. T. (1980). TREMOR IN THE BLOOD: USES AND ABUSES OF THE LIE DETECTOR. New York: McGraw-Hill. **425, 447**

LYKKEN, D. T. (1982). Research with twins: The concept of emergenesis. THE SOCIETY FOR PSYCHOPHYSIOLOGICAL RESEARCH, *19*, 361–373. **490**

LYKKEN, D. T. (1984). Polygraphic interrogation. NATURE, *307*, 681–684. **424**

LYONS-RUTH, K., CONNELL, D. B., ZOLL, D., & STAHL, J. (1987). Infants at social risk: Relations among infant maltreatment, maternal behavior, and infant attachment behavior. DEVELOPMENTAL PSYCHOLOGY, *23*, 223–232. **495**

MAASS, A. & CLARK, R. D., III (1983). Internalization versus compliance: Differential processes underlying minority influence and conformity. EUROPEAN JOURNAL OF SOCIAL PSYCHOLOGY, *13*, 45–55. **773**

MAASS, A., & CLARK, R. D., III (1984). Hidden impact of minorities: Fifteen years of minority influence research. PSYCHOLOGICAL BULLETIN, *95*, 428–450. **772**

MACCOBY. E. E. (1980). SOCIAL DEVELOPMENT: PSYCHOLOGICAL GROWTH AND THE PARENT-CHILD RELATIONSHIP. New York: Harcourt Brace Jovanovich. **103**

MACCOBY, E. E. & JACKLIN, C. N. (1974). THE PSYCHOLOGY OF SEX DIFFERENCES. Stanford: Stanford University Press. **102, 103**

MACCOBY, E. E., & MARTIN, J. A. (1983). Socialization in the context of the family: Parent-child interaction. In P. H. Mussen (Ed.). HANDBOOK OF CHILD PSYCHOLOGY (Vol. 4). New York: Wiley. **115, 500, 501**

MACKENZIE, B. (1984). Explaining race differences in IQ: The logic, the methodology, and the evidence. AMERICAN PSYCHOLOGIST, *39*, 1214–1233. **484**

MADDI, S., & COSTA, P. (1972). HUMANISM IN PERSONOLOGY: ALLPORT, MASLOW, AND MURRAY. Chicago: Aldine. **572**

MAHER, B. A. (1966). PRINCIPLES OF PSYCHOTHERAPY: AN EXPERIMENTAL APPROACH. New York: McGraw-Hill. **647, 660, 662**

MAIER, S. F., & SELIGMAN, M. E. P. (1976). Learned helplessness: Theory and evidence. JOURNAL OF EXPERIMENTAL PSYCHOLOGY: GENERAL, *105*, 3–46. **274**

MAIN, M., & CASSIDY, J. (1988). Categories of response to reunion with parents at age 6: Predictable from infant attachment classifications and stable over a 1-month period. DEVELOPMENTAL PSYCHOLOGY, *24*, 415–426. **497**

MAIN, M., & SOLOMON, J. (1986). Discovery of an insecure-disorganized/disoriented attachment pattern: Procedures, findings and implications for the classification of behavior. In T. B. Brazelton, & M. Yogman (Eds.), AFFECTIVE DEVELOPMENT IN INFANCY (pp. 95–124). Norwood, NJ: Ablex. **495**

MALINOWSKI, B. (1927). SEX AND REPRESSION IN SAVAGE SOCIETY. London: Humanities Press. **539**

MALOF, M., & LOTT, A. J. (1962). Ethnocentrism and the acceptance of Negro support in a group pressure situation. JOURNAL OF ABNORMAL AND SOCIAL PSYCHOLOGY, *65*, 254–258. **761**

MALONEY, L. T., & WANDELL, B. A. (1986). Color constancy: A method for recovering surface spectral reflectance. JOURNAL OF THE OPTICAL SOCIETY OF AMERICA, *3*, 29–33. **188**

MALT, B. C. (1985). The role of discourse structure in understanding anaphora. JOURNAL OF MEMORY AND LANGUAGE, *24*, 271–289. **296**

MANDLER, G. (1982). MIND AND EMOTION. New York: Norton. **447**

MANDLER, J. (1983) Representation. In P. H. Mussen (Ed.) HANDBOOK OF CHILD PSYCHOLOGY (Vol. 3). New York: Wiley. **94**

MANUCK, S. B., KAPLAN, J. R., & MATTHEWS, K. A. (1986). Behavioral antecedents of coronary heart disease and atherosclerosis. ARTERIOSCLEROSIS, *6*, 1–14. **592**

MANUCK, S. B., & KRANTZ, D. S. (1986). Psychophysiologic reactivity in coronary heart disease and essential hypertension. In K. A. Matthews, S. M. Weiss, T. Detre, T. M. Dembroski, B. Falkner, S. B. Manuck, & R. B. Williams J. (Eds.), HANDBOOK OF STRESS, REACTIVITY, AND CARDIOVASCULAR DISEASE. New York: Wiley. **601**

MARBLY, N. (1987) But you weren't there. In T. Williams (Ed.) POST-TRAUMATIC STRESS DISORDERS: A HANDBOOK FOR CLINICIANS. Cincinnati, OH: Disabled American Veterans. **585**

MARCIA, J. E. (1966). Development and validation of ego identity status. JOURNAL OF PERSONALITY AND SOCIAL PSYCHOLOGY, *3*, 551–558. **508**

MARCIA, J. E. (1980). Identity in adolescence. In J. Adelson (Ed.), HANDBOOK OF ADOLESCENT PSYCHOLOGY New York: Wiley. **508**

MARCUS, J., HANS, S. L., NAGLER, S., AUERBACK, J. G., MIRSKY, A. F., & AUBREY, A. (1987). A review of the NIMH Israeli Kibbutz-city study. SCHIZOPHRENIA BULLETIN, 13, 425–438. 657

MARDSEN, G. (1971). Content analysis studies of psychotherapy: 1954 through 1968. In A. E. Bergin & S. L. Garfield (Ed.), HANDBOOK OF PSYCHOTHERAPY AND BEHAVIOR CHANGE. New York: Wiley, 562

MARKMAN, E. M. (1979). Classes and collections: Conceptual organization and numerical abilities. COGNITIVE PSYCHOLOGY, 11, 395–411. 92

MARKMAN, E. M. (1987). How children constrain the possible meanings of words. In U. Neisser (Ed.), CONCEPTS AND CONCEPTUAL DEVELOPMENT: ECOLOGICAL AND INTELLECTUAL FACTORS IN CATEGORIZATIONS. New York: Cambridge University Press. 351

MARKUS, H. (1977) Self-schemata and processing information about the self. JOURNAL OF PERSONALITY AND SOCIAL PSYCHOLOGY, 35, 63–78. 716

MARKUS, H., & NURIUS, P. (1986). Possible selves. AMERICAN PSYCHOLOGIST, 41, 954–969. 645

MARLATT, G. A., BAER, J. S., DONOVAN, D. M., & KIVLAHAN, D. R. (1988). Addictive behaviors: Etiology and treatment. In M. R. Rosenzweig & L. W. Porter, (Eds.), ANNUAL REVIEW OF PSYCHOLOGY (Vol. 39). Palo Alto, CA: Annual Reviews. 233

MARR, D. (1982). VISION. San Francisco: Freeman. 165, 174, 201

MARRON, J. E. (1965). Special test preparation: Its effects on college board scores and the relationship of effected scores to subsequent college performance. Office of the Director of Admissions and Registrar. U. S. Military Academy, West Point, NY. 467

MARSHALL, G., & ZIMBARDO, P. G. (1979). Affective consequences of inadequately explained physiological arousal. JOURNAL OF PERSONALITY AND SOCIAL PSYCHOLOGY, 37, 970–988. 423

MARTIN, C.L., & HALVERSON, C.F. (1983). A schematic processing model of sex typing and stereotyping in children. CHILD DEVELOPMENT, 52, 1119–1134. 106

MASLACH, C. (1979). The emotional consequences of arousal without reason. In Izard, C. E. (Ed.), EMOTION IN PERSONALITY AND PSYCHOPATHOLOGY. New York: Plenum. 423

MASLOW, A. H. (1967). Self-actualization and beyond. In J. F. T. Bugenthal (Ed.), CHALLENGES OF HUMANISTIC PSYCHOLOGY. New York: McGraw-Hill. 549

MASLOW, A. H. (1970). MOTIVATION AND PERSONALITY (2nd ed.). New York: Harper and Row. 547, 548

MASSON, J. M. (1984) THE ASSAULT ON TRUTH. New York: Farrar, Straus & Giroux, Inc. 536

MASTERS, W. H., & JOHNSON, V. E. (1966). HUMAN SEXUAL RESPONSE. Boston: Little, Brown. 20

MASUDA, M. & HOLMES, T. H. (1978). Life events: perceptions and frequencies. PSYCHOSOMATIC MEDICINE, 40, 236–261. 581

MATAS, L., AREND, R. A., & SROUFE, L. A. (1978). Continuity of adaption in the second year: The relationship between quality of attachment and later competence. CHILD DEVELOPMENT, 49, 547–556. 498

MATHES, E. W. (1975). The effects of physical attractiveness and anxiety on heterosexual attraction over a series of five encounters. JOURNAL OF MARRIAGE AND THE FAMILY, 37, 769–773. 736

MATTHEWS, D. F. (1972). Response patterns of single neurons in the tortoise olfactory epithelium and olfactory bulb. JOURNAL OF GENERAL PHYSIOLOGY, 60, 166–180. 155

MATTHEWS, K. A., WEISS, S. M., DETRE, T., DEMBROSKI, T. M., FALKNER, B., MANUCK, S. B., & WILLIAMS, R. B., JR. (Eds.) (1986). HANDBOOK OF STRESS REACTIVITY AND CARDIOVASCULAR DISEASE. New York: Wiley. 615

MAYER, R. E. (1983). THINKING, PROBLEM SOLVING AND COGNITION. New York: Freeman. 369

MCALISTER, A., PERRY, C., KILLEN, J., SLINKARD, L. A., & MACCOBY, N. (1980). Pilot study of smoking, alcohol and drug abuse prevention. AMERICAN JOURNAL OF PUBLIC HEALTH, 70, 719–721. 775, 776

MCBURNEY, D. H. (1978). Psychological dimensions and the perceptual analysis of taste. In E. C. Carterette, & M. P. Friedman (Eds.), HANDBOOK OF PERCEPTION (Vol. 6). New York: Academic Press. 156

MCCARTHY, R. A., & WARRINGTON, E. K. (1987a). The double dissociation of short-term memory for lists and sentences. BRAIN, 10, 1545–1563. 296

MCCARTHY, R. A., & WARRINGTON, E. K. (1987b). Understanding: A function of short-term memory? BRAIN, 110, 1565–1578. 296

MCCARTNEY, K., & PHILLIPS, D. (1988). Motherhood and child care. In B. Birns & D. Hay (Eds.), DIFFERENT FACES OF MOTHERHOOD. New York: Plenum. 498

MCCAULEY, C. (1989). The nature of social influence in groupthink: Compliance and internalization. JOURNAL OF PERSONALITY AND SOCIAL PSYCHOLOGY, 57, 250–260. 781

MCCLELLAND, J. L., & RUMELHART, D. E. (1981). An interactive model of context effects in letter perception: Pt. 1. An account of basic findings. PSYCHOLOGICAL REVIEW, 88, 375–407. 178

MCCLELLAND, J. L., RUMELHART, D. E., & THE PDP RESEARCH GROUP (1986). PARALLEL DISTRIBUTED PROCESSING: EXPLORATIONS IN THE MICROSTRUCTURE OF COGNITION (Vol. 2). Cambridge, MA: Bradford Books/MIT Press. 177

MCCLINTOCK, M. K. (1971). Menstrual synchrony and suppression. NATURE, 229, 244–245. 154

MCCLOSKEY, M., WIBLE, C. G., & COHEN, N. J. (1988). Is there a flashbulb-memory system? JOURNAL OF EXPERIMENTAL PSYCHOLOGY, 117, 171–181. 310

MCCLOSKEY, M. & COHEN, N. J. (1989). Castastrophic interference in connectionist networks: The sequential learning problem. In G. H. Bower (Ed.). THE PSYCHOLOGY OF LEARNING AND MOTIVATION (Vol. 24, pp. 109–164). New York: Academic Press. 305

MCCONAGHY, M. J. (1979). Gender permanence and the genital basis of gender. Stages in the development of constancy of gender identity. CHILD DEVELOPMENT, 50, 1223–1226. 102

MCCRAE, R. R., & COSTA, P. T., JR. (1987). Validation of the five-factor model of personality across instruments and observers. JOURNAL OF PERSONALITY AND SOCIAL PSYCHOLOGY, 52, 81–90. 531

MCDOUGALL, W. (1908). SOCIAL PSYCHOLOGY. New York: G. P. Putnam's Sons. 408

MCELREE, B. & DOSHER, B. A. (1989). Serial position and set size in short-term memory: The time course of recognition. JOURNAL OF EXPERIMENTAL PSYCHOLOGY: GENERAL. 118, 346–373. 296

MCFARLAND, D. (1985). ANIMAL BEHAVIOUR: PSYCHOBIOLOGY, ETHOLOGY AND EVOLUTION. Menlo Park, CA: Benjamin-Cummings. 415

MCGHIE, A., & CHAPMAN, J. (1961). Disorders of attention and perception in early schizophrenia. BRITISH JOURNAL

OF MEDICAL PSYCHOLOGY, *34*, 103–116. **647, 649**

MCGRAW, M. B. (1975). GROWTH: A STUDY OF JOHNNY AND JIMMY. New York: Acno Press (Originally published 1935). **74**

MCGUFFIN, P., SARGEANT, M., HETT, G., TIDMARSH, S., WHATLEY, S., & MARCHBANKS, R. M. (1990). Exclusion of a schizophrenia susceptibility gene from the chromosome 5q11-q13 region. New data and a reanalysis of previous reports. AMERICAN JOURNAL OF HUMAN GENETICS. *47*, 524–535. **652**

MCGUIRE, W. J. (1964). Inducing resistance to persuasion: some contemporary approaches. In L. Berkowitz (Ed.), ADVANCES IN EXPERIMENTAL SOCIAL PSYCHOLOGY (Vol. 1). Academic Press. **775**

MCGUIRE, W. J., & PAPAGEORGIS, D. (1961). The relative efficacy of various types of prior belief-defense in producing immunity against persuasion. JOURNAL OF ABNORMAL AND SOCIAL PSYCHOLOGY, *62*, 327–337. **775**

MCKENNA, R. J. (1972). Some effects of anxiety level and food cues on the eating behavior of obese and normal subjects. JOURNAL OF PERSONALITY AND SOCIAL PSYCHOLOGY, *22*, 311–319. **386**

MCKENZIE, B., & OVER, R. (1983). Young infants fail to imitate facial and manual gestures. INFANT BEHAVIOR AND DEVELOPMENT, *6*, 85–95. **78**

MCNALLY, R. J. (1990). Psychological approaches to panic disorder: A review. PSYCHOLOGY BULLETIN, *108*, 403–419. **633**

MCNEAL, E. T., & CIMBOLIC, P. (1986). Antidepressants and biochemical theories of depression. PSYCHOLOGICAL BULLETIN, *99*, 361–374. **644**

MCNEILL, D. (1966). Developmental psycholinguistics. In F. Smith & G. A. Miller (Eds.), THE GENESIS OF LANGUAGE: A PSYCHOLINGUISTIC APPROACH. Cambridge, MA: MIT Press. **353**

MEANEY, M. J., AITKENS, D. H., BERKEL, C., BHATNAGAR, S., SARRIEAU, A., & SAPOLSKY, R. M. (1987). POST-NATAL HANDLING ATTENUATES AGE-RELATED CHANGES IN THE ADRENOCORTICAL STRESS RESPONSE AND SPATIAL MEMORY DEFICITS IN THE RAT. Paper presented at the 17th Annual Meeting of the Society of Neuroscience, New Orleans. **589**

MECHANIC, D. (1962). STUDENTS UNDER STRESS. New York: Free Press. **610**

MEDCOF, J., & ROTH, J. (Eds.) (1988). APPROACHES TO PSYCHOLOGY. Philadelphia: Open University Press, Milton Keynes. **30**

MEDNICK, S. A., CANNON, T., PARNAS, J., & SCHULSINGER, F. (1989). 27 year follow-up of the Copenhagen high-risk for schizophrenia project: Why did some of the high-risk offspring become schizophrenic? (Abstract) SCHIZOPHRENIA RESEARCH, *2*, 14. **657**

MEDNICK, S. A., MACHON, R., HUTTUNEN, M. O., & BONETT, D. (1988). Fetal viral infection and adult schizophrenia. ARCHIVES OF GENERAL PSYCHIATRY, *45*, 189–192. **655**

MEGARGEE, E. I. (1972). THE CALIFORNIA PSYCHOLOGICAL INVENTORY HANDBOOK. San Francisco: Jossey-Bass. **558**

MEICHENBAUM, D. H. (1985). STRESS INOCULATION TRAINING. New York: Pergamon. **615**

MEICHENBAUM, D. H., & JAREMKO, M. E. (Eds.) (1983). STRESS REDUCTION AND PREVENTION. New York: Plenum. **615**

MEIER, R. P. (1991). Language acquisition by deaf children. AMERICAN SCIENTIST, *79*, 60–76. **355**

MELAMED, B. G., & SIEGEL, L. J. (1975). Reduction of anxiety in children facing hospitalization and surgery by use of filmed modeling. JOURNAL OF CONSULTING AND CLINICAL PSYCHIATRY, *43*, 511–521. **680**

MELTON, A. W. (1963). Implications of short-term memory for a general theory of memory. JOURNAL OF VERBAL LEARNING AND VERBAL BEHAVIOR, *2*, 1–21. **289**

MELTZOFF, A. N., & MOORE, M. K. (1977). Imitation of facial and manual gestures by human neonates. SCIENCE, *198*, 75–78. **78**

MELTZOFF, A. N., & MOORE, M. K. (1983). Newborn infants imitate adult facial gestures. CHILD DEVELOPMENT, *54*, 702–709. **78**

MELVILLE, J. (1977). PHOBIAS AND OBSESSIONS. New York: Coward, McCann, & Geoghegan. **625**

MELZAK, R. (1973). THE PUZZLE OF PAIN. New York: Basic Books. **159, 160**

MELZAK, R. (1990). The tragedy of needless pain. SCIENTIFIC AMERICAN, *262*, 27–33. **158, 159**

MERVIS, C. B., & PANI, J. R. (1981). Acquisition of basic object categories. COGNITIVE PSYCHOLOGY, *12*, 496–522. **336**

MERVIS, C. B., & ROSCH, E. (1981). Categorization of natural objects. In M. R. Rosenz & L. W. Porter (Eds.), AN-

NUAL REVIEW OF PSYCHOLOGY (Vol. 21). Palo Alto, CA: Annual Reviews. **335**

MESSICK, S., & JUNGEBLUT, A. (1981). Time and method in coaching for the SAT. PSYCHOLOGICAL BULLETIN, *89*, 191–216. **467**

METALSKY, G. I., HALBERSTADT, L. J., & ABRAMSON, L. Y. (1987). Vulnerability to depressive mood reactions: Toward a more powerful test of the diathesis-stress and causal mediation components of the reformulated theory of depression. JOURNAL OF PERSONALITY AND SOCIAL PSYCHOLOGY, *52*, 386–393. **598**

MEYER, J. P., & PEPPER, S. (1977). Need compatibility and marital adjustment in young married couples. JOURNAL OF PERSONALITY AND SOCIAL PSYCHOLOGY, *8*, 331–342. **740**

MICHOTTE, A. (1963). THE PERCEPTION OF CAUSALITY. New York: Basic Books. **173**

MILES, L. E., RAYNAL, D. M., & WILSON, M. A. (1977). Blind man living in normal society has circadian rhythm of 24.9 hours. SCIENCE, *198*, 421–423. **210**

MILGRAM, S. (1963). Behavioral study of obedience. JOURNAL OF ABNORMAL AND SOCIAL PSYCHOLOGY, *67*, 371–378. **21, 762, 764, 768**

MILGRAM, S. (1974). OBEDIENCE TO AUTHORITY: AN EXPERIMENTAL VIEW. New York: Harper & Row. **21, 762, 763, 765, 766, 769, 784**

MILLER, A. (1984). A transitional phase in gender constancy and its relationship to cognitive level and sex identification. CHILD STUDY JOURNAL, *13*, 259–275. **106**

MILLER, D. T., & ROSS, M. (1975). Self-serving biases in attribution of causality: Fact or fiction? PSYCHOLOGICAL BULLETIN, *82*, 213–225. **645**

MILLER, G. A. (1956) The magical number seven plus or minus two: Some limits on our capacity for processing information. PSYCHOLOGICAL REVIEW, *63*, 81–97. **293**

MILLER, G. A., & GILDEA, P. M. (1987). How children learn words. SCIENTIFIC AMERICAN, *257*, 94–99. **351**

MILLER, P. H. (1989). THEORIES OF DEVELOPMENTAL PSYCHOLOGY (2nd ed.). New York: Freeman. **123**

MILNER, B. (1964). Some effects of frontal lobectomy in man. In J. M. Warren & K. Akert (Eds.), THE FRONTAL GRANULAR CORTEX AND BEHAVIOR. New York: McGraw-Hill. **52**

MILNER, B., CORKIN, S., & TEUBER, H. L. (1968). Further analysis of the hippocampal amnesic syndrome: 14-year follow-up study of H. M. NEUROPSY-

CHOLOGIA, *6*, 215–234. **290**

MINARD, R. D. (1952). Race relations in the Pocahontas coal field. JOURNAL OF SOCIAL ISSUES, *8*, 29–44. **732**

MISCHEL, W. (1966). A social learning view of sex differences in behavior. In E. E. Maccoby (Ed.), THE DEVELOPMENT OF SEX DIFFERENCES. Stanford: Stanford University Press. **102**

MISCHEL, W. (1968). PERSONALITY AND ASSESSMENT. New York: Wiley. **526, 565**

MISCHEL, W. (1973). Toward a cognitive social learning reconceptualization of personality. PSYCHOLOGICAL REVIEW, *80*, 272–283. **543**

MISCHEL, W. (1993). INTRODUCTION TO PERSONALITY (5th ed.). Fort Worth: Harcourt Brace Jovanovich. **572**

MISHKIN, M., & APPENZELLER, T. (1987). The anatomy of memory. SCIENTIFIC AMERICAN, *256*, 80–89. **165**

MISHKIN, M., MALAMUT, B., & BACHEVALIER, J. (1984). Memories and habits: Two neural systems. In G. T. Lynch, J. L. McGaugh & N. M. Weinberger (Eds.), NEUROBIOLOGY OF LEARNING AND MEMORY. New York: Guilford Press. **313**

MITA, T. H., DERMER, M., & KNIGHT, J. (1977). Reversed facial images and the mere-exposure hypothesis. JOURNAL OF PERSONALITY AND SOCIAL PSYCHOLOGY, *35*, 597–601. **738**

MITCHEL, J. S., & KEESEY, R. E. (1974). The effects of lateral hypothalamic lesions and castration upon the body weight of male rats. BEHAVIORAL BIOLOGY, *11*, 69–82. **381**

MOERMAN, D. E. (1981). Edible symbols: The effectiveness of placebos. In T. A. Sebok & R. Rosenthal (Eds.), THE CLEVER HANS PHENOMENON Annals of the New York Academy of Sciences (Vol. 364). New York: New York Academy of Science. **242**

MOLDIN, S., GOTTESMAN, I. I., ERLENMEYER-KIMLING, L., & CORNBLATT, B. A. (1990). Psychometric deviance in offspring at risk for schizophrenia. PSYCHIATRY RESEARCH, *32*, 297–322. **657**

MONAHAN, J. (1976). The prevention of violence. In J. Monahan (Ed.), COMMUNITY MENTAL HEALTH AND THE CRIMINAL JUSTICE SYSTEM. Elmsford, NY: Pergamon Press. **671**

MONEY, J. (1980). Endocrine influences and psychosexual status spanning the life cycle. In H. M. Van Praag (Ed.), HANDBOOK OF BIOLOGICAL PSYCHIATRY (Part 3). New York: Marcel Dekker. **403, 405**

MONEY, J. (1987). Sin, sickness, or status? Homosexual gender identity and psychoneuroendocrinology. AMERICAN PSYCHOLOGIST, *42*, 384–400. **405**

MONEY, J. & LAMACZ, M. (1989). VANDALIZED LOVEMAPS: PARAPHILLIC OUTCOME OF SEVEN CASES IN PEDIATRIC SEXOLOGY. Buffalo, NY: Prometheus. **398**

MONEY, J., SCHWARTZ, M., & LEWIS, V. G. (1984). Adult heterosexual status and fetal hormonal masculinization and demasculinization: 46, XX congenital virilizing adrenal hyperplasia and 46, XY androgen-insensitivity syndrome compared. PSYCHONEUROENDOCRINOLOGY, *9*, 405–414. **403**

MONEY, J., WIEDEKING, C., WALKER, P. A., & GAIN, D. (1976). Combined antiandrogenic and counseling programs for treatment of 46 XY and 47 XXY sex offenders. In E. Sacher (Ed.), HORMONES, BEHAVIOR AND PSYCHOPATHOLOGY. New York: Raven Press. **395**

MONSELL, S. (1979). Recency, immediate recognition memory, and reaction time. COGNITIVE PSYCHOLOGY, *10*, 465–501. **296**

MONTAIGNE, M. de (1580/1943). Of the inconsistency of our actions. In D. M. Frame (Trans., Ed.), SELECTED ESSAYS. Roslyn, NY: Walter J. Black. **565**

MOOK, D. C. (1987). MOTIVATION: THE ORGANIZATION OF ACTION. New York: Norton. **409, 415, 447**

MOORE, B. C. J. (1982). AN INTRODUCTION TO THE PSYCHOLOGY OF HEARING (2nd ed.). New York: Academic Press. **163**

MOOS, R. H. (1988). COPING RESPONSES INVENTORY MANUAL. Social Ecology Laboratory, Department of Psychiatry, Stanford University and Veterans Administration Medical Centers, Palo Alto, CA. **603**

MORAY, N. (1969). ATTENTION: SELECTIVE PROCESSES IN VISION AND HEARING. London: Hutchinson. **185**

MORELAND, R. L., & ZAJONC, R. B. (1979). Exposure effects may not depend on stimulus recognition. JOURNAL OF PERSONALITY AND SOCIAL PSYCHOLOGY, *37*, 1085–1089. **738**

MORRISON, D. M. (1985). Adolescent contraceptive behavior: A review. PSYCHOLOGICAL BULLETIN, *98*, 538–568. **116**

MORROW, J., & NOLEN-HOEKSEMA, S. (1990). Effects of responses to depression on the remediation of depressive affect. JOURNAL OF PERSONALITY AND SOCIAL PSYCHOLOGY, *58*, 519–527. **604**

MOSCOVICI, S. (1976). SOCIAL INFLU-ENCE AND SOCIAL CHANGE. London: Academic Press. **771**

MOSCOVICI, S., LAGE, E., & NAFFRECHOUX, M. (1969). Influence of a consistent minority on the responses of a majority in a color perception task. SOCIOMETRY, *32*, 365–379. **772**

MOSCOVICI, S., & ZAVALLONI, M. (1969). The group as a polarizer of attitudes. JOURNAL OF PERSONALITY AND SOCIAL PSYCHOLOGY, *12*, 125–135. **779**

MOSKOWITZ, H. R., KUMRAICH, V., SHARMA, H., JACOBS, L., & SHARMA, S. D. (1975). Cross-cultural difference in simple taste preference. SCIENCE, *190*, 1217–1218. **155**

MOTT, F., & HAURIN, R. (1988). Linkages between sexual activity and alcohol and drug use. FAMILY PLANNING PERSPECTIVES, *20*, 128–137. **113**

MOVSHON, J. A., & VAN SLUYTERS, R. C. (1981). Visual neural development. ANNUAL REVIEW OF PSYCHOLOGY, *32*, 477–522. **197**

MOWRER, O. H. (1947). On the dual nature of learning—A reinterpretation of "conditioning" and "problem-solving". HARVARD EDUCATIONAL REVIEW, *17*, 102–148. **273**

MUNROE, R. H., MUNROE, R. L., & WHITING, B. B. (Eds.) (1981). HANDBOOK OF CROSS-CULTURAL HUMAN DEVELOPMENT. New York: Garland STPM Press. **523**

MURDOCK, B. B., JR. (1962). The serial position effect in free recall. JOURNAL OF EXPERIMENTAL PSYCHOLOGY, *64*, 482–488. **297**

MURPHY, G. E., & WETZEL, R. D. (1980). Suicide risk by birth cohort in the United States, 1949 to 1974. ARCHIVES OF GENERAL PSYCHIATRY, *37*, 519–523. **638**

MURPHY, G. L. & MEDIN, D. L. (1985). The role of theories in conceptual coherence. PSYCHOLOGICAL REVIEW, *92*, 289–316. **334**

MURPHY, K. R. & DAVIDSHOFER, C. O. (1991). PSYCHOLOGICAL TESTING: PRINCIPLES AND APPLICATIONS (2nd ed.). Englewood Cliffs, NJ: Prentice Hall. **486**

MURSTEIN, B. I. (1972). Physical attractiveness and marital choice. JOURNAL OF PERSONALITY AND SOCIAL PSYCHOLOGY, *22*, 8–12. **739**

MUSSEN, P. H. (Ed.) (1983). HANDBOOK OF CHILD PSYCHOLOGY (4th ed.). New York: Wiley. **123**

MUSSEN, P. H., CONGER, J. J., KAGAN, J., & HUSTON, A. C. (1990). CHILD DEVELOPMENT AND PERSONALITY (7th ed.). New York: Harper &

Row. **123**

MYERS, D. G. (1990). SOCIAL PSYCHOLOGY (3rd ed.). New York: McGraw-Hill. **727, 746, 779, 784**

MYERS, D. G., & LAMM, H. (1976). The group polarization phenomenon. PSYCHOLOGICAL BULLETIN, *83*, 602–627. **779**

NAKAYAMA, K., & TYLER, C. W. (1981). Psychophysical isolation of movement sensitivity by removal of familiar position cues. VISION RESEARCH, *21*, 427–433. **172**

NARANJO, C., & ORNSTEIN, R. E. (1977). ON THE PSYCHOLOGY OF MEDITATION. New York: Penguin. **249**

NATHANS, J., THOMAS, D., & HOGNESS, D. S. (1986). Molecular genetics of human color vision: The genes encoding blue, green, and red pigments. SCIENCE, *232*, 193–202. **141**

NEALE, M. C., & STEVENSON, J. (1989). Rater bias in the EASI temperament scales: A twin study. JOURNAL OF PERSONALITY AND SOCIAL PSYCHOLOGY, *56*, 446–455. **490**

NEBES, R. D., & SPERRY, R. W. (1971). Cerebral dominance in perception. NEUROPSYCHOLOGIA, *9*, 247. **55**

NEGRETE, J. C., & KWAN, M. W. (1972). Relative value of various etiological factors in short-lasting, adverse psychological reactions to cannabis smoking. INTERNAL PHARMACOPSYCHIATRY, *7*, 249–259. **231**

NEISSER, U. (1981). John Dean's memory: A case study. COGNITION, *9*, 1–22. **299**

NEISSER, U. (Ed.) (1982). MEMORY OBSERVED: REMEMBERING IN NATURAL CONTEXTS. San Francisco: Freeman. **298, 309, 328**

NEISSER, U. (Ed.) (1986). THE SCHOOL ACHIEVEMENT OF MINORITY CHILDREN. Hillsdale, NJ: Erlbaum. **484**

NEUGARTEN, B. (1968). Adult personality: Toward a psychology of the life cycle. In B. Neugarten, (Ed.), MIDDLE AGE AND AGING. Chicago: University of Chicago Press. **120**

NEWCOMB, M. D., & BENTLER, P. M. (1988). CONSEQUENCES OF ADOLESCENT DRUG USE. Newbury Park, CA: Sage. **233**

NEWCOMB, T. M. (1943). PERSONALITY AND SOCIAL CHANGE. New York: Dryden Press. **511, 514**

NEWCOMB, T. M. (1961). THE ACQUAINTANCE PROCESS. New York: Holt, Rinehart & Winston. **740**

NEWCOMB, T. M., KOENING, K. E., FLACKS, R., & WARWICK, D. P. (1967). PERSISTENCE AND CHANGE: BENNINGTON COLLEGE AND ITS STUDENTS AFTER TWENTY-FIVE YEARS. New York: Wiley. **511, 514**

NEWELL, A., & SIMON, H. A. (1972). HUMAN PROBLEM SOLVING. Englewood Cliffs, NJ: Prentice-Hall. **362, 369**

NEWPORT, E. L. (1990). Maturational constraints on language learning. COGNITIVE SCIENCE, *14*, 11–28. **355**

NEZU, A. M., NEZU, C. M., & PERRI, M. G. (1989). PROBLEM-SOLVING THERAPY FOR DEPRESSION: THEORY, RESEARCH, AND CLINICAL GUIDELINES. New York: Wiley. **603**

NICKLAUS, J. (1974). GOLF MY WAY. New York: Simon & Schuster. **235**

NILSON, D. C., NILSON, L. B., OLSON, R. S., & MCALLISTER, B. H.(1981). THE PLANNING ENVIRONMENT REPORT FOR THE SOUTHERN CALIFORNIA EARTHQUAKE SAFETY ADVISORY BOARD. Redlands, CA: Social Research Advisory & Policy Research Center. **610**

NININGER, H. H. (1933). OUR STONE-PELTED PLANET. Boston: Houghton Mifflin. **246**

NISAN, M., & KOHLBERG, L. (1982). Universality and variation in moral judgment: A longitudinal and cross-sectional study in Turkey. CHILD DEVELOPMENT, *53*, 865–876. **91**

NISBETT, R. E. (1968). Taste, deprivation, and weight determinants of eating behavior. JOURNAL OF PERSONALITY AND SOCIAL PSYCHOLOGY, *10*, 107–116. **387**

NISBETT, R. E. (1972). Hunger, obesity, and the ventromedial hypothalamus. PSYCHOLOGICAL REVIEW, *79*, 433–453. **385**

NISBETT, R. E., & ROSS, L. (1980). HUMAN INFERENCE: STRATEGIES AND SHORTCOMINGS OF SOCIAL JUDGMENT. Englewood Cliffs, NJ: Prentice-Hall. **713, 715, 747**

NOLEN-HOEKSEMA, S. (1991). Responses to depression and their effects on the duration of depressive episodes. JOURNAL OF ABNORMAL PSYCHOLOGY, *100*, 569–582. **603**

NOLEN-HOEKSEMA, S., & LYUBOMIRSKY, S. (1992). Effects of ruminative and distracting responses on problem-solving and attributions. Manuscript submitted for publication. **606**

NOLEN-HOEKSEMA, S., & MORROW, J. (1991). A prospective study of depression and distress following a natural disaster: The 1989 Loma Prieta earthquake. JOURNAL OF PERSONALITY AND SOCIAL PSYCHOLOGY, *61*, 105–121. **604, 605, 606**

NOLEN-HOEKSEMA, S., PARKER, L., & LARSON, J. (1992). Psychosocial predictors of depression in family members of the terminally ill. Manuscript submitted for publication. **605, 611**

NORMAN, R. (1975). Affective-cognitive consistency, attitudes, conformity, and behavior. JOURNAL OF PERSONALITY AND SOCIAL PSYCHOLOGY, *32*, 83–91. **733**

NORMAN, W. T. (1963). Toward an adequate taxonomy of personality attributes: Replicated factor structure in peer nomination personality ratings. JOURNAL OF ABNORMAL AND SOCIAL PSYCHOLOGY, *66*, 574–583. **531**

NORTH, C. (1987). WELCOME SILENCE. New York: Simon and Schuster. **647, 650, 665**

NUCCI, L. (1981). The development of personal concepts: A domain distinct from moral or societal concepts. CHILD DEVELOPMENT, *52*, 114–121. **93**

O'DONNELL, J. A., & CLAYTON, R. R. (1982). The stepping stone hypothesis: Marijuana, heroin, and causality. CHEMICAL DEPENDENCIES, *4* (No. 3). **233**

OFFIR, C. (1982). HUMAN SEXUALITY. San Diego: Harcourt Brace Jovanovich. **383, 394, 396, 415**

OGBU, J. U. (1986). The consequences of the American caste system. In Neisser, U. (ed.), THE SCHOOL ACHIEVEMENT OF MINORITY CHILDREN. Hillsdale, NJ: Erlbaum. **485**

O'HARA, M. W., NEUNABER, D. J., & ZEKOWSKI, E. M. (1984). Prospective study of postpartum depression: prevalence, course and predictive factors. JOURNAL OF ABNORMAL PSYCHOLOGY, *93*, 158–171. **595**

OHMAN, A., FREDRIKSON, M., HUGDAHL, K., & RIMMO, P. (1976). The premise of equipotentiality in human classical conditioning: Conditioned electrodermal responses to potentially phobic stimuli. JOURNAL OF EXPERIMENTAL PSYCHOLOGY: GENERAL, *105*, 313–337. **631**

O'LEARY, K. D., & WILSON, G. T. (1975). BEHAVIOR THERAPY: APPLICATION AND OUTCOME. Englewood Cliffs, NJ: Prentice-Hall. **682**

OLTON, D. S. (1978). Characteristics of spatial memory. In S. H. Hulse, H. F. Fowler, & W. K. Honig (Eds.), COGNITIVE PROCESSES IN ANIMAL BEHAVIOR. Hillsdale, NJ: Erlbaum. **279**

OLTON, D. S. (1979). Mazes, maps, and memory. AMERICAN PSYCHOLOGIST, *34*, 583–596. **279**

OLWEUS, D. (1969). PREDICTION OF AGGRESSION. Scandanavian Test Corporation. **561**

ORLINSKY, D. E., & HOWARD, K. I.

(1987). A generic model of psychotherapy. JOURNAL OF INTEGRATIVE AND ECLECTIC PSYCHOTHERAPY, 6, 6–27. **696**

ORNE, M. T., & HOLLAND, C. C. (1968). On the ecological validity of laboratory deceptions. INTERNATIONAL JOURNAL OF PSYCHIATRY, 6, 282–293. **766**

ORTONY, A., CLORE, G. L., & COLLINS, A. (1988). THE COGNITIVE STRUCTURE OF EMOTIONS. Cambridge: Cambridge University Press. **447**

OSHERSON, D. N. (1976). LOGICAL ABILITIES IN CHILDREN: Vol. 4. REASONING AND CONCEPTS. Hillsdale, NJ: Erlbaum. **340**

OSHERSON, D. N., (1990). INVITATION TO COGNITIVE SCIENCE. Cambridge, MA: MIT Press. **26, 31**

OSHERSON, D. N., KOSSLYN, S. M. & HOLLERBACH, J. M. (1990). AN INVITATION TO COGNITIVE SCIENCE (Vol. 2). Cambridge, MA: MIT Press. **201**

OSHERSON, D. N. & LASNIK, H. (1990). AN INVITATION TO COGNITIVE SCIENCE (Vol. 1). Cambridge, MA: MIT Press. **369**

OSHERSON, D. N. & SMITH, E. E. (1990). AN INVITATION TO COGNITIVE SCIENCE (Vol. 3). Cambridge, MA: MIT Press. **344**

OSHERSON, D. N., SMITH, E. E., WILKIE, O., LOPEZ, A., & SHAFIR, E. B. (1990). Category based induction. PSYCHOLOGICAL REVIEW, 97, 185–200. **369**

OSOFSKY, J. D. (Ed.) (1987). HANDBOOK OF INFANT DEVELOPMENT (2nd ed.). New York: Wiley. **123**

OVERMEIER, J. B., & SELIGMAN, M. E. P. (1967). Effects of inescapable shock upon subsequent escape and avoidance responding. JOURNAL OF COMPARATIVE AND PHYSIOLOGICAL PSYCHOLOGY, 63, 28. **586**

PAICHELER, G. (1976). Norms and attitude change: Pt. 2. The Phenomenon of Bipolarization. EUROPEAN JOURNAL OF SOCIAL PSYCHOLOGY, 6, 405–427. **772**

PAICHELER, G. (1977). Norms and attitude change: Pt. 1 Polarization and styles of behavior. EUROPEAN JOURNAL OF SOCIAL PSYCHOLOGY, 7, 5–14. **772**

PALLIS, C. A. (1955). Impaired identification of faces and places with agnosia for colors. JOURNAL OF NEUROLOGY, NEUROSURGERY, AND PSYCHIATRY, 18, 218–224. **187**

PALLONE, N. J. (1961). Effects of short- and long-term developmental reading courses upon SAT verbal scores. PERSONNEL AND GUIDANCE JOURNAL, 39, 654–657. **467**

PALMER, F. H., & ANDERSON, L. W. (1979). Long-term gains from early intervention: Findings from longitudinal studies. In E. Zigler, & J. Valentine, (Eds.), PROJECT HEAD START: A LEGACY OF THE WAR ON POVERTY. New York: Free Press. **481**

PALMER, J. A., HONORTON, C., & UTTS, J. (1989). REPLY TO THE NATIONAL RESEARCH COUNCIL STUDY ON PARAPSYCHOLOGY. Journal of the American Society for Psychical Research, 83, 31–49. **243**

PALMER, S. E. (1975). The effects of contextual scenes on the identification of objects. MEMORY AND COGNITION, 3, 519–526. **182**

PAPAGEORGIS, D., & MCGUIRE, W. J. (1961). The generality of immunity to persuasion produced by pre-exposure to weakened counterarguments. JOURNAL OF ABNORMAL AND SOCIAL PSYCHOLOGY, 62, 475–481. **775**

PATEL, V. L., & GROEN, G. J. (1986). Knowledge based solution strategies in medical reasoning. COGNITIVE SCIENCE, 10, 91. **365**

PATTERSON, F. G. (1978). The gestures of a gorilla: Language acquisition in another pongid. BRAIN AND LANGUAGE, 5, 72–97. **357**

PATTERSON, F. G., & LINDEN, E. (1981). THE EDUCATION OF KOKO. New York: Holt, Rinehart & Winston. **357**

PATTERSON, G. R. (1976). The aggressive child: Victim and architect of a coercive system. In L. A. Hamerlynck, L. C. Handy, & E. J. Mash, (Eds.), BEHAVIOR MODIFICATION AND FAMILIES: 1. THEORY AND RESEARCH. New York: Brunner/Mazel. **562**

PATTERSON, G. R., & LITTMAN, R. A., & BRICKER, W. A. (1967). Assertive behavior in children: A step toward a theory of aggression. MONOGRAPHS OF THE SOCIETY FOR RESEARCH IN CHILD DEVELOPMENT, (Serial No. 113), 5. **443**

PAUL, G. L. (1967) Insight versus desensitization in psychotherapy two years after termination. JOURNAL OF CONSULTING PSYCHOLOGY, 31, 333–348. **699**

PAUL, G. L. & LENTZ, R. J. (1977). PSYCHO-SOCIAL TREATMENT OF CHRONIC MENTAL PATIENTS: MILIEU VERSUS SOCIAL LEARNING PROGRAMS. Cambridge, MA: Harvard University Press. **679**

PAULHUS, D. (1982). Individual differences, self-presentation, and cognitive dissonance: Their concurrent operation in forced compliance. JOURNAL OF PERSONALITY AND SOCIAL PSYCHOLOGY, 43, 838–852. **735**

PAULUS, P. B., & MURDOCK, P. (1971). Anticipated evaluation and audience presence in the enhancement of dominant responses. JOURNAL OF EXPERIMENTAL SOCIAL PSYCHOLOGY, 7, 280–291. **751**

PAVLOV, I. P. (1927). CONDITIONED REFLEXES. New York: Oxford University Press. **255, 287**

PECHURA, C. M. & MARTIN, J. B. (Eds.) (1991). MAPPING THE BRAIN AND ITS FUNCTIONS. Washington, D.C.: National Academy Press. **47**

PECK, J. W., & NOVIN, D. (1971). Evidence that osmoreceptors mediating drinking in rabbits are in the lateral preoptic area. JOURNAL OF COMPARATIVE AND PHYSIOLOGICAL PSYCHOLOGY, 74, 134–147. **376**

PEDERSEN, N. L., PLOMIN, R., MCCLEARN, G. E., & FRIBERG, L. (1988). Neuroticism, extraversion and related traits in adult twins reared apart and reared together. JOURNAL OF PERSONALITY AND SOCIAL PSYCHOLOGY, 55, 950–957. **505**

PEELE, S. (1988). Fools for love: The romantic ideal, psychological theory, and addictive love. In R. J. Sternberg, & M. L. Barnes (Eds.), THE PSYCHOLOGY OF LOVE (pp. 159–188). New Haven, CT: Yale University Press. **741**

PELLEGRINO, J. W. (1985). Inductive reasoning ability. In R. J. Sternberg (Ed.), HUMAN ABILITIES: AN INFORMATION-PROCESSING APPROACH. New York: Freeman. **476**

PENNEBAKER, J. W. (1990). OPENING UP: THE HEALING POWER OF CONFIDING IN OTHERS. New York: William Morrow and Company. **607**

PENNEBAKER, J. W. & BEALL, S. K. (1986). Confronting a traumatic event: toward an understanding of inhibition and disease. JOURNAL OF ABNORMAL PSYCHOLOGY, 95, 274–281. **604**

PENNEBAKER, J. W. & O'HEERON, R. C. (1984). Confiding in others and illness rates among spouses of suicide and accidental-death victims. JOURNAL OF ABNORMAL PSYCHOLOGY, 93, 473–476. **607**

PEPLAU, L. A., RUBIN, Z., & HILL, C. T. (1977). Sexual intimacy in dating relationships. JOURNAL OF SOCIAL ISSUES, 33, 86–109. **400**

PERLMUTTER, M., & HALL, E. (1985). ADULT DEVELOPMENT AND AGING. New York: Wiley. **123**

PERRIN, F. A. C. (1921). Physical attractiveness and repulsiveness. JOURNAL

OF EXPERIMENTAL PSYCHOLOGY, *4*, 203–217. **736**

PERRY, D. G., & BUSSEY, K. (1984). SOCIAL DEVELOPMENT. Englewood Cliffs, NJ: Prentice-Hall. **102**

PERRIS, C., BLACKBURN, I. M., & PERRIS, H. (Eds.) (1988). COGNITIVE PSYCHOTHERAPY: THEORY & PRACTICE. New York: Springer-Verlag. **709**

PETERSEN, A. C. (1988a). Adolescent development. In M. R. Rosenzweig, & L. W. Porter (Eds.), ANNUAL REVIEW OF PSYCHOLOGY (Vol. 39). Palo Alto, CA: Annual Reviews. **112, 113**

PETERSEN, A. C. (1988b). Pubertal change and psychosocial development. In D. L. Baltes, R. M. Featherman, & R. M. Lerner (Eds.), LIFE-SPAN DEVELOPMENT AND BEHAVIOR (Vol. 9). New York: Academic Press. **114**

PETERSON, C. (1988). PERSONALITY. San Diego: Harcourt Brace. **30**

PETERSON, C., & SELIGMAN, M. E. P. (1984). Causal explanations as a risk factor for depression: Theory and evidence. PSYCHOLOGICAL REVIEW, *91*, 347–374. **598, 642**

PETERSON, C. & SELIGMAN, M. E. P. (1987). Explanatory style and illness. Special illness: personality and physical health. JOURNAL OF PERSONALITY, *55*, 237–265. **598**

PETERSON, C., SELIGMAN, M., & VAILLANT, G. (1988). Pessimistic explanatory style as a risk factor for physical illness: a thirty-five-year longitudinal study. JOURNAL OF PERSONALITY AND SOCIAL PSYCHOLOGY, *55*, 23–27. **598**

PETERSON, S. E., FOX, P. T., SNYDER, A. Z., & RAICHLE, M. E. (1990). Activation of extrastriate and frontal cortical areas by visual words and word-like stimuli. SCIENCE, *249*, 1041–1044. **347**

PETTIGREW, T. F. (1959). Regional differences in anti-Negro prejudice. JOURNAL OF ABNORMAL AND SOCIAL PSYCHOLOGY, *59*, 28–36. **732**

PETTY, R. E., & CACIOPPO, J. T. (1977). Forewarning, cognitive responding, and resistance to persuasion. JOURNAL OF PERSONALITY AND SOCIAL PSYCHOLOGY, *35*, 645–655. **775**

PETTY, R. E., & CACIOPPO, J. T. (1981). ATTITUDES AND PERSUASION: CLASSIC AND CONTEMPORARY APPROACHES. Dubuque, IA: Wm. C. Brown. **776, 784**

PETTY, R. E., & CACIOPPO, J. T. (1984). The effects of involvement on responses to argument quantity and quality: Central and peripheral routes to persuasion. JOURNAL OF PERSONALITY AND SOCIAL PSYCHOLOGY, *46*, 69–81. **776, 777**

PETTY, R. E., & CACIOPPO, J. T. (1986). Elaboration likelihood model of persuasion. In L. Berkowitz, (Ed.), ADVANCES IN EXPERIMENTAL SOCIAL PSYCHOLOGY (Vol. *19*, pp. 123–205). New York: Academic Press. **776**

PETTY, R. E., CACIOPPO, J. T., & GOLDMAN, R. (1981). Personal involvement as a determinant of argument-based persuasion. JOURNAL OF PERSONALITY AND SOCIAL PSYCHOLOGY, *41*, 847–855. **777**

PETTY, R. E., HARKINS, S. G., WILLIAMS, K. D., & LATANÉ, B. (1977). The effect of group size on cognitive effort and evaluation. PERSONALITY AND SOCIAL PSYCHOLOGY BULLETIN, *3*, 575–578. **759**

PETTY, R. E., OSTROM, T. M., & BROCK, T. C. (1981). Historical foundations of the cognitive response approach to attitudes and persuasion. In R. E. Petty, T. M. Ostrom, & T. C. Brock (Eds.) COGNITIVE RESPONSES IN PERSUASION. Hillsdale, NJ: Erlbaum. **773**

PHILLIPS, J. L., JR. (1981). PIAGET'S THEORY: A PRIMER. San Francisco: Freeman. **123**

PHILLIPS, J. L., JR. (1992). HOW TO THINK ABOUT STATISTICS (revised ed.). New York: Freeman. **31**

PHOENIX, C. H., GOY, R. H., & RESKO, J. A. (1968). Psychosexual differentiation as a function of androgenic stimulation. In M. Diamond (Ed.), REPRODUCTION AND SEXUAL BEHAVIOR. Bloomington: Indiana University Press. **404**

PIAGET, J. (1932/1965). THE MORAL JUDGMENT OF THE CHILD. New York: Free Press. **88**

PIAGET, J. (1952) THE ORIGINS OF INTELLIGENCE IN CHILDREN. New York: International Universities Press. **411**

PIAGET, J. (1962). PLAY, DREAMS AND IMITATION. New York: Norton. **78**

PIAGET, J., & INHELDER, B. (1969). THE PSYCHOLOGY OF THE CHILD. New York: Basic Books. **84**

PILIAVIN, I. M., RODIN, J., & PILIAVIN, J. A. (1969). Good Samaritanism: An underground phenomenon? JOURNAL OF PERSONALITY AND SOCIAL PSYCHOLOGY, *13*, 289–299. **757**

PILLIMER, D. B. (1984). Flashbulb memories of the assassination attempt on President Reagan. COGNITION, *16*, 63–80. **310**

PINKER, S. (1984). LANGUAGE LEARNABILITY AND LANGUAGE DEVELOPMENT. Cambridge, MA: Harvard University Press. **369**

PINKER, S., & PRINCE, A. (1988). On language and connectionism: Analysis of a parallel distributed processing model of language acquisition. COGNITION, *28*, 71–193. **354**

PION, G. M. (1991). Psychologists wanted: employment trends over the past decade. In R. R. Kilburg, Ed., HOW TO MANAGE YOUR CAREER IN PSYCHOLOGY. Washington, D.C.: American Psychological Association. **23**

PIRCHIO, M., SPINELLI, D., FIORENTINI, A., & MAFFEI, L. (1978). Infant contrast sensitivity evaluated by evoked potentials. BRAIN RESEARCH, *141*, 179–184. **194**

PLATT, J. J., YAKSH, T., & DARBY, C. L. (1967). Social facilitation of eating behavior in armadillos. PSYCHOLOGICAL REPORTS, *20*, 1136. **749**

PLOMIN, R. (1986). DEVELOPMENT, GENETICS, AND PSYCHOLOGY. Hillsdale, NJ: Erlbaum. **65**

PLOMIN, R. (1990). NATURE AND NURTURE. Pacific Grove, CA: Brooks/Cole. **523**

PLOMIN, R. (1991). Behavioral genetics. In P. R. McHugh & V. A. McKusick (Eds.), GENES, BRAIN, AND BEHAVIOR. New York: Raven Press. **62**

PLOMIN, R., & BERGEMAN, C. S. (1991). The nature of nurture: Genetic influence on "environmental" measures. BEHAVIORAL & BRAIN SCIENCES, *14(3)*, 373–427. **479**

PLOMIN, R., & DANIELS, D. (1987). Why are children in the same family so different from one another? BEHAVIORAL AND BRAIN SCIENCES, *10*, 1–60. **506**

PLOMIN, R., DEFRIES, J. C., & LOEHLIN, J. C. (1977). Genotype-environment interaction and correlation in the analysis of human behavior. PSYCHOLOGICAL BULLETIN, *84*, 309–322. **503**

PLOMIN, R., DEFRIES, J. C., & MCCLEARN, G. E. (1989) BEHAVIORAL GENETICS: A PRIMER (2nd ed.). New York: Freeman. **69, 665**

PLOMIN, R., & DUNN, J. (Eds.). (1986). THE STUDY OF TEMPERAMENT: CHANGES, CONTINUITIES AND CHALLENGES. Hillsdale, NJ: Erlbaum. **523**

PLOMIN, R., PEDERSEN, N. L., MCCLEARN, G. E., NESSELROADE, J. R., & BERGEMAN, C. S. (1988). EAS temperaments during the last half of the life span: Twins reared apart and twins reared together. PSYCHOLOGY AND AGING, *3*, 43–50. **490, 491**

PLUTCHIK, R., & KELLERMAN, H.

(Eds.) (1980). EMOTION: THEORY, RESEARCH, AND EXPERIENCE (Vol. 1). New York: Academic Press. **447**

POLIVY, J., & HERMAN, C. P. (1985). Dieting and binging: A causal analysis. AMERICAN PSYCHOLOGIST, *40*, 193–201. **388**

POPE, K. S., & SINGER, J. L. (Eds.) (1978). THE STREAM OF CONSCIOUSNESS. New York: Plenum. **249**

PORTER, H. (1939). Studies in the psychology of stuttering: Pt. 14. Stuttering phenomena in relation to size and personnel of audience. JOURNAL OF SPEECH DISORDERS, *4*, 323–333. **758**

POSNER, M. I. (1989). FOUNDATIONS OF COGNITIVE SCIENCE. Cambridge, MA: MIT Press **31, 201**

POSNER, M. I., & KEELE, S. W. (1967). Decay of visual information from a single letter. SCIENCE, *158*, 137–139. **292**

POSNER, M. I., & MARIN, O. S. M. (Eds.) (1985). MECHANISMS OF ATTENTION: Vol. 11. ATTENTION AND PERFORMANCE. Hillsdale, NJ: Erlbaum. **201**

POSNER, M. I., PETERSEN, S. E., FOX, P. T., & RAICHLE, M. E. (1988). Localization of cognitive operations in the human brain. SCIENCE, *240*, 1627–1631. **47**

POST, R. M., KOTIN, J., GOODWIN, F. K., & GORDON, E. (1973). Psychomotor activity and cerebrospinal fluid amine metabolites in effective illness. AMERICAN JOURNAL OF PSYCHIATRY, *130*, 67–72. **644**

POWLEY, T. L., & KEESEY, R. E. (1970). Relationship of body weight to the lateral hypothalamic feeding syndrome. JOURNAL OF COMPARATIVE AND PHYSIOLOGICAL PSYCHOLOGY, *70*, 25–36. **381**

PREMACK, D. (1959). Toward empirical behavior laws: Pt. 1. Positive reinforcement. PSYCHOLOGICAL REVIEW, *66*, 219–233. **269**

PREMACK, D. (1971). Language in chimpanzees? SCIENCE, *172*, 808–822. **357**

PREMACK, D. (1985) "Gavagai!" Or the future history of the animal language controversy. COGNITION, *19*, 207–296. **280**

PREMACK, D., & PREMACK, A. J. (1983). THE MIND OF AN APE. New York: Norton. **280**

PRESSLEY, M., LEVIN, J. R., & DELANEY, H. D. (1982). The mnemonic keyword method. REVIEW OF EDUCATIONAL RESEARCH, *52*, 61–91. **318**

PRIEST, R. F., & SAWYER, J. (1967). Proximity and peership: Bases of balance in interpersonal attraction. AMERICAN JOURNAL OF SOCIOLOGY, *72*, 633–649. **737**

PRINTZMETAL, W., & BANKS, W. P. (1977). Good continuation affects visual detection. PERCEPTION & PSYCHOPHYSICS, *21*, 389–395. **168**

PROTHRO, E. T. (1952). Ethnocentrism and anti-Negro attitudes in the deep South. JOURNAL OF ABNORMAL AND SOCIAL PSYCHOLOGY, *47*, 105–108. **732**

PULKKINEN, L. (1982). Self-control and continuity from childhood to adolescence. In P. B. Baltes & O. G. Brim Jr. (Eds.). LIFE-SPAN DEVELOPMENT AND BEHAVIOR (Vol. 4, pp. 63–105). New York: Academic Press. **501**

PUTNAM, F. W., JR. (1984). Cited in R. M. Restak THE BRAIN. New York: Bantam. **209**

RAAIJMAKERS, J. G., & SHIFFRIN, R. M. (1981). Search of associative memory. PSYCHOLOGICAL REVIEW, *88*, 93–134. **308**

RAAIJMAKERS, J. G. (1992). The story of the two-store model. In D. E. Meyer & S. Komblum (Eds.) ATTENTION & PERFORMANCE XIV: A SILVER JUBILEE. Hillsdale, N.J.: Erlbaum. **297**

RACHLIN, H. (1980). Economics and behavioral psychology. In J. E. R. Staddon (Ed.), LIMITS TO ACTION. New York: Academic Press. **276**

RACHMAN, S. J., & HODGSON, R. J. (1980). OBSESSIONS AND COMPULSIONS. Englewood Cliffs, NJ: Prentice-Hall. **627**

RACHMAN, S. J., & WILSON, G. T. (1980). THE EFFECTS OF PSYCHOLOGICAL THERAPY (2nd ed.). Elmsford, NY: Pergamon Press. **695**

RAMACHANDRAN, V. S. & GREGORY, R. L. (1991). Perceptual in filling of artificially induced scotomas in human vision. NATURE, *350*, 699–702. **137**

RAMEY, C. T. (1981). Consequences of infant day care. In B. Weissbound & J. Musick (Eds.), INFANTS: THEIR SOCIAL ENVIRONMENTS. Washington, DC.: National Association for the Education of Young Children. **498**

RANDI, J. (1982). FLIM-FLAM! PSYCHICS, ESP, UNICORNS AND OTHER DELUSIONS. Buffalo: Prometheus Books. **247**

RAPAPORT, D. (1942). EMOTIONS AND MEMORY. Baltimore: Williams & Wilkins. **309**

RAPOPORT, J. L. (1989). THE BOY WHO WOULDN'T STOP WASHING. New York: Dutton. **627, 635, 665**

RAVUSSIN, E., & collaborators (1988). Reduced rate of energy expenditure as a risk factor for body-weight gain. THE NEW ENGLAND JOURNAL OF MEDICINE, *318*, 467–472. **386**

RAY, W. J., & RAVIZZA, R. (1988). METHODS TOWARD A SCIENCE OF BEHAVIOR AND EXPERIENCE (3rd ed.). Belmont, CA: Wadsworth. **30**

RAYNER, K. (1978) Eye movements in reading and information processing. PSYCHOLOGICAL BULLETIN, *85*, 618–660. **183**

REGAN, D., BEVERLEY, K. I., & CYNADER, (1979). The visual perception of motion depth. SCIENTIFIC AMERICAN, *241* (No. 1), 136–151. **172**

REGAN, D. T., & FAZIO, R. (1977). On the consistency between attitudes and behavior: Look to the method of attitude formation. JOURNAL OF EXPERIMENTAL SOCIAL PSYCHOLOGY, *13*, 28–45. **734**

REGIER, D. A., BOYD, J. H., & collaborators. (1988). One-month prevalence of mental disorders in the United States. ARCHIVES OF GENERAL PSYCHIATRY, *45*, 977–986. **617, 623**

REICHER, G. M. (1969). Perceptual recognition as a function of the meaningfulness of the material. JOURNAL OF EXPERIMENTAL PSYCHOLOGY, *81*, 275–280. **178**

REISENZEIN, R. (1983). The Schachter theory emotion: Two decades later. PSYCHOLOGICAL BULLETIN, *94*, 239–264. **426, 434**

REISER, B. J., KIMBERG, D. Y., LOVETT, M. C., & RANNEY, M. (1989). KNOWLEDGE REPRESENTATION AND EXPLANATION IN GIL, AN INTELLIGENT TUTOR FOR PROGRAMMING. Technical Report 37, Cognitive Science Laboratory, Princeton University. **16**

RESCORLA, R. A. (1967). Pavlovian conditioning and its proper control procedures. PSYCHOLOGICAL REVIEW, *74*, 71–80. **259**

RESCORLA, R. A. (1972). Informational variables in Pavlovian conditioning. In Bower, G. H. (Ed.), PSYCHOLOGY OF LEARNING AND MOTIVATION (Vol. 6). New York: Academic Press. **259**

RESCORLA, R. A. (1980). Overextension in early language development. JOURNAL OF CHILD LANGUAGE, *7*, 321–335. **351**

RESCORLA, R. A. (1987). A Pavlovian analysis of goal-directed behavior. AMERICAN PSYCHOLOGIST, *42*, 119–129. **265**

RESCORLA, R. A. & SOLOMON, R. L. (1967). Two process learning theory: Relations between Pavlovian conditioning and instrumental learning. PSYCHOLOGICAL REVIEW, *74*, 151–182. **273**

RESCORLA, R. A., & WAGNER, A. R. (1972). A theory of Pavlovian conditioning: Variations in the effectiveness of reinforcement and non-reinforcement. In P. H. Black & W. F. Prokasy (Eds.). CLASSICAL CONDITIONING II. New York: Appleton-Century-Crofts. **261**

REUBENS, A. B. & BENSON, D. F. (1971). Associative visual agnosia. ARCHIVES OF NEUROLOGY, *24*, 305–316. **186**

REYNOLDS, D. V. (1969). Surgery in the rat during electrical analgesia induced by focal brain stimulation. SCIENCE, *164*, 444–445. **160**

RHEINGOLD, H. L., & COOK, K. V. (1975). The content of boys' and girls' rooms as an index of parent behavior. CHILD DEVELOPMENT, *46*, 459–463. **102**

RICE, B. (1978). The new truth machine. PSYCHOLOGY TODAY, *12*, 61–78, **425**

RICH, C. L., FOWLER, R. C., FOGARTY, L. A., & YOUNG, D. (1988). San Diego suicide study. ARCHIVES OF GENERAL PSYCHIATRY, *45*, 589–592. **639**

RICHARDSON, J. L., SHELTON, D. R., KRAILO, M., & LEVINE, A. M. (1990). The effect of compliance with treatment in survival among patients with hematologic malignancies. JOURNAL OF CLINICAL ONCOLOGY, *8*, 356. **613**

RIESE, M. L. (1987). Temperament stability between the neonatal period and 24 months. DEVELOPMENTAL PSYCHOLOGY, *23*, 216–222. **83**

RIESEN, A. H. (1947). The development of visual perception in man and chimpanzee. SCIENCE, *106*, 107–108. **196**

RIMM, D. C., & MASTERS, J. C. (1979). BEHAVIOR THERAPY: TECHNIQUES AND EMPIRICAL FINDINGS (2nd ed.). New York: Academic Press. **680**

RINGELMANN, M. (1913). Research on animate sources of power: The world of man. ANNALES DE L'INSTITUTE NATIONAL AGRONOMIQUE, 2E SERIE-TOME XII, 1–40. **759**

RIORDAN, C. A., & TEDESCHI, J. T. (1983). Attraction in aversive environments: Some evidence for classical conditioning and negative reinforcement. JOURNAL OF PERSONALITY AND SOCIAL PSYCHOLOGY, *44*, 683–692. **743**

RIPS, L. J. (1983). Cognitive processes in propositional reasoning. PSYCHOLOGICAL REVIEW, *90*, 38–71. **340**

RIPS, L. J. (1988). Deduction. In R. J. Sternberg & E. E. Smith (Eds.), THE PSYCHOLOGY OF HUMAN THOUGHT. New York: Cambridge University Press. **341**

ROBINS, L. N. (1966). DEVIANT CHILDREN GROWN UP. Baltimore, MD: Williams & Wilkins. **664**

ROBINSON, D. L., & WURTZ, R. (1976). Use of an extra-retinal signal by monkey superior colliculus neurons to distinguish real from self-induced stimulus movement. JOURNAL OF NEUROPHYSIOLOGY, *39*, 852–870. **189**

ROCK, I. (1983). THE LOGIC OF PERCEPTION. Cambridge, MA: MIT Press. **169, 170, 201**

RODIN, J. (1981). Current status of the internal-external hypothesis of obesity: What went wrong? AMERICAN PSYCHOLOGIST, *36*, 361–372. **383, 387**

ROEDIGER, H. L. (1990). Implicit memory: Retention without remembering. AMERICAN PSYCHOLOGIST, *45*, 1043–1056. **316**

ROFF, J. D., & KNIGHT, R. (1981). Family characteristics, childhood symptoms, and adult outcome in schizophrenia. JOURNAL OF ABNORMAL PSYCHOLOGY, *90*, 510–520. **657**

ROFFWARG, H. P., HERMAN, J. H., BOWER-ANDERS, C., & TAUBER, E. S. (1978). The effects of sustained alterations of waking visual input on dream content. In A. M. Arkin, J. S. Antrobus, & S. J. Ellman (Eds.), THE MIND IN SLEEP. Hillsdale, NJ: Erlbaum. **217**

ROGERS, C. R. (1959). A theory of therapy, personality, and interpersonal relationships as developed in the client-centered framework. In S. Koch (Ed.), PSYCHOLOGY: A STUDY OF A SCIENCE: VOL. 3. FORMULATIONS OF THE PERSON AND THE SOCIAL CONTEXT. New York: McGraw-Hill. **545**

ROGERS, C. R. (1951). CLIENT-CENTERED THERAPY. Boston: Houghton Mifflin. **545**

ROGERS, C. R. (1963). The actualizing tendency in relation to motives and to consciousness. In M. Jones (Ed.), NEBRASKA SYMPOSIUM ON MOTIVATION (pp. 1–24). Lincoln: University of Nebraska Press. **545**

ROGERS, C. R. (1970). ON BECOMING A PERSON: A THERAPIST'S VIEW OF PSYCHOTHERAPY. Boston: Houghton Mifflin. **545, 688, 709**

ROGERS, C. R. (1977). CARL ROGERS ON PERSONAL POWER. New York: Delacorte Press. **573, 709**

ROGERS, C. R., & STEVENS, B. (1967). PERSON TO PERSON: THE PROBLEM OF BEING HUMAN. New York: Pocket Books. **573**

ROGERS, T. B., KUIPER, N. A., & KIRKER, W. S. (1977). Self-reference and the encoding of personal information. JOURNAL OF PERSONALITY AND SOCIAL PSYCHOLOGY, *35*, 677–688. **716**

ROHN, R. D., SARTES, R. M., KENNY, T. J., REYNOLDS, B. J., & HEALD, F. P. (1977). Adolescents who attempt suicide. JOURNAL OF PEDIATRICS, *90*, 636–638. **639**

ROITBLAT, H. L. (1986). INTRODUCTION TO COMPARATIVE COGNITION. New York: Freeman. **287**

ROLAND, P. E., & FRIBERG, L. (1985). Localization of cortical areas activated by thinking. JOURNAL OF NEUROPHYSIOLOGY, *53*, 1219–1243. **360**

ROOK, K. (1984). The negative side of social interaction: impact on psychological well-being. JOURNAL OF PERSONALITY AND SOCIAL PSYCHOLOGY, *46*, 1097–1108. **610**

ROSCH, E. (1974). Linguistic relativity. In A. Silverstein (Ed.), HUMAN COMMUNICATION: THEORETICAL PERSPECTIVES. New York: Halsted Press. **339**

ROSCH, E. (1978). Principles of categorization. In E. Rosch & B. L. Lloyd, (Eds.), COGNITION AND CATEGORIZATION. Hillsdale, NJ: Erlbaum. **333**

ROSE, J. E., BRUGGE, J. F., ANDERSON, D. J., & HIND, J. E. (1967). Phase-locked response to lower frequency tones in single auditory nerve fibers of the squirrel monkey. JOURNAL OF NEUROPHYSIOLOGY, *309*, 769–793. **149**

ROSEMAN, I. J. (1984). Cognitive determinants of emotions: A structural theory. In P. Shaver (Ed.), REVIEW OF PERSONALITY AND SOCIAL PSYCHOLOGY: VOL. 5, EMOTIONS, RELATIONSHIPS, AND HEALTH. Beverly Hills, CA: Sage. **427**

ROSENBLITH, J. F., & SIMS-KNIGHT, J. E. (1989). IN THE BEGINNING: DEVELOPMENT IN THE FIRST TWO YEARS (2nd ed.). Newbury Park, CA: Sage. **123**

ROSENBLOOM, P. S., LAIRD, J. E., NEWELL, A., & McCARL, R. (1991). A preliminary analysis of the foundations of Soar. ARTIFICIAL INTELLIGENCE, *47*, 289–325. **282**

ROSENHAN, D. L. & SELIGMAN, M. E. P. (1989). Abnormal Psychology (2nd ed.). New York: W. W. Norton. **649, 665**

ROSENMAN, R. H., BRAND, R. J., JENKINS, C. D., FRIEDMAN, M., STRAUS, R., & WRUM, M. (1976) Coronary heart disease in the Western Collaborative Group Study: Final follow-up experience of 8-1/2 years. JOURNAL OF THE AMERICAN MEDICAL ASSOCIATION, *233*, 878–877. **601**

ROSENTHAL, R. (1966). EXPERI-MENTER EFFECTS IN BEHAVIORAL RESEARCH. New York: Appleton-Century-Crofts. **242**

ROSENTHAL, R. (1984). META-ANALYTIC PROCEDURES FOR SOCIAL RESEARCH. Beverly Hills, CA: Sage. **242**

ROSENZWEIG, M. R., & LEIMAN, A. L. (1989). PHYSIOLOGICAL PSYCHOLOGY (2nd ed.). Lexington, MA: Heath. **69, 415**

ROSS, L. (1977). The intuitive psychologist and his shortcomings: Distortions in the attribution process. In L. Berkowitz, (Ed.), ADVANCES IN EXPERIMENTAL SOCIAL PSYCHOLOGY (Vol. 10). New York: Academic Press. **722**

ROSS, L., AMABILE, T. M., & STEINMETZ, J. L. (1977). Social roles, social control, and biases in social-perception processes. JOURNAL OF PERSONALITY AND SOCIAL PSYCHOLOGY, 35, 485–494. **725**

ROSS, L., BIERBRAUER, G., & HOFFMAN, S. (1976). The role of attribution processes in conformity and dissent: Revisiting the Asch Situation. AMERICAN PSYCHOLOGIST, 31, 148–157. **760, 761**

ROSS, L., & NISBETT, R. E. (1991). THE PERSON AND THE SITUATION: PERSPECTIVES OF SOCIAL PSYCHOLOGY. New York: McGraw-Hill. **747**

ROSS, M., & SICOLY, F. (1979). Egocentric biases in availability and attribution. JOURNAL OF PERSONALITY AND SOCIAL PSYCHOLOGY, 37, 322–336. **727**

ROVEE COLLIER, C., & HAYNE, H. (1987). Reactivation of infant memory: Implications for cognitive development. In H. W. Reese (Ed.), ADVANCES IN CHILD DEVELOPMENT AND BEHAVIOR (Vol. 20). New York: Academic Press. **81**

ROY, A. (1981). Role of past loss in depression. ARCHIVES OF GENERAL PSYCHIATRY, 38, 301–302. **640**

ROYCE, J. R., & MOS, L. P. (Eds.) (1981). HUMANISTIC PSYCHOLOGY: CONCEPTS AND CRITICISMS. New York: Plenum. **30**

RUBIN, D. C. (Ed.). (1986). AUTOBIOGRAPHICAL MEMORY. New York: Cambridge University Press. **312**

RUBIN, Z. (1973). LIKING AND LOVING. New York: Holt, Rinehart & Winston. **737, 738, 741**

RUCH, J. C. (1975). Self-hypnosis: The result of heterohypnosis or vice versa? INTERNATIONAL JOURNAL OF CLINICAL AND EXPERIMENTAL HYPNOSIS, 23, 282–304. **236**

RUCH, J. C., MORGAN, A. H., & HILGARD, E. R. (1973). Behavioral predictions from hypnotic responsiveness scores when obtained with and without prior induction procedures. JOURNAL OF ABNORMAL PSYCHOLOGY, 82, 543–546. **237**

RUCK, B. (1980). Biofeedback: Issues in Treatment Assessment. National Institute of Mental Health Science Reports. **611**

RUDERMAN, A. J. (1986). Dietary restraint: A theoretical and empirical review. PSYCHOLOGICAL BULLETIN, 99, 247–262. **386**

RUMELHART, D. E., & MCCLELLAND, J. L. (1987). Learning the past tenses of English verbs: Implicit rules or parallel distributed processing? In B. MacWhinney (Ed.), MECHANISMS OF LANGUAGE ACQUISITION. Hillsdale, NJ: Erlbaum. **354**

RUMELHART, D. E., MCCLELLAND, J. L., & THE PDP RESEARCH GROUP (1986). PARALLEL DISTRIBUTED PROCESSING: EXPLORATIONS IN THE MICROSTRUCTURE OF COGNITION. VOLUME 1: FOUNDATIONS. Cambridge, MA: Bradford Books/MIT Press. **177, 201**

RUSHTON, J. P., JACKSON, D. N., & PAUNONEN, S. V. (1981). Personality: Nomothetic or idiographic? A response to Kenrick and Stringfield. PSYCHOLOGICAL REVIEW, 88, 582–589. **568**

RUSSEK, M. (1971). Hepatic receptors and the neurophysiological mechanisms controlling feedback behavior. In S. Ehreupreis (Ed.), NEUROSCIENCES RESEARCH (Vol. 4). New York: Academic Press. **379**

RUSSELL, D. E. H., & HOWELL, N. (1983). The prevalence of rape in the United States revisited. JOURNAL OF WOMEN IN CULTURE AND SOCIETY, 8, 688–695. **582**

RUSSELL, M. J. (1976). Human olfactory communication. NATURE, 260, 520–522. **80, 154**

RUSSELL, M. J., SWITZ, G. M., & THOMPSON, K. (1980). Olfactory influence on the human menstrual cycle. PHARMACOLOGY, BIOCHEMISTRY AND BEHAVIOR, 13, 737–738. **154**

RYLE, G. (1949). THE CONCEPT OF MIND. San Francisco: Hutchinson. **316**

SACHS, J. D. S. (1967). Recognition memory for syntactic and semantic aspects of connected discourse. PERCEPTION AND PSYCHOPHYSICS, 2, 437–442. **299**

SACKEIM, H. A., PORTNOY, S., NEELEY, P., STEIF, B. L., DECINA P., & MALITZ, S. (1985). Cognitive consequences of low dosage ECT. In S. Malitz & H. A. Sackeim (Eds.) ELECTROCONVULSIVE THERAPY: CLINICAL AND BASIC RESEARCH ISSUES. Annals of the New York Academy of Science. **703**

SALAMY, J. (1970). Instrumental responding to internal cues associated with REM sleep. PSYCHONOMIC SCIENCE, 18, 342–343. **217**

SALAPATEK, P. (1975). Pattern perception in early infancy. In L. B. Cohen & P. Salapateck (Eds.), INFANT PERCEPTION: FROM SENSATION TO COGNITION (Vol. 1). New York: Academic Press. **195**

SALK, L. (1973). The role of the heartbeat in the relationship between mother and infant. SCIENTIFIC AMERICAN, 228, 24–29. **81**

SANDERS, G. S. (1984). Self-presentation and drive in social facilitation. JOURNAL OF EXPERIMENTAL SOCIAL PSYCHOLOGY, 20, 312–322. **754**

SANDERS, G. S., & BARON, R. S. (1975). The motivating effects of distraction on task performance. JOURNAL OF PERSONALITY AND SOCIAL PSYCHOLOGY, 32, 956–963. **754**

SANDERS, G. S., & BARON, R. S. (1977). Is social comparison irrelevant for producing choice shifts? JOURNAL OF EXPERIMENTAL SOCIAL PSYCHOLOGY, 13, 303–314. **780**

SAPOLSKY, R. M. (1990). Stress in the wild. SCIENTIFIC AMERICAN, 262, 116–123. **592**

SARASON, I. G. & SARASON, B. R. (1989). ABNORMAL PSYCHOLOGY: THE PROBLEM OF MALADAPTIVE BEHAVIOR (6th ed.). Englewood Cliffs, NJ: Prentice-Hall. **626, 633, 665**

SATINOFF, E., & RUTSTEIN, J. (1970). Behavioral thermoregulations in rats with anterior hypothalamic lesions. JOURNAL OF COMPARATIVE AND PHYSIOLOGICAL PSYCHOLOGY, 71, 72–82. **375**

SATINOFF, E., & SHAN, S. Y. (1971). Loss of behavioral thermoregulation after lateral hypothalamic lesions in rats. JOURNAL OF COMPARATIVE AND PHYSIOLOGICAL PSYCHOLOGY, 72, 302–312. **375**

SATTLER, J. M. (1988). ASSESSMENT OF CHILDREN. San Diego: Jerome M. Sattler. **462, 463, 486, 487**

SAUNDERS, D. R. (1985). On Hyman's factor analyses. JOURNAL OF PARAPSYCHOLOGY, 49, 86–88. **244**

SAVIN-WILLIAMS, R. C., & JAQUISH, G. A. (1981). The assessment of adolescent self-esteem: A comparison of methods. JOURNAL OF PERSONALITY, 49, 324–336. **562**

SAXE, L., DOUGHERTY, D., & CROSS, T. (1985). The validity of polygraph testing. AMERICAN PSYCHOLOGIST, 40, 355–366. **425**

SCARR, S. (1988). How genotypes and environments combine: Development and individual differences. In N. Bolger, A. Caspi, G. Downey, & M. Moorehouse (Eds.), PERSONS IN CONTEXT: DEVELOPMENTAL PROCESSES (pp. 217–244). New York: Cambridge University Press. **503, 504, 506**

SCARR, S., & MCCARTNEY, K., (1983). How people make their own environments: A theory of genotype-environment effects. CHILD DEVELOPMENT, *54*, 424–435. **503, 504, 506**

SCARR, S., PHILLIPS, D., & MCCARTNEY, K. (1990). Facts, Fantasies and the future of child care in the United States. PSYCHOLOGICAL SCIENCE, *1*, 26–35. **499**

SCARR, S., & WEINBERG, R. A. (1976). IQ test performance of black children adopted by white families. AMERICAN PSYCHOLOGIST, *31*, 726–739. **478, 485**

SCARR, S., WEINBERG, R. A., & LEVINE, A. (1986). UNDERSTANDING DEVELOPMENT. San Diego: Harcourt Brace Jovanovich. **509**

SCHACHTEL, E. G. (1982). On memory and childhood amnesia. In U. Neisser (Ed.), MEMORY OBSERVED: REMEMBERING IN NATURAL CONTEXTS. San Francisco: Freeman. **313**

SCHACHTER, S. (1971). EMOTION, OBESITY, AND CRIME. New York: Academic Press. **422**

SCHACHTER, S., & SINGER, J. E. (1962). Cognitive, social and physiological determinants of emotional state. PSYCHOLOGICAL REVIEW, *69*, 379–399. **423**

SCHACTER, D. L. (1989). Memory. In M. Posner (Ed.), FOUNDATIONS OF COGNITIVE SCIENCE. Cambridge, MA: MIT Press. **311, 316**

SCHAFER, R. (1976). A NEW LANGUAGE FOR PSYCHOANALYSIS. New Haven: Yale University Press. **540**

SCHAIE, K. W., & WILLIS, S. L. (1986). Can decline in intellectual functioning in the elderly be reversed? DEVELOPMENTAL PSYCHOLOGY, *22*, 223–232. **120**

SCHAIE, K. W., & WILLIS, S. L. (1991). ADULT DEVELOPMENT AND AGING (3rd ed.). New York: HarperCollins. **120**

SCHIFF, W., & FOULKE, E. (Eds.) (1982). TACTUAL PERCEPTION: A SOURCEBOOK. Cambridge: Cambridge University Press. **163**

SCHIFFENBAUER, A., & SCHIAVO, R. S. (1976). Physical distance and attraction: An intensification effect. JOURNAL OF EXPERIMENTAL SOCIAL PSYCHOLOGY, *12*, 274–282. **738**

SCHIFFMAN, H. R. (1990). SENSATION AND PERCEPTION: AN INTEGRATED APPROACH (3rd ed.). New York: Wiley. **163**

SCHLEIFER, S. J., KELLER, S. E., MCKEGNEY, F. P., & STEIN, M. (1979 March). The influence of stress and other psychosocial factors on human immunity. Paper presented at the 36th Annual Meeting of the Psychosomatic Society, Dallas. **593**

SCHLESINGER, A. M., JR. (1965). A THOUSAND DAYS. Boston: Houghton Mifflin. **780**

SCHMITT, B. H., GILOVICH, T., GOORE, N., & JOSEPH, L. (1986). Mere presence and social facilitation: One more time. JOURNAL OF EXPERIMENTAL SOCIAL PSYCHOLOGY, *22*, 242–248. **754**

SCHNEIDER, A. M., & TARSHIS, B. (1986). AN INTRODUCTION TO PHYSIOLOGICAL PSYCHOLOGY (3rd ed.). New York: Random House. **69**

SCHNEIDER, D. J., & MILLER, R. S. (1975). The effects of enthusiasm and quality of arguments on attitude attribution. JOURNAL OF PERSONALITY, *43*, 693–708. **723**

SCHNEIDERMAN, N. S., & TAPP, J. T. (Eds.) (1985). BEHAVIORAL MEDICINE: THE BIOPSYCHOSOCIAL APPROACH. New York: Erlbaum. **615**

SCHNEIDMAN, E. A. (1985). DEFINITION OF SUICIDE. New York: Wiley. **638**

SCHRADER, W. B. (1971). The predictive validity of College Board Admissions tests. In W. H. Angoff (Ed.), THE COLLEGE BOARD ADMISSIONS TESTING PROGRAM: A TECHNICAL REPORT ON RESEARCH AND DEVELOPMENT ACTIVITIES RELATING TO THE SCHOLASTIC APTITUDE TEST AND ACHIEVEMENT TESTS. New York: College Entrance Examination Board. **468**

SCHUCKIT, M. A. (1989). DRUG AND ALCOHOL ABUSE: A CLINICAL GUIDE TO DIAGNOSIS AND TREATMENT (3rd ed.). New York: Plenum. **223, 249**

SCHULTZ, D. (1987). A HISTORY OF MODERN PSYCHOLOGY (4th ed.). New York: Academic Press. **30**

SCHWARTZ, B. (1989). PSYCHOLOGY OF LEARNING AND BEHAVIOR (3rd ed.). New York: Norton. **266, 271, 277, 287**

SCHWARTZ, B. & REISBERG, D. (1991). LEARNING AND MEMORY. New York: Norton. **287**

SCHWARTZ, G. E. (1975). Biofeedback, self-regulation, and the patterning of physiological processes. AMERICAN SCIENTIST, *63*, 314–324. **611**

SCHWARZ, C. S. (1983, April). Infant day care: effects at 2, 4, and 8 years. Paper presented at the meeting of the Society for Research on Child Development, Detroit. (Abstract published by ERIC Clearinghouse on Elementary and Early Education, #PS013805). **499**

SEARS, D. O., PEPLAU, L. A., & TAYLOR, S. E. (1991). SOCIAL PSYCHOLOGY (7th ed.). Englewood Cliffs, NJ: Prentice-Hall. **746, 784**

SEARS, R. R. (1943). Survey of objective studies of psychoanalytic concepts. SOCIAL SCIENCE RESEARCH COUNCIL BULLETIN, No. 51. **540**

SEARS, R. R. (1944). Experimental analyses of psychoanalytic phenomena. In J. M. Hunt (Ed.), PERSONALITY AND THE BEHAVIOR DISORDERS (Vol. 1, pp. 306–332). New York: Ronald. **540**

SEARS, R. R., MACCOBY, E. E., & LEVIN, H. (1957). PATTERNS OF CHILD REARING. New York: Harper & Row. **539**

SEEMAN, J. (1949). A study of the process of nondirective therapy. JOURNAL OF CONSULTING PSYCHOLOGY, *13*, 157–168. **687**

SEGAL, M. W. (1974). Alphabet and attraction: An unobstrusive measure of the effect of propinquity in a field setting. JOURNAL OF PERSONALITY AND SOCIAL PSYCHOLOGY, *30*, 654–657. **737**

SEIDEN, R. H. (1966). Campus tragedy: A study of student suicide. JOURNAL OF ABNORMAL PSYCHOLOGY, *71*, 388–399. **638**

SEIFERT, C. M., ROBERTSON, S. P., & BLACK, J. B. (1985). Types of inferences generated during reading. JOURNAL OF MEMORY AND LANGUAGE, *24*, 405–422. **323**

SEKULER, R., & BLAKE, R. (1985). PERCEPTION. New York: Knopf. **163**

SEKULER, R., & GANZ, L. (1963). A new aftereffect of seen movement with a stabilized retinal image. SCIENCE, *139*, 1146–1148. **172**

SELFRIDGE, O., & NEISSER, U. (1960). Pattern recognition by machine. SCIENTIFIC AMERICAN, *203*, 60–80. **178**

SELIGMAN, M. E. P. (1971). Phobias and preparedness. BEHAVIOR THERAPY, *2*, 307–320. **631**

SELIGMAN, M. E. P. (1975) HELPLESSNESS. San Francisco: Freeman. **260, 274, 586**

SELIGMAN, M. E. P. & BINIK, Y. M. (1977). The safety signal hypothesis. In H. Davis & H. Hurwitz (Eds.), PAVLOVIAN OPERANT INTERACTIONS. Hillsdale, NJ: Erlbaum. **580**

SELIGMAN, M. E. P. & JOHNSTON, J. C. (1973). A cognitive theory of avoidance learning. In F. J. McGuigan & D. B. Lumsden (Eds.), CONTEMPORARY AP-PROACHES TO CONDITIONING AND LEARNING. Washington, D.C.: Winston-Wiley. **273**

SELYE, H. (1979). THE STRESS OF LIFE (rev. ed.). New York: Van Nostrand Reinhold. **589**

SEWELL, W. H., & MUSSEN, P. H. (1952). The effects of feeding, weaning, and scheduling procedures on childhood adjustment and the formation of oral symptoms. CHILD DEVELOPMENT, 23, 185–191. **539**

SHAFER, L. F. (1947). Fear and courage in aerial combat. JOURNAL OF CONSULTING PSYCHOLOGY, 11, 137–143. **419**

SHAPIRO, A. K., & MORRIS, L. A. (1978). The placebo effect in medical and psychological therapies. In S. L. Garfield, & A. E. Bergin (Eds.), HANDBOOK OF PSYCHOTHERAPY AND BEHAVIOR CHANGE, (2nd ed.) New York: Wiley. **698**

SHAPIRO, D. A., & SHAPIRO, D. (1982). Meta-analysis of comparative therapy outcome studies: A replication and refinement. PSYCHOLOGICAL BULLETIN, 92, 581–604. **695**

SHAPLEY, R., & LENNIE, P. (1985). Spatial frequency analysis in the visual system. ANNUAL REVIEW OF NEUROSCIENCES, 8, 547–583 **175**

SHAVER, P., HAZAN, C., & BRADSHAW, D. (1988). Love as attachment: The integration of three behavioral systems. In R. J. Sternberg, & M. L. Barnes (Eds.), THE PSYCHOLOGY OF LOVE (pp. 68–99). New Haven, CT: Yale University Press. **744**

SHAW, D. W., & THORESEN, C. E. (1974). Effects of modeling and desensitization in reducing dentist phobia. JOURNAL OF COUNSELING PSYCHOLOGY, 21, 415–420. **680**

SHEEHY, G. (1976). PASSAGES. New York: Dutton. **120**

SHEINGOLD, K., & TENNEY, Y. J. (1982). Memory for a salient childhood event. In U. Neisser (Ed.), MEMORY OBSERVED: REMEMBERING IN NATURAL CONTEXTS. San Francisco: Freeman. **5, 313**

SHEKELLE, R., NEATON, J. D., JACOBS, D., HULLEY, S., & BLACKBURN, H. (1983). Type A behavior pattern in MRFIT. A paper presented to the American Heart Association Council on Epidemiology Meetings, San Diego. **601**

SHELDON, W. H. (1954). ATLAS OF MAN: A GUIDE FOR SOMATOTYPING THE ADULT MALE AT ALL AGES. New York: Harper & Row. **526**

SHEPARD, R. N., & COOPER, L. A. (1982). MENTAL IMAGES AND THEIR TRANSFORMATIONS. Cambridge, MA: MIT Press, Bradford Books. **359, 361, 369**

SHEPOSH, J. P., DEMING, M., & YOUNG, L. E. (1977, April). The radiating effects of status and attractiveness of a male upon evaluating his female partner. Paper presented at the annual meeting of the Western psychological Association, Seattle. **737**

SHERMAN, A. R. (1972). Real-life exposure as a primary therapeutic factor in the desensitization treatment of fear. JOURNAL OF ABNORMAL PSYCHOLOGY. 79, 19–28. **678**

SHERRINGTON, R., BRYNJOLFSSON, J., & collaborators (1988). Localization of a susceptibility locus for schizophrenia on chromosome 5. NATURE, 336, 164–167. **652**

SHWEDER, R. A. (1984). Anthropology's romantic rebellion against the enlightenment, or there's more to thinking than reason and evidence. In R. A. Shweder, & R. A. LeVine (Eds.), CULTURE THEORY: ESSAYS ON MIND, SELF, AND EMOTION (pp. 27–66). Cambridge: Cambridge University Press. **97**

SIDEL, R. (1986). WOMEN AND CHILDREN LAST. New York: Penguin Books. **499**

SIEGEL, S. (1979). The Role of Conditioning, Drug Tolerance and Addiction. In J.D. Keelu (Ed.), PSYCHOPATHOLOGY IN ANIMALS: RESEARCH AND CLINICAL IMPLICATIONS. New York: Academic Press. **258**

SIEGEL, S. (1983). Classical conditioning, drug tolerance, and drug dependence. In Y. Israel, F. B. Glaser, H. Kalant, R. E. Popham, W. Schmidt, & R. G. Smart (Eds.). RESEARCH ADVANCES IN ALCOHOL AND DRUG PROBLEMS (Vol. 7). New York: Plenum. **258**

SIEGLER, R. S. (1986). CHILDREN'S THINKING. Englewood Cliffs, NJ: Prentice-Hall. **123**

SIGALL, H., & LANDY, D. (1973). Radiating beauty: The effects of having a physically attractive partner on person perception. JOURNAL OF PERSONALITY AND SOCIAL PSYCHOLOGY, 31, 410–414. **737**

SILVERMAN, I. (1964) Self-esteem and differential responsiveness to success and failure. JOURNAL OF ABNORMAL AND SOCIAL PSYCHOLOGY, 69, 115–119. **644**

SILVERMAN, I. (1971). Physical attractiveness and courtship. SEXUAL BEHAVIOR, 1, 22–25. **739**

SILVERMAN, L. H. (1976). Psychoanalytic theory: The reports of my death are greatly exaggerated. AMERICAN PSYCHOLOGIST, 31, 621–637. **540**

SILVERMAN, L. H., & WEINBERGER, J. (1985). Mommy and I are one: Implications for psychotherapy. AMERICAN PSYCHOLOGIST, 40, 1296–1308. **540**

SILVERSTEIN, L. B. (1991). Transforming the debate about child care and maternal employment. AMERICAN PSYCHOLOGIST, 46, 1025–1032. **499**

SIMMONS, J. V. (1981). PROJECT SEA HUNT: A REPORT ON PROTOTYPE DEVELOPMENT AND TESTS. Technical Report 746, Naval Ocean Systems Center, San Diego. **268**

SIMMONS, R. G., & BLYTH, D. A. (1988). MOVING INTO ADOLESCENCE: THE IMPACT OF PUBERTAL CHANGE AND SCHOOL CONTEXT. New York: Aldine. **112**

SIMON, H. A. (1985, June). Using Cognitive Science to Solve Human Problems. Paper presented at Science and Public Policy Seminar, Federation of Behavioral, Psychological, and Cognitive Sciences. **366**

SIMON, H. A., & GILMARTIN, K. (1973). A simulation of memory for chess positions. COGNITIVE PSYCHOLOGY, 5, 29–46. **364**

SIMPSON, J. A., CAMPBELL, B., & BERSCHEID, E. (1986). The association between romantic love and marriage: Kephart (1967) twice revisited. PERSONALITY AND SOCIAL PSYCHOLOGY BULLETIN, 12, 363–372. **741**

SINGER, J. L., & SINGER, D. G. (1981). TELEVISION, IMAGINATION AND AGGRESSION. Hillsdale, NJ: Erlbaum. **445**

SIQUELAND, E. R., & LIPSITT, J. P. (1966). Conditioned head-turning in human newborns. JOURNAL OF EXPERIMENTAL CHILD PSYCHOLOGY, 3, 356–376. **80**

SIZEMORE, C. C., & PITTILLO, E. S. (1977). I'M EVE. Garden City, NY: Doubleday. **208**

SKINNER, B. F. (1938). THE BEHAVIOR OF ORGANISMS. New York: Appleton-Century-Crofts. **253, 287**

SKINNER, B. F. (1948). "Superstition" in the pigeon. JOURNAL OF EXPERIMENTAL PSYCHOLOGY, 38 168–172. **274**

SKINNER, B. F (1971). BEYOND FREEDOM AND DIGNITY. New York: Knopf. **253**

SKINNER, B. F. (1981). Selection by consequences. SCIENCE, 213, 501–504. **10**

SKYRMS, B. (1986). CHOICE AND CHANCE: AN INTRODUCTION TO INDUCTIVE LOGIC. Belmont, CA: Dickenson. **340, 342**

SLOANE, R. B., STAPLES, F. R., CRISTOL, A. H., YORKSTON, N. J., & WHIPPLE, K. (1975). PSYCHOTHERAPY VS. BEHAVIOR THERAPY. Cambridge, MA: Harvard University Press. **696**

SLOBIN, D. I. (1971). Cognitive prerequisites for the acquisition of grammar. In C. A. Ferguson, & D. I. Slobin (Eds.), STUDIES OF CHILD LANGUAGE DEVELOPMENTS. New York: Holt, Rinehart & Winston. **353**

SLOBIN, D. I. (1979). PSYCHOLINGUISTICS (2nd. ed.). Glenville, IL: Scott, Foresman. **338, 358**

SLOBIN, D. I. (Ed.) (1985). THE CROSS-LINGUISTIC STUDY OF LANGUAGE ACQUISITION. Hillsdale, NJ: Erlbaum. **353**

SLOMAN, S. & RUMELHART, D.E. (1992). Reducing interference in distributed memories through episodic gating. In A. Healy, S. Kosslyn, & R. Shiffin (eds.) FROM LEARNING THEORY TO CONNECTIONIST THEORY: ESSAYS IN HONOR OF W.K. ESTES. Hillsdale, NJ: Erlbaum. **305**

SMETANA, J. G. (1988). Concepts of self and social convention: Adolescents' and parents' reasoning about hypothetical and actual family conflicts. In M. R. Gunnar & W. A. Collins (Eds.), THE MINNESOTA SYMPOSIA (Vol. 21). Hillsdale, NJ: Erlbaum. **114**

SMILANSKY, B. (1974). Paper presented at the meeting of the American Educational Research Association, Chicago. **482**

SMITH, C. A., & ELLSWORTH, P. C. (1985). Patterns of cognitive appraisal in emotion. JOURNAL OF PERSONALITY AND SOCIAL PSYCHOLOGY, *48*, 813–848. **427**

SMITH, C. A. & ELLSWORTH, P. C. (1987). Patterns of appraisal and emotion related to taking an exam. JOURNAL OF PERSONALITY AND SOCIAL PSYCHOLOGY, *52*, 475–488. **427**

SMITH, D., KING, M., & HOEBEL, B. G. (1970). Lateral hypothalamic control of killing: Evidence for a cholinoceptive mechanism. SCIENCE, *167*, 900–901. **440**

SMITH, E. E. (1989). Concepts and induction. In M. I. Posner (Ed.), FOUNDATIONS OF COGNITIVE SCIENCE. Cambridge, MA: MIT Press. **333**

SMITH, E. E., ADAMS, N., & SCHORR, D. (1978). Fact retrieval and the paradox of interference. COGNITIVE PSYCHOLOGY, *10*, 438–464. **308**

SMITH, E. E., LANGSTON, C., & NISBETT, R. E. (1992). The case for rules in reasoning. COGNITIVE SCIENCE, *16*, 1–40. **344**

SMITH, E. E., & MEDIN, D. L. (1981). CATEGORIES AND CONCEPTS. Cambridge, MA: Harvard University Press. **369**

SMITH, G. M. (1986). Adolescent personality traits that predict adult drug use. COMPREHENSIVE THERAPY, *22*, 44–50. **233**

SMITH, M. B., BRUNER, J. S., & WHITE, R. W. (1956). OPINIONS AND PERSONALITY. New York: Wiley. **729**

SMITH, M. L., GLASS, G. V., & MILLER, T. I. (1980). THE BENEFITS OF PSYCHOTHERAPY. Baltimore: Johns Hopkins University Press. **694, 695**

SMUTS, B. B. (1986). Gender, aggression, and influence. In B. Smuts, D. Cheney, R. Seyfarth, R. Wrangham, T. Struhsaker (Eds.), PRIMATE SOCIETIES. Chicago: University of Chicago Press. **439**

SNODGRASS, J. G., LEVY-BERGER, G., & HAYDON, M. (1985). HUMAN EXPERIMENTAL PSYCHOLOGY. New York: Oxford University Press. **30**

SNOW, C. (1987). Relevance of the notion of a critical period to language acquisition. In M. H. Bornstein (Ed.), SENSITIVE PERIODS IN DEVELOPMENT: INTERDISCIPLINARY PERSPECTIVES. Hillsdale, NJ: Erlbaum. **355**

SNYDER, M. L., & URANOWITZ, S. W. (1978). Reconstructing the past: Some cognitive consequences of person perception. JOURNAL OF PERSONALITY AND SOCIAL PSYCHOLOGY, *36*, 941–950. **325**

SNYDER, M. L., STEPHAN, W. G., & ROSENFELD, D. (1976). Egotism and attribution. JOURNAL OF PERSONALITY AND SOCIAL PSYCHOLOGY, *33*, 435–441. **726**

SNYDER, M. L., TANKE, E. D., & BERSCHEID E. (1977). Social perception and interpersonal behavior: On the self-fulfilling nature of social stereotypes. JOURNAL OF PERSONALITY AND SOCIAL PSYCHOLOGY, *35*, 656–666. **722**

SNYDER, S. H. (1980). BIOLOGICAL ASPECTS OF MENTAL DISORDERS. New York: Oxford University Press. **654**

SORENSEN, R. C. (1973). ADOLESCENT SEXUALITY IN CONTEMPORARY AMERICA. New York: World. **113**

SPANOS, N. P. (1986). Hypnotic behavior: A social-psychological interpretation of amnesia, analgesia, and "trance logic". THE BEHAVIORAL AND BRAIN SCIENCES, *9*, 449–502. **239**

SPANOS, N. P., & HEWITT, E. C. (1980). The hidden observer in hypnotic analgesia: Discovery or experimental creation? JOURNAL OF PERSONALITY AND SOCIAL PSYCHOLOGY, *39*, 1201–1214. **239**

SPEARMAN, C. (1904). "General intelligence" objectively determined and measured. AMERICAN JOURNAL OF PSYCHOLOGY, *15*, 201–293. **471**

SPEATH, J. L. (1976). Characteristics of the work setting and the job as determinants of income. In W. H. Sewell, R. M. Hauser, & D. L. Featherman (Eds.), SCHOOLING AND ACHIEVEMENT IN AMERICAN SOCIETY. New York: Academic Press. **468**

SPENCE, K. W. (1964). Anxiety (Drive) level and performance in eyelid conditioning. PSYCHOLOGICAL BULLETIN, *61*, 129–139. **242**

SPERRY, R. W. (1968). Perception in the absence of neocortical commissures. In PERCEPTION AND ITS DISORDERS (Res. Publ. A.R.N.M.D., Vol. 48). New York: The Association for Research in Nervous & Mental Disease. **55**

SPIEGEL, D. (1991). Mind matters: Effects of group support on cancer patients. JOURNAL OF NIH RESEARCH, *3*, 61–63. **613**

SPIEGEL, D., BLOOM, J. R., KRAEMER, H. C., & GOTTHEIL, E. (1989). Psychological support for cancer patients. LANCET, *II*, 1447. **612**

SPIELBERGER, C. D., JOHNSON, E. H., RUSSELL, S. F., CRANE, R. S., JACOBS, G. A., & WORDEN, T. J. (1985). The Experience and Expression of Anger: Construction and validation of an anger expression scale. In M. A. Chesney & R. H. Rosenman (Eds), ANGER AND HOSTILITY IN CARDIOVASCULAR AND BEHAVIORAL DISORDERS. New York: Hemisphere/McGraw-Hill. **601**

SPOEHR, K. T., & LEHMKUHLE, S. W. (1982). VISUAL INFORMATION PROCESSING. San Francisco: Freeman. **201**

SPRINGER, S. P., & DEUTSCH, G. (1989). LEFT BRAIN, RIGHT BRAIN (3rd ed.). San Francisco: Freeman. **57, 69**

SQUIRE, L. R. (1987). MEMORY AND BRAIN. New York: Oxford University Press. **40, 69, 329**

SQUIRE, L.R. (1992). Memory and the hippocampus: A synthesis from findings with rats, monkeys, and humans. PSYCHOLOGICAL REVIEW, *99*, 195–231. **48, 306**

SQUIRE, L. R., & BUTTERS, N. (Eds.) (1984). THE NEUROPSYCHOLOGY OF MEMORY. New York: Guilford Press. **329**

SQUIRE, L. R., COHEN, N. J., & NADEL, L. (1984). The medial temporal region and memory consolidations: A new hypothesis. In H. Weingardner and E. Parker (Eds.), MEMORY CONSOLIDATION. Hillside, N J: Erlbaum. **306**

SQUIRE, L. R. & FOX, M. M. (1980). Assessment of remote memory: Validation of the television test by repeated testing during a seven-day period. BEHAVIORAL RESEARCH METHODS AND INSTRUMENTATION, *12*, 583–586. **306**

SQUIRE, L. R., ZOLA-MORGAN, S., CAVE, C. B., HAIST, F., MUSEN, G, & SUZUKI, W. A. (1990). MEMORY: ORGANIZATION OF BRAIN SYSTEMS AND COGNITION. In Symposium on quantitative biology, the brain. Vol. 55, Cold Spring Harbor Laboratory, Cold Spring Harbor, NY. **315**

STAATS, A. W. (1968). LANGUAGE, LEARNING AND COGNITION. New York: Holt, Rinehart & Winston. **253**

STALLER, S. J., DOWELL, R. C., BEITER, A. L., & BRIMACOMBE, J. A. (1991). Perceptual abilities of children with the Nucleus 22-channel cochlear implant. EAR HEAR, *12*, (supplement) 34–47. **152**

STANLEY, B. G., ANDERSON, K. C., GRAYSON, M. H., & LIEBOWITZ, S. F. (1989). Repeated hypothalamic stimulation with neuropeptide Y increases daily carbohydrate and fat intake and body weight gain in female rats. PHYSIOLOGY AND BEHAVIOR, *46*, 173–177. **382**

STASSER, G., TAYLOR, L. A., & HANNA, C. (1989). Information sampling in structured and unstructured discussion of three- and six-person groups. JOURNAL OF PERSONALITY AND SOCIAL PSYCHOLOGY, *57*, 67–78. **779**

STASSER, G., & TITUS, W. (1985). Pooling of unshared information in group decision making: Biased information sampling during discussion. JOURNAL OF PERSONALITY AND SOCIAL PSYCHOLOGY, *48;* 1467–1478. **779**

STAYTON, D. J. (1973, March). Infant responses to brief everyday separations: Distress, following, and greeting. Paper presented at the meeting of the Society for Research in Child Development. **495**

STEERING COMMITTEE OF THE PHYSICIANS' HEALTH STUDY RESEARCH GROUP (1988). Preliminary report: findings from the aspirin component of the ongoing Physicians' Health Study. NEW ENGLAND JOURNAL OF MEDICINE, *318*, 262–264. **243**

STEFFY, R. A., ASARNOW, R. F.,

ASARNOW, J. R., MACCRIMMON, D. J., & CLEGHORN, J. M. (1984). The McMaster-Waterloo High-Risk Project: Multifacted strategy for high-risk research. In H. F. Watt, E. J. Anthony, L. C. Wynne, & J. E. Rolf (Eds.), CHILDREN AT RISK FOR SCHIZOPHRENIA. New York: Cambridge University Press. **657**

STEIN, J. A., GOLDING, J. M., SIEGEL, J. M., BURNAM, M. A., & SORENSON, S. B. (1988). Long-term psychological sequelae of child sexual abuse: the Los Angeles epidemiologic catchment area study. In G. E. Wyatt & G. J. Powell (Eds.), LASTING EFFECTS OF CHILD SEXUAL ABUSE. Newbury Park: Sage Publications. **582**

STEINBERG, L. (1985). ADOLESCENCE. New York: Knopf. **123**

STEINBERG, L. (1987). Impact of puberty on family relations: Effects of pubertal status and pubertal timing. DEVELOPMENTAL PSYCHOLOGY, *23*, 451–460. **114**

STEKETEE, G. and WHITE, K. (1990). WHEN ONCE IN NOT ENOUGH. Oakland, CA: New Harbinger Publications. **679**

STELLAR, E. (1954). The physiology of motivation. PSYCHOLOGICAL REVIEW, *61*, 5–22. **380**

STELLAR, J. R., & STELLAR, E. (1985). THE NEUROBIOLOGY OF MOTIVATION AND REWARD. New York: Springer-Verlag. **408, 415**

STERN, D. B. (1978). Phenomenology of obsessive-compulsive neurosis. BRITISH JOURNAL OF PSYCHIATRY, *132;* 233–234. **627**

STERNBACH, R. A. (Ed.). (1986). THE PSYCHOLOGY OF PAIN (2nd ed.). New York: Raven. **163**

STERNBERG, R. J. (Ed.) (1982). HANDBOOK OF HUMAN INTELLIGENCE. New York: Cambridge University Press. **487**

STERNBERG, R. J. (Ed.) (1984). HUMAN ABILITIES: AN INFORMATION-PROCESSING APPROACH. New York: Freeman. **487**

STERNBERG, R. (1986). A triangular theory of love. PSYCHOLOGICAL REVIEW, *93* 119–135. **744**

STERNBERG, R. J. (1985). BEYOND IQ: A TRIARCHIC THEORY OF HUMAN INTELLIGENCE. New York: Cambridge University Press. **475, 477**

STERNBERG, R. J. (1986). INTELLIGENCE APPLIED: UNDERSTANDING AND INCREASING YOUR INTELLECTUAL SKILLS. San Diego: Harcourt Brace Jovanovich. **487, 744**

STERNBERG, R. J. (1990). METAPHORS

OF MIND: CONCEPTIONS OF THE NATURE OF INTELLIGENCE. New York: Cambridge University Press. **487**

STERNBERG, R. J., & SMITH, E. E. (Eds.) (1988). THE PSYCHOLOGY OF HUMAN THOUGHT. Cambridge: Cambridge University Press. **369**

STERNBERG, S. (1966). Highspeed scanning in human memory. SCIENCE, *153*, 652–654. **295**

STERNBERG, S. (1969). Memory-scanning: Mental processes revealed by reaction-time experiments. AMERICAN SCIENTIST, *57*, 421–457. **295**

STERNBERG, S. (1975). Memory scanning: New findings and current controversies. QUARTERLY JOURNAL OF EXPERIMENTAL PSYCHOLOGY, *27*, 1–32. **295**

STERNGLANZ, S.H., & SERBIN, L.A. (1974). Sex-role stereotyping in children's television programs. DEVELOPMENTAL PSYCHOLOGY, *10*, 710–715. **104**

STEUER, F. B., APPLEFIELD, J. M., & SMITH, R. (1971). Televised aggression and the interpersonal aggression of preschool children. JOURNAL OF EXPERIMENTAL CHILD PSYCHOLOGY, *11*, 422–447. **445**

STEVENS, S. S. (1957). On the psychophysical law. PSYCHOLOGICAL REVIEW, *64*, 153–181. **130**

STILES, W. B., SHAPIRO, D. A., & ELLIOTT, R. (1986). Are all psychotherapies equivalent? AMERICAN PSYCHOLOGIST, *41;* 165–180. **695**

STIPEK, D., & MCCROSKEY, J. (1989). Government and workplace policies for parents. AMERICAN PSYCHOLOGIST, *44*, 416–423. **499**

STOKES, D. M. (1987). Theoretical parapsychology. In S. Krippner (Ed.), ADVANCES IN PARAPSYCHOLOGICAL RESEARCH (Vol. 5). Jefferson, NC: McFarland. **246**

STONER, J. A. F. (1961). A COMPARISON OF INDIVIDUAL AND GROUP DECISIONS INVOLVING RISK. Unpublished masters' thesis, Massachusetts Institute of Technology. **778**

STRACK, F., MARTIN, L. L., & STEPPER, S. (1988). Inhibiting and facilitating conditions of the human smile: A non-obtrusive test of the facial feedback hypothesis. JOURNAL OF PERSONALITY AND SOCIAL PSYCHOLOGY, *54*, 768–777. **433**

STRAUSS, J. S. (1982). Behavioral aspects of being disadvantaged and risk for schizophrenia. In D. L. Parron, F. Solomon, & C. D. Jenkins (Eds.), BEHAVIOR, HEALTH RISKS, AND SOCIAL

DISADVANTAGE. Washington, DC: National Academy Press. **655**

STREISSGUTH, A. P., CLARREN, S. K., & JONES, K. L. (1985). Natural history of the fetal alcohol syndrome: A 10-year follow-up of eleven patients. THE LANCET, *2*, 85–91. **223**

STRICKER, E. M. (1983). Thirst and sodium appetite after colloid treatment in rats: Role of the renin-angiotensin-aldosterone system. BEHAVIORAL NEUROSCIENCE, *97*, 725–737. **382**

STRICKER, E. M., ROWLAND, N., SALLER, C. F., & FRIEDMAN, M. I. (1977). Homeostasis during hypoglycemia: Central control of adrenal secretion and peripheral control of feeding. SCIENCE, *196*, 79–81. **378**

STRICKER, E. M., & VERGALIS, J. G. (1988). Hormones and behavior: The biology of thirst and sodium appetite. AMERICAN SCIENTIST, *76*, 261–268. **376**

STROEBE, W., INSKO, C. A. THOMPSON, V. D., & LAYTON, B. D. (1971). Effects of physical attractiveness, attitude similarity and sex on various aspects of interpersonal attraction. JOURNAL OF PERSONALITY AND SOCIAL PSYCHOLOGY, *18*, 79–91. **737**

STRONG, S. R., HILLS, H. J., KILMARTIN, C. T., DEVRIES, H., LANIER, K., NELSON, B. N., STRICKLAND, D., & MEYER, C. W., III (1988). The dynamic relations among interpersonal behaviors: A test of complementarity and anti-complementarity. JOURNAL OF PERSONALITY AND SOCIAL PSYCHOLOGY, *54*, 798–810. **740**

STUART, R. B., & DAVIS, B. (1972). SLIM CHANCE IN A FAT WORLD. Champaign, IL: Research Press. **682**

STUNKARD, A. J. (1982) Obesity. In M. Hersen, A. Bellack, A. Kazdin (Eds.), INTERNATIONAL HANDBOOK OF BEHAVIOR MODIFICATION AND THERAPY. New York: Plenum. **385**

SUAREZ, E. C., & WILLIAMS, R. B. (1989). Situational determinants of cardiovascular and emotional reactivity in high and low hostile men. PSYCHOSOMATIC MEDICINE. *51*, 404–418. **601**

SUDDATHG, R. L. CHRISTISON, G. W., TORREY, E. F., CASANOVA, M. F., & WEINBERGER, D. R. (1990). Anatomical abnormalities in the brains of monozygotic twins discordant for schizophrenia. NEW ENGLAND JOURNAL OF MEDICINE, *322*, 789–794. **655**

SUEDFELD, P. (1975). The benefits of boredom: Sensory deprivation considered. AMERICAN SCIENTIST, *63*, 60–69. **411**

SULLIVAN, H. S. (1953). THE INTERPERSONAL THEORY OF PSYCHIATRY. New York: Norton. **119**

SUINN, R. M. (1990). ANXIETY MANAGEMENT TRAINING: A BEHAVIOR THERAPY. New York: Plenum Press. **709**

SUOMI, S. J., HARLOW, H. F., & MC KINNEY, W. T. (1972) Monkey psychiatrist. AMERICAN JOURNAL OF PSYCHIATRY, *28*, 41–46. **410**

SUPER, C. M. (1976). Environmental effects on motor development: A case of African infant precocity. DEVELOPMENTAL MEDICINE AND CHILD NEUROLOGY, *18*, 561–567. **75**

SVENSON, O. (1981). Are we all less risky and more skillful than our fellow drivers? ACTA PSYCHOLOGICA, *47*, 143–148. **644, 727**

SWETS, J. A. & BJORK, R. A. (1990). Enhancing human performance: An evaluation of "new age" techniques considered by the U. S. Army. PSYCHOLOGICAL SCIENCE, *1*, 85–96. **321**

SWINNEY, D. A. (1979). Lexical access during sentence comprehension: Consideration of context effects. JOURNAL OF VERBAL LEARNING AND VERBAL BEHAVIOR, *18*, 645–659. **347**

SWINNEY, D. A. ZURIF, E. B., & NICOL, J. (1989). The effects of focal brain damage on sentence processing: An examination of the neurological organization of a mental module. JOURNAL OF COGNITIVE NEUROSCIENCE, *1*, 25–37. **357**

SYER, J., & CONNOLLY, C. (1988) SPORTING BODY SPORTING MIND: AN ATHLETE'S GUIDE TO MENTAL TRAINING. Englewood Cliffs, NJ: Prentice Hall. **234, 249**

SYMONS, D. (1990). On the use and misuse of Darwinism in the study of human behavior. In J. Barkow, L. Cosmides, & J. Tooby (Eds.), THE ADAPTED MIND: EVOLUTIONARY PSYCHOLOGY AND THE GENERATION OF CULTURE. Oxford University Press. **27**

TALLENT, N. (1992). THE PRACTICE OF PSYCHOLOGICAL ASSESSMENT. Englewood Cliffs, NJ: Prentice-Hall. **573**

TANENHAUS, M. G., LEIMAN, J., & SEIDENBERG, M. (1979). Evidence for multiple stages in the processing of ambiguous words in syntactic contexts. JOURNAL OF VERBAL LEARNING AND VERBAL BEHAVIOR. *18*, 427–441. **347**

TANNER, J. M. (1970). Physical growth. In P. H. Mussen (Ed.), CARMICHAEL'S MANUAL OF CHILD PSYCHOLOGY, (3rd ed, Vol. 1). New York: Wiley. **111**

TARLER-BENLOLO, L. (1978). The role of relaxation in biofeedback training. PSYCHOLOGICAL BULLETIN, *85*, 727–755. **611**

TART, C. T. & DICK, L. (1970). Conscious control of dreaming: Pt. 1. The post-hypnotic dream. JOURNAL OF ABNORMAL PSYCHOLOGY, *76*, 304–315. **217**

TARTTER, V. C. (1986). LANGUAGE PROCESSES. New York: Holt, Rinehart & Winston. **369**

TAVRIS, C. (1984). ANGER: THE MISUNDERSTOOD EMOTION. New York: Simon & Schuster. **447**

TAVRIS, C., & SADD, S. (1977). THE REDBOOK REPORT ON FEMALE SEXUALITY. New York: Dell. **400**

TAYLOR, S. (1986). Stress and development of illness. In S. E. Taylor, HEALTH PSYCHOLOGY. New York: Random House. **591, 615**

TAYLOR, S. E. & BROWN, J. D. (1988). Illusion and well-being: A social psychological perspective on mental health. PSYCHOLOGICAL BULLETIN, *103*, 193–210. **644, 645**

TAYLOR, S. E., & THOMPSON, S. C. (1982). Stalking the elusive "vividness" effect. PSYCHOLOGICAL REVIEW, *89*, 155–181. **715**

TEDESCHI, J. T. & ROSENFELD, P. (1981). Impression management and the forced compliance situation. In J. T. Tedeschi (Ed.) IMPRESSION MANAGEMENT THEORY AND SOCIAL PSYCHOLOGICAL RESEARCH. New York: Academic Press. **735**

TEITELBAUM, P., & EPSTEIN, A. N. (1962). The lateral hypothalamic syndrome: Recovery of feeding and drinking after lateral hypothalamic lesions. PSYCHOLOGICAL REVIEW, *69*, 74–90. **380**

TELLEGEN, A., LYKKEN, D. T., BOUCHARD, T. J., JR., WILCOX, K. J., SEGAL, N. L., & RICH, S. (1988). Personality similarity in twins reared apart and together. JOURNAL OF PERSONALITY AND SOCIAL PSYCHOLOGY, *54*, 1031–1039. **490**

TELLER, D. Y., MORSE, R., BORTON, R., & REGAL, D. (1974). Visual acuity for vertical and diagonal gratings in human infants. VISION RESEARCH, *14*, 1433–1439. **194**

TEMPLIN, M. C. (1957). CERTAIN LANGUAGE SKILLS IN CHILDREN: THEIR DEVELOPMENT AND INTERRELATIONSHIPS. Minneapolis: University of Minnesota Press. **351**

TENNANT, C., SMITH, A., BEBBINGTON, P., & HURRY, J. (1981). Parental loss in childhood: Relationship to adult psychiatric impairment and contact with psychiatric services. ARCHIVES OF GENERAL PSYCHIATRY, *38*, 309–314. **640**

TERKEL, J., & ROSENBLATT, J. S. (1972). Humoral factors underlying maternal behavior at parturition: Cross transfusion between freely moving rats. JOURNAL OF COMPARATIVE AND PHYSIOLOGICAL PSYCHOLOGY, *80*, 365–371. **407**

TERRACE, H. S., PETITTO, L. A. SANDERS, D. J., & BEVER, T. G. (1979). Can an ape create a sentence? SCIENCE, *206*, 891–902. **358**

TESSER, A., & BRODIE, M. (1971). A note on the evaluation of a "computer date." PSYCHONOMIC SCIENCE. *23*, 300. **736**

TETLOCK, P. E., & LEVI, A. (1982). Attribution bias: On the inconclusiveness of the cognition-motivation debate. JOURNAL OF EXPERIMENTAL SOCIAL PSYCHOLOGY, *18*, 68–88. **727**

THIGPEN, C. H., & CLECKLEY, H. (1957). THE THREE FACES OF EVE. New York: McGraw-Hill. **208**

THOM, M. (Ed.) (1987). LETTERS TO *MS*. 1972–1987. New York: Holt. **583**

THOMAS, A., & CHESS, S. (1977). TEMPERAMENT AND DEVELOPMENT. New York: Brunner/Mazel. **83**

THOMAS, A., & CHESS, S. (1986). The New York longitudinal study: From infancy to early adult life. In R. Plomin, & J. Dunn (Eds.), THE STUDY OF TEMPERAMENT: CHANGES, CONTINUITIES AND CHALLENGES (pp. 39–52). Hillsdale, NJ: Erlbaum. **492**

THOMAS, A., CHESS, S., BIRCH, H., HERTZIG, M., & KORN, S. (1963). BEHAVIORAL INDIVIDUALITY IN EARLY CHILDHOOD. New York: New York University Press. **492**

THOMAS, E. L. & ROBINSON, H. A. (1982). IMPROVING READING IN EVERY CLASS. Boston: Allyn & Bacon. **321**

THOMPSON, L. A., DETTERMAN, D. K., & PLOMIN, R. (1991). Associations between cognitive abilities and scholastic achievement: genetic overlap but environmental differences. PSYCHOLOGICAL SCIENCE, *2*, (3), 158–165. **478**

THOMPSON, R. A., LAMB, M., & ESTES, D. (1982). Stability of infant–mother attachment and its relationship to changing life circumstances in an unselected middle-class sample. CHILD DEVELOPMENT, *53*, 144–148. **497**

THOMPSON, S. K. (1975). Gender labels and early sex role development. CHILD DEVELOPMENT, *46*, 339–347. **105**

THOMPSON, W. R. (1954). The inheritance and development of intelligence. PROCEEDINGS OF THE ASSOCIATION FOR RESEARCH ON NERVOUS AND MENTAL DISEASE, *33*, 209–231. **65**

THORESEN, C. E., TELCH, M. J., & EAGLESTON, J. R. (1981). Altering Type A behavior. PSYCHOSOMATICS, *8*, 472–482. **601**

THORNDIKE, R. L., HAGEN, E. P., & SATTLER, J. M. (1986). STANFORD-BINET INTELLIGENCE SCALE: GUIDE FOR ADMINISTERING AND SCORING THE FOURTH EDITION. Chicago: Riverside. **460**

THORNDYKE, E. L. (1898). Animal intelligence: An experimental study of the associative processes in animals. PSYCHOLOGICAL MONOGRAPHS, *2* (No. 8). **265**

THURSTONE, L. L. (1938). Primary mental abilities. PSYCHOMETRIC MONOGRAPHS, No. 1. Chicago: University of Chicago Press. **472**

THURSTONE, L. L., & THURSTONE, T. G. (1963). SRA PRIMARY ABILITIES. Chicago: Science Research Associates. **474**

TIENARI, P., SORRI, A., LAHTI, I., NAARALA, M., WAHLBERG, K., et al. (1987). Interaction of genetic and psychosocial factors in schizophrenia. The Finnish adoptive family study: A longitudinal combination of the adoptive family strategy and the risk research strategy. SCHIZOPHRENIA BULLETIN, *13*, 477–484. **657**

TIME (1983, August 15). Babies: What do they know? When do they know it? (p. 5). **79**

TOLMAN, E. C. (1932). Purposive Behavior in Animals and Men. New York: Appleton-Century-Crofts. (Reprinted, 1967. New York: Irvington.) **258, 279, 287**

TOMKINS, S. S. (1962). AFFECT, IMAGERY, CONSCIOUSNESS: VOL. 1 THE POSITIVE AFFECTS. New York: Springer. **433**

TOMPKINS, S. S. (1980). Affect as amplification: Some modifications in theory. In R. Plutchik & H. Kellerman (Eds.), EMOTION: THEORY, RESEARCH AND EXPERIENCE (Vol. 1). New York: Academic Press. **434**

TORGERSEN, S. (1983) Genetic factors in anxiety disorders. ARCHIVES OF GENERAL PSYCHIATRY, *40*, 1085–1089. **633**

TREISMAN, A. (1969). Strategies and models of selective attention. PSYCHOLOGICAL REVIEW, *76*, 282–299. **185**

TREISMAN, A., & GORMICAN, S. (1988). Feature analysis in early vision: Evidence from search asymmetries. PSYCHOLOGICAL REVIEW, *95*, 15–48. **175**

TREISMAN, A., & SCHMIDT, H. (1982). Illusory conjunctions in the perception of objects. COGNITIVE PSYCHOLOGY, *14*, 107–141. **186**

TRINDER, J. (1988). Subjective insomnia without objective findings: A pseudodiagnostic classification. PSYCHOLOGICAL BULLETIN, *103*, 87–94. **214**

TRIPLETT, N. (1898). The dynamogenic factors in pacemaking and competition. AMERICAN JOURNAL OF PSYCHOLOGY, *9*, 507–533. **749**

TRUAX, C. B., & MITCHELL, K. M. (1971). Research on certain therapist interpersonal skills in relation to process and outcome. In A. E. Bergin & S. L. Garfield (Eds.), HANDBOOK OF PSYCHOTHERAPY AND BEHAVIOR CHANGE: AN EMPIRICAL ANALYSIS. New York: Wiley. **562, 688**

TULVING, E. (1974). Cue-dependent forgetting. AMERICAN SCIENTIST, *62*, 74–82. **301**

TULVING, E. (1983). THE ELEMENTS OF EPISODIC MEMORY. New York: Oxford University Press. **328, 329**

TULVING, E. (1985). How many memory systems are there? AMERICAN PSYCHOLOGIST, *40*, 385–398. **316**

TULVING, E., & PEARLSTONE, Z. (1966). Availability versus accessibility of information in memory for words. JOURNAL OF VERBAL LEARNING AND VERBAL BEHAVIOR, *5*, 381–391. **301**

TULVING, E., SCHACTER, D. L., & STARK, H. A. (1982) Priming effects in word-fragment completion are independent of recognition memory. JOURNAL OF EXPERIMENTAL PSYCHOLOGY: LEARNING, MEMORY, AND COGNITION, *8*, 336–342. **315**

TURIEL, E. (1983). THE DEVELOPMENT OF SOCIAL KNOWLEDGE: MORALITY AND CONVENTION. Cambridge: Cambridge University Press. **93, 123**

TURKHEIMER, E. (1991). Individual and group differences in adoption studies of IQ. PSYCHOLOGICAL BULLETIN, *110* (3), 392–405. **484**

TVERSKY, A., & KAHNEMAN, D. (1973). On the psychology of prediction. PSYCHOLOGICAL REVIEW, *80*, 237–251. **343**

TVERSKY, A., & KAHNEMAN, D. (1983). Extensional versus intuitive reasoning: The conjunction fallacy in probability judgment. PSYCHOLOGICAL REVIEW, *90*, 293–315. **343**

TYHURST, J. S. (1951). Individual reactions to community disaster. AMERICAN JOURNAL OF PSYCHIATRY, *10*, 746–769. **435**

TYLER, H. (1977). The unsinkable Jeane Dixon. THE HUMANIST, *37*, 6–9. **246**

ULLMAN, S. (1989). Aligning pictorial descriptions: An approach to object recognition. COGNITION, *32*, 193–254. **360**

ULRICH, R. E., STACHNIK, T. J., & STAINTON, N. R. (1963). Student acceptance of generalized personality interpretations. PSYCHOLOGICAL REPORTS, *13*, 831–834. **554**

URSIN, H. (1978). Activation, coping, and psychosomatics. In H. Ursin, E. Baade, & S. Levine (Eds.), PSYCHOBIOLOGY OF STRESS: A STUDY OF COPING MEN. New York: Academic Press. **590**

U.S. BUREAU OF LABOR STATISTICS. (1987). STATISTICAL ABSTRACT OF THE UNITED STATES (107th ed.). Washington, DC: U.S. Department of Commerce. **498**

UTTS, J. (1986). The gansfeld debate: A statistician's perspective. JOURNAL OF PARAPSYCHOLOGY, *50*, 393–402. **243**

VALLIANT, G. (1977). ADAPTATION TO LIFE. Boston: Little, Brown. **120**

VAN EEDEN, F. (1913). A study of dreams. PROCEEDINGS OF THE SOCIETY FOR PSYCHICAL RESEARCH, *26*, 431–461. **217**

VAUGHN, B. E., LEFEVER, G. B., SEIFER, R., & BARGLOW, P. (1989). Attachment behavior, attachment security, and temperament during infancy. CHILD DEVELOPMENT, *60*, 728–737. **496**

VEITH, I. (1970). HYSTERIA: THE HISTORY OF A DISEASE. Chicago: University of Chicago Press. **708**

VELMANS, M. (1991). Is human information processing conscious? BEHAVIORAL AND BRAIN SCIENCES, *14*, 651–726. **206**

VINTER, A. (1986). The role of movement in eliciting early imitations. CHILD DEVELOPMENT, *57*, 66–71. **79**

VIORST, J. (1986). NECESSARY LOSSES. New York: Faucett Gold Medal. **709**

VISINTAINER, M. A., VOLPICELLI, J. R., & SELIGMAN, M. E. P. (1982). Tumor rejection in rats after inescapable or escapable shock. SCIENCE, *216*, 437–439. **593, 594**

VON LANG, J., & SIBYLL, C. (Eds.) (1983). EICHMANN INTERROGATED (R. Manheim, Trans.). New York: Farrar, Straus & Giroux. **762**

WAGNER A. R. (1981). SOP: A model of automatic memory processing in animal behavior. In N. E. Spear & R. R. Miller (Eds.), INFORMATION PROCESSING IN ANIMALS: MEMORY MECHANISMS. Hillsdale, NJ: Erlbaum. **261**

WAGNER, M. W., & MONNET. M. (1979). Attitudes of college professors toward extrasensory perception. ZETETIC SCHOLAR, *5*, 7–17. **247**

WALD, G., & BROWN, P. K. (1965). Human color vision and color blindness. COLD SPRING HARBOR SYMPOSIA ON QUANTITATIVE BIOLOGY, *30*, 345–359. **143**

WALDROP, M. M. (1987). The workings of working memory. SCIENCE, *237*, 1564–1567. **317**

WALKER, C. E., HEDBERG, A., CLEMENT, P. W., & WRIGHT, L. (1981). CLINICAL PROCEDURES FOR BEHAVIOR THERAPY. Englewood Cliffs, N.J: Prentice-Hall. **679**

WALKER, E. (1978). EXPLORATIONS IN THE BIOLOGY OF LANGUAGE. Montgomery, VT: Bradford Books. **395**

WALLACH, M. A., KOGAN, N., & BEM, D. J. (1962). Group influence on individual risk taking. JOURNAL OF ABNORMAL AND SOCIAL PSYCHOLOGY, *65*, 75–86. **778, 780**

WALLACH, M. A., KOGAN, N., & BEM, D. J. (1964). Diffusion of responsibility and level of risk taking in groups. JOURNAL OF ABNORMAL AND SOCIAL PSYCHOLOGY, *68*, 263–274. **778**

WALLACH, M. A., & WALLACH, L. (1983). PSYCHOLOGY'S SANCTION FOR SELFISHNESS. San Francisco: Freeman. **551**

WALSTER, E., ARONSON, E., ABRAHAMS, D., & ROTTMANN, L. (1966). Importance of physical attractiveness in dating behavior. JOURNAL OF PERSONALITY AND SOCIAL PSYCHOLOGY *4*, 508–516. **736**

WALZER, M. (1970). OBLIGATIONS. Cambridge, MA: Harvard University Press. **771**

WARRINGTON, E. K., & WEISKRANTZ, L. (1978). Further analysis of the prior learning effect in amnesic patients. NEUROPSYCHOLOGIA, *16*, 169–177. **314**

WASON, P. C., & JOHNSON-LAIRD, P. N. (1972). PSYCHOLOGY OF REASONING: STRUCTURE AND CONTENT. London: Batsford. **341**

WATERMAN, A. S. (1985). Identity in the context of adolescent psychology. In A. S. Waterman (Ed.), IDENTITY IN ADOLESCENCE: PROGRESS AND CONTENTS: (NEW DIRECTIONS FOR CHILD DEVELOPMENT, NO. 30). San Francisco: Jossey-Bass. **510**

WATERMAN, A. S., & WATERMAN, C. K. (1972). The relationship between freshman ego identity status and subsequent academic behavior: A test of the predictive validity of Marcia's categorization system for identity status. DEVELOPMENTAL PSYCHOLOGY, *6*, 179. **118**

WATERS, E., WIPPMAN, J., & SROUFE, L. A. (1979). Attachment, positive affect, and competence in the peer group: Two studies in construct validation. CHILD DEVELOPMENT, *50*, 821–829 **499**

WATSON, D. & PENNEBAKER, J. W. (1989). Health complaints, stress, and distress: exploring the central role of negative affectivity. PSYCHOLOGICAL REVIEW, *96*, 234–254. **596**

WATSON, D. L., & THARP, R. G. (1989). SELF-DIRECTED BEHAVIOR: SELF-MODIFICATION FOR PERSONAL ADJUSTMENT (5th ed.). Belmont, CA: Wadsworth. **709**

WATSON, J. B. (1930). BEHAVIORISM (Rev. ed.). New York: Norton. **72**

WEAVER, E. G. (1949). THEORY OF HEARING. New York: Wiley. **149**

WEBB, W. B. (1975). SLEEP THE GENTLE TYRANT. Englewood Cliffs, NJ: Prentice-Hall. **210**

WECHSLER, D. (1939) THE MEASUREMENT OF ADULT INTELLIGENCE. Baltimore: Williams and Wilkins. **463**

WECHSLER, D. (1955) MANUAL FOR THE WECHSLER ADULT INTELLIGENCE SCALE. San Antonio: The Psychological Corporation. **463**

WECHSLER, D. (1958). THE MEASUREMENT AND APPRAISAL OF ADULT INTELLIGENCE. Baltimore: Williams. **471**

WECHSLER, D. (1974). WECHSLER INTELLIGENCE SCALE FOR CHILDREN, REVISED. New York: Psychological Corporation. **463**

WECHSLER, D. (1981) MANUAL FOR THE WECHSLER ADULT INTELLIGENCE SCALE—REVISED. San Antonio: The Psychological Corporation. **463**

WECHSLER, C. (1991) WECHSLER INTELLIGENCE SCALE FOR CHILDREN, REVISED. San Antonio: The Psychological Corporation. **463**

WEGNER, D. M., SCHNEIDER, D. J., CARTER III, S., & WHITE, L. (1987). Paradoxical consequences of thought suppression. JOURNAL OF PERSONALITY AND SOCIAL PSYCHOLOGY, *53*, 1–9. **607**

WEIGEL, R. H., VERNON, D. T. A., & TOGNACCI, L. N. (1974). Specificity of the attitude as a determinant of attitude-behavior congruence. JOURNAL OF

PERSONALITY AND SOCIAL PSYCHOLOGY, *30*, 724–728. **734**

WEINER, E. (1972). THEORIES OF MOTIVATION: FROM MECHANISM TO COGNITION. Chicago: Rand McNally. **598**

WEINSTEIN, N. D. (1980). Unrealistic optimism about future events. JOURNAL OF PERSONALITY AND SOCIAL PSYCHOLOGY, *39*, 806–820. **645**

WEINSTEIN, S. (1968). Intensive and extensive aspects of tactile sensitivity as a function of body part, sex, and laterality. In D. R. Kenshalo (Ed.), THE SKIN SENSES. Springfield, IL: Thomas. **157**

WEISS, J. M., GLAZER, H. I., POHORECKY, L. A., BRICK, J., & MILLER, N. E. (1975). Effects of chronic exposure to stressors on avoidance-escape behavior and on brain norepinephrine. PSYCHOSOMATIC MEDICINE, *37*, 522–534. **589**

WEITZMAN, L. (1985). THE DIVORCE REVOLUTION. New York: Free Press. **499**

WERTHEIMER, M. (1912/1932). Experimentelle Studien uber das Sehen von Beuegung. ZEITSCHRIFT FUER PSYCHOLOGIE, *61*, 161–265. **167**

WERTHEIMER, M. (1987). A BRIEF HISTORY OF PSYCHOLOGY. (3rd ed.). San Diego: Harcourt Brace. **30**

WEST, C., & ZIMMERMAN, D. H. (1983). Small insults: A study of interruptions in cross-sex conversations between unacquainted persons. In B. Thorne, C. Kramarae, N. Henley (Eds.), LANGUAGE, GENDER, AND SOCIETY. Rowley, MA: Newbury House. **725**

WEST, M. A. (Ed.) (1987). THE PSYCHOLOGY OF MEDITATION. New York: Oxford University Press. **249**

WESTON, D., & TURIEL, E. (1980). Act-rule relations: Children's concepts of social rules. DEVELOPMENTAL PSYCHOLOGY, *16*, 417–424. **93**

WETZLER, S. E. & SWEENEY, J. A. (1986). Childhood amnesia: An empirical demonstration. In D. C. Rubin (Ed.), AUTOBIOGRAPHICAL MEMORY. New York: Cambridge University Press. **312**

WHITE, C. (1977). Unpublished Ph.D. dissertation, Catholic University, Washington, DC. **387**

WHITE, G. L., FISHBEIN, S., & RUTSTEIN, J. (1981). Passionate love and the misattribution of arousal. JOURNAL OF PERSONALITY AND SOCIAL PSYCHOLOGY, *41*, 56–62. **743**

WHITE, G. L., KIGHT, T. D. (1984) Misattribution of arousal and attraction: Effects of salience of explanations for arousal. JOURNAL OF EXPERIMENTAL SOCIAL PSYCHOLOGY, *20*, 55–64. **743**

WHITE, R. W., & WATT, N. F. (1981). THE A NORMAL PERSONALITY (5th ed.). New York: Wiley. **640**

WHITING, B. B., & EDWARDS, C. P. (1988). CHILDREN OF DIFFERENT WORLDS: THE FORMATION OF SOCIAL BEHAVIOR. Cambridge, MA: Harvard University Press. **507, 523**

WHITING, B. B. & WHITING, J. W. M. (1975). CHILDREN OF SIX CULTURES: A PSYCHOCULTURAL ANALYSIS. Cambridge, MA: Harvard University Press. **507, 523**

WHITING, J. W. M., & CHILD, I. (1953). CHILD TRAINING AND PERSONALITY: A CROSS CULTURAL STUDY. New Haven: Yale University Press. **507, 523**

WHYTE, W. H. (1956). THE ORGANIZATION MAN. New York: Simon & Schuster. **778**

WHORF, B. L. (1956). Science and linguistics. In J. B. Carroll (Ed.), LANGUAGE, THOUGHT AND REALITY: SELECTED WRITINGS OF BENJAMIN LEE WHORF. Cambridge, MA: MIT Press. **338**

WIEBE, D. J. & MCCALLUM, D. M. (1986). Health practices and hardiness as mediators in the stress-illness relationship. HEALTH PSYCHOLOGY, *5*, 425–438. **599**

WIESEL, T. N., & HUBEL, D. H. (1974). Ordered arrangement of orientation columns in monkeys lacking visual experience. JOURNAL OF COMPARATIVE NEUROLOGY, *158*, 307–318. **196**

WIGDOR, A. K., & GARNER, W. R. (Eds.) (1982). ABILITY TESTING: USES, CONSEQUENCES, AND CONTROVERSIES. Washington, DC: National Academy Press. **487**

WILCOXIN, H. C., DRAGOIN, W. B., & KRAL, P. A. (1971). Illness-induced aversions in rat and quail: Relative salience of visual and gustatory cues. SCIENCE, *171*, 823–828. **263**

WILKES, A. L., & KENNEDY, R. A. (1969). Relationship between pausing and retrieval latency in sentences of varying grammatical form. JOURNAL OF EXPERIMENTAL PSYCHOLOGY, *79*, 241–245. **348**

WILKINS, W. (1984). Psychotherapy: The powerful placebo. JOURNAL OF CONSULTING AND CLINICAL PSYCHOLOGY, *52*, 570–573. **698**

WILLIAMS, D. C. (1959). The elimination of tantrum behavior by extinction procedures. JOURNAL OF ABNORMAL AND SOCIAL PSYCHOLOGY, *59*, 269. **267**

WILLIAMS, M. D., & HOLLAN, J. D. (1981). The process of retrieval from very long-term memory. COGNITIVE SCIENCE, *5*, 87–119. **319**

WILLIAMS, R. (1989). THE TRUSTING HEART: GREAT NEWS ABOUT TYPE A BEHAVIOR. New York: Random House. **602**

WILLIAMS, R. B., JR., BAREFOOT, J. C., HANEY, T. L., HARRELL, F. E., BLUMENTHAL, J. A., PRYOR, D. B., & PETERSON, B. (1988). Type A behavior and angiographically documented coronary atherosclerosis in a sample of 2,289 patients. PSYCHOSOMATIC MEDICINE, *50*, 139–152. **601**

WILLIS, S. L. (1985). Towards an educational psychology of the older adult learner: Intellectual and cognitive bases. In J. E. Birren & K. W. Schaie (Eds.), HANDBOOK OF THE PSYCHOLOGY OF AGING (2nd ed.). New York: Van Nostrand Reinhold. **120**

WILLSHAW, D. J. (1981). Holography, associative memory, and inductive generalization. In G. E. Hinton & J. A. Anderson (Eds.), PARALLEL MODELS OF ASSOCIATIVE MEMORY. Hillsdale, NJ: Erlbaum. **305**

WILSON, E. O. (1963). Pheromones. SCIENTIFIC AMERICAN, *208* (5), 100–114. **154**

WILSON, W. R. (1979). Feeling more than we can know: Exposure effects without learning. JOURNAL OF PERSONALITY AND SOCIAL PSYCHOLOGY, *37*, 811–821. **738**

WINCH, R. F., KTSANES, T., & KTSANES, V. (1954). The theory of complementary needs in mate selection: An analytic and descriptive study. AMERICAN SOCIOLOGICAL REVIEW, *29*, 241–249. **740**

WINSON, J. (1990). The meaning of dreams. SCIENTIFIC AMERICAN, *262*, 86–96. **219**

WINTEMUTE, G. J., TERET, S. P., KRAUS, J. F., & WRIGHT, M. W. (1988). The choice of weapons in firearm suicides. AMERICAN JOURNAL OF PUBLIC HEALTH, *18*, 824–826. **638**

WIRTZ, P. W., & HARRELL, A. V. (1987). Effects of postassault exposure to attack-similar stimuli on long-term recovery of victims. JOURNAL OF CONSULTING AND CLINICAL PSYCHOLOGY, *55*, 10–16. **582**

WISNIEWSKI, E. J. & MEDIN, D. L. (1991). Harpoons and longsticks: The interaction of theory and similarity in rule induction. In D. Fisher, M. Pazzani, & P. Langley (Eds.), CONCEPT FORMATION: KNOWLEDGE AND EXPERI-

ENCE IN UNSUPERVISED LEARNING. San Mateo, CA: Morgan-Kaufman. **337**

WOLFE, D. A. (1985). Child-abusive parents: An empirical review and analysis. PSYCHOLOGICAL BULLETIN, *97*, 462–482. **407**

WOLMAN, B. B., DALE, L. A., SCHMEIDLER, G. R., & ULLMAN, M. (Eds.). (1986). HANDBOOK OF PARAPSYCHOLOGY. New York: Van Nostrand & Reinhold. **249**

WONG, D. F., PEARLSON, G. D., TUNE, L. E., YOUNG, C., ROSS, C., VILLEMAGNE, V., DANNALS, R. F., YOUNG, D., PARKER, R., WILSON, A. A., RAVERT, H. T., LINKS, J., MIDHA, K., WAGNER, H.N. & GJEDDE, A. (1989). Update on PET methods for D2 dopamine receptors in schizophrenia and bipolar disorder (Abstract). SCHIZOPHRENIA RESEARCH, *2*, 115. **654**

WONG, D. F., PEARLSON, G. D., TUNE, L. E., YOUNG, C., ROSS, C., VILLEMAGNE, V., DANNALS, R. F., YOUNG, D., PARKER, R., WILSON, A. A., RAVERT, H. T., LINKS, J., MIDHA, K., WAGNER, H. N., & GJEDDE, A. (1986) Positron Emission Tomography reveals elevated D2 dopamine reception in drug-naive schizophrenics. SCIENCE, *234*, 1558–1563. **654**

WOOD, G. (1986). FUNDAMENTALS OF PSYCHOLOGICAL RESEARCH (3rd ed.). Boston: Little, Brown. **30**

WOOD, W., WANG, F. Y. & CHACHERIE, J. G. (1991). Effects of media violence on viewers' aggression in unconstrained social situations. PSYCHOLOGICAL BULLETIN, *109*, 371–383. **445**

WOODRUFF, D. S., & BIRREN, J. E. (1983). AGING: SCIENTIFIC PERSPECTIVES AND SOCIAL ISSUES (2nd ed.). Belmont, CA: Wadsworth. **123**

WOODY, R. H., & ROBERTSON, M. (1988). BECOMING A CLINICAL PSYCHOLOGIST. Madison, CT: International Universities Press. **708**

WORD, C. O., ZANNA, M. P., & COOPER, J. (1974). The nonverbal mediation of self-fulfilling prophecies in interracial interaction. JOURNAL OF EXPERIMENTAL SOCIAL PSYCHOLOGY, *10*, 109–120. **721**

WORLEY, P. F., HELLER, W. A., SNYDER, S. H., & BARABAN, J. M. (1988). Lithium blocks a phosphoinositide-mediated cholinergic response in hippocampal slices. SCIENCE, *239*, 1428–1429. **702**

WORTMAN, C. B., BREHM, J. W.

(1975). Responses to uncontrollable outcomes: An integration of reactance theory and the learned helplessness model. ADVANCES IN EXPERIMENTAL AND SOCIAL PSYCHOLOGY, *8*, 277–236. **587**

WRIGHT, L. (1988). The Type A behavior pattern and coronary artery disease, quest for the active ingredients and the elusive mechanism. AMERICAN PSYCHOLOGIST, *43*, 2–14. **601**

WRIGHT, W. D. (1946). RESEARCHES ON NORMAL AND COLOR DEFECTIVE VISION. London: Henry Kimpton. **140**

WYNNE, L. C., SINGER, M. T., BARTKO, J., & TOOHEY, M. L. (1977). Schizophrenics and their families: Research on parental communication. In J. Tanner (Ed.), DEVELOPMENTS IN PSYCHIATRIC RESEARCH. London: Hodder & Stoughton. **656**

YAGER, T., LAUFER, R., & GALLOPS, M. (1984). Some problems associated with war experience in men of the Vietnam generation. ARCHIVES OF GENERAL PSYCHIATRY, *41*, 327–333. **585**

YALOM, I. D. (1985). THE THEORY AND PRACTICE OF GROUP PSYCHOTHERAPY (3rd ed.). New York: Basic Books. **709**

YARBUS, D. L. (1967) EYE MOVEMENTS AND VISION. New York: Plenum. **184**

YERAGANI, V., BALON, R., & POHL, R. (1989). Lactate infusions in panic disorder patients and normal controls: Autonomic measures and subjective anxiety. ACTA PSYCHIATRICA SCANDINAVICA, *79*, 32–40. **633**

YESAVAGE, J. A., LEIER, V. O., DENARI, M., & HOLLISTER, L. E. (1985). Carry-over effect of marijuana intoxication on aircraft pilot performance: A preliminary report. AMERICAN JOURNAL OF PSYCHIATRY, *142*, 1325–1330. **231**

YOST, W. A., & NIELSON, D. W. (1985). FUNDAMENTALS OF HEARING (2nd ed.). New York: Holt, Rinehart & Winston. **148, 163**

YOUNISS, J., & SMOLLAR, J. (1985). ADOLESCENT RELATIONS WITH MOTHERS, FATHERS, AND FRIENDS. Chicago: University of Chicago Press. **114**

YU, B., ZHANG, W., JING, Q., PENG, R., ZHANG, G., & SIMON, H. A. (1985). STM capacity for Chinese and English language materials. MEMORY AND COGNITION, *13*, 202–207. **293**

ZAJONC, R. B. (1965). Social facilitation. SCIENCE, *149*, 269–274. **750**

ZAJONC, R. B. (1968). Attitudinal effects of mere exposure. JOURNAL OF PERSONALITY AND SOCIAL PSYCHOLOGY,

Monograph Supplement *9* (No. 2), 1–29. **738**

ZAJONC, R. B. (1980). Compresence. In P. B. Paulus (Ed.), PSYCHOLOGY OF GROUP INFLUENCE. Hillsdale, NJ: Erlbaum. **429, 750**

ZAJONC, R. B. (1984). On the primacy of affect. AMERICAN PSYCHOLOGIST, *39*, 117–123. **429**

ZAJONC, R. B., HEINGARTNER, A., & HERMAN, E. M. (1969). Social enhancement and impairment of performance in the cockroach. JOURNAL OF PERSONALITY AND SOCIAL PSYCHOLOGY, *13*, 83–92. **751**

ZAJONC, R. B., MURPHY, S. T., & INGLEHART, M. (1989). Feeling and facial efference: Implications of the vascular theory of emotion. PSYCHOLOGICAL REVIEW, (in press). **429, 434, 435**

ZALUTSKY, R. A., & NICOLL, R. A. (1990). Comparison of two forms of long-term potentiation in single hippocampal neurons. SCIENCE, *248*, 1619–1624. **42**

ZAMANSKY, H. S., & BARTIS, S. P. (1985). The dissociation of an experience: The hidden observer observed. JOURNAL OF ABNORMAL PSYCHOLOGY, *94*, 243–248. **238, 239**

ZIEGLER, H. P., & LEIBOWITZ, H. (1957). Apparent visual size as a function of distance for children and adults. AMERICAN JOURNAL OF PSYCHOLOGY, *70*, 106–109. **196**

ZELAZO, P. R., ZELAZO, N. A., & KOLB, S. (1972). Walking in the newborn. SCIENCE, *176*, 314–315. **74**

ZELNIK, M., & KANTNER, J. (1977). Sexual and contraceptive experience of young unmarried women in the United States, and 1971. FAMILY PLANNING PERSPECTIVES, *9*, 55–71. **113**

ZELNICK, M., & KANTNER, J. (1980). Sexual activity, contraceptive use, and pregnancy among metropolitan-area teenagers: 1971–1979. FAMILY PLANNING PERSPECTIVES, *12*, 230–237. **113**

ZHANG, G., & SIMON, H. A. (1985). STM capacity for Chinese words and idioms: Chunking and acoustical loop hypothesis. MEMORY AND COGNITION, *13*, 193–201. **292**

ZIGLER, E., & BERMAN, W. (1983). Discerning the future of early childhood intervention. AMERICAN PSYCHOLOGIST, *38*, 894–906. **481**

ZILLMANN, D. (1984). CONNECTIONS BETWEEN SEX AND AGGRESSION. Hillsdale, NJ: Erlbaum. **742**

ZILLMANN, D., & BRYANT, J. (1974). Effect of residual excitation on the emotional response to provocation and delayed aggressive behavior. JOURNAL OF PERSONALITY AND SOCIAL PSYCHOLOGY, *30*, 782–791. **423, 742**

ZIMBARDO, P. G. (1970). The human choice: Individuation, reason and order versus deindividuation, impulse and chaos. In W. J. Arnold & D. Levine (Eds.), NEBRASKA SYMPOSIUM ON MOTIVATION (Vol. 16). Lincoln: University of Nebraska Press. **752, 754**

ZOLA-MORGAN, S. M., SQUIRE, L. R., & AMARAL, D. G. (1989). Lesions of the hippocampal formation but not lesions of the fornix or the mamalary nuclei produce long-lasting memory impairments in monkeys. JOURNAL OF NEUROSIENCE, *9*, 898–913. **306**

ZOLA-MORGAN, S. M. & SQUIRE, L. R. (1990). The primate hippocampal formation: Evidence for a time-limited role in memory storage. SCIENCE, *250*, 228–290. **306**

ZUBEK, J. P. (1969). SENSORY DEPRIVATION: FIFTEEN YEARS OF RESEARCH. New York: Appleton-Century Crofts. **411**

ZUCKERMAN, M. (1979a). SENSATION SEEKING: BEYOND THE OPTIMAL LEVEL OF AROUSAL. Hillsdale, NJ: Erlbaum. **411**

ZUKERMAN, M. (1979b). Attribution of success and failure revisited, or: The motivational bias is alive and well in attribution theory. JOURNAL OF PERSONALITY, *47*, 245–287. **644**

ZUCKERMAN, M., & NEEB, M. (1980). Demographic influences in sensation-seeking and expressions of sensation-seeking in religion, smoking and driving habits. PERSONALITY AND INDIVIDUAL DIFFERENCES, *19*, 197–206. **412**

ZURIF, E. B. (1990). Language and the brain. In D. N. Osherson & H. Lasnik (Eds.) AN INVITATION TO COGNITIVE SCIENCE: LANGUAGE (Vol. 1). Cambridge, MA: MIT Press. **346**

ZURIF, E. B. CARAMAZZA, A., MYERSON, R., & GALVIN, J. (1974). Semantic feature representations for normal and aphasic language. BRAIN AND LANGUAGE, *1*, 167–187. **357**

# Index

Page numbers in italics refer to figures; those followed by "t" refer to tables; those followed by "n" refer to notes.

Ability tests: aptitude versus achievement, 451–453, 452; generality versus specificity, 454–455; group differences in test performance, 468–469, 469t; individual versus group tests, 464, 465; and mental abilities, 451–455; perspective on, 482–484; in placement of schoolchildren, 482–483; predictive validity of, 466–470; test scores and academic performance, 466–468, 467; use of, to predict performance, 469–470

Abnormal psychology: antisocial personality, 659–664; anxiety disorders, 624–635; and classification of abnormal behavior, 619–624, 620t–621t; definition of abnormality, 617–618; and definition of normality, 618–619; generalized anxiety disorder, 624–625, 625t; insanity as legal defense, 662–663; and lifetime prevalence rate of selected disorders, 623, 623t; mood disorders, 635–645; obsessive–compulsive disorders, 626–629; panic disorders, 625; personality disorders, 658–664; phobias, 625–626; schizophrenia, 645–658. See also Psychotherapy

Abnormality: behavioral perspective on, 623; biological perspective on, 623; classification of, 619–624, 620t–621t; cognitive perspective on, 623; compared with normality, 618–619; definition of, 617–618; lifetime prevalence rate of, 623, 623t; psychoanalytic perspective on, 623; vulnerability-stress model of, 624

Absolute motion, 172

Absolute thresholds, 128–129, 128, 132, 148, 148

Abstract concepts, and cognitive maps, 279–280

Academic performance, and test scores, 466–468, 467, 469–470

Accommodation, 84

Acetylcholine (ACh), 39–40

ACh. See Acetylcholine (ACh)

Achievement tests, 451–453

Acoustic buffer, 292, 292

Acoustic coding, in short-term memory, 291–292

Acquired Immune Deficiency Syndrome. See AIDS

Acquisition: in classical conditioning, 255–256, 255

ACT. See American College Test (ACT)

ACTH. See Andrenocorticotrophic hormone (ACTH)

Action potential, 37–38

Acuity, visual, 193–195, 194

Acupuncture, 158

Additive mixture, of color, 140–141, 141

ADH. See Antidiuretic hormone (ADH)

Adler, Alfred, 537, 545

Adolescence: alcohol use during, 221–223, 223; college versus family during, 510–511; conflict with parents during, 114–115; development during, 111–116; drug use during, 220; and hormonal control of sexuality, 394–395, 394; identity development during, 115; identity statuses during, 508–510, 509, 510t; personality during, 508–511; physical changes during puberty, 111; pregnancy during, 116–117, 117; psychological effects of puberty, 112–113; sexual development during, 111–113; sexual standards and behavior during, 113–114, 113t

Adolescent growth spurt, 111, 111

Adrenal–cortical system, 588

Adrenal glands, 61

Adrenaline, 61, 588

Adrenocorticotrophic hormone (ACTH), 61, 588, 589

Adulthood: aging years, 118t, 120–121, 120; continuity of personality during, 512–518, 514t; discontinuity in personality during, 519–520; early adulthood, 118t, 119; Erikson's psychosocial stages of, 118t, 119–121; longitudinal studies of personality throughout, 512–513; maladaptive personality patterns in, 515–518; middle adulthood, 118t, 119–120; midlife crisis during, 119–120

Aerobic exercise, 612

Age regression, and hypnosis, 239

Aggregated score, 568

Aggression: in animals, 439–440; behavioral perspective on, 9; biological approach to, 9, 439–441, 534; and children's viewing of television violence, 5, 6, 444–446, 445; cognitive perspective on, 10–11; as drive, 438–441, 442; as emotional reaction, 437–446; expression of, and catharsis, 443–446; frustration–aggression hypothesis, 585; imitation of, 442–443, 442, 443; as learned response, 438, 441–443, 442, 443; reinforcement of, 443; and stress, 585. See also Violence

Aging: as developmental stage, 118t, 120–121, 120; statistics on, 120

Agnosia, 186–187

Agonists, 226

Agoraphobia, 626, 678

AIDS (Acquired Immune Deficiency Syndrome), 113, 117, 225, 228–229, 400

Ainsworth, Mary, 493

Albinism, 63

Alcohol: and alcoholism, 223–224, 223t; blood alcohol concentration, 221, 222; effects of, 221, 222; usage of, 221–223, 223

Alcoholics Anonymous, 691, 691t

Alcoholism, 223–224, 223t

All-or-none principle, 38

Allport, Gordon, 527–528, 545, 553, 566–567

Alpha waves, 212

Altered state of consciousness, 203

Alternate form reliability, 552

Alzheimer's disease, 315

Ambiguous stimulus, 182, *182*
Ambiguous words, 346–347
Ambivalence, 539
American College Test (ACT), 464
American Sign Language (ASL), 355
Ames room, 190–191, *190, 191*
Amino acids, 378–379
Amnesia: anterograde amnesia, 312–313; childhood amnesia, 5, *5*, 8, 312–313, 313; definition of, 312; memory in, 312–314; posthypnotic amnesia, 238–239, *240*; retrograde amnesia, 313; and short-term versus long-term memory, 290; skills and priming in, 314. *See also* Forgetting
Amphetamines, 40, 226–227, 654
Amygdala, 306, 429
Anal personality, 536
Anal stage, of psychosexual development, 535
Androgen, 395, 404
Androgenization, 404
Anger, and stress, 585
Angiotensin, 376
Angular gyrus, 56–57
Angular movement, 160–161
Anorexia nervosa, 5, 389–392
Antagonists, 226
Anterograde amnesia, 312–313
Antianxiety drugs, 699–700
Antidepressant drugs, 642, 701–702
Antidiuretic hormone (ADH), 376
Antipsychotic drugs, 653–654, 700–701
Antisocial personality, 659–666
Anxiety: classical conditioning theory of, 542; "free-floating" anxiety, 625; psychoanalytic theory of, 535, 540, 596–597, 629–630; and stress, 584–585
Anxiety disorders: behavioral perspective on, 630–632; biological perspective on, 633–635; cognitive perspective on, 632–633; generalized anxiety disorder, 624–625, 625t; obsessive-compulsive disorders, 626–629; panic disorders, 625; phobias, 625–626; psychoanalytic perspective on, 629–630
Apathy, and stress, 586–587
Aphasia, 56, 357
Apnea, 214, 216
Aptitude tests, 451–453
Arendt, Hannah, 762
Aristotle, 6
Armed Services Vocational Aptitude Battery (ASVAB), *465*
Arousal: and emotion, 418–422; and lie detection, 424–425
Arousal level, 413
*Art of Love* (Ovid), 742
Articulatory codes, 56
Artificial ears and eyes, 152–153, *153*
Asch, Solomon, 759–761, *760*
ASL. *See* American Sign Language (ASL)
Assertiveness training, 681
Assessment. *See* Psychological tests
Assimilation, 84

Association areas, of brain, *51*, 52
Associative agnosia, 186
Associative learning, 264–265
ASVAB. *See* Armed Services Vocational Aptitude Battery (ASVAB)
Asylums, 667–668
Attachment: ambivalent insecure attachment, 495–496; assessment of, 493–495; avoidant insecure attachment, 494–495; definition of, 493; disorganized attachment, 495; to fathers, 496–497; and infant temperament, 496; of infants to parents, 99–101; and later development, 497–499; secure attachment, 494; and sensitive responsiveness, 495–496; Strange Situation research on, 493–497
Attention: and conjoining features, 186; mood congruence in, 436; role in recognition, 183–186; selective attention, 183–186
Attitudes: and behavior, 732–735; and cognitive dissonance theory, 734–735; consistency of, 726–729; definition of, 725–726; ego-defensive function of, 730–731; functions of, 729–732; instrumental function of, 729–730; knowledge function of, 730; social adjustment function of, 731–732; value-expressive function of, 730
Attraction. *See* Interpersonal attraction
Attributional styles, 598
Attributional theory, 641–642
Auditory area, of brain, 51, *51*
Auditory sense: artificial ears, 152–153, *153*; and components of the ear, 146–148, *147, 148*; decibel ratings of common sounds, 146t; hearing pitch, 149–151, *150*; hearing sound intensity, 148–149, *148*; of infants, 77; minimum stimulus for, 128t; selective listening, 184–185; sound waves, 145–146, *145*; and Weber's constant, 129–130, 130t
Authoritarian parents, 500–501, *501*
Authoritarian personality, 730–732
*Authoritarian Personality* (Adorno), 731
Authoritative parents, 500, *501*
Authority, obedience to, 762–769
Autobiographical memory, 298
Autonomic nervous system, 43, 58, 59, 60, 588, 661
Aversive conditioning, 272–273
Avoidance learning, 273
Avoidant coping strategies, 604

BAC. *See* Blood alcohol concentration (BAC)
Baldness, 63
Barbiturates, 221
Base–rate rule, 342
Basilar membrane, 147, 148
Beck, Aaron, 641, 641t, 642ʼ
Beers, Clifford, 668–669
Behavior, and attitudes, 732–735
Behavior rehearsal, 680–681

Behavior therapies: assertiveness training, 682; behavior rehearsal, 680–681; modeling, 680; self-regulation, 682, 683t, 684; for stress management, 611–612; systematic desensitization and exposure, 678–679; systematic reinforcement, 679; techniques of, 676–678
Behavioral coping strategies, 603
Behavioral medicine, 591
Behavioral perspective: on abnormality, 623; on anxiety disorders, 630–632; on depression, 640; on psychology, 6, 9–10; on stress, 597
Behaviorism, 9–10, 203–204
Békésy, Georg von, 150–151
Belief-driven learning, 284
Bem, Daryl, 723
Benzodiazepines, 635, 699–700
Binet, Alfred, 84, 458–460, 470
Binocular disparity, 169
Binocular parallax, 169
Biofeedback training, 611
Biogenic amines, 642
Biological constraints: on classical conditioning, 262–263, 263t; on operant conditioning, 275–278
Biological perspective: on abnormality, 623; on aggression, 439–441; on antisocial personality, 661; on anxiety disorders, 633–635; autonomic nervous system, 58–60; brain asymmetries, 52–58; brain structure, 44–48; cerebral hemispheres, 48–52; endocrine system, 60–61; genetic influences on behavior, 62–67; on homosexuality, 402–403; on maternal behavior, 407–409; on mood disorders, 642–644; nervous system components, 35–42; nervous system organization, 42–43; on psychology, 6, 7–9, 12; on schizophrenia, 651–655, *652*. *See also* Brain; Genetics
Biological psychology, *22*
Biological therapies: electroconvulsive therapy, 702–703; psychotherapeutic drugs, 642, 653–654, 699–702; underlying assumptions of, 698
Bipolar cells, 137
Bipolar disorders, 637–638, 642
Blind spot, *136*
Blocking, 260, 260t
Blood alcohol concentration (BAC), 221, *222*
Body image, 390–391, *390, 391*
Body movement, and orientation, 160–161
Body senses: kinesthesis, 160; orientation and body movement, 160–161
Bottom processes, 322–323
Bottom-up processes, 181
Bowlby, John, 493
Brain: and anxiety, 634–635, *634*; association areas of, *51*, 52; asymmetries of, 52–58, *53, 54, 57*; auditory area of, 51, *51*; and biological perspective on psychology, 7–9; central core of, 44–45, *44*;

concentric layers of, *44*; cortical areas and their functions, 50–52, *51*; and emotional expressions, 434–435; and facial expressions, 432–433; feature detectors in, 174–175, *174*; hemispheres of, 4, *4*, 8, 48–58, *49*, *51*, *53*, *54*, 432–433; and hunger, 380–382; and language, 56–57, *57*, 356–357; limbic system of, *44*, 45, 48; motor area of, 50, *51*; picture of living brain, 46–47; and schizophrenia types, 655; and sensory coding, 130–131; sensory inputs to two hemispheres, 53–54, *53*; and sexuality, 396; somatosensory area of, 50–51, *51*; and split-brain perception, 54–55, *54*; structure of, 44–48, *44*, *45*; visual area of, 51, *51*
Brain-scanning techniques, 360
Brightness, of color, 139
Broca's aphasia, 357
Broca's area, *51*, 52, 54, 56, 356
Bulimia, 392–393
Bystander intervention: and definition of situation, 755–756; and diffusion of responsibility, 756–757, *757*; and murder of Kitty Genovese, 754–755; role of helping models in, 757–758; role of information in, 758

CA. *See* Chronological age (CA)
CAI. *See* Computer-assisted instruction
California Psychological Inventory (CPI), 558
Cancer, 612–613
Cannabis, 221t, 230–231
Cannon, Walter, 421
Cardinal dispositions, of personality, 528
Case histories, 22
Castration, 395
Castration anxiety, 536
CAT. *See* Computerized axial tomography (CAT)
Catatonic immobility, 651
Categorization, 332
Catharsis, 443, 444
Cattell, Raymond, 529, *529*, 531, 554–555
Causality, and social beliefs, 722–725
Causality heuristic, 344
Cause-and-effect relations, 19
CCK. *See* Cholecystokinin (CCK)
Central core, of brain, 44–45, *44*
Central dispositions, of personality, 528
Central executive, 292, *292*
Central fissure, 50
Central nervous system, 42
Cerebellum, 44, *44*
Cerebral cortex, 48, 50
Cerebral hemispheres, 4, *4*, 8, 48–58, *49*, *51*, *53*, *54*, 432–433
Cerebrum, 48, *49*, 50
CHD. *See* Coronary heart disease (CHD)
Checking compulsion, 627–628
Chemical castration, 395
Child abuse, 407, 410
Childhood: cognitive development in,

83–97, 85t; daycare during, 498–499; gender identity and sex typing in, 101–111; Head Start programs during, 480–481; language development in, 350–359; and maternal employment, 498–499; moral judgments in, 88–89, 92–93; parental childrearing practices during, 499–502, 507–508, 507t; personality development during, 489–508; social development in, 97–111. *See also* Infants
Childhood amnesia, 5, *5*, 8, 312–313, *313*
Childrearing, 267, 499–502, 507–508, 507t, 546–547. *See also* Parents
Chlorpromazine, 41
Cholecystokinin (CCK), 379, 633
Chromosomes, 62, *62*, *63*
Chronological age (CA), 458, 460
Chunking, 293, 317–318, *317*
Cilia, 154, *154*
Circadian rhythm, 210
Clairvoyance, 240
Classical concepts, 333
Classical conditioning: acquisition and extinction of conditioned response, 255–256, *255*; biological constraints on, 262–263, 263t; contiguity and predictability in, 258–260; in different species, 256; and discrimination, 257, *257*; and drug tolerance, 258; emotion and predictability in, 260–261; ethological approach to, 262; experimental variations of, 255–256; of fear, 257–258, 597, 630–632; and generalization, 256, *257*; models of, 261; Pavlov's experiments, 254–255, *255*; of personality, 542; and phobias, 630–632; predictability and cognitive factors in, 258–262, *259*, 260t; reward learning in, 277–278; second-order conditioning, 256–257
Client-centered therapy, 545–546, 685–688, *687*
Clinical psychology, clinical psychologists, 24, 672
Closure, in grouping 167
Cocaine, 40, 227–229, *228*
Cochlea, 147, *147*
Cochlea implant, 152–153, *153*
Cocktail party phenomenon, 185
Codeine, 224
Coefficient of correlation, 17–18, *18*, 456
Cognition, and emotion, 422–428. *See also* Mental abilities; Thought; and headings beginning with Cognitive
Cognitive appraisals, 422–423, 427–428
Cognitive behavior therapy, 612–613, 683–685, 685t
Cognitive consistency, 726
Cognitive coping strategies, 603
Cognitive development: in childhood, 83–97, 85t; evaluation of Piaget's cognitive stages, 90–93; information-processing approaches to, 94; knowledge-acquisition approaches to, 94–96; moral

development, 88–89; Piaget's stage theory of, 83–90, 85t; sociocultural approaches to, 97
Cognitive–developmental theory, of gender identity, 104–109;
Cognitive dissonance theory, 723, 734–735
Cognitive economy, 331–332
Cognitive impairment, and stress, 587
Cognitive maps, and abstract concepts, 279–280
Cognitive models of classical conditioning, 261–262
Cognitive perspective: on abnormality, 623; on anxiety disorders, 632–633; on depression, 641–642, 641t; on gender identity, 104–109; on psychology, 6, 10–11
Cognitive response theory of persuasion, 773–777
Cognitive science, 26, *26*
Cognitive skills, and amnesia, 314
Cognitive techniques, of stress management, 612–613
Cognitive triad, 641, 642
Cold receptors, 158
Colds, and stress, 592–593, *593*
Coleridge, Samuel, 361
Color: additive mixture, 140–141, *141*; appearance, 139–140, *139*, *140*; brightness of, 139; color circle, *142*; color solid, 139, *139*; constancy of, 188; deficiency, 141, *143*; hue of, 139; mixture, 140–141, *141*, *142*; opponent–color theory of, 143–144, *144*; saturation of, 139; seeing, 138–145, *139–145*; and solar spectrum, 138–139, *139*; subtractive mixture, 140–141, *141*; theories of color vision, 141–145, *143–145*; two–stage color theory of, 144–145, *145*
Color blindness, 141, *143*
Color constancy, 188
Color opponent cells, 144
Common traits, of personality, 528, 553
Communication: by chimpanzees, 355–359; of emotional expressions, 430–431; and language, 344–349. *See also* Language
Community Mental Health Centers Act, 669–670, 703
Companionate love, 741–744
Comparison process, in intelligence, 475
Complex cells, 174–175
Complex learning: cognitive maps and abstract concepts in, 279–280; insight learning, 280–282; and mental representations, 278–279; prior beliefs in, 282–285
Compulsions, 627, 630
Computer axial tomography (CAT), 654
Computer simulation, 365–367, *367*
Computer–assisted instruction, 16, *16*
Computerized axial tomography (CAT), 46

Concepts: acquisition of, 335–337; combination of, 338–339; development of words and concepts, 350; functions of, 331–332; hierarchies of, 334–335, *334*; linguistic relativity hypothesis of, 338–339; prototypes, 333–334

Concordance rates, 642

Concrete operational stage, of cognitive development, 89

Conditioned fear, 4–5, 9, 257–258, 597, 630–632

Conditioned reinforcers, 268–269

Conditioned response (CR), 255, *255*, 542

Conditioned stimulus (CS), 255–263, 542

Conditioning: classical conditioning, 254–263, 542; in language learning, 352–353; learning by, 8; operant conditioning, 264–278, 541–542; of personality, 541–542; prepared conditioning, 631

Conduction loss, 148

Cones, 135–137, *136*

Conformity to majority, 759–761, *760*

Conjoining features, 186

Conjunction rule, 342

Connectionism, 26

Connectionist models: of memory, 304–305, *304, 305*; of recognition, 176–178, *176–178*

Consciousness: altered state of consciousness, 203; aspects of, 203–206; and controlling, 205; divided consciousness, 207–209; hypnosis, 235–240; introspective method for study of, 203; meditation, 231–235; and monitoring, 204–205; preconscious memories, 205–206; psi phenomena, 240–247; and psychoactive drugs, 219–231; sleep and dreams, 210–219; unconscious, 206

Conservation, 86–87, *87*, 92–93, 95–96, *95*

Conservation of energy, 535

Construct validity, 552

Constructive memory: schemata, 325–326; simple inferences, 323–324; stereotypes, 324–325; and top–down processes, 322–323

Contingency learning, 274–275

Contraceptive use, 116–117

Control group, 16, *16*

Controlling, and consciousness, 205

Copernicus, 537

Coping skills: behavioral strategies of, 603; cognitive strategies of, 603; defense mechanisms as emotion–focused coping, 606–610; distraction strategies of, 604; emotion–focused coping, 602, 603–606; negative avoidant strategies of, 604; problem–focused coping, 602–603; ruminative strategies of, 603, 604–605

Core properties, 335–336

Cornea, of eye, 135, *135*

Coronary heart disease (CHD), 591–592, 601–602

Corpus callosum, 53

Correlation coefficient, 17–18, *18*, 456

Correlational method: cause–and–effect relations in, 19; coefficient of correlation in, 17–18, *18*; naturally occurring differences in, 17; tests in, 18–19

Cortex, 174–175, *174*

Corticotropin–releasing factor (CRF), 61

Counseling psychology, counseling psychologists, 24– 25, 672

Counterconditioning, 678

CPI. *See* California Psychological Inventory (CPI)

CR. *See* Conditioned response (CR)

Crack, 227

Creativity, visual, 361

CRF. *See* Corticotropin–releasing factor (CRF)

Crisis intervention, 704–705

Criterion validity, 552

Criterion measure, 456

Criterion method of test construction, 555

Criterion problem, 552–553

Critical periods: of development, 76, 197; in language learning, 355

*Crowd* (LeBon), 752

CS. *See* Conditioned stimulus (CS)

CT. *See* Computerized axial tomography (CAT)

Cultural influences: on childrearing practices, 507–508, 507t; and incest taboo, 539; on Oedipal conflict, 539–540; on personality, 506–508

Cultural truisms, 775

Curiosity motives, 410–412


Darwin, Charles, 72, 429, 430–431, 457, 537, 543

Data collection: and schemata, 715–718; sources of data, 714; and theories, 718; and vividnes, 714–715

Data–driven learning, 284

Deaf persons, language learning of, 354–355

Decibels, 146, 146t

Decision making, in groups, 778–781

Deductive reasoning, 340–341, *341*

Defense mechanisms, 535, 540, 606–610

Degradation, 39

Deindividuation, 752–754

Deinstitutionalization, 669

Delirium tremens (DTs), 224

Delta waves, 212

Delusions, 623, 648

Delusions of grandeur, 648

Delusions of influence, 648

Delusions of persecution, 648

Demand curves, 276–277, *277*

Dendrites, 36

Denial, 609

Deoxyribonucleic acid (DNA), 62, *63, 64*

Dependent personality disorders, 659

Dependent variable, 14–15

Depolarization, 37

Depressants, 221–224, 221t

Depression: antidepressant drugs for, 642,

701–702; behavioral perspective on, 640; biological perspective on, 643–644; cognitive distortions in, 641, 641t; cognitive perspective on, 641–642, 641t; electroconvulsive therapy for, 306, 703; post–partum depression, 595; psychoanalytic perspective on, 639–640; and stress, 586–587; and suicide, 638–639; symptoms of, 635–637; therapy for, 683–685, 685t; vulnerability to, 644–645

Depth cues, in perception, 168–169, *169*, 189–190, *189*

Depth perception, 169, *170*, 195–196, *195*

Descartes, Rene, 191

Development: adolescent development, 111–116; basic questions about, 71–76; cognitive development in childhood, 83–97, 85t; critical periods of, 76, 197; early sexual development, 404–406; emotional development, 428; Erikson's psychosocial stages, 116–118, 118t, 537; Freud's psychosexual stages, 101–102, 535–536; of language, 350–359; as lifelong process, 116–121; perceptual development, 191–199; of perceptual–motor coordination, 198–199, *198*; rearing with controlled stimulation, 196–199; social development in childhood, 97–111; stages of development, 75–76

Developmental psychology, 23–24

Diabetes, 67 ✓

*Diagnostic and Statistical Manual of Mental Disorders* (DSM–III–R), 620t–621t, 621–623

Diathesis–stress model, 624

Dieting, 387–388

Difference reduction, in problem solving, 362

Difference threshold, 129

Differential reinforcement, 257

Diffusion of responsibility, 756–757, *757*

Direct observation, 19–21

Discrimination: and classical conditioning, 257, *257*; in operant conditioning, 266, 269–270

Discrimination (prejudice), 726

Discriminative stimulus, 267

Disease. *See* Health; and names of specific illnesses

Dishabituation, 77

Displacement, 293–295, *294*, 585, 609–610

Dispositional attribution, 722

Disruption: and emotion, 435–436, *435*

Dissociation, 207–208

Distance: in grouping, 168; perceived distance, 189

Distance perception, 168–170, *169, 170*

Distraction–conflict theory, of social facilitation, 752

Distraction coping strategies, 604

Divided consciousness, 207–209

Dizygotic twins, 65–66, *66. See also* Twin studies

DNA, 62, *63, 64*

Dominant genes, 63–64
Dopamine, 41, 653–654, 700
Dopamine hypothesis, 653–654
Double–blind procedure, 698
Dream analysis, 674–675
Dreams: awareness of being in dream state, 217; content of, 217–219, 674–675; control of content of, 217; differences in dream recall, 216; Freud on, 217–219; and implicit predream suggestion, 217; length of, 216–217; lucid dreams, 217; and posthypnotic predream suggestion, 217; precognitive dreams, 245–246; theories of dream sleep, 218–219
Drive reduction, 413
Drives, 534; aggression as, 438–441, *442*
Drug therapy. *See* Psychotherapeutic drugs
Drug tolerance, 258
Drugs. *See* Psychoactive drugs; Psychotherapeutic drugs
DSM–III–R. *See Diagnostic and Statistical Manual of Mental Disorders* (DSM–III–R)
DTs. *See* Delirium tremens (DTs)
Dual–memory model, 297–298, *297*
Duodenum, 379
Duverney, Joseph Guichard, 150

Ear, structure of, 146–148, *147*, *148*
Eardrum, 147, *147*
Early adulthood: as developmental stage, 118t 119
Early selection, 185
Eating disorders: anorexia, 389–392; bulimia, 392–393. *See also* Obesity
Ebbinghaus, Hermann, 293
Eclectic approach, to psychotherapy, 688, 689t, 690
ECT. *See* Electroconvulsive therapy (ECT)
Educational psychology, 25
EEG. *See* Electroencephalogram (EEG)
Ego, 358, 534, 537, 540, 597, 673
Ego–defensive function, of attitudes, 730–731
Ego defensiveness, 730
Eidetic images, 292, *292*
Elaboration, and encoding, 319
Electroconvulsive therapy (ECT), 306, 702–703
Electroencephalogram (EEG), 57, 211, *211*
Electroshock therapy, 702–703
Emmert's experiment, 189–190, *189*
Emotion: aggression as emotional reaction, 437–446; and arousal, 418–422; blood flow and body temperature in, 434–435; brain localization of facial expressions for, 432–433; clinical implications of cognitive appraisals of, 427–428; and cognition, 422–428; components of, 417–418, 426, *426*; differentiation of, 420–422, *421*, 433–435; dimensions of, 426–427; distinguished from motives,

417; energy and disruption as reaction to, 435–436, *435*; and facial expression, 429–435; and forgetting, 309–311; general reactions to, 435–437; intensity of, 419–420, 433–435; and lie detection, 424–425; and mood congruence in attention and learning, 436; and mood effects in evaluation and estimation, 437; and overeating, 386–387; physiological basis of, 418–419, 419t; precognitive emotions, 429; and predictability, 260–261; "primary" emotions, 426–427, 427t; and spinal cord lesions, 420, *420*; without cognition, 429
Emotion–focused coping, 602, 603–606
Empathy, in therapy, 687
Empirical method of test construction, 555
Empirical validity, 552
Empiricism, 191
Encoding: and elaboration, 319; encoding–retrieval interactions in, 307–309; and imagery, 318; and intelligence, 475; in long–term memory, 299–300; in short–term memory, 291–292; as stage of memory, 289, *289*
Endocrine system, 60–61, *60*
Endorphins, 40, 226, 588
Energy: conservation of, 535; and emotion, 435–436, *435*
Engineering psychology, 25
Enkephalin, 40
Epinephrine, 61, 588
Episodic memory, 316
Erikson, Erik, 116–118, 118t, 508, 537, 545
Escape learning, 273, 276–277
ESP. *See* Extrasensory perception (ESP)
Estimation, and mood effects, 437
Estrogen, 395
Estrous cycle, 396
Ethical issues: in Milgram's obedience experiments, 768–769; in psychological research, 20–21
Ethology, 262, 408–409
Ethyl alcohol, 221
Evaluation, and mood effects, 437
Evocative interaction, between personality and environment, 503
Evocative interaction, to consistency of personality, 569
Evoked potentials, 193
Evolution, theory of, 72
Evolutionary psychology, 26–27
Excitatory connections, in networks, 176, *176*
Exemplar strategy, 336
Exercise: and obesity, *388*
Expectancies: in operant conditioning, 273
Experimental design, 15–16
Experimental group, 16, *16*
Experimental method: control of variables in, 14–15; definition of, 14; experimen-

tal design in, 15–16; measurement in, 16–17
Experimental psychology, *22*
Explicit memory, 290–291
Exploration, as motive, 410–411
Expressive aphasia, 56
Extinction: in classical conditioning, 255–256, *255*; in operant conditioning, 266; and systematic desensitization, 678–679
Extracellular fluid, 376
Extrasensory perception (ESP), 240, 247
Extraversion–introversion, 530
Eye, structure of, 135–137, *135–137*
Eye color, 63
Eye movements, in selective looking, 183–184
Eyesight. *See* Visual sense
Eysenck, Hans, 530, *530*, 531

Facial expression: and emotion, 429–435
Facial feedback hypothesis, 433
Facilitation. *See* Social facilitation
Facilitator interneurons, 265
Factor analysis, 471, 472t, 529
Factor–analytic theories, of personality, 528–531, *529*, *530*, 531t
Factorial approach, to intelligence, 471–474, 472t
Familiarity, and liking, 738
Family therapy, 692–693
Fat cells, 378–379, 385
Fathers, attachment to, 496–497. *See also* Parents
Fear: biological perspective on, 12; cognitive perspective on, 10; conditioned fear, 4–5, 9, 257–258, 597; phobias as anxiety disorders, 625–626; "stranger anxiety" of infants, 98–99, *98*; symptoms of, 419t
Feature detectors, 174–175, *174*
Features: behavioral indicators of, 175, *175*; conjoining features, 186; of natural objects, 179–180, *179*, *180*; recognition of, 174–176, *174*, *175*; relations between, 175–176, *175*
Fechner's law, 130, *130*
Feeding center, in brain, 380
Females. *See* Mothers; Sex differences; Women
*Feminine Mystique* (Friedan), 550
Fertility, 396
Festinger, Leon, 734–735
Fetus: hormones' effect on, 402–405
Fetus, development of, 72–73
FI schedule. *See* Fixed interval (FI) schedule
Fight–or–flight response, 419, 588–589, *589*
Figure–ground organization, *166*, 167
File–drawer problem, 244
Fittest responses, survival of, 266
Fixations, 183, 536
Fixed–action patterns, 408
Fixed interval (FI) schedule, of reinforce-

ment, 271
Fixed ratio (FR) schedule, of reinforcement, 270–271
Flashbulb memories, 309–310
Flooding, 679
Follicle–stimulating hormone (FSH), 395
Follicles, 395
Foreclosure, 508, *509*, 509, 510t
Forgetting: emotional factors in, 309–311; evidence for retrieval failures, 300–301; as function of time, *302*; and interference, 301–302; and long–term memory, 300–303; repression hypothesis of, 311; in short–term memory, 293–295, *294. See also* Amnesia; Memory
Formal operational stage, of cognitive development, 89–90
Fovea, 136–137
FR schedule. *See* Fixed ratio (FR) schedule
Fraternal twins, 65–66, *66. See also* Twin studies
Free association, 533, 674
"Free–floating" anxiety, 625
Free–recall experiment, 297, *297*
Frequency theory, of pitch perception, 149
Freud, Anna, 537
Freud, Sigmund: on aggression, 438; on anxiety, 596–597, 629; on childhood amnesia, 5, 312; cocaine use by, 227–228; dogmatism with colleagues, 536–537; on dreams, 217–219; on ego defensiveness, 730; modifications of theories of, 536–537; office of, *674*; on phobias, 630; picture of, *11*; psychoanalytic techniques of, 673–676; on psychoanalytic theory of personality, 533–538, 543; on psychological factors of mental illness, 668; on repression, 208, 606–607; on stages of psychosexual development, 101–102; on the unconscious, 11, 206
Freudian slips, 206, 533
Friedan, Betty, 550
Fromm, Erich, 537
Frontal association areas, of brain, 52
Frontal lobe, of brain hemispheres, 50
Frustration, 585
Frustration–aggression hypothesis, 438, 585
FSH. *See* Follicle–stimulating hormone (FSH)
Fundamental attribution error, 566, *722–725, 725*, 767
Fuzzy concepts, 333

g factor, in intelligence, 471–472, 531
GABA. *See* Gamma–aminobutyric acid (GABA)
Galton, Sir Francis, 457–458
Galvanic skin response (GSR), *256*, 257, 661
Gamma–aminobutyric acid (GABA), 41
Ganglia, 264

Ganzfeld procedure, 241, *241*
Gardner, Howard, 476–477
Gechner, Gustav, 130
Gender constancy, 105–109
Gender identity: cognitive–developmental theory of, 104–109; definition of, 101; gender schema theory of, 109–111; of hermaphrodites, 405–406; hormones versus environment in, 405–406; and prenatal hormones, 402–403, 404–405; psychoanalytic theory of, 101–102; social learning theory of, 102–104; of transsexuals, 406
Gender schema theory: of gender identity, 109–111
General paresis, 668
Generalization: and classical conditioning, 256, 257; in operant conditioning, 269
Generalized anxiety disorder, 624–625, 625t, 630
Generativity, 119
Genes, 64–64, *64*
Genetics: chromosomes and genes, *62–64*, 62–64; environmental influences on gene action, 67; genetic studies of behavior, 65–66; and intelligence, 478–480, 478t; and interaction between nature and nurture, 72–75; and mood disorders, 642–643; and obesity, 383–386; and schizophrenia, 651–655, *652*; selective breeding, 65, *65*; and twin studies, 65–66, *66*
Genital stage, of psychosexual development, 536
Genotypes, 489
Genovese, Kitty, 754–755
Genuineness, in therapy, 687
Geons, 179–180, *179, 180*
Gestalt psychology, 166–168, *166–168*, 171–172, 175
Gestalt therapy, 689t
Glial cells, 37
Glucose, 378
Glutamate, 41
Glycerol, 379
GMAT. *See* Graduate Management Aptitude Test (GMAT)
Gonadotropin–releasing factors, 394
Gonadotropins, 394–395
Gonads, 394–395
Good continuation, in grouping, 167, *168*
Graduate Management Aptitude Test (GMAT), 466
Graduate Record Examination (GRE), 466
Grain size, 361
Grammatical morphemes, 346
"Gray matter," 48
GRE. *See* Graduate Record Examination (GRE)
Group ability tests, 464, *465*
Group decision making, 778–781
Group polarization, 778–780
Group therapy, 690–691, 691t

Grouping of objects, 167–168, *167, 168*
Groupthink, 780–781, *780*
GSR. *See* Galvanic skin response (GSR)
Gustation, 155–156, *156. See also* Taste

Habituation, 77, 253, 264, *265*
Hair cells, 147
Halfway houses, 704
Hallucinations: and hallucinogens, 229–230; positive and negative hallucinations in hypnosis, 239–240; in schizophrenia, 623, 648–649
Hallucinogens, 221t, 229–230
Handwriting analysis, 554–555
Hartman, Heinz, 676
Hartshorne, 565, 566–567
Hashish, 230
HD. *See* Huntington's disease (HD)
Head Start programs, 480–481
Health: effect on stress on, 591–596; stress and illness, 590–591
Hearing. *See* Auditory sense
Hearing loss, 148
Hearing pitch, 149–151, *150*
Hello–goodbye effect, 694
Helmholtz, Hermann von, 150, 169
Helplessness, learned, 586–587
Hemophilia, 63
Heredity. *See* Genetics
Hering, Ewald, 143, 144
Heritability, 479
Hermaphrodites, 405–406
Heroin, 224–226, *226*
Heuristic theory of persuasion, 776–777
Heuristics, 341, 342–344, 776
Hidden–observer phenomenon, in hypnosis, 238–239
Hierarchy of needs, 547–548, *547*
Hippocampus, 8, 48, 306
Hippocrates, 6, 525, 530, 667
Holmes–Bates stereoscope, *170*
Home sign, 354
Homeostasis, 44, 373–377, *374*
Homosexuality, 45, 400–404, 402t
Honorton, Charles, 241–242
Hormones: and endocrine system, 60–61, *60*; and homosexuality, 402–403; prenatal hormones, 402–405; and sexuality, 394–396, *395*; and thirst, 376; versus environment in sexual development, 405–406
Horney, Karen, 537, 676
House, William, 152
Hue, of color, 139
Human factors engineering, 25
Humanistic psychology, 544–548
Humanistic therapies, 685–688
Hunger: brain mechanisms for, 380–382; as motivation, 377–382; satiety detectors for, 379; variables of, 378–379
Huntington's disease (HD), 63–64, 315–316, 652–653
Hyman, Ray, 241–242
Hypnotherapy, 689t

Hypercomplex cells, 175
Hyperoptic vision, 135
Hypnosis: and age regression, 239; characteristics of hypnotized state, 236–237; control of movement as hypnotic suggestion, 237–238; definition of, 235; Freud's use of, 533; and hidden–observer phenomenon, 238–239; hypnotic suggestions, 237–240; individual differences on hypnotizability, 237, *237*; induction of, 236–237; and positive and negative hallucinations, 239–240; posthypnotic amnesia, 238–239; posthypnotic predream suggestion, 217; posthypnotic response, 238
Hypothalamus, 44–45, *44*, 61, 374–376, 379–382, 385, 396, 418–419, 439, 588

ICSH. *See* Interstitial–cell stimulating hormone (ICSH)
Id, 358, 534, 540, 596–597, 673
Ideal self, 546, 563
Identical twins, 65–66, *66*. *See also* Twin studies
Identification, Freud on, 102
Identity: development during adolescence, 115; Erikson on, 118
Identity achievement, 508–510, *509*, 510t
Identity crisis, 508
Identity diffusion, 508, 509, *509*, 510t
Identity statuses, 508–510, *509*, 510t
Ill–temperedness, 515–518
Illness. *See* Health; and names of specific illnesses
Illness–behavior model, of stress, 596
Illusion, and well–being, 644–645
Illusions, 190–191, *190*, *191*
Imagery: and encoding, 318; and perception, 359–360
Imaginal thought, 359–361
Imitation: of aggression, 442–443, *442*, *443*; and infants, 78–79; in language learning, 352–353
Immune system, 592–595
Immunocompetence, 592
Implicit memory, 290, 311–316
Impossible figures, 184, *185*
Imprinting, 408
Incest taboo, 539
Incus, 147, *148*
Independent variable, 14
Induced–compliance experiment, 723, *723*, 735
Inductive reasoning, 342–344
Indulgent parents, 501, *501*
Industrial psychology, 25
Infants: and attachment, 99–101, 493–499; capacities of newborns, 76–83; cocaine–exposed infants, 228; discrimination by, 192–196; hearing of, 77; and imitation, 78–79; instincts and maternal–infant behavior, 408–409; learning of, 80–82; memory of, 80–82; motor development of, 73–75, *73*; and object permanence, 91–92, *91*; premature infants, 72–73; research methods for study of, 77, 192–193; sleep of, 210; smell as sense of, 80; social behavior of, 97–99, *98*; taste as sense of, 80; temperament of, 82–83, 489, 496; vision of, 78–80, *80*
Inferences, 323–324
Influence. *See* Social influence Information–processing approaches: to cognitive development, 94; to intelligence, 474–477, 475t
Informational influence, 779
Informed consent, in psychological research, 20–21
Inhibitory connections, in network, 177, *177*
Innate releasers, 408, 409
Innateness, 408
Inner ear, 147, *147*
Insanity, as legal defense, 662–663. *See also* Abnormal psychology
Insight, 675, 697
Insomnia, 214
Instincts: and maternal–infant behavior, 408–409
Instrumental function, of attitudes, 729–730
Intellectualization, 609
Intelligence: aspects of, 477–478; componential model of, 475–476, 475t; environmental influences on, 480–482; factorial approach to, 471–474, 472t; genetic influences on, 478–480, 478t; information–processing approach to, 474–477, 475t; multiple intelligences, 476–477; nature of, 470–478; and race, 484–485. *See also* Mental abilities
Intelligence quotient (IQ), 460, *460*, 462, 466, 467, *467*
Intelligence tests: Binet's method of, 458–460; coaching and test sophistication, 466–467; historical background on, 457–458; item selection for, 458–459; as mental–age scale, 458–460; predictive validity of, 466–470; for specific mental abilities, 460–463; Stanford–Binet Intelligence Scale, 459–460, 461t, 463, 466–467; test scores and academic performance, 466–468, *467*; Wechsler Intelligence Scales, 462–463, 462t, *463*, 467
Intensity, changes in, 129–130, *129*, *130*, 130t
Interaural intensity, 149
Interdisciplinary approaches, to psychology, 25–27
Interjudge reliability, 552
Internal consistency, 552
Interneurons, 37
Interpersonal attraction: and familiarity, 738; liking, 736–740; love, 740–744; and marriage, 741; passion through misattribution, 742–743; passionate and companionate love, 741–744; and physical attractiveness, 736–737; and proximity, 737–738; and similarity, 738–740; triangular theory of love, 744, 744t
Interpersonal influence. *See* Social influence
Interpretation, 675
*Interpretation of Dreams* (Freud), 217–218, 533
Interscorer agreement, 552
Interstitial–cell stimulating hormone (ICSH), 395
Interval schedules, of reinforcement, 271–272
Intracellular fluid, 375
Introspections, 7
Introspective method, for study of consciousness, 203
Introversion–extraversion, 530
Investigation, as motive, 410–411
Ion channels, 37
Ion pumps, 37
IQ, 460, *460*, 462, 466, 467, *467*

James, William, 76, 420–421
James–Lange theory, 421, 434
Janet, Pierre, 207–208
Janis, Irving, 780, 781
Jet lag, 210–211
*Journal of Parapsychology*, 241, 244
Jung, Carl, 530, 537, 545
Just noticeable difference, 129, *129*

Kant, Immanual 191
Kelly, George, 548–549, 551, 563–564
Key–word method, 318, 319t
Kibbutzim, 482
Kinesthesis, 160
Knowledge–acquisition approaches, to cognitive development, 94–96
Knowledge function, of attitudes, 730
Kohlberg, Lawrence, 90–91, 90t
Köhler, Wolfgang, 280–282

Language: and brain, 56–57, *57*; brain areas associated with, 356–357; chimpanzees' learning of, 355–359; and communication, 344–349; comprehension of, 345, 348–349, *349*; critical periods in language learning, 355; development of, 75, 350–359; effects of context on comprehension and production, 348–349, *349*; hypothesis testing in language learning, 353–354; innate factors in language learning, 354–355; language units and processes, 345–348; learning processes for, 352–354; levels of, 345, *345*; primitive to complex sentences in, 351–352; production of, 345, 348–349, *349*; properties of, 345; sentence units in, 347–348, *348*; speech sounds in, 345–346; and thought, 338–339; word units in, 346–347; words and concepts, 350
Late selection, 185–186
Latency period, of psychosexual development, 536

Latent content, of dreams, 218
Lateral fissure, 50
Lateral hypothalamus (LH), 380–382
Law of effect, 265–266
Law of large numbers, 344
Law School Admissions Test (LSAT), 466
Learned helplessness, 586–587
Learning: associative learning, 264–265; aversive conditioning, 272–273; avoidance learning, 273; belief–driven learning, 284; by conditioning, 8; classical conditioning, 254–263; cognitive maps and abstract concepts in, 279–280; complex learning, 278–285; computer–assisted instruction, 16, 16; of concepts, 335–337; contingency learning, 274–275; data–driven learning, 284; definition of, 253; escape learning, 273, 276–277; through experience, 336–337; habituation as, 253, 264, 265; of infants, 80–82; insight learning, 280–282; of language, 352–354; mood congruence in, 436; neural basis of elementary learning, 264–265; operant conditioning, 264–278; perspectives on, 253–254; prior beliefs in, 282–285; reward learning, 276–278; sensitization as, 264, 265; state–dependent learning, 309; types of, 253; vicarious learning, 441
LeBon, Gustave, 752
Left hemisphere of brain, 50, 53, 55–58. See also Cerebral hemispheres
Lens, of eye, 135, 135
Lesbians, 402, 403–404
Levels of analysis, 26
LH. See Lateral hypothalamus (LH); Luteinizing hormone
LH syndrome, 380–382
Libido, 535
Lie–detector test, 424–425
Life Events Scale, 580t, 581
Light: adaptation to, 137–138, 138; seeing, 137–138, 138; sensitivity to, 137, 137; and vision, 134–135
Lightness constancy, 187–188
Liking: and familiarity, 738; love and, 740–741; and physical attractiveness, 736–737; and proximity, 737–738; and similarity, 738–740
Limbic system, 44, 45, 48, 419, 653
Linear movement, 160
Linear perspective, 168, 169
Listening. See Auditory sense
Lithium, 41
Localization: definition of, 165; distance perception, 168–170, 169, 170; figure–ground organization, 166, 167; grouping of objects, 167–168, 167, 168; motion perception, 170–173, 171, 173; segregation of objects, 166–168, 166–168
Location constancy, 188–189
Lock–and–key action, 38
Locke, John, 72, 191
Logical rules, 340, 342

Long–term memory: and addition of meaningful connections, 299–300; and context, 308–309, 308; definition of, 298; emotional factors in forgetting, 309–311; encoding in, 299–300; encoding–retrieval interactions in, 307–309; and organization, 307–308, 307; retrieval in, 300–303; storage in, 306; transfer from short–term memory to, 297–298; versus short–term memory, 290
Long–term potentiation (LTP), 41–42, 42
Longitudinal studies, of personality, 512–513
Love: infatuated love, 744; liking and, 740–741; and marriage, 741; passion through misatribution, 742–743; passionate and companionate love, 741–744; romantic love, 741, 744
LSAT. See Law School Admissions Test (LSAT)
LSD, 41, 229
LTP. See Long–term potentiation (LTP)
Lucid dreams, 217
Lunch–line effect, 205
Luteinizing hormone (LH), 395

MA. See Mental age (MA)
Magnetic resonance imaging (MRI), 46–47
Majority, conformity to, 759–761, 760
Males. See Fathers; Men; Sex differences
Malinowski, Bronislaw, 539–540
Malleus, 147, 148
Manic–depression, 637
Manifest content, of dreams, 218
Manipulation, as motive, 410–411
Mantra, 233
MAO inhibitors, 642
Marijuana, 15, 15, 221t, 230–233
Marital therapy, 692
Marriage, and love, 741
Maslow, Abraham, 547–548, 547, 550–551
Maternal behavior. See Mothers
Matramudra, 233
Maturation, 72
MCAT. See Medical College Admissions Test (MCAT)
McGuire, William, 774–775
Mean, in statistics, 16
Means–ends analysis, in problem solving, 362
Measurement, in the experimental method, 16–17
Mechanisms of defense, 535, 540
Medical College Admissions Test (MCAT), 456, 466
Meditation: concentrative meditation, 232; definition of, 231; effects of, 234–235; opening–up meditation, 232; for relaxation, 233–234; traditional forms of, 232–233
Medulla, 44
Memory: in amnesia, 312–314; and practicing retrieval, 321, 321; autobiographi-

cal memory, 298; biological approach to, 8; and childhood amnesia, 5, 5; chunking and memory span, 317–318, 317; connectionist models of, 304–305, 304, 305; constructive memory, 322–326; context and retrieval, 319; dual–memory model, 297–298, 297; elaboration and encoding, 319; encoding stage of, 289, 289; episodic memory, 316; explicit memory, 290–291; flashbulb memories, 309–310; imagery and encoding, 318; implicit memory, 290, 311–316; of infants, 80–82; long–term memory, 290, 298–311; and marijuana, 15, 15; of meaning of message, 13; and organization, 319–320, 320; PQRST method for, 321–322; preconscious memories, 205–206; repressed memories, 208; retrieval stage of, 289, 289; semantic memory, 316; short–term memory, 290, 291–298; stages of, 289, 289; storage stage of, 289, 289; techniques for improvement of, 317–322; transfer from short–term memory to long–term memory, 297–298; types of, 290–291
Memory list, 295
Memory span, 293, 317–318, 317
Men, ill–tempered, 516–518
Menarche, 111
Menopause, 396
Mental abilities: and ability tests, 451–455; aptitude versus achievement in testing, 451–453, 452; generality versus specificity in testing, 454–455; group tests for, 464, 465; nature of intelligence, 470–478; predictive validity of tests of, 466–470; primary mental abilities, 473, 474t, 531; sex differences in, 470–471; testing for specific mental abilities, 460–463; tests of intellectual ability, 457–466. See also Intelligence; Thought; and headings beginning with Cognitive
Mental age (MA), 458, 460, 466
Mental computation, 26
Mental disorders. See Abnormal psychology; and specific abnormalities
Mental health: community mental health centers, 669–670, 703; community resources for, 704–705; and crisis intervention, 704–705; enhancement of, 703–707; paraprofessionals for, 705; promotion of own emotional well–being, 705–707
Mental hospitals, 669–671, 670
Mental medium, 361
Mental model, 341
Mental practice, 321, 321
Mental representations, 26, 86, 278–279
Mental rotation, 360, 360, 361
Meta–analysis, 242
Metabolic rate, 386
Methadone, 226, 226
Method of loci, 318
Middle adulthood, as developmental

stage, 118t, 119–120
Middle ear, 147, *147*, *148*
Midlife crisis, 119–120
Milgram, Stanley, 762–769
*Mind That Found Itself* (Beers), 668–669
Mindguards, 781
Minimal risk, in psychological research, 20
Minnesota Multiphasic Personality Inventory (MMPI), 555–558, 556t *557*
Minority, persuasive influence of, 771–773
Misbehavior, in operant conditioning, 275
Mischel, Walter, 565
MMPI. *See* Minnesota Multiphasic Personality Inventory (MMPI)
M'Naghten Rule, 662
Mnemonic systems, 318, *318*
Modeling, 441–443, 680, 757–758
Molecular psychology, 40–41
Monamine oxidase (MAO) inhibitors, 701
Monitoring, and consciousness, 204–205
Monoamine oxidase (MAO) inhibitors, 642
Monozygotic twins, 65–66, *66*. *See also* Twin studies
Montaigne, Michel de, 565
Mood. *See* Emotion
Mood congruence, 436
Mood disorders: behavioral perspective on, 640; biological perspective on, 642–644; bipolar disorders, 637–638; cognitive perspective on, 641–642; definition of, 635; depression, 635–637; psychoanalytic perspective on, 639–640; and vulnerability and stress, 644–645
Moral development, 88–89, 92–93
Moral realism, 89
Moral reasoning, stages of, 90–91, 90t
Moratorium, 508, 509, *509*, 510t
Morpheme, 346–347
Morphine, 224
Mothers: biological determinants of maternal behavior, 407–409; employment of, 498–499; environmental determinants of maternal behavior, 409–410; infants' attachment to, 99–101, 493–499; infants' social behavior toward, 97–99, *98*; instincts and maternal–infant behavior, 408–409; maternal behavior of, 407–410
Motion: absolute motion, 172; and event perception, 173, *173*; in grouping, 168; induced motion, 171–172; perception of, 170–173, *171*, *173*; real motion, 172–173; relative motion, 172; stroboscopic motion, 171, *171*
Motion after–effect, 172
Motion parallax, 168
Motivation: adult sexuality, 393–404; common principles for different motives, 413; curiosity motives, 410–412; distinguished from emotion, 417; exploration and manipulation as, 410–411; hunger, 377–382; maternal behavior as, 407–410; obesity and anorexia, 382–393;

sensory stimulation as, 411–412; survival motives and homeostasis, 373–377; temperature regulation, 374–375; thirst, 375–377
Motor area, of brain, 50, *51*
Motor development: of infants 73–75, *73*; and perceptual–motor coordination, 198–199, *198*
Motor neurons, 37
Motor skills, and amnesia, 314
MRI. *See* Magnetic resonance imaging (MRI)
Müller, Johannes, 134
Multiple intelligences, 476–477
Multiple personality, 208–209, *208*
Multiple sclerosis, 38
Multivariate experiments, 16
Munsell, Albert, 139
Munsell system, of color, 139
Myelin sheath, 38
Myopic vision, 135

Naltrexone, 226, *226*
Narcissistic personality disorder, 659
Narcolepsy, 214
Narcotics. *See* Opiates
Nasal cavity, 154, *154*
Nativism, 191
Natural object recognition, 179–183, *179–183*
Nature and nurture, interaction between, 72–75
NE. *See* Norepinephrine (NE)
Needs, hierarchy of, 547–548, *547*
Negative avoidant coping strategies, 604
Negative hallucinations, 239–240
Neglecting parents, 501–502, *501*
Nerves, 37
Nervous system: action potentials, 37–38; autonomic system, 43, 58, *59*, 60, 588, 661; central nervous system, 42; components of, 35–42, *36–39*, *42*; neurons and nerves in, 35–37, *36*, *37*; neurotransmitters and neuroreceptors, 39–42, *42*; organization of, 42–43; parasympathetic nervous system, 58, 418; peripheral nervous system, 42–43; somatic system, 43; sympathetic nervous system, 58, 418, 588; synaptic transmission, 38–39, *38*, *39*; underreactive autonomic nervous system, 661. *See also* Brain
Networks: augmented networks of recognition, 177, *177*; simple networks in recognition, 176–177, *167*; with top–down activation for recognition, 177–178, *178*
Neurobiology, 8
Neurons, 8, 35–37, *36*, *37*, 130
Neuroreceptors, 38, 41–42, *42*
Neuroses, 622
Neurotic anxiety, 596, 629
Neuroticism, 530
Neurotransmitters, 36, *38*, 39–42, *42*, 61, 226, 265, 434, 634, 642–643, 703

Newborns. *See* Infants
Nigrostriatal bundle, 382
NMDA receptors, 41–42, *42*
Non–REM sleep, 212–213, 219
Nonconscious–conscious continuum, 206
Nondirective therapy, 685–688
Noradrenaline, 61
Norepinephrine (NE), 40–41, 61, 588, 642–643, 701, 703
Normal distribution curve, 460, *460*
Normality, definition of, 618–619
Normative influence, 779
Nose. *See* Smell
Noun phrases, 347
NREM sleep, 212–213, 219
Nuclear magnetic resonance, 46–47
Null results, 244
Nurture and nature, interaction between, 72–75

Obedience to authority, 762–769
Obesity, 5, 9, 10, 382–389, *387–389*
Object permanence, 86, *86*, 90–92, *91*
Object recognition, 179–183, *179–183*
Object relations theory, 537
Objective anxiety, 596, 629
Observational method: case histories, 22; direct observation in, 19–21; survey method, 21
Obsessions, 626–627, 630, 632
Obsessive–compulsive disorders, 626–629, 630, 632–633, 635
Obsessive–compulsive personality, 629
Occipital lobe, of brain hemispheres, 50
Odor. *See* Smell
Oedipal conflict, 102, 536, 539, 606, 630
Olfaction: evolutionary significance of, 151–154; olfactory system, 154, *154*; sensing intensity and quality, 155. *See also* Smell
Olfactory bulb, 154, *154*
Operant conditioning: aversive conditioning, 272–273; biological constraints on, 275–278; and child rearing, 267; contiguity versus control in, 274; contingency learning in, 274–275; control and cognitive factors in, 274–275; definition of, 264–265; and demand curves, 276–277, *277*; discrimination in, 269–270 269–270; economics of reward in, 276–277, *277*; escape and avoidance, 273; expectancies in, 273; experimental variations in, 266–267; generalization in, 269; and law of effect, 265–266; and misbehavior, 275; of personality, 541–542; punishment in, 272–273; reinforcement in, 268–272, *271*, 276–277, *277*; response–reinforcer constraints on, 275–278; schedules of reinforcement in, 270–272, *271*; shaping in, 267–268, *267*, *268*; Skinner's experiments, 266–267; Thorndike's experiments, 265–266
Operational stages, of cognitive development, 85t, 89–90

Opiates, 40, 221t, 224–226, *225, 226*
Opinion molecules, 728–729
Opioid receptors, 226
Opium, 224
Opponent–color theory, 143–144, *144*
Optic nerve, 137
Oral personality, 536
Oral stage, of psychosexual development, 535
Organizational psychology, 25
Orientation, and body movement, 160–161
Osmoreceptors, 376, 377
Osmosis, 376
Outer ear, 147, *147*
Outline of Psychoanalysis (Freud), 533
Oval window, 147, *148*
Overeating, and obesity, 386–387
Ovid, 742
Ovulation, 396

PACE. *See* Professional and Administrative Career Examination (PACE)
Pain: gate control theory of, 160; phasic pain, 158; as sensory process, 158–159, *159*; tonic pain, 158
Panic disorders, 625. *See also* Anxiety disorders
Parallel processing, 177
Paranoid, 648
Paraphilias, 398–399
Paraprofessionals, in mental health, 705
Parapsychology, 240–247
Parasympathetic nervous system, 58, 418
Parents: attachment of infants to, 99–101, 493–499; authoritarian, 500–501, *501*; authoritative, 500, *501*; childrearing practices of, 499–502, 507–508, 507t; conflict with adolescents, 114–115; and gender identity of children, 102–104; indulgent, 501, *501*; infants' social behavior toward, 97–99, *98*; as influence on antisocial personality, 661–664; as influence on schizophrenia, 656–657; neglecting, 501–502, *501*; and Rogers's unconditional positive regard, 546–547; teenage parents, 116–117. *See also* Mothers
Parietal lobe, of brain hemispheres, 50
Parkinson's disease, 382
Partial reinforcement, 270
Partial–reinforcement effect, 270
Passionate love, 741–744
Path analysis, 517, *517*
*Pattern and Growth in Personality* (Allport), 527
Pattern completion, 305
Pattern recognition, 165
Pavlov, Ivan, 254–255, *254*, 543, 668
PCP, 229–230
Peak experience, 548
Perceived distance, 189
Perception: and absence of stimulation, 196–197; and amnesia, 314; and con-

stancies, 187–191, 196; and controlled stimulation, 196–199; definition of, 127; of depth, 195–196, *195*; depth cues in, 168–169, *169*; development of, 191–199; discrimination by infants, 192–196; of distance, 168–170, *169, 170*; figure–ground organization, *166*, 167; of forms, 193–195; functions of, 165–166; grouping of objects, 167–168, *167, 168*; and imagery, 359–360; of letters and words, 178, *178*; and limited stimulation, 197, *197*; localization, 166–173; of motion, 170–173, *171, 173*; perceptual–motor coordination, 198–199, *198*; recognition, 173–187; segregation of objects, 166–168, *166–168*
Perceptual constancies: lightness and color constancy, 187–188
Peripheral nervous system, 42–43
Permission rule, 341
Personal construct theory, 548–549
Personal constructs, 548
Personal dispositions, of personality, 528, 553
Personality: during adolescence, 508–511; during adulthood, 511–520; aggregation solution to consistency paradox of, 568; assessment of, 551–561; and attachment, 493–499; California Psychological Inventory, 558; during childhood, 489–508; consistency paradox of, 564–570; continuity of, during adulthood, 512–518, 514t; cultural influences on, 506–508; definition of, 489, 525; discontinuity in, 519–520; environmental influences on, during childhood 493–502; evocative interaction with environment, 503; genetic influences on, during childhood, 489–492; genotype–environment correlation in, 502–503; in humanistic psychology, 544–548; and identity statuses, 508–510, *509*, 510t; interaction solution to consistency paradox of, 569–570; interactions with environment, during childhood, 502–506; longitudinal studies of, 512–513; maladaptive personality patterns, 515–518; and parental childrearing practices, 499–502; person–centered solution to consistency paradox of, 566–567; personal construct theory of, 548–549; phenomenological approach to, 544–551; phenomenological assessment of, 562–564; proactive interaction with environment, 504; psychoanalytic approach to, 533–540; psychoanalytic assessment of, 558–561; reactive interaction with environment, 503; social–learning assessment of, 561–562; social–learning approach to, 540–544; and stress, 597–602; trait approach to, 525–533; trait assessment of, 553–558; Type A pattern, 599–602, 600t, 613–614; type theories of, 525–526

*Personality* (Allport), 527
Personality assessment: computer software for handwriting analysis, 554–555; general considerations on, 551–553; Minnesota Multiphasic Personality Inventory, 555–558, 556t, *557*; personality inventories, 554–555; personality ratings, 553; phenomenological assessment, 562–564; psychoanalytic assessment, 558–561; Q sort, 553–554, 562–563; reliability of, 552; *Role Construct Repertory Test*, 563–564, *564*; Rorschach Test, 558, 558–559, *559*, 561; Sixteen Personality Factor Questionnaire, 554–555; social–earning assessment, 561–562; and testimonial validity, 554–555; Thematic Apperception Test, 560–561, *560, 561*; trait assessment, 553–558; validity of, 552–553
Personality disorders, 658–664
Personality inventories, 554–555
Personality psychology, 24
Personality ratings, 553
Personality types, 525–526
Persuasion: central versus peripheral routes of, 776–777; cognitive response theory of, 773–777; and forewarning, 775; heuristic theory of, 776–777; inoculation against, 774–775; one–sided versus two– sided communication in, 774; persuasive influence of minorities, 771–773; and practical applications, 775–776
PET. *See* Positron emission tomography (PET)
Pettigrew, Thomas, 732
Phallic stage, of psychosexual development, 102, 535
Phasic pain, 158
Phenomenological approach to personality: evaluation of, 550–551; humanistic psychology, 544–548; personal construct theory, 548–549; portrait of human personality in, 549–550
Phenomenological assessment of personality, 562–564
Phenomenological perspective, on psychology, 6, 11–12
Phenomenology, 11–12, 544
Phenothiazines, 700
Phenylketonuria (PKU), 63, 652–653
Pheromones, 153
Phobias, 625–626, 630–632, *630*; therapy for, 678–679, *680*. *See also* Fear
Phonemes, 345–346, 350
Photoreceptors, 137
Physical attractiveness, 736–737
Physical dependence, on psychoactive drugs, 220
Physiological psychology, 22
Physiology, 6
Piaget, Jean, 83–93, 85t, 411
Picrotoxin, 41
Pictorial cues, 168, *169*

Pinel, Philippe, 667
Pitch and frequency, 149–151, *150*
Pituitary gland, 61, 588
PK. *See* Psychokinesis (PK)
PKU, 63
Place theory, of pitch perception, 150–151
Placebo response, 698–699
Placebos, 698
Plato, 6
Pleasure principle, 534
Pluralistic ignorance, 755
Poison ivy susceptibility, 63
Polygenic traits, 65
Polygraph, 424–425, *424, 425*
Pop-out effect, 175
Population, 479
Positive hallucinations, 239–240
Positive regard, unconditional, 546–547
Positron emission tomography (PET), 47, 654
Positrons, 47
Post-partum depression, 595
Post-traumatic stress disorder, 584–585
Posterior association areas, of brain, 52
Posthypnotic amnesia, 238–239, *240*
Posthypnotic predream suggestion, 217
Posthypnotic response, 238
Power of situations, 767–768
PQRST method, 321–322
Pragmatic rules, 341
Precognition, 240
Precognitive dreams, 245–246
Precognitive emotions, 429
Preconscious memories, 205–206
Preferential looking method, 192–193
Pregnancy: cocaine use during, 228; teenage pregnancy, 116–117, *117*
Prejudice, 726, 730–731
Prenatal hormones, 402–403, 404–405
Preoperational stage, of cognitive development, 85t, 86–88
Preoptic area, of hypothalamus, 376
Prepared conditioning, 631
Pressure, 157–158, *157*
Primacy effect, 717, *717*
Primary mental abilities, 473, 474t, 531
Priming, 314
Prior beliefs, in complex learning, 282–285
Privacy rights, in psychological research, 21
Proactive interaction, between personality and environment, 504
Proactive interaction, to consistency of personality, 569–570
Probability, 343
Problem-focused coping, 602–603
Problem solving: computer simulation of, 365–367, *367*; definition of, 361–362; experts versus novices in, 364–365; and representing the problem, 363–364; strategies for, 362–363
Professional and Administrative Career Examination (PACE), 464

Projection, 609
Projective tests, 558–561
Prosopagnosic, 432–433
Prostheses, 152–153
Prototypes, 333–334, 335–336
Proximity: in grouping, 167, *167*; and liking, 737–738
Psi phenomena: anecdotal evidence for, 245–246; debate over evidence for, 241–244; definition of, 240; experimental evidence for, 241; file-drawer problem in research on, 244; inadequate controls in research on, 243–244; replication problem in research on, 242–243; skepticism about, 246–247; types of, 240
Psychedelics. *See* Hallucinogens
Psychiatric nurses, 673
Psychiatric social workers, 672–673
Psychiatrists, 672
Psychoactive drugs: adolescents' use of, *220*; amphetamines, 226–227; biochemical effects of, 220; and brain chemistry, 40–41; cannabis, 221t, 230–231; cocaine, 227–229, *228*; depressants, 221–224, 221t; drug dependence, 232–233; and drug tolerance, 258; and drug-abuse medications, 226, *226*; hallucinogens, 221t, 229–230; history of use of, 219–220; LSD, 229; marijuana, 230–231; opiates, 221t, 224–226, *225, 226*; PCP, 229–230; stimulants, 221t, 226–229, *228*; and withdrawal symptoms, 220
Psychoanalysis, 673–676
Psychoanalysts, 672
Psychoanalytic assessment: problems with projective tests, 561; projective tests in, 558–559; Rorschach Test, 558–559, *558, 559*, 561; Thematic Apperception Test, 560–561, *560*, 516
Psychoanalytic theory: of abnormality, 623; of aggression, 438–441, *442*; of anxiety disorders, 629–630; of depression, 639–640; evaluation of, 539–540; Freud's approach, 533–538; of gender identity, 101–102; modification's of Freud's theories, 536–537; of personality, 533–540; personality development in, 535–536; personality dynamics in, 535; personality structure in, 534; portrait of human personality, 537–538; in psychology, 6, 11; of stress, 596–597; unconscious in, 11, 206
Psychoanalytic therapies, 676
Psychoimmunology, 592
Psychokinesis (PK), 240
Psychological dependence, on psychoactive drugs, 220
Psychological determinism, 533
Psychological development. *See* Development
Psychological tests: ability tests, 451–455; aptitude versus achievement, 451–453, *452*; characteristics of a good test, 455–457; coaching and test sophistication, 466–467; and correlational method,

18–19; generality versus specificity, 454–455; group tests, 464, *465*; personality assessment, 551–561; phenomenological assessment, 562–564; psychoanalytic assessment, 558–561; reliability of, 455–456, 552; social-learning assessment of personality, 561–562; for specific mental abilities, 460–463; trait assessment, 553–558; uniform procedure for, 457; validity of, 456, 552–553. *See also* Ability tests; Intelligence tests; Personality assessment
Psychologists, 672
Psychology: behavioral perspective on, 6, 9–10; biological perspective on, 6, 7–9, 12; cognitive perspective on, 6, 10–11; correlational method in, 17–19; definition of, 4, 13; employment settings for, 23t; ethical issues in research, 20–21; experimental method in, 14–17; interdisciplinary approaches to, 25–27; methods of, 13–22; observational method in, 19–22; origins on psychological perspectives, 6–7; perspectives in, 6–13, 7; phenomenological perspective on, 6, 11–12; psychoanalytic perspective on, 6, 11; scope of, 4–5; specializations within, 22–25, 23t–24t; women in, 24t. *See also* Abnormal psychology; Biological perspective; Personality; Social psychology; and specific psychological concepts
*Psychopathology of Everyday Life* (Freud), 533
Psychophysical methods, 128
Psychoses, 622
Psychosexual development, stages of, 101–102, 535
Psychosocial stages, 116–118, 118t, 537
Psychosomatic disorders, 590–591
Psychotherapeutic drugs, 642, 653–654, 699–702
Psychotherapy: behavior therapies, 676–683; client-centered therapy, 545–546, 685–688, *687*; cognitive behavior therapies, 612–613, 683–685, 685t; common factors in psychotherapies, 695–698; comparison of psychotherapies, 695; definition of, 673; eclectic approach to, 688, 689t, 690; effectiveness of, 693–698; and enhancement of mental health, 703–707; evaluation of, 693–695; Gestalt therapy, 689t; group therapy, 690–691, 691t; historical background on, 667–673; humanistic therapies, 685–688; hypnotherapy, 689t; marital and family therapy, 692–693; nondirective therapy, 685–688; and placebo response, 698–699; professions involved in, 671–673; psychoanalysis, 673–676; psychoanalytic therapies, 676; rational-emotive therapy, 689t; reality therapy, 689t; transactional analysis, 689t
Psychotic behavior, 623
Psychoticism, 530

Puberty, 111–113, 394–395, *394. See also* Adolescence
Punishment: of aggression, 443; definition of, 272n; in operant conditioning, 272–273
Pupil, of eye, 135, *135*

Q sort, 512–513, 553–554, 562–563

Race, and intelligence, 484–485
Rap centers, 704
Rape, 582–583
Rapid eye movement (REM) sleep, 212–213, 216, 218–219
Rate of response, 267
Ratio schedules, of reinforcement, 270
Rational–emotive therapy, 689t
Rational method of test construction, 555
Rationalization, 607–608
Reaction formation, 539, 608
Reactive interaction, between personality and environment, 503
Reactive interaction, to consistency of personality, 569
Real motion, 172–173
Real self, 563
Reality principle, 534
Reality therapy, 689t
Reasoning: deductive reasoning, 340–341, *341*; definition of, 339–340; inductive reasoning, 342–344
Rebellion, 768–771
Receiver–operating–characteristic curve (ROC curve), 133, *133*
Receptive aphasia, 56
Receptors, 36–37
Recessive genes, 63–64
Recognition: and augmented networks, 177, *177*; breakdown of, 186–187; early stages of, 174–176, *174, 175*; of features, 174–176, *174, 175*; as function of perception, 173; matching stage and connectionist models of, 176–178, *176–178*; of natural objects and top–down processing, *179–183*, 179–183; and networks with top–down activation, 177–178, *178*; pattern recognition, 165; role of attention in, 183–186; and simple networks, 176–177, *177*
Recovery, Inc., 691, 691t
Reduced stimulation studies, 411
Reductionism, 12
Rehearsal, 291
Reinforcement: of aggression, 443; in classical conditioning, 255; conditioned reinforcers, 268–69; differential reinforcement, 257; negative reinforcement, 272n; in operant conditioning, 266, 268–272, *271*, 276–277, *277*; partial reinforcement, 270; in personality development, 541–542; positive reinforcement, 272n, 276–278; and punishment, 272–273, 272n; relativity of, 269; schedules of, 270–272, *271*; systematic rein-

forcement, 679
Relative height, 168, *169*
Relative motion, 172
Relative size, 168, *169*
Relaxation training, 233–234, 611
Releasers, 408, 409
Reliability, 455–456, 552
Reliability coefficient, 456
REM sleep, 212–213, 216, 218–219
Remembering. *See* Memory
Renin, 376
Rep Test. *See* Role Construct Repertory Test
*Report on the Banality of Evil* (Arendt), 762
Repression, 208, 535, 606–607
Repression hypothesis, 311
Rescorla–Wagner model, 261
Research: case histories in, 22; correlational method in, 17–19; direct observation in, 19–21; and errors in intuition, 566–567; ethical issues in, 20–21, 768–769; evoked potentials method of, 193; experimental method in, 14–17; Ganzfeld procedure for, 241, *241*; habituation and dishabituation, 77; longitudinal studies, 512–513; observational method in, 19–22; in parapsychology, 241–244; preferential looking method of, 192–193; survey method in, 21
Reserpine, 41
Resistance, 674
Reticular system, 45
Retina, of eye, 135–136, *135, 136*
Retrieval: and context, 319; encoding–retrieval interactions in, 307–309; evidence for retrieval failures, 300–301; in implicit memory, 315–316; and interference, 301–302; in long–term memory, 300–303; models of, 303, *303*; practice of, 321, *321*; as search process versus activation process, 303, *303*; in short–term memory, 295–296, *295*; as stage of memory, 289, *289*
Retrieval cue, 301
Retrograde amnesia, 313
Reuptake, 39, 642, 701
Reward learning, 276–278
Right hemisphere of brain, 50, *53*, 55–58. *See also* Cerebral hemispheres
ROC curve. *See* Receiver–operating–characteristic curve (ROC curve)
Rods, 135–137, *136*
Rogers, Carl, 545–547, *545*, 550–551, 562–563, 685–688, *686*
Role Construct Repertory Test, 549, 563–564, *564*
Rorschach Test, 558–559, *558, 559*, 561
Ruminative coping strategies, 603, 604–605
Rutherford, Lord, 149

*s* factors, in intelligence, 472
S–R psychology. *See* Stimulus–response psychology

Safety signal hypothesis, 580
Sanford, E. C., 298
SAT. *See* Scholastic Aptitude Test (SAT)
Satiety center, in brain, 380
Satiety sensors, 376–377, 379
Saturation, of color, 139
Scanning mental images, 360–361, *361*
Scapegoat theory, of prejudice, 730–731
Schedules of reinforcement, 270–272, *271*
Schema (schemata), 84, 325–326, 715–718
Schematic processing, 716, *717*
Schizophrenia: antipsychotic drugs for, 653–654, 701; biological perspective on, 651–655, *652*; case study of, 646; characteristics of, 646–651; definition of, 645–646; diagnosis of, 619–620; dopamine hypothesis of, 653–654; drug therapy for, 41; and family relationships, 656–657; hereditary component of, 67; psychotic episode of, 650; social and psychological perspective on, 655–657; types of, 655; vulnerability for, 657–658
Scholastic Aptitude Test (SAT), 453, 453t, 454t, 464, 466–468, *469*, 483, 552
School psychology, school psychologists, 25
Second–order conditioning, 256–257
Secondary dispositions, of personality, 528
Secondary sex characteristics, 111
Sedatives. *See* Depressants
Seeing. *See* Visual sense
Segregation of objects, 166–168, *166–168*
Selective adaptation, 172
Selective attention, 183–186
Selective breeding, 65, *65*
Self–actualization, 12, 548, 549t
Self–attributions, 723–724, 726–727
Self–concept, 546
Self–efficacy, 684–685
Self–help groups, 691, 691t
Self–ideal discrepancy, 563
Self–perception theory, 723
Self–perceptions, 735
Self–presentation theory, of social facilitation, 752
Self–regulation, 684
Self–schema, 623, 641
Semantic memory, 316
Semi–circular canals, 161
*Sensation Seeking Scale* (SSS), 411–412, *412*, 412t
Sensitivity, 127–130, *128–130*, 128t, 129t
Sensitization, 264, *265*
Sensorimotor stage, of cognitive development, 85t, 86
Sensory coding, 130–131, 134, *134*
Sensory leakage, 243–244
Sensory neurons, 36–37
Sensory processes: absolute thresholds for, 128–129, *128*; auditory sense, 145–151; body senses, 160–161; decision processes in detection, 132–133; definition of, 127; detecting changes in intensity, 129–130, *129, 130*, 130t; properties of,

127–134; and sensitivity, 127–130, *128–130*, 128t, 129t; sensory coding, 130–131, *134*, 134; skin senses, 157–160, *157*, *159*, *160*; smell, 151–155; taste, 155–156, *156*; visual sense, 134–145
Sensory–neural loss, 148
Sentence units, 347–348, *348*
Sentences, primitive to complex, 351–352
Serial search, 295
Serotonin, 41, 642–643, 701, 703
Set points, 380–382, 385
Sex differences: in ill–temperedness, 516–518; in mental abilities, 470–471
Sex education, 108–109
Sex hormones, 394–395
Sex–linked disorders, 64
Sex–linked genes, 64, *64*
Sex of offspring, 64
Sex–role stereotyping, 102–109, 519
Sex typing, 101. *See also* Gender identity
Sexism: in childhood, 108–109; and sex education, 108–109
Sexual abuse, 582–583
Sexual development: hermaphrodites, 405–406; hormones versus environment in, 405–406; and prenatal hormones, 402–403, 404–405; transsexualism, 406
Sexual perversions, 398–399
Sexuality: in adolescence, 111–114, 113t; adult sexuality, 393–404; and contraceptive use, 116–117; cultural influences on, 399–400; early experiences of, 397–399; experiments with monkeys, 397–399; homosexuality, 400–404, 402t; hormonal control of, 394–396, *395*; hormonal effects on desire and arousal, 395–396; and hypothalamus, 45; neural control of, 396; premarital intercourse, 113–114, 113t, 399–400, *400*; research on, 20–21; teenage pregnancy, 116–117, *117*; transsexualism, 406; variables influencing sexual preference, 402t
Sexually transmitted diseases, 113, 117
Shadow (repetition), 185
Shakespeare, William, 526
Shape constancy, 188, *188*, 189
Shaping, 267–268, *267*, *268*
Sheldon, William, 526
Short–term memory: acoustic coding in, 291–292; chunking in, 293; dual–memory model, 297–298, *297*; encoding in, 291–292; forgetting in, 293–295, *294*; limited capacity of, 292–293; retrieval in, 295–296, *295*; storage in, 292–295; and thought, 296; transfer to long–term memory from, 297–298; versus long–term memory, 290; visual coding in, 292
Sight. *See* Visual sense
Signal detection, theory of, 132–133
Similarity: in grouping, 167–168; and liking, 738–740
Similarity heuristic, 343
Simon, Théophile, 458

Simple cells, 174, *174*
Simple inferences, 323–324
Simple phobia, 625
Simulation. *See* Computer simulation
Sine wave, 145, *145*
Single–cell recording, 131, *131*
Situational attribution, 722
Sixteen Personality Factor Questionnaire, 554–555
Size constancy, 189–191, *189–191*
Size–distance invariance principle, 190
Skin senses: minimum stimulus for touch, 128t; pain, 158–159, *159*; pressure, 157–158, *157*; temperature, 158; Weber's constant for touch, 129–130, 130t
Skinner, B. F., 72, 266–267, *266*
Skinner box, 266, *266*
Sleep: advice for good night's sleep, 215t; depth of, 211–213; disorders of, 214, 216; and dreams, 216–219; schedules of, 210–211; stages of, 212–213, *212*; theories of dream sleep, 218–219
Smell: and Weber's constant, 129–130, 130t; evolutionary significance of, 151–154; infants' sense of, 80; minimum stimulus for, 128t; olfactory system, 154, *154*; sensing intensity and quality, 155
Social adjustment function, of attitudes, 731–732
Social beliefs: data collection about, 714–718; detecting covariation in, 718–722; and fundamental attribution error, 722–725, *725*; inferring causality in, 722–725; intuitive approach to, 713–714; and self–attributions, 723–724; and stereotypes, 716, 719–722
Social development: in childhood, 97–111; of infants, 97–99, *98*
Social facilitation, 749–752, *750*, *752*
Social impact theory, 758–759
Social influence: cognitive response theory of persuasion, 773–777; conformity to majority, 759–761; forms of, 749; obedience to authority, 762–769; persuasive influence of minorities, 771–773; power of situations, 767–768; rebellion, 768–771
Social–learning assessment, of personality, 561–562
Social–learning theory: of aggression, 438, 441–443, *442*, *443*; of gender identity, 102–104; of personality, 540–544
Social norms, 749, 764–765
Social phobias, 626
Social psychology: attitudes, 725–735; bystander intervention, 754–758; cognitive response theory of persuasion, 773–777; conformity to majority, 759–761; definition of, 713; deindividuation, 752–754; group decision-making, 778–781; group polarization, 778–780; groupthink, 780–781, *780*; interpersonal attraction, 736–744; interpersonal influence, 759–777; obedience to authority, 762–769;

persuasive influence of minorities, 771–773; power of situations, 767–768; profession of, 24; rebellion, 768–771; and social beliefs, 713–725; social facilitation, 749–752, *750*, *752*; social impact theory, 758–759
Sociocultural approaches, to cognitive development, 97
Sociopaths. *See* Antisocial personality
Socrates, 6
Somatic system, 43
Somatosensory area, of brain, 50–51, *51*
Somatotypes, 526
Sound. *See* Auditory sense
Sound intensity, 148–149, *148*
Sound waves, 145–146, *145*
Spatial context, 182, 183
Spatial frequency, 194, *194*
Spatial localization, 165
Spearman, Charles, 471–472, 531
Species specificity, 408
Specific nerve energies, 134
Speech. *See* Language
Speech sounds, 345–346
Sperry, Roger, 54
Spinal cord, 43
Split–brain perception, 4, *4*, 8, 54–55, *54*
Spock, Benjamin, 533
Spontaneous activity, 131
Spontaneous remission, 693
Sports psychology, 234–235
Spurious associations, 283
Stages of development, 75–76; Erikson's psychosocial stages, 116–118, 118t, 537; Freud's psychosexual stages, 101–102, 535
Stanford–Binet Intelligence Scale, 459–460, 461t, 463, 466–467
Stapes, 147, *148*
State–dependent learning, 309
Statistical significance, 16–17, 242
Statistics, definition of, 16
Stereoscope, 169, *170*
Stereotypes, 324–325, 716, 719–722, 726
Stern, William, 460
Stimulants, 221t, 226–229, *228*
Stimulation, absence of, 196–197
Stimulaton–produced analgesia, 158
Stimulation seeking, as motive, 411–412
Stimulus: conditioned stimulus, 255–263; discriminative stimulus, 267; unconditioned stimulus, 255–263
Stimulus–response psychology, 9, 540
Storage: in implicit memory, 315–316; in long–term memory, 306; as stage of memory, 289, *289*
Storage, in short–term memory, 292–295
Stradonitz, Friedrich Kekule von, 361
Strange Situation, 493–497
Strategy, in complex learning, 279
Stress: and anger and aggression, 585; and anxiety, 584–585; and apathy and depression, 586–587; behavioral theory of, 597; causes of, 577–578; and challenging

Stress (continued)
life events, 580–581, 580t; characteristics of stressful events, 578–583; and cognitive impairment, 587; and controllability, 579, 593–595; coping skills for, 602–610; and coronary heart disease, 591–592; and defense mechanisms as emotion–focused coping, 606–610; definition of, 577; and depression, 644–645; effect of family and friends on, 610–611; effects on health, 591–596; emotion–focused coping for, 602, 603–606; and hardiness of personality, 598–599; and health behaviors, 596; and illness, 590–591; illness–behavior model, 596; and immune system, 592–595; and internal conflicts, 581–583; on Life Events Scale, 580t, 581; management of, 610–614; and personality style, 597–602; physiological reactions to, 587–591, 589; and predictability, 579–580; problem–focused coping for, 602–603; psychoanalytic theory of, 596–597; psychological reactions to, 583–587; and schizophrenia, 656, 657–658; and traumatic events, 578; and Type A pattern, 599–602, 600t, 613–614; vulnerability–stress model, 595
Stress management: aerobic exercise, 612; behavioral techniques of, 611–612; biofeedback training, 611; cognitive techniques of, 612–613; and effect of family and friends, 610–611; relaxation training, 611; for Type A behavior, 613–614
Stress responses, 577
Stressors, 577
Stroboscopic motion, 171, 171
Subtractive mixture, of color, 140–141, 141
Suicide, 638–639
Sullivan, Harry Stack, 537
Superego, 358, 534, 540, 542, 597, 673
Superposition, 168, 169
Suppression, 606–607
Survey method, 21
Survival motives, and homeostasis, 373–377
Survival of the fittest, 266
Sympathetic nervous system, 58, 418, 588
Synapse, 36, 36, 38–39, 38, 39, 265
Synaptic gap, 36, 38
Synaptic terminals, 36
Synaptic vesicles, 38
Syntactic analysis, 348
Systematic desensitization, 678–679
Systematic reinforcement, 679

Taste: and Weber's constant, 129–130, 130t; gustatory system, 155–156, 156; infants' sense of, 80; minimum stimulus for, 128t; and obesity, 387, 387; sensing intensity and quality, 156; as sensory process, 155–156, 156
Taste aversion, 262

Taste buds, 156, 156
TAT. See Thematic Apperception Test (TAT)
Teenagers. See Adolescence
Telegraphic sentences, 351
Telepathy, 240, 246
Telephone hot lines, 704–705
Television violence, 5, 6, 444–446, 445
Temperaments, 82–83, 489. See also Personality
Temperature regulation, as homeostasis, 374–375
Temporal context, 182, 182
Temporal lobe, of brain hemispheres, 50
Temporal stability, 552
Temporal theory, of pitch perception, 149
Terman, Lewis, 459–460
Test anxiety, 587
Test of Primary Mental Abilities, 473
Test–retest reliablity, 552
Testimonial validity, 554–555
Testosterone, 395, 402–403, 404, 440–441
Tests. See Psychological tests
Texture gradient, 170, 171
Thalamus, 44, 44
Thematic Apperception Test (TAT), 560–561, 560
Theophrastus, 525–526
Theories, 718. See also specific theories
Therapy. See Psychotherapy
Thirst, as homeostatic system, 375–377
Thorndike, E. L., 265–266
Thought: concepts and categories, 331–339; imaginal thought, 359–361; linguistic relativity hypothesis of, 338–339; problem solving, 361–367; reasoning, 339–344; and short–term memory, 296. See also Mental abilities; and headings beginning with Cognitive Thought stopping, 684
Three Faces of Eve, 208
Thurstone, Louis, 472–473, 474t, 531
TM. See Transcendental Meditation (TM)
Token economies, 679
Tonic pain, 158
Top–down processes: in concept learning, 336–337, 337; and constructive memory, 322–323; in networks for recognition, 177–178, 178; and recognition of natural objects, 181–183, 182–183
Touch. See Skin senses
Trait approach to personality: Allport's theory of, 527–528; evaluation of, 532–533; factor–analytic theories, 528–531, 529, 530, 531t; personality traits, 526–527; personality types, 525–526
Trait assessment, 553–558
Tranquilizers, 221, 699–700
Transactional analysis, 689t
Transcendental Meditation (TM), 233
Transference, 675
Transsexualism, 406
Traumatic events, and stress, 578

Trial–and–error behavior, 266
Trichromatic theory, of color vision, 141–143, 143
Tricyclic antidepressants, 642, 701
Triplett, Norman, 749
Twin studies: on anxiety disorders, 633; on intelligence, 478–480, 478t; on mood disorders, 642; on obesity, 383–385; on personality, 489–493, 504–506; on schizophrenia, 651; uses in research, 65–66, 66
Two–point threshold, of pressure, 157, 157
Two–stage color theory, 144–145, 145
Type A pattern, 599–602, 600t, 613–614
Type B pattern, 601
Type theories, of personality, 525–526
Typicality, and prototypes, 333

UCR. See Unconditioned response (UCR)
UCS. See Unconditioned stimulus (UCS)
Unconditional positive regard, 546–547
Unconditioned response (UCR), 255
Unconditioned stimulus (UCS), 255–263, 542
Unconscious, 11, 206
Unconscious inference, 169–170
Underreactive autonomic nervous system, 661

Validity, 456, 552–553
Validity coefficient, 456, 552
Value–expressive function, of attitudes, 730
Variable interval (VI) schedule, of reinforcement, 271–272
Variable ratio (VR) schedule, of reinforcement, 271
Variables, in experimental method, 14–15
Venereal diseases. See Sexually transmitted diseases
Ventromedial hypothalamus (VMH), 380–382
Verb phrases, 347
Vestibular sacs, 160
Vicarious learning, 441
Violence on television, 5, 6, 444–446, 445. See also Aggression
Visual acuity, 193–195, 194
Visual buffer, 292, 292
Visual cliff, 195–196, 195
Visual coding, in short–term memory, 292
Visual creativity, 361
Visual neglect, 359–360
Visual sense: and Weber's constant, 129–130, 130t; artificial eyes, 153; brain area for, 51, 51; and components of the eye, 135–137, 135–137; critical period of development of, 76; of infants, 78–80, 80; and light, 134–135; minimum stimulus for, 128t; seeing color, 138–145, 139–145; seeing light, 137–138, 137–138; selective looking, 183–184, 184, 185
VMH. See Ventromedial hypothalamus

(VMH)
VMH syndrome, 380–382
VR schedule. *See* Variable ratio (VR) schedule
Vulnerability–stress model, 595, 624

WAIS. *See* Wechsler Adult Intelligence Scale (WAIS)
Warm receptors, 158
Washing compulsion, 627–628
Watson, John B., 9, 72, 203, 543
Weak methods, of problem solving, 363
Weber, Ernst, 129
Weber's constant, 129–130, 130t
Weber's law, 129
Wechsler, David, 462–463, 471
Wechsler Adult Intelligence Scales
(WAIS), 463, 568
Wechsler Intelligence Scale for Children (WISC), 463, 480
Wechsler Intelligence Scales, *463*, 467
Weight. *See* Obesity
Weight control programs, 388–389, *389*
Wernicke, Carl, 56
Wernicke–Geschwind model, 56–57, *57*
Wernicke's area, 51, 56, 356
Wertheimer, Max, 167, 171
WISC. *See* Wechsler Intelligence Scale for Children (WISC)
Withdrawal symptoms, 220
Women: employment of, 498–499; ill-tempered females, 516–518; in psychology, 24t. *See also* Mothers
Word units, 346–347
Words and concepts, 350
Working backwards, in problem solving, 363
Working through, 676

X chromosome, 64

Y chromosome, 64
Yoga, 232
Young–Helmholtz theory, of color vision, 141–143, *143*
Youth centers, 704

Zajonc, Robert, 750
Zen, 232